Asian Mythologies

Asian Mythologies

Compiled by

YVES BONNEFOY

Translated under the direction of

WENDY DONIGER

by Gerald Honigsblum,
Danielle Beauvais, Teresa Lavender Fagan, Dorothy Figueira,
Barry Friedman, Daniel Gold, Louise Guiney, John Leavitt,
Michael Sells, Bruce Sullivan, and David White

The University of Chicago Press • *Chicago and London*

YVES BONNEFOY,
a scholar and poet of world renown, is professor of comparative poetics, Collège de France. Among his many works to have appeared in English, two have been published by the University of Chicago Press—a volume of poetry, *In the Shadow's Light* (1991), and a work of criticism, *The Act and Place of Poetry* (1989), both translated by John T. Naughton.

WENDY DONIGER
is the Mircea Eliade Professor in the Divinity School, and professor in the Department of South Asian Languages and Civilizations, the Committee on Social Thought, and the College, at the University of Chicago. Under the name of Wendy Doniger O'Flaherty she has written, among other books, *Women, Androgynes, and Other Mythical Beasts* (1980), *Dreams, Illusion, and Other Realities* (1984), and *Tales of Sex and Violence: Folklore, Sacrifice, and Danger in the Jaiminīya Brāhmaṇa* (1985), all published by the University of Chicago Press.

The University of Chicago Press, Chicago 60637
The University of Chicago Press, Ltd., London

Printed in the United States of America

02 01 00 99 98 97 96 95 94 93   5 4 3 2 1

This paperback is drawn from *Mythologies*, compiled by Yves Bonnefoy, translated under the direction of Wendy Doniger, and published by the University of Chicago Press in 1991. That work was originally published as *Dictionnaire des mythologies et des religions des sociétés traditionnelles et du monde antique*, sous la direction de Yves Bonnefoy publié avec le concours du Centre National des Lettres, © 1981, Flammarion, Paris.

The preparation of the complete English edition was supported by grants from the French Ministry of Culture, the Andrew W. Mellon Foundation, and the National Endowment for the Humanities.

This book is printed on acid-free paper.

Paperback ISBN: 0-226-06456-5

Library of Congress Cataloging-in-Publication Data

Dictionnaire des mythologies et des religions de sociétés traditionnelles et du monde antique. English. Selections.
Asian mythologies / compiled by Yves Bonnefoy ; translated under the direction of Wendy Doniger by Gerald Honigsblum . . . [et al.].
p. cm.
Translation of selections from: Dictionnaire des mythologies et des religions des sociétés traditionnelles et du monde antique.
Includes bibliographical references and index.
1. Mythology, Asian—Encyclopedias. I. Title.
BL1005.D5313 1993
291.1'3'095—dc20   92-39077
CIP

Contents

PART 3   SOUTHEAST ASIA

PART 4   EAST ASIA AND INNER ASIA

Preface to the Paperback Edition

This is one of four paperback volumes drawn from the full, clothbound, two-volume English-language edition of Yves Bonnefoy's *Mythologies*. These paperback volumes are not an afterthought but were part of the publication plan from the beginning. Indeed, one of the reasons why we restructured the original French edition as we did was to make these separate volumes ultimately available. For although there is a sweep and majesty in the full edition, both in French and in English, a breathtaking scope that is the true raison d'être of the work as a whole, there is also, in the English edition, a pattern that allows readers to focus on one culture at a time. And it is with such readers in mind that the University of Chicago Press has issued these paperbacks. Together, they cover almost all of the full edition: along with the present volume, the series includes *Roman and European Mythologies*, *Greek and Egyptian Mythologies*, and *American, African, and Old European Mythologies*. Each contains, in addition to the culturally specific material, the prefaces and the general introductory section of the full work, which deal with methodological issues relevant to any part of it.

Since each culture poses different problems, and each section of essays embodies the work of a different group of French scholars, each section has its own methodological flavor and makes its own contribution to the more culturally specific study of mythology. "Asia" is a word that, like almost all words designating groups of people, has some problematic political echoes. It designates in common usage precisely the groups of cultures covered in this volume: South Asia, Iran, Southeast Asia, East Asia (China and Japan), and Inner Asia. Indeed, there are problems even with these apparently inoffensive terms. "Inner Asia" is a catchall term, not really adequate to cover Tibetans as well as Turks, Mongols, Finno-Ugrian, and Siberians (to say nothing of Abkhaz and Ubykh). "South Asia" should, rightly, designate Sri Lanka and Pakistan as well as India, but there is hardly anything here about South Asia outside of India. And to use the nongeographical term "Buddhism" in the company of all the other, geographical terms is awkward, but one of the strengths of the articles on Buddhism in this collection is precisely their unusual ability to span Buddhism across cultures, from India through Tibet to China.

Another strength of this particular group of essays on Asian mythologies is its treatment of the mythologies of several obscure peoples about whom little has appeared in English (such as the Turks and Mongols), and others (in Southeast Asia) about whom the available literature has always taken an imperialist slant—imperialist in two very different senses, which we might call Asian and European. When the French and the Dutch had only recently stopped living in trees and caves, Asian imperialism had already begun in Southeast Asia: the political and religious hegemony of Hinduism and Buddhism (and, later, Islam) was already felt over Indonesia and Indo-China and Java. European scholarship has reflected that imperialism, generally treating the mythologies of Southeast Asia as variants of Indian mythology, transformations of Hinduism and Buddhism. What is particularly valuable about this volume, therefore, is the way in which it deals primarily with indigenous (what the French call "autochthonous") mythologies. These are to the mythologies of Hinduism and Buddhism what the Native American mythologies of North and South America are to the mythologies of the Puritans and of the African slaves. Not that Hindu and Buddhist strains are neglected, for they are an inextricable part of the mythologies of the culture that now tells the stories. But here, for the first time in English, is a balanced picture of the full span of the mythologies of Vietnam and Java and Madagascar, the complex braid of Hindu/Buddhist, "autochthonous," and, finally, European themes and images.

This second imperialism, that of Europe, must also be taken into account. The European presence is strongly felt in these articles, both as an object, as one of the actors in the history of Southeast Asia (and in Asia in general), and as the subject who looks back upon the history it has helped to create. It is surely not surprising that the French have produced such extensive and valuable scholarship about Vietnam and Indo-China, far better than that of British or German scholars (though not, perhaps, better than that of Dutch scholars). The depth of the French knowledge of Asia results in large part from the political presence of the French in Southeast Asia (and, to a lesser degree, in India). But is this a good thing or a bad thing? Whatever they might have to answer for as colonizers, the French are, I believe, to be thanked for their work as scholars, preserving records of traditions even when other branches of their culture were destroying those traditions. It is an ambivalent gift, to be sure, and nowadays political imperialism is regarded as inseparable from academic or intellectual imperialism. For many have argued that colonial scholarship itself is polluted and invalidated by the political situation of the scholars who produced it. Readers will have to judge this issue for themselves.

Wendy Doniger

Preface to the English Edition of the Complete Work

Yves Bonnefoy in his preface (which follows this preface) explains why he organized his book—and after all, this is his book—as he did. He had good reasons, and he is eloquent in their defense. But it remains for me to explain the ways in which the English edition differs from the French in more than the language in which it is expressed, since some of what M. Bonnefoy will say does not in fact apply to this edition at all, particularly in what concerns the arrangement of the articles.

M. Bonnefoy graciously if reluctantly allowed me to restructure his work. As he put it, "Of course I will miss the formula of the dictionary, for the reasons that I indicate in my preface (the rupture with all the apriority of classification, the possibility of surprising juxtapositions, in short, the irony), *but I absolutely do not oppose* your choice, which is in response to very good reasons, and which is better adapted to the English-speaking world in which your edition will appear. I therefore give you carte blanche, with the understanding that you will publish my preface as is. For it is a good idea to point out that the book was originally what I indicate in that preface—this will bring in a supplementary point for reflection."[1] On another occasion,[2] he remarked that there was another consideration (one that, I must confess, had not occurred to me) that had persuaded him to organize his original version of the book in what he termed "the random way," while we might be able to rearrange our version in "the more organized way": French students, he pointed out, have only limited access to open stacks in the French libraries (since there is not enough room to accommodate them) and few of the bookstores are quiet enough to read in. French students therefore have apparently not formed the habit of browsing—except in a dictionary.

Without denying the validity of his arguments, let me state my reasons for the reorganization. And in order to justify the changes, I shall first state my conception of the strengths and weaknesses of the French work itself.

The Strengths and Weaknesses of the French Edition

To begin with, even in its French form, with all the articles arranged alphabetically, it is not a dictionary, nor even an encyclopedia, nor a dispassionate fact-book even for those topics that it covers (and many major items are omitted). It is a quirky and idiosyncratic set of essays, long and short, by a particular group of mythologists, most of whom are French and all of whom participate in the French school of mythology in its broadest sense. The patent omissions and biases have prompted a certain amount of criticism leveled at the French edition,[3] criticism of imbalances, of inconsistencies (in the selection of topics, in the manner of their treatment, in the style, in the methodologies, etc.), and of the choice of illustrations, as well as more substantive criticisms of the interpretations.

Some of these criticisms are just; some are not. The arguments about what *is* there (what is said about the mythologies that are discussed) are interesting; the arguments about what is *not* there are, I think, beside the point. Many of the scholars involved in the project chose not to write about what other people (including certain reviewers) regarded as "central" or "basic" themes of the mythologies they treated; they wrote long essays on the subjects they cared about personally, and gave short shrift to subjects to which other scholars might have given pride of place. The reader who continues perversely to look for ways in which the glass is half empty rather than half full will notice immediately, for instance, that there is almost nothing about Islam or Judaism in the book. This is primarily because Yves Bonnefoy had originally intended to save this material for another volume, on the mythologies of monotheistic religions—a volume that has not yet materialized. It might be argued that this justification is disingenuous, for some of the very best material in the extant volume is on Christianity, which is by most standards monotheistic. But on closer inspection it is quite clear that while the book does treat the appropriation of classical mythology by Christianity, and the incorporation of "pagan mythologies" into what might be called "rural Catholicism," it rightly does not treat mainstream, monotheistic Christianity as a mythology. Moreover, to have dealt with the central traditions of Islam and Judaism in this way would certainly have been tantamount to a betrayal of what the adherents of those religions regard as their basic tenets. Yet this Jewish and Islamic silence is also in part accounted for by the simple fact that the authors who were assembled to prepare this book did not choose to write articles on these subjects. Similarly, the African articles deal almost exclusively (though hardly surprisingly) with Francophone Africa; yet these articles constitute superb paradigms for the study of other African mythologies. So, too, there are only two articles on Buddhism per se, and there is virtually nothing about Buddhism (or Islam, for that matter) in Southeast Asia (though there is a great deal of wonderful material about indigenous Southeast Asian religions, and those two articles on Buddhism are fascinating). On the other hand, there is extensive coverage of the Turks and Mongols, whose mythologies are relatively unknown to Western readers. This sort of imbalance might be regarded as a kind of mythological affirmative action.

This is, therefore, certainly not an encyclopedia. In a famous painting by the surrealist René Magritte, a caption in his neat script, under a painting of what is clearly a pipe, declares, "This is not a pipe." I would have liked to write on the cover of this book, "This is not a dictionary of mythologies." Rather like the ugly duckling that turned out to be a terrific swan, as a dictionary this book leaves much to be desired, but as a book of mythologies it is superb, indeed peerless. If it is not a dictionary, what *is* it, then? It is a most exciting (far more exciting than an encyclopedia ought to be) collection of essays on *some* aspects of *some* mythologies, written by a group of brilliant and philosophically complex French scholars. It is highly opinionated and original, and should inspire hot, not cold, reactions. Like all multiauthored works, it is a mixed bag; there is some jargon, some wild theorizing, some boring surveys, some overclever interpretation, and some of what I would regard as simple errors of fact, but there is also an overwhelming proportion of very sound and/or brilliant articles about mythology in general and about a number of mythologies in particular. This is not primarily a book, for instance, to consult for all the stories about Apollo; one has Robert Graves for that (though this is a far better book with which to begin to formulate some ideas about the meaning of Apollo). It is, however, a book in which to discover the delightful and useful fact that in the ritual celebration of the Brazilian god Omolu, who is of Yoruba origin but came to be syncretized with Saint Lazarus, people dance to a beat called "he kills someone and eats him." I was thrilled to come upon a hauntingly sad and beautiful Inuit myth about the cycle of transmigration of a mistreated woman, a myth that agrees, in astonishing detail, with certain complex myths of transmigration that I know from medieval Sanskrit philosophical texts. Other readers will undoubtedly stumble upon strange stories that are curiously familiar to them—stumble upon them quite by chance, just as Yves Bonnefoy intended them to do.

But if the selection is not as complete as a dictionary should ideally be, neither is it as arbitrary as a nondictionary can be. Most of the great mythological traditions are covered, and within those areas most of the important myths are treated. But this is not the point. What is treated very thoroughly indeed is the problem of *how to understand a mythology*, what questions to ask, what patterns to look for. More precisely, this is a book that demonstrates what happens when a combination of two particular methodologies, those of Georges Dumézil and Claude Lévi-Strauss, is applied to *any* mythology. It is, as its title claims (in English as in French), not so much a book about myths (sacred narratives) as a book about mythologies (whole systems of myths, or even systems of ideas about myths). It is that rare and wonderful fusion, a book about methodology that simultaneously puts the methodology to work and shows you just what it can and cannot do. It is a mythodology.

Many of these articles tell the reader how to study mythology in general and, more important, how to study each particular body of mythology, how to solve (or, more often, to approach) the particular problems that each mythology presents. Some tell the reader why it is not possible to write an article about that particular mythology at all (a consideration that does not, however, prevent the author from writing the article in which this assertion is made). The most hilarious example of this (I will leave the reader to decide which article it is) is almost an unconscious satire on the pusillanimity of scholars in certain fields; in it, the author goes on for pages and pages (it is one of the longest articles in the book) telling us, over and over, why there are insufficient data, why the data that we have are skewed, why the extant interpretations of the data are skewed, why all hypotheses and generalizations about the data are worthless, why in fact it is impossible to make any valid statement about the mythology at all. This is in its way a masterpiece, a kind of Zen nonarticle on a nonsubject, a surreal piece of nonscholarship worthy of Samuel Beckett. And yet even this article has its value here as a striking example of one particular methodology, one approach to the subject, that argues in great detail, and rightly, the obstacles that oppose any truly responsible survey of the subject.

But this is the exception, not the rule. The book teems with marvelous primary material, both myths and rituals (with which many myths are inextricably linked), using the materials and the methodological considerations to animate one another, the soul of data within the body of theory, and the soul of theory within the body of data. Sometimes the methodology is in the foreground, sometimes the data; usually they are in a fine balance. In the Greek and European sections, for instance, there are startling reinterpretations of well-known stories, or new emphases on previously overlooked details in well-known stories; many of the articles on the Greeks demonstrate the cutting edge of French structuralism. As Arthur Adkins has remarked, "The dictionary in its French version is a truly remarkable work. The Greek section in particular is quite unlike any other dictionary known to me. [It] for the most part presents the views of the Paris school, and the writers come out fighting. The Paris school is undoubtedly producing the most interesting work in the field at present. . . . [The work] represents more of a *parti pris* than the title 'Dictionary' may suggest."[4] The Vietnamese section, by contrast, abundantly documents a fascinating mythology that is virtually unknown to the English-speaking world, and presents it, moreover, in the context of an enlightened political awareness that is almost unprecedented in scholarly treatments of mythology anywhere (but that is also a notable virtue of the articles in this volume that deal with the Americas and Oceania).

If this is a book as much about method as it is about myths, what is the method? It is a masterpiece of what might be called trifunctional structuralism, a joint festschrift for Claude Lévi-Strauss and Georges Dumézil, a vision of the world of mythology seen through their eyes, *la vie en* Lévi-Strauss and Dumézil. To combine the methodologies of these two scholars is in itself a most extraordinary and fruitful achievement. If I may oversimplify both approaches for a moment, Lévi-Strauss's basic method, a variant of Hegelian dialectic, is to seek the intellectual or logical framework of the myth in binary oppositions that are mediated by a third term; the Dumézilian approach is to gloss the main figures of a myth in terms of three functions that have social referents: religion and government, defense, and material production. These two theories are in no way contradictory, especially if one resolves the potential conflict between Dumézilian tripartition and Lévi-Straussian bipolarization by taking into account the mediating third term and thus making Lévi-Strauss, too, tripartite. In this sense, both of them operate with triads, though very different triads. Furthermore, they complement rather than contradict one another because they focus on different levels (Lévi-Strauss on abstract intellectual concepts, Dumézil on social functions). Combined as they are in this volume, they are startlingly innovative.

Indeed, the beauty of the book is that it is not doctrinaire in its application of the theories of these two great scholars, but rather creative and imaginative. Dumézil's trifunctional analysis of Indo-European mythology is applied, quite loosely to be sure, even beyond the bounds of the Indo-European world (where it is, properly speaking, no longer trifunctional but tripartite), and a general way of thinking in terms of oppositions and inversions forms the armature of many analyses in which the name of Lévi-Strauss is not actually invoked. The search for tripartitions of both sorts is the driving force behind many of the analyses in this book.

The book is so very French that I thought seriously of putting the word "French" in the title of the English edition: *Mythologies According to the Contemporary French School*, or *The View from France*, or *Essays in the French Style, A French Collection, A Paris Collection, The French Connection*, and so forth. Yves Bonnefoy's remarks, in his preface, explaining why he chose primarily French scholars are delightfully, if unconsciously, Francophile. He has maintained elsewhere that the preponderance of French scholars was simply a natural outcome of choosing to organize the scholarship from the geographical center of the project, Paris, rather than to range over the world at random. But as anyone who has ever had the privilege of working at the Sorbonne will immediately realize, most French scholars think that the only people who know anything are other French scholars. In this instance, at least, they would be right: such is the hegemony of French scholarship in the field of mythology right now that a well-read American or British mythologist would probably draw on precisely these same "French" approaches.

This is one of the great values of the book: it represents, as few other works in any field do, the achievements of the *crème de la crème* of an entire generation of French scholarship in a large and important field. Yves Bonnefoy himself has remarked that he loves the book because it freezes a moment in time, in history, and in space; it is the embodiment of the beauty of the Ecole Pratique.

But in a way, the guiding spirit of the book is not just that of the twin gods, Dumézil and Lévi-Strauss. It is the spirit of Yves Bonnefoy himself. This is, after all, a book put together by a poet, not by a philologist. The editor of this nondictionary is also, let me hasten to say, a scholar of the first rank, but he is at heart a poet. The reader who keeps this in mind is more likely to get from the book what it has to give than the reader who picks it up hoping that it will be a kind of mythological Guinness book of records.

The Restructuring of the English Edition

We decided to restructure the book in order to minimize its weaknesses, emphasize its sometimes hidden strengths, and make it useful to the English-speaking reader in new ways. Its primary weakness is, as I have admitted, that it is not a true encyclopedia. If the English edition were arranged alphabetically, as the French edition is, readers might look for things and not find them and get mad, as some of the French reviewers did; and, on the other hand, readers might overlook a lot of strange and beautiful essays that no one would ever dream of looking up on purpose at all.

Bonnefoy in his preface explains why he wanted to use a dictionary format: to avoid all prearranged categories, to let the reader find things by chance, to allow accidental juxtapositions to give rise to unexpected ideas. But to some extent this argues for a false naïveté on the part of the reader and even, perhaps, on the part of the editor, for both of them *are looking for something*. In choosing the arbitrariness of alphabetical order, Bonnefoy is indeed shuffling the deck; but he does still have a deck, which, like all decks, is highly structured. The alphabetical shuffle conceals the true order but does not destroy it. Thus, for instance, all the articles on a certain subject are written by a single author, an expert on that subject. Clearly the articles were originally commissioned in this way, and they are still listed this way in the front of the French edition. And each author does have his methodological presuppositions, which the reader encounters every time he or she wanders (arbitrarily, accidentally) into that territory. Bonnefoy chose to conceal the patterns that he saw in the material in order to let readers discover them by chance; I have chosen to set out in the open the patterns that I see, and to let readers decide whether or not they want to follow those patterns. The difference lies in what sort of browsing is encouraged, cross-cultural (through the French edition's physical juxtaposition of the major articles on creation or on sacrifice) or intracultural (through the English edition's grouping of all the Siberian or Celtic articles).

Several of the translators, the Honigsblums in particular, arranged the work according to geographic areas or cultures, which made it easier to check the consistent use of technical terms. Gradually it occurred to us that this arrangement would also be useful to readers. Bonnefoy chose to mix the cultures together to encourage cross-cultural *aperçus;* I chose to separate out each culture to encourage consecutive reading in each tradition. (Another, related advantage of the present arrangement lies in the fact that this arrangement will make it possible in the future to publish sections of the work as individual books, making them available to specialists in particular cultural fields.) For the overall structure I decided to use a kind of geographical swing: beginning with Africa, then traveling up through the Near East, the ancient Mediterranean, the Indo-European world; remaining in place geographically but moving forward in time to later European culture, then back in time to South Asia; on in both space and time to Southeast Asia, East Asia, Inner Asia; across the Bering Strait to North America, South America; and finishing the journey paradisiacally in the South Pacific. Within each category of culture (Greek, Celtic, etc.), I have put the long, meditative, general essays first, and the shorter, more straightforward dictionary entries second. Several pathbreaking essays that are not tied to a particular culture, and that immediately establish the Dumézilian and structuralist stance of the book, form an introductory sequence.

Of course, since both the French and the English editions have detailed indexes, and the French edition has an outline listing the articles according to cultures, it comes down to a matter of emphasis, for in either edition the reader can find materials that are arranged alphabetically (both in the index and in the body of the work in the French edition, and in the index in the English edition) as well as materials that are grouped according to the culture (in the outline of the French edition, and in the body of the work in the English edition). In the restructured English edition, the reader can still use the index as Bonnefoy suggests the French index might be used, to find his or her favorite Naiad or Norse god, and also to find all the articles on, say, creation, or sacrifice, which cut across methodological lines. This is, after all, the same book, and can ultimately be used in all the same ways.

New problems arise out of this rearrangement, however, for some cultures don't really fit into any of the large categories—Turks and Mongols, Armenians and Albanians, Ossets and Georgians, Siberians, Malagasy, Maghreb—and so I had to settle for putting them where they seemed least out of place. Another disadvantage of my rearrangement is the fact that it exposes repetitions, necessary in an encyclopedia (where the author of any one article, who cannot assume that the reader will have read any other article, may therefore have to resupply a certain amount of basic material), but rather jarring in a book such as this (where the reader may well find it annoying to read the same story, or the same theory, almost verbatim in consecutive articles). A good example of this recycling is provided by the very first part, on West Africa, with its recurrent motifs of twinning and sexual mutilation; another occurs in the South Asian section, which pivots around the sacrificial pole and the avatar.

I decided not to cut any of these repetitions, however, for several reasons. First of all, I decided not to abridge or revise (a decision I will attempt to justify below). Second, some readers may only pick up isolated articles and will therefore need the basic information that also appears in other articles. And, finally, these repetitions demonstrate how certain scholars always think in terms of a limited number of particular myths, dragging them into whatever other subject they are supposed to be discussing. For scholars, like their native informants, do just what Lévi-Strauss says they do: they continually rework the same themes in a kind of academic bricolage, and no two variants are ever *quite* alike.

For the most part, I think the rearrangement is a positive move. For one thing, it makes it possible to *read* the book, instead of merely browsing in it or looking things up in it (though, as I have said, readers can still engage in both of these activities in the English edition). For another, it may prove more useful in this form not only to mythophiles and area specialists, but to people interested in French anthropology and philosophy.

The book is therefore *re*structured, because of course it was originally highly structured, ideologically if not organizationally. Its English title, *Mythologies,* to me echoes the wonderful books by Roland Barthes and William Butler Yeats, both with the same title, and further resonates with the French title of the great Lévi-Strauss trilogy, *Mythologiques* (treacherously translated in one English edition as *A Science of Mythology*). *Mythologies* has, finally, the advantage of being simultaneously an English and a French word, a last attempt at bilinguality before the Fall into the English version.

The English Translation

This edition was prepared "under my direction" in not nearly so important a sense as the original was "sous la direction de Yves Bonnefoy." Certain parallel procedures probably exacerbated rather than minimized the inevitable slip twixt French cup and English lip, and one of these was the employment of a team of English scholars to translate the text that was originally composed by a team of French scholars.

Gerald Honigsblum translated the entire second volume of the French edition, with the editorial assistance of Bonnie Birtwistle Honigsblum. The first volume was translated by a group of professional translators (Danielle Beauvais, Teresa Lavender Fagan, Louise Guiney, Louise Root, Michael Sells) and another group consisting of some of my students in the history of religions (Dorothy Figueira, Barry Friedman, Daniel Gold, John Leavitt, and David White). Their initials follow those of the original authors of the French articles. Bruce Sullivan did the bibliographies.

The translated articles were then checked for accuracy (in the transliteration of names, technical terms, and so forth) by specialists in each of the particular fields. Arthur Adkins did by far the most difficult task, working painstakingly and courageously through the enormous and often very tricky articles on the Greeks and Romans. Lawrence Sullivan vetted Africa and the Americas for us; Robert Ritner, Egypt; Walter Farber, Mesopotamia; Dennis Pardee, Semites; Richard Beal, Hittites; Laurie Patton, Celts; Ann Hoffman, Norse; Zbigniew Golab, Slavs; Frank Paul Bowman, Richard Luman, and David Tracy, early Christianity; Anthony Grafton, medieval and renaissance Europe; Françoise Meltzer, modern Europe; Charles Keyes, Southeast Asia; Anthony Yu and Jane Geaney, China; Gary Ebersole, Japan; Bruce Cummings, Korea; Matthew Kapstein and Per Kvaerne, Tibet; Robert Dankoff, Turks and Mongols. I did the South Asian and Indo-Iranian sections.

There are thus several levels at which inconsistencies—in style, in format (citations of texts, abbreviations), in transliteration, in ways of dealing with specific untranslatable concepts—could have slipped in: differences between the technical languages (not to say jargons) and the methodologies employed by the various academic guilds that regard themselves as the proprietors of each culture (anthropologists in Africa, Sanskritists in India, archaeologists in Sumer, and so forth); differences between the approaches of individual French authors, between our several translators, between our experts; and, over the long haul, differences in my own decisions at particular stages of the final supervision, and in the decisions of our copyeditors at the Press. We have tried to minimize the inconsistencies, but we know that many remain.

We left the bibliographies basically in their original form, with the following exceptions: in some cases we have substituted English editions for French editions, or extended the dates of continuing series, and in several cases we have added supplementary bibliographies (clearly designated as such and distinguished from the original French text). But many bibliographies and articles still cite the French editions of texts that have subsequently appeared in English.

We did not follow the usual practice of citing standard English translations of Greek or Latin or Sanskrit works that the French, naturally enough, cited in French. Instead, we translated the French translation of the classical text into English. At first glance this procedure may seem unwise, but we found it necessary because the French version of the classical text (and the subsequent analysis, which depended upon that version) often differed so dramatically from any extant English translation that the sense of the discussion would be totally obscured by the introduction of such a translation. We made an occasional exception, using a standard English translation where there were long quotations not directly analyzed in the French text, or where the available English translation was very close to what the French author had made of the original. (We were also, unfortunately, forced to translate back into English a few citations from English primary and secondary sources that time and other constraints prevented us from obtaining in the original form, and to retranslate several entire French articles that we know were originally written in English, because the English originals were for one reason or another no longer available to us.)

We decided to give Greek and Roman names, wherever possible, in the form used by the *Oxford Classical Dictionary*, which unfortunately is inherently inconsistent. The *OCD* has the advantage of avoiding pedantry by spelling most names in the way that people in English-speaking countries are used to seeing them. This means Latinizing most of the familiar Greek names (not, of course, substituting Roman names: thus we have Heracles, not Herakles, for the Greek god, but Hercules only for the Roman god), but not Latinizing the unfamiliar Greek names, and not Romanizing any of the Greek words when they are not names. All words, including proper names, that are printed in the Greek alphabet in the French edition have here been transliterated. No accents are indicated, and macrons are used not to distinguish long and short *a*, *i*, and *u*, but only on *e* and *o*, to distinguish epsilon from eta and omicron from omega.[5]

We also sought to standardize the transliteration of non-Greek names and terms, such as Gilgameš (vs. Gilgamesh) and Śiva (vs. Shiva), and we used the Pinyin system for most Chinese names.[6] But this general policy was sometimes overruled by the demands of a particular article. We strove for consistency within each article—using English titles for Greek works where the meaning was needed and traditional Latinized titles where it was not, full citations or abbreviations as appropriate, and so forth. Assuming, perhaps snobbishly, that anyone who couldn't read French couldn't read Greek or Latin, I have translated many titles and quotations that my sanguine French colleague, Yves Bonnefoy, had left in their classical splendor. Except for the titles of certain works generally known to English speakers in their original form, and terms that either are familiar to readers or have no English equivalent, I have translated everything, even terms like *polis* (for the most part), and *savoir faire*, and, sometimes, *par excellence*. I fear that this may insult some readers, but I suspect that it will be a welcome (and in any case probably invisible) crutch to *hoi polloi*.

Despite everything, the book remains idiosyncratic, but the idiosyncrasies are in large part a true reflection of the original French edition. In general, we have not *corrected* the original text at all, since, as I noted above, the work is valuable not only for the information and ideas that it contains but for being *what it is*, a moment frozen in time, a fly in amber, an incarnation of the École Pratique as it was in 1981, warts and all. The warts include matters of style and politics, such as sexist and occasionally racist language in the original text. These problems were sometimes ameliorated and sometimes exacerbated by the transition from French to English. Thus, to ameliorate, we often chose to translate *homme* as "human" rather than "man"; but the English "savage" (often more apt than "wild" or "primitive") exacerbates the negative connotations of *sauvage*, which the French often use in a positive sense.

Our respect for the integrity of the French text made us resist the temptation to correct what we regarded as errors in that text. (Of course, we made our own errors, and unfortunately the reader who does not have the French edition will not know, if he or she finds a mistake, which side of the Atlantic it originated on.) We certainly made no attempt to correct such major problems as wrongheaded (in my opinion) opinions, nor to decipher the impenetrable semioticisms in one or two articles or to excise the unreadable lists in others. At the other end of the spectrum, however, we did correct typographic errors and a few outright howlers (such as a reference to the *Iliad* when the *Odyssey* was clearly intended). It was trickier to decide what to do about the middle ground: infelicities of expression, repetitions, and so forth. Of course we tried to clarify unclear thoughts, though we certainly did not always succeed. But for the most part, we respected our French colleagues' right to live with their own sins.

At first we made no attempt to smooth out the English, striving only to make the French thought accessible in English, leaving it awkward when it was awkward. We did try, however, to say well in English what was well said in French. In the end, however, our collective gorge rising again and again in response to such massive proportions of translatorese and the fatal attraction of the *cliché juste*, we did try to relax the translation a bit.

By and large, I opted for fidelity over beauty. This is rather a shame, for the original French text is, on the whole, very beautiful. Not for the first time I take comfort in Claude Lévi-Strauss's famous dictum that, whereas poetry may be lost in translation, "the mythical value of myth remains preserved through the worst translation."[7] I fear that we have lost much of Yves Bonnefoy's poetry; I can only hope that we have found, for the English reader, most of Yves Bonnefoy's mythology.

Wendy Doniger

NOTES

1. YVES BONNEFOY, personal communication, 28 June 1984.
2. Notes on a meeting with Yves Bonnefoy, 6 June 1988.
3. As, for example, by ROBERT TURCAN, in "Mythologies et religions: Notes Critiques, à propos du *Dictionnaire des Mythologies* . . . ," in *Revue de l'Histoire des Religions* 200, no. 2 (April–June 1983): 189–98.
4. ARTHUR ADKINS, personal communication, 2 March 1988.
5. Our attempt to follow, consistently, the above rule resulted in the following apparent inconsistencies. A distinction is made between the treatment of two forms of the same word when it is used both as a name and as a noun: thus we have Eros (the god) and *erōs* (the emotion), Cyclops (plural: Cyclopes) for the individual and *kuklops* for the class of creature. Exceptions to the general Latinization occur in certain familiar spellings particularly with regard to *clk* (Clytemnestra, following the regular policy, but Kronos, following general usage); to *-osl-us* (Pontus, following the rule, but Helios, following general usage); and to certain plurals (Kronides, but Oceanids and Atreidae; Melissae, but Moirai). In general, upsilon is transliterated as *y* in Latinized names, such as Polyphemus, but as *u* in nouns, such as *polumētis*. And so forth.
6. For the Yoruba names, we chose to follow the French edition in using a simplified transliteration, for the system that is technically, and politically, correct is extremely cumbersome and incompatible with the methods used in other parts of the work.
7. CLAUDE LÉVI-STRAUSS, *Structural Anthropology* (New York 1963), 210.

Preface to the French Edition of the Complete Work

I

A few words of introduction, not in justification of the enterprise, but in order to clarify certain of its intentions and various points of method.

One of our primary convictions was of the need to adopt the dictionary format. Encyclopedias, invariably too lengthy to be read in a single sitting, are usually approached through the index, thereby functioning like dictionaries but with certain disadvantages that dictionaries do not have. For one thing, readers of encyclopedias are deprived of those sudden juxtapositions that alphabetical order can effect between two topics that may have something in common but occur in different contexts: chance encounters from which fresh insights can emerge. And for another thing, an encyclopedia, no matter how rationally intended the order of its contents, cannot but reflect the preconceptions of the time when it was written; it thus rapidly becomes dated and, even, from the very moment of its conception, imposes certain constraints on its readers. We have only to think of the treatises of the not very distant past and their way of drawing distinctions between the Mediterranean world and what is loosely referred to as the Orient, as if western Europeans lived at the center of the world! Progress has been made in this respect, but potentially dangerous prejudices are undeniably still at work in our thinking today. "Any classification of religions . . . will always in some way be factitious or one-sided; none is susceptible to proof," wrote Henri-Charles Puech.[1] Only alphabetical order, arbitrary by definition, can eliminate hidden dogmatism or prevent the consolidation of an error as yet unperceived as such.

Furthermore, and as a corollary to its primary task of rational organization, an encyclopedia also tends toward a kind of unity—if not homogeneity—of discourse; and because any work of this kind attempts to say the most in the least possible number of pages, there will be—in order to achieve coherent exposition of the most important material—an attenuation of what, in a monograph, would remain undiminished or would even be enhanced: diversity of viewpoint, the clash of ideas and methods, to say nothing of the irreconcilability of different scholars' feelings, aspirations, and temperaments. Even when there is consensus on some point, we cannot believe that this disparity, the nutrient on which all scholarship thrives, will have lost its seminal value. The advantage of a dictionary, which allows free rein to a greater number of authors, and which facilitates the juxtaposition of both detailed analysis and broad synthesis, is that it can more comfortably, or more immediately, accommodate a living science whose very contradictions and even lapses into confusion serve as a lesson that can inspire, and on which we can reflect. We might say that a dictionary can aspire to a totalization which, because it is still only potential, is less subject to the perils of dogmatic deviation. Within a dictionary's open-ended structure, every aspect of scientific research—classification or comparison, hypothesis or explanation, discovery of a law or conjecture as to its significance—will be allowed to reveal its specificity and find its own level. We may, therefore, regard the dictionary format as the most adequate expression of today's scholarship, which is suspicious of all systems, instinctively realizing the complexity and pluralities inherent in its objects of study as well as the interaction between these objects and its own methods.

There is, in short, a kind of spirit or "genius" in what might simply appear to be the way the subject matter is arranged; and in direct consequence of this conception came the following decision: that in making the choices rendered necessary by the limited space, preference would be given to the process of discovery rather than to what has already been discovered; to new challenges, new departures, and new divergences rather than to the syntheses of the past, even those still found acceptable today. In deciding what to include in the dictionary, our preference has been, in other words, for new problems rather than old (and hence overfamiliar) solutions, even major ones. *Research,* the only endeavor, today, to which we habitually apply the word "pure," has been our true objective. In this book the reader will find what are at this very moment the pivotal points being debated in regard to this or that myth or religious festival, and not a mere enumeration—the comprehensiveness of which would in any case be difficult to establish—of points already settled in the past. And let us remark in passing that, by so doing, we are merely making public, for the sake of a more general reflection, a practice that has already proved itself in certain scientific circles, but only to a privileged few. The introduction to the *Annuaire* of the École des Hautes Études (section V, religions), states that the teaching dispensed by the professors of this institution is a science "in process" and that "those responsible for teaching others will find no better way to exercise their function as the initiating and motivating force behind their students' research than by sharing . . . the results of their own, even if this means admitting to failures." In this dictionary we have not always been quite so radical as these admirable words advise, but we, too, have attempted not to "transmit what is already known, but to demonstrate as concretely as possible how knowledge is acquired, and how it grows."[2]

It should therefore come as no surprise to the reader that some of the assignments normally charged to works on mythology were eliminated from our project at the outset, notably those detailed accounts of demigods, nymphs, demons, genies, and heroes that occupy the forefront of less recent or more conventional studies. Insofar as these figures do not appear prominently among those chosen by contemporary scholars for reevaluation, merely to have listed them and added a few perfunctory remarks about each one—which, as there are thousands of them, is the best we could have done—would have been once again, and once too often, to present only the chaff instead of getting at the grain deep within, to rethrash the oversimplifications of yesteryear with an outward show of scientific objectivity. Apart from a few minor protagonists of Greek myth—retained because of their artistic or literary importance, through centuries of survival or revival or nostalgia for the gods of antiquity—we have chosen to deal, rather, with the innumerable minor characters in the drama of creation and the cosmos within the context of broader-based articles concerned primarily with *structures:* creation, cosmos, sacrifice, the divinity of the waters, divine animals or ancestors, etc.—the structures that modern science has taught us better to discern beneath the apparent disorder of myths. For only through these more active concepts, these more all-encompassing frameworks, can we realize the ultimate meaning of something that has always been only an element in the symbolic totality arising from man's desire to know; only in this way will we be able to perceive the differences, similarities, resonances, and, what is more, the perhaps hidden truth, the quality of mystery, even the power to terrify, that underlies figures who became, in the mirror of classical paintings or in the *Mythologies* of our grandparents, elegant Marsyas or lovable Flora. The reader will, however, be able to find the information that our articles do dispense about many of these tiny sparks from the larger fire, by referring to the index, where many names that he may have regretted not finding more prominently displayed in the columns of the text have been assembled.

We have, on the other hand, been generous in allotting space—and sometimes a great deal of space—to what at first glance might appear to be an excessively specific or technical development on a minor point in a remote religion, or an almost unknown tribe. We have done so because some important aspect of the most recent research in the field is thereby revealed, is therein at work, and the essay is therefore being offered, indirectly, as a concrete example of today's practical methods. In a situation of overwhelming possibility, the guiding principle presiding over the choices we did in fact make was consistently to prefer the illuminating example over the supposedly exhaustive enumeration; except on those occasions when a truly extensive, minutely scrupulous coverage of a field narrow enough to be included in the book in its entirety could also be made to serve as one of our major exemplary cases. This dictionary is in large measure a *network of examples,* each with some bearing on a particular level or category of religious experience or scientific method; if we have included a study of sacrifice in a religion in which sacrifice is especially important, we have deliberately omitted an article on sacrifice for another region of the world in which, by the same token, animals or the presence of the dead have been selected from a mythic narrative in which they are felt to be essential. The advantage of this principle is that it allows us to plumb the depths, which is one way to achieve universality and thus to speak of everything, despite the occasional appearance of superficiality. The reader will note that our articles are seldom very short; allowing for the stylistic terseness characteristic of dictionaries, we strove for an average length that would permit us to publish what are actually brief monographs; I am pleased to note that the present enterprise has served as the occasion for much research, some of it completely new, either in subject matter or in approach. The reader will thus be a witness to the creative process in action.

And if he should be annoyed because he cannot find in our table of contents or even our index some name or subject to which several lines have been devoted in the *Oxford Classical Dictionary* or the *Real-Encyclopädie,* he should also bear in mind the intellectual character of our endeavor, and should listen in the depths of our pages for the stirrings of research in process, that catalyst through which, from the womb of needs as yet unsatisfied, hypotheses as yet unproved, oppositions and even conflicts, are born the research projects, innovations, and ideas that tomorrow will provide the material for new articles in the still open dictionary and, later, for a whole new volume. Any dictionary worthy of the name must affirm, with real fervor, that it will continue thus; that is, that it will turn into a serial appearing twelve times a century, an institution whose past becomes future, a rallying ground that will help keep a discipline alive.

II

What is this discipline, exactly, in our own case? And how did we define or, rather, how were we able to recognize the subjects appropriate to our dictionary?

It is entitled *Dictionary of Mythologies and Religions in Traditional Societies and in the Ancient World*—thus, apparently, introducing two distinct subjects. What really is the subject, and what, in terms of specific content, will the reader find in the book?

Let us state at the outset that what our French publisher wanted was a "Dictionary of Mythologies," explanation enough in itself, because it refers to a specific area and one abundantly rich in problems of great scientific interest today. To quote again from section V of the *Annuaire:* the current tendency for the science of religion to assume a central place in anthropological studies is due to "the increasing importance being accorded to 'myth' for the interpretation and comprehension of the human phenomenon. On this point, the most diametrically opposed schools of contemporary thought are undivided. Religious myths have attained highest priority as objects of study by the most disparate scientific disciplines and schools of philosophy, whether they are regarded as images or projections of a system of communications among men; as manifestations of archetypes of the psyche; or as the special objects of a phenomenology of human consciousness . . ."[3] Certainly we no longer believe, as did the Socrates of Plato's *Phaedrus,* that there is no need to study myth because the important thing is to know ourselves—rather the reverse. Mythology appears to us ever more clearly as one of the great aspects of our relationship with ourselves, as well as being a conception of the world and the terrestrial environment that has been undoubtedly useful; we therefore ought to draw up a balance sheet—however provisional—of the discoveries made by the present century in the various chapters of man's reflection on myth. That there is still not complete agreement among scholars as to how myth should be defined matters little; that the problem of definition may even be premature also matters little, precisely because the plurality inherent in the enterprise of a dictionary as defined above actually makes the juxtaposition of contradictory propositions seem natural and allows them to be compared with one another. Neither in this introduction nor in the body of the book, where the actual choices have been made, will the reader find a definition of myth decreed as law, as if the die were cast. Our only methodological limitation, one that in our view safeguards the rights both of the study of myths as archetypes and of the methods appropriate to myths approached as systems of communication, is to apprehend myth on the level of collective representations, where, as one of our contributors writes, myth is "the form in which the essential truths of a particular society are articulated and communicated." Despite what may be the apparent freedom of the narrative, our task must be to seek within it a body of collective knowledge in contradistinction to the ephemeral creations of the individual consciousness, no matter how impressive these may be in great novels or poems. Apart from a few fleeting insights, included solely that we might better understand and recognize the limitations we have set for ourselves, there are in our dictionary none of the "personal myths" that come from art and the free play of imagination and that perhaps belong to a dialectic entirely different from those that unite human beings under the sign of their communications in the real world, of their confrontation with real necessities, and that are accompanied and made possible by rituals and beliefs. We have similarly omitted from the book what are sometimes referred to as "modern myths," representations that are circulated by popular literature or the media, myths that do indeed touch many spirits but that differ from the great majority of mythic narratives in that they are not so much the expressions of a society as they are the expressions of a yearning for a different society, or of the fear of forces that the structures of our societies have not integrated. In our view, the place for the study of these is, rather, in a dictionary devoted to the basic categories of religious experience as such, in particular, transcendence, eschatology, and salvation.

In short, the myths in this book have been culled only from the mouths of societies or groups. This does not indicate a refusal to study the connection between myth and the deep structures of the human psyche; it merely delimits, in order to avoid any confusion, an object of thought that could then be connected with others, or analyzed in other ways than has been done here. The one form of individual creativity we did consider appropriate to include, at least through a few major examples, is the reflection of those who, although they may have relied on highly subjective spiritual or philosophical preconceptions, nevertheless attempted—as did Plato, for example, or Cicero—to understand myths as society produces them or assumes them. Objective as contemporary scholarship aspires to be, there are a few preconceptions similar to theirs still at work today, perhaps; so who can tell if in these ancient interpretations of myth there is not some lesson that could be of use to future investigations either of myth as the expression of social relationships, or of mythological figures as spearheads cutting through local custom and belief toward more universal spiritual forms?

But assuming nothing about the essence or function of myth except its relationship to a society does not necessarily mean that erecting the boundaries for a dictionary of mythologies presents no further problems. For no myth exists in isolation; none is a narrative drawing only on itself for its terms and its conventions. We still had to decide what, precisely, from a given society or culture, and from among all its conscious or unconscious communal acts, ought to be included in the book so that none of the discussion or information would be elliptical or too allusive. In other words, what complementary studies must be integrated into a dictionary of mythologies to ensure that the overall statement that it makes will not be hobbled, giving only an impoverished and therefore dangerous idea of the field?

Here is where we can justify the ambiguous precision of our title, in which the word "religion" appears next to the word "mythology." Proceeding empirically, at no great philosophical risk, we may hold as evident that in every human society mythical narrative and religious practice are closely related; and thus, that everywhere, or almost everywhere, it is the historian or analyst of religions who also studies mythologies. As a corollary to this, surely we can affirm that it makes little sense to classify and analyze myths without reference to those aspects of religion that have determined them and will certainly clarify them. And, further, if we do so, in order to make room for this additional material we should also be prepared to sacrifice some of the data about myths properly speaking: what is lost in comprehensiveness will largely be regained in the comprehension of the place and the meaning of myth. This book deals with religions as well as with myths; or, rather, it stands at the intersection where the two roads meet—always with the proviso, however, that each of our contributors has been left free to decide for himself how to apportion the two concerns in practice, taking account of the vastly different forms that the same scientific goal can assume in areas as diverse as Indonesia, for example—that huge complex of societies, languages, and religious influences, where current research is still at the stage of amassing data that must subsequently be put in order—or Vedic India, or Greece, which we know plenty about.

We do not mean that all things religious are therefore in a relationship of complicity, or even of continuity, with the production of myths and the sometimes evanescent, sometimes enduring, figures of myth; there is a dividing point at which one must take sides; the consequences are bound to be great and it is important to justify them. It may come as a surprise to the reader that the religions of Sumeria, Egypt, and Persia are included in the book, while Judaism, Christianity, and Islam are not; that the divinities—if that is the right word—of Buddhism are included, but that no reference is made to the spiritual essence of this major religious experience as it occurs in China, Japan, or elsewhere. It may also cause surprise that, more specifically, the studies of the religions which have been included do not mention what has often made them forms of transcendental experience, mysteries, quests for the Absolute, arenas of soteriological ambition for the yearnings or the nostalgia of individuals or of sects. This is because, during such phases in a religion's development, the religious principle—in its essence, perhaps, a contradictory one—turns against the mythic narrative by which it is at other times nourished. When this happens, the spirit is no longer content to rest at the level of the gods but aspires to a transcendence that it senses as amounting to something more than the representations of it provided by myth; it rejects myth or creates in place of it a gnostic system to uncover its secret meaning. And the effort thus made by the religious spirit to reach the divine within mythical manifestations that it regards as paradoxical or imperfect consequently determines that this aspect of the religious experience has no place in a dictionary of myth and of the rituals and beliefs associated with myth. We have not taken into consideration here the aspect of religion that fights the gods, the mediating powers, that holds them to be paganisms; this aspect in itself is so complex and so rich that it would take another book at least the size of this one to do it justice. The reader will therefore not find among the religions introduced in this volume those whose essential vocation is—let us try to be succinct—the direct experience of transcendent divinity; nor those which tend to have a universal message, addressed to all people everywhere, no matter what their culture or where they live; not even those religions whose moorings in the history of a specific society or a specific people have enabled them, through a founder, a theophany, a prophet, or their reform of a previous paganism, to attach to themselves legends or histories closely resembling myths. In practice, we have excluded from this book the great religions of a Word, a Promise; and especially the mystery religions, Judaism, Christianity, Islam, Gnosticism, Taoism, and the legacies of the Buddha. The one exception to this rule consists of certain incursions justified by the "pagan" nature of some of their minor aspects, such as the cult of the saints in our own churches or the gods and demons of Buddhism.

Let us hope that these religions will one day form the subject of another dictionary, one dealing, as it were, with divinity, as opposed to gods; with universal theologies and experiences of unity, in contrast to the rivulets of myths, rituals, and holy places. Upon further reflection, we ought also to reserve for another volume certain problems of boundaries, such as the way in which past and present evangelistic missionaries have regarded the myths of societies they set out to convert, not without repercussions on Christian doctrine; or—to come closer to home—the way in which at certain moments Christianity itself has played the role of a myth: a myth of truth, or progress, even at the price of relinquishing a good part of its aptitude for genuine communion. As one of our authors writes, myths are never recognized for what they are except when they belong to others; it is therefore our duty to apply to our own behavior as people of the Western world the same methods that our science reserved only yesterday for so-called primitive societies. But a great religious experience must first be described before we can go beyond it and begin the task of distinguishing its ambiguities.

And yet certain religions which might be said to represent a quest for the Absolute as obvious as any other—those of India, for instance, and perhaps also of Egypt—have been included; but this is because in their search for unity they involve myth in a very intimate, almost ultimate, manner, if only in an initial stage and as one more form of illusion. We have not used the word "polytheism" to designate the religions whose myths are dealt with in this dictionary, despite its apparent reference to the differentiation, the polymorphy, of the divine. For although there are resolutely polytheistic religions, such as those of ancient Greece or Rome, in other cultures and other lands there are religions based on more complex intuitions, in which the multiplicity of representations at once clear-cut and diffuse exist in a sort of breathing of the spirit that seems to refute our own exaggerated distinctions between entity and nonentity, between the one and the many. Might we not, perhaps, call these religions "poetic" or "figurative," since an artist knows well the imaginary nature of the figures that, nevertheless, alone can express, in the artist's vision, the essential reality? In any case, such religions belong in this dictionary by virtue of their massive and continuing recourse to the logic of myth.

III

And now for a few words of clarification concerning the geographical and historical area covered by our enterprise. Or rather—since this dictionary by definition covers all terrestrial space and every era of terrestrial history—concerning the relative proportions we decided upon for the various parts of our inquiry.

First, one remark that may be useful: if we have designated and defined myth in the context of an inquiry that by rights extends to the farthermost regions of the globe, this in no way means that we wish to affirm, by emphasizing the most powerful of these mythologies—whose links with the languages in which they are expressed are obviously close—that there is any uniformity on earth in this mode of consciousness. As has frequently been pointed out, the word *myth* itself comes from the Greek, and the concept that we project into this word, although adjusted to accommodate overlappings and overflowings, also has a logic, a coherence, and still bears the mark of its origin; there is therefore no foundation for believing that what some other ethnic group has experienced under the forms that we call myth corresponds to the same laws with which we are familiar. Perhaps there are societies that do not tend to integrate their myths into some meaningful whole but leave them as fragments that flare up and then are extinguished without, in passing, casting any light on what we ourselves are tempted to look for or to find everywhere: the outline, if only a rough one, of the vault of a universe. If in these cases we can often see nothing but an incoherent babble opening the way to higher forms of consciousness, might it not also be possible for us to sense in them an entirely different mode of consciousness, one in which the discontinuous, the partial, the forever incomplete would themselves be perceived as the very being of human meaning? Could we not see them as an ontology of the superficiality of our inscription on the world—an ontology that the planet's recent history would tend rather to confirm than to deny—somewhere beyond the ruin of our own aspirations? The representation of the divine can obey laws as diverse as those of artistic representation, which extends from the controlled irrationality of a Poussin, who was, in fact, an heir to the Greeks, to the fugitive traces on the gray wall of some works of art of our time.

This should remind us if need be that a dictionary like ours, if it is to fulfill its task of describing the variety of mythologies, must supplement its descriptions of the religious data with additional material on the cultures, mental structures, languages, and functionings of the social collectivity. To the extent that myth is one of the forms of asking questions about mystery, it represents a relationship between the human consciousness—in its cognitive functions, its praxis, its historical memory, or its exploration of the outside environment—and the culture as a whole. Recent research has clearly demonstrated that myth's manifest complexity makes it one of the most useful tools for an archaeology of the imagination, of philosophy, or of science. It was therefore essential to the present undertaking that myth appear not only as an act of speech about the divine, but as a text in which the divine is infinitely embedded in signifiers; and it is the task of the ethnologist, the sociologist, and the linguist to decipher and analyze these signifiers. A background in the social sciences is much more than an imperative for this book; it is its natural and inevitable locus, and one from which many of our contributors, either explicitly or implicitly, have strayed but little. But this consideration even further restricts the space available for the purely mythological material within the finite number of pages at our disposal. When the whole world demands to be heard, the time for each part to speak must be allotted sparingly.

How to mitigate this disadvantage? It would have been tempting to reverse ethnocentric custom and to eliminate at a stroke every trace of exclusiveness, every hierarchy; to relinquish forever the specious charm of the old Greco-Roman monopoly, and its belated acceptance of Egypt and the Near East; and thus to have offered to each separate part of the world an equal number of pages. But rational and fair as this was in principle, we knew that in practice it could never be other than a utopian ideal, at least for the foreseeable future. The first and major reason is that the analysis of myths that is most familiar to us is the work of scholars who write or read in French, English, Italian, German, and more rarely in other languages, still mostly Western ones. With all of its virtues and all of its limitations, this linguistic given constitutes an intangible fact that we must first examine before our own consciousness can be raised, before it can be made to apprehend from within how to circumscribe its own difference so as to be more receptive to categories other than its own. If the mythology of Africa or of ancient Japan is an object of study for our language, the myths and divinities of Greece and Rome, not to mention those of the Celtic and Germanic worlds, survive through hidden symbolisms, overt conditionings, artistic or philosophical references, even—and above all—through concepts, in the most intimate being of mythology, that operate on the very level on which our language apprehends and analyzes the object. And these components, all too familiar but never sufficiently explored, never sufficiently distanced, therefore demand an almost excessive attention if we in the West are ever to achieve a valid understanding of the other civilizations of the world.

This invaluable opportunity to psychoanalyze our methods, we felt, should not be sacrificed by unduly abbreviating that portion of the book dealing with our own origins; so, an important place, even though in a most attenuated manner, should once again be given to the cults and mythologies of more or less classical antiquity and to their later effects on the religious, artistic, and intellectual life of Europe, of which we, of course, are a product. And because for other parts of the world we have also had to take into account the very variable degree of progress in the field, so that it would have been unfortunate to weigh each contribution equally, we have resigned ourselves without compunction to being biased in our allocation of space, believing that to define where we stand does not—or at least so we may hope—imply a valorization of what lies nearest to us or any dogmatism. We have reserved almost half the work for the Mediterranean world, the Near and Far East, and for the historical relations between their mythologies and the European consciousness, as demonstrated by such phenomena as the survival of the classical gods or the fascination with Egypt after the Italian Renaissance. The other half of the book is for the rest of the world, here again, however, taking into account the actual importance that one region or another may have today assumed in a field that naturally is not static and that will have fresh insights to contribute to future supplements to the present volume. It is unfortunately only too true that the vast societies of Africa and Asia have in our columns once again been given less space than the tiny population of Greece. But a particular problem concerning a particular, vanishing society in Vietnam has, on the other hand, merited more of our attention than many perhaps expected aspects of our classical world. We can only hope that the reader will not find our distribution of the materials too misinformed.

IV

Here now is some practical information to help the reader find his way through the labyrinth of the dictionary. [The rearrangement of articles in the English-language edition obviates the problems discussed in this paragraph, which we have therefore abridged.] Certain religions or cultures to which, regretfully, we could only allot a few pages are represented by a single article that can easily be found under the name of the country or geographical area, thus, *Albania* or *Crete*. Generally speaking, however, our contributors had more space at their disposal and were able to address various questions that they considered not only basic but exemplary, in articles spread throughout the book. A list of the names of all the authors, in alphabetical order of their initials, allows the reader to go from the initials at the end of each article to the complete name of the author.

This same list also indicates the academic affiliations of the hundred or so scholars who were willing to contribute to the dictionary; it will be noted that most of them teach at the Collège de France, the École Pratique des Hautes Études, or in French universities. Why this preference for the French, in a century when intellectual exchange is so abundant, between some countries at least, and in which we see so many publications—of, for example, papers delivered at colloquia—that mix together in their abstracts the names of professors from Tübingen or Yale with those from Tokyo or Nairobi? It may at once be pointed out that contributions to this type of publication are usually printed in the language in which the original paper was delivered, obviously requiring of the reader that he be made aware of the linguistic and conceptual apparatus presiding at their conception. French scholars know that, in dealing with ideas originally conceived in German, or in English, they must undertake the task of recognizing schools of thought, cultural or religious conditionings or customs, the influence exerted by the words themselves—since every language has its own semantic nodes, as complex as they are uncompromising; and they also know this task may take a long time, demanding further reading or travel abroad. They further understand that it is only in connection with these vast extratextual areas that they will be able to identify and appreciate the meaning of the text itself. It is of course always possible to translate, and to read a translation. But we must not forget that it takes more than a mere rendering of sentences into a new language for these backgrounds to be revealed and for the underlying meaning to be made clear.

This is precisely the risk that prevails when an enterprise such as ours is opened to authors who think and write in different languages—which would have to be many in number for all the major trends in international scholarship to be represented as they deserve. We believed that scholars who thus had to express themselves through translation would find their work deprived of a part of its significance at the very moment when we would seem to be listening to it. Moreover, the converse is also true: problems can best be differentiated, and even antagonistic methods best be revealed, through the widest possible deployment of the unity and diversity—the cluster of potentialities simultaneously contiguous and concurrent—that is embodied in a single language at a precise moment in its history. We therefore deemed it preferable to call primarily on French scholars and, since those responding to our call number among the most eminent and the most representative, thus to offer to the reader, as an adjunct to our panorama of mythologies and religions, a matching panorama of the contemporary French schools of history, sociology, and religious studies, all of which are of the first rank and deserve to be known as such. To sum up: while a few of the original contributions to the *Dictionary of Mythologies* were translated from languages other than French, for the most part the material can be viewed as a whole, produced by a single society—an ever evolving one, to be sure, and one not inattentive to other cultures—at a crucial juncture in the development of a scientific discipline that is still young. This dictionary is French, the expression of a group of scholars all working within reach of one another, as sensitive to their areas of disagreement as they are gratified by their points of convergence. It is our hope that, if it should be translated, the translator will find it vast enough to allow for the emergence, here and there within its mass, of the unstated concept of implied bias not readily discernible in briefer texts; and that these underlying elements will be revealed in a translation offering the reader, and serving as the basis for future debate, an intellectual effort seen whole: not just the visible tip of the iceberg, but its hidden, submerged bulk as well.

V

Such were the guiding principles determining how our work should be organized. It is only proper to add, however, that despite the great trust which it was the present editor's pleasure to encounter in his authors—who sometimes produced material for him equivalent in volume to a small book—the above principles are primarily the expression of his own concept of what scholarship is, and what it is that scholars are attempting to do. Only he can be held directly responsible for them.

I have just used the word "trust." Going back to the source from which all trust springs, however, I should rather have said "generosity," because this word, glossing "trust," better characterizes both the reception that I as editor was given by specialists in their fields who could so easily have refused to credit any but one of their own, and the quality of their contributions, which to me seems patent. I see this now that the enterprise has been achieved. Most of these scholars, all of them with many tasks competing for their time, have been with our project from the beginning, when, responding to my appeal, they consented to represent their respective disciplines in a dictionary that was still just an idea—an idea to which they themselves had to give meaning. Most of them also agreed to oversee the illustration of their articles, thereby enriching the text with a variety of often rare, sometimes previously unpublished, documents directly relevant to the text. Whenever minor vicissitudes befell the project thereafter, decisions were always made in a spirit of mutual understanding and cooperation. I am extremely grateful to all the authors of this book, and to those eminent individuals who were kind enough to advise me when initial decisions had to be made. Indeed, my only great regret is that I am unable to express this gratitude today to two men who are no longer with us, two men who possessed consummate wisdom, foresight, and discipline, and whose example will stand as an enduring one. Historian Eugène Vinaver's masterly command of Arthurian Romance, a borderline topic standing between myth and literature, is well known. So, too, is Pierre Clastres's intense involvement with the Indian civilizations of South America; the articles by him that we are publishing here were the last pages he ever wrote.

I now have the pleasure of thanking Henri Flammarion and Charles-Henri Flammarion, who wanted this dictionary to exist, and who showed such keen interest in the questions with which it deals. My thanks also to those who transformed typescripts, photographs, and graphics into the reality of the present book. First on the list of these is Francis Bouvet, a man attached to the project from the moment of its inception and now, regrettably, only a memory, but a cherished one. My thanks to Adam Biro, who took over the same functions and brought to them the same understanding and the same invaluable support. Thanks to Claire Lagarde, who from start to finish, and with intuitive devotion and unfailing good humor, sent out requests, acknowledged receipts, sent out requests again, read, filed, saved, and expedited contracts, typescripts, documents, and proofs, even at times when her other duties were pressing. And, finally, thanks to Pierre Deligny, who, simply because he was asked, since we had no legitimate claim to his assistance, unhesitatingly accepted in his own name as well as in that of Denise Deligny and Danielle Bornazzini the crushing responsibility for correcting three successive sets of proofs, with their intricate web of unfamiliar names, cross-references, rearrangements, accent marks, and emendations, and who brought the job to a successful conclusion, with Mesdames Deligny and Bornazzini specifically undertaking responsibility for compiling the index. Yes, to these other authors of the *Dictionary of Mythologies*, many thanks, in the name of the authors of the text.

Yves Bonnefoy/l.g.

NOTES

1. Preface, *Histoire des religions*, vol. 1 (Paris 1970) (Encyclopédie de la Pléiade).
2. *Annuaire* of the École des Hautes Études, Paris, vol. 83, no. 1 (1975–76), p. 4.
3. Ibid., p. 3.

Contributors

A.L.-G André Leroi-Gourhan, professor, Collège de France.

A.P. Arshi Pipa, professor, University of Minnesota.

C.Ma. Charles Malamoud, directeur d'études, École pratique des hautes études, Ve section (sciences religieuses).

C.P. Christian Pelras, chargé de recherche, Centre national de la recherche scientifique.

D.L. Denys Lombard, directeur d'études, École des hautes études en sciences sociales.

F.M. François Mace, professor, Institut national des langues et civilisations orientales.

F.-R.P. François-René Picon, maître de conférences, University of Paris V.

G.C. Georges Charachidzé, professor, University of Paris III and École pratique des hautes études, IVe section (sciences historiques et philologiques).

H.O.R. Hartmut O. Rotermund, directeur d'études, École pratique des hautes études, Ve section (sciences religieuses); director, Centre d'études sur les religions et traditions populaires du Japon.

J.D. Jacques Dournes, chargé de recherche, Centre national de la recherche scientifique.

J.-L.M. Jean-Luc Moreau, professor, Institut national des langues et civilisations orientales.

J.-P.R. Jean-Paul Roux, directeur de recherche, Centre national de la recherche scientifique; professor, École du Louvre.

J.Sc. Jacques Scheuer, member, Centre d'études indiennes en sciences sociales, Paris.

J.V. Jean Varenne, professor, University of Lyon.

L.Be. Laurence Berthier, chargée de conférences, École pratique des hautes études, Ve section (sciences religieuses).

L.D. Laurence Delaby, documentalist, Centre national de la recherche scientifique.

L.O. Li Ogg, professor, University of Paris VII, section des études coréennes.

L.O.M. Tu Chuong Le Oc Mach, tutor in Vietnamese, Institut national des langues et civilisations orientales.

M.Bi. Madeleine Biardeau, directeur d'études, École pratique des hautes études, Ve section (sciences religieuses).

M.D. Marcel Detienne, directeur d'études, École pratique des hautes études, Ve section (sciences religieuses).

M.El. Mircea Eliade, professor in the Divinity School, University of Chicago.

M.K. Maxime Kaltenmark, directeur d'études, École pratique des hautes études, Ve section (sciences religieuses).

M.-L.R. Marie-Louise Reiniche, maître assistant, École des hautes études en sciences sociales.

P.K. Per Kvaerne, professor, University of Oslo.

R.A.S. Rolf A. Stein, professeur honoraire, Collège de France.

S.T. Solange Thierry, directeur d'études, École pratique des hautes études, Ve section (sciences religieuses).

PART

1

Introduction: The Interpretation of Mythology

Toward a Definition of Myth

From Plato and Fontenelle to Schelling and Bultmann, philosophers and theologians have proposed numerous definitions of myth. But all the definitions have one thing in common: they are based on Greek mythology. For a historian of religions, this choice is not the happiest one. It is true that myth, in Greece, inspired epic poetry and theater as well as the plastic arts; yet it was only in Greek culture that myth was subjected to prolonged and penetrating analysis, from which it emerged radically "demythologized." If the word "myth," in all European languages, denotes "fiction," it is because the Greeks declared it to be so twenty-five centuries ago.

An even more serious mistake in the eyes of the historian of religions is that the mythology that Homer, Hesiod, and the tragic poets tell us about is the result of a selective process and represents an interpretation of an archaic subject which has at times become unintelligible. Our best chance of understanding the structure of mythical thought is to study cultures in which myth is a "living thing," constituting the very support of religious life—cultures in which myth, far from portraying *fiction,* expresses the *supreme truth,* since it speaks only of realities.

This is how anthropologists have proceeded for more than half a century, concentrating on "primitive" societies. Reacting, however, against an improper comparative analysis, most authors have neglected to complement their anthropological research with a rigorous study of other mythologies, notably those of the ancient Near East, primarily Mesopotamia and Egypt; those of the Indo-Europeans, especially the grandiose and exuberant mythology of ancient and medieval India; and finally that of the Turco-Mongols, the Tibetans, and the Hinduized or Buddhist peoples of Southeast Asia. In limiting research to primitive mythologies, one risks giving the impression that there is a gap between archaic thought and that of peoples considered "of history." This gap doesn't exist; indeed, by restricting investigation to primitive societies, one is deprived of the means of measuring the role of myth in complex religions, such as those of the ancient Near East or of India. For example, it is impossible to understand the religion and, more generally, the style of Mesopotamian culture if one ignores the cosmogonic myths and the myths of origin that are preserved in the *Enūma Eliš* or in the epic of Gilgameš. Indeed, at the beginning of each new year, the fabulous events recounted in the *Enūma Eliš* were ritually reenacted; at each new year the world had to be re-created—and this requirement reveals to us a profound dimension of Mesopotamian thought. The myth of the origin of man explains, at least in part, the characteristic vision and pessimism of Mesopotamian culture: Marduk drew man out of the earth, that is, out of the flesh of the primordial monster Tiamat, and out of the blood of the archdemon Kingu. And the text specifies that man was created by Marduk in order to work the land and to ensure the sustenance of the gods. The epic of Gilgameš presents an equally pessimistic vision by explaining why man does not (and must not) have access to immortality.

Historians of religions therefore prefer to work on *all categories* of mythological creations, both those of the "primitives" and those of historic peoples. Nor do the divergences that result from too narrow a documentation constitute the only obstacle to the dialogue between historians of religions and their colleagues in other disciplines. It is the approach itself that separates them from, for example, anthropologists and psychologists. Historians of religions are too conscious of the axiological differences in their documents to put them all on the same level. Attentive to nuances and distinctions, they cannot be unaware that there are important myths and myths of lesser importance, myths that dominate and characterize a religion, and secondary, repetitive, or parasitic myths. The *Enūma Eliš,* for example, could not be placed on the same level as the mythology of the female demon Lamashtu; the Polynesian cosmogonic myth has a completely different weight from the myth of the origin of a plant, since it precedes it and serves as its model. Such differences in value do not necessarily command the attention of the anthropologist or the psychologist. Thus, a sociological study of the nineteenth-century French novel or a psychology of the literary imagination can make equal use of Balzac and Eugène Sue, Stendhal and Jules Sandeau. But for the historian of the French novel or for the literary critic, such mixing is unthinkable, for it destroys their own hermeneutic principles.

In the next generation or two, perhaps earlier, when we have historians of religions born of Australian or Melanesian tribal societies, I have no doubt that they, among other critics, will reproach Western scholars for their indifference to the scales of *indigenous* values. Let us imagine a history of Greek culture in which Homer, the tragic poets, and Plato were passed over in silence, while the *Interpretation of Dreams* by Artemidorus of Ephesus and the novel by Heliodorus of Emesa were laboriously analyzed under the pretext that they better clarified the specific characteristics of the Greek spirit, or helped us understand its destiny. To return to our subject, I do not believe it possible to understand the structure and function of mythic thought in a society in which myth still serves as a foundation without taking into account both the *body of mythology* of that culture and the *scale of values* that it implies or declares.

Indeed, wherever we have access to a still living tradition that is neither strongly acculturated nor in danger of disappearing, one thing immediately strikes us: not only does mythology constitute a kind of "sacred history" of the tribe in question, not only does it explain the totality of reality and justify its contradictions, but it also reveals a hierarchy in the sequence of the fabulous events it relates. Every myth tells how something came into existence—the world, man, an animal species, a social institution, etc. Because the creation of the world precedes all others, cosmogony enjoys particular prestige. As I have tried to show elsewhere (see, for example, *The Myth of the Eternal Return*, New York, 1954; *Aspects du mythe*, Paris 1963), the cosmogonic myth serves as a model for all myths of origin. The creation of animals, plants, or man presupposes the existence of a world.

Of course, the myth of the origin of the world is not always cosmogonic in the technical application of the term, like Indian and Polynesian myths, or the myth told in the *Enūma Eliš*. In a large part of Australia, for example, the cosmogonic myth in a strict sense is unknown. But there is still a central myth which tells of the beginnings of the world, of what happened before the world became as it is today. Thus one always finds a *primordial history*, and this history has a *beginning*—the cosmogonic myth properly so called, or a myth that introduces the first, larval, or germinal state of the world. This beginning is always implicit in the series of myths that tell of fabulous events that took place after the creation or the appearance of the world, myths of the origin of plants, animals, and man, or of death, marriage, and the family. Together these myths of origin form a coherent history, for they reveal how the world has been transformed, how man became what he is today—mortal, sexual, and obliged to work to sustain himself. They also reveal what the Supernatural Beings, the enculturating Heroes, the mythical Ancestors, did and how and why they moved away from the Earth, or disappeared. All the mythology that is accessible to us in a sufficient state of conservation contains not only a beginning but also an end, bounded by the final manifestations of the Supernatural Beings, the Heroes or the Ancestors.

So this primordial sacred history, formed by the body of significant myths, is fundamental, for it explains and justifies at the same time the existence of the world, of man, and of society. This is why myth is considered both a *true story*—because it tells how real things have come to be—and the exemplary model of and justification for the activities of man. One understands what one is—mortal and sexual—and one assumes this condition because myths tell how death and sexuality made their appearance in the world. One engages in a certain type of hunting or agriculture because myths tell how the enculturating Heroes revealed these techniques to one's ancestors.

When the ethnologist Strehlow asked the Australian Arunta why they celebrated certain ceremonies, they invariably replied: "Because the [mythical] Ancestors prescribed it." The Kai of New Guinea refused to modify their way of living and working and explained themselves thus: "This is how the Nemu [the mythical Ancestors] did it, and we do it the same way." Questioned about the reason for a certain ritual detail, a Navajo shaman replied: "Because the Sacred People did it this way the first time." We find exactly the same justification in the prayer that accompanies an ancient Tibetan ritual: "As has been passed down since the beginning of the creation of the earth, thus we must sacrifice. . . . As our ancestors did in ancient times, so we do today" (cf. *Aspects du mythe*, pp 16ff.). This is also the justification invoked by Hindu ritualists: "We must do what the gods did in the beginning" (*Śatapatha Brāhmaṇa*, 8.2.1.4). "Thus did the gods; thus do men" (*Taittirīya Brāhmaṇa*, 1.5.9.4). In sum, the governing function of myth is to reveal exemplary models for all rites and all meaningful human activities: no less for food production and marriage than for work, education, art, or wisdom.

In societies where myth is still living, the natives carefully distinguish myths—"true stories"—from fables or tales, which they call "false stories." This is why myths cannot be told indiscriminately; they are not told in front of women or children, that is, before the uninitiated. Whereas "false stories" may be told anytime and anywhere, myths must be told only *during a span of sacred time* (generally during autumn or winter, and only at night).

The distinction made between "true stories" and "false stories" is significant. For all that is told in myths *concerns the listeners directly*, whereas tales and fables refer to events which, even when they have caused changes in the world (for example, anatomical or physiological peculiarities in certain animals), have not modified the human condition as such. Indeed, myths relate not only the origin of the world and that of animals, plants, and humans, but also all the primordial events that have resulted in humans becoming what they are today, i.e., mortal, sexual, and societal beings, obliged to work for a living, and working according to certain rules. To recall only one example: humans are mortal because something happened in the beginning; if this event hadn't occurred, humans wouldn't be mortal, they could have existed indefinitely, like rocks, or could have changed their skin periodically, like snakes, and consequently would have been able to renew their life, that is, begin it again. But the myth of the origin of death tells what happened *in illo tempore*, and in recounting this incident it explains *why* humans are mortal.

In archaic societies, the knowledge of myths has an existential function. Not only because myths offer people an explanation of the world and of their own way of existing in the world, but above all because in remembering myths, in reenacting them, humans are able to repeat what the Gods, the Heroes, or the Ancestors did *ab origine*. To know myths is to learn not only how things have come into existence, but also where to find them and how to make them reappear when they disappear. One manages to capture certain beasts because one knows the secret of their creation. One is able to hold a red-hot iron in one's hand, or to pick up venomous snakes, provided one knows the origin of fire and of snakes. In Timor, when a rice field is growing, someone goes to the field at night and recites the myth of the origin of rice. This ritual recitation forces the rice to grow beautiful, vigorous, and dense, just as it was when it *appeared for the first time*. It is *magically forced to return to its origins*, to repeat its exemplary creation. Knowing the myth of origin is often not enough; it must be recited; knowledge of it is proclaimed, it is *shown*. By reciting myths, one reintegrates the fabulous time of origins, becomes in a certain way "contemporary" with the events that are evoked, shares in the presence of the Gods or Heroes.

In general one may say:

—that myth, such as it is lived by archaic societies, constitutes the story of the deeds of Supernatural Beings;

—that the story is considered absolutely *true* (because it refers to realities) and *sacred* (because it is the work of Supernatural Beings);

—that myth always concerns a "creation"; it tells how something has come into existence, or how a way of behaving, an institution, a way of working, were established; this is why myths constitute paradigms for every meaningful human act;

—that in knowing the myth one knows the "origin" of things and is thus able to master things and manipulate them at will; this is not an "external," "abstract" knowledge, but a knowledge that one "lives" ritually, either by reciting the myth ceremonially, or by carrying out the ritual for which it serves as justification;

—that in one way or another one "lives" the myth, gripped by the sacred, exalting power of the events one is rememorializing and reactualizing.

To "live" myths thus implies a truly "religious" experience, for it is distinct from the ordinary experience of daily life. This experience is "religious" because it is a reenactment of fabulous, exalting, meaningful events; one is present once again at the creative works of the Supernatural Beings. Mythical events are not commemorated; they are repeated, reiterated. The characters in myth are brought forth and made present; one becomes their contemporary. One no longer lives in chronological time but in primordial Time, the Time when the event *took place for the first time*. This is why we can speak of the "strong time" of myth: it is the prodigious, "sacred" Time, when something *new*, something *strong*, and something *meaningful* was made fully manifest. To relive that time, to reintegrate it as often as possible, to be present once again at the spectacle of divine works, to rediscover the Supernatural Beings and relearn their lesson of creation—such is the desire that can be read implicitly in all ritual repetitions of myths. In sum, myths reveal that the world, man, and life have a supernatural origin and history, and that this history is meaningful, precious, and exemplary.

M.El./t.l.f.

The Interpretation of Myths: Nineteenth- and Twentieth-Century Theories

If we fail to trace its outline clearly at the outset, the subject we discuss here risks either being merely a collection of rather curious interpretations accepted in their own periods, or else getting lost in the underbrush of the most varied hermeneutic enterprises. There are two indispensable points of reference. We must, first of all, distinguish interpretation from exegesis. We will define the latter as a culture's incessant but immediate commentary on its own symbolism and practices, its most familiar stories. There is no living tradition without the accompanying murmur of its exegesis of itself. Interpretation, on the other hand, begins when there is some distance and perspective on the discourse of a tradition based on memory. Its starting point is probably, as Todorov suggests, the inadequacy of the immediate meaning, but there is also the discrepancy between one text and another, from which the strangeness of the first can become evident. For, in the work of interpretation, it is the prefix *inter* of the Latin word *interpretatio* that designates the space of deployment of hermeneutic activity. In the Western tradition, from the Greeks to ourselves by way of the Romans and the Renaissance, the first hermeneutics appears in the gap opened up by what a new form of thought decided to call *muthos,* thus inaugurating a new form of otherness which makes one text the mythologist of the next. But this interpretive path required one more marker to give it its definitive orientation. From Xenophanes and Theagenes in the sixth century B.C. to Philo and Augustine, hermeneutics took as its privileged object the body of histories that a society entrusts to its memory, what today we call a mythology. But the play of allegory often based itself on nothing more than a name, a word, or a fragment of a text, on which it could graft the bourgeoning symbolism whose discourse became all the more triumphant when, with the affirmation of Christian doctrine, the certainty of possessing the truth unleashed the audacities of a hermeneutics like that of the *City of God.* It is only with Spinoza—as Todorov has recently stated—that a theory of interpretation takes shape on which our modern readings still largely depend. It was he who formulated rules whose mere application was enough to uncover the truth of a meaning, inside the text and within the bounds of a work. But before it could become philology in the nineteenth century, this theory of interpretation, which Spinoza applied to Scripture, still needed the presence of a cultural object with a clearly defined shape—mythology—understood as a discourse that is other, with its own distinctive traits.

Within these limits and for both of these reasons, an archaeology of theories of the interpretation of myth can restrict itself to the nineteenth and twentieth centuries. Travel accounts since Jean de Léry have traced an axis of otherness whose two poles are the savage and the civilized, between which the Greeks serve as mediator. It is the exemplary values of Greece that are evoked, in good Renaissance style, and Lafitau (1724)—while orienting it toward a deciphering of the present by the past—was merely to systematize the path already beaten, throughout the seventeenth century, by Yves d'Évreaux, Du Tertre, Lescarbot, and Brébeuf. One of the best understood differences—the importance of which has been shown by Michel de Certeau—is that between nakedness and clothing. The detour via the Greeks allows the naked body, which a purely and simply Christian education leads one to reject as belonging to paganism and noncivilization, to be made an object of pleasure, and it may also allow the surprise of a return to oneself. Savages are so handsome that they can only be virtuous. And men's stature, the proportion of their limbs, their nakedness in the midst of the forests, in the beauty of a nature not yet offended by civilization, remind most of these voyagers of the lineaments of Greek statues and the natural privilege which distinguished, in their eyes, the heroes of Homer and Plutarch. As a Jesuit father wrote in 1694, "We see in savages the beautiful remains of a human nature that is completely corrupted in civilized peoples." Nothing could be more like an American savage than a Greek of Homeric times. But this splendid animal, whose development has known no obstacles, whose body is not deformed by labor, evokes the citizen of Sparta or the contemporary of the Trojan war only on the moral and physical level. There is no meeting on an intellectual level; all that the travelers of the seventeenth century expected from savages was that they bear witness to a natural religion of which they were the last trustees. Never, it seems, is the mythology of Homer or Plutarch compared with the stories of these first peoples of nature. One reason is probably that classical mythology, thoroughly moralized, had by then been integrated into a culture dominated by belles lettres. Myths would remain masked as long as they were not assigned their own space.

The nineteenth century saw the discovery of language as the object of a comparative grammar and a renewed philology. In this linguistic space, which is to the highest degree that of the sounds of language, mythical discourse suddenly appeared. It did so in the modality of scandal, which would feed the passionate discussions and theories of two rival schools of the second half of the nineteenth century: the school of comparative mythology, and the anthropological school. As the Sanskritist and comparative grammarian Max Müller wrote, "The Greeks attribute to their gods things that would make the most savage of the Redskins shudder." Comparison defines the nature of the scandal. It is as if it were suddenly discovered that the mythology of Homer and Plutarch was full of adultery, incest, murder, cruelty, and even cannibalism. The violence of these stories, which seemed to reveal themselves brutally as "savage and absurd," appeared all the more unbearable since they were being read at the same time as the stories of distant lands, lands that colonial ethnography was both inventorying and beginning to exploit. The scandal was not that the people of nature told savage stories, but rather that the Greeks could have spoken this same savage language. For in the nineteenth century all that was Greek was privileged. The romantics and then Hegel affirmed this enthusiastically. It was in Greece, they said, that Man began to be himself; it was Greek thought that opened up the path leading from natural consciousness to philosophical consciousness; the Greek people were believed to have been the first to have attained "the uttermost limits of civilization," in the words of a contemporary of Max Müller, the anthropologist Andrew Lang. From the moment that the mythology of Greece could resemble the language spoken by "a mind struck temporarily insane" (Lang), neither our reason nor our thought is definitively safe from an unforeseeable return of the irrational element which, the voice of the savages teaches us, is buried at the very heart of those stories that once seemed so familiar.

The mythology that is subjected to the trial of interpretation is, primarily, nothing but an absurd, crazy form of speech which must be gotten rid of as quickly as possible by assigning it an origin or finding an explanation to justify its oddness. On this point, Max Müller and Andrew Lang are in full agreement. Their divergence appears from the time when the presence of those insane statements at the heart of language and in mythic discourse has to be justified. For Max Müller, a contemporary of the discovery of comparative grammar, the only possible explanation was a linguistic one. And his *Science of Language* argues that a stratigraphy of human speech reveals a mythopoeic phase in the history of language. Since 1816, when Franz Bopp published the first comparative grammar, language had been understood as a set of sounds independent of the letters that allow them to be transcribed; a system of sonorities, animated with its own life, endowed with continual activity and traversed by the dynamism of *inflection*. In the history of language, after what is called a thematic stage, in which terms expressing the most necessary ideas are forged, and what is called a dialectal stage, in which grammar definitively receives its specific traits, an age begins that Max Müller designates as mythopoeic, in which myths make their appearance in very specific circumstances.

At the beginning of its history, humanity possessed the faculty of uttering words directly expressing part of the substance of objects perceived by the senses. In other words, things awakened sounds in humans which became roots and engendered phonetic types. Humans "resonated" at the world, and thus had the privilege of "giving articulated expression to the conceptions of reason." As soon as the individual lost the privilege of emitting sounds at the spectacle of the world, a strange disease fell upon language: words like "night, day, morning, evening" produced strange illusions to which the human mind immediately fell victim. For as long as humans remain sensitive to the meanings of words, these first sonic beings are conceived of as powers, endowed with will, and marked by sexual traits, though the physical character of the natural phenomena designated by the words is not forgotten. As soon as the double meaning becomes confused, the names of the forces of nature break free: they become proper names, and from a spontaneous expression like "the sky rains," a myth abruptly emerges based on "Zeus makes the rain fall." There is an excess of meaning at the source of mythopoeic creation, an uncontrolled surplus of signification, which tricks the speaker, prey to the illusions of a language within which the play of these "substantive verbs" produces, in a burgeoning of images, the strange and often scandalous discourse of myths.

To this theory, which based the metaphors of language on natural phenomena and declared that a good mythologist should possess a "deep feeling for nature," without which linguistic knowledge is futile, the anthropological school immediately objected that comparative grammarians seemed to have forgotten somewhere along the way that "the Redskins, the Australians, and the lower races of South America" continued even today, in the forests and savannas, to tell the same savage tales, which can hardly be explained as the unwonted result of a few misunderstood phrases. The road the anthropological school would follow led in the opposite direction from that of the grammarians. It was no longer the past or origins that were to explain the present, but rather the mythology of contemporary savages that could account for the "savage" stories of the past. And Lang attempted to show that what shocks us in the mythology of civilized peoples is the residue of a state of thought once prevailing in all humanity. In contemporary primitives we can see the power of this state of thought as well as its coherence. At the same time, anthropologists began to investigate these gross products of the primitive human mind and to discover that things which to our eyes seem monstrous and irrational were accepted as ordinary events in everyday life. They soon came to the conclusion that whatever seems irrational in civilized mythologies (the Greco-Roman world, or India) forms part of an order of things that is accepted and considered rational by contemporary savages.

This position led to two orientations, which anthropology attempted to explore in parallel. For the first, which leads from Frazer to Lévy-Bruhl, mythology remains the discourse of madness or mental deficiency. In 1909, before he published the thousands of pages of *The Golden Bough*, the prolegomena to a history of the tragic errors of a humanity led astray by magic, James George Frazer wrote a small book (*Psyche's Task*) in which he asked how folly could turn to wisdom, how a false opinion could lead to "good conduct." And at the center of his reflection Frazer places a paradox:

primitive superstitions were the foundation of what now seems desirable to us in society: order, property, family, respect for life. Prejudice and superstition in fact served to strengthen respect for authority and thus contributed to the rule of order, the condition of all social progress. Frazer had given hundreds of examples in his already published works, and in this slim volume he is no less enthusiastic an admirer of the conduct of the son-in-law in a primitive society who avoids speaking to or being alone with his mother-in-law, surrounding her with taboos, as if these people, not yet capable of elaborating a thought-out set of laws, still had a sense that an intimate conversation between these two people could easily degenerate into something worse, and that the best way to prevent this from happening was to raise a solid wall of etiquette between them. Without knowing it, and almost reluctantly, primitive thought, even in its most obstinate errors, prepared the way for the triumphs of morality and civilization.

For Lucien Lévy-Bruhl, who published *Les fonctions mentales dans les sociétés inférieures* in 1910, primitive societies differed from ours in their mental organization: their thought, constituted differently from our own, is mystical in nature; it is ruled by a "law of participation" that makes it indifferent to the logic of noncontradiction on which our own system of thought is based. Lévy-Bruhl finds the characteristics of primitive thought, which surrenders itself to affectivity and to what he calls "mysticism," among both schizophrenics and children, who also think in an affective way and establish commonalities between things and beings whose mutual distinctiveness is obvious to the intelligence of a civilized adult. Lévy-Bruhl would increasingly identify this "prelogical" stage with "mystic experience," and Van der Leeuw, who extended his analysis, would try to show that primitive thought survives in every human mind, that it is a component of all forms of reason, an indispensable element whose symbolic load and image-making power help to balance the conceptual development of our thought. In the *Notebooks,* which were published after his death, Lévy-Bruhl found it necessary to revise his position on the mental and intellectual gap between ourselves and "savages." But his work, in profound accord with that of Frazer, seems to us today to be part of a fencing in of savage thought (*la pensée savage*), confining it in the prelogical and thus avoiding any contamination which might threaten our own reason.

At the very moment when these armchair anthropologists were interning primitive thought, others were setting out on voyages of discovery to Africa and Oceania, and so were discovering, alive and functioning, the rationality of a form of thought that operates through and in myth—a rationality different from our own, but no less impressive for that. The great living mythologies of the Pacific or the Sudan fulfill an indispensable function in these simpler cultures. Revealing a distinctive reality, guaranteeing the effectiveness of worship, myths codify the beliefs, found the moral rules, and determine every practice of daily life. When Marcel Griaule brought back the Dogon cosmology, with its astonishing architectures of symbolic correspondences, there could no longer be any doubt that mythology was indeed the keystone of archaic societies, the indispensable horizon of all cultural phenomena and of the whole pattern in which society is organized. Myths not only constitute the spiritual armature of human lives; they are bearers of a real "theoretical metaphysics." For the first time, then, myths came to be studied in their entirety, a study in which every detail, even the most insignificant, found its place in a holistic interpretation, an interpretation so rich, so exhaustive, that the ethnographer, once introduced into this polysymbolic world, is in serious danger of "having nothing more to say about Dogon society than the Dogon say themselves" (Pierre Smith, 1973).

In 1903, before Frazer and Lévy-Bruhl had begun their investigations, Marcel Mauss, following the French sociological school, set forth in a few pages a program of which Georges Dumézil would one day prove to be the master craftsman. Three points seem essential. 1. To determine the mechanism of the formation of myths means to seek some of the laws of the mental activity of man in society. 2. Mythology can be reduced to a small number of myths, and each type is made up of a certain number of combinations. 3. The apparent illogicality of a mythic narrative is itself the sign of its distinctive logic. For Mauss, Durkheim's nephew and collaborator, myths are social institutions, that is, ways of acting and thinking which individuals find already established and, as it were, ready to hand; they form a fully organized pattern of ideas and behaviors which imposes itself more or less forcefully on the individuals inscribed in a society. Myth is above all *obligatory* in nature; it does not exist unless there is a sort of necessity to reach agreement on the themes that are its raw material and on the way these themes are patterned. But the constraint comes solely from the group itself, which tells the myth because it finds its own total expression in it.

A symbol through which society thinks itself, mythology informs experience, orders ritual and the economy, and gives archaic societies their categories and classificatory frameworks. For the Durkheimian school, myths—which, incidentally, are hardly mentioned in the *Année sociologique*—are of the same order as language, "a property of which the proprietor is unconscious"; and, inseparable from this, just as a language continues to bear centuries-old vocabulary and syntax, mythology implies a certain traditional way of perceiving, analyzing, coordinating. The analogy is even more precise: like language, mythology is tradition itself, it is the symbolic system that permits communication beyond words; it is the historical unconscious of the society. In this perspective, the importance of myths derives from the common nature that links them to the most archaic element of language, in that domain where sociology hoped to discover some of the fundamental laws of the mind's activity in society.

It was Mauss once again who, against Lévy-Bruhl, in 1923 defended the thesis that considerable parts of our own mentality are still identical to those of a large number of societies called primitive. But it was first Marcel Granet, then Louis Gernet, who developed a sociological analysis of religion with its legends and myths. For the Sinologist Granet, attempting to proceed from language to the fundamental frames of thought, the mythology of the Chinese provided material in which the emotions characteristic of ancient festivals were recorded. Behind the legendary and mythic tales were ritual dances and dramas from which imaginative schemas emerged that imposed themselves on the mind and on action. Farther along, social contexts and great technical feats that crystallize the productions of the imaginary order could be glimpsed. For the Hellenist Gernet, in a break with the established positivist history that was content to note the gratuitous play of the imaginary, myths reveal a social unconscious. Just as semantic analysis gives access to the great social fact of language, the study of legends and of certain mythic themes allows one to go back to transparent or explicit social practices. The mythic image thus offers the most convenient means of access, not to a timeless memory, but to archaic behaviors and social actions and—going far beyond the social data that have, as Gernet puts it, "a direct relation to myth"—to fundamental phenomena of mental life, those that determine the most general forms of thought.

The specificity of the Greeks pointed Gernet in yet another direction. Myths, in their fragments, shining splinters, offer not only the prehistoric behaviors that were their reason for being; they are at the same time part of a global way of thinking, whose categories, classifications, preconceptual models exert a major influence on positive thought and its various advances. Thus Gernet, starting from a series of traditions about types of precious objects, attempts to show how money and the economy emerge from a set of behaviors linked to the mythical notion of value—a notion that involves domains which, though separate nowadays, used to overlap or merge together: the religious, the political, the aesthetic, the juridical. Mythology is thus part of a global religious system that is symbolic in character, with a web of multicorrespondences from which law, philosophy, history, and political thought will emerge and become progressively distinct. But since Gernet thought of myths as raw material for the thought that arose with and in the Greek city, in the space of the polis, he examined the mythic element only in terms of what was beyond it, in a break with its own nature and its functioning. By failing to separate mythology either from language or from the institutional system, the sociological model of myth culminated in the paradox of sometimes losing sight of the very object that seemed finally to have been recognized and legitimated.

More serious, certainly, was the misunderstanding between Freudian psychoanalysis and the anthropological problematic, which seems to give access to a form of the unconscious inscribed in myth. In his self-analysis, as recounted in his letter to Fliess of October 15, 1897, Freud discovers that his libido awoke between the ages of two and two and a half, and turned toward *matrem* (confessors' Latin for the name of the mother). Freud refers this desire for the mother to a Greek tragedy, *Oedipus the King*, a reference both cultural and paradigmatic. The first thing that Sophocles' Oedipus gives Freud is a better understanding of himself—but the choice of a Greek paradigm already announces the universal character of Freud's discovery of the heart of the matter. The early hypothesis, that little Sigmund is *like Oedipus*, shifts toward the Freudian thesis that Oedipus marrying his mother *must have been the same as ourselves*. While Freud's enterprise, by showing that there is no essential difference between the mentally ill person and the healthy person, seems to invert the separation marked by Lévy-Bruhl, it does assume, from the beginning, a segregation of Greek myths from those of other peoples. For Freud, *Oedipus the King* still excites us and exerts a profound effect on us because every man, always and everywhere, feels love for his mother and jealousy of his father; and from the day Freud first adopted this view, the Greek myth was invested with a new privilege: that of translating better than any other "an instinctual attraction which everyone recognizes because everyone has experienced it."

It was to Greek mythology that Freud would continue to turn in his quest for successive proofs of the reality of the unconscious, comparing the discourse of dreams and fantasies with the legends of Olympus, which his successors, stubbornly but not without fidelity, were to proclaim as the language in which we can most easily read the drives and works of desire. In asking for an admission of guilt within the Oedipal configuration, psychoanalysis indeed marks a return to myth and the religious; but in seeing both of these as merely the visible tip of the iceberg of the "Unconscious," forgetting that analytical space is that of free association, it has condemned mythology to being nothing but the symbolic and obsessive repetition of a few unconscious representations centered on sexuality.

It was in the direction opened up by Maussian sociology that theoretical work on myth became involved in the first structural analyses. Resuming the project of comparative mythology that had been wrecked by the excesses of Max Müller and his disciples, Georges Dumézil, thanks to a decisive discovery, founded the comparative study of Indo-European religions by ceasing to rely on purely linguistic concordances between divine names and adopting instead the more solid base of articulated sets of concepts. A factual discovery—in Rome, the three *flamines majores* corresponding to the Jupiter-Mars-Quirinus triad; in Iran, the tripartition of social classes—opened the way to structural analysis of the Indo-European world: the tripartite schema was an essential structure in the thought of the Indo-Europeans. Every organized society is based on the collaboration of three distinct but complementary functions: sovereignty, martial power, fecundity. Parallel to this, the gods form a functionally weighted triad, within which the Sovereign, the Warrior, and the group of divinities who preside over fecundity mutually define one another. Since there was never any question of reproducing a definitely Indo-European myth or ritual, Dumézil had to use precise and systematic correspondences to trace a ground plan of the chosen myth or ritual, indicating its articulations, its intentions, its logical significations, and then, on the basis of this schematic figure, projected into prehistory, to try to characterize the divergent evolutions which have led to analogous and diverse results in different places: Indian myth, Roman myth, Scandinavian myth, or Vedic ritual in relation to the Latin rite. For Dumézil, religions are whole patterns in which concepts, images, and actions are articulated and whose interconnections make a sort of net in which, by rights, the entire material of human experience should find its distribution.

By focusing his examination on the concept and on organized patterns, Dumézil radically parts company with a history of religions that thought in terms of genesis and affectivity. For historians like H. J. Rose and H. Wagenvoort, all religion is rooted in the sense of the "numinous" that the human race experiences spontaneously when confronting the phenomena of nature: there is no divine power who was not first one of these *numina*, in which magico-religious force, diffused in the natural world, is concentrated. For Dumézil, by contrast, the observer never reaches isolated facts, and religion is not a form of thought soaked in emotionality. It is in their mutual relations that the various elements can be apprehended, and there always remains, virtually or in action, a representation of the world or of human action that functions on different levels, under a particular type on each level. The religious system of a human group is expressed "first of all in a more or less explicit conceptual structure, which is always present, if sometimes almost unconscious, providing the field of forces upon which everything else comes to be arranged and oriented; then in myths, which represent and dramatize these fundamental intellectual relationships; and then, in turn, in rituals, which actualize, mobilize, and use the same relations." Independently of these gains in the Indo-European domain, Dumézil's method affirmed the virtues of the concept that can equally inform a myth or underlie a ritual. From this point on, "the surest definition of a god is differential, classificatory," and the object of analysis becomes the articulations, the balances, the types of oppositions that the god represents. Against the historians of genesis, Dumézil affirms the primacy of structure: the essential problem is not to determine the precise origin of the various elements that have been fitted together but to accept the *fact* of the structure. The important thing, Dumézil declares, is to bring the structure itself to light, with its signification. It would seem to follow that structures are there, that it is enough to be attentive to them, to avoid forcing them, and to show a little skill in disengaging them. Thus it is not necessary to construct structures as one would elaborate a model of the set of properties accounting for a group of objects. In a sense, structuralism is still in the age of hunting and gathering. Myths, for Dumézil, are the privileged theater that makes visible fundamental conceptual relations. But in the spirit of Mauss's sociology, to which he owes a curiosity for "total social facts" that causes him to explore simultaneously all the works produced by the human mind, myths cannot be deciphered until they have been put back into the totality of the religious, social, and philosophical life of the peoples who have practiced them. The mythology posited by the earlier comparativism of Frazerian inspiration as separate from language, as a more or less autonomous object, endowed with permanence and chosen to locate the common themes elaborated by the Indo-Europeans, was referred back to the language of which it formed a part and, through this language, to the ideology that grounds it and runs through it.

The structural analysis developed by Lévi-Strauss was established under the same kind of conditions as the comparative and philological analysis of the nineteenth century. The gratuitous and insane character of mythic discourse was again the point of departure. For Max Müller this was shocking; for Lévi-Strauss it was a challenge. He took up the challenge after he had shown that kinship relations, in appearance contingent and incoherent, can be reduced to a small number of significant propositions. If mythology is the domain in which the mind seems to have the most freedom to abandon itself to its own creative spontaneity, then, says Lévi-Strauss, to prove that, on the contrary, in mythology the mind is fixed and determined in all of its operations is to prove that it must be so everywhere. The structural analysis of myths thus finds its place in a wider project, which aims at an inventory of mental constraints and postulates a structural analogy between various orders of social facts and language.

This whole approach to myth applies to a new domain the methods of analysis and principles of division developed for linguistic materials in the methods theorized by the Prague school and more particularly by Roman Jakobson. But while myth is assimilated to a language from the outset, it is not identical either to the words of a text or to the sentence of communicative discourse. Mythology is a use of language in the second degree; it is not only a narrative with an ordinary linguistic meaning: myth is in language and at the same time beyond natural language. In the first stage of an ongoing investigation ("The Structural Study of Myth," 1955), Lévi-Strauss tries to define the constituent units of myth in relation to those of structural linguistics. Mythemes are both in the sentence and beyond it. In this perspective, the constituent unit is a very short sentence, which summarizes the essential part of a sequence and denotes a relation: "a predicate assigned to a subject." But this sentence is not part of the explicit narrative; it is already on the order of interpretation, the product of an analytical technique. These sentence relations, then, are distributed on two axes: one horizontal, following the thread of the narrative, the other vertical, in columns, grouping together relations belonging to the same "bundle." It is on the level of these bundles of relations that the real mythemes are located. At the same time, structural analysis poses two principles as essential to its practice: there is no authentic version of a myth in relation to others that are false; correlatively, every myth must be defined by the whole set of its versions. There thus takes shape the project of ordering all the known variants of a myth in a series forming a group of permutations.

The next stage of his investigation ("The Story of Asdiwal," 1958) led Lévi-Strauss to propose that myth makes full use of discourse, but at the same time situates its own meaningful oppositions at a higher degree of complexity than that required by natural language. In other words, myth is a metalanguage and, more precisely, a linked sequence of concepts. Attention will be turned, therefore, to registering the various levels on which myth can be distributed. The cutting up of the mythic narrative which in the first phase (1955) seemed to be entrusted to the whim or ingenuity of the model-builder, is now subject to testing—indispensable to all formal analysis—in terms of the *referent:* "the ethnographic context," which the later transformational orientation of the *Mythologiques* would cease to pursue. The surveying of pertinent oppositions in a mythic sequence thus finds the fundamental guarantee of its legitimacy in previous knowledge of an organized semantic context, without which the myth is in principle incomprehensible. Ritual practices, religious beliefs, kinship structures: the whole of social life and social thought is called upon to define the logical relations functioning within a myth, and at the same time to establish the different types of liaison between two or more myths. In the four-volume *Mythologiques* (1964–1971), the progressive analysis continues to show relations between myths, the social life of those who tell them, and the geographical and technological infrastructure, but it does not restrict itself to this back-and-forth between levels of signification and an ethnographic context that reveals the philosophy of a society. The meaning of a myth is no longer inscribed in its structures' reference to a social infrastructure; rather, the position the myth occupies in relation to other myths within a transformation group is henceforth the vector of an analysis that reveals the autonomy of a mythic thought in which every narrative refers back in the first instance to another, picking up and organizing its elements in a different way. Just as each term, itself without intrinsic signification, has no meaning other than a positional one in the context in which it appears to us, in the same way each myth acquires a signifying function through the combinations in which it is called upon both to figure and to be transformed. It is these transformations which, in the last analysis, define the nature of mythic thought.

It has been objected that this practice of mythological analysis makes a choice for syntax against semantics; and, likewise, that while it has been possible to apply the practice successfully to the mythologies of so-called totemic societies, since these are rich in classificatory structures, it excludes Semitic, Hellenic, and Indo-European societies from its field of interest, societies whose mythological thought is marked by renewals of meaning and by a semantic richness that exceeds the powers of structural analysis. One can reply, on the one hand, that for this type of analysis, which gets at the meanings of myths by multiplying the formal operations that allow us to uncover the logical framework of several narratives, the semantics of myths is necessarily enriched through the inventorying of the syntax. On the other hand, the practice of structural analysis is hardly alien to our familiar mythologies, such as that of the Greeks; one may, indeed, be surprised at the remarkable similarities between the way the Greeks themselves thought their mythology and the method used by ethnologists in approaching myths told by nonliterate peoples. More pertinent objections have come from anthropologists such as Dan Sperber, who denounces the semiological illusion of structuralism as well as the distance between the linguistic models invoked and an intuitive practice whose specific procedures, unlimited in number and nature, offer knowledge of the intellectual operations from which the stories we call "myths" are woven.

M.D./j.l.

BIBLIOGRAPHY

The titles listed are in the order and within the limits of the problems formulated by this article.

T. TODOROV, *Symbolisme et interprétation* (Paris 1978). M. DE CERTEAU, "Ethno-graphie: L'oralité, ou l'espace de l'autre," in Léry, *L'écriture de l'histoire* (Paris 1975), 215–48. G. CHINARD, *L'Amérique et le rêve exotique dans la littérature française du XVIIe au XVIIIe siècle* (Paris 1934). M. DETIENNE, "Mito e Linguaggio: Da Max Müller a Claude Lévi-Strauss," in *Il Mito: Guida storica e critica* (2d ed., Bari and Rome 1976), 3–21 and 229–31, with bibliography. H. PINARD DE LA BOULLAYE, *L'étude comparée des religions*, 1 and 2 (Paris 1925). J. DE VRIES, *Forschungsgeschichte der Mythologie*, Orbis Academicus, 1, 7 (Munich 1961). K. KÉRÉNYI, *Die Eröffnung des Zugangs zum Mythos* (Darmstadt 1967). G. VAN DER LEEUW, *L'homme primitif et la religion*, Étude anthropologique (Paris 1940). P. SMITH, "L'analyse des mythes," *Diogène* 82 (1973): 91–108. M. MAUSS, *Œuvres*, V. Karady, ed., 3 vols. (Paris 1968–69). L. GERNET, *Anthropologie de la Grèce antique* (Paris 1968). S. C. HUMPHREYS, "The Work of Louis Gernet," *History and Theory* 10, 2 (1971). J. STAROBINSKI, "Hamlet et Freud," preface to French trans. by E. Jones, *Hamlet et Œdipe* (Paris 1967), IX–XL. S. VIDERMAN, *La construction de l'espace analytique* (Paris 1970). S. FREUD, "Zur Gewinnung des Feuers," in *Gesammelte Werke* (London 1932–39), also in English. G. DELEUZE and F. GUATTARI, *L'anti-Œdipe* (Paris 1972), "Psychanalyse et familiarisme: La sainte famille," 60–162. H. FUGIER, "Quarante ans de recherches dans l'idéologie indo-européenne: La méthode de Georges Dumézil," *Revue d'histoire et de philosophie religieuse* 45 (1965): 358–74. M. MESLIN, *Pour une science des religions* (Paris 1973), "Psychanalyse et religion," 113–38. P. SMITH and D. SPERBER, "Mythologiques de Georges Dumézil," *Annales E.S.C.*, 1971, 559–86. J.-P. VERNANT, "Raisons du mythe," in *Mythe et société en Grèce ancienne* (Paris 1974), 195–250. P. RICŒUR, s.v. "Mythe (3. L'interprétation philosophique)," in *Encyclopædia Universalis* (Paris 1968), 11:530–37. CL. LÉVI-STRAUSS, *Structural Anthropology*, 2 vols. (New York 1963, 1976), originals in French; *Mythologiques*, 4 vols. (Paris 1964–71), = *Introduction to a Science of Mythology*, 4 vols., entitled *The Raw and the Cooked* (New York 1969), *From Honey to Ashes* (London 1973), *The Origin of Table Manners* (New York 1978), and *The Naked Man* (New York 1981).

Myth and Writing: The Mythographers

The word *mytho-logy* is but one instance of many in which the proximity of myth and writing inevitably results in a kind of violence, its victim an original word, sacred in nature and condemned to fixity by a profane order. Beyond the words which by their very texture bear witness to this phenomenon (such as *mythography*), Greek privilege has held fast. When strange and unforgettable stories, which sounded very independent and yet bore obvious resemblances to the mythology of antiquity, were brought to us from all continents, early anthropologists turned instinctively to Greece, where a few centuries earlier great minds from Xenophanes to Aristotle had faced the problem of limiting the dominion of myths and had resolved it within their own intellectual activity by drawing a boundary at which mythical thought fades away before the rationality of scientists and philosophers. The split between the land of myth and the kingdom of *logos* served as a precedent for the decision made by Tylor and his disciples to impose a historical limit on the reign of mythology over the human mind. This opposition between two forms of thought and two stages of human intelligence, the latter canceling the former, took the form of a sharp contrast between reason, which used all the resources of the written, and a mythological activity tuned to the fantasy of an incessant babbling.

Henceforth, never the twain shall meet. For those practicing historians who tend to favor written traces, oral discourse has become so totally inaudible that it is quite illegible whenever it manifests itself as writing—a contrived writing, which masks the incoherence of traditions sustained through memory by imposing a factitious order of mythographical classifications. For others, the Greeks so thoroughly ensured the triumph of reason and *logos* that they ruined their former system of thought for good, allowing only frail remains to survive as witnesses of a lost state to which only two possible roads of access still remain: one is the discovery, by an ancient traveler in a forgotten village, of a tale saved from the contamination of writing thanks to a few natives unaware of the progress of culture; the other is the less hazardous road of historical and geographical investigation through which one gains access to a long-deferred vision of a landscape that authenticates the narrative or the myths of which it is the guarantor, the recovered witness.

Within this framework, the truth of the myth is enclosed in a speechlike nature, which writing more or less obliterates, at times by shackling the freedom of a self-expressive memory with the constraints of an interpretation subject to foreign rules; and at other times, more often than not, by reducing the myth's own speech to silence in order to speak on its behalf and to condemn it to an absolute otherness. In an attempt to rectify this division, structural analysis introduced a summary separation between cold and warm societies, the former deprived of a temporal dimension, the latter open to history and to the continual renewals of meaning that writing facilitates. The border thus drawn appeared all the more definite as it seemed to reiterate the distinction between oral and written literature, a distinction reinforced, if not justified, by the decision made by this type of analysis to look for the essential of the "myth" not in the narration but in the story transmitted by memory, a story whose narrative form was left to the discretion and talent of each narrator.

Yet another issue arises, for which the Greek model inspires a formulation that suggests the progressive emergence of writing in a traditional society. Since the time E. A. Havelock first published his studies, the Homeric epic, which Milman Parry had recognized as belonging to oral practice, can no longer be considered an enclave of a living tradition that made room for a culture of the written. The introduction of an alphabetical writing technique caused no immediate changes, nor did it produce any profound upheaval. Greece experienced not a revolution of writing but, rather, a slow movement with uneven advances depending on the areas of activity; by the turn of the fourth century, writing prevailed mentally and socially. Until the end of the fifth century, Greek culture had been essentially of the oral type. It entrusted to its memory all traditional information and knowledge, as do all societies unacquainted with written archives. And it is here that we must revise the notion of *mythology*, with which the Greeks encumbered us as a consequence of their entanglement with *logos*. For the unified concept "myth," which nowhere seems to be defined as a discrete literary genre, must fade away in favor of a set of intellectual operations fundamental to the memorizing of narratives that together make up a tradition. Claude Lévi-Strauss suggests the term *mythism* for the process by which a story, initially personal and entrusted to the oral tradition, becomes adopted by the collective mode, which will distinguish between the crystal clear parts of the narrative—that is, the levels that are structured and stable because they rest on common foundations—and the conjectural parts—details or episodes amplified or neglected at each telling, before being doomed to oblivion and falling outside the bounds of memory. Every traditional society develops, with varying success, a widely shared creative memory, which is neither the memory of specialists nor that of technicians. The narratives we agree to call myths are the products of an intellectual activity that invents what is memorable.

When writing appears, it neither banishes traditional memory to a state of decay nor sustains an oral practice in imminent danger of becoming extinct. Writing occurs at different levels and in different orders, but always at the encounter between an act of remembering and the works that memory creates. Writing was to introduce a new memory, word-for-word memory, which comes with the book and with education through the study of written texts. Competing ever so slowly with the former kind of memory, mechanical memory alone is capable of engendering the idea, familiar to us, of the *correct* version, a version which must be copied or learned exactly, word for word. In Greece between the sixth and fifth centuries, the first historians, those whom the Greeks call "logographers," selected writing as the instrument of a new kind of memory that would become an integral part of thought and political action. This new way of remembering was constructed on the boundary between a type of oral tradition with its remembrances, spoken narratives, and stories circulating by word of mouth, and, on the other side, the dominant obsession of the new investigators, who respected as knowledge only what had been seen, and who would ultimately condemn, without appeal, those who accepted traditions of the past that were transmitted without precise terminology or rigorous proof. This was the battleground, the wide open space of writing, for the confrontation between variants that became different versions of the same myth, usually examined from within the confines of a city in quest of self-image or political identity.

Elsewhere, other routes were taken that linked writing to the production of myths whose successive variations were inseparable from the hermeneutic activity of scribes and interpreters devoted to textual exegesis. From the moment the traditional narratives of the Bible, the Book of the Hebraic world, were committed to writing, they were swept away by the inner workings of a system of writing which, though initially consonantal, in its hollows called for a vocalic complement to bear its meaning, since one cannot read a consonantal text unless one understands it, that is, unless one attributes to it a meaning set apart from other possible meanings. In the continuity of interpretation thus opened up, the hermeneutics that was focused on the mythical accounts of Israel claimed a privileged place, which made it more sensitive to the permanence of fundamental themes endlessly revived and reevaluated, but also forced it to be the infinite exegesis, forever interned within its own symbolic wealth.

M.D./g.h.

BIBLIOGRAPHY

R. FINNEGAN, *Oral Poetry: Its Nature, Significance and Social Context* (Cambridge 1977). J. GOODY and J. WATT, "The Consequences of Literacy," *Comparative Studies in Society and History*, 1963, 304–45. J. GOODY, "Mémoire et apprentissage dans les sociétés avec et sans écriture: La transmission du Bagre," *L'homme*, 1977, 29–52. E. A. HAVELOCK, *Preface to Plato* (Cambridge, MA, 1963). R. KOENIG, "L'activité herméneutique des scribes dans la transmission du texte de l'Ancien Testament," *Revue de l'Histoire des Religions*, 1962, 141–74. CL. LÉVI-STRAUSS, *Mythologiques* 4 (Paris 1971): 560 (translated as *Introduction to a Science of Mythology*, New York 1969–). L. SEBAG, *L'invention du monde chez les Indiens Pueblos* (Paris 1971), 472–85. J. VANSINA, *De la tradition orale: Essai de méthode historique*, Musée royal de l'Afrique centrale (Tervuren 1961).

Some mythographic texts of ancient Greece: APOLLODORUS, *The Library*, J. G. Frazer, ed. (London 1921). DIODORUS OF SICILY, *The Library*, vol. 4, C. H. Oldfather, ed. (London 1935). ANTONINUS LIBERALIS, *Metamorphoses*. HYGINUS, *Astronomica*, B. Bunte, ed. (Leipzig 1875). HYGINUS, *Fabulae*, H. I. Rose, ed. (Leiden 1933). *Mythographi graeci*, 5 vols., R. Wagner, Martini, A. Olivier, and N. Festo, eds., Bibl. Script. graec. Teubneriana (Leipzig 1896–1926). *Mythographi Vaticani*, G. H. Bode, ed., vols. 1–2 (1834; reprinted Olms 1968). ACUSILAUS OF ARGOS, PHERECYDES OF ATHENS, and HELLANIKOS OF LESBOS, in *Fragmente der griechischen Historiker*, F. Jacoby, ed., I: *Genealogie und Mythographie* (Leiden 1922; 2d ed., 1957).

PREHISTORIC RELIGION

To speak of "prehistoric religion" without specifying time and place is tantamount to assimilating under modern thought facts and contexts that came to light at very different times and places, tantamount to creating a kind of average image that can only be validated by the judgment of our own way of thinking projected onto some arbitrarily chosen facts. Prehistoric religion no longer occasions a debate in which either pro- or anticlerical convictions are at stake. The science of prehistory has been enriched by much new data and major changes in methodological approaches. Rather than arguing about whether the atheist brute evolved first into the magician and then into the priest, scientists have given priority to inquiries that bring out the deep connections among play, aesthetics, social behavior, economic realities, and practices that rest on a metaphysical framework. The proofs that can be proliferated from a so-called religious approach are largely derived from the realm of the unprecedented, from the presence of peculiar facts found in a context where they are least expected, such as the discovery, on a Mousterian site inhabited by Neanderthal man, of fossil shells, which he collected and brought back to his dwelling place, or the discovery that he gathered red ocher or buried his dead. These diverse elements do not fit in with our vision of Neanderthal man. Yet how could there not be a striking contrast between this primal brute with his bulky brow ridges and the subtle quality of a religiosity polished by two millennia of Christianity and all of ancient philosophy? Neanderthal man was not, in the final analysis, as short of gray matter as was long believed, though the metaphysical level of his cultic activities was certainly very different from ours (at least, as we imagine ours to be).

What matters is the existence of practices within a psychological realm not directly tied to techniques of acquisition, manufacture, or consumption, even if these practices do flow back into material life. Man acquired religious behavior when he developed the whole system of symbolic thought, which cannot be separated from language and gesture as it works out a network of symbols that present a counterimage of the outside world. That Neanderthals had already developed this network of symbols is beyond doubt, but whether one can go on to distinguish evidence of a primordial religion or an extremely diffuse symbolic complex remains questionable. The gathering of magical shells and ocher supports the view that the pump had been primed for the simultaneous evolution of the fields of art, play, and religion, three fields which to this day cannot be separated.

Homo sapiens picked up where Neanderthal man left off, with regard to the gathering of "curios" (shells, fossils, crystals, iron pyrites, stalactite fragments, etc.) sometimes found together in the same pile. Ocher became much more plentiful. The first use of manganese dioxide, a black dye, coincided with the production of a greater number of drawings engraved on bone or stone surfaces. By the Aurignacian period, these drawings took the form of rhythmic incisions and figurative tracings. By 30,000 B.C., figurative art had developed to the point at which subjects could be divided into the following groups: female sexual symbols (sometimes also male), figures of animals, and regularly spaced incisions or punctuations. These themes predominated throughout the development of Paleolithic art, a subject to which we shall return.

Burial Grounds and the Cult of Bone Remains

Neanderthals buried their dead. The practice of inhumation is attested by several obvious tombs and, statistically, by the numerous finds of skeleton fragments. Shanidar in Iraq is the site of the only discovery of a Neanderthal laid out on a bed of flowers, from which a great number of fossilized pollens were found. In Monte Circeo (Italy), in a similarly convincing find, a skull was placed in the center of a cave chamber. In the face of such striking testimony, it is difficult not to ascribe to the immediate predecessors of humankind as we know it today sentiments analogous to our own regarding the afterlife in a parallel universe, a universe which may have been as inexplicit as that of the average subject of any of today's major religions. Difficult as it may be, given the available evidence, to describe Neanderthal man's attitude toward the supernatural, it is even more difficult to demonstrate the meaning of what falls into the category of the "cult of bone remains." Because bone is the only physical element (human or animal) that survives decomposition, any bones found as evidence in an unusual situation could have played a part in a cult. Whether with respect to Neanderthal man or to *Homo sapiens,* we have some evidence that can be explained in terms that are not at variance with an interpretation based on the supernatural. Separated by several scores of millennia, the skulls of Monte Circeo (Mousterian) and the skull from Mas-d'Azil (Magdalenian) attest the special character of the head (the whole head or merely the skull). Although the idea of "graves" of animals has been advanced repeatedly, it seems that natural phenomena were more often at issue than man himself, especially in the case of the remains of cave bears.

The burial graves of fossil *Homo sapiens* are rare, and hardly a single grave dating from the Upper Paleolithic Age (30,000–9000) has been excavated either with care or with all the technical means that would have assured its documentary value. We do, however, have a certain number of facts at our disposal (graves; bodies, either curled up or stretched out; a head protected by a stone; ocher dusting; and funereal household objects, including, at the least, clothing and ornaments worn by the dead person). In addition, the double children's tomb at Sungir, north of Moscow, where hundreds of ornamental elements adorn the bodies and large spears made of mammoth ivory were found in the grave, bears witness to the development of the concern to equip the dead, a development that occurred at a remote phase of the Upper Paleolithic Age. Obviously, graves do not all reflect identical religious intentions, nor can we be certain what kind of sentiments led to these emotional displays. Mortuary furniture is ordinarily less sumptuous. In several cases we might even speculate that the presence of certain vestiges was connected with accidental conditions surrounding the filling of the grave. But a rather constant factor is the presence of ocher, which varied according to the population's wealth in dyes. Ocher gave the soil and the skeleton that it covered a reddish coloration. This practice, common during the Upper Paleolithic Age, is the indisputable sign of acts whose meaning goes beyond a simple natural emotion. If the use of ocher supports various interpretations according to habitat, the sheer fact of its being brought into a grave where a body had been laid constitutes the most distinct feature of the belief in an afterlife, since the dead person was considered still capable of using what he was offered.

Personal Adornments

Jewelry appeared in the West around 35,000 B.C. Its prior origin is unknown. Throughout Europe, its appearance coincided with the first manifestations of the Upper Paleolithic Age. During the Châtelperronian epoch (35,000–30,000), it appears already quite diversified: at that same time we find annular pendants carved out of bone, as well as teeth from various animal species (fox, wolf, marmot, aurochs, etc.), made so that they could be hung by means of a perforation of the root or a slit. Fossil shells were treated in the same way. It may seem far-fetched to regard ornamental pendants as anything other than purely aesthetic objects, and, in fact, some may have had exclusively decorative functions. However, among the hundreds of pendants acquired from European sites, the majority reveal a preoccupation with magic at one level or another. Those that unambiguously represent male and female sexual organs must surely have had some sort of symbolic value (fig. 1). The cylindrical fragments of stalactite and points of belemnites designed to hang may have a meaning of the same order. This symbolic function of sexual images may have been extended to include fragments of shattered assegai spears that were perforated but otherwise untreated (see the symbolism of the assegai below). The role of teeth designed to hang must have been rather complex, at least in the early stages, for the teeth of some animals, the marmot for example, do not seem to have the characteristics of a trophy or a talisman. This is not true of the atrophied canines of reindeer, which even today are symbols of masculinity and

Pendants with genital designs. Left: series of female symbols; right: phalloid symbol. 7.5 cm. Isturitz (Pyrénées district). (Fig. 1)

were imitated in bone or soft stone when pendants first appeared.

The same applies to shells. For the most part they seem to have a purely aesthetic function, but the rather frequent discovery of porcelain (Cyprea), universally attested in prehistoric and historic times as a protective female symbol, makes it highly probable that the collection of shells served as talismans. In short, having gone beyond a strictly decorative function, long and oval pendants encompassed both the aesthetic and the religious realms, and probably the social realm as well, although we still have too little data to clarify the matter.

The Occurrence of Wall Painting

The development of personal adornments does not diminish the importance of the collections of natural curiosities; rather, it was an added feature that prevailed until the end of the Upper Paleolithic Age, ca. 9000. Adornments evolved throughout this period. But in the Aurignacian and the Perigordian Ages, the main event was the spread of pictorial works. Between 30,000 and 20,000, certain forms began to appear in engravings. These first forms were executed on blocks and probably on the walls of rock shelters as well. Despite their crudeness, they shed light on the concerns of their creators. The repertoire of these works is very limited; representation of the female genitalia, highly stylized, is the most widespread. A few representations of the male genitalia can be found, but they were apparently replaced quite early by abstract symbolic figures: dotted lines or bar lines that seem to accompany explicitly female figures. There are also highly geometrical figures of animals, parallel to one another and often juxtaposed or superimposed on one another. The Aurignacian-Gravettian bestiary includes the horse, the bison, the ibex, and other imprecise figures indicating that from the very beginning art made use of two clearly defined registers: human figures symbolically rendered, starting with the representation of the entire body and progressing, by way of genital figures and animals, to geometric figures. During the ensuing 20,000 years, the details may have varied but the basic figures, human and animal, remained in the same relationships. These relationships cannot easily be established on the basis of the engraved blocks alone; displacement in the course of time and, especially, following excavations has destroyed the spatial ties that might have guided us to their meaning. But something happened, perhaps by the Gravettian Age but certainly around 15,000: penetration deep into caves and the execution of paintings or engravings, sometimes more than a kilometer from the opening. This boldness on the part of Paleolithic men is of immediate interest to us because the works produced at such locations preserved their positions with respect to one another and with respect to the wall itself. We can therefore raise questions about the possible religious ideology of the creators of these figures. What motives could have inspired the Magdalenians of Niaux or Pech-Merle to their speleological adventure? It is hard to believe that it was just a matter of curiosity, and one is inclined to think that in their eyes the cave must have seemed a mysterious amalgam of female forms. Direct evidence is furnished by the numerous oval cavities or cleft lips painted on the inside in red ocher (Gargas, Font-de-Gaume, Niaux). The execution of numerous genital symbols in deep side passages indirectly reinforces the hypothesis of the woman-cave. To date, explicit male symbols are rare but one may find, on Aurignacian blocks, for instance, signs made up of series of dots or rods accompanying oval or triangular figures depicted with different degrees of realism. All stages of development come together, with regional nuances, from the whole female figure to the pubic triangle rendered as an empty rectangle. This tendency of male and female signs to conceal themselves behind abstract graphics may well have been a response to taboos of a socioreligious character. This hypothesis becomes all the more plausible as other figurative anomalies give evidence of the same meaning. Not only is there no known instance of human or animal mating anywhere in Paleolithic art, but sexual organs are explicitly represented on relatively few figures. At Lascaux (where, however, the bulls have obvious sexual characteristics), two figures appear (fig. 6): the "jumping cow" in the Axial Diverticulum and an engraved horse in the Passage, both of which have their hooves turned in such a way that the underbelly on both animals is visible and completely empty. This strange mannerism in figure drawing is not easily explained, but it does show the complexity of Paleolithic thought. Curiously, secondary sexual characteristics (the antlers of the cervidae, the thick withers of the bovidae, and

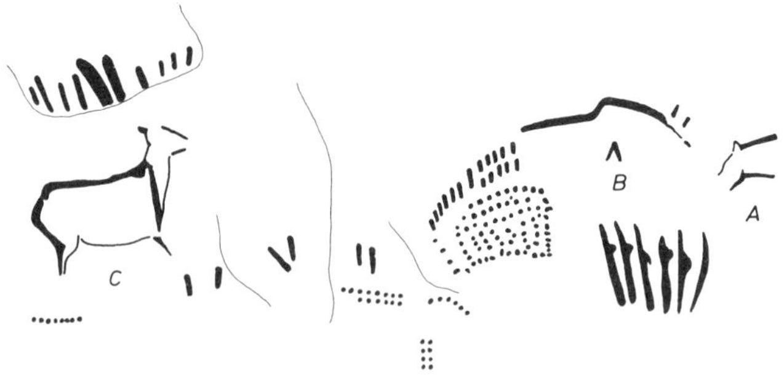

Middle part of the first great panel of the Cave of Pindal (Asturias). Animals A and B (horse and bison) are reduced to the minimal identifiable size: dorsal line and horns for the bison, which also bears a scar from a wound in the shape of an inverted V; central portion of the head and the neck and withers for the horse. Above the bison and the horse, S^2 line of the so-called claviform type (see fig. 5). The photograph includes only the right side of a series of red and black paintings. Between group A-B and the doe (C), there are several groups of S^1 and S^3 signs. The doe is 85 cm long. (Fig. 2)

the horns of the ibex) are rendered very exactly; and, moreover, the animals are frequently depicted in couples, the female in front and the male behind. It is certain that the figures basically connote what might be thought of as a "fertility cult," a generally banal statement that takes on a subtlety in the present instance by virtue of the apparent contradiction of the representation.

Animals

Paleolithic materials yield other peculiar data. The hundreds of figures that cover the walls of caves seem at first glance to defy any kind of order. Even though the idea of a coherent whole emerges from the way the figures are arranged, few prehistorians have used this possible organization to delve further into the ideology of the artists. One rather surprising fact stands out: the fauna that are represented display variations that seem to reflect the environment. In some caves the bison, together with the horse, is the principal subject (Font-de-Gaume, Niaux, Altamira), whereas in others the aurochs plays the main role (Lascaux, Ebbon). But in all the cases cited above, the complementary bovid (bison or aurochs depending on the site) is represented by one or more figures separated from the rest. Another point should also be mentioned: the reindeer that figure in great numbers among the food wastes of the hunters at the time of these works occupy little space in the iconography of certain grottoes such as Lascaux, Niaux, or Altamira. At Lascaux, rather paradoxically, though the bony remains of reindeer make up almost all the animal wastes, only one figure can be attributed to the reindeer, and even that is somewhat doubtful. Thus the fauna depicted do not always correspond to what Paleolithic man hunted. This fact is important because, if it were confirmed, it would lead us to conclude that at least some of the animals represented played a role unconnected with the food that people then lived on. The number of sites for which it was possible to draw up a list of the animals depicted and a parallel list of the animals consumed as meat is unfortunately too limited to verify this hypothesis.

Groupings

We referred above to groupings of animal figures and signs, starting with the Aurignacian Age (30,000). The most frequent, almost exclusive animal grouping is of horses (100%) and of bison (56%) (or of aurochs, 39%, in other words, 95% for bovidae). This initial dyad, moreover, occupies the center of all surfaces used, and may be repeated several times in the same cave. The groupings in wall paintings have a complexity that derives from the diversity of the caves in which the decorations appear. So, too, geographical location and chronological evolution are reflected in various applications of the initial figurative formula and in the more or less pronounced use of natural forms. In any case, it is likely that the cave or the surface of the shelter wall was the object of a deliberate choice, and that the figures were not piled one on top of another haphazardly.

The horse(A)-bovid(B) twosome appears at all sites (fig. 7.1). Although we must allow for the possibility of caves or shelters that might not fit the basic AB formula, practically speaking the AB group is always present and dominates the groupings both numerically and topographically. But rarely does the AB group appear alone. Another category of animals intervenes, namely, group C (stag, mammoth, and occasionally chamois and reindeer). Among the wall painting groups, the ibex is most often the accompanying animal, but the stag, hind, mammoth, and reindeer also play the same role, most often on the sidelines, on the outer perimeter of the central panel groupings, or in the intermediary sections. The most frequent formula is thus AB + C, making up a triad with one interchangeable element: the ibex at Niaux, the mammoth at Rouffignac, the stag at Las Chimeneas. In the same cave, we can also see "moving" animals, or the following: at Niaux, the stag marks the deepest part of the large painted surface, the rather numerous ibexes framing the AB figures; at Lascaux, the situation is similar—ibexes appear three or four times immediately to the side of a group of animals, stags being equal in number but farther to the side. In a cave like the Combarelles, in which the figures number into the hundreds, the "third animal" is represented by the reindeer, the ibex, and the mammoth, which are concentrated in the general area of the side panel of each decorated gallery.

Finally, there is also a D category to which fierce animals belong: the rhinoceros, the bear, and the big cats. The bear is a relatively rare animal in Paleolithic iconography and has no clearly defined place, but the rhinoceros and the big cats are marginal animals, most often situated in the deepest or most peripheral parts of the figured group. At Lascaux, Font-de-Gaume, the Combarelles, to cite only a few, the big cats are in this position. In these three places, the rhinoceros occupies an analogous position: at Lascaux, at the bottom of the Well; at Font-de-Gaume, at the end of the main gallery next to the big cat; and at the Combarelles, superimposed over the "lioness" from the end of the second gallery. The complete formula for the grouping is C + AB + C (+ D) in the case of a cave with a single composition, one that forms part of a series. In extreme cases, as in Lascaux or Combarelles, one may encounter a series of groupings with the basic formula repeated time and again.

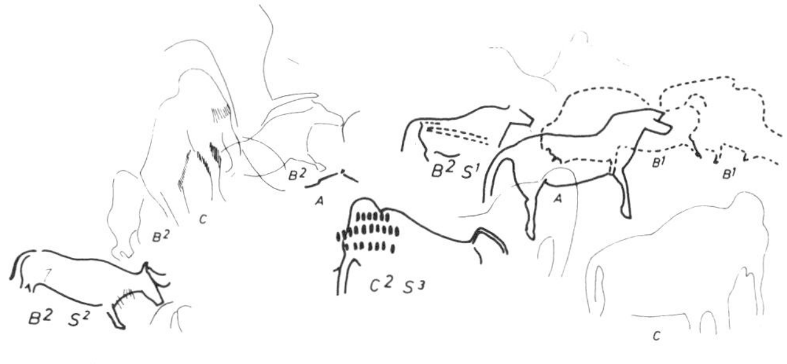

Cave of Pech-Merle (Lot). Middle and left of the great frieze painted in black. Two groups of animals can be seen: the group on the left and the group on the right each include a horse (A) and two bison on the right, two aurochs on the left. The mammoths present in both groupings make up group C. Between the two groupings, there are also three animals marked by signs: (1) a bull (B^2) bearing a sign (S^1) with a male connotation on his side (see fig. 5); (2) a cow (B^2) marked by wounds (S^2); (3) diagonally across from both animals, a mammoth bearing three rows of thick red dashes. The figures are between 60 and 120 cm long. (Fig. 3)

Signs

Signs seem to follow the same general patterns as animal figures. They fall into three categories (fig. 5). The first is made up of male symbols (S^1) ranging from the human body depicted in its entirety to a simple little stick. In between are sometimes very abstract transitions (lines branching out with two extensions at the base, as in Lascaux). The signs of the second group (S^2) correspond to female symbols. Like the signs of the first group, they range from a complete female representation to an empty or partitioned rectangle. The third group (S^3), in comparison with the other two, is homologous to the animals of group C or CD. It is made up of aligned dots or a series of little sticks aligned or clustered. In several cases, the S^3 signs are repeated at the beginning and the end of the figurative series. This phenomenon is quite evident at Lascaux, where the aligned dots are found at the entrance and at the far end of the Axial Diverticulum, between the Passage and the Nave, at the bottom of the Well, and at the end of the Diverticulum of the Big Cats. The signs of the third group, therefore, occupy a position rather set back, most often in the background, as at Font-de-Gaume, Pech-Merle, and El Castillo.

The relationship between signs and animals corresponds to the following broad lines: the S^1S^2 group is found juxtaposed with the animals of groups A and B (fig. 2), as in the case of the Diverticulum of the Big Cats at Lascaux (fig. 6), in which the S^1S^2 signs are in the central panel, right across from an AB group (horse-bison). But the signs may be independent of the animal figures, grouped in a separate diverticulum. Good examples can be found at Niaux (Black Room), at El Castillo, at La Pasiega, and, notably, at Cougnac. The relationship between animals and signs may thus be defined by the following formula:

$$\begin{array}{c} C + AB + C + D \\ S^3 + S^1S^2 + S^3 \end{array}$$

or

$$\begin{array}{ccccccc} C & + & AB & + & C & + & D/S^1S^2, \\ & & S^3 & & & & S^3 \end{array}$$

Both formulas can even be found in the same cave (La Pasiega).

This complex arrangement must have encompassed an ideology whose elaborate character may be perceived through the arrangement. The situation is further complicated, however, by the role played by the cave itself. Natural caves have many accidental features that evoked, for Paleolithic man, sexual forms, generally female. These natural structures, fissures or stalagmitic formations, sometimes underscored in red (Gargas, Niaux), are also frequently completed with an S^1 sign (little sticks or dots: Gargas, Combel de Pech-Merle, Niaux), proving that the natural phenomenon was considered equivalent to S^2. This is particularly clear in Niaux, where two fissures in the inner gallery were marked at the entrance by a sign of male connotation (branching sign) accompanied in one of the two cases by a horse with its head extended in the direction of the fissure.

In the course of millennia and in a territory as vast as that of Paleolithic cave art, figurative traditions must have undergone numerous variations, and it is remarkable that we should come across an ideographic system that is so well constructed. Yet two rather important questions, concerning the role of wounds on animals and the role of hands, remain largely unresolved.

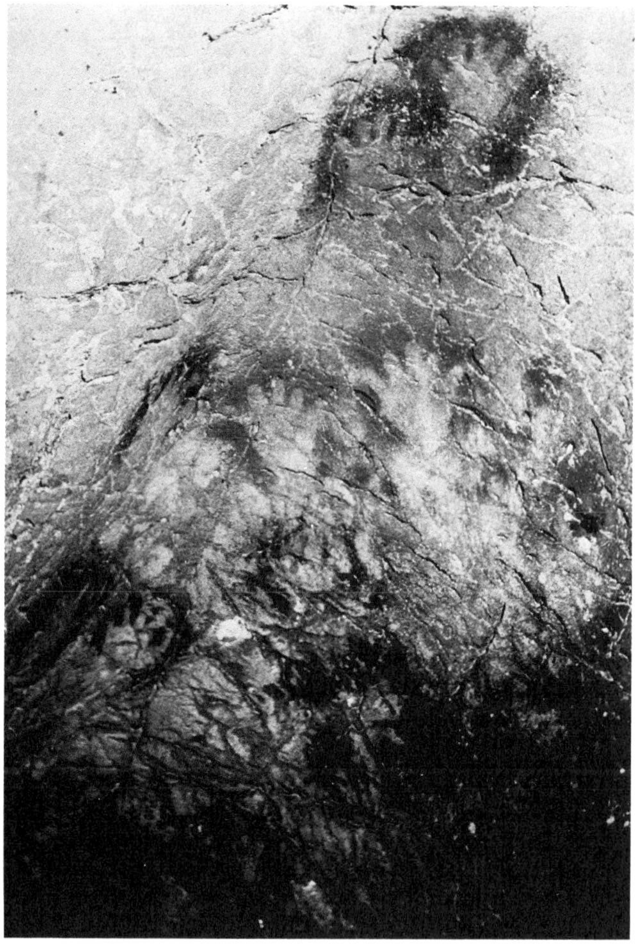

Cave of Gargas (Hautes-Pyrénées). Panel showing "negative" hands with "mutilated" fingers. Most such hands, colored red or black, are grouped in twos by subject, and appear to have been executed by folding in the fingers or by applying a stencil. (Fig. 4)

Wounds

In art objects as well as mural art, we find animals with wounds. Ever since research on prehistoric religion began, this detail has been thought to reveal the practice of magic spells. This explanation is not altogether impossible, but certain elements lead us to believe that it does not resolve the problem entirely. In fact, 96% of the animal figures on file (between 2,500 and 3,000) show no wounds. We might ask ourselves if the two series, animal and sign, really belong to the same symbolic system, or if two lines of symbols might have existed without any organic ties between them. Signs do seem to have played their role at the same times and in the same places as animals. What is more, both evolved synchronically, and both underwent parallel stylistic transformations. It is very unlikely that signs were slipped in among animals, with no connection to them, in the course of various rituals; too many signs are connected to animals by their position for the relationship not to be a close one, as the Pech-Merle paintings show (fig. 3). This does not preclude the claim that signs are sometimes independent, as at Altamira, where the signs and the animals of the Great Ceiling make up two distinct clusters; or as at El Castillo or La Pasiega, where, for one important portion, the painted

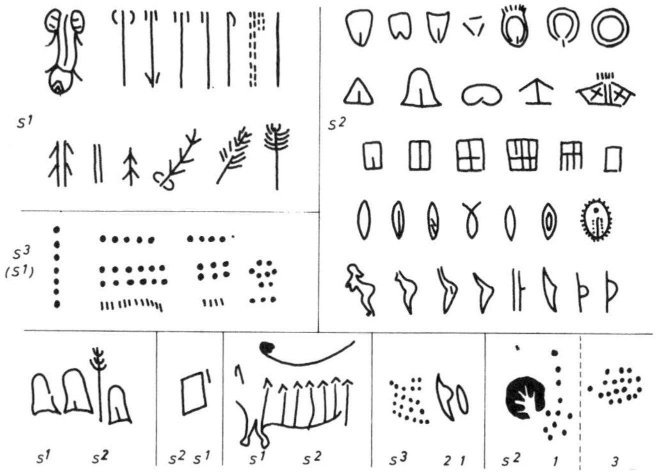

Geometrization of male and female symbols. S^1: phalloid derivatives. S^2: principal series of vulvar derivatives. S^3: rows of punctuation (dotted lines) and barred lines. Below, from left to right: S^1-S^2 groupings. El Castillo (Santander): triangle derivatives and branching sign. Lascaux (Dordogne): maximal geometrization and abstractions (empty rectangle and bar). Lascaux: crooked bar (S^1) and seven aligned wounds (S^2). S^1, S^2, S^3 groupings. Niaux (Ariège): bar (S^1), claviform (see same S^2 figure), cloud of dots (S^3). Pech-Merle (Lot): at the entrance of a deep side passage, three figures that appear to correspond in value to S^1: dotted line with four lateral dots (see same S^3 figure). The negative hand probably corresponds to S^2, and the cloud of dots, farther into the passage, probably corresponds to S^3. (Fig. 5).

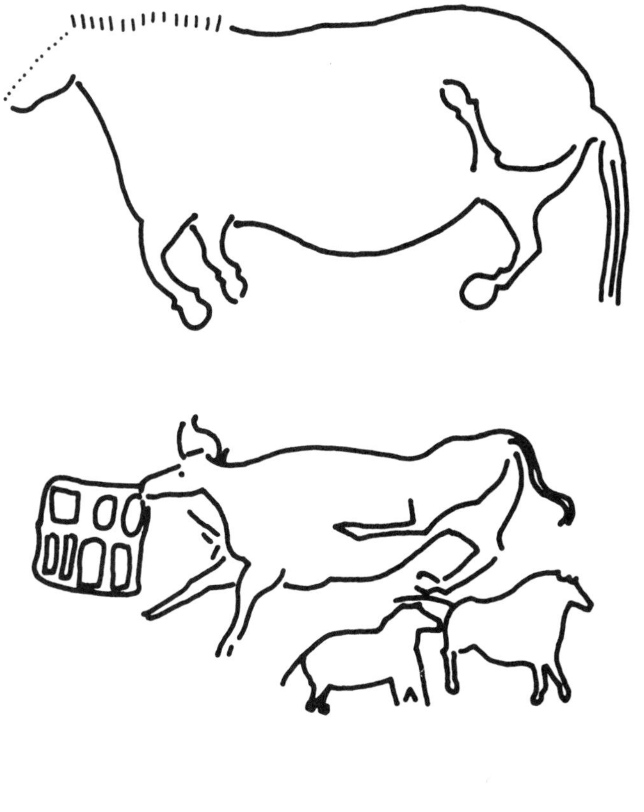

Lascaux (Dordogne): (1) Engraved horse with rump turned such that the perineal region is exposed but devoid of primary sexual characteristics. 60 cm. (2) Paintings from the axial gallery, central part of the righthand wall. Aurochs in the same posture as the horse in front. Secondary sexual characteristics (general profile) are attributable to a cow, but primary characteristics, notably the udder, are invisible. This figure is included in the grouping formula A-B S^1-S^2 (horse-aurochs, bars, gridlike sign; see fig. 5). 1.70 m. (Fig. 6)

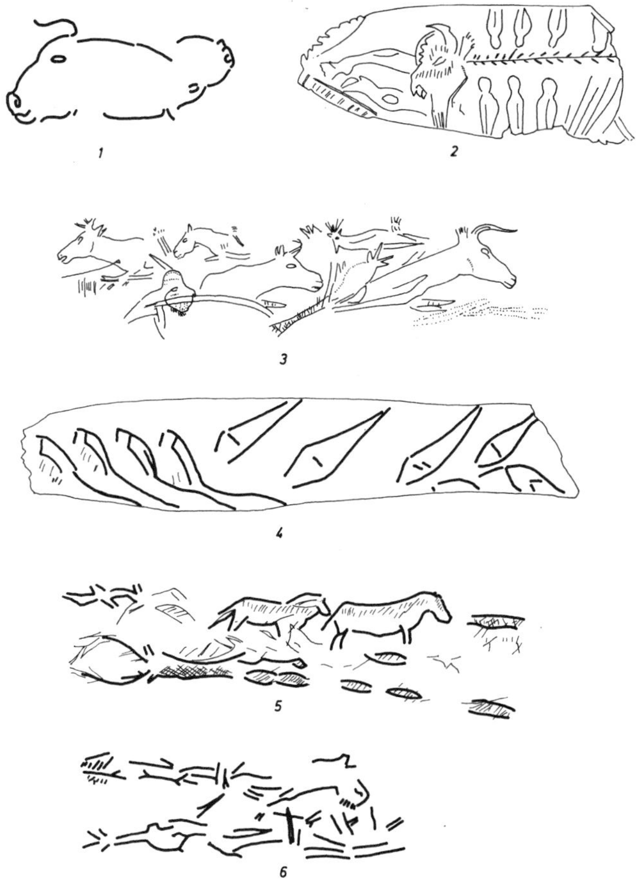

Gourdan (Haute-Garonne). The principle of association of animals A and B may also be applied to portable objects. This engraving on bone plaquette represents the aurochs-horse twosome with the heads of both animals assembled like the faces on playing cards. About 6 cm from nose to nose. (2) Raymonden (Dordogne). Partial pendant (or fish spatula). A scene of a religious nature seems to be unfolding: six or seven persons (perhaps more) are lined up on either side of a line resembling barbed wire at the end of which is the severed head of a bison and two paws with ill-defined hooves. Near the knee, one of these legs bears a "chestnut," a horny growth that is the vestige of the multifingered hoof of the ancestors of the *equidae*. It may indeed be a horse leg, and this grouping with its sacrificial look may refer to the A-B model. (3) Torre (Guipuzcoa). Roll of fine engravings around a bone tube. From left to right: stag, man, horse, chamois, two small ibex with frontal horns, and aurochs. This series of animals referring to A-B model + C is of more than purely artistic interest: between the subjects are abstract tracings (parallel or crossed strokes, beginnings of spherical figures, clouds made of fine dots, etc.) which must have ensured that Magdalenians could "read" this mythogram. (4) Mas-d'Azil (Ariège). Bone plaquette engraved with horses and fish, already strongly geometrized. Mythographic theme born out by several examples. (5) El Valle (Santander). Bone tube with engraved bird. Subject related to preceding one: two horses, one behind the other, a stag facing forward, numerous features with no apparent meaning, perhaps a snake, and some oval figures, probably fish. (6) El Pendo (Santander). Bone tube engravings, like the preceding ones, but virtually uninterpretable. There remains a part of the head and neck of a horse and a herbivore with visible horns (or antlers) and ears borne by a very long neck. Note that these two figures occupy the same situation as those of the El Valle tube. (Fig. 7)

signs are collected in a side passage; or at Cougnac (Lot), where S^1 and S^2 signs are located in a side alcove away from the animal figures, while the S^3 series occurs in the figured panels.

Whether these are two series of symbols executed simultaneously and experienced as forming the frame of a single ideological block, or whether they are two separate series with elements that were to enter one another on synchronic but distinct levels—either case presupposes a highly complex intellectual content, intimately tied to an elaborate social system. Could they be symbols of the propagation of humans and animals, a cosmogony that calls into play the complementary forces of male and female? It is difficult to reach a conclusion without going beyond the available data, but certainly we are in the presence of something quite different from what was long imagined about "the Paleolithic savages."

Of the 4% of animals showing wounds in the thoracic or the neighboring abdominal areas, if we do a percentage count by species, the greatest number goes to the bison (8%), then to the horse (2.5%), with zero or less than 1% for all other species. There is yet another striking fact. Although wounded animals are encountered throughout the Franco-Cantabrian region, most cases occur in the Ariège sector of the Pyrenees, with the greatest number represented at Niaux (25% of figured animals). The value of the wound as a testimony to magic spells for game might be merely an accessory phenomenon, but the hunting symbolism to which it refers is certain. The fact that wounds appear essentially only on the bodies of the basic twosome is perhaps connected with the AB = S^1S^2 equation, the wounds being the equivalent of S^2, that is, the female connotation. Three pieces of evidence may be invoked to support this contention: a horse at Lascaux bearing seven wounds on its body and an S^2 sign (fig. 5) on its neck and withers; a bison at Bernifal whose shoulder has an oval wound flanked by two little sticks; and a bison at Niaux engraved on clay, which has three wounds and two little sticks on its side. These parallel sticks belong to the highly varied portion of masculine symbols. One of the best examples of the relationship between signs and animals is that of the great panel of Pech-Merle (fig. 3) made up of two groupings that share the same C animal (C^2 mammoth). One is the aurochs-horse (AB^2), and the other the horse-bison (AB^1). Between the two groupings of figures are three animals: a bull, a cow, and a mammoth. Each bears different signs. The bull bears a double line of dashes with lateral extensions (S^1, of male character). The cow is riddled with wounds that seem to play the role of S^2 signs. The mammoth is covered with red spots aligned to form the equivalent of the S^3 sign. From this evidence we can hypothesize that "wounds" have the value of a female symbol. Establishing this symbolism would open a vast realm of possibilities for the symbolic system of Paleolithic art, one that involves the alternation of symbols of life and death.

Hands

While the problem of wounds allows us to do no more than hint at some kind of metaphysical solution, *positive* hand imprints (in which a hand is smeared with color and pressed flat against the wall) and *negative* hand imprints (in which a hand is laid flat against the wall and outlined in color) raise questions equally resistant to clear answers. Positive hands are substantially rarer than negative hands and show up infrequently in groupings, but the Bayol cave in the Ardèche region has a good example. It shows six positive hands in a grouping that includes an aurochs, two horses, and one big cat, all treated in a very particular style.

There are several types of negative hands, probably corresponding to several different traditions. The first category is made up of hands integrated in a grouping that includes, notably, dottings; this is the case in Pech-Merle, where in six instances hands are associated with dotted lines in close proximity to the two crisscrossed horses and once with eleven dotted lines above the opening of a very low side passage (fig. 5). The same arrangement of animal figures and dottings is found in El Castillo. In the Périgord, negative hands appear in isolation (one at Font-de-Gaume, one at Combarelles, several grouped at Bernifal, etc.). At Roucadour (Lot), the hands are superposed over the animals, and they have long pointed fingers incised on a black background. The Pech-Merle hands give the impression of being inserted in an arrangement where they play an important role, surely as important as the S^2 signs with their female connotation.

The hands in the cave of Gargas (Hautes-Pyrénées), like those in the neighboring grotto at Tibiran, are very different in nature (fig. 4). Repeated scores of times in different panels and hollows of the cave, they have the special feature of cut-off or, more likely, bent-in fingers. The various combinations of fingers might have been part of a kind of symbolic code of the animals most commonly represented in figurative art (horse, bison, ibex, etc.). The same digital formula appears again in side-by-side hands repeated twice and alternating between red and black (fig. 4). Examples can also be found at the openings of niches or fissures, in the position normally occupied by animals or signs of CD and S^1 groups. As strange as it may seem, the "mutilated hands" of Gargas, which include many children's hands, are not missing all five fingers. They seem to correspond to a fairly rational application of signals involving variably bent fingers, gestures that can still be observed today among certain groups of hunters, notably the Bushmen. Aside from the monumental aspect of the connections between the groups of hands and their natural support, the ideographic aspect is extremely impressive.

Animal and human figures make up the ground on which our tentative explanation of wall painting rests. This explanation calls on data which, in the way they are assembled, suggest a complex ideological construct. To what extent can objects that are found not on walls but on sites of living quarters corroborate this claim?

Objects

Caves contain particularly precious data, if only because the images have preserved their location on walls. A no less precious source of information, however, may be found on the surfaces of Paleolithic floors strewn with objects that bear human and animal figures. Some of these objects are fairly soft fragments of stone or fragments of bone on which figures have been incised or sculpted. No practical function can be attributed to them, and we are struck by their resemblance to the figures on walls. Given their iconographic content, we ask whether they could have played the same role in living quarters as the figures played in the cave, and whether they were used to reproduce the same combinations. These questions are difficult to answer decisively, for the possibilities of iconographic combinations are extremely varied. The figures (statuettes, plaquettes or blocks, weapons or tools, personal adornments) may have been assembled in a meaningful way (according to the C-A-B-C + D model), a configuration that may presuppose, for example, either several plaquettes each bearing one figure, or several plaquettes each bearing several animal figures. Unfortunately rare are the cases where portable objects are found in their functional places, and even rarer are sites where the excavators took the trouble to record the exact position of the relics. Yet we can begin by assuming that, since caves existed only in a limited number of areas while vast territories lent themselves only to open-air settlements, the plaquettes of stone, ivory, or bone or the statuettes which sometimes abound at such sites fulfilled the role that otherwise devolved upon cave walls.

We may also assume that the other decorated objects reflect, in whole or in part, the same ideological scheme that is displayed by the grouping of the figures on the walls.

Statuettes

Statuettes of animals are relatively rare in the Paleolithic art of western Europe. The cave of Isturitz (Basses-Pyrénées) stands out as an exception with its numerous animals (bison, horses, bears) incised in soft rock. The true domain of animal figures in round relief is central and eastern Europe. The pictorial repertory of Europe east of the Rhine is mostly made up of statuettes molded in clay mixed with powdered bone (Moravia), incised in bone or in mammoth ivory; and figurines of mammoth, horse, bison, and big cats. The functions of these statuettes are as yet unclear, but since they must have assumed the same role as that played by the engravings and paintings in the caves, they must have the same symbolic ranges.

One category of figures is made up of female statuettes, inaccurately called "Venus" figures, that appear in various forms depending on the stages of the Paleolithic epoch and the regions in which they were executed. The items discovered at Kostienki (on the Don River), on Ukranian sites, at Predmost in Moravia, Willendorf in Austria, and at Brassempouy and Lespugue in southwestern France show in the details of their execution that they belong to the same pictorial traditions. Were the religious traditions that they were supposed to illustrate of the same nature? That is hard to answer, for the good reason that female statuettes can only symbolize a limited number of functions, generally relating to fertility. Based on what we know today, it would be difficult to say any more about them, except perhaps that the statuettes discovered in living quarters may have played an identical role to that of the signs in the groupings of figures on the walls. Male figures by their very scarcity seem to have occupied a much more modest place.

In brief, plaquettes, which are far more numerous in the West than statuettes, and statuettes, which are more numerous than plaquettes in central and eastern Europe, seem to have had the same functions. Given the resemblances between portable art (on plaquettes and statuettes) and mural art, we can ascribe identical functions to them and assimilate them to the same religious process. Unfortunately, this does not entirely clarify the details of the process that we know to have borrowed the same basic symbols throughout all of Europe for twenty thousand years. The formula A-B, C, D + S^1, S^2, S^3 did not necessarily have the same ideological implications in the Urals as it did on the banks of the Vézère. The hundreds of plaquettes of engraved schist from Gönnersdorf (dating from the Magdalenian epoch ca. 10,000) left lying on the ground may not have had the same function as the heavy engraved blocks of the Aurignacian epoch around 30,000.

It seems possible nevertheless to discern in the groupings of art objects and mural art alike the systematic presence of two animals A-B, often associated with one or two animals from group C. Human figures and male and female symbols are also present, as they are in wall paintings. The specialized use of certain objects may have influenced the choice of the figures that were drawn on them. There were relatively few decorated objects during the first millennia; realistic figures, at least, were rare. It is not until the middle and late Magdalenian Age, from 12,000 to 9000, that objects made of reindeer horn and bone begin to be covered with figures. Propelling devices—hooked pieces probably designed to hurl assegais at game—most often depict a single animal, close to the hook. On objects in this category the most eclectic assortment can be found: horse, bison, mammoth, ibex, reindeer, big cat, fish, bird. The propelling devices (their real use is still unknown) thus fall in the same iconographic category as plaquettes and statuettes.

Perforated Sticks

Perforated sticks are a different story. A kind of lever made of reindeer horns, the stick consists of a cylindrical handle with a bifurcation at one end in which a hole three centimeters in diameter has been pierced at the thickest point. Its real use was to straighten out, while hot or cold, the long assegai spears that had kept the curvature of the horns from which they had been made. The class of perforated sticks includes a large number of carefully decorated objects. In a significant proportion of them, the handle is sculpted in the shape of a phallus. Sometimes both extensions of the head of the object have this decoration. There are also many perforated sticks that bear the A-B grouping (horse-bison) or the third animal, in the form of a stag, a reindeer, or an ibex. A whole series of perforated sticks are decorated on their lateral extensions with two heads of bison, highly geometrized and often reduced to two sets of parallel bars. This decorative element can be found from the Asturias to Switzerland. Some perforated sticks feature realistic scenes, such as the one at Dordogne in Laugerie-Basse, which on one side shows a man knocked over by a bison and on the other side a horse; or the one in La Madeleine, which has a man, a snake, and two horses on one side, and two bison on the other. Certainly these animals were not grouped in a fortuitous manner: the H-B + A formula (Human-bison + horse) is the same formula as in the famous scene on the Well at Lascaux (a man knocked over by a bison, with a horse on the opposite wall). The second scene, however, must refer to another mythic content, for its formula, H-A + B (+ S) (Human-horse + bison [and snake]), has no known equivalent, but it does highlight the imperative character of the representation of the complementary animal: in the first case, the horse; in the second, the bison. We should also note that, as at Lascaux, the second animal is on the side opposite to the one with the scene.

Assegais

Assegais make up a category of particularly expressive decorated items. The ornamentation on these spears appears relatively early, around 20,000, and consists of geometric patterns, sometimes of a highly simplified animal figure. These markings may correspond to different hunters in the same group. But as time went by, the animal figures multiplied on some of these assegais. During the late Magdalenian era, some were covered with rows of horses on a raised field, which suggests that they served as instruments for parades or rituals rather than as effective weapons. The ends of assegais are often perforated to make them into pendants. Such pieces may have been part of a particular assegai that was lucky in its hunting and thereby served as a "talisman." The numerous pendants found in the Upper Paleolithic Age are largely inspired by sexual symbolism (cowrie shell, oval pendants, stag canines, etc.). It is thus likely that the assegai played a dual symbolic role. A few indices seem to support this contention, namely, the probable assimilation in mural art of male symbols with the assegai and female symbols with the wound. Many details from the natural relief of walls, such as oval niches painted red and the wounds on certain animals, support such a hypothesis. But it is difficult to consolidate the ideological aspects of this symbolic frame of reference.

Other decorated objects that might shed light on the religious thought of Paleolithic man require an even more sensitive interpretation. Harpoon points with realistic decoration are extremely rare. Conversely, we do have a considerable number of spatulas in the shape of fish, often highly geometrized. They may bear symbolic meaning, but at what level? The scale of values may range from a representation of a primarily aesthetic character to an instrument indispensable for the execution of a ritual. The same may be said of the rings of bone, three or four centimeters in diameter, with a very eclectic range of animal engravings on both sides. The fish spatula with its inevitable iconographic base (usually a species of *Salmonidae*), and the rings of bone on which all species are represented (including the human species) provide us only with a basic assumption and certainly not with evidence for an entire superstructure of beliefs. It is therefore by reference to the figures on walls and plaquettes that the iconography of portable objects can be analyzed. We may also want to view in the same spirit the so-called silhouette outlines, small pendants carved out of a hyoid bone, of which there are many known examples showing heads of horses as well as a group of eighteen ibex heads and one bison head, which may remind us of the triad horse-bison-ibex, the model of wall depiction.

One last category of materials is made up of groupings of figures engraved mostly on cylindrical objects (tubes of bird bone, assegai shafts, etc.), similar to the perforated sticks referred to above. Some of these objects bear explicit figures, like the bone tube of Torre (Spain), which in the space of fifteen centimeters depicts a series of busts including a stag, man, horse, chamois, ibex, and aurochs (fig. 7.1). This grouping, which may also incorporate signs in parallel or converging lines cross-hatched inside with ladders, is not far removed from certain wall groupings, such as the diver of Portel (Ariège), whose middle part is occupied by a horse, a bison, and male and female signs, while the periphery is occupied by the third sign (S^3), an ibex, and a stag. It would be hard not to regard these various assembled animals as the protagonists of a mythical story, a mythogram rather than a catalogue of the presumed victims of a spell of hunting magic. But whatever the figures may designate precisely, we cannot yet afford to go outside the realm of fact to venture an explanation. Thus we have a whole series of groupings on cylinders or plaquettes, graphically explicit but just as mysterious as ever, such as the strange object found in Les Eyzies on which eight hunters carrying assegais on their shoulders seem to be parading in front of a bison, or another item from Chancelade (fig. 7.2) on which seven human silhouettes appear to surround a bison's head and severed front hooves. These two examples, probably variants of the same theme, show how the discovery of new versions might help us to decipher an increasingly important part of the Paleolithic message.

A significant number of specimens (figs. 7.4, 7.5, 7.6) bear an ornamentation that is very difficult to identify: a row of curves and ovoid figures including a recognizable horse here and there or a highly simplified stag, or sometimes a fish. Given the constancy with which geometric motifs replace explicit figures, we could almost speak of ideograms, though we need not see in these semigeometric figures the elements of "writing." We can assume that the geometrized symbols preserved their meaning, so that a grouping like "chevrons-broken lines" could be equivalent to, for instance, "horse-snake," chevrons being the tail end of a row of horses, and the broken line being the geometrization of the snake's body: both cases exist in an explicit form.

It might seem surprising to hear so little said about "prehistoric religion." As far as practices are concerned, our knowledge consists mainly of gaps. We may imagine that the caves were shrines in which highly elaborate rituals took place, but all we *have* is wall decorations. The fact that the dead were buried with ocher and, at least in some cases, with funerary personal effects, leads us to ascribe to Upper Paleolithic man some notion of an afterlife, but we know nothing about its modalities in any detail. The tablets or engraved blocks tell us about iconographic activities that must have had a religious purpose, but we are far from being able to assert what kind of purpose it was. The same applies to decorated objects (perforated sticks, propelling devices, spatulas, etc.) of which we cannot even claim to know the exact usage. Nevertheless, the wealth of the iconography and the constancy of certain relationships between figures and between figures and the surfaces on which they appear make it possible for us to sketch the bare outlines of a system of religious thought, though its background is still very murky. The complexity and quality of these groupings express feelings (with nuances tied to places and times) that reflect simultaneously the aesthetic and religious life of Paleolithic man.

A.L.-G./g.h.

BIBLIOGRAPHY

H. BREUIL, *Quatre cents siècles d'art pariétal* (Montignac 1952). P. GRAZIOSI, *L'arte dell'antica età della pietra* (Florence 1956). A. LAMING-EMPERAIRE, *La signification de l'art rupestre paléolithique* (Paris 1962). ANDRÉ LEROI-GOURHAN, *Préhistoire de l'art occidental* (Paris 1965); *Les religions de la préhistoire* (Paris 1971); "Les signes pariétaux de Paléolithique supérieur franco-cantabrique," *Simposio intern. de arte rupestre* (Barcelona 1968), 67–77, fig.; "Considérations sur l'organisation spatiale des figures animales dans l'art pariétal paléolithique," *Actes del Symposium intern. de arte prehis.* (Santander 1972), 281–308; "Iconographie et interprétation," *Val Camonica symposium 72* (Capo di Ponte 1975), 49–55. ARLETTE LEROI-GOURHAN, "The Flowers Found with Shanidar IV, a Neanderthal Burial in Iraq," *Science* 190 (1975): 562–64. L. MEROC, "Informations archéologiques, Circonscription de Toulouse, Mas d'Azil," *Gallia Préhistoire* 4 (1961):256–57.

"Nomadic Thought" and Religious Action

> When the rainy season comes, the mendicant monk stops wandering and heads back to his monastery.[1]

For some years now, nomadic societies have awakened strong and renewed interest among ethnologists. On an intuitive level, these societies scattered over the globe seem to be mutually comparable, and attempts have been made to construct models of such societies, that is, to go beyond the empirical diversity that science seeks to overcome. These attempts at synthesis, notably the collective work published under the direction of Lee and De Vore[2] on hunter-gatherers, and the works of B. Spooner[3] on pastoral nomads, are evidence of the special position that nomadic societies occupy today in ethnology.

The term "nomadism" covers quite diverse phenomena: hunter-gatherers and pastoral nomads move over greater or lesser distances, more or less frequently; hunter-gatherers make use of wild objects, and pastoral nomads domestic objects, to mediate their relation with the natural environment. Although nomadic societies differ among themselves in their type of economy and in the breadth and frequency of their movements, as a group they contrast with societies that do not move, settled societies, and it is in this light that we shall consider them for the purposes of this study, setting aside the ways in which the group could be subdivided. Dissimilar in many ways, both social and economic, these societies share not only itinerant behavior but also certain characteristics, which we will examine in order to determine whether they are reflected at the level of thought and worldview. Starting with a limited amount of work done on this subject, we can but suggest a direction of study and posit some hypotheses for research. To find pantheons common to nomads, if such a thing were possible, would require far more concerted and exhaustive studies. But it may already be possible to isolate from its various contexts an attitude to the supernatural world and religion that is common to nomads, and to define a framework within which we might study their mythology.

"Free, individualistic, subject to no state nor to any tyranny," such is the "traditional stereotype" of the pastoral nomad.[4] But it is also an objective piece of information to the extent that it is derived from the image that the nomad has of himself. When this self-image comes into close contact with settled societies, it may even be more pronounced, thus affirming in a deliberate way the difference between nomadic and settled ideologies. Pastoral nomads have a realistic vision of the world and a rather meager ceremonial life. They practice a great deal of divination but little witchcraft. Religion is centered on the individual rather than on the group; indeed, a pantheon comprising a great number of divine figures seems to be more common among farmers. If nomads show little interest in religion, and if they refer to manifestations of the supernatural in "stoic terms," this does not mean that they are any more "secular"[5] than any other group. The cosmology of pastoral nomads in the Middle East, for example, tends to be expressed in Islamic terms. Through this filter, as Spooner points out, it should be possible to see those elements of cosmology that antedate Islam or are not integral to it. When these are compared with other cosmologies from nomadic populations in regions lacking such a culturally dominant ideology, it may be possible to isolate the elements that derive from the nomadic adaptation.[6]

The mythology of hunter-gatherer societies presents notable similarities. The myths that retrace the origins of a society are apparently universal and come out of the same mold. In these myths, the culture hero creates mankind and its customs; he domesticates fire, teaches arts and crafts, and shapes the landscape and animals. In the cosmology, spirits are not gods: culture heroes or creator spirits no longer intervene in the affairs of men, and that is why they are not worshiped. They have to do with existential ideology and not with normative ideology. Just as the accent is placed on the person in nomadic society, so the world of spirits is strongly individualized; egalitarianism within the group is reflected in the absence of any hierarchy among the spirits. The individual deals directly with the world of the supernatural. Except for the shaman/doctor, there is no reliable mediation by specialized individuals.[7] The culture hero who offers the world to humans after he has created them is not totally absent from nomadic societies; but probably more characteristic of such societies is the strongly existential aspect of the ideology as well as egalitarianism. The absence of authoritarian chiefs and of a certain type of power excludes certain types of divine figures. Moreover, nomadic hunters pay little attention to what does not involve them directly. Accordingly, the Mbuti are more concerned with the present than with the past or the future. They are practical people. They eschew all speculation about the future or the hereafter on the grounds that not having been there they do not know what it is like and not knowing what it is like they cannot predict what their behavior will be. They say that to try to look into the future is to "walk blindly."[8] Knowledge is considered a way of living rather than a rule. And it is precisely in their behavior in the face of—rather than by the content of—myth or the supernatural that the clear outlines of a way of thinking peculiar to nomads begin to emerge. We see in hunter-gatherers certain features already observed in the pastoral nomads, and profoundly different from the religious attitudes of settled societies. Before we describe nomadic societies as nonreligious or hardly religious, we might first ask whether ethnologists hold too narrow a conception of ritual and symbolic behavior, and whether their analytic tools may be too closely tied to the categories of settled societies, which would hamper their perception of religious phenomena among nomads.

Among the Basseri, pastoral nomads of Iran, the paucity of ritual activity is striking;[9] they are indifferent to metaphysical problems and to religion. But is this really a lack, or are the descriptive categories that are being used incapable of describing the reality of the situation? The central rite of the society is migration itself. For the Basseri, migration is laden with meaning, though not expressed by means of technically unnecessary symbolic acts or exotic paraphernalia. The Basseri respond not to the utilitarian aspects of activities but to movement and its dramatic forms, to the meanings implicit in the sequence of their activities.[10] Is it not rather ethnocentric to assume that an activity that is important from an economic point of view cannot also be important from a ritualistic or symbolic point of view? The migrations of nomads are more than mere business trips; they are also ritually motivated and determined, and our difficulties in observation seem to be due to our conflation of these two domains.

In this discussion of the relationship between religious attitude (taken in a rather broad sense) and nomadism, societies with seasonal variations are both exceptional and typical because they are alternately nomadic and settled. The gathered habitat of the winter season contrasts with the scattered habitat of the summer season, with its mobility and the splintering of the group into families in the narrowest sense of the word. There are two ways of occupying land, but there are also two ways of thinking: "This contrast between life in winter and life in summer is reflected not only in rituals, festivals, and religious ceremonies of all sorts. It also profoundly affects ideas, collective representations, in a word, the whole mentality of the group.[11] . . . In summer, life is somewhat secularized."[12] The ecological constraints to which the group is subject make nomadism necessary, and the group's requirements come to restrict religious thought and practice. But just as we must consider the role of adaptation to the environment, we must also refine our categories of analysis, and when appearances evoke secularization, we must understand that the foundation has yet to be deciphered. The mobility that characterizes nomadic societies is indeed the central feature of their organization, but it is also the main obstacle to our understanding.

"We must beware of any tendency to treat fixed and permanent ties linking together aggregates of people as normal, and loose, impermanent bonds as abnormal and requiring special explanation."[13] The migrations of hunters or pastoral nomads by far exceed those that would be required by the demands of the natural environment and of access to natural resources. The fluidity and the constant coming and going, both of groups and of individuals within the groups, have a political function: they make it possible to ensure order, the resolution of conflicts, and, paradoxically, cohesion, because the lines of fusion and fission of groups and individuals do not necessarily follow the lines of kinship. Among nomads, social relations become activated through changes of place: proximity or distance are not relevant, and space is in a sense negated. Finally—and, in our view, this is an essential point—the changes of place have a religious function: they are highly valued, so highly that Barth sees them as the central rite among the Basseri. It is movement that leads nomads "into closer recognition of the one constant in their lives, the environment and its life-giving qualities. Under such conditions of flux where band and even family relations are often brittle and fragmentary, the environment in general, and one's own hunting territory in particular, become for each individual the one reliable and rewarding focus of his attention, his loyalty, and his devotion."[14] In other words, the nomad "does not have the impression of inhabiting a man-made world. . . . He is controlled by objects, not persons. . . . There is not an anthropomorphic cosmos. Hence there is no call for articulate forms of social intercourse with nonhuman beings and no need for a set of symbols with which to send and receive special communication."[15] The nomad does not seek to improve the environment in which he lives. In this sense, he is controlled by objects and a world that are *wild*, and he is in direct touch with nature. The domestic animals through whose intervention he exploits the wild objects, if he is pastoral, serve only to mediate this relationship with nature. Whether he is a hunter-gatherer or a shepherd, he does not impose his Culture on Nature as do settled peoples. Mobility and fluidity of groups and within groups; decentralized societies, or rather societies with multiple centers; egalitarianism; direct contact with nature—such are the poles that may affect the ideology of nomads and that may be reflected in collective representations and in rituals.

With a few examples, we have sought to come to terms with nomadism and its underlying ideology as a "certain type of behavior,"[16] rather than as a mode of economic production or as a variable determined by environment. This particular attitude, in the face of the supernatural and the symbolic world, is governed by what we might call a nomadic way of thinking that participates in the "primitive/wild/*sauvage*" way of thinking but preserves its own characteristics within it. The analysis of the content of the myths of various nomadic societies may indeed highlight the lines of force around which "nomadic thought" is organized, and will finally allow us to spell out the specificity of a way of thinking in which what is normal is not what is fixed, and the fluid and the moving are order and not chaos.

F.-R.P./g.h.

NOTES

1. M. MAUSS, "Étude de morphologie sociale," in *Sociologie et anthropologie* (Paris 1966), 472.
2. R.-B. LEE and I. DEVORE, eds., *Man the Hunter* (Chicago 1968).
3. B. SPOONER, "Towards a Generative Model of Nomadism," *Anthropological Quarterly* 44, no. 3 (1971): 198–210; "The Cultural Ecology of Pastoral Nomads," in *Addison-Wesley Module in Anthropology,* no. 45 (Reading, MA, 1973).
4. B. SPOONER, "Cultural Ecology of Pastoral Nomads," 35.
5. Ibid., 39.
6. Ibid.
7. E. R. SERVICE, *The Hunters* (Englewood Cliffs, NJ, 1966).
8. C. M. TURNBULL, *Wayward Servants* (Garden City, NY, 1965), 247.
9. F. BARTH, *Nomads of South Persia* (Boston 1961), 135.
10. Ibid.
11. M. MAUSS, "Étude de morphologie sociale," 447–48.
12. Ibid., 444.
13. J. WOODBURN, "Stability and Flexibility in Hadza Residential Groupings," in *Man the Hunter,* Lee and DeVore, eds., 107.
14. C. M. TURNBULL, "The Importance of Flux in Two Hunting Societies," in *Man the Hunter,* Lee and DeVore, eds., 137.
15. M. DOUGLAS, *Natural Symbols* (London 1970), 60–61; cited in Spooner, "Cultural Ecology of Pastoral Nomads," 40.
16. CL. LÉVI-STRAUSS, "Hunting and Human Evolution: Discussion," in *Man the Hunter,* Lee and DeVore, eds., 344.

PART

2

South Asia, Iran, and Buddhism

The Religion and Mythology of Vedic India

Of Vedic India we know nothing but the language and the religion. The only documents that this culture has left are texts, and the texts are religious in inspiration, tone, and destination. Here no object remains for the archaeologist's gaze; there is no external testimony to give the historian a point of support, a chronological reference. Between the end—a violent end, it is generally thought—of the Indus civilizations (whose dating is uncertain, and of which nothing is left but material remains) and the beginnings of Buddhism, followed by the first Greek accounts, what we know about India comes down to what we can learn from the Vedas. The Vedas, however, are sacred books that speak only of the sacred. It has been possible to identify certain hymns out of this mass which are secular in tone (such as the hymn "to the frogs," *Ṛksaṃhitā* 7.103). But these are only isolated cases; and while it is true that in these cases the playful element of religion carries more weight than its serious side, it is nonetheless true that the rare poems that can be termed profane emanate like all the others from sacerdotal sources.

The texts that Indian tradition groups under the name of *Veda*, "knowledge," form as a set what the same tradition designates as *śruti*, "revelation," literally "hearing": extraordinary figures, human beings, yet endowed with virtues and powers that place them above the gods, the *ṛṣis* (Louis Renou translates this term as "prophet") had a vision, in the time of origins, of particular portions of this knowledge and transmitted this vision to mankind. (One should note the succession of metaphors: the *ṛṣis saw* the Vedas, but they bequeathed them to posterity in the form of a text to be heard—and repeated.) Where did this revelation come from? Two types of answers to this question have been offered: for followers of certain Indian doctrines, the Vedic texts are the work of a divinity, and even the work of a personal god. For others—and notably for followers of the *Pūrva-mīmāṃsā*—the Veda is *apauruṣeya:* it has no personal author; what is more, it is uncreated, eternal, and unalterable, notwithstanding the fact that particular mythic events were the occasions for the *ṛṣis'* discovery of the different parts and different versions of the Vedic text. An idea that came to be accepted in the post-Vedic period is that the whole of the original Veda was concentrated into certain syllables, or even into a single syllable, and that the task of Vyāsa, the prototype and patron of all the *ṛṣis*, was to unfold and explicate (but at the same time to dilute) the Veda by giving it the form in which the world knows it.

The *śruti* is also called *trayī vidyā*, the "triple science." For Indian tradition, the Vedic text is made up of three vast collections: the *Ṛgveda*, "Veda of Verses"; the *Sāmaveda*, "Veda of Melodies"; and the *Yajurveda*, "Veda of Ritual Formulas." To these has been added a fourth Veda, perhaps a more recent one, and in certain respects of lesser dignity: the *Atharvaveda* (its name comes from the *ṛṣis* to whom it was revealed), which for the most part contains prayers and incantations of a specifically magical character. Verses, melodies, formulas, incantations: this division really applies only to the oldest layer of these three-plus-one Vedas. Each of them in fact consists of several strata which correspond to distinct "literary genres."

a. The *Saṃhitās*. Each Veda has as its original kernel one or more collections of "composed" poems which consist almost entirely of hymns and prayers. The *Saṃhitā* of the *Ṛgveda*, or *Ṛksaṃhitā*, is a collection of more than a thousand poems grouped into ten books or "circles" (*maṇḍalas*). On the basis of formal criteria and, more arbitrarily, content, modern exegetes distinguish an earlier part (*maṇḍalas* 2 through 7) and a later part within the *Ṛksaṃhitā* itself. It is now generally agreed that the earliest poems of the Veda are contemporary with the entry of the *ārya* invaders into India, that is, these poems took on the form in which they have been fixed around the fifteenth century B.C. But comparison with the Avesta (to mention only the Iranian domain, which is extremely close) shows that many traits of this archaic poetry have been inherited from a period before the separation between the *āryas* who were to become the Iranians and those who would move into India. On the other hand, the work of elaborating and fixing the Veda took place on Indian soil over many long centuries, until roughly the middle of the first millennium B.C. The *Saṃhitā* of the *Sāmaveda* consists mainly of verses drawn from the *Ṛksaṃhita* and adapted for recitation in song. The *Saṃhitā* of the *Yajurveda* (divided into the White and Black *Yajurvedas*) includes formulas, in prose or in verse or in mixed prose and verse, directly connected with the ritual and arranged in the order in which they were used in the ceremonies. Finally, the *Saṃhitā* of the *Athar-*

vaveda, quite composite in content, contains on the one hand, as noted, spells for long life, against sickness, against possession by demons, for gaining love or wealth—but also some long hymns in which the exaltation of a particular detail of the ritual is the point of departure for grandiose cosmic evocations.

b. To each of these *Saṃhitās* is assigned one or several *Brāhmaṇas.* The object of these prose treatises is *brahman,* that is, sacred knowledge. They are presented as kinds of theological observations on the rite: they describe the main articulations of the rite (whose different modalities they present and sometimes discuss), provide its mythological justification, and reveal its symbolic implications. The descriptive or prescriptive part of the *Brāhmaṇas* is made up of *vidhis,* "injunctions"; the rest consists of *arthavādas,* "explications," developments meant to stimulate the desire and imagination of the person performing the *vidhi.* The richest and most voluminous of the *Brāhmaṇas* is the *Śatapatha Brāhmaṇa,* "*Brāhmaṇa* of the Hundred Paths." It belongs to the White *Yajurveda.*

c. The *Āraṇyakas,* "forest (books)," follow the pattern set by the *Brāhmaṇas,* to which they form appendixes of a sort. But the rites that provide their theme lend themselves more specifically to a symbolic interpretation. The "*āraṇyaka*" reading of the rite leads directly into truths about the nature of man and the correspondences between macrocosm and microcosm—truths judged to be so charged with meaning that they belong to the domain of *rahasya,* the "esoteric." Too dangerous, in a way, to be pronounced or studied within the village community, they can be uttered only in the solitude of the forest.

d. Finally, the *Upaniṣads.* This term, which properly signifies "showing equivalences," designates a class of texts that are also extensions of some *Brāhmaṇas* or *Āraṇyakas.* The *Upaniṣads,* at least the oldest among them (which are in prose for the most part, unlike the later *Upaniṣads*), develop and systematize the speculative implications of the earlier texts. The ritual point of departure is often lost sight of or reduced to a mere pretext. What is aimed at is a "metaritualism," which, drawing the ultimate conclusions from the correspondence between the human person and the world, leads ultimately to the identification of *ātman,* the individual soul, and *brahman,* which from this point on will be none other than the Absolute: an identification presented both as a truth to be discovered and a goal to be attained.

e. To the Vedas strictly speaking, whose components have just been listed, are added the *Vedāṅgas,* (auxiliary) "limbs" or appendixes of the Vedas: technical treatises composed of *sūtras,* extremely concise aphorisms on how in practice to perform the *vidhi.* This definition particularly fits the *Kalpasūtras,* aphorisms on the rite, which are divided into *śrautasūtras,* instructions on the public ritual, and *gṛhyasūtras,* instructions on the domestic ritual. Another part of the *Vedāṅga* is made up of the *sūtras* of phonetics (*śikṣā*), which teaches the proper articulation of the Vedic text; the *sūtras* of grammar (*vyākaraṇa*); *sūtras* that analyze the metrical structures of Vedic poetry (*chandas*); those that formulate the etymology of Vedic words (*nirukta*); and, finally, *sūtras* on astronomy (*jyotiṣa*).

The *Saṃhitās,* the *Brāhmaṇas,* the *Āraṇyakas,* and the *Upaniṣads* together make up the *śruti;* the auxiliary limbs of *Vedāṅga* belong to *smṛti,* "remembered tradition." But what forms the most essential part of *smṛti* is the imposing ensemble of *dharmasūtras* and *dharmaśāstras,* prose aphorisms or more lengthy verse treatises on dharma, the religious, juridical, and social "law" (among the *dharmaśāstras,* the most famous is the collection of the "Laws of Manu"). Dharma is in principle eternal, but the texts that reveal it, unlike those that constitute *śruti,* belong to human culture: thus *smṛti* is not the object of the same reverence as is *śruti.* But the two are closely connected: a *smṛti* text is necessarily assigned, more or less artificially, to a particular Veda; indeed, a *smṛti* teaching is not fully valid unless it is based on an authority depending on *śruti.*

Together *śruti* and *smṛti* serve, even today, as the reference for Brahmanical orthodoxy. To be within the fold of Brahmanism means, on the level of doctrine, to recognize the truth of what is taught in these two classes of texts. We should add that the lineages of Brahmans are defined not only by the ancestors from whom they are descended, but also by the Vedic "branch" or school (that is, the subdivision of the Veda), and so the founding *ṛṣi,* with which they are associated: a man should marry within his caste but outside his *gotra,* the community which by family tradition is identified with the same *ṛṣi* as himself. But we must not think that the Vedic texts, passed down over the centuries from generation to generation with remarkable exactitude and fidelity, and used in ceremonies to this day, continued to be understood throughout this entire period, nor even that their text was studied. By the end of the Vedic period, the hymns of the *Ṛksaṃhitā* in particular had become for the most part a dead letter; this is understandable considering the archaism of the language of these texts, their extraordinary poetic violence, their morphological and semantic exuberance, the boldness of their syntax and rhetoric, and finally their deliberate hermeticism. In the fourteenth century, at Vijayanagar, in Mysore, a group of learned exegetes led by Sāyana prepared commentaries for nearly the whole of the Veda: these glosses, infinitely precious for the more recent parts of the Veda, were an unquestionable aid to the first Western Vedists. But once this stage was passed, they found themselves able to progress only through a critique of Sāyana. It has been repeated many times, and the arrogance of the claim does not make it any less true: it was Western philology that restored an understanding of the Vedic hymns to India.

Within the *śruti* itself, we have seen that a first distinction is called for by the very form of the texts: there is first of all the initial burst of the *Saṃhitā*—and then all the rest, which in one way or another is commentary or secondary development. For the Indian tradition, however, the dividing line is somewhat different: on the one hand it recognizes *mantras,* hymns, parts of hymns, or isolated formulas, in verse or prose, which have the common characteristic of being uttered in the rite and so constitute a part of the rite; and on the other hand what the tradition encompasses under the general rubric of *brāhmaṇa* (the word being used here in a broader sense); didactic and discursive rather than directly performative texts, these are commentaries or meditations on the rite but not elements of the rite itself. There is also another classification, this one also proposed by the Indian tradition, with the doctrinal content of the texts as its criterion: it distinguishes the *karmakāṇḍa,* the "section of acts," which mainly covers the *Brāhmaṇas,* from the *jñānakāṇḍa,* the "section of knowledge," which coincides with the *Upaniṣads,* understood as *Vedānta,* "completion of the Veda" (the *Āraṇyakas,* which occupy an intermediate position between the *Brāhmaṇas* and the *Upaniṣads,* are generally classed with the *jñānakāṇḍa*). The *Brāhmaṇas* are indeed oriented toward the "act" par excellence, the rite (and more precisely the sacrifice); they teach us how to perform it correctly, how it is to be understood, and the immediate or deferred boon that will be its result. The *Upaniṣads,* on the other hand, teach us that knowledge relegates action to the background; more, that knowledge (of the connections that may be glimpsed through meditating on the rite) is itself a means for us to free ourselves from the chain of births and deaths into which the act (including the ritual act) necessarily locks us. In this way the *Upaniṣads* are the source of inspiration to those who seek deliverance (*mokṣa*), whereas the *Brāhmaṇas* guide those who wish to follow the path of the meritorious act, which leads to heaven (*svarga*).

For any historian who is interested in mythology and ritual and who wonders about Vedism as a unity rather than about the relations between Vedism and the religious forms that followed it, what counts, of course, is not so much the articulation of the *jñānakāṇḍa* and the *karmakāṇḍa* as the relation between the hymns of the oldest part of the *Ṛgveda* on the one hand and the *Brāhmaṇas* on the other. At the time that the most archaic hymns were taking form, the *ārya* population occupied only the northwestern part of the subcontinent, Kashmir and the Punjab. The landscape of the *Brāhmaṇas*, on the other hand, is the Doab between the Ganges and the Yamuna, and the Gangetic Plain up to and past Banaras. In the *Brāhmaṇas* the social structure has changed, the distribution of activities, functions, and statuses among the different classes (*varṇas*) and castes (*jātis*) has become more complicated and at the same time more rigid. Even the language has changed. The Sanskrit of Vedic prose is extremely close to classical Sanskrit, and in the new conditions the culture as a whole, particularly the religion, had to be transformed through its contact with conquered populations (although it is a dangerous temptation, which has been yielded to all too often, to attribute all innovations, real or apparent, to the influence of non-Aryan populations—about which, after all, we have no definite knowledge).

As for the pantheon, the myths, and the theory and practice of the ritual, the chief difficulty in any attempt to write history or in any evaluation of historical shifts is not so much our ignorance of the events as the fact that the documents for the beginning of the period (the archaic kernel of the *Ṛgveda*) and the mass of later *Saṃhitās* and *Brāhmaṇas* are completely different in both character and significance.

The *Ṛgveda* consists of poems whose religious matter is not strictly speaking exposed but is rather evoked in a staggering web of metaphors. How much is stereotyped formula, how much topical description, and how much personal invention in the poet's eulogy to the divinity? The formulas that seem to sketch the characteristic and differential traits of a god melt into one another or collapse into others that are applied without distinction to any divine figure: a Vedic god, whatever his function and mythology, is always celebrated as a supreme, all-powerful god, the source or motive force of all cosmic processes. The myths, which provide the framework for the poems, figure in them only as fragments or allusions. Enigma is a procedure which not only Vedic poetics but also Vedic theology makes use of frequently; the obscure text is the symbol of the mystery of the cosmic reality to which it refers. The rite is an essential theme of these poems, in the sense that the moments and aspects of the sacrifice, the human participants, the utensils, and the material of the offering are exalted with the same ardor and the same refinement as the divinity itself (indeed, Bergaigne could claim that everything in the *Ṛksaṃhitā*, down to the tiniest detail, was based on the rite: the Vedic poem interweaves cult and myth, both of which have the function of representing, making explicit, and thus perpetuating the great phenomena of nature). But while in these texts the *ṛṣis* give us an idea of the eminent value that they attributed to the rite, they do not make it possible for us to visualize the concrete performance of a ceremony. In the *Ṛgveda*, the discourse on the rite is subject to the same ellipses, the same symbolizations, and the same transfigurations as is mythical discourse; and, as we might expect, myth and rite symbolize each other. Thus the work of understanding the Veda consists not only of deciphering the text but of reconstructing from the fragments that it offers us the totality—mythology, ritual, and the system of correspondences between the two—from which these fragments seem to have been detached or diverted. What materials can we use to fill in the enormous gaps that remain?

Three schools of Vedists (at least) confront one another: for some the *Ṛksaṃhitā* can be explained by what precedes it; for others, by what comes after it; for yet others, it can be explained only by itself. Members of the first school of thought see a profound break between the religion of the *Ṛgveda* and Brahmanism (and even more between the *Ṛgveda* and Hinduism): conceived, if not composed, by *ārya* bards before they settled in India, the older part of the *Ṛgveda* bears witness to the religion and world view of the Indo-Iranians; comparison with the earliest attested forms of the religions of other Indo-European peoples permits a kind of etymological reconstruction of the religion of the Veda. For the adversaries of these comparativists, on the other hand, the *Ṛgveda* is already a totally Indian work: the fauna and flora are those of India; and in the same way the religion should be treated as the point of departure for a tradition which becomes more explicit as it develops. If not going so far as to accept the *Brāhmaṇas'* claim to be a direct commentary on the *mantras*, one should at least consider the religious conceptions of these two parts of the *śruti* as homogeneous. A third group, finally, sees the Vedic hymns as a solitary block; light must be sought, they maintain, in an unflagging analysis of the text itself, and the text alone (and there is no doubt that it is this truly ascetic doctrine that has been behind the most decisive advances in Vedic philology, if not in our understanding of Vedic religion).

Problems of an entirely different nature confront someone who wishes to study the religion of the *Brāhmaṇas*. This is a very dry prose which, while far from limpid, at least aims at didactic clarity: the purpose of the *Brāhmaṇas* is not to use all the resources of poetry to evoke various divinities and powers toward whom human rites and prayers ascend; it is rather to explain to men why and how they should say these prayers and celebrate these rites. Here what is most disconcerting is the overabundance of explanations or, more precisely, of justifications. The rite required of men is always to some extent the consequence of a mythical event: it reproduces it, commemorates it, or seeks to rectify or limit an evil that came into being in the time of origins. And this causal connection, over and above the analogy between the cosmos and the sacrificial ground, concerns not only the major rituals as wholes: every detail of the rite is founded in mythology, and in such a way that their explanations frequently overlap and entangle one another.

The question that arises is this: how old and how authentic are these stories that come in at a certain point to give a reason for some ingredient or moment of the sacrifice, then disappear never to be heard of again? Take, for instance, the rule forbidding Kṣatriyas (members of the *varṇa* whose privilege is military and political power) to drink the soma that they are enjoined to offer to the gods—while the Brahmans who participate in the same sacrifice are entitled to a share of the drink (cf. *Aitareya Brāhmaṇa* 7.27ff.). Why this exclusion? It is, the *Brāhmaṇa* teaches, because the god Indra, as punishment for his numerous misdeeds, was himself denied the soma (a drink he coveted) by the other gods; this is why the Kṣatriyas, who in a sense have Indra as their patron, must also abstain from soma; later the interdiction was lifted for the god but not for the human group, which continues to serve, and by this very fact to commemorate, the sentence that the gods pronounced long ago against the fiercest and most powerful of their number. The myth appears in this form only in connection with this ritual prescription. In the developed, autonomous version of the myth, it is not the other gods who inflict this punishment on Indra; instead, the father of one of his victims excludes him from the soma sacrifice in which he is involved. This narrative, at least, can be connected with a well-attested set of myths. But what status can we attribute to the story's sequel? Deprived of soma, the Kṣatriyas have as their special sacrificial food the boughs and fruit of the *nyagrodha* tree, whose branches grow toward the earth. Why is this? As is often the case, the origin myth is really the story of a rite performed in the time of origins: when, thanks to their sacrifice, the gods became able to ascend toward the sky, their movement knocked over some cups of soma set out on the ground. These cups became the *nyagrodha,* and the thin streams of liquid that poured out of them became its branches.

These weak legends, which Bergaigne says "seem to have been made up after the fact to explain formulas that were no longer understood" (*La religion védique,* 3, p. 280), and which Dumézil (*Mythe et épopée,* 1, p. 150) calls pseudomyths, appear not only to justify ritual practices and the social organization and values which it is the explicit purpose of the rites to make known. They are also invoked when it is necessary (a common digression in discussions of the rite) to tell why the human body is made the way it is and why the rite must be performed if we want the body to be maintained harmoniously in its state. For what reason, in the *agnihotra* ceremony, must an offering of milk be made first to Agni (the god of fire) and only afterwards to Sūrya (the sun god) and Vāyu (the wind god)? Because it was Agni whom Prajāpati created first of all, making him come out of his own mouth. But also because (1) milk naturally belongs to Agni, since the milk of the cow is Agni's sperm—this is why it comes warm out of the cow's udder; and (2) it is thanks to this offering that Agni reproduces his own seed; and on the model of Agni, the man who offers the *agnihotra* is reproduced from his own seed. Why is it that human embryos survive and develop when no one feeds them? It is because "the sun, when it sets, enters like an embryo into the womb of fire . . . and along with the sun, all creatures become embryos: they lie down and are satisfied. If night wraps up the sun, it is because embryos are also wrapped up (in the womb). And if the *agnihotra* is offered in the evening, after sunset, this is for the sake of the sun when he is in an embryonic state: it is because of this that embryos survive without having to be fed . . ." (*Śatapatha Brāhmaṇa* 2.3.1.1ff.).

The rite and its mythic justification also explain why the nasal septum separates man's two eyes; why his palms and forehead are smooth and hairless; why his skin has no fur; his feet no hooves; why his fingers are both interdependent and independent. The myths also deal with speech: the form of nouns is always "motivated"; either their etymology is transparent, i.e., the object that they designate got its name because when it was created it was the origin, result, or site of an action designated by the verbal root from which the noun is derived; or else the etymology is opaque, and the myth explains by what malicious decision of the gods a phoneme was modified or displaced in such a way that the link between the derived form and the root ceased to be apparent.

What is interesting in this invention of mythic motifs that are ceaselessly returned to, reshaped, and accumulated (one could hardly list all the variants of the creation of the world—each quite different from all the others—that the *Brāhmaṇas* propose when the need arises) must be sought, we suggest, not principally in the myths thus fabricated, but rather in the ends that they serve. What is it that requires explanation and justification? It is man's relations with his own body, his language, and the fundamental constraints (physical or social)—so obvious that one forgets to notice them—that inform even his smallest movements.

There is thus a considerable difference between the inspiration, goals, and style of the hymns and those that can be observed in the *Brāhmaṇas.* But is the difference so great as to make pointless any comparison between the mythological contents of these two parts of the *śruti?* Certainly not. The same gods, after all, are in both. But the importance of each and their configuration has changed. While it is true that in the *Brāhmaṇas* Indra maintains the primacy that was his from the beginning (in the older part of the Veda, Indra is the greatest of the gods, the largest number of hymns are dedicated to him, and the most glorious feats are attributed to him), and while it is true that Soma and Agni, being both gods and elements of the sacrifice (soma, the matter of the oblation; fire, the vehicle of the offering), remain at the center of the religious structure, other divine figures nonetheless become blurred or altered. Varuṇa, originally the guardian of cosmic order, is now the punisher of ritual faults and the guardian of oaths. A more serious transformation affects the notion of *asura.* In the earlier parts of the *Ṛgveda,* the most powerful gods are called *asuras:* Mitra, Varuṇa, Aryaman, Agni, Rudra, the goddess Uṣas ("dawn"), Indra, the whole group of the Ādityas. What these divinities have in common is the possession of *māyā,* the art of fabricating forms, of creating wonders or spinning illusions. In the *Brāhmaṇas,* on the other hand, the *asuras* are demons, the perennial adversaries of the gods: gods and *asuras* battle one another for the possession of heaven and the control of the sacrifice. But the gods and the *asuras* are both sons of Prajāpati: here again is the main innovation of the later Vedas: the emergence of a primordial divinity who, from his own body, creates living beings, the sacrifice, the articulated pattern of time.

As an example we will present myths concerning Soma as they appear in connection with the ritual in various texts of the later part of the Veda.

C.Ma./j.l.

BIBLIOGRAPHY

Publications on various aspects of Vedic studies are listed and classified in L. Renou's *Bibliographie védique* (Paris 1931) and continued according to the same principles in R. N. Dandekar's *Vedic Bibliography,* 1 (Bombay 1946), 2 (Poona 1961), 3 (Poona 1973).

A. BARTH, *Les religions de l'Inde* (Paris 1879), in *Encyclopédie des sciences religieuses,* by Lichtenberger; reprinted in *Quarante ans d'Indianisme,* the works of Auguste Barth, vol. 1 (Paris 1914). A. BERGAIGNE, *La religion védique d'après les hymnes du Rig-Veda,* 3 vols. (Paris 1878–83). M. BLOOMFIELD, *The Religion of the Veda: From Ṛg-Veda to Upanishads* (New York 1908). W. CALAND and V. HENRY, *L'Agniṣṭoma, description complète de la forme normale du sacrifice de "Soma" dans le culte védique,* 2 vols. (Paris 1906, 1907). G. DUMÉZIL, *Aspects de la fonction guerrière chez les Indo-Européens* (Paris 1956); *Les dieux souverains des Indo-Européens* (Paris 1977); *The Destiny of the Warrior* (Chicago 1970), originally in French (Paris 1969); *Mythe et épopée,* 1–2 (Paris 1968, 1971). P.-E. DUMONT, *L'Agnihotra* (Baltimore 1939); *L'Aśvamedha* (Paris 1927). K. F. GELDNER, *Vedismus und Brahmanismus* (Tübingen 1928). J. GONDA, *Change and Continuity in Indian Religion* (The Hague 1965); *Die Religionen Indiens,* 1: *Vedismus und älterer Hinduismus* (Stuttgart 1960), also in French; *The Savayajñas* (Amsterdam 1965). J. C. HEESTERMAN, *The Ancient Indian Royal Consecration: The "Rājasūya" Described according to the Yajus Texts and Annotated* (The Hague 1957). V. HENRY, *La magie dans l'Inde antique* (Paris 1904). A. HILLEBRANDT, *Ritual-Litteratur* (Strasbourg 1897); *Vedische Mythologie,* 1–2 (2d ed., Breslau 1927–29). A. B. KEITH, *The Religion and Philosophy of the Veda and the Upanishads* (Cambridge, MA, 1925); *Vedic Index of Names and Subjects,* 2 vols. (London 1912). S. LÉVI, *La doctrine du sacrifice dans les Brâhmaṇas* (Paris 1898; 2d ed., Paris 1966, with preface by L. Renou). H. LOMMEL, *Altbrahmanische Legenden* (Zurich 1964). H. LÜDERS, *Varuṇa,* 2 vols. (Göttingen 1951–59). A. A. MACDONELL, *Vedic Mythology* (Strasbourg 1897). A. A. MACDONELL, A. B. KEITH, and J. MUIR, *Original Sanskrit Texts,* 5 vols. (London 1872–74). H. OLDENBERG, *Die Religion des Veda* (3d ed., Stuttgart 1923); *Vorwissenschaftliche Wissenschaft: Die Weltanschauung der Brāhmaṇa-Texte* (Göttingen 1919); "Zur Religion und Mythologie des Veda," Nachrichte von der Kgl. Gesellschaft der Wissenschaften zu Göttingen, Philosophische-historische Klasse (1915), 167–235, 361–403. R. PISCHEL and K. F. GELDNER, *Vedische Studien,* 3 vols. (Stuttgart 1889–1901). W. RAU, *Staat und Gesellschaft im alten Indien nach den Brāhmaṇa-Texten dargestellt* (Wiesbaden 1957). L. RENOU, *Anthologie sanskrite* (Paris 1947); *Les écoles védiques et la formation du Veda* (Paris 1947); *Études védiques et pāṇinéennes,* 17 vols. (Paris 1955–69); *Hymnes et prières du Veda* (Paris 1938); *Hymnes spéculatifs du Veda* (Paris 1956); *Les maîtres de la philologie védique* (Paris 1928); *Poésie religieuse de l'Inde antique* (Paris 1942); *Religions of Ancient India* (London 1953). L. RENOU and J. FILLIOZAT, *L'Inde classique, manuel des études indiennes,* 1 (Paris 1947), 2 (Hanoi 1953). B. SCHLERATH, *Das Königtum im Rig- und Atharvaveda* (Wiesbaden 1960). H. P. SCHMIDT, *Bṛhaspati und Indra: Untersuchungen zur vedische und Kulturgeschichte* (Wiesbaden 1968); *Vedisch vratá und avestisch urvāta* (Hamburg 1958). P. THIEME, *Der Fremdling im Ṛgveda: Eine Studie über die Bedeutung der Worte ari, arya, aryaman und ārya* (Leipzig 1938); "Mitra und Aryaman," *Transactions of the Connecticut Academy of Arts and Sciences* 41 (New Haven 1957). J. VARENNE, *Mythes et légendes extraits des Brāhmaṇas* (Paris 1967); *Le Veda* (Paris 1967), an anthology. M. WINTERNITZ, *History of Indian Literature,* 3 vols. (Calcutta 1920–33), originally in German.

Translations

Ṛgveda: K. F. GELDNER, *Der Rig-Veda aus dem Sanskrit ins Deutsche übersetzt und mit einem laufenden Kommentar versehen,* 4 vols. (Cambridge, MA, 1951–57).

Atharvaveda: D. W. WHITNEY, *Atharva-Veda saṁhitā: Translated with a Critical and Exegetical Commentary,* 2 vols. (Cambridge, MA, 1905).

Taittirīyasaṁhitā: A. B. KEITH, *The Veda of the Black Yajus School Entitled Taittirīya Saṁhitā Translated from the Original Sanskrit Prose and Verse,* 2 vols. (Cambridge, MA, 1914).

Śatapathabrāhmaṇa: J. EGGELING, *The Śatapatha-Brāhmaṇa according to the Text of the Mâdhyandina School,* 5 vols. (Oxford 1882–1900).

Aitareyabrāhmaṇa and Kauṣītakibrāhmaṇa: A. B. KEITH, *Rigveda Brahmanas: The Aitareya and Kauṣītaki Brāhmaṇas of the Rigveda, Translated from the Original Sanskrit* (Cambridge, MA, 1920).

Aitareya-Āraṇyaka: A. B. KEITH, *The Aitareya Āraṇyaka Edited . . . with Introduction, Translation, Notes, Indexes . . .* (Oxford 1909).

Soma as Sacrificial Substance and Divine Figure in the Vedic Mythology of Exchange

The sacrificial substance called soma and the divine figure Soma together form indissolubly the theme of a mythology that reveals its full meaning only in connection with the ritual that corresponds to it.

The sacrifices that use as the material of their oblations the plant called soma are the most prestigious form of the Vedic ritual. A considerable number of texts are devoted to the minute description as well as the glorification of the soma ceremonies (notably all of book 9 of the *Ṛksaṃhitā*). Despite all that has been said about it, we know very little about the nature of this plant. Its botanical identity remains uncertain, and controversies have surrounded it since the beginnings of Indian studies (see Wasson 1968), but have led to nothing but hypotheses. The plant seems far more important for what can be made of it in the cult and for what can be said of it poetically in the hymns than for what it actually is. Several species have probably borne the same name and served the same ends, and a text as early as the *Śatapatha Brāhmaṇa* lists the plants that can be used as substitutes for soma per se. The typical soma is above all a plant, *the* plant par excellence, that grows wild in mountainous regions, "in the north," whence it is brought with great difficulty. The part of the soma plant that is used in rituals consists of its stems, from which, when they are crushed, a brownish juice flows. When filtered ("clarified"), the juice is called soma too; it provokes in the men (and gods) who drink it a kind of euphoric exaltation that the texts take great pains to distinguish from ordinary intoxication and that in certain ways suggests the effects of hallucinogenic substances (as, for instance, in Ṛgvedic hymn 10.119).

The ritual of the soma plant is thus the history of the transformation that it undergoes between the time when it is picked and the time when its juice is squeezed out and consumed. The consequences of the ritual are twofold: immediate effects on the psyche of individuals, men and gods alike, who have the right to partake of this delicious beverage, whence they draw strength and exhilaration; and cosmic effects: the soma that flows in the sacrificial vats is the image and in a way the cause of all liquids, of all saps that carry life throughout nature. The earthly soma has a celestial counterpart whose receptacle is the moon: this is the *amṛta,* the liquor of immortality that the gods drink when the moon is full and the dead drink at the new moon (Gonda 1962, p. 84; Keith 1925, p. 166).

From the time of the *Brāhmaṇas* it has been taught that soma and the moon are one and the same, and the word soma later becomes one of the usual names for the moon in classical Sanskrit. What facilitates this close correspondence, to the point of identification, is the way in which both the planet and the plant are characterized by changes in their form and volume. The stems of soma that swell when they are immersed before being crushed are analogous to the crescent moon.

In the series of changes that the successive phases of the ritual impose on the soma plant, the Ṛgvedic hymns to the god Soma refer mainly to operations ranging from pressing (the stems are crushed with stones, and the stones themselves are glorified in hymns) to decanting and then to final clarification. The juice thus extracted is collected in vats and filtered in woolen sieves, and the melodious din of the soma splashing against the walls of the containers and the noise of the drops falling one by one through the filter are also constantly repeated poetic themes. The *Brāhmaṇas* go back farther into time and develop at great length what might be called the prehistory of the *soma pavamāna*, or the soma "in process of clarification." They discuss the ceremonies that precede or constitute the introduction of the soma into the sacrificial apparatus, notably the rite known as "the purchase of the soma." The mythology of the soma is essentially connected with the preliminary part of the ritual. The basic theme of the mythology is the "abduction" of the soma, or of Soma, by the gods. Men's efforts to obtain the soma and make it come to the sacrifice are presented in the *Brāhmaṇas* in such a way as to assign a symbolic function to them: to commemorate and transpose to the world of men the stratagems that the gods resort to in their attempts to secure soma for themselves. Each of these sequences, the mythical sequence and the ritual sequence, has its own coherence; in addition, the two sets cannot be superimposed on one another. Certain elements of the myth (of the different variants of the myth) are not translated in the ritual, and the ritual contains sections that are not found in the myth.

But the facts that are especially worth noting are the complexity of the mechanism of transposition and the mythical function (the function of a myth of origin) that the ritual assumes in connection with the actions of profane life: the myth justifies the ritual, and the ritual justifies the social institutions and behavior. In the myth, (the) Soma while already on his way toward the camp of the gods is diverted, somehow, by the Gandharvas, and the gods must repurchase him by paying a ransom that is none other than Speech (*vāc*). But the most dramatic moment of the rite of the introduction of the soma is a mock purchase: a strange dramatization requires the celebrants, already in possession of the soma stems, to hand them over to a man of low caste who assumes the role of "soma merchant." They "buy" the soma from him at the end of a violent but carefully orchestrated session of bargaining. This ritual transaction is overdetermined in the sense that several reasons for its existence are clearly indicated in the text:

1. It commemorates the myth: the soma merchant plays the part of the Gandharva; the cow that will eventually be the purchase price represents Speech which the gods gave to the Gandharva to regain possession of Soma, etc.

2. The soma obtained by the men is destined to be pressed on the sacrificial site. This pressing is a murder, the murder of a god: "Truly, they kill the Soma when they press him" (*Taittirīya Saṃhitā* 6.6.7.1; see S. Lévi 1898, p. 170). Just as one must take all sorts of precautions in order to circumscribe and reject the evil inherent in killing the victim of a blood sacrifice, so one must attribute to a stranger the crime of introducing Soma, simultaneously a god and an oblatory substance, into the system that will ultimately result in his killing. The soma merchant is wicked on two scores: first because he "represents" the Gandharva who retains Soma, and second as the scapegoat whom the celebrants and the sacrificer saddle with the sin of having procured the soma that they are about to offer.

3. The purchase of the soma, the purchase of a god, and a divine king at that, because once it is bought, the soma is welcomed as a royal guest, and Soma is frequently designated as a king, the only king that the Brahmans recognize (see Heesterman 1957, p. 75ff.), is in turn the prototype of the eminently profane social practice known as commerce. More precisely, the texts that deal with this connection between the purchase of and bargaining for the soma and commerce in general use the poetic figure of the a fortiori: "because one bargains to buy King Soma, everything is for sale here on earth" (*Śatapatha Brāhmaṇa* 3.3.3.1) . . . "Because the celebrant and then the seller first bargain and then come to an agreement, people here on earth do the same whenever anything is for sale; they too begin by bargaining and then come to an agreement" (ibid. 4).

The purchase of the earthly soma by the celebrants is an imitation of the repurchase of the celestial soma. The *Brāhmaṇas* show that between the mythic repurchase and the ritual purchase that repeats it and results from it there is a connection that is precisely the one that Benveniste points out in the history of Indo-European institutions: the repurchase, whose objective is the recovery of a living person, is the original form of purchase, the acquisition of material goods (see *Vocabulaire des institutions indo-européennes* [Paris 1969], vol. 1, p. 129ff.). But the transaction itself is a deception in two ways. The soma merchant is artificially incited by the celebrants, who pretend to buy from him what they in fact already have. And even this fiction is not fully carried out, since according to certain texts at least (among them *Āpastamba Śrauta Sūtra* 10.27.6ff.), all the negotiating ends with a brawl, or a mock brawl, during which the soma merchant is beaten with a bludgeon and the cow given to him in exchange for his soma is brutally taken back from him (see Gonda 1962, vol. 1, p. 185). This dramatization, quick dialogue, dramatic progression, and final reversal may have resulted in the notion that the origin of Indian theater is to be found in this part of the soma liturgy (see Hillebrandt 1927, vol. 1, p. 258). A rather fragile hypothesis, and an answer to a question that may not have any meaning; but one cannot help but be struck by all the "representation" that this ritual contains.

This set of preliminary actions constitutes what we might call the *dīkṣā* of the soma: wrapped in linens, the packets of soma stems are like fetuses surrounded by their membranes. This embryonic phase also characterizes the sacrificer during the *dīkṣā*, that is, the consecration that gives him the new body that he will use during the sacrifice per se. (For details on the *dīkṣā* of the soma which, however, is prepared to be not the sacrificer but the victim, see *Śatapatha Brāhmaṇa* 3.3.3.12.) The ritual actions performed during this preparation and this introduction of the soma serve not merely as the model or condition for the possibility of commerce; the Brāhmaṇa commentary goes further into abstraction and into the search for the basis of any activity that implies a comparison between a model and its replica. There comes a time in the course of these operations when the soma stems, displayed on a piece of linen, must be measured with one's fingers, alternately stretched and folded. "It is because one measures King Soma that measuring exists both among men and in general" (*Śatapatha Brāhmaṇa* 3.3.2.9). Exchange, simulation, measurement: here as in so many other examples, what establishes the elementary actions of men and gives them meaning is the fact that the actions first had to be performed in the ritual.

The following are the principal articulations of the myth in which the gods take possession of the soma, as it is told in the *Taittirīya Saṃhitā* 6.1.6.1ff., the *Aitareya Brāhmaṇa* 3.25, and the *Śatapatha Brāhmaṇa* 3.6.2.2ff.

1. In the time of the origins, Soma was in the celestial world, and the gods were here on earth. They wanted to have him come to them so that they could offer him in sacrifice. To that end, they produced two female creatures (protagonists of a separate mythology, who appear here as two "fictions"), two *māyās*, Kadrū and Suparṇī. Kadrū is the Earth; Suparṇī is Speech.

2. Kadrū and Suparṇī are rivals. "Whichever one of us," they decided, "has the best eyesight will triumph over the other and take over the other's person (*ātman*)." Suparṇī says, "I see on the other side of the ocean a white horse tied to a post." "I," replies Kadrū, "can see the wind moving the horse's tail." Kadrū and Suparṇī rush forward to see: Kadrū was right; she wins and takes over the *ātman* of her rival.

3. But Kadrū gives Suparṇī a chance to repurchase herself: "Go and seek Soma for the gods. Soma is in heaven. If you bring him back, I shall return your *ātman* to you." Suparṇī had children, the metric forms (*chandas*) of the Veda. She says, "This is why parents have children, to repurchase their *ātman*" (a reference to the theory that man is indebted to his ancestors and repays this debt by engendering descendants). She therefore charges her children with this task.

4. The metric forms are transformed into birds (their mother Suparṇī has a name meaning "well-winged"), and the *jagatī* is the first to take flight. (The *jagatī* is a stanza with twelve syllables in each line. But the narrative is also a myth of the origin of the metric forms: how did the stanzas come to have their present form? In the version in the *Aitareya Brāhmaṇa,* these metric forms are originally identical, although they bear different names: their differences are potential, and it is because of the events of the myth that the differences are actualized. The *jagatī,* like the other meters, is thus conceived as having originally been made of four-syllable lines.) After covering half the distance, she grows tired and sheds three syllables. After becoming monosyllabic, she is unable to reach Soma and returns to the gods, bringing back two elements that are essential to the sacrifice, the *dīkṣā,* the preliminary consecration of the sacrificer, and *tapas,* ascetic energy. (In the *Taittirīya Saṃhitā* version, the meters are from the beginning different both from one another and from what they will become later. When the *jagatī* takes flight, she consists of fourteen syllables. On the way she loses two syllables, but brings back the *dīkṣā* and the *paśus,* the animal victims.)

5. Now it is the turn of the *triṣṭubh* (a stanza with lines of eleven syllables; but originally, according to the *Aitareya,* the lines had four syllables.) The *triṣṭubh* must also shed a syllable—but only one—retrace her steps, and bring back the *dakṣiṇā,* that is, the sacrificial honoraria. (In the version in the *Taittirīya Saṃhitā,* she has thirteen syllables when she sets out and she loses two.)

6. The gods turn to the *gāyatrī* stanza, with eight syllables in each line. (The *gāyatrī* is the noblest meter because it is the metric formula of the *sāvitrī,* i.e., the prayer to the god Savitṛ, who is considered the quintessence of the Veda.) She reaches the soma, succeeds in frightening the guardians, and seizes the soma with her claws and her beak. She also takes possession of the two syllables dropped by the *jagatī* and the one syllable abandoned by the *triṣṭubh:* she thus becomes octosyllabic, the form we know today. (The same narrative is told in the *Taittirīya Saṃhitā,* which adds that the *gāyatrī* succeeded where the other meters had failed because she was accompanied by a female goat, *ajā.* But the *Śatapatha Brāhmaṇa* 3.3.3.9 says that *ajā* means "she who fetches," and the form *ajā* was originally the esoteric name of the goat. The *Taittirīya Saṃhitā* also says that because of this exploit the *gāyatrī,* the smallest of the meters, is also the most glorious meter.)

7. The part of the soma that the *gāyatrī* squeezes in her right claw is what later becomes in sacrifice the morning pressing; the part that she squeezes in her left claw is the noon pressing. But on the return flight, she sucks up the share of soma that she carries in her beak. Emptied of its juice, this part of soma is inferior to the previous ones. To cancel this difference, the gods decide to add "cattle" to the third pressing; and, in addition, the evening soma is mixed with milk, and the offering is followed by an offering of butter and an immolation of animal victims.

8. The meters that had failed in their attempts claim from the *gāyatrī* the lost syllables that she acquired. The *gāyatrī* refuses: the syllables belong to her because she found them. This judgment is confirmed by the gods: and that is why, even today, one can claim to be the owner of something one has found. The line of the *gāyatrī* thus has eight syllables, that of the *triṣṭubh,* three, and that of the *jagatī,* one. The *gāyatrī* reserves for herself the privilege of helping with the morning pressing and entrusts this task to the other two meters for the pressings of noon and evening. Unable to fulfill her duty, the *triṣṭubh* asks the *gāyatrī* for help. The *gāyatriī* intervenes in the noon pressing, joins the *triṣṭubh,* and from this combination is born a new *triṣṭubh* with eleven syllables. The process is repeated for the *jagatī,* which had become monosyllabic: adding the eleven syllables from the new *triṣṭubh,* she assumes her definitive form with a line of twelve syllables.

9. But before these adjustments take place among the meters, one event interrupts Soma's voyage toward the gods. The soma is intercepted by the Gandharva Viśvāvasu (this phase of the myth is told by the *Taittirīya Saṃhitā* and the *Śatapatha Brāhmaṇa*). The gods plot to take back Soma. "The Gandharvas," they say, "love women. Let us send them Speech, who is a woman." According to the *Taittirīya Saṃhitā,* the gods transform Speech into a one-year-old woman. Speech returns with the soma, but the unhappy Gandharvas follow her to the gods and complain: "Take back the soma, but let us keep Speech." The gods propose to let Speech decide. The gods and the Gandharvas enter into a competition to seduce Speech: the Gandharvas try to please her by reciting the Veda, but the gods, better advised, invent the lute and make music. They win, and Speech returns to their camp. That is why to this day women love music, dance, and frivolous songs. So goes the *Śatapatha Brāhmaṇa* version. The *Taitirīya Saṃhitā* version differs only in one detail: after serving as ransom for the soma, Speech takes the form of a gazelle and flees from the Gandharvas but does not return to the gods. The Gandharvas and the gods agree to compete to attract her. The *Taittirīya Saṃhitā* specifies that in the ritual the cow with which the soma is bought from the merchant represents Speech, and that it must be one year old, just like the Speech woman whom the gods gave to the Gandharvas to repurchase Soma from them. And the text also adds that Speech was one year old, and that is why humans speak when they reach the age of one. Moreover, just as the gods sought to please Speech, so the sacrificer and the celebrants must try to please the cow destined first to pay the soma merchant. They make an appropriate offering to him. And just as Speech chose the side of the gods, so the soma cow chooses the side of the sacrificer and the celebrants, who take her away.

With Speech and the soma at their disposal, the gods and men—each of these groups on the level appropriate to it—can now proceed to the immolation of their royal guest. But men do not limit themselves to a pure imitation, nor even to a transposition, of what the gods do; for, although the gods have given men the model of the quest for the soma, men give the gods the substance of the sacrifice. It is in drinking the soma prepared by men and transformed by the ritual into ambrosia that the gods are immortal.

C.Ma./g.h.

BIBLIOGRAPHY

In the bibliography at the end of the article "The Religion and Mythology of Vedic India," the following works refer particularly to Soma: BERGAIGNE, 1878, especially pp. 148–235. CALAND-HENRY, 1906–7. GONDA, 1962, especially pp. 81–86 and 184–91; 1965, pp. 38–70. HEESTERMAN, 1957, passim, especially pp. 69–90. HILLEBRANDT, 1927–29, especially 1:193–498. See also H. LOMMEL, "König Soma," *Numen* 2 (1955). L. RENOU, *Études védiques et pāṇinéennes* 9 (Paris 1961). U. SCHNEIDER, *Der Somaraub des Manu, Mythus und Ritual* (Wiesbaden 1971). R. G. WASSON, *Soma, Divine Mushroom of Immortality,* Ethnomycological Studies 1 (New York 1968).

VEDIC COSMOGONY

The Vedic hymns provide a great quantity of cosmogonic themes, but most are in the form of allusions or dispersed fragments, in which images recur of unfolding space, of the prop that holds earth and sky apart, etc. The myth of Indra is perhaps the only exception to this, and it is not by chance that it is taken up again in classical Hinduism, and in an interesting way, since in the intervening time the relations between Indra and Viṣṇu had changed. The Brāhmaṇas, by contrast, present myths with greater continuity; among these are accounts of cosmogonic value, more or less inchoate, which are related to some sacrificial rite. The principal myths were later taken up under the form of the avatars of Viṣṇu: the Fish, the Turtle, the Boar, and the Dwarf. These will be dealt with in the article on the avatar, for it is not by chance that these incomplete cosmogonic accounts could realize their callings by becoming transformed into myths of avatars, with their heroes becoming forms of Viṣṇu.

There is nevertheless a Vedic hymn that must be placed on a level completely distinct from all others, as much for its form as a well-articulated cosmogony as for its simultaneously diffuse, omnipresent, and highly structured posterity: this is the *Puruṣa Hymn* (RS 10.90), which we must cite in its entirety here (after the translation by Louis Renou, *Hymnes speculatifs du Veda,* Paris 1956):

> The Man has a thousand heads; he has a thousand eyes, a thousand feet. Completely covering the earth, he overflows it by ten fingers.
>
> The Man is none other than this universe, that which is past and that which is to come. He is the master of the immortal domain, because he grows beyond food.
>
> Such is his strength, and even more vigorous than this is the Man. All of the beings are one-quarter of him; the Immortal in the sky, the (other) three-quarters.
>
> With three-quarters the Man placed himself on high; the fourth had his birth here below. From there he spread in every direction, toward things that eat and things that do not.
>
> From him is born the (creative) Energy, from the (creative) Energy the Man was born. Once born, he stretched himself beyond the earth as far to the front as to the rear.
>
> When the gods performed the sacrifice with the Man as oblatory substance, the spring served as (ritual) butter, the summer as firewood, the autumn as offering.
>
> On the (sacred) palanquin they sprinkled the Man (that is,) the sacrifice that was born in the beginning. Through him the gods performed the sacrifice along with the Saints and the Seers.
>
> From this sacrifice offered in its total form, the speckled (ritual) fat was drawn off. From this were made the animals of the air, those of the desert, and those of the clusters.
>
> From this sacrifice offered in its complete form were born the verses, the melodies; the meters were also born from this, the (liturgical) formula was born from this.
>
> From this (sacrifice) were born the horses and all beasts with two rows of teeth. The bovines were also born from it, and from it were born the goats and the lambs.
>
> When they had dismembered the Man, how did they distribute his parts? What became of his mouth? What became of his arms? His thighs, his feet, what name did these receive?
>
> His mouth became the Brahman, the Warrior was the product of his arms, his thighs were the Artisan (better: "the man of the land" M.B.), from his feet was born the Servant.
>
> The moon was born from his consciousness, from his gaze was born the sun, from his mouth Indra and Agni, from his breath was born the wind.
>
> The atmospheric region came from his navel, from his head evolved the heaven, from his feet the earth, from his ear the celestial quarters: thus the worlds were determined.
>
> Seven were the planks of the palings, three times seven were made the burning logs, when the gods performed the sacrifice, having bound the Man as victim.
>
> The gods sacrificed the sacrifice by the sacrifice. Such were the first institutions. These powers had access to the firmament, in which are found the Saints, the original gods.

The poet is less concerned with a proper cosmogony, i.e., with an explanation of the universe that tells a story beginning with a chaos or a zero point, than with the organization of all that exists around two key ideas that are well identified: the Puruṣa and the sacrifice. The Puruṣa is above all the Male, but this is a Male whose form is undoubtedly human: in the same way *puruṣa* would become the common word designating man, but specifically the immortal aspect of transmigrating man, which is promised deliverance. But *puruṣa* would also become one of the names for the Absolute, and particularly of Viṣṇu, and this name would be given to a more "personal" Absolute than that of the *brahman.* The Puruṣa of the hymn is at once identified with our world and with the universe that envelops and transcends it, with the mortal and with the immortal. Its function as the origin of everything is accentuated by the reciprocal engendering that takes place between it, the Male, and the Female Energy: there is an implicit refusal to claim a precedence of one over the other, even if the Puruṣa is clearly the more essential principle. But a couple is thus formed that would become the Puruṣa and the Prakṛti—or Śakti—the original Male with the female energy which he projects outside of himself to produce the world. These two principles would give Hinduism its god/goddess opposition, in which the goddess, closer to the world, if only by her essential nature, would always exist as the active hypostasis of the god; she would be the god in action, whereas the god himself would always tend toward inaction, not by virtue of a "natural tendency" that he had from the start, but in order to incarnate those values that appeared in Hinduism.

Nevertheless, the creation of the world is not carried over into a sexual engendering. It is not a question of Energy—unless it is precisely the energy of the sacrifical activity, or the fertile female aspect of the sacrificial activity that is above all identified with the Puruṣa. The sacrifice lies at the base of everything; the Puruṣa is the sacrifice and also the sacrificial victim. Nothing is said about the person who offers the sacrifice (the gods generally serve as technicians, or officials), but to say that the Puruṣa is the sacrifice is also a way of identifying him with the person who sacrifices. Here we touch on what was undoubtedly the most profound intuition of the Vedic poets, one that would be at the root of innumerable mythic or other speculations in Hinduism: there is never a sacrifice that is not of one's self; if one sacrifices something to the gods, it must be something of oneself, something of value. In other words, the victim offered in sacrifice is nothing other than a substitute for the sacrificer. Thus each time that we see a man (or his son) appear in the position of sacrificial victim, in a myth or symbolically in a rite, one must not jump to the conclusion that this was originally a human sacrifice: in each case this is a reminder of the symbolic equivalence of the sacrificer and the sacrificial victim.

The emphasis thus placed upon the sacrifice in the Vedic hymn can mean only one thing: what it tells us about the Vedic state of the religion is centered upon the sacrifice. It is through the sacrifice that not only the organization of the human world but also the establishment of the rest of the universe is to be realized, including the forest animals and all that lies beyond this earth. This organizing principle would never be questioned—even when the Vedic sacrifice became outmoded in practice—but it would reappear transformed and relativized in the interior of the Hindu world.

Let us recall the four great "classes"—*varṇas*—of human beings born from the Puruṣa and the way in which they are connected to him. The Brahman, priest and cleric, is his mouth. The warrior-prince—Kṣatriya—is his arm. The Vaiśya—whose name indicates a close relationship with the land, with the earth that he inhabits, and whose class includes the agriculturalist, the pastoralist, and the merchant—comes from his thigh. And the Śūdra, the whole group of the service castes, is his feet. There is thus an implied hierarchy in this choice that goes from the head to the feet of the Puruṣa: note that, on the level of the Vedic gods who are later enumerated, Indra and Agni are his mouth. The sacrifice is first of all the food of the gods, a nourishing stream that constantly rises from the earth to the sky and that Indra, the king of the gods, causes to return to earth in the form of beneficent rain. Indra is both the king of the gods and the regulator of the rains that fall upon the earth, two apparently disparate functions that cannot be understood unless they are taken together. Agni is Fire, and above all the sacrificial Fire who is also called "the mouth of the gods," because he is charged with bringing to the gods, with his smoke, the sacrificial food that men feed to him: melted butter, the fat of the victim. But the Brahmans themselves are the gods of the earth, whom other men are required to feed. Feeding Brahmans—sacrificial priests and others—is part of the sacrificial rite, and this even comes to take the place of the whole of the rite, of the sacrifice itself. The Brahman is thus, like Agni or Indra, the mouth of the Puruṣa. His place in the cosmos as ordained by the sacrifice consists in part of receiving gifts, above all gifts of food: this becomes a part of the classical definition of the Brahman.

The Warrior is the arm of the Puruṣa: the arm as symbol of strength is obvious, but it may have a more complex significance, since the Kṣatriya is at once prince and warrior, warrior because he is prince. His arm is an arm of punishment, which is the essence of the prince, who carries out military campaigns on the exterior and polices the interior for the general peace. It is in these ways that the warrior exercises his classical function of protecting his subjects. The authority of his arm allows him, among other things, to collect taxes, which is essential to his administration and especially to his religious role: the protection of his subjects requires an abundance of sacrifices interspersed with general gifts to Brahmans.

If the Vaiśya is the thigh of the Puruṣa, this is probably by virtue of a play on words that was to be exploited for all it was worth. The man of the Viś is the man of the soil, the inhabitant of the country whose activity produces wealth, the preeminent royal subject on whom the king assesses taxes to cover his ritual and nonritual obligations. He thus has an essential connection with the earth, the ground of the kingdom, which is the source of all wealth. One of the names for the earth is *urvī*, "the wide," "the extended" (the feminine of *uru*), whereas the thigh is called *ūru*. In fact classical mythology pays little attention to the Vaiśyas, and the thigh as a symbol of the earth reappears sometimes in connection with Brahmans (like Aurva) and sometimes with Kṣatriyas (like Duryodhana).

As for the Śūdra, the lower castes whose sole duty is to serve the three higher *varṇas*, the only part of the Puruṣa which he could possibly be is the feet. The foot is the lowest part of a person: for this reason to place one's foot on someone's head is the most extreme humiliation, but to touch another's feet with one's head is an act of total submission and a recognition of one's own inferiority. The Śūdra is excluded from any participation in the sacrifice, and it is remarkable that the cosmic Puruṣa, the Puruṣa-sacrifice, nevertheless includes this group. This is an implicit recognition of the fact that the sacrificial system could not exist if the Śūdra refused to fulfill his functions, and for this reason he is incorporated into a cosmic order centered upon the sacrifice.

Indra, Agni, Sūrya the Sun, Candramas the Moon (masc.), and Vāyu the Wind are among the most important Vedic gods. With the exception of Indra, they are not individualized in complete myths. Classical Hinduism would convert them into guardians of the cardinal points, but here they are essentially recipients of sacrifice. Inhabitants of heaven, they occupy the highest level of a world in which earth, atmosphere, and the sky are superimposed.

Whatever may have been the concrete reality of the society of castes in the period in which this cosmogony was composed, every Hindu can recognize in it what for him constitutes the order of the world and can find in it the place assigned to him alone: what would come to be called dharma.

M.Bi./d.w.

BIBLIOGRAPHY

F. B. J. KUIPER, "Cosmogony and Conception: A Query," *History of Religions* 10, no. 2 (1970).

The Mythologies of Hindu India

This study of Indian mythologies will be restricted to Hinduism: Buddhism emigrated from India about ten centuries ago, and its Indian mythology owes a great deal to Hinduism. The same can be said about Jainism, a branch of Brahmanism that diverged at about the same time as Buddhism, and that survives in India to this day. We will leave aside tribal religions which, from north to south and from east to west, are all embedded within Hinduism: they are the religions of populations living apart from Hindu society, but are strongly influenced by this encompassing presence.

Hindu mythology is certainly one of the lushest and most complex that humanity has produced. At first glance it defies any attempt to order it, as well as any attempt to describe it exhaustively. But the various dictionaries and indexes have always emphasized monographic descriptions of divinities and rites, giving preference to enumeration and seeking exhaustivity. They have thus risked increasing the impression of extreme diversity, of gratuitous and uncontrolled fantasy. Our position will be the opposite of this: we will sacrifice exhaustiveness in favor of intelligibility, positing both a deep unity beneath the diversity and the possibility of grasping this unity through an appropriate method. This is why, in particular, this new collection is not meant to be a simple addition to the others, and does not hesitate to turn to the others for information (see bibliography). In most cases we will rather try to illuminate mythic data, not to speak of a new light.

We will not be dealing with myths *and* rituals, which would be an almost infinite task, but will use rituals as one of the sources for our understanding of myths (not the only one, for there is far from a one-to-one correspondence between myth and ritual). On the other hand, we will focus on the myth as the unit of study rather than its characters, motifs, or phases of composition: it is the myth that bears the meaning that engendered it, and it is therefore the myth that can provide the keys to interpretation, if we ask the right questions. We must, given the limits of brief articles, leave our preliminary work to some extent in the dark, and, in particular, almost completely ignore any comparison between different versions of the same myth. Yet all the great Indian myths present a multiplicity of versions, which we refuse to dissect according to the pseudohistorical principle of interpolation: for it is often the confrontation of these versions that provides us with the single global meaning of all of them, or of some obscure detail in its specific context, or that allows us to distinguish the basic myth from some sectarian inflection. The story that is chosen for presentation carries along with it the understanding attained by this preliminary labor: it is never just an innocent summary. References to the different texts will allow the reader to discover at least partially the elements of the interpretation. Such a method presumes that we leave the historical dimension out of consideration, and that all the versions of a single myth be taken ideally as synchronic. Mythic data is in fact neither dated nor datable, since its fixation in writing presupposes a more or less long oral tradition. When we can perceive an evolution it is usually so superficial that we can safely ignore it.

Nevertheless, India presents itself to us, through its texts, its monuments, and its still living practices and beliefs, with a historical depth of more than three thousand years. In spite of the lack of precise dates and in spite of the explicit will to immutability, decisive changes have certainly taken place in the course of these three millennia, changes that myths can register in the absence of datable events. Moreover, a complex social organization, hierarchical in principle, adds a sociological density to this historical depth, a density that is bound to be refracted in the myths in which the society expresses itself: the myths and rituals must in one way or another take account of a hierarchical principle that is always at work. Finally, this complex and stable society, whose unity has never been realized politically or linguistically, stretches over an extremely vast geographical area: though Hinduism appears unified in its deep structure, it is evident that we must find, alongside pan-Indian myths and cults, complex local allegiances which are also inscribed in the deep structure and belong to it just as fundamentally as aspects that are geographically coextensive with Hindu society. We will then, even before considering the specifically religious values around which the myths are organized, note three kinds of division that in themselves give them a characteristic form, if not a particular content. On this level we already know, without any possible hesitation, that we are within the Hindu fold, since the forms, while not equivalent to the contents, are themselves translations of more or less conscious values that are found again on the level of content.

The first division particularly concerns classical Hinduism in its most Brahmanical form, the form explicated by the Brahmans, agents of the transmission of all normativity. It is,

Nartamalei. Photo M. Biardeau.

(Left) Lingarāja (early twelfth century). Photo by Jarrige.

paradoxically, historical in nature, in a universe that privileges atemporal unity, and is expressed entirely in the opposition between Revelation, *śruti* (literally, "hearing"), and Tradition, *smṛti* (literally, "remembering"). For classical Hinduism, i.e., the religious state that is found already constituted in the two great Sanskrit epics and in the socioreligious law codes, the Veda is considered the supreme norm, the basis of all else. Yet not only do the Vedic texts, from the earliest to the most recent, present states of the language that differ greatly from classical Sanskrit, compelling us to assume their historical anteriority; in addition, the state of the religion that they describe cannot be viewed as if it had an unbroken linear development in classical Hinduism, which nevertheless claims the Veda as its basis. There is a real break between the two, and it is likely that the received canon has been constituted as such largely because of this break: Revelation has been endowed with distance, strangeness, even unintelligibility, and at the same time absolute superiority. The canon consists entirely of texts that have left no trace on the ground: collections of hymns in verse, *saṃhitās;* mythico-ritual texts, *brāhmaṇas,* in which the hymns are broken up and scattered, transformed into formulas, and incorporated in the rite; and more or less esoteric speculations on the rites and myths, *upaniṣads* and *āraṇyakas,* which diverge widely from the rites and myths while at the same time maintaining them as intangible points of departure. When the oldest texts of Tradition—the *sūtras*—comment on the *brāhmaṇas,* one already has the impression of a great distance between the two types of texts. We are no longer dealing with quite the same state of the religion; the two may even be incompatible. But the intangibility of the Revelation—the real raison d'être of the Brahmans—means that the Vedic universe will continue to exist in an integral, if not perfectly intact, form within the new universe that is coming into being. Certain myths are privileged witnesses to the transcendence of the Veda in classical Hinduism. Better than any datable event, they help us to understand the enormous transformation of Hindu consciousness, a transformation partly contemporaneous with the birth of Buddhism and Jainism and therefore the expression of a period of intense socioreligious vitality. Several of the myths presented in this collection have been chosen precisely for the way that they mutually articulate Revelation and Tradition: cosmogonic narratives in the first place, the foundation myths of the religion; but also the story of Indra, which takes on a new dimension in its passage from the Veda to the epic; or the story of Dakṣa's sacrifice, whose classical posterity cannot be predicted from its Vedic origins.

The sociological division corresponds to the self-image of a hierarchical society. The high castes are recognized in certain values, precisely those that distinguish them from the lower castes. The lower castes, for their part, unabashedly express their subordination to the superior castes by elucidating their own values, held to be inferior. As a first approximation we can say that the high castes are characterized by practices that are considered pure (vegetarianism), while the lower castes follow the contrary practices (meat eating). But here we must be on guard against taking the formal opposition as a unidimensional one; the myths show that it is pervaded by the most diverse meanings: it is at work in particular in the innumerable narratives that bring together Brahmans and royal castes, the two components of the superior society who cannot live without one another. The pure practices of the Brahman, as opposed to the impure practices of the king, have a hierarchical connotation, since the king must submit to the Brahman's advice in all things; but it is the impurity of the king that makes it possible for the Brahman to do his own duty, that is, to stay pure. In the same way it is the serving castes, at the bottom of the social scale, whose impure practices make it possible for the supposedly superior castes to fulfill their own requirements. The myth does not stop there: there is no "impure-in-itself." Hinduism redeems impurity, and even transforms it into purity, by introducing a new variable into the social hierarchy, a sort of outsider who relativizes everything inside society with regard to his own values. Thus the hierarchical division is no longer anything but a formal aspect of a complex discourse in which all the values of Hinduism are at play—the very values that allow the articulation of Revelation and Tradition. It is not a question of opposing a superior to an inferior religion, even if the gods of some are not to the same extent the gods of others: Hinduism is the whole within which the small and the great of this world have their place and their chance for salvation, in which all are assured of finding the divinity appropriate to their heart, status, and lineage. From the point of view of the organization of research, this means that we must abandon the traditional opposition between the classical Indianist and the field ethnologist. Neither of these can do without the problematic of the other. What is really involved, in fact, is a single problematic, at work both in normative texts, mythical or otherwise, and in religious practice as it has been observed for almost two hundred years.

Collaboration between the specialist in classical religion and the ethnologist, whose experience is highly localized, is equally indispensable for the third division that Hindu mythology reveals: the great gods Viṣṇu and Śiva are found everywhere in the Hindu area, whereas other divinities, equally important in the devotion of the worshipers, are much more limited in extent. Sometimes we find gods whose sovereignty is recognized over an entire region—these may also be goddesses—and this territorial sovereignty takes material form in a regional pilgrimage site. Sometimes we find divinities linked to the locality itself, to the village; although the same names are found from one village to the next, as in the case of the "village deities"—*grāmadevatās*—of Andhra Pradesh, the worshipers associate them with the protection of their village alone and do not worry about whether two *grāmadevatās* with the same name are identical. On this level, we speak of "popular" religion, but in a sense that does not confine it exclusively to the lower castes, as was possible with the sociological division: for the local divinities group around themselves all the local castes, just as the sovereign divinity of a larger territory protects the territory's population as a whole. The annual festival of this divinity is really everyone's festival. This is why we will not oppose what has sometimes been called the "great" and "little traditions." The same people worship Viṣṇu and/or Śiva, and the sovereign god of their region, such as Subrahmaṇya, Narasiṃha, or Khaṇḍobā, and the local guardian deity. This geographical distinction provides yet another form to which the myths give a religious content and which reappears in the structure of the pantheon. Reference to classical texts may not be sufficient for the correct articulation of these different levels of the divine, for the geographical organization of forms of the divine takes on other meanings. This is why we have tried to give at least one localized example of the mythico-ritual complex that makes up the religion of a village. It would have been better to have many soundings of this kind, to reveal the enduring framework on which infinite variations are worked. The problem of the god-goddess relationship, for instance, arises particularly from the geographical register. There seem to be no "pan-Indian" goddesses apart from the consorts of Viṣṇu and Śiva, and in this case the role of the consort is not dissociated from that of the god. Yet on the regional or local level there seems to be a rivalry between god and goddess (sister, mother, or wife) which can be resolved in complementarity. The myth must also account for this reality, inscribed as it is in the religious geography of India.

Without the organizing principles that we have just enumerated, Hindu myths would remain discourses floating in the air without any directly intelligible connection with the people who have elaborated them. Yet these principles never appear as such in the myths themselves. To facilitate the understanding of the myths without having to repeat these principles of decipherment, we will present them in three types of articles. Some, dealing with the most fundamental myths, will stress the great structures of Hinduism. In these cases we will not hesitate to supplement the mythical narrative with data of various sorts that can bring the meaning to the surface. Other articles will use the myths to explicate the symbolic value of a particular object or, in contrast, the symbolic substitutes for an object that is highly charged ideologically: these articles should help the reader to penetrate the coded text that is a myth. Finally, we will discuss important myths in which these structures and symbols are at work, reducing the interpretation to a minimum. Here the goal, which must probably remain an ideal, is to make available for any reader the instruments for a rational decipherment of any Hindu myth: but decipherment remains an infinite task, which always leaves a residue behind it.

M.Bi/j.l.

BIBLIOGRAPHY

M. BIARDEAU, *Clefs pour la pensée hindoue* (Paris 1972). M. BIARDEAU and CH. MALAMOUD, *Le sacrifice dans l'Inde ancienne* (Paris 1976). C. DIMMITT and J. A. B. VAN BUITENEN, *Classical Hindu Mythology* (Philadelphia 1978). J. DOWSON, *A Classical Dictionary of Hindu Mythology and Religion, Geography, History and Literature* (10th ed., London 1961). L. DUMONT, *La civilisation indienne et nous* (1964); *Homo hierarchicus: Essai sur le système des castes* (Paris 1966). E. W. HOPKINS, *Epic Mythology* (1st Indian reprint, Varanasi and Delhi 1968; originally Strasbourg 1915). S. LÉVI, *La doctrine du sacrifice dans les Brâhmaṇas* (reprint, Paris 1966). A. A. MACDONELL, *The Vedic Mythology* (1st Indian reprint, Varanasi 1963). A. A. MACDONELL and A. B. KEITH, *Vedic Index of Names and Subjects*, 2 vols. (3d reprint, Delhi 1967). E. MOOR, *The Hindu Pantheon* (reprint, Varanasi and Delhi 1968). J. MUIR, *Original Sanskrit Texts on the Origin and History of the People of India, Their Religion and Institutions*, 5 vols. (reprint, Amsterdam 1967). W. D. O'FLAHERTY, *Hindu Myths* (Baltimore 1975). V. R. RAMACANDRA DIKSHITAR, *The Purāṇa Index*, 3 vols. (Madras 1955). L. RENOU, *Hymnes spéculatifs du Veda* (Paris 1956). Y. P. TANDON, *Purāṇa-viṣayasamanukramanikā: A Concordance of Purāṇa-Contents* (Hoshiarpur 1952). J. VARENNE, *Mythes et légendes extraits des Brâhmaṇa* (Paris 1967); *Le Veda, premier livre sacré de l'Inde*, 2 vols. (Paris 1967), an anthology; *Upanishads du Yoga* (Paris 1971). VETTAM MANI, *Purāṇic Encyclopaedia* (Delhi and Varanasi 1975).

The *Yūpa* (Sacrificial Post) in Hinduism

Sacrifice is a form of ritual so universal that Hubert and Mauss once devoted an entire *Essay* to it in an attempt to identify its common mechanism across various religious systems. It is at the core of the oldest form of Indian religion, what we call Vedic literature. Although the practice of Vedic sacrifice became increasingly rare very early, and although it was preserved only in a few great royal rituals, the notion of sacrifice has never stopped controlling the organization of the Hindu world and was actualized in renewed sacrificial forms still observable in India today.

In a world like that of Hinduism, where the polarization between the pure and the impure reaches a maximum tension, speculation on sacrifice can only bring out the internal contradiction of this ritual: designed to ensure the prosperity of everyone, it can do so only by including a harmful element of execution, the destruction of the victim. Moreover, it ensures the prosperity of the world that practices it only by opposing it to the wild, disorganized, and hostile world and by controlling the connections between the two worlds. It is therefore not surprising that there was much speculation about the *yūpa,* the sacrificial post. For the *yūpa* is situated on the edge of an altar of the sacrificial arena, half inside, half outside, thus symbolizing its function as frontier guard and communicator with the outside. It is the place where the victim is tied before being put to death. Finally, its verticality gives it the obvious role of a cosmic pillar. A hymn in the *Atharvaveda* (10.8) associates it closely with the *araṇis,* the two pieces of wood that ritually produce sacrificial fire by friction. It is fitting that this Veda, the least prestigious because its hymns have no connection with the solemn Vedic ritual, is the one that brings us one of the earliest speculations on the sacrificial post as a symbol of the totality of the sacrifice: the post embodies the very principle of all sacrificial activity, along with the essential tension that dwells in it. But it is also possible that its mythical fertility was a direct result of its ritual devaluation. We do not know when it stopped being actually functional: a Vedic hymn shows it soiled with the victim's blood, but the descriptions of the Vedic ritual imply the opposite: that the victim is not killed at the sacrificial post, though it is first tied to it. The *yūpa* could perhaps all the better play its role as a symbol: Hindu mythic thought has expounded at length on this theme, on the myth itself, the ritual, and the iconography. On the other hand, the *yūpa* is designated by all kinds of substitutes, mythical, iconographical, and linguistic (almost every term referring to a post or pillar in classical Sanskrit may be used symbolically to evoke the sacrificial post). All the variations on the sacrificial post are of course perfectly integrated into the Hindu universe of *bhakti* without ever losing sight of its original Vedic meaning. That is, it is associated first with Rudra-Śiva, since the Vedic Rudra is identified with the *yūpa,* but also with the Trimūrti, the trinity that the supreme deity divides into when it turns to the creation of our universe at the dawn of a new cosmic era. At this level, Rudra-Śiva has as his partners Brahmā and Viṣṇu, each of whom has his own function, complementary to that of the other two. Brahmā, the personification of Vedic knowledge and practice, the fertile aspect of the sacrifice, is the agent of creation. Viṣṇu, who is the sacrifice itself insofar as he is inseparable from the prosperity of the world (Śrī or Lakṣmī), is the guarantor of cosmic order. And Rudra-Śiva, because of his identification with the sacrificial post, the

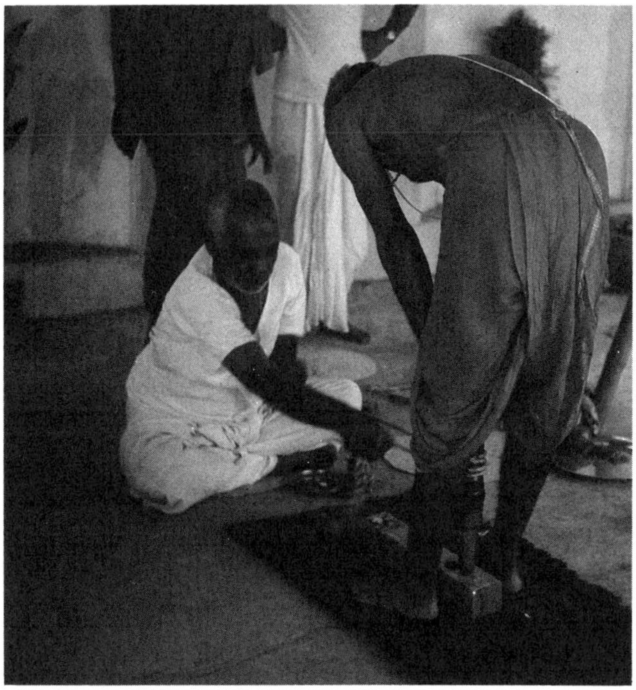

Lighting the sacrificial fire by rubbing two pieces of wood. Photo M. Biardeau.

Linga in disuse, showing its three component parts—square, octagonal, and round. Photo IFI 33–7.

symbol of destruction, controls the destruction of the world when the moment for it comes (the indispensable complement of this sacrificial structure is provided by the renunciation of the world of sacrifice: Rudra-Śiva is thus *simultaneously* the preeminent yogi and the sacrificial post).

There is no question of exhausting the subject here. But we will limit ourselves to emphasizing the main variations on the theme of the sacrificial post. The most important and the most obvious, although perhaps the most ignored, variation is that of Śiva's linga, the virtually exclusive ritual representation of the god. The classical linga was mounted on a rounded or sometimes square pedestal called a *yoni,* "womb" or "vulva," depending on the context. It is therefore perfectly legitimate to see in the linga a phallic symbol. From there it is just a short step to making it the Indian version of a primitive phallic cult, a step that was taken with alacrity and is still taken, viewing Rudra-Śiva as a primitive, "non-Aryan" god, a latecomer into the Hindu constellation, where he encountered difficulties in being accepted. But, in the first place, the idea of a non-Hindu or non-Vedic Rudra-Śiva is a pure fiction that would be hard to support with archaeological evidence (even if we take into account one seal from the Indus civilization that might represent this figure); indeed, his connection with the Vedic world is as clearly defined as that of Viṣṇu and neither more nor less ancient than that connection. Beyond that, there have been attempts to misrepresent as history, in the Western sense of the term, stories that sought to explain a structure in the narrative mode. Therein lies the most common error in the interpretation of myths in general. Rudra-Śiva is not an upstart in Hinduism; rather, he is the part of the danger and impurity that Hinduism had to integrate as part of its system starting with the Veda, in order to make it viable. He is the requisite complement of Viṣṇu, the negative side of whatever Viṣṇu is the positive side of.

If, instead of reconstructing a hypothetical history based on data that are by definition ahistorical, we start from the Rudra-Śiva that is given by the oldest Vedic testimony, we see in the linga first a transposition of the sacrificial post. The problem is then how we moved from the meaning "post" to the meaning "phallus," or, more exactly, "copulation." But we are guided here by two factors: first, the profusion of myths, too long a subject to examine here; and second, the fact that this is a general problem in Hinduism: the sacrificial post is perceived as a "terrible" and impure representation of the god, of Rudra rather than Śiva. The devotion of a high-caste Hindu—and the frequenting of Śivaite temples by Brahmans is in itself a sign of nobility—seeks a benevolent and placated god, one who dispenses favors and brings deliverance, preferably a pure god who does not allow murder in his vicinity. The terrible function of Rudra, which cannot be annulled, goes back to the subordinate gods who surround him or to the Goddess with her bloody ritual, whom the lower castes more often worship. In a pure Hindu temple (with a vegetarian ritual), the sanctuary per se is the *garbhagṛha,* the "house of the embryo," in other words a womb, a place where the world is in its germinal state, where it constantly creates itself, whether the deity is Viṣṇu or Śiva. In the case of the representation of Śiva, the transition from post to phallus—meanings that remain, both of them, largely subconscious for most Hindus—seems to have resulted in a double iconographic modification. The oldest lingas that have been found are cylinders, which probably had no yoni as a pedestal. The classical linga, on the other hand, is found only in association with its yoni. Furthermore, nothing emerges but a portion of a cylinder, the upper part of the linga, which specifically represents Śiva. Immediately below and at the level of the yoni, and therefore not visible, is a portion of an octagonal section that represents Viṣṇu (the royal Viṣṇu watching over the eight cardinal points), while the square base (the four Vedas as well as the four cardinal points delimiting the world) is Brahmā. The phallic representation of Śiva thus embodies the very structure of Hindu divinity turned to the creation of the world. The linga-yoni combination presupposes that Śiva in this case is the supreme god, and no one else (to the extent that the linga is still a transposition of the sacrificial post). But it is represented at the level where it appears to be triple, the level of the Trimūrti that is tied to the creation of the world.

It is thus not by chance that one of the best-known myths about the linga features the three gods of the Trimūrti for the greater glory of Śiva. It is the myth of the "apparition of the linga," or *liṅgodbhava,* of which there are many Purāṇic versions (*Vāyu Purāṇa* 1.55; *Brahmāṇḍa Purāṇa* 1.26; *Śiva Purāṇa, Rudra Saṃhitā Sṛṣṭi Khaṇḍa* 15; *Liṅga Purāṇa* 1.17; *Skanda Purāṇa* 1.16.131–32, 1.3.9–15, 3.1.14, etc.). It is of particular interest since it brings out in all of its versions the meaning of the sacrificial post without emphasizing the phallic meaning, aside from attributing to Śiva the function of supreme creator. The narrative describes Brahmā and Viṣṇu disputing the question of who came first and who has the function of creating the world. The function of creator is understood here as meaning the function of the supreme deity and not the function attributed to Brahmā at the level of the Trimūrti. The quarrel therefore turns on the question of who is the supreme deity. Brahmā has no claim to this, and some versions of the myth stress Brahmā's incapacity. On the other hand, the Śivaite sects proclaim the absolute primacy of Śiva, in opposition to the claims both of the nonsectarian Hindu tradition and of the Vaiṣṇava sects.

Potu Raju from Mallavaram in front of a temple of the goddess. Photo M. L. Reiniche.

While Brahmā and Viṣṇu boast of their respective merits, a flaming linga appears, with no visible base or top. Brahmā then takes on the form of a *haṃsa* (the bird that symbolizes him because of a Sanskrit play on words) to go to find the top, and Viṣṇu transforms himself into a boar so that he may dig into the ground in order to try to find the base. Brahmā goes toward the sky, toward deliverance; Viṣṇu reverts to the role of sacrificial boar that he plays in Purāṇic cosmogony or else to one of the avatar forms that allow him to retrieve the earth from the bottom of the ocean of the flood. When both of them fail to achieve their ends, they worship the greatness of Śiva, whom the iconography depicts in all his glory inside the linga bursting open in a diamond-shaped split. Several versions pit the humility of Viṣṇu (who bows down with no resistance) against the deception of Brahmā, who claims to have reached the top of the linga. It is this lie that excludes Brahmā forever from the right to be worshiped by devotees.

Śiva's linga here is able to give a deliverance higher than Brahmā's and, at the same time, represents the salvific sacrifice more fundamentally than Viṣṇu. The linga is simultaneously the cosmic pillar, with no beginning or end, the sacrificial post (whose meaning is reinforced by its fiery nature, fire being the other destructive element of sacrifice, the one by which Rudra destroys the worlds), and the abstract representation of the Great Yogi. No single value is stressed because it embodies them all, wherein lies its transcendence. When Brahmā and Viṣṇu have failed in their active quest, they attain knowledge of Śiva through meditation.

We can therefore distinguish two principles with regard to the symbolism of the sacrificial post which allow us first to identify it and then to interpret it. We must of course handle these principles with care, in context, and not apply them mechanically. First: in a mythical narrative or in a visual representation, when an element, preferably unitary, is asserted through its verticality (there is even a unicorn Śiva), one can see in it a sacrificial symbol. Here are a few examples, which we cannot analyze further here: the lotus stem that comes out of the navel of Viṣṇu as he rests on the ocean or on the serpent Śeṣa and that bears an open lotus flower in which the four-faced Brahmā is enthroned; the tusk of the sacrificial boar on which he retrieves the earth; the single tusk of Gaṇapati; Viṣṇu's club; the palace pillar from which Narasiṃha emerges. One could go farther than this: the left leg of Vāmana-Trivikrama is raised to the point of verticality starting from a certain date in the history of art (eighth century?), as Śiva's leg is raised when he dances the *ūrdhva-tāṇḍava* (the "terrible" dance). This may well happen because the meaning of the "sacrificial post" is not far away. Finally, on a more down-to-earth level, we may decipher this same notion in the *daṇḍna,* the staff that symbolizes royal power.

Second: if in fact this vertical element—often in a totally anecdotal and trivial aspect—is the outcropping of the meaning "sacrificial post," we should attribute to it a function that we might call "Rudraic," after the "terrible" name of Rudra-Śiva. In every circumstance it manifests the inescapable part of violence, of murder and impurity, that is implicit in the very existence of the cosmos, and it impresses upon its bearer the Rudraic function that it signifies.

M.Bi./g.h.

BIBLIOGRAPHY

J. FILLIOZAT, "Les images de Śiva dans l'Inde du Sud. 1: L'image de l'origine du liṅga (*liṅgodbhavamūrti*)," *Arts Asiatiques* 8, fasc. 1 (1961).

Rudra/Śiva and the Destruction of the Sacrifice

I. Vedic Revelation

Sacrifice

The most ancient texts of the Veda are grouped into collections called *Saṃhitās* and include especially hymns to the many deities of the pantheon. On the level of the texts that came next, the *Brāhmaṇas,* the entire religion is organized around the sacrifice. The gods, to whom the invocations and oblations are addressed, are no longer the center of attention. Rather, the process (the "course") of sacrifice, the mechanism of sacrifice, has become the main point, and sacrifice has become an end in itself. It produces and organizes the cosmos. It is identified with Prajāpati, the author and master of all living creatures, a rather abstract Lord, beyond the deities of the pantheon. The focus shifts from the gods to the ritual. The *Brāhmaṇas* describe the rites, explain their hidden meaning, and shed light on their supposed origin and the meaning attributed to them in connection with etymologies, legends, and fragments of myths.

Sacrifice, an object of speculation by the Brahmans, is the foundation of the universe, the guarantor of good order and cosmic and social harmony, and the source of all prosperity. But it brings into play hidden and dangerous forces that must be handled carefully, that only the learned Brahman ("he who knows . . .") knows how to handle because he is a specialist in rituals and formulas and holds the key to their meaning. Even if it is performed correctly in full awareness of the facts, sacrifice always involves a portion of violence, of contact with death, and therefore a portion of danger and impurity. The animal victim is slain, the stalks of soma are crushed, and the seeds are pounded. During these violent but necessary operations, it is the sacrifice itself that is put to death: "Indeed, one kills the sacrifice when one lays it out" (*Śatapatha Brāhmaṇa* 2.2.2.1). It is therefore hardly surprising that they attribute to the sacrifice the intention to escape. It must be approached with all the wiles of a hunter: "The sacrifice has the nature of game" (*Pañcaviṃśa Brāhmaṇa* 6.7.10–11). Is it to ensure control over it that the *dīkṣita,* the one who submits to the preparatory consecration of the sacrifice (*dīkṣā*), wears a black antelope skin (*Śatapatha Brāhmaṇa* 1.1.4.1; see also 6.4.1.6)?

The Role of the Brahman

Since the animal is put to death by suffocation or strangulation with a noose, bodily lacerations and other damage to the victim caused during the offering are kept to a minimum. It is agreed that the necessary violence, evil, and danger are concentrated in a tiny part of the animal (*Śatapatha Brāhmaṇa*

1.7.4.5, 10). It is sometimes explicitly stated that the damaged part of the animal is the size of a grain of barley (*Taittirīya Saṃhitā* 2.6.8.4). But this minuscule morsel of meat is potentially quite dangerous. The imprudent gods discover it to their peril. "When these gods laid out the sacrifice, they offered the first separated share to Savitṛ; it cut off his hands . . . they offered it to Bhaga; it destroyed his eyes . . . They offered it to Pūṣan; it broke his teeth . . ." (*Kauṣītaki Brāhmaṇa* 6.13). How shall it be disposed of? What place, what priest will be able to neutralize this threat? For some, this task is incumbent upon Indra. He alone is able to absorb the shock. "'Indra is the strongest and mightiest of the gods; therefore offer it to him,' they said to one another; and so they did. He appeased it with the ritual formula" (*Kauṣītaki Brāhmaṇa* 6.14). Indra is the most vigorous of the gods. But his power, as has been noted, is not that of the warrior but of one who knows the ritual formulas (*brahman*). It is therefore no surprise that in other versions of the myth, Bṛhaspati (or Brahmaṇaspati), the "master of the formula," is mentioned in place of Indra: "They brought it to *Bṛhaspati;* it did him no harm; and thenceforth it was appeased" (*Śatapatha Brāhmaṇa* 1.7.4.8; see also *Taitirrīya Saṃhitā* 2.6.8.5).

Bṛhaspati is the priest of the gods. His counterpart or representative on earth, on the sacrificial site, is the priest called the Brahman (*Kauṣītaki Brāhmaṇa* 6.13). He is the most discrete but in a sense the most important of the officiants. He alone conducts half of the sacrifice (ibid. 6.11). The other priests recite formulas, sing, move about continuously, and perform all the operations of the ritual. The Brahman is immobile and virtually silent. He observes and oversees all that is said and done on the sacrificial site. Being the one who knows the texts and rites best, he intervenes when an error has been committed. As a physician, he "heals" the sacrifice (ibid. 6.12). He does this by resorting to Viṣṇu, because "Viṣṇu is the sacrifice" (*Śatapatha Brāhmaṇa* 1.7.4.20). The Brahman priest is therefore the one who, on earth and in the image of Bṛhaspati, harmlessly consumes the wounded part of the victim (1.7.4.13–17). To protect himself, he does this "through the mouth of Agni," fire.

The Slaying

The Brahman priest abolishes the wound, heals the sacrifice, and neutralizes the danger. Who then was responsible for the actual slaying? The sacrificer (*yajamāna*), the patron of the sacrifice, is not involved in the slaying, nor are any of the principal celebrants in charge of killing the animal. It is the *śamitṛ,* the executioner, of whom virtually nothing is known (does he belong to the caste of Brahmans?), that is charged with this vile and dangerous chore. One of the explanations of his name is that he must "appease" (*śamayati*) the victim, after obtaining its consent or at least without letting the animal moan audibly.

The Origins of Rudra

In the myth, Rudra is the one to whom the gods appeal to do their dirty work. Rudra is represented as living on the margin of the civilized world, as one coming from outside, as an intruder. He comes from the mountain; he emerges from the forest. He is a hunter. He stands for what is violent, cruel, and impure in the society of gods or at the edge of the divine world. The following is an account of the "birth" of Rudra. He is associated with fury and born of the tears of Prajāpati. "This is why the *Śatarudrīya* (oblation) is made. When Prajāpati was dismembered, the deities went away from him. Only one god did not leave him: Manyu, Fury. He felt himself stretched out inside. He (Prajāpati) wept (*rud-*) and the tears that poured from him landed on Manyu. He became Rudra . . . Rudra with a hundred heads, a thousand eyes, a hundred quivers, arose, his bow bent . . . looking for food. The gods were frightened" (*Śatapatha Brāhmaṇa* 9.1.1.6). To appease him, one offers him the *Śatarudrīya,* while reciting this litany: "We bow before your fury, O Rudra, before your arrow, your two arms . . . ! (*Vājasaneyī Saṃhitā* 16).

According to the *Kauṣītaki Brāhmaṇa,* Rudra is the product of a particularly dangerous and reprehensible union, an act of incest. "Prajāpati, desiring offspring, practiced intense austerities. As he became ardent, five were born from him: Agni (fire), Vāyu (wind), Āditya (the sun), Candramas (the moon), and Uṣas (dawn) as the fifth . . . Uṣas took the form of an *apsaras* (nymph) and appeared before them. Their spirits all flew out of their bodies toward her. Their seed fell" (ibid. 6.1). Prajāpati made a golden cup and collected the seed in it. Out of it came a creature with a thousand eyes and feet, bearing a thousand arrows. Prajāpati gave him eight terrible names: Bhava, Śarva, Rudra, Paśupati . . . (ibid. 6.2–9). Similarly, in the *Śatapatha Brāhmaṇa* (6.1.3.7–8), incest produces a young boy (*kumāra*) who is born weeping (*rud-*). This Kumāra is fire. The first of his eight names is Rudra: "Rudra is indeed Agni" (ibid. 6.1.3.10).

According to other versions, it is Prajāpati himself who commits incest with his daughter. Taking on the form of a male antelope, he mates with his daughter turned female antelope. The gods seek someone who can punish him, but find none among themselves. They pool the most terrible parts of themselves to produce "this god," that is, Rudra, but people avoid naming him. In exchange for dominion over domestic animals (*paśus,* see below), he pierces Prajāpati with his arrow (*Aitareya Brāhmaṇa* 3.33; see also *Maitrāyaṇī Saṃhitā* 4.2.12; *Jaiminīya Brāhmaṇa* 3.261–62). The theme recurs in the *Śatapatha Brāhmaṇa,* where the gods condemn Prajāpati's incest. They ask that "the gods who rule over the *paśus*" pierce Prajāpati. When the wrath of the god has been appeased, they heal him: "Prajāpati is indeed the sacrifice" (ibid. 1.7.4.1–4).

In the eyes of the gods, Prajāpati's incest is a sin or an evil, but a necessary evil, since Prajāpati-Sacrifice is the origin of the world and its inhabitants. Rudra is always associated with this dangerous moment in the career of Prajāpati (or of his sons). Sometimes he appears as the product of incest, and at other times the gods use him or even produce him in order to "punish" Prajāpati.

Mṛga/paśu

Rudra is a game hunter (*mṛga-vyādha,* meaning "one who pierces wild animals") and master of cattle (*paśu,* designating both domestic animals and sacrificial victims). This double qualification of Rudra is indeed important for understanding the myth, but it is not easy to follow all of its implications. By committing incest, Prajāpati places himself outside (or on this side of?) the norms. By becoming a male antelope, a wild animal (*āraṇya*) and no longer *paśu,* he ceases to be a normal sacrificial victim (since only *paśus* are used for sacrifice; *Śatapatha Brāhmaṇa* 13.2.4.3: *apaśur . . . āraṇyaḥ*); he enters a realm that is beyond the control of the gods, who must resort to Rudra, the god who regulates the outside world, the game hunter. The wound that Rudra inflicts on Prajāpati-Sacrifice corresponds to the wounded part of the animal victim, that damaged and dangerous part that the Brahman priest alone may consume (*Śatapatha Brāhmaṇa* 1.7.4.9). Rudra thus maintains ambiguous ties with the sacrifice. His presence is indispensable but dangerous. He represents the violent,

Bhairava. Private collection. Photo Dominique Champion.

unappeased aspect of fire and presides over the slaying of the victims. According to certain texts (*Aitareya Brāhmaṇa* 3.33; *Maitrāyaṇi Saṃhitā* 4.2.12), he obtains from the gods control over the *paśus* in exchange for his services. An ambiguous force, he has power over life and death, and since he exercises this right when the *paśu* is the sacrificial victim, it is necessary to keep him auspicious (*śiva*) so that he will spare and protect the cattle (and even humans, for man is also a *paśu* and Rudra may strike men as well as cattle).

The theme of incest expresses two ideas: one is the cosmogonic value of sacrifice, the first creative act, in which the "lord of living creatures" (*prajā-pati*) has no recourse other than to project out of himself a female creature, hence a daughter, and to mate with her; the other is the dangerous character inherent in all sacrifice, since it implies killing. Incest is reprehensible, and sacrificial killing is an impurity that one must rid oneself of. Precisely because life (of the cosmos) comes from death (of the victims and of all the substance of the oblations), the sacrifice (in which the sacrificer, the victim, and rite itself are identified) seeks to flee in the form of a game animal that is not suitable for sacrifice (see above) in order to escape from the gods. This can be translated: the sacrifice is what imposes order on the cosmos by opposing it to the world of the forest, uninhabited, hostile to man, and always menacing. If it is not properly performed, if its dangerous character is not overcome, the humanized space is taken over by savage space, and the world of the gods dissolves into disorganization. The gods must therefore resort to Rudra because his connection with the forest and with game makes him fit to circumscribe the limits of the two worlds, to neutralize the harmful aspects of sacrificial violence.

Rudra's Share

The *Śatapatha Brāhmaṇa* teaches that one must appease Rudra by granting him his share of the offering, without which he is liable to destroy the entire sacrifice: "The gods, by means of sacrifice, ascended into heaven" (ibid. 1.7.3.1); but the god who rules over cattle (*paśu*) was left behind. Seeing that he was excluded from the sacrifice (see *Gopatha Brāhmaṇa* 2.1.2; *Pañcaviṃśa Brāhmaṇa* 7.9.16), he pursued the other gods and threatened them with the weapon he was brandishing: "Reserve a share of the oblation for me!" The gods agreed and assigned him a supplementary offering, with what was left of the sacrifice (see *Aitareya Brāhmaṇa* 3.34.3). In the ritual, this is the last offering, the oblation to Agni Sviṣṭakṛt, fire that "makes good oblations." Again there is the association between Rudra and fire: "Agni is indeed this god (Rudra)" (*Śatapatha Brāhmaṇa* 1.7.3.8). Just as one says, "Viṣṇu is indeed the sacrifice," so one says, "Rudra is Agni" (e.g., *Śatapatha Brāhmaṇa* 1.7.3.8; 6.1.3.10; 9.1.1.1). This simply means that Rudra is the destructive and terrifying aspect of fire. Agni conveys the offerings to the gods, but precisely by destroying them and consuming them. The devouring fire frightens Prajāpati himself (*Śatapatha Brāhmaṇa* 2.2.4.1–6). All of Rudra's names are terrible when unappeased; only Agni is his propitious and appeased name. This may be why the offering to Rudra Paśupati, the terrible hunter who threatened the gods, is made in the name of Agni Sviṣṭakṛt. And care is taken that this supplementary offering to Rudra should not come into contact with cattle (*paśu*,) for fear that they may fall under the harmful power of Rudra (ibid. 1.7.3.21; see also 1.7.4.12; 12.7.3.20; *Pañcaviṃśa Brāhmaṇa* 7.9.18).

Rudra's Function

The myth from the *Śatapatha Brāhmaṇa* has more than once been presented as the reflection of a historical conflict. In this view, Rudra was a deity alien to the Vedic world, a deity whose origin was tribal, Dravidian, or even Hamitic, whose supporters were only able to introduce him into the Brāhmaṇic pantheon and ritual at the price of a lengthy struggle. But the absence of historical documents makes it virtually impossible to verify such hypotheses. How necessary are they? According to Vedic literature, Rudra represents one of the aspects and dimensions of all sacrifice. "Viṣṇu is the sacrifice." He embodies its harmonious process, its continuity, its promise of prosperity. Rudra, the hunter, the savage god, stands on the edge of the sacrifice. He is called *Sthāṇu*, from the name of the post to which the sacrificial animal is tied, situated at the border between the liturgical terrain and the outside world. But for all his marginality, Rudra(-Śiva) is no less indispensable to the proper function of the sacrificial mechanism. No sacrifice without killing, without violence, without impurity. Rudra is the catalyst for this dangerous side of sacrifice; he limits and controls it. If anyone forgets to offer him the share in the sacrifice that belongs to him, if anyone refuses to "give the fire its share" (sacrificing something to save the rest), the violence that he represents, far from being controlled and circumscribed, would invade the entire sacrificial site and destroy it.

II. The Epic Revivals

Rudra's threatening but indispensable presence continued to impose itself on later literature, both epic (*Mahābhārata*) and Purāṇic. The *Mahābhārata* (MBh) is the story of an eighteen-day war between the incarnations of the *devas* (gods) and *asuras* (antigods). Roughly speaking, this merciless war symbolizes the opposition between *dharma* and *adharma,* law and anomie, the order of the world and chaos. What is more, the MBh places this epic story within the framework of a cosmic cycle. The extermination at the end of the war is the image of the dissolution (*pralaya*) of the world at the end of time.

The Story

In this vast epic, we find at least four versions of a myth that might be called "the destruction of the sacrifice (of Dakṣa) by Rudra." Two of these versions have virtually no direct connection with the central story: the one in book 12, close to the *Vāyu Purāṇa,* and the one, in book 13, that echoes the narrative in book 7. For example, this is a summary of the version in book 10: The gods decide to offer a sacrifice and determine the distribution of the offerings. Unaware of Rudra's true nature, they do not assign any share to him. But "he" (Rudra), dressed in an antelope skin and with a bow in his hand, arrives furious on the site of the sacrifice. The earth trembles; the sun and fire lose their brilliance; the gods are terrified. Rudra aims an arrow at the Sacrifice and pierces it; it is transformed into a *mṛga* and takes flight. As if in play, he breaks Savitṛ's arms, destroys Bhaga's eyes and Pūṣan's teeth, and reduces all the gods to impotence. The gods and the Sacrifice beg for Rudra's protection, hoping to propitiate him. Rudra agrees to cast the fire of his wrath into the water. He heals the gods who were mutilated and restores the integrity of the Sacrifice and the harmony of the universe. The gods assign all the oblations to him.

A few preliminary remarks are in order. Depending on the version, the Sacrifice is offered by "the gods" or by Dakṣa. Dakṣa's name connotes the active mind, the ability to accomplish, the efficacious will, and finally sacrificial competence. The *Śathapatha Brāhmaṇa* identifies Dakṣa with Prajāpati (2.4.4.2). Later tradition makes him one of the sons of Brahmā, who is in many ways the heir of Prajāpati. The epic narrative has some abridging and displacements. Rudra, excluded from the oblations (see *Śatapatha Brāhmaṇa* 1.7.3), pierces the Sacrifice (ibid. 1.7.4) and himself mutilates the gods who in the *Brāhmaṇas* are wounded by the *prāśitra,* the damaged part of the victim. There is no longer anything about Prajāpati's incest, but the sacrifice continues to escape in the form of a *mṛga.* During the sacrifice in book 7, Rudra is given "a special share"; in book 10, the gods assign him "all the oblations."

How do these new versions of the myth fit both into the framework of the epic and into the extension of Vedic literature?

Book 7: The Sacrifice of Battle

Arjuna, the hero of the camp that represents the interests of the gods and dharma, has a vision that he alone is privileged to see. An individual shining with energy runs through the battle camp. The weapon that he brandishes does not leave his hand, but out of it come a thousand arrows that strike the enemy; Arjuna only strikes warriors that are already slain. The *ṛṣi* Vyāsa explains that this mysterious person is Rudra. He urges Arjuna to pay homage to this god and to sing praises from the *Śatarudriya* hymn. He recalls two or three myths about Rudra, especially the myth of the destruction of the sacrifice.

Arjuna's vision is certainly not a mere transposition of the myth of the destruction of the Sacrifice. There are certain constants in the role of Rudra. In countless passages the MBh lets it be known that war is a sacrifice in which any warrior—but especially the king—is simultaneously the sacrificer, the priest, and, if he dies in combat, the victim. In the MBh, Arjuna is not the titular king, but more than any other character in the epic, he represents the image of the ideal king. The vision that closes book 7 makes him discover that, in the sacrifice of war, it is not he who kills the enemy victims. The perfect warrior is only an instrument in the hands of the deity: Rudra does the slaying before him and for him. The Vedic texts made a connection between the damaged part of the victim and the arrow with which Rudra pierced Prajāpati-Sacrifice. Here, in a martial context and a martial language, Rudra performs the office of executioner. And the text suggests that victims who have fallen on the battlefield are "Rudra's share."

Book 10: The Eschatological Sacrifice

The war is over. After eighteen days of combat, Arjuna and his brothers, guided by Kṛṣṇa, the avatar of Viṣṇu-Nārāyaṇa, have achieved victory. In the enemy camp only three survivors remain. But one of them is of such size that the final outcome is not yet settled: Aśvatthāman, a warrior Brahman, a partial incarnation of Rudra, whose composite birth naturally evokes the Vedic myths of the origin of the god. Aśvatthāman was born "of the combination of Mahādeva (Rudra-Śiva) and Antaka (death), of Krodha (wrath) and Kāma (desire)" (MBh 1; see *Śatapatha Brāhmaṇa* 9.1.1.6 for Manyu; *Aitareya Brāhmaṇa* 3.33 for the combination of the terrible forms of all the gods). This Rudraic patrimony is reflected in a nocturnal ceremony during which Aśvatthāman offers himself up to Rudra-Śiva by immolating himself in the sacrificial fire. Rudra enters him and possesses him. Aśvatthāman then attacks the camp of the victors at night when they are asleep. He kills his principal adversaries not with the sword or arrows, but "like Rudra who personally strikes the *paśu.*" His two acolytes light three fires and burn down the entire camp, transforming it into a vast sacrificial area with its three great liturgical fires. The only survivors of this total destruction are Arjuna and his brothers, whom Kṛṣṇa had the foresight to bring to shelter. And when Aśvatthāman puts the finishing touch on his masterpiece of death by killing all the embryos in the dynasty of the victors, in the lineage of dharma, it is once again Kṛṣṇa who gives life back to the stillborn heir, Arjuna's grandson. Viṣṇu, of whom Kṛṣṇa is the avatar, must represent the continuity of the sacrifice and the stabilization or reestablishment of dharma. When Aśvatthāman is finally neutralized and condemned to exile and wandering (in the image of Rudra, the hunter, the savage god), Kṛṣṇa asserts that this warrior Brahman owes to Rudra his ability to unleash such destructive power. Kṛṣṇa then concludes with two myths, including the myth of the destruction of the sacrifice.

What connection is there between this last myth and book 10 of the MBh? A detailed study of the nocturnal carnage perpetrated by Rudra's Brahman incarnation, by the warrior possessed by Rudra, would clearly show many points of contact with the story of the destruction of the sacrifice, particularly in its epic and Purāṇic versions. Does this mean that the myth of the destruction of the sacrifice served as a model for book 10 of the MBh? The truth of the matter is more complex than that.

We must return to what was suggested above: the epic is not just a heroic story; it is also an image of the dissolution (*pralaya*) of the world at the end of a cosmic cycle. When the time of death approaches, Rudra destroys the world by fire, dissolves it, and reabsorbs it. The supreme deity in this phase of destruction is both sacrificer and yogi. Destruction by fire is interpreted as a sacrifice of cosmic dimensions for which Rudra-Śiva is both sacrificer and performer. But in this destructive enterprise with all its violence and death, the divine yogi acts with detachment and even indifference. The ideal king, to whom the message of the MBh and of the *Bhagavad Gītā* is addressed, finds in him the model of his own action, often cruel and violent, but indispensable for the good of the world. For the king and the warrior who act as yogis, detached from the fruit of action, war is a sacrifice that, rather than making them impure and prisoners of their passions, becomes a school of detachment and a way to deliverance.

Rereading the Vedic Myth

The entire context of epic and Purāṇic mythology sheds light on Aśvatthāman's intervention in book 10 and his connection with the sacrifice of Dakṣa. Despite all its sacrificial symbols, the story of the night massacre and the destruction of the camp is not merely the transposition of the myths of Rudra and Prajāpati in the *Brāhmaṇas*.

The myths or fragments of myths from the *Brāhmaṇas* were intended to justify certain liturgical rules that assured the correct functioning of the sacrifice by carefully delimiting the dangerous part, that is, Rudra's share. The destruction of the sacrifice and the mutilation of the gods here appeared to be a threat or a hypothesis: without Rudra, the sacrifice is impossible or destroys itself; if Rudra is not given his share, if he is willfully excluded from the sacrifice, then impurity, violence, and destructive fire take over the sacrificial site and the whole sacrifice.

Within the epic context, it is no longer merely a threat or hypothetical destruction in the event of a mistake during the ritual. It is a real and inevitable destruction. The myth of the destruction of Dakṣa's sacrifice takes on all of the symbolism of the periodic dissolution of the cosmos. The myth has in common with the burning of the camp of the victors an eschatological meaning that it did not have in the Vedic context: war ends with a universal conflagration that allows the survival only of the minimum number of creatures needed to ensure the start of a new era. The earthly crisis—a framework chosen to teach the king his duty—is a miniature of the cosmic crisis. War is the sacrifice appropriate to the warrior-king, just as the dissolution of the world is a monstrous cosmic sacrifice placed under the aegis of Rudra-Śiva. The theme of the destruction of Dakṣa's sacrifice by Rudra thereby logically takes on eschatological connotations that give the holocaust of Aśvatthāman its nobility and make explicit its true meaning in the epic drama.

The Purāṇas

This inquiry could be extended into Purāṇic literature. Many of the *Purāṇas* contain a version of the destruction of Dakṣa's sacrifice. The setting has become wider: all classes of beings and all the worlds are present. Rudra-Śiva duplicates himself by sending before him Vīrabhadra, the expression of his fury, and multiplies himself in troops (*gaṇas*) of cruel and repulsive creatures. The Goddess in the form of Kālī participates in the punitive expedition. Elements of this dramatization have influenced the composition of book 10 of the MBh. As for its global importance, a few brief remarks will have to suffice. Several versions tend to oppose Śiva to Viṣṇu in a sectarian way, either to ridicule Viṣṇu or to make him recognize the superiority of Śiva. Dakṣa becomes the model of the man who refuses, or shows that he is unable, to recognize that superiority. But what certain versions criticize in Dakṣa is at a deeper level the blind confidence in ritual (*karman*), whereas salvation is the fruit of knowledge (*jñāna*) and especially of devotion (*bhakti*). The questions that the myth attempted to answer in the *Brāhmaṇas* are progressively lost from sight. But the myth pursues its forward thrust.

J.Sc./g.h.

Purāṇic Cosmogony

The Purāṇas are a class of texts belonging to the *smṛti* tradition in India. They were transmitted over a long period of time and were established in a fixed form only after centuries of changes, additions, and omissions whose history is quite impossible to reconstruct. If we include in this group, besides the eighteen "great Purāṇas," the secondary and sectarian Purāṇas, the caste Purāṇas, and those Purāṇas connected with pilgrimage sites, they constitute an enormous body of literature, which has retained up to the present its capacity to be enriched. As their name indicates, they deal first, although not exclusively, with things of the past, and the account of the origins of the world figures in most of the "great Purāṇas." It is surprising that these texts, as diverse as they are, share a single account of creation, in which textual variations are almost insignificant. This must therefore be a fundamental narrative, which expresses the stability of a structure in which the Hindu world recognizes itself.

There is another surprise: one must both remember the Puruṣa hymn in which Vedic cosmogony is expressed, because its elements recur, and forget it, because a totally new organization emerges, sustained by new elements, in which the old elements are reinterpreted. This discontinuity constitutes a primary testimony to the impossibility of passing linearly from the Vedic world to the universe of classical Hinduism.

The essential difficulty in explaining the Purāṇic cosmogony is that it cannot be done solely in terms of myths. This is not only because of the complexity of the whole and the interpretive work that it demands, but also because this cosmogony sets up the fundamental values of Hinduism, many of which resist being cast into mythic or ritual forms of expression. Within the Vedic world itself, and within those higher castes that had the greatest interest in the sacrificial religion, a debate developed about the ritual. We find this is formulated in the Upaniṣads and the Āraṇyakas—texts that still belong to the *śruti,* to Revelation. It appears in the form of esoteric speculations on the ritual or, within the ritual itself, in the form of debates between Brahmans and kings, in teachings made by a husband to his wife (BAU), a father to his son (ChU), the Vedic god of death Yama to the obstinate Naciketas (KU), etc. The ensemble of values that emerge from this contention become mythologized in the restructuring of Purāṇic cosmogony. This results in a narrative of a type which, although it is somewhat unusual, especially in the first part, is easy to decipher. In addition, the Upaniṣadic debate itself and the values that flow from it are expressed through a certain number of concepts that the myth never explicates as such, even when they are its ultimate referents. These include yoga, renunciation, dharma, and bhakti, terms that must be introduced into the mythic account but defined without the aid of that account. Such is the price that must be paid for a culture that, although it is rich in myths, is only so by virtue of having developed a complex ideology in a complex society, an ideology that is clearly expressed in codes of laws or conceptual treatises parallel to the myths. One could almost say that mythic symbols and narratives are rich only in their conceptual richness, even if their uncommon language lends them another function, more didactic or "popular."

Cosmogony is thus composed of two quite distinct parts. We shall call the first "primary cosmogony or creation," in opposition to the other which will be called "secondary." Neither constitutes an absolute beginning, since this is a cyclic time that has two different levels of eternally recurring cycles (and there is even a third). The two accounts of creation correspond to temporal cycles of different lengths, and each period of creation has a corresponding period of the dissolution of the world, or of cosmic night, of equal duration, which itself gives rise to two separate accounts. The perfect logic of the whole makes it necessary to treat cosmic nights as inseparable segments of the cosmogonies. It is the same myth, unfolding in several episodes.

Primary Creation

At the beginning of a primary creation, we again encounter the Vedic Puruṣa, who is now known either as the supreme Puruṣa, *puruṣottama,* or as the supreme Ātman, *paramātman,* or as the supreme Brahman *parabrahman*—all three significant designations. But he is also called *mahāyogin,* the great yogi, which is for this period the most important aspect of the primal divinity, who is no longer a sacrificial victim: it is by an act of yoga that he will first set the universe in motion, in placing outside of the Male the primal Energy, the original nature—the *avyakta* (nondifferentiated), *pradhāna* or *prakṛti*—which draws all of its being from him. Once this first jolt in the immobility of Being has taken place, Nature will evolve through a prescribed series of forms, but her evolution is possible only through the immanent presence of the Puruṣa at each stage, even though that Puruṣa remains immutable and inactive, a yogi, detached from the world.

At this point, we may place the stages of primary cosmogony in a pattern, along with the corresponding stages of the "ascension" that the yogi undergoes, turning away from the world in order to rise up to the supreme Puruṣa, according to the *Kaṭha Upaniṣad* (3.10–11 and 6.7–8, with the variants indicated):

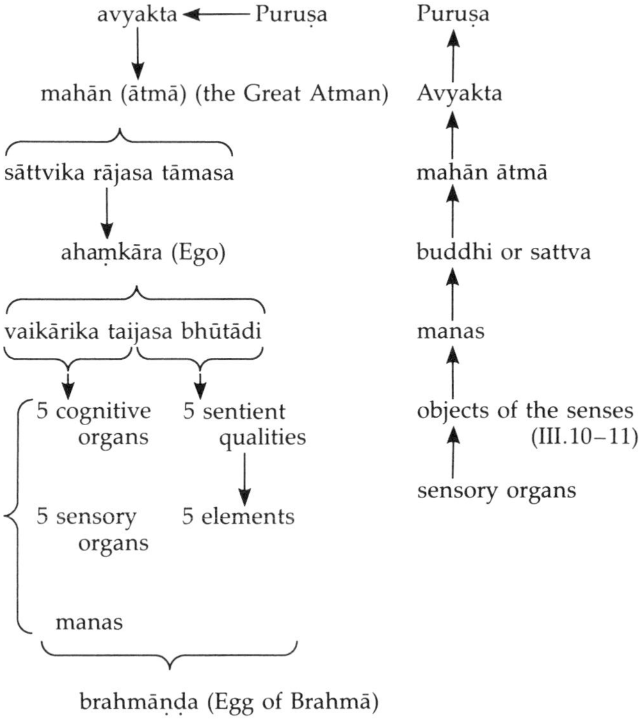

On one side we have the stages of a cosmic manifestation beginning with the Puruṣa and the Avyakta or Prakṛti, until the formation of an Egg of Brahmā; on the other side, the stages of ascension of the individual yogi toward the identification with the Puruṣa (who in the KU is named Viṣṇu). The direction of movement is inverted, but the stages are comparable, especially if we reduce the differences that might exist: the sensory organs and the objects of the senses are placed on an upward-tending line in the KU, whereas they constitute two parallel descending lines of evolution in the Purāṇas. This is in keeping with the role played in the Purāṇas by the three components of being, *sattva, rajas,* and *tamas,* below the Great *Ātman:* they are too functional to be left out of a description of the manifestation of the cosmos. The *rajas* is the active component, which, agitating itself, creates a disequilibrium in the whole and allows evolution to follow in a more linear fashion. The *sattva* (a term that designates being in general) is the pure, luminous, transparent, peaceful component, while the *tamas* ("darkness") is its opposite, all that is heavy, opaque, obtuse, and that represents the heaviness of Nature. The Puruṣa lies beyond these components, but its pure light (or consciousness) can be reflected in the transparency of the *sattva.* The *Avyakta* holds them in equilibrium, so long as none of the components becomes excessive. Starting from the *mahān* (*ātmā*), the triplicity of Nature permits the formation of a knot that is decisive for further evolution. The Great Ātman should not be taken as the universal Ātman (only the Puruṣa is worthy of this title), but rather as an Ātman, a "Self," who has not yet been limited by a sense of self. The *mahān ātmā* of the KU must be understood in the same way: as the stage at which the yogi crosses the limits of his empirical individuality. For this reason, the following stage in the cosmogony is the constitution of an ego, of a sort of cosmic individual who, drawing on his three components, will form on the one hand the equivalent of a human psyche and on the other the (objective and subjective) material world, sentient bodies, and impressions. The Great Yogi is at first Puruṣa in name only, but in the course of the evolution that will lead to the cosmos, he recovers the form of the cosmic man that he had in the hymn to Puruṣa. This is the inverse of the movement of the KU yogi through his human determinants to the Great Ātman, then to the Nondifferentiated, and finally to the supreme Puruṣa who is Viṣṇu.

On the other hand, if in the creative process we do not encounter the three stages mentioned in the yogic ascension (*manas, buddhi, mahān ātmā*), it is because the Purāṇic account in fact identified *mahān* (*ātmā*, the term *ātman* being generally omitted), *buddhi* ("Intellect"?), *sattva*, and even *manas*. In Hindu psychology, the *manas* plays the role of a "communal sense." It is through it that all the internal and external sensory elements pass, in order that they may be communicated to the *ātman*, that Self in which the equivalent of our "soul" may be seen, if it were not impossible for it to say "I" about itself. The Purāṇas thus treat the *ātman* either as the direct emanation of the *avyakta* or as an eleventh sense. There is no point in wondering what these stages could represent for the yogi. It is, however, significant that the process of the emanation of the cosmos passes over some of them and introduces an ego in their place. This is not an invention of the Purāṇas; it is to be found in the oldest Upaniṣads. It orients itself totally toward evolution as it reconstitutes the cosmic man.

What does this cosmogony mean? In the beginning was yoga, and no longer the sacrifice. The Absolute is that of the yogi, that is, the man who has renounced society, the sacrifices that ensure his prosperity, and all the activities of men. To renounce the world is first of all to contest the sacrificial rite, the idea that that rite, performed in order to obtain well-being in this world and in the beyond, binds man into a cycle of rebirths that is endless because its results are always produced in the future. Renunciation is thus release from rebirths. But it is not enough to leave the society in which one is living in order to reach that end: renunciation has its own logic, which draws man ever further away from the conditions of all empirical life; and yoga is offered itself precisely in order to help the renunciant to leave behind his concrete humanity, to turn his attention away from desirable objects, from desire itself, to turn toward what is beyond all things, which will release him.

Yoga thus becomes the supreme value, and the Absolute is that of the yogi.

Cosmogony itself is not the creation of renunciants; it can only be the discourse of men searching to explain the existence of this world and to ensure its essential parts. But these men knew of the yogi and of his speculations. The starting point for everything, the ground zero of cosmogony, thus takes the form of a projection of the yogi into the absolute. The cosmogonic Puruṣa is first of all the Great Yogi. It is more difficult to understand the cosmogonic inversion of yogic ascension, since the end of yoga is to extricate oneself from the world. But the KU itself says that "yoga is surging and disappearing"; it is a recurrent, and not continuous, experience. The yogi passes through phases of concentration in which the universe disappears from his senses, and phases of return into ordinary empirical consciousness. He does not deny the existence of the world; he merely alters his interest in it, reabsorbing his senses and their objects into himself to turn himself toward the interior world. Hence the transposition: the Great Yogi, in his state of concentration, reabsorbs the whole universe into himself, whereas he causes it to emanate outside of himself when he engages in the conditions of empirical life and makes himself into an ego. The alternation of cosmic days and nights is the same as the alternation of the yogic phases of the supreme Puruṣa. This also enables us to understand why cyclic time is necessary in Hinduism: the universe is perpetually tied to the perpetual yoga of the Puruṣa, who creates only for the good of creatures, as he is himself perpetually released. He could remain collected into himself and nothing would happen. But he agrees to return to ordinary life, to be reborn as it were, in order that beings might exist and strive for release.

The Trimūrti

The moment in which the *Avyakta* begins to evolve is regarded as the birth of Brahmā into a new life. Until this point, it has been as if the Puruṣa sacrifice of the Puruṣa hymn were placed in parentheses. The creation of a cosmic ego that causes the Puruṣa to recover a human form is a hint that the sacrifice has not completely disappeared. The account of the primary creation stops when an Egg of Brahmā has been constituted. This is a further step in the same direction.

Who is this Brahmā, who is now said to be reborn for a new life of one hundred years (the ideal duration of life in India, but Brahmā's years are not the same as human years)? The most elevated social category is that of the Brahmans: the Brahman, who is in theory a priest, is in charge of the Vedic sacrifice and is an expert in Vedic knowledge. He is so called because he knows the formulas—*brahman*—and their manipulation. The term *brahman* in the neuter comes to designate all of the Veda and all Vedic knowledge. It is also the name given to the function and power of Brahmans. In the masculine, the term designates the Vedic sacrificial priest who oversees the whole of the rite without doing or saying anything. The Brahmā (masc.) who is born in the primary creation in order to inaugurate a period known as a *mahākalpa* is apparently connected with this *brahman:* that is, with the Veda and the sacrifice for which it stands as charter. The proof of this will emerge in the secondary cosmogony. For the moment, it is the connection between the *brahman* and the supreme Puruṣa that must be defined. It has been stated that the Puruṣa was present and immanent at each moment of cosmic emanation. At the level of the Egg of Brahma, from which the world will emerge, it is he who takes the name and the form of Brahmā. But this is only one of the three forms that he takes on at this level, for there is a triplicity in which we again encounter the three components enumerated previously. Brahmā is the creative aspect, because knowledge and Vedic practices are the mover of the world in which we live; because he is eminently active, he is composed of *rajas*. At the same time, the Puruṣa is Viṣṇu, he who preserves and conserves the world by virtue of the *sattva* that is dominant in him; and he is Rudra(-Śiva), the destroyer, he who is charged with *tamas*. The ensemble makes up the Trimūrti ("Triple Form"), and each of these aspects operates in the myth.

There is a source of confusion at this point, because the supreme Puruṣa may also, according to the Purāṇas, be called Viṣṇu or Śiva, or even the supreme Brahman (neuter): the levels must be kept separate. In his nonmanifest, ultimate form, the Puruṣa is never Brahmā (masc.), and to be the supreme Brahman (neuter) does not prevent him from being called Viṣṇu or Śiva. Those are the only two proper names for the supreme Puruṣa.

Curiously, the Egg of Brahmā concludes the account of primary creation. We are told that the worlds are contained in it and that the Puruṣa resides in its center, but we never see this egg hatch, because secondary cosmogony follows a completely different set of rules. The chaos-egg is an Upaniṣadic image. The choice of this form, which is also found in other myths, seems to be connected with the fact that the Sanskrit word for bird is *dvi-ja,* "he who is twice born," because it is oviparous. This is also the name of the members of the three highest *varṇas,* because they are born a second time during the initiation ceremony, but it comes to be especially applied to Brahmans. It is thus normal to have the birth of Brahmā take place from an egg.

Secondary Creation

Secondary creation does not take up where the primary left off: it takes place, not at the beginning of a life of Brahmā, but at the beginning of a day of Brahmā or a *kalpa,* and explicitly presupposes the night that preceded it, of equal duration. There are 360 days in a year of Brahmā, and he lives for 100 years: there will thus be 36,000 cycles of the world or *kalpas* repeating secondary creation within a *mahākalpa* or life of Brahmā. Beyond this, the *kalpa* or day of Brahmā contains 1,000 *mahāyugas* or *yugas* of the (Vedic) gods, which are themselves separated, no longer by cosmic nights, but by "twilights." Knowing that a *mahāyuga* is made up of 12,000 divine years, and that one divine year is equal to 360 human years, we may conclude that the edifice of the Purāṇic double cosmogony with its symmetrical dissolutions of the world carries only the weight of theory, with no practical consequence for contemporary man, who has moreover taken care to situate himself at a comfortable distance from any cosmic catastrophe. Man occupies the center of a cosmic period, just as he is the center of creation.

The narrative is brief: Nārāyaṇa awakens on the one ocean, into which the earth, and even the triple world (hell, earth, heaven), have disappeared. He is described (*Viṣṇu Purāṇa* 1.4–5, *Kūrma Purāṇa* 1.6–7, *Vāyu Purāṇa* 1.6) in the terms that the Puruṣa hymn uses for the cosmogonic Puruṣa. Nārāyaṇa is the form of the Puruṣa during the cosmic night that separates two *kalpas.* When he awakens, he becomes Brahmā, who becomes Vāyu (Wind, but also the vital breath) in order to move and then transforms himself into a Boar to go to search for the Earth at the bottom of the water and to put it back on its supports.

Here ends the colorful part of an account that draws upon a cosmogonic theme found in the Vedic texts (notably *Taittirīya Saṃhitā* 7.1.5.1, *Kāṭhaka Saṃhitā* 8.2), in which it is Prajāpati who transforms himself successively into Wind and Boar and then unites with the Earth that the Boar has pulled out of the water. It is Brahmā who in the Trimūrti inherits the functions of the Vedic Prajāpati. It is important to specify this, because each of the three aspects of the Trimurti is, in its own way, identified with the sacrifice: thus Brahmā is a "Lord of Creatures," *prajā-pati,* while Viṣṇu is the guarantor of cosmic order, dharma, and of general prosperity, *śrī.* Śiva is identified with the fire that consumes victims and with the post to which they are bound when they are put to death. He is thus allied with the fatal and somber aspects of the sacrifice. We can already see that the cosmogony and dissolution that take place at the level of the Trimūrti are assimilated into a sacrificial act.

It is for this reason that every Purāṇic text identifies the Boar, who plunges into the ocean of the flood (see below) to pull out the Earth, with the sacrifice. There can no longer be any doubt that in moving from the primary cosmogony to the secondary cosmogony we have moved from the realm of yoga to the realm of the sacrifice. But the same Puruṣa is at work in the cosmic manifestation, which is another way of saying that the sacrifice occurs in the interior of yoga, and no longer as its antagonist but as its subordinate. The Hindu universe has grown by inserting the Vedic universe into the universe that the renunciants know and teach.

Brahmā—whose four faces evoke his identity with the four Vedas—continues the work of creation, once the earth has been set at the center of the triple world. But the character of the second part of the account, which is once again completely charged with ideology but with minimal detail, reconciles it with the primary cosmogony. Immediately after the completion of the two accounts follows an obligatory recapitulation of the stages of creation from the *mahān* (*ātmā*) to the final stage of secondary creation, without any interruption. This recapitulation does away with the imagery of the two accounts: the Egg of Brahma, Nārāyaṇa who awakens on the ocean and becomes Brahma, Vāyu, the Boar. It must be admitted that without such imagery the cosmogonic accounts lose much of their intelligibility. The images may be omitted only after their meaning has been acquired in the context of the whole. Even so, not everything in the second part is clear, as will be seen.

Brahmā begins by creating the quintuple *avidyā,* metaphysical Ignorance, which makes the creation of individual beings possible, because it allows them to be unaware of their identity with the Puruṣa. The creation of Ignorance by Brahmā is explicitly connected with his desire to create beings of every kind. After this a primary creation follows, in which the predominance of *tamas* is such that beings are immobile and unconscious and do nothing (*asādhaka*): these are the plants. Brahmā, unsatisfied, begins again. This time the four-footed animals appear, but they still have too much *tamas,* so if they move, it is generally to follow an evil path. Brahmā, discontented with his work, then creates the (Vedic) gods who live in the skies, that is, the uppermost part of the triple world. But the gods have such a predominance of *sattva* that they are completely satisfied with their lot and do nothing. Brahmā is pleased with this creation, but pushes his work further in order to obtain "effective" beings—(*sādhaka*). These are men, who have within them *tamas, sattva,* and *rajas* in such abundance that they are subject to suffering and must act to escape it. The following stage of creation seems to describe the kind of help, of "grace," that each category of beings receives; but the text is obscure, and one has the impression of confronting realities that are as inaccessible to us as were the yogic stages of ascension of the *Kaṭha Upaniṣad.*

Significantly, it is at the human level that *rajas,* the active component of which Brahmā himself is made, reappears. *Rajas* is connected with those activities that characterize men, the only creatures who are capable of studying the Vedas and sacrificing. This is the secret complicity between Brahmā and men: men are the sole agents of what Brahmā represents, the sacrificial act—*karman.* But—and this point changes everything—the ritual activity of men has as its sole motivation the suffering that must be escaped, and no longer the positive search for terrestrial happiness. Their goal becomes the same as that of the yogi when he wants to escape the world of rebirths conceived as a world of suffering. To be a *sādhaka,* according to Brahmā and according to all of classical Hindu thought, is to take the path that leads to the attainment of the Absolute; that is, release from all suffering: it is to take the path of yoga, for which the term is *siddhi,* "realization" of the Absolute. But the *sādhaka* is the one who, from the beginning, undertakes the ritual activity patronized by Brahmā. Instead of being an obstacle to release, ritual becomes a means to it, and metaphysical Ignorance becomes a precondition for access to the supreme Knowledge. Thus, ritual seems already to belong to the world of yoga. The cosmogonic account is not further explained with regard to these implications, though they allow us to glimpse an integration of yoga with ritual that leaves neither one nor the other wholly intact. This interpenetration of these two sets of values constitutes what in Hinduism is called *bhakti,* the religion of devotion. It is essentially around *bhakti* that the whole of classical mythology is composed, whether it be sectarian or nonsectarian. But the symmetrical account of the dissolution of the world will help make the structure and meaning of the whole more precise.

The Dissolution of the World

At the end of a day of Brahmā (*kalpa*), the world enters a period of night, the sleep of creatures. This period is inaugurated by a cosmic catastrophe—*pralaya,* "dissolution," "reabsorption"—of which the account includes two principal phases and an introduction. This account, which, like that of creation, is actually based in Purāṇic literature (*Viṣṇu Purāṇa* 6.3, *Agni Purāṇa* 368–69, *Kūrma Purāṇa* 2.45, *Bhāgavata Purāṇa* 12, *Matsya Purāṇa* 165, *Vāyu Purāṇa* 1.7.18ff.), has so deeply structured Hindu thought, right up to the present, that it is important to set it forth in all its complexity and discuss the different levels of interpretation that it offers.

a) The Cosmic Fire

In the "picturesque" account that describes the *pralaya* in most of the Purāṇas, it all begins with a prolonged drought that progressively weakens all the creatures. Then the sun burns more brightly, is divided into seven, and draws all of the moisture out of the triple world before setting it on fire. The fire rages from the earth to the hells and then to the sky, until the whole becomes a mere incandescent ball, and resembles the back of a tortoise once again. The monstrous sun that sets fire to the worlds is called by diverse names: it is Kāla-Agni, the Fire of Time, or Kāla-Agni-Rudra, Rudra the Fire of Time, or Agni-Saṃvartaka, the destructive fire. The *Viṣṇu Purāṇa* clearly states that Viṣṇu (here the supreme Puruṣa) takes the form of Rudra, because he wants to reabsorb the world into himself.

mahākalpa (= life of Brahmā)	Supreme Purusa: Viṣṇu or Śiva	
		Brahmā (*rajas*) + Brahman (day) (night)
kalpa (= day of Brahmā)	Trimūrti	Viṣṇu or Puruṣa + Nārāyaṇa (day) (*sattva*) (night)
		Rudra, (*tamas*)

Note: Rudra is the "terrible" name of Śiva (= "the Beneficent")

Translation: the Puruṣa—who in the great Vaiṣṇava Purāṇa is called Viṣṇu—takes the *tāmasic* form of Rudra in the Trimūrti in order to burn up the world. The destructive role of Rudra is thus connected with his Vedic character: identified with the fire that consumes the victims, he is qualified to burn up the worlds, but at the same time he makes the fire into a sacrifice in which the three worlds are the victims. On the other hand, one must take literally Viṣṇu's desire to reabsorb the world into himself: at the level of the *mahākalpa* (the life of Brahmā), the rhythm of cosmic days and nights was assimilated to the rhythm of the yoga of the Puruṣa. The same holds on the level of the *kalpa:* it is by virtue of his yoga, but at a lower stage of yogic experience, that the Puruṣa periodically reabsorbs the worlds into himself and emits them. This lower stage is limited to the contents of the Egg of Brahmā, but these contents are more complex than they at first appear. The burning of the world is thus as much an effect of the *tapas* of Śiva as it is a sacrifice. The yogic character of the cycle of the *kalpa* (day of Brahmā) is irrefutably confirmed when it is further understood that the sleep of Nārāyaṇa on the cosmic ocean, from which secondary creation arises and with which it terminates at the end of the account, is really a yogic sleep, during which all of creation is reabsorbed into him. The dissolution of the world that the fire inaugurates is thus both a sacrifice by Rudra and an act of yoga by the divinity.

This double interpretation of the first act of the *pralaya* becomes more specific with respect to the fate of creatures in this catastrophe. In all the variants, the sky is emptied of its inhabitants when the fire reaches it: either they betake themselves to the higher spheres of their own will, or the heat of the fire drives them there. Those who inhabit the sky are primarily the gods, the great Seers of previous ages, the Perfected Ones—*siddhas,* those who have reached the culmination of the yogic experience, i.e., the renunciants—but also the members of the higher *varṇas* of normal human society who have fulfilled their dharma, along with their retinue. There is a logic here: renunciants no longer have any right to a special fate, because yoga and the sacrifice are no longer regarded as being in opposition. They are thus associated in the sky with all those who are there at the moment of *pralaya* and are promised release. Among these are the heads of high-caste families and apparently those who have served them properly and have thus properly fulfilled their duty, their own dharma. In the perspective of the renunciant at odds with the ritual world, the sky was a world into which one was reborn, a transmigratory world like all the others, a fruit of the ritual. It remains so to a certain extent, outside of the moment of *pralaya,* but at the same time it becomes an obligatory stage on the way to release, even for the renunciant. There is another transformation: in the original perspective, release applied only to members of the upper castes—because to become a renunciant was to renounce one's sacrificial fires—but in the Purāṇic view, release seems to include all of the world. Salvation is promised to all. Finally, release is not an individual process, even if the merits of each person continue to play a role. It takes place collectively for all those who happen to be located in the sky at the desired moment.

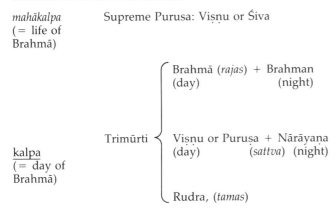

All of the inhabitants of the sky at the moment of *pralaya* are thus destined for release: they will not be reborn again. Their ascent above the sky results in the appearance of other spheres: *maharloka* (here *loka* means "world" and *mahas* means "strength, power," and irresistibly evokes for the mythographer the *mahān ātmā*), *janaloka* (the world of those destined for rebirth, if one derives *jana* from the root *jan-,* "to be born"), *tapoloka* (the world of ascetic heat—*tapas*), and the *brahmaloka.* This is the highest sphere, the end of the odyssey of creatures liberated at the end of a *kalpa.* But this ascension is far from immediate and linear: creatures oscillate between two of these spheres situated beyond the transmigratory cycle for ten *kalpas* before they are able to reach the Brahmaloka. When they finally arrive there, they enjoy absolute independence, all are equal, and they have perfect happiness.

The arrival at Brahmaloka is the part of this account that is the most clearly stated. This world of Brahmā or of Brahman (neuter) is a reminder of the fact that release takes place within the Egg of Brahmā—in the terminology of the primary cosmogony—that is, in the part of the universe where the sacrificial values hold sway. The universe of *bhakti*, which up to this point has had a temporal structure, now unfolds spatially. But the Brahmaloka, the site of release, cannot merely be the world of Brahmā, if Brahmā is first of all the god of the sacrifice. Its description—the absolute equality between all who have been liberated, the absence of a ruler, that is, the reverse of the terrestrial world—appears to be the mythic transposition of release as it is conceived by the "orthodox" renunciant. This is the high-caste renunciant who withdraws from a world governed by ritual to effect his own salvation, the renunciant at odds with the ritual world: the solitary *sannyāsin* ("renouncer"). For him, release from rebirths is the final stage of a process more "gnostic" than yogic: he is to reach an intuitive, experiential consciousness, the total identity of his *ātman*—of his Self, of his own being divested of an ego—with the Brahman. It is possible for the supreme form of the divinity to receive the name of "supreme Brahman," but this is merely a secondary designation for him, given as a reminder of the fact that he has within himself the Brahman of the *sannyāsin*. The Absolute that is defined by its being beyond the rite, that repudiates it by presupposing it, is by preference given the name of Brahman (or Ātman, since the two terms are interchangeable): the best that may be said is that the terrestrial Brahman is a projection of this, and that this Absolute cannot be dissociated from the *brahman* that it renounces. But contrary to the Brahman of the *sannyāsin*, the Brahmaloka is not the supreme level: it is situated at the level of the Trimūrti.

If Brahmaloka is truly the mythic "place" of release according to the conception of the *sannyāsin*, then it is possible to decipher step by step the rest of the odyssey of those who are released. Note first that they escape the cosmic fire: but in a society where the higher castes have recourse to the burning of the dead—a rite conceived as a sacrifice, the last in which the fire is ignited with the sacrificial fire of the deceased—the fact of being spared the cosmic fire evokes the treatment given to *sannyāsins* alone. Not only are they inhumed and not burned, but their death involves no impurity for those near them. That is, they are at no time associated with the dangerous world of "the departed"—*pretas*—not only because they no longer have a sacrificial fire in which to be burned, but because they have already observed their funeral rites by entering *sannyāsa*. At the same time, like all who die, they are subject to an intermediate period, which usually ends on the eleventh day, between inhumation and the final rites. This could well be the explanation for the curious oscillation of those who have been released, between two spheres above the world of transmigration, but below the Brahmaloka, over a period of ten *kalpas* (ten days of Brahmā).

Before taking up the fate of transmigratory creatures, we may quickly complete our description of the second phase of release, which takes place at the level of the *mahākalpa*, thus at the end of a life of Brahmā. From the point of view of the cosmos, reabsorption into the Puruṣa takes place in exactly the opposite order from that of cosmic emission, and thus tells us nothing more. As for those who are released from the Brahmaloka, they too are reabsorbed with Brahmā into the Puruṣa, where they will remain forever. No account specifies what they gain from this ultimate stage of release in relation to the first. But other myths describe this final residence of the released in the supreme Puruṣa as the paradise of Viṣṇu, Vaikuṇṭha, or Śiva, Kailāśa, according to the name that they give to the supreme divinity.

An account of the cosmic fire would not be complete if it did not specify the fate of those who are to be reborn. These are those who were living in the two lower spheres of the triple world at the moment of the fire. The fire of Rudra or Kāla reduces them, as well as the three worlds, to ashes, but their *ātmans*, the transmigratory part of them, escape in order to pass the cosmic night in a place where they are to be reborn with their *karman:* their refuge is the Janaloka. The name of the sphere that shelters them is a good indication of what awaits transmigratory beings, even if it is itself beyond transmigration.

It is evident, from all this symbolism, that the fire is a sacrifice, a sacrifice in which the fire is Rudra, i.e., in which the destructive aspect is primary. But the cosmic fire is also conceived as the funeral pyre of ordinary beings, of those who have not been promised release. The *ātmans* of these beings have to be conserved somewhere. The Janaloka is thus chosen for them.

Whatever their origins are, and by whatever means these cosmic spheres that appear only in the account of *pralaya* came into being, it seems clear—according to a process that recalls the stages of the primary cosmogony—that these are cosmological transpositions of seven ritual exclamations, of which the first three, in common usage, had a cosmological import from the start. The *Vāyu Purāṇa* (2.39.18b–27, 31b–34) attributes the creation of the seven worlds (*bhūr, bhuvas, svar, mahas, jana, tapas, satya = brahman*) to seven words of Brahmā. The three lower worlds form the "triple world," that of transmigration, even after the Purāṇas have replaced the intermediary space—*bhuvas*—with hell in order to lodge there the antigods, the *asuras*. When they are used on numerous ritual occasions, they are obviously meant to designate the three worlds. The rest is less clear, but we may note certain rituals in which the seven exclamations take the place of the three. These are the texts of the tradition (*smṛti*) that appear to be the most direct commentaries on the Vedic ritual that discuss these terms; it is thus nearly certain that the Purāṇic authors were aware of this, and that their account is an intended transposition. Whether or not they invented the cosmic spheres corresponding to the last four exclamations, the seven exclamations were never used together except in the ceremony of entry into *sannyāsa* and in the burial of *sannyāsins*.

This also confirms the hypothesis that the first phase of *pralaya*—the one that, moreover, determines the fate of transmigratory as well as released beings—follows a pattern inspired by the world of the orthodox *sannyāsin*, of the high-caste renunciant who regards the Absolute as Brahman rather than as Viṣṇu or Śiva. We must now complete the lesson taught by the account of secondary creation: henceforth yoga would regulate not only sacrificial values but every form of renunciation that proceeded from it directly. Release as defined by the *sannyāsin* becomes no more than a first stage toward final release. The Brahman of Brahmaloka is not the ultimate resting place of the one who is released, and, correlatively, the one who is released is not necessarily the *sannyāsin* in the strict sense of the word. The latter loses his prerogatives and is forced to allow into his company those he thought he had left behind for all time when he renounced his worldly existence. It is for this reason that the expanded universe developed in the primary creation and its corresponding reabsorption must be characterized as the universe of bhakti, of the religion that broke through the bonds of brahmanical orthodoxy decisively (in technical terms, the bonds of the *varṇāśramin*) to offer salvation to all. However, the continued use of "orthodox" categories at the same time shows that these have been not abolished but more safely preserved within that which encompasses them.

b) The Flood

When the three worlds have been consumed by the fire fanned by the breath of Rudra—or by the breath of the serpent Śeṣa (*Viṣṇu* 6.3.24) whom we will encounter again—the breath once again comes into play, that of Viṣṇu Janārdana (the "Oppressor of Creatures"), or more simply, the Wind, in order to pile up the clouds and start the rain that extinguishes the fire and submerges the rest of the three worlds in the one ocean. When the deluge has finished the work of the fire, the Wind appears again, this time to dissipate the clouds and end a rain that has continued for over one hundred years (like the initial drought). Then, on the ocean where everything else has disappeared, Viṣṇu lies asleep. He has the name of Vāsudeva or Nārāyaṇa, the two names that make him the container of all of the creatures: it is thus in him that, in the account of the *pralaya* between two *kalpas,* one must imagine the existence of the four spheres that lie above the triple world of transmigration. He either sleeps directly on the cosmic ocean (*Viṣṇu* 6.37–41) or on the serpent Śeṣa (*Vāyu* 2.4.4). All is plunged into darkness, but this Nārāyaṇa is none other than Brahmā, the god who at the dawn of a new day recreates everything.

The flood narrative (see *Matsya* for a different account) thus brings the universe back to the state from which secondary cosmogony began. The cycle of the *kalpa* is thus completed, and the cycle of the *mahākalpa* is also seen coming full circle with the completion of a life of Brahmā and the end of the journey of those who have been released. In the world of the narrations of the destruction of the world, sometimes the theme of the cosmic fire predominates and sometimes the theme of the flood. Both themes are used here: the first, corresponding to the first phase of the dissolution of the world, serves to determine the fate of the creatures; the second would be unexpected if it did not make it possible to return the cosmos to the state from which secondary creation began. Should this simple superposition of two themes be seen as a redundancy or as a mythic necessity?

The first part of an answer is given by the change in the divinity who controls the scene. Rudra disappears with the Fire, as does Janārdana (which is a "terrible" name of Viṣṇu-Kṛṣṇa). From this point on it can only be Nārāyaṇa or Vāsudeva, who is none other than Brahmā the creator but who for the time being sleeps on the cosmic ocean. The god made of *tamas* has given way to the god made of *sattva.* When Viṣṇu is associated with the preservation of the worlds, we think of his association with the sacrifice that ensures the prosperity of the three worlds; but he is also the one who preserves the worlds, or more exactly the creatures, during the cosmic night. To say that he is made of *sattva* is to restore to *sattva* its proper meaning of being in general, or the totality of beings (the Sanskrit abstract noun has both senses). Viṣṇu in the form of Nārāyaṇa (or Vāsudeva) thus carries all of the creatures in himself, both those awaiting rebirth and those who are released to the level of Brahmaloka. As already noted in connection with the *mahākalpa* and the ultimate form of the Great Yogi, the emission and reabsorption of the worlds are tied to the rhythm of divine yoga. We find this same pulsation on the level of the *kalpa.* The sleep of the god on the ocean is a yogic image, mentioned in the Purāṇic account (for example, *Kūrma* 45.55; *Viṣṇu* 6.4.6), and its most famous mythic use occurs when the Goddess appears, at the time of his awakening, as the personification of his yogic sleep, *yoganidrā* (a feminine noun, luckily). It is sufficient to specify that this yogic repose is not so deep as the sleep of the god between two *mahākalpas,* since it allows the creatures to survive as a trace in the divine consciousness. The theme of yogic sleep occurs again at another level—in which the image does not reveal its meaning so easily—with regard to the epic Kṛṣṇa: each time that he is called upon for a crucial appearance, he is found asleep on his couch. He thus seems to be not only an avatar of Viṣṇu but also a reincarnation of the *ṛṣi* Nārāyaṇa.

A second part of the answer is that the ocean of the flood is a universal image of the return of the world to chaos. But the most commonly described scene puts the serpent Śeṣa between the ocean and Nārāyaṇa: the great coiled serpent is another image of the unformed, of chaos, but this serpent is named Śeṣa, "the remainder," which gives him a much more precise meaning. Śeṣa is most precisely what remains of the cosmic sacrifice, the incandescent ball that the breath of Viṣṇu and the clouds save from total annihilation. The meaning of this remainder lends itself to two complementary interpretations. Every Brahman knows that he should eat only the "remainder" of the sacrifice: in practice all food to be consumed should be sacrificial food. Thus it is necessary for a portion of it to be offered to the gods, who may also be represented by any guest who might have arrived unexpectedly. The remainder of the sacrifice is thus the condition for all pure life, for all prosperity. Here, in the context of the *pralaya,* it is the promise of a future rebirth. The sacrificial circle continues, and on the cosmic level where we exist it merges with the cycle of the *kalpa.* Nārāyaṇa the yogi sleeps on the sacrificial remainder of the world. Yoga and sacrifice join to ensure the continuity of the world, and the sacrifice is once again subordinated to yoga.

The meaning of the serpent—*nāga*—which echoes the cosmic sacrifice, also requires a more precise interpretation of the ocean. The *nāgas,* in Hindu mythology, live in a subterranean aquatic world. There is thus a connection between Śeṣa and his natural milieu, the ocean. Beyond this, however, we are reminded of funerary rites, for an aspect of these rites is transposed in the cosmic fire. After incineration, the ashes of the dead are collected and at least some of them are thrown into the Ganges to ensure a heavenly rebirth or release for the dead (the waters of the river mingle with those of the ocean at its mouth, just as the individual *ātmans* melt into the Brahman): the heavenly resting place (the Vedic world beyond) and eternal release, as we have seen, are no longer placed in opposition, and the Ganges is the river of salvation, of all salvation. Every river becomes the Ganges or is mysteriously connected to the Ganges, and the cremation grounds of India are always put on the bank of a river. The theme of the flood is thus put to another logical use. The disappearance of the residue of the cosmos in the ocean—the symbolic meaning of the sacrificial residue is borne here by the serpent Śeṣa—corresponds to the phase of the immersion of the ashes and promises a happy future for everyone: heavenly rebirth, in the popular consciousness, is merely the collateral for good future rebirths, and this is all that is asked of the Ganges for the individual, as it is asked of the flood for the three worlds.

M.Bi./d.w.

BIBLIOGRAPHY

M. BIARDEAU, "Études de mythologie hindoue," parts 1–3, *BEFEO* (1968–71). CH. MALAMOUD, "Observations sur la notion de 'reste' dans le brâhmanisme," *Wiener Zeitschrift für die Kunde Südasiens* (1972).

Abbreviations

BAU	*Bṛhad-āraṇyaka-upaniṣad*
ChU	*Chāndogya-upaniṣad*
K	*Kūrma-purāṇa*
KU	*Kaṭha-upaniṣad*
V	*Vāyu-purāṇa*
Vi	*Viṣṇu-purāṇa*

The Hindu God with Five Heads (*Pañcamukha*)

The number five is one of the most widely used numbers in classical Hinduism. It would probably be impossible to bring all of its uses together into a single pattern of meaning. It is nevertheless a recurring theme in both classical and modern iconography, in which its meaning is clear and its structure well defined. The theme is a representation of divinities with five heads or five faces—*pañcamukha*—though the mythology gives no account of this fivefold multiplication of the heads of divinities and generally assumes that divinities have only one head. Among the gods of the sanctuary proper, we find the multiplication by five only for the linga of Śiva, which becomes curiously transformed into a *pañcamukha-liṅga:* Śiva is the only divinity whose mythology includes the mention of five heads (see below). On the other hand, five-headed figures can be found on processional images and frequently on the reliefs that adorn walls and pillars. Thus we have Gaṇapatis, Hanumāns, Bhairavas, Goddesses, Viṣṇus, and Narasiṃhas with five heads. But we must exclude from this list Brahmā, who never has more than four heads (see below), Dattātreya, who often has three as the incarnation of the Trimūrti, and Skanda, who has either one or six. Most of the time the five heads are not on the same plane. The most frequent arrangement is of four heads placed according to the four cardinal directions around a central pivot (the linga, for example) with a fifth placed on top. When the five heads are on the same plane, the central head marks the highest point of the curve formed by their crowns. The five heads thus become (with some exceptions) four heads plus one.

This representation would seem to be the generalization of a theme that has its basis in a specific myth, or rather in two myths that are connected to one another, but of which the first may have come into existence only because of the second. The first concerns Brahmā exclusively. The classical Brahmā, heir to the Vedic Prajāpati, is still associated with the theme of incest that quite logically characterizes the progenitor of all creatures. But the theme is used in a new way. The account that the *Matsya Purāṇa* (3.30–41) gives of this is very clear in its brevity: Brahmā, wanting to create beings, divided in two so as to form a couple, but the woman who issued from this division appeared to be his daughter because she was born from his body. As soon as he sees her, he falls in love with her beauty and desires her violently, despite the protests of the *ṛṣis* (led by Vasiṣṭha) who are born of him and consider her their sister. The woman has the

Five-headed Bhairava. Chariot wood. Madras Museum special collections. Photo IFI 298–51.

name of Sāvitrī, Sarasvatī, Gāyatrī, Brahmāṇī, and Śatarūpā ("having one hundred forms"), and it is she whom we meet again as the consort of Brahmā: the *gāyatrī* (or *sāvitrī*), for example, is only a Ṛgvedic verse that the Brahman must recite each day at sunrise, but it ends up, like all the other names of this series, designating the Vedic Speech personified and the feminine energy that ensures Brahmā's fertility, the energy through which Vedic knowledge may be expressed and communicated. Without her there would be no ritual, and thus no viable creation.

Sāvitrī, once created, shows her respect for her father by walking around him to the right (*pradakṣiṇa,* i.e., clockwise). Brahmā, ashamed but overwhelmed with desire—*kāma-ātura,* "sick with desire," the text says—so badly wants to follow her with his eyes that a new head appears to the right, then another to the rear, and then a fourth to the left. His incestuous desire makes him lose all the merits he acquired by the asceticism that he had practiced to create beings. Then he grows a fifth head on top, which he covers with an ascetic's topknot, and he orders his sons to create beings (in his place?).

Brahmā thus has four heads plus one. The first four are absorbed in watching and desiring the beauty of Sāvitrī, with whom he would create the world; for does not everything arise from the Veda and thus from Brahmā? But because of this desire he has exhausted the merits of his asceticism and his creative capacity. The fifth head, with its ascetic's topknot and its gaze turned upwards, returns to its earlier austerities and leaves the work of creation to Brahmā's sons. The symbolism of this account is complex: in it we find first of all the Vedic idea of the exhaustion that is provoked by the creative act and the ritual act—always identified—and that calls for a regeneration of lost powers. But Hinduism greatly enriched this theme, which meanwhile had passed through Upaniṣadic reflections: between the Brahmā who is sick with desire and the fifth head with its ascetic's topknot there is clearly the same tension that is found between the sacrificial values that underlie all of creation and the renunciation of the world that is the final end of creation. The religion of ritual is henceforth assimilated to the world of desire: one performs a ritual only out of a desire for a certain result, and Brahmā is sometimes identified with Kāma, the god of love. But the Upaniṣads were very quick to make the distinction between the inferior *brahman*—the Veda, the science of ritual, the Vedic Speech—and the supreme Brahman, that which transcended ritual and word, the absolute of the renunciant. Here apparently the first four heads of Brahmā operate on the level of ritual—the driving desire behind the ritual act becoming the desire for the beauty of Sāvitrī, for creative Speech, and for creation as a whole. There are four heads because there are four Vedas, and because the terrestrial world, the world of desire and the world of acts—*karmabhūmi*—is symbolized by the four cardinal points. As for the fifth head, this is the symbol of the supreme Brahman, the one in which the renunciant seeks his ultimate deliverance from rebirths, and which is found again in Hindu cosmology as Brahmaloka, "the world of Brahmā," but also "of the Brahman."

Five-headed Viṣṇu seated on five Brahmās. Temple of Sattanadar at Nagapattinam (South India). Photo IFI 6680–3.

Yet Brahmā is never represented with anything but the first four heads. We know, on the other hand, that he is the only one of the three divinities of the Trimūrti who is not considered to be a god of *bhakti;* that is, who has not been raised to the supreme level of cosmology, as Śiva and Viṣṇu have been. He remains closely tied to the sphere of the Veda and of the ritual, even in his renunciant dimension, which is an effective way to take account of the relationship that the high-caste renunciant retains with the ritual world that he has left behind. Brahmā is not the god of grace, as a god of bhakti should be. All he knows how to give is favors—*vara*—which reward the ascetic efforts of an individual, preferably of an *asura* or an evil prince with suspect motives: he never leaves the circle of retribution of *karman,* even when the *karman,* "ritual action," becomes *tapas,* "austerities," "ascetic heat." He is not the god of the unearned boon.

This is what the second myth undertakes to explain, in permanently depriving Brahmā of his fifth head. It is Śiva, or one of his terrible emanations, who takes charge of the execution, which gives the myth the misleading appearance of being a Śaiva sectarian myth: to cut off one of Brahmā's heads, in short, to sacrifice it, is automatically to commit Brahmanicide, one of the most detestable crimes of Hindu dharma. Who but Śiva could undertake such a task in the world of bhakti? The myth is recounted many times (*Vāmana Purāṇa* 2; *Kūrma Purāṇa* 2.31, etc.), with multiple variants and more or less disastrous consequences for Śiva, whose sufferings we shall here summarize. The outline of the account is very simple: Rudra-Śiva and Brahmā quarrel. Brahmā believes in his own superiority and angers Rudra with remarks made by his fifth head. Rudra then gives himself five heads so as to be equal to Brahmā, but Brahmā's fifth head still refuses to recognize Rudra's superiority, until Rudra cuts it off with a stroke of his fingernail (or commands Bhairava to do this). Rudra goes away, but because this head remains stuck to his hand—where it becomes his begging bowl (the begging bowl of his Kāpālika devotees, the men "with a skull")—he has to make a long pilgrimage to rid himself of it.

What is interesting here is that Śiva gives himself five heads to become the "physical" equal of Brahmā: the five heads are as widely known in Hinduism as the four heads of Brahmā. Each head has a name that is attested in the *Mahā-nārāyaṇa Upaniṣad* (which can hardly be suspected of Śaiva sectarianism), and they are also designated by the generic term of *pañcabrahma,* "the five *brahmans,*" "the five ritual formulas," as the five names are given in ritual invocations transmitted by the Upaniṣads. As for the *pañcamukha-liṅga,* its most widespread form is that of a linga with an anthropomorphic face on each of its four sides, oriented to the cardinal directions, while the fifth is simply the upper extremity of the linga, rising above the four faces. It is evident that the five faces of Śiva are not of the same order as the five faces of Brahmā in the first myth. The end of the linga symbolizes the supreme form of the god, unmanifested, the form related to release, while the four faces recall the bond that unites Śiva with the world of Vedic ritual (as well as Śaiva ritual, which is merely a continuation of the Vedic ritual).

We also know representations of Viṣṇu with four or five heads, but here the lateral heads are generally the heads of animals that recall the theriomorphic avatars of Viṣṇu: boar, lion, fish. On the other hand, the sectarian Vaiṣṇava concept of the four *vyūhas,* the four "unfoldings" of the god, which, through successive levels, allow him to pass from the supreme nonmanifest state to the manifest state (the names of the *vyūhas* are borrowed from the mythology of Kṛṣṇa and appear in the MBh), remained sectarian and was not translated into iconography. This may be a supplementary confirmation of the nonsectarian character of the myth of the decapitation of the fifth head of Brahmā. Given the position of Viṣṇu with regard to sacrificial values, he naturally takes the title of the supreme Brahman, and no one dares to contest his title. He has no need to debate with Brahmā over a superiority that is recognized to be his from the start (except for the exigencies of Śaiva mythology).

The generalization of the iconographic theme of five-headed divinities is not a chance occurrence: it expresses the fact that every Hindu god, no matter what his level in the pantheon, represents for his devotee the totality of bhakti, the impossible summation of prosperity in this world: *bhukti,* and deliverance in the other world: *mukti.* If it is a relatively secondary divinity like Bhairava or Hanumān (who have the function of "guardians of the territory" of the superior god), he more or less implicitly takes on the role of intermediary to the higher god on behalf of the devotees who appeal to them.

M.Bi./d.w.

Deva/Asura: Celestial Gods and "Demons" in Hinduism

The opposition between the *devas*—celestial gods—and the *asuras* (is "demons" the correct translation?) is less a myth than an omnipresent motif in Indian mythology, a motif that merits a clarification of meaning.

The theme is already present in Vedic literature, although it is difficult to tell how the two were originally distinguished from one another, since the god Varuṇa, for example, is often considered to be an *asura.* The *devas* and *asuras* have the same father: Prajāpati, the primordial Progenitor, but the *asuras* are the older and stronger sons. They would invariably be victorious in the conflicts in which they fight the gods if the gods did not resort to a ruse or a benefactor (such as Viṣṇu, with his three steps) to defeat them. But it is clear that, in spite of the strength of the *asuras,* it is the gods who are to receive the sacrifice, who are the keepers of sacrificial knowledge, and whose place in the ritual assures the order of the world. Yet on the Vedic level, where *deva* and *asura* seem to be associated with the sky, their opposition is limited to the ritual domain. This fundamental relationship will not vary; it will become more detailed through various types of oppositions, but these oppositions will leave intact the neutral "nature" of the *devas* and *asuras* when they are taken individually. If *deva* is translated as "god," it is tempting to translate *asura* as "demon," but this opposition has for us a moral connotation that is not appropriate in the Indian context.

This becomes even clearer in classical Hinduism, where the war between the *devas* and *asuras* is a recurrent theme (avatar myths, epics). Their relationship thus remains, collectively, one of hostility. The gods become the sole legitimate occupants of heaven—*svarga*—while the *asuras* inhabit the infernal regions. The space that divides the higher luminous sphere from the kingdom of darkness is occupied by the earth inhabited by men—which logically becomes the place where the hereditary enemies meet in battle. The society of the gods is organized like the society of the *asuras,* after the model of human society: there is no mention of castes, but there is a king of the gods—always Indra—and a royal chaplain, Bṛhaspati ("the master of the ritual formula"), of the Aṅgiras family. Similarly, there is a king of the *asuras* whose name varies from one myth to another, and a chaplain of the *asuras*—who is as much a Brahman as the chaplain of the gods—named Śukrācārya, of the family of the Bhṛgus, to whom are attributed powers that exceed those of Bṛhaspati and who is the real source of the might of the *asuras.* When the triple world—*trailokya*—is in order, the celestial gods receive the sacrificial offerings of men: this is the state of dharma in which the hierarchy of beings is respected. When the *asuras* defeat the gods, they drive them out of heaven and receive the sacrificial offerings in their place. The normal order is reversed, and catastrophe is inevitable, for the triple world cannot continue under these conditions. At such times Viṣṇu "descends" to reestablish dharma and to return everyone to his proper place, with the *devas* above and the *asuras* below. But Viṣṇu is no longer a simple Vedic god of the sacrifice, a *deva* in the ordinary sense. His divinity is of the highest order, and it is to him that the oblations that men offer to the *devas* ultimately go. Correspondingly, the *devas* have lost their role as the models of human sacrificial activity. Meanwhile, on earth the Vedic sacrifice has practically disappeared, and sacrifices (*yāga* and no longer *yajña*) are offered in temples to the gods of bhakti: to Viṣṇu, Śiva, the Goddess, and all the great regional gods connected with Viṣṇu or Śiva.

There is a new element in the *deva/asura* conflicts that expresses this new universal dimension: even when the king of the *asuras* succeeds in occupying the throne of Indra, it is possible for a particular *asura,* preferably his heir, to refuse the fait accompli, more from devotion to Viṣṇu and to dharma than devotion to the *devas.* The gods become mere terms of a series which also includes Brahmans, cows, and the Vedas—that is, they become parts of the dharma of which Viṣṇu is the sole guarantor. Prahlāda, son of Hiraṇyakaśipu, king of the *asuras* and a great devotee of Viṣṇu, was to reign over the underworld after his father was killed by Narasiṃha and Indra was reinstated on his throne. Vibhīṣana, the brother of Rāvaṇa, was to rule over Laṅkā, the kingdom of the *rākṣasas* (a variant of *asuras* in the classical mythology: Rāvaṇa is the reincarnation of Hiraṇyakaśipu), when Rāma killed Rāvaṇa and won back Sītā. Prahlāda and Vibhīṣaṇa are good *asuras-rākṣasas.*

The strength of the *asuras* may be connected with that of their chaplain (as in the myth of Yayāti), but the most frequent theme is that of the boon that Brahmā gives to the king of the *asuras* which guarantees him nearly total invulnerability; yet Viṣṇu will continually rely on trickery to strike the heel of this Hindu Achilles. Śukrācārya and Brahmā are clearly equivalent terms here. They establish a connection between the power of the *asuras* and the ritual, since Śukra is the Brahman priest of the *asuras,* whereas Brahmā represents precisely the knowledge and power of the ritual. They thus illustrate the possible deviation from the ritual order (and from retribution for actions) that is not integrated into the order of bhakti—in which Viṣṇu is all-powerful—and the necessity to integrate the ritual order into the comprehensive order of bhakti. The triple world is no more than a small part of the universe, even if it is the only part in which anything actually happens, but the dharma that guides it becomes finely tuned with the rest of the universe.

On the level of popular mythology, i.e., the one that is current and locally diversified, the theme of the opposition of the *devas* and the *asuras* has an application that also presupposes the intervention of bhakti: the king of the *asuras* can transform himself into a *bhakta* at the moment when he is killed by the great local god (a form of Śiva or Viṣṇu) or by the Goddess. His death in battle with the god becomes a warrior's sacrifice that assures him of his salvation. He thus becomes the guardian of the great god in his temple. This is a motif that makes it possible to integrate an inferior, impure divinity (the king of the *asuras* has by definition the rank of a Kṣatriya, is carnivorous, and requires blood sacrifices) into a pure temple; to transpose in the temple the hierarchical relationship that unites the pure and impure castes. And this is not the only mode of articulation of the pure and the impure within the Hindu pantheon.

M.Bi./d.w.

BIBLIOGRAPHY

G. DUMÉZIL, *Mitra-Varuna: Essai sur deux représentations indo-européennes de la souveraineté* (4th ed., Paris 1948); *The Destiny of the Warrior* (Chicago 1970). J. GONDA, *The Vedic God Mitra* (Leiden 1972). F. B. J. KUIPER, "The Basic Concept of Vedic Religion," *History of Religions* 15, no. 2 (1975); *Varuṇa and Vidūṣaka: On the Origin of the Sanskrit Drama* (Amsterdam, Oxford, and New York 1979). H. LUDERS, *Varuṇa*, 2 vols., 1: *Varuṇa und die Wasser* (Göttingen 1951); 2: *Varuṇa und das Ṛta* (Göttingen 1959). A. A. MACDONELL, *Vedic Mythology* (Indian reprint, Varanasi 1963).

Vasiṣṭha/Viśvāmitra and the Separation of the Priestly and Royal Functions

Vasiṣṭha and Viśvāmitra are two *ṛṣis* that a very rich mythology usually portrays as two enemies. From the Vedic period, one of them was known as the best Brahman priest (one of the celebrants of the Vedic sacrifice, the one who presides) and the other as a *ṛṣi* of royal origin who is nevertheless accepted as the chaplain of a king, and a great number of Vedic hymns are attributed to him. The Vedic information is fragmentary and does not form a coherent whole. But in classical Hinduism, beginning with the epics, Vasiṣṭha is a symbol of the pure Brahman, son of Brahmā himself or of the Vedic gods Mitra and Varuṇa. Viśvāmitra, on the other hand, is the "upstart," who, born a Kṣatriya, sought to acquire the quality of a Brahman, which is normally acquired only by birth. The confrontation between the two individuals has consequently been interpreted for a long time as one of the echoes of a historical conflict between Brahmans and Kṣatriyas, when the Kṣatriyas rebelled against the superiority of the Brahmans. The meaning of these mythic stories is mainly ideological, even if Vasiṣṭha and Viśvāmitra did once exist. The confrontation, which is found elsewhere, is the expression of a very particular balance that regulates the relationship between Brahmans and Kṣatriyas. Although they are deprived of all material power, Brahmans are superior because they are the experts in the Vedic sacrifice, the source of all wealth in this world, and because they have a very pure way of life. What the Kṣatriyas have is strength, but even that strength would be denied them if the Brahmans did not sacrifice on their behalf and receive their gifts, thereby sanctifying the obligatory impurity of Kṣatriya customs. The equilibrium of society rests on the strict separation of the priestly and royal functions, which involves a parallel separation of the social categories performing those functions: a Brahman can only be a Brahman and cannot rule over a kingdom; a Kṣatriya can only be a king and warrior and cannot be his own priest or keep his wealth for himself. It is characteristic that the alleged revolt by the Kṣatriyas expressed in the myths consists, not in denying the power appropriate to Brahmans, but in envying it and claiming it, in other words, in combining the two powers. The sacrosanct separation is thus removed and there is chaos.

We know that the (historical?) exception represented by Viśvāmitra led to an abundant literature. His confrontation with Vasiṣṭha is concretized in several different accounts that are generally given in isolation. There are many epic and Purāṇic versions, and they are rather divergent, though the message seems to be always the same. We have chosen here the version of the *Rāmāyaṇa*, which has the advantage of giving in a single account the principal episodes of the struggle between the two *ṛṣis* by joining them with a common thematic thread. In the *Rāmāyaṇa*, Vasiṣṭha is the chaplain and counselor of King Daśaratha, the father of Rāma. Daśaratha receives a visit from Viśvāmitra (1.18), who asks him to entrust Rāma to him for a brief period of time, but Vasiṣṭha must intervene to secure Daśaratha's consent. At this point the two *ṛṣis* are at last reconciled. A few chapters later (1.51–65), however, their quarrels are reported to Rāma.

Viśvāmitra, the son of King Gādhi, goes around the world with his army. He arrives at Vasiṣṭha's hermitage, where he is received with hospitality. They strike up a conversation. Vasiṣṭha asks his guest if his kingdom is prospering. He then insists on feeding the entire army. To do so, he calls his cow Śabalā, who provides him with all that he needs for a sumptuous feast. The dazzled Viśvāmitra offers Vasiṣṭha one hundred ordinary cows in exchange for Vasiṣṭha's cow. Vasiṣṭha refuses, because all of his activity as a Brahman depends on the cow, since he cannot sacrifice without her. Viśvāmitra makes an even better offer, which is still rejected. Viśvāmitra then tries to take the cow away by force, but at Vasiṣṭha's bidding she emits warriors who proceed to destroy Viśvāmitra's army. Viśvāmitra's hundred sons attack Vasiṣṭha, who reduces them to ashes in a fit of rage.

Viśvāmitra then leaves his kingdom to his only surviving son, withdraws into the forest, and practices austerities in honor of Śiva, who appears to him and asks him what he wants. Viśvāmitra replies that he wants the knowledge of all weapons, including magic weapons. Armed with this panoply, he presents himself at Vasiṣṭha's hermitage more boastful than ever and begins by setting it on fire. All Vasiṣṭha has

Ascetic among his five fires. Photo P. Amado.

to do is counter with his Brahman's stick—the *brahmadaṇḍa*—to annul the effect of Viśvāmitra's weapons. Viśvāmitra realizes that the power of the Kṣatriya is nothing next to that of the Brahman. He must purify himself in order to become a Brahman. He goes south with his principal wife and devotes himself to great austerities. At the end of a thousand years, Brahmā appears to him and bestows on him the title of royal *ṛṣi*. Viśvāmitra is not satisfied and begins a new period of asceticism.

At this moment, the pious king Triśaṅku takes it into his head to offer a sacrifice in order to ascend to heaven with his human body. Vasiṣṭha, his chaplain, tells him this is impossible. Vasiṣṭha's sons are asked and also refuse to perform this sacrifice, which their father has declined to undertake. Triśaṅku threatens to go to see another priest. Vasiṣṭha's sons then condemn him to be a *caṇḍāla* (untouchable). He is abandoned by all. Triśaṅku calls on Viśvāmitra, who is moved by compassion when he sees him. The fallen king protests his innocence and asks for his help. Viśvāmitra agrees to undertake the sacrifice and to summon other *ṛṣis* to help him: Triśaṅku will ascend to heaven in his human form. Viśvāmitra dispatches his sons to search for the other *ṛṣis* and bring them back. They all come except for Vasiṣṭha's sons, who consider the sacrifice even more impossible now, with a Kṣatriya celebrant and an untouchable sacrificer. Viśvāmitra reduces them to ashes (with the fire of his anger) and condemns them to be reborn seven hundred times as untouchables. His curse is effective. He then undertakes the sacrifice, but when he invites the gods to receive their share, they abstain. Then, confident of the power that he was given for his ascetic ardor (*tapas*), Viśvāmitra interrupts the sacrifice and sends Triśaṅku to heaven by his own power. Triśaṅku ascends, but Indra sends him away, because he has been cursed by his teacher (Vasiṣṭha and his sons) and does not merit the rewards of heaven. Triśaṅku calls on Viśvāmitra to help. Viśvāmitra breaks Triśaṅku's fall and sets out to create another heaven for his protégé, beginning with another Big Dipper to the south. The gods intervene and stop him from pursuing his work. Viśvāmitra explains that he has promised Triśaṅku and he cannot go back on his word. He convinces the gods to let the constellation he has created remain in the sky and to let Triśaṅku live in it, shining like a star. The sacrifice is completed, and they all return to their respective dwelling places (another version of the story of Triśaṅku appears in *Harivaṃśa* 1.12–13).

Viśvāmitra leaves the south, where his austerities have been prevented from achieving their purpose. He settles in Puṣkara and begins to practice *tapas* again. At that moment, King Ambarīṣa of Ayodhyā begins to perform a sacrifice. But the sacrificial victim is stolen by Indra. The celebrant directs the king to replace the victim quickly, for the disappearance of a designated victim is a serious sin. The king searches for a victim and is ready to buy one at the price of thousands of cows. He encounters the *ṛṣi* Brahman Ṛcīka with his wife and children and offers to buy one of his sons for one hundred thousand cows, in order to make the child into the sacrificial victim. Ṛcīka does not want to sell his oldest son, and his wife does not want to be separated from her youngest son. The middle son, Śunaḥśepa, volunteers to be the victim, and his father receives the one hundred thousand cows and a pile of gold coins. Ambarīṣa takes Śunaḥśepa with him. On the way, he stops at Puṣkara to rest. There Śunaḥśepa meets Viśvāmitra, his maternal uncle, and asks him to free him and to allow Ambarīṣa to achieve his desires in another way. Viśvāmitra asks his sons to take Śunaḥśepa's place. The sons refuse. The father curses them and condemns them to be reborn on earth as untouchable dog eaters for one thousand years, like Vasiṣṭha's sons. He advises Śunaḥśepa to let himself be tied to the sacrificial stake and to sing praises to Indra and Viṣṇu. He will then be freed. He does so and Indra grants him a life of one thousand years and Ambarīṣa is rewarded for his sacrifice. Viśvāmitra resumes his austerities for another thousand years (another version of the story of Śunaḥśepa appears in *Aitareya Brāhmaṇa* 7.13–18).

One thousand years elapse and Brahmā and all the gods come to reward Viśvāmitra by giving him the title of *ṛṣi*. Viśvāmitra continues his austerities because this does not satisfy him. After a long time, the nymph Menakā comes to bathe in the lake at Puṣkara. The *ṛṣi* falls in love with her and lives with her for ten years, thus wiping out all the fruits of his austerities. Viśvāmitra realizes that this is a trick that the gods have played on him. He dismisses Menakā and sets out for the mountains in the north.

The gods are frightened by his new austerities. They ask Brahmā to reward him with the title of *maharṣi* (great *ṛṣi*). Viśvāmitra asks Brahmā if this means that he has finally mastered his senses. The answer is no; he will have to prolong his *tapas* once again. During the summer, he sits between four fires, under the sun that acts as the fifth fire; he remains unprotected during the monsoon rains and lives in the water during the winter. This goes on for a thousand years. The gods and their king Indra are worried. They send the nymph Rambhā to Viśvāmitra, but because she fears the wrath of the ascetic, Indra promises her help in the form of a cuckoo with a spellbinding song. Viśvāmitra senses a trap; he angrily curses Rambhā and turns her into a stone statue, but he promises her that a very glorious Brahman (Vasiṣṭha) will free her. Yet he has once again consumed all the merit of his *tapas* in the fire of his anger.

Viśvāmitra resolves never to get angry again and not to speak or eat or even to breathe for hundreds of years, until he has reached the status of Brahman. To that end, he settles in the east. This time he does not allow himself to be distracted from his vow, even by Indra who comes to tempt him, disguised as a Brahman. Smoke comes out of his head, which disturbs the three worlds. All the inhabitants of heaven ask Brahmā to put an end to his *tapas* for fear that he will set the worlds on fire. He must be granted his wish. Brahmā therefore goes to inform him that he has now become a Brahman and grants him long life. Viśvāmitra then asks that Vasiṣṭha recognize him as a Brahman. Vasiṣṭha accedes to the gods' request and proclaims that Viśvāmitra is a *brahmarṣi*. That is how Viśvāmitra became a Brahman and the greatest ascetic of them all.

The exception proves the rule: Viśvāmitra had to spend thousands of years practicing harsh austerities to attain the status of a Brahman. He was delayed when, not fully master of himself—which is supposed to be the virtue of a Brahman, on the model of the yogi—he was on several occasions tempted to abuse the power acquired through his *tapas* to perform remarkable feats or else simply yielded to the temptation of love or anger. He covered the entire spectrum of possible downfalls before attaining perfect mastery of himself. The slow ascension described in the *Rāmāyaṇa* did not win everyone's approval, for Viśvāmitra appears in a less flattering light in other myths. See, for example, the story of Hariścandra in *Mārkaṇḍeya Purāṇa* 1.7–9, in which Viśvāmitra is depicted as merciless; the story of King Kalmāṣapāda in *Mahābhārata* 1.174–76; and the story of the river Sarasvatī, ibid. 9.42, in which Vasiṣṭha is the paragon of all virtues, especially patience, in the face of the odious Viśvāmitra. In every way, this upstart Brahman retains something of his Kṣatriya origin.

M.Bi./g.h.

The Main Myth of the *Mahābhārata*

The *Mahābhārata* (MBh), the longer of the two Sanskrit epics, has been translated or adapted into several of the modern languages of India and plays an enormous role in the traditional education of the Hindu consciousness even today. There is a single myth that unfolds throughout the course of its eighteen sections. But it is filled with secondary myths meant to illustrate a point of doctrine or to bring consolation. There are also many didactic discourses, and books twelve and thirteen consist essentially of the teaching given by Bhīṣma to Yudhiṣṭhira.

Only the principal myth in its most significant articulations will be discussed here, with an emphasis on what it shares with the myth of the *Rāmāyaṇa* (R); for there is a clear parallelism between the two epics. Both give an account of the duties of a perfect king devoted to Brahmans—and from this, the duties of all categories of human beings—and have as their narrative theme the myth of an avatar: Rāma in the R, and Kṛṣṇa in the MBh. However, whereas the R presents the story of the exploits of Rāma, the perfect prince and incarnation of Viṣṇu, the MBh has a much more complex narrative plot, duplicating the avatar Kṛṣṇa in himself and in Arjuna, the ideal prince. The MBh is far less the tale of the epic deeds of Kṛṣṇa than the tale of the epic deeds of the five Pāṇḍava brothers; Kṛṣṇa is present only to guarantee by his presence and by his advice the ultimate victory of the Pāṇḍavas and its profound import for the triumph of dharma. The *Harivaṃśa*, the supplement to the MBh, traces the epic deeds of Kṛṣṇa beginning with his birth.

The simplified account that will be given here necessarily refers to the complicated genealogical ties that unite heroes and heroines, ties that contribute to the originality of the MBh in relation to the other epic. Bear in mind that the system of kinship in the epic involves preferential cross-cousin marriage (a man's marriage to the daughter of his mother's brother or his father's sister). Cross-cousin marriage has as a corollary the importance of the relationship between brothers-in-law (and cross-cousins), a very close relationship indeed, and of the role of the mother's brother and (eventually) the father's sister: two brothers-in-law (the husband and the brother of the same woman) are allies and can count on one another in all circumstances. Normally a man and his mother's brother also give mutual assistance; failure to do so implies a serious disorder. This system of kinship, sketched here only in broad terms, is still known and practiced in South India.

From the myth of the avatar the MBh gets its "date," at the juncture between two yugas, but this chronological framework is very loose and has no effect on the unfolding of the plot, which mainly takes place on earth. In fact, the two yugas, the Dvāpara and the Kali (the two worst), are transformed into *asuras* who become incarnate, one (Kali) as the usurping prince Duryodhana, the son of the blind Dhṛtarāṣṭra, and the other as his mother's brother Śakuni, who will be his tool. Duryodhana has ninety-nine brothers, all *rākṣasas* (demonic and cannibalistic beings) who have become incarnate. He challenges the kingship of the five Pāṇḍava brothers, who represent dharmic kingship. Though the five brothers are regarded as the sons of Pāṇḍu, when a curse prevented Pāṇḍu from uniting with his two wives, Kuntī and Mādrī, the first three sons were actually engendered in Kuntī by the gods Dharma, Vāyu, and Indra (the king of the gods), while the last two, the twins Nakula and Sahadeva, were engendered in Mādrī by the twin gods called the Aśvins. These are thus divine incarnations. When Pāṇḍu dies young and his second wife, Mādrī (the sister of an incarnate *asura*, Śalya), ascends his funeral pyre, the Pāṇḍavas are raised at the court of Hāstinapura, the capital of the dynasty of the Kurus, with their cousins, the Kauravas, the hundred sons of Dhṛtarāṣṭra. Their mother, Kuntī, also takes shelter in Hāstinapura. Dhṛtarāṣṭra, the older brother of Pāṇḍu, must take the place of his dead brother, but he assumes a kingship for which he is not qualified because of his blindness. Furthermore, he is placed under the moral authority of his uncle Bhīṣma, the Kṣatriya who renounced both throne and marriage and whose complete detachment assures his perfection, and of Bhīṣma's younger brother Vidura. Bhīṣma is the incarnation of Dyaus, the sky, whereas Vidura, whose status is inferior because his mother is a Śūdrā, is the incarnation of Dharma.

From the very start, the situation is explosive. The tutelary presence of Bhīṣma (associated with the name of the capital, Hāstinapura, "the elephantine city"—which could also be the heavenly capital, since King Indra has an elephant for his mount) seems to create a heaven on earth. Thus, Hāstinapura could be heaven, normally inhabited by the gods and placed under the sovereignty of Indra. But there, next to the gods who are incarnate in the Pāṇḍavas and Vidura, are the one hundred demonic sons of Dhṛtarāṣṭra, placed in a position of superiority because of the role assumed by their father. At first Dhṛtarāṣṭra exercises an

Memorial to a warrior killed in combat in the company of his wife. Hampi Museum (Karnataka). Photo M. Biardeau.

impartial rule, with the help of Bhīṣma and Vidura, but the appetites of his elder son, Duryodhana, soon cause him to deviate from his course. This, if we have deciphered it correctly, sets the scene for a war between the *devas* and the *asuras* in which the *devas* will inevitably be routed from their domain, heaven, but which will ultimately end in their favor, thanks to the intervention of the avatar.

However, the other theme dear to the myths of the avatar, the confrontation between Brahman and Kṣatriya, is not absent. When Prince Drupada and the Brahman Droṇa study the Veda together under the watchful eye of Droṇa's father, they become friends. When Drupada becomes king, Droṇa the Brahman, who is so poor that he cannot find milk for his son, comes to ask Drupada for help on the basis of their former friendship. Droṇa is also ambitious and would really like to be called the king's friend. To this end, he obtains arms and becomes proficient in their use under the tutelage of the Brahman warrior Paraśurāma. But a Brahman cannot be a warrior. In addition, Drupada refuses to remember the former friendship, which became impossible as a consequence of their insuperable differences. Droṇa appears to have no intention of serving the king as chaplain or minister, which would have been appropriate for a Brahman, and the friendship that he claims would exclude such subordination. The problem is posed in such a way that it is no more Droṇa's fault than Drupada's. Rather, it is the divine order that from behind the scenes uses men to play its own game. It was the divine order that made Pāṇḍu disappear and placed the Pāṇḍavas at the mercy of their paternal uncle.

Droṇa, repulsed and still poor, goes to take refuge with his brother-in-law, the Brahman warrior Kṛpa (another symptom of a crisis situation), who is the master-at-arms of the cousins at the court of Dhṛtarāṣṭra. Droṇa in turn becomes their master-at-arms and quickly singles out the Pāṇḍava Arjuna as his best student. As his honorarium, he makes the princes promise to make a secret vow come true on the day when their military education is completed. Droṇa's vow is that the cousins wage war on Drupada to avenge him. The promise is fulfilled; the victory over Drupada is effected mainly by Arjuna, who brings Drupada to his master, bound hand and foot. Droṇa, magnanimous in his way, sets Drupada free and gives him half the kingdom, keeping the better half for himself. His dream of equality thus comes true, and he offers Drupada his friendship a second time. But Drupada can think only of vengeance; he will perform a sacrifice to get a son who can defeat Droṇa. He knows that the power of a Kṣatriya alone cannot get the better of a Brahman who combines his own power with that of a warrior. From Drupada's sacrifice is born not only a son, Dhṛṣṭadyumna, the incarnation of the sacrificial fire (the god Agni), but also a daughter, Kṛṣṇā Draupadī, the incarnation of Śrī or of Śacī, the wife of Indra. From that time on, Drupada dreams of having Arjuna himself for his son-in-law. And indeed Draupadī becomes the wife of the five Pāṇḍavas.

Finally the avatar himself becomes one of the protagonists, although he explicitly delegates his tasks to the Pāṇḍavas, depending on the circumstances. His special tie with the Pāṇḍavas is expressed in terms of kinship: Kuntī, the mother of the three elder sons, is his father's sister; she is also known as Pṛthā, a name that makes her related to the earth—Pṛthivī. But Kṛṣṇa has a much closer tie with Arjuna, the third Pāṇḍava, since the two of them are incarnations of the two inseparable *ṛṣis*, Nara and Nārāyaṇa. Since Nārāyaṇa is a name of Viṣṇu, of whom Kṛṣṇa is the avatar, it was necessary to work through the creation of these two *ṛṣis* (ascetic "visionaries," assuring communication between the world of men and the invisible world) in order to forge the profound unity of the pair Arjuna/Kṛṣṇa. In times of crisis, it is not only Viṣṇu-Nārāyaṇa who becomes incarnate, says the MBh; it is Nārāyaṇa who divides himself into Nara and Nārāyaṇa in order to come down among men when it is time to fight. Arjuna is the incarnation of Nara, whereas Kṛṣṇa is the incarnation of Nārāyaṇa. Since they are incarnations of *ṛṣis*, the asceticism of the renunciant is never far from them: Kṛṣṇa remembers that he is a yogi and Arjuna is associated with this yoga. To seal this tie in terms of kinship, it is logical for Kṛṣṇa to give his sister Subhadrā to Arjuna in marriage. Thus they that were cross-cousins become brothers-in-law.

This ontological identity between Kṛṣṇa and Arjuna clarifies the relationship between the first three Pāṇḍavas: the eldest, the son of the god Dharma, is normally the king at the explicit level of the narrative. But it is clear that his sovereignty is of a special type: a mediocre warrior who leaves the most difficult tasks for his brother, he is always tempted to renounce power and retire into the forest. His sovereignty is the sovereignty of the value that he represents, dharma. Together the five brothers constitute a sovereignty that is subordinate to dharma. This is symbolized by the fact that Yudhiṣṭhira, also known as the Dharmarāja, "the king of dharma" or "King Dharma," is at their head. It is also significant that Dharma and Dharmarāja are names of Yama, the god of death. The group of Pāṇḍavas is on earth for the sole purpose of making sure that the earth and the Kuru dynasty weather the crisis that threatens to sink them. The entire group is there to wage war, even if Arjuna is more specifically in charge by virtue of his relation to the avatar. The second brother, Bhīma, the son of Vāyu, is in radical opposition to his older brother. Vāyu, the wind, is characterized by strength, and so is Bhīma. But Vāyu is also the breath of life, the first and last manifestation of all life. And Bhīma is the advocate of all that allows the world to remain alive and well. He can be brutal if this is necessary to dispel a threat, and he believes in the value of desire as a motive for action, whereas his brothers preach detachment. His qualities of violence and blindness are such that he readily gives in to Draupadī's every whim (she is the common wife of the five brothers). He is as close to the interests of this world as Yudhiṣṭhira is removed from them, but he always submits to his older brother and even to Arjuna.

If Arjuna comes third in line, though he appears to be the most important, it is because his role assumes submission to the opposed values represented by his older brothers. For therein lies the role of the king, to make it possible for all his subjects to live in peace according to their dharma and their wishes (including the renunciants in the forest). For that purpose, he must be perfectly disinterested but an invincible warrior. Arjuna, who is not the king in the epic, actually represents the ideal of the king.

Everything makes the twins, Nakula and Sahadeva, inferior to their older brothers, even though they identify themselves with them in all of their undertakings and serve them, Sahadeva being closer to Yudhiṣṭhira, and Nakula being closer to Arjuna and Bhīma. The hierarchical structure of society requires the existence of faithful executors without a will of their own. The twins at the same time represent all that in the society of the three worlds is inferior to the Brahmans and the Kṣatriyas (and, hence, the gods). It is not by accident that the twins have a mother's brother who is an *asura*. This recalls that the *asura* is evil, not by nature, but only if he refuses his inferior position.

Open animosity between the cousins soon breaks out, all the more because Yudhiṣṭhira wins the affection of everyone and Dhṛtarāṣṭra quickly designates him crown prince: as the eldest son of Pāṇḍu, the deceased king, Yudhiṣṭhira has a legitimate claim to the throne. But Pāṇḍu, while he was still alive, went to the forest in order to let his blind older brother, despite his handicap, take power in his name. Duryodhana does not give up. He is all the less resigned because he has a ferocious appetite for power that he pits against the detachment of Yudhiṣṭhira. Childish pranks are soon followed by criminal outrages. When, thanks to Vidura's warnings, the Pāṇḍavas escape from the burning house of lac, they undergo an initial period of clandestine life in the forest. Bhīma kills his first *rākṣasas*, and he even inherits a *rākṣasa* son after living for a while with the sister of one of his victims. This is a valuable alliance. The five brothers and their mother take refuge with a Brahman. Dressed as young Brahman students, they do not leave until they have liberated the area from a *rākṣasa*. On the way they join a troop of Brahmans who are heading for the celebration of the *svayaṃvara* of Draupadī: the princess is called upon to "choose" a husband for herself, and Drupada, her father, has designed a test that he believes only Arjuna can pass. The winner of the contest is the one that Draupadī must "choose." As expected, Arjuna wins the contest while still disguised as a Brahman and without being recognized. This Kṣatriya, whom Droṇa had equipped with a *brahmāstra* (a magical weapon that symbolizes the power of the Brahman), thus claims to possess a power superior to that of an ordinary Kṣatriya. He combines within himself something of the power of the Brahmans and something of the power of the Kṣatriyas, which must assure his invincibility and at the same time make him the privileged defender of the Brahmans and the Brahmanic order, in other words, of dharma.

It is on the occasion of the *svayaṃvara* that Kṛṣṇa appears for the first time in the narrative, along with his older brother Balarāma. It is also at this point that the mysterious Karṇa appears among the competitors, the adopted son of a Sūta (an inferior caste, "mixed," from the union of a Brahman and a Kṣatriya). He is really the son that Kuntī bore to Sūrya, the sun god, before her marriage and that she abandoned after she gave birth to him in secret. He will not know his origin until after he has firmly committed himself to the faction of Duryodhana. Nor will the Pāṇḍavas find out that he is their brother until after his death on the battlefield. On the day of the *svayaṃvara*, Draupadī refuses to let him try his luck because he is not a Kṣatriya. Duryodhana makes him a king on the spot, but this kingship in itself is not sufficient to give him the quality of a Kṣatriya: this is a violation of dharma and Draupadī will not be satisfied with such an artifice.

Arjuna therefore wins Draupadī, the incarnation of Śrī or Śacī, and she will always secretly favor him. But as a result of an involuntary decision made by Kuntī, Draupadī must marry all five brothers, an anomaly that the myth must justify in several ways, but that also underscores the unity of the five brothers. The brothers from then on possess the woman who is the incarnation of Śrī, the prosperity of a kingdom governed according to dharma, and they have as a brother-in-law the incarnation of Agni, the sacrificial fire. They have also already chosen a Brahman chaplain, so they are in a position to assume power, at least in normal times. A supplementary dimension takes account of the time of crisis, the time of the avatar, which is the time of the epic. In the course of a solitary pilgrimage around India, Arjuna meets Subhadrā, Kṛṣṇa's sister, with whom he immediately falls in love. Kṛṣṇa gives him permission to take his sister away, and Arjuna persuades Draupadī to accept this secondary wife by introducing her as his servant, dressed as a cowherd, a *gopālikā*. After this marriage, Draupadī bears a son to each of her five husbands, and Subhadrā also has a son by Arjuna.

Yudhiṣṭhira celebrates his coronation with the solemn sacrifice of the *rājasūya* (the consecration of the king). The sacrifice is preceded by the more or less compulsory submission of all the surrounding peoples and also by the death of King Jarāsandha, an enemy of Kṛṣṇa whom Kṛṣṇa had reserved as a victim for Bhīma. At this point the two parts of the biography of Kṛṣṇa are joined in the *Harivaṃśa*. Yudhiṣṭhira is at the height of his splendor, and Duryodhana's jealousy is at its peak. In order to obtain through deceit what he cannot get in any other way, Duryodhana plots with his mother's brother Śakuni, with Karṇa, and with his brother Duḥśāsana. A dice game is organized at the court of Dhṛtarāṣṭra (the ritual of the *rājasūya* itself includes a dice game) in which Yudhiṣṭhira must play against Śakuni, who plays on behalf of his nephew Duryodhana. Yudhiṣṭhira is inexperienced, and Śakuni, a clever and dishonest player, is sure to win. During the first round, the Dharmarāja loses all his possessions, including his brothers, himself, and their common wife. But she refuses to become Duryodhana's slave: Did Yudhiṣṭhira have the right to gamble her away? No one dares to answer her question, and tension is high in the assembly, when suddenly ominous noises are heard, which make Dhṛtarāṣṭra, Duryodhana's father, decide to free Draupadī and to grant her a wish. She quickly asks for freedom for her husbands. But a second round of dice is organized immediately, and this time the stakes are victory or a twelve-year exile in the forest, followed by a year-long period during which the five brothers and their wife would have to live completely incognito. If they should be recognized, they would have to leave for the forest for another twelve years. Śakuni wins again, and Duryodhana fervently hopes never to allow Yudhiṣṭhira the opportunity to seize power again. This day marks the beginning of his reign. In fact, the crucial turn is at the end of the first round of dice when Draupadī annuls its results: after this, her fate remains tied to that of her five husbands. She goes into exile with them, scorning Karṇa's suggestions and Duryodhana's advances. Śrī—the prosperity of the kingdom, inseparable from dharma—goes away with the Pāṇḍavas, thus signifying that they have lost power only temporarily and that Duryodhana will be unable to rule. The narrative could not express Draupadī's personal choice: it is she who saves the Pāṇḍavas by deciding to follow them.

So they depart for the forest, the long sojourn into the wilderness assigned to the renunciant (but also to the hunter-king), in which the Pāṇḍavas live a life that is a mixture of the life of ascetics (in particular, they live in sexual abstinence despite the presence of their wife) and the life of hunter-kings. It is a sojourn marked by significant events, among them an attempted abduction of Draupadī by the brother-in-law of the enemy cousins, during which each of the brothers affirms his own role and prepares himself for what is to follow: it is clear that the exercise of kingship cannot do without this renunciation, even if in reality it does not necessarily include living in the forest but takes more inward forms. The main event is the five-year period that Arjuna spends in heaven with Indra, his father, after he has gained access to heaven through harsh asceticism and the grace of Rudra-Śiva. In *svarga* (heaven), Arjuna prepares himself for his earthly role by triumphing over the *asuras,* the enemies of the gods, with the weapons given him by the gods: this is the role of an avatar. Everything moves toward a war between the cousins, in which the fate of dharma is at stake.

The thirteenth year is the crucial one, since, if they are recognized, the five brothers and their wife will have to go back into the forest again. But they have the promise that they will overcome this trial. All six of them appear at the court of Virāṭa, king of the Matsyas ("fish"), in various disguises that serve to hide them and at the same time reveal their individual characters: Yudhiṣṭhira has become a Brahman proficient at dice, and the whole court of Virāṭa spends the entire year playing dice, to the great triumph of Yudhiṣṭhira. Bhīma is a cook, a butcher, and a wrestler. As for the twins, one cares for horses and the other, cows. Draupadī is the queen's maid in charge of hairdressing and the preparation of perfumes and ointments. The most important disguise is that of Arjuna, who presents himself as a eunuch. Eunuchs could not be warriors—and in any case the brothers hid their weapons before they arrived, separately, one by one, at the court of Virāṭa. Arjuna has a woman's name (through which his true identity is transparent: Bṛhannalā, under which can be read Bṛhan-nara, "the great Nara"); he has long, flowing hair; and he is the dancing and singing master to Virāṭa's daughter Uttarā. But Uttarā will become the wife of Abhimanyu, the son of Arjuna and Subhadrā; thus Abhimanyu is Kṛṣṇa's nephew, and the son born to him and Uttarā will inherit the dynasty. As a eunuch, Arjuna maintains a relationship with the princess that will make it possible to weather the crisis; he becomes a symbol of the world that keeps on living and is reborn, a world that is identical with divine play—*māyā* or *līlā*. Arjuna dances and causes the world to dance, like the divinity itself; and it is through this that his royal role becomes apparent.

This entire period, during which Duryodhana's efforts to discover his cousins are all in vain, is a preparation for the war that will follow. The language is that of sacrifice: the war will be a sacrifice of warriors, and the sojourn in disguise at the court of Virāṭa is the requisite period of consecration —*dīkṣā*—during which the sacrificer acquires a divine body for the period of the sacrifice. The *dīkṣā* is conceived as a return to the womb and a rebirth. The period of living in hiding is the passage through the womb, as the narrative notes on two occasions. The year ends with the brilliant reappearance of Arjuna as a warrior. Virāṭa, after losing his general (whom Bhīma secretly killed for pursuing Draupadī too assiduously), is attacked by the Trigartas and the Kauravas. While Virāṭa takes four of the Pāṇḍavas to fight against the Trigartas and wins thanks to them, the Kauravas attack his deserted capital, where Virāṭa's son, Uttara, has been left behind with the eunuch Bṛhannalā (Arjuna). Thus, Arjuna soon finds himself the lone warrior—with Uttara as his charioteer—facing all the great Kaurava warriors: Duryodhana and Karṇa, as well as Droṇa and Bhīṣma. He routs them and takes back the herds of Virāṭa, which they had taken. But now he must reveal his true identity, since the year of probation has just come to an end. At this point, all the Pāṇḍavas acknowledge who they are, and Uttarā marries Abhimanyu.

Duryodhana does not want to relinquish even the smallest part of his kingdom to Yudhiṣṭhira. After last-minute negotiations, war breaks out. The Pāṇḍava side raises seven armies, and Dhṛṣṭadyumna, the brother of Draupadī and the incarnation of Agni (the deified sacrificial fire), serves as commander-in-chief on all fronts, although Arjuna remains technically above him. On the Kaurava side are eleven armies (11 + 7 = 18; there are 18 sections in the MBh, 18 chapters in the *Bhagavadgītā,* and the battle lasts 18 days), and Bhīṣma is the first commander-in-chief. At the end of the tenth day, Bhīṣma is disabled and is replaced by Droṇa, who is killed five days later, after he has killed Drupada. Bhīṣma and Droṇa have never stopped hoping that the Pāṇḍavas will win, but since Bhīṣma is the incarnation of Heaven, and Droṇa is the incarnation of the chaplain of the gods, they must appear in the Kaurava camp in order to symbolize the occupation of heaven by the *asuras.* Both consider themselves Duryodhana's prisoners. When Karṇa, the third commander-in-chief, is killed by Arjuna, he is replaced by Śalya; although he is an incarnate *asura,* Śalya is the mother's brother of the twins; he has contributed to Karṇa's defeat and wants to help his nephews. The victory is won at the cost of some infractions of dharma, the most famous one being the lie that Yudhiṣṭhira must tell to bring about the death of Droṇa, the invincible Brahman warrior: he tells him that his son Aśvatthāman has been killed. The infractions are always either suggested or approved by Kṛṣṇa as being necessary in the crisis of dharma. Kṛṣṇa himself does not fight: he is Arjuna's charioteer and does what Arjuna asks him to do. It is in this capacity that he preaches the *Bhagavadgītā* at the dawn of the first day of battle. The charioteer—*netṛ*—is not only the driver of the chariot but also a guide and counselor. The avatar has delegated his violent function to Arjuna and teaches him spiritual matters. Symmetrically, he has granted Duryodhana the support of his troops (magical?), whom Arjuna annihilates in a great carnage.

Just as the war is thought to be over—only three warriors are left of the Kauravas: the Brahman Kṛpa; the Brahman Aśvatthāman, the son of Droṇa and nephew of Kṛpa; and the Kṣatriya Kṛtavarman, since Duryodhana has died on the battlefield—a last bloody episode ensues. Aśvatthāman, with the aid of Kṛpa and Kṛtavarman, goes to set the Pāṇḍavas' camp on fire during the night and to kill all the survivors. With foresight, Kṛṣṇa had already made the

Bhīṣma on his bed of arrows. Temple of Halebid (Karnataka). Photo Michel Defourny.

Pāṇḍavas leave, but among the victims are Dhṛṣṭadyumna, the murderer of Droṇa, and Draupadī's five sons. Aśvatthāman takes his vengeance. The role of Kṛṣṇa (who withdraws) and of Rudra (who "possesses" Aśvatthāman); the apparition of a hideous black woman, the "Night of Time"; the fire; the holocaust of all the occupants—all of this evokes the end of the world. The episode makes the war the symbolic transposition not only of a conflict between the *devas* and the *asuras* but also of an end of the world at the end of a cosmic cycle. Total annihilation is just barely avoided, but there must be a "remnant" of the sacrifice: with a magic weapon, Aśvatthāman kills all the embryos carried by the women of the Pāṇḍava camp. He also kills Abhimanyu's son, whom Uttarā is carrying in her womb and who now represents the only hope of the dynasty. Kṛṣṇa promises to revive him when Uttarā gives birth to the dead child, thus playing the role of Viṣṇu in the destruction of the world. All lamentations are in vain in the face of so many disappearances. There are not even any guilty parties; the divine order had willed it since the beginning.

The narrative is then interrupted for a long time to make room for the teachings of Bhīṣma—who never seems to finish dying—teachings directed at his grandnephews on kingship, deliverance, and other subjects crucial to dharma. The MBh is a veritable *summa* of Hindu ideology.

The narrative resumes with the great horse sacrifice celebrated by Yudhiṣṭhira, immediately preceded by the birth of Parikṣit, the stillborn child whom Kṛṣṇa, his great-uncle, revives. A penance for sins committed (but they are not really sins), a ritual reprise of the war-sacrifice, and a reaffirmation of Dharmarāja's kingship—the sacrifice is all of these things. Yudhiṣṭhira's brothers reappear beside him with their common spouse and their mother; the others are there too: the blind Dhṛtarāṣṭra and his wife; Kṛpa, the Brahman who also had to fight on Duryodhana's side (probably the incarnation of the Rudras, the celestial host in which Rudra-Śiva is duplicated, and thus closely tied to Aśvatthāman, his nephew, an incarnation of Rudra, of Death, of Anger, etc.); and Vidura, who did not fight. Order is restored, and Parikṣit must grow up (the chronology surrounding the final events fluctuates, to say the least). But the characters of the drama leave the stage one by one. First, Dhṛtarāṣṭra, his wife, Kuntī, and Vidura retire into the forest. Vidura (an incarnation of dharma) dies during a strange encounter with Yudhiṣṭhira where he pours himself out, so to speak, into his nephew, the Dharmarāja. The other three then die in a forest fire accidentally ignited by the sacrificial fire of Dhṛtarāṣṭra. This is once again the theme of fire as a reprise of the funeral pyre. Then comes the turn of Kṛṣṇa and his brother, Balarāma. The members of the clan kill one another at Dvārakā, where they had retreated to be among their own people. Both die as yogis: Balarāma reassumes his form as a serpent (he is the reincarnation of the serpent Śeṣa), while Kṛṣṇa is killed by a stray arrow shot by the hunter Jara ("old age"). Dvārakā is flooded by the waters of the ocean. Arjuna then notices that his weapons have no strength left; his role is finished along with Kṛṣṇa's. This is a signal. After setting the affairs of the kingdom in order and giving the kingship to Parikṣit, the Pāṇḍavas set out together, along with Draupadī, on the road to heaven. Draupadī and four of the brothers die one after the other on the way. Yudhiṣṭhira alone reaches the gate of heaven, accompanied by a dog who has been following him since the beginning of his journey and from whom he refuses to be separated in order to enter heaven. This dog turns out to be the form taken by Yudhiṣṭhira's father, Dharma, in order to put his son's virtue to a final test. In heaven, Yudhiṣṭhira is reunited with all of the warriors killed during the battle, after a brief vision of hell to make him expiate his few sins.

M.Bi./g.h.

BIBLIOGRAPHY

Translations

The Mahābhārata of Krishna-Dwaipāyana Vyāsa, translated by P. C. Roy and K. M. Ganguli, 12 vols. (Calcutta 1883–96). *The Mahābhārata,* translated and edited by J. A. B. van Buitenen (Chicago 1973–78), 3 vols. = Parvans 1–5; also *The Bhagavadgītā in the Mahābhārata* (Chicago 1981).

Studies

M. BIARDEAU, "Études de mythologie hindoue IV et V," *Bulletin de l'École française d'Extrême-Orient,* 1976 and 1978. G. DUMÉZIL, *Mythe et épopé,* 1: *L'idéologie des trois fonctions dans les épopées des peuples indo-européens* (Paris 1968); *Mythe et épopé,* 2: *Types épiques indo-européens: Un héros, un sorcier, un roi* (Paris 1971). H. GEHRTS, *Mahābhārata, das Geschehen und seine Bedeutung* (Bonn 1975). A. HILTEBEITEL, *The Ritual of Battle: Krishna in the Mahābhārata* (Ithaca, NY, 1976).

Abbreviations

MBh *Mahābhārata* (edition of Citrashala Press, Poona)
R *Rāmāyaṇa* (edition of Gita Press, Gorakhpur)

The *Rāmāyaṇa*

Shorter than the *Mahābhārata* (MBh), the *Rāmāyaṇa* (R) is attributed to the *ṛṣi* Vālmīki, although the various Sanskrit versions known to date are sufficiently divergent for the oral tradition to have had an impact on it, as it has on the MBh. It has been adapted or translated into several modern Indian languages. The most widely known non-Sanskrit versions in India are the version of Tulsīdās in Hindi and the version of Kamban in Tamil.

The R seems to be older than the MBh, which mentions the adventure of Rāma on several occasions and gives a summary of it. This is not the case the other way around. However, the story of Rāma Jāmadagnya, the oldest versions of which appear in the MBh, is well known to the *Rāmāyaṇa.* It is true that Paraśurāma appears in the first section of the R, which is thought to be of more recent date than the rest. But it would be difficult to set this section aside in order to bring out the basic structure of the poem—which constantly refers back to it—and we will here consider it as significant as the rest. The same principle guides the analysis of the MBh. In any case, it is more fruitful to compare the two epics than to wonder which came first, since we know that they were both composed over a span of several centuries. The fact that the MBh deals with the lunar dynasty and the R deals with the solar dynasty expresses the complementarity of the two works: the two dynasties together represent the traditional and theoretical division of the Kṣatriyas.

The R is far less didactic in form than the MBh, and the symbolism that it uses emphasizes much less the typical structure of an avatar myth: notably, there is no allusion to the point at which two yugas join to "date" the narrative, as is expected of a descent of Viṣṇu to the earth. This does not mean that the epic ignores this structure, since the account of the fall of Laṅkā and the death of Rāvaṇa makes ample use of images of the end of the world identical to those of the MBh, and since the narrative as a whole is ordered with respect to that moment, but the conception as a whole may have a less powerful and less carefully detailed symbolism. There is no doubt, however, that the ultimate purpose of the R, besides the amusement that it provided for the princes, is the same as that of the MBh: to teach what a good king should be.

The R is the story of Rāma, the perfect prince, the model of a king, and to this day, *rāmarājya,* "the kingship of Rāma," is the highest reference to good government (the term was notably part of Gandhi's vocabulary). But the prince is also an avatar of Viṣṇu. Therein lies the first major difference from the apparent structure of the MBh. Whereas the MBh puts the entire weight of the action on the five Pāṇḍava brothers and gives the avatar Kṛṣṇa the role of counselor to Arjuna, the R features the Rāma avatar as the central character. And the avatar is himself a king, while Kṛṣṇa is not. This is not, however, a simple avatar. The story of his birth at the same time as the birth of his three brothers heralds a well-known theme of later Viṣṇuism and provides an example of an omnipresent motif in Hindu mythology.

King Daśaratha of Ayodhyā, who has three wives but no descendants, celebrates a great sacrifice in order to obtain offspring. At the same time, the gods are harassed by the *rākṣasa* Rāvaṇa, king of Laṅkā. Laṅkā (Sri Lanka) represents the far south as opposed to Ayodhyā, Daśaratha's capital, north of the Ganges, not far from the Himalayas. Since the north is always superior to the south, this particular north-south structure is the substitute for the heaven-hell opposition when the adversary of the gods is the king of the *asuras.* The epics do not make a strict distinction between *rākṣasas* and *asuras.* The first are cannibalistic, but there are good *rākṣasas* just as there are good *asuras,* as long as they enter into the service of dharma in their legitimate place, which is inferior to that of the gods. The gods therefore address Brahmā, the cause of their plight, since it is he who made Rāvaṇa invincible. However, Rāvaṇa in his contempt for men did not include them in the list of creatures who are not to be capable of killing him. Brahmā and the gods therefore ask Viṣṇu to become incarnate among men in order to deliver them from Rāvaṇa. Viṣṇu accepts, and when Daśaratha's sacrificial fire blazes up, an extraordinary creature rises from it and hands the king a bowl of magic porridge, which he must give to his wife to obtain a son. Daśaratha apportions the porridge among his three wives. The first, Kauśalyā, gets half of it; she will give birth to Rāma, the rightful heir. Of the remaining half, he gives one half (that is, a quarter of the whole) to his second wife, Sumitrā, and half of what is left (i.e., one-eighth of the total) to his third wife, Kaikeyī, and the remaining eighth to Sumitrā again. Kaikeyī gives birth to Bharata, and Sumitrā gives birth to twins, Lakṣmaṇa and Śatrughna (the births take place in that order). Since they are all "portions" of Viṣṇu, it is known right away that they will form a unified block, despite the bad queen Kaikeyī; but the theme of twins, which is also found in the MBh, recalls a familiar structure: Rāma and Bharata will occupy positions in the forefront, with Bharata totally devoted to Rāma, whereas the twins will serve Rāma and Bharata, respectively, in the capacity of confidants, devotees, and assistants. This is in keeping with the principle that in India a man, particularly a man of high standing, cannot alone fulfill the totality of the role given him. The hierarchical relationship must appear in one way or another. If there are only four forms of Viṣṇu,

Offering to Hanumān. Katmandu. Photo Catherine Jarrige.

and not five, as there are five Pāṇḍavas, it means that the supreme form of Viṣṇu, which makes up the fifth comprehensive term, remains unmanifested. There are four brothers, just as later there are four *vyūhas* ("deployments") of Viṣṇu, the number four recalling the four Vedas as well as the four cardinal points, that is, the realm of human action.

While in the MBh the five Pāṇḍavas are sons of different celestial gods and Kṛṣṇa is Viṣṇu's avatar (doubled also by the Brahman *ṛṣi* Vyāsa, and also consubstantial with the Pāṇḍava Arjuna), the R has recourse to what seems to be an altogether different assignment of roles. Indeed, Viṣṇu is not the only one in the R to become incarnate, but this time the gods become incarnate not among men but among monkeys (and secondarily bears, but these may be dismissed for our purposes since their role is not distinct from that of the monkeys, and they are never in the forefront). The divine incarnations are ultimately more numerous than in the MBh, but Rudra is missing (Purāṇic mythology turns Rāvaṇa himself into a devotee, a *gaṇa* of Rudra-Śiva). Bṛhaspati, Kubera, Viśvakarman, Agni, the Aśvins, Varuṇa, and Parjanya are explicitly said to be the fathers of different monkeys, but the essential roles, those that require special attention, are incontestably those of Hanumān, the son of Vāyu, Vālin, the son of Indra, and Sugrīva, the son of Sūrya. Here we recognize deities whose incarnations play prominent roles in the MBh. They will appear later as the action unfolds (*Kiṣkindhā kāṇḍa*, or book 4). Some thought must be given to the need for these divine partners and to the choice of monkeys as their incarnations. But the conjunction of the worlds of men and of monkeys precludes the well-informed ties of kinship that, in the MBh, symbolically fuse alliances and solidarities.

Vasiṣṭha, Daśaratha's chaplain, performs the traditional rites for all four sons as they grow up in such a way as to confirm their hierarchy and accentuate the primacy of Rāma. They are already adolescents, experts in arms as well as in the Vedas, when the *ṛṣi* Viśvāmitra arrives at the court of Daśaratha. Viśvāmitra asks Daśaratha to lend him his son Rāma, who alone will be able to rid him of the *rākṣasas* who keep him from completing his sacrifice by defiling it. These *rākṣasas* are to no one's surprise minions of Rāvaṇa, and the incapacity with which Viśvāmitra is struck is only one aspect of the insults that the all-powerful Rāvaṇa inflicts on the three worlds. According to Viśvāmitra, only Rāma can kill the *rākṣasas* and make possible the fulfillment of the sacrifice. This is the first trial of Rāma in his role of defender of the Brahmanic order and proves his quality as an avatar. The express approval of Vasiṣṭha is required for Daśaratha to consent to let his son leave with Viśvāmitra, accompanied by Lakṣmaṇa. On the way, Viśvāmitra teaches them magic formulas that will make them invincible. This is also the occasion for their apprenticeship in living in the forest; they spend one night in a hermitage that was occupied by Rudra, the very spot where Rudra reduced the god Kāma ("love") to ashes. They must also kill Tāṭakā, the mother of one of the *rākṣasas* who are oppressing Viśvāmitra. Then Viśvāmitra equips them with an impressive array of magic weapons, some of which evoke the destruction of the world. When Rāma reaches Viśvāmitra's hermitage, he has no trouble ridding it of the *rākṣasas* while Viśvāmitra himself performs his sacrifice.

This is only a preparation for what is to follow. Instead of returning home, Rāma and Lakṣmaṇa are invited by Viśvāmitra and his entourage of *ṛṣis* to continue their journey to Mithilā, where King Janaka has an extraordinary bow. This bow is the one that Rudra used previously to threaten the gods during the sacrifice of Dakṣa, because he had been forgotten in the distribution of the shares in the sacrifice. But the gods had propitiated him in time, and he had given them his bow. No one can string the bow. In fact, Rāma, escorted by powerful Brahmans, has to go to a *svayaṃvara* analogous to that of Draupadī in the MBh, because Janaka has decided to give his daughter in marriage only to a prince who can string and bend Śiva's bow. The comparison with the MBh is relevant especially in view of the fact that Sītā's birth is just as marvelous as that of Draupadī. Her father Janaka ("the begetter") saw her rise from the furrow (*sītā*) that he was digging with his plow to prepare the sacrificial area. She was thus born, like Draupadī, not from a human womb but from the earth sanctified for the sacrifice. Rāma, who has been well prepared by Viśvāmitra, easily bends the bow to the point of breaking it. He obtains Sītā's hand in marriage. At the same time, Lakṣmaṇa also gets a wife, Sītā's sister, and the other two brothers marry the two daughters of Janaka's younger brother. All four weddings are therefore celebrated by Vasiṣṭha at the same time in Mithilā in the presence of

Viśvāmitra, who then disappears from the epic, never to appear again.

It is apparently important that the alliance with Janaka be solidly established, although this plays virtually no part in the rest of the narrative. The king, already well known in the Veda for his piety, is sometimes referred to as the king of Mithilā (in the northeast of the Indus-Ganges plain, on the border of the Himalayas) and sometimes as the king of Videha. He is also called the Videha ("the bodiless"), and he is in possession of the bow with which Rudra-Śiva, contrary to the most commonly known versions of the myth, refused to destroy the sacrifice of Dakṣa. Before he gets home Rāma stops at the hermitage where Rudra, engaged in the austerities of a yogi, reduced to ashes Kāma, the god of love, who had come to seduce him. The text explicitly cites this episode as the reason for Kāma's other name, Anaṅga ("the bodiless"). The two facts invite comparison. Janaka's daughter is born of the sacrificial area of "the bodiless" one who had become the "begetter." Is it possible that Śiva allowed this sacrificial act to become fertile in anticipation of the crisis of the world, just as Draupadī was born of a dangerous sacrifice that her father had performed in order to get a son who could kill his enemy Droṇa? The role of Viśvāmitra, the Brahman born a Kṣatriya, helps to load the situation with hidden and disquieting meanings, while Vasiṣṭha's presence makes it certain that dharma is observed. Sītā is not explicitly given as the incarnation of Śrī, but she is described as such, and all throughout the epic she is compared or assimilated to Śrī (for instance when Hanumān finds her in the *aśoka* woods at Laṅkā, 5.16.6ff.).

Another trial: on the way back to Ayodhyā, the retinue of Daśaratha and his family encounters Paraśurāma. This Brahman, a great destroyer of Kṣatriyas, challenges Rāma (could he be the new avatar?) by challenging him to bend Viṣṇu's bow, which he is holding in his hands. Rāma bends it with such ease that Paraśurāma admits defeat and bows to Rāma as if he were Viṣṇu in person.

Rāma earns the affection and admiration of all. In the absence of his brother Bharata and of Śatrughna, Daśaratha decides to anoint him crown prince. Everyone agrees except of course Queen Kaikeyī, Bharata's mother, who seeks to ensure the kingship for her son. The preparations for the ceremony of consecration are quickly completed, and on the eve of the event Rāma must undergo rites of purification. Meanwhile, Kaikeyī reminds Daśaratha that she had once saved his life and that he had then promised her a reward of her choice. The time has come to grant her wish. Daśaratha must send Rāma into exile in the forest for fourteen years and consecrate Bharata as crown prince. Kaikeyī believes that in fourteen years the people will have forgotten Rāma. After a night of vain supplications, Daśaratha is forced to yield so as not to go back on his word, given so long ago. If he refused, Kaikeyī would commit suicide. The day when Rāma was to be consecrated turns into the day of his departure for exile. Disinterested and virtuous, he submits with joy, seeking above all to allow his father to keep his word. But Sītā, whose exile was not expected, refuses to remain in Ayodhyā. She determines to follow her husband into exile, for she cannot live without him. She imposes her decision on her husband. They leave in the company of the faithful Lakṣmaṇa, and Daśaratha dies of a broken heart soon after. Bharata is summoned to be consecrated as king, since the kingdom cannot remain without a king. When he arrives, Bharata learns of his mother's scheming at the same time as he learns of his father's death. He refuses to rule in place of Rāma, whom he considers the rightful heir to the throne. So he goes off to the forest in search of his brother to tell him of their father's death and to persuade him to return to Ayodhyā and assume the throne; Bharata asserts that he will refuse the kingship in any case. But Rāma is of the opinion that his father's death does not invalidate his promise. He will therefore spend fourteen years in exile with Sītā and Lakṣmaṇa. Bharata then pledges to carry on the administration of the kingdom while awaiting the return of his brother, and he enthrones Rāma's sandals to symbolize his brother's reign. He will venerate them and ask them for orders every day, and he will live the life of an ascetic for the entire period.

The differences from the plot of the MBh are obvious. The wicked queen's plan fails, and there are not two camps fighting over the throne of Ayodhyā. During Rāma's absence, the royal function will be reduced to a minimum, and its ascetic component will be dominant. This will be a time of latency, of waiting and trial, the meaning of which will become more precise but once more will shed light on the importance of detachment and renunciation for the perfect exercise of kingship. Bharata's asceticism symbolizes his refusal to "enjoy" ruling the kingdom in his brother's place. Another crucial fact is Sītā's departure with Rāma. Like all princesses of royal rank, she symbolizes the kingdom and its prosperity. Because she is Śrī, she can only be on the side of dharma, and her departure from Ayodhyā signifies both the period of latency about to befall the kingdom and the future return of Rāma. As a result, the reign of the wicked Duryodhana in the MBh and the regency of the virtuous Bharata in the R are symbolically identical. The presence of Draupadī and Sītā in the forest is a sign of that. The ensuing events will place Sītā at the center of the drama much more clearly. Looming on the horizon are the threat posed by Rāvaṇa and the role given to Rāma, the avatar of Viṣṇu. Along with the obvious differences between the MBh and the R at the most superficial level, there is also a strict parallelism in the construction of the first three books of both epics. The first book gives the myth of the births, the first ordeals, and marriage; the second, in the MBh, is the royal consecration of Yudhiṣṭhira followed by the disastrous dice game and the departure for the forest; in the R, the second book describes how the consecration of Rāma as crown prince is replaced by his condemnation to exile in the forest. Finally, the third book of both epics corresponds to the time of exile in the forest. From that point on, the structural differences noted up to this point at the level of the narrative will bring about differences in the development of the plot.

The forest where Rāma settles is called the Daṇḍaka (forest of punishment); the use of power to punish the wicked outside as well as inside the kingdom is, for Brahmanic ideology, the very essence of royal power. Rāma finally sets up his hermitage at Pañcavaṭī (the site of "the five banyans") near the source of the Godāvarī River (the site of modern Nasik in the state of Maharashtra). But from the moment that he enters the forest, it becomes clear that he will not live the life of an ascetic like the others. All the *ṛṣis* who live in the hermitages that he visits count on him for protection from the *rākṣasas* who threaten their peace and their ascetic practices. He will therefore keep some of what, in a manner of speaking, constitutes the essence of the royal function, as the very name of the forest foreshadows. Sītā does not understand. Should he not be giving himself over wholly to asceticism and nonviolence? No, answers Rāma, he is a Kṣatriya, and he cannot refuse the *ṛṣis* (Brahmans) the protection that they ask for. His dharma has not changed. In the MBh, the period of exile in the forest is marked by the death of some *rākṣasas* too, but Bhīma is always the one to take charge of it; Yudhiṣṭhira devotes himself more willingly to asceticism, while Arjuna prepares for war in the heaven of Indra. And Draupadī too reminds Yudhiṣṭhira of his dharma as a Kṣatriya, which he seems to forget. Here Rāma alone is king, and his function cannot completely disappear. It is even asserted in this period of exile, which also will be the time of struggle against the enemies of dharma.

The first serious skirmish with the *rākṣasas* is the result of the visit to the hermitage by Śūrpaṇakhā, Rāvaṇa's sister and a terrible *rākṣasī*, who has the power to take on a seductive form. She falls in love with Rāma, wants to take him away from Sītā, and promises him all sorts of delights that will make him forget his dreary ascetic life. We recognize here the theme of the temptation of ascetics in order to subvert their virtues and the power that the virtues confer upon them. Rāma is, however, unshakable. He is as faithful to Sītā as Sītā is to him. The perfect king and Śrī are inseparable. Lakṣmaṇa rids his brother of the bothersome demoness by cutting off her nose and ears. Disfigured, she goes to complain to Khara ("rude," and also "ass"), another one of her brothers who is camped nearby with fourteen thousand *rākṣasas*. War breaks out and Rāma kills all the *rākṣasas* including Khara. Śūrpaṇakhā's love has turned to hatred, and she goes to seek vengeance in a highly feminine form heavily laden with symbolic implications.

Śūrpaṇakhā goes to Laṅkā to see her brother Rāvaṇa, not so much to speak to him about Rāma, who killed their brother Khara, and about the danger that he represents for them, as to extol Sītā's incomparable charm. Śūrpaṇakhā is so eloquent that Rāvaṇa is seized with an intense desire to take Sītā for himself and searches for a way to do this. With some difficulty he convinces his friend Mārīca (whose name evokes a "mirage") to accompany him to Pañcavaṭī in order to put his plan into action. The plan calls for Rāvaṇa to hide and for Mārīca to take the form of a golden deer so splendid that Sītā will covet it and Rāma will pursue it eagerly. The deer will have to carry Rāma a suitable distance away, and then it will imitate Rāma's voice to call Lakṣmaṇa to the rescue and thus force Lakṣmaṇa to leave Sītā by herself in the hermitage. Rāvaṇa will then take advantage of Lakṣmaṇa's absence to carry Sītā away. Everything goes according to plan. When Rāma finally kills the deer, it reverts to its *rākṣasa* form. Lakṣmaṇa, hearing his call, is not taken in: this cannot be Rāma's voice. Unfortunately, Sītā, ignorant like all women and given to momentary impulses, thinks that she recognizes Rāma's call and forces Lakṣmaṇa to run to his rescue. Rāvaṇa wastes no time in appearing. He tries in vain to seduce Sītā and then carries her off into the air, dragging her by the hair. He must first mortally wound the vulture Jaṭāyu, who tries to prevent the abduction and warns Rāvaṇa that he is making a serious mistake. Before he dies, Jaṭāyu has just enough time to tell Rāma and Lakṣmaṇa what has happened. This is the beginning of the wanderings of the two brothers in their touching quest for Sītā, which will take them first to the kingdom of monkeys and then to Laṅkā.

The abduction of Sītā by the king of the *rākṣasas* has no counterpart in the MBh. It is, however, clear that his desire to take for himself the princess who represents Śrī on earth is analogous to Duryodhana's desire for Draupadī during the dice game. The differences between this successful abduction and the scorned propositions of the Kaurava usurper are practically nonexistent. Rāvaṇa will imprison Sītā on Laṅkā in a garden of his harem and will each day attempt to seduce her, alternating between threats and promises but resolved not to use force. Sītā's absolute faithfulness is her only safeguard, but every Hindu knows that there is nothing that a faithful woman cannot obtain. Her character as a *satī*, or perfect wife, is her most inviolable protection. At a deeper level, it is impossible for a nondharmic king to possess Śrī.

Rāma and Lakṣmaṇa have therefore left Pañcavaṭī in search of Sītā. They leave in a southward direction on Jaṭāyu's instructions. On the way, they meet the monkeys Hanumān and Sugrīva and quickly become friends with them. Each tells his story. Sugrīva's story is not absolutely transparent. He was the king of Kiṣkindhā, but he was dispossessed of both his throne and his wife (they go together, as we know) by his brother Vālin. Sugrīva is the younger brother of Vālin, and Vālin was king quite legitimately. However, one day in the forest Sugrīva came in good faith to believe that his brother had disappeared and would never return. He therefore returned to their capital and succeeded his brother on the throne, fully enjoying the privileges of his new high position: feasts, banquets, women, nothing lacking, until the day when Vālin unexpectedly reappeared, drove Sugrīva out, and reclaimed the power; he kept his brother's wife at the same time. With the last detail, Vālin is of course at fault, but can he really be regarded as a usurper? The situation is not very clear. But the two monkeys are in possession of jewels that Sītā had dropped from the air on her way to Laṅkā, and Hanumān, Sugrīva's favorite advisor, immediately demonstrates great devotion to Rāma and gets along splendidly with Lakṣmaṇa. A pact is concluded: Rāma will help Sugrīva recover his kingdom while Sugrīva will place his troops of monkeys at Rāma's disposal in order to retrieve Sītā from Rāvaṇa.

Sugrīva's cause is not altogether just, and we may see in this equivocal situation one of those bendings of dharma from which the MBh does not recoil whenever it turns out to be necessary for the final victory. But the episode has another dimension. We know that Vālin is Indra's son, while Sugrīva is Sūrya's son, and Hanumān is Vāyu's son. We thus find in the monkeys the divine incarnations that the MBh puts among the Pāṇḍavas and Karṇa, Kuntī's secret elder son. Arjuna is Indra's son, Bhīma is Vāyu's son, and Karṇa is Sūrya's son. We may recognize in Arjuna the figure of the ideal king—as his father Indra is king of heaven—while Bhīma has inherited from his father his strength and lust for life. As for Karṇa, he embodies the sun when it deviates from its normal course and burns the world at the end of a cosmic period. He is the enemy of Arjuna, who can only rule over a world ordered by dharma. Karṇa-Sūrya has been made king on the spur of the moment by Duryodhana-Kali, while Arjuna-Indra is not a king at all in the MBh. This is what brings us to the narrative structure of the R: to be sure, Rāma's exploits have not yet spoken explicitly of the end of the world, of the cosmic crisis; the overall setting has not insisted on this framework peculiar to the myth of the avatar. But the respective positions of the two kings of the monkeys could be a transposition of that framework: the sovereignty is denied to Indra's son, who would otherwise have a rightful claim to it, and is given to Sūrya's son, whose legitimacy is doubtful and who will lead his army into great carnage. This son of Sūrya has the son of Vāyu at his service. Sūrya and Vāyu are closely associated in the myth of the dissolution of the world at the end of a cosmic period; the wind fans the fire set by the sun. It is logical that it should be Rāma, the avatar dedicated to destruction for the sake of dharma, who kills Vālin-Indra to make room for Sugrīva-Sūrya.

But why monkeys? Rāma and Lakṣmaṇa needed an army to help them retrieve Sītā, without whom they could not reenter Ayodhyā (the period of exile was drawing to a close).

Hanumān. Private collection. Photo Dominique Champion.

The monkeys, headed by Hanumān, turn out to be excellent and humble devotees and elucidate the bhakti that must be addressed to the human king as well as to the avatar of Viṣṇu that he represents. However, to this day Hanumān has countless shrines almost everywhere in India, which make him the protector of the places where he is worshiped. There he is not the ecstatic devotee that is represented in Rāma's temples, hands joined before the god, but rather an unarmed monkey running with a mountain in one hand and trampling on a demon. If one is to judge by what Hanumān says about himself to his half-brother Bhīma in the MBh, what Hindu consciousness remembers about monkeys is above all their vegetarianism, synonymous with nonviolence (Hanumān reproaches Bhīma for his unreasoned violence). The most frequent name applied to monkeys in the R is that of *vānara,* evoking the forest—*vana.* These swift and strong creatures fight with no weapons, using only rocks and uprooted trees (as Bhīma does on occasion). We may therefore advance the hypothesis that monkeys (and probably bears for the same reason) were chosen to form Rāma's troops because they also evoke the values of self-denial and self-sacrifice that are required of the perfect warrior. Their bhakti is merely the expression of these values and of the link that they necessarily imply with the supreme divinity.

Hanumān is the first to set foot on the island of Laṅkā after crossing the sea in one leap. He finds Sītā and promises her an early rescue. All by himself, he could undoubtedly abduct Sītā and even defeat the *rākṣasas,* but Sītā persuades him to save this glory for Rāma. Vāyu's son therefore contents himself with setting a fire in Rāvaṇa's capital so as to leave signs predicting the impending disaster, taking pains to spare the palace of Vibhīṣaṇa, a brother of Rāvaṇa, in whom he has discovered a good *rākṣasa.* Indeed, Vibhīṣaṇa, unable to convince Rāvaṇa to surrender Sītā to Rāma and to make an alliance with him, leaves the island and puts himself at Rāma's service with full devotion. From this moment on, it is certain that he will be chosen to succeed Rāvaṇa on the throne of Laṅkā after Rāvaṇa's death. Starting with this first fire of Laṅkā, the evocation of the Fire of Time or of the end of a yuga becomes as frequent in the R as it is in the MBh. This is not a simple poetic image; it is the entire symbolism of the myth of the avatar that is once again developed. Viṣṇu becomes incarnate only when a crisis of dharma makes inevitable a bloody war in which the good and the wicked must perish in the sacrifice of battle so that dharma may be restored. The war is a reduced form of the end of the world.

After forewarning Rāvaṇa of what to expect, Hanumān reports on his mission to Rāma and Sugrīva. They immediately decide on an expedition during which many monkeys will meet their death, as will Rāvaṇa's older son, Indrajit, even though he had been strong enough to defeat Indra; and finally Rāvaṇa himself will be killed by Rāma. Laṅkā is again set on fire, but this time from top to bottom. Rāvaṇa, before the power of his enemy, sees the truth: Rāma may well be Nārāyaṇa in person. Vibhīṣaṇa is immediately installed on the throne of Laṅkā, having abundantly proved his devotion to Rāma, to the point of making war against his own brother.

The reunion of Rāma and Sītā is less touching than one would have expected from the scenes where they lament their separation. To keep dharma safe, Rāma consents to take Sītā back only after she has undergone an ordeal of fire, from which she emerges victorious: she entered the fire and it refused to burn her, a sure sign that Rāvaṇa did not touch her and that Śrī is intact. Only then can the couple return to Ayodhyā, their period of exile completed, and Bharata arranges a triumphant welcome by the entire population.

Thus, unlike the MBh, in which war follows the period of exile because Duryodhana refuses to return his kingdom to Yudhiṣṭhira, the R includes the war in the period of exile. Because the overall setting is symbolically less clear (Bharata awaits his brother's return to the position of head of the kingdom), the war Rāma must wage has a more subtle symbolic meaning. On the level of narrative, it is not his kingdom that Rāma must wrest from the *rākṣasas,* but his wife, Śrī incarnate, without whom he cannot be king. By taking Sītā away from him, Rāvaṇa takes away the one who symbolizes the kingdom along with the prosperity ensured by good government, carefully performed sacrifices, and respect for Brahmans. Sītā's abduction is like the duplication of the theme of exile, both being signs of the disorder embodied in Rāvaṇa's power, and reveals its meaning, because a good king must be like a yogi in the world, a prince capable of complete detachment with regard to his reign, and at the same time capable of self-sacrifice in the service of his kingdom. Rāma's return to Ayodhyā had to go by way of Laṅkā, the kingdom of the *rākṣasas.* The ordeal saved the cause of dharma (as the fire's refusal to burn Sītā shows), and Rāma has fulfilled the duties of an avatar.

The last part of the R, like the first, is considered to be a later addition. Whereas the first part seems indispensable for understanding the work as a whole, the last part is disconcerting in content. Our inability to account for it is what makes us think of it as a false conclusion. But let us guard against those pseudohistorical reconstructions designed to account for an apparent difficulty in the narrative.

After his return to Ayodhyā, Rāma is again seized with doubts about Sītā, and he sends her into exile in the forest, where she finds refuge in the hermitage of Vālmīki (the presumed author of the R). This is where she gives birth to twins, Kuśa and Lava, the sons of Rāma. When, after a long separation, Rāma is led by his sons to recognize Sītā's innocence, she is summoned back from exile and asks the earth, from which she was born, to take her back. The earth opens and swallows her. Many Vaiṣṇava devotional texts assert that Rāma reigned for one thousand years after his return to Ayodhyā, which seems to run counter to the sense of this tragic end.

A comparison with the MBh may help to reconcile this ending of the story with the "authentic" R, despite everything. In any case, simply to regard it as an extra piece tacked on is a sure way to deprive it of any meaning. The last books of the MBh are not the most successful. Obviously, the epic authors had to solve a difficult problem on the narrative level. The Pāṇḍavas, and similarly the pair Kṛṣṇa and Arjuna, came down to earth for the time of the crisis and to save dharma. Once their task is accomplished, they must withdraw. This is how the population of Dvārakā kills itself off, Balarāma and Kṛṣṇa die, and Dvārakā is soon after submerged under the ocean. This first catastrophe, which concerns the avatar himself, is the signal for the Pāṇḍavas to depart for heaven. The *Uttara Kāṇḍa* (section 7) of the R probably tries to solve the same problem. Rāma has rid the world of the *rākṣasas* and reestablished dharma. He must then withdraw. Just as the rest of the R is centered on Sītā's fate, so the disappearance of the heroes, once their task is accomplished, is symbolized by the disappearance of Sītā, who simply returns to her place of origin. The Śrī whom she embodies—just as Draupadī embodies Śrī in the MBh—is not the Śrī of peacetime. Not only must she put up a superhuman resistance to the demon who wishes to possess her, but she must also insist that the act of killing the demon be reserved for her husband alone. Rather than accept an abrupt intervention by Hanumān who would materially resolve the problem, she unmistakably chooses war, being a true princess. She came to earth for that purpose, like Rāma himself. The surest signs of this, from the beginning, are her birth from the sacrifice of Janaka and the role Śiva's bow plays in the choice of her husband. The R does not say, as the MBh says of Draupadī, that she was born to destroy many Kṣatriyas, but the entire epic implies that she was born to destroy the evil *rākṣasas* and many good monkeys. Hanumān sees in her the cause, and indeed the worthy cause, of all that has happened. When she disappears, the continuity of the dynasty is assured. Thus the last section of the R may be awkward; it may even be surprising at first sight, but it is not as devoid of meaning as one might believe. *Exeunt omnes.*

M.Bi./g.h.

BIBLIOGRAPHY

G. COURTILLIER, trans., *La légende de Rama et de Sita extraite du Ramayana de Valmiki* (Paris 1927). M. N. DUTT, trans., *The Ramayana,* trans. into English prose from the original Sanskrit of Valmiki, 4 vols. (Calcutta 1891–94). T. H. GRIFFITH, trans., *The Ramayan of Valmiki,* trans. into English verse (Varanasi 1963). C. RAJAGOPALACHARI, *Ramayana* (Bombay 1976). M. L. SEN, trans., *The Ramayana,* a modernized version in English prose, 3 vols. (Calcutta). H. P. SHASTRI, trans., *The Rāmāyaṇa of Vālmīki,* 3 vols. (London 1952–59).

Abbreviations

MBh *Mahābhārata*
R *Rāmāyaṇa* (Gita Press, Gorakhpur)

VIṢṆU AND ŚIVA, THE SUPREME GODS OF HINDU BHAKTI

Viṣṇu and Śiva are the two supreme gods of Hindu bhakti. All the other gods that one finds in myth and ritual are related to them as avatars or sons. There are two essential reasons for treating them together here: the first is that they are usually seen as mutually exclusive, supreme gods of different and antagonistic sects. Without ignoring either the historical and still current reality of the sects or their mythical creations, we must note the limits of their influence on most devotees (we must distinguish the major Vaiṣṇava and Śaiva sects from the more limited groups of disciples of a spiritual master or guru, who adopt their chosen deity), and we must also reverse the order of logical priority: sects are understood only as choices made within a system of beliefs in which Viṣṇu and Śiva are given together, which we shall designate by a term borrowed from the Sanskrit: the Hinduism "of the Tradition." Within this system, each god has a place and a set of characteristics that define him and are found in all myths, even in sectarian concepts.

The second reason is that the emergence of the two gods out of the Vedic pantheon has often been regarded as entirely contingent: two minor gods at the level of Vedic sacrifice, they appear as the great gods of the yogi starting with the Upaniṣads (Viṣṇu in the *Kaṭha Upaniṣad* and Rudra-Śiva in the *Śvetāśvatara Upaniṣad*), and later as the great gods of bhakti, or Hindu devotion, starting with the epics. But the contingency is greatly reduced when we note that ever since Vedic literature the two gods have had a basic connection with sacrifice, and that this connection, different for the two, is what determines their later promotion. The Vedic Viṣṇu can be seen in the epic and Purāṇic Viṣṇu, just as the Vedic Rudra can be seen in the Hindu Rudra-Śiva.

The Vedic literature on the subject is too vast and too dispersed to give exact references here. Basically, all the mythical data mentioned here can be found in the *Śatapatha Brāhmaṇa,* which may serve as a starting point for more intensive study. It should be remembered that at this level the myths are more fragmentary than they are in Hinduism, and that one must juxtapose them and seek their unity in the meaning rather than try to reconstitute a narrative unity that may never have existed.

Almost everywhere in the *Brāhmaṇas,* Viṣṇu is identified

Pool of the Temple of Mahākuteśvara (Karnataka). Photo M. Biardeau.

(Right) Ardhanārīśvara, Temple of Kodumbalur (South India). Photo M. Biardeau.

with the sacrifice as a global operation with all its agents and instruments but above all with the sacrifice as the source of all prosperity in this world, with the glorious and triumphant sacrifice. In this respect he is associated with Śrī, that shining glory and prosperity that sacrifice, and sacrifice alone, can give to the earth.

It is also because he is identified with sacrifice, which in the Vedic hymn to Puruṣa takes on a human form, that the gods make him stretch out on the ground to delimit with his body the sacrificial area: Viṣṇu is the creator of liturgical space, consequently of all ordered space, of all the cosmos. This second feature led to the idea of associating him with Indra, the king of the gods, in order for him to open the space for his strides; he takes three strides, as there are three worlds, one on top of another, with the sky as the highest level. This creation of ordered and sanctified space expresses Viṣṇu's general connection with the cosmic order that will be called dharma. The order is controlled by sacrifice.

Another aspect seems surprising at first: the gods are united against Viṣṇu and cut off his head with the tip of his bow. Within a ritual context in which the victim is not decapitated but suffocated, the meaning is not immediately obvious. But whatever the contemporary practice may be, Vedic ritual attaches great importance to the heads of the victims, without saying explicitly how one is to procure the heads (indeed, without even saying that they are victims): they are placed in the fire altar (the head of a goat, a horse, etc., and even of a human). Although nothing is known of the practice that preceded the suffocation of the victims, it is known that blood sacrifice in later Hinduism is always performed through decapitation and that the head is generally the only part of the victim that is offered to the deity. It is therefore not unreasonable to propose that Vṣṇu, beheaded by his own bow, is there identified with the victim of the sacrifice. The cosmogonic Puruṣa supplies the model for such identifications (sacrificer-victim-sacrifice), and Viṣṇu has a vocation to become this Puruṣa, which he will indeed become when Puruṣa becomes the supreme god and the Great Yogi.

But it is not known how he became the Great Yogi at the same time as he became the supreme Puruṣa, unless the two meanings—the meaning of the yoga embodied in the Great Yogi and the meaning of the sacrifice symbolized by the Puruṣa—were inseparable very early. The name of Puruṣa Nārāyaṇa, which appears in the *Śatapatha Brāhmaṇa* with no reference to Viṣṇu, bears witness to this coalescence of the two aspects; the *Kaṭha Upaniṣad,* however, merely calls Puruṣa Viṣṇu. Whereas the Absolute also takes on the name of Brahman, which evokes the totality of knowledge and of Vedic practices, this epithet is also often coupled with the name of Viṣṇu (or Śiva), reverting to the image of the cosmogonic Puruṣa (the Man-Sacrifice). Viṣṇu is the supreme Brahman, the god of deliverance that is promised to the yogi.

Conversely, Rudra remains from one end of Vedic literature to the other the terrible god whom one must render propitious (*Śiva*) by an appropriate ritual. We shall not stress here his terrible aspect, which comes to him from his essential association with the deadly and dangerous aspects of sacrifice: the stake to which the victim is tied and the fire that consumes him. We must, however, note the connection that causes so many apparent contradictions, the connection between the dreaded aspect of the god and his nature as the Great Yogi. In fact it is easier to grasp what predisposes the Rudra of the sacrifice to become Rudra-Śiva who is the Great Yogi than it is to understand the transformation of Viṣṇu into the Great Yogi. Rudra is the mountain dweller, the god of the wild places that are uninhabited or are inhabited by outlaws or wild animals. In the *Śatarudrīya,* for instance, he is represented as accompanied by all sorts of unsavory characters, humans or animals or unclassifiable creatures, who together catalyze all that Hindu consciousness finds most disturbing. But the renunciant is also at least in theory one who left the village for the forest, and when he abandons life in society, he draws closer to the life of the wilderness. That is why there are in the forest both hunters (impure, since they kill animals)—Rudra is a hunter—and renunciants. At the present time the temples of great regional divinities located on mountains accommodate both the hunter-god and the yogi god. The mountain partakes of the same symbolism as the forest. Rudra-Śiva, the terrible god who looks with "favor" on his devotees, is logically associated with the yogi and becomes a yogi himself.

This has important implications for the connection with Viṣṇu: because he is the luminous god-sacrifice and the dispenser of all prosperity, his yoga must add something more to the purity required of the man in the world who sacrifices. When a man becomes a yogi, he makes a meticulous search for anything that keeps him from impurity: he keeps a vegetarian diet, he filters his water to avoid swallowing tiny animals, he abstains from using fire, which also kills insects, etc. The renunciant of the Brahman caste, the only one who has the right to be called a *sannyāsin,* has as his deity Nārāyaṇa, the yogic form of Viṣṇu most often represented in the great Vaiṣṇava temples. The Śaiva ascetic or the sectarian Śaiva may also seek a rigorous purity; such is the case, for instance, in the Śaivasiddhānta in South India. But the attitude toward the pure and the impure is rather that of someone who has placed himself outside these categories for good. Since the pure and the impure are distinctions that govern the society of castes, the renunciant places himself beyond the pure and the impure. He shows this by representing Śiva in his impure aspects (hunter, god of cremation grounds, etc.), and by adopting practices considered impure. The Kāpālikas used to drink from and receive alms in a human skull; they used to dress in rags that they picked up from the cremation grounds. The Śaiva renunciant is more a yogi than a *sannyāsin* (literally, renouncer); he may also come from non-Brahman castes and generally does.

When Viṣṇu and Śiva appear as gods of bhakti (which they are in the Hindu Tradition as well as in the sects), these differential features appear too. Viṣṇu is at the head of the ordered world. He therefore logically has a royal aspect that never leaves him. Even the reclining Viṣṇu of the great temples who presents the theme of the yogic sleep of Viṣṇu during the cosmic night, or, more precisely, his reawakening at the dawn of a new day of the world, wears a royal diadem. The cosmogonic myth of the Purāṇas is taken up by the cultic iconography with a visual variant (given particularly in the *Mahābhārata* 3.272): Viṣṇu lies on the serpent Śeṣa who is coiled on the ocean. Out of his navel comes a long-stemmed lotus that holds in its petals a four-headed Brahmā, who represents the first stage of the creation of the world. At his feet is Śrī, who has become his wife.

There is no doubt that in nonsectarian Hinduism Viṣṇu is the supreme god. He appears in both epics which, to be sure,

Inside the shrine of Śiva at Mahākuteśvara (Karantaka). Photo M. Biardeau.

do not ignore Rudra-Śiva. That is why it is he—the pure god, both yogi and king, the symbol of the union of the two highest *varṇas,* Brahman and Kṣatriya—who according to the theory must descend to earth. The classic list of avatars connects them solely with Viṣṇu. Another consequence of the primacy of Viṣṇu is his essential connection with the Goddess, who is generally and too hastily considered to be Śaiva. Although she is Śiva's wife, she is Viṣṇu's sister, and this double connection, formulated especially in South India, is in itself a denial of sectarianism, since it makes Viṣṇu and Śiva brothers-in-law. Finally, Viṣṇu's wife, Śrī or Lakṣmī, often splits into Śrī and Bhū (the Earth), and the Earth, which cannot exist without Śrī, needs the Goddess to watch over her.

As for Śiva, in his great temples he is both the terrible god of sacrifice and the yogi. His ritual representation in the form of a linga is the source of much incoherent writing about the primitive aspects of this phallic god. There is no doubt about the sexual interpretation of Śiva's linga: the male organ is inserted in the yoni, the female organ, in an act of procreation. This is for Śiva the symbolic equivalent of the reclining Viṣṇu, whose awakening causes a lotus to emerge from his navel, a lotus that bears Brahmā. We may even safely assert that the lotus stem has the same symbolism as Śiva's linga. Clearly the deity of the shrine is the one that brings the worlds to the seminal state and makes them blossom each in its own way. During his cosmic sleep, Viṣṇu carried the creatures within him, and he emits them in the form of a lotus that reveals Brahmā among its petals. For Śiva, it is his connection with the sacrificial post that serves as the theme: the *sthāṇu* ("erect pole," one of Śiva's names) is also, in the "terrible" mode, a promise of fertility for the world at the same time as it is a threat of death for the victim that is tied to it. Moreover, through the simplicity of its structure, it gives a representation of the god as close as possible to the unmanifest, as unanthropomorphic as possible. When Śiva is represented in human form (in shrines where he is in a subordinate position, or on mural decorations), he always wears his hair in a bun, like an ascetic; he is always the yogi, the form of the deity that is in charge of the dissolution of the worlds, who sacrifices the world at the end of a cosmic period in a great conflagration. All of this is what is echoed in the linga. The most ancient lingas that have been found do not seem to have been associated with a yoni. The yoni must have been added to make the sacrificial post tolerable as a ritual form in order to eliminate any deadly connotation and to assert the improbable fertility of a god who is a yogi. The sexual symbol thus formed is the solution to the double contradiction that haunts Rudra-Śiva and that his devotees remain aware of: a contradiction between the deadly aspect associated with impurity and death, and the consecrated fertility of the creator (for in his great temples Śiva is considered to be a supreme god, and the worlds emanate from him); and a contradiction between the chaste ascetic and "procreation" necessary for the birth of the worlds. We could not understand this choice if we did not go back first to the Vedic sacrificial post and then to the role played by Rudra-Śiva in the myth of the dissolution of the worlds, in which it is as a yogi that he burns up the three worlds. In the final analysis, all of this was possible only from the perspective of Vedic conceptions, in which the god who presides over the death of sacrificial victims (Rudra is Paśupati, "master of the cattle" and/or "master of sacrificial victims") must be alien to the inhabited world, living as he does in the forest like the yogi.

M.Bi./g.h.

BIBLIOGRAPHY

J. GONDA, *Viṣṇuism and Śivaism: A Comparison* (London 1970). W. D. O'FLAHERTY, *Asceticism and Eroticism in the Mythology of Śiva* (London 1973).

Popular Hinduism

By popular Hinduism is meant the religion as it can be observed in the representations and practices of the whole Hindu population of a given region of India. Briefly, what is involved is a transition from myth to ritual: in the context of the religion of a great civilization like that of India, this means a transition from the Hinduism of the texts—originally and generally in Sanskrit, but often translated as so many versions in an orally transmitted or even written corpus in the various vernaculars of the subcontinent—to its expression as it is actualized in the cults and the pantheon specific to a region. Here we touch on one of the first problems in the observation of Hinduism: the diversity and variety of religious practices from one region to the next, in spite of many common traits and a social system characteristic of all Hindus, i.e., the caste system, based on, among other things, the essentially religious principle of the distinction between pure and impure.

Regional diversity combines with another source of difficulty for an understanding of the whole: some of the religious practices of the middle and lower castes, generally nonvegetarian, seem very different from and incompatible with Hindu orthodoxy and the practices of the upper castes, generally vegetarian, especially with those of the Brahmans. The divinities of the lower castes, served by non-Brahman priests, receive meat offerings and demand blood sacrifices; their cult seems to reveal principles opposed to the Brahmanical ideals of nonviolence and purity.

This apparent contradiction was systematized and transformed by an entire current of thought into a dichotomy whose terms were irreconcilable because they were explained on the basis of a pseudohistorical origin that linked Hinduism with the Aryans alone and attributed any practices judged deviant to the indigenous peoples whom the Aryans conquered. While anthropological studies of recent years have helped us to go beyond this historicism, they have still not entirely broken with the old dichotomous view of popular religion. Yet the study of the organization of the pantheon and the cults in a particular region, as well as the study of the representations expressed in myths locally associated with them, reveal a global structure whose fundamental principles are those of classical Hinduism. This proposition will be illustrated on the basis of a general study done in Tamil Nadu in the district of Tirunelveli, a region at the southern end of the Indian subcontinent.

I. Inferior Divinities (or Deified "Demons")

Divinities of low status are innumerable; they are found throughout India under the most varied names; they are of both sexes, but male divinities, always associated with a barely personalized feminine principle (sister or consort), are dominant in Tirunelveli. In this region their sanctuaries are very distinctive: they are made up of groups of little columns in the shape of truncated pyramids, each of which is the seat and representation of the divinity; a statue in the god's image completes, or sometimes replaces, them. No matter how many seats form it, any sanctuary is supposed to include twenty-one gods, an expression of wholeness. In Tamil this type of holy place is called *pēy-kōvil*, "sanctuary of demons" (from the Sanskrit *preta*, "deceased"). This name tells us something about this category of divinities: they are malevolent creatures, sharing as a group characteristics that hardly distinguish them from demons (among whom are classified the unsatisfied dead); they are transformed into gods and made benevolent from the moment when, after their seat is erected, they are worshiped.

A *pēy-kōvil* can be located either inside or outside the village; sometimes there are two of them; in any case, the divinity who presides over it has a sanctuary of localized reference somewhere in the district. This may be situated within the grounds of one of the main temples of the god Śāstā. Generally speaking, each of these lower divinities can be found in a subordinate position either in a temple of Śāstā or in a temple of the Goddess (see § III below, "Śāstā and the

Amman koḍai of the untouchables of Pallar: those possessed by Pallar walk around the whole village. Photo M.-L. Reiniche.

Goddess"). In this way their sanctuaries are connected in a kind of network across Tirunelveli.

The sanctuary of a lower god belongs in principle (for there are extensions and exceptions) to the kin group descended patrilineally from the ancestor who contracted the relationship with the divinity and built his seat. This relationship, called *aḍimai* ("being at the feet," devotion, slavery), is woven from extremely particular but quite stereotyped circumstances, whose history is sometimes connected directly to the myth of the divinity concerned. In most cases the cult develops following an accidental death or an occasion (a mistake) which allowed the divinity to "follow" the ancestor and impose himself on him and his family by bringing evil (sickness, death), until he is recognized and worshiped.

The various stories telling how the *aḍimai* relationship was contracted reveal two important points. On the one hand, the divinity in his demonic form always comes from somewhere else; it is what is not one's own. Evil is the other, and otherness is expressed in different ways: the demon is generally the god of another group of a different caste; he is also a haunter of open spaces—external and opposed to the special space of the village—and especially the forest and cremation grounds; it is in these places that he attacks the wretch whom he has chosen and whom he pursues (in normal times, the *extra muros* sanctuaries of these divinities are always dangerous places to frequent).

On the other hand, the notion of sacrifice, which keeps returning in various forms, seems essential. A tragic death at the hands of a demon is the sacrifice necessary for a foundation: in giving the cult its basis, it gives the worshiping group the indispensable base that, in circumstances and social contexts that are specific to each case, allows it to define its own identity and develop. (In other regions of India it may be the unsatisfied dead person himself who, by being worshiped, becomes a protective divinity.)

The demon, transformed into a benevolent divinity, continues to manifest his presence on certain occasions through possession. For a given kin group, to possess a god, that is, to have a sanctuary that belongs to him and to worship him there periodically, also means to be possessed: while the

A *pēy-kōvil* outside a village, shown eight days after the *koḍai,* Photo M.-L. Reiniche.

One possessed by the "demon" Çudalai MāḍaN. A temple outside the village of Minkulam (South India). Photo M.-L. Reiniche.

Mariyamman koḍai. One of the possessed and a *Kaniyar.* Photo M.-L. Reiniche.

term *aḍimai* puts the accent on subordination, it also expresses an identity between the group and its god, as well as a relationship of reciprocity from which bargaining is not excluded. Possession, like the ritual, is transmitted from father to son.

The festivals, called *koḍai,* "gift," that celebrate these divinities generally take place once a year, at dates fixed according to each sanctuary's custom, mainly in the hot, dry season from January to August. The *koḍai,* which lasts for three days, is a highly institutionalized affair in Tirunelveli and requires a large number of specialists. Even though it concerns lower gods, in all cases except for untouchables a Brahman priest consecrates and purifies the sanctuary. But the culminating point of the festival is the offering of meat and the sacrifice of male goats. The possessed, those who by heredity "dance the god," are present at all the main stages in the festival, but especially during the sacrifices. Under the effect of a fast begun eight days earlier and in a state of extreme purity, they keep themselves apart from village life for the whole time of the festival, living outside the village;

they are temporarily compared to renouncers. Since they become the god whom they dance but continue to be members of the group offering the sacrifice, they express the identity of the divine and the human and are at the same time indispensable intermediaries for an effective sacrifice. During these festivals specialists sing the story of the god who is being celebrated.

II. Myths

Among all the lower divinities, there is one category particularly in evidence in Tirunelveli: the *māḍaN*. The local myths of two of them are significant in showing how the cults described above should be understood within the larger context of Hinduism.

1. The Story of Takka RājaN

King TakkaN (the Tamil form of the Sanskrit name Dakṣa, a well-known figure in the classical myths) performs *tapas* to obtain a daughter. Śiva, won over by his asceticism, sends Pārvatī to be his daughter; but when the goddess reaches the age of sixteen, he comes to take her back just as TakkaN is about to give her in marriage to a king. TakkaN, enraged, makes a great sacrifice (*yāga*) which so heats up Kailasa, where Śiva and Pārvatī reside, that they cannot stand it any longer. Pārvatī sends her first two sons, Subrahmaṇya and Gaṇeśa, to plead with her father, but to no avail. Śiva then creates VērvaiputtiraN—the "son (born) of sweat"—(in the classic myth, Vīrabhadra) and sends him to destroy TakkaN's sacrifice. In his carnage, VērvaiputtiraN cuts off TakkaN's head and replaces it with the head of a bovine (*māḍu*). When TakkaN is expelled from heaven, he descends to earth to a mountainous place in the west of Tirunelveli district near the source of the Tambraparni, where there is an important regional temple of Śāstā (see § III below, "Śāstā and the Goddess"), the temple of Sorimuttu. TakkaN, now the god Taḷavāy MāḍaN, has a sanctuary there; he then goes on a pilgrimage the length of the valley. Wherever he stops, there is now a place of worship. He finally arrives at another Śāstā temple; this Śāstā keeps him near himself, on the bank of the reservoir: Taḷavāy MāḍaN, the "war chief" of Śāstā, splits in two and becomes Karaiyadi MāḍaN as well, "he who is at the foot of the bank."

After this the story becomes more specific and tells how the god, through a series of crimes against men, is able to impose his worship on one or more local groups.

The following story has many points in common with the preceding one. In both cases, the reference to Dakṣa lays more or less explicit stress both on the destruction of the sacrifice and on the destructive sacrifice, and the rest of the story can be understood as a development of the same theme. In addition, both of the stories include both an extraterrestrial episode and a terrestrial one; it is thus clear that we are dealing with a form of the descent of the divinity, which reproduces at a certain level—that of the immediate interests of man and local society—the function of the avatar.

2. The Story of Çuḍalai MāḍaN

Pārvatī, after doubting the omnipotence of her husband Śiva, is condemned to become the daughter of Dakṣa until Śiva comes to reclaim her and marry her. Pārvatī, also called Brahmaśakti, asks for a child. Śiva sends her to the infernal regions, where the fire of final destruction is kept, to gather a spark from a sacred lamp in the hem of her clothing. The spark then turns into a shapeless mass (*muṇḍam*, "[shaved] head" or "trunk without a head"). When Pārvatī complains, Śiva makes the lump into a child, but instead of feeding him on milk the goddess gives him nectar; the starving child goes and eats from a corpse that is being burned at the cremation ground (*cuḍalai*).

The corpse eater, henceforth called *çuḍalai māḍaN* or *çuḍalai muṇḍaN*, cannot remain in Śiva's paradise and goes down to earth. But before leaving, he imposes conditions: he asks to be given a female counterpart, and he wants a cult (*bali*). The gods prepare this on the cremation ground, and the MāḍaN demands meat offerings, animal victims, and alcohol; he also asks for a *narabali* (human sacrifice). Śiva causes the birth of the Kaniyar singers and dancers, who are ready to offer their blood in place of, or as if it were, a *narabali* (here the myth describes a *koḍai;* the Kaniyar sometimes offer their blood at them). MāḍaN, satisfied, goes to earth to receive the offerings of men.

The first part of the myth is full of reminiscences of more classical texts and elements that in various ways stress the notion of sacrifice. By his birth MāḍaN is associated with the fire of destruction, and logically he is a corpse eater like the cremation fire: he is comparable to Śiva in his terrible form. On the other hand, it is not insignificant that Çuḍalai MāḍaN is first born as a *muṇḍam* (on the level of the sanctuary, the split *māḍaN-muṇḍaN* is often represented by two divinities). *Muṇḍam* can refer both to the ball of food offered to the divinity and to the severed head of the sacrifice. The presence in the sanctuary of *muṇḍaN* next to Çuḍalai MāḍaN, like the "bovine" head (*māḍu*, which may be the source for *māḍaN*) on the shoulders of Taḷavāy MāḍaN—alias Dakṣa—tells us that each of these divinities symbolizes the sacrifice in the double sense of the one who offers the sacrifice and the sacrificial victim. Also note MāḍaN's relation to the goddess as *śakti*, which sometimes, in the text, goes so far as to identify them.

The second part of the myth describes the demon's wanderings on earth. He descends at Kāśi (Banaras), the holy city of Hinduism on the Ganges, and from there goes to Madurai, formerly the political and religious capital for the whole of the far south of India. He worships the goddess of the great temple of the city, becomes known to the local Brahmans, and then departs for Tirunelveli. He crosses the district and even pays a visit to Kerala country, which borders the district to the west. While on the one hand he worships the higher divinities of the great sanctuaries, at the same time he oppresses the people at every step of his journey until they worship him: he possesses the women as if he were their husband, feeds on the fetuses of pregnant women, kills men, burns down houses, and uses disguise and illusion to spread confusion.

Then Çuḍalai MāḍaN goes to Śāstā's sanctuary in Sorimuttu, which is situated near the source of the Tambraparni in the Ghats. He settles near there on the finest tree in the forest, a *vaNNi maram*, the "fire" tree; Brahmaśakti is on top of it and the demons are all around it. At this point carpenters come to cut down the tree for the great temple of Subrahmaṇya at Tiruchendur, in the eastern part of the district. They are supposed to turn it into a "flag tree," the pole at the entrance to the sanctuary, on which the divinity's banner is hoisted at festivals to be carried in processions. As soon as the carpenters start their work, MāḍaN makes them all kill one another in a great bloodbath. After thus forcing recognition of his hegemony, he demands worship, and the tree cannot be cut down until he gets it. Finally there is a processional return to Tiruchendur; MāḍaN is celebrated in blood sacrifices, including sacrifices of buffaloes, and Subrahmaṇya grants him the right to receive offerings in this world because he has the power to subdue evildoers.

Çudaḷai MāḍaN in human form, at Gopalasamudram (South India). Photo M.-L. Reiniche.

The various episodes of this tale simply repeat over and over again the necessity of the destructive sacrifice whose victim is, finally, man. The necessity is accompanied by a mutual and hierarchical acknowledgment between the higher values represented by the great gods and the values of blood sacrifice demanded by the deified demons.

The myth's geographical frame corresponds more or less to Tirunelveli and highlights the east-west axis of the Tambraparni River with Sorimuttu and Tiruchendur—Śāstā and Subrahmaṇya—as its two poles. On the regional level, the main sanctuaries of the divinities are spatially opposed. The sanctuary of Sorimuttu, located both in the mountains and in the forest, is the ideal place to polarize all the values associated with *kāḍu*, open space, the "forest," in opposition to *grāma*, inhabited space. The forest tree, the "fire" tree that is the dwelling of both the demon born of the fire of the sacrificial lamp and the goddess, slayer of powers that disturb the world order, must be transported from its wild place to the pure and separate place of the great temple of Subrahmaṇya. Made into the "flag tree," it becomes the symbol of the manifestation of divinity and of the positive sacrifice that must be performed for the good of the worlds. But the passage from one place to the other, which can be understood as a separation between the negative (dangerous) and positive aspects of the sacrifice, cannot be accomplished without a consecration of the destructive aspects: these ground and make fertile the positive sacrifice of the great temple, since this cannot take place until the values represented by the inferior divinity have been recognized.

This separation, on the level of representation and worship, between the ideals of nonviolence and purity and the recognition that any act required for the maintenance of life is indissociable from violence and impurity, is transposed to the society itself. As in the myth, it is primarily non-Brahmans, and especially members of the lower castes, who are the demons' prey; in relation to the higher castes, their vulnerability is indissociable from their impurity, and their ignorance makes them "stupid beings" (*māḍaN*), which assimilates them to the divinity of the same name. Individually all men (including Brahmans) are impure and stupid because they are composed of both life and death. In this system, nevertheless, the Brahmans are the guardians of the positive sacrifice because of their knowledge and the purity that they are in a position to preserve. The ignorance and impurity attributed to the lower castes makes them the exact antithesis of the Brahmans; they are the preeminent agents and victims of the destruction and negation of life, as well as of its fertility. Just as the positive and negative aspects of the sacrifice are complementary, the lower castes are as indispensable as the Brahmans for the maintenance of society and the prosperity of the world.

All of the inferior divinities are connected more or less explicitly with Śiva (or with the Goddess). This is to be understood in connection with the destructive aspects of the god, and more precisely with his relation to the sacrifice, especially its impurities and dangers: there is an equivalence between MāḍaN and the terrible form of Śiva; both of them haunt cremation grounds, and the villagers do not hesitate to identify them. There is also a distance between them. Cuḍalai MāḍaN is born as a shapeless mass, evoking either the severed head of the sacrifice or the ball of food of the offering, but in either case it is the symbol of the sacrificial victim. Furthermore, he is not essentially different from Taḷavāy, MāḍaN, or Dakṣa, sacrificed by Śiva with the help of Vīrabhadra, who comes forth out of Śiva. MāḍaN is both Śiva and Śiva's sacrificial victim; at the same time he is an intermediary between Śiva and men, the manifestation of the god (in his terrible aspects if they are not properly recognized) on this earth.

The splitting in two of Śiva and his delegate reflects another splitting: that which takes place during the festival between those who offer the *koḍai* and those who are possessed. Both of these belong to the same kin group, but the possessed person is separated from the group and, going outside the dwelling area to seek a state of abstinence and purity, finds himself temporarily in a situation of renunciation. During the principal moments of worship, he dances the god, and, like Śiva's dance, the dance of possession is a dance of destruction, and its presence is particularly necessary at the moment of blood sacrifice. It is as if the possessed person's particular state of purity and identification with the god made it possible for him to handle the dangerous aspects of the sacrifice, and consequently to make its benefits fall back upon the group of which he never ceases to be a member.

III. Śāstā and the Goddess

The hierarchically superior position of Śāstā and the Goddess, to whom the inferior divinities are subordinate, serves to express a different, more general, level of religious and social reality. Throughout the south of Tamil Nadu, the god Śāstā (also often known under the name of AiyaNār) and the Goddess, while they have separate places of worship, are always associated, to the extent that locally they are complementary from various points of view.

We can take the example of a village of Tirunelveli: depending on its importance, it will have at least one, and usually several, sanctuaries of goddesses. One or two may be common to the village as a whole; the other belongs to the area of a local group of a caste or subcaste. With their different names, the various goddesses are always forms of the great Goddess, and their equivalence is expressed by saying that they are eight sisters. Two of them, however, are distinguished. She who dwells at the "north gate" is supposed to be responsible for the foundation of the village: as such, she is considered the eldest of all the sisters, and she is also called *brāhmacāriṇī:* the notion of celibacy gives her a dimension of renunciation. The other goddess is the figure of the supreme wife, the wife of the great god, here Śiva, and she has all the auspicious traits of female destiny. Both of these, the one because she is a renouncer, the other because she is a wife, receive only vegetarian offerings. In this they are opposed to all the other goddesses of the locality, closer to the terrible form of Durgā or Kālī, who demand blood sacrifices during festivals that, like those of the inferior divinities, are called *koḍai.* In one of their sanctuaries, shared by the entire locality, the first male goat sacrificed to the goddess is offered in the name of the community as a whole by the most important person in the village in terms of authority and wealth, generally a non-Brahman, but always a member of a high caste in which the rules of orthodoxy and vegetarianism can be strictly followed. Finally, these goddesses have their hereditary possessed mediums, members of the group to whom the sanctuary principally belongs.

Festival at the temple of Śiva. Photo M.-L. Reiniche.

In this region of Tamil Nadu, the Goddess appears above all as a goddess of the locality, as closely connected to the habitat itself as to the people who live there. Her functions are connected with the prosperity and well-being of the group, and above all its health: as is the case elsewhere in India, the Goddess both gives and cures illness in general and smallpox in particular. The myths associated with her are not especially distinctive. They echo the main theme of the *Devī Māhātmya:* the Goddess's struggle against the *asura.* On the popular level, sickness is directly associated with her: because the Goddess rid the world of *asuras,* they say, the Lord granted her the boon of spreading smallpox. The myth expresses, not without paradox, the fact that all forms of evil are interconnected.

The cult of the local goddess is sometimes associated with the cult of Śāstā in the same cycle of festivals. This is rarely the case in Tirunelveli. However, at the time of the Goddess's *koḍai* (as well as during the festivals of the lower divinities), the story of Śāstā is always sung before the story of the divinity who is being celebrated.

The preeminence of Śāstā over the Goddess is due both to his status as a male divinity and to the fact that he is generally a vegetarian god—although there remains a certain ambiguity on this point, to which we shall return. Moreover, in Tirunelveli it is explained by saying that he always receives the first homage because he is the god of the *kula.* This term, which designates a corporate group, has a greater or lesser extension depending on the context. In this case it means the patrilineal descendants of a distant ancestor, and every *kula* of whatever caste is supposed to celebrate the Śāstā of the ancestor's place of origin, thus associating the origin of what may be called a clan or a lineage with a given locality and territory. Elsewhere in India such a divinity is usually found only among the high castes, Brahmans or aristocratic Kṣatriya lineages; it goes with status, prestige, and a certain form of authority, none of which the middle and lower castes have; among middle and lower castes in Tirunelveli, genealogical memory is short and the lineage structure relatively weak. In this context, the extension of which Śāstā is the object as the *kula* god probably results from historical factors that are difficult to account for, but also from certain characteristics of the god and his cult.

Śāstā's sanctuaries are innumerable; generally situated outside the locality, they are often found on the bank of a reservoir: the god has something to do with the arrival of water and the fertility of the fields; as a result, every Śāstā is the god of those who hold traditional rights over the land irrigated by a reservoir. At the same time, he is a hunting god; he commands the beasts and demons and rules over the wild space that is in opposition with the inhabited space of the village. More locally, one or more Śāstās are associated with the territory that depends on and defines an agglomeration. Their sanctuaries are usually only of local interest, with the exception of a small number of them, including the sanctuary of Sorimuttu for Tirunelveli and that of Sabarimalai in Kerala; both are located in the mountains.

In Tirunelveli the festival of Śāstā is celebrated in March on Panguni Uttaram, a date of the Hindu calendar reserved for Subrahmaṇya in other parts of Tamil Nadu. In Tirunelveli district this is the occasion for a displacement of the population: everyone goes to worship his ancestral Śāstā; on this occasion every sanctuary brings together people not only of different castes but from different localities. A distinction is nevertheless maintained, among both the devotees and the divinities of a sanctuary, between vegetarians and nonvegetarians. The services on the morning of the festival are strictly vegetarian; Śāstā is honored above all others and receives honors from everyone, including the Brahmans and the orthodox high castes. But with the approach of night Śāstā seems to be forgotten in favor of the inferior divinities who are subordinate to him. The festival starts to look like a *koḍai* offered by non-Brahmans, with meat offerings, blood sacrifice, and dances of possession.

Every Śāstā sanctuary is thus the site for the operation of one of the fundamental principles of Hinduism, that of the distinction between vegetarian and carnivorous (gods and men); this overlaps with other essential oppositions: nonviolence-violence, pure-impure, etc. At the same time, Śāstā, chief of the demons, sanctions blood sacrifices, but not without ambiguity, since while every devotee says that he is raising a male goat to offer to his Śāstā on Panguni Uttaram, when the time comes he will dedicate it to an inferior divinity. In this sense, a Śāstā sanctuary is also the site where the relationship between inferior and superior is symbolically expressed: just as the deified demons are subordinate to Śāstā, who at the same time guarantees them a certain legitimacy, so the great majority of non-Brahmans are subordinate to the traditional holders of status, authority, and superior rights over the land. These non-Brahmans are devotees of the inferior divinities, and it is these who are their *kula* gods; but they always refer to the superior power, in this case to Śāstā.

The relationship that unites Śāstā to the inferior divinities can be specified in at least one case. The divine personality of the god is not easily defined, and there is a certain diversity in his iconography, his attributes, etc. Sometimes he seems to resemble Vīrabhadra, who was produced by Śāstā to destroy Dakṣa's sacrifice; this trait is confirmed in Tirunelveli at a certain number of sanctuaries: whenever Talavāy-Karaiyaḍi MāḍaN, alias Dakṣa, the divinity with a bovine head, is near Śāstā, the god, even if not recognized as such by his devotees, is basically Vīrabhadra. We can surmise that at least in this particular case (although it is likely that the attribution can be generalized to a certain extent) Śāstā assures the functions of Vīrabhadra—and so of Śiva-Rudra—in connection with the sacrifice.

Although Śāstā has often been taken for a modest village divinity of Dravidian origin, and although his cult is restricted to South India (Kerala and part of Tamil Nadu), he must not be confused with the inferior divinities: he is their master but does not belong to their category. Among his names, *aiyaN, aiyaNār, aiyappaN,* from Sanskrit *ārya,* "Lord, master," and *śāstā,* from Sanskrit *śāstr,* "he who punishes, governs, teaches," all refer to both the Brahman and the king.

The myth of his birth, well known among the villagers, is taken directly from various Purāṇic versions. A *rākṣasa* performs *tapas,* and through his asceticism he obtains from Śiva the ability to burn or cut whatever he touches with his finger. Hardly has he received this gift when he wants to try it out on Śiva himself, who is forced to flee. Viṣṇu intervenes in his seductive female form of Mohinī and gets the *rākṣasa* to destroy himself. Śiva wants to see Viṣṇu in the form of a young woman; he lets himself be seduced in turn, and from his seed AiyaNār is born.

The Purāṇa tells nothing more than this; in its relative simplicity, the symbolism of this myth—and notably the complementarity of the two great gods in a single act of creation—is probably sufficient in itself. Yet the story is continued in regional texts. As in the case of the inferior divinities, the second part of the story takes place on earth: Śāstā is also a form of divine descent.

One of the versions, the one that is sung during festivals in Tirunelveli, does not explain the descent; but the version presented in the myth of Śāstā from Sabarimalai is entirely Purāṇic and takes up a well-known mythic theme: Śāstā is sent to earth as the adopted son of a king of Kerala country, for he is the only one who can kill the female buffalo-*asura, mahiṣi.* From this point on, the two stories are comparable: the god is both literate and expert in the use of arms. In the Tirunelveli version he presents himself to the king of Madurai and stands out among all the king's warriors (this recalls Tirunelveli's political dependence on Madurai). As the result of a plot hatched by the king's entourage, he is sent to the forest to get tiger's milk to cure the queen's pretended headaches. In the Kerala version, Śāstā takes advantage of this opportunity to kill the female buffalo *mahiṣi.* Then in both versions he returns to the royal city with tigresses; he sows terror, confounds the wicked, and reveals his divine nature. After this he withdraws to a mountain—to Sabarimalai or Aryankavu—where he has his sanctuary: here he is represented as a yogi (whereas in the plain he is usually accompanied by two wives).

The myth simultaneously affirms Śāstā's royal characteristics and his Brahmanic ones (he is literate and a renouncer). Everything takes place on the level of a particular kingdom. The divinity imposes himself through his warlike and superhuman aspects, but he does not reign directly over society; it is the territory as a whole that he protects. Śāstā is associated more with external space; he is a hunter and yogi: hunting and renunciation are both associated with the forest; since he dominates the wild world, he commands the demons, but he is also concerned with the fertility of the fields and with the water that they need. He embodies the potentialities of external space in relation to the socialized space of the village.

Although on the cosmic level Śāstā is the destroyer of the *asura,* on the earthly level of the kingdom he restores order, and he does this by introducing the values of the forest (since in the last analysis the ultimate value is renunciation) into the organized world of the royal city. The struggle against the *asura* remains the model and justification for divine intervention among men, as well as the means of transmitting the message of Hinduism: salvation through devotion and renunciation.

In a way the complementarity of Śāstā and the Goddess is what unites the two spaces and the values associated with them. While the goddess of the locality (she can also have other dimensions) is connected with the habitat, Śāstā is connected with the territory as a whole, which includes the village. This is also a complementarity in function with regard to the different needs of the group, more or less comparable to the complementarity of men and women in Indian society.

We must not, however, be too rigorous in defining the spheres of influence of the two divinities. We have seen that the legend of Śāstā from Sabarimalai, in giving a mythical reason for the birth, takes up a theme that is generally associated with the Goddess: the destruction of the buffalo *asura*. While the goddess battles the buffalo demon *mahiṣa*, Śāstā deals with the feminine form, *mahiṣi*. This is probably a case of the appropriation of a well-known theme by the followers of the famous AiyappaN of Sabarimalai. Nevertheless, the use of this theme, with its reversal of masculine and feminine roles, is not without significance and tends to suggest a certain functional equivalence of the forms of descent of the god and those of the goddess. On the level of the manifestation, the masculine and feminine aspects of the divine vary by complementing one another.

IV. Divine Hierarchy and Social Hierarchy

Both Śāstā and the Goddess, like the inferior divinities on another level, can be regarded as forms of descent of the supreme divinity; even the goddess, the personalized and projected "energy" (*śakti*) of the god, is viewed in this way in local myths. In the context of rural life, these forms of descent are closer to human interests in their main aspects: the complementary functions of Śāstā and the Goddess are more closely connected with the territory and its prosperity, as well as with the health and well-being of the resident group; those of the inferior divinities are connected with the fertility of the kin group.

Every village has these two categories of divinities. If the agglomeration is important enough, moreover, the supreme form of the god (Śiva or Viṣṇu) is also present in a great Brahmanic temple. On this level, too, the cult and the festivals concern the general prosperity of the locality, especially the maintenance of the sociocosmic order of which the local order is the projection. In Tirunelveli, in sum, simplifying the complexity of the pantheon a bit, we can distinguish three categories of temples corresponding to three main categories of divinities.

On the local level of each of these sanctuaries, we are in the universe of the ritual, of either vegetarian or blood sacrifice, that is, of the effective act, whose goal is the good of the worlds, and so of man; the universe of the ritual corresponds to that of society. But it is also important to note that no divinity is limited to this universe; each of them participates in the ultimate values of renunciation, which lie beyond specifically social values. The demonic dimension of the inferior divinities has in it something comparable to the values of renunciation, if only in a negative sense; and this whole set of values (renunciation, danger, something beyond the pure and the impure) is associated in Hindu symbolism with the same space, that of the outside, the world of the forest, opposed to the social space of the village, the space of the strict separation of pure and impure and the distinction of castes. While in the end it is the values of renunciation and devotion that orient the religion of the ritual, in a parallel way the values associated with the demonic forms of the divine (violence, impurity) seem in the last analysis indispensable for making the ritual fruitful and gaining the goods of this world that are necessary for the reproduction of any life and any society.

The dichotomous series introduced by the opposition of vegetarian and carnivore, pure and impure, etc., is reproduced both in the pantheon and among men; in a way the vegetarian divinities are those of the Brahmans and the other high castes, whereas the meat-eating divinities are those of the lower castes. This overly one-sided view must, however, be qualified. To meet a crisis, even a Brahman will occasionally offer (vegetarian) worship to an inferior god; on the other hand, the superior divinities are the objects of everyone's devotion. But the multiplicity of representations is definitively resolved in the affirmed unity of the divine.

Similarly, the relationship between pantheon and society is complex and cannot be reduced to a vague reflection. The three divine categories of the local pantheon correspond to the three main divisions of the society, more or less assimilable to the *varṇas* of the classical tradition; this equivalence operates on the level of the functions that each category, divine and social, assumes. On the one hand, the Brahmans hold the knowledge of the world order as it is and should be, and therefore also purity; by their status, they are close to the superior form of divinity. By contrast, the population of the non-Brahmans, the Śūdras, is entirely involved in tasks of service for the higher *varṇas*. Between these two extremes, those who have both wealth and authority over men take on, locally and regionally, the functions of the Kṣatriya *varṇa*—whether or not they really come from it. On the one hand, they compete with the Brahmans in maintaining the social order according to dharma; on the level of the great temple, they are the ideal practitioners of the function of sacrificer, reproducing in this way the function of royalty. On the other hand, because of their authority and the protection that they are supposed to provide, they work with the Śūdras to maintain local prosperity; it is they who order blood sacrifices to the local goddess. Their intermediate position and their functions correspond to those of Śāstā and the Goddess.

It is on this level that the various oppositions are resolved, in particular the opposition between nonviolence and blood sacrifice. The function of power sanctions the necessity of this always violent act for the prosperity of the world and, in the last analysis, for the preservation of the Brahmanic ideals of nonviolence and purity. The structure of the local pantheon involves a complete construction of the world that includes a model for society and its reproduction.

M.-L.R./j.l.

Avatars

Classical mythology knows only of avatars (*avatāras*) of Viṣṇu, but there are also local avatars of Śiva. And alongside the avatars of Śiva and of Viṣṇu, the two sons of Śiva also appear on the scene, and one of them at least, Skanda-Subrahmaṇya, seems to have a function in South India that is quite similar to that of an avatar, namely, the function of a great god who is sovereign over a given territory. By contrast, nowhere is there a son of Viṣṇu. But classical mythology, even if it introduces Gaṇapati only quite late, knows Skanda very well from the time of the epics. It is important to pay attention to these differences, and this is one of the problems that the myths of avatars should help to resolve.

On the other hand, at least on the mythic level, the avatar of Viṣṇu is always related to a cosmic period, the yuga. The Supreme Puruṣa emits the world for the period of one *mahākalpa* (one life of Brahmā or one hundred years of Brahmā), and within one *mahākalpa* there are one hundred times three hundred sixty days of Brahmā or *kalpas,* which are so many cycles in which the triple world, under the guardianship of the Trimūrti, undergoes a period of emission and a period of reabsorption, a cosmic day and night. Each *kalpa* is measured by one thousand *mahāyugas* or "divine" yugas, each *mahāyuga* being composed of a series of four yugas in decreasing order: the Kṛta Yuga, in which dharma, the sociocosmic order, is in a perfect state, is measured by four thousand "divine years" and is flanked by two "twilights" (but not "nights," as are periods of greater duration) of four hundred years each; the Tretā Yuga, in which dharma is reduced by one-fourth, has a length of only three thousand divine years and two twilights of three hundred years; during the Dvāpara Yuga, dharma is cut in half, and the duration is two thousand years, with twilights of two hundred years. Finally, the Kali Yuga, the most evil yuga and the one in which we live—as it should be—retains only one-fourth of dharma and one thousand years of duration, with twilights of one hundred years. When these are added up, a *mahāyuga* lasts for twelve thousand divine years, a figure that must be multiplied by three hundred sixty to get the corresponding number of human years. Here we are in a temporal unit which concerns us more than the *kalpa,* not only because of its duration, but also because it involves dharma, for which man is responsible above all. Also, the yuga (and the *mahāyuga*) is operative only in our triple world, and the cosmic crises that constitute the twilights affect only the three worlds between which the creatures transmigrate. Whatever may have been the origin of the yugic structure, it is not insignificant that in Hindu mythology the four yugas borrow their names from the game of dice.

According to the theory—which was already taking form in the epic—an avatar is a "descent" of Viṣṇu into the triple world when, at the end of a yuga, dharma is in such a bad state that a divine intervention is needed to reestablish it. They go so far as to say that Narasiṃha, the half-man, half-lion avatar, appeared at the end of the last Kṛta Yuga, that Rāma was the avatar at the end of the Tretā Yuga, and that Kṛṣṇa was the avatar of the end of the Dvāpara. This attractive ordering is not without its problems: it is difficult to understand how Viṣṇu intervenes in order to reestablish dharma when the following yuga is in fact inferior in dharma to the one that preceded it. Devotion to Kṛṣṇa cannot tolerate the idea that Kṛṣṇa could have remained in the world during the Kali Yuga, and has this yuga begin with the death of Kṛṣṇa: but Kṛṣṇa descended to earth at the end of the Dvāpara with the precise purpose of restoring dharma. On the other hand, it would be hard to find an account of a cosmic twilight like those given in the Purāṇas for the creation and dissolution of the cosmos. There are various accounts, for each avatar, but although they all bear witness to an identical deep structure and make use of stereotyped characters, one would still be hard-pressed to speak of *the* myth of the avatar or of *the* twilight between two yugas in the same way as we spoke of *the* Purāṇic cosmology and *pralaya.* In short, although we can conceive of a temporal cycle on the order of a *kalpa,* it would be on the level of the *mahāyuga,* of the group of four yugas, rather than that of the yuga: at the end of the Kali Yuga, a catastrophe permits the passage to a new Kṛta Yuga and reestablishes the integrity of dharma. And this eventuality is foreseen for the end of our Kali Yuga, when Viṣṇu will intervene in the form of the Kalkin avatar. But in any case, this temporal cycle—which must be essential, since it is the unit by which the greater cycles were determined—no longer corresponds to a rhythm of divine life or divine yoga. There is thus a rupture between the cycles of Purāṇic cosmogony and the yugas, with which epic mythology seems more preoccupied than with *kalpas.*

Another difficulty arises from the ambivalence that the universalism of bhakti introduces with regard to dharma: the Kali Yuga is the preeminent age of bhakti, because with dharma disappearing, devotion to Viṣṇu must compensate for it; thus Śūdras and women, those forgotten by high-caste society, may find salvation during this yuga by means of devotion—including performance of their duties as women and Śūdras. Divine grace does the rest. Is it so necessary, then, to reestablish a Kṛta Yuga, the age in which salvation is most difficult to obtain? Apparently divine grace allows sin to flourish, since even the wicked can obtain salvation if their last words are for Viṣṇu. They even tell the story of the evil man who, in his hour of death, called to his son just before dying; his son was named Nārāyaṇa, which is also the name of the god, and this was enough to save him. But the salvation of individuals does not prevent social disorder from increasing, so one must wait for the inevitable return of a golden age. The confusion is increased when one remembers that devotion is preferentially given to the avatars of Viṣṇu who come to reestablish dharma: Rāma and Kṛṣṇa are the principal objects of Vaiṣṇava bhakti (at least in northern India). This is simultaneously the reinforcement of dharma by bhakti and the mutual opposition of the two.

What then is the meaning of the divine intervention, of the new form taken by the supreme Puruṣa? The classic list of the ten avatars—which even today allows certain variants—does not tell us much more. The list contains an anomalous assemblage of themes, of which some are cosmogonic themes taken from the Veda (the Fish, the Tortoise, the Boar, the Dwarf), while others are much more enigmatic, and since they occur today as the ruling divinities of certain regions, we may well imagine that it was their cultic position which made them avatars. In any case, this sidesteps the question that remains to be resolved, for this incarnating god had the gift of inspiring theologico-comparative innovations.

If we bear in mind that it is the epics that speak to us of these divine descents for the first time (in stories in which Viṣṇu is accompanied on earth by a certain number of heavenly gods, the ancient Vedic gods, or other superhuman beings) and center their story around these descents, we may expect them to throw some light upon the problem. The main difficulty then becomes the enormity of the works to be dealt with, the MBh especially; yet it is the MBh, in which didactic passages are constantly mingled with the narrative, that is the most apt to give us the answer to our question. It strikes us immediately that the narrative is explicitly located at the junction between the Dvāpara Yuga and the Kali Yuga, but that two of its characters are, also explicitly, incarnations of Dvāpara and Kali, who have become *asuras* to fit the demands of the myth. The chronological framework of the junction between the two yugas is quite fuzzy, and there continues to be debate today about the point in the narrative where one yuga gives way to the other. On the other hand, the fact that the incarnation of Kali becomes the usurping king who, in order to take control of the royal house, goes to war against the five brothers who represent righteous kingship, thus precipitating the catastrophe foretold from the start, is fundamental. This is because at several points the epic does not hesitate to call a bad king a Kali, and this epithet develops into the more formal idea that it is the king who makes the yuga (MBh 5.132; 12.69–70) or, as is said in the *Laws of Manu* (9.301–2), that it is the king who is the

The wild-boar avatar of Viṣṇu saving the earth. The Temple of Alagarkoil (Madura). Photo M. Biardeau.

Rāma, the avatar of Viṣṇu and the hero of the *Rāmāyaṇa*. Private collection. Photo Dominique Champion.

yuga. In other words, the state of the world, that is, the state of dharma, depends essentially upon the governing king.

But in the *Rāmāyaṇa*, the Rāma avatar is the legitimate king. When he is exiled he recovers his kingdom only after the conquest of Laṅkā; that is, after a war in which the enemy must be killed at any cost. In the MBh the intrigue is more complex, for the Kṛṣṇa avatar acts as though his past as an avatar were behind him and offers himself as a model for the representative of the ideal king, who also stands as his own double. The avatar thus recovers in himself something of the yogi Puruṣa when he contents himself with counseling and guiding without engaging in battle, yet he ensures the victory of his close friend Arjuna when he takes the initiative in all the twisting of dharma, i.e., of the code of battle, that he makes in order to win: what matters here above all else is making war and winning the victory in order to save the world. Avatar and king are undoubtedly connected, and they are on earth to make war; the MBh says this explicitly.

If Hindu mythic structures have reserved such an important place for the avatars of Viṣṇu, it is not only because the character of the king is pivotal to Hindu society. It is also and especially because his role and the ethic that it presupposes are opposed on the one hand to those of the Brahman and on the other to those of the renunciant. To express it in religious terms, it is because he is excluded from salvation. The fact that it is the epic genre that introduces us to the avatar is sufficient proof that war is central to the debate. The king is considered to be above all the possessor of power and the one who uses power to administer punishment within the kingdom. This is not his only role, but it is this role that concerns the ideology.

Without repeating the whole debate on *ahiṃsā*, "nonkilling," we may summarize what appears to have been the fundamental approach of the Hindu tradition, which was based on a revelation that centered on the sacrifice *and* on its negation: the sacrifice, of which the Brahman is the officiating priest, implies by definition the destruction of the oblatory substance, either animal or vegetable (every great Vedic sacrifice includes both kinds of oblation). Every destruction is a death, every death a stain, a sin of impurity that constitutes a danger to the sacrificer as well as to the officiating priest. The ritual takes account of this and takes every precaution to wipe out the stain inherent in sacrifice and even all impurity: since it is possible to say "killing in sacrifice is not killing" (*Manu* 5.39), it then suffices to transform every activity into a sacrifice in order for every killing, even the most insignificant and the most inevitably joined to life, to be expiated. The renunciant who refuses the sacrifice also refuses this facility and becomes fastidious about the canons of ahiṃsā. Apparently we owe to the renunciant the adoption of a vegetarian diet by the Brahman and his imitators and correlatively the very rapid abandonment of official Vedic sacrifices, for which purely vegetable offerings were substituted. The ideal of the renunciant commanded the attention of the man of the world at the same time as the Absolute became the Great Yogi. Conceived as superior, he evidently first made his mark on the Brahman, who became and remains to the present day the champion of *ahiṃsā*. Within the bhakti tradition, the Brahman is no more than the one who must live under the shelter of royal protection and can practice the trade of officiating priest only by keeping himself pure of all "violence." In particular, he may not defend himself.

But the Hindus—whom we mistakenly imagine to be forever lost in contemplation and unable to deal with material necessities—did not, for all this, shut out the Kṣatriya, the king and warrior, from the realm of values. They are too convinced of the need for strong government. Only the Kṣatriya can encourage, and if necessary constrain, each individual to follow his dharma (even the renunciant, who became a role model for society). The distinction and complementarity of the two superior *varṇas,* Brahmans and Kṣatriyas, already mentioned in the Puruṣa hymn, becomes all the stronger for this. The more the Brahman becomes "nonviolent," the more the king must be able to make war. And since the Supreme Puruṣa, as the Great Yogi, is the guarantor of Brahmanic values (in which the sacrifice becomes subordinated to yoga), he must also have a form that guarantees royal values: this is the avatar. The avatar has not forgotten that he was a yogi, but he also knows that he has descended into a world in which the sacrifice is the sole driving force, a world whose cyclic renewal is conceived as a total sacrifice. It is easy to see how war could become the warrior's perfect form of sacrifice, a sacrifice in which he would have only a marginal need for the Brahman officiating priest and in which he might offer himself as victim with the hope of substituting the person of the enemy in the course of battle. And if this sacrifice, as murderous as any other, is performed with indifference, "for the good of the worlds," it carries with it no pollution because it requires no attachment.

The epic conceptions are accompanied by a complete transformation of the doctrine of *karman*—of action, notably of ritual action. The renouncer of the Revelation (*śruti*) is first of all the one who condemns all action, particularly ritual acts, because they produce results in an indefinite number of rebirths. The *Bhagavad Gītā*—whose inclusion within the MBh is all too often forgotten—disputes the validity of this form of renunciation: Kṛṣṇa (the avatar) explains to Arjuna (the figure of the ideal king) how it is impossible to live without action and consequently to live without killing, if only imperceptible animalcules. But the counterpart of this is that it is not the act that pollutes but attachment to the results of the act, the fact that the act is wanted in order to produce a desired fruit. If one suppresses this attachment and substitutes for it concern for the good of the worlds, which may be termed a royal concern, then not only does every act become good and productive of deliverance, but the man who performs it imitates the divinity who, while a yogi and insofar as he is a yogi, perpetually "acts" in order to keep the worlds in existence. When the warrior kills enemies who threaten dharma, he is the image of the yogi god who reabsorbs the worlds into himself: this is the meaning of the terrible vision of himself that Kṛṣṇa gives to Arjuna in the *Gītā* (11). The avatar, the warrior form of the divinity, is only an image of the Great Yogi who reabsorbs the worlds into himself at the end of the *kalpa* or the *mahākalpa.* Similarly, the king who is at war against evil enemies, and who kills them for the good of the worlds and through his adherence to the order of the worlds desired by the divinity, is the replica of the avatar and thus the lesser image of the Great Yogi whose yoga produces the sacrifice of the worlds.

In practice, the myths of the avatars are generally placed in opposition to the divine incarnation of one or many *asuras* who, under one form or another, try to take control or have taken control of a power which does not belong to them and by which they establish in the world a state of disorder—*adharma.* A typical scenario is that of the battle of the *devas* and the *asuras,* in which the *asuras* are victorious and dislodge the *devas* from heaven. The inhabitants of the infernal regions, occupying heaven, receive in the place of the gods the oblations coming from the earth: the cosmic order is turned upside down, and the gods go to ask the help of Viṣṇu, who "descends" to restore the only viable order. Often the story includes a favor bestowed by Brahmā upon the king of the *asuras,* the baneful consequences of which he finds he is unable to control. Another scenario sets the stage on earth, where the fate of the three worlds (heaven, earth, hell) unfolds: here it is a Kṣatriya, a king, who fails to make dharma reign in his kingdom. Whatever the nature of his bad conduct, the result is always that the Brahmans are wronged, and this harms even the gods, who need harmony between Brahmans and kings in order to receive their portion of the sacrifice and to be nourished with it. The evil Kṣatriya is always finally considered an incarnate *asura,* and the disorder always takes the form of the encroachment of royal power upon the power of the Brahmans.

M.Bi./d.w.

BIBLIOGRAPHY

M. BIARDEAU, "Études de mythologie hindoue," part 4, *BEFEO* (1976).

Abbreviations

MBh	*Mahābhārata* (Poona 1930: Citrashala Press edition)
R	*Rāmāyaṇa* (Gorakhpur edition)

NARA/NĀRĀYAṆA

Nārāyaṇa is well known as a name of Viṣṇu. He seems to appear in the form of the *ṛṣi* Nārāyaṇa and is thus inseparable from the *ṛṣi* Nara. The *ṛṣi,* an omnipresent character in Hindu mythology, is a man of bygone times (the seven great *ṛṣis* of the origins are Brahmā's first creatures) whose ascetic life in the forest and extreme purity (connected with a scrupulous practice of daily rituals) developed his knowledge and power in an extraordinary way. Simultaneously an ascetic in the forest and a householder with his wives and his sacrificial fires, he provides the mythic model for the *vānaprastha,* the one who has settled in the forest, the theoretical stage in every human life between the stage of the householder and that of the total renunciant. He is the watchful intermediary between gods and men. Among the best known *ṛṣis* are Nārada, Vyāsa (the other incarnation of Nārāyaṇa, the one who brought the Veda to men, as well as the MBh and the Purāṇas), Agastya, Vasiṣṭha, and Viśvāmitra. It is, however, unusual to see the supreme god himself take the form of an *ṛṣi*, and we must still take into account the way he splits into Nara and Nārāyaṇa. Because it is truly a splitting: the *Śatapatha Brāhmaṇa* (a text of the Vedic canon) contains what may have been the basis of this mythic creation. In 13.6.1, in the context of the (human) sacrifice to the Puruṣa, the Puruṣa is referred to as Puruṣa Nārāyaṇa. We know that *puruṣa* and *nara* are synonyms (meaning "man"), and it seems clear that *Nārāyaṇa* is the mythical transformation of the expression *puruṣāyaṇa*, which occurs in one Upaniṣad. Puruṣa Nārāyaṇa—who at this stage is still not explicitly Viṣṇu—is the proper name of the supreme deity associated with *Nārāyaṇa*, a name that is patronymic in form. One only has to cut this name in two and put *nara* back in place of *puruṣa* to obtain two characters, one of whom will be called Nara and the other Nārāyaṇa.

This creation seems to be tied to the MBh: it may have been motivated by the splitting of the avatar into Kṛṣṇa and Arjuna, the avatar himself (Nārāyaṇa) and the ideal human king who must play the role of the avatar on earth (Nara). Since it was impossible to read this dichotomy directly into Nārāyaṇa the supreme god, it was hypostasized in a pair of inseparable *ṛṣis*. But these two *ṛṣis* merely constitute the intermediate stage that makes it possible to pass from Viṣṇu to Kṛṣṇa and Arjuna. So their mythology, though rich, is fragmentary.

The epic (7.201.86) tells us that Nara was born of the asceticism of Nārāyaṇa, who is the son of Dharma. In 12.334.8–9, it speaks of Nārāyaṇa, the son of Dharma, who has taken a quadruple form: Nara, Nārāyaṇa, Hari (another name of Viṣṇu), and Kṛṣṇa. Purāṇic literature makes Ahiṃsā (Nonviolence) the mother of both *ṛṣis*. Invariably their hermitage is in Badarī, in the Himalayas, which is identified with modern Badrinath, a pilgrimage site dedicated to Viṣṇu and located on the upper Ganges.

These two *ṛṣis*, of such a special nature, maintain a privileged position among all the others, a position that evokes their ties to the supreme Puruṣa: they do not bow before Brahmā himself, and since the other *ṛṣis* and the heavenly gods are surprised by this offhand manner, Brahmā tells them who the *ṛṣis* are. The gods understand this so well that they immediately ask for their help in their struggle against the *asuras* (MBh 5.49): both of them are present to fulfill the function of an avatar of the supreme Puruṣa.

But their ontological identity does not create any confusion of their roles. When Nara accompanies Nārāyaṇa, Nārāyaṇa remains much closer to the Puruṣa, the perfectly immutable yogi, whereas Nara is the active character, the one who fights and whose duty it is to carry out particular tasks dealing with dharma, the cosmic order that must be preserved. This arrangement recalls the roles of Kṛṣṇa and Arjuna in the MBh. These dual roles are also expressed in the mythology peculiar to the two *ṛṣis*, notably in the story of King Dambhodbhava (MBh 5.96), which Paraśurāma tells at the court of Dhṛtarāṣṭra in order to bring the Kauravas to a better sense of reality. King Dambhodbhava, whose name indicates his extreme vanity, reigned over all the earth and deemed himself superior to all creatures. This incurred the wrath of the Brahmans (a king cannot be superior to a Brahman). They tell him cleverly that he is surely not the equal of the ascetics Nara and Nārāyaṇa and that he should measure himself against them to verify his own superiority. Dambhodbhava provokes the two *ṛṣis* in their hermitage. They try to calm him down but they do not succeed. Nara then vows to fight the king and his army alone. Total defeat ensues, and the king falls at the feet of Nara, who advises him to adopt a more dharmic attitude. Nārāyaṇa is content to be present at the scene without participating in it.

The epic also introduces the two *ṛṣis* in the story of the churning of the sea of milk, in a context where Nārāyaṇa is in fact Viṣṇu himself (MBh 1.19). Viṣṇu asks Nara to help him give the ambrosia to the gods, and the two of them then fight with the gods against the *asuras*. Nara blocks the road to heaven with rocks cut from the mountains with his arrows, thus forcing the *asuras* to retreat to the earth and the waters. The gods also give him the task of guarding the elixir of immortality, and the text gives him the title of *kirīṭin* ("diademed"), an attribute specific to Arjuna throughout the epic. In the Nara/Nārāyaṇa pair, Nara has a role that strongly evokes that of the earthly king, the keeper of dharma.

Behind the distinction between the two *ṛṣis* stands the image from the *Muṇḍaka Upaniṣad* of two birds perched on a tree, one of which eats the fruit of the tree while the other watches him but does not eat. The aim of this text is not to contrast the Puruṣa with the king but to contrast the liberated Ātman with the creature caught inside the web of earthly activities: the image is thus applicable to every man. But the ideal king can be symbolized by Nara, "Man," because, in fact, he also represents the ideal man.

M.Bi./g.h.

Matsya: The Fish and the Flood in the Work of the Mythic Imagination

Matsya, the Fish, is the name of one of the classical avatars of Viṣṇu. This myth has a Vedic prehistory in which the principal role is played by Manu, the legislator and mythical ancestor of the two great royal dynasties of the Tradition. It is the Indian version of the myth of the flood.

The *Śatapatha Brāhmaṇa* (1.8.1.1–10) gives a complete account of the Vedic myth, in which there is no mention of Viṣṇu at all. Manu is brought water for his morning ablutions. In this water is a little fish, who asks Manu to protect him, promising in return to save Manu from an imminent flood. Fearing that he will be swallowed by other fish, the little fish asks for shelter. Manu first puts the fish in a pot full of water, and then, as it continues to grow, he transfers it into a ditch and then finally into the ocean, once it is big enough to escape all danger. The fish reveals to Manu the date of the flood, and counsels him to call him when he has finished building a boat. When Manu appears in his boat, the fish draws near and allows Manu to attach his boat to his horn; then he leads him to the north slope of the mountains where he will watch over the receding waters. As the sole survivor of the flood, Manu must engender a new human race, and for that purpose he practices austerity and performs sacrifices.

This flood is thoroughly Indian, despite the universal character of the theme. Manu is a *prajāpati,* a progenitor of the human race who alone escapes the flood. His boat is not the equivalent of Noah's Ark, though it is still the symbol of salvation: it is what enables one to cross over. The Himalayas, which border India on the north, are the impassable frontier that separates ordinary mankind from the world of salvation. The land of salvation lies beyond the mountain to the north, and the fish will guide the boat there, thereby indicating that Manu is saved from the flood.

Why a fish? Clearly the flood theme calls for one, and it is risky to apply to the Vedic myth what would be true for the classical period. The text does, however, tempt us to do so, since the fish evokes the danger of being devoured by another fish: classical India indeed speaks of the "law of the fishes" to designate what we would call the "law of the jungle." The law of the fishes is set against the order imposed by a good king, an order in which the weak are protected from the strong and in which dharma rather than individual force is the organizing principle. Manu, who is in essence the legislator and the father of the traditional royal dynasties, has an obvious connection with royal power (though he cannot be reduced to this function alone). Thus it is logical that the little fish should appeal to him in order to escape the law of the fishes.

But this is not just any fish. Its horn designates it a bearer of sacrificial values, and it is undoubtedly as such that it is able to guide Manu toward the region of salvation and allow him to recreate the human race through sacrifice. Its identity, however, is not precisely defined except by the symbolic trait of its horn.

The version of the myth provided by the *Mahābhārata* (3.187) identifies the fish with Brahmā. This text's reference to the law of the fishes is even more explicit than that in the Vedic account. As for the flood, it is clearly described as the advent of the cosmic night. Manu must bring aboard with him the seven *ṛṣis* and all the known grains. Guided by the fish during the stormy flood, his boat represents "the remnant" that must survive the cosmic night to make possible the dawn of a new cosmic era. After the waters have receded, Manu recreates living beings through his acts of austerity.

It is not necessary to arrange the different versions of the myth in historical order to see how clearly the mythical imagination works in the myth of the Fish: Brahmā is close to Viṣṇu; in the Purāṇas, Viṣṇu becomes Brahmā when he awakes to create the world. But the epic does not yet make the fish into an avatar of Viṣṇu. In the *Matsya Purāṇa* 1.12ff., this step is finally taken. Manu recognizes Viṣṇu Vāsudeva in the Fish, and the Fish, speaking of the flood to come, evokes the end of a yuga, which he describes as the end of a *kalpa* complete with fire and flood. The fish avatar is always equipped with a horn of salvation. Manu no longer has to build his boat, which the gods provide for the salvation of creatures, and he must bring aboard all living creatures. A little further into the text he only has to take every species of grain with him. By spiritual concentration on the divine Fish he ties his boat to the horn, and the mooring rope is made of the snake Ananta (Śeṣa, the serpent that symbolizes the cosmic residue between two *kalpas*).

The theme of the avatar is rendered entirely banal in the *Bhāgavata Purāṇa* 8.24.7–58, when the story of Manu and the flood receives a heavenly preamble: while Brahmā is asleep, the *asura* Hayagrīva takes advantage of the situation to steal the Veda. Viṣṇu then becomes incarnate as a fish. The story takes place in a previous *kalpa,* and Manu, the son of Vivasvat (the Sun), is replaced by one of his predecessors in the role of Manu, the royal *ṛṣi* Satyavrata. This is the typical pattern of an avatar narrative, where the disappearance of dharma is provoked by an *asura* who takes what does not belong to him. Viṣṇu alone can reestablish the cosmic order, and he does this in the form of a fish. And Manu clearly has a royal function that associates him with the work of the avatar.

We thus have an exemplary myth: at the Vedic level, it can be seen as a cosmogony, as one of the many cosmogonic accounts of Revelation. But the Tradition has regarded it as secondary in comparison with the myth of Puruṣa and has used it again at the level of the avatar, where the cosmogonic theme is subordinated to the salvific function of Viṣṇu's "descents." Moreover, the story of creation per se is not told and indeed becomes unnecessary as the royal character of Manu enables him to establish dharma and not to beget Brahmans. Although there is no explicit combat with the *asura,* the martial function of the king lies just beneath the surface, and that is why Manu must be king.

M.Bi./g.h.

Narasiṃha, the Man-Lion

Narasiṃha, the avatar of the Man-Lion, is one of the "descents" of Viṣṇu that have no Vedic antecedent. His myth features two *asuras* instead of one, father and son: the first is the king of *asuras,* eager to reign in place of Indra in heaven; the second is just the opposite, a great devotee of Viṣṇu, highly respectful of dharma. There is an inherent tension between, on the one hand, the god of bhakti, dispenser of a universal salvation, the calm yogi, and, on the other hand, the avatar, who is devoted to safeguarding dharma, the socioeconomic order, and thus to the destruction of the evil *asuras* and thereby to violence. In this myth, that tension reaches its highest level.

And since in the classical myth Narasiṃha's appearance on earth is limited to the moment when he suddenly emerges in a half-human, half-leonine form to kill the *asura* Hiraṇyakaśipu, a split is also introduced between the myth and the ritual: the great temples of bhakti cannot enthrone the terrible form of a god, so they substitute for the murder scene either Lakṣmī-Narasiṃha, in which the god is seated and holds his wife (Śrī or Lakṣmī, the usual consort of Viṣṇu, though the myth doesn't say a word about her) on his left knee, or, quite often, Yoganarasiṃha, in which the half-human, half-leonine form, strangely enough, assumes a posture of yoga. This form of the descent of the god recalls that he is above all the Great Yogi and the god of bhakti, the god of all mercy. That is what the myth also says in another way, a way that has no recourse to any elements of the biography of the god.

Lakṣmī Narasiṃha. Probably from Gujarat. Private collection. Photo D. Ċhampion.

We shall follow here the version of the *Bhāgavata Purāṇa* (7.3–8), sometimes using the variants introduced by the *Viṣṇu Purāṇa* (1.17–20), the two Purāṇas providing the two fundamental broad outlines on which the different versions are based.

Hiraṇyakaśipu is the king of the *asuras.* He is filled with hatred for Viṣṇu and with contempt for his sectarian devotees, and he seeks to escape the rhythm of the *kalpa* that the god of bhakti imposes by his yoga. He therefore devotes himself to appalling austerities (*tapas*) in order to obtain equal status with Brahmā and the possibility of substituting his own order for the dharma. The gods, made uncomfortable by the heat of his *tapas,* complain to Brahmā, who appears to Hiraṇyakaśipu to ask him what he wants. Hiraṇya asks for invulnerability (that he may not be killed either by a man or by an animal, either by one of Brahmā's creatures or by anyone who is not one of Brahmā's creatures, either by day or by night, either in the air or on the ground, etc.), equal status with Brahmā, and a *tapas* that cannot be diminished. Brahmā grants it all. Hiraṇya immediately takes advantage of this to overthrow Indra and become the sovereign of the three worlds (heaven, earth, and hell). He receives the sacrificial oblations in place of Indra. This time, the worlds and the gods complain to Viṣṇu.

The setting is precisely that of a myth of an avatar: it is classical in that Brahmā grants an *asura* a dangerous favor that the *asura* will misuse. Here the theme is stressed: if Brahmā grants favors so easily, it is because he does not really have a choice. As the personification of the ritual power of the Brahmans, he can demonstrate the efficacy of the ritual only by rewarding the *asura* for it. Here *tapas* is only an extreme variant of the ritual. This ascetic technique of producing heat is manipulated by the *asura* as a ritual designed to satisfy a desire and not as a practice of renunciation: the heat that emanates from the *tapas* is capable of setting the world on fire in a conflagration that would appear to be a "normal" (conforming to the norm) end of the world. It is like a threat of holocaust without any counterpart for the worlds. And the gods are well aware of this, since they have a direct interest in the smooth running of the "triple world" on which their lives depend.

But Brahmā is also, in classical mythology, the personification of the impersonal absolute, Brahman, the Absolute particularly of those who do not accept the gods of bhakti and instead seek deliverance outside ritual but within its extended dimension. The Brahman is the Absolute of Brahmans who might be called orthodox, who refuse salvation through bhakti, in which the privilege of birth and ritual is abolished through divine grace, and reject the gods who are its guarantors, especially Viṣṇu. This Absolute also occurs in Purāṇic literature in the form of the Brahmaloka, the "world of the Brahman" or "of Brahmā." The myth emphasizes this orthodox—but too orthodox—aspect of Hiraṇyakaśipu: he wants equal status with Brahmā (like those who have been released in the Brahmaloka); he does not want to submit to the alternating phases of emission and reabsorption of the world that characterize bhakti and that the "orthodox" refuse. The *Harivaṃśa* makes him a *brahma-bhakta,* a sectarian devotee of Brahmā or the Brahman to the exclusion of the great gods of bhakti. He does not limit himself to rejecting devotion to Viṣṇu: he lays claim to a state that the orthodox Brahmanic conception reserves only for Brahmans. In other words, he wants to add to his royal power a privilege of the Brahmans, a crime difficult to pardon.

Viṣṇu's answer to the gods is unexpected. He announces that he will "descend" to punish the wicked *asura,* according to the usual scenario of the myth of the avatar, but he subordinates this descent to the ill treatment that Hiraṇya will inflict upon his son, the devotee Prahlāda. What is unusual is the merging within one character—Prahlāda, the good *asura*—of the values of bhakti and dharma that the avatar must save. Viṣṇu's words are unambiguous: "When someone hates the gods, the Veda, cows, Brahmans, and the 'perfected ones,' when he hates the dharma and myself, he quickly perishes. When Hiraṇya hurts his own son Prahlāda, who is calm and free of hostility, strengthened though Hiraṇya may be by the favors (of Brahmā), I shall make him perish." Viṣṇu then sings the praises of Prahlāda: he is a perfect *bhakta,* and this perfection obviously includes respect for dharma, for the sociocosmic order, as well as for Viṣṇu's love. The terms that Viṣṇu listed—gods, the Veda, cows, Brahmans, etc.—form an indissoluble whole: bhakti, or the love of Viṣṇu, is incorporated within dharma, while reciprocally dharma does not exist without that which exceeds it, namely, that very bhakti. Prahlāda symbolizes the fusion of the orthodox universe with the universe of bhakti. The dharma of the Brahmans is henceforth guaranteed by Viṣṇu, but it must in return open itself to what is beyond it, by admitting, for example, that an *asura,* an inhabitant of the infernal (inferior) regions, may be a perfect devotee and may be saved. Thanks to this identification, Viṣṇu will descend to save dharma by saving his *bhakta* from the claws of his father.

In fact, Hiraṇyakaśipu fails in his effort to turn his son away from his devotion to Viṣṇu. He therefore attempts to kill him, but in vain. Here the *Viṣṇu Purāṇa* is more explicit than the *Bhāgavata*. Prahlāda's hands and feet are tied, he is thrown into the sea, and rocks are piled on him. Held prisoner at the bottom of the water, he enters into *samādhi* (the mystical state) and experiences oneness with Viṣṇu, whereupon his bonds fall away and he rises to the surface alive and well. Viṣṇu asks him what he wants. Nothing more than always to be the devotee of Viṣṇu, and the pardon of his father. When Hiraṇyakaśipu sees his son reappear, he repents, but he is quickly killed by Viṣṇu, who appears in the form of Narasiṃha.

The scene in which Prahlāda is thrown into the sea and there experiences oneness with Viṣṇu is symbolic: the devotee is released by his god from the ocean of rebirths. The chains of servitude fall, and he is united with his god. The scene is symmetrical with the one in which Hiraṇyakaśipu asks Brahmā for a parody of release. The emphasis on this aspect of the intervention of Viṣṇu results in the weakening of the central theme of the myth of the avatar: the murder of the *asura*. The narrative dismisses it in one line and implies that Hiraṇya is released.

On the other hand, the *Bhāgavata Purāṇa* does not introduce an account of Prahlāda's release but tells the well-known scene of the murder of Hiraṇyakaśipu by Narasiṃha. Hiraṇya wants to kill his son, who resists all his attempts to seduce him, and he defies him to prove that his god is ubiquitous: Can he emerge from the pillar of his palace (which he kicks)? The response is immediate: Narasiṃha (neither man nor beast) cracks open the pillar at twilight (neither by day nor by night) and kills Hiraṇya whom he suspends across his thighs (neither on earth nor in the air, but the thighs symbolize the earth, through a Sanskrit play on words). It is more than likely that the pillar of the palace of Hiraṇyakaśipu here symbolizes the sacrificial pole, transforming the scene of the murder quite appropriately into a blood sacrifice, a martial sacrifice: Hiraṇya struggles with Narasiṃha before he is killed, and he dies as a warrior. As for Viṣṇu, by assuming a leonine form he has taken on a royal appearance that makes him fit to fight against a king.

The difference between the two versions illustrates the tension that exists between the two points of view, that of bhakti and that of the avatar, despite their reconciliation in the character of Prahlāda. The god of bhakti can only be good, the giver of grace, as calm as any yogi. The avatar can only be terrible, since he comes to kill. The myth has to be scattered in complementary versions in order to say all that it has to say. Correlatively, the temples of Narasiṃha differ, ranging from rather inaccessible sanctuaries on top of a mountain to their counterparts at the foot of the same mountain. The temple above most often (perhaps always) houses a terrible form, symbolizing the protection that the avatar extends to the whole territory, while the temple below should contain a kindly and calm form of the god.

M.Bi./g.h.

Paraśurāma

The myth of the Brahman warrior known as Rāma "with the ax" resembles the myth in which Vasiṣṭha and Viśvāmitra oppose each other. This is an echo of the many historical conflicts in which Brahmans and Kṣatriyas oppose each other. Paraśurāma, also known by the name of Rāma Jāmadagnya, the son of Jamadagni, is a great destroyer of Kṣatriyas, so great that Daśaratha, the father of Rāma the hero of the *Rāmāyaṇa,* grew pale when he saw him arrive to put his son to a test. However, in the MBh and even more clearly in the Purāṇas, he is one of Viṣṇu's avatars. He has a very rich mythology, with popular extensions in all of the Deccan, thanks to his mother, Reṇukā, who plays an important though passive role in the myth. His unusual status as a Brahman warrior (of which there are some other examples in the MBh) brings fully to light the opposition between Brahmanic purity (represented by his father and even more by his four older brothers) and the impurity of the warrior, which he takes on himself. In one way or another, this opposition is always present in the avatar. For example, it is found in the same form in the myth of Kalkin, the avatar of the future. Moreover, in all the versions that have evolved, the myth involves the decapitation of his mother, Reṇukā, which pushes violence to its highest point. In general, myth tends to describe extreme situations that make meaning more apparent. In the MBh, it is parallel cousins, that is, brothers, who fight for the sovereignty of the earth. Here the mission of the avatar seems to take place through the murder of his mother—the account of which is at first sight loosely tied to the rest of the myth. But the meaning is not necessarily the same as in the MBh. In particular, we must not forget that Reṇukā, the Goddess of the Deccan, is represented sometimes only by a head, sometimes by a headless body (she can appear in both forms in the same locality, one for the pure castes, the other for the impure). She has a counterpart in the north of India, where the Tantric goddess Chinnamastā ("with her head cut off") cuts off her head to let all creatures (and her own head) drink her blood. There seems to be in this a theme of the beheaded Goddess, which theoretically appears only in very veiled and indirect forms. The myth of Paraśurāma may help us to approach this theme and to put it in the proper perspective.

We shall follow here the version given in the MBh 3.115–17 (other versions can be found in MBh 12.49, *Bhāgavata Purāṇa* 9.15–16, *Brahmāṇḍa Purāṇa, Reṇukā Māhātmya,* etc.). Arjuna Kārtavīrya, king of the Haihayas, received a thousand arms and a heavenly chariot from Dattātreya, who wanted to make him a protector of dharma. But Kārtavīrya (we will call him this to avoid confusing him with the Pāṇḍava Arjuna) lets his strength go to his head and oppresses the gods, the *ṛṣis,* and all creatures. He goes so far as to disturb Indra when he is intimately engaged with his wife. The gods and the *ṛṣis,* with Indra at their head, complain to Viṣṇu, who consults Indra to find a way to get rid of the abusive king.

Then King Gādhi (in some versions the incarnation of Indra) has a daughter, Satyavatī, whom he marries to the Brahman *ṛṣi* Ṛcīka, a descendant of Bhṛgu. Ṛcīka prepares two bowls of rice porridge for his wife and his mother-in-law, which they must drink in order for his wife to conceive a Brahman and his mother-in-law to conceive a Kṣatriya. But as the result of a confusion (or an intentional exchange made by the mother of Satyavatī, according to some versions), the two bowls of porridge are switched. Satyavatī, married to a Brahman, will conceive a son who will have in him the power of the Kṣatriya, while her mother, a Kṣatriyā married to a Kṣatriya, will have a son endowed with the power of a Brahman; his name will be Viśvāmitra. This is such a catastrophe for Satyavatī that she begs her husband to postpone this curse and bring it on her grandson rather than her son. In fact, she gives birth to the Brahman Jamadagni ("consuming fire"), who in turn will marry Princess Reṇukā. Reṇukā will bear five sons, four pure Brahmans (four like the Vedas) and a fifth, Rāma, who will have a talent for warfare as well as for learning the Veda. This version of the myth does not state clearly that he is the incarnation of Viṣṇu, but he proves to be the one whom Viṣṇu has destined to save dharma from Kārtavīrya's attacks.

The theme of the "mixing of the *varṇas*" (the four *varṇas* are the categories serving to classify castes) is thus strongly expressed. Whereas in "normal" society (in compliance with the norm) a Brahman man can only marry a Brahman woman, a Kṣatriya man only a Kṣatriyā woman, here the two generations present a mixture—and always in the right direction, since the husband is of a higher status than the wife. We may thus expect that the sons born of this mixture will have special characteristics: that Jamadagni ("consuming fire") is the son of a Brahman and a princess is not an accident, and this mixture surely has some repercussions on his conduct toward his wife and sons, as we shall see. But the mixture is aggravated in the next generation by the ritual error made at the moment of the conception of Jamadagni and Viśvāmitra, of which the result is visited upon the generation of the grandson. All these detours were needed to produce the warrior Brahman Rāma Jāmadagnya, whose profound ambiguity makes him an ideal figure of an avatar. He will be a violent Brahman—a contradiction in terms—but he will put all of this violence to the exclusive service of the Brahmans and thus of dharma. This is the paradox that the myth poses for the prince who is destined to protect dharma, but whose pride leads him to stray from the right path.

This is when, at least in this version, the episode of the beheading of Reṇukā takes place, a princess who had become the pious wife of an ascetic Brahman. One day as she goes to fetch water for her husband's ritual needs, she lingers behind at the river to watch a prince frolicking in the water with his women, regretting what she will undoubtedly never know with her Brahman husband. Jamadagni guesses why she is late and in a fit of fury asks his sons to cut off her head. The first four refuse, and their father strikes them dead with his powerful ascetic's glance. Paraśurāma, on the other hand, agrees; he decapitates his mother with one blow of an ax. Satisfied, Jamadagni asks him what he wants as a reward. He hastens to ask for the resurrection of his mother and his brothers. His wish is granted. The *Bhāgavata Purāṇa* even asserts that he agreed to kill his mother because he knew that his father could bring her back to life.

Here ends this episode. Then Kārtavīrya suddenly makes his entrance. He arrives at Jamadagni's hermitage while his sons are away. Though he is treated as he ought to be by Reṇukā, he is not satisfied and forcibly takes away the calf of Jamadagni's cow, Homadhenu, and breaks the trees of the hermitage. Other versions are more explicit: he is received sumptuously by Jamadagni and his wife thanks to their cow, who supplies whatever is wanted. The king is jealous of the Brahman for having such a cow and asks to have it. In the *Reṇukā Māhātmya* the cow defends herself by producing armies from her body. When Rāma finds out what has happened, he kills Kārtavīrya after cutting off his thousand arms. The sons of Kārtavīrya avenge their father by killing Jamadagni. Rāma then swears that he will rid the earth of all its Kṣatriyas, beginning with Kārtavīrya's sons and close relatives. He does it over and over again, twenty-one times. Some versions put the beheading of Reṇukā between the murder of Kārtavīrya and the slaughter of all the Kṣatriyas.

After the carnage, Rāma fills five holes with the blood of his victims and performs a ritual in honor of his ancestors. His grandfather Ṛcīka appears to him and stops him, undoubtedly disapproving of the excessive bloodshed and the bloody ritual. Rāma then offers a sacrifice to Indra and gives the land to the officiating Brahmans and a golden altar to Kaśyapa; then he retires to Mount Mahendra, where he is said to be still living today.

The versions that take the narrative further all show the catastrophic result of the disappearance of the Kṣatriyas: the earth must be quickly restored to them in order for it to survive, for the Brahmans are incapable of governing themselves without a king. Rāma's work was therefore essentially destructive, too destructive. He becomes so completely carried away by his wrath that in each version he must be stopped by the intervention of his ancestors. There has to be at least the possibility of a rebirth of the Kṣatriyas so that the earth may be assured of a fresh start. However, the myth is constructed much like the myth of an avatar, in which the destruction, which takes on the aspect of the end of the world, proves to be necessary for rebirth. Certain versions send Rāma to Rudra-Śiva in search of weapons. The *Reṇukā Māhātmya* makes Kārtavīrya an *asura* incarnate, which brings the myth closer to the prototype.

This is the framework in which one must view the beheading of Reṇukā. The *Reṇukā Māhāmya* makes her an avatar of Pārvatī, that is, the Goddess (Jamadagni becomes an avatar of Śiva). Even without this ultimate development, it is possible to perceive the Goddess in Reṇukā, in the sense that the Goddess is close to the earth and its interests. The Princess Reṇukā, tempted by the games of the prince, mother of the warrior avatar, preserves something of the king's wife that she was meant to be. And the king's wife always symbolizes the kingdom, the land over which her husband rules, and in particular its prosperity. When Rāma slaughters the Kṣatriyas, he deprives the earth of those who are literally at its head: the beheading of Reṇukā foreshadows the decapitation of the earth.

This episode is not just a somewhat redundant segment of the narrative. When we know the importance of the theme of the head or of the beheaded Goddess in the cult of the Goddess, we are led to seek the meaning of the theme of the Goddess per se. Death by decapitation is above all a sacrificial theme, closely tied to "the sacrifice of battle" of which the MBh speaks. The buffalo that is traditionally offered to the Goddess is beheaded in front of her, as warriors have their heads cut off on the battlefield. In the sacrifice of battle, as in any sacrifice, the victim is first and in reality the sacrificer himself, the one who offers the sacrifice. The victim that he offers is a substitute for himself. The same applies in battle—especially in the battle that, according to the myth, the Goddess wages with the buffalo-demon. This is even more true of battle, for the warrior (man or woman), who goes off to war makes a sacrifice of his life. He gives himself in sacrifice and will be the victim if he is killed. On the other hand, if he is victorious and kills the enemy, he offers the enemy as a victim, a substitute for himself. The Goddess who decapitates the buffalo-demon has by implication offered herself for decapitation. Her warrior's sacrifice is what saves the world. Reṇukā is first sacrificed by her son in a sacrifice that would be more monstrous than self-sacrifice. She is then replaced by substitute victims, the Kṣatriyas who proved to be dangerous to the well-being of the cosmic order, dharma. The theme of the beheaded Goddess thus explained could account for the mysterious affinities that seem to draw the Goddess close to the demon that she kills.

M.Bi./g.h.

Abbreviation

MBh *Mahābhārata* (Citrashala Press, Bombay)

Vāmana, the Dwarf

Vāmana, the dwarf, is one of the incarnations of Viṣṇu. The *Śatapatha Brāhmaṇa* (1.2.5.1–9) tells how the gods, conquered by the *asuras,* try to obtain a share of the earth that the *asuras* are apportioning among themselves. They go to see the *asuras,* placing Viṣṇu at their head, Viṣṇu who is the sacrifice. But Viṣṇu is a dwarf. When they ask the *asuras* for a share of the world, the *asuras* grant them a plot as large as Viṣṇu can cover with his body. The gods accept and with the appropriate ritual, of which Viṣṇu is the center, they obtain the entire earth. Several times elsewhere, reference is made to the three strides taken by Viṣṇu to open the space where Indra is supposed to reign. These two themes together form the classic myth of the dwarf. Curiously, the treatises on iconography retain the original duality of the myth using the name of Vāmana for the dwarf who tricks King Bali with his small size and Trivikrama ("he of the three strides") for the same dwarf when he assumes a gigantic size and measures the universe with his three steps.

The *Rāmāyaṇa* (1.31.4–20) gives a well-developed version of the classic myth: Bali, the king of the *asuras,* has made himself master of the three worlds in place of Indra. He makes a sacrifice. The gods, led by Indra, come to see Viṣṇu and ask him to take advantage of this golden opportunity, in which Bali is disposed to make gifts to all who present themselves to him. Viṣṇu becomes incarnate in the womb of Aditi (thus becoming Indra's younger brother, who will serve his older brother), and is born in the form of a dwarf who is a Brahmanical student equipped with an umbrella and a water jug. He appears before Bali, who grants him an amount of land equivalent to three strides. Viṣṇu then becomes master of the three worlds with his three strides, confines Bali to the kingdom of hell, and returns sovereign power over the three worlds to Indra.

The *Bhāgavata Purāṇa* (8.15–23) clearly states that Bali was made invincible by the Brahmans of the family of Bhṛgu, notably his tutor and chaplain Śukrācārya, who revived him after Indra had killed him. The same chaplain watches over Bali and wants to prevent him from giving in to the apparently modest request of the dwarf who presents himself to him, for he recognizes Viṣṇu in him and sees through his scheme. The pious Bali feels guilty of a grievous error: by keeping the promise he made to the dwarf, he disobeys his tutor and grants the three strides worth of land. Śukrācārya therefore curses him: he will quickly lose his prosperity. Indeed, although all the good omens increase, Viṣṇu grows and grows. In one stride he covers the earth and the atmosphere. With a second step he covers the sky, and with a third stride he steps beyond the upper spheres of the universe and finds no place to put his foot down. Bali, cursed by Śukra for wanting to keep his promise, is now reproached by Viṣṇu for not being able to keep it: Viṣṇu does not know where to take his third step and condemns Bali to rule in hell. But Bali, full of devotion, offers his head for Viṣṇu to put his foot on, a sign of complete submission. The deposed king thus receives the promise that he will be reborn as Indra in a future age of the world. For the moment, Indra resumes his celestial sovereignty.

The reuse of a Vedic theme as an avatar myth is easy. All the added details (the character of the king of the *asuras* and his tutor, the resurrection of Bali through the power of his tutor) are expected. The ambivalence of the *asura* is more interesting, especially as it appears in the *Bhāgavata Purāṇa:* of course he is guilty of dethroning Indra, but he tries to keep his word against the will of his tutor, which is a virtue peculiar to ascetics and the perfected ones, and his ultimate submission to Viṣṇu makes him a *bhakta,* a devotee who deserves to be reborn as Indra one day. This ambiguity in the myth is a live issue today: in Kerala, Bali is considered the king of the Golden Age, and each year they celebrate his brief return to earth from the netherworld in which Viṣṇu keeps him confined. Bali is also the grandson of Prahlāda, the *asura bhakta* of the myth of Narasiṃha. It is clear that he is no demon per se, for an *asura* may be a good *asura* if he submits to the will of Viṣṇu and to the order of the world to which he is guarantor, to the point where he can imagine "legally" leaving his inferior position of *asura* one day and becoming a *deva.* Bali is put in a situation such that his piety makes him commit two faults in spite of himself: disobeying his tutor and failing to keep his promise to Viṣṇu. But his attitude of perfect humility redeems him. He will expiate his faults, but he will also have his reward. The order of the world will be safe and Viṣṇu will not have failed in any way in his job of avatar.

In the myth of Narasiṃha, the abusive *asura* and the devout *asura* are two antagonistic characters, father and son. These two characters here form a single figure, who must be connected with the Kerala myth of Bali, king of the Golden Age. What surfaces in the myth is a fact peculiar to Hinduism that has been underestimated: quite often in India the names of places indicate that the land belongs to the local *asura,* whom the avatar deity brings under subjection, generally by killing him and granting him salvation at the moment of his death. This situation is explicit in an indefinite number of local myths that all resort to the theme of the avatar who kills the *asura.* What is expressed in this way is the opposition, basic to Hindu society, between the so-called pure castes, Brahman and others, and impure castes, inferior to the pure castes, which include the royal caste or the dominant local caste. Even if in certain cases the dominant caste adopts the vegetarianism of the Brahmans (it may occasionally be made up of Brahmans, but this is not the situation treated by the theory), the general schema stands. Hindu thought knows that this world cannot exist without resorting to impure violence, which is symbolized by the meat diet (Bali's name means "the strong one"). It is the duty of the king to resort to force, and the "impurity" of his position is made tolerable by subordinating it, in status, to the purity of the priestly castes of the Brahmans. The impure castes play the role of *asuras* on earth, while the Brahmans represent the *devas.* Viṣṇu is always on the side of the Brahmans and purity, even when he descends to punish the wicked and put the *asuras* back in their place. He is the model of the good king devoted to the Brahmans, who maintains the cosmic order against the wicked *asura* kings. India has never had any illusions: the strongest will always be tempted to rise out of their subordinate position and assert their strength. Hence the abundance of local myths in which the *asura* is master of the earth, but in which he is forced to bow before his superiors, the heavenly gods and their eminent master, Viṣṇu. One might almost reconstruct the actual social hierarchy from this myth.

M.Bi./g.h.

The Childhood and Adulthood of Kṛṣṇa

Paradoxical as it may seem, the superabundant classical and modern Hindu literature dealing with Kṛṣṇa is deceptive from a mythological point of view. It is as if bhakti in its most affective dimension had erased the fundamental structure of the myth in order to multiply and juxtapose occasions to wax ecstatic over the marvelous child and the untiring slayer of *asuras;* or better still, as if it had to be proved that Kṛṣṇa indeed became an avatar by accumulating superhuman exploits. At best, he is made into a kind of professional knight-errant. There are, however, an appreciable number of *asuras* whose names include a reference to Kāla, Time, the fundamental element of the myth of the avatar, or to the Earth, which the *asura* oppresses. Since the symbolism operates on the second or third level, one has the impression that there is nothing but a series of tales, and that dharma is nothing but the distant horizon of wonders wrought by this Indian Don Quixote. We may compare this to the grandiose claims made by certain apocryphal gospels of the first centuries of Christianity.

This observation is in a way connected with a problem raised by European Indology, but one that must be recognized as strictly a product of Western scholarship of the last century: in view of what the texts presented, they asked, how many different characters had contributed to the formation of the god Kṛṣṇa? Not a single Hindu would accept such atomization, even if it were only a dichotomy. Kṛṣṇa is Kṛṣṇa, and he could not be a god of pastoral tribes (to account for the fact that Kṛṣṇa was raised among the cowherds) telescoped together with a Kṣatriya hero (the Kṛṣṇa who is the friend of Arjuna in the MBh), and then enlarged somehow to the dimension of an avatar of Viṣṇu. Whatever the apparent disparity of these characters may be for us, it is necessary to keep them together and to see how they are organized from the Hindu point of view as one and the same god, the avatar of Viṣṇu. Not only is the historical amalgam of disparate characters highly unlikely, but the texts do not favor such an amalgam: Kṛṣṇa the cowherd is just as much, if not more, an avatar of Viṣṇu as is the epic Kṣatriya (see below). And meanwhile, Western scholarship (except for a few latecomers) completely rejected the historical value of the epic, which it saw as only a myth.

Rather than relating minutely all the exploits of Kṛṣṇa, which after all vary with the texts, we will attempt to discover how the two essential parts of his "biography" fit logically together: on the one hand his birth and youth, and on the other his adulthood and his participation in the adventures of the Pāṇḍavas. We will principally consider the MBh and the three great texts of nonsectarian Vaiṣṇava bhakti: the *Harivaṃśa* (section 2), regarded as an appendix of the MBh; the *Viṣṇu Purāṇa* (5); and the *Bhāgavata Purāṇa* (10). The MBh tells how Kṛṣṇa died but does not deal with his birth. The *Harivaṃśa* tells how he was born but fails to say

Kṛṣṇa as cowherd, avatar of Viṣṇu. Theophany of Kṛṣṇa on the mountain. Manuscript of the *Bhāgavata Purāṇa,* Pahari School, ca. 1750. New Delhi, National Museum. Photo Catherine Jarrige.

how he died, integrating from the MBh only the axial episode of the murder of Kaṃsa and the confrontation with Jarāsandha, while the *Bhāgavata Purāṇa* follows him from his birth to his death, devoting much space in his biography to his relationship with the Pāṇḍavas. It is not a matter of reconciling these data, nor even of bringing out the fundamental structure of *one* myth of the avatar, because it is precisely the structure that happens to be blurred, albeit presupposed, by the accidents of literary history—the creation of the MBh. Rather, it is a matter of retracing the steps taken by the mythographers who seem to have used a theme of the avatar to make something else out of it. Obviously this reconstitution remains largely hypothetical; its sole merit is to introduce a little intelligibility into an otherwise confusing overall picture.

One must start from the MBh, without necessarily putting it chronologically before the HV; on the contrary, the logical necessity of a myth of Kṛṣṇa's birth and youth will visibly emerge out of the epic narration. It matters little when the myth took on a literary form if its idea belongs to the epic itself.

Unlike the *Rāmāyaṇa,* the MBh centers its narrative not on the avatar but on the character of the ideal earthly king, who must imitate the avatar and be tied to him by a devotion that goes as far as ontological identity. The plot in its quasi entirety must thus be reserved for Arjuna (and his brothers), while keeping the rank of avatar unequivocally for Kṛṣṇa. Kṛṣṇa is a Kṣatriya of the same "lunar" dynasty as the Pāṇḍavas; he even belongs to the older branch of this dynasty, which assures him of a superiority over the Pāṇḍavas; but because of a curse the older branch, going back to Yadu, the elder son of Yayāti, was condemned never to reign. This explains why Kṛṣṇa is not a king in the epic, not even in his own city of Dvārakā, where King Ugrasena owes his power to him, and why the "universal" royal functions are reserved for the Pāṇḍavas, descendants of the youngest son of Yayāti, whose father enthroned him as his successor.

None of this alters the fact that from one end of the epic to the other, Kṛṣṇa—flanked by his older brother Balarāma, the incarnation of Śeṣa—affirms that he is, and is recognized as, the avatar of Viṣṇu, as well as the incarnation of the *ṛṣi* Nārāyaṇa. Since Balarāma is the earthly incarnation of the serpent Śeṣa, his relationship to Kṛṣṇa is analogous to the relationship between Bhīma and Arjuna. Like the avatar, the king upholds (hence the relation of younger to elder) the values of this world, the values of dharma and its indispensable accessories, *artha* and *kāma,* what could be called the values of life (Bhīma is the son of Vāyu, the wind, and also the breath of life). The assertion of Kṛṣṇa as avatar is, however, set more on the level of discourse (the *Bhagavad Gītā* is the best example of this) than in the sphere of action. There is only one minor exception: during the war of extermination that the opposed cousins wage on one another, the peacetime dharma is more than once set amiss by the heroes of the camp of dharma themselves. They have to kill Bhīṣma, the common ancestor; Droṇa, their tutor, whose extreme virtue they recognize; and their parallel cousins, who, despite being demons incarnate, are no less their brothers. They will even discover after the battle that they have killed Karṇa, their half-brother. Arjuna has difficulty accepting this situation, whence his name of Bībhatsu, "he who is loath"; the *Bhagavad Gītā* is the teaching of Kṛṣṇa, who justifies the murders perpetrated on the battlefield for the triumph of dharma. In our terms this would be a case of the means justifying the end. India prefers to speak of "dharma for hard times"—*āpad-dharma.* But it is significant that all the responsibilities are thus borne by the avatar himself by virtue of his qualifications, since in the *Gītā* he offers himself explicitly as a model to follow. He is not the "ideologue" of the camp of dharma; he is its ideology incarnate and the assurance of its victory. It is because of him that the epic drama takes its form, and that one recognizes in the deeds of the Pāṇḍavas, and particularly of Arjuna, the structure of an avatar myth. In a serious crisis the extent of the royal power is laid bare, revealing what is most exorbitant about it. Hindu mythic thought could not find a better symbol of this situation than the time of the avatar. At the same time, making Kṛṣṇa Arjuna's charioteer throughout the battle is an inspired invention. There were not many ways of expressing the dual position of servant (of the good of the worlds) and leader (of the worlds), which is simultaneously the dual position of the avatar and the king.

The role of the supreme master—who is at the same time on the narrative level the one who pulls the puppet-strings—allows Kṛṣṇa a certain inactivity, or at least a certain distance from the main action. There one can see at every moment his profound nature as a yogi, the essential dimension of the avatar, since it excludes any striving for the sake of personal interest and substitutes for it the sole pursuit of the "good of the world": every time that Kṛṣṇa's presence or help is suddenly required he seems to be found asleep on his bed. Clearly, Kṛṣṇa's bed and slumber are reminders of Nārāyaṇa's yogic sleep on Śeṣa and the ocean of the cosmic flood. The dichotomy that the MBh sets up between the avatar and the king rather paradoxically makes the yogic dimension all the more evident, since Kṛṣṇa preaches a yoga of action. Nor does he disdain to act at critical moments like a deus ex machina, as the supreme god that he really is: hence the resurrection of the stillborn child of Uttarā, bearer of all the hope of the lunar dynasty.

Thus the MBh is the text that best makes it possible to situate the character in all his breadth and purity of lineage, with relative discretion as to the display of his power. It is also the only text to make systematic use of the tradition according to which Arjuna and Kṛṣṇa are incarnations of the two *ṛṣis* Nara and Nārāyaṇa and not only the descents of

Dance of Kṛṣṇa and the Gopīs. Manuscript of the *Bhāgavata Purāṇa,* Kulu school, ca. 1794, Banaras, Bhavat Kala Bhavan. Photo Catherine Jarrige.

Indra and Viṣṇu. This invention is connected with the necessity to express the intimate link between the king and the avatar. Beyond this, the epic does not allow us to sketch a biography of Kṛṣṇa. His interventions are sporadic but situated at the critical moments of the narrative, such as the eighteen-day battle. We learn that he had a bone to pick with Śiśupāla, notably over his wife Rukminī, which allows him to kill Śiśupāla, the reincarnation of Hiraṇyakaśipu and of Rāvaṇa, who refuses to give him precedence at the time of Yudhiṣṭhira's royal consecration. Śiśupāla is, like the Pāṇḍavas, his cross-cousin, but he represents the attitude that is the complement to bhakti, perfect hatred, which wins salvation for him when Kṛṣṇa kills him. It is also known that his absence from the scene of the game of dice was motivated by his struggle against the incarnate *asura* Śālva, king of Saubha. Śālva was said to be the husband that Ambā had chosen for herself. Ambā, the eldest daughter of the king of Kāśī, refused to marry Vicitravīrya, Bhīṣma's half-brother, on whose behalf Bhīṣma had abducted her. One of the traits of the "avataric" actions of Kṛṣṇa appears here: the actions often form a counterpoint to the episodes of the epic, more or less symbolic depending on the case.

But it is in connection with the murder of Kaṃsa (perpetrated by Kṛṣṇa and reported by him) and the murder of Jarāsandha (which he left to Bhīma) that his role of avatar seems to be asserted in action. Kṛṣṇa killed Kaṃsa, the king of the Bhojas at Mathurā and his maternal uncle, who had been abandoned by his kinsmen. Kṛṣṇa himself tells of this murder and proposes his action as a model for the sages of the court of Dhṛtarāṣṭra, notably Bhīṣma and Droṇa, who were supposed to have sacrificed Duryodhana in order to avoid a war. When Jarāsandha, the father-in-law of Kaṃsa and the king of the Magadhas, attacked Mathurā to avenge the death of his son-in-law, Kṛṣṇa preferred to refuse to fight with him and to transfer the entire population of Mathurā, with its king Ugrasena (the father of Kaṃsa and usurper of Kaṃsa's throne), to Dvārakā, on the coast of Saurāṣṭra. This event is surely of great importance. For one thing, at that point Kṛṣṇa leaves Mathurā, situated in the middle of Madhya-deśa, the land of the Bhāratas, to transfer his residence to the outer limits of the earth, to a city whose name implies that it is an "entrance," a "gate": but a gate to what? The land of the Bhāratas that eluded the dharmic princes and needs to be reconquered? The gate of salvation? But this comes to the same thing. We must bear in mind that one never enters a place through the gate to attack it, but through "what is not the gate"—*advāra*. This supplies all the symbolic weight of the name of Kṛṣṇa's residence, which is already his own when he appears in the MBh.

On the other hand, when Yudhiṣṭhira wants to receive the royal consecration, Kṛṣṇa tells him that he must first get rid of Jarāsandha, whom he himself cannot kill. What follows is an extraordinary nocturnal expedition of three men, Kṛṣṇa, Arjuna, and Bhīma, who take the form of false Brahmans to enter through "what is not the gate," into the capital of Jarāsandha. Kṛṣṇa already emerges as the leader. He has in him the *nīti*, the art of leadership, of governing (the charioteer is the *netṛ*, from the same root), whereas he attributes victory to Arjuna and force to Bhīma. It is Bhīma who is charged with liquidating Jarāsandha, the enemy of the kings and the devotee of Rudra Paśupati. Has he not begun to collect in this prison kings whom he means to sacrifice to Paśupati when he has collected a hundred of them? The name Jarāsandha, which a myth of birth accounts for, evokes the decline of the world (*jarā* means "old age"). He is the one who has made a pact with the decline, or who has vowed the decline of the world, for the sacrifice of the one hundred kings expresses a totality that would leave the world kingless, and thus headless and destined for death. It is logical that Bhīma, the son of the breath of life, is charged with carrying out the sacrifice. In place of the hundred kings Bhīma sacrifices Jarāsandha, who is of course the incarnation of an *asura*. By murdering Jarāsandha, Bhīma gives the earth a renewal of life that makes possible the royal consecration of Yudhiṣṭhira. But when one learns that Kaṃsa is only the incarnation of the *asura* Kālanemi—a mythic variant on the well-known expression *kālacakra*, "the wheel of time"—one thinks of the way that the stage of the MBh is set at the junction of the two worst yugas, the Dvāpara and the Kali, in which two of the protagonists are the incarnations of the *asuras* Kali and Dvāpara. This new contrapuntal play in the narrative is now duplicated: Kṛṣṇa is the agent in the murder of Kaṃsa, and he fully assumes his role of avatar by allowing the world to overcome the crisis that threatened its existence (the wheel of time always has an inauspicious connotation). It is this model that he proposes to the epic heroes. In the murder of Jarāsandha, whom he voluntarily abandoned because of his concern for Bhīma and Arjuna, he transfers his responsibilities to the Pāṇḍavas.

In other words, in order for Kṛṣṇa to be able to emerge fully as an avatar, he must at some time justify the incarnation through his acts. By making earthly heroes the protagonists of the action, the epic must project back into Kṛṣṇa's past his active role of avatar, which seems to culminate in the murder of Kaṃsa. The murder of Kaṃsa and by correlation the story of Kṛṣṇa's childhood, which Kaṃsa entirely decreed, thus become logical parts of the horizon of the MBh, and it is necessary to evoke them for the credibility of the avatar. In this way, the epic is laden with the myth of Kṛṣṇa's birth and childhood, but does not deal with it except in passing. This is why the HV, which is the first text to furnish the myth, appears as the complement of the MBh.

We will not dwell on the mythical prehistory of Kṛṣṇa in the HV, but it is interesting that before his descent among men, he battled with the *asura* Kālanemi on behalf of the gods, in the combat known as the combat of Tārakā (more precisely, "made of Tārakā"—of "her who gives deliverance"). So there is a heavenly counterpart to the battle between Kaṃsa (Kālanemi) and Kṛṣṇa. Immediately after the victory of Viṣṇu over Kālanemi, which is thus a duplication, the earth comes to Brahmā and in the presence of all the gods complains of the burden crushing her; here the myth of the avatar type takes shape. Brahmā asks Viṣṇu to become incarnate, and in an innovation full of insights, Viṣṇu now asks for the collaboration of the Goddess, who, we learn, is merely his *yoga-nidrā*, his yogic sleep. Within Viṣṇu, she keeps him asleep with the world reabsorbed in him; outside of him, she becomes Devī, Māyā ("Divine Illusion"), Līlā ("Divine Play" in creation), in short all the feminine energy of the deity, which is the web of the life of the world. Viṣṇu will be content to descend into the womb of Devakī, the sister of Kaṃsa, but all the manipulations are left to the care of the Goddess, including her own "sacrifice."

Meanwhile, on earth, Nārada, the "busybody" of the gods, informs Kaṃsa that his sister's eighth child will kill him. Kaṃsa therefore decides to place Devakī and her husband Vāsudeva under close guard. As an added precaution, he himself takes charge of killing the newborn babies one by one. For the first six, the solution is simple. Viṣṇu goes to get six *asuras* who are waiting in hell in the form of six "embryos." These are the six sons of Kālanemi himself, so the father (Kaṃsa) will kill his own children by killing the six firstborn children of Devakī. They owe their unfortunate fate to the curse of Hiraṇyakaśipu, and the solution is in the end to their benefit, for they will thus be quickly delivered from the curse and will be able to enjoy in peace the protection that they have obtained from Brahmā. The case of the seventh embryo is more complicated. At the end of the seventh month of pregnancy, the Goddess is charged with transferring the embryo carried by Devakī into the womb of Rohiṇī, another wife of Vāsudeva, whom Kaṃsa does not distrust. This embryo will become Balarāma, also known as Saṅkarṣaṇa. As for the eighth, who is the incarnation of Viṣṇu, the Goddess must play an even more delicate role for him. When he descends into the womb of Devakī, she is to "descend" into the womb of Yaśodā, the wife of the cowherd Nanda, who lives at Gokula, near Mathurā, on the Yamunā River. Both of them will be born at the same time (at night), and Vāsudeva, duly warned, is to transport his newborn son immediately to Gokula and substitute him secretly for the daughter of Yaśodā, whom he will bring back to Mathurā. The next day, Kaṃsa learns the news of the birth of the eighth child and, despite its sex, seizes it and smashes it to death on a rock (*śaila:* we know that Pārvatī, "the daughter of Parvata, the mountain," is also called Śailajā, one of the synonyms of *Pārvatī*). The Goddess then escapes into the air, announcing to Kaṃsa that his murderer is already born. Kaṃsa will look for him in vain, for he cannot suspect that he is the alleged son of Nanda and Yaśodā (*yaśo-dā*, "giver of glory," is a name that echoes *śrī* or *lakṣmī*, as well as *rādhā* and *rukmiṇī*).

Balarāma, the son of Rohiṇī, will also be entrusted to Nanda to be raised with Kṛṣṇa ("the black"), and Vasudeva himself will take charge of the rites that mark the birth and childhood of his two sons; this is an important detail, for it confirms their Kṣatriya nature. But they are raised at the *vraja*, the grounds of the herdsmen, among cowherds, like the children of cowherds. Nanda and Yaśodā believe that Kṛṣṇa is their son. Of course Balarāma, but especially Kṛṣṇa, performs all sorts of marvelous feats that we will not describe in detail now, and they kill their first *asuras*, who are sent by Kaṃsa or are enemies of the cows that they bring to graze in the forest. Kṛṣṇa is the favorite of the cowherd women, the *gopīs*, who have maternal feelings for him until the child has grown sufficiently for maternal love to turn into plain love. Rādhā, the favorite *gopī,* the lover of Kṛṣṇa, will appear much later in Kṛṣṇa literature.

The importance of the theme of the *gopīs* is one of the elements that could contribute to a digression from the avatar myth if one were to forget that the avatar only forms a unity with the god of bhakti, and that he is often the preferred form in which devotees worship him. In fact, bhakti recounts a certain number of sentiments that the *bhakta* can have for his god and that assume that he has a human form. Among these, maternal love in particular shows the extraordinary development of the myth and iconography of the childhood of Kṛṣṇa: thus they speak of Bāla-Kṛṣṇa, "the child Kṛṣṇa" (the one who plays with a butterball stolen from his mother, a butterball that symbolizes the earth that has become the substance of the oblation). But this is also a theme that runs through all of Hindu bhakti: there is a Bāla-Subrahmaṇya, a Bāla-Dattātreya, a Baṭuka-Bhairava ("little Bhairava"), in which childhood also obviously implies sexual abstinence. The love between two lovers is another such sentiment, and this produces the *gopīs* of the *rāsa-līlā,* "the game made of *rasa*" (or of the *rāsa-maṇḍala,* "the circle made of *rasa*"), in which each *gopī,* in love with Kṛṣṇa, thinks that she has Kṛṣṇa all to herself: the play of god in his creation and with his creatures. But hatred is also one of the recounted sentiments, which makes possible the salvation of Śiśupāla, who is assured definitive deliverance after his decapitation by Kṛṣṇa in the MBh.

However, the major problem raised by Western critics, although it has never troubled Hindu consciousness, is the transformation of Kṛṣṇa and his brother into cowherds. It is true that this is not a simple episode of transition, since it is as cowherds that the two brothers are called to Mathurā by the suspicious Kaṃsa. After their exploits among the cowherds, he wants to match them against adversaries of his choice who can kill them. The test rebounds to embarrass him and then destroy him. Kṛṣṇa and Balarāma kill their adversaries and then Kaṃsa himself. They are recognized as the Kṣatriyas that they never stopped being, and Kṛṣṇa is offered the kingship of Mathurā, which he refuses in order to put his maternal great-uncle Ugrasena back on the throne. It is then that the two brothers become initiated as warriors and bring the son of their guru back to life after he has been killed by the sea monster Pañcajana ("the five nations"); this favor serves as their traditional tuition gift to their teacher. Kṛṣṇa, moreover, wins the famed Pāñcajanya conch shell, which he generally carries in his upper left hand (when he is represented with four arms) and which is a symbol of the group of peoples who live under the same Brahmanic dharma. A little later the threat of Jarāsandha takes form. His troops are repulsed several times, but he is invincible. The people abandon Mathurā for the first time, moving toward the south under the leadership of Paraśurāma. Kṛṣṇa and Balarāma receive Viṣṇu's weapons and a mission to ensure the victory of the gods. When Jarāsandha appears he is defeated and takes flight. But after a few turns of fortune in which there is talk of Rukmiṇī and Śiśupāla—Kṛṣṇa finally carries off Rukmiṇī (an incarnation of Śrī) after he is installed in Dvārakā—Kṛṣṇa and Balarāma return to Mathurā and decide to take shelter from Jarāsandha in Dvārakā, on the seashore (note that Paraśurāma had been exiled to the end of the earth, that is, to the seashore, when his role of avatar had come to an end). The moment when Kṛṣṇa emigrates to Dvārakā marks both a farewell to the world of the cowherds of his childhood and in a way a farewell to his active role as avatar: he hands over the power to the Pāṇḍavas.

The child Kṛṣṇa. Detail of a shrine column at Akkiripalli (Andhra Pradesh). Photo M. Biardeau.

This may explain the repetitious character of the episodes that constitute the second part of Kṛṣṇa's biography in the HV. One *asura* succeeds another. Not that the episodes are without meaning; for example, the intervention of Śiva and the Goddess in the fight against Bāṇāsura is interesting in more than one respect, and one can hear echoes of the MBh in it. Similarly, the fight against Narakāsura recalls that in the epic Karṇa is regarded as an incarnation of that Naraka, and so forth. But the accumulation of motifs that brings nothing new expresses an unbridling of the mythical imagination as it pursues its relentless course. The avatar myth loses in purity of line what it gains in proliferation of motifs. It is the *bhakta*'s love that is at work rather than his intelligence.

To return to the central problem, the child Kṛṣṇa is a clandestine avatar. He must therefore wear a kind of disguise that, like the disguises of the Pāṇḍavas during their year of clandestine life with King Virāṭa, must simultaneously hide and reveal his true nature. He is disguised as a cowherd, and one may recall the disguise of a cowherd that is worn by the last of the Pāṇḍavas, Sahadeva, the expert in *nīti,* in the MBh. Is this so strange and unexpected when we know the symbolic role of the cow in the scheme of Brahmanic values? In the MBh, Arjuna would rather violate an agreement made with his brothers than ignore the call for help from a Brahman whose cow was stolen. Karṇa is cursed by a Brahman for having killed his cow entirely by accident, a sure sign that he is not worthy of royalty. When one lists all that the avatar and the good king are supposed to protect, the cow is always there next to the Brahman and dharma, to the point that there is an expression *go-brāhmaṇa* that designates either Brahmans and cows as an inseparable whole, or Brahmans who are characterized by their cows (as opposed to other castes which seek to set themselves apart from Brahmans, but claim their status). Starting with the Vedic hymns, the epithet *go-pati,* "master of cows," characterizes Indra especially and is connected with his royal status, whereas *go-pa* designates any protector and not only a cowherd. The king as master of cows is also their protector, the one who can give them to the Brahmans. If one holds that the avatar is the image of the ideal king, both of them must be protectors of cows, and their role becomes sufficiently defined by this symbol.

But why is Kṛṣṇa a clandestine avatar? Why this recourse to a disguise? Here is where the logical link with the MBh appears to be essential. For one thing, Kṛṣṇa is not supposed to be king, in order to leave this function to another, but he has to be a Kṣatriya in order to be a valid model for the king. Note that the epic reinforces the equal status of Kṛṣṇa and Arjuna through bonds of kinship. With this as a starting point, a framework must be established that will permit the avatar to prove his nature, to kill an *asura* who endangers the world. But the secrecy imposed on Kṛṣṇa in his disguise as a cowherd answers to yet another necessity, the source of which is also found in the epic: in order to accede to an incontestable kingship, the Pāṇḍavas must suffer an exile in the forest, a symbol of renunciation, and a period of living incognito, conceived as a preparatory consecration for the sacrifice of war. The childhood of Kṛṣṇa among the cowherds is the symbolic echo of this dual necessity. The cows of the *vraja* graze in the forest, and the two brothers cleanse the forest of its *asuras* for the good of the cows and their guardians, just as Bhīma kills several *rākṣasas* during his exile (among them the *asura* Baka, during the first exile, to save a family of Brahmans). The two brothers strike camp when Kṛṣṇa thinks they should, to find a forest with richer pasturage; to instigate this move, he produces wolves from his body to cause damage and create panic among the cowherds—a curious echo of a world crisis, in which one must destroy in order to start over again. Soon after this migration, Kṛṣṇa imposes his superiority upon Indra. The prodigal son is thus simultaneously hidden, humble, and close to the cowherds whose life he shares, but he is orchestrating the game. His life unfolds for the most part in the forest, the place where the cows pasture; in a parallel development, when Duryodhana wants to gloat over the sight of the Pāṇḍavas condemned to an ascetic life in the forest, he uses the pretext of checking on his father's herds nearby. Finally, since the period of childhood is connected with sexual abstinence, Kṛṣṇa lives at Gokula as a young *brahmacārin* (a Brahmanic student sworn to absolute chastity). He marries Rukmiṇī—and a few others—only at Dvārakā. In brief, the childhood of Kṛṣṇa seems to be a brilliant invention that can respond to all aspects of the problem: it paves the way for Kaṃsa's murder, which is the culmination of his active role as avatar. Although Kaṃsa was duly warned about what awaited him, this is because Kṛṣṇa must undergo both a period of ascetic life and a period in hiding, to symbolize both the dimension of renunciation and the preparatory consecration for the sacrifice that consists in the murder of Kaṃsa.

Thus the biography of Kṛṣṇa is made up of two or even three rather heterogeneous parts, of which the first two at least fit together perfectly: the child Kṛṣṇa grows up among

Kṛṣṇa and Rādhā. Manuscript of the *Gītagovinda* of Manaku, 1730. Lahore, Pakistan, Central Museum. Photo Catherine Jarrige.

the cowherds until the day when he asserts himself as avatar by killing Kaṃsa. The Kṛṣṇa of the MBh, detached from his role as savior of the world, shows the ideal king how to become a savior; he continues to pull the strings offstage, since he is still the supreme god incarnate, who gives victory to the defender of dharma. Finally, the biography of Kṛṣṇa at Dvārakā, which the HV attempts to construct in parallel to the events in the MBh but without any major connection between them, is less successful, because it is largely superfluous. From one end of his myth to the other Kṛṣṇa is indeed the avatar of Viṣṇu, one and the same person, conceived first for the role that he plays in the epic.

One can cite as an example of the profound unity of the three parts of the life of Kṛṣṇa the three episodes that describe his relationship with Indra. In the myth of childhood, Kṛṣṇa teaches the cowherds to substitute for the sacrifice to Indra the sacrifice to cows, to the mountain, and to Brahmans. He asserts that he is identical with the mountain, which accounts perfectly for his ritual role as the god who is sovereign over the territory. The unhappy Indra sends cascades of water down on Mount Govardhana ("the one that makes the cows thrive") and upon the cowherds and their herds. Kṛṣṇa then lifts up the mountain with his finger to give shelter to man and beast. Indra is forced to admit defeat and to recognize that the supremacy of Kṛṣṇa is for the good of the worlds. We know that the avatar's mission is to deliver the gods from the *asuras,* who by definition are stronger than the gods. One of the characteristics that qualifies him as an avatar is his capacity to defeat "even Indra," which makes him at least the equal of the *asuras.*

The same theme appears in the epic. This time it is actually Arjuna who, while preparing for his role as a king who in fact is another avatar, braves Indra's anger together with Kṛṣṇa to please Agni, the sacrificial fire, and to allow him to burn the Khāṇḍava forest where a few of Indra's friends live. In the epic this episode is referred to frequently to show that Arjuna can defeat Indra. But he defeated Indra only in association *with Kṛṣṇa.* And Indra, Arjuna's father, congratulates both heroes when they succeed, but the action is attributed to Arjuna rather than to the avatar. Finally, during Kṛṣṇa's stay in Dvārakā, he has his celebrated confrontation with Indra for possession of the *pārijāta,* a tree in Indra's heaven that assures him prosperity and grants him all he desires. Kṛṣṇa's favorite wife, Satyabhāmā, wants to have the tree, which is the property of Indra's wife, Śacī. Indra refuses to give it up and the two gods fight. Indra is clearly beaten, and the *pārijāta* will remain on earth for one year, according to some versions, or for as long as Kṛṣṇa lives, according to others. Underlying this episode is the rivalry between Rukmiṇī and Satyabhāmā, Kṛṣṇa's two principal wives, and Satyabhāmā's jealousy of Rukmiṇī, to whom Nārada brought a flower of the *pārijāta* from heaven. Whatever may be the symbolism associated with the two wives (Rukmiṇī is Śrī) and with the *pārijatā,* this episode cannot be said to be necessary. Kṛṣṇa has already done the work of an avatar; he no longer needs to prove his superiority over Indra, and the *pārijāta* will continue to belong to Śacī. The theme here thus seems simultaneously to undergo a kind of degradation and to become redundant.

M.Bi./g.h.

BIBLIOGRAPHY

G. DUMÉZIL, *Mythe et épopée* 1: *L'idéologie des trois fonctions dans les épopées des peuples indo-européens* (Paris 1968); *Mythe et épopée* 2: *Types épiques indo-européens—un héros, un sorcier, un roi* (Paris 1971). A. HILTEBEITEL, *The Ritual of Battle: Krishna in the Mahābhārata* (Ithaca 1976). H. H. WILSON, trans., *The Vishnu Purana: A System of Hindu Mythology and Tradition* (London 1840; reprint, Calcutta 1961). J. M. SANYAL, trans., *The Srimad-Bhagavatam,* 5 vols. (Calcutta, n.d.). M. A. LANGLOIS, trans., *Harivansa ou histoire de la famille de Hari,* 2 vols. (Paris 1834–35).

Abbreviations

MBh *Mahābhārata*
HV *Harivaṃśa*

Gaṇapati

Purāṇic mythology makes Gaṇapati the brother of Skanda, since Śiva and Pārvatī are his parents and the two gods are symmetrically arranged on each side of the sanctuary in a number of temples of Śiva or the Goddess. But their symmetry and kinship should not create an illusion: although they are two, they are not identical, but together they form a significant whole.

When Gaṇapati (also called Gaṇeśa) appears alone in one of the innumerable sanctuaries that are consecrated to him throughout India, he is not worshiped on the same level as Skanda-Subrahmaṇya in the South. He is only *gaṇa-pati* (or *gaṇa-īśa*), commander of Śiva's *gaṇas,* while his brother is *devasenā-pati,* commander of the armies of the gods, which is unquestionably a nobler, more royal status. On the other hand, Gaṇapati may be compared with Hanumān, the god who covers all of North India and much of the Deccan with his sanctuaries. Both of them are often represented very crudely, on a prominent rock in which the figure is barely outlined and invariably smeared with a layer of red lead: this last detail always seems to symbolize the function of a guardian in the service of a superior and royal deity or of a transcendent order, dharma. This is also what the myths of the birth of Gaṇapati indicate, myths essentially Purāṇic and relatively late.

So popular a god must have an abundant mythology, the essential point of which concerns his birth and his elephant head. This will be presented here only synthetically, since an abundance of narrative is not necessarily the sign of a richer mythology. The most significant versions of his birth can be roughly divided into two groups: those in which he is born from Śiva and those in which he is born from Pārvatī, for his birth is no more "normal" than Skanda's. The versions in which he has both Śiva as father and Pārvatī as mother are the least interesting, for they give a poorer account of the god's peculiarities.

When Śiva creates Gaṇapati, it is always at the request of the gods and *ṛṣis* who want a distinction to be made between good and evil; not only must the success of auspicious enterprises and the failure of evil ones be assured, but the wicked must be prevented from performing meritorious actions and the good must be protected and guided in pious actions, a challenge in which the *asuras* and the *devas* and the cause of dharma loom large. This is why Gaṇapati is also called Vināyaka, "the one who removes (obstacles)," and Vighneśvara, "lord of obstacles." The obstacles may be the work of those malicious and alarming *gaṇas* of Śiva's that Gaṇapati is responsible for controlling.

The son that Śiva emits from himself is handsome, like another self. He seduces all the women around him, which offends the ascetic disposition of Pārvatī: So she condemns him to have the head of an elephant and a large belly, in other words, to be ugly. There are other examples in Hindu myths of ugliness signifying "terrible." The fatherhood of Śiva, the ugliness inflicted by Pārvatī associates the god thus formed with the terrible *gaṇas* that he controls. These factors also seem to commit him to celibacy, but his own qualities are sometimes cast in the form of two wives—two abstractions without myth but significant in themselves: Buddhi: Wisdom, and Siddhi: Success. His vehicle, the rat, is associated with the same qualities.

In the versions in which Gaṇapati is born from Pārvatī, the Goddess sometimes wants to procure an absolutely trustworthy guardian for her door, and sometimes the gods and *ṛṣis* whom Śiva sends to her petition her to prevent the success of the wicked and to guarantee success for the good. In both instances, it is his function as guardian—of the Goddess, that is, of the Earth and the manifested Universe, or of dharma, the cosmic order: it is all one—that is imperative.

Here the versions diverge: according to the *Śiva-Purāṇa,* when Pārvatī decides to procure a reliable guardian for her door—in particular to avoid the untimely visits of her husband Śiva—she creates him from the secretions of her skin, that is, from her natural impurities. Vighneśvara (he is not yet *gaṇa-pati*) then assumes his functions and mounts guard at the door of his "mother," until the inevitable day when Śiva comes to see his wife when she is not receiving visitors—she is in her bath. Vighneśvara makes no exception: he blocks the door. Śiva wants to be received and instead receives several blows. Śiva then unleashes against him his *gaṇas,* but Vighneśvara subdues them. Viṣṇu and Subrahmaṇya try in their turn without result. Pārvatī emits two subordinate goddesses who come to the aid of her guardian. Viṣṇu finally resorts to his *māyā* (magic illusion) to create confusion on all sides, which enables Śiva to cut off Gaṇapati's head. Pārvatī, furious, sends a thousand goddesses to harass the gods and will let herself be appeased only if her son is resuscitated. Śiva sends the gods toward the north, ordering them to cut off the head of the first living being who appears, to replace Gaṇapati's head (Where had it gone?). It is an elephant that appears, with a single tusk: it is therefore an elephant's head with one tusk that is attached to the body of the Goddess's guardian, which proves satisfactory. She presents her son to Śiva: a reconciliation for the greatest triumph of cosmic order. Vighneśvara submits to Śiva, who makes him *gaṇa-pati.*

Several well-known themes appear in this account, to which so brief a summary does not do justice. First there is the "impure" origin of the god, from the secretions of the Goddess's skin, which recognizes the necessary participation of the impure in the order of the cosmos. This factor assigns Gaṇapati, at the start, to the class of inferior gods and those who are devoted to potentially polluting tasks. But the situation does not remain so simple: it is Śiva's unexpected visit that has induced the Goddess to create her guardian. The detail of the bath is revealing: there is no doubt that the

Gaṇapati. Private collection. Photo Dominique Champion.

Goddess here is the Creation, which according to an image that is well known but inverted by classical philosophy escapes from the sight of the Primordial Male, in which she risks destruction. The Goddess who does not want to be seen in her nakedness denies herself reunion with the world of release, affirms the value of this world, and desires its well-being. This suggests that Gaṇapati, as guardian of the Goddess, oversees *bhukti,* the auspicious progress of earthly affairs, rather than *mukti,* deliverance.

The battle with Śiva, its consequences, Viṣṇu's decisive intervention, and the decapitation of Vighneśvara evoke other well-known themes: first note Viṣṇu's collaboration in Śiva's enterprise by the subterfuge of his power of illusion: the same *māyā* enables him to outwit the vigilance of the *asuras* during the churning of the ocean of milk, from which the gods secure the elixir of immortality (in the same myth, Śiva consumes the poison produced by the churning in order to neutralize its effect on the world). Viṣṇu's *māyā* is in a sense also the Goddess, the Earth, the Primordial Creation, whatever one wishes to call it—the feminine form of the divine that deludes creatures and makes the world exist; but

Viṣṇu's power produces the cosmos only to allow it to achieve release. As for the decapitated Vighneśvara, he becomes in this way a sacrificial victim. His own head necessarily disappears, since it constitutes the sacrificial offering in the Hindu (and no longer Vedic) animal sacrifice. This transition through the sacrifice evokes the case of so many *asuras* whose original wickedness is obliterated at the moment of their sacrificial death and who are transformed into the guardians of superior divinities: this "sacrifice" of Vighneśvara by Śiva may be what enables this impure creature to reach the world of dharma, by placing him in the service of pure causes. The elephant's head symbolizes power, and often royal power, but this meaning is effaced here; however, it is not just any power: like Hanumān the Monkey, the elephant combines power with a vegetarian regimen. He therefore unites in himself what is required to make a good guardian and the purity that is needed for being auspicious (Bhairava, Śiva's guardian, could not play the same role). Moreover, his single tusk, unexplained in the myth, is an evocation of the sacrificial stake, while his trunk may suggest the fertile sexual organ, the tusk and trunk uniting in a double symbolism of Śiva's linga: the iconography shows the trunk poised on a dainty morsel held in his left hand, or even on the sexual organ of a goddess seated on his left thigh. The sacrificial meaning of the decapitation is confirmed by the transformation that Gaṇapati undergoes. He is thereafter submissive to Śiva: *bhukti,* without renouncing its rights, acknowledges the transcendence of *mukti.* This submission consummates his inclusion in the Hindu sacrificial system and renders him fit to control the adverse forces that may create obstacles to the success of the virtuous.

The orientation of Gaṇapati toward the world of *bhukti* also appears in a version of his myth in the *Skanda Purāṇa:* this time the initiative comes from the gods, but Śiva is the guilty party. Did he not grant salvation to all those, good and evil, who visit his temple at Somnath? Heaven is overpopulated, and not just by people of good society: by Śūdras, women, etc. The gods are nearly turned out of the gates of heaven by this excess population. They therefore go to complain to Śiva about the disastrous effects of his grace. But he cannot break his promise. The gods must appeal instead to Pārvatī. The Goddess, praised and propitiated by the gods, who invoke her in particular as Kālarātrī—the "Night of Time"—takes pity on the gods and by rubbing her skin produces a Vighneśvara with four arms and the head of an elephant. He is ordered to remove the Somnath devotees, except those who worship him.

This version of the myth, less rich than the preceding one, evokes other well-known themes: the overpopulation of heaven, and especially the fact that all beings may be found there, is an attenuated form of the theme of the occupation of heaven by the *asuras.* But this situation is created by *bhakti*: the Hindu conscience continually collides with the contradiction between the universality of salvation afforded by devotion to a great god like Viṣṇu or Śiva and the necessity of maintaining the Brahmanical order, without which the world cannot endure. One cannot accord salvation to Śūdras and women and at the same time maintain dharma, the sociocosmic order with all its hierarchies and exclusions. Gaṇapati must act as a filter: from the guardian of the Goddess he has become the guardian of the gate of heaven. This new Saint Peter has no keys, but he can place obstacles where necessary or remove them from the path for those who merit it. Since it is a matter of guaranteeing the auspicious operation of dharma, the worship of Gaṇapati that the Goddess establishes symbolizes above all obedience to dharma, the cause of success in this world and in the other (even for Śūdras and women): it is for this reason that Gaṇapati adorns the lintels of many sanctuary doors. He shares this honor with Gaja-lakṣmī, the goddess of prosperity, who is framed by two elephants who sprinkle her with their trunks. The same two divinities figure alternatively on the door lintels of traditional high-caste homes.

Thus traits that are deemed impure and have a function in the service of Brahmanical purity are again seen combined in the same divinity. We can also understand what renders this god both "popular" and the jealous property of the Brahmans who officiate for him. He is the god of every beginning: his blessing must be obtained if an enterprise is to be brought to a successful conclusion. Evidently "popular" piety retains above all the guarantee of success that he offers to his devotees and that tends to distinguish two representations: the most common one shows the trunk turned toward the left, because it is normally to the left of a god that his wife or the Earth, whom he protects, is situated, and the Earth is represented in his hand by a dainty morsel. But there is a form that is more refined, with a more elaborate ritual, that is called Siddhi-vināyaka, "the one who removes (obstacles) to success," or "the one who leads to success," or, in Tamil, Valampuri-vināyaka, "Vināyaka (with his trunk) turned toward the right." The end of his trunk is coiled from left to right, clockwise. This direction, which is also followed in circumambulating a sanctuary, is considered particularly auspicious. This form of Gaṇapati captures only his aptitude for bestowing success.

M.Bi./b.f.

BIBLIOGRAPHY

A. GETTY, *Gaṇeśa, a Monograph on the Elephant-Faced God* (2d ed., New Delhi 1971).

SKANDA, A GREAT SOVEREIGN GOD OF SOUTH INDIA

Skanda is one of the most ancient figures of pan-Indian mythology, since the MBh gives several versions of his myth, and iconography also bears witness to him at an early date. The *Chāndogya Upaniṣad* at least knows his name. But it is in South India that he has been recognized until the present as a great sovereign god—one might even say *the* great sovereign god, were it not for AiyaNār-Śastā, who has the same function. Skanda, better known in his shrines as either Subrahmaṇya or Ṣaṇmukha ("the six-headed one"), seems to hold the position that Rāma and Kṛṣṇa, the two great avatars of Viṣṇu, hold in the north. Skanda is regarded as the son of Śiva (as is AiyaNār), although the myths of his birth make the paternity rather indirect. Furthermore, the iconography of the south, at least at a certain period, insists on depicting the group known as Somaskanda, "(Śiva) with (his wife) Umā and Skanda," although Skanda was not born of Pārvatī-Umā.

To simplify an extremely rich and complex mythology, we shall limit ourselves to the evidence given by the great epic. The MBh provides two distinct myths, both of which narrate both Skanda's birth and his confrontation with an *asura*, and these two passages may be considered the reference myths of the numerous Purāṇic variants. We cannot talk about one without talking about the other, since the two shed mutual light on each other. Although the general arrangement of the avatar myths prevails here, the insistence on the myth of birth and its complexity show how formidable Rudra-Śiva's offspring was to the gods: there was thus a basic opposition between Viṣṇu's avatars, who are "descents" of the supreme god at the request of the heavenly gods, and Śiva's son, who must earn the trust of the gods and virtually imposes himself on them through his great power. He is *su-brahmaṇya*, that is, as devoted to the triumph of the gods and of the Brahmanic order as the avatars are. Skanda's relationship with the avatars of Viṣṇu is somewhat like the relationship between Rudra-Śiva and Viṣṇu. Viṣṇu is unquestionably the sovereign god in the Epic, the one whom the devotee addresses freely. Rudra-Śiva remains the terrible god to whom prayers are addressed in very specific circumstances: prayers to get weapons, to wreak vengeance on someone, to acquire a power not sanctioned by dharma; but in the last resort, all of this also serves a dharma whose total design escapes mankind. Similarly it may be possible to discern features peculiar to the *asuras* whom Skanda opposes, although *asuras* inimical to the gods seem at first sight to have very few special features.

In the third book of the MBh (223ff.) the setting is wholly classical. The gods have been defeated in a fight with the *asuras*, and Indra, worried, searches for a good "general of the army of the gods" (*devasenāpati*), that is, one who can defend the inhabitants of heaven against their hereditary enemies. He meets a young woman abducted by the *asura* Keśin, and he rescues her. Her name is Devasenā ("army of the gods"), and she asks Indra to give her a husband (*pati*) who will protect her. Indra consults with Brahmā, and both agree that a son born of Agni (the sacrificial fire) would make an ideal *devasenāpati*, simultaneously general of the army of the gods and husband of Devasenā.

Indra then goes to the place where the divine *ṛṣis* are conducting a sacrifice and have invited Agni to participate. Agni falls in love with the wives of the *ṛṣis*, and as he sits comfortably in one of the sacrificial fires, he looks at them at his leisure. However, his despair over not being able to possess the wives of the *ṛṣis* drives him to abandon his body (the concrete sacrificial fire) and take refuge in the forest. He is followed there by Svāhā (the personified invocation that accompanies any oblation to the gods as it is poured into the fire). She is in love with him, and in order to unite with Agni she takes the form of six of the seven *ṛṣis'* wives in succession. Six times Svāhā collects Agni's seed in her hand and brings it to the White Mountain that is covered with a forest of reeds. She deposits it there in a golden pot, from which a child is born—Skanda Kumāra, an infant with six heads, who reaches adult size by his sixth day of life. His sixth head is that of a goat.

He frightens everyone, and there are disputes about his birth and parentage. Only Viśvāmitra, who has secretly followed Svāhā, knows whose child he is and is the first to "take refuge" in Skanda (the fixed formula of both Hindu bhakti and Buddhist piety). The gods advise Indra to kill him, for Skanda might try to take his place, but Indra declares his impotence. He dispatches the *Mātṛs* (mothers of the worlds) to go to see the child, but on seeing his strength, they too take refuge in him and adopt him as their son. His goat head is especially dear to them. Agni comes to see him with his goat head (the goat is the paradigm of the sacrificial victim), and then come groups of unsavory characters, the Gaṇas, who also appear around Rudra-Śiva. Indra finally visits him with all the gods. Before Skanda's obvious superiority the gods forsake Indra and take refuge in Skanda. Indra has to do the same after attempting to put up a fight. Śrī then comes to live with him. The Brahmans worship him and the *ṛṣis* propose that he become the new Indra. But Skanda refuses the kingship. He would rather be Indra's servant, so Indra asks him to be the general of the army of the gods and gives him Devasenā for his wife.

At this point the text specifies that Skanda is Rudra's son, since Agni is Rudra. He has many mothers: the *ṛṣis'* wives claim this title, as do the Mātṛs and Svāhās. Skanda gives the Mātṛs the power to inflict all sorts of pain and sorrow on children up to the age of sixteen. He has a whole court of demons and demonesses, the Kumāras and the Kumārīs, the Grahas ("kidnappers") who symbolize all the misfortunes reserved for children.

Rudra comes in his turn to see Skanda, who meets him halfway and assures Rudra that he is at his command. The *asuras* attack and the buffalo *asura* Mahiṣa charges Rudra's chariot. Rudra refrains from killing him in order to leave this task to Skanda, who splits Mahiṣa's head in half with his *śakti* (a magical or real weapon that symbolizes his power to act in the world). The falling head clears a passage in the mountain and opens up an access road to the Uttara-Kuru, the "Kuru of the North," a paradisiacal country. The *asuras* are defeated, and Rudra advises the gods to regard Skanda as another form of Rudra.

The MBh 13.84–86 narrative about Skanda is inserted in a speech glorifying gold. We should note that, for the Hindus, gold is solid fire and therefore closely connected not only with the sacrificial fire and sacrifice (sacrificial fees of gold and cows are the most highly valued) but also with Śrī.

Rudra married Rudrāṇī (a name that the Goddess takes on) and they remain in a long sexual embrace until the gods, afraid of the offspring that would result from such a union, ask Śiva to abstain from procreating; they argue that the world could not bear a son born of him. Rudra consents and henceforth practices complete sexual abstinence. The furious Goddess curses the gods and condemns them to be childless themselves. Agni (the sacrificial fire) is absent at the moment of this curse, but some of Rudra's seed has fallen to earth, into the fire.

At the very same moment, the gods are harassed by the *asura* Tāraka and seek counsel from Brahmā, who has granted invulnerability to Tāraka. Brahmā believes that only a son of Agni can oppose the demon. They set out to find Agni, who has vanished in order to sleep. Betrayed by a series of indiscretions, he keeps changing his hiding place until the gods finally find him in the *śamī* tree. The gods make their request, and Agni agrees to help them.

Agni unites with Gaṅgā and deposits within her an embryo (the seed obtained from Śiva). But Gaṅgā is unable to bear the embryo, which carries within it all the heat of Agni. Suffering greatly and against her will she deposits it on Mount Meru. It looks like a gleaming piece of pure gold that illuminates the whole mountain. Everybody rushes to see it and is set aglow by its brightness.

After completing the task assigned him by the gods, Agni disappears with Gaṅgā. The embryo develops in a forest of reeds. The Kṛttikās (wives of the *ṛṣis*, who are identified with the Pleiades) see him and nurse him.

Procession statues of Subrahmaṇya and his two wives. Tiruttani (South India). Photo IFI.

After an interruption, the narrative resumes: the Kṛttikās give birth simultaneously to six parts of the embryo, which they reduce to one, but with six heads. The child takes refuge in a grove of reeds where the Kṛttikās nurse him.

All the creatures, headed by the Trimūrti and the celestial gods, come to see him. The gods think that the *asura* Tāraka is already doomed. They appoint Guha (one of Skanda's names) general of their armies and tell him about the trouble that Tāraka is causing them. Guha kills Tāraka with his infallible *śakti*.

The two stories begin in very different ways, but with an identical narrative process. In one case the defeated army of the gods needs a general, and the youthful Devasenā, harassed by an *asura,* asks for a husband. In the second version the gods ask Rudra not to procreate, which causes them to be cursed with sterility. The double sterility immediately becomes the demon Tāraka, who afflicts the gods and from whom they must be freed. The first part of the second story must be structured in this way, partly because of the name of the *asura* (Tāraka, "he who delivers") and also because of the subsequent corollary: Agni has vanished to go to sleep, which implies a suspension of all sacrificial activity on earth and thus a threat of cosmic death. By asking Rudra to observe perpetual continence, in fear of his offspring, the gods send the Great Yogi back to his yoga without allowing him to alternate the phases of cosmic emission and reabsorption. They thus condemn the world to final deliverance without any hope of a new beginning. So terrible a prospect must take the form of an *asura,* and the favor granted by Brahmā to the *asura* is merely another form of this inconsiderate step of the gods. The two stories open on an avatar theme, the first in a classical manner, the second with unusual details. At issue is more than a mere reversal of the normal cosmic order that needs to be reestablished. The very existence of the cosmos is at stake. It may be said that the first account is at the junction of two yugas, while the second tells of the threat of a definitive end to the world. But this threat is obviously idle, since some of Rudra's seed has escaped from him and has been collected in fire on earth. The seed is the "remnant" necessary for every new beginning of the world.

The second account immediately places Rudra in the forefront, and the seed that Agni deposits inside Gaṅgā is Rudra's; this is not said explicitly, but as in the first account, Rudra and Agni are identified. The theme of linear descent is thus substituted for the theme of the avatar, and Rudra appears instead of Viṣṇu. There is probably a connection between this choice and the particular character of the *asura,* who is none other than the terrible aspect of Rudra, the one with which he annihilates the world, and also the one that makes him the god of deliverance for the yogi. It remains to show that the Mahiṣa of the first account (the *asura* usually seen in connection with the Goddess) is different from the *asura* who confronts the avatar. Here we can only offer some rather indirect hints, which the myth of the *Devī Māhātmya* does not corroborate. This remains an open issue.

The first account insists less on the connection between Rudra and Skanda. We are reminded almost by conspicuous silence that Agni is identical to Rudra, and that Skanda is consequently Rudra's son. Only at the end does Rudra explicitly charge Skanda with the task of slaughtering Mahiṣa, and only then does he give him his blessing. On the other hand, the gods have every reason to be frightened by the child and his extraordinary power, and their fright is much like the one that they experience in the second account at the thought of Rudra having a son. Skanda is soon surrounded by *gaṇas* ("troops") that in Śaiva mythology turn out to mean all kinds of disquieting creatures, collective or individual, including *asuras* that are devotees of Rudra, as they are of Skanda in this case. Skanda is also associated with the Mātṛs ("the mothers"). There is no reason to believe that these are identical with the *saptamātṛkās* of the *Devīmāhātmya,* but their function is made clear. In popular worship, Skanda has the reputation of being a god "who kidnaps" children, but also a god to whom people pray to have children. That is probably why he has six heads: he is associated with the goddess Ṣaṣṭhī ("sixth"), who presides over the sixth day after birth, the period regarded as crucial to the survival of a newborn child. In the epic myth, his "kidnapping" function seems to be given over to the Mātṛs, and even more characteristically to the Kumāras and the Kumārīs who surround him and who bear one of his names, Kumāra ("the young boy, the young man"). This name connotes at least mythically the state of an unmarried young man who has taken a vow of chastity, which accords with Skanda's residence in the mountain. In some parts of India women are not allowed inside his temples for that reason. The Kumāras and Kumārīs thus participate in his asceticism, and there is a connection between the divine yoga and the power that the god has to reabsorb all creatures within him.

Moreover, Skanda Kuāra is born on a mountain covered with a forest of reeds. This motif appears elsewhere. The Brahman warrior Kṛpa and his twin sister Kṛpī, the future wife of Droṇa in the MBh, are born in a clump of reeds on which the seed of their ascetic father has fallen. Kṛpa ("pity") is more expert in warfare than in the Veda, although he is a Brahman, and his brother-in-law Droṇa is also a warrior Brahman. Kṛpa is an incarnation of the Rudras (a group of lesser deities associated with Rudra), and his nephew Aśvatthāman, the son of Droṇa, is an incarnation of Rudra, Antaka (death), Krodha (wrath), and Kāma (desire). The reeds (*śara-vana*) evoke arrows (*śara*), and this theme, which all the myths of Skanda associate with birth, gives him simultaneously the character of a warrior and of an ascetic, and connects him indirectly with Rudra. Skanda thereby evokes Rudra, the terrible ascetic, and may himself presage the end of the world. Skanda, who had such difficulty being born because of his illustrious and complex parentage, is logically associated with the fate of earthly children. There is there no need to posit two Skandas or two traditions about Skanda (the problem of AiyaNār-Śāstā is posed in very similar terms): his character as a terrible ascetic connected with Rudra gives him his reputation as a kidnapper; an adapted cult is enough to transform the threat that he constitutes into a blessing. A god so dangerous and at the same time so essential to the world's salvation naturally finds Viśvāmitra an ideal devotee.

Skanda is rather far from the character of the avatar. Although in his great shrines his function is very close to that of Viṣṇu's avatars, he cannot be confused with any of these "descents," and his connection with Śiva remains essential. Closer to the demons than any avatar (including the Goddess), within the myth he fulfills a more permanent function then they do, since he is the general of the armies of the gods. The order over which he watches is the same as the dharma connected with the avatar, but he cannot be considered a model king. He consecrates or illustrates Rudra-Śiva's participation in the Brahmanic order, as well as the participation of lesser deities and demons. This ascetic receives no less than two wives, Devasenā in the MBh and Vaḷḷi, a daughter of the mountain and huntress, both of whom undergo infinite variations within Purāṇic mythology. A god interested in the order of the world cannot do without a wife any more than he can do without demons who are subordinate to him. Skanda Kumāra has the same ambiguity as Rudra-Śiva, yogi and spouse of Pārvatī, and the Goddess, virgin and spouse of Śiva. The renunciation of the world always governs the order of the world and is closely implicated in the order of the world.

M.Bi./g.h.

BIBLIOGRAPHY

P. K. AGRAWALA, *Skanda Kārttikeya: Study in the Origin and Development* (Banaras 1967). A. K. CHATTERJEE, *The Cult of Skanda-Kārttikeya in Ancient India* (Calcutta 1970). F. L'HERNAULT, *L'iconographie de Subrahmaṇya ou Tamilnad* (Pondicherry 1978).

Abbreviations

MBh *Mahābhārata* (edition: Citrashala Press, Poona)
DM *Devī-māhātmya* (edition and translation: "Les Belles Lettres")

DEVĪ: THE GODDESS IN INDIA

Devī: the Goddess. She is given this name in order to encompass all the individual proper names that are given to her in the great temples and village sanctuaries of India. No matter what level her function may be situated at, it is always the same. Sometimes associated with a great god, usually a form of Śiva, sometimes independent, she cannot be mistaken: she is the Goddess who confers the favors necessary to a happy earthly existence and leads to the god of final release. She is a benevolent goddess for her devotees, but her anger is terrible. She carries off children and gives children to sterile parents, unleashes epidemics and cures diseases. By the evils that she unleashes she is close to the *asuras;* but she also kills the buffalo-*asura* for the gods and thus ensures the prosperity of the triple world. She gives victory to Kṣatriyas who pray to her. She is also sometimes called Yogeśvarī and thus participates in the function of the Great Yogi: for in order to attract the attention of Śiva, whom she wanted to marry, it was necessary for her to become an ascetic and to rival in her austerities the one whom she desired. She is often considered a virgin as well, when she is alone in her temple. In the form of Satī, she dies because of the quarrel between her father Dakṣa and her husband Rudra, and thus becomes the model for wives who commit suicide on their husband's funeral pyres.

When we pass from *bhakti* to Śāktism (the nuances of the transition from the one to the other are infinite), she becomes the preeminent divinity, the Śakti who is superior to Śiva, and this reversal of the usual hierarchy is accompanied in a few cases by a reversal of dharma: what was prohibited becomes permitted, the impure becomes pure, and mundane objects of pleasure become instruments for salvation.

In every way, even when she presides over release, she is closer to earthly values than the god is, more attentive to the prayers and needs of her devotees; but she is also more apt to make use of the violence without which the earth could not live. It is thus not surprising that one of the myths of her birth, the least developed and also the least interesting, has her born from Parvata, "the mountain," which makes her Pārvatī, the daughter of the mountain. Here the mountain evokes both the mythic support of the world that makes the world habitable and the Himalayan dwelling of Rudra-Śiva, which is inhabited by the solitary yogis.

There is a tendency to simplify the Goddess by making her into a Śaiva goddess, the wife of Śiva—even when she is alone, independent, and a virgin in her own sanctuary—in opposition to Śrī or Lakṣmī, who would be the Vaiṣṇava goddess. The two must be distinguished: Śrī is never the warrior goddess, except in certain regions of India where she is found with the name of Mahālakṣmī; but in this case she is merely the Goddess. Śrī in the strict sense is always associated with Viṣṇu, just as prosperity is associated with the sacrifice; this is another way of saying that she is always on the side of dharma. As a goddess she is also closer to worldly concerns than the god is: incarnate as Draupadī or as Sītā in the epics, she is the catalyst for the plot. It is for her and at her instigation that people fight. She is thus not as completely opposed to the Goddess as might have been thought.

The main reason we cannot set the Vaiṣṇava goddess and the Śaiva goddess in opposition is that the Goddess has a tie with Viṣṇu which is as essential as her tie with Śiva. When the myth makes her a daughter of Dakṣa, she is related to the sacrifice and thus to Viṣṇu. But the two most important myths about her origin associate her directly with Viṣṇu. In the *Harivaṃśa*, the book of the acts of Kṛṣṇa and the appendix to the *Mahābhārata* (2.2), Viṣṇu asks Nidrā, the "sleep" of Time—i.e., the sleep of the cosmic night, whose name is feminine in Sanskrit—to "descend" to the earth to undo the criminal designs of Kaṃsa. She is to descend into

Durgā, the buffalo killer. Probably from Gujarat. Note the buffalo head on the pedestal, at the right. Private collection. Photo Dominique Champion.

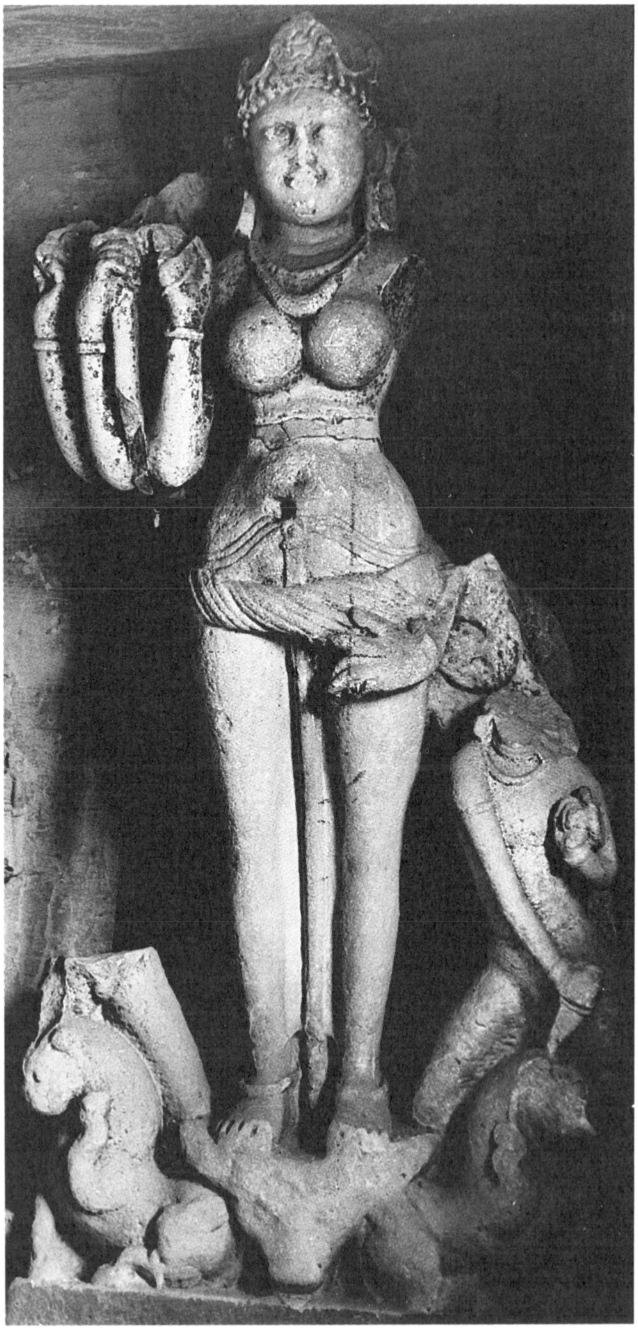

Durgā standing on the head of a buffalo. Bisnagar, Gwalior Museum. Photo O. Divaran.

the womb of Yaśodā, the wife of the cowherd Nanda, and he will descend into the womb of Devakī, the wife of Vasudeva and the paternal aunt of Kaṃsa, the incarnate *asura,* who kills his aunt's progeny as soon as they are born. At the time of birth, in the night, the two newborn infants are exchanged. Kaṃsa then takes her away to kill her by crushing her against a rock (an echo of the theme of birth from a mountain), from which she flies up into the sky. Viṣṇu then describes her in terms that make it easy to recognize the Goddess in her: like him, she is black, dressed in dark blue and yellow silk, and she lives in the Vindhya Mountains, where she is devoted to celibacy. This goddess Nidrā thus comes to be associated with the function of an avatar of Viṣṇu, and is elevated to the level of great Goddess. This myth is the source of the common belief that the Goddess is the sister of Viṣṇu.

The *Devīmāhātmya,* a famous poem to the glory of the Goddess which is found within the *Mārkaṇḍeya Purāṇa,* specifies who Nidrā is, and in doing so brings her even closer to Viṣṇu. It must be recalled that during the cosmic night Viṣṇu sleeps in a yogic sleep on the serpent Śeṣa, and that at the dawn of a new cosmic day a lotus bearing Brahmā emerges from his navel. The DM adds to this scenario the presence of two *asuras,* Madhu and Kaiṭabha, born from Viṣṇu's earwax, who attempt to kill Brahmā. In order to awaken the still sleeping Viṣṇu, Brahmā then sings the praises of Yoganidrā, the goddess who lives in the eyes of Viṣṇu and keeps him asleep. We recognize her as the Nidrā of Time of which the HV spoke. This Nidrā is the yogic sleep of Viṣṇu, identical with the sleep of Time, whence comes her name of Yoganidrā. Brahmā praises her as the cause of the creation and dissolution of the worlds; in other words, she is the projection of the yogic activity of the god. She is the double of the god as the supreme Puruṣa who is immutable and collected into his yoga, and as the female energy by which he comes out of his yoga to preside over the fate of the worlds by emitting and reabsorbing them in turn. Praised by Brahmā simultaneously as the Night of Time—Kālarātri—which provokes the yogic sleep of Viṣṇu and his absorption of all creatures and as Mahāmāyā, the cosmic illusion that, once outside of Viṣṇu, makes the world appear and allows it to exist by blinding it to its own nature, Yoganidrā goes out of Viṣṇu, thus making the god wake up and confront the two *asuras,* whom he finally destroys.

We have here, in mythic terms, all of the elements of the Goddess's complexity, both as a power that causes the delusion of all creatures and as an instrument for their salvation. As such, she is essentially bound to Viṣṇu before she is connected with Śiva. This reason alone would seem to constitute a very solid argument for taking the Hinduism of the *smṛti* tradition to be logically prior to the sects. It is normal that the tie with Viṣṇu should be more fundamental than the relationship with Śiva—she is or is not the wife of Śiva—to the degree that it is Viṣṇu who is the supreme god of Hinduism of the *smṛti* tradition, especially as it is presented in the epics. Furthermore, it is for the benefit of Brahmā, and thus apparently for the whole Brahmanic order, that she awakens Viṣṇu. His intervention is beneficial for the creation that has been endangered by the *asuras.*

But the *Devīmāhātmya* is mostly the account of the victory of the Goddess over the buffalo demon Mahiṣāsura. Although other demons combat her after Mahiṣa, the story is clearly centered upon Mahiṣa. The ritual iconography of this form of Durgā is immense: its popularity would be hard to explain if it were not connected with the annual sacrifice of one or more buffalos to the Goddess which took place until recent times, whenever she was the protectress of a kingdom or locality. This is far from the Vedic sacrifice, at least apparently. The victim is an *asura,* an evil being whom one must get rid of, who must be killed by an untouchable and eaten by untouchables. It is no longer an individual sacrificer who offers the sacrifice but the whole local community led by its chief, king, or local equivalent, and all the castes are associated with the event, even if they do not all participate in it physically. The ritual is extremely varied, but we may point out a particularly revealing trait found in the buffalo sacrifice as it is performed in most of the villages of Andhra Pradesh (the eastern coastal region north of Madras): the severed head of the buffalo is offered to the Goddess, whose image is a temporary one made of clay for the occasion, and is then carried, along with the clay image of the Goddess, to the outer limit of the village lands. The victim represents an evil that must be gotten rid of, and this evil seems also to be connected with the Goddess, whose image is also expelled. The buffalo sacrifice takes place, depending on the region, at the time of the annual temple festival, at the beginning of spring, or for the autumn Navarātri. But the Goddess's victory over the buffalo is itself invariably celebrated at Vijayādaśamī, the day following the nine nights of Navarātri, the "tenth" day of "the Victory."

The myth itself very much resembles a myth of an avatar which has been edited and corrected by the epic: when

Durgā, the buffalo killer. Private collection. Photo Dominque Champion.

Mahiṣa, the buffalo-*asura,* is the king of the *asuras,* the gods and the *asuras* wage a long war; the *asuras* are victorious and Mahiṣa becomes the king of heaven in Indra's place. The gods, led by Brahmā, go to the dwelling of Śiva and Viṣṇu and tell the two gods what has happened. From each of the great gods, from Brahmā and from each of the celestial gods, great rays of light shoot out and unite into one light and take a feminine form. Each then gives her a weapon. The Goddess shakes the world with her roar. A battle begins between her and Mahiṣa; it will end in the victory of the Goddess and the death of Mahiṣa. The Goddess drinks heavily during the battle. The account continues with a description of her victories over other *asuras,* Śumbha and Niśumbha, who have occupied heaven once again. This scenario is even simpler: the gods go directly to the Himalayas (where the Goddess lives under certain forms) and sing the praises of the one they call Viṣṇumāyā. This is of course still the same Goddess. They ask her to rid them of Śumbha and Niśumbha. Śumbha tries to win the Goddess for his wife (in Karnataka, she is sometimes considered the wife of the buffalo that is sacrificed to her), but she slips away from him and provokes the insolent *asura* into battle. The lion that is her vehicle, her terrible Kālī form, which she emits from her

Durgā of the Durgāpūjā in Bengal. Photo Pierre Amado.

Durgā. Shrine at Kalo. Photo Pierre Amado.

angry forehead, and the *śaktis* (female energies) of the gods Brahmā, Śiva, Skanda, Viṣṇu, and Indra, lend her strength. Viṣṇu's *śakti* in fact divides into two parts, one the female replica of Viṣṇu—Vaiṣṇavī—and the other the female replica of the sacrificial boar of Hindu cosmogony. To these are added the *śakti* of Narasiṃha—Nārasimhī—another form of Viṣṇu. These together form the group of the "Seven Mothers"—*saptamātṛkās*—who are well known in iconography. The Goddess sends Śiva as a messenger to Śumbha and Niśumbha to demand that they restore heaven to Indra. Thus it is again the whole divine community, along with the supreme gods and the celestial gods, who take part, just as on earth it is the whole local community that assembles for the sacrifice of the buffalo to the Goddess. The *asuras* refuse, which is the signal for a great battle. The Goddess devours all those who fall to earth, which puts the whole army of the *asuras* to flight. Then the *asura* Raktabīja rises up, and from every drop of his blood as it falls on the ground a new *asura* is produced. Thousands of *asuras* are thus produced, to the despair of the gods. The Goddess therefore commands Kālī to collect in her open mouth all the blood that flows from Raktabīja and to devour the new *asuras* born from his blood. The long digressions which follow add nothing to the structure of the whole, apart from a repetition of the carnage that leads to the final victory.

The Goddess—who calls the battle, as in the epic, "the sacrifice of battle"—fears neither blood nor wine; in other words, she fears neither impurity nor violence, when they are for the good of the gods and the worlds. She can support the great god in the eternal battle against the demons, and her aid is necessary because in his temple the great god is always a pure god who avoids all killing. The violence of the Goddess, however, eventually becomes transformed in her ritual into blood sacrifices and offerings of wine. This brings her very close to the demons that she kills: this is why the mythic motif of the avatar of the god—whose ideological justification lies elsewhere—must be duplicated by the Goddess who kills *asuras*. The low tasks are left to the Goddess so that the purity of the god may be maintained; and extreme Tantrism, known as Śaktism, only glorifies her role and cleanses it of any suspicion of impurity. This phenomenon is thus not a vulgar return of "mundane" appetites rebelling against renunciation, but the affirmation, carried to its furthest limits, that the world must exist in order for there to be release from the world.

M.Bi./d.w.

BIBLIOGRAPHY

Célébration de la Grande Déesse (Devī-māhātmya), Sanskrit text translated and commented upon by Jean Varenne (Paris 1975).

Abbreviations

DM *Devī-māhātmya*
HV *Harivaṃśa* (Citrashala Press, Poona)

Kāmadhenu: The Mythical Cow, Symbol of Prosperity

Kāmadhenu (or Kāmaduh) is the most common, virtually generic, name of the cow that symbolizes in India the source of all prosperity; she is the cow "from whom all that is desired is drawn." The proper names that she is given, such as Śabalā (the spotted one) and Kapilā (the red one), do not prevent her from also receiving the epithet Kāmadhenu. All the values that the Hindus attach to the cow in general are projected onto the Kāmadhenu.

The Kāmadhenu of myth is always closely associated with the Brahman, whose entire wealth she represents. The Brahman is the priest of the Vedic sacrifice, and the first prerequisite for a sacrifice is the material oblation of cow's milk and its derivatives, particularly clarified butter, which is poured on the sacrificial fire as an offering. Kāmadhenu sometimes becomes Homadhenu, the one "from whom oblations are drawn." Thus in myths it is common to find the function of the Brahman associated either with the cow or with milk. Sacrificial payments were once measured in cows, and even today it is an act of piety to give a cow to a Brahman. It is commonly said that a Brahman without a cow is not a Brahman. From all of this, one can understand how it is that the cow is associated with everything that defines the Brahmanical order: respect for the cow is a corollary to the respect that is given to Brahmans, gods, and dharma in general, that is, to the sociocosmic order.

The sociocosmic order (dharma) can be maintained only through sacrifice, which nourishes the gods of heaven, who in turn cause rain to fall on the earth at the right time; it is thus as a result of sacrifice that plants grow and that animals—notably the cow—and men can be nourished, and that they can prosper, and that they can offer sacrifices. This order is a closed circuit that should function forever if everyone respects it, and the cow occupies a preeminent place in it by virtue of its role in the sacrifice. The sociocosmic order, on which the prosperity of the world depends, since it is founded on the principle of sacrifice, would not exist without the cow. That is why the cow is the symbol both of the Brahman's power and of all wealth, since the prosperity of the world springs from the oblation of clarified butter.

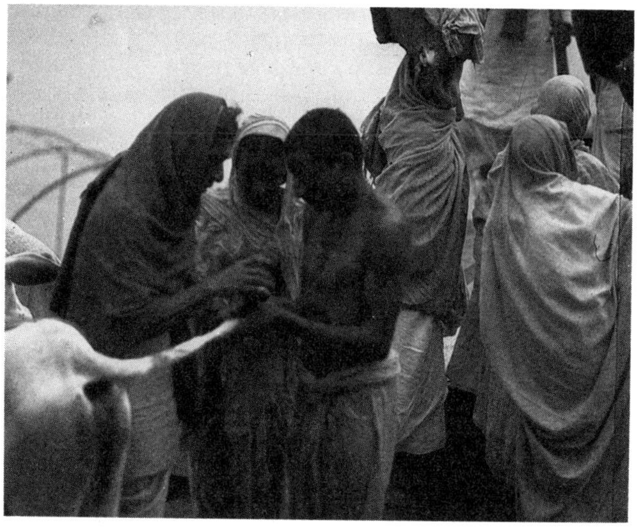

Gift of a cow at Banaras. Photo Pierre Amado.

By the same token, the mythical cow Kāmadhenu is very close to the fertile earth, and in Sanskrit, "cow" is a word frequently used for "earth." Furthermore, the cow, a feminine agent, is necessarily related to the Goddess who is also at least partially related to the earth. As a possession of the Brahman whose status forbids him to defend himself and who relies on the prince's protection, the cow becomes the Brahman's best protection in the event that he is attacked by an abusive prince seeking to deprive him of his power. As a goddess, the cow can become a warrior or at least produce the armies needed to protect herself and her owner.

M.Bi./g.h.

Symbols of the Earth in Indian Religion

Contrary to widespread ideas about Hindu spirituality and the desire for deliverance that all Hindus supposedly share, the earth, and above all the land of India, stands at the very center of all mythico-ritual speculations in India. The theoretical foundation of its perpetuity and the guarantee of its prosperity are issues of prime concern. This concern was, perhaps from the very beginning (if the notion of historical origin has a meaning in this context), compounded with the values symbolized by the renunciants. In broad outline, the earth is the world of sacrifice and transmigration, while renunciants represent what lies beyond sacrifice, which the world of sacrifice must integrate to ground itself in the absolute.

Moreover, the cosmological representations of the Hindus do not allow us to isolate a precise image of the earth. Except for their concept of seven islands surrounded by seven oceans, they are more preoccupied with situating the earth within the vertical hierarchy of the worlds, or with isolating in one of the seven islands the land of India, the land of the Middle—*madhyadeśa* (not because the Aryans actually occupied and settled the center of the plain between the Ganges and Indus rivers, but because the land of the Bhāratas, as they call themselves, must by definition be the center of the world). The land of men is located between the netherworld and the sky, and there the fate of the triple world is sealed by the joint effect of sacrifice and renunciation. But in another sense, the earth of the myths may also be this triple world, which is entirely swept away in the cosmic catastrophe at the end of an age of the world and is reborn after a cosmic night. When the earth figures symbolically in a myth, it does not matter whether it is the earth itself or the triple world, since they are interdependent. For instance, the bad government of a king on earth reveals an invasion by the inhabitants of the lower worlds and threatens the peace of the gods in heaven; the absence of sacrifices on earth causes a famine among the gods, which in turn results in a drought on earth.

Consequently the symbols used in myths to signify the earth are determined, not by physical representations of the earth, but rather by the values by which its fate is acted out.

First of all, although the primordial male, the supreme Puruṣa, soon emerges as the hypostasis of release, the one toward whom creatures freed from rebirth aspire, the Goddess at the opposite end of the spectrum is the world that emanates from the deity, the world of transmigration, the earth in the broadest sense. Since release is on the side of renunciation, while transmigration is based on sacrifice, the Goddess has to be closely associated with sacrifice. She is therefore sometimes black—Kālī, Kṛṣṇā, Nīlā, Tillotamā, Śyāmā, all names for the Goddess or related mythical individuals meaning "black"—and sometimes gold: then she is called Lakṣmī or Śrī. These two colors of the Goddess are also the colors of fire, which is *kṛṣṇavartman* (the black-traced one) and in its solid form appears as gold. The two features complement each other: Lakṣmī is prosperity, which sacrifice can bring, and gold is the best symbol for this prosperity. The thirst for gold that Hindus still have today has its roots in this concept. Of course, it is not possible to separate gold from its economic value. The young groom who brings his wife into the house also brings in Lakṣmī. The new bride must have a sari with at least one gold brocade border, and she is covered with gold jewels. These jewels are her personal property and remain in the house so long as circumstances allow her to keep them, for they are signs that Lakṣmī is present.

But prosperity is never there once and for all. It must constantly be made through sacrificial rites, in which fire also plays a destructive role: without the permanent consumption of the victims by fire—that is, their consumption by the gods—the earth could not survive. This destructive aspect of fire constantly confronts the earth with the darkness that threatens the world, but fire is in itself "dark" (*tāmasic:* since it is associated with killing; this accounts for the dark complexion of the goddess: Kālī, the name of one of her bloodiest forms, is also the Vedic name of one of the seven tongues of the sacrificial fire. There is a continuity between this meaning of the color black and a common example used by classical Indian philosophy that indicates that the earth, naturally black, turns red through the action of fire; potter's earth is not normally black.

By extension, when a text stresses the dark complexion of a mythical woman who is not identified with the Goddess, one can suspect the presence not only of the meaning "Goddess" but also of the meaning "earth" (feminine beauty implies, by contrast, a fair complexion, a sign of high caste). The same can be said about odor: since odor is the characteristic property of the earth, the property that reveals the presence of the element earth wherever it may be, when a text stresses a woman's fragrance (or bad smell), her symbolic link with the earth becomes apparent. Thus Satyavatī, who was born of a female fish, has the smell of fish but then loses that smell and receives a penetrating fragrance on the day that she conceives a Brahman, the *ṛṣi* Vyāsa (also called Kṛṣṇa, and dark in complexion like his mother), the promulgator of the Vedas (*Mahābhārata* 1.105).

But the earth also appears under less transparent symbols, whose common feature is a more or less direct association with the sacrifice or the sacrificial fire. Because the earth is above all an anisotropic space, whose cardinal points assume complementary values, a square object easily evokes it. This object can be complex in itself: when, after beheading his mother and making his father revive her, Paraśurāma destroys all the Kṣatriyas on earth and then gives the earth to the Brahmans, his gift of the earth to the Brahmans, who must set it back in motion, is symbolized by a golden altar, which he gives at the end of a great sacrifice to the principal celebrant, Kaśyapa, one of the progenitors in Hindu mythology. The sacrificial altar, the *vedī*, is not generally square, but at this highly complex level of Hindu symbolism the shape of the *vedī* probably merges with the square shape of the sacrificial fire in which the oblations are offered (each solemn Vedic sacrifice has three main fires). In the present-day ritual of the temples, the oblations are made into a square hearth next to a *vedī* that is also square. The golden altar that Paraśurāma offers is the earth purified by the sacrifice of the Kṣatriyas. The square base of the linga, which represents Brahmā and his four Vedas, in all likelihood also evokes the world organized according to the four cardinal points in the Vedas.

Since forms take on value only insofar as they are signs, there is no paradox in also seeing the earth as symbolized by all kinds of spherical objects: the ball of sweets placed in Gaṇapati's left hand is one example; others are the balls with which so many princes and princesses of the epic play, and the ball of butter that the child Kṛṣṇa steals from his foster mother. This symbolism is more complex, and the nuance that separates balls of food from balls in games should be appreciated. The guiding idea that lies behind the entire sacrificial economy and that specifically informs the concept of the cosmogonic Puruṣa is that in any sacrifice, the true victim is the one who offers the sacrifice, and the victim actually put to death is only a substitute. This idea, reworked by the epic to elaborate the notion of a sacrifice appropriate to the warrior, reappears in the mythical theme of the beheaded goddess: the warrior-goddess, victorious over the buffalo-demon, can triumph over her enemy only because she offered herself in sacrifice at the start of the combat. She would have been beheaded if she had not beheaded him. And perhaps she beheads herself by beheading her enemy, who is only a part of her since she is the mother of the universe.

The earth lives only by sacrifices. She is more or less identifiable with the Goddess, and thus constantly finds herself in the position of a sacrificial offering. But there is a difference: whereas the Goddess is often represented in her shrine as a bodiless head—or more rarely as a headless body—the earth symbolized by the myth is more often assimilated to a ball of food, since any sacrificial offering is food for the gods and since the ball of food figures explicitly in the ritual for the ancestors beginning with its Vedic forms. Kṛṣṇa's ball of butter instead evokes the melted butter that fuels the sacrificial fire. The ball of sweets is another version of this and gives its name to the episode of the Khāṇḍava forest in the *Mahābhārata* (1.222ff.); *khāṇḍava* is the name of a candy, and the forest that Agni, the sacrificial fire, devours with the help of Kṛṣṇa and Arjuna is an image of the earth consumed by the cosmic conflagration at the end of one of the ages of the world: the fire that devours the Khāṇḍava had been made ill by the excess of clarified butter and seeks a cure by a change of diet. This is thus an opposition between butter and candy. The candy, substituted for butter when the sacrificial mechanism is derailed, recalls the ball-shaped food for the ancestors, or better still, the funeral sacrifice of which the cosmic fire is a transposition.

The balls that princes and princesses play with in crucial episodes—the Kaurava princes during the arrival of Droṇa, Devayānī and Śarmiṣṭhā in the Yayāti myth, and Kuntī when her father Śūra gives her to King Kuntibhoja—recall that the fate of the earth is in the hands of the princes. The king's principal wife symbolizes his kingdom, and her attachment to the king symbolizes her attachment to his kingdom. The element of play introduced by the ball connects the king closely with the deity who plays with his creation: this is the Hindu image of gratuitous activity. Just as the deity has no need of creation but creates in a spirit of play (but also for the good of creatures), so the king must rule his kingdom without pursuing his own personal interest. At the same time, the play has a sexual connotation: the Puruṣa and the Devī, the king and his wife, the ruler and his kingdom, are all united according to a set of interrelated connections. If gratuitous activity and sexual relations are taken together, this is close to the guiding idea of *śākta* Tantrism: to control pleasure through the exercise of pleasure.

Finally, there seems to be a simple play on words at the origin of yet another image of the earth, which seems at first glance to be aberrant: *urvī*, one of the terms for the earth, means "the broad one," "the one spread out" (as does the word *pṛthvī*, or *pṛthivī*). This is the feminine form of the adjective *uru*. The word *ūru*, with a long *ū* in the first syllable, means "thigh." This may explain why Aurva is born from his mother's thigh, where he had hidden to escape the massacre of the Bhṛgu Brahmans by the descendants of the Kṣatriya Kṛtavīrya. It is also why Narasiṃha lays Hiraṇyakaśipu across his thighs to kill him, because Hiraṇyakaśipu could not be killed on the ground or in the air: Narasiṃha's thighs thus offer a perfect solution.

M.Bi./g.h.

Ganges and Yamunā, the River of Salvation and the River of Origins

Although the mythology of the Gaṅgā (the Ganges) is infinitely richer than the mythology of the Yamunā, it would be an error in perspective to treat one separated from its connection with the other. Although the Gaṅgā, the white river, is the river of salvation, the Yamunā, the black river, is the river of origins. Their confluence at Prayāga (near modern Allahabad) is one of the most sacred sites in India.

Moreover, to speak of the Gaṅgā and the Yamunā is to speak of Viṣṇu and Śiva; the relation of the two gives rise to a third term: Viṣṇu and Śiva evoke Brahmā, the necessary complement of the Trimūrti; while the Gaṅgā and the Yamunā give rise to the Sarasvatī (which is supposed to be present but visible only to yogis at the confluence at Prayāga). This similarity is no accident: Gaṅgā and Yamunā personified are also have a connected with Viṣṇu and Śiva, while Sarasvatī is one of the names of the consort of Brahmā. In the *Mahābhārata*, Gaṅgā is the mother of Bhīṣma, the hero who sets in place the protagonists of the drama that will save the world by provoking a great massacre, while the Yamunā (the unpersonified river) is the birth place of the Brahman *ṛṣi* Vyāsa, the promulgator of the Vedas (the necessary prelude to a creation of the world) and one of the incarnations of Viṣṇu in the epic. Eventually, the Sarasvatī traverses Kurukṣetra, where the great battle of eighteen days takes place. In the ancient temples of northern India, the opposition of the two rivers is found on the doorjambs of the sanctuary, where Gaṅgā, on one side, is mounted on a *makara*, while Yamunā, on the other, rests on a tortoise. The *makara*, a mythical crocodile with a constantly gaping mouth, symbolizes the time of salvation, the cosmic night when the divinity "swallows" the world, whereas the tortoise is a cosmogonic theme known from Vedic literature. Gaṅgā and Yamunā are associated in the same way as the two kinds of grace that are embodied in the god of the sanctuary: the grace that bestows salvation (*mokṣa* or *mukti*) and the grace that bestows the benefits of this world (*bhukti*). The complementarity of the two rivers is therefore necessary to symbolize the duality of the god, at once yogi and creator.

Nevertheless, the Yamunā hardly occurs in the mythology in a personified form. She preserves her character as a river, and it is necessary to pay attention to all the events that take place on the banks of the Yamunā or on her waters (such as the conception of Vyāsa and the childhood of Kṛṣṇa). But Vedic literature presents her as the sister of Yama, the god of death, identified later with Dharma. She may be seen as the female and therefore fertile complement of the god whose function is to empty the earth of its excess human beings. Yamunā is charged with assuring the renewal of the multitude of creatures, but this is barely suggested; it is inferred, rather, like her connection with the Gaṅgā, from the place that the Yamunā, as a river, has in various myths.

Gaṅgā has a broadly diffused myth, with multiple variants, which must account for her ritual role: she is the river in which the ashes of a dead person must be immersed in order to assure him salvation. All kinds of beliefs are connected with the sojourn of the ashes in the river, but all these beliefs recognize the Gaṅgā as the river of salvation. It is probable (see below), but not proved, that the river's powerful course, which terminates with a delta into a vast ocean, distinguishes it as the type of river that the Upaniṣads evoke when they compare the disappearance of individual *ātmans* into the one Brahman with the disappearance of multiple rivers into a single ocean. But salvation in India, where one always hesitates between the pleasure of favorable rebirths and absorption into the Absolute without return, is an eminently ambiguous thing. It is even more ambiquous when one passes from individual to collective salvation, for this may signify the end of the world, which no one wants. The myth of the Gaṅgā—which will be treated separately—bears the mark of this ambiguity. We will cite the narrative from the *Mahābhārata* (3.106ff.) here, but the *Rāmāyaṇa* (1.42–43) tells a similar version of the myth.

The Gaṅgā has not always flowed on the earth; her myth is the story of her descent from heaven (or from Viṣṇu's big toe, as Purāṇic tradition maintains). This story is in turn connected with the story of the sons of Sagara, the Sāgaras (*sāgara*, "ocean").

The good king Sagara had two wives, evidently too proud (*darpita*) of their beauty, for he had no descendants from them. He had to propitiate Śiva with harsh austerities in order to obtain progeny: Śiva granted him sixty thousand sons from one of his wives, arrogant (*darpita*) warriors destined to perish all together, and a single son from his other wife, who would assure the continuity of the line. The sixty thousand sons apparently could not be born in a normal manner: their mother was delivered of a kind of gourd whose seeds had to be extracted so they would grow in pots

Devprayag. The confluence, in the Himalayas, of the two rivers that form the Ganges. Photo Pierre Amado.

Kedarnath. Sanctuary to Śiva at the sources of the Ganges. Photo Pierre Amado.

filled with clarified butter (which had the effect of transforming them into oblatory material). These sixty thousand sons of Sagara soon behave in such a manner that the gods request Brahmā to rid them of these warriors: the gods need not fear, the Sāgaras will perish quickly. From his other wife, Sagara has had a better son, whom he has had to exile, but by whom he obtains a pious grandson, Aṃśumān, the continuator of his line.

Sagara offers a horse sacrifice and, in conformity with the ritual, releases the sacrificial horse, ordering his sixty thousand sons to protect it during its year of wandering (the idea being that wherever the horse might freely wander, even if at the cost of battle by his guardians, the sacrificing king is acknowledged as sovereign). But at a certain moment the horse disappears and the Sāgaras return to their father to relate their misadventure. He enjoins them to search everywhere for the horse and not to return without it. The Sāgaras scour the earth, and finally go underground to gain access to the subterranean world. In doing this, they overpower the inhabitants of the infernal regions as they have overwhelmed gods and men. In the end, they find the horse in the depths of the lower regions (assimilated eventually to the bottom of the ocean that had been drained previously by Agastya: he had consumed all its water to make it possible for the gods to kill an *asura*); the horse is grazing quietly near a *ṛṣi* resplendent in meditation: Kapila in person, a form of Viṣṇu. The Sāgaras, taking Kapila for the thief, begin to insult him. The sage, disturbed in his meditation, glances at them and reduces them to ashes on the spot. Nārada, the messenger of the gods, goes to inform Sagara of what has happened. The king sends his grandson to recover the horse in order to make it possible for him at least to finish his sacrifice and thus to save himself from the lower regions. Aṃśumān conciliates Kapila so completely that he obtains not only the return of the horse but the promise that his grandson by the grace of Śiva will succeed in causing the Gaṅgā to descend to earth to purify the ashes of his uncles and to assure their future in the beyond.

This is a theme of the avatars, although Kapila is not included in the list of the ten classical avatars. It is clearly Viṣṇu who intervenes to save Sagara and the Sāgaras. Moreover, the Gaṅgā, in descending to earth, will fill the ocean, covering the ashes of Sagara's sixty thousand sons, who will thereafter be able to partake of salvation: there is therefore an explicit link between the descent of the Gaṅgā to earth and the emptying of her waters into the ocean; and the identification of the waters of the river and of the ocean may well be one of the mythical transformations of the comparisons of salvation with the flowing of rivers into the sea.

The son of Aṃśumān will try in vain to obtain the purification of the Sāgaras, and it is his grandson Bhagīratha who accomplishes this feat: he goes to the Himalayas to practice austerities in order to propitiate Gaṅgā, who eventually appears to him and promises him what he desires. She will come to earth to purify the sons of Sagara and to fill the ocean. But the violence of her current means that the earth will not be able to withstand the shock. Bhagīratha must therefore devote himself to further austerities on Mount Kailāsa, this time to obtain Śiva's mediation: Śiva agrees to receive the Gaṅgā on his head when she descends from heaven. The river falls on his head, is split into three streams of water (the three Himalayan torrents that unite to form the Ganges), and asks Bhagīratha to show her the course she must take. Bhagīratha accompanies her to the dried-up ocean where the ashes of the Sāgaras await their purification.

The myth therefore establishes a double connection, between the Gaṅgā and the ocean, on the one hand, and between Viṣṇu(-Kapila) and Śiva on the other hand, in which structures known from other sources are encountered again. That Śiva the destroyer here plays the part of mediator is not surprising. His function as "swallower" of the worlds is apparently transferred to the Gaṅgā, which receives the ashes of the dead, but his intervention signifies the first act in the drama of salvation. There must be death, the funeral pyre, and ashes—all things connected with Śiva—in order that the second phase, salvific immersion in the waters of the deluge or of the Gaṅgā, may unfold. Moreover, it is Śiva's yogic power that makes it possible for him to receive the violent flood that has come down from heaven.

The iconographic career of this myth attests its importance: recall the immense stone relief of Mamallapuram, to the south of Madras, that illustrates the descent of the Ganges, and the representation of Śiva as the "bearer of Gaṅgā"—*gaṅgādharamūrti*. Moreover, it might be very instructive to make an exhaustive survey of all the rivers in India that have received a compound name terminating in *-gaṅgā*. In the final analysis, every river and every temple pond is Gaṅgā.

M.Bi./b.f.

BIBLIOGRAPHY

M. E. ADICÉAM, "Les images de Śiva dans l'Inde du Sud," 15: "Gaṅgādharamūrti," *Arts Asiatiques* 32 (1976). O. VIENNOT, *Les divinités fluviales Gaṅgā et Yamunā aux portes des sanctuaires de l'Inde* (Paris 1964).

PRE-ISLAMIC IRAN

During the third millennium B.C., various Indo-European tribes emigrated from their original habitat in eastern Europe and reached Central Asia, where they remained for a time. They then gradually moved south, and at the beginning of the second millennium their presence can be detected on the Iranian plateau and in the mountains of Afghanistan. Some of these tribes, starting from Kashmir and the Punjab, undertook the conquest of India, while others took over all of Iran up to the confines of the Caucasus and Mesopotamia. Around 1800 B.C., a vast Iranian domain had thus come into being, extending from Zagros to Transoxiana.

As they settled into the various provinces of this territory, the conquering tribes maintained a certain distinctiveness, especially in their dialects, but they also shared a sense of community, like the Greeks, who considered themselves Greek despite the rivalries among their cities. The Medes occupied the northwest,the Persians settled in the southwest, while the east was held by tribes of unknown name, closely related to the tribes that occupied the Punjab. In the extreme north, the Scythians led a nomadic life and spread their influence from the Ukraine to Siberia. On several occasions they attempted to penetrate Iran and India, where they managed to found a dynasty in the first century B.C. At the same time, other Iranian tribes, particularly the Parthians, appeared in Persia and in India, where from time to time powerful empires were constituted that contributed to the cultural unification of these peoples.

The Aryans

It is also significant that these tribes all called themselves Aryans (in Sanskrit: *ārya;* in ancient Iranian: *aĩrya*), in contrast with the native populations who are considered "barbarians" (that is, incapable of speaking correctly) and more or less as "demoniacs" (because they worshiped false gods). The word refers both to an ethnic reality, in which men with fair skin conquered darker native peoples, and to a socioreligious community, in which people practiced similar rites and organized their social life in analogous ways. Even today the country is officially called "the domain of the Āryas" (in Persian, *īrān shahr,* a transposition of the ancient formula *aĩryānām vaejo,* which has the same meaning).

Of course, there is no exception here to the rule of religion as the main piece in the cultural edifice of civilizations at this level; indeed, it is religion that gives this community of interests its reason for existing and its basic justification. Equally, it is religion that provides the ideology on which the very notion of being Aryan is based. This can be seen in the fact that the Aryans understood the conquest of territory as the sacralization of ground considered profane prior to the first lighting of the ritual fire. This remained true in Iran up to the ending of the Sassanian empire in the seventh century under the blows of Islam. Likewise, any individual introduced into the Aryan community had to be "adopted" by the fire god, to whom he was solemnly presented. Thus, the assimilation of indigenous populations could be carried out on a grand scale, because in the final analysis the decisive criterion was the adherence of the newly introduced person to the religion of the "masters."

And, in fact, this is what happened in Iran as in India: only a few centuries after the settling of Indo-Europeans in these two countries, all the inhabitants had converted; this made intercommunal marriages permissible and led to a general mixing of populations. At all levels of society, the same religion was practiced, the same language spoken, the same customs observed. When the first authentic historical evidence appears, Iran has already completed its cultural unification, even without political unity. It should be said, however, that we do not know this religion well, mostly because of the disparate nature of the sources that we can use in our attempt to understand it.

Strangely enough, it is only with Herodotus that we have the first description of Iranian religious customs. From him we learn that the Persians did not build temples but worshiped their gods in the open air, that they had no statues of the gods, that sacrifices were made in the presence of fire and included the killing of animals whose flesh was consumed, and finally that they did not bury or cremate corpses but rather exposed their dead on hills, where they were devoured by vultures. All these characteristics are truly Iranian, but as an explanation of the whole, the description falls short. About the gods themselves Herodotus is even more vague: he sees them as natural forces and elements and as what he calls "the Sky."

Less than a century before, Darius had had an inscription engraved in which the name of this god of the Sky is revealed: Ahura Mazdā. King Artaxerxes II (405–359) boasts in another inscription of being the protégé not only of Ahura Mazdā but also of Mithra and the goddess Anāhitā. From this period on, the available documentation increases considerably: thanks to the bas-reliefs we have some idea of the costumes, the ritual gestures, and the shape of the altars and of some liturgical instruments, notably the mortar that is used to pound the *haoma.* The god Ahura Mazdā appears in the form of a winged disk (perhaps symbolizing the Sun), sometimes crowned with the bust of a bearded figure, and often accompanied by imaginary animals: winged lions, bull-men, scorpion-men, etc. Many of the scenes remain a mystery, lacking as they do any explanatory inscriptions. Much later there finally appears the name of Zarathustra (the "Zoroaster" of the Greeks), whose doctrine becomes the official religion of the Iranian Empire starting from the third century A.D. (the Sassanian dynasty). We will see below what problems are raised by this belated victory of the Zoroastrian prophet, all the more since it is at about the same period that the mysteries of Mithra start to spread in the Roman Empire, along with the diffusion of the cult of this god in western India; but Mithra is only given a modest position in Zoroastrianism itself!

The Avesta

It would be very difficult to piece together all these apparently contradictory factors if we did not have the Avesta, the sacred book of Zoroastrianism. In this book, the archaeology and religious history are made clearer, rites are described, formulas to be recited given in extenso, etc. At the heart of this collection is a unique section, differentiated from the rest of the work by style, the dialect in which it is written, and literary genre. It is composed of hymns of medium length (fifteen or so strophes) attributed to Zarathustra himself and called simply "Songs" (*gāthās*). Other, longer, hymns, written in a different dialect, constitute together with the Gāthās what by convention is called the Yasna ("the sacrifice," that is, texts suitable for recitation during the sacrifices). There are also about twenty liturgical poems that are different from the preceding ones and that the Avesta groups according to the "characteristic of the time" for a particular prayer (the Yasht). Finally, the section called Vidēvdāt ("against demons") concerns ritual impurities and the means of avoiding them or effacing them. Here there are directions concerning daily life and considerations about the destiny of the soul after death. Several chapters of lesser interest complete this certainly archaic collection.

Indeed, philological comparison shows that the dialect of the Gāthās is of the same linguistic stratum as that of the Veda, estimated to have been composed about 1500 B.C., if not several centuries earlier. The other dialect, that of all the Avesta (except the Gāthās), is a little more modern and resembles the Sanskrit of the year 1000 B.C. Thus with the Avesta one has arrived at an Iranian religion in the full sense of the word, a religion that took shape once the Aryans, who had been settled in the country for several centuries, finally brought about the cultural unity of their "domain" (*vaejo*). Unfortunately the precious testimony of the Avestan hymns is flawed by a twofold misadventure that befell the sacred text: on the one hand, the book that we have is truncated, representing only one-fourth of the original Avesta; on the other hand, Zarathustra, acting as a reformer, overturned the theology and contributed to the disappearance of important information about the former religion.

We must therefore realize that the Avesta took its definitive form only under the Sassanians, when Zoroastrianism had been consecrated as the "national faith." The priests of that time, by their own admission, retained from the former traditions only what seemed to them to be suitable to the practice of the reformed religion and of the rest gave us a sibylline summary, just enough to render appreciable the extent of the loss. From the third and fourth centuries on, and even more after the Islamic conquest, Zoroastrian theologians composed exegetical treatises for the priests that were designed to preserve the spirit of what they called "the Good Religion." Thanks to these works composed in old Persian and then in classical Persian, many aspects of the tradition are revealed to us, for example the domestic cult that the Avesta does not mention at all; what is more, the mythology is clarified by these encyclopedic instructions. As examples we can cite from among these books the *Dēnkart*, dating from the tenth century, the *Zartusht Nāma* (thirteenth century), which narrates the legendary life of the Prophet, and the *Rivāyāt*, letters exchanged around the seventeenth century between the Zoroastrians of Iran and their brothers who had emigrated to India.

It can be seen from this brief overview that the sources that we have at our disposal for the study of the Iranian religion are often disappointing, because they are fragmentary and reformational in intent. Modern scholarship, however, has succeeded in giving an order to these heterogeneous pieces of information, and has discovered behind their impartiality the essentials of what can be called the original theology. This work was begun at the end of the eighteenth century when the French scholar Anquetil-Duperron succeeded in having some Parsis (Iranians who had emigrated to India) transmit the Avesta to him; these Parsis, however, had only a passing knowledge of the Avesta, and Anquetil's contribution would have been negligible if the text he brought back from India had not been correctly deciphered by nineteenth-century philologists, notably Burnouf, who in 1833 constructed his first key to the Avestan language with the first translation of the Yasna.

Having recognized the relationship of the Iranian dialects to Sanskrit, Greek, Latin, Germanic, and the other Indo-European languages, the linguists of the nineteenth century kept refining the study of Avestan vocabulary and syntax until another French scholar, J. Darmestéter, managed to complete a translation of the sacred scriptures of the Zoroastrians (*L'Avesta*, 1892, republished in 1960). In this monumental work, authoritative even today, the only weakness was the interpretation of the Gāthās. The considerable progress of comparative grammar in the first half of the twentieth century made it possible for J. Duchesne-Guillemin (*Zoroastre*, 1948) and H. Humbach (*Die Gāthās des Zarathustras*, 1959) to make translations that can be considered definitive.

At the same time, the study of religion was being organized in a similar fashion by the systematic comparison of the main elements of Iranian religion with those elements that form the basis of our knowledge of Indo-European beliefs. For the most archaic period, the most important point of reference was obviously Vedic India, with which the linguistic connection was extraordinary, especially for religious vocabulary: *daeva/deva*, *ahura/asura*, *mithra/mitra*, *haoma/soma*, *daenā/dhenā*, *yasna/yajña*, etc.; it was easy for specialists to show that the realities expressed by the words also coincided, with some allowance being made for local distortions. For the classical and later periods, the autonomous development of Iranian religion made the comparison with India less and less meaningful, but it did make possible some connections with the beliefs of the Romans and the Greeks, as well as with the lesser-known beliefs of the Scythians and the Slavs.

The crowning achievement of this comparative effort can be seen today in the work of Georges Dumézil, who must be given credit for demonstrating the trifunctional structure of Indo-European ideology; by means of this key, the Iranian pantheon, which had once seemed chaotic, recovers its harmonious order and its coherence. Thus we can under-

Temple of fire, a structure known as the Kabba of Zarathustra. Naqshi-i Rustam, near Persepolis. Photo Lucien Hervé.

stand how the populations of this region of Asia could have remained attached to their gods for such so long (three millennia); and Henri Corbin has shown how even Islam has been affected by that pantheon, as in the Iranian version (Shiism) and particularly in the Sufism of a Sohrawardī. These diverse considerations have given rise to so many historical references that we should say something about the evolution of the Zoroastrian religion before proceeding to analyze it in detail.

Historical Background

When the Aryan tribes undertook the conquest of Iran and India, they had in common a whole collection of beliefs and rituals that had remained close to those of their Indo-European ancestors; the Veda (composed during the second millennium B.C.) gives a very complete picture of these. On both sides of the Hindu Kush, the pantheon was divided between Asura gods (in Iran, *Āhura*) and Deva gods (Iranian, *daeva*), sacrifices were offered (*yajña/yasna*), and people hoped to be admitted after death to the celestial dwelling place of the perpetual Light; to do this, one had to act according to the good (*ṛta/arta*) and reject evil (*druh/druj*), etc. The parallelism must have been even closer than we can imagine, and the evolution of both religions would probably have taken very similar paths if a major event had not totally upset the situation in Iran—the preaching of Zarathustra and the gradual conversion of the Iranians to the teachings of the Reformer. The whole thing remains something of a mystery.

Keeping to the least doubtful probabilities, the Prophet can be assumed to have lived in Chorasmia (south of the Aral sea) or in Sogdiana (the upper basin of the Amu Darya) at an indeterminate time. The later Zoroastrian tradition gives the dates 628 and 551 B.C., but seems to confuse the birth of the Reformer with the fall of the Achaemenid Empire; moreover, the language of the Gāthās is so archaic and so close to that of the Ṛg Veda (eighteen hundred B.C.) that one hesitates to ascribe such a recent date to the birth of Zarathustra. Whatever the solution may be, the man must have had a strong personality, considering the radical nature of his reform and the passion that infused the hymns that he composed. As a priest (*zaotar;* in India: *hotṛ*), he seems to have been able to impose the values of his caste at the expense of those of the warrior aristocracy: for example, he attacked the practice of blood sacrifices and the rites of the *haoma* (Sanskrit, *soma*), which were the preserve of the gods of the warriors function.

In India, their chief was called Indra, "king of the *devas*"; it is significant that in Zoroastrian theology, the *daevas* are "demons" and that Indra was the name of one of these "demons." Inversely, the deities of the priestly function were often called Asuras in the Ṛg Veda, and Zarathustra chose to name Ahura Mazdā ("the Wise Lord") the supreme God, whom he recommends as the exclusive object of worship. This last characteristic is remarkable in an ideological context such as that of ancient Iran, and we can understand why the message was badly received. Persecuted, Zarathustra had to leave his country and take refuge further south, probably in Seistan (the south of what is now Afghanistan). He is said to have converted a minor local king, the *kavi* (prince) Vishtāspa, who had given him asylum and devoted himself to the diffusion of the doctrine of the Prophet, by arms if necessary. The Prophet was nevertheless assassinated at an advanced age (seventy-seven years, according to tradition).

If we recall that Zoroastrianism became the official religion of Iran only during the third century A.D., we realize that the reformed faith was propagated very slowly; some scholars think that the Iranians never adhered to it unanimously. In proof of this they cite the fact that, at the time of the Roman Empire, it was not the cult of Ahura Mazdā that was spread in western Europe but that of Mithra, whom Zarathustra had repudiated as he had all other gods but the Wise Lord. The doctrine of the Prophet seems first of all to have won over the Medes with whom the tribes of Sogdiana were in permanent contact. From Herodotus we know that the priestly function among the Medes was in the possession of the clan of the magi (*maga*), who enjoyed great prestige throughout the entire Iranian domain. Their conversion therefore added greatly to the fame of the Reformer. At the time of Plato, the Greeks already associated magic ("the wisdom of the magi") with Zoroaster, whom they considered to be a demigod (he was called "the son of Ahura Mazdā").

In light of this special situation, it is noteworthy that the Iranians should have rejected the reformed religion for so long: that rejection indicates that polytheism was deeply rooted in people's minds, doubtless because it corresponded better to the structure of the society. It will be shown below that triumphant Zorastrianism "recovered" the essential part of the archaic religion, at the price of changing its perspective. The organization, in the third century, of a veritable Zoroastrian church with a sort of pontiff at its head was most certainly a defensive reaction against Christianity and Manichaeanism, which were also organized in churches. The Iranian religion at least managed to gain the upper hand over its two rivals and gave way only before Islam, which seized political power in two centuries starting in 635 and succeeded in converting a very great majority of the population.

Little Zoroastrian communities survived in the southeast of the country, and there are still five active temples of fire in the region of Kerman (with about twenty thousand worshipers called "Ghebers," from an Arabic word for non-Muslims). Other Zoroastrians emigrated to India, to the region of Surat (north of Bombay), where there were Iranian trading posts. They prospered there, and in the nineteenth century their community played an important role in the economic life of the British colony. It was to these Parsis (as the Indians called them) that Anquetil-Duperron went in search of the Avesta. The religion that they were practicing then had become highly formalistic, because they no longer understood the text, though they recited it scrupulously and in its entirety during their religious ceremonies. Today the situation has improved a little because, thanks to European philologists, the Avesta has been rendered intelligible and translated, its content explained by comparison with other forms of religion, etc. This is what J. Duchesne-Guillemin called "the response of the West to Zoroaster." Nevertheless, the Parsi community remains so reduced in number (less than a hundred thousand worshipers) in relation to the enormous mass of the Hindu population (more than six hundred million) that it has a tendency to remain closed in on itself and thus to accentuate the formalism of its religion. This can be especially noted in the refusal of external conversion, even in the case of marriage, an attitude obviously opposed to the teachings of the Prophet, who had hoped that the entire world would belong to the Good Religion. There is thus little to be learned from the Parsis; yet they can be admired for their faithfulness to their ancestral religion (even if they retained nothing of it but the letter).

The Rites

The study of the beliefs and practices of pre-Islamic Iran remains thus in the purview of the historian of religions, who relies essentially on philology, with some help from archaeology. Following a proper method, such a historian will differentiate rites, mythology, and theology and present them in this order, as all religion is first of all orthopraxy. As we begin to analyze the Iranian ritual we are struck by the fact that it is centered on fire: there is no religious ceremony, public or private, official or domestic, that does not require the presence of a hearth, around which the ceremony is organized.

Fire-centeredness is characteristic of Indo-European liturgies, but it is unusually well developed by the Indo- Iranians, to such an extent that the Parsis have often mistakenly been called "fire worshipers," when in fact they worship only Ahura Mazdā. It is true that a perpetual fire burns in their temple, and the priests recite their prayers in front of it, but for modern Zoroastrians the flame is only the symbol, the perceptible sign of the purity and beauty and light of the Wise Lord. Nevertheless, far in the past fire was indeed a deity and, as such, an integral part of the pantheon into which the divine society was organized, rich in individuals of both sexes. A modest god, at first sight, because he was without the mythological pomp enjoyed by the Rulers and the Warriors, he nevertheless occupied a position of the greatest strategic importance because of his special role in the ritual.

The Sacrifice

For the ancient Iranians, as for the Vedic Indians, the gods were able to keep their immortality only to the degree that mortals nourished them with oblations, just as mortals won their place in Heaven by preparing their offerings and consuming them together with their divine guests. The question arises, however, as to the contact between the world on high and this world: invisible, untouchable, radically nonhuman, how can these "absolute others" hear the invitation that we address to them to come to us and share our meal? A mediation is necessary, and Indo-Europeans all agree that this task devolves upon fire, either through force (the Promethean myth of the theft of the divine fire) or through the free choice of the deity whose external form is fire. The Indo-Iranians tend to the latter and never cease thanking the fire god for having consented to come to live among men. Moreover, only a part of the activity of this deity is thought to be exercised here below: there is a fire in the sky (which is the sun), a fire in the atmosphere (lightning), and lastly, a fire on earth (the one that glows in our hearths and on our altars).

No matter what the form of the myth, the point remains that the fire god has established his dwelling on earth among men and that he fully assumes his role as intermediary between his peers, the other gods of the pantheon, and the worshipers. Thus, when a ritual ceremony is to be celebrated, a sacred ground, rectangular in form, is marked out by a furrow on the cleared earth at some distance from the village. Herodotus noted this fact with surprise; but this was because he knew nothing about the religion of his distant ancestors: they too venerated the gods in the open air, away from their dwelling places, in clearings and glades; they too regarded the sacrifice as a cosmic drama that concretely enacted the junction of the sky (that luminous dome over their heads) with the earth (the ground lying fallow under their feet). That was the norm in the Indo-European period, and remained so in India until the demise of Vedic religion.

The Greeks and Romans, by contrast, very early assumed the habit of building temples sheltering the dedicated images of the deities. As for Iran, it moved in a different direction: the Zoroastrian reform made the spread of religious images impossible, and it was to fire itself that the honor of a special building was reserved. From the Achaemenid period on, there were fire temples (pyrea) throughout all of Iran, from Susa to Bactria, and even nowadays Zoroastrians build them; they can be seen in some areas in southeastern Iran, as well as in India among the Parsis of Bombay. The buildings all contain a square room in which the sacred fire burns in perpetuity. The worshipers can see the flame through openings, and at certain periods, notably under the Sassanians, the raised hearth was constructed on top of elevated areas from which it shone as the sign of imperial power and of the "Aryanization" of the conquered territories. It must be remembered that in Rome, in a similar manner, the temple of Vesta sheltered the national hearth that was guarded by consecrated virgins.

It is important to note that the sacrifice was celebrated, not in or in front of this hearth, but at a distance, in another spot, where a rectangular room, carefully oriented, reconstituted the sacrificial arena of ancient times: one or several fires were lit there, for ritual use only, an additional sign of the fundamental distinction between the fire as symbol, a terrestrial image of the Wise Lord (Ahura Mazdā), and the fire as eater of offerings, whose mythological function is to assure and maintain relations between the world of men and that of the gods. To the first fire personal prayers and hymns of praise are dedicated, while the second fire is asked to assemble the deities to whom the sacrifice is dedicated and to transmit to them the food specially prepared for them. The one is thus a great god, while the other seems to be only a simple messenger, almost a servant. A messenger, indeed, but also a witness and thus perhaps a judge.

This new mythological appearance of the fire god makes it possible to understand why the Indo-Iranians never really dissociated the two aspects of a deity that they knew to be singular. Here too it is the sacrificial ritual that has provided the key to the problem: if Fire can receive offerings and distribute them to those for whom they are meant, it is because Fire is capable (perhaps the only one capable?) of hearing the request made by the one who sacrifices at the beginning of the ceremony and then, as the ceremony unfolds, interpreting the words of the person making the invocation. When, for example, an offering is presented to Mithra (Vedic, Mitra) the *zaotar* (Vedic, *hotṛ*) throws it in the hearth placed before him, saying, "This is for Mithra!"; the flame is believed to understand the meaning of these words; when the oblation has been consumed, it is in fact "carried" by the fire god to his friend Mithra, to whom the Messenger bears witness to the sacrificer's correct intention and to the fact that his gestures conformed precisely to the ritual protocol. In addition, the prayers, sometimes public but often secret (that is, mental, not expressed), are transmitted at the same time to the one for whom they are meant, which implies that the fire god has the power to read the hearts of men. This shows the importance of the *zaotar*, the priest of both the oblation and the invocation, whose role is essential in the practice of the religion, as he is the one who represents humans (and notably the one who sacrifices) before the fire god, just as the latter represents the deities of the pantheon to mortals. Zarathustra was a *zaotar* by profession, which assured him of constant dealings with Fire, and this explains why he never ceases to invoke the flame as witness to the purity of his intention of reform. This is also why he has chosen Fire as the favored symbol of the majesty of Ahura Mazdā, who has been promoted to the rank of sole god in his theological system. A certain equivocation remains in the religion of Zarathustra himself, and even more so in that of his followers. In many respects the impression remains that Fire has retained something of its role of mediator in the emotions of these worshipers: the priests who are seen officiating before the flame in innumerable Iranian bas-reliefs are in all likelihood waiting for Atar ("Fire") to transmit their prayer to the Wise Lord, who can be seen in the sky in the form of a winged disk suspended above the hearth. The reverence accorded to this "angel messenger" is so great that one must bathe and change one's clothes before approaching him and address him only if a cloth has been placed in front of one's mouth, for fear of contaminating him with impure breath. In their houses today, Zoroastrians keep a sacred fire burning (often in the form of a simple oil lamp), and it is here that they recite their daily prayers, in conformity to an ancient custom.

The Domestic Cult

This presence of Fire in the very heart of the dwelling place is moreover necessary for the celebration of the domestic cult and especially of the sacraments that provide the rhythm for the life of the individual: the giving of the name, initiation, marriage, funeral. For the Indo-Europeans, religion was primately a family affair. At first there was no priest, but the head of the family presided, perhaps assisted by a liturgist, that is, by a ritual technician whose role did not go beyond that of a paid adviser. The ceremonial, even when extended to the clan, the tribe, or the "city," remains astonishingly faithful to its domestic origins, as it always includes preparing a meal, which the patron (the one who sacrifices, himself as an absolute rule the head of a family) offers to the gods and to those mortals whom he has invited to share the food that the Fire-Messenger has not consumed in the name of the divine guests.

Gradually, however, the ceremony becomes more complicated; in India and Iran, the technical experts of the sacrifice assume an increasing role and tend to form a sacerdotal caste. We know that the post-Zoroastrian religion has at its disposal a veritable clergy in the magi, whose privileges become very substantial under the Sassanians. Nevertheless, the fundamental structure of the ritual, even in this case, remains what it was in the beginning: the sacred texts (the Veda in India, the Avesta in Iran) teach categorically that the priest is merely the servant of the lay person offering the sacrifice, who is the sole patron of a rite that without him would not exist.

Thus, the *zaotar* is nothing unless he has been hired by the head of a family, and we know what an anguished search Zarathustra conducted, going the length and breadth of Iran looking for a prince who would accept him as chaplain despite his heretical positions. In fact, the Reformer was

A traditional representation of Ahura Mazdā as an eagle with wings extended. Photo Lucien Hervé.

unable to preach his doctrine until Vishtāspa had become his patron. Everything therefore leads back to the family and to its head and more particularly to the domestic hearth, where the sacred Fire burns in perpetuity. Hence, all the sacraments will appear as stages in the life of the family ("incarnated" in some sense in each of its members) and will take place in the home in front of the hearth.

One of the most important of these liturgical moments is the *naojote* ("new birth"), which marks, at the ending of childhood, around the age of twelve, the entry into the world of adults. In the beginning, the rite concerned only boys and inaugurated their professional apprenticeship, which would be completed by the marriage that was obligatory for everyone. From a theological point of view, biological birth conferred on the ancient Iranian nothing more than a bare existence inferior even to that of animals: this is because man is a being with a spiritual essence, and his passage on earth is like that of an exile. In order to regain his heavenly homeland, he must have the spiritual seed quickened in him so that he can, throughout his life, make it grow and blossom. If he is successful, he will be "delivered" and win the realm of unextinguishable light, the Dwelling of Song (*Garō Demānā*), in a word, the Paradise whose name (*pairidaēza*, the "Other Country") was borrowed by the Bible from the Avesta.

The *naojote* is thus an initiation, normally conferred by a father on his son. Stripped of his childhood clothes, the young man puts on a new tunic (*surdēh*) and girds himself with a belt (*kūsti*). He then learns his true name, which has been kept secret until then, and he is presented to the Fire, which literally "recognizes" and "adopts" him. For the first time he recites his prayers before the witness god and from then on the head of the family can die in peace, because the continuity of the family line has been assured. The girls, for their part, received their initiation from their husbands during the marriage ceremony, because their real existence (and thus their spiritual blossoming) began only at the moment when they were adopted by the Fire of their father-in-law. This must be put in the past tense, however, because, at an unknown but relatively recent time, they were admitted to the *naojote*. In any case this is the custom of Zoroastrians today, in India as in Iran. The important element is the relation to Fire, which is felt to be both a factor of spiritual development (one can reach Heaven only through sacrifice, which requires the ministry of the mediator god) and as a guarantee of the perennial duration of the succession (for the Fire adopts new members: sons born to the family, daughters from the outside who enter through marriage).

The marriage ceremony itself is conducted around the family hearth: it is in the presence of the domestic Fire that the father designates the two messengers who are to go to request the hand of the young girl that he wishes to marry to his son. It is in front of the Fire of the future family-in-law that the messengers are received and that the sacramental "yes" is pronounced by the father of the fiancée. When the actual wedding is celebrated, the Fire again is witness, receives the propitiatory offerings, and thus makes himself the guarantor of the union. It should be emphasized that only the father and his child have a role to play in the *naojote*, and likewise only the respective fathers and the others concerned are sufficient to perform the marriage ceremony. As customs evolved and religious studies fell into disuse, the liturgists were transformed from mere counselors into officiating priests: nowadays many Zoroastrians think that the *dasturs* ("priests") are necessary for the regular administration of the sacraments. However, one has only to listen to the texts that they are reciting to realize that they are nothing but spokesmen, in the literal sense of the term, for their lay patrons.

As for funerals, the Fire no longer played its mythological role of psychopomp after the Iranians, breaking with Indo-European tradition, stopped cremating their dead. This change took place fairly far in the past, since Herodotus remarks on it already in the fifth century B.C. For fear of soiling the elements that make up the universe, the bodies of Zoroastrians are neither burned, submerged in water, nor buried, but are abandoned on boulders or cliffs where beasts of prey devour them. Often (and this is the rule today) circular enclosures are built (the *dakhma*, known in the West as "towers of silence") where bodies are brought and placed out of sight to be torn to pieces by vultures. This absence of the mediator god is unusual and corresponds in all likelihood to an abandoning of the tradition. Modern theologians try to justify it by stating that death is a complete defilement, capable of contaminating even Fire; but how is it possible to believe that he who is the ultimate Purifier could be affected by the death (so necessary to the maintenance of cosmic order) of any individual? Moreover, the intimate relations between the head of the family and his hearth seem to be broken off at that most decisive moment when the deceased will have to undertake the difficult eschatological voyage: it is a great aberration for him not to receive the provisions for the journey from his regular protector.

The Zoroastrians of today are profoundly conscious of this feeling of abandonment, foresakenness, and solitude. Such a situation, combined with the prospect of what will happen to the body in the *dakhma*, overwhelms the worshipers and arouses in their consciousness a kind of despair, countering the optimism that is usually and rightly attributed to the Zoroastrian religion, which is entirely oriented toward the enhancement of life, the celebration of light and happiness, the striving after earthly prosperity, the promise of Paradise, etc. Of all this, fire—glowing, warm, crackling (which is referred to as "singing")—is the central symbol, along with the Sun. Its absence from funeral ceremonies can only be an accident and does not in any way hinder its prestige or the Zoroastrians devotion to it.

The *Haoma*

There remains, in the domain of ritual, the difficult problem of *haoma* ("juice"; in India, *soma*). It is known that in the distant past certain solemn sacrifices (that is, those outside the domestic ritual) included the preparation of a "drink of immortality," which the worshipers consumed after pouring the part that they owed to the gods into the fire. This practice is found throughout the Indo-European realm and seems to be linked to a form of esoteric cult, one reserved for certain individuals who received a special initiation that gave them access to it. The idea is that drinking the potion assures immortality and makes one an "almost god," a hero in the Greek sense of the word. It is even thought that the gods are what they are because they have drunk ambrosia, and that they retain their divine status only under the express condition of continuing to drink it. This *haoma* had been stolen from the gods and given to man (a variation of the Promethean myth): an eagle had brought it to them to enable them to become gods too. From this time on, the members of the pantheon are tributary to mortals: if mortals were to lose their faith, if they should cease to "press out the *haoma* for the gods," according to the consecrated formula, the Immortals would know death and disappear. This "twilight of the gods" would bring on the end of the world.

Such a theology has certainly never been "popular," for it undermines the foundation of devotion and impairs the respect and fear that the worshipers feel toward their gods. Nevertheless, the magical enchantments of the *haoma* must have enjoyed great prestige, above all in the aristocracy, because the sacrifice of the *haoma* tends progressively to become the norm of the "solemn" liturgy (that is, the liturgy of the king and the chiefs of the clan). In the beginning, this type of ceremony probably belonged to the special initiation of warriors and to its renewal each time a military mission was being prepared or had been achieved. Furthermore, in Iran as in India, the dominant religion became that of the prince, especially when the first empires were constituted. The other classes of society then required, and soon obtained, the right to participate in the ritual of the *haoma*. Thus during the "classical" period of the Vedic and Avestan religions (around the tenth century B.C.), every important sacrifice included the pressing out and the drinking of the *haoma/soma*.

It should be noted that the "juice" in question was no ordinary drink. Its consumption, according to the ancient texts, brought on a sort of drunkenness or ecstatic trance, which was said to be a "foretaste of the celestial delights." At the same time, it was stated that, by drinking the *haoma*, warriors acquired strength, courage, and above all that "furor" (*aēshma* in Avestan, *furor* in Latin, *hubris* in Greek) by virtue of which they could accomplish great exploits on the battlefield and impose victory even on an enemy of greater numbers. It is not known from what plant this juice was extracted, but, to judge from the effects that its absorption produces upon the minds of the worshipers, it seems likely that it was a hallucinogen. Alcohol must be excluded as a possibility, as the texts state that alcohol must be reserved for profane feasts. Hashish has been considered (*bhanga* in Iranian, *bhangā* in Sanskrit), but a passage from the Dēnkart seems to contradict this suggestion, for we read that Zarathustra's patron, King Vishtāspa, drank one day a cup of *haoma* mixed with hashish (*hōm ut bhangh;* see Widengren, p. 89); so the two ingredients could not have been the same. Recently, R. G. Wasson has put forth the intriguing hypothesis that the preparation was based on the *Amanita muscaria* (fly-killing amanita, or false orange mushroom). Approved by considerable men of learning, with Claude Lévi-Strauss in the front rank, this theory seems to take account of all the difficulties and to resolve them convincingly.

In any event, it was a toxic beverage, a drug whose use was made part of an aristocratic liturgy of a "Dionysian" character in contrast to the "Apollonian" serenity of the domestic rites. It is to be observed, however, that throughout the Indo-European domain, "mysteries" of this type aroused the hostility of the priestly circles, in the name of the morality and dignity of the religion. This explains why the secret of the "nectar of the gods" was lost during the historic period in the West, notably for the Romans and Greeks, who retained of it only a mythical memory. It did remain in the possession of very closed circles, as was the case, for example, among the Celts and the Germans until the advent of Christianity. In Iran, Zarathustra was the incarnation of this hostility, which he expressed with a violence that says much about the resistance his reform encountered. In one of the Gāthās (Yasna 48), he does not hesitate to call the *haoma* "filth" and accuses it of causing warriors to lie and to commit cruelty and gratuitous violence (strophes 10 to 12), which make them "bad princes" in his eyes. Carrying out a measure that will meet with similar success in India, the Prophet in his reprobation associates the killing of animal victims with the enchantments of the *haoma*. In doing this, he says explicitly that these two aspects of the religion of his fathers are closely united and that they must be rejected together in order to establish the Good Order (*Arta* or *Asha*) that is both religious and political, the Empire (*kshatra*) in which men will be able to dedicate themselves to the peaceful breeding of cattle while venerating the unique god Ahura Mazdā.

This last recommendation obviously implies the rejection of all the deities of the Indo-European pantheon, leveled by Zarathustra to the rank of pernicious demons. It will soon be seen that the force of popular sentiment and the dexterity of the theologians made it possible for the aforementioned deities to survive clandestinely in the Zoroastrianism, in the same way that the *haoma* was reintegrated into the body of the ritual. This could of course only be done at the cost of softening the ritual, which was reduced to a primarily verbal ceremony with little place for gestures or manipulations. Nowadays, and it has probably been thus since the time of the Arsacids (third century B.C.), the Zoroastrian ritual (*mazdā-yasna*) has excluded the killing of animal victims: it is enough to offer as an oblation a very small quantity of fat at a certain moment during a ceremony consisting essentially of the recitation of the entire Avesta.

The *haoma* has been replaced by a substance that keeps the same name but with the explicit indication that it is only a substitute (*parā-hōm*). Moreover, the priests consume only a few drops of it, as though to emphasize the henceforth symbolic character of the rite thus preserved (which "keeps in memory" the *hōm* pressed out by Yima, the first man, at the beginning of time). The plant used for this purpose by the Parsis of Bombay is the *Ephedra vulgaris;* a few sprigs of it are powdered in a mortar together with some pomegranate grains; the whole is "drowned" in a proportionately much greater quantity of holy water. It goes without saying that such a drink has no toxic effect at all; yet for this harmless substitute for the former ambrosia the Zoroastrian priests have still chosen a plant whose essence (ephedrin) could eventually produce a kind of intoxication if it were extracted and prepared to this end and in sufficient quantity.

To permit the reintegration of *haoma* into the reformed religion, a mythological hymn had to be composed and a place found for it in the definitive compilation of the Avesta that was made just before the Islamic invasion. This hymn was the Hōm Yasht, in which the Prophet engages in a dialogue with the "genies" of *haoma* and concludes by recognizing in him a "just one . . . who keeps death away and procures long life." The form taken by this justification reminds us that during the Indo-European period every element of the sacrifice was regarded as the tangible manifestation of the power of a particular god. The pre-Zoroastrian *haoma* thus began as a deity, worthy of being the object of a cult, like the god Soma in India, whose praises the poets of the Ṛg Veda never tire of singing.

Because the reform of the Iranian religion effected by Zarathustra excluded all forms of polytheism, it was no longer possible to detect the presence of a god in the plant that gives eternal-life. But people continued to see it (and especially its sap) as a manifestation of the power and bounty of the Wise Lord, a manifestation whose guardian could be a genies or an angel. This was how the Zoroastrian theologians reasoned, and this was how they justified the retention in the liturgy of strophes such as the following (Yasna 9.17): "I ask you for wisdom, golden Haoma! I ask you for vigor, for victory in battle, for physical health and prosperity, for power and glory, for learning! I ask you for the power that will let me reign over the earth, to make order reign there, to keep Evil away from it." Such passages, which closely resemble parts of the Veda, surely had their origin in the hymns that the first Iranians recited in order to propitiate the *haoma* in its aspect as divine person; but they carry little weight, for the theologians cleverly succeeded in making such invocations "inoffensive," so to speak, by interpolating "modern" notations into them whose presence alone was sufficient to demote the *haoma* to the rank of creature (and servant) of the one God. Thus the sixteenth verse of Yasna 9 says: "The Haoma is good because it has been created good [*hudhātō*]"; and elsewhere (Yasna 10, verse 10): "Haoma, it is the good God who has made you [*tatakhshat*]." Many more examples could be given; all imply that Ahura Mazdā has made the plant, given it special virtues, and used the Power (which he has given it) to make his goodness shine out for those men who merit it.

The Myths

The recognition of this state of affairs makes it possible to appreciate the breadth and complexity of the problem (for it is one) posed by Iranian mythology. Strictly speaking, Zoroastrian orthodoxy permits of no mythology, in the proper sense of the term, within the framework of the religion, anymore than there can be a mythology, theoretically, in the Judaism of the prophets, for example. Nevertheless, the Indo-European traditions were sufficiently lively in Iran (as has been seen for the ritual) for the concept of the world to remain the same even after the preaching of the Reformer. Moreover, we must not forget that Zarathustra never ceased to affirm his fidelity to *ārya* ideas: he had come, he said, to reestablish the "Good Religion," which he judged to have become decadent, and not to abolish it. Bearing this affirmation in mind, Western observers, from Eugène Burnouf (*Commentaire sur le Yasna*, 1832) to Jacques Duchesne-Guillemin (*La religion de l'Iran ancien*, 1962) have detected and brought to light the survival of former patterns in the new construction erected by the Prophet of Ahura Mazdā.

To date, the most convincing work of synthesis is that of Georges Dumézil (*Naissance d'archanges*, 1945). Using the facts furnished by specialists in Iranian culture and comparing them systematically with those collected by specialists of other Indo-European religions, Dumézil has shown how Zarathustra, as a skilled theologian, was able voluntarily and consciously to rearrange the cultural patrimony that he had inherited. The mysterious Destiny (Latin, *fatum;* Greek, *anankē;* Sanskrit, *daivam*) was something to which the gods submitted, just as did all living things, as well as the universe itself; it was sufficient to see it as a conscious will, a Wisdom, in order to transform it from an archaic polytheism into a monotheism: this Will, this Wisdom, could be nothing other than the "essential" attribute of a divine personality (necessarily unique) to which the Prophet gave the name of Wise Lord, that is, "the God in whom Wisdom is incarnated," or, if you like, "Wisdom in the form of Power." This Will manifests itself in the world in various ways, according to circumstances and need: here it will be creative, there destructive, elsewhere it will preside over the germination of plants and the growth of animals; it will grant victory to one army over another, make the sun rise, inspire ideas in respectable men; it is through this Will that fire heats, water quenches thirst, cows give milk, and so on, ad infinitum. Since his contemporaries believed that an agent was necessary for each of the cosmic functions, Zarathustra explained to his disciples that these so-called deities were in fact only genies ("angels") created by Ahura Mazdā to play the role of responsible guardians.

This is what happened, as has been seen above, to the genie of the Haoma, even though its integration into the mythical edifice of Zoroastrianism certainly came long after the preaching of the Prophet. In this way, a good number of deities who had enjoyed a most prestigious status of personal autonomy (with a name, a function, and a special resting place) in the archaic religion, henceforth saw themselves limited to the subaltern position of zealous (and therefore "adorable": *yazatas*) servants of the Wise Lord.

Daevas and Ahura

This "recovery" affected only a part of the divine personnel of the ancient mythology. Another group of gods, however, was put into the camp of the adversaries—necessarily demonic—of the Good Religion. To understand this surprising discrimination, it must be remembered that the Indo-Iranians of the second millennium B.C. had inherited from their Indo-European forefathers a concept of divine society whose principal characteristic was its complexity. Far from conceiving of the pantheon as a serene and pacific world, they took pleasure in telling of its intrigues, rivalries, and combats, whether singular or collective. Even though many aspects of this situation are closed to us for lack of documentation, the general outline is clear.

This situation is essentially a struggle for universal power, in the most concrete sense of the term: who will be consecrated "king of the gods"? In Greece, Zeus wins this title by assassinating his own father; in India, Indra obtains it after eliminating Vṛtra, who had been keeping back the waters necessary to life, etc. Behind such incidents (which have something of the "duel" about them) are confrontations between definite groups: the Titans against the gods, according to the Greek terminology; the Asuras against the Devas, according to that of the Indo-Iranians. The battle is indecisive and terrible; in Greece it is the gods who gain the upper hand, in India the Devas. Or at least they gain an advantage that is always contested and always in peril. Classical Indian mythology is filled with the continuously renewed tumult of battle between Asuras and Devas. Later Hinduism, although unfaithful in many respects to Vedic religion, still maintains this outline: Kṛṣṇa can play his role of avatar only after having eliminated several Asuras; Durgā accedes to the rank of sovereign goddess only when she has killed the Asura Mahiṣa, etc.

But it is remarkable that these adversaries of the established gods are never confused with demons as such. They are clearly recognized as also belonging to the world on high by their nature; it is remembered that in the beginning they were "above" the gods, but that, when the occasion arose, they made unfortunate choices. Deprived of their celestial nobility, they attempt in vain to reconquer it. Condemned to err, they never stop making mistakes and instinctively, one could say, form their ranks behind the banner of Falsehood, Lies, Disorder, Darkness, and thus of Evil. Inversely, the gods struggle to inaugurate (or to safeguard) Good Order, Truth, Light, and thus the Good.

What counts in the final analysis are not the "virtues" specific to one side or the other but rather the free choice that they make between the eternally existing Good and Evil. It is a necessary choice, because this coexistence cannot be peaceful: the universe is a battlefield, and the destiny of each being, mortal or immortal, is sealed by the place he takes in the struggle. Moreover and above all, the universe survives only insofar as Order wins out over Disorder thanks to the valiant efforts of those engaged on the right side. The Indo-Europeans conceived of the world as formed of a multitude of parts combined to form a whole; the Good was thus the right adjustment (*arta* in Iranian, *ṛta* in Sanskrit) of these constituent elements; Evil was their dissociation (*anṛta* in Sanskrit). On the ethical level, always emphasized by the Iranians, the *arta* (also called *asha*) is the true Reality of things, their Truth, to which is opposed the *druj* (in Sanskrit: *druh*), "deceit, lies, falseness, unreality."

However, in contrast to what can be seen throughout the Indo-European domain, and especially in India, Zarathustra professed that the Daevas (the gods; in Sanskrit, Devas) had opted for the *druj*, while the Ahura par excellence, promoted to the rank of supreme deity, Ahura Mazdā, the Wise Lord, made himself the champion of the *arta*. The magnitude of the Reform can be seen: not only has the perspective been inverted (one must curse the Daevas rather than offer them veneration and sacrifices), but in addition even the mythology has been literally "erased," since the whole camp of the ancient Indo-Iranian Asuras has been absorbed into the one, solitary, all-powerful person of the Ahura, who represents Perfect Wisdom. Far from the dualism which it is often thought to be, Zoroastrianism is a pure monism, for what can the obscure forces do when faced with the radiant majesty of the Creator?

The unhappy Daevas, leveled to the rank of inferior demons, must content themselves with tormenting men, tempting them, and deceiving them with lies, in order to bring them to act against the Good Religion, etc. But simple exorcisms are enough to keep them away: moreover, the Avesta includes a particular section called Vidēvdāt (or Vendidād, "Law against the Demons"), in which there is a list of the gestures to be made and the formulas to be recited on the various occasions when the demons might appear. Thus armed, the worshiper has nothing to fear from the agents of the *druj*, if only, of course, he does not let himself be tricked by them, and always makes the "Good Choice," that is, follows the precepts of the Law scrupulously and always labors on behalf of justice (another meaning of the word *arta*), as Zarathustra himself says (Yasna 30, verse ll):

> If you men understand the instructions that the Wise One [that is, Ahura Mazdā] gave: well-being and punishment, long torture for the wicked and health for the just, all will be henceforward for the best!

Angra Manyu

This famous text, which greatly exalts the necessity of the Right Choice, nevertheless poses an additional problem: the Prophet here makes reference to a Spirit of Evil who is no longer only the *druj* (an abstract entity, a negative value) but a divine personage, an antagonist of his homologue the Holy Spirit.

> In the beginning (explains Zarathustra in the third strophe of this same Yasna 30), the two Spirits are twins, one the Good, the other the Evil, in thought, word, and deed. Of these two, the wise choose the right one, but not the fools.

What is new here is the affirmation of the existence of two Spirits (*Manyu*), placed on the same level of existence, and what is more, twins. Are they from the same mother? Do they become enemy brothers in a rivalry for the inheritance of the sovereignty over the universe? Or do they coexist for all eternity? It can be said, without fear of exaggeration, that all of Zoroastrian theology is one long dispute over these questions. For some, Spenta Manyu (the Holy Spirit) is another name of Ahura Mazdā (also called, in the Avesta, Vohu Manyu, "the Good Thought, the Spirit of Good"); from this, Angra Manyu, "the Spirit of Evil," appears as a rival of equal rank, since he is the twin brother of the Wise Lord.

In this perspective, the existence of dualism seems impossible to refute: there is neither one god, nor several, but two, and only two. It is thus neither polytheism nor monotheism but an original system, one perhaps unique in the history of religions and moreover without a name. Foreign observers (Greeks especially) believed that the opposition between Ohrmazd (a late form of the name of Ahura Mazdā) and Ahriman (for Angra Manyu) were fundamental to Iranian religion and that the worshipers considered them equal in power. The Gnostics and the Manichaeans inherited this vision and combined it with the Christian idea of Satan as "Prince of this World." Nevertheless, it does not seem that the Zoroastrians had ever professed a radical dualism. For the orthodox, Ahura Mazdā is the only sovereign god: the two Spirits are a projection of his omnipotence into two opposed but complementary forces. Just as there cannot be heat without cold (or dry without wet, light without darkness, etc.), so also one cannot imagine the Good without its contrary, Evil. At least not in this "lower world" that is by nature subject to the tensions of duality (whereas the world on high where the just go after their death is the world of unity).

Such a view involves the idea of conflict (*druj/arta*) and choice. There may even be here too the division of the divine community (Daevas/Ahura), which would entail the following sequence of events: Angra Manyu fighting with the Daevas for the triumph of the *druj*, against Spenta Manyu fighting with the angels of Ahura Mazdā for the safety of the *arta*. But we can see the imbalance of a system that cannot integrate the Ahura par excellence (the sole Ahura: Mazdā) in opposition to the Daevas, on pain of falling back into the "sin" of dualism.

An original solution to the problem of the "paternity" of these twin Spirits is said to have been proposed by certain Iranian theologians, at least if Greek evidence can be believed on this subject (Eudemus of Rhodes, cited by the neo-Platonist Damascius). In the beginning, said these priests, there was nothing but infinite Time (*Zurvān akarana*), from which came Light and Darkness, Ohrmazd and Ahriman, and, eventually, all living beings. An odd doctrine, at first view, but one that recalls Greek traditions about Kronos and Vedic traditions that exalt Kāla (time) and Prajāpati, the first god, in whom the Great Year becomes incarnate. There is, however, no formal proof that the cult of Zurvān ever had a significant existence in Iran; still it is troubling to note that Mani chose to call by this name the great god of the religion that he founded in the third century A.D.

The Ameshas Spentas

However these problems are to be solved, Zoroastrianism remains a religion marked more than many others by the belief that Evil is powerful, that it is a Spirit (that is, a cosmic energy, a divine power), and that the dynamism of his actions makes necessary a constant struggle to contain him. And there is the corollary idea that things do not always work out for the best in this battle: the order of things has a tendency to degenerate because the ranks of the just diminish. Evil, however, will not triumph, because at the end of time, just when Evil will think himself victorious, Renewal will break forth, a kind of Parousia or, better, a restoration of the golden age. This is an old Indo-European theme that Zarathustra took up for his own purposes and to which he gave a prophetic form of expression, one useful for his moral preaching. In addition, the Prophet explains that men are guided, inspired, and upheld in their salutary choice by semidivine entities (a species of angels) raised up by the Wise Lord to this end. These "Immortal Saints" (*Ameshas Spentas*) are seven in number, and the Avesta lists them explicitly in a hierarchy: at the head, Spenta Manyu (the Holy Spirit), then Arta (or Asha, Justice, Good Order, etc.), and Vohu Manyu (Good Thought, Right Inspiration); in fourth position, Kshatra (Empire), then Sarvatāt (Corporal Integrity, Good Health, Prosperity, etc.); in sixth position, Amretāt (Immortality, Eternal Life); in seventh and final place, Armaïti (Devotion).

The very names of these Immortal Saints show that they are not at all personal gods, but rather "values" that are so many "forces" or, if one prefers, "aspects" of divine Wisdom. Moreover, their respective places in the hierarchy constitute in themselves a veritable theology lesson, since it is obvious that the holy spirit, the cosmic order, and right inspiration are factors in the establishment of a kingdom in which the just will know a life without end dedicated to the service of the Lord; inversely, it is by starting with devotion that the faithful person will gain life everlasting, physical integrity, the realm, and the harmonious cohabitation with the Spirit of God. Yet other combinations are possible (and, for example, the central position of the Empire indicates the importance that Zarathustra attaches to the establishment of a "Zoroastrian state"), but it is evident that no real mythology is possible with such angels. From this, some historians of religion have concluded that Zarathustra was a kind of Calvinist before his time.

Zurvān and the two spirits: the evil spirit and the good spirit. Portion of the head of a pin in the shape of a disk. Bronze. Louristan. New York, Harramaneek collection. Photo Giraudon.

But one can avoid this anachronism by examining the list of the Ameshas Spentas in the light of the works of Georges Dumézil. The reference to the tripartite ideology common to all Indo-European peoples then appears very clearly; the three first powers obviously come from the first function (magicoreligious sovereignty), the Empire belongs no less clearly to the second (the war function, the exercise of temporal power), while the last three evoke the notions of prosperity, happiness, and health, which are typical of the third function. In fact, this analysis can be narrowed down further by taking into consideration the fact that the first and the third functions are usually "two-headed" (in India, Mitra and Varuṇa for the first, the Nāsatya twins for the third), while the second is represented by a single personage (in India, Indra). Elsewhere, the list of major gods thus hierarchized includes in the first rank a "god of beginnings," often ambivalent (in Rome, Janus of the two foreheads), and, at the end, an "all-purpose" goddess whose influence is felt on all levels.

From this we would have, at the very beginning, Spenta Manyu (a veiled designation of the Twin Spirits Spenta and Angra, as two faces of the same power, which is simultaneously good and bad), and then, to represent the first function, Arta (in India, Varuṇa, foremost guardian of the Ṛta) and Vohu Manah (in India, Mitra, the juridical sovereignty, legislative rectitude); the second function offers no problem (Kshatra replaces the god of war, in India, Indra); on the third level: physical integrity and immortality (in India, the wonder-working Nāsatya twins); and at the end of the list, the goddess Armaïti, whose devout spirit should, according to Zarathustra, inspire all actions, no matter what the level on which they are situated.

This view of things is all the more likely to be correct, since it happens that the Avesta sometimes substitutes the name of Anāhitā, a river goddess and female genie of fecundity, for that of Armaïti, thus betraying the mythological origin of

Armaïti. One can only admire the work of transposition undertaken by the Prophet and his theologians to safeguard the purity of Zoroastrian doctrine (Ahura Mazdā the only Lord) even while adjusting to the profound feelings of the worshipers of the time, steeped as they were in the polytheistic ideology of their fathers. It is, moreover, significant that a good number of the gods of the ancient religion had to be integrated into the main part of the religious source in the form of "adorable" genies (*yazatas*) who were attendants of Ahura Mazdā.

If we consult the list of Yashts, those liturgical hymns that appear in the Avesta, we notice a whole series of names that directly evoke the archaic Indo-Iranian divinities. Besides Haoma, already cited, we find the Sun, the Moon, the goddess of horses, Anāhitā, Mithra, Vāyu, Verethraghna, Fortune, the Daenā, the Fravashis, then several "moral" powers comparable to the Ameshas Spentas: Rectitude (Arshtāt), the Light of Holiness (Khvarenah), Conscience (Chistāt). It is interesting that this section of the Avesta contains the names of Indo-European deities that seem to do double duty with those of the homologous entities: what is the use of making Mithra an autonomous *yazata* when the worshiper is invited elsewhere to venerate Vohu Manah? What is the function of Verethraghna (a former god of war, homonym of the Vedic Vṛtrahan, one of the divine names of Indra) when one already has Kshatra? What is the use of Vayu and Anāhitā, when one already has Manyu and Armaïti?

The Zoroastrians have no answer to these questions, on the one hand because they see no clear correspondence between the Ameshas Spentas and the other *yazatas*, and, on the other, because the multiple "angels of the Lord" seem natural to them. But to the outside observer it is clear that this is a late "recovery," designed to make it possible to rally to the Zoroastrian reform those people who had remained faithful to the gods of their ancestors. Indeed, hardly any of these *yazatas* appears in the text of the liturgical songs (Gāthās) attributed to Zarathustra himself. Impossible to date, this "recovery" may have been carried out in the last centuries B.C.; in any case, it took its definitive form during the definitive compilation of the Avesta, under the Sassanians (around the third century A.D.).

Something of the ancient hymns has been preserved in the Yashts, but this has been done by placing it in a new framework: the Prophet is imagined questioning the Lord in order to know, for example, who Vāyu is (or Mithra, Haoma) and the answer is given in the form of a litany of divine names just like those in the Veda:

> I am called Vāyu, O holy Zarathustra! . . . I am called He-who-controls-everything . . . I am called He-who-does-good . . . I have the name He-who-goes-forward; I have the name He-who-goes-backward.

Dozens of "names" are thus cited in an uninterrupted series, until the point where Vayu explains to the Prophet that their recitation will protect him in all circumstances (and notably in battle). Zarathustra then asks:

> What sacrifice shall I offer you? What sacrifice shall I have offered to you? By what sacrifice shall your worship be accomplished?

At the end of this Yasht, Vayu promises:

> If you honor me with a sacrifice, I will tell you Words: created by Mazdā, they are Glorious and Healing! So that neither Angra Manyu nor the sorcerers (*yātus*) will be able to harm you, nor their agents, be they men or Daevas!

It is evident from this example that the Avesta does not hesitate to celebrate the virtues of sacrifice to the ancient Indo-Iranian gods, if it is conceded that these liturgical gestures will have, in addition to their intrinsic worth (for example, safety in battle, normal when dealing with a "violent" god like Vayu), the advantage of procuring for the worshiper a deepening of his intimate knowledge of the Wise Lord (here, for example, Vayu will reveal formulas of exorcism against the agents of the Evil One). But all of this is true only according to the perspective of strict Zoroastrian orthodoxy; outside this group, the *yazatas* behave like real gods: this was the extraordinary destiny of Mithra, in the first centuries A.D., throughout the entire Roman Empire.

Eschatological Myths

Nevertheless, no religion can do entirely without mythology, and whatever may have been the efforts of Zoroastrian theologians to purge their religion of it, the Avesta preserves at least the memory of certain myths. Almost all of these belong to the domain of eschatology, which is hardly surprising if we recall that every religious undertaking must regard itself as salvational. Man, in all latitudes and in all eras, asks first of "those who know" what will be his fate after death, for he believes that what he does today has meaning only in relation to his destiny in the other world. But of course this implies the belief in a hereafter and the certitude that the being that dies does not completely disappear. Gradually, a view of the world is organized in which the evolution of the universe must be taken into account: cosmogonies and apocalypses cannot be dissociated from thoughts of death and the hereafter. It would therefore be necessary to have at our disposal a great number of mythical narratives in order to reconstitute with some coherence the eschatological system of the Iranians. But we have already said that this is not the case, and we must resign ourselves to having only a partial and unsatisfactory view of this system.

This situation arises as soon as one examines, for example, the Zoroastrian concept of the human being. The human being was composed of three parts: body, spirit, and soul. This first part was strongly emphasized: as a divine creation, the body was entitled to every care, and its physical integrity was, along with its beauty, the sign of special protection by the powers on high (one of the Ameshas Spentas was named Sarvatāt and presided over the full development of the physical personality). From numerous indications it can be surmised that the ancient Zoroastrians regarded sickness as a punishment (or a trial) that employed the malevolent services of the agents of the *druj*. As a corollary, the image of the decomposition of the corpse appeared as absolute Evil, the work of a particular demon named Druj-i-Nasush. Thus it seems that death was the manifestation of a triumph of the Evil One, determined, by nature, to destroy the Good Creation, the work of the Wise Lord. This is a scandalous situation which can only be accepted if it is held to be provisional. From this comes the belief in the resurrection of bodies that many historians regard as the fundamental characteristic of the Zoroastrian religion—often adding that this belief was probably inherited by Christianity from this source. This resurrection was, moreover, supposed to take place not immediately after death, in a Paradise similar to our world, but at the end of time at the Great Renewal awaited by the Zoroastrians.

The second element of the human being is the Manah (or Manyu; in Sanskrit, *manas* or *manyu*). More than "thought," this Manah is a force of life, a quasi-divine Power through which man is radically separated from the animals and recognizes himself as a member of the Community of the Just (*artāvan:* "those who belong to the *arta,*" the Sovereign Good). This is thus the Spirit in the full sense of the word; a Spirit capable of doing Evil to others as much as Good, like the two divine Manyus who act either for the *arta* (this being Spenta Manyu, the Holy Spirit) or for the *druj* (this is Angra Manyu, the Evil Spirit). Man is thus responsible for his acts by virtue of the Manah with which he is provided, and these acts determine the fate of the third human element in the world beyond, at least for the period which precedes the Great Renewal.

This third element bears the name of Fravarti (or Fravashi) and corresponds more or less to the notion of "soul" in the Christian sense of the term. Like the Christian soul, the Fravarti is created by the Lord, is immortal, and is destined either to suffer in Hell or to rejoice in Paradise according to a particular judgment that it must undergo immediately after the death of the individual it inhabits. It seems, nevertheless, that Zoroastrians also believed that the soul, during life, played the role of guardian angel. As a witness of the actions inspired by the Manah, the Fravarti blames or approves, suffers or rejoices, like the conscience in certain forms of popular Christianity. Moreover, the ancient texts leave us to understand that the "souls of those of the dead who are just" watch over the interests of the living. One can thus pray to them and even worship them, as is indicated by a Yasht that is dedicated to them, in which these Fravartis are said to assist the Wise Lord in his role as guardian of the universe:

> If I had not given assistance to the powerful Fravartis of the just, I would not have the herds and the men that are here. . . But power would belong to the *druj,* and so would the empire, and so would the corporeal world. (Yasht 13, verse 12)

Thus the soul of a given individual becomes, after death and according to the acts accomplished on this earth, either a demon agent of the *druj* or an angel of the Lord. And so the more of the just there are, the more help and assistance the Lord will have. The reason the universal order is constantly degenerating, according to the Zoroastrians, is that the worshipers of the Good Religion are becoming less and less numerous. The hope nevertheless remains that the situation will be radically modified because the worst will be succeeded by the best at the final Renewal.

At the time of death the soul undertakes a difficult journey: a path leads it to a precipice spanned by a bridge. If the soul manages to cross over, the way will be opened toward the "House of Songs" where the just reside; if it cannot, it falls to the bottom of a ravine into the dark and icy dwelling place of the souls of the wicked. But at the beginning of the bridge the soul sees a young girl in whom it recognizes its "double," the Daenā (Sanskrit, *dhenā*). A mysterious entity, this Daenā is, in essence, the moral value of the existence lived by a given individual: if his actions were mostly good, the Daenā will be young, pretty, well dressed, perfumed, etc.; if, on the contrary, the life was bad, the Daenā will resemble a sinister witch, stinking and dressed in rags. Moreover, the Daenā seizes "the hand" of the Fravarti and leads him onto the bridge: naturally, the pretty young girl helps the soul to cross it without difficulty, while the old witch throws it into the infernal hole. According to one variation, it is the bridge itself that makes the selection (it is called Chinvat, the bridge of the Selector); it widens itself for the just and narrows for the wicked, to the point of being no more than a razor's edge! Finally, according to a third form of the mythical story, the decisive trial consists of an actual act of judgment: the soul must plead its cause before a tribunal presided over by Mithra assisted by two assessors: Sraosha and Rashnu. Yet elsewhere it is said that it is Ahura Mazdā alone who decides, after weighing the merits and demerits of the dead person.

Comparison with other sectors of the Indo-European domain demonstrates that these diverse conceptions were able to coexist without difficulty. In Greece, too, the soul was to make a dangerous crossing (the river Acheron) and to confront the judgment of Minos, Eachus, and Rhadamanthe. In India, too, there was a reception of souls by young girls, the crossing of a bridge, and the judgment (given by Yama, the first of mortals), as there was among the ancient Germans and the Scandinavians. In fact, beyond the picturesque quality of certain details (everywhere one finds the theme of the guard dogs: Cerberus, Saramā), what remains is the idea of the responsibility of the soul and the clairvoyance of the soul's judges. Zoroastrianism, because of its own special character, was obliged to insist on this aspect: did it not place Right Choice at the very center of its ideology?

Paradise (*parādesha,* or *païrideza*—the Bible borrowed this word from the Indo-Iranian) is celestial and luminous: the soul of the just person "rises to the sky," where a perpetual light (*lux perpetua*) shines, where "no shadow is made," it is said. There on high the soul tastes delicious foods and sings the praises of the Lord before the throne of gold in which he is seated (this is the source of the name of "House of Songs" frequently given to the Zoroastrian paradise). Furthermore, the Avesta has foreseen the fate of souls which are neither good nor evil: such mediocre souls await the final Renewal "in neutral ground"; like those in the Greek Limbo, they neither suffer nor rejoice but live like larvae in a gray and indistinct world. The idea of Renewal, so important in the "cosmic" eschatology of Zoroastrianism, is evidently linked to the notion of cyclical time. Like the Greeks and Indians, the Iranians believed that in the beginning, the world was perfect (the age of gold, according to Hesiod; the perfect age, according to the Veda), but that a slow process of involution made it travel the successive stages of a route leading to final decrepitude (according to Hesiod, the age of gold, then silver, then bronze, then iron). When this last age is reached, the Wise Lord brusquely reestablishes the initial situation: this return to the age of gold constitutes the Renewal that the Zoroastrians of today are awaiting impatiently.

Of course, a mutation of this dimension is bound to be accompanied by cataclysms: that which is bad must first be destroyed so that the good may unfold and blossom. Fire usually presides over this labor: it is said, for example, that a river of fire will flow over the universe, purifying everything in its path, Hell itself will then be abolished and the worst demons will become angels (again) "in three days." Over the course of time, Zoroastrians developed a tendency to regard this Renewal as definitive, whereas the Avesta sees in it the reestablishing of an age of gold that will be ineluctably succeeded by a new age of silver, etc. But "modern" theologians (those of the last ten centuries) believed that this would be a limitation of the omnipotence of Ahura Mazdā. In our day, it seems that the majority of Parsis (contemporary

Zoroastrians) conceive of the Renewal as a definitive Parousia.

But "travel accidents" could occur in the course of the ages. The best known of these events concerns Yima, the father of the first humanity. In the beginning, it is taught, the sun god Vivahvant (in India, Vivasvant), who is, in the Zoroastrian perspective, one of the privileged servants of the Wise Lord, engendered (or created from many elements) the first man, to whom the name of Yima is given (Yama in the Veda). Now the word *yama* means "twin," which implies that what was created was in fact two personages, a male and a female (in India, Yama and Yamī), who coupled and engendered in their turn innumerable human beings. Zoroastrians see in this initial incest the justification of consanguine marriages, which they advocate within the Community of the Just (the Zoroastrian church).

Yama was thus the king of the age of gold and became on his death a God (or an archangel); during his reign, says the Avesta (Yasna 9, verses 4 and 5):

> There was neither excessive cold nor heat, nor old age, nor death, nor envy created by the demons. The fathers, like the sons, had the appearance of young men of fifteen, as long as Yima, son of Vivahvant, reigned, he of the beautiful flocks!

Nevertheless, the multiplication of beings is such (because there is no death) that Ahura Mazdā must enlarge the earth three times. Finally, the situation degenerates to such an extent that the Lord warns the faithful Yima that a Great Winter is about to occur:

> First the cloud will snow from the highest mountains to the deepest valleys . . . water will flow in great waves and it will be impossible to cross over those places where now the tracks of sheep may be seen! (Vidēvdāt, chapter 2)

Little by little everything will be submerged, and all beings will perish except for a pair from each species, which Yima is invited to hide in a fort that he is to build on the highest mountain. In this enclosure, as a reserve from the age of gold, the seeds of the future will subsist along with Yima until the anger of the Wise Lord will have been calmed. At the end of the Flood, Yima will open the doors of the enclosure and the earth will be repopulated anew. According to certain traditions, the Fort of Yima still stands: it constitutes what is called Paradise; the souls of the just will await the end of time there. When this world has become irremediably evil and is destroyed, the Enclosure of Yima will be enlarged to cover the dimensions of the entire earth and a new age of gold will be installed as a Great Renewal. This notion of a remainder from which a new world is constructed is found throughout the Indo-European domain and notably in India.

Conclusion

Zoroastrian religion clearly presents a dual character: on the one hand, it has remained intrinsically faithful to the ideology of the *āryas* (and remains so even to our day, when Iranians, even though converted to Islam, constantly give prominence to their national identity), and on the other hand, because of the preaching of Zarathustra, the Zoroastrian religion is distinguished from this Aryan ideology in many aspects. The rejection of mythology is surely the most striking of these fixed "reformist" positions, but it is not the only one. There is also the repudiation of blood sacrifices and the correlative repudiation of the enchantments of the Haoma. There is, finally, the constant reference to the merciless struggle that will be waged in this world by the two Spirits for the triumph of Good (or Evil). Asked to take sides in the battle, warned that his fate in the other world depends on the choice he will make, the worshiper is led to reduce his religion to simple moralism. And in fact, many Zoroastrians today are content to recommend to their children the exercise of three virtues—"good thoughts, good words, good acts" symbolized by the three red candles lighted on feast days. One of the eleven verses of the Zoroastrian Credo (the prayer called Fravarāne, after its first word) says, in its own terms:

> I proclaim myself the adorer of Mazdā, disciple of Zarathustra, pious and believing! I praise Good Thought; I praise the Good Word; I praise Good Action; I praise the Good Religion of Mazdā . . . who is the greatest, the most beautiful of creatures, past, present, and to come; she is the follower of Ahura, the follower of Zarathustra!

But the same ambiguity that has already been noted so often above can be seen again here: if the Good Religion is a "creature," should we not see in her a female angel, an "almost goddess"? Thus the polytheism so ferociously exorcised by the Reformer makes a clandestine reentry. Mithra, Anāhitā, Verethraghna, the Fravartis, Yima are an integral part of the mental universe of the Parsis, who, it must be said, are not terribly interested in knowing the theological status of these divine beings; they are content to know that these beings are beneficent, that one can ask for their help, and that the just will meet them, up there in Paradise, after their death.

Moreover, the modern Zoroastrian, in this respect following his ancestors, is a happy worshiper: unless he shows some excess of cruelty and a deliberate will to act in an evil way, he considers himself to be assured of salvation. The ceremony of the *naojote* has introduced him into the Community of the Just, that is, into that cosmic "reserve" whose place is by right in the Enclosure of Yima. He can be excluded from it only by some abominable crime of which he would refuse to repent. Beyond this, the priests teach him that creation is intrinsically good, because it is the work of Ahura Mazdā: his duty is thus to integrate himself into it with gratitude and joy and to do his part in making it prosper. The souls of the just are invited after the death of the individuals to help the Lord in his cosmic tasks; in the same way, the believer has the duty of working, here below, toward the prosperity of everyone, beginning with himself. Thus the Parsis consider it legitimate to accumulate riches, when this is possible; we know that in the nineteenth century, in India, the community engaged thoroughly in industrialization and became in this way one of the richest and most powerful social groups of the British Empire. By acting in this way, it was following in every detail the teaching of the Prophet, and beyond this in the spirit of Indo-Iranian religion, which also invited its followers to work with confidence towards the collective prosperity.

Nor is this in contradiction with the belief in the ineluctible end of the world in which we live, because work is above all an endeavor of personal salvation. Ignoring monasticism and asceticism, Zoroastrian religion is essentially a doctrine of action; it was thus before Zarathustra, and remained so after the Reform, because that reform, like so many others, was more of a restoration than a revolution. This emphasis on action gives Zoroastrianism a modern aspect that is prized by the Parsis and compensates in their eyes for the small number of followers of the Good Religion.

J.V./t.l.f.

BIBLIOGRAPHY

Iran before Islam

R. GHIRSHMAN, *Iran, from the Earliest Times to the Islamic Conquest* (New York 1954), originally in French. HUART and DELAPORTE, *L'Iran antique* (Paris 1953). R. GHIRSHMAN, *Perses, Parthes et Sassanides,* 2 vols. (Paris 1962).

Zoroastrian Texts

ANQUETIL-DUPERRON, *Le Zend-Avesta* (1771), first edition of the sacred text, now obsolete. J. DARMESTETER, *Le Zend-Avesta* (1892), reedited in three volumes under the corrected title *Avesta* (Paris 1960); English translation in *Sacred Books of the East* series. J. DUCHESNE-GUILLEMIN, *Zoroastre* (Paris 1948), the authoritative French translation of the *Gâthâs.* H. HUMBACH, *Die Gâthâs des Zarathushtras,* 2 vols. (Heidelberg 1959). H. LOMMEL, *Die Yashts des Avestas* (Göttingen 1927). J. DE MENASCE, *Une encyclopédie mazdéenne, le Dênkart* (Paris 1928). I. GERSHEVITCH, *The Avestan Hymn to Mithra* (Cambridge 1959).

Zoroastrian Religion in General

J. DUCHESNE-GUILLEMIN, *La religion de l'Iran ancien* (Paris 1962). G. WIDENGREN, *Les religions de l'Iran* (Paris 1968). H. S. NYBERG, *Die Religionen des alten Irans* (Leipzig 1938). J. H. MOULTON, *Early Zoroastrianism* (London 1913). R. C. ZAEHNER, *The Dawn and Twilight of Zoroastrianism* (London 1961). M. MOLE, *Culte, mythe et cosmologie dans l'Iran ancien* (Paris 1964).

Zarathustra

ZARATHUSTRA (Darmstadt 1970), a collection of studies and articles. J. VARENNE, *Zarathushtra et la tradition mazdéenne* (Paris 1966; 2d ed., 1977). P. DU BREUIL, *Zarathoustra et la transfiguration du monde* (Paris 1978). W. B. HENNING, *Zoroaster* (Oxford 1951). A. V. W. JACKSON, *Zoroaster, the Prophet of Ancient Iran* (New York 1899).

Specific Studies

E. BENVENISTE, *The Persian Religion according to the Chief Greek Texts* (Paris 1929). BIDEZ and CUMONT, *Les mages hellénisés,* 2 vols. (Paris 1938; reprinted 1975). F. CUMONT, *Textes et monuments relatifs aux mystères de Mithra,* 2 vols. (Brussels 1899). G. DUMÉZIL, *Naissances d'Archanges* (Paris 1945). J. DUCHESNE-GUILLEMIN, *Ormazd et Ahriman* (Paris 1953). R. C. ZAEHNER, *Zurvan, a Zoroastrian Dilemma* (Oxford 1955). S. WIKANDER, *Vayu* (Lund 1942). H. W. BAILEY, *Zoroastrian Problems in the Ninth-Century Books* (Oxford 1943).

The Parsis

H. HAUG, *Essays on the Language, Writings and Religion of the Parsis* (London 1907; reprinted Amsterdam 1971). D. MENANT, *Les Parsis* (Paris 1898; reprinted Paris 1972). D. K. KARAKA, *History of the Parsis,* 2 vols. (London 1884). J. J. MODI, *The Religious Ceremonies and Customs of the Parsees* (Bombay 1937; reprinted 1951).

Influences on Iranian Islam

BAUSANI, *La Persa religiosa* (Turin 1959). H. CORBIN, *Terre céleste et corps de résurrection* (Paris 1960); *En Islam iranien,* 4 vols. (Paris 1977).

AHURA MAZDĀ (OR OROMAZDES, OHRMAZD)

The Indo-Iranians inherited from their Indo-European ancestors a theological system in which the divine powers were divided into three vast, hierarchically arranged realms: magicoreligious sovereignty, the exercise of physical forces, and the production of riches. The gods, who were very numerous, acted for the good of the world—that is, for the protection of the Cosmic Order—in one or the other of these sacred areas. The first function, for example, was taken care of by two great deities (aided by several others): Mitra and Varuṇa. Mitra inspired and secured ventures which brought peace (treaties, alliances) and goodwill (administration of the law). Varuṇa watched over the people, scrutinizing their behavior with his innumerable eyes and intervening in combat so that right would triumph; to do this he struck evil people with paralysis or madness; and all magic powers *(māyā)* belonged to him. In Varuṇa's presence, one was struck with sacred terror, but the just man could turn to him, as well as the repentant sinner, whom he readily forgave. Mitra presided over the day (and thus directed the course of the sun), while Varuṇa reigned over the night and the secret world of the stars.

Ahura Mazdā. Cast of a Sassanian intaglio. Paris, Bibliothèque nationale, Cabinet des Médailles. Photo BN.

At some point—we do not know precisely when—this order was somewhat abused by certain Iranians, who replaced the duality of powers with the idea of a single sovereign at once both majestic and terrible, following a pattern reminiscent of that followed by both the Greeks and the Romans, for whom Jupiter-Zeus alone assumed the function of the king of the gods and of the world. As Mitra and Varuṇa belonged to the class of Asuras (in Iranian,

Ahuras), the Supreme God became the Ahura par excellence, the Single Ahura, the Wise Lord: Ahura Mazdā. Somewhat later, perhaps towards the eighth century B.C., Zarathustra preached a veritable monotheism, which relegated all the other gods to a subordinate role as the assistants of the Lord. Ahura Mazdā was the only eternal god, said Zarathustra, the others having been created by him at the same time as other living creatures: "in the beginning." Thus these *yazatas* ("worthy of being adored") were, in his eyes, only "angels," beneficent genies, and Ameshas Spentas ("Immortal Saints"). Zarathustra also attributed to Ahura the beneficent, serene, and luminous traits of sovereignty: the Lord created a perfect Order (*arta*), just and peaceful, in which all creatures were promised a prosperous life on earth and happiness after death in a Paradise filled with light, joy, and song. The only requirement was to remain faithful to the Good Religion, to stay an *artāvan* (one of the "just"). This apparently led to the problem of Evil: how could it be that any creature would not follow the paths of the Lord? Zarathustra was satisfied by the existence of a genie of Evil, the Druj, whose role was to "trick" men. But, faithful to his original position (radical monotheism), the Prophet did not develop any mythology of antagonism between *arta/druj*. He taught that these two entities waged a constant battle under the influence of the two Spirits (*manyus*), the Wicked (Angra Manyu, or Ahriman) and the Holy (Spenta Manyu), and that men must rally under the banner of the Holy Spirit. The Good Choice is the condition of salvation, since the Wise Lord does not abandon those who are faithful to Justice (*arta*).

It must be added that the religious sensibility of the Iranians was for a long time loath to embrace such a system entirely: Zoroastrianism did not become the national religion of Iran until the third century A.D. The "Varuṇian" aspect of the sovereign function came to be attributed to Mithra, who remained extremely popular, probably because his mythology was filled out with elements taken from that of Mazdā. It is certainly not an accident that there were mysteries of Mithra (whose success outside Iran is well known) and not of Ahura Mazdā. Cleverly, the compilers of the Avesta retained certain hymns dedicated to gods such as Mithra, Vayu, Haoma, and Anāhitā and represented them as acolytes of the Wise Lord. It was in this way, surely, that they could triumph over and (much later) convert all of Iran. Today, for the Parsis, Ahura Mazdā is a figure as mythologically colorless as God the Father for Christians, majestic, sovereign, creative, intrinsically good, but distant and "without a story."

J.V./d.b.

Anāhitā (or Anahid)

Zoroastrianism gives only a very small place to female deities. In this it resembles Vedic religion (and in general, all Indo-European religions). After one has mentioned the Fravartis (or Fravashis), that is, the "souls of the just," and the Daenā (the personification of the conscience), the topic is almost exhausted; a "goddess of the horses," Drvāspā, could be included (but this may be only the name of the "power" of the god Gāush) and Vanuhi Dāïtyā (or Veh Dātīg), the female spirit of the river Araxe. The Druj (Evil, Disorder, Trickery), does not seem to have ever been personified. Thus the only Iranian goddess in the full sense of the term appears to have been Anāhitā (called Anaïtis by the Greeks) or, more precisely, Ardvā Sūrā Anāhitā ("the High, the Powerful, the Immaculate"). Her anthropomorphic traits are clearly indicated in the Avestan hymn that honors her (Yasht 5): we learn (verses 126 on) that she looks like a young girl with swollen breasts; and, we are told, "she has cinched in her waist to give more charm and fullness to her bosom." Clothed in a gold brocade coat, crowned with stars and beams of light, she also wears otter furs and splendid jewels: dangling earrings, necklaces, belt. The many statuettes found at Susa confirm the accuracy of this description. Upon seeing her heavy breasts and the richness of her apparel, some Greeks were reminded of Aphrodite; others, because of her name and her priestly bearing, supposed that Anāhitā was the Iranian Artemis. In fact, it was Athena they should have thought of; as various modern scholars (notably Georges Dumézil) have shown, the goddess was known for her wisdom (she gave advice to Zarathustra and taught him a certain type of sacrifice) and for her participation in the fight for justice.

Anāhitā first appears, however, in the Avesta as a goddess of the waters: the very first verse of the Yasht that is dedicated to her formally assimilates her to the liquid element in general: purifying and life-giving water in the form of rivers, lakes, and seas, and among living creatures in the form of sperm, vaginal secretions, and milk. Rain, on the other hand, is not mentioned, as it is a natural attribute of the storm god. From this starting point, Anāhitā became a spirit (female) of prosperity in Zoroastrianism, lending her effective aid to the Wise Lord's work of creation and to the maintaining of Cosmic Order. If we add to this task Anāhitā's responsibility to fight for justice and to give liturgical lessons, we can see that she was a "tri-functional" goddess, inspiring the three major classes of activity that correspond to the three divisions of Iranian society, according to the Dumézilian interpretation of the basic Indo-European ideology. This may be why Zoroastrian theologians were unable to avoid incorporating Anāhitā into their religious system, even into the strictly monotheistic framework of the Zoroastrian reform. Anāhitā was furthermore the planet Venus, the morning star, the brightest in the sky. There are many indications that the worship of the goddess was constant throughout the vast Iranian realm and remained so until the establishment of Islam.

J.V./d.b.

Mithra (or Mihr, Mihir, Meher)

Homologous to the Vedic god Mitra, the Iranian Mithra is a person of the utmost importance, a sovereign whose majesty may well have equaled that of Ahura Mazdā and may even have surpassed it at various times in certain regions of Iran (notably in the extreme west). Furthermore, one can read in the Avesta (Yasht 10, stanza 1): "I created him to be as worthy of sacrifice, as worthy of prayer, as myself, Ahura Mazdā." Moreover, it is the cult of Mithra and not that of the Wise Lord that spread throughout the Roman Empire and northwest India during the third century A.D.

Etymologically Mithra's name evokes contractual alliance, so that he is the guardian of loyalty, the guarantor of sincere friendship, and the preeminent witness. The same *Yasht* in stanza 2 says: "Never break a contract, no more the one that you seal with a wicked man than the one that you seal with a just man, for the contract is binding on both parties!" Those who violate this rule are called *mithro-druj,* meaning both "cheats" and "enemies of Mithra." The God who sees all ("He has ten thousand spies," one reads in stanza 24) strikes them with a stupor ("You deprive their arms of strength, their feet of agility, their eyes of sight, and their ears of hearing": ibid., stanza 23), though the just come through without difficulty to the end. Conversely, the truthful, the loyal, the "true friends" (another meaning for the word *mithra*) are assured of gaining prosperity: "You enlarge their houses, you give beautiful women, beautiful chariots . . . to the just who offer sacrifice to you by calling you by your name with the appropriate words" (stanza 30).

Such promises explain the adjective that is frequently coupled with his name: *vourugauyaoiti,* "possessing vast pastures." Not that Mithra is an agrarian deity to whom one should pray so that crops may grow, but rather that he is a fighting god who brings the victory that makes it possible for the *āryas* to get control of new territories. As the same hymn (stanza 4) says: "We sacrifice to Mithra-of-vast-pastures, thanks to whom the Aryan nations receive stable and happy establishments." It is therefore a matter of placing oneself under the protection of Mithra or better still of placing oneself under his banner in order to obtain (or to maintain) through violence those material goods that Zoroastrianism considers "desirable" (stanza 33: "Grant us the favor that we implore of you . . . wealth, might, and victory!"). The vocabulary is consistently military, with references to the god's chariot, to his white hair, and to his weapon (a mass of steel as resplendent as gold and covered with sharply pointed studs). This weapon bears the name of *vazra* (stanza 96), the exact equivalent of the *vajra* with which Indra, the Vedic god of war, is equipped.

This raises the problem of the exact role of Mithra in the Zoroastrian theological system. Georges Dumézil has shown that among the Indo-Europeans (and especially among the Indo-Iranians) the administration of the sacred in its highest form, magico-religious sovereignty, was assigned to two deities (assisted by a third deity and by a few others) named Mitra and Varuṇa in the Veda. Preeminent *asuras,* these two share the task between them: one (Mitra) has shining benevolence, "solar" peace, and mercy; the other (Varuṇa) has the punishment of the wicked, "nocturnal" violence, and magic. It happens, however, that the Iranian Mithra (like Týr, to a lesser extent, his counterpart among the ancient Germans and Norsemen) has taken on numerous elements that normally belong to the second function, the one that governs the force of war. To preserve a just alliance one must sometimes wield a sword, and Mithra does not hesitate to do so. One must also fight if one wishes to give the just, in this case the Aryans, "vast pastures."

Thus progressively Mithra became a violent god, while remaining a solar god, a personification of the sun. An archer like Apollo, impossible to conquer (*Sol invictus*), he was worthy of trust, since his faithful followers knew that he would help them effectively. Simultaneously, the other Ahura was becoming the supreme (and only) god of Zoroaster, which probably allowed Mithra to inherit certain other roles of Varuṇa, starting with magic. In combat Mithra is the one who paralyzes the army of the wicked, a function which the Veda assigns, with more likelihood, to Varuṇa. Some have maintained that Mazdā was promoted in opposition to Mithra—the rivalry of functions evolving into a true conflict. When, for example, Zoroaster forbids the sacrifice of bovines and the consumption of the *haoma,* he probably points to (without actually naming it) the cult of Mithra, who requires the slaughter of animal victims and the drinking of *haoma.* Though this is altogether possible, it must be noted that the Prophet blames the *daevas* exclusively, and Mithra could not be taken for one of them. Moreover, the constant identification of this god with light (and most especially with the light of the sun) had to make him a priori a sympathetic figure to the Zoroastrians, for whom light was the most important symbol of the "Sovereign Good."

This is undoubtedly why the worship of Mithra was "recovered" by the Zoroastrians, who succeeded in separating it from the mythical elements that were too overtly connected with warfare by bringing them back to the god's coadjutors: Rashnu, Sraosha, and especially Verethraghna. Since he had become a simple servant of the Wise Lord (within the framework of orthodox Zoroastrianism), notably charged with the judgment of the souls of the dead, Mithra had to keep on some of the faithful who were more or less heretical. It is through them that we know such other aspects of the mythology of Mithra as the slaughter of the bull, the visit in the cave where water runs and magical plants grow, etc. These traits are not easy to interpret from the Iranian point of view because we lack explicit documents. Through comparison we may be able to think of the cave as the dwelling place of the sun, since in the Veda it is said that the killing of Vṛtra by Indra (known henceforth as Vṛtrahan, equivalent to Verethraghna in Iranian) allowed the waters to run, the plants to grow, and (especially) the sun to shine for the first time. They were all enclosed in a rock which the god split open to "let there be light." The killing of the bull brings to mind the elimination of the dragon Vṛtra by Indra. The comparison is not misleading if one bears in mind that in post-Vedic Hinduism the adversary dragon becomes a bull (*mahiṣa*), which the goddess Durgā must kill in the name of the gods. Nor should we forget that Mithra inspired a brotherhood of young warriors organized into an initiation society (*haênâ*). Perhaps the sprinkling of blood in the mysteries of Mithra was a reminder of the trials endured by the candidates.

J.V./g.h.

Vayu (or Vay, Vai)

In an important hymn (Yasht 15), the Avesta celebrates a homologue of the Vedic god Vayu. Both gods preside over atmospheric movements: the wind (the first meaning of the word *vayu*) is the outward sign of their power. In a broader sense, all that is "breath" belongs to them, notably the breath of life that animates creatures and the world itself conceived as a living organism. Such a function was bound to ensure for Vayu a choice place within the religious system born of the Zoroastrian reform. In fact, the second stanza of the hymn says that Ahura Mazdā himself offered a sacrifice to Vayu, asking if "he would be so kind as to destroy the creatures of the spirit of evil and protect those of the holy spirit," a surprising formulation within the monotheistic perspective of the Avesta and one that seems to be a vestige of a time (or of theological circles) in which Vayu the Soul of the World occupied the place of supreme deity.

But a closer examination of the Avestan hymn indicates that Vayu's military role is what is most important here: he is invincible, armed with a spear, a golden helmet, a belt, boots, etc. (stanza 57); and he fights from a chariot, spreading terror among the enemies of the Aryans. Various acolytes assist him, among them Yima and Thraētaona (the dragon-slaying god). He himself bears the epithet of Rāma-Hvāstra (the name of one of Mithra's lieutenants), because he brings "pleasure" (*rām*) to the Zoroastrians by ensuring them "good (*hu*) establishments (*vāstra*)," i.e., vast pastures. This is the essential point of the praise of Mithra, and it is certain that Vayu has more or less melted into the mythical image of this deity. If he has not done so entirely, it is probably because Vayu retains a certain ambiguity. The hymn must recognize that there are indeed two contradictory sides to this character, "a good and an evil Vayu," or more exactly, "one part that belongs to the holy spirit and one part that belongs to the spirit of evil." All indications are that Vayu as the breath of the Universe was originally identified with the spirit (*manyu*).

Responsible for all thoughts, all inspirations, and all passions, the god impelled all creatures both toward the Good (the cosmic order or *arta*) and toward Evil (actually disorder). But before the time of Zarathushtra's preaching and even more after that, worshipers obviously were accustomed to distinguishing between two spirits (Spenta Manyu and Angra Manyu) in keeping with a tendency toward dualism that remains one of the basic characteristics of Iranian religion. In the end, formally distinguished from the two Manyus and reduced to his originally secondary role of fighter, Vayu survives in the Avesta only as an effective and fierce lieutenant of the Wise Lord, ensuring his victory over the henchmen of the Druj (Evil). We should note that certain later texts attribute to this *yazata* (deity worthy of worship) the role of a psychopomp. Depending on the works accomplished by the deceased during his life, Vayu leads him to the House of Songs (the Zoroastrian paradise) or casts him into hell.

J.V./g.h.

Verethraghna (or Varahran, Bahram)

The Avesta has preserved a liturgical hymn (Yasht 14) dedicated to the fighting god Verethraghna, a homologue of the Vedic god Indra Vṛtrahan, who in turn owes his name to the fact that he put to death (*han*) the demon Vṛtra, a kind of dragon (or serpent) who guarded the access to an enclosure (a hollow mountain or a cave) in which the waters, the plants, and the sun were being kept prisoners. After his victory, Indra splits the rock and frees the vital elements, thus allowing the universe to come into existence. Such a cosmogonic myth could not survive within Zoroastrian religion, since it was essential to Zarathushtra's preaching to give Ahura Mazdā alone all the credit for a creation deemed to be perfect. Given that circumstance, Verethraghna is but a "fighter for justice," i.e., for the preservation of the Good Order (*arta*) that was put in place in the beginning by the Wise Lord. In such a perspective, it is not surprising that the killing of the dragon was attributed to Thraētaona (an acolyte of Vayu): the objective was evidently to remove from Verethraghna any connection with the cosmogonic enterprise. The prestige of this god did, however, remain great within the aristocratic caste, as is witnessed by the many Iranian princes who took names in which his name occurs (for instance Varhrān I, who had Mani executed in the third century).

The Avestan hymn presents a further anomaly, unique in all the of Zoroastrianism: the god manifests himself in ten different forms. These avatars are, in order, the Wind (stanza 2), the Bull (stanza 7), the Horse (stanza 9), the Camel (stanza 11), the Boar (stanza 15), the Young Warrior (stanza 17), the Raven (stanza 19), the Ram (stanza 23), the Buck (stanza 25), and the Man in the Prime of Life (stanza 27). All is not clear in this list. For instance, the Raven of stanza 19 could be a kite; stanza 39 may refer to an eleventh incarnation, the River. In each case, however, it seems as if the authors sought to present a symbol of virile strength. We are also reminded of the labors of Hercules, the metamorphoses of Jupiter, and of course the successive incarnations of Viṣṇu (several are identical, such as the Boar and the two warriors). With regard to the Ram, we may also think of the "dreaded" fire (savanna fire used to flush out the enemy) extolled in the Veda. But since we have no mythical narratives, it remains very difficult to account for these forms of Verethraghna. We should add that the cult of the god enjoyed a great vogue in the second and third century A.D., along with the cult of Mithra in the western part of the Iranian domain, particularly among the Parthians and as far away as Armenia.

J.V./g.h.

Buddhist Mythology

I. General Remarks

Although it was first a philosophy and a physical, spiritual, and mental technique for salvation, Buddhism received a pantheon and mythical narratives that increased in number and importance in proportion as ritual played a greater and greater role. These gods and narratives were in large part borrowed from various currents of Hinduism. In Hīnayāna Buddhism, the great Brahmanical gods accompany the Buddha, serve him or guard him, and various kinds of minor divinities populate space and involve both the communities of monks and the laity. In Mahāyāna Buddhism (from about the first or second century A.D.) metaphysical Buddhas and Bodhisattvas appear who look a lot like great divinities. Their bearing owes much to the non-Buddhist models. At the same time, Hindu gods and goddesses increase in number and play a more important role now as acolytes of the Buddhas and the Bodhisattvas. But it is especially in Tantrism (*gsan-snags* in Tibetan, *mizhong* in Chinese, *mikkyō* in Japanese), from the sixth or seventh century on, that the pantheon includes a considerable number of divinities and that the narratives are more numerous. Moreover, the borrowings were made above all from Śaivism, and violent, terrible, and excessive aspects became particularly apparent.

Born in India, Buddhism developed there for some fifteen hundred years (from Hīnayāna to Mahāyāna, then to Vajrayana or Tantrism), in multiple currents according to regions (from Kashmir and Assam in the north, to Ceylon in the south), thus offering a great variety and absorbing into itself, notably in the mythology and the pantheon, many Hindu elements (Brahmanical, Śaiva, Vaiṣṇava, etc.). At the same time, it spread into many foreign countries, northern Central Asia, China, Korea, and Japan in the east, Indochina and Indonesia in the southeast. According to the historical circumstances of each particular time and region, Buddhism assumed different forms. These forms derived not only from exported materials, which differed according to the school, the date, and the region of Indian origin and were subject to the contingencies of the means of communication, the rarity of manuscripts, etc., but, even more, from the inevitable fusion with indigenous elements native to the country that received them and assimilated them over centuries. As a result, in India and even more in the foreign countries where Buddhism was implanted, there arose a series of variations of forms, inversions, and mutations.

II. Method

These transformations pose a problem. The simplest, most widespread method has the merit of bringing a certain order to the mass of forms: they are classed chronologically (by epochs), geographically (by countries), or sociologically (by environments, schools, etc.). This historic view can only record the transformations, however; it cannot explain them.

In this connection, there is generally talk of evolution, and a number of monographs have been devoted to certain divinities, narratives, and rituals. But the word "evolution" is inappropriate: it implies that the form that is passed on is effaced and surpassed in the course of ages or migrations. The resulting transformation would be a distortion, a deformation—in short, the original would have been left far behind. The new form resulting from a syncretism, from an amalgam of the original element with elements from the foreign country, would be some sort of bastard form, especially if it belonged to the "popular" milieu of the lay believers, a milieu more or less distanced from the orthodoxy of a church or the authority of canonical texts.

A number of authors have tried to explain certain transformations simply as the result of historical circumstances or various contingencies. Or else they have blithely cited exterior influences, or confusions due to bad readings of texts, misunderstood words, etc. This purely historical and philological point of view often neglects the problem of understanding why such a new form has appeared, while arguing for its late or popular character (which generally implies a deformation lacking any value or interest). It is true that one cannot always explain all the details, nor should one deny the contingent factors that could have contributed to the transformation. But the attitude just referred to is simplistic and a bit lazy; it evades deeper analysis and abandons research.

One could postulate and demonstrate, with the help of some examples, a network of relations, a coherent group with connections not only between elements of the same period and milieu but even between prior and later forms, between the aspect peculiar to the country of origin and the one it took from its neighbors. The least one could say is that such a grouping becomes apparent to the observer who is considering a more or less recent culmination of the process in such and such a country of adoption. The situation is self-explanatory: the individuals, generally anonymous but often known, who elaborated recently transmuted forms, had in their memory, consciously or unconsciously, the sum of all the previous elements, of different dates and origins, that they could know (either orally or in writing) and that we rediscover simply by looking into all the available sources.

The later aspects of the divinities of the pantheon and the new groups that they form in a particular country are not the result of random selection, irregular deformation, or an interpretation that would be rated as "false" in comparison with the orthodox and older model. One would hardly dare say (to use a common but rather unscientific phrase) that "it's as if" the developments or the later transformations were programmed in advance or logically in embryo in the earlier forms (any more than a later event can be predicted in history). But one can say, a posteriori, that a more recent transformation maintains a certain connection with the earlier forms and is integrated into a group that is subject to a kind of internal "logic"[1] of forms that are bound to certain functions and structures. Despite important changes throughout history and across different countries, there is often a great stability and even a perpetuation of old representations and their connections. Often, instead of being distanced from the point of departure by a kind of irreversible evolution, recent forms recover former models that have fallen into disuse. We may know the reasons for such a renewal or at least may locate the source that has been used, but often we have no idea how later authors, distant from the ancient model, could have been familiar with it.

This stability is certainly due in part to ecclesiastics' care in maintaining a tradition while conforming to the orthodox prescriptions that they knew. But, in spite of the desire of Buddhists in different countries to keep the adopted religion pure and authentic, they could not entirely resist the tendency of all representation and all oral or written "discourse" to undergo conscious or unconscious transformations while passing from one person to another, from an earlier to a more recent period, from one country or environment to its neighbor. The priests or the worshipers reflected upon the available texts and the visual representations. Certainly they could misunderstand and reinterpret a particular form that had become incomprehensible. But they could also sense, or clearly discover, the connections between diverse characters of the pantheon after an analysis analogous to the one we are able to remake. In following the meanderings of these connections, they could take up again characteristics or characters that had fallen out of use. They could also innovate by originating substitutions, superimpositions, identifications, amalgams, or reassemblances. Having done this, they could hardly keep in mind the historical identity of the characters or their provenance. What interested them were types; what they retained for their combinations were sometimes names or formal characteristics, motifs, or themes, connections or functions in isolation, sometimes several of these elements at once. They proceeded by analogy or by taking account of their categories of classification. But although the various elements that were combined may have had different origins or belonged to varied contexts, the choice the worshipers made implies that they recognized a connection between forms and contents.

III. Buddhist Concepts of the Pantheon

In research on the relationship between the diverse individuals of the pantheon, the contemporary scholar can and should bear in mind certain general principles of classification that the Buddhist authors were perfectly conscious of. Certainly, the classifications made in the course of centuries in various schools often complied with doctrinal preoccupations that involved a certain degree of arbitrariness, but they can be a useful indicator of the role assigned to characters, their place in the group, and their interrelationships.

The most universally applied principle is that of "incarnations" (corresponding to the "avatars"—the word signified "descent to earth"—of Hinduism). The word "incarnation" chosen by the European translators is inadequate because it designates not only the flesh-and-blood characters who live in our world but also the divinities in their apparitional form. Three Bodies for each Buddha are generally distinguished: the Dharma Body (*dharmakāya*), a kind of "form" of the Absolute; the Enjoyment Body (*sambhogakāya*), an intermediary stage permitting manifestation through acts; and the Artificial Body (*nirmāṇakāya;* Tibetan *sprul-sku,* commonly called *tulku;* Chinese *huashen*), which is the "incarnation" in an apparently material form. Indo-Tibetan Tantrism adds to these the Supreme Body, said to be of Nature itself or of Bliss (at the top of the hierarchy), and distinguishes between a peaceful, pure form and a terrible form (*krodha*). Sino-Japanese Tantrism takes a further step downwards with a Body of Assimilation (Chinese *tongliu;* Japanese *tōru*), which represents the terrible and "demonic" form that a Buddha can take to subjugate demons or bloodthirsty non-Buddhist divinities by assuming their form and acting against them. In India and Tibet, the connections between diverse figures of the pantheon are multiplied since each Buddha is believed capable of having emanations or Artificial Bodies according to the three modes of existence (Body, Speech, and Thought). Further, the notion that each primordial Buddha has his Bodhisattva who corresponds to the Enjoyment Body (for example, Buddha Amitābha → Bodhisattva Avalokiteśvara) is added to the classification according to the Three Bodies. Moreover, the peaceful Bodhisattvas have a terrible form that appears as the Body of Assimilation (for example, Avalokiteśvara → the terrible form: Hayagrīva). Finally, especially in Japan, a Buddha or a Bodhisattva, a Buddhist character, is regarded as the original Form (Japanese *honji*), whereas an indigenous divinity or one whose origin is known to be Hindu is the descended "trace" (avatar: Japanese *suijaku*).

An iconographic characteristic often marks the connection. Avalokiteśvara carries in his headdress an image of Amitābha. In China and Japan, Hayagrīva ("horse's neck") is marked by a horse's head above Avalokiteśvara (Guanyin, Kan-non). He was identified in this form with the Goddess of Silkworms (a young girl who was enveloped by the skin of the horse that she had killed and skinned). In this function, he took the form of the Bodhisattva Aśvaghoṣa (a famous theologian) because of his name ("horse's voice," Ma-Ming). Dressed in white like a female form of Avalokiteśvara (Baiyi, Guanyin), Aśvaghoṣa sits on a white lotus placed on a white horse.

A second principle allows us to spot some of the connections between certain characters of the pantheon. Consciously formulated in Indo-Tibetan Tantrism, it corresponds in fact to the Body of Assimilation of Sino-Japanese Tantrism, whose origin is unknown. According to this principle, the subduer takes the form of the subdued, and according to the ancient commentaries of Indo-Tibetan Tantrism (eighth to tenth centuries), "The name of the subdued becomes that of the subduer," or: "The subduers, heroes, or heroines, take the same aspect and the same name as the 'terrible ones' (the subdued) and trample on them." Thus Yama, the god of Death, has a buffalo's head or a bull's head. Yamāntaka ("Killer of Yama"), his subduer, has the same head. The divinities who subdue the demon Rudra have the same accoutrements as the subdued demon. The subduers of Śiva and Umā, whom they trample under foot, carry in their hands the same weapons and insignia as the subdued.

To follow all the forms of the numerous divinities of this pantheon across the ages and the lands is out of the question. We therefore offer only a few examples illustrating what has been noted above. We proceed in the order of logical priority, since chronological priority is not relevant in all cases; for the Hindu data, for example, we have used iconographic characteristics and narratives of diverse dates. Thus we begin with India and Hinduism, which provided the models—the choice of characters that we have selected as a result of our understanding of the role they played later and elsewhere.

R.A.S./d.f.

NOTE

1. This term may appear to be wrong. By employing it, we would not want to imply precision in reasoning, or rationality. It is employed here as in common parlance to designate a "coherent series," a "coherent, regular, and necessary sequence" (*Dictionnaire Robert*). It is in this way that Jean-Pierre Vernant speaks of "the logic that presides over the organization of a pantheon" (*Mythe et pensée chez les Grecs,* 1:128).

BIBLIOGRAPHY

P. DEMIÉVILLE and J. FILLIOZAT, *Le Bouddhisme,* in L. Renou and J. Filliozat, *L'Inde classique,* vol. 2 (Hanoi 1953). H. DORÉ, *Recherches sur les superstitions en Chine* (Shanghai 1929). R. LINOSSIER, "Mythologie du bouddhisme dans l'Inde," in Hackin, ed., *Mythologie asiatique illustrée* (Paris 1928). J. HACKIN, "Mythologie du lamaïsme," in ibid.; "Mythologie du bouddhisme en Asie centrale," in ibid. A. GETTY, *The Gods of Northern Buddhism* (Oxford 1928). B. BHATTACHARYA, *The Indian Buddhist Iconography* (Calcutta 1958); *An Introduction to Buddhist Esoterism* (Varanasi 1964). S. B. DASGUPTA, *An Introduction to Tantric Buddhism* (Calcutta 1958). E. SENART, *Essai sur la légende du Buddha, son caractère et ses origines* (Paris 1882).

The Guardian of the Gate: An Example of Buddhist Mythology, from India to Japan

The following article presents, as an example and in some detail, one feature of Buddhist mythology in its development and ramifications through various countries and times, beginning with India and Hinduism, which provided the model. We should emphasize at the outset that as far as the Hindu point of view goes, the choice of documents we have made does not pinpoint the precise models that might have been borrowed at a given date by Buddhists from other countries. Rather it aims to reveal the connections among the characters of the myth within the coherent framework of Hinduism alone.

I. Hinduism

Śiva, his wife, and their two sons are the heroes of a highly complex mythology and of a great number of stories. It is impossible for us to include here all of the details and variants of this mythology. Wendy Doniger O'Flaherty has devoted an exhaustive work to them, which shows the principal theme that underlies them: the ambivalence and alternation of asceticism and sexuality in the life of the yogi and in married life, as well as the resulting ambiguity in the attitudes of both the god and the goddess.

Two brothers, Skanda (the younger) and Gaṇeśa (the elder), are the children of Śiva (also called Rudra or Mahādeva or Maheśvara) and his wife Pārvatī (Umā). In most accounts, however, they are created separately, on the sole initiative of the father-god or mother-goddess. They form a pair of opposites. This bipartite structure is evident from their iconographical forms. Skanda is a handsome and chaste young man, while Gaṇeśa is fat and gluttonous. But they are inseparable, each being the inversion of the other; they draw upon the very same sexual theme and have parallel and similar functions. They appear as the mirror image of their parents' relationships, both antagonistic and complementary. The parental couple may be replaced by the one character of Śiva in a bipartite form called Ardhanārīśvara, "the lord who is half-woman" (hermaphrodite). Śiva alone also represents the ambiguity of sexual power: unbridled passion versus abstinence (asceticism). Skanda is called Kumāra (young man), Subrahmaṇya (the pure conduct of a young Brahman) and Kārttikeya (because of the women who intervene in the process of his birth). The legend goes as follows. The gods (*devas*) are in need of a general or warrior to defeat the demons (*asuras*). They persuade Śiva to give up the asceticism to which he has devoted his life and to marry Pārvatī or Umā in order to beget this general. But Śiva, good ascetic that he is, remains in sexual union for one thousand years without ejaculating. The gods, fearing that a child born of such a union would be too powerful and harsh, interrupt the coitus (notably through Agni, the god of fire). Umā remains childless and calls down the curse of sterility on the wives of the gods. Śiva is momentarily distracted and ejaculates in spite of himself. His sperm is entrusted to fire (the god Agni). Agni cannot consume it and throws it into the water (the River Gaṅgā). Or else the sperm falls directly into the water. It is finally entrusted to the reeds on a white mountain (Śveta). In some accounts the sperm is Agni's; and one or six women (the Kṛttikas, or Pleiades, bathing in the Ganges) receive it and deposit it, and a child with six heads and twelve arms is born from it. In other accounts the sperm or the embryo (received six times) remains for six days in an urn (hence his epithet of *guha,* meaning "secret") or in a reed (on a white mountain). One pseudoscientific etymology explains Skanda as meaning "gush of semen," but in yoga, Skanda is the power of sexual abstinence. According to a treatise by a Brahman converted to Buddhism (translated into Tibetan, ca. 1000), Skanda is called *brahmacārya* (pure conduct) because, like his father, Śiva, he is capable of having a wife and playing with her without getting excited. This is said to be the asceticism known as "the sword (of the *makara*)." Now this sea creature (who has an elephant's trunk) is the emblem of the god of love (Kāma; the same emblem was adopted in Tantric Buddhism for the god Rāga, "passion-desire"). It was in fact Kāma who on Brahmā's orders incited Śiva the ascetic to desire his wife and to lose his sperm. To punish him, Śiva reduced him to ashes with the burning gaze of his third eye.

In contrast to Skanda (Śiva's double), Gaṇeśa is the representative of Pārvatī, although some stories at the same time show the affinity of the two brothers. According to one of these accounts, the gods are in need of a general to fight the *asuras.* Since Śiva is engaged in asceticism and Umā has made their wives sterile, they beget Skanda-Kārttikeya by the mating of Agni (fire) with Gaṅgā (water). It is also for the purpose of conquering the *asuras,* who are at first victorious, that the gods (*devas*) receive from Śiva a part of his power in the form of a handsome creature (delivered from Pārvatī's womb). This is Gaṇeśa, also known as Gaṇapati (lord of the "troops" or *gaṇas,* obese and dwarflike creatures) or Vighneśvara or Vināyaka (lord of obstacles; he creates them and dispels them). But elsewhere it is clear that this perfect son was made by Śiva merely by glancing at Pārvatī (and without her participation). He is at first a dashing, good-looking young man who seduces all the women. But Umā becomes vexed with him and curses him, giving him an elephant's head and a fat belly. In another narrative, Pārvatī is disturbed by her husband while she is bathing. Displeased, she decides she needs a faithful doorkeeper (*dvārapāla*). With the "impurities" from her ablutions, she creates a handsome young man, who is to allow no one to enter. Śiva tries to force his way in, but Gaṇeśa stops him. Śiva calls in the troops, Viṣṇu (and Skanda) are repelled, but by means of a trick, the creation of a beautiful woman named Māyā who momentarily distracts the guard, the assailants cut off Gaṇeśa's head. Pārvatī is furious and creates goddesses who attack the gods. She finally agrees to make peace on condition that her "son" be brought back to life. Śiva cuts off the head of an elephant that *has only one tusk* and puts it in place of Gaṇeśa's severed head. He entrusts him with the command of the armies (his own "troops" or *gaṇas*). According to another Indian version, Parvatī disposes of her impurities in the River Gaṅgā. A she-demon with the head of an elephant (probably a *makara,* a sea monster with an elephant's trunk) swallows them and gives birth to a child with five elephant heads. Pārvatī takes him and Śiva accepts him as his child. The variant referred to above, told by a Brahman who converted to Buddhism, stresses the sexual theme as it is connected with the elephant god. Having severed the fifth head of Brahmā, who was guilty of incest with his daughter, Maheśvara devotes himself to an asceticism that consists of carrying skulls, to cleanse himself of his sin. Later, however, he wants to arouse the desire of the wives of the hermits (*ṛṣis*). While the hermits are away, he pays the wives a visit and exposes his erect penis. The women are aroused. Upon

Tibetan Mahākāla mbon-po Ben. Fifteenth to sixteenth century. Boston, Museum of Fine Arts (Bigelan). Museum photo.

Daikoku. Japan. Paris, Musée Guimet. Photo Musées nationaux.

their return, the *ṛṣi* curse him: his penis drops off, and he turns into an elephant living in the forest. A god appeases the *ṛṣis* with gifts, picks up the penis, and returns it to Śiva; we are not told whether or not he remains an elephant. Śiva then has intercourse with his wife Umā, but as a result of an "obstacle" (*vighna*) his sperm falls to the ground. Umā puts the head of the elephant (or of "an" elephant) into the sperm (we are not told whose head was severed), and from this is born Vināyaka (that is, Gaṇeśa, the creator and vanquisher of "obstacles").

The single tusk forms the subject of other stories. One day when Gaṇeśa has eaten too many offering cakes (*modaka*), he goes riding on his mount, which happens to be a rat. A large snake blocks the road. The rat rears up in fear, Gaṇeśa falls, his big stomach bursts open, and the cakes are scattered about. Gaṇeśa puts them back into his stomach and to prevent them from falling out again through a remaining slit in his stomach, he uses the snake as a belt. This spectacle provokes the laughter of the Moon and his wives, the twenty-seven constellations. Gaṇeśa is furious. He cuts off one of his tusks and throws it with a curse. The Moon is struck and goes dark. The gods appease Gaṇeśa, who forgives the Moon, but only halfway: he is forced to disappear periodically. According to another account, Kṛṣṇa wants to return Śiva's battle-ax to him. But Śiva is making love with Pārvatī, and the closed door to their room is guarded by Gaṇeśa. Kṛṣṇa throws the ax at him, and Gaṇeśa consents to receive the blow on one of his tusks, which breaks.

Gaṇeśa is worshiped (like Śiva) in the form of a shapeless stone, painted red, placed along thoroughfares (roads, rivers), but at an early date he became a guardian of the gate at the entrance of temples.

Another aspect of Gaṇeśa is his function as god of intelligence. In one story, when the author of the *Mahābhārata* epic dictates his poem to Gaṇeśa, the latter *pulls out a tusk* and uses it as a pen to write the poem down with superhuman speed. (In a Tantric variant, he writes down the Tantras dictated by Śiva.) In another story, Gaṇeśa is in competition with his brother Skanda to take a wife. Śiva and Pārvatī decide that whoever goes around the world faster will marry first. Subrahmaṇya (Skanda) takes off at great speed, but Gaṇeśa first salutes his parents with seven circumambulations because, according to the Vedas, the merit of this ritual is equivalent to going around the world seven times (the theme of cunning). Gaṇeśa thus gets two wives, Buddhi (intelligence) and Siddhi (success). Finally, whereas Skanda has six mothers (the Pleiades, who gathered up Śiva's sperm),

Gaṇeśa is identified with the seven mothers in the temples of Śiva, while elsewhere these seven mothers are preceded by Tumburu (Śiva) and followed by Vināyaka (Gaṇeśa).

Without claiming to list all aspects and all variations, the following table summarizes the oppositions or inversions and the connections between the two brothers:

Skanda	Gaṇeśa
represents the father (Śiva, the ascetic: sexual power/abstinence)	represents the mother (Umā, Pārvatī, wife: chastity/sterility)
born of sperm (→fire [Agni]) →water [Ganges]→six mothers	born of intimate ablutions (water, menstrual blood, impurities→water [Ganges]) associated with the seven mothers
six heads, one body	six elephant heads, one body
handsome	(handsome >) ugly (dwarf, pot-belly, elephant head, single tusk)
pure young man (sexual abstinence)	glutton (pleasure of eating)
general of the *devas* (in the fight against the *asuras*): red standard	general of the Gaṇas, Śiva's troops, red
called Guha (secret)	guardian of the door (secret of the alcove or of intimate toilet)
swift (in reality)	swift (metaphorically: knowledge and inspiration)

The sexual theme is clearly indicated (psychoanalysts will undoubtedly see castration in the loss of a tusk connected with the son's opposition to his father in defense of his mother). In Hindu Tantrism, sexual rites (*kaula*) are secret to the point that they must not even be mentioned in the presence of Skanda and Gaṇeśa. Two Purāṇas show a transformation of the myth of the guardian of the sexual secret. When the gods interrupt the union of Śiva and Pārvatī, *two* sons are born of the lost drops of sperm. They must guard the door against any further interruption, but due to an oversight by Pārvatī, it is they who see her scantily clad and are condemned to be reborn as men with the faces of monkeys. In any event, the mythology of Śiva is largely characterized by themes of incest (of which Brahmā, his "father," was guilty), by themes of opposition between father and son, and by themes of castration (Brahmā's severed head and Śiva's loss of his sexual organ).

Conversely, the woman's role is ambiguous. Her particular connection with Gaṇeśa is sometimes transferred to Śiva. According to the legend of one Purāṇa, Pārvatī must choose a spouse from among an assembly of gods. Śiva is transformed into a baby and hides in her lap, but she recognizes him and carries him off. In a fertility rite in which Parvatī is associated with Gaṇeśa, we are told that Śiva hides under her skirt. Sometimes Pārvatī holds Skanda on her lap while Gaṇeśa plays by her side. Sometimes Umā holds a little Gaṇeśa in one hand and a *linga* (phallus, that is, Śiva) in the other. In other cases, it is Gaṇeśa who replaces the *linga*. According to one account noted by a Dutchman in 1672, Gaṇeśa had sexual relations with Parvatī and was punished by the jealous Śiva. Conversely, according to one Purāṇa, Skanda's purity is explained in a curious manner. His mother, Pārvatī, at first advises him to play at his leisure. Skanda then seduces the gods' wives. To stop these misdeeds, Pārvatī sees to it that each woman with whom he wants to have intercourse will take the form of his own mother. Overcome by shame (or retreating before inevitable incest), Skanda becomes "without passion." The male sexual theme is thus duplicated on the female side. The goddess is shown to be simultaneously the mother and the wife of the same man.

II. Buddhism

Keeping a secret (*guha*) is characteristic of other individuals who share some of the traits of Gaṇeśa: the *gaṇas* (dwarfs) and the *yakṣas* (pot-bellied dwarfs, guardians of treasures and secrets, who live in caves and hence are called *guhyakas*). In Buddhism, the best known among these *yakṣas* is Vajrapāṇi, guardian of the Buddha (see below). On the other hand, the type of pot-bellied dwarf that is portrayed by Gaṇeśa is essentially a god of wealth. But he also includes the second of the three Indo-European functions described by Georges Dumézil, that of the warrior. Skanda is considered to be Śiva's youngest son. Elsewhere, this lastborn is Mahākāla (sometimes a pot-bellied type associated with wealth and food; sometimes, as in Tantric Buddhism, a fierce warrior, though still pot-bellied). The Chinese Buddhist form of Skanda is characterized by a stick or a studded sword resting *horizontally* on his arms with his hands joined in prayer; a Tibetan Buddhist form of Mahākāla (mGon-po Beṅ) has the same distinctive trait. There are other common features, especially if one takes into account forms specific to Buddhism, which accepted both brothers separately into its pantheon. The "young man" (Kumāra) type of Skanda served as a model for Mañjuśrī (raised sword held in his right hand, book of Prajñāpāramitā [the mother] in his left hand), a Bodhisattva of wisdom and intelligence, which are the traits of Gaṇeśa.

The son or double of Śiva, Mahākāla has the same features as Gaṇeśa. In the Hindu Tantras he is fierce, and he holds a stick, a club, or the trident of Śiva and of the yogi; but he is also a pot-bellied child, dressed in red. Tantric Buddhism retained all these features. His identification with Śiva is known among the Tibetans: he is for them the warrior-god (*dgralha*) of the gods, needed for the battle of the *devas* against the *asuras*. He clothes himself in many forms: red (fierce, warrior), white (peaceable, wisdom, with Gaṇeśa's elephantine features), brother-sister (lČam-dral, lČam-sriṅ, warrior). The Chinese Buddhists also recognized his identity with Śiva (Maheśvara). He is sometimes surrounded by the Seven Mothers (Gaṇeśa is associated with them too). In Nepal, both Gaṇeśa (on the left) and Mahākāla (on the right) appear as guardians of the gate of Buddhist monasteries, whereas in northern India and in Turkestan this function is guaranteed by the couple Mahākāla (on the right) and the goddess Hārītī (on the left). Among numerous aspects that we cannot possibly broach here, Mahākāla's role as god of the kitchen is particularly significant.

In Tibet, China, and Japan, the name Mahākāla has been understood to mean Great Black (it could also mean Great Time). In China and Tibet, he is the fierce deity we have just mentioned. But in Japan he has become a popular god of wealth and happiness. He is known as Daikoku, a little man standing on two bags of rice and carrying a mallet and a bag on his shoulders. The same term also designates the main pillar of the kitchen, of which he is the deity. This god, popular and authentically Japanese in appearance as he is, was nevertheless imported from India as early as the beginning of the ninth century by the founders of Japanese Tantrism (which does not exclude the possibility that this foreign model may have been superimposed on a native deity of the same type, although the existence of the latter has never been attested). For once, in this particular case, we need not imagine obscure resurgences. A written Chinese source, well known among all educated Japanese Buddhists, gives us the model: the Chinese pilgrim Yijing, who lived in northern India in the seventh century, reports in his travelogue that in Indian monasteries it was the custom to place a small statue of Mahākāla carrying a golden bag next to the pillar in the kitchen or in front of the pantry door. The name of the god probably derives from the fact that the statue was regularly anointed with oil, which turned it black. He was worshiped before every meal. The leftovers from the meal, however, were given to the goddess Hārītī, who also stood near the monastery kitchen (or refectory) or by the main entrance. She was a child-eating ogress whom the Buddha converted by taking away one of her five hundred children. He returned the child to her at the moment of her conversion. She holds a child in her arms, and three or five more play at her feet.

The feature of nourishment (abundance and wealth) and the feature of guarding the door revert back to the figure of Gaṇeśa. But instead of the male couple of two brothers, we find here a couple made up of both sexes.[1]

The goddess Hārītī (devourer and giver of children) has enjoyed great success in Buddhism from India through central Asia to the Far East. In China, she was identified with a native figure, the "Mother of Demon-Children" (Guizi mu) or the "Mother of the Nine Children" (Jiuzi mu). But like Skanda and Gaṇeśa, she has been treated as an independent and isolated individual. For all these deities, the couple has been dislocated, but, as we shall see, it has reemerged in different forms. In India, Hārītī is the wife of Pañcika (also called Kuvēra). We shall encounter her again in Chinese Buddhism. Let us first consider the husband, Pañcika, who appears here as a variant of Mahākāla in the couple placed by the door or in the kitchen.

Pañcika fits perfectly into the war/wealth or handsome young man / pot-bellied dwarf binary system. Sometimes he is the general of Kuvēra (Kubera), the lord of the north; sometimes he is identified with him (he carries a spear and a purse). Both are of the type of the dwarf, *yakṣa*, the guardian of wealth (notably of the monastery). In the art of Gandhāra he reminds one of a Greek Silenus.

Kuvēra resembles the kitchen Mahākāla: he is naked, obese, and obscene, and he carries a purse or a bag made of mongoose skin, overflowing with treasures. His double in this same aspect is Jambhala (a god of wealth, although he also has a fierce form): the purse is often replaced by a rat (Gaṇeśa's mount), or by a mongoose or ichneumon spitting out treasures. Kuvēra means "ugly body" (he has three legs, only eight teeth, a cast in one eye, and a big belly). He is one of the great *guhyakas* (guardians of secrets or of caves). But this side of him always calls to mind his other side. Kuvēra is identified with Vaiśravaṇa, whether (as in India) of the pot-bellied type or (as in central Asia and Japan) as the great warrior of the Iranian type, standing and holding a spear in his right hand and a stupa in his left, appearing as a young man, guardian of the north, god of war and wealth. According to Foucher, Kubera and Gaṇeśa often make a pair at the entrance to temples.

A site at the bottom of a lake surrounded by mountains was made habitable by boring a large hole through which the water drained out (the legend of Khotan and the valley of Kathmandu). The author of this deed is sometimes Kuvēra, sometimes Vaiśravaṇa (with their spears), but often Mañjuśrī (with his sword), all three of them types of the handsome young man. Mañjuśrī is sometimes referred to as Pañcaśikha or Five Tufts of Hair, and he is the protector (the tutelary deity) of the Mahā Cīna country (upper Asia, but not China; later, however, Mañjuśrī became the patron of China, known at that time as Mahācīna, and lives there on the Wutai shan, the "Five-Peak Mountain").

It is said with good reason that he looks like the Brahmanic Skanda-Kārttikeya or is modeled after him (Lamotte). Pañcika also means something like Five Peaks, and he is the *yakṣa* protector of China. He is connected with the rooster, which is Skanda's emblem. He has been seen as a doublet of Vajrapāṇi (Lamotte). The Chinese have in fact identified Weituo (< Skanda) with Vajrapāṇi (see below). Mañjuśrī too has been assimilated to Skanda and associated with Vajrapāṇi.

All of these are familiar members of the Buddhist pantheon from northwestern India and central Asia to the outer reaches of the Far East. Because it is so widespread, the type of the pot-bellied dwarf has caught the attention of archaeologists and art historians. A monograph on this subject by Scherman and Foucher reviews all the specimens from the Greek Silenus to the laughing, pot-bellied Buddha of the Chinese and Japanese (Miluo, see below). But most works, like N. Péri's monograph on Weituo, *isolate* these characters and merely trace the evolution of the forms, ignoring the system or the binary structure that alone can explain the various rearrangements effected in the course of time in different countries.

III. Sino-Japanese and Tibetan Buddhism

We have already named some of the individuals in this group to underscore certain relationships. But before moving on toward purely Chinese and Japanese forms (more or less popular), it would be useful to group some of them together, namely, those who appear to be transformations of the couple, which we have rather arbitrarily left behind. We hasten to add that this does not mean that the deities treated here belong exclusively to Chinese and Japanese Buddhism. They are also attested in Indian and Tibetan Buddhist texts, notably in the *sādhanas* and the Tantras, some of which have been translated into Chinese.

The two brothers, Skanda and Gaṇeśa, both sons of Maheśvara (Śiva), were known to Buddhists as Hindu deities (an example from the sixth century can be seen on the frescoes of Dunhuang). But, as we have already stated, this couple has been split up, and each of the partners has been treated individually, taking on a Buddhist aspect before entering into new binary combinations of various forms.

In Tibet and in China, Skanda does not play a major role as such. In Chinese sutras (starting in the fifth century), he appears in lists of deities next to Guhyaka, alias Vajrapāṇi (in Chinese Miji jingang, Vajra of the Secret Traces), or to Sarasvatī, or else as one of the many *yakṣas*. But for some reason the correct transcription of his name, Jian tuo, disappears in China under the Tang (seventh through ninth centuries) through a scribal error that turns it into Weituo (the characters "jian" and "wei" look alike).

The Chinese monk Daoxuan made this figure known in this specific form of Weituo or a certain General Wei, a form that philologically obscures the Hindu model of Skanda.

Skanda and Gaṇeśa below their father Maheśvara. Detail of Dunhuang, China. Paris, Musée Guimet. Photo Musées nationaux.

According to Daoxuan himself, it was during a series of visions in 667 that, in response to certain questions he put to a deity, he came to know him. Rejecting the gods' desires and adopting a chaste way of life (*brahmacārya*), this young man (*kumāra*) is a general who protects Buddhism. His protection, however, covers only three parts of the world, excluding the north (where, according to him, Buddhism is not widespread) but including, especially, the south.[2] During the same period, Weituo is identified with Vajrapāṇi (Guhyapada) and with the future Buddha Rucika.

In a sixth-century sutra translated into Chinese (and later into Tibetan), two women are contrasted to each other: one has a thousand sons who all become Buddhas (the thousandth being Rucika), while the other has only two, of whom the second becomes Miji jingang (Vajrapāṇi), who protects those thousand Buddhas. Quite early, this second protector was assigned to the post of guardian of the gate, and he was immediately split into two guardians posted at either side of the gate, each simply bearing half the name: Jingang (Vajra) and Lishi ("athlete," an epithet of Miji jingang = Jingang lishi). This reminder of bipartition connected with the door (Skanda-Gaṇeśa) may have been encouraged or reinforced by the existence of an ancient and purely Chinese god of the door, sometimes regarded as a single figure, Yulei, at other times as two, Yu and Lei. Bipartition is so persistent that the couple soon splits into two separate and isolated members, each of whom has his own double. There is a double form for Vaiśravaṇa, the handsome warrior, as well as for Gaṇeśa or Gaṇapati, the round-bellied elephant. The first forms a pair of back-to-back warriors, the second (Huan-hsï t'ien, god of pleasure) a couple consisting of a man and a woman, each with the head of an elephant, embracing face to face. We shall have more to say about these new forms of regrouping and these tendencies toward doubling. But to return to Weituo (< Skanda): not only did he become guardian of the monastery gate in China from the seventh century on (not alone, but associated with a pot-bellied type, as we shall see later), but in Chan monasteries his statue was also placed in the kitchen to ensure food for the community. Thus he fulfills the same function as his pot-bellied double, Mahākāla (> Japanese Daikoku). This role does not occur accidentally. Mañjuśrī, another figure of the type of the young man (though distanced from this role, as an important Bodhisattva of wisdom), was also placed in the refectory. And, as might be expected, in this role he was soon associated with a type of old glutton, the famous *arhat* (saint) Piṇḍola, whom we shall discuss later.[3]

Let us return to the Buddhist Weituo of China and Japan. While becoming independent of his model Skanda, he retains one of the latter's characteristic features and receives a transferred feature vaguely allusive to his brother Gaṇeśa, from whom he has been disssociated. He is famous for being a fast runner (which is in keeping with the Hindu legend of Skanda). But the Buddhist legend finds a new motivation for him. In an early version, probably dating back to the seventh century, the dying Buddha promises Indra one of his teeth as a relic. The god takes two (a "couple" of teeth), but two very swift demons steal them from him (the word "swift" is used here to translate the term *yakṣas,* creatures dependent on Vaiśravaṇa, with Vajrapāṇi as their chief). Whereas Weituo was identified with Vajrapāṇi in China, in thirteenth-century Japan he was the son of Vaiśravaṇa. A hundred years later, a Japanese legend tells that on the death of the Buddha, a demon named Swift stole *one* of his teeth and sped away. But Weituo (Japanese Idaten) pursued him and retrieved the tooth (he was even swifter). This strange apparition of the feature of the single tooth or two teeth obtained by the swift Weituo (< Skanda) appears to be a recollection of the broken tooth of his brother Gaṇeśa.

We now turn to the place and role of female characters. In the Hindu couple of Skanda/Gaṇeśa, the first is linked to the father (sperm retained through asceticism, but released involuntarily); the second to the mother (intimate ablutions). In the Indian Buddhist couple of the guardians of the gate, the refectory, or the kitchen, Mahākāla (borrowing the formal features of Gaṇeśa), guarantor of abundant food, is associated with Hārītī (the devourer and then giver of children, fertility). This Hārītī is also the wife of Pañcika (the double of Kuvēra, himself the replica of Mahākāla). For Foucher, the role of Hārītī was taken up in China and Japan by the goddess Guanyin, giver of children. So much for the potbelly type. The other type, that of the young warrior, in the form of Vaiśravaṇa, also has a wife: her name is Sarasvatī, the goddess of eloquence and intelligence (Benzaiten in Japanese), associated with water, or sometimes Śrī (Kijoten in Japanese). Although he looks like a warrior and sometimes functions as one, Vaiśravaṇa is a god of wealth. Śrī (fortune) is also Kubera's wife. The personality of these two characters is brought out by a Tibetan Buddhist ritual that associates the two. In it, Vaiśravaṇa is called *brahmā-kumāra,* an epithet that marks his status as a chaste young man (like Skanda). Kuvēra is called Maheśvara (Śiva).

Another representative of the type of the young man, Mañjuśrī (related to Pañcika through certain formal features), is generally alone (wisdom, speech), but despite his appearance as a young man, he is regarded as the mother of all the Buddhas (Prajñāpāramitā), symbolized by the book in his left hand, while his right hand holds the sword of wisdom.[4] We have seen how this young man (connected with his mother as was, inversely, his pot-bellied counterpart Gaṇeśa) became the keeper of the refectory (in place of the pot-bellied Mahākāla) and was then associated with Piṇḍola.

The ambiguous connection, often hard to perceive, between the two types of gods and a goddess is expressed in a few stories and in various regroupings of the characters. Archaeologists and historians of iconography have surmised that by withdrawing from the scene the goddess Hārītī, giver of children, served as a model for the Chinese goddess Guanyin, who has the same function. It is possible that this prototype played a role, but not directly. In this particular function, Guanyin is depicted as dressed in white and holding a single child in her arms, while Hārītī's formal characteristic of numerous children was transferred to a god depicted as a jolly pot-bellied monk (Miluo, see below). Above all, the goddess Guanyin (in Japan, Kan-non) is the transformation of the male Avalokiteśvara (Guanyin), and the highly complex question of the date of and motivation behind this transformation has yet to be resolved.

The role, place, and nature of the goddess help us understand new transformations of the group under consideration here. The goddess serves as a signifier for both the sexual theme and the nourishment theme, and she appears in both cases with the chaste young warrior and with the pot-bellied glutton.

A Chinese story that was taken up relatively late on the "popular" level (which is to say that its possible literary source—if it had one—is unknown, as is its historical time span) associates the goddess Guanyin with the guardian of monasteries, Weituo, in connection with a temple (Jietai si, near Peking), whose main chapel (at the northern end) is occupied by Guanyin with a Thousand Arms (and a thousand eyes), while the sides are adorned with five hundred *arhats* (a group of saints, usually sixteen or eighteen in number).[5] An abbot of this temple once had an empress as his faithful donor. One day, he places his alms bowl in front of the statue of Weituo so that it may be filled miraculously. By the power of this guardian god (guarantor of nourishment and wealth, the heir to Skanda, renowned for his great speed), the bowl flies off to the empress and returns filled with jewels by courtesy of this lady. The miracle is repeated daily. But one day the bowl arrives when the lady is still in bed (intimacy). Annoyed, she cries out, "Maybe you would like me to give you five hundred virgins for your five hundred monks?" Henceforth, the bowl never returns. The abbot explains that Weituo (< Skanda, chaste young man) is vexed, but that—since lying is the worst of sins—the empress had to keep her word. She therefore proceeds to send the five hundred most beautiful girls. The abbot enjoins the monks to resist their charms, but they all succumb. The abbot condemns the monks and the girls to be burned. But when the flames reach the couples, Guanyin (of whom there are forms associated with carnal love in China, as there are for Tārā in Tibet) saves the five hundred girls and five hundred monks with her thousand arms (as many as there are *arhats* flanking the goddess [Rousselle]). We lack sufficient documents to trace back the chain of transformations that have evolved into this story. But it obviously combines some features of the legends of Skanda and Gaṇeśa: the woman annoyed at being disturbed during sexual intimacy, the guardian's chastity offended and opposed to sexual license.[6] The Buddhist adaptation takes into account the functions of the guardian of the gate and kitchen that are assumed by the equivalent figures of Mahākāla/Hārītī or Pañcika (Kuvēra)/Hārītī. But the feature of abundance (wealth and fertility) is transferred from the pot-bellied type to the young man type. The assimilation of Skanda and Mañjuśrī, due to their common features, takes place in the *Mañjuśrīmūlakalpa,* a text of Indo-Tibetan Tantrism; in it, the god Kārttikeya-Mañjuśrī is placed by the second gate of a *maṇḍala* (but this god is merely a doublet of Skanda, and the Chinese translation speaks of "Kumāra *and* Mañjuśrī").

The story of Weituo becomes clearer when set against a rare ritual of the end of the seventh century that did not survive beyond the tenth century. It concerns a Mañjuśrī with a thousand arms and a thousand bowls (one in each hand). These thousand bowls contain a thousand Śākyamuni Buddhas, who multiply into millions. In another ritual, Śākyamuni performs a miracle: he makes the bowls fly in order to save creatures from their sufferings. These features must be connected with the function of Mañjuśrī, the guardian of refectories.[7] We have seen that in this function he is associated with one of the sixteen *arhats,* Piṇḍola. Now, Piṇḍola represents the second type of guardian: the glutton. The young man type does not include the feature of the bowl. Conversely, the pot-bellied type (otherwise in opposition to the young man type, as, for instance, Piṇḍola as an old man) is characterized by a receptacle or some symbol of food. The Tantric Gaṇeśa, pot-bellied and stocky, holds a skull rather than a bowl in his left hand, and pokes his trunk into it. The rare form of Mañjuśrī with a thousand arms and a thousand bowls is obviously a doublet of Guanyin with a thousand hands and a thousand eyes. These two figures face each other on the right and the left of a Dunhuang painting representing a paradise of the Buddha of Medicine. The connection between these two characters may explain the story of Weituo, since Guanyin with a thousand hands and a thousand eyes includes in the background a sexual theme (although worshipers may not have been conscious of it).

Just as we have been able to find a few isolated landmarks of the sexual type between the goddess and a god of the chaste young man type, the same sexual theme reappears as if by a necessary complementarity in a story and a ritual from the beginning of the eighth century which identify Guanyin, the goddess, not with Weituo (< Skanda) or with Mañjuśrī, but with the pot-bellied type Gaṇeśa.

Maheśvara (Śiva) has three thousand sons by his wife Umā. Fifteen hundred of them (whose leader is Vināyaka, the creator of obstacles and of ritual faults, but who can also remove them) do evil. The others (whose leader is Senāyaka, a name formed in contrast to the first) do good. This second leader is an incarnation of Guanyin (Avalokiteśvara with Eleven Faces). To overcome the wicked Vināyaka, he (or rather she) takes on the same wicked aspect as his and vanquishes him by uniting with him to form a couple called "Older Brother–Younger Brother, Husband-Wife." Their statue shows them embracing. It was placed in the bedrooms of the laity, and it was not allowed to be placed in a Buddhist temple. Translators point out that the story of this submission by coupling was based on an unidentified sutra, but that both ancient and modern masters had preserved only its mantra.

Statues of this kind, depicting two deities, male and female, with elephant heads, embracing, are attested from the middle of the seventh century. This double form of Gaṇeśa is called Nandikeśvara, "lord of pleasure" (in Chinese, Huanxitian; in Japanese, Kangiten). It was kept secret because of its sexual character, but it still serves today in Japanese Tantrism as the guardian of the entrance gate to the most secret rite, that is, to the room in which monks receive the supreme consecration (*abhiṣeka*). The secret statue is generally accompanied by the statue of Guanyin (in Japanese, Kan-non).[8] Each of the two spouses has an intact left tusk, but the right one is broken (like that of the Hindu Gaṇeśa, a reminder of the theme of the defense of woman's intimacy), but the two are distinguished by opposite characteristics: the woman is on the left, the man on the right, and there are, according to Getty, other oppositions: mouth open/closed, like the two Vajrapāṇi guardians of the gate; crowned/uncrowned; short tusks and trunk / long tusks and trunk; eye small/big. The epithet of "pleasure" also designates the round cake (a ball of rice) that Gaṇeśa Gaṇapati (Vanāyaka) holds (in his left hand, a female symbol) at the same time as he holds a turnip and a radish (in his right hand, a male symbol), a doublet of the broken tusk. The cake recalls the gluttony of the Hindu Gaṇeśa, whose large stomach bursts open and is tied together with a snake. A late Japanese account takes up this theme and tells of a king who ate so much meat that he exhausted all supplies (first all the oxen, then dead humans, and finally live humans). The title of Dasheng (Great Saint) given to the figure of Gaṇeśa, who has split into a sexual couple, is also attributed to Vaiśravaṇa (the young warrior). Protector of the north, he is the only one of the guardians of the four regions to bear this title. A third "Great Saint" also becomes part of this group. He is known as the "Monk of the Community" (*saṃgha*, Sengjia heshang). Another monk, Wanhuei (who runs fast like Skanda), learns that he is a reincarnation of Guanyin. He vanquished a "mother of the water," a "holy mother." In a temple of popular Taoism, the guardian god (Wang lingguan) is flanked by the "Great Saint" (on the left) and Guanyin (on his right).

Thus we see the goddess (in this case, Guanyin, the female form of Avalokiteśvara, himself a transformation of Śiva) associated now with one, now with the other of the two guardians, and associated simultaneously with the two themes of sex and food. In the case of Huanxitian (Nandikeśvara), she combines the two Indian pairs: the older and younger brothers and the husband and wife.

Whether we are dealing with affirmed sexuality or refuted sexuality (chastity), the relationship between Guanyin and the chaste young man Weituo is well attested in modern China. The statues of Weituo and Guanyin are often found together, along with a third pot-bellied individual, at the entrance of temples. On the road to Kangding, in the outlying Sino-Tibetan regions, the bridge crossing the Tadu River connects a temple of Guanyin with the mountain of Weituo on the opposite bank. They have a cult of two stones there, one elongated, the other one round, which are regarded as the sexual organs of the two deities.[9] According to one tradition (Lessing), a formal feature of Weituo can be explained by the relationship between the goddess and the god. In most cases, but particularly when in front of Guanyin, the young warrior joins both hands in prayer, holding horizontally across his arms a studded stick (a kind of mace or a doublet of the *vajra*). In other cases, his stick stands upright on his right palm or is pointed toward the ground, while his left hand (when he is standing) or his right hand (when he is sitting) rests effortlessly on the pommel (which represents a ball or a jewel). In the absence of precise and complete evidence, nothing can be confirmed. It is, however, possible that the horizontal position of Weituo's stick is a relevant feature indicating a relationship with the goddess characterized by respect and chastity.

We shall now return to the elephant-god, one of the partners of the couple whose transformations we are tracing. He has his own existence in Buddhist Tantrism (India, Tibet, China, Japan), sometimes as the vanquisher of and protector against obstacles (Vināyaka or Vighnāntaka, a god), at other times as the vanquished creator of obstacles (Vināyaka, a demon trampled under the feet of his vanquisher). It is not our purpose here to examine the multiple forms and functions of this elephant-god. But we do have to present the collection of features that becomes part of the bipartite system we are dealing with and shows further transformations.

When Vināyaka is the vanquished demon, the vanquisher is sometimes Tārā, but according to a Chinese account at the end of the seventh century, based on the statements of an Indian monk, it is Avalokiteśvara with a thousand arms and a thousand eyes, the same who vanquished Vināyaka (Gaṇeśa) by becoming his wife; sometimes it is Amṛtakuṇḍali ("Production of *amṛta*"), or Ucchuṣma. His Tibetan and Chinese name means "accumulated filth." In Chinese, a homophonic variant turns the name into "filthy traces" (Huei-chi). In both cases, his epithet is Vajra. He is also called Vajra with a Head of Fire, and he is identified with Vajra-yakṣa. According to one legend, he was once a man full of sexual passion, which manifested itself as a fire throughout his whole body. He became a Buddha by transforming this fire of passion into a fire of wisdom. He then took on the form of an athlete (*lishi*) and is known as Mahābala ("Great Force"). We have already seen that one of the guardians of the gate, Vajrapāṇi, split into two in China in the form of Jingang (Vajra) and Lishi (athlete). Ucchuṣma, a great athlete, thus appears as a doublet of Vajrapāṇi (who is also known as "Secret Traces" in Chinese). A Tibetan ritual of lustration has preserved a tradition that regarded Ucchuṣma as an incarnation of Vajrapāṇi Guhyapati ("Lord of Secrets"), a son of Maheśvara and Umā. Thus we find

Kangiten, Japan. Paris, Musée Guimet. Photo Musées nationaux.

again the characteristic feature of the Hindu Gaṇeśa (filth and the guarded secret). In modern Nepal, the entrance to Hindu and Buddhist temples is guarded by Gaṇeśa and Mahākāla (Snellgrove). According to a Tibetan historian of the seventeenth century, in the reign of the first king (ca. 650) the gate to the temple of Lhasa was protected by two guards, Vajrapāṇi on the right and Ucchuṣma on the left. Ucchuṣma is also regarded as the fierce form of Jambhala, a god of wealth of the pot-bellied type (like Mahākāla). In this case, he tramples on Kuvēra, king of wealth (vanquisher over vanquished). Instead of spitting out jewels, his mongoose expels them through its anus. In a cycle of Tibetan stories too lengthy to analyze here, Ucchuṣma is the transformation of excrements and other filth resulting from the submission of the demon-god Rudra-Maheśvara (through impalement) and of his wife (through coitus): his name is then Vajra-Kumāra (Young Man). He either transforms the filth that he represents into *amṛta*, or he eliminates it by means of his fire. In this last capacity, he plays the same role as another terrible warrior full of fire, Acala ("Immobile," Fudō in Japanese). Appropriately, Ucchuṣma is employed as a guardian of latrines and bathrooms, thus returning to the theme of Gaṇeśa born of the impurities from his mother's intimate bath.

Associated with Vajrapāṇi (who was identified with Weituo < Skanda) and represented as a young warrior, Ucchuṣma is also classified in the north as the other two types of gods of wealth, Vaiśravaṇa (warrior) and Kuvēra (ugly, fat). But the motif of filth relates him, instead, to the pot-bellied type of Gaṇeśa, who, under the name of Vināyaka, is depicted as vanquished by him both in the paintings of Dunhuang and in Sino-Japanese Tantrism.

In the Dunhuang paintings, two of which are clearly dated by inscriptions (A.D. 943 and 981), the vanquisher and the vanquished are depicted doubled on the right and on the left by Avalokiteśvara with a thousand hands and eleven heads (the one who vanquished Vināyaka by becoming his wife). The vanquisher is doubled by yet another related form, itself doubled on the left and on the right. Except for some cases in which the places are inverted (inversions that can be noted in other elements of this scene, without any regularity or discernible reason), they appear as follows: On the left, a form of Vajrapāṇi, whose throat is blue as a result of having swallowed poison, but whose body is red. He is called Blue Poison Vajra (homophonic variant: Vajra who dispels poison, Bidu jingang) or Blue-faced Vajra (Qingmian jingang). He may be identified with Kuṇḍali Yakṣa (Waley) or rather Amṛtakuṇḍali ("producer of *amṛta*"). He is accompanied by another form of Vajrapāṇi, "Secret Traces" (Miji jingang), whose body is blue. Facing him on the right is a form of Ucchuṣma known as Vajra with a Head of Fire (Huotou jingang) or Red-faced Vajra. He is accompanied by another fierce vanquisher with a red skin, Vajra Great God (Mahādeva) or Trailokyavijaya (vanquisher of the three worlds). The main vanquishers are seen at his feet, on the left a demon with the head of a pig, called Vinākaya, "Demon-Mother," and on the right a demon with the head of an elephant, called Vināyaka, "demon-father." We have here a form of Gaṇeśa. The variant of the head of the pig, brought in for the sake of symmetry (left/right; mother/father), may be explained both by the form (his extended snout replacing the trunk) and by the content (in China, pigs feed on excrement). Later, a double of Vajrapāṇi characterized by these inverted forms may be found. It should again be noted here that these representations go back to well before the tenth century.

A ritual translated into Chinese in the middle of the seventh century is devoted to Vajragarbha, a doublet of Vajrapāṇi (here he is the Lord of Secrets, and by the sixth century he sometimes replaces Vajrapāṇi, opposite Avalokiteśvara, on either side of the Buddha). He is surrounded by fourteen Śaiva deities, among whom we find Ucchuṣma, Amṛtakuṇḍali, and Śankara (generally, it is Śiva, but here it is a woman, the elder daughter of Vajragarbha). Amṛtakuṇḍali dispels obstacles (Vināyaka). He is blue, but has fiery red hair. He tramples on an elephant-headed demon, holding a turnip in his right hand and a "cake of joy" (*huanxi tan, modaka*) in his left hand (Gaṇeśa). Ucchuṣma too is blue with hair red as fire. He seems to be distinct from the two related characters, Vajra with a Head of Fire, who vanquishes demons, and Blue-faced Vajra, who is represented as a *yakṣa* with a blue body, trampling on a demon and surrounded by four *vajrayakṣas*. We can see that the filth of Ucchuṣma forms a counterpart to the poison of Vajrapāṇi, which, once digested and neutralized, becomes *amṛta* in his doublet Amṛtakuṇḍali.

The characteristic of gluttony of the Hindu Gaṇeśa and its connection with filth (through his mother) thus reappear in Buddhism among its gods who are vanquishers. They are particularly well illustrated by an altogether different figure known only in Tibetan Tantrism. This is a ritual object, either a mask that serves as a receptacle to light a fire, or a hollow statuette that is used to get medicine into the mouth of a sick patient: the medicine is placed in the mouth of the god, travels through his stomach, and comes out through his anus. This object does not, therefore, come under the general rubric of the guardian-gods that we are discussing. But it is appropriate to mention it because this particular form highlights the connections between the two guardians, Vajrapāṇi and Ucchuṣma.

The bodiless mask shows only one face of the fierce deity, a wide open mouth (though a rare variant at the Leiden Museum transforms the mouth into the trunk and tusks of an elephant, reminiscent of Gaṇeśa or Gaṇapati). The statuette is more pertinent. The god is of the dwarf type, with short legs and pot-belly (like a *gaṇa* or *yakṣa*). The identity of this god varies according to the source. He is a form of Vajrapāṇi called Vajraḍāka ("Walking Vajra," probably swift like Skanda) or, in Tibetan, Za-byed ("Eater," also an epithet of fire). This god helps the worshipers to cleanse themselves of their sins, which he swallows and digests with his fire (digestion being conceived of as a kind of combustion). When he is not the object of a ritual, but a member of the pantheon, he tramples on (vanquishes) a prostrate Gaṇeśa. He thus plays the same role as Ucchuṣma (the Lama Kazi Dawa Samdup in fact identified him with this god, but his source remains unknown). Be that as it may, we can see here another example of the transfer of characteristics: the warrior-guardian takes on features of the glutton (Vajrapāṇi = Vajraḍāka), while the warrior Ucchuṣma has retained the features of the bath and filth that were characteristic of the gluttonous Gaṇeśa. In Sino-Japanese Tantrism, Ucchuṣma is assimilated into another form, Vajrayakṣa (whereas in Tibet Vajrapāṇi reappears in the form of a *yakṣa*). Both vowed to eat filth. In both cases, we find in the background the theme of *amṛta* in opposition to the poison swallowed and transformed, a theme that is connected with Śiva > Avalokiteśvara as well as with Indra > Vajrapāṇi.[10] Two legends (poorly attested, to be sure—oral versions of unknown origins brought by European travelers) illustrate this theme. Whereas generally it is Śiva who swallowed the poison that appeared at the same time as the *amṛta* (hence his blue neck and his name Nīlakaṇṭha), according to one of the legends of Tibetan origin it is Vajrapāṇi (whom Buddhists identify with Indra) who has a blue neck because he had to drink the urine of Rāhu, who had stolen the *amṛta* (and then threatened to swallow the sun and the moon). Finally, according to another legend of Mongolian origin, Indra pursued Rāhu as he was swallowing the sun and the moon and slit open his belly so that he had to let them pass "through his bottom." This legend intends to explain the figure of Vajrapāṇi-Vajraḍāka, who swallows a pill and gives it back through his anus.

We now turn to the other pot-bellied types who have taken the place of Gaṇeśa among the guardian couples. First among them is Piṇḍola, who was associated (in the eighth century; see above) with the young Mañjuśrī to the left of the refectory. This function was attributed to him by the fourth-century Chinese monk Daoan, who also launched the cult of the future Buddha Maitreya. He saw the saint in a dream in the form of an old man with white hair and long eyebrows, who asked him for a meal (or in the form of a small boy who asked him for a bath). In India, his function as a guardian of the refectory is attested in the eighth century at the latest and his cult by the seventh century. On the occasion of religious meals, he would be offered a meal and a bath, while the leftovers from the meal were given to the goddess Hārītī. Piṇḍola is one of the sixteen or eighteen saints (*arhats*) and one of the four principal ones among them. These saints await Maitreya's coming on earth. They must protect Buddhism, each living on his own mountain and protecting a different country (we saw them earlier, surrounding Weituo and Guanyin).

The Tibetans translated the name of Piṇḍola as "seeker of alms" (beggar, *piṇḍāra*), and the Chinese as "immobile" (*acala*). According to S. Lévi, it means "food leftovers" (*piṇḍoli*). Indeed, *piṇḍa* designates a round mass, a ball, notably of food (rice, meat), hence: alms, quantity.[11] Various accounts illustrate his connection with abundant food, but there is also reference to his intelligence and knowledge. He learns the three Vedas and excels in triumphing over heretics in controversies, which is why his statue is also placed in the preaching room.

As a result of a sin committed in a previous life (according to a Japanese version, he broke his vow of chastity in his youth), he is always hungry and gluttonous to the point of eating tiles and bricks. In another story, he was a Brahman and had an unbearable wife. His seven daughters and their husbands demanded that he feed them. Unable to do so, he was disgusted and became a disciple of the Buddha. Or else, when the Buddha is invited to a sermon by the daughter of his patron, Piṇḍola remains sitting on his mountain, busily sewing his robe. Remembering his duty, he sticks the needle into the ground and takes flight to join the Buddha, but the mountain is dragged along with him by the thread of the needle, and a pregnant woman dies of fright at the spectacle. For this mistake, the Buddha expels Piṇḍola from the community. He must wander throughout the world and may no longer eat with the other monks. The commonest account (in several versions) attributes this punishment to the fact that he exhibited his power to perform miracles (something a saint must not do without a good reason) in order to respond to a challenge from a heretic: to catch, without touching it, a bowl made of precious sandalwood, suspended out of reach. In one of the versions, the bowl is filled with sugar and "pills of joy" (S. Lévi, *modakas,* "pellets of pleasure"), which the Buddha accepts while refusing the bowl. These pellets (*huanxu* in Chinese) are the very ones that characterize Gaṇeśa, especially in his dual form of a sexual couple (Huanxitian). According to another version, Piṇḍola performs miracles to convert a woman who refuses to believe in the Buddha or to give the monks anything to eat. Overcome by his magic, she first gives a small ball of rice, which grows bigger and bigger. She then consents to give him one small ball of rice from her own supply, but all the others follow behind the first. Piṇḍola orders the woman to bring them all to the Buddha. They are sufficient to feed all 1,250 monks of the community, and there are still some leftovers.

Whereas the bowl, the gluttony, and the abundance of cakes or balls of rice are features characteristic of Gaṇeśa, the bowl also refers us back to the forms of the young man (Weituo, Mañjuśrī). A woman plays only an obscure role in their adventures. Gaṇeśa, having doubled into a sexual couple (with Guanyin), is called "Great Saint" (*dasheng* in Chinese), and Piṇḍola "Saint-Monk" (*shengseng*). According to a Chinese Buddhist work of the early eleventh century, Chinese monasteries included three chapels (of guardian deities), one for demons (Kuei or, in one commentary, Guizi mu, "Mother of Demons," a variant of Hārītī), another for the god of the community (Chinese Qielan, Sanskrit *saṃgharama,* a variant of the "Great Saint," the *saṃgha* monk), and yet another for Piṇḍola. The latter's association with Hārītī shows once again his link with the pot-bellied type (he replaces Mahākāla > Daikoku, stocky and carrying a bag; associated with Hārītī, who receives the leftovers of food). In a little Kyoto temple dedicated to Guanyin with Eleven Faces, to whom one prays for successful childbirth, Piṇḍola is seated outside, to the right of the door, carrying a little ball of rice in his hand. In another temple of Guanyin (Tokyo, Ueno, Kiyomizu Kan-non), Kan-non (with naked stomach and breasts, giver of children, like Hārītī), on the right, is flanked by Piṇḍola (Japanese Binzuru) on the left. We have already seen the (five hundred or sixteen) *arhats* associated with a story of Weituo (< Skanda) and Guanyin. Whereas Piṇḍola was assigned to guard the refectory or the preaching room, another of the sixteen *arhats,* Bhadrapāla, was chosen to be the guardian of the bathroom (while Piṇḍola when invited for a ritual leaves behind traces on the ground, on the bed, and in the bathroom).

Another *arhat* takes on the features of Piṇḍola and brings us back to the prototype of Gaṇeśa/Gaṇapati. This is Gavaṃpati, "chief or king of the bulls," a name that the Chinese also translated as "trace of the bull" or "look of the bull." He has the hoof of a bull and he chews the cud after eating, rechewing what he has eaten in excess. For five hundred lives preceding this one, he was a bull. Such was the retribution for a sin committed long ago that may appear rather insignificant: while picking a stalk of wheat, he dropped a few grains on the ground. Like other *arhats,* he lived in heaven so long that he was not aware that the Buddha had already entered into Nirvana, and he performed miracles.

His connection with Gaṇeśa was made specific in Burma and Thailand, where both characters are depicted back to back, their hands over their eyes. His name connects him to Śiva, whose mount is the bull Nandin and who is called Paśupati, "lord of cattle." Nandin and Gaṇeśa figure among the twelve gods in Śiva's retinue. And, most significantly, if Gaṇeśa is the guardian of the intimacy of his mother Pārvatī, Nandin (and not Skanda) often plays the role of guardian of the door of Śiva when Śiva has intercourse with Pārvatī.

Gavaṃpati was not kept as a guardian, but he is said to have sat in the preaching room of the gods (like Piṇḍola). Like Piṇḍola, he is characterized by the theme of excessive

Weituo with a mace carried horizontally. Japan. Paris, Musée Guimet. Photo Musées nationaux.

food. The Gaṇeśa type whom we compared with Piṇḍola is thus effectively realized for Gavaṃpati; this formulation also hints of the link with Śiva (and perhaps the sexual code).

The gluttonous characteristics have been rearranged in another way in two new transformations. One is Tibetan: Ha-shaṅ, the monk of the masked dances; the other is Chinese: Budai heshang, the "Monk with the Canvas Bag," and Miluo, the fat, laughing Buddha. The choice of the name Miluo (= Maitreya) is not accidental. We have just seen how by the fourth century the cult of this future Buddha spread at the same time as that of Piṇḍola. The *arhats* (saints) have been awaiting this future Buddha by remaining in our world ever since the time of our own Buddha, Śākyamuni. They are therefore very old. Thus the formal opposition of the handsome young man and the pot-bellied gluttonous dwarf gives way to a variant: the handsome young man in opposition to the grotesque old man. Appropriately, the fat, laughing monk (Heshang, Tibetan Ha-shaṅ) was added to the series of sixteen *arhats* next to a certain Dharmatala (an old man carrying a broom, with a tiger coming out of his knee), who seems to be a variant on Bodhidharma (who in Japan became a comic and grotesque figure). The question of this list of sixteen *arhats* and the individuals who constitute it is too complicated to be broached here.

The Monk with the Canvas Bag and the pot-bellied Buddha are related characters. We do not know which one is the transformation or variant of the other (nor do we know the chronology of these forms, although they are attested by the ninth or tenth centuries at the very least). Among the stucco figurines that came from central Asia (and are dated from the sixth to the tenth centuries according to the Delhi Museum), we can see pot-bellied individuals, naked, laughing, holding their belly with their right hand, their left hand resting on a canvas bag. According to a Chinese catalog of the eighth century, there appeared as early as the first century a translation of a sutra called "The transformation of Miluo (Maitreya) into a Woman's Body." In A.D. 690, a woman, the empress Wu zetian, was declared to be the incarnation of Miluo, and already in 602 another empress was considered to be an incarnation of Avalokiteśvara.

In a remarkable spirit of inference or in a more or less conscious response to the connections inherent in the features of this coherent whole, the fat Buddha Miluo and the fat monk (Heshang, Ha-shaṅ) are both depicted surrounded by little children who climb all over them and play with them. This feature is illogical at first glance and incomprehensible in such characters as the comical, pot-bellied old men, but it is perfectly justified for the role of the woman who is the giver of children and for the iconographic prototype of Hārītī surrounded by five hundred children (associated as a guardian with Mahākāla > Daikoku, pot-bellied and holding the bag that means abundance). The ambiguous, obscure place of the goddess and the transfer of her features to the pot-bellied type respond both to the variation between the brother couple and the husband-wife couple and to the particular connection between the pot-bellied guardian (Gaṇeśa) and his mother.

The Monk with the Canvas Bag (Budai, Hotei in Japanese) was not kept as a guardian of the gate (unless he is to be identified with Miluo). But the Japanese clearly felt that he belonged to the group of deities we have been studying. Toward the fifteenth and sixteenth centuries, they formed a group of Seven Deities of Happiness that included only one woman, Benzaiten (Sarasvatī, wife of Vaiśravaṇa, a young warrior type), Bishamon (Vaiśravaṇa), two very long-lived old men (of Chinese origin), Hotei, Daikoku (Mahākāla with his bag of rice), and Ebisu (a Japanese god associated with fish).[12]

Chinese authors tried to identify Budai with a historical character (Tang, Song, or Yuan). It matters little which, for we are dealing with a *type* of saint. One art historian (Scherman) recognized in him the type of the dwarfish and obese *yakṣa* and even the popular figure of Silenus, the friend of children (Buddhists knew him from the art of Gandhāra, in which Greek models were used to represent Buddhist characters). Another author (Lessing) thought of Diogenes and his bag. But the laughter, clowning, and grotesque and paradoxical attitudes of the saint are characteristic of Chan (Zen) and Tantrism. The Chinese *arhats* are all represented as grotesque characters of the caricatured Indian type (large nose, dark complexion, and so forth). Similarly, the Tibetans made the Indian saint (*ācārya*) into a clown mask used in masked dances (the *acaras*).

Certain specific features of "Gaṇeśa" figures (sometimes taken up by his young man counterpart) can be found in the figure of the pot-bellied old saint. The Monk (Budai heshang) stuffs everything into his canvas bag; for this bag is inexhaustible and contains the three worlds. He tastes everything he receives and puts the leftovers in his bag (Hārītī gets the food leftovers), even wastes, even stones and bricks (the "foods" of the eternally famished and gluttonous Piṇḍola). In so doing, he is said to be "full of pleasure and supremely at ease" (*huanxi zicai*), an expression that echoes Gaṇeśa's double (Huanxitian) with his cakes (*huanxi*). Curiously enough, the same features can be found in India. For the sect of Gāṇapatyas (worshipers of Gaṇeśa), the elephant-god's cake is the "seed of life," and his pot-belly is a vast space containing millions of cakes, which are all the human seeds of the universe. In China, the bag of Miluo or Budai is called "the mother of breaths" (*qimu*) because it contains the primordial breath of life, the seed of all past worlds.

As interesting and amusing as these new forms of pot-bellied types may be, both of them are, like their Indian model, charged with the function of wealth, abundance, and fertility. But their existence as separate individuals is not really surprising. These characters have been used in Japan for a group of gods of happiness (wealth, ripe old age, abundance of food and children). In Tibet, in the masked dances, the Monk (*Heshang* > Ha-shan in Tibetan) plays the role of a clown and is believed to recall the famous Monk (the Mahāyāna *ha-shaṅ*) who sustained a theological debate with the Indian masters.

Interestingly, in modern China the fat and laughing Miluo is placed at the entrance of temples. A great Sinologist (Maspero) found this surprising: "We do not know why or when this particularly ugly type was chosen to welcome visitors at the entrance of Buddhist temples." The choice does not seem so arbitrary to us. We have seen that the fat Mahākāla and his counterpart Ucchuṣma (filth) were placed as guardians in the same place. Better still, their Hindu prototype Gaṇeśa is placed at the southern end of the temple, right by the entrance, looking southward, whereas his mount, the rat, looks northward. We can see immediately that this is what characterizes the position of the fat Miluo.

What Maspero does not say is that at this place and in this function, Miluo is never alone. He is always associated with a second guardian, and in most cases that second guardian is Weituo, the young warrior. Despite the dissociation of the Hindu couple of Skanda/Gaṇeśa and despite the transformations and new regroupings of each of these two characters separately in the course of history and in various countries, it was nevertheless possible—amazingly—very late and only in China, to reconstitute the couple of the young warrior and fat glutton in this new form as guardians of the gate leading to the holy of holies, to the "secret." Did the authors of this innovation somehow sense or stumble upon the system, or did they proceed lucidly through a deliberate analysis analogous to ours and based on extensive reading? It would be hard to say. But now let us examine in some detail the way the guardian couple of the temple gates has been depicted in "modern" China (for four centuries, and sometimes even for as many as eight or nine centuries).[13]

Of course, in so vast a country we are bound to encounter a great many variants. The Miluo/Weituo couple is not the only couple to act as guardians. Historical reasons, contingencies of all kinds, associations of different ideas have all resulted in other combinations. We shall give only a few examples.

In the most pertinent and undoubtedly the most widespread case, Miluo, the Buddha with the pot-belly, squatting and laughing, and Weituo, the young warrior standing, are placed back to back at the entrance of temples. Given the normal orientation of Chinese temples, where the principal deity is seated at the north end looking southward (like the emperor), and where the entrance gate opens to the south, Miluo looks southward, that is, to the outside, and Weituo northward, to the inside. It will be recalled that Weituo rules over the three points of the compass other than the north, and especially over the south, while the north is guarded by Vaiśravaṇa (sometimes with a double, the two warriors seated back to back, whereas the two Gaṇeśas, Huanxi tian, the male/female couple, embrace face to face). Sometimes Weituo (on the left) and Vaiśravaṇa (on the right) flank the main deity. As we have said, Weituo (< Skanda) was regarded as a form of the athletic guardian Vajrapāṇi (whom we will see, *doubled*, at the entrance gate). As early as the sixth century, and especially in the Tantrism of the eighth and ninth centuries, Vajrapāṇi is contrasted to and associated with Guanyin (in his male aspect, Avalokiteśvara). But what distinguishes him from Weituo (at least in the iconography of modern China) is that Vajrapāṇi brandishes his weapon while Weituo keeps his "in repose" (especially, perhaps, when he is associated with Guanyin). In modern China, the female Guanyin is found either alone looking northward, or back to back with Weituo (looking northward); or else Guanyin (with children) is at the north end, and Weituo, with his back to her, looks toward the south, where he is preceded by Miluo. Or, again, at the entrance we may find the Miluo/Weituo couple back to back, and, farther, in another couple, this time Guanyin/Weituo, also back to back.

In a pagoda devoted to Guanyin, the entrance is guarded by Qielan (the guardian of the monastery, see below) looking southward and, back to back, Weituo looking northward, but the scene is repeated in the holy of holies (at the northernmost end of temples) where Guanyin is seated, wearing the crown of Vairocana (the Buddha of the Center), with Miluo. In the preceding room, we can see Vairocana at the far end, then the young Buddha, and in front of him the couple called Huo and He, of whom we shall speak later. In another temple, we can see the same group (Vairocana, the young Buddha, and Huo and He), all facing south, but Guanyin has her back to them and faces north.

We also find, back to back, Guanyin (facing north) and Vairocana; Guanyin (facing north) and the Buddha; Guanyin and Amitābha; Weituo and Samantabhadra; and Weituo (facing north) and Dipamkara. Despite variations in which certain theological speculations intervene, there is a persistent individual link between Weituo and Guanyin and between the features connected with the back-to-back position and the northward position.

A particularly interesting case is that of the Guanyin temple on the island of Putuo, which is her most important holy place (Potalaka). Behind the entrance hall, we can see Weituo looking northward, facing Guanyin. But there is a second Weituo with his back to her, looking toward the main room devoted to Guanyin.

This doubling or splitting in two is a common way of achieving a necessary bipartite structure. In the case of Guanyin, in addition to recalling the ambiguous place occupied by a goddess who is associated sometimes with one and sometimes with another of the two members of the couple, the Chinese succeeded in finding a historical precedent for her function as a guardian. In his account of his travels in India, Xuanzang (mid-seventh century) describes the site of the Bodhi tree of enlightenment in Bodhgaya, the (immobile) "Vajra seat" on which Śākyamuni became the Buddha. The northern and southern limits of this site are marked by two statues of Avalokiteśvara (male, Guanzizai) sitting and looking eastward. It was believed that the end of the Buddha's religion would be signaled when these two statues had sunk into the ground, and at that time the one at the south is said to have already disappeared down to its navel.

For certain figures who were put in the place of the fat Miluo, the reason for assigning them the role of guardian of the gate is clear. The most frequent doublet is the god Qielan (Saṃgharama, "community" or "monastery"). We saw above that by the eleventh century, three guardian deities were needed in a monastery: Hārītī, Qielan, and Piṇḍola. It is significant that this model was not followed. Hārītī with her children gave her features both to Guanyin and to Miluo. An important pair of opposites was reconfigured by reintroducing the type of the young warrior. In the late legend of Guanyin of the South Seas (Miaoshan), Qielan sweeps the house clean for Guanyin (the theme of filth). In the iconography of modern China, he holds a purse in his left hand; the purse is also a feature of the god of wealth (Chinese), of another Chinese guardian of the gate (Jiantan), and sometimes of Miluo (or Budai heshang), who holds it instead of his usual bag. It may be recalled that this purse appears as a feature of Kuvēra-Vaiśravaṇa (variant: a rodent spitting or defecating jewels), and of Jambhala (whose fierce form is Ucchuṣma, filth), while the bag (of Budai) appears as a feature of Mahākāla, guardian of the refectory and the gate, who became the Japanese Daikoku (god of wealth and of the kitchen, but not of the gate). The gate god Qielan (Saṃgharama) has a doublet in the Monk Saṃgha (community), of whom we have already spoken, who bears the title of "Great Saint" (*dasheng*), like Gaṇeśa (doubled into a male/female couple, an elephant and Guanyin) and Vaiśravaṇa (doubled into two back-to-back warriors). According to the legend of the Great Saint (attested in the beginning of the twelfth century), he was a monk who discovered a statue of the Buddha Dipaṃkara at the site of an ancient monastery called Accumulated Fragrances (a euphemism for the kitchen and the supplies of the monks, but also the name of the Gandhamādana mountain connected with Mañjuśrī, who played the role of guardian of the gate beside Piṇḍola). He had a hole in the top of his head, which he plugged with cotton. At night when he removed the plug, fragrances would come out. The water in which he bathed his feet cured the sick. At his death, the monk Wanhuei ("Swift") stated that this saint was an incarnation of Guanyin. Speed is a characteristic feature of Weituo (and of his model Skanda), whom modern Chinese tradition regards as a disciple of Dipaṃkara (the Buddha of the past, Maitreya > Miluo being the Buddha of the future). We surmise that the Weituo/Miluo couple may have been replaced by the Weituo/Dipaṃkara couple. The swift runner Wanhuei does not appear by accident. According to the modern legend, Weituo is responsible for introducing the Buddhas invited to a great feast given by the Buddha, while Wanhuei is one of the guests invited to the feast of the Chinese goddess Xiwang mu (who gives the peach of immortality). Around the twelfth century, he is represented with disheveled hair and a smiling face, like one of those grotesque monks of the Budai heshang type, and he is identified with a popular Chinese god named Huohe ("Harmonious Union," a god of happiness), unless this god is split into two as the pair of brothers Huo and He (much like Skanda and Gaṇeśa).

According to an old Chinese custom, a god who has a double form or a double function is commonly represented as a couple. His name is then divided into two parts: we have already come across Yulei = Yu and Lei, god of the gate; another one is Xihe = Xi and He, the time-keeping god. This is also what happened to Huohe: he is either a couple of young children referred to by the formula *huantian xidi* (joy-pleasure heaven-earth, Huantian like the double Gaṇeśa), or a couple of elderly men of the *arhat* type, or a couple of fat, almost naked monks (like Miluo). Huohe is the technical term designating the harmony of the community of monks (*saṃgha-samarga*). The Huo and He couple has been identified with two famous monks, "buffoons" of the *zhan (zen)* type, known as Hanshan and Shide (regarded as incarnations of Mañjuśrī and of Samantabhadra), the former always laughing, the latter characterized by the food leftovers that he collects and the other carries away. We shall not follow their fate any farther, nor that of Huohe, because they were not kept as Buddhist characters in charge of guarding the gate, the kitchen, or the bath. Suffice it to point out their formal connections with the deities with whom we are concerned.

Let us now return to the Great Saint, the Monk "Community" or "Monastery" (Qielan), and quickly sketch his character as god of the soil, guardian of the dwelling place and of the group that dwells there. It is this quality of his that is operative when his statue, made up of himself coupled with Weituo, is replaced by that of the purely Chinese and popular god of the soil (Tudi).[14] His most common form (a dignified old Mandarin with his wife) is not pertinent for our purposes. He does, however, also have a form analogous to characters of the Buddhist milieu: an old man with thick eyebrows, white face and beard, holding a studded stick (the form is attested as far back as the twelfth century). It is the same form as Piṇḍola, and it emphasizes his function of guardian of the dwelling place. It is also typical of the saints (*arhats*) who stay here on earth and get to be very old, and as such it is widespread in Tibet and Mongolia in the person of the Old White Man (in Tibetan sGam-po dkar-po, in Mongolian Čaghan ebügen). Sometimes identified with a form of Mahākāla (White Protector) and often confused with the Chinese god of longevity (Shouxing, in Tibetan Mi che-rin), he was introduced into the masked dances beside the jolly "Monk" (Hashaṅ) surrounded by children. The variant of the Tudi/Weituo couple, which seems at first glance to be wholly contingent, may be explained in a fashion that is admittedly rather allusive and obscure if one bears in mind the associations of ideas and the formal features of the entire spectrum of characters we are dealing with here.

One final representation of the guardian of the gate remains to be looked at. In China, in addition to the couple Miluo/Weituo and its variants, or sometimes in its absence, one can always find on either side of the temple gates the Vajrapāṇi in two parts, of whom we have had occasion to speak earlier—Jingang (Vajra) and Lishi (athlete). He is, as it were, an echo of Weituo, with whom he has been identified. In Tibet, we saw Vajrapāṇi (in Chinese, "secret traces") and Ucchuṣma (in Chinese, "filthy traces") at the gate. We have already stated that Vajrapāṇi was at first a *yakṣa* standing

Avalokiteśvara. Painting from Dunhuang. Paris, Musée Guimet. Photo Musées nationaux.

next to the Buddha to protect him. According to Indian monastic rules (translated into Chinese in the seventh century), the two sides of the gate were supposed to be guarded by two *yakṣas* carrying sticks. In Indo-Tibetan and Sino-Japanese Tantrism, Vajrapāṇi became the "lord of secrets" (receiving and keeping the secret teachings). He is said to be a *yakṣa* called Secret. He is swift (like Skanda > Weituo). In certain sutras translated as far back as the sixth century, he listens to and understands the secrets of the Buddhas, or he writes down the words and acts of the Buddha (motifs characteristic of the Hindu Gaṇeśa, as we pointed out earlier). In China, starting at the end of the tenth century, two Vajrapāṇis appear at the gate of the monastery. But as ornaments or in famous caves, a variant of two athletes (the two kings, in Japanese Ni-Ō) appears as early as the sixth century.

We saw earlier that in Dunhuang paintings (tenth century), a Vajrapāṇi with a blue head is coupled with a Ucchuṣma with a red head, on the left and on the right of Avalokiteśvara, and that this symmetry is extended to the Gaṇeśas whom they vanquish. Other formal features underscore this bipartition. The two doublets of Vajrapāṇi also show symmetrical and inverted configurations. The first, on the left, Secret Traces (Guhyapada), raises his right arm and lowers his left arm (left leg bent, right leg stretched); the second, on the right, Great-God, does the opposite, but, in both, the hand on the raised arm is open and the hand on the lowered arm is closed into a fist.

In China and in Japan, these two athletes are often though not always shown with an additional formal feature that underscores their bipolarity: open mouth / closed mouth (in Japan, they are the guardians of the two opposite and complementary *maṇḍalas,* placed to the east and to the west). This feature has been interpreted as symbolic of the two monosyllabic mantras, A (open mouth) and Hūṃ (closed mouth), or else A and Vam, the mantras of the two *maṇḍalas.* Generally speaking, we may see Vajra (open mouth) and Athlete (closed mouth). But while they are always opposites, their respective places on the left and right are not fixed and may be inverted. In addition, while these two athletes are surely transformations of the doubled Vajrapāṇi or of the two *yakṣas* who guard the gate, they more precisely represent two rare guardians referred to in the *Mahāvairocanasūtra* (translated at the beginning of the seventh century); they are distinguished by the feature of the left hand open/closed. They are best known in Japan under the name of Fukaotsu ("Unsurpassable") and Sōkō ("Facing"), names taken from the Chinese sutra. In Japan, a further step was taken (in the Shūgendō tradition), making them into two demons who were vanquished by the holy founder (En-no gyōja, a yogi or Tantrist) and became his acolytes or servants. They are then put in opposition as a male (holding an ax = war) and a female (holding a vase = wealth), mouth open (A) and closed (Hūṃ), red eye and yellow mouth. In China, the two warriors took on the modern popular form of Heng (< Hūṃ) and Ha (< A) explained as the exhalation ("blower") and inhalation ("sniffer") of breath. The meaning varies depending on the doctrine. The formal features serve mainly to underscore the bipartition or polarity (opposition and complementarity). With the doubling of Vajrapāṇi, we return to the procession of couples we have seen marching past.

We have reached the end of a long voyage through time and space, from India to Japan and from Hinduism to Buddhism, in the context of a particularly significant group that is easy to discover. We venture to summarize what we can learn from this play of the imagination as it proceeds through constant transformations.

First there is the known history, the written documents and conscious interventions, dated and localized, of priests who were simultaneously traditionalist and innovative. Judging by the few available documents, the known prescriptions of the learned priests have been followed only partially or temporarily.

The Indian model indicated by Yizing (seventh century), Mahākāla (pillar, black) and Hārītī (kitchens, storehouses, entrance gates), is unknown in Tibet (Vajrapāṇi and Ucchuṣma), and partially followed in Nepal (Mahākāla and Gaṇeśa). By contrast, it used to be well known in China and Japan but has not been retained in those countries. In China neither the god nor the goddess played any role, even separately; in Japan, Mahākāla alone became important. First selected by a priest to be a protector of the temples of Tantrism (but not to stand at the gate nor in the kitchen), and then forming a triad with Vaiśravaṇa and Sarasvatī in the same setting, he finally became a popular god of the kitchen even outside Buddhism. The second Indian model known to the Chinese and Japanese through written documents (Piṇḍola and Mañjuśrī in refectories) was imposed in China by an imperial decree in 769, but did not last beyond the ninth or tenth century, whereas the cult of Piṇḍola in the refectory was already common in the fifth century. These two saints were replaced by Weituo (< Skanda) and Miluo (or variants), despite another written source (ca. A.D. 1000), which was read everywhere, that said monasteries should have three chapels, one each for Hārītī, Saṃgharama, and Piṇḍola (thus reverting back to the goddess hinted at in the seventh century, but replacing Mahākāla with Piṇḍola). Here again, only Piṇḍola was retained in Japan (but he was placed outside the preaching room), while in China it was Saṃgharama, god of the soil, who survived. Conversely, Vajrapāṇi—clearly attested in Indian Buddhism as the personal guardian of the Buddha—was doubled in China into Lishi (athlete) and Jingang (Vajra), starting in the sixth century (he appears in a festival of the end of the year), and was maintained in China and in Japan in this form or in its variants of Two Kings or of Heng and Ha at the entrance gate to temples. The Indian model only called for two *yakṣas* at this place, but Vajrapāṇi was known to have been at first a *yakṣa*.

None of the known models called for the couple of guardians at the gate that was conceived only in China (Weituo/Miluo, the chaste young warrior and the fat and smiling saint). This innovation corresponds to the Hindu couple Skanda/Gaṇeśa not only in its form, but also in its content (purity/gluttony; abstinence/abundance, and so forth) and in its function (guarding the gate or the secret). Various Buddhist characters (Pañcika, Kuvēra, Vaiśravaṇa, Hārītī, and so forth) had the same forms and functions, but not always the same content and certainly not at the same time. The most recent and the most remote innovation seems to be explained only through a kind of return to the prototype that is least consciously acknowledged. Not only is this prototype Indian, which is quite normal; it is Hindu rather than Buddhist.

Is the reference to Hindu representations justified? Chinese, Indian, and Tibetan Buddhists may well have known them. Aside from oral transmission (possible but not provable) by Indian travelers and residents in China and Tibet, and vice versa, learned priests knew a good many Hindu traditions through Buddhist works that mentioned them critically. They sometimes adopted them and gave them a Buddhist form. They could also see images. Working in China between 693 and ca. 706, an Indian monk, the translator of a Buddhist ritual, founded a Hindu temple in his host country. Between 1200 and 1400, the Indian community of Zhenjiang (Zayton) left behind Śaiva and Vaiṣṇava sculptures.

The function of guardian of the gate is all the more readily granted to a couple in that the very character of a gate implies a leaning toward bipartition (by the symmetry of right and left). This couple may be obtained either by doubling a single character (with opposite and symmetrical features) such as the warrior (*yakṣa*, Vajrapāṇi), or by the association of two characters of opposite features (thin and fat, man and woman). But the fundamental idea of a door is not in and of itself the only condition necessary for doubling. This process also applies to seemingly isolated individuals who have other functions (Gaṇeśa, Vaiśravaṇa). Their bipartition is both formal and functional. Each of them is simultaneously a god of war and a god of wealth, thin and fat.

Instead of being distinct as they are in Dumézil's Indo-European schema of the three functions, these functions are interchangeable and simultaneous. The third function, the priesthood, appears to be absent. It may have been transformed into the function of the secret (revealed and to be guarded), of inspiration, and of intellectual keenness.

Bipartition sometimes gives way to a tripartition obtained through the figure of a woman. Her status is ambiguous. By associating now with one and now with the other of two opposite and complementary characters, she may serve to bring about a new transformation and a return to bipartition, to a sexual couple.

R.A.S./g.h.

NOTES

1. As has been said, in Tibet there is a particular form of Mahākāla, called Brother-Sister (lČam-dral, lČam-sriṅ), who is a single warrior god. However, in the school of Sa-skya-pa, this single god became a goddess named dKar-mo ñi-zla, White Sun-Moon (necklace of a thousand suns and moons; diadem of skulls, surmounted by sun and moon).

2. It will be recalled that the protector of the north is either Vaiśravaṇa, of whom the type is the same as that of Skanda, or Kubera, who is pot-bellied like Gaṇeśa. Curiously, a Tamil legend (twelfth century) makes Skanda a kind of violent rogue who turns the universe upside down with his tricks and usurps the throne of the Supreme Deity. In Buddhism, Vaiśravaṇa had a son, Nuocha (Naṭa), who became the same type of turbulent god in popular Chinese legends. As for the pot-bellied type, it should be noted that Maitreya, the Buddha placed in the north, became in China the smiling Miluo with the big belly.

3. We are dealing here with an innovation, apparently arbitrary, which emphasizes the historic intervention of an individual at a definite date. But this unique and contingent event has only unleashed a process of transformation that is inherent in the system. It was in 769, at the request of the great translator and propagator of Tantrism in China, the Indian Amoghavajra, that the emperor gave the order to worship Mañjuśsrī as a divinity of refectories and to place him above Piṇḍola. The author of the request based it on an Indian model and on classic texts in which the great Bodhisattvas are seen at the side of the Buddha, feather-duster in hand, while the saints of the Hīnayāna stand behind him, broom in hand. The goal was clearly political. According to another seventh-century monk, in India Mañjuśrī was placed in the refectories of Mahāyāna monasteries, and Piṇḍola in those of Hīnayāna (no examples of this are known). This seems primarily to mean that Amoghavajra affirmed the superiority of the Mahāyāna. The plan failed. In China, the cult of Piṇḍola dates from the fourth century, and his presence in the refectory is attested at the latest in the seventh century. It is maintained there until the tenth, while that of Mañjuśrī seems not to go beyond the ninth century.

4. In other cases, Prajñā is also the consort of Mañjuśrī.

5. In a fourteenth-century temple (at Hebei) devoted to Guanyin with Eleven Heads, this individual (who is not specified as male or female) is flanked by sixteen *arhats;* there are more than two guardian warriors (Vajrapāṇi) at the temple door.

6. The tale alludes, in the form of a joke, to doctrinal controversies on the nature of the saint (in the Mahāyāna and Tantrism): the necessity of asceticism opposed to the total freedom of the one who has realized the Absolute. A famous tale in the Mahāyāna depicts one monk who strictly observes the vows (repression of desires) and another (named "Sense of Pleasure," Hi-ken) who acts spontaneously and freely without rejecting the world (freedom to act even in the passions). The first falls into hell, the second becomes a Buddha in a paradise. In Hinduism, the same opposition is inherent in the ambiguous nature of the yogi Śiva: sexual power and asceticism. An Indonesian tale illustrates this opposition by representing the traits of a pair of brothers. One of these brothers is named Glutton, is the type of yogi free to do anything, lives in the east, and attains the supreme heaven of Śiva. The other is named Withered Trunk, is of the ascetic type (lean, emaciated), lives in the west, and receives only a small part of the celestial joys (Bosch).

7. In an isolated ritual, translated into Chinese in the eighth century, the Buddha Śākyamuni is flanked by Mañjuśrī, seated and offering him a bowl with both hands (to the left), and by the terrible Vajrapāṇi, standing, twirling his *vajra* (to the right).

8. The conscious explanation bespeaks rather another function of this elephant-god: to dispel the obstacle-demons (*vighnas*) who might disturb the rite. But there are forms of this god in which he is alone (trampling on Gaṇeśa; this is Vighnāntaka). The choice of the form of the sexual couple seems to imply the motif of marital intimacies. Elsewhere, in Hinduism, Nandikeśvara is the name of one of Śiva's guardians, Nandin, the bull. It will be seen that Nandin is associated with Gaṇeśa.

9. This popular interpretation, which inverts the negative sign of sexuality (chastity) into a positive one, though it initially appears incorrect or distorting, is not isolated or contingent. The other type of pure young man (*kumāra*), Mañjuśrī, has also taken an aspect of this genre. A red Mañjuśrī of Indo-Tibetan Tantrism is a doublet of the Indian god of love, Kāma (he has his bow and arrows). Another form of Mañjuśrī (as Vajrasattva) alone (*ekavīra*) is characterized by his erect, but concealed, penis. Despite the sublime status of Prajñā or Prajñāpāramitā, to whom Mañjuśrī is doubly connected (at once mother and wife), this goddess also receives in late Indo-Tibetan Tantrism (twelfth century?) a sexual coloration: a beautiful young maid of sixteen years, she holds with both hands a lotus on which the manual of eroticism, the *Kāmaśāstra,* reposes. Similarly, in the popular culture of "modern" China and Japan (i.e., for many centuries), Guanyin (Kan-non), a goddess, has had expressly sexual traits and functions. Two other forms of Mañjuśrī, proper to Indo-Tibetan Tantrism, have a marked sexual character. These are Dharmadhātu Vāgīśvara (Master of Speech) and Mahārāga or Vajrarāga Mañjuśrī (Great Passion). Each has his female consort on his left knee. Their principal hands hold the sword of wisdom and the book *Prajñāpāramitā*. The other hands hold a bow and arrows (symbolic of the god of love, Kāma, Rāga), a *vajra,* and a bell (sexual symbolism).

10. In Tantrism, the five *amṛtas* are excrement, urine, sperm, blood (especially menstrual), and human flesh.

11. The Chinese translation of his name, "Immobile" (*acala*), remains unexplained. This epithet is normally the name of a warrior god, Acala (Japanese Fudō), who destroys impurities with fire (like Ucchuṣma) and eats food leftovers. He is sometimes a form of Vajrapāṇi (Tibet, Japan). Wild in appearance, he is depicted as a young man, fat and stocky. The same form (as fierce as fire, pot-bellied youth, red) characterizes Mahākāla in Hindu Tantra.

12. In this group, the most pertinent triad had been created previously by the priests of Japanese Tantrism in the form of a Daikoku with three faces, representing Daikoku in the center, Benzaiten to the left, and Bishamon to the right. This triad recalls the opposition of the young warrior—doubled by his wife--and the fat man (see above).

13. The persons in question here are represented in high relief on two great stupas at Zhenjiang (the Zayton of European travelers) reconstructed in 1228–38, but constructed previously in 1145, according to a preserved inscription, and taking as its model the bronze stupas of the tenth century. Depicted there are the two Vajras, guardians of the gate, Weituo, Piṇḍola, Gavaṃpati, Budai hezhang, Hanzhan, and Che-tö. But other individuals may have been added during restoration (sixteenth century) so that no certain date may be assigned to a particular representation.

14. Another case of replacement by a purely Chinese god is Guandi (face to the south), back to back with Weituo. Guandi is a warrior like Weituo. He is at the same time the god of war and god of wealth, like Vaiśravaṇa (back to back), and this from two points of view: formal and functional. Guandi, for his part, often forms a couple with the goddess Guanyin.

BIBLIOGRAPHY

H. DORÉ, *Recherches sur les superstitions en Chine* (Shanghai 1929). A. FOUCHER, *L'art gréco-bouddhique du Gandhāra,* École française d'Extrême-Orient, vol. 5 (Paris 1905). A. GETTY, *Gaṇeśa* (Oxford 1936). W. A. GROOTAERS, "Temples and History of Wanchuan," *Monuments serica* 13 (1948); "Rural Temples around Hsuan-hua (South Chahar)," *Folklore Studies* 10, 1 (1951). J. HACKIN, *Mythologie asiatique illustrée* (Paris 1928). W. KIRFEL, "Der Mythus von der Tārā und der Geburt des Buddha," *Zeitschrift der Morgenländischen Gesellschaft* 102, 1 (1952): 46–50. M. LALOU, "Mythologie indienne et peintures de Haute-Asie," 1: "Le Dieu bouddhique de la fortune," *Artibus Asiae* 9 (1946). E. LAMOTTE, "Mañjuśrī," *Toung Pao* 48, 1–3 (1961); "Vajrapāṇi en Inde," in *Mélanges de sinologie offerts à Monsieur Paul Demiéville,* vol. 1 (Paris 1966). L. DE LA VALLÉE POUSSIN, "Avalokiteśvara," in Hastings, *Encyclopedia of Religion and Ethics,* vol. 2 (1909). S. LÉVI and E. CHAVANNES, "Les 16 arhat protecteurs de la loi," *Journal asiatique,* 2d series, 8 (1916). H. MASPERO, "Mythologie de la Chine moderne," in Hackin, ed., *Mythologie asiatique illustrée.* WENDY DONIGER O'FLAHERTY, *Asceticism and Eroticism in the Mythology of Śiva* (New York 1973). N. PÉRI, "Le Dieu Wei-t'o," *Bulletin de l'École française d'Extrême-Orient* 16, 3 (1916). J. PRIP-MOLLER, *Chinese Buddhist Monasteries* (2d ed., Hong Kong 1967). G. T. A. RAO, *Elements of Hindu Iconography* (New York 1968). E. ROUSSELLE, "Die typischen Bildwerke des buddhistischen Tempels in China," *Sinica* 8, 2 (1933). L. SCHERMAN, "Die beiden Dvārapāla Figuren im Museum Rietberg," *Artibus Asia* 25, 1 (1962).

PART 3

Southeast Asia

Austroasiatic, Vedic, and Brahmanic Myths of Southeast Asia

The definition of the mythologies of Southeast Asia presupposes an investigation of great complexity. Such an inquiry is dependent on a socioreligious context that, from Burma to Vietnam, presents elements that are specific from the point of view not only of their geographic and ethnic localization but also of their historical development.

It is known, in a general way, that the countries of southern Asia between India and China are set in the framework of a cultural substratum which has been given the names Austroasiatic, Austric, or Austronesian, and that the features of this basic civilization, which existed before the historical contributions of India and China, have been brought to light by the joint researches of specialists in human geography, paleontology, prehistoric archaeology, linguistics, and ethnology.

Dazzled at first by the richness of the documents from India, by the architectural beauty of the temples, by the sculpture, and to a lesser extent by the graphic art of Brahmanic and Buddhist inspiration, European Orientalists of the end of the nineteenth and beginning of the twentieth century applied themselves essentially to the study of philosophico-religious thought, to the study of artistic forms that resulted from that vision of the world and of the texts that expounded it.

Thus oriented toward India, researchers saw the mythology as overlaying and bringing together every problem posed to man: the explanation of the world, the definition of cosmic and ritual order, the birth of the gods, the themes of their abundant iconography, the exploits of each god, and the profound meaning of the sacrifice that binds the gods to human society. All was mythology in that sum of knowledge that India conceived as revealed truths, "seen" by the *ṛṣis,* the great sages of Vedic tradition.

But Southeast Asia did not remain on the outside of this long and complex tradition. She integrated it partially, made selections and transpositions, here and there culled scraps of the mythological thought, adapted divine or epic characters to the point of rendering them indigenous, or was content to use Brahmanic names for local spirits.

There is no question here of analyzing what the peoples to the east of India were able to receive and recreate, from the time when Indian civilization began to be propagated and implanted abroad, according to the diverse modalities of Indianization.

Around the beginning of the Christian era, contacts by maritime and land routes between the peoples of the Indian subcontinent and those of Southeast Asia had brought about a confrontation of two great orders of civilizations: on the one hand, an "Indianness" entering into history, attested by writing and art; and on the other hand, a civilization "of the South Seas" or of the monsoons, a veritable mosaic of peoples without writing, peoples of the plains and deltas, peoples of the forests and mountains, who all, in their way, had to different degrees acquired the mastery, or more exactly the technology, of harmony with the natural environment. Rice growers with dry, flooded, or irrigated rice fields, seafarers, gatherers, peddlers, makers of implements of stone, metal, and wood, potters, weavers, people who originally gathered and burned weeds, seminomads who gradually settled in densely or sparsely populated habitats, closed in on themselves or, on the contrary, open to the outside—these people were, from the first centuries A.D., at a period roughly corresponding to the Kushana and then to the Gupta dynasty in India, and to the Han dynasty in China, engaged in a process of development at once technological, political, economic, and religious, that is, cultural in the largest sense.

It is known that China made its mark mainly in the north of the Indo-Chinese peninsula, in particular on the civilization of the Dai-Viet in the delta of the Red River. It was obviously at the height of Hue that China directly confronted the civilization called Indianized, at a time when the Chinese command of Je-nan, recovering the lands of the Viet, had an uncertain frontier, continually challenged by Lin-yi, the country of the Cham, an Austronesian people from the coast of Annam. Until the end of the fifteenth century, the kingdom of Champa, the builder of the temples of My-Son, represented the outpost of Indianized Southeast Asia, facing a Sinicized Indochina.

If we begin with a schema a little too rigid to correspond to reality, it is to the period from the first to the thirteenth through fifteenth centuries that the first great phase should be assigned, the phase of the formation of the ancient

The goddess Umā Bhagavati in the ruins at Angkor. Photo Leclère.

The *Phnom* of Phnom Penh (mountain shrine). Includes a Buddhist pagoda as well as figures from Brahmanic mythology and earth spirits.

Head of a dragon-naga with crested head and wings at the base of its neck, mounted on the head of a crocodile. Wood, painted red and green. Laos, Sithadone province, Khong region.

kingdoms and of their evolution in the framework of institutions marked by India: the Mon kingdoms of Burma, of the north of the Malay peninsula, and of Dvāravati and Haripuñjaya in Thailand; the kingdom of Funan, so named by Chinese travelers as early as the second century, in the delta of the Mekong, along the length of the Gulf of Thailand, and in the territory of present-day Cambodia; the Cham kingdom of Champa, from the north of Hue as far as the present area of Phan-Rang and Phan-Thiet. Then the Pyu kingdom of Burma, or Srikshetra; the Khmer kingdom of the Kambujas, called Chen-La by the Chinese, the Angkorian kingdom from the ninth century; the great kingdom of Srivijaya in Indonesia and in the south of the Malay peninsula.

What had taken place, from the point of view that concerns us here? Each of the peoples settled in the area of Southeast Asia at that time had its own socioreligious structures. Each belonged to one of the linguistic families called Mon-Khmer, Tibeto-Burman, Tai-Kadai, Miao-Yao, or Austronesian. Each transmitted orally its myths, its accounts of the beginnings, the names of its tutelary powers, and its own system of the invisible. But the constitution of kingdoms and principalities, the appearance of certain forms of urbanization, the adoption of writing, the establishment of dynastic rituals where various types of chiefdoms or clan societies existed, that is, the entry of these societies into a new framework, half-imposed, half-developed in a long symbiosis, modified the style of these peoples very profoundly. There was then what might be called a "borrowed culture": the theocratic monarchies came from India, the Brahmanic gods in whom the kings of Angkor and Champa placed their trust came from India, iconographic models came from India, the Sanskrit of epigraphical texts came from India, and the alphabet, from various writing systems and multiple relays, came from India.

Nevertheless, each new kingdom was composed of ethnic groups that did not abandon their local organization and their fundamental beliefs. And there was the beginning of a profound brew, with innumerable motifs, where the indigenous and the foreign intermingled and fertilized one another.

From the twelfth to thirteenth centuries, the Tai peoples reestablished in Southeast Asia the Khmer grandeur of Angkor. The Tai kingdom of Sukhothai, then the kingdom of Ayutthaya, and the Lao kingdoms of Luang Prabang and Vientiane entered the cultural scene in turn. Buddhists from south China, the Tai assimilated the contributions of the Mon and the Khmer. In Burma, Burman unity took on a bloody character as the Mon and Shan played their own game, but Burman culture was finally elaborated; Burman culture was also Indianized by means of a Buddhism accepting of the *nats*, the local spirits.

When the West intervened in the destiny of Southeast Asia, first in the sixteenth century through Portuguese and Spanish activities, it did not understand the great cultures there: India, China, Khmer, Mon, Tai, Brahmanism, Buddhism—and such Buddhism—spirits of the earth, ogres, demons, ghosts, oral myths, written myths, local legends, legends from the great Sanskrit epics, etc. How can one find one's bearings, and above all how can one distinguish what comes from the Vedism of archaic Aryan India, from the Brahmanism of preclassical and classical India, from Mahāyāna Buddhism, and from Hīnayāna or Theravāda Buddhism, and how can one separate this from what constitutes the native ground, that is, the complex of particular forms of animism emerging from the "culture of vegetation" to which south Asia bears witness?

Thus, in approaching the mythology of this part of the world, the principal insight is that it is not a question of creating an arbitrary, arid, and lifeless division between the contribution of the religions of India and the local supernaturalism, but of perceiving the whole, deeply implicated in collective representations.

In the course of centuries, beginning with the Austroasiatic substratum, a system of relationships between man and the invisible was formed that integrated Buddhism but was not dependent on it alone. The old Mon, Khmer, and Cham peoples, and then the Burmans, Tai, Lao, were as if inseminated by the enormous germination of myths and epics from India. They acquired its gods and chose among them. They followed the teaching of the Buddha, adapting it to their own inclinations: accumulated merit leads to a happy rebirth rather than to extinction; the Buddha fulfills our desires by accepting our offerings rather than teaching us to desire nothing! His footprints are stamped here and there in the ground, in Burma and in Thailand. His statues emit light, leave their places, and perform miracles. The mythology of Buddhism, whether Mahāyāna or Theravāda, was born, paradoxically, not from speculation but from collective practice at the level of the village community.

Altar decorated with bamboo poles, erected in the fields at the time of the feast of the spirits who protect the paddy. Paris, Musée de l'Homme collection. Photo Matras.

And it is also in the village community that syncretism takes place and is lived. It is there that the god Indra intervenes at the time of ordination of a monk, and that a spirit of the earth must be propitiated in the precincts of a monastery. It is there that the acquired patrimony dissolves into an amalgam in which nothing is felt to be contradictory or incompatible. Certainly a few kings of Siam and Laos have thought it expedient, in order to preserve Buddhist orthodoxy, to promulgate edicts against the *phi*, genie or spirits in the Tai domain, particularly King Pothisarath in 1527. This was an admission of the intensity of their active presence at the heart of the official religion.

In order to introduce a little order and clarity into an account devoted to the mythology of Indianized Southeast Asia, we will single out a few striking themes, significant on some level, without isolating them from their context. It is within this perspective that we will first consider some myths of nature and of the gods. A second development gives us access to the domain of earth spirits, the *neak-tā* of Cambodia, the *nats* of Burma, and the *phi* of Laos and Thailand. Finally, a third panel of the triptych evokes the image of a Buddhism in which myth flourishes even today, of heroes, saints, living persons with supernatural powers whose legends and cult continue after their death and who are in the process of forming a kind of new Buddhist pantheon, the *luang pho* of Thailand.

The mythological material of Southeast Asia will not be exhausted, and the three groups of accounts and facts that are considered here serve only to highlight the three orders that go beyond them: the myths of Vedism and Brahmanism, the Austroasiatic myths, and the Buddhism of the Great and of the Little Vehicle. It is the selection, the integration, and the interpretation that Southeast Asia has given to these that comprise its originality in this domain and its special contribution to the religious vision of the world.

S.T./b.f.

BIBLIOGRAPHY

C. ARCHAIMBAULT, "Une cérémonie en l'honneur des génies de la mine de sel de Ban Bo (Moyen Laos): Contribution à l'étude du jeu de Ti-K'i," *BEFEO* 48, no. 1 (1956); *Structures religieuses lao: Rites et mythes* (Vientiane 1973). D. BERNOT, "Les Nats de Birmanie," in *Génies, anges et démons* (Paris 1971), 297–341. J. BOISSELIER, *Le Cambodge: Asie du Sud-Est* (Paris 1966). *Cérémonies des douze mois: Fêtes annuelles cambodgiennes* (Phnom Penh). G. COEDÈS, "La légende de la Nāgī: Études cambodgiennes," 1, *BEFEO* 11, nos. 3–4. G. COEDÈS and C. ARCHAIMBAULT, *Les trois mondes: Traibhūmi Braḥ Rvaṅ* (Paris 1973). G. CONDOMINAS, "Notes sur le bouddhisme populaire en milieu rural lao," *Archives de sociologie des religions* 25–26 (1968): 81–150. J. DE FELS,

Somdet Phra Chao Tak Sin Maharat, le roi de Thonburi, 2 vols. (diss., Paris 1976). M. Giteau, "Le Barattage de l'océan au Cambodge," *Bull. de la Société des Études indochinoises,* n.s., 26. P. Lévy, "Ti-Khi: Un jeu de mail rituel au Laos," *Annuaire de l'EPHE, Sciences religieuses,* 1952–53, 3–15. P. Mus, "Barabudur: Les origines du stūpa et la transmigration," *BEFEO* (1932–34; reprinted New York 1978). A. R. Peltier, *Introduction à la connaissance des hlvṅ ba de Thaïlande* (diss., Paris 1976). Phouvong Phimmasone, "Cours de littérature lao," *Bull. des Amis du royaume lao,* nos. 4–5 (1971), 5–70. E. Porée-Maspero, "Kroṅ Pali et rites de la maison," *Anthropos* 56 (1961): 179–929; *Étude sur les rites agraires des Cambodgiens,* 3 vols. (Paris 1962–69). E. Porée-Maspero and S. Bernard-Thierry, *La lune: Croyance et rites du Cambodge,* 264–65; *La lune: Mythes et rites* (Paris 1962), 263–87. P. A. Rajadhon, "The Phi," *Journal of the Siam Society* 61, no. 2: 153–78; "The Kwan and Its Ceremonies," ibid. 50, no. 2. A. Souyris-Rolland, "Contribution à l'étude du culte des Génies tutélaires ou 'Neak-Ta' chez les Cambodgiens du Sud," *Bull. de la Société des Études indochinoises,* n.s., 26, no. 2 (1951): 160–73. J. S. Tambiah, *Buddhism and the Spirit Cults in North-East Thailand* (Cambridge 1970). R. C. Temple, *The Thirty Seven Nats: A Phase of Spirit-Worship Prevailing in Burma* (London 1906). M. Zago, *Rites et cérémonies en milieu bouddhiste lao* (Rome 1972).

Southeast Asian Origin Myths and Founding Myths

The origin myths among the majority groups of Southeast Asia are no longer "pure" in the ethnologists' sense of the term. Only the minorities have preserved intact (as far as we can tell) oral narratives of their birth and settlement, which are inextricably connected with the birth of mankind and the organization of society, and these myths have been preserved only to the extent that they succeed in transmitting fully their explanation of the world.

I. The Flood

An echo of the flood type of Genesis can be heard in the *Nithan Khun Borom* (or the *Nidāna Khun Parama,* according to the transliteration from the Pali), a great text that is simultaneously mythical, cosmogonic, historical, and gnomic; it tells of the origins of the Lao.

This long narrative includes the story of the flood, which was caused by an argument among the gods that put an end to an early phase of humanity. Following this cataclysm, three giant gourds (only two according to some versions) started growing to enormous size from a creeper growing out of the nostrils of a buffalo. The noise heard coming from inside was so great that the gods, the *khun* "lords of heaven," opened them up: one of the *khun* stabbed the gourds with a chisel and a branding iron. A multitude of men sprang out of the gourds: those who came out through the cuts made by the branding iron were black and wore their hair tied up: they were the Kha; those who came out through the cuts made by the chisel were fair-skinned and wore their hair short: they were the Tai Lao. Animals also jumped out of the gourds, and the whole crowd spread and soon multiplied and proliferated.

The *khun* taught the Sons of the Gourd how to till the land and build houses. They taught them the marriage and funeral rituals and the duties of respect for parents and ancestors. But soon men became ungovernable, and the *khun* could not manage them. They complained to the Phaya Then, Indra, the king of the heavenly realm, who sent them reinforcements in the persons of two other *khun.* But these *khun* turned out to be unable to handle men, and the god recalled them to heaven.

Then a new phase of this extraordinary story began: the god of heaven sent men his own son, Khun Borom, or Parāma, the "supreme lord." Khun Borom's descent to earth, in which he landed on a "small, flat paddy field," is undoubtedly one of the most striking mythological texts of Southeast Asia. Heaven and earth were able to communicate without difficulty at that time: some versions state that the two realms were contiguous, and others claim that they were tied together by rattan cords. Later, Indra had the rattan bridge that joined the two realms cut, "and since then, gods and men no longer communicate with one another."[1]

A gigantic creeper started growing as Khun Borom was organizing the earth. It obscured the sky and cold settled in. An elderly couple who had descended with the demiurge hero whom Laotians call the Pu Yoe Ya Yoe (also known as Pu Thao Yoe and Mē Ya Ngam) came forward spontaneously and offered to cut down the enormous creeper, which crushed them as it fell. The sun began to shine upon the world again. The two ancestors, benefactors of creation, became objects of a cult: in the festivals and processions that mark the new year in Laos, they appear in the form of monstrous masks with enormous jaws and bulging eyes. The dance of the old man and the old woman kneaded the earth and renewed the original cultivation. What we loosely call land management, or, better, the organization of space, is on the mythical level the separation of heaven and earth and the progressive creation of the earth to meet the needs of mankind.

The myth does not stop there but continues with the description of the partitioning of the new territory among the seven sons of Khun Borom. Here we enter into a very particular category of texts, characteristic of the countries in question, in which historical data are quite naturally connected with legendary origins.

In fact, the designations of the seven provinces each granted to one of the princes are geographically very precise and by and large correspond to later Laotian principalities, at least in part. For the carving out of *Nithan* out of frontier history goes beyond the historical boundaries of the country of Lan Xang (Laos) and encompasses the neighboring lands of southern China, Vietnam, Thailand, and lower Burma, as though the natural extension of the great story of the origins, conceived as the origin of men on earth, inevitably resulted in the hegemony of the Tai groups on the Indo-Chinese peninsula, uniting all the sons of the mother-gourd under the same essentially divine power.

II. Accounts of the Founding of Angkor

Many other examples of this genre of text can be found in the Annals, dealing with the founding of kingdoms and cities, whether in Khmer, Tai, or Burman territory. The numerous toponymic legends sometimes have mythological overtones. This is notably the case with the accounts of the founding of Angkor, which began with the evocation of five *devis,* or goddesses that live in Indra's paradise. They took

One of the ancestors' masks, here representing the Pu Ngoe Nga Ngoe of Laos, mythic first couple. Laos, Luang Prabang. Paris, Musée de l'Homme collection.

flight and came down to frolic on earth. One of them stole a flower and was sentenced by Indra to live a human life for six years and became the wife of a poor gardener. A remarkably talented weaver, she made marvelous silk fabrics and thus made her husband rich. Soon they had a son, who also had exceptional talents: he could dig, build, and draw all sorts of pictures on the ground. When the six years were up, his mother ascended to Indra's heaven again as the god had prescribed.

The son, however, came to be known as a semidivine person, the heavenly architect. His name in Sanskrit was Viśvakarman, "the one who makes everything, who creates everything." But in Southeast Asia, this name underwent a number of transformations and was apparently assimilated to the name of the god Viṣṇu, since in Cambodia he became Braḥ Bisnukar, which is transcribed Viṣṇukarman.

The story of the founding of Angkor tells that the son of the *devi* sets out to seek his mother. He finds her, is carried away by her into heaven, and is introduced to the god Indra. "My son," says the goddess, "is particularly ingenious at tracing figures, at sculpting, and at building temples or fortresses that are the envy of men."[2] Indra then orders the boy to join the *devaputras,* or sons of god, in his heavenly workshops. "He learned to draw, to sculpt, to make music; he learned to build ships that sail on the solid earth. He engraved gold and silver, and he learned the blacksmith's trade; he discovered the solutions to pour on clay to turn it into stone."

Satisfied with this knowledge, Indra decided that from then on Viśvakarman or Bisnukar would be the master of artisans, artists, and master craftsmen. "Every human builder will be expected to make an offering to Popusnokar. . . . If a man undertakes a work of some importance and does not make the offering to Popusnokar, may his eyes close to the light of day."[3]

A second development of the story involves Indra's own son, Braḥ Khet Mālā, whom he makes invulnerable and endows with long life by immersing him in a pool seven times a day for a week, while Brahma recites incantations over the prince and sprinkles him "to give him a life of four hundred years."

This prince inherits the kingdom of Cambodia. Indra gives it to him and suggests that he have a monument built to his liking that will remind him of the celestial palaces of his father. The prince replies that he could do nothing in his new kingdom that could equal in beauty the dwelling place of Indra, and that he would be content with an edifice as splendid as his cattleshed.

Viśvakarman is then dispatched to earth in a chariot to build the monument of the son of Indra in the kingdom of Cambodia. The legend describes him at work, embarking on a junk to search for shells with which to make lime to coat the stones; this episode is the occasion for a mythical explanation for the existence of the piles of shells found on the site of Samong Sen.

He then goes to find sesame seeds and makes from them a magical preparation to cover the earthen model that he has built. The monument turns to stone, "without beams or rafters," without joints, and finally he decorates it with marvelous sculptures.

The end of the story shows the heavenly architect still smelting iron and forging a sword with a blade as thin as a rice leaf. Until quite recently, no blacksmith in Cambodia—least of all the Kuy of the Phnom Dek region—would begin his work without first paying homage to Braḥ Bisnukar and making offerings to him.

Thus the gods and demigods, or the sons of the gods, play a part in the daily life of the people of Southeast Asia, even though they are Buddhists and even though the monastery coordinates religious activities in each village. The myths, even when they are incomplete or forgotten, prolong their existence through precise rituals or diffuse beliefs. Some now have the flavor of tales, the tales of "whys and wherefores," in which explanations are given of the origins of animals, plants, and natural phenomena.

The corpus of myths about the birth of the serpents, for instance, has never been explored; nor has the entire corpus of legends about rice and betel. The origins of tigers, cats, and mosquitoes, which are narrated in the light of popular tales designed more to entertain than to teach, are nonetheless based on a mythology of nature and the gods. We shall see that some of these gods of Brahmanism, such as Gaṇeśa with his elephant head, have become "earth spirits."[4]

This initial overview of the myths of nature and the gods may give an idea of the richness of such a long tradition. The boundaries between what came from India and "what came from the ancestors" are nonexistent in the view of the villagers. Even those who are literate, although they know that an ancient culture came to them through Sanskrit and Pali texts, tend to integrate, assimilate, and supply local exegeses. And it is evident that the moon and the sun, the *devatās* of the sky and the sea, the animals and plants, the "lords" Śiva, Viṣṇu, Brahmā, and Indra, and many others are here the deities of the Khmer, Burmans, and Tai. Demiurges like Khun Borom and divine builders like Viṣṇukarman belong to the country where they have worked.

But even more native to the locality and children of the country are the earth spirits, the *nats* of Burma, the *phi* of the Tai, and the *neak-tā* of Cambodia.

S.T./g.h.

BIBLIOGRAPHY AND NOTES

1. PHOUVONG PHIMMASONE, "Cours de littérature lao," *Bulletin des Amis du royaume lao*, nos. 4 and 5 (1971), 49.

2. G. H. MONOD, *Légendes cambodgiennes que m'a contées le Gouverneur Khieu* (Paris 1922), 140–41.

3. Ibid., 141.

4. For origin legends, see the *Recueil d'histoires khmères anciennes, Prajum ryoen bren khmêr* (Phnom Penh 1967–72). In particular, see vols. 7 and 8.

Earth Spirits in Southeast Asia

1. The *Nats* of Burma

"The mountain, by definition, is a place that the *nats* enjoy."[1] This idea of the favorite dwelling place of the local spirits is consistent with one of the defining characteristics of Austroasiatic culture: everywhere the mountain is considered a sacred place. The mountain is inhabited by invisible beings. In Burma, the famous Mount Poppa is peopled by *nats*. But spirits also abound in the forest, the world of wonders.

If we try to classify the earth spirits of Burma, or *nats*, according to their habitat, we find that our classification corresponds both to the elements of nature—the aquatic, terrestrial, and heavenly worlds—and to the parts of the house. In other words, although the *nats* appear to be first the primal inhabitants of the land, they are also inside dwellings built by men. They are, moreover, sometimes inside the bodies of men.

The legal oath[2] enumerates all the possible habitats of *nats*: "rivers, streams, and brooks, lakes and torrents, waterfalls and whirlpools, forests and trees; the sun and the moon, stars and meteors, clouds, wind, fog, and mist." There seems to be a difference between the idea of the spirits of distant and imaginary heavenly worlds or the guardians of the cardinal points, and the very vital notion of the spirits of rivers and trees frequented by men, which are experienced as a living presence. Thus, the Burmans distinguish the "lords of the river," *khyong shang*, from the "lords of the mountain," *tong shang*.[3] Yet despite this distinction, it is maintained that some *nats* have multiple habitats. A *nat* may, for example, have its seat on a mountain, like Lady Min Mahagiri, and also be found in a house, hidden high on an interior post, with its name changed. Denise Bernot, citing U Hting Aung, offers historical reasons for the double habitat. "The ritual in the home has evolved as a successor to the ritual to the *nat* on the mountain (Min Mahagiri); on the mountain, it was the object of a popular cult from before the time of Anorahta (Aniruddha); under Kyanzittha (Cançitça), 1084–1112, the cult took on an official character and continued to flourish for five centuries. In our day, the Lord of the Great Mountain has become the Lord of the Great Mountain within the Home: *eindwing min Mahagiri*."[4]

This fact certainly reinforces the impression of the omnipresence of *nats* among men. The earth spirits are essentially guardians of a god, and they appear as simultaneously good and evil, depending on the way in which they are—or are not—worshiped. However, some *nats* seem to be rather bad and dreadful, inclined to play tricks, and others are naturally good and "respectful of the law."

One belief, which seems to belong to another order and to evoke evil spirits rather than earth spirits, concerns the "sixty-six classes of *song*." The *song* are invisible beings, sometimes taking human form or revealing themselves in a gust of wind, who are by nature dangerous, capable of tormenting, devouring, and causing sickness and death.

Nats are protectors of the village, field, and home; they are "guardians of the sea," "guardians of the forest," and "guardians of the mountain." They also exercise their protective role over ancient temples and present-day monasteries.

It is when one learns about the "history" of each *nat* that their composite origin is seen. Indeed, some are men and women who lived in the past and died a violent death at the king's command. We know, for example, that king Kyanzittha had the architect of Pagan's Ananda Temple buried alive. He then became the *nat* guardian of the monument, "and this took place as late as the middle of the nineteenth century, during the construction of Mandalay, where the guardian spirit was represented by four stone statues, armed with clubs, one at each corner of the building."[5]

The blacksmith and his sister, who figure in the official enumeration of the Thirty-seven *Nats*, had a similar origin: they were burned alive on the order of the king, who feared the power of the blacksmith. And many examples can be found of nobles and generals promoted to the status of *nat* after being sent to a brutal and unjust death by their sovereign or after suffering unjust treatment.

Other *nats* have a totally different origin and derive from the Indian pantheon, like Kuvera, who is Kubera of India, the god of wealth, and the *nats* Wirupakkha, Wirulaka, Dattaratha, and Manimekhala, whose names, more or less transformed from Sanskrit, are found throughout all of Indianized Southeast Asia.

Finally, the very nature of the *nats* has been influenced by Theravada Buddhism, for some of them have become spirits as a result of accumulating exceptional merit while alive. The mythology of these *nats* also takes on the appearance of history: one of the *nats*, the protector of the city of Thaton, long ago received orders from two Buddhist missionaries to drive away evil spirits from the city. Another is called Shin Upago, a Burmese adaptation of the name of the celebrated disciple Upagupta. Having become a *nat*, or "little Buddha," he is believed to have vanquished and converted the demon

Māra. Still others are guardians of the relics of the Buddha.

In other words, the confusion or assimilation of the heroes of Buddhist legend with the *nats* vividly shows that the boundary between the Indian contribution and native beliefs is no more precise than the line between the gods and the divinities of nature.

The multiplicity of the *nats* can be surprising when it is learned that the Burmese speak freely of the "Thirty-seven," whom they name and consider historical beings. But the *nats* who figure in different lists are not always the same thirty-seven; thirty-seven is important as a mythic, theoretical number. Indra is the foremost of the Thirty-seven that gradually became established between the beginnings of the kingdom of Pagan and the seventeenth century, receiving their official and definitive consecration from the minister Myawadi at the end of the eighteenth century. But it was then no longer Indra who was recognized as their supreme chief but a Buddhist devotee named Çeja. The battle of King Anorahta in the eleventh century to maintain Buddhist orthodoxy, particularly through the destruction of *nat* shrines, remained inconclusive. For the sovereign himself finally decided to regroup the *nats* and entrust them to a patron subject to the law of the Dhamma, thus subjecting them to the Buddha all at once.

There is much to be said about the Burman and Mon earth spirits, some deriving from ancestral localities and some drawn from Brahmanic sources or integrated with Buddhism. The ideal number of thirty-seven schematizes an increasing multitude and seems to be an attempt to delimit and define it better. It seems that these hordes are sometimes arranged in a hierarchy in the image of Burmese or Thai society, according to their power and the size of the territory that they protect. But the hierarchy is also consistent with cosmogonic themes in which the levels of the heavens correspond to categories of supernatural beings superior or inferior to one another.

Whatever their origins, habitats, and names may be, how do these omnipresent *nats* intervene in human life? This is no longer a matter of mythology in the narrow sense, but of ritualized relationships. Yet there is a constant dialogue between men and *nats,* for men know that *nats* have the power to procure for them immediate happiness, health, wealth, and luck and to preserve them from dangers. The *nats* present both a higher organization of protection and the fearsome apparatus of a power that bestows favors and refuses them. Men depend partly on the attitudes of *nats,* who can be persuaded by invocations, prayers, offerings, dances, and feasts given in their honor. Mediums address themselves to *nats* by means of the trance, which marks the entrance into a relationship with an invisible being who is invited and questioned. During certain collective ceremonies, the villagers sacrifice animals and then gather in haunted places—the confluence of two rivers, for example—while singing piously of their desires: good rice crops, good health for the family, vows to "the Lady of the River" and the "Noble Lord of the Forest."

The modalities of these relationships are numerous, varying according to the place and the particular personalities of the different spirits. But it is clear that there is a system of close bonds, a familiar cooperation among occupants of the same territory, the prosperity of some dependent on the goodwill of others. Buddhism "dresses" the whole without contradicting it, *nats* involved in the same universe as men, men in turn able to become *nats* through the effect of their efforts or their merits.

2. The *Phi* of Thailand and Laos

Like their neighbors the Burmese *nats,* the *phi* of Thailand are innumerable and populate nature. In Laos, the *phi* intervene constantly in everyday life, to such an extent that few acts, individual or collective, are accomplished without them: they are feared, they are invoked, they are consulted.

Altars called *Ho Phi* are erected to them, either in the village or within the home. According to Nithan Khun Borom, "formerly each village had for all of its inhabitants a great *Ho Phi* dedicated to its tutelary spirit, and each villager had a little *Ho Phi* inside his house where he made offerings to the *phi* of his ancestors, to the *phi* who protected the house, and even to the evil spirits like the *phi mot* and the *phi pop.*"[6]

For the Laotian author cited here, Vongkot Rattana, the term *phi* includes the spirits of the land, manes of the ancestors, and "spirits" in general, good and bad. Indeed, this term seems to encapsulate for him all nondivine supernatural beings, all beings that do not derive from the essence of Indra or Buddha. But though these beings do not share the nature of those divinities, they surpass them in strength and in "magic powers," and, at a level superior to men, direct the affairs of the territory.

It is striking how the commentators on Tai and Lao religion need to show the *phi* entering into the course of history. "Generation upon generation, this cult has been practiced from remote times, probably since the reign of Khoun Kan Hang, one of the first kings of Xieng Dong-Xieng Thong."[7] And in 1359 King Fa Ngum, the founder of the kingdom of Lan Xang, dismantled the cult of the *phi* and established Theravāda Buddhism as the official religion. But actually, "the majority put shrines in their homes to venerate the Buddha, while saving the *Ho Phi* to honor the spirits."[8]

Two hundred years later, in 1527, King Photisarath faced a religious situation in which the cult of the *phi* had assumed such importance that he felt obliged to interfere: by royal ordinance he transformed the shrines, the *ho,* into dwellings for *uposat,* that is, for those who lived according to the precepts and intended to become monks.

But no steps taken have ever prevailed against the *phi.* They have continued to be present and to manifest themselves not only in the country and the villages but also among princes, at the court, and within monastery walls. *Ho* were constructed in gardens, notably in the palace park of the crown prince at Luang Prabang, in the mountains, at the confluence of rivers, in certain forested areas, at the borders of the country, and finally on land belonging to Buddhist monasteries.

Far from having disappeared or weakened after the royal ordinance of the sixteenth century, the cult of the *phi* was made official, since the governor of every province received each year a sum of silver from the royal treasury, silver that he was to distribute to the keepers of the altars to organize a great annual offering ceremony on the eighth day of the waxing moon of the seventh month. Once every three years a buffalo was offered to the spirits, probably a replacement for human sacrifice.

Thus, according to Georges Condominas, "in the cult of the *phi* one is dealing with an ancient Tai animist base enriched with the cults of the first proto-Indo-Chinese inhabitants and assimilated by their conquerors."[9]

The principal characteristic of the *phi* is that they are the masters and guardians of the soil. Or more precisely, this significance of the term shows most clearly their specific role and how they are connected to the animist religion that existed before Buddhism. The *phi muang* is the one who watches over the collectivity and is its ageless master. The *phi ban* is the village *phi*, also called *phi laksa ban*, that is, "the one who guards the village," or *phi hak ban*, "the one who loves the village." In these invisible characters, materialized through their *ho*, the sacred is concentrated in its chthonic aspect.

In Tai country the spirits of the land seem never to have been the object of systematization; nor were they reduced to an enumeration that ideally limited their number and let them be represented as historical persons. But each of them has his own mythology, involving pseudohistorical facts, or "historical legends," and most of the time a hierarchy can be discerned among them. Given the abundance of variants, we must limit ourselves to two examples, one from Laos and the other from Thailand.

The first example is the "spirits of salt" studied by Charles Archaimbault.[10] The author takes us to Ban Bo, about sixty miles north of Vientiane, where there are salt pits that the villagers exploit. The layer of salt water that feeds them is pumped out and put into great heating vats where it is brought to a boil. After the water has evaporated, the salt is collected and packed. In the village of Ban Bo there is a *ho* perched on piles above the pits: this is the *Ho Bo*, the dwelling of the guardian spirits and protectors of the salt works.

As in all places thus guarded by invisible masters, a series of taboos governs comings and goings, indeed, the very behavior of the men who settle there. The transgression of these taboos entails punishment by the *phi* and always necessitates rites of propitiation—offerings performed through the *cam*, the guardian and servant of the spirits.

Charles Archaimbault stresses the fact that the *phi* of the salt are strongly hierarchized, and that they form a society whose structure, though schematic, faithfully reflects that of the ancient royal administration: at its head presides Cao P'a Satt'ong, the monarch of the spirits of the salt. Serving directly under him are the viceroy P'ia Ong and his assistant P'ia O. These dignitaries transmit the orders of the king to the two "chiefs of the march," Ai Dan S'ai and Ai Dan K'ua. "Important works" are finally entrusted to the executioners Bak Ham and Bak K'am.[11]

We thus see an organization of the invisible, a supernatural administration of a territory exploited by men with the permission of its real masters, the *phi*. All the relationships between the spirits and the villagers illuminate both this subordination of men to a powerful order beyond them and the terms of a contract continually renewed by rituals and festivals, especially the festival called Boun Teto Ti-K'i. During this festival, where formerly a ball game known as *ti k'i*[12] was played, the important people of the village invited the spirits to be present at the rite and prepared resting places, water jugs, and betel for them. The people made offerings to the *phi* while beseeching them to protect the community: "We ask you to keep us in good health! Protect all the residents, all the traders!" The days that followed saw individual offerings accompanied by vows, then the final confrontation of two ball teams, the villagers' team and the spirits' team, the latter always emerging victorious: "Through the victory of the priestly clan, the Ti K'i confirms a previous right. It ratifies the property rights of the spirit, who long before the exploitation of the pits had already been in possession of them; the villagers' rights on the land were only rights acquired later and maintained through the benevolence of the spirit."[13]

A second type of Tai spirit is modeled on the mythic person of a king who has become a *phi:* an actual king, because we are speaking of Somdet Phra Chao Taksin, king of Thonburi after the fall of Ayutthaya to Siam in 1767, before the foundation of Bangkok in 1782. Nothing is more normal than that this sovereign should be considered a hero of spiritual renewal after the destruction of the prestigious capital by the Burmans. But King Taksin has entered into the mythology, as Jacqueline de Fels has ably shown in a recent thesis.[14] On the day that his memorial was inaugurated in Thonburi in April 1954, the Brahmans of the court performed the ceremony "inviting the soul" of the king to be present. Everywhere sanctuaries were set up and offerings of flowers were piled up at the foot of his image. Whatever the historical accounts of his death—madness, assassination, plots—King Taksin plays a part in the religious life of the Thai: "Even though the image before which they prostrate themselves most often represents the king of Thonburi in his martial aspect, it is not so much the defender of the fatherland that they now invoke as a protector who is their own, whose power can help them in their everyday life."[15]

The notion of the lord of a temporal realm has given way to that of a *phi muang*, the tutelary spirit of the kingdom: "the guardian of a land of which he is still the sovereign, he always insures its defense. He can bring good fortune and long life to everything living there—men, animals, and plants—while remaining the stern master who punishes offenses. And many residents of Thailand today place themselves under the protection of this *phi muang*."[16] In this respect they differ little from the residents of the thirteenth-century capital city of Sukhothai. In his celebrated inscription, King Rama Kamheng, while placing all the inhabitants of his kingdom "under the law of the Buddha," did not hesitate to evoke the tutelary spirit of the *muang*, "superior to all the spirits of the country. If the prince who is sovereign over the Muong Sukhot'ai offers him proper worship and presents ritual offerings to him, then the land is stable and prospers; but if he does not offer him the prescribed worship and does not present him with ritual offerings, then the spirit of the hill will no longer protect or respect the country that is falling into decay."[17] Georges Coedès, who cites this passage, makes it clear that it refers to the spirit "P'ra Khap'ung," Lord of the Summit: "This name also evokes that of the Nat or Burman spirit Mahāgiri, who lives on Mount Poppa, the holy mountain located to the southeast of Pagan."[18]

We will see comparable phenomena illustrated as we move into the Khmer domain.

3. The Cambodian *Neak-tā*

The belief in the existence of "earth spirits" or "spirits of the soil" is common to all the people of Cambodia, whether they are from towns, villages, or the countryside. Everywhere, the presence of a *neak-tā* is marked by a mixture of respectful fear and familiarity.

When we try to define the characteristic traits of the many spirits, we find a number of apparently incoherent, indeed contradictory, facts. The term *neak-tā*, sometimes written *ana'k-tā*, is recognized and understood all over the country, and means "someone, a certain individual" (*neak* or *ana'k*), "old" (*tā*). The term *tā*, moreover, is more a term of address than an epithet, and connotes familiarity, as when we say "Uncle."

But this common usage denotes individuals who can appear very different from one another. Some have a per-

Guardian *nats* in the precincts of the pagoda of Schwezigon. Burma, valley of the Irrawaddy-Nyaung-U. Paris, Musée de l'Homme collection. Photo S. Karpelès.

(Above right) Statues of *nats* in the precincts of the *Shwe Dagon*. Burma, Rangoon. Paris, Musée de l'Homme collection. Photo S. Karpelès.

sonal name, a name of their own, while others are referred to only as *neak-tā* or *lok cā's*, "old gentlemen"; some are unique, while others appear in a group; some seem to "govern" a territory and so are found in an organized, hierarchical system, while others, who live in a tree or an abandoned place, seem to have ill-defined relationships with the inhabitants of the region. Finally, some spirits are materialized in an object that is somehow permanent—a rock, a statue, or a piece of a statue—while others, more numerous, are content to be present invisibly, "dwelling" in a tree, on a hillock, in a termite hill, in a body of water or a confluence of waters—marked only by the offerings placed near their supposed habitat.

One major fact, however, remains constant: the essentially tutelary role of the spirit. Whether he is territorial or merely local, the spirit watches over, guards, and protects—as long as he is offered the appropriate worship. Here again there is an invisible tutelary organization that must be conciliated by honoring it with the customary ritual.

We have already noted that certain spirits of the land have their own names. Most of the time the name is borrowed from the place where they live, a mountain, for example, a rice field, a pond, or a particular tree: *neak-tā* of Angkor Borei (Nagara Puri), *neak-tā* of Phnom Chisor, *neak-tā* Ben of Kompon Cham, *neak-tā* of Phnom, a sacred hill in Phnom Penh. Other *neak-tā*, in addition to the term that identifies their locality, carry another designation: such is the case with the protecting *neak-tā* of the city of Pursat, south of the Great Lake, who is characterized as *neak-tā khlang muang Bodhisat,* that is, "spirit center of the province of Pursat." In other places too, the Thai word for "territory," or "province," *muang,* replaces the corresponding Khmer term, *sruk.* It is interesting that the tutelary spirit is regarded as the "center" of the territory that it protects and "governs." It is situated there within an order of cosmogonic thought well attested in

Nats at the east entrance to the temple of Thatbyinnyu. Burma, valley of the Irrawaddy. Paris, Musée de l'Homme collection. Photo S. Karpelès.

India and in the Indianized domain: the mountain is the center and the axis of the world, the seat of the divinity. We know that in Cambodia, during the centuries of Angkorian power—the ninth to the thirteenth centuries A.D.—the idea of the temple-mountain developed, simultaneously the seat of the "patron" god of the reigning king and the center of the capital. Similarly, the *neak-tā* "center of the province," *khlang muang,* makes use of the notion (unless he was the one who originated it) of a power fixed at the center, at the very axis of a particular territory, a province, a city, a hamlet—or the world.

A second notion appears in the names given to spirits: the notion of age and antiquity, already included in the word *tā*. Some spirits are called *cā's sruk,* "the old one of the country," a name that suggests two orders of questions: Are local spirits regarded as the former inhabitants of the Khmer country, the first to have governed it, in prehistory? And what are the relations that unite the *neak-tā* with the dead? The answers to these two questions are far from being settled.

Indeed, although certain spirits seem to have been established at a particular place since time immemorial, many others, by contrast, have a history that places them in a temporal context and makes them a type of "ancient dead." This is true for the *neak-tā khlang muang* of Pursat, who is certainly the most universally known to Cambodians: "Toward the end of the sixteenth century, King Cei Cedsda'r found himself in Bantay Cei, the Citadel of Victory, several miles from the present-day city of Pursat. The war against the Siamese was raging, and with the rout of the Cambodian troops the king had been placed in great danger. It was then that the governor of Pursat decided to sacrifice himself. He had a pit dug, in which he placed all sorts of weapons. Then, after saying his prayers, he jumped into it; he was followed by his wife, who did not want to survive him. The pit was then immediately filled in. A few days later, the Siamese laid siege to the citadel. But a great noise filled the night, and the Siamese fell like flies, killed by a disease: this was the work of troops of ghosts that the governor had gone to search for in the kingdom of the shades in order to save Cambodia."[19] Since then, every year people commemorate the sacrifice of the former governor who became the tutelary spirit of Pursat.

Some *neak-tā* are said to be dead children; others, men who died a violent death, like the *neak-tā* of Khone islet.

In another category—if indeed it is right, as it is convenient, to speak here of categories—are the *neak-tā* who have the names of Brahmanic divinities. The most striking of these is the *neak-tā* Gaṇeśa, the protector of diverse *sruk* of Cambodia. In the Brahmanic mythology of India, Gaṇeśa is the son of the god Śiva and the goddess Pārvatī. We know that he has the head of an elephant, that he is frequently represented together with a rat, and that he holds a pot of honey into which he dips his trunk. In India, Nepal, and Sri Lanka, he is the god of skill, intelligence, cleverness, and knowledge. In Cambodia he has become a tutelary *neak-tā,* assimilated to the land, born of the Khmer patrimony. Here is an example of the integration of a Brahmanic divinity into the mythological pantheon of the country. This example is by no means isolated. But instead of bearing a recognizably Indian name, the spirit is called by an epithet that makes it possible

(Right) *Phi* tree (a sacred tree covered by *ex-votos* and offerings) on a village street. Thailand, Krung Thep (Bangkok). Paris, Musée de l'Homme collection. Photo G. Fouquet.

Two spirits of the *nā'k-tā*. A village altar. Cambodia, near Angkor, on the Banteay Shrérï trail.

to identify him with one or another Indian divinity. Thus the *neak-tā kraham ga,* the "rednecked" spirit, to cite only one, seems to be Śiva himself, often evoked in Indian hymns by the deep color of his neck. In other cases, the original name is masked by a distortion, on which a popular etymology has been superimposed: the spirit Me Sar of Ba Phnom is known as the "white chief" or the "white mother," but it is more likely that its name results from the contraction of one of the names of the goddess Durgā, the wife of Śiva: that is, the destroyer of the buffalo demon, Mahiṣāsura.

These names, of forgotten Brahmanic origin, do not imply that the spirits in question correspond in their personalities, actions, or final appearance to the divinities whose patronymics they have received. But we have good reason to believe that "where they are found there were once temples at which these divinities were honored. Very often, moreover, we see in the hut of a *neak-tā* fragments of ancient statues that prove the existence of temples that have disappeared."[20]

Popular stories depict spirits who have no name but "the *neak-tā* of the village," usually described as "very powerful." Often their dwelling places—huts, "pagodas," or trees—are alluded to, and sometimes also their animal familiar, like the crocodile of the story of Suk the Sweet and Suk the Wicked,[21] a creature who lived nestled under his master's house, next to the river. The story of the man who dug up crabs presents a picture of a special place: the earth under the timbers of the foundation of the pagoda of the *neak-tā,* where the hero of the story, "marked" from the beginning by good luck deriving from his past merits, each day dug up crabs that he sold to make his living.[22]

Finally, still other spirits demand attention: those called by nicknames that are often crude, like *ā'c chkē,* "dog excrement," or *prahok,* "fish sauce." A termite hill that grows on top of the uncremated corpse of someone who died a violent death is often both the origin of these spirits and their place of residence.

Whatever they are named, it is clear that the *neak-tā* are everywhere intensely alive: they live together with men in a way that is simultaneously ancestral and immediate, since one event or another can lead to the birth of a new *neak-tā.* It is enough to find some material support—a rock, a newly discovered statue, a termite hill—to invite a wandering spirit to settle there permanently and thus to become the guardian and protector of the place. And the tutelary function, though constantly attested, shows a number of variants.

Some *neak-tā* are thought to be givers of rain, like the Trañol spirit of Prei Kra-bas. Others are used to find lost livestock. They are invoked in case there are animal diseases, epidemics, and collective calamities. According to oral traditions, the rites performed in their honor once used to include blood sacrifices, in certain cases human sacrifices, often replaced by sacrifices of buffaloes. The *neak-tā* Krol of Kompong Thom seems to have received human victims until about 1904. In other cases the presence of the spirit is celebrated with dances regarded as "fertility dances": songs and dances for children, livestock, rain, health, abundance, and prosperity. The women of the village sometimes mime a sexual union with the stone that represents the *neak-tā.* Firecrackers, the shooting of guns, and offerings of vegetables, cloth, and money accompany these cults, which vary from place to place. Everywhere, however, the monks of the Buddhist monastery of the place participate, to "Buddhicize" the ceremony and because the coexistence of the earth spirits with Buddhism is always accepted and experienced without friction. Similarly, the head of the province, representing

The *nā'k-tā* (temple of the earth spirit; a small straw hut); in the foreground, a pile of ritual stones. Cambodia, province of Kratie, Sambok. Paris, Musée de l'Homme collection. Photo J. Dournes.

political authority, formerly royal authority and divine right, is present at the rite in honor of the *neak-tā.* Integrated into the temporal administrative system, he comes to give his supernatural homologue the homage that consecrates the harmony between the two orders of power.

Finally, the *neak-tā* sometimes speak, to give oracles through the mouths of *rūp,* "possessed persons," generally women, who temporarily receive the *neak-tā* into themselves. The word *rūp,* from the Sanskrit *rūpa,* "form," denotes the medium as well as an apparition or concrete image of the spirit.

The fact that all Cambodia is inhabited by *neak-tā* only confirms the permanence of the Austroasiatic Mon-Khmer substratum, as much among the Khmer majority as among the minority groups of the forests and mountains. But the two most striking characteristics of this "organization of protection" are, first, its coexistence with Buddhism—the pagodas of the *neak-tā* within the walls of monasteries, the monks reciting prayers at festivals of the *nā'k-tā*—and, second, its hierarchical aspect.

A spirit is more or less powerful according to the importance of its territory. A city, for example, may have other spirits subordinate to the protecting spirit, who are thought of as "ministers" or are given the military title of *sena.* One might ask if the tutelary *neak-tā* of the city or province are not sometimes somehow assimilated to the guardian spirits of doors, or to the guardians of the directions of space, which derive from Indianized mythology. But the *neak-tā* are not satisfied with those places: the bonds that unite them with human society are ceaselessly put into question, tightened or relaxed, according to events and to how men honor them. A system of gift and countergift is evident here, and the contract between the invisible society and the country's inhabitants—the one as real as the other—is constantly renewed, according to the norms and requirements of territorial and collective life.

At the end of this general review of the earth spirits of Burma, Thailand, and the Mon-Khmer country, it is easy to note the repetitions and parallelisms, as well as the identical character of the fundamental schemata of the myths and the rituals that concern them. All the spirits—masters of the earth, ancestral guardians, the undisputed owners of the land—dispense wealth on condition of being served. They speak and heal through mediums, or punish and torment. They represent a hierarchy superimposed upon the human hierarchy. But all of them are also subject to Buddhist law, and whether they have Indra or Çeja for their mythic sovereign does not change the fact that they constitute part of an environment profoundly marked by Theravada Buddhism. The "syncretism" that joins their cult to the practice of Buddhist observances—often to the point of making them inseparable—should not be interpreted exclusively as a one-way influence of Buddhism on the ancient religion. For in its conception of the world and in its vision of creatures, Buddhism itself gives the spirits and supernatural beings a place. This is a constant theme of Buddhist cosmogonies—especially of the Traibhūmi or Trai Phum, one of the most celebrated texts of the "explication of the world" in Southeast Asia.

S.T./d.g.

BIBLIOGRAPHY AND NOTES

1. D. BERNOT, "Les Nat de Birmanie," p. 309 in *Génies, anges et démons* (Paris 1971), 297–341.
2. Cited by D. BERNOT, "Les Nat de Birmanie," 307–8; see R. C. TEMPLE, *The Thirty Seven Nats: A Phase of Spirit-Worship Prevailing in Burma* (London 1906).
3. D. BERNOT, "Les Nat de Birmanie," 309, note 10.
4. Ibid., 309–10.
5. Ibid., 311.
6. R. VONGKOT, "Les rites du culte des Phi, au Ho Vang-Na à Luang-Prabang," *Bulletin des Amis du royaume lao* 6, 2 (1971): 95.
7. Ibid., 95.
8. Ibid.
9. G. CONDOMINAS, "Notes sur le bouddhisme populaire en milieu rural lao," *Archives de sociologie des religions* 25, 1 (1968): 85.
10. CH. ARCHAIMBAULT, "Une cérémonie en l'honneur des génies de la mine de sel de Ban Bo (Moyen Laos) (Contribution à l'étude du jeu de Ti-K'i)," *BEFEO* 48, 1 (1956); cited here from the same article reprinted in *Structures religieuses lao (rites et mythes)*, Documents pour le Laos (Vientiane 1973), 2:1–16, plates 6–9.
11. Op. cit., 3.
12. See P. DE LÉVY, "Ti-khi: Un jeu de mail rituel au Laos," *Annuaire de l'École pratique des Hautes Études, Sciences religieuses* (1952–53), 3–15.
13. ARCHAIMBAULT, "Une cérémonie en l'honneur des génies de la mine de sel de Ban Bo," 78.
14. J. DE FELS, *Somdet Phra Chao Tak Sin Maharat, le roi de Thonburi*, 2 vols. (diss., Paris 1976).
15. Ibid., 2:360.
16. Ibid., 2:361.
17. G. COEDÈS, *Les États hindouisés d'Indochine et d'Indonésie* (Paris 1964), 377–78.
18. Ibid., 377, note 2.
19. *Cérémonies des Douze Mois, fêtes annuelles cambodgiennes*, Commission des moeurs et coutumes du Cambodge (Phnom Penh n.d.), 29.
20. Ibid., 27.
21. F. MARTINI and S. BERNARD, *Contes populaires inédits du Cambodge* (Paris 1946), 138.
22. Ibid., 106.

SOUTHEAST ASIAN MYTHS AND RITUALS OF THE MOON

From the very first studies of lunar myths in Southeast Asia, it was evident that local ideas were interwoven with legends that came from India and China. In the context of this theme, the deeply composite character of the tradition, as it is received, transmitted, and lived, appeared with sudden brilliance.

In India, the moon is generally a male deity. The Vedic hymns occasionally give the moon the name of Soma, which is otherwise usually the name of the sacred plant that allows communication with the divine. The Brahmanic legends refer to the marriage of this moon god with a daughter of the sun. In China, myths evoke the moon as a female being. But in a country like Cambodia, it seems that both sexes are attributed to the moon, prevailing alternately. Thus, sometimes male, sometimes female, it is Lord Moon (Braḥ Chan), Lord Month (Braḥ Khê), or the deified month of the lunar calendar, with whom an earthly girl may fall in love; or it may be Somā, in the feminine, identified with the Nāgī, the serpent-woman, daughter of the wet and the cold, the ophidian wife of the Brahman Kaundinya, according to the Sanskrit tradition of the founding of the kingdom of Funan, or the wife of Prince Braḥ Thoṅ, the sun king and founder of the first Khmer dynasty, according to the oral tradition.

The union of lunar princesses and solar princes is the favorite theme of the dynastic legends of ancient Cambodia. The legend of the Nāgī Somā was told countless times, inscribed on stone, and narrated in the Annals. Whether it is the Brahman Kaundinya who came from India or Prince Braḥ Thoṅ, one of them meets at the seashore the daughter of the king of the Nāgas, the sovereign of the country and the lord of the land. He marries her and "founds a royal race." It is likely that the salutations to the moon that used to be celebrated at the royal palace in Phnom Penh symbolized a mystical marriage between the solar prince and the stars of the night. Each year, according to the thirteenth-century Chinese chronicler Chou Ta-kuan, the king of Angkor united with a symbolic Nāgī, thus reviving the alliance of the origins.

It is thus evident that the lunar myth, included here in the dynastic legends, is complex, since it comes to be associated with the myth of the serpent-woman, and thus with the myth of the Nāgas, half-human, half-snake, who own the land. The lunar myth is also integrated into the dualist system which opposes sun and moon, dry and damp, bird and snake, and which can be traced throughout the mythico-social universe of ancient Cambodia in conjunction with other complementary oppositions.

But the moon has been given other names. The name of Somā, made feminine by the lengthening of the final vowel of the original Indian noun Soma, may represent a scholarly and royal tradition, probably introduced by the Brahmans. In orally transmitted legends one almost always finds the name Chan, which comes from the Sanskrit *candra,* "moon." The Lord Braḥ Chan sits on his throne in heaven, where he forms a couple with the sun. A legend widespread in Cambodia tells the story of Bimān Chan, whose name means "sojourn of the moon." The story refers to the love that unites the Lord Braḥ Chan of the sky with a young girl from earth, Bimān Chan, whom he takes with him to the firmament.

The sequel to the story shows the interweaving of other themes, notably that of beheading. Badly advised by the other two wives of the Lord Moon, Bimān Chan asks her husband to carry her away higher and higher into the sky. But the wind blows hard in the high altitude and tears off the young woman's head, which falls into the pond of a monastery, while the body continues to live in the sky. Soon the head is picked up and placed before the Buddha of the pagoda. Then, after many episodes, notably the restoration of the body, the young woman becomes Bimān Chan again and marries an earthly prince, Suryavaṅ, whose name means "of the race of the sun."

These variations on the luminous couples, mixing the divine, the astral, and the royal, evoke the distant echo of the Vedic hymns to the moon and the sun, even while the Buddha appears in them. The rural tradition first emphasizes the beneficent role of the moon, male or female, depending on the story. The moon scatters the rain, which in turn fertilizes the rice fields. It marks the passing of time, dividing the month into the "bright fortnight" and the "dark fortnight." Between the two, the full moon marks the high point of good fortune, when the fates are in balance. The observation of the moon develops into a science of prediction, into the reading of the mysteries of germination, prosperity, and calamities. Treatises on divination copy this language throughout all the countries of Southeast Asia.

The moon is light and movement, as the Khmer represent it: "The moon takes upon herself the task of lighting the world during the night and of safeguarding human lives as best she can. She mounts a chariot of precious stones, covered on the outside with a layer of silver. The chariot is forty-nine *yojanas*[1] in length. The moon lights the three worlds. From any one of the four cardinal points, the moon projects her light for a distance of at least nine hundred thousand *yojanas*. The moon moves around the three worlds ceaselessly, all through the night. Together with the sun, she revolves around Mount Somer;[2] she performs the *pradakshina*. Her journey is less rapid than the sun's. From time to time, one overtakes the other, and then the sun passes his companion. When the moon disappears, the sun comes out, and when the sun disappears, the moon comes out. The two of them sustain the life of humanity."[3]

Throughout the oral narratives, it appears that most of the time the moon and the sun had human forms before becoming the heavenly bodies of the day and the night. One legend specifically states that the sun, fire, thunder, wind, rain, the star Rāhu, and the moon were seven brothers, the moon being the youngest of them all. Another legend depicts the sun, the moon, and Rāhu as three brothers; Rāhu became the monster of eclipses, the one who swallows the sun or the moon.

The myths of eclipses, in Thailand as well as in Laos and Cambodia, always show Rāhu swallowing the moon in his

The god Surya, the sun, on a ceremonial fan from Thailand. Paris, Musée de l'Homme collection. Photo Destable.

enormous mouth, which has only an upper jaw, from either unquenchable anger or brotherly affection. In any case, eclipses are terrifying and inspire taboos and propitiations.

Finally, it is essential to note similar myths that are inseparable from royal or rural rituals. The ceremonies at Angkor are never described in detail. But the festivals of greeting the moon, synchronized with the agrarian cycle, continue to thrive even today. In about 1850, King Ang Duang lent all his prestige to the great ritual that followed immediately after the Festival of the Waters, in October-November, that is, during the eighth month of an ordinary year or the ninth month of an intercalary year. The king would greet the stars at the royal palace to the sound of marine shells. Installed in his floating house connected to the bank by a pontoon, he could contemplate the reflection of the rays on the surface of the waters of Four Arms at Phnom Penh. A *baku,* that is, a descendant of Brahmanic priests of older times, would come to present him with lustral water in a shell inlaid with gold, enameled in various colors, and set in a golden bowl. The king would wet his palms, lift his hands to the moon, moisten his face, contemplate, pay homage, and then sprinkle the royal children, using a leaf from the *bilva* tree (*Aegle marmelos*). The Buddhist monks were invited to dine in the throne room, thus marking the presence of Buddhism at the very heart of these rituals, which are a part of both the Brahmanic tradition and the agrarian cycle.

In the countryside, on the village squares or more often in the courtyards of monasteries, the festival included the offering of new rice that was lightly roasted and crushed with a pestle, the construction of temporary pavilions, and the burning of candles and incense when the moon was at its zenith. From the drops of wax that fell onto the banana leaves that were arranged below, one could predict the abundance or shortage of rainfall, and from the shapes of the spots formed by the wax, one could see revelations of the health of men and animals and the prosperity of the country: "O Braḥ Chan, great, magnificent, proud, and splendid, more beautiful than a diamond, clearer than crystal, O Braḥ Chan, I salute you!" Variants from village to village would have one constant: the presence of Buddhist priests, who would chant the Chanda Parittam, a prayer in Pali to the glory of the moon. It is not uncommon in some places to see them sprinkle the soil of the monastery, thus symbolizing the fertilizing rain.

Whether the king sprinkles his children, the monks sprinkle the ground, or country people offer or scatter rice or drip candle wax, the essential meaning of these rituals is clearly to perform a fertility rite, in which the moon and water are closely associated.

Finally, another cycle is worth noting. Buddhist Southeast Asia has explained the festival of greeting the moon by reference to the Jātakas, the tales of the Buddha's former lives. According to the *Sasa-jātaka*, in one of his former lives the Buddha was reincarnated in the form of a hare and from compassion and "extreme charity," he gave his flesh to a famished traveler. Since then, the image of the hare, often called the "rabbit of the moon" in popular stories and traditions, seems to be imprinted on the lunar disk, where he can be distinguished on clear nights.

Thus, from dynastic legends to village rites and Buddhist tales, the myth of the moon unfolds its rich and complex motifs, through which we can read a whole religious history that is closely tied to social behavior.

S.T./g.h.

BIBLIOGRAPHY AND NOTES

1. The measurement of the itinerary, corresponding to about two geographical miles, would be a little less than three kilometers.
2. Mount Meru of Indian cosmogony, center of the universe, became Sumeru, Somer, or Men, in Southeast Asia.
3. E. PORÉE-MASPERO and S. BERNARD-THIERRY, "La lune, croyances et rites du Cambodge," 264–65, in *La lune, mythes et rites* (Paris 1962), 263–87 *(coll. Sources Orientales, 6).*

The Acculturation of the Divinities of Hinduism in Southeast Asia

I. The Earth

We have studied several nature myths. But the Southeast Asian mythology of nature involves many other characters as well. A particularly important one is the Earth, who, under the name of Dharaṇī or Braḥ Dhar(a)ni (pronounced Thorani), appears as a young woman kneeling, twisting her long hair in both hands. We know that the goddess Earth is a figure in the Indian epics. The great Vedic hymns celebrate her under the name of Aditi, bearer of all plants and animals, mother of all beings. At the end of the Sanskrit *Rāmāyaṇa*, the Earth comes to find Sītā, the wife of Rāma, who was born from a furrow, and swallows Sītā up in her depths while Rāma rises to heaven. In Buddhist legend, the Earth rises up to engulf the armies of Māra the tempter, who is trying to turn the Buddha away from his meditations. And this is the aspect under which Southeast Asia has adopted this essentially benevolent goddess: from the coil of hair she twists an abundant river flows. Her name of Dharaṇī, "she who bears," or who supports, comes from the Sanskrit, but in Southeast Asia her legend makes her an accomplice of the Buddha in his search for supreme Enlightenment. The bronze casters, the image makers of Thailand, Burma, Laos, and Cambodia, have everywhere represented her as a lithe and smiling young woman, helpful and auspicious.

II. The Devatās

In a general way, nature is populated with divinities, *devatās*, a word whose pronunciation varies from country to country, *thēvoda, debta,* etc. These supernatural beings must not be confused with the earth spirits who have been discussed already. They constitute a pantheon originally from India, but in some sense "domesticated" or acculturated.

From the great god Brahma, ordinarily considered a single being, there arose in Southeast Asia a multitude of *brahmas* or *prohms*, immaterial beings inhabiting the various celestial levels. They are not inaccessible, in the sense that they are included in the system of transmigration and are part of the "wheel of existence." In other words, the *prohms* are not reincarnations, since they are disembodied, but the new condition of beings who, in an earlier life, were men or animals.

The *devatās* of the sky, the clouds, the sea, and the trees are usually anonymous, with the exception of certain goddesses, fairies, or nymphs such as, for example, Manimekhala, associated with the myths of the sea and lightning, and Deb Pranam, a divinity portrayed in a praying position, hands joined to make the *añjali* greeting in homage to Buddha. We could also cite Mera, called an *apsara,* a celestial dancer, who in one of the dynastic traditions of Cambodia is supposed to have married the ascetic Kambu to found the kingdom of the Kambuja.

In fact, nearly all the mythological characters of Indian legend have passed into Southeast Asia: *kinnaris,* bird-women who come to frolic on earth, on the edges of lakes, in forest clearings, and who sometimes marry ordinary humans; *gandharvas,* celestial musicians; *yakṣas,* ogre-like beings endowed with remarkable powers like flying or walking on the sea; above all, the *nāgas* and *nāgīs,* ophidian beings, half-human, half-serpent, who range over almost all of southern Asia, and who belong both to the Indian heritage and to indigenous belief. The *nāgas* are regarded as the owners of the land, and their kings have different names depending on the text and the place: Bhuvajan, Bhujon, dwelling in the deep lakes of the kingdom of Patala; or Krun Bāli, the great serpent living underground, who must be propitiated whenever a house is built.

Bird-woman, or *kinnari,* from the shadow theater of Thailand. Paris, Musée de l'Homme collection.

Two half-woman–half-bird creatures, or *kinnari.* Temple of the dawn, or "Vatarun." Thailand, Krung Thep (Bangkok). Paris, Musée de l'Homme collection. Photo Pourcher.

Besides this divine multitude, who, according to the tales and legends, are very familiar and very close to humans, some of the great gods of Brahmanism have also had remarkable careers in Southeast Asia.

III. The Great Gods of Brahmanism: Śiva, Viṣṇu, and Indra

We know that the ancient kingdoms of Angkor, Champa, and Śrivijaya consecrated most of their major sanctuaries to the gods Śiva and Viṣṇu. Śiva the creator, the powerful god, was represented both inside and outside the temples in the form of a linga, a more or less realistic or ornamented phallic symbol. The kings who built the temples were fused with him after their deaths in a ritual of apotheosis, and during their lives were identified with his power, both divine and royal, as king of the gods, *devarāja,* interpreted as "god-king."

Śiva survived after the Hinduized monarchies ended. Today one can still see the linga, decorated with garlands of flowers, on the edges of the Buddhist stupas of certain pagodas in Thailand. In Cambodian tales he is called "the Lord," Braḥ Iśvara, Braḥ Isūr, and he figures in the origin myths of the creation of animals. He also appears, but in the aspect of his wife Umā, on the ritual candlesticks of Cambodia, small bronze leaves called *babil,* "popil," used especially in marriage rites. The popil with its lighted candle is supposed to originate in the vulva of Umā and the phallus of Śiva, and thus continues the great Indian mythological theme of the linga and the yoni, the myth of fertilizing creation and of the alliance that generates prosperity.

As for the god Viṣṇu, to whom the temple of Angkor Wat is dedicated and whose name of glory was taken by the king Sūryavarman II, he is associated with epic themes drawn from the *Viṣṇupurāṇa* and the *Bhāgavatapurāṇa.* One of these themes is illustrated in one of the famous bas-reliefs of Angkor Wat, that of the Churning of the Ocean. "It is probably the Vaiṣṇava character of the myth that made it one of the favorite motifs of the Khmers, among whom the cult of Viṣṇu seems always to have been extremely popular, even during periods when Śaivism was preponderant" (Madeleine Giteau, 1951).

Viṣṇu, the god of order, permanence, and stability, who in India inspired particular movements of devotion and whose cult has spread throughout continental and insular Southeast Asia, is assimilated to the protecting king, the guardian of order. The work of the sovereign is set in parallel with the churning of the ocean of milk. Let us here briefly summarize the main myth. Exhausted by their constant battle against the *asura* demons, the gods, *devas,* come to ask Viṣṇu, also

Giants at the Wat Phra Keo, Krung Thep (Bangkok). Paris, Musée de l'Homme collection. Photo Gruault.

Apsaras: Dancers of the paradise of Indra. Cambodia, Angkor Wat. Paris, Musée de l'Homme collection. Photo Martel.

called Bhagavat, for help. Viṣṇu advises them to join together to churn the great ocean of milk; each group should pull on its own side to turn the churning stick, the *devas* in one direction and the *asuras* in the other. The stick of the cosmic churn is Mount Mandara, while the rope to turn it is none other than Vasuki, the king of the serpents. At the very beginning, an incident opposes the two groups of partners, since the *asuras* want to pull from the side of the serpent's head: Mount Mandara plunges under the waters. Viṣṇu turns into a gigantic tortoise and dives into the sea to support the mountain-pivot. The churning is about to start again when Vasuki vomits a black poison that threatens all creatures with death. The god Śiva, filled with compassion upon seeing this, absorbs the poison to save the world of the living.

After these two setbacks, the sublime and marvelous churning starts again, opposing and uniting in a single rhythmic effort benevolent and malevolent forces, which join together in a single creation. The sea foams and bubbles, and from its waves emerge successively the cow who gives clarified butter, the horse, the king of elephants with four tusks, the jewel, the tree, the *apsaras,* the goddesses Śrī and Varuṇī, and finally the drink of immortality, the *amṛta* nectar.

From this ensemble the Khmer image makers composed a fresco in which Viṣṇu appears not only as his tortoise avatar to support the churning stick, but also as the supreme master who directs the operation and is seated at the top of the stick, which becomes a pillar or a tree. He is Nārāyaṇa, the Braḥ Narāy of the Khmers. In these representations the churning has undergone iconographic variations that do not affect its deep significance and its integration into royal mythology: from the second half of the tenth to the beginning of the thirteenth century, it made it possible for the kings who were building and organizing the kingdom to be assimilated to the image of Viṣṇu directing the *devas* and the *asuras,* who make nectar spring from the ocean. Like the god, the king makes prosperity and continuity spring forth for his city in whose center the temple-mountain rises. This is probably an unwarranted simplification and schematization of the meaning of the myth in the realm of Angkor, but what is important to understand is that only certain myths were selected out of the enormous mass of Indian texts, and they were chosen for purposes of local reinterpretation in the country's sociohistorical framework. In this context the myth seems to have served as the explanation for power and at the same time as an expression of a contract between the king and his people.

The various forms of Viṣṇu, his avatars, his reincarnations in Rāma and Kṛṣṇa, have also become entirely accessible to the countries of Southeast Asia and have been used abundantly in art. But it is Rāma in particular who has undergone the most significant transformations. There was an enormous proliferation of versions of the Sanskrit *Rāmāyaṇa*, first in the vernaculars of India and then throughout the languages of all of Southeast Asia. The Indian text gives Rāma the essence of a god, Viṣṇu-Nārāyaṇa, and at the end of this immense tale transforms him into the giver of justice and the vanquisher of the demonic and the too human in order to have him return to heaven, gloriously escorted by the Vedic and Brahmanic gods. The Tai, Laotian, and Khmer texts, on the other hand, transform the hero into a much more human character, although he has superhuman aspects. While he remains the prince who conquers the demons and their chief Rāvaṇa, he does this either by magic power, stratagems, illusions, as in the *Braḥ Lak Braḥ Lam* of Laos, or by Buddhistic merit in the fullest sense, since he is sometimes called the "bud of Buddha," particularly in the Cambodian Reamker, which means that he is assimilated to a Bodhisattva, a "being to be awakened," or a future Buddha.

Performances in dance or mime, shadow theater, and recitations have long had the sacred character of magico-religious drama. The *Rāmāyaṇa*, conceived as a great myth of divine and demonic forces and their complementary interplay, has today become an entertainment, a novel of adventures and love. But certain village troupes still mime the high deeds of Rāma and his monkey allies to get rain. If the essential thing for the public is that he be reunited with his wife Sītā, he still remains a model whose temporary presence restores and revives the auspicious influences within the group.

Finally, another god plays a considerable role in the mythical perspective of Southeast Asia: this is the god Indra, the great god of the Vedas, king of heaven, wielder of the thunderbolt. The ancient hymns already describe the protective aspect of this god, who from the heights of his sovereign dwelling oversees what is happening on earth. When he moves into the lore of the Southeast Asian countries, Indra loses his majesty but keeps his attentive solicitude. He intervenes in human affairs as the deus ex machina who recognizes meritorious heroes who are worthy of being rescued and elevated. He appears in a great many tales, seated on a throne which has the property of getting hot when an unusual event occurs on earth, because of the extreme virtue, the Buddhist "mark," of such a character. The god "casts his divine eye," discovers the hero, and intervenes in his favor.

Indra is not absent from Buddhist texts, since it is he who, under the name of Sakka, takes on a human form to tempt and test the prince Vessantara, the hero of charity and of the perfect gift, the next-to-last incarnation of the Buddha.

In the person of a dancer, Indra sometimes takes part in village festivals. He is also the hero of a group of texts called "prophecies of Indra," which combine cosmogony, formulas for happiness, and the science of foretelling the future.

While far from exhaustive, this summary shows the presence of the great gods and secondary divinities of the Hindu pantheon in myths, legends, folktales, and rituals. Not only did these gods not die in the course of their expatriation from India; to a certain extent they were recreated in Southeast Asia and came to form an integral part not only of the iconographic heritage but also of the religion conceived as a system of relations between men and gods.

S.T./j.l.

BIBLIOGRAPHY

M. GITEAU, "Le Barattage de l'Océan au Cambodge," *Bulletin de la Société des études indochinoises*, n.s., 26, 2 (1951): 141.

The Mythic Themes of Theravāda Buddhism in Southeast Asia

One might be surprised to see mythology mentioned in connection with Hīnayāna or Theravāda Buddhism, that is, Buddhism "of the Lesser Vehicle," or of the Southern Church, which was predominant in the countries discussed here from the thirteenth century and which much earlier coexisted there with Mahāyāna, or Buddhism of the Greater Vehicle. It is well known that wherever Mahāyāna was implanted, mythological themes and a multifaceted pantheon were developed. The great "redeemers," the *bodhisattvas*, or the "beings to be awakened," were reclothed in the Buddhist countries of the north in forms and functions that assimilated them to the divinities who gave help. But the Hīnayāna or Theravāda, the authority for the original teaching of the Buddha, theoretically distanced itself from all that did not concern the one Buddha, his Law, and his Community, the Triple Gems.

If there is, nevertheless, any mythology here, it is because, on the one hand, Buddhism and the religion of the earth spirits are closely associated, and, on the other hand, mythical themes sprang up locally.

These particular aspects of Buddhism can be considered briefly on two planes: that of the textual traditions of the interpretation of the world and its phenomena and that of Buddhist legends proper. In Southeast Asia, these legends join the "popular" religion, transforming the statues and relics into sources of magical efficacy, introducing ancestral motifs into festivals of Buddhist commemoration or inaugurations of pagodas, and creating new saviors to dispense favors.

I. The Organization of the World

The History of the Three Worlds, *Traibhūmikatha*, is a complex text, of which a number of versions exist in Southeast Asia. One of these, under the title of *Traibhūmi Braḥ Rvaṅ*, was written in Thai by one of the kings of the Thai dynasty of Sukhothai, Lidaiya or Lu Thai, in 1345. Others were recast, sometimes fragmentarily, notably by King Taksin in the eighteenth century.

The work in question is a Buddhist cosmological treatise, and although it has a scholarly character, it was known equally well in a way that went beyond the circle of mere learned men or Buddhist priests. The description of the universe that is set out in detail in that text gave rise to iconographic representations, and the characters that were developed there entered into the popular tradition to a greater or lesser extent.

The Three Worlds in question are, in the Buddhist perspective, the World of Desire, the World of Form, and the World without Form. Each of these Worlds is composed of "lands." For example, in the divisions of the First World, the Kāmabhūmi, eleven lands or domains are enumerated and described, including hells, the land of animals, the land of the *pretas,* or "damned," the land of *asuras,* or "demons," the land of men, the land of the four great Guardian Kings of the four directions, the land of the "thirty-three," etc. In the World of Form the superimposed "lands," which we would call "heavens," are placed in rows one above the other, where the Brahmans, the "gods of inferior brilliance," the "gods of unlimited brilliance," and the "radiant gods" are enthroned. In the World without Form, the "domain of infinite space" and the "domain of nothingness" open out.

This general vision of the world is augmented by the list of the modes of generation, the modes of rebirth according to the law of transmigration. Throughout this group more or less abstract Buddhist conceptions are combined with descriptions full of imagery: "The guardians of this hell are armed, some with lances and sabers, others with hammers of red iron from which flames shoot forth; the guardians pursue them, chase them, prick them, lacerate them, beat them, and push them until they fall in a pit of burning coals . . ."[1] "At the foot of Mount Meru is a large pond named Simbali . . . All around it is spread a forest of false cotton plants, all of the same height . . . and the sight of their delicate greenery gladdens and enchants . . . The shores of the lake are the home of all of the Garudas."[2]

In other words, the entire mythological universe unfolds its landscapes and inhabitants. Hells and heavens and natural and supernatural beings are inscribed in a vast Buddhist context, which seems to come from a much older foundation. Mount Meru, center of the world, the celestial tiers and the cosmic mountain, far from being elements of an inaccessible metaphysics, have found in the very architecture of Southeast Asia their figurations and their functions: the temple-mountain of Angkor, in Cambodia, is after all the cosmos in miniature. Gods and demons, spirits, *nāgas,* monsters of eclipses and all the "forms" are present in this immense fresco to which the art and literature of Southeast Asia so often refers. The mythology of Buddhism here identifies itself with the global description of the universe and of the karmic condition.

Statue of the national heroine Suranari, to whom a ritual is dedicated even today by Thais, Loatians, and Chinese. Paris, Musée de l'Homme collection. Museum photo.

II. The New Saviors

The sources which have ceaselessly inspired sculptors and exegetes and which have animated the scenes of theater and dance and given life to the shadow plays have not tarnished with age. Although the symbolism of the monuments and the great mythical themes associated with royal power have died away, the celebrations still call forth the memory of ancestors and gods. The water festivals, the festivals of the New Year, of the first furrow marked in the earth at the beginning of farming, and many others, illustrate myths drawn from a long-standing tradition.

Moreover, the "Golden Legend" of the Buddhist countries is not yet closed. Innumerable works on the gods, the Buddhas, the Saints, the sites of pilgrimage marked by the footprints of Viṣṇu or of the Buddha, the miraculous peregrinations of statues like the Emerald Buddha, or those of Phra Keo or Phra Bang,[3] the accounts of the voyages of Saint Malay in the hells and heavens, all of this together constitutes a mythology peculiar to Southeast Asia.

This mythology continues today, at least in certain places. Just as the earth spirits seem to have kept their vitality, so too the "miracle" caused by the abundance of merits still flourishes and suggests the myth and the ritual. It is difficult to distinguish here between devotion and mythology. But it is certainly tempting to see in the cult of the *hlvṅ ba* (or *luang pho,* according to a more traditional transcription) which is now being developed in Thailand, the continuation of a process of the creation of legends.

The *luang pho* of Thailand that A. R. Peltier studied[4] are Buddhist monks, living or dead, whose supernatural powers are manifested through cures, feats, and multiple miracles; they also distribute the supernatural. Their biographies, which reveal exceptional behavior, divine interventions, and metamorphoses, beginning in early childhood, unfold as divine myths. Their name of *luang pho* signifies "august father" or "royal father." The figure of four hundred is noted by A. R. Peltier: "Anyone who begins to be interested in this category of monks is also surprised to perceive that more and more of the believers set up statues of monks, living or dead, to be revered; sometimes they are specially built in the enclosure of the monastery, sometimes in a reception room of the pagoda. It is finally surprising that there are 'uncovered' more and more footprints in stone left by these monks, prints which, like those of the Buddha's foot, are now the object of pilgrimages."[5]

All of the data that we have mentioned, from the distant influence of Vedism and Brahmanism to present-day Buddhism, which rests primarily on the ancient foundation of beliefs in chthonic forces, may give a misleading impression of incoherence. It is the particular distinction of the Indianized lands of Southeast Asia to have been able to create out of this rich and complex heritage a mythology expressed in art, literature, and institutions, as well as in daily life through rituals and beliefs.

S.T./d.f.

BIBLIOGRAPHY AND NOTES

1. G. COEDÈS and CH. ARCHAIMBAULT, *Les trois mondes: Traibhūmi Braḥ Rvaṅ* (Paris 1973), 35.

2. Ibid., 49.

3. R. LINGAT, "Le culte du Bouddha d'Émeraude," *Journal of the Siam Society* 27 (1934): 9.

4. A. R. PELTIER, "Introduction à la connaissance des hlvṅ ba de Thaïlande" (diss., Paris 1976).

5. Ibid., 11.

The Religions and Myths of Insular Southeast Asia

The vast Malay archipelago constitutes an incomparable field for the mythologist. Close to Melanesia and Polynesia, it is still rich in a great number of oral traditions; close to the Asiatic world, where writing has played an essential role, it is equally rich in numerous religious and epic literatures in which the influence of Indian mythology and Islam have left traces. It is a crossroads area in which the oral and written coexist and in which prehistoric migrations left various substrata, which came to be modified to a greater or lesser degree in the historical period by the great civilizations of India, China, Islam, and Europe.

Studies of mythologies in the proper sense of the word are nevertheless still few and are carried out in dispersion, which may perhaps be explained by the extreme diversity of terrains and by the encyclopedic knowledge that an all-encompassing analysis would demand. The earliest studies on mythology were done by missionaries eager to convert "marginal" populations that had escaped Islam (Kruyt and Adriana among the Toraja, Arndt on Flores, and Schärer among the Ngaju of Kalimantan), followed by the Western, Indonesian, and Japanese ethnologists, who sometimes applied comparative or structuralist methods (Tobing among the Batak, Suzuki on Nias, Berthe among the Bunaq of Timor). The inventory is far from being completed, but the little that we know already poses fascinating problems. In a brilliant study of myths about the origins of cereals, Mabuchi suggested a possible connection with more northern mythologies in Taiwan or Japan; the studies of van Wouden on the social structures of eastern Indonesia demonstrated the value of comparison with more eastern mythologies, from Melanesia or elsewhere in the Pacific. We are just beginning to see the potential benefits of a comparative study of Indonesian and Malagasy mythologies.

For obvious reasons, the analysis of written literature (which fell within the guidelines of the philological method), especially of Javanese and Balinese literatures, which are strongly influenced by India (and written down in scripts inspired by Indian prototypes), and of Bugis and Malaysian literatures (the latter written in Arabic characters), was done by Orientalists who, while they sometimes had a good knowledge of their area, were usually looking for Indian, Persian, or Arabic influences. They therefore had difficulty in seeing how imported nomenclatures—such as that of Sanskrit—often did nothing but "dress up" earlier indigenous myths. Their scholarly publications and translations (often in Dutch) nevertheless placed a considerable corpus at the disposal of mythologists, a corpus of which the analysis has barely begun. Special mention should be made of Rassers, who, in studying the Javanese myth of Pañji, attempted to highlight those elements that were pre-Indian.

Although there are still few syntheses, we nevertheless have at our disposal some that are truly remarkable, and these allow a view of insular Southeast Asian mythologies as a whole in which numerous convergences are certainly the result of more than chance.

I. An Immense Archipelago

The religious situation in insular Southeast Asia (Malaysia, the Philippines, and Indonesia) is particularly complex.

1. In Indonesia, the great majority of the approximately 147 million inhabitants claim to be Muslim, but there are also:

—Two and one-half million Balinese Hindus, who are especially localized on Bali and western Lombok, but a few colonies have recently settled in southern Sumatra and central Celebes; furthermore, a revival of Hinduism has been observed in Java since 1965, which accounts for nearly 300,000 Hindus there by 1970.

—Buddhists, especially in Java and in certain large cities where there are large Chinese minorities. Their number is uncertain—perhaps a few hundred thousand?

—Approximately 7 million Christians of all denominations, spread over the whole country, but especially represented in certain regions or certain ethnic groups, such as the center and east of Java, among the Toba Batak, and on Nias (Sumatra), in northern Celebes, in the Central Moluccas (near Ambon), and on Timor and Flores.

—An indeterminate number of adherents of traditional (tribal) religions that have kept their full vitality only among the Karo Batak (Sumatra), among certain populations of the interior of Kalimantan (Borneo), and among the Toraja of Celebes; tribal religions are also practiced among various other small groups of the Celebes, the Moluccas, and the Lesser Sunda Islands.

But the preceding schema hardly accounts for the fluidity of the real situation, since the boundaries are not very clear. Among a great number of the followers of the great religions, archaic beliefs and practices persist, sometimes with only those modifications which are necessary to attenuate the most flagrant contradictions. This is why some observers suppose that although 90 percent of Indonesians are Muslims, perhaps no more than 30 percent are orthodox practitioners—those who are called *santri* in Java, as opposed to the *abangan,* whose popular religion is only superficially Muslim and incorporates numerous pre-Islamic elements. But this judgment is still too categorical, since many of the *santri* undoubtedly remain attached to a view of the world that is properly Indonesian, whereas many of the *abangan* attest to a real and profound attachment to Islam, even if

Infernal punishments inflicted upon adulterers and fornicators, according to Hindu-Balinese religious teachings. Detail from the decoration of the painted ceiling of the Court of Justice in Klungkung, Bali. Photo Marcel Bonneff.

they jealously preserve traditions that are in fact contradictory to it.

It is among the *abangan,* but not among them alone, that many devotees to spiritual movements (*kebatinan*) are recruited. These movements flourish especially in Java, and there are a great variety of them; some of them manifest some hostility toward Islam and seek a return to traditional or Hinduized sources, while others, on the contrary, accommodate very well to Islam and are associated with the mystical Muslim brotherhoods (*tarekat*).

2. In Malaysia, the religious situation is further complicated by the multinational character of the society, in which large Tamil, and even larger Chinese, minorities live alongside the Malays (there are almost as many Chinese as Malays in western Malaysia).

If one limits oneself to indigenous peoples (approximately 5 million people), the situation in Malaysia is somewhat comparable to that in Indonesia, with a strong Muslim majority (4.5 million), found mainly among the Malays, who are 100 percent Muslim, as well as among certain indigenous populations of Borneo (Melanau in Sarawak, Bajau in Sabah). A strong Muslim proselytism is exercised among the aboriginal populations of western Malaysia and among certain peoples of Sabah. But the traditional religions still hold solid positions in the interior of Sabah, Brunei, and Sarawak.

3. In the Philippines, the advance of Islam, which in the sixteenth century had reached the port of Manila, was halted by the Spanish colonization. It is now retrenching in a large part of Mindanao and the Sulu archipelago, where it has approximately 1.5 million followers who are still closely attached to their Malay neighbors, especially those of Sabah. Elsewhere, there was a great Christianization, so that out of a population of 38.5 million inhabitants, 29.5 million are Christian, of whom 3 million belong to a Christian church that belongs to the Philippines, the Aglipayan Church, named for its founder, Gregorio Aglipay. There are nonetheless large pockets of pagans, some 7.5 million people.

In fact, what was said above about the Muslims of Indonesia (which may to a large extent be applied to Malaysia) also holds for the Christians of the Philippines: popular religion remains permeated with native traditions.

II. The Traditional Systems

The fact that the great majority of inhabitants follow one of the great religions, Hinduism, Islam, or Christianity, does not reduce the study of the ancient religious systems to a purely historical endeavor, as these systems have had a profound influence on contemporary thought and practice; the old systems coexist alongside orthodox Islam or Christianity, persist in the form of popular traditions, or result in a true syncretism, as on Bali and, to a certain extent, Java.

1. *Cosmologies and cosmogonies.* As W. Stöhr has shown in *Les religions d'Indonesie,* the cosmological systems of Malaysia may be grouped together, despite their diversity—and despite lacunae in our knowledge—and with few exceptions, into three principal types.

a. The first, especially widespread in eastern Indonesia, is based on a dualist view of the cosmos merged with the supreme Divinity, whose unity depends on the union of two opposed and complementary principles. This is the meaning, in the central Moluccas, of the union of the male principle, Upo Lero ("Grandfather Sun"), with Upu Nusa ("Grandmother Earth"), the female principle. In the southeastern Moluccas, the union is that of a solar divinity and a lunar divinity (which is nevertheless connected with the earth). Elsewhere (Tanimbar, Adonara, Pantar, eastern Flores), there is more stress on the idea of a supreme Divinity that is simultaneously lunar and solar (as is Lera Wulan on Flores), that brings together in itself both male and female characteristics, but that is also set in opposition to a chthonic divinity of lower status.

This fundamental dualism (which may be schematized as a Male-Female or Upstream-Downstream opposition) is the basis for a general classificatory system, which is found elsewhere in regions that have long been subjected to a great religion which came from outside: Hinduism in Bali, Christianity in Ambon. By virtue of this system there is on the one hand an association of the notions of sky and Ouranian divinities, sun, day, male ancestors, younger brothers, east, upstream or the interior of a country, upper, high, right side, above, in front of, inside, contents, the ancients; on the opposite side are the notions of the earth and indigenous divinities, moon, night, female ancestors, older brothers, west, downstream or on the seacoast, lower, low, left side, below, behind, outside, container (the list may contain local variants). At the same time it should be noted that such a dualism corresponds not so much to a distribution of things into two closed classes as to a universal bipolarization which gives rise to relative oppositions: the earth, which is female in relation to the sky, is male in relation to the sea; the sun, male in relation to the moon, at the same time has a female aspect (the setting sun) which is opposed to a male aspect (the rising sun); in the same way, the moon, female in relation to the sun, also has both a male aspect (the waxing moon) and a female aspect (the waning moon). On Bali, although the demons appear upstream in relation to the gods who are downstream, the gods may nevertheless be classified as both Ouranian and chthonic gods, an opposition symbolized by the pair of Mahadewa and Dewi Sri.

It must nonetheless be stressed that, despite its negative character, the lower world is absolutely necessary to the cosmic balance. In the same way, the divinity of the lower world is fundamentally as important as that of the upper world, and the missionaries who sometimes took the name of the latter to translate the Christian idea of God did not make the best choice.

b. A second kind of cosmological system, very widespread in all the rest of Malaysia, is founded on the existence of three worlds, the higher and lower, but also the intermediate level, which is that of mankind. This last level may have been created following a battle between the higher gods and the lower gods, as among the Ngaju of Kalimantan, the inhabitants of Nias, and the Toba Batak of Sumatra; on the other hand, among the Bugis and the Toraja of Celebes, the Iban of Borneo, and the Ifugao of northern Luzon, this world seems to be as old as the other two, and apparently the most important task of the gods was to give them form, by making the earth emerge out of the middle of the primeval waters and by sending the first humans there.

In connection with this system, the number three is often preeminent in the organization of space and the house and in the political and social systems; but there is no classificatory system based on the number three that can compare with the dualist system presented above, which is latent at all times. One may thus surmise that the tripartite systems are only a particular development of the dualist system (in the same way as, in Java, the system called *moncapat* is based on four elements plus one).

c. A third type of cosmological system, much less widespread than the preceding two, is that of the original female divinity who comes from a stone and gives birth spontaneously after being fertilized by the wind, either to a son whom she then marries (Minahasa in Celebes, Rioug on Flores), or to a pair of twins who unite with one another (Nias). Or this may be conceived as a simple variant on the theme of duality in unity.

In all of these systems, a theme which appears persistently is that of the cosmic tree, the bond between sky and earth and the symbol of the whole. This theme is perpetuated in very diverse cultural contexts, as may be seen in the figure of the *kayon* in the Javanese shadow theater (or *wayang*) and in the frequent presence of sacred trees, generally the Ficus, as the central point of a village compound, or the center of a city for groups still attached to their traditional religion, as on Nias, as well as in Hindu Bali and Muslim Java—which emphasizes very well the permanence of the Malaysian concept of inhabited space as a microcosm that reproduces a macrocosm.

A meaning that is identical to that of the cosmic tree is also expressed in an equally widespread way through the union, at times in the form of a banner, of a lance, or another cold steel weapon—a masculine symbol—with cloth—a feminine symbol.

The chthonic female principle also appears very frequently in the form of a serpent or of a *nāga,* of which the masculine/Ouranian equivalent is a bird, sometimes a cock, but much more often a hornbill. Representations of these two associated beings, which form one composite being (sometimes in the form of a boat), have the same meaning as the banner and the cosmic tree.

2. *Origin myths.* The origin of men and the origin of food plants are closely associated in the myths.

a. As far as the origin of mankind is concerned, three principal (sometimes overlapping) themes may be distinguished:

—The theme of the first humans born by mistake, as the chance consequence of the activity of the primordial divinities. Thus, on Kalimantan, a battle takes place in the cosmic tree between the male hornbill and the female hornbill. Woman is born from the remains of the tree knocked down by the female hornbill, and man from the moss vomited by the male hornbill. However, in other Ngaju texts, this birth is said to be willed by the higher Divinity.

—The theme of the first humans fashioned by a divine demiurge from earth (Murut), or, less often, from bark (Bahau) or from gold (Toraja).

—The theme of the first humans born from a divine couple (Batak, Nias, Bugis, Bunaq, Ifugao).

The first humans are generally "celestial humans," who

Public reading of the Koran in Parit Mukuasang, Johore state, Malaysia. Photo Christian Pelras.

The cover of a modern Javanese work on the history of Rama with a representation of a *kayon* or *ganungan*. This accessory from the shadow theater is sometimes considered a symbol of both the "cosmic mountain" and the "tree of life."

are then supposed (or whose children are supposed) to descend to the intermediate world. The descent sometimes corresponds to the establishment of the world as an inhabitable territory, which is often shown as emerging from the primordial waters or as floating on them; this is followed more or less directly by an episode which accounts for the break in physical relations between the human world and spiritual worlds.

b. It is usually soon after the descent of the first men onto the earth that the myths recount the appearance of death and the origin of food plants.

Toichi Mabuchi gave evidence of the existence in insular Southeast Asia of three types of myths, of which two are particularly well represented in Malaysia:

—Myths of the first type tell of the celestial origin of food plants that may either have been produced at the same time as men (Batak, Toraja) or received as a gift (Ifugao, western Toraja, Ceram, Sumba, Tetun, Bali), or stolen (western Toraja, Minahasa, Ngaju).

—The second type is the one according to which food plants come from the body of a hero, and especially that of a heroine, whose death is often the first death in this world, whether the person dies naturally (Bugis, Sumba), or is killed (Banggai, Tempasuk, Ceram, Adonara), or has voluntarily sacrificed himself (Java, Sunda) or has been allowed to sacrifice (western Toraja, Tetun, Atoni, Sika, Lamaholat, Adonara, Alor).

—The third type, according to which the cultivated plants were taken or received from the lower world, is rarely found in Malaysia. Mabuchi gives only one example of this, from Kei. In fact, this type only appears in the area in which myths of the second type are more strongly represented, i.e., in eastern Indonesia and Java, where the sacrificed individual is always connected with the lower, female half of the cosmos. On the other hand, rituals of human sacrifice and headhunting, connected with the cultivation of rice, were reserved, as van Wouden has shown, for the male half.

So we note, in spite of some overlap, a definite contrast between eastern insular Southeast Asia (the Moluccas, the Lesser Sunda Islands, and Java), in which myths that assert the chthonic aspect of rice predominate, and western insular Southeast Asia (Sumatra, Kalimantan, Celebes, Philippines), in which, by contrast, myths that affirm the celestial origin of rice predominate.

An analysis of the relations between the two systems and of their distribution among the various ethnic groups still remains to be done.

Often grafted upon the diverse origin myths are the adventures of certain culture heroes (such as Mau Ipi Guloq for the Bunaq of Timor, Sawerigading for the Bugis of

Celebes, Sese nTaola for the Bare'e Toraja, also of Celebes, or of Borneo, Seraguntung for the Iban, and Silai for the Ngaju), which furnish the societies in question with a kind of archetype of the ideal hero, but which serve just as often as foundations for ritual and for the rules of social organization (particularly for marriage rules).

3. *Myths of social and political organization.* Throughout Malaysia, there are myths that connect the traditional forms of social and political organization with the events that befell the first ancestors.

For eastern Indonesia, these myths (at least those published before 1935) were analyzed by van Wouden in his study of the social structures of the region. They account for the origins of clans, their hierarchy, and their political functions, which correspond, according to van Wouden, to a double dualism: a functional dualism, founded on the opposition between a male moiety, connected with the earth and with warlike activities, and a female moiety, connected with the lower world and with agriculture; and a cosmic dualism that set in opposition a celestial moiety, devoted to spiritual matters, and a terrestrial moiety, devoted to profane matters.

When the two dualisms are superimposed, this is translated into the political sphere through the existence of a double rule: one chief, qualified as "feminine" (even though the chief is a man), who is either the master or the superintendent of the soil, is charged with the relations with the divine world and with certain agrarian rites and is considered the elder; and a "masculine" chief, who is the real holder of direct power, is charged with political matters and is responsible for the conduct of war; he is considered the younger (Sumba).

When the two dualist systems intersect instead of being superimposed, one finds more complex political systems. For example, to an (elder) spiritual chief two (younger) profane chiefs may be set in opposition, one feminine and connected with agriculture and the other masculine and connected with war.

For the other regions, there are no overall studies. It nevertheless appears that there is quite a broad variety of types of myths in this sphere, as a function of each society's type of organization.

In the unilinear societies of western Indonesia, the existence of different clans may be connected with the appearance of a certain number of ancestors, generally brothers, who were born on earth of the first parents of celestial origin (Batak), or who descended simultaneously from the sky onto different points in the region (Nias). The clans that result from them each have their own mythic histories, but they are not basically hierarchical, and their dualism is not as clear as in eastern Indonesia.

In the bilateral societies that are found in most cases (Java, part of Sumatra, Malaysia, Borneo, Celebes, the Philippines), it is mainly a matter of accounting for the boundaries of territorial units and, in extreme cases, of justifying the existence of a social hierarchy and of a certain type of political organization.

Among the Ngaju of Borneo, the nobles (*utus gantong*) are connected with Mahatala and the upper world, and the common people with Jata and the lower world. Among the Bugis, by contrast, all of humanity has its origin in the spiritual world (as much higher as lower); but the nobility comes from "white-blooded beings," *tomanurung* (descended from the sky) or *totompo'* (arisen from the depths), while the common people descend from the servants who accompanied the first *tomanurung*, Batara Guru, to earth. The *toma-*

Statue of Durga, called *Loro Jonggrang*, "the slender young woman," in the temple of Prambanan (Central Java). An offering left at the base of the statue can be seen in the photo, though the inhabitants of the area are officially adherents of Islam. Photo Christian Pelras.

A Javanese family on pilgrimage at a consecrated burial place. Kramat. Note the incense burner and the flower petals scattered on the tomb. Photo Marcel Bonneff.

nurung and *totompo'* are also the source of the principal estates, of which they were the first lords, and of which the continuity is marked by the *regalia* which are supposed to have descended from the sky with them and which are the hereditary wealth of the collective group and the guarantor of its continuity and prosperity (*arajang*): swords, banners, cloth, plows, etc.

III. The Impact of the Great Religions

Since the fifth century, but especially from the seventh century to the fifteenth, the Malay archipelago experienced a penetration which historians have called an Indianization. Perhaps following the closing of the Central Asian route (in the period of the great invasions), certain elements of Indian society (Brahmans, Kṣatriyas, and merchants) sailed in the direction of the Southeast Asian shores and contributed to the development of Indianized kingdoms, which were generally based on the cultivation of irrigated rice and which were strongly influenced by the great religions of Indian origin: Hinduism and Buddhism. The kingdoms are known to us now especially through the great temples that they left and through a rich epigraphy, sometimes in Sanskrit and always in scripts derived from Indian models.

This was a phenomenon of particularly long duration (nearly a millennium) and great complexity, which looked very different in different periods and which should in no case be considered a colonization of the region by India (which never had political control there). It should also be pointed out that although the Indianization also touched several regions of the Indo-Chinese peninsula (especially Cambodia, where the kingdom of Angkor flourished from the ninth century to the fourteenth), it took in only a few islands of the archipelago, essentially Bali and Java, as well as certain regions of Sumatra. Elsewhere Indian civilization echoed, in a more and more muted way, through the intermediary of Java. Although it is attenuated, the echo is sometimes encountered far away and in unexpected places. In 1971 in the southern Philippines a completely isolated people was discovered who had a very primitive technology: the Tasaday. People were all ready to congratulate themselves for having found a veritable "isolate," a witness to prehistoric times, until it was discovered that they designated some supernatural force by the term *dewata,* which is derived from the well-known Sanskrit term for "divinity."

The effect of the arrival of the great Indian religions was to change earlier mythologies; the pantheons were restructured as the Indian heroes—especially those of the great epics—gained a footing on the islands. On the one hand, the *wayang* ("shadow theater"), which must originally have been a ritual to evoke the ancestors, was enriched by the entire mythology of the *Rāmāyaṇa* and especially of the *Mahābhārata;* on the other hand, a written literature appeared which sought to adapt into the vernaculars (Javanese and Balinese) the great legendary themes of the Indian subcontinent. Thus there was a *Rāmāyaṇa* in Old Javanese from the ninth century, and an adaptation, also in Old Javanese, with the title of *Bharatayuddha,* of the story of the fratricidal war between the Pandawas and Kuruwas, from the twelfth century. A quite complex ritual syncretism developed in a parallel fashion.

In no case is this a simple importation of Indian mythologies; the indigenous element remained very much present under the new facade. So it is that the fourteenth and fifteenth centuries saw a development of the cult of Bima, regarded as a savior hero, of whom only a few characteristics were borrowed from India. Parallel to this, it seems that Sadewa (the twin brother of Nakula, who in the *Mahābhārata* plays quite a self-effacing role) also enjoyed a great popularity in this period. In a general sense, at the end of Majapahit there is a renaissance of mythologies from the indigenous substratum, and it is probably around this date that the famous myth of Pañji—which may be a resurgence of an ancient myth of social organization common to the whole eastern part of the archipelago—takes shape and spreads as far as Cambodia and Siam. Far from abolishing the substratum, the greatest effect of Indianization was to dress it up and brighten it with sumptuous colors. Many of the gods of ancient Java, such as Semar and even Ratu Kidul, survived without damage and even benefited from the prestigious transposition.

What complicates the matter somewhat is the fact that this Indianized stratum is no longer directly accessible today, except perhaps on the little island of Bali, on which Hinduism has continued to develop by itself, thus revealing amalgams in a discourse of Indian tonality, with certain chunks torn out in prehistory. Elsewhere a new layer came to cover the Hindu layer in a general way; starting in the thirteenth century (in northern Sumatra), and especially from the fourteenth century onward, Islam moved silently onto all of the shores of the archipelago and from there spread widely into the interior. On Java, the very old Indianized kingdoms were remodeled, even as they preserved a large part of their ancient mythology; the *wayang* was largely preserved intact, and certain collective rites of the preceding period were conserved until now, with, as in the case of the *garebeg,* for example, very few modifications. Elsewhere Islam took root directly in the substratum and, as in many other regions of the Muslim world, was able to adapt very well in assimilating many of the pagan rituals. The *kramat,* or sacred, i.e., miraculous, tombs, the objects of numerous pilgrimages, recall the cult of the saints or Maraboutism, well known elsewhere; here it represents a considerable concession to the cult of the ancestors, immanent throughout the archipelago and always near. The Islamic fast overlays a notion that already existed and is called *puasa,* which is nothing but a variant of the Sanskrit term *upavasa;* circumcision (*sunat*) also existed in more than one region at an earlier time. As for ritual prayer, in Indonesia this is often called *sembahyang,* "to place one's hands together before the *yang,*" i.e., before the paranatural force that the *wayang* already intended to evoke. Here too there was syncretism and often conservatism. It was only in the beginning of the twentieth century that an orthodox tendency, stimulated by pan-Islamicism, sought to purify Indonesian Islam by removing all of the "dross" from it.

Christianity played only a minor role in Indonesia. The Dutch prohibited the "Papists" from proselytizing and were not interested in converting those under their jurisdiction. Things changed slightly toward the end of the nineteenth century, and a few Catholic and Protestant missionaries were able to convert to their religion certain regions that had generally remained outside of Islam. Here too there was often syncretism; in Java sacred history was portrayed in the form of the *wayang;* in Toraja country, a paper cross was put between the horns of the buffalo sacrificed to the ancestors.

Also to be noted is a complete messianic mythology, still alive now, and, since the time of independence (1945), the setting up of a "national" mythology that brings together a collective pantheon and, through the intermediary of an ad hoc committee, all the "national heroes" (*pahlawan nasional*) who worked in various provinces in the anticolonial struggle and to bring modern Indonesia into existence.

D.L. and C.P./d.w.

BIBLIOGRAPHY

W. STÖHR and P. ZOETMULDER, *Les religions d'Indonésie* (Paris 1968).

1. The Traditional Systems

P. ARNDT, Mythologie, Religion und Magie im Sikagebiet. östl. Mittelflores (Endeh, Indonesia, 1932). R. F. BARTON, *The Mythology of the Ifugaos* (Philadelphia 1955). L. BERTHE, *Bei Gua, Itinéraire des Ancêtres, Mythes des Bunaq de Timor* (Paris 1972). J. DERAEDT, "Religious Representations in Northern Luzon," *St. Louis Quarterly* 2, 3 (1964). E. JENSEN, *The Iban and Their Religion* (Oxford 1974). A. E. JENSEN, *Die drei ströme: Züge aus dem geistigen und religiösen Leben der Wemale* (Leipzig 1948). P. E. DE JOSSELIN DE JONG, ed., *Structural Anthropology in the Netherlands: A Reader* (The Hague 1977). T. MABUCHI, "Tales concerning the Origins of Grains in the Insular Area of Eastern and South Eastern Asia," *Asian Folklore Studies* 23, 1 (1964). CH. MACDONALD, "Mythe de création Palawan," *Archipel* 8 (1974): 91–118. W. MÜNSTERBERGER, *Ethnologische Studien an Indonesischen Schöpfungsmythen* (The Hague 1939). C. H. M. NOOY-PALM, "Introduction to the Sa'dan Toraja People and Their Country," *Archipel* 10 (1975): 53–92. H. SCHÄRER, *Ngaju Religion: The Conception of God among a South Borneo People* (The Hague 1963). P. SUZUKI, *The Religious System and Culture of Nias* (The Hague 1959). PH. L. TOBING, *The Structure of the Toba-Batak Belief in the High God* (Amsterdam 1956). J. A. J. VERHEIJEN, *Het Hoogste wezen bij de Manggareijers* (Vienna 1951). F. A. E. VAN WOUDEN, *Types of Social Structure in Eastern Indonesia* (The Hague 1968).

2. The Impact of the Major Religions

B. R. O'G. ANDERSON, *Mythology and the Tolerance of the Javanese* (Ithaca, NY, 1965). M. BONNEFF, "Le renouveau d'un rituel royal: Les Garebeg à Yogyakarta," *Archipel* 8 (1974): 119–46. M. COVARRUBIAS, *Island of Bali* (New York 1938) (numerous editions). G. W. J. DREWES, *Drie Javaansche Goeroes; hun leven, onderricht en messiasprediking* (Leiden 1925). C. GEERTZ, *The Religion of Java* (Glencoe, IL, 1960). R. GORIS, *Bijdrage tot de kennis der Oud-Javaansche en Balinesche theologie* (Leiden 1926). K. G. P. H. HADIWIDJOJO, "Danse sacrée à Surakarta: La signification du Bedojo ketawang," *Archipel* 3 (1972): 117–30. HARDJOWIROGO, *Sedjarah Wajang Purwa* (Jakarta 1965). K. A. H. HIDDING, *Gebruiken en godsdienst der Soendaneezen* (Batavia 1935). C. HOOYKAAS, *Āgama-Tīrtha: Five Studies in Hindu-Balinese Religion* (Amsterdam 1964). J. KATS, *Het Javaansche toneel* (Weltevreden 1923). CL. LOMBARD-SALMON, "A propos de quelques cultes chinois particuliers à Java," *Arts asiatiques* 26 (1973): 244–48. MANGKUNEGORO VII, *On the Wayang Kulit (Purwa) and Its Symbolic and Mystical Elements* (Ithaca, NY, 1957). TH. PIGEAUD, *Javaansche Volksvertoningen* (Batavia 1938). R. M. NG. POERBATJARAKA, *9 Pandjiverhalen onderling vergeleken* (Bandung 1940). J. J. RAS, "The Panji Romance and W. H. Rassers' Analysis of Its Theme," *BKI* 129 (1973): 411–56. W. H. RASSERS, *De Pandji-Roman* (Antwerp 1922); *Pañji, the Culture Hero* (The Hague 1959). D. A. RINKES, "De heiligen van Java," six articles in *TBG* 53–55 (1911–13). SENO SASTROAMIDJOJO, *Renungan tentang Pertunjukan Wajang Kulit* (Jakarta 1964). P. J. VAN LEEUWEN, *De Maleise Alexander Roman* (Utrecht 1937). P. WIRZ, *Der Totenkult auf Bali* (Stuttgart 1928). R. WINSTEDT, *A History of Classical Malay Literature* (2d ed., Oxford 1969). P. ZOETMULDER, *Kalangwan: A Survey of Old Javanese Literature* (The Hague 1974).

Divine Totality and Its Components: The Supreme Deity, the Divine Couple, and the Trinity in Indonesian Religions

Although the traditional religions of insular Southeast Asia have highly diverse pantheons, and although each has an original character that should not be underestimated, it is nonetheless possible to highlight certain constants and in particular to distinguish several types of deities.

Some deities probably represent totality, both divine and cosmic, while others represent the components of that totality, in the form of a divine couple in systems that are fundamentally dualistic, or of a trinity where the tripartite system prevails.

I. Various Examples

Among the Toba Batak of Sumatra, for example, the primordial deity, Mula Jadi na Bolon, was interpreted by P. L. Tobing as the expression of totality, encompassing the upper world, the middle world, and the lower world, in which it is manifested in the persons of three deities: Ompunta Tuan Bubi na Bolon, Raja Pinangkabo, and Naga Padoha (the serpent of the lower world). Its symbol is the cosmic tree that links the three worlds together. Out of the eggs of a bird created by the totality emerges a second trinity that is entrusted with the responsibility of governing the world. It consists of Batara Guru (the deity attached to the upper world), Soripada (the deity attached to the middle world), and Mangalabulan (the deity attached to the lower world). A fourth deity, Debata Asi-Asi (the "compassionate god"), is said to incarnate the totality of the triad. For Tobing, this triad also symbolizes the three basic clans of the marriage system of generalized exchange: Soripada represents a man's clan of reference (*dongan sabutuha*), Batara Guru represents the clan from which he receives his women (*hula-hula*), and Mangalabulan, the one to which he gives his women (*boru*). In this interpretation, Debata Asi-Asi represents society in its totality, a world parallel to the cosmos.

On Nias, a primordial divine couple is made up of Lature Danö and Lowalangi. Lature Danö, the deity of the lower world, is associated with the negative aspects of the cosmos—evil, darkness, death—with the color black and the moon, and is symbolized by the snake. Lowangali, the deity of the upper world, is associated with the positive aspects of the cosmos—good, light, life—with gold and the sun, and is symbolized by the cock or the hornbill. These two deities are considered brothers, but the myths about their origins differ widely. In northern Nias, they are said to have been born from the cosmic tree (*toro'a*), from which seven other spirits also came. In southern Nias, their mother is said to be Inada Samadulo Hosi (they have no father), who came out of a rock which was the body of the first entity, Inada Samihara Luwo. In a third story, however, where they have the names of Bauwa Danö and Luo Mewöna, they are the sons of the primordial god Sirao. Lature Danö and Lowalangi are simultaneously opposed and closely linked. According to P. Suzuki, this unity within duality is symbolized by the ambiguous character of Silewe Nazarata, simultaneously the sister and the wife of Lowalangi, but also allied with Lature Danö, simultaneously benevolent and disturbing and sometimes represented by a two-faced and bisexual statue. The priests and priestesses are her disciples, and it is she who taught men the rituals of war and introduced the use of statues (*adu*).

Among the Ngaju of Borneo, the primordial divine couple is formed by Jata and Mahatala. Jata (whose complete name is Bawim Jata Balawang Bulan) is the female deity of the

In the main enclosure of Balinese temples, in the most prestigious corner, oriented in relation to the mountain toward kaja-kangin (generally northeast), it is increasingly common to find an oratory in the shape of an empty throne, as above. This oratory, formerly dedicated to Surya, the solar deity, is now usually designated as Sang Hyang Widi Wasa, the undifferentiated Divine Totality. Photo Christian Pelras.

lower world, symbolized by the water snake (hence her former name, Tambon), the moon, or the sacred cloth. Mahatala, the male deity of the upper world, appears in the form of the hornbill (Tingan), the sun, or the sacred spear. She reigns at the bottom of the primordial waters, he on top of the sacred mountain (or else she is on top of the Mountain of Gold and he on top of the Mountain of Diamonds). The union of Jata and Mahatala corresponds to the supreme deity Tambon Haruei Bungai, "the water snake which is one with the hornbill," represented by the mystical boat shaped like the body of a snake, with its prow and stern shaped like the head and tail of a bird. This deity is also symbolized by the red and white banner, the union of the sacred spear and the sacred cloth; by the *sanggaran* or the *keramen,* poles erected during funerary festivals and head-hunting rituals, poles that stand next to the representations of the hornbill and the snake; and, finally, by the three-branched tree of life or cosmic tree. In the cosmic tree at the beginning of time there was a bitter struggle between a male and female hornbill, the emanation of the double deity, out of which the first human couple was born.

The mythology of the southeastern Moluccas is dominated by the divine couple Upu Lero and Upu Nusa. Upu Lero ("grandfather sun") corresponds to the male principle, Upu Nusa ("grandmother earth") to the female principle, and the world was engendered by their union, commemorated each year by the great communal feast of *porka*. The supreme deity, It Matromna, much more remote and never addressed directly, must surely be seen as representing divine totality, and the fig tree by which the rites and sacrifices of the *porka* used to take place, as well as the banner raised on that occasion, must be symbols of that totality.

Among the Lamaholot of the islands of eastern Flores, Adonara and Solor, the relationship between duality and unity is less clearly defined. Their principal deity is Lera Wulan, whose name means "Sun-Moon," but it is not clear whether this double name expresses an original duality. This is a male celestial deity whose female counterpart is Tana Ekan, Mother Earth, born of the primordial waters, whose union with Lera Wulan was at the origin of the world.

Among the Iban of Borneo, we can again clearly see the existence of a dialectical relation between a deity of totality that differentiates itself and acts in the form of a divine couple. One version of the Iban myth states that the primordial deity Entala, sometimes called Gantallah, is a spirit "without limbs" which of its own will created two birds, one male and one female, sometimes called Ara and Irik, who fly over the primordial waters. One created the earth, the other the sky. But the earth was a little too big, and as Ara and Irik compressed it to make it fit into the sky, they made mountains burst out. Plants grew, and Ara and Irik created the first human couple. Another version says that they were created by Entala himself, but in both cases, after men appear on earth, Entala no longer participates in the subsequent acts of creation, which are then entrusted to the two Petaras, who may be another expression of the divine couple of the cosmology.

The kinship between this Iban myth and certain myths of the Philippines is rather striking, since several northern Luzon groups also know a primordial deity named Batala or Lumawig and express the idea of the creation of the world by the intercession of two birds. Nevertheless, the overall data from this region give the impression of much less clearly structured systems. In particular, while it is possible to recognize the existence of primordial deities similar to the Entala of the Iban retired into inactivity, we see no sign of deities that reflect a dualist or tripartite system.

For instance, the inhabitants of Palawan (another island of the Philippines) have a supreme deity called Ampuq, lord of the world, who has not intervened in the world since creation. At the request of the "Man of Dust," and with the help of his golden scarf, Ampuq created the earth and the sky, light, water, stars, the sea, air, and wind, and with the help of his betel quid he created man and all living creatures, whom he entrusted to the Man of Dust. In another version, he uses some earth and animates with his breath first the intercessor Diwata and then the first human couple. In yet a third version, he entrusts to the Man of Dust the task of creating Diwata, who is the protector of humanity; it is from him that the shamans draw their power and with him that they establish contact.

II. Tutelary Deities

This brings us to a third type of deity, the tutelary deities, who are often thought to be at the origin of the first humans, or at least linked to men from the very start, and with whom men have a much closer relationship than with the primordial deities. As we have seen, this is true of the Diwata of Palawan. Among some other groups in the Philippines, a similar role is attributed to Kabunian.

In fact, for some of the peoples of northern Luzon (Philippines), among them the Kalinga and the Nabaloi of Kabayan, Kabunian is the name of the principal deity, who is male, the initiator of rituals and of culture, and the guarantor of ethical laws. Among the Nabaloi he is often associated with, but never confused with, Akou, the solar deity connected with the funeral rites, and he stands in opposition and complementarity to Kabigat, another male deity, who dispenses wealth and is connected with agrarian cults and head-hunting. Kabunian, by contrast, is credited with putting an end to this practice. For the Tinguian, Kabunian is a tutelary deity, distinct from god the creator, Kadaklan, and subordinate to him. On the other hand, among the western Nabaloi and the Kankanay, *kabuniyan* is only a general term for "deity," while the Ifugao use it to designate the celestial world as a whole.

Similarly, for the Toraja of the south Celebes (Indonesia), Puang Matua, the "Old Master," "god of the center of the firmament, lord of the rising sun," is not the first god. He is the son of the goddess Simbolon Manik and the god Usuk Sangbamban, who was born of a rib of Gauntikembong, lord of the celestial world. According to another version, his mother's name was Puang Tudang, and his father, Puang Basi-Basian, was born of the union between the sky and the earth, for originally sky and earth touched one another. He is nevertheless the most important deity for humans, and myths tell how his wife, Arrang Dibatu, who was born from a rock, sent him west to look for the gold which was used to make a pair of bellows for a piston-operated forge (*sauan sibarrung*) that he used to make his own creation: by putting a fistful of pebbles in the bellows, he made the sun, the moon, and the stars; then, using flakes of gold in the same way, he created animals, plants, water, iron, rice, and finally Datu Laukku, the celestial ancestor of man. One of his children, Pong Mula Tau, was the first man to descend to earth, and he brought with him the original ritual (*aluk*).

Finally, certain deities are felt to be even closer to men because they lived among them during a certain time in their history. This is particularly true of the female deities at the time of the origin of food plants, which in a way are the earthly aspect of the primordial female deity.

We can judge the importance accorded to such deities by the survival of the cult of Roro Kidul or Ratu Kidul in Java, despite Islam. She is the "queen of the south" (*ratu,* "queen"; *roro,* or *loro,* "young woman"; *kidul,* "south"), the pre-Indian female deity who is reputed to have ruled over the southern coast of Java, where the currents and shifting sands are extremely dangerous and harbors are rare. Like another Lorelei, she lures imprudent sailors to her and is worshiped by fishermen, as well as by collectors of swallow nests, who risk their lives climbing down a rope alongside a cliff to gather the precious product. She has such a cult at Karang Bolong (fifty kilometers east of Cilacap), where offerings are placed in front of her "bed" before each new harvest. One carefully avoids wearing green garments near the coast because they would offend the queen.

But the influence of Roro Kidul is not felt only at this popular level. According to a well-established tradition, confirmed by chronicles dating back to the seventeenth century, the founder of the current Mataram dynasty, the famous Senapati (1575–1601), deliberately sought an alliance with the queen and with all the evil spirits that obey her. One night as he was meditating near the sea at a place called Parang Tritis, south of Yogyakarta, she appeared to him and they coupled. Since then, Roro Kidul continues to lend her unfailing support to Senapati's descendants, who alone have the privilege of seeing her. Several particularly sacred rituals are observed in the courts of central Java to this day to

Rite of *labuhan* celebrated in 1972 at Parang Kusuma, near Parangtritis, southern coast of Java. Immersion of offerings to Roro Kidul, a female spirit who rules over the "South Sea." Photo Marcel Bonneff.

commemorate this hierogamy. On the anniversary of his accession to the throne, the king attends a sacred dance called *bedoyo ketawang*, with nine female dancers and Roro Kidul, whom he alone sees. On the king's birthday, one of his garments is solemnly carried to Parang Tritis and cast into the water (*nglabuh*). Finally, the queen comes to visit humans with all her retinue, and her passage is manifested by a particularly violent storm (*lampor*).

D.L. and C.P./g.h.

The Origin of Humanity and the Descent to Earth of the First Human Beings in the Myths of Indonesia

One of the important episodes in the "geneses" of insular Southeast Asia is the one that tells of the first settlement of the ancestors of mankind on earth. Whether the first human beings were created inadvertently or were begotten by a primordial couple, many myths tenaciously affirm their divine descent.

This is evident, for example, in the Batak myth that ascribes the origin of humanity to the goddess Si Boru Deak Parujar, the daughter of the deity of the upper world, Batara Guru. Her older sister, Sorbayati, was supposed to marry Raja Odap-Odap, the son of Mangalabulan, the brother of Batara Guru and the god of the lower world. But Odap-Odap preferred the younger sister, Si Boru Deak Parujar, and out of shame, Sorbayati threw herself off the roof of Batara Guru's house during a dance. From her body, bamboo and rattan were born. Eager to escape from Raja Odap-Odap, who looked like a lizard, Si Boru Deak Parujar descended into the middle world among the primordial waters, and with the help of the supreme deity, Mula Jadi na Bolon, she arranged the first earth, fixing it solidly onto the back of the snake of the depths, Naga Padoha. Then she agreed to marry Raja Odap-Odap, who had finally taken on a human form. From their union (although other traditions claim that it was "from a mushroom born of the tears of Si Boru Deak Parujar," or "from a bird's egg from which the principal deities emerged") was born the first human couple, the twins Si Raja Ihat Manisia and Si Boru Ihat Manisia. When these two grew up they married, their parents returned to heaven, and the link that once united the middle and upper worlds was broken. The first human couple settled in the village of Si Anjur Mula-Mula at the foot of Mount Pusuk Buhit, to the west of Lake Samosir, and founded a family. One of their children, Si Raja Batak, was the ancestor of all the Batak. He received the first *tunggal panaluan,* the magic wand of the Batak diviner, which symbolizes the unity of the three cosmic principles and of the three primary colors. He had two sons, Guru Tatea Bulan and Raja Isumbaon, the ancestors of the two phratries into which Batak society is ideally divided; both were specialists, one in sacred matters and the other in profane matters. They were associated with the moon and the sun, respectively. From them came the eight fundamental Batak clans (five from the first and three from the second), on which the total of approximately three hundred present-day *margas* (subclans) is based.

On Nias, the mythical ancestors of the inhabitants of the island, to whom one can trace back all genealogies, are Daeli, Gözo, Hia, and Hulu. The points where they descended from heaven are marked by a temple and a sacred tree, where their descendants gather together periodically to celebrate the community festival of Börö N'adu. Hia was the first to come down, and he landed in the south, which made the earth tilt; then Gözo landed in the north, and this area also sank under the primordial waters, while the middle of the island was raised. Hulu and Daeli then came down, and the earth finally flattened out. As for their origin, one tradition claims that they were the children of the god Sirao and the half brothers of Bauwa Danö (Lature Danö) and Luo Mewöna (Lowalangi). However, according to other traditions mankind came either from the goddess Inada Dao or from a first couple that were born from the division of a child without limbs, who had been born to Lowalangi and a daughter of Lature Danö. In fact, these contradictory versions probably express the same idea: that mankind participates in divine and cosmic totality, and that it harbors within itself simultaneously the contradictory aspects of a basic dualism.

A similar interpretation may also be given to the myth of the Ngaju, where the battle fought by a male and a female hornbill (a symbol of duality) in the cosmic tree (a symbol of totality) triggers the birth of the first woman (born of fragments from the tree felled by the female) and the first man (who arose from the foam vomited by the male). The village where they settled, Batu Nindan Tarong, in the middle of the primordial waters, was naturally not yet of our world, but was rather a prototype of villages to come. The real first man was the couple's last child, Maharaja Buno. He came down to earth and became the ancestor of human beings after he created a wife out of clay. The fact that he was the brother of the ancestors of pigs, dogs, chickens, and spirits shows to what extent mankind is felt to be in close communication with nature as well as with the supernatural.

In these myths, the first earth upon which the first human beings settled seems to spring up from the middle of the primordial waters. The aquatic theme is sometimes replaced by the theme of the flood, in which one should not be too quick to see any Western influence.

Thus, in the story of Bugan and Wigan, the first couple and the ancestors of the Ifugao of northern Luzon in the Philippines, one version claims that they are the children of Kabigat and Bugan, two deities of the upper world (*kabunian*). Eager to populate the middle world (*pugao*), they sent their two children into the forest to pick tubers and then unleashed a flood that took them upstream (*daiya*) into this world. In order to ensure their survival, they sent after them a house with a granary of rice, pigs, chickens, cats, dogs, and full jars. At the start, the couple respected the prohibition against incest, but one day Bigan had sexual relations with his sister while she was asleep. At first their heavenly parents were angry, but then they consented to the marriage, from which four daughters and five sons were born. In order to lead them to perpetuate the line of descendants, the sons and daughters were brought up in separate villages. When they reached adulthood, they married, but after that marriages between brothers and sisters were forbidden. In another version, Kabigat and Bugan are the first couple, born of the supreme deity known as the celestial Wigan. Their progeny became so numerous that the earth was overpopulated, whereupon the celestial Wigan unleashed a flood, of which the only survivors were two of the children of Kabigat and Bugan, here named Balitok and Bugan.

Among the Iban of Borneo, we also find the story of Dayang Raca, the sole survivor of a flood that drowned all the rest of the original humans. Impregnated by the flame of

Shrine in the shape of a tomb, known as Puang Sanro, South Celebes. Here worshipers commemorate the reascent to heaven of Batara Guru, who rose again from this spot and was the first man, son of the prince of gods, in Bugis mythology. Photo Christian Pelras.

a fire that she had lit (which was nothing but a manifestation of Kucok, the spirit of fire), she gave birth to a child that had only half a body, and she named it Simpang Impang ("Half-gone"). When he grew up and despaired of his infirmity, Simpang Impang tried to drown himself but was pulled out of the water by a strange creature, Indai Jebua, who turned out to be the spirit of vermin. When he had lived with her for a while, he left her; she gave him a present of three enormous grains of rice, but the wind made them fall, and they broke into small pieces the size of actual grains of rice.

The myth of origin of the Bugis of the Celebes, at least as it has come down to us, contains far fewer elements susceptible to a "cosmic" interpretation (although it refers to a union between the upper world and the lower world). According to the Bugis texts, the first man to come down from heaven was not the ancestor of all of humanity but only the ancestor of the princely families. The myth describes how the deities of the upper and lower worlds decided one day to people the middle world (the earth), so that there might be human beings to recognize their divinity and serve them. The principal deity of the upper world, Patoto'e ("he who fixes destinies"), designated for this mission his oldest son, La Toge 'langi', who has the title of Batara Guru. Placed inside the hollow part of a bamboo tube, Batara Guru, during his descent and in accordance with his father's instructions, gave form to the earth and disseminated plant and animal species. After landing on earth at Luwu' on the Gulf of Bone, he first submitted to two weeks of asceticism and fasting, and then servants who came from heaven helped him to break the soil and plant the first crops. After three months, his wives descended to earth, together with his palace and the mass of his commoner subjects, who constituted the first generation of humans (thus also of heavenly origin, but from the very beginning of lower rank). Then, as he had been promised, out of the waters of the sea emerged his first cousin We Nyili' Timo, the daughter of the principal deity of the lower world, who became his principal wife.

The first child of Batara Guru, born of one of his secondary wives, was a daughter who died within seven days. From her body rice was born, whose spirit was from then on revered under the name of Sangiang Serri. Other children were born of his other wives, and finally We Nyili' Timo gave birth to the one who would inherit the kingdom of Luwu', Batara Lattu. When he reached adulthood, Batara Lattu married his cousin We Opu Sengngeng, the princess of Tompo' Tikka' (the land of the rising sun), whose father and mother, just like his own, had come down from the upper world and up from the lower world, respectively. From this marriage was born a set of twins: a boy, Sawerigading, who was the future culture hero of the Bugis, and a girl, We Tenriabeng. On the day when the two children were solemnly placed in their suspended cradle (the ceremony that marks the entrance of all Bugis children into society), Batara Guru's reign on earth ended. He returned to the upper world, followed by his wives, and Batara Lattu took his place as king of Luwu'.

D.L. and C.P./g.h.

Culture Heroes of Insular Southeast Asia

Throughout the entire world of insular Southeast Asia, every single ethnic or social group identifies itself with a particular culture hero. The exemplary adventures of these figures are first told in connection with the basic myths of each group, to whom they represent in some way an ideal personification transported back to a period when the divine world and the human world still maintained a special relationship.

The disappearance or the replacement of old religious or cultural systems by new ways of thinking does not necessarily presuppose their dismissal. They can survive and even maintain a surprising vitality under the convenient cover of tales of a national character (such as Sawerigading among the Islamized Bugis for three and a half centuries), or a popular character (like Pañji among the Javanese). But new culture heroes can also be born and can incarnate, next to the old, new values or ideals. Such is the case, in Indonesia and in Malaysia, with certain Islamic heroes, images of the ideal Muslim, but also introducers and guarantors of a new order, just as the ancient culture heroes had introduced fundamental rituals guaranteeing the fertility of men and crops. And one may wonder whether the new *pahlawan nasional* ("national heroes") are not, in their own way, additional culture heroes. Let us therefore distinguish between four types of heroes.

I. Heroes of Oral Myths

The first, dearest to anthropologists, is the hero of oral myths—of whom we will not, in such a restricted space, present a detailed analysis; rather it will suffice to evoke a few representative examples.

One such example is Mau Ipi Guloq. He is the culture hero of the Bunaq of Timor, the first man to domesticate the buffalo. He and his brother Asan Paran had trapped two wild sows, who then transformed themselves into women. But his brother kept them for himself, and in anger Mau Ipi Guloq went his separate way. One day, using the golden blowpipe that Asan Paran had lent him, Mau Ipi Guloq was hunting a crow that had been bothering his buffalo. He wounded the bird, and it flew away with a golden arrow in its body. Setting out to look for it, Mau Ipi Guloq descended into the lower world, whose ruler was ailing. Offering to take care of him, Mau Ipi Guloq noticed that his arrow was the cause of the illness. He succeeded in retrieving the arrow and replacing it with a bamboo arrow soaked in his betel pouch. As payment, he was given two oranges from a tree of the lower world, which changed into princesses.

Asan Paran proposed exchanging one of his wives for one of the princesses; when his brother refused, he plotted his murder and finally succeeded in killing him by making him fall to the bottom of a ravine. Mau Ipi Guloq's wives found him and were able to resuscitate him by using oil brought from the lower world. He went home refreshed and rejuvenated. Asan Paran asked that a bath also be prepared for him that would make him look like his brother; pretending to do what he asked, Mau Ipi Guloq's wives scalded him to death. Mau Ipi Guloq then married his sisters-in-law. He became one of the principal ancesters of the Bunaq.

Adventures which are similar, though inverted because they concern the upper world, are attributed to Sese nTaola, the culture hero of the Bare'e Toraja of central Celebes. As a child he has such a voracious appetite that his horrified parents consider killing him. So he leaves home and after various adventures arrives at the seashore with some companions acquired on his journey. After several months of swimming across the sea, and after killing the monster that barred their passage, they reach the other side (which probably represents the upper world). In the first village lives a cannibal couple whom they succeed in overcoming. Later they encounter other villages where Sese nTaola's companions one after another find wives for themselves. In the last village there rages a *guruda,* a gigantic bird who devours all the inhabitants. Here, Sese nTaola discovers a young girl hidden in a drum; she is Lemo nTonda, the sister of Datu of the Wind, who had followed him all the way from the cannibals' village. Despite her warnings, Sese nTaola attacks Guruda and his six children. He succeeds in killing all of them, but at the end of his last battle with Guruda himself, he is killed. Lemo nTonda revives him but he immediately falls asleep, and during his sleep, which lasts a month, Lemo

Illustration from a Javanese manuscript recounting the story of Pañji: the hero is received at the palace of Daha. Document Marcel Bonneff.

Bugis manuscript of the *La Galigo* cycle: drawing the ship of Sawerigading. Photo Christian Pelras.

nTonda is taken away by Datu nTo Wawo Yangi (the "Prince of the Sky"). When he awakens, Sese nTaola challenges the Datu to single combat, kills him, takes Lemo nTonda back, but again falls asleep for a month, and his companion is again taken away by Datu nTo Mato Eo (the "Prince of the Rising Sun"). This same sequence is repeated six more times, the subsequent kidnappers being Datu nTo Kasoyao (the "Prince of the North"), Datu nPayompo Yangi Sambiranya (the "Prince of the South"), Torokuku mBetu'e (the "Bird of the Stars"), and finally Momata Tibu (the "Cross-eyed"). While killing the latter, he again loses his life, and Lemo nTonda revives him again, as well as the villagers whom Guruda had killed. Then the two of them make their way back to Sese nTaola's country aboard a copper vessel that his double (*tanoana*) had constructed while Sese nTaola was asleep, during his visits to his grandfather, Toranda Ue ("he who lives in the water"). In the course of their crossing, Sese nTaola must again fight six battles, is killed in the last one, and is revived by Lemo nTonda. When he arrives in his village, he finds that his parents have died. They are resuscitated, but they must pay a fine for the hardships endured by their son.

More fundamental to the Iban of Borneo, perhaps because they are explicitly linked to the origins of rituals, are the adventures of Seragunting. Sometimes also called Surong Gunting, he is the son of the warrior Menggin (or Siu) and the celestial nymph Endu Dara Tincin Temaga (or Endu Sudan Galiggan Tincin Mas), the daughter of the god Singalang Burong.

Tincin Temaga married Menggin, who in the course of a hunt had taken possession of her feathered robe, on condition that he would never touch another bird. Soon after the birth of Seragunting, he involuntarily breaks the interdiction, and Tincin Temaga leaves him. In the company of his son, Menggin goes to look for her. He crosses the sea and reaches the land of Calaos (Tansang Kenyalang) where he finds Tincin Temaga in the stream where she bathes. She describes the path to Singalang Burong's house and explains how to avoid the traps awaiting him. Flies will show him where to put his feet so as to avoid the daggers planted in the path; another fly will settle on the dish that he should eat; a glowworm will show him under which mosquito net he should sleep, etc.

Thus Menggin stays on the veranda of the house where his father-in-law lives until his son becomes old enough to walk and talk. When this time comes, Seragunting goes to take his place at the side of Singalang Burong, who is furious and refuses to recognize him as his grandson if he does not succeed (which he does) in a series of trials: top contests, wrestling, hunting; collecting a large quantity of pearls scattered under the house; retrieving oil spread on the surrounding terrain; and finally, going to look for honey in a hive in the forest. Seragunting sends the bees from the hive after Singalang Burong, who has to seek shelter in the granary. He will not come down until he has recognized his grandson. Seragunting and his father then return to life among human beings in order to avoid meeting the celestial husband of Tincin Temaga, whose return from headhunting is announced.

Later, Seragunting returns to his grandfather's house to ask him how to succeed in farming and headhunting. On the way, he encounters the Pleiades and Orion's Belt, who show him how to use the stars in agriculture. Then Singalang Burong teaches him the art of reading omens from the flight of birds, as well as the rituals of the principal ceremonies. During his stay, Seragunting impregnates his young aunt Dara Cempaka Tempurong Alang, a crime which should be punished by death, but for which the sacrifice of a pig is sufficient. This will be the occasion to teach human beings the degrees of relationship prohibited for marriage.

II. Heroes of Written Accounts

Although Iban culture may appear to be reserved for ethnological study, Javanese civilization has long been of interest to Orientalists. The difference in cultural climate between the two types of society and between the scholarly approaches to them should not mask the existence of deep affinities between the great civilizations of insular Southeast Asia and seemingly more primitive cultures. This is what is shown by the study of a second type of culture hero, who appears this time in written narratives, apparently more profane, and who is sometimes composed of borrowed elements. One such hero is Pañji, the hero of a cycle of Javanese origin, who seems to have been important in the fourteenth and fifteenth centuries. He was also known in other areas of the archipelago (there are versions in Malay and in the languages of Sumatra, Celebes, and Lombok) as well as on the Indo-Chinese peninsula (Thailand, Cambodia). Western mythologists have been particularly interested in him and have given him an unusual fate; it is surely not paradoxical to say that he is better known today among anthropologists and other specialists than in Java, where other figures are popular. But there was a time when stories of Pañji inspired a particular genre of shadow theater (*wayang gedog*) as well as masked dances.

The interpretation of the "myth of Pañji" is difficult first because of the large number of accessible versions, which require laborious philological discussion. Aside from the Javanese and Balinese (*Malat*) versions, there are at least three Malayan versions designated by the names under which Pañji appears in each one of them: *Hikayat Cekel Wanengpati, Hikayat Pañji Kuda Semirang,* and *Hikayat Pañji Semirang*. The Javanese scholar R. M. Ng Poerbatjaraka devoted himself to a painstaking study of the texts and believes that they date from the end of the Majapahit period (as opposed to C. C. Berg, who believes them to be older).

The story tells of the quest of Pañji, a hero of divine origin, incarnated as the Prince of Koripan under the name of Raden Inu Kertapati, searching for his true love (his own sister, in fact), incarnated as the Princess of Daha, under the name of Candra Kirana. After a series of mishaps and adventures which take both of them all over Java, they succeed in finding each other and celebrate their wedding with much ceremony; Pañji, who meanwhile has triumphed over all his enemies, is declared the one and only king of the whole island.

In 1922, W. H. Rassers presented a paper in Leiden which was to cause a great stir, entitled *De Pandji-roman.* According to Rassers, the story was actually an adaptation of a much older myth which was found in the east of the archipelago; Pañji and Candra Kirana were transpositions of the sun and the moon; and in the Koripan/Daha contrast were found the representation of two totemic and exogamous moities. Pañji's quest was the representation of an ancient initiation, and the solemn wedding that ends the story was the transposition of the ceremony that concluded the initiation. All of this without putting into question certain Indian influences evident elsewhere (Pañji clearly appeared as a reincarnation of Wisnu, and Candra Kirana as a reincarnation of Dewi Sri). The more recent works of S. O. Robson, and especially of J. J. Ras (who connects the myth of Pañji with a myth of creation highly esteemed among the Ngaju of Kalimantan), seem to confirm certain proposals of Rassers. This shows in any case the importance of not separating the Javanese domain from the rest of the archipelago.

One can say as much about the Bugis domain; open to external influences, Islamized since the beginning of the seventeenth century, and even taxed by certain of the "fanatic Muslims," very actively involved in agriculture, navigation, and trade, characterized by the existence of a most elaborate political system, proud of a rich written literature, the Bugis at first seem far removed from the world of primitive Indonesia. But their monumental national epic, the cycle of *La Galigo,* harbors, under many epic or romantic episodes, an undeniably mythical base, above all in its key figure, Sawerigading, whose character remains essential for the Bugis of today.

Sawerigading is the son of the king of Luwu, Batara Lattu, and the grandson of Batara Guru, the first man descended from the sky. His adolescent adventures are related to a series of journeys which lead him all around Celebes, to the Moluccas, and to Sumbawa, as well as to countries with unidentifiable names, which could be either real or mythical places. He visits, among other places, the island where the cosmic tree (Pao Jengki, the "mango of Zanj") grows, whose branches rise up into the sky and whose roots go down as far as the lower world; he sees in the middle of the ocean the whirlpool by which the waters of the sea connect with that world. He also penetrates twice into the Land of the Dead, but must decide on the first visit not to marry We Pinrakati, a young princess who had just died, and on the second to bring back among the living Welle ri Lino, to whom he was engaged.

Upon returning to Luwu, Sawerigading meets his twin sister, We Tenriabeng, from whom he had been separated at birth. He falls in love with her and decides to marry her. All of the remonstrances of his entourage as well as of We Tenriabeng herself are in vain. Finally, his twin sister tells him of the existence, in the land of Cina, of one of their cousins, We Cudai, who resembles her exactly. And she gives him a strand of her hair, one of her bracelets, and one of her rings which will make him sure of her. Sawerigading embarks once again on a vessel carved out of the trunk of a gigantic tree, the Welenreng, which grew in the land of Luwu. After engaging in numerous battles at sea and after numerous mishaps, he succeeds in marrying We Cudai, who would give birth to, among others, a son, La Galigo (whose name was given to the cycle), and a daughter, We Tenridio, who was to become a *bissu* (shaman or medium).

After the marriage of his grandson, La Tenritatta, Sawerigading, who had broken his promise never to return to Luwu, is engulfed by the waves along with We Cudai. They replace Guri ri Selleng and his wife as rulers of the lower world, while We Tenriabeng and her husband Remmang ri Langi' inherit the throne of the upper world. All the princes of divine origin then disappear from the earth, with the exception of a daughter of Sawerigading and a son of We Tenriabeng who get married and rule over Luwu. As soon as they have a son, communications between the earth and the supernatural worlds are broken; after that, mankind is on its own.

But not entirely. For a Bugis saying now proclaims: "The Orient swallowed him; the West makes him rise again." The West is Mecca; and the mysterious Sun which had disappeared into the eastern seas in the form of Sawerigading suddenly rose once again on the western horizon, but this time in the name of the prophet Muhammad.

Thus do the Bugis affirm their dual attachment both to their ancestral personality and to their new faith.

III. Heroes Linked to Successive Acculturations (India, China, Islam)

This leads us to culture heroes of a third type, heroes whose backgrounds—if not their basic functions—are very different. They are heroes connected with the different acculturations that occurred in the historical period, most importantly Indianization, Sinicization, and Islamization. Here are a few notable figures for each:

1. *Aji Saka* is the Javanese culture hero to whom are attributed the innovations brought about by Indianization. King Saka (*aji,* "king") is said to have landed on Java with two loyal companions, Dora and Sembodra. The country was at that time under the authority of a terrible ogre who regularly demanded a tribute of human flesh (an allusion to the cannibalism of the first inhabitants?). Aji Saka offers himself as a sacrifice, but on condition that the ogre first grant him a plot of land the size of his handkerchief. The monster willingly agrees, but soon the magic handkerchief takes on an enormous size and covers the entire island. Out of vexation, the ogre jumps into the sea and turns himself into a giant tortoise. Aji Saka then opens up the forest and creates the first kingdom of Mendangkamulan, with the first cultivation of the land and the first villages. One day he wanted to get back his *keris* (kris), which he had entrusted to Dora with orders not to give it to anyone else, and sent Sembodra to retrieve it. Dora pretended to know nothing about it and the two loyal servants ended up by killing one another. To commemorate the sad event, Aji Saka carved into a tree twenty symbols corresponding to the following twenty syllables: *ha-na-ca-ra-ka da-ta-sa-wa-la pa-da-ja-ya-nya ma-ga-ba-ta-nga,* which in Javanese means: "There were two messengers, a dispute arose, equal were their merits, they both perished." He thus created the Javanese syllabary which, adapted from Indian models and transformed several times, has been maintained up to the present. According to the same tradition, he established on the same occasion "the Saka era," according to which the entire epigraphy of the Indianized period is dated (the Saka era whose beginnings correspond to 78 A.D. is known elsewhere, in India and in most of the Indianized world).

2. *Sampo.* The famous maritime expeditions across the "Southern Seas" (*Nanyang*) and the Indian Ocean, all the way to Mecca and the African coast, launched at the beginning of the Ming Dynasty by the emperor Yong Luo and under the direction of the admiral Zheng He from 1405 to 1433, are well known to us from Chinese sources, and correspond to an important moment in the commercial politics of the Chinese empire. In the Chinese communities of Southeast Asia, particularly in Java, their memory has been considerably embellished, giving rise to a whole series of local traditions centering around the character of Sampo (Zheng He was also called San Bao) or his "pilots," who are said to have landed and founded a family line on Java. Although the first Chinese communities settled on Java before the fifteenth century, and it is improbable that Zheng He himself ever actually set foot on the northern coast of Java, Sampo thus became a kind of culture hero, the initiator of the whole Chinese presence on the island.

Today remembrances of him are maintained primarily in

three places: In Djakarta a shrine is dedicated to him in the temple in Ancol, near the coast. In the beautiful Chinese temple of Cirebon, which in its present state dates from the end of the eighteenth century, a huge iron anvil is preserved which is said to come from one of the great Captain's junks. And finally, in Semarang, a little west of the city, are a cave and a temple where Sampo's memory is preserved. In Ancol, as in Semarang, a Muslim tomb is shown which is thought to be that of one of Sampo's pilots who was married to a woman of the region and who died on Java. In Semarang a big commemorative procession still takes place annually during which Sampo's statue is carried, and "his" horse is led by its bridle. On Bali, several traditions dealing with a certain Dampu Awang evoke Sampo, and in the Philippines, on Jolo, they honor a certain Pen Dao Gong, who is also thought to have belonged to Zheng He's crew.

3. Islam was introduced into Java progressively and peacefully largely by way of the ports of the northern coast (the Pasisir) from the beginning of the fifteenth century until the end of the sixteenth century. Popular beliefs hold that the conversion was essentially due to "nine messengers," or Wali Sanga (pronounced *songo*), who had come from across the sea and by their force of persuasion and their miracles were able to win over the people, who had until then been followers of *agama Boda* (a kind of mixture of Buddhism and Hinduism). The term *wali* is found in old Javanese where it denotes a certain category of dignitary; the word has undoubtedly been confused with the Arab *wali* which denotes the "representative." The number of *wali* is regularly fixed at nine (Javanese *sanga*), but the lists vary noticeably according to the region. The graves of these illustrious men—whose historical reality is certainly not always evident—are scattered from the east to the west along the Pasisir and are the goals of very frequent pilgrimages (*kramat*). There is a series of legends about these *wali* which form an integral part of the folklore.

The first *wali* are remembered in the region of Surabaya, where Islam was first introduced. The oldest is Malik Ibrahim, who is also the most historical, for he was a merchant from Gujurat whose tomb, dated from A.H. 822 (A.D. 1419), has been discovered. In the Ampel Denta quarter, in the heart of the Arab quarter in Surabaya, is the tomb of Raden Rahmat, also known as Sunan Ampel; he was thought to be the nephew of a princess of Campa, the wife of one of the last kings of Majapahit, and had gathered around him a great many disciples. Two of his sons, Sunan Drajat and Sunan Bonang (who could walk on water), are considered to be *wali*, as was one of his best pupils, Sunan Giri, who one day threw his *kalam* at some infidels who were attacking him, and the *kalam* immediately turned into krises. The prestige of these heroes spread quite rapidly among merchants, and the descendants of Sunan de Giri, who settled on a promontory (*giri*, "mountain") near Surabaya, exercised great influence all the way to the Moluccas and maintained their authority until the seventeenth century.

The figure of Sunan Kali Jaga is inseparable from the implantation of Islam into the region of Demak (the central region of the Pasisir, just to the east of what is now the city of Semarang). He had summoned all the other *wali* in order to construct a great mosque in Demak in only one night and had also assembled the "council" in charge of condemning to the pyre the impudent Siti Jenar, one of the *wali* who had committed the error of revealing the esoteric part of the doctrine. And it was Sunan Kali Jaga who managed to convert Kyai Ageng Podanarang, the regent of Semarang. By

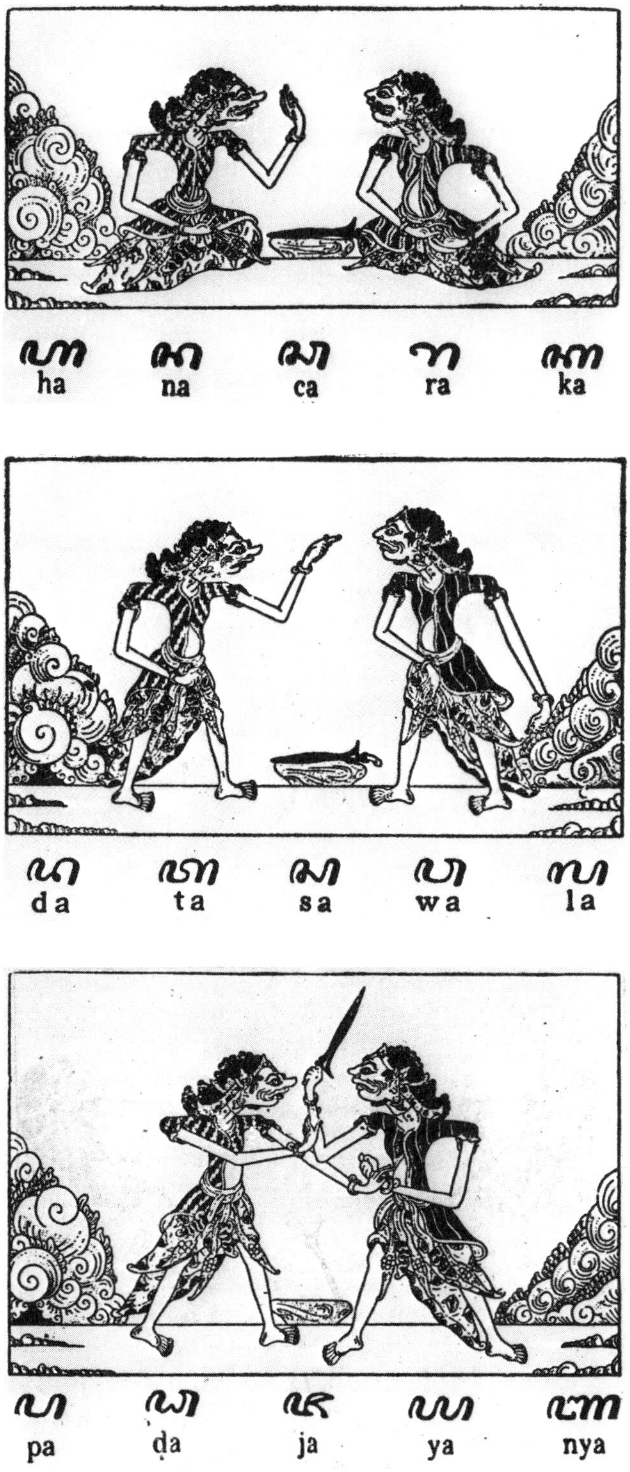

Javanese alphabet book in which the signs for the various syllables are illustrated by the dispute between the two envoys of Agi Saka.

Tomb, in Gresik (East Java), of Malik Ibrahim, one of the nine *wali*, the earliest propagators of Islam in Java. Photo Marcel Bonneff.

transforming gold into earth, and vice versa, in front of his eyes, he was able to convince Kyai Ageng of the vanity of earthly things; the regent abandoned his wealth and went off to preach the new religion in central Java. Like the other *wali*, he convinced the pagans through his miracles—putting his hand in fire without getting burned, causing a spring to arise, etc. He finally settled on a hill near Yogya, in the place called Tembayat; he was buried there and has remained famous under the name of Sunan Bayat.

Continuing further west, on the north coast of Java one finds the tomb of Sunan Panggung (in Tegal) and, most importantly, the great necropolis of Gunung Jati, to the north of Cirebon, where on the uppermost level is found the tomb of Sunan Gunung Jati (d. ca. 1570)—the most important *wali* of west Java.

Outside of Java a legend comparable to Ulakan is encountered in Minangkabau country (western Sumatra), where the tomb of Syaikh Burhanuddin—who was also believed to have introduced Islam into the region—is the object of a very important pilgrimage (especially during the month of Safar).

The introduction of Islam also had the effect of disseminating in the archipelago a completely new cycle of wonders borrowed from the myths and legends of the Arab and Persian worlds and from the Orient in general. Some of the legendary heroes were not received simply as common fictional heroes, but became totally naturalized to the point of taking a place among the local cultural heroes. We will give three such examples here: Alexander, the Macedonian hero; Amir Hamzah, the uncle of the Prophet Mohammad; and Muhammad Hanafiah, the half brother of the Shiite martyrs Hasan and Husayn.

Iskandar Zulkarnain. Known as "Alexander the Two-Horned," the conquerer of the world whose legend spread all the way to the far west in the Middle Ages is found in most of the Muslim world, where he was "recovered" as a culture hero, bringing the light of the true religion to every continent. Thus one finds "Stories of Alexander" in Arabic, Turkish, Persian, Hindi, Malay, Javanese, and Bugis. The Malay version, which has been studied by van Leeuwen, first tells in epic style about Alexander's conquests (Andalus here is notably assimilated to Andalas, another name for Sumatra), then recounts the stages of a more philosophic quest during which the hero seeks the fountain from which the water of eternity is drawn (somewhat like Bima); this search even leads him to dive to the bottom of the oceans in a sort of bathyscaphe to explore the lower worlds.

Elsewhere Iskandar was introduced into the myth of the origins of Malay rulers and he is notably linked to the region of Palembang (where his tomb can be seen at the foot of Mount Siguntang).

Amir Hamzah. In the history of the beginnings of Islam, Amir Hamzah is the uncle and one of the staunchest partisans of the prophet Muhammad. But in the Malay archipelago he is a marvelous hero at the center of an extremely rich cycle whose episodes are told not only in Malay, but also in the principal regional languages: Javanese, Balinese, Sundanese, and Bugis. The first Malay versions certainly date from before the beginning of the sixteenth century; a very famous Javanese version called *Menak*, "The Knight" (an epithet given to the hero), was recorded in central Java toward the end of the eighteenth century. Van Ronkel has shown that at the origin of the *Hikayat Amir Hamzah*, "The Story of Amir Hamzah," there was a Persian text that borrowed certain themes from the *Shah Nameh*, but the Indonesian versions were considerably amplified, using indigenous motifs.

The story, which is very long (a Malay version has 1,845 pages), recounts the entire life of the hero, from his birth in Mecca (where he miraculously escapes from a massacre of the innocents) to his apotheosis in the paradise of Allah. Just like Iskandar Zulkarnain, Amir Hamzah is presented as a champion of Islam who converted his enemies to the true religion, but this theme is not essential; somewhat like Pañji, who tried to find his fiancée Candra Kirana, Amir Hamzah tries to win the hand of the beautiful Mihrnigar, the daughter of King Nusyirwan, of whom he immediately becomes enamoured. This "quest" serves as a framework for a series of episodes, of war or of gallantry, for while he is waiting the hero has other amorous adventures and ends up with a large number of descendants. He often comes up against the jealousy and the hostility of unscrupulous rivals such as Gustehem or Bekhtek, who try to get rid of him, but he can count on the loyalty of certain companions, such as his namesake Amir, the son of Omayya (a servant of his father) born the same day as he, or, in the Javanese version, two clownish servants who recall the *punakawan* of the *wayang*, Marmaya and Marmadi.

On Java, the episodes of the *Menak* were taken up again by the *wayang golek*.

Muhammad Hanafiah. A hero of the Shiite Muslim tradition, Muhammad Hanafiah's exploits are recounted in an important Malay text, the *Hikayat Muhammad Hanafiyyah*, which was probably adapted from the Persian during the fifteenth century. The text is known through at least thirty manuscripts and a lithographed edition in Singapore. The story is no longer popular today, but it is extremely interesting in that it attests to a Shiite presence in the Malay world at the very beginning of Islamization.

The half brother of the "martyrs" of Shiism, Hasan and Husayn, Muhammad Hanafiah appears here as a brave warrior who seeks to avenge them. After the death of Husayn on the battlefield of Karbala, Yazid prepares to put his prisoners to death. But Muhammad Hanafiah gathers together the partisans of Ali and takes up the battle again. Yazid is forced to seek help from the four Oriental kings (Frankish, Chinese, Abyssinian, and Zanj); Muhammad Hanafiah is captured, and is going to be burned alive, but he is saved at the last minute and his severed arm is miraculously rejoined. Yazid tries to escape but is killed in the flames. All the prisoners are liberated, and Muhammad Hanafiah restores Zainal Abidin, the son of Husayn, to the throne. Muhammad Hanafiah then learns that Yazid's followers have gathered in a cave to prepare their revenge, and he goes there and massacres a large number of them. But a mysterious voice orders him to stop, and the door to the cave quickly closes on him. His companions mourn him for three days and three nights.

Traces of Shiism are evident elsewhere in Sumatra and in Java, where the date of the battle of Karbala, the tenth day of the month of Muharram (Asyura), was commemorated by the preparation of a special kind of pulp (*bubur suren*). Even today in Priaman, on the west coast of Sumatra, Asyura is still celebrated by throwing into the sea a cenotaph (*tabut*) which is thought to be that of the martyr Husayn, but it is possible that this ritual was introduced more recently (in the eighteenth century).

Portrait of Prince Diponegoro, leader of a revolt against the Dutch in the nineteenth century, who has been accorded the rank of "national hero" in independent Indonesia. Photo Marcel Bonneff.

IV. Modern Heroes

A last type of culture hero, which will merely be mentioned here, is perhaps not as far removed from the preceding heroes as one might think; these are the national heroes that the independent states of insular Southeast Asia have chosen to symbolize the birth of a new society: Rizal and Aguinaldo for the Philippines, and Hasanuddin, Kartini, and Imam Bonjol for Indonesia. Although they are historical, each of these figures has his myth—simplified official biographies, widely disseminated, particularly through schools—his commemorative ritual, his stereotyped iconography, etc.

The frequency with which they are mentioned shows how much modern societies, from that point of view, have traits in common with so-called primitive societies.

D.L. and C.P./t.l.f.

BIBLIOGRAPHY

W. H. RASSERS, *De Pandji-Roman* (Antwerp 1922); summarized in English in the article by J. J. Ras cited below. *Pañji the Culture Hero* (The Hague 1959); translation of articles only loosely connected with the myth of Pañji. R. M. NG. POERBATJARAKA, *Pandji-verhalen onderling vergeleken* (Bandung 1940); Indonesian translation by Zuber Usman and H. B. Jassin (Jakarta 1968). R. O. WINSTEDT, "The Panji Tales," *JMBRAS* 19, 2 (1941): 234–37. C. C. BERG, "Bijdragen tot de kennis der Pandji verhalen," *BKI* 110, 3–4 (1954). TJAN TJOE SIEM, "Masques javanais," *Arts Asiatiques* 20 (1969): 185–208. S. O. ROBSON, *Wangbang Wideya* (The Hague 1971). J. J. RAS, "The Panji Romance and W. H. Rassers' Analysis of Its Theme," *BKI* 129, 4 (1972): 411–56. P. J. VAN LEEUWEN, *De Maleise Alexander Roman* (Utrecht 1937). L. F. BRAKEL, *The Hikayat Muhammad Hanafiyyah: A Medieval Muslim Malay Romance* (The Hague 1975).

Communal Festivals in Insular Southeast Asia

Communal festivals in insular Southeast Asia are generally annual. They plunge society back into the mythical time of origins by recreating the unity of the cosmos in order to purify it from all evil influences and to ensure its vitality and fertility through the ensuing period.

At Kalimantan, among the Ngaju, groups of villages celebrate the *tiwah* in this way, in the name of the entire Ngaju people, on the occasion of lesser funerals which are generally collective, sometimes for as many as sixty dead. The public ceremonies last seven days. The first four days, which are marked by strict prohibitions, center on funerary rituals and involve two ceremonies whose purpose is to make the spiritual soul (*liau*) and the corporeal soul (*liau karaban*) of the dead pass, under the guidance of Tempon Telon, the psychopomp spirit, to the land of the dead (*lewu liau*), where they are reunited and reawakened to a new life. Parallel to this, their remains, which had been brought to the village and cremated to begin the festival, are now brought in vessels (*sandong*) intended for them. On the principal day, the fifth, which is marked by many delegations from neighboring villages bearing offerings, the prohibitions are lifted. On this day the ancestors visit the living, and the people return to the time of origins through the ritual. The final two days are set aside for the purification of the participants.

The great festival of the Iban, which is related to headhunting, is the *gawai kenyalang* or *gawai burong;* it concerns all the inhabitants of the village (which may merely correspond to a longhouse). A great number of participants are invited from outside, and much rice beer (*tuak*) is drunk. As with other Iban ceremonies (*gawai batu,* the ceremony before the clearing of the land; *gawai benih,* before sowing; and *gawai antu,* festivals of the dead among the Saribas Krian Iban), it includes among its rites augury (*beburong*), propitiary sacrifices of chickens or pigs (*ginselan*), cockfights (*sabong*), offerings (*piring*), and incantations (*pengap*).

In Sumatra, every Batak territorial unit had an annual festival of purification, called *bius.* It centered on a buffalo sacrifice and involved many mock battles.

In Nias, the *börö n'adu* was celebrated every seven or fourteen years in the various parts of the island in which the first ancestors descended from the sky; each of the places was marked by a temple (*osali*) and a sacred tree (*fösi*). It brought together many villages which were themselves grouped into cultural communities (*öri*); it lasted five days and included songs, dances, and offerings. According to P. Suzuki, the festival carried with it the idea of a periodic renewal of the cosmos, whose annihilation is first symbolized by simulated battles and by throwing into deep water the statues that each *öri* has brought. It also symbolizes rebirth through the offering of food to a sacred pig which is to remain intact for the following seven years. Through this periodic return to the time of origins, the union of men with the divine world is also clearly celebrated.

In spite of great differences in details, all of the festivals—as well as the *bua' kasalle* of the Toraja of South Celebes, the *reba* of the Ngada of Flores, the *porka* of the Southwest Moluccas, etc.—are concerned with well-defined territorial and even political units, whose integrity they attempt to ensure when they appeal for fertility and prosperity for their populations, their harvests, and their herds.

The introduction of the great religions in places where the local religion was already old did not make the latter disappear completely. One can regard the *galungan* festival of the Hinduized Balinese, and perhaps even the Muslim Javanese *garebeg,* as continuations of these.

Galungan is one of the most important Balinese festivals. As it has no direct correspondence with original Hinduism, it should probably be related to a pre-Hindu tradition. According to tradition, it was instituted to commemorate the victory that the people of Bali gained over the magician king Maya Danawa with the help of the army of the gods led by Indra. It is celebrated on the Wednesday of the eleventh week of the liturgical year of 210 days. This is a case of a true "national" festival in the strongest sense, in which the alliance of the gods with men is renewed by making the latter depositaries and life tenants of the earth, of which the former are the true lords.

A few days before the festival, temples and family sanctuaries are first purified, and some rituals take place to appease the Galungan "demon" (*buta*), the incarnation of Batara Kala, who is supposed to descend to earth on this occasion.

Yogyakarta (central Java): the royal ritual of the *garebeg.* Symbolic offerings of food in the form of mountains (*gunungan*), indications of harmony between the ruler and the people, are carried in a huge procession from the palace to the great mosque. The ceremony is made up of a number of elements of pre-Indian origin, yet today it takes place three times a year on the principal Muslim feasts. In the foreground, the female *gunungan,* and in the background, the male *gunungan.* Photo Marcel Bonneff.

Ceremonies are organized on the day of Galungan. These take place in every temple of the village: the temple of origin (*pura puseh*), the principal temple (*pura desa* or *pura agung*), the temple of the dead (*pura dalem*); in every temple of the kingdom: the mountain temple (*pura panataran*) and the marine temple (*pura segara*); in every family sanctuary (*sanggah*); and in every site considered important to the house and the territory: beds, hearths, granaries, courtyards, stables, entryways, streets, intersections, gardens, canals, lakes, rivers, springs; and, finally, in all the cemeteries where the dead await cremation. After this, everyone visits family and friends to offer their good wishes. Ten days of festivities follow, which are marked by an atmosphere of rejoicing, with dancing and theatrical presentations, ending with the day of Kuningan. This is a day of introspection that is dedicated principally to honoring divinized ancestors who are supposed to descend to earth on this day to receive homage and the offerings of men and to reciprocate with their blessing on the world of the living.

R. Goris showed very convincingly that in earlier times the

liturgical cycle must have begun on the day following Kuningan. Moreover, the name *galungan* seems to be related to the root *guling,* "turn," "make a revolution." This thus seems to be an ancient rite of the "regeneration of time," representing the death and rebirth of a universe that is conceived as fundamentally dualistic.

As for the *garebeg,* this is a great Javanese collective ritual which makes it possible for the ruler (the sultan of Yogyakarta, sunan of Surakarta, or sultans of Cirebon) to assert his power in renewing the bond that ties him to his people. The festival has been attested since the time of Majapahit, but has been greatly Islamized. Today there are three *garebegs,* fixed according to the Islamic calendar (*G. Mulud, G. Sawal,* and *G. Besar,* the last corresponding to Idul Adha); the most important is the first, which falls on the anniversary of the birth of the Prophet (*Mulud*). The people from the countryside converge upon the capital at this time, and a great fair takes place; this is also the time when taxes are paid, generally in the form of rice. The rice is then partially cooked and prepared in the form of "mountains" (*gunungan*). On the appointed day, the ruler appears in all his majesty before his functionaries and his subjects, and the *gunungan* (one considered male and the other female) are brought out with great pomp (the primary meaning of *garebeg* is "procession"). After a short trip to the mosque (to receive the blessing of the *pangulu*), the *gunungan* are given to the crowd, which falls on them to get a piece.

D.L. and C.P./d.w.

Indonesian Rites of Passage

Despite the diversity of rituals in insular Southeast Asia, the cycle of rites of passage is remarkably similar from one ethnic group to another.

Before birth, most often in the seventh month, but sometimes as early as the third or fifth month, there is a ceremony that the Malays call *lenggang perut:* a ceremonial massage of the future mother's belly, with or without propitiatory offerings. After birth, for several days, it is customary for the mother of the newborn to stay close to the fire all the time, and everywhere this time is marked by a period of taboos that ends only with the ritual purification of mother and child.

A whole series of ceremonies marks the recognition of the infant as a new member of the community and his progression to adult status: naming, cutting a lock of hair, piercing the ears (for girls), and first contact with the earth, all of which occur in the course of the first months. Then, at adolescence, circumcision (not only for Muslims), filing the teeth, and in some regions tattooing (though this has often fallen into disuse).

The filing of the teeth—a rite of passage once found among most ethnic groups in insular Southeast Asia, and performed on marriageable young men and women—involved filing down the ends (and sometimes even the whole) of the incisors and/or the canines of the upper jaw. On Bali, the ceremony is supposed to rid people of the *sadripu*—the "six enemies," or six evil spirits that personify the fundamental faults of human nature. It constitutes a step on the road that leads humans from the world below to the world above, the last step of which will be cremation. It must therefore normally take place before marriage; and if people die before they undergo this ritual, a surrogate rite precedes cremation.

Marriage rites are often highly elaborate and present many local differences; the differences depend especially on the role played by marriage alliance in the society and also on the extent to which the rites include Muslim or Christian rites. The rites also have elements common to many ethnic groups. The union of the couple is above all manifested by the public performance of an act done together: eating together, sitting solemnly together, etc. To this are added the ritual acts that mark the establishment or confirmation of an alliance between the families, which consist essentially in an exchange of customary gifts. In societies in which the alliances follow a system of generalized exchange, the goods offered by those who give the bride often include fabrics, and those coming from the groom's side include weapons. Among the Batak, the two groups even have the names of *ulos* (fabrics) and *piso* (knives), respectively; these two elements apparently represent the female and the male aspects of totality.

As for funeral practices, all techniques are or have been represented in Indonesia: besides inhumation, which is the most widespread because of Muslim and Christian influences (but which already existed almost everywhere even before), the dead are put in man-made or natural caves (southern Toraja), lie in state (Bali Aga), or are abandoned (forest nomads of Punan), inserted into a crack of a tree that will close up again over the body (Ot Kayam, Toraja), put in a coffin in the branches of a tree or on top of a post (Nias, Ngaju), buried in rock containers (north Celebes), temporarily buried with subsequent retrieval of the bones (Ngaju, north Nias), or cremated (Bali, Ngaju, Maajan); there may even be some endocannibalism (Batak, Ot Pari). But of all these funeral rites, cremation is undoubtedly one of the most spectacular.

In insular Southeast Asia, it is above all the Balinese Hindus who are known for practicing cremation, but in reality this ritual is performed by several other non-Hindu ethnic groups in Sumatra (Batak Karo), in Borneo (Ngaju), and formerly in Celebes (Bugis); in Bali itself, numerous pre-Hindu elements are apparent and indicate that we are dealing here as elsewhere in insular Southeast Asia with a double funeral ritual.

In most cases the dead are first buried and only their bones (which are sometimes even cleaned) are burned. It even happens that burial may have taken place so long ago that they must be satisfied with collecting a little earth from the tomb and burn only an effigy (*adegan*) of the dead person. Usually the ashes are scattered in a river, after they have been honored, but they may also be preserved in special urns. The general schema behind the ritual is therefore parallel to the one found among the Ngaju of Kalimantan and the one that the Batak used to practice. In all cases, the second funerals are intended to raise the dead person to the rank of ancestor (*pitra,* in Bali).

In Bali, dead princes are not buried; their bodies are preserved, as in the Toraja region, in many layers of fabrics. However, twelve days after cremation, a second ceremony takes place (*ngerorasin* or *mitra yadnya*) during which the recalled and symbolically fed soul lives in an effigy (*puspa*). The effigy will be burned after the soul has been sent back

In the Sundanese region (western Java) the circumcised child, dressed like a hero in the traditional theater, is paraded through the village. Photo Marcel Bonneff.

(Right) In the state of Johoe, young Malay newlyweds enthroned (*bersanding*) like "regents for a day," before gathered guests. Photo Christian Pelras.

Bali: for cremation, the remains of the deceased are placed in the replica of a psychopomp animal, which varies according to the caste. This bull—for a nobleman—is carried to the site of the pyre by a group of men spinning around to chase away the evil spirits. Photo X.

(*merelina*) to join the ancestors. In this particular case (which has a parallel among certain non-Islamic peoples of eastern Java), we can also speak of double funerals.

Beyond the diversity of particular cases, the double funerals are the most characteristic and constant feature of insular Southeast Asia; second funerals, often more modest than first funerals, are designed to cut definitively the ties that bind the dead to the world of the living and to make him a part of the world of ancestors; the second funerals have been perpetuated in Java in the form of the *kenduri arwah,* a votive meal that takes place forty days after burial (and double funerals remain very important in Madagascar).

The community festivals that used to take place in many ethnic groups were closely connected to ancestor worship and sometimes to funeral rites. But in many areas, they have fallen into disuse, either because of recent Islamization or Christianization, or simply because they were very costly and the local administration discouraged the practice.

On the other hand, simple agrarian rites performed within the home have survived very well until now, even in regions that have long been Islamized; the principal ones are associated with planting and harvesting the staple food (generally rice). This is also true of fishing rites in the coastal regions and of construction rites everywhere. Elements of the various rites can be found in virtually all areas. Let us cite among others the communal meals, food offerings, and sacrifices.

In Java, the communal meal is called a *slametan* and is very much in use among those known as *abagan* ("the red ones"), that is, among those for whom Islam has not eliminated many old beliefs and practices. The *slametan,* whose purpose

A Toraja funeral, in South Celebes, involves the sacrifice of many water buffalo. At the end of a cycle of ceremonies that may last for several years, the coffins are placed in cavities dug out of cliff faces. Photo Gilbert Hamonic and Christian Pelras.

is to obtain general welfare (*slamet*) for the participants, takes place before any important collective act, or sometimes after it, in order to give thanks. The meal is eaten in the traditional way, on the ground on a mat; it is preceded by a prayer or the recitation of a formula by a pious man invited for the occasion; the food, generally "yellow rice" (*nasi kuning*), rice colored with turmeric, is eaten with the fingers. In areas where Malay is spoken, they speak rather of *kenduri*. These meals, often accompanied by offerings of food to the ancestors or guardian spirits, also have a clearly sacrificial aspect; the sacrificed animals are chickens, goats (pigs for non-Muslims), or water buffaloes, depending on the importance of the occasion.

Particular cases of blood sacrifices are the cockfights (the meaning is quite clear in Bali; it is less clear elsewhere, where the sporting aspect has become dominant) and headhunting. According to Stöhr, headhunting probably represented the original murder by which food plants were introduced into the world; and it appears certain that it had something to do with fertility rites.

In many traditional religions in insular Southeast Asia, headhunting is a ritual of great importance, and it was apparently once practiced by all the peoples of the archipelago, for whom it represented the highest form of blood sacrifice, next to animal sacrifice (in ascending order of value: chickens, dogs, hogs, and water buffaloes). It was of course suppressed as soon as the colonial administration established its authority over the regions where it was still practiced. The heads that the community needed for certain rites were obtained by surprise attacks, most often on isolated and defenseless individuals (women and children) of neighboring and unfriendly communities. The heads were welcomed in the village by shouts of rejoicing.

Although there was great diversity, it seems that the heads were primarily necessary for the performance of the funeral rites that enabled the dead to reach the status of ancestors and enabled the community to be completely purified. The proper performance was a precondition for the celebration of the agrarian rites of the community and a guarantee of fertility. There is probably a connection with the numerous myths of the origin of rice and other cultivated plants, linking their appearance with the death of an original semi-divine person.

The way that headhunting was practiced limited it in practice to peoples who lived in small autonomous communities (the interior of Kalimantan and of Celebes, Ceram, Timor, etc.). Wherever there was a form of supraterritorial political unity, it tended to be replaced by sacrifices either of slaves or of water buffaloes; but although the warriors were no longer head-hunters, they remained "beheaders" for a long time.

D.L. and C.P./g.h.

A Myth of the Origin of Grains: Hainuwele in Ceram, Indonesia

W. Stöhr proposes to group under the heading of the myth of Hainuwele a series of beliefs, frequent in the Malay archipelago, which connect the appearance in the world of the first food plants (very often rice) with the death of a hero or, more frequently, of a heroine.

Hainuwele, whose name has been used to characterize this theme, is the central character of an origin myth of the Wemale (Ceram, Indonesia).

In the olden days, when the nine clans of the first humans still live on the sacred mountain of Nunusaku, the hero Ameta discovers, while chasing a boar, a fruit then unknown to him, the coconut. Soon after it has been planted, the coconut becomes a mature tree. Ameta wants to cut short its inflorescence in order to collect the sap from which palm wine is made, and he cuts his finger. From the mixture of his blood with the sap a baby girl is born whom he names Hainuwele ("palm frond"). After three days, Hainuwele, already nubile, is invited to participate in the great *maro* dance: the men of the nine original human families form a spiral, and the women sitting in the center offer them betel. But things are different with Hainuwele, as on the second night she offers them corals; on the third, Chinese porcelains; on the fourth, large porcelain dishes; on the fifth, machetes; on the sixth, a copper betel service; on the seventh, gold earrings; and on the eighth, magnificent gongs. These goods of increasing value come from the metamorphosis of her excrement. Moved by jealousy, the first men dig a hole in the middle of the dancing area and on the ninth night make Hainuwele fall into it and bury her alive. Surprised that his daughter has not come home, Ameta goes out to search for her and finally digs her up, dead: this is the first death in this world. Ameta then cuts the body of Hainuwele into pieces and buries them: these produce the tubers (yams, taro), which are staples of the Wemale diet. Furthermore, in her wrath at the murder, Mulua Satene, the woman who ruled over the first men, strikes them with one of Hainuwele's arms. Some are transformed into pigs, deer, birds, or fish; others remain human, but become mortal. Then Mulua Satene goes to live on Mount Saluhua, one of the two sacred mountains of Ceram, where she will reign over the souls of the dead.

There is general agreement that Mulua Hainuwele and Mulua Satene are two aspects of the female divinity, of which the other manifestations are Mulua Dapie Bulane (the Moon) and Tapele (the Earth). The male counterpart of the female aspect is Tuwala Lia Matai (the Sun), Lanite (the Sky), Mabitu (the Creator), who has as his home the sacred mountain of Nunusaku. As is the case elsewhere in Southeast Asia, these two entities represent the two opposite and complementary aspects upon which the cosmic whole rests. This assimilation is all the more plausible in that one finds many parallels to it throughout the rest of the archipelago.

According to one interpretation, the Dewi Sri of the Balinese corresponds only superficially to the Śrī of Hinduism, the former being a personification of the primordial chthonic and lunar female divinity, in whom are reunited the contradictory and indissolubly linked forces of death and fertility, and who is also known as Dewi Danuh, the divinity of the waters. Under the name of Sri, she becomes the goddess of ripening rice and of the monsoon; under the name of Uma, she is the divinity of germination; under the name of Durga, she is the goddess of the dead and the mistress of the *butukala* who threaten future harvests with diseases and pests; under the name of Ibu Pertiwi, she is the goddess of terrestrial fertility; finally, under the name of

Two views of the cult of Sri, the rice goddess in Indonesia. *Left:* in Celebes, in the Bugis region, an offering of popcorn (the food of the gods) from the first sheaves of the harvest, the embodiment of Sangian Serri. Photo Christian Pelras. *Right:* in Bali, a symbol of Dewi Sri, hanging in a rice field as protection. Photo Marcel Bonneff.

Giriputri, she is the goddess of the sacred mountain of Gunung Agung, from which comes the holy water that blesses the harvest, while the masculine deity of Gunung Agung is Mahādeva, a name which designates the male, heavenly, and solar god who is also hidden behind the names of Surya and Siwa.

But a Javanese account allows us to establish an even more striking parallel between Dewi Sri and Hainuwele. This account relates that from a jewel brought from the netherworld by the serpent Antaboga, a young girl named Tisnawati was born. The heavenly god Batara Guru wants to marry her. She resists his advances and dies. From her body, buried in the earthly kingdom of Mendang Kamulan, various plants come into being: the coconut palm from her head; rice from her sex organ; the banana tree from the palms of her hands; corn from her teeth. The king of Mendang Kamulan, while visiting his rice fields, sees a great serpent, which at his approach turns into a young girl who tells him she is a metamorphosis of Dewi Sri, the wife of Wisnu, who will become incarnate as his own wife.

For the Sundanese, the neighbors of the Javanese, the rice divinity Nyi Pohaci (also known as Sanghyang Sri) was hatched from an egg produced from the tears of the serpent of the netherworld, Dewa Anta or Antaboga. Dewa Wenang, fearing that the sky god Batara Guru may marry her, has her eat the fruit of the tree of paradise. Unable to tolerate other food any longer, she ends up dying of hunger. Various useful plants appear on her tomb: the coconut palm, born from her head; rice from her eyes; bamboo from her thighs, etc. The plants are brought to King Siliwangi, who instructs one of his wives, the celestial (lunar) nymph Dewi Nawang Sasih, to take care of the rice, and she teaches the people how to cook it. In those days, one spike of rice was sufficient, when cooked, to feed a hundred people. But Siliwangi broke the taboo against touching the kitchen utensils, and since then rice no longer multiplies with cooking, because Dewi Nawang Sasih has returned to the sky.

In these two accounts, there is an implicit equivalence—noted by Rassers with respect to the Javanese myth—between Dewi Sri and the semidivine female character who becomes the wife of the king. Both appear as personifications of this female lunar goddess from the netherworld, an idea found in Ceram as well as Bali.

In other regions, where outside influences were less important, the character of Sri has a more secondary place in the myth, although there are many resemblances to the preceding accounts.

Thus, for the Bugis, rice arose, in the time of origins, on the tomb of the daughter of the first being who descended from the sky. This being, La Toge' langi' Batara Guru, is the son of the principal god of the upper world, whose wife comes from the netherworld. He descends to earth to populate it, and he fathers a little girl named We O'dangriu, who dies after seven days. He ascends to the sky to share his sorrow with his father, who tells him that his child has become rice, in order that the subsistence of man may be made secure. Since then, she has been known as Sangiang Serri.

In Flores, too, it is the children of the original couple whose bodies, cut into pieces, become transformed into food plants.

D.L. and C.P./d.w.

The *Wayang* (Ritual Theater) and Its Myths in Java and Bali

The *wayang* is a very important ritual in Java and Bali, which became a performance (shadow play) only recently and under the influence of Westernization. It is also performed in certain regions influenced by Indo-Javanese culture, such as the Banjar region (southern Kalimantan), Palembang, and the state of Kelantan (on the Malay peninsula).

The shadow play, *wayang kulit,* functions as a veritable conservatory of oral tradition (Java, Bali, Kelantan in Malaysia). In these performances, whose quasi-ritual nature is still quite evident, the *dalang* (puppeteer) plays the role of a medium between the world of ancestors and that of the living. The layout is typical of the Javanese *wayang:* on the left, the character of Bima dominates the stage; on the right is the "tree of life" (*gunungan* or *kayon*). Photo Marcel Bonneff.

Originally it was probably a ritual designed to evoke the ancestors. The word is formed on the root *yang,* which designates all that belongs to the supernatural world. The evocation always takes place at a difficult moment in the life of the family or group (birth, circumcision, epidemics among humans or livestock, etc.). The officiant, or *dalang,* generally performs for nine hours straight and always at night (from 9:00 P.M. to 6:00 A.M.). This synchrony with cosmic order is always obligatory (midnight represents a crucial moment when the balance of nature is in question).

This ritual took shape partly during the period of Indianization and integrated a number of elements borrowed from the epics and the pantheon of India, notably the figures of numerous heroes in the *Mahābhārata* and the *Rāmāyaṇa,* and the themes from several episodes or *lakons.* Attested by the tenth and eleventh centuries, the shadow theater (or *wayang kulit*) was sustained and even enriched after Islamization. Certain parallel forms even developed (*wayang kelitik,* with flat figurines made of wood; *wayang golek,* with marionettes sculpted in the round; *wayang wong,* with actors of flesh and blood); even certain heroes of Islam have been integrated, such as Amir Hamzah.

A considerable repertory was developed that was based especially on native elements, but also on elements that were Indian and to a certain extent Islamized, which serve as a true frame of reference in daily life. To this day, no Javanese is considered cultivated by his peers unless he has assimilated and mastered this enormous mythological corpus, which must be read at several levels, for many episodes certainly have an esoteric meaning.

The *dalang* is ordinarily accompanied during each evocation by a gamelan orchestra and a few singers (*pesindén*), but he alone manipulates and recites. He has at his disposal eighty to a hundred leather figurines that he animates successively on a screen and that he can eventually set down in the trunk of a banana tree placed horizontally at the bottom of the screen.

Most of the leather figurines correspond to various characters, positive characters (*halus*), placed to the right of the *dalang,* and negative characters (*kasar*), demons, ogres, and others, placed to his left. But the *dalang* also uses some accessories, notably a very special object called a *kayon* or *kekayon* (based on the root *kayu,* "tree") or else *gunungan* (based on the root *gunung,* "mountain"). It involves a leather figurine, rectangular at the base but pointed at the top, rather like a poplar leaf. In the center is the closed door of a palace guarded by two giants; the rest represents the thick foliage of a forest. The *dalang* uses this to punctuate certain episodes. Positioned in the middle of the screen, the *kayon* symbolizes the absence of action. When it leans slightly to the right on the screen, it indicates that the story is in progress. Finally it serves to evoke the forest, as well as fire (for this purpose, the other side of the silhouette is painted red). Much has been said about the origin and meaning of this accessory, which appears to be very old. Basing his speculation on the name of *gunungan,* Stutterheim thought it might be an evocation of Mahāmeru, the cosmic mountain, the axis mundi. Rassers saw in the door painted in the middle a representation of the men's house, where initiations used to take place in the past. Brandes, Aichele, and Hidding have in turn insisted, not without reason, that there may have been a connection with the "tree of life" that figures prominently in several mythologies of the archipelago.

I. The Gods

Several gods are among the leather figures used by the *dalang,* but two are particularly important: Batara Guru and Semar.

Batara Guru, "the divine master" (*batara* is a special title reserved for the gods), is assimilated to Śiwa. He also has the name of Manikmaya. He has four arms and stands on the bull Andini. Alone among all the figures, he is shown with his feet pointing outward, to the left and right. The effigy representing Guru is the object of special respect on the part of the *dalang,* and no one would dare to sit on a box that contains it.

Semar is an ambiguous character endowed with great powers. He is not of Indian origin but almost always appears as the servant of the five Pandawas. His name can be traced to the root *samar* ("hazy, indistinct"), and indeed he speaks in allusions or ambiguous words (*wangsalan*). He is also known by the name of Batara Ismaya.

Semar is Batara Guru's brother. Both are sons of Sang Hyang Tunggal ("the unique"), who decided that Semar would come to earth to watch over the welfare of men and, more particularly, over the welfare of the Pandawas, who are always definitely the favorites of the gods. Since then Semar has lost his original imposing bearing. He appears as an old potbellied man, with short legs and a prominent rump, often with tears in his eyes and a running nose. Behind this mediocre and almost ridiculous exterior is hidden his divine power, and although he speaks modestly to his masters, he addresses the gods as his equals.

He rarely appears alone but is generally accompanied by minor characters, usually three: Bagong, who is considered the living shadow of Semar himself, and Nalangareng and Pétruk, who are his sons. All together they form the group of *punakawans,* "servants." Like the *vidūsaka* in Indian drama, they lighten the atmosphere by their clever tricks and refer to current events. Sometimes, however, they become the heroes of important *lakons.* In *Pétruk dados ratu* (Pétruk becomes king), for instance, we see Pétruk get hold of the *Kalimasada,* the talisman of the Pandawas, and attain supreme dignity, but only temporarily, for no one can change the social order, and he must soon return to his rank as servant.

II. The Kurawas and Pandawas

Many *lakons* are borrowed from the *Bharatayuddha,* which is a Javanese adaptation of the *Mahābhārata,* or rather the characters are borrowed, for many of the plots are original. We shall focus on the five Pandawas, who always play a key role.

1. *Yudistira*

In the Indian *Mahābhārata,* as in the Javanese *wayang,* Yudistira is the oldest of the five Pandawa brothers. He is the archetype of the just king. He never gets angry, which makes people say that his blood is white. He never raises his voice or refuses a request. When he is young, he has the name of Raden Puntadewa, and the leather figurine that represents him at that age has a few bracelets and pendants, as it does for other princes, but once he has become king, he is shown without any jewelry at all.

He is, strictly speaking, the Pandita Ratu, simultaneously knowledgeable and wise (*pandita*) and a ruler (*ratu*). Unlike his brothers, who assert their personalities in combat, Yudistira is in no way a warrior. His strength is not in his magical weapons but in a sacred text, the *Kalimasada,* which contains all the secrets of the universe. By his royal virtue, he attracts many people to his new capital city of Ngamerta, an open city in the heart of the forest, and he fosters prosperity. He is married to the faithful Dewi Drupadi, who bears him a son, Raden Pancawala.

Despite all his qualities, Yudistira is swept away by his passion for gambling and falls into the trap set for him by his cousins, the Kurawas. He plays dice and loses his kingdom, his own freedom, and the freedom of his wife and his brothers. This fatal error sets off the fratricidal war and leads to the end of the whole tribe (only Parikesit, the grandson of Arjuna, manages to survive). On the day after the massacre, the five brothers and Drupadi make their way to the home of the gods, but only Yudistira reaches the goal. The others have fallen by the wayside, exhausted by all the bloodshed. But Yudistira intercedes on their behalf, and in the end they all enter into heaven.

One tradition explains that *Kalimasada* (or *Kalimahusada*) is in fact nothing but *Kalimah syahadat* (the profession of faith of Muslims) and adds that there is therefore no interruption between the Hinduized period and Islam. According to this same tradition, Yudistira was immortal until the arrival of the

Punakawans are servants who act as both counselors and "jesters" to heroes of the *wayang purwa* (epic repertory of Hindu origin). They are supposed to portray popular Javanese common sense, and represent an important indigenous contribution to mythology of Hindu origin. From right to left: Pétruk, Bagong, Nalagaréng, and Semar. Semar is the father of the other three, himself the son of the supreme god Sang Hyang Tunggal. Illustration from a Javanese manuscript in the Jakarta Museum. Photo Marcel Bonneff.

first *walis;* he did not die until after he had understood the true meaning of their secret and was buried behind the great mosque of Demak, where there is still a tomb said to be his.

2. Bima

Second among the Pandawas, Bima is the son of Prabu Pandu and Dewi Kunti. In the *wayang,* and more generally in Javanese mythology, he appears as a major hero, a symbol of strength, courage, and righteousness. He is also named Bratasena or Bayusuta (in his youth) and Werkudara (when he is older).

One of the oldest *lakons* that we have evidence of, the tenth-century *lakon* known as *Bima bungkus,* mainly tells of his marvelous birth: Bima is imprisoned by a particularly resistant and constricting placenta until he is set free by an elephant called Sena.

Here too, the hero of the Indian epic has taken on several characteristics that belong to much older figures. R. Goris has shown how wind, lightning, and other forces of nature become incarnate. Bima is presented as the adopted son of Sang Hyang Bayu (the wind), and as the brother of Hanuman, Begawan Maenaka, and Liman Sena, who are like his emanations. All five are represented wearing loincloths decorated with the *poleng* motif (black and white checks), which attests both to their bonds of kinship and, for our purposes, to their membership in the substratum. W. F. Stutterheim also claims to have found in the fourteenth and fifteenth century elements of what he would call a "cult of Bima"; certain iconographic details in the temple of Sukuh (near the modern city of Yogyakarta) indicate this, notably a large statue representing the hero (now in a private collection in Surakarta). This piece of evidence, together with certain popular traditions, leads us to think that Bima was honored as a benevolent deity during the waning days of the Indianized period, shortly before the people converted to Islam.

His righteousness and courage notwithstanding, Bima has something of the demoniac in him by virtue of his stature. His weapon is the *pancanaka,* a single extremely blunt nail with which he stabs all his enemies. Through his unions he also participates in the parallel world of monsters. His first wife is Dewi Nagagini, daughter of the snake Antaboga. (The five Pandawas encounter her when they flee the palace fire set by the Kurawas and take refuge deep in the seventh underground world.) She bears Bima his first son, the divine Antasena. His second wife is Dewi Arimbi, sister of the ogre Prabu Arimba, herself an ogress, who bears him a second son, the valiant Gatotkaca.

Bima also appears in *lakons* whose philosophical content reveals his extraordinary power. One of the most famous is the *lakon* called *Dewa Ruci* (or *Bima suci*), which tells of his quest for perfect knowledge. Durna, the counselor of the Kurawas, orders him to search for the water of immortality (*Toyamarta*) in the hope that he will lose his life during the search. Bima sets out courageously and heads toward Mount Candramuka, where he triumphs over the two monsters Rukmuka and Rukmakala, but finds nothing. Durna then advises him to search in the middle of the ocean. Bima goes off again, triumphs over the serpent Nemburnyawa, and finally meets his master, the dwarf Dewa Ruci, who looks just like him and who advises him to enter into him to find supreme wisdom. "I look smaller than you," he tells him, "but in fact the whole world is within me." In another *lakon* called *Sena Rodra* (Angry Bima), Bima boasts of a supernatural knowledge that comes from the countries of the West (*saking tanah brang kilen*). The gods are very uneasy when they see that he possesses and distributes the kind of knowledge, here called *Sastra Jendra,* of which they alone had previously had the secret. Bima and his family are arrested and detained for a time in a corner of paradise, but the gods are attacked by giants and must call on him. Then he is freed and returns to reign in Java.

In popular imagery there is often an image of Bima, notably a depiction of the scene where he fights with the serpent Nemburnyawa in the middle of the sea. There are even some paintings on glass depicting the same episode. Popular belief also recognizes the silhouette of Bima in the southern part of the Milky Way (*lintang Bima sekti*).

The memory of Bima remains even in modern life. The fast train that runs daily between Djakarta and Surabaya was christened "Bima" (an allusion to the swiftness of the hero who flies "like the wind"), and the three-masted boat used by the Indonesian navy as a teaching vessel was christened "Dewa ruci."

The myth of Bima can also be found in eastern Sumbawa island, where a small Sultanate used to have that name.

3. Arjuna

Arjuna is the third of the Pandawas and one of the main heroes of the Indian *Mahābhārata* and the Javanese *wayang.* Like Bima, he is a brave warrior, but with a much more

Illustration of a libretto in Indonesian telling the story of Arjuna. He is represented here as a *wayang* puppet, surrounded by the seven *bidadari* temptresses.

delicate complexion than his older brother. He is as handsome as a god, and his amorous conquests are countless. He has been called the Javanese Don Juan, but in fact it is often the women who, seduced by his charms, pursue him. He also goes by other names: Parta, Margana, Panduputra, Kuntadi, Palguna, Danajaya, and especially Janaka and Pamade.

Arjuna has a slight defect, an extra finger on his right hand, an index finger that once belonged to King Prabu Palgundi, but which Druna gave him with the talisman it was wearing, the Ampal ring, whose power is without equal. Arjuna also has other extraordinary magical weapons: the Pulanggeni kris and the Sarotama arrow. All of this makes it possible for him to gain the victory during the single combats he engages in on the occasion of the Bharatayuddha; and notably it allows him to triumph over his half brother Adipati Karna, whom he loves but who has joined the ranks of the Kurawas.

His character is, as it were, inseparable from his many wives. The two most famous are Dewi Sumbadra and Dewi Srikandi. The first is the archetype of the modest and faithful wife. She resists Burisrawa's advances and prefers to kill herself (she is later revived). She is the mother of Angkawijaya (or Abimayu), whose son, Parikesit, is to be the only survivor of the terrible fratricidal war. She triumphs over Resi Bisma, one of the champions of the Kurawas. Among the wives of the second rank, we should also mention Dewi Srimendang, a princess; Rarasati, a simple attendant, the daughter of a shepherd; and Dewi Ulupi, the daughter of a hermit. But we must not forget the beautiful Banowati, the legal wife of Suyudana, king of the Kurawas and the adversary of the Pandawas. After her husband's death, Banowati takes refuge with Arjuna.

Arjuna has one final feature that complements the others. He can control his passions and impulses perfectly, and he knows how to intensify his power and strength through asceticism. This is one of the fundamental features of Javanese philosophy: a retreat into the forest allows one to commune from time to time with supernatural forces and to "recharge" one's own energy. A famous eleventh-century poem in Old Javanese, the *Arjunawiwaha,* tells the story of Arjuna's retreat on Mount Indrakila. He takes the name of Bengawan Mintaraga and suffers the assaults of seven celestial creatures (the *bidadaris*) sent by the gods to tempt him and distract him from his meditation. The gods are in fact threatened by the giant Niwatakawaca and want to ask Arjuna's help. The hero finally overcomes the monster and receives a part of the celestial kingdom as a reward.

4. *Nakula and Sadewa*

In Java as in India, the twins who complete the team of Pandawas play a secondary role. We should, however, note that, like Bima, Sadewa must at one time have enjoyed the privilege of being considered a benevolent hero. Several fourteenth- and fifteenth-century bas-reliefs depict him battling the entire army of evil spirits that the dreadful Durga commands.

D.L. and C.P./g.h.

BIBLIOGRAPHY

J. KATS, *Het javaansche toneel* (Weltevreden 1923). HARDJOWIROGO, *Sedjarah Wajang Purwa* (Djakarta 1965); in Indonesian, catalog of the characters of the *wayang.* J. R. BRANDON, *On Thrones of Gold: Three Javanese Shadow Plays* (Cambridge, MA, 1970).

Concerning the *kayon:* W. F. STUTTERHEIM, "Oost-Java en de Hemelberg," *Djåwå,* 1926, pp. 333ff. W. AICHELE, "Bijdrage tot de Geschiedenis van de Wenschboom," *Djåwå,* 1928, pp. 18ff. K. A. H. HIDDING, "De Betekenis van de Kakajon," *TBG* 71 (1931): 623–62.

Concerning the character of Bima: R. GORIS, "Storm-kind en geestes zoon," *Djåwå* 7 (1927): 110–13. W. F. STUTTERHEIM, "Een oud-Javaansche Bhima-Cultus," *Djåwå* 15 (1935): 37ff. H. OVERBECK, "Bima als goeroe," *Djåwå* 19 (1939): 12–21. A. PANNEKOEK, "Een merkwaardig Javaansch sterrebeld," *TBG* 69 (1929): 51ff.

THE *RĀMĀYAṆA* IN INDONESIA

The story of Rāma reached insular Southeast Asia relatively early. There is a ninth-century Javanese version, and the main episodes can be found depicted on the bas-reliefs of the Hindu temple of Prambanan (ninth century, near Yogyakarta), and later in Panataran (fourteenth century, east Java). As in Thailand and Cambodia, certain Javanese court dances are directly inspired by the *Rāmāyaṇa.* But side by side with this tradition, which is rather close to the classical model, is another, substantially different one, which takes up several themes that have nothing to do with Vālmīki's *Rāmāyaṇa.*

The *Hikayat Sri Rama* ("History of the divine Rāma") is an old Malay text that illustrates the parallel tradition well. From Mandudari, whom he found in a bamboo, King Dasarata had two sons: Rāma and Lakṣamaṇa. The giant Rāvaṇa, king of Langka, heard of Mandudari's beauty and came to ask Dasarata for her. From the secretion from her skin (Malay *daki*), Mandudari made a frog that transformed itself into a beautiful woman in her likeness. This double, called Mandu-daki, was given to Rawana. Dasarata, however, managed to sleep with Mandu-daki first; she later gave birth to a daughter, named Sita Dewi. Following a prediction that Sita would marry Rawana's victorious opponent, Rawana got rid of the infant by abandoning it in a chest drifting downstream. Sita was saved, was raised by an ascetic, and later married Rāma. Rāma and Sita swam in a magic lake and found themselves transformed into monkeys; this is how they conceived Hanuman, who was "transferred" into the womb of Dewi Anjani, who carried him and gave birth to him. Rawana abducted Sita, but Rāma retrieved her with the help of Hanuman.

D.L. and C.P./g.h.

BIBLIOGRAPHY

W. STUTTERHEIM, *Rāma Legenden und Rāma-Reliefs in Indonesien,* 2 vols. (Munich 1925). A. ZIESENISS, *Die Rāma Sage bei den Malaien, Ihre Herkunft und Gestaltung* (Hamburg 1928). P. L. AMIN SWEENEY, *The Ramayana and the Malay Shadow-play* (Kuala Lumpur 1972).

Two Javanese views of Rāma: on a bas-relief of the temple of Prambanan (expedition against Lanka, with the help of Hanumān and his army of monkeys); and as performed by a dancer at the court of Yogyakarta.

Recent Forms of Eschatology and Messianism in Insular Southeast Asia

If it is the case that the mythologies of insular Southeast Asia are particularly rich in myths about origins—the origin of the world, of men, of cultivated plants—then it may be asked whether a mythology also developed about the future and the last things. This phenomenon is well-attested in some places: Kalimantan and Nias, and especially Java, where numerous popular movements have been colored by millenarianism. Some recent studies, notably those of Professor Sartono Kartodirdjo of Yogyakarta, have drawn attention to precisely these marginal ideologies, which are perhaps influenced by time-oriented religions (the "end of the world" of Christianity, the *kiamat* of Islam) and exacerbated by social and colonial oppression.

At present, a great number of predictions (*ramalan, pralambang*) are attributed to a certain Jayabaya (pronounced Joyoboyo), who is a sort of Javanese Nostradamus. Collections of his predictions circulate among the people from time to time, especially when the political situation deteriorates and social tensions increase. This mythical figure, of ill-defined appearance, is sometimes assimilated to King Jayabhaya of Kediri, whose existence is certified by inscriptions dating from 1135 and 1141 and whose name figures in a colophon of the *Bharatayuddha,* a sacred text which told of the fratricidal battle between the Pandawas and the Kurawas, and which has inspired a great many *lakons* of the *wayang.*

In fact, Jayabaya's reputation may not be very old. It is said that his predictions were cast into a definite form by the famous poet Ranggawarsita who flourished in the nineteenth century (d. 1873), but his success was assured especially after the beginning of the twentieth century. Following the war in the Pacific, there was much commentary on the

Cover of a work about the predictions of Jayabaya.

prediction according to which "Java would be occupied by dwarfs who came from another island for a time equal to the life of a corn plant" (an allusion to the Japanese occupation); and the work of a certain Tjantrik Mataram, who attempted to connect the *ramalan* of the diviner with the phases of the Indonesian revolution, was immensely successful.

Although the figure of Jayabaya is definitely quite recent, the Javanese people's taste for the *pralambang* is certainly older. Brandes published a text of this genre which is certainly from before 1715, and since the eighteenth century there have been numerous testimonies to a latent messianism. The predictions generally announce that after a particularly troubled period (*zaman edan*, "period of madness") would come a new golden age marked by the coming of a *Ratu adil*, "King of Justice." This "Ratuadilism," as historians who have studied it name it, underlaid many of the peasant uprisings and other popular movements that erupted in Java throughout the nineteenth century.

D.L. and C.P./d.w.

BIBLIOGRAPHY

J. L. A. BRANDES, "Iets over een oudere Dipanegara in verband met een prototype van de voorspellingen van Jayabaya," *TBG* 32 (1889): 368–430. TJANTRIK MATARAM, *Peranan Ramalan Djojobojo dalam Revolusi kita* (3d ed., Bandung 1948). SARTONO KARTODIRDJO, *Protest Movements in Rural Java* (Singapore 1973). IDWAR SALEH, "Agrarian Radicalism and Movements of Native Insurrection in South Kalimantan (1858–1865)," *Archipel* 9 (1975): 135–54.

Desacralization from Myths to Tales in Java

What is probably the most interesting aspect of insular Southeast Asia from the standpoint of the study of myths is that in many cases the myths remain alive and continue to sustain social organization and daily ritual. We must, however, hasten to add that in several places in the archipelago, Islam and Western thought have also made their presence felt, encouraging the development of critical thinking and true rationalism. In Java and especially in the Sundanese region in western Java, everything that has not been recovered at one time or another in the hallowed conservatory of the *wayang* has necessarily fallen prey to this criticism. People have stopped believing in it, while continuing to appreciate its "charm." One can compare this process to the literary recovery of our own tales and legends. In the twentieth century, certain talented authors, such as the Sundanese writer Ajip Rosidi, have rewritten ancient legends, and collections have appeared in scholarly editions for young students. Echoes of Mme d'Aulnoy and Charles Perrault!

We shall give four examples of this literature of folk tales (*dongeng* or *cerita rakyat*), two borrowed from Javanese legends and two others borrowed from Sundanese legends. Mythologists will find here what he is looking for, since the structures of these stories come from far away, but the ethnologist would be wrong to compare them indiscriminately with the myths of the Far East, for example, for their social function has nothing in common with them.

I. Jaka Tarub

The story of Jaka Tarub (pronounced *Joko*) takes place in Java, but closely related versions can be found in other regions of the archipelago (Madura, central and northern Celebes), and even outside insular Southeast Asia, in Japan, for example. In a way, the legend bears a kind of resemblance to the French legend of Mélusine.

Jaka Tarub (in Madura, the hero's name is Aryo Menak) is strolling one night in the forest and discovers several maidens bathing in a pond. They are *bidadari*, or celestial creatures, who have left their winged garments on the bank. Jaka Tarub makes away with one of the garments, and he marries the *bidadari*, who is unable to fly away with her female companions; this spirit's name is Nawangwulan, and she bears him a daughter named Nawangsih. Nawangwulan is extraordinary in that she is able to feed her family with a single grain of rice at each meal, but she does this only on condition that Jaka Tarub will not come near the cooking pot. One day when she is away her husband wants to get to the bottom of the matter; he lifts the cover and sees only a single grain of rice. When she returns, Nawangwulan realizes what has happened, for there is still only one grain of rice and the spell is broken. She thus starts to hull the rice each time she prepares it, just like the other women, and the reserves are quickly used up. One day she discovers in the bottom of the

Javanese naive painting illustrating an episode from the tale of Jaka Tarub. The *bidadari* Nawangwulan, after returning to the heavenly world, comes back to visit and suckle her child. Marcel Bonnoff document. Photo Flammarion.

Cover of a comic book in Indonesian, telling the story of Sang Kuriang, the Sundanese Oedipus.

granary the winged garment that Jaka Tarub had hidden away. She puts it on and disappears.

Modern Indonesian painting has also appropriated this theme, and one often sees representations of the scene of Jaka Tarub surprising the *bidadari.*

II. Damar Wulan

Dama Wulan is a Javanese hero whose story takes place toward the end of the time of the kingdom of Majapahit, at a time when its power is tottering and the crown is worn by a princess. Originating in eastern Java, the story was probably introduced into central Java toward the end of the seventeenth century. It is never represented in Javanese shadow plays, but it is sometimes presented with flat wooden marionettes (*wayang kelitik*) or with actors (*ketoprak,* a kind of theater quite widespread in eastern and central Java). The plot goes as follows:

The kingdom of Majapahit is once again threatened, this time by the armies of Menak Jingga ("Red Knight"), who rules over the region of Balambangan (the easternmost part of the island of Java). The generals are powerless and the queen grieves; finally she promises her hand (and the crown) to whoever will save the situation. Damar Wulan, a modest gardener, offers to try his luck. He sets out toward the Menak Jingga's capital city and slips into his harem. Because of his noble bearing, he quickly manages to seduce the many wives of the old man. Two of them in particular have managed to steal from their husband his secret weapon, the famous *Wesi Kuning,* a mace made of "yellow iron." The next day, Damar Wulan has no trouble conquering his adversary. He cuts off Menak Jingga's head and returns to Majapahit triumphant. In order to attenuate whatever excessively "social" dimension the story may have (the unstoppable rise of a young commoner), certain versions point out that even though Damar Wulan was actually reduced to cutting grass in the gardens of Majapahit, he was really the son of a minister, but, because he had been abandoned, he had forgotten his noble birth.

III. Sang Kuriang

The legend of Sang Kuriang is associated with the center of the Sundanese region (western Java), and more particularly with the region of Bandung. It has caught the attention of comparativists who have made Sang Kuriang the Oedipus of insular Southeast Asia.

Princess Dayang Sumbi hit her young son, Sang Kuriang, on the head with a spoon and left him with a scar. Sang Kuriang leaves the village, wanders for many years, and one day returns by accident. He has become an adult and falls madly in love with Dayang Sumbi, whom he does not recognize and who has retained her youth. Dayang Sumbi is about to agree to the marriage when she recognizes the scar. To avoid incest, she asks Sang Kuriang first to meet a condition which she believes to be impossible: she asks him to transform the region into a lake overnight and to build a boat that will allow her to ride around in it. Sang Kuriang agrees to the condition and begins to work as soon as the sun has set. With the help of the spirits, he succeeds in damming the river Ci Tarum and creating a lake, and then he begins to build the boat. The worried Dayang Sumbi resorts to a stratagem to make the sun rise sooner. She unfurls a magic fabric (called *boéh larang*) and causes a rain of marvelous leaves to fall (*daun kingkilaban*). The cocks crow, day breaks, and the frustrated Sang Kuriang overturns the unfinished boat; this is said to be the origin of the name of the nearby volcano near Bandung: Tangkubanperahu, "overturned boat."

IV. Lutung Kasarung

This is a myth known in the western region of Java (Sunda and the area around Banuymas). The king of Pasir Batang has seven daughters; the oldest, Purbararang, vows an undying hatred for her youngest sister, Purbasari, whose charm and beauty inspire her jealousy; finally she gets rid of her by exiling her in the forest. The poor little girl soon finds a companion, a big monkey called Lutung Kasarung (*lutung*, "monkey"), who is in fact a temporary metamorphosis of the god Guriang Tunggal (or Sang Hiang Tunggal). He has dreamed of a bride who resembles his mother, and his mother, the venerable Sunan Ambu, has sent him into the middle world, promising him that he will find there what he is looking for. Lutung Kasarung begins by building a magic palace for Purbasari, and then he helps the unhappy young girl with the trials that Purbararang continues to impose on her. Purbasari thus manages to fill a pit and triumphs over her sister by quickly cultivating a *huma*, or dry field. The frustrated Purbararang then proposes a beauty contest between Lutung Kasarung and Indrajaya, her own fiancé. Lutung Kasarung resumes his divine bearing, and Purbararang is forced to admit defeat. Purbasari returns to the kingdom and succeeds her sister on the throne; a great feast is held, and Purbararang becomes the guardian of the poultry yard. This legend has been the object of a celebrated Sundanese *pantun* that has been studied by C. M. Pleyte (*VBG* 58, Batavia [Djakarta], 1910), and by the Sundanese author Ajip Rosidi.

D.L. and C.P./g.h.

Tha Mythology of the Highlands of Madagascar and the Political Cycle of the Andriambahoaka

I call, I call
The male gods and the female gods
God who made man smell sweet
God who made hands and feet
The twelve mountains,
The four cardinal points and the fifth middle point
Halfway between heaven and earth,
The south and the north,
The east and the west,
The earth and the sky support each other so that
What is on high may come down and what is down below may rise.
. . .
We are calling you, O gods who reside on high
and all those who are here below.

—Decary, 124–25

Although the existence of Malagasy mythology has sometimes been denied, it appears to be a highly promising field of research, however complicated it may be by virtue of its being inseparable from the great mythologies of the Indian Ocean. This factor cannot be ignored, but given the present state of our knowledge of the subject, this article discusses only the most obvious comparisons; others that are no less interesting have merely been indicated in the few notes at the end of the chapter.

Throughout the Middle Ages of the Indian Ocean—extending, for our purposes, from the eighth or ninth century to the beginning of the sixteenth century, which was marked by the arrival of the Portuguese—men who had come directly or indirectly from southern Arabia, from the Persian Gulf, and from India and Indonesia, using already well-known sea routes, forged ahead beyond the coast of East Africa and, by way of the Comorian archipelago, reached Madagascar. Given this complexity, I cannot present a general Malagasy mythology. Such a mythology, following the religions, would necessarily reflect distinct facets of different heritages. A preliterate "Creole" civilization, the civilization of Madagascar is doubly syncretic in that the syncretisms that were elaborated there had already been largely primed on the distant shores of Southeast Asia, or closer, on the coast of East Africa, even before those who were destined to become the Malagasy landed on Madagascar.

The conditions of the settlement probably account for the absence of a pantheon or even a unified religion. In the different regions of the island, religion reveals elements of the cults of East African or Indonesian ancestors, combined with the one God of Islam or even with Indo-European gods.

Since I am not trying to draw up an inventory of so rich and varied a folklore (and one that reflects the great Semitic, Indian, and Indonesian mythologies of the Indian Ocean), I have chosen to limit my essay to certain established systems. Thus, the new problem will rely on a mythology that is both widespread enough to be representative of the whole island and at the same time sufficiently restricted to remain "typically" Malagasy, without going beyond any boundary of Madagascar.

A good example of this transregional type is offered by the settlement traditions of the "Arab-Persian" Antalaotra, already strongly Africanized and accompanied by their African allies. Whether Malagasy or Comorian, these traditions are inseparable from their Shirazi counterparts on the east coast of Africa and are merely the historicized version (for a period between the tenth and the early sixteenth centuries) of a myth from southern Arabia and the Persian Gulf: the myth "of the seven brothers," about the legendary destruction of the kingdom of Sheba in Yemen.[1]

The myth of I/bonia/masi/bonia/manoro, Ibonia for short, appears, on the other hand, to be unquestionably and fundamentally Malagasy.[2] Known throughout Madagascar in many different versions, it has been integrated into a cycle in the highlands that could be called the "cycle of the Andriam/bahoaka," "the princes of the people," or, with greater precision (if R. P. Webber's hypothesis is correct), "the princes of the universe" (Webber 739), for in the Indian or Indianized tradition of sacred kingship they are universal sovereigns.

There is little doubt that the Andriambahoaka cycle is connected with the first Malagasy dynasty, that of the Andriambahoaka Raminia, who, according to their traditions, came "from Mekke and Mangalore" and landed on the northern coast of Madagascar at the end of the twelfth century or the beginning of the thirteenth century (COAM 8: 12–14; Leitão 201–2). The newcomers colonized the eastern coast and, penetrating into the interior early on, introduced in most of the island new political concepts that consisted essentially of the concept and the prestigious title of Andriambahoaka, the universal sovereign, a god-king in the best Indian (or Indianized) tradition. At the beginning of the seventeenth century, the title of Andriambahoaka of the Raminia sovereigns of the eastern side is attested in the kingdom of Imamo (*Firaketana* 45–47) close to the kingdom of Imerina in the heart of the highlands. Even today those who are possessed in the royal cults of the southwest invoke this title in their trances. Clearly the concept of *Andriana* in itself conveys the whole hierarchical conception of the world and society insofar as the *andriana* claim a divine origin in order to set themselves apart from all other mortals.

One of the first functions of the Andriambahoaka cycle consists in explaining within the myth a claim to hegemony that has its origin in an unusual marriage of Heaven and Earth. Later, on the basis of this prior claim, princes belonging to different dynasties were drawn into the politics of expansion that were logically meant to result in the political unification of Madagascar. In three centuries of relentless effort, from the sixteenth century through the eighteenth, the Maroserana rulers in the south and west came very close to achieving this result, but it was the rulers of Imerina, the heirs of the Vazimba princes, who finally completed this task. In the process, they managed to convert the myth into history, even while they were slaughtering their eastern cousins.

This political saga calls attention to what may be called the "utilitarianism" of the Malagasy rulers, who literally bring Heaven to Earth, and in the absence of this impossible pantheon, simply clothe their mythology in history.

The myth of Ibonia and the cycle of the Andriambahoaka thus follow the fortunes of the Malagasy dynasties. Both of them seem to come directly or indirectly from the fortunes of the Raminias and become differentiated from one another step by step as the princes come to take into account the institutions, customs, and fundamental beliefs in different regions and among dissimilar populations: the Africans, Malays, and Africanized Arab-Persians on whom the princes impose their domination. However, just as the new dynasties that developed in the south, the center, and the west do not repudiate any of their essential heritage, so too these same myths, which are nothing but the political ideology of the rulers, preserve under the guise of an apparent surface diversity the essentials of the original framework and the original message. The Zatovo princes from the south and west "whose hands and feet were not created by God" are undeniably marked by African cultural traditions. But at the same time, like their Indianized Indonesian cousins from the highlands, they are no less Andriambahoaka.[3]

Thus it is strictly for the sake of brevity at this quite preliminary stage of the study of Malagasy mythology that I limit myself to the historical and cultural milieu of the highlands during a period approximately from the beginning of the fourteenth century to the end of the sixteenth century. Historically, we are dealing with the Vazimba period and the beginning of the Merina period (for the Imerina).

With the supernatural tales that, like Andrianoro, deal with the conditions that preceded sovereignty on earth, Ibonia constitutes a kind of crowning point within the cycle of the Andriambahoaka. Building on earlier tales, it introduces a real theory of power and sovereignty. With the marriage between a human and a princess of Heaven, Andrianoro illustrates the theme that the "sovereign has no family," in the sense of blood relatives, and that in the relentless struggle for power (as attested by bloody interregnums until well into the nineteenth century) he finds his support in his wife, who is a sign of the continuity of his lineage, and in his people. The Princesses of Heaven, strange Green Princesses whose strangeness could not be diminished by Gérard de Nerval's *Voyage en Orient*, play a central role. By contrast, the people remain significantly in the background but nonetheless always present. Such a scheme ties the cosmic and social balance to the person of the sovereign, so that he must benefit from so unusual a union. Combined, the two genealogies are ordered as follows:

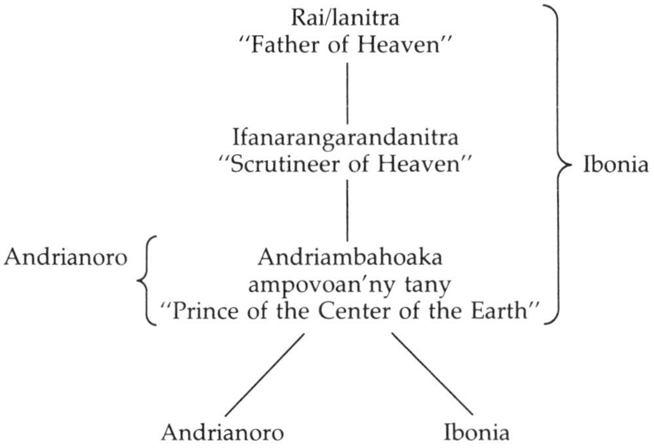

The Arabic root *nūr* (Malagasy *noro*) may explain Andrianoro, "the prince of Light," but it is no longer understood in this sense; it evokes the idea of happiness and joy, but a particular happiness, always associated with circumcision, an institution fundamentally royal in origin. Like Andrianoro, Ibonia is rendered as "son" of the Prince of the Center (from the Arabic *'ibun*, "son"?). Of the five Andriambahoaka, the one in the center and those in the four cardinal points, only the Prince of the Center has a vocation to become a universal prince. In the historical period under discussion here, it is only a matter of vocation. Several times Ibonia, after the unconditional surrender of his cousins, the four Andriambahoaka of the cardinal points, refuses the sovereignty that they offer him, content to accumulate the merits of a considerable ancestry. The historical sovereigns of the Merina dynasties make the most of this moral asset, not just within the myth but actually within history, the history of the gradual unification of the greater part of Madagascar.

Let us begin with the myth of Andrianoro, first because it logically precedes that of Ibonia, and second because its themes (some treated thoroughly, others merely skimmed over) reappear in most of the supernatural tales of the cycle of Andriambahoaka.

Andrianoro, the son of the Prince of the Center, refuses the marriages that he is offered until finally, with the help of Ranakombe the soothsayer and through trickery and magic, he secures for himself a heavenly nymph who had come to a lake to bathe. She warns him that "as a man of earth," he will not be able to live in Heaven where the words of her father are as thunderbolts, and that if her lips should touch even a drop of alcohol, she will instantly die.

The nymph imposes dangerous trials on her husband, the implications of which her in-laws do not grasp. Taking

King Merina Radama I. Tananarive, Queen's Palace Museum. Paris, Musée de l'Homme collection.

advantage of their son's absence, they break through the sevenfold wall that protects their village and force their hated daughter-in-law to drink the fatal alcohol.

Alerted by premonitory dreams, Andrianoro returns in haste, and in his grief can only arrange for a second, proper funeral. The tomb is opened, the shroud enveloping the body is unrolled, and to the astonishment of those who are present, the Princess of Heaven appears alive but with a strange diaphanous green color. Full of wrath, Andrianoro banishes his parents and warns that if they do not disappear immediately he will have them put to death by the people, "who henceforth hate them."

But the story does not end there. Grieved to hear the endless rumbling of Heaven that bears witness to the pain of her parents, the celestial wife insists on paying them a visit. Despite the tears of his younger sister and his affection for her, Andrianoro foolishly decides to accompany his wife, though he is fully aware of the terrible trials that await him.

Against all odds, he triumphs, with the complicity of his wife and the assistance of animal allies. After that, the Celestial Father recognizes the union that he had denied. The happy couple returns to earth, but in the interim, the beloved sister has died of sorrow (*Anganon'ny Ntaolo A. N.* 79–84).

Andrianoro and the Green Princesses

Andrianoro foretells most of the themes that occur in the rest of the corpus and that generally revolve around the trials undergone by heroes bold enough to disavow blood ties and endogamous marriage in favor of an infinitely more hazardous union with a princess who belongs, in every sense of the word, to another world.

When Andrianoro's beloved younger sister dies of grief, her death, by breaking away the affective register of a structural reality that turns the marriage bond into a strong link, finally severs the last bond that connects the hero to what sociologists call his family of orientation. In the masculine mode with Andrianoro and the lastborn heroes and in the feminine mode with the Green Princesses, a whole subset of marvelous tales deal with the same theme that we have already mentioned: "The sovereign has no family." In the fierce competition for political power, the closest relatives, generally brothers or father's brothers, are the most formidable opponents. The wife, in the cycle of the Andriambahoaka, always a single wife of superior essence, is both the pledge and the assurance of the continuity of the line. One can understand that the aggression of the brother, even of the father, against the Prince, which is motivated in the first place by jealousy, complies in fact with more deeply rooted motives. What is at stake is the breaking of the line through the assassination of the sovereign or his wife, and thus the dishonored rival kingdom is doomed "to a heritage of dogs and boars"—that is, the escheated property is left for anyone to claim. All of this explains the harshness of the punishment that Andrianoro does not hesitate to inflict on his parents, a punishment worse than death, since as a result of the banishment that condemns them to wander in misery, their remains are scattered far from the family tomb.

At the start, the wicked deeds that overtake heroes or heroines either directly or through the lives of their spouses are motivated by the resentment inspired by certain qualities that are inherent in heroes, that is, that belong to their very nature. It is never a matter of unimportant qualities but of the real qualifications for the exercise of sovereignty. The older relatives of Imbahitrila do not forgive him for the goodness and compassion that induce him to redeem and free trapped animals (making an implicit pact that all the kites and rats will remember; *A.N.* 104). Ramanongavato and the young prince of *Ny niandohan'ny vonoan'olona* (the origin of executions) show qualities of boldness and courage that explain both their popularity among the people and their elder brothers' resentment (Renel 1.1–8; *A.N.* 69–74). For heroines the image is different, and the attribute that is by far the most detested is the primary characteristic of these Mélusines: fertility. [Mélusine, in French folklore, was cursed to become a serpent from the hips down every Saturday. When her husband broke his promise never to look at her on a Saturday, she disappeared forever.—Ed.] This fertility is often outrageously excessive, such as that of the last and favorite wife of the Andriambahoaka, who boasts of having given birth "in one fell swoop" to two boys and a girl. This maternity occurred, unfortunately for her, during the absence of the Prince (*Haitraitra an'olombelona, Zaka an'nanahary:* "Man proposes but God disposes"; *A.N.* 64–69).

The ill-advised bragging in front of co-wives who suffer from barrenness (the worst of curses)[4] gives evidence that these Princes and Green Princesses, somewhat in the style of the Zatovos in the south and the west, "seek out misfortune," if only through the hatred that their mere presence is able to provoke. Between them and their rivals there is a structural opposition of traits of character and personality: popular versus "bitter-skinned" (unpopular), courageous versus cowardly (the theme of false heroes is often encountered), sympathetic versus cruel, fertile (to excess) versus sterile, etc.

With the exceptions of Ibonia and Andrianoro, who are only sons since they are paradigmatic sons, all the heroes, male or female, are lastborn children. Exceptions are rare. In a myth about the Green Princesses, the heroines are the last wives, a status that is hard to distinguish from that of lastborn daughters, especially since there is often sororal polygyny.[5] These heroes, whatever their sex may be, have another characteristic in common: abnormality through excess or transgression. They are either highly gifted heroes, like Ibonia and most of the other Princes, who are introduced from the beginning as sons of Andriambahoaka, or conversely they are weak heroes, usually afflicted with a physical defect. The Princess of the King of the Center has a marvelous beauty, enough to eclipse her two sisters, but her feet are paralyzed (Renel 1.46–49). The same applies to Faralahy (Renel 1.65–76). This defect is particularly aggravated for Im/bahitr/ila, "he whose side is numb" (*A.N.* 104–16), and I/silak/olona (*A.N.* 116–22), the "splinter (of wood) man," both of whom are man on one side and tree on the other side, clearly monstrous. And the defects or handicaps provide the siblings (always of the same sex) with pretexts that force their parents to abandon the unfortunates in deserted shacks outside the village or in the heart of thick forest. But the wicked deed produces the inverse effect, for the heroines are soon rescued and adopted by sympathetic monsters, while the lastborn sons are visited by the sons of God who become their friends. From that point, it becomes clear that the situation is totally reversed. The heroes rejected and scorned at the onset now magically come into wealth and power and are able to marry, and not infrequently their close kin receive the exemplary punishment of being demoted to the status of servants, or worse yet, of being transformed into dogs or put to death.

The development of the intrigues in the case of the Green Princesses, who are co-wives persecuted by their elder rivals (the Malagasy term *rafy* means both female rival and co-wife), is always the same, forming the framework of the narrative. The last co-wife at the start, she becomes the sole wife of the Andriambahoaka at the end. The husband-wife relationship develops to a higher degree the naturally close tie that generally exists between relatives of different sexes. We have seen the antagonisms that prevail between father and son as well as between siblings of the same sex. By contrast, although Ibonia is his father's murderer (one does not know exactly how), his affection for his mother never falters and is an index of the profound identity of nature that quite obviously exists between a mother and a son when they face the same trials. Andrianoro's hatred for his older sister, in contrast with the warm affection that binds him to his younger sister, is all the more understandable because the elder sister, through her function as sworn enemy of the Heavenly Princess, seems to the Princess more like a co-wife than a sister-in-law. Following Andrianoro, several marvelous tales (among them the myth of Ibonia) illustrate the theme of married love. Ibonia is the story of the exploits of a hero determined at all costs to find his wife again, even though he knows full well that "the search for one's wife can lead to death." It is indeed death itself that Ra/Zatova encounters when, in despair, he commits suicide on the body of his beloved; the two lovers become reincarnated as *vorondreo,* birds of good omen (*Leptosomus discolor*) (Renel 1.26–31). Male heroes are not the only ones who enjoy such all-encompassing feelings, for I/toeram/bola/fotsy ("she whose nature is silver"), in order "not to abandon her husband in his misfortune," confronts a formidable ogre and manages to obtain at the risk of her life the spells and the magic formula that will allow her to bring her chosen husband back to life after he has been mortally wounded by a rival (*A.N.* 93–98).

These qualities of altruism and absolute devotion confirm the overvaluation of the marriage bond, which must entail a symmetrical devaluation of blood ties,[6] a characteristic of the Andriana order. This being the case, the behavior of the Princes and the Green Princesses toward their biological or adoptive parents remains quite dissimilar. The banishment that Andrianoro inflicts can be justified by the murder of his wife. What is more, the lastborn handicapped sons act against their cruel fathers and brothers only in self-defense. The same does not hold true for the female side. Andrianoro's wife might be considered abnormally attached to her heavenly parents were it not for the fact that she does not hesitate to become her husband's accomplice against them. In other tales, the bias is even clearer, with some of the daughters of God flagrantly deceiving their father to steal from him the rice that they will introduce on earth. But the worst ingratitude is that of the Green Princesses, the natural or adopted daughters of monsters, whom they abandon at their first opportunity to follow the Andriambahoaka. Is it the monstrous nature of the mothers that authorizes the Princess with the paralyzed feet to participate in the killing of the sympathetic monster? (She kills him as monsters are often killed, piercing him with a white-hot trident; Renel 1.46–49).[7] Should we see here, in contrast with the irreproachable behavior of the males, the discrete expression of a thinly veiled disapproval?

These unusual marriages are not without their difficulties. Schematically, the Andriambahoaka Princes submit to tests in which they actively mobilize their forces to obtain extraordinary wives, and, on the other hand, the extraordinary princesses passively "endure"—this is the expression used by Andrianoro's wife—tests in order to succeed in marrying a man (perhaps a Prince) of the earth.

The males' trials take place on earth and in heaven, while the Green Princesses are tested on earth. The males' trials assume strength, determination, and personal valor among the heroes. They may require the use of talismans, but that is not absolutely necessary, and most often the champions act alone, relying solely on their courage. Their dangerous adversaries are from here below: crocodiles, wild bulls, hippopotamuses. Sometimes, however, the line between the familiar and the extraordinary is difficult to trace, and often after they have encountered the animal adversaries, preferably in the auspicious north or east, the Princes confront even more formidable challenges to the south and to the west. This time there are more or less anthropomorphic monsters, of which there is a long list, including the Trimos: ogres and ogresses, sometimes complete with tails, creatures unlike any others, capable of removing their eyes or armed with a razor-sharp tail that glows in the dark, etc.

The tests in heaven are divided into tests of strength and tests of intelligence (*Rabenimiehaka A.N.* 84–89). The first that are imposed by the same Rabenimiehaka, the highly demanding father-in-law, are tests of "the battle with life," and consist of difficult tasks (clearing forests and swamps, setting up rice plantations), tasks for men among migrant farm workers, in the same way as the tasks imposed on the Green Princesses (weaving, basket making, etc.) are women's tasks. The tests of intelligence, of the "battle with the mind" (ibid.), are based on the astonishing identity of the inhabitants of heaven, which we will discuss later. These tests consist in having to distinguish the daughters from the mother or the lastborn daughter from her sisters, or else to identify the cow that produced the herd in the pastures of God.

The tests of the "battle with life" in heaven are usually insurmountable; severe in themselves, they cannot be accomplished within the given period of time. Often the unfortunate candidate has to clear, irrigate, plant, and harvest on the same day. Having to distinguish between creatures who resemble one another perfectly also exceeds human capacities. At that point, the magical helpers intervene. Animal allies suddenly appear at a given moment to cut or dig, or even more valuable helpers, real intelligences, appear on the spot, the daughters (wives) or sons of God.

The outside contests, like that of Ranakombe, are all that can reverse the normal course of things, and the unexpected victory that they bring to the heroes results in a radically new reversal. The sons-in-law are accepted, the couple returns to earth together with their wealth and a whole people of a superhuman origin who, when they do not come down from heaven, may come out of the sea driving a herd of sea cattle,[8] or they may suddenly emerge, in front of Ramanongavato, from an abyss that has direct communication with the lower world (Renel 1.1–8).

The tests that are imposed on the Green Princesses by their rivals, tests somewhat curtailed by the cruel but only temporary penalty given by their adoptive mother, are less violent. The Princesses must above all "endure" their fate, but this characteristic is not general, and it may happen that the Princesses, for instance, Itoerambolafotsy or the very willing mother of Ibonia, become actively engaged just like the male heroes, with whom, in this case, they tend to identify. The tale points out that Itoerambolafotsy ties around her waist, in the masculine fashion, the loincloth stained with the blood of her husband; she also blackens her face, and, still apparently like the male champions, disguises herself as an old woman (the last subterfuge permits her to reach the bedside of her dying husband). This is a macabre version of the device of the Donkey Skin that recurs incessantly in the tales, practiced by such heroes as Ibonia, the young Prince of *Ny niandohan.*

As soon as he emerges from the lower world into which his brothers had thrown him and at the last moment severs the creeper that he was using to climb back to the light, Ramanongavato is recalled to life again and called "the very black one." Is this an attempt to hide a brilliance that would immediately reveal his essence of Andriana? How else can we explain those charred or tarred faces, the dazzling clothing discarded in favor of soiled or bloodstained rags, and finally those strange disguises under the skins of old people?

Furthermore, the theme of flaying recurs repeatedly. In heaven it presents no problem, since the inhabitants remove their skins as they would remove their clothing. On earth, it is a disguise or even a penalty when the monstrous and mocked mothers of the Green Princesses tear the skin off their faces and remove their eyes.

There is a complete dichotomy between the two situations: real or imagined death (flaying alive revealing blind skeletons) followed, without any transition, by the achievement of the height of honors: sovereignty for the men and the status of the monogamous wife of the sovereign for women.[9] This reversal has all the characteristics of a rite of passage and initiation.

All along this transitional phase, the phase of passage, the actors can be recognized by their voices, their bearing, and also by the emotions that they inspire. The fate of the Green Princesses is still more cruel, since in their pitiful state they can only suffer the mockery of their rivals and endure this to the bitter end: having to appear in public in front of the people, who are summoned to admire the beauty of their rivals. Until the last second, they remain hidden, masked beneath a veil that is supposed to hide their shame, so that suddenly, to the consternation of all, they can appear at the peak of their beauty, acclaimed by the people while their dishonored rivals are shamefully chased away or in their confusion jump from a precipice. Symmetrically, the recognition of the male heroes, now rid of the soot or tar that had covered their faces and having cast off their old men's skins, takes place in the same way: publicly, in front of the people. The fratricidal brothers take flight or are put to death.

Gods and Men

The very idea of a "Prince of the Center of the Earth" involves a symbolism of space, which is itself inseparable from a political intention: to found a dynasty outside of the common order, the necessary prerequisite for sovereignty on earth. This purpose presupposes an exogamous marriage as distant as possible, since this is no more or less than an alliance with a princess of heaven, or even a daughter of God.

It is as though the Andriambahoaka were taking into consideration this structure of the center and the cardinal on the political level, by affirming (pending the time when they would make them into vassals) their dominance over their surrounding cousins, only to reject the same structure on the matrimonial level. For throughout the myths of Andrianoro, Ibonia, and many other supernatural tales, it is clear that this same structure also symbolizes the endogamous marriage with patrilateral parallel cousins, the daughters of the brothers of the Father, the Prince of the Center. Thus, through this marriage they bring about on a human scale the theme of the marriage of heaven and earth, which, like the theme of war, presupposes a previous separation, the condition of all classification, even of the creation of the world that put an end to chaos. The theme of war is treated directly in numerous etiological tales that seek to explain the origin of the earth's configurations, the height of the mountains and the depressions of valleys (all the earth did not rise up at the same time in an assault against heaven). For our purposes, the hostile relations between the two worlds reappear in the latent antagonism that opposes human beings to the supernatural. On the one hand, there is the fear of men before forces that they do not understand and that always assume in their eyes the strangest or most terrifying forms. On the other hand, there is a lack of confidence, an uneasiness in the Daughters of Heaven, who are ready to flee at the least suspicious sign that gives them an inkling of the tricks and traps of men. These well-founded worries in fact foreshadow their capture. For, however imperceptibly, the princesses allow themselves to be won over and seduced by their abductors, whose principal helpers they frequently become. Originally this was a premeditated or more innocent abduction resulting from a chance encounter when the Prince wandered far away from home in pursuit of wild birds (Renel 1.37).

This last reference is not gratuitous, for we shall see that, in the same way, the main characters of the myths and supernatural tales are predisposed by their ambiguity to the role of mediator that they assume. They find themselves in places of passage between the earth and the suprahuman worlds: certain out-of-the-way places, dense forests, lakes, entrances to abysses, and even the sandy beaches at the boundary between the earth and the waters.[10]

It is sometimes an explicit or implicit question of the worlds above and below, such as the explanation of eclipses given in 1616–17 by the Raminia princes to an incredulous Portuguese missionary (COAM 2.163)[11] or better yet the explanation for the god of the kingdom of the dead (though what we have here is an abridgment by Renel: Renel lexicon 2, 323–24). In practice, the three-way opposition, earth/lower world/upper world (heaven), can be reduced to a simple dual opposition (right/left, God/human, masculine/feminine) that reinforces the opposition between heaven and earth.

The world of heaven as it is represented in Malagasy mythology and folklore is difficult to define. But it seems to be conceived on the model of the worlds of Indonesian spirits (for example, Alkema and Bezemer 203; Jensen 93, 105, 109, etc.), characterized from the start by systematic inversions. For example, thin cows graze in rich pastures, and fat cows feed on sterile laterite. Men of the earth who visit heaven must also conform to the inversions. They must eat green bananas, drink muddy water, cross waterfalls without going around them. Besorongola's brothers, who are not aware of these prescriptions, are changed into dogs. Another imperative is not to be surprised by or to laugh at such unexpected sights as the inhabitants of heaven removing their lips or their skin, ridding themselves of their bones (so as not to break them), legs without bodies; that is, to guard against any unseemly and noisy reaction that might deny the "normality" of the situations they witness (*A.N. Imbahitrila* 112–13; Renel 1, *Besorongola* 58–64; *Faralahy* 71–74).

On the instructions of his wife, Andrianoro counteracts the treacherous invitations of his father-in-law. In an effort to outbid the latter, who has invited him not only to take the place of honor at the north end of the house, but indeed to sit on his own throne of gold, Andrianoro accentuates his humiliation in reverse by assuming the status of a servant, choosing to squat in the southeast corner of the house, which is reserved for fowls and servants. In another story, the hero, who has been ordered to go west to cut wood or to pick bananas, goes east, thus avoiding the thunderbolt that strikes in order to destroy him (*A.N.* 122–23).

In the case of Andrianoro, this inversion of behavior, dictated by his refusal to accept a false and deceitful reciprocity, is justified on two counts. He is a man of earth in the kingdom of heaven, but he is also the son-in-law in the presence of his unwelcoming father-in-law. In other words, in the Malagasy tradition of the highlands (consistent with the Indonesian tradition on every point in this matter), he is a debtor and forever beholden to his father-in-law, who in his capacity as a wife giver (however reluctant) is superior to the wife takers.[12]

In the eyes of God, this de facto marriage which results from a rape is no marriage at all, having been made without the indispensable consent that in any event would not have been given, since in Malagasy tradition the marriage of a high-ranking Princess with an inferior always remains unthinkable. This indicates the nature of the emotions that one should feel toward the impudent young man whose scandalous marriage will not be recognized de jure until after he has passed certain tests that would normally prove fatal to him.

The God of Ibonia compels respect in the image of that great beyond where "all love one another like brother and

The royal palace and house of noblemen. Tananarive, Queen's Palace Museum. Paris, Musée de l'Homme collection.

sister," in contrast with the cheating that is widespread on earth (Becker 42). The God of Andrianoro is different: starting with the traps he sets; the celestial father of his wife is a cheat. Tied all the same to heaven, to light, he reveals himself through lightning, the most dazzling expression of this same light, through thunder, and also through his insidiously treacherous maneuvers, to be a dangerous and frightening god. His word is effectively lightning and thunder, which, though they constitute his normal mode of expression, such as the rumblings that express his grief at being separated from his daughter, nonetheless each time cause the hero to faint.

Formidable as he is, this Rai/lanitra, "Father of Heaven," is also known as Zanahary, the creator god, "he who molds feet and hands," and also as Andria/manitra, "the sweet-smelling Prince," a quality that he transmitted to humans, if we are to believe the invocation text reported by Decary (ibid.). Yet the Trimos and other monsters (who thereby establish themselves as Trimos, i.e., ogres) shout *maimbo olombelona* ("This reeks of human!") when they suspect the presence of humans. The Webber dictionary gives the following definition for the root *imbo:* a strong and unpleasant odor such as tar, resin, *smoke, onions* (italics mine). That onions are abhorred by idols is one of the most common taboos. As for smoke, it is one of the elements that most annoys God, and incorrigible humans, aware of this, do not fail to smoke him out (Renel 3.69–74 and 119–21).

Nevertheless, God's attitude is not systematic, and whatever his wrath is, as soon as the trials are overcome, his attitude changes radically, and the couple is showered with gifts. Since that time, by matrilineal descent, the basic traits and attributes of his own nature pass on to members of his half-divine, half-human line of descendants, i.e., the Andriana, who will be demigods before they are worshiped as the *Andriamanitra hita maso* ("gods that one sees with one's own eyes") or, as Ibonia proclaims, the "gods on earth."

This brings us to the crux of the matter: the intrinsic nature, the essence of these inhabitants of heaven, namely, "brilliance" and what might be called their permanent and complete identity.

The creatures of heaven are creatures of light whose beauty, especially that of the women, is always described as dazzling, in the strict sense of the term. Their marvelous beauty unsettles the mind of humans, who are incredulous in the face of such apparitions, the likes of which do not exist on earth. Their complexions are luminous and white unless they appear to be that strange diaphanous green; their eyes are like mirrors; their long black hair, sometimes green for certain girls of the water, flows down over their shoulders; they are as beautiful as the rising sun. The literature is very rich in expressions of the ineffable feelings that they inspire. Although less is said about the beauty of the Princes, the Andrianoro and Iboniamasiboniamanoro bear within their names the mark of this light.

I have now come to the other fundamental characteristic that permeates all the physical and psychological aspects of the creatures of heaven: their complete identity, what may be called their continuity, their transitivity in space and time. They are immutable and permanent in every sense of the terms.

Their identity is first understood as a physical identity that makes them completely indistinguishable from one another if they are of the same sex. This is the source of the previously mentioned theme of the tests of recognition: to know how to identify the daughter as distinct from the mother is obviously impossible, since the Princesses are called Ra/manaha/dreny or Ra/mitovi/aman/dreniny, meaning "the equal or likeness of her mother" (*A.N.* 84; Ferrand 103). The same test can also be applied to the herds, which indicates that in the kingdom of heaven, identity extends to all beings.[13]

The psychology of gods as well as of all supernatural beings (including monsters) is marked by the same permanence and stability, which as a result makes all their behavior entirely predictable, allowing humans to practice all the tricks that they will not fail to indulge in. This is fairly clear as far as dealings with the gods are concerned; but, it should be pointed out, if humans have to trick the gods, they generally trick them with deference, never ridiculing them as they do monsters. As a matter of course, monsters are represented as stupid and their behavior as perfectly mechanical. When the Green Princesses flee with their lovers, they gain time by scattering on their path such goods as seeds, which their fierce adoptive mothers never fail to pick up and invariably bring home before resuming their pursuit (*A.N.* 76–77; Renel 1.38–41). The monsters provoke laughter as a result of their imbecility and their candor, like the ogresses who, at Isilakolona's demand, persist in fetching water in fishing nets (*A.N.* 119).

There is yet another difference. Directly grappling with the monsters, the heroes deceive them without showing them any kindness and kill them as soon as they can. With God, by contrast, they use trickery only through the mediation of interposed helpers: the soothsayer Ranakombe or more frequently the wife or the son of God. There is constant recourse to animal allies, acquired at the very start of the narratives through a sympathetic attitude. It also happens, and Andrianoro is an example of this, that the help of animals is directly solicited and that cattle are sacrificed to seal the contract. In all cases, the most decisive help comes from the daughters or sons of God who reveal the fundamental rules to which humans will have to conform.

Identity and permanence persist in time. Unlike humans, the creatures of heaven are exempt from the pains of birth, life, and death. The beauty of mothers is entirely equal to that of their daughters, since no distinction is possible.

This whole set of characteristics, the distinctive attributes of the creatures of heaven, tends to contrast them with humans, who live in a state of discontinuity and who, like "all those whose gates face west," are aware of the cycle of life and death. Several tales represent death as the result of a choice proposed to men by God: instead of the death of the moon which is reborn, men apparently preferred the death of the banana tree, which does not disappear until it has perpetuated itself with its shoots (Renel 3.54–55, 75–76).

Although the gods are "identical," humans are above all dissimilar in their appearance, their clothing, and their social statuses, i.e., in their nature and their psychology, these two aspects being inseparable. But although they act according to their nature and in this context, it is possible to distinguish differential psychologies that correspond to the sexes, or even more, to social groups. There is always something unpredictable about them, an unpredictability well expressed by the proverb that compares the vagaries of human beings to the zigzags that eels trace in water (Houlder 1). In the Andriambahoaka cycle, this mobility and lack of attachment to a firm base makes possible the victory of human heroes, laughable in their weakness, over infinitely more powerful beings. Their victory is consecrated by the successful marriage with a princess from the other world, who thereafter will give birth to a new category between gods and men, the category of the Andriana.

Ibonia: Between Men and Gods: The Andriana

I call, I call
. . .
The other cardinal points and the middle,
the fifth point halfway between heaven and earth
. . .

(ibid.)

Refusing the endogamy of the four cardinal points, the sons of the Princes of the Center seek out the Princesses of Heaven. We have seen that Ibonia may mean "the son," a son who admittedly owes nothing to his father, the Prince of the Center, since he is reputed to be born of a talisman, a magical grasshopper that by itself penetrated the body of his mother through the top of her head, lodged in her womb, coiled up there, and became a fetus (Becker 27–28). This is why, in contrast with Zatovo who is "not created by God," Ibonia is reputed to be "not created by men."

The entire myth of Ibonia underscores his miraculous nature. "God on earth," the hero has many affinities with the Indo-European god of sovereignty, who in India is Indra, the warrior champion of the gods, often compared to a bull, and also a god of rain. The correspondences (I will not underscore them systematically) are unsettling. In hymn 4.18 of the *Ṛg Veda,* Indra has decided to come into the world through his mother's side, and the narrators try in vain to dissuade him:

Narrators: Here is the tried and true way by which all the gods experienced birth. This is the way that he must be born already grown [the gods are born as adults]. He must not throw his mother into this evil death.

Indra: I shall not come out this way. It is a bad passageway. I want to come out sideways, through the side. I have many things to do that have not been done, to fight against one, to make a pact with the other. (Renou 1901: 16–17)

Long before his birth, Ranakombe had warned the hero's mother about his deadly character:

Child of misfortune, of calamity, of curse . . . lightning . . .
on earth fatal to his father, in the womb, fatal to his mother.

To which the latter retorts

It is better than having no children to inherit from the fathers. (Becker 22)

We know the stakes: sovereignty, its exercise, and above all, its continuity. Consistent with the inauspicious prediction, Ibonia remains in his mother's womb for ten years. Indra had been carried for "one thousand months and as many autumns" (Renou ibid.).[14]

The myth pursues a parallel line and is not explicit about the parricide of Ibonia, which is decidedly more mysterious than that of his illustrious model. On the other hand, his birth verifies the somber predictions of Ranakombe. When he is about to be born, by his command his mother makes a fantastic cosmic tour of the highest summits, the darkness of the forests, and the depths of waters and the sea, before returning to the house that is the center of the world. Then, on the verge of birth, he asks his mother to swallow a razor blade in a banana, adding, "For I will come out neither climbing nor descending, but I will come out through your womb" (Becker 43).[15]

However, the Prince of the Center, the husband of the mother of Ibonia, who had already refused to give his barren wife a rival (ibid. 21), is not convinced, and, before forging the fatal blade, he cries out again, "Is this not precisely what I do not want?" (ibid. 43), but he bows before the reasons of state when his wife, the guarantor of the perpetuation of his line of descent, reminds him of them. The sun is at the zenith. Ibonia is born by opening his mother's side, and leaps directly onto the golden throne on the top of his house. His mother dies. He turns his face toward the east (ibid. 44).

Ibonia's birth is marked by a frightful cosmic upheaval: "All living beings had their thighs broken, rocks split, the earth tottered, and thunder filled the skies" (ibid. 44). This correspondence is constant throughout the myth. The slightest shift in movement of the hero and, before him, of his mother, and even of the Andriambahoaka princes, is accompanied by a noise and by phenomena never before seen: "The earth rises and falls; the skies capsize, the rocks resound." Ibonia is quite aware of this and often evokes these cosmic extensions of his personality:

I straighten up, and the skies break open;
I stoop down, and the earth breaks open;
I lean sideways, and the eastern forest burns,
I kick the earth, and it dissolves into mud.

(ibid. 126–27)

A particular link unites him with light, fire, and water. I will return to this link with fire in connection with baths in a brazier of live coals. Using a curious weapon in the form of a cross (as his name indicates), Ibonia throws it with such violence that it leaves behind it a trail of fire (ibid. 120–21). His link to water, to all the waters of heaven and earth, is fundamental, for it is one of the essential characteristics of the Andriambahoaka sovereigns and, after them, of the Malagasy sovereigns. In 1653, after defeating the Raminia Andriambahoaka, Flacourt saw a delegation of noblemen and chiefs coming toward him at Port Dauphin. They asked him to "make the rains fall," since drought was threatening the crops (COAM 9.184–85). In the myths, the "Princes of the Rivers" (Andrian/ony or Andria/nady, on the basis of the Malagasy and Sanskrit terms) are numerous. For Ibonia this intimacy with waters is strange. Before his birth, his mother penetrates the waters twice, and later, on the advice of Ranakombe, in order to discipline himself for war in view of the approaching fight against his rival, Ibonia dives in with his talismans, from sunset to sunrise (Becker 88). Later, like another Moses, he orders the waters of the river of "the Center" to open to let him pass through (ibid. 129). Finally, shortly before his death, he warns his mother that, on certain days, rain will fall continuously "like tears" (ibid. 132).

The "works" of Ibonia are inseparable from certain questionable actions of a kind that prompt him, as he is waist deep in dried mud, to "encircle" his paternal village, piercing with his assegai spears the loads carried by the people, but—and this is made very clear—he does stop short of killing. These misdeeds are repeated four times over. Eager to kill him, his father sends people against him who successively stone him, spear him, and shoot him with a rifle and finally fire cannonballs at him. All is to no avail, as Ibonia remains invulnerable, and every time it is his mother's intervention that channels his energy in a useful direction, making him battle monsters and then sending him to battle his two most powerful cousins. These recognize his superiority and for different reasons offer him their power, which the hero declines, satisfied to have established his preeminence (ibid. 95–106). These restricted and limited misdeeds merely herald the excellence of the reign of a civilizing sovereign.[16]

Ibonia, it will be recalled, marks a second phase in the Andriambahoaka cycle; the first, the creation of an incomparable dynasty through an exceptional marriage, was completed by Andrianoro. In the second phase, however, the theme of the rejection of the cousins of the cardinal points is recalled and developed. Ibonia rejects all offers of marriage, just like Andrianoro, but with much more violence and in a manner particularly insulting to his mother's brother (the principal political rival whom "the uterine nephews stabbed in the back"; Délivré 269 and 401, note 81). The hero's vehemence can perhaps be explained by the fact that, unlike Andrianoro, whose first and only union is monogamous, Ibonia is married even before he is born. It is in his mother's womb that he designates Iampelasoamananoro as his wife, whom he several times promised "to die, rather than to be left on earth and alive for any rival." Yet she was raped by his archrival. Ibonia, who unlike Indra "does not see his wife dishonored," is determined to find her again.

We have seen how important the concept of identity is for the inhabitants of heaven. If Ibonia, born of a talisman, does not accept the offers of marriage, this can certainly be related to a refusal of the polygamous marriage but also to a refusal of what he considers to be of an essence other than that of the Prince of the Center and of his cardinal brothers. In this frame of reference, his predestined wife can only be identical to him. In fact, this identity is already apparent in the simple juxtaposition of names: I/bonia/masi/bonia/manoro and I/ampela (woman)/soa/mananoro, which contain the qualifiers *masi(na), noro, soa,* invariably associated with circumcision (see Cousins 8–13 and Rainandriamampandry 88–93).

In the logic of the society under study, this identity, stronger than the identity that results from belonging to the same Andriana order, can only be one of royal marriages, the most eminent form of which remains the marriage of a brother and sister. According to the legend, such a marriage was made by the two children of Ramini, the ancestor of the dynasty (COAM 8.82), and according to history, a marriage was also probably made by a Sakalava sovereign with his half-sister (Guillain 26).[17] If Ibonia's refusals are examined in terms of the degrees of relationship, it turns out that the only dynastic (thus, endogamous) marriage he does not reject is the marriage with his matrilateral parallel cousin. A parallel marriage, of the children of sisters "who could not have been contained in the same womb," is today absolutely banned in Madagascar and regarded with horror as the most completely incestuous union.[18] However, the second version of Ibonia presents the hero and his wife as the children of two sisters and as promised to each other even before their birth (*A.N.* 34.34–39). The royal wedding par excellence outside the realm of myth was that Radama II (who reigned from 1861 to 1863), the son of the much feared Ranavalora I; he married the future Rasoherina, his mother's sister's daughter.

This apparent digression brings us back to Andrianoro and to the ambiguity of the hero who, though Prince of the Earth, nevertheless displays many traits that connect him with the realm of heaven. In fact, his excessive determination to marry a Princess of Heaven, his obstinacy in provoking his heavenly father-in-law by his mere presence, would be acts of madness if they were not basically founded, however vaguely, on that very identity of nature that the dreadful father-in-law is not long in grasping. As we have seen, Andrianoro's insistence is in itself unacceptable, because it runs counter to the Malagasy hierarchical conception that condemns hypogamous marriage. In this frame of reference, Andrianoro would be guilty of *misavi-drazana,* i.e., he would be seeking to arrogate divine ancestors for himself (which is not all that inaccurate!) (Cousins 29).

His wife's rank as a celestial nymph captured in a lake provides an explanation reinforced by the isomorphism of the Green Princesses, who are indiscriminately daughters of heaven, of the water, of the sea, or of the underworld, and are all Mélusines.

In Malagasy folklore, the prototype of the Mélusines is incontestably Ranoro, "the holy Vazimba," who is represented as an Andriana princess sitting in the middle of the water on a large lotus leaf. Behind her one can frequently see the rocks from which she is said to have jumped into the Mamba River when her ill-advised husband transgressed the (Mélusine) condition of their union by uttering the word "salt."[19] However, in a short study devoted to the explanation of several etymologies, M. Randria presents Ranoro as a daughter of God who is offended (for the same reason) and disappears never to return, fleeing not to the Mamba River but, appropriately, into a lake, Lake Andrianoro, east of Antananarivo (Randria 26–28).

This lucky encounter confirms the identity of the names Ra/noro, Andria/noro, and beyond that, as we have seen, with Ibonia and his wife, an even more fundamental identity of essence. This version grounds the mysterious selective affinity that draws toward one another the Green Princesses and the Princes of the Center, whose boldness is thereby justified.

Curiously, if one bears in mind that Andrianoro is the son of the Prince of the Center, Javanese symbolism adds a further supporting argument. In fact, it qualifies (and thereby assimilates) the center of the same structure of four cardinal points as *langit* (sky), a word that is, moreover, close to Malagasy *lanitra.* What is surprising about this assimilation of the Princes of the Center to the Princes of Heaven? Ibonia declared:

> Neither my hands nor my feet are the work of men;
> I am the one who looks after the earth; God looks after the heavens;
> He is God up Above, and I am God on Earth.
> . . .
> I am the one and only one who fills the earth.
> (Becker 39)

This is nothing more nor less than a claim to the status of universal sovereign of the Indianized kingdoms that are evoked by many characteristics of the architecture of the royal palaces and cities, such as sevenfold protective walls and symbolic roads through the kingdom (Heine-Geldern 1–14). At this point it is sufficient to keep in mind the notion of "God on earth" that will be attached to the Malagasy sovereigns, who were reputed to be *Andriamanitra hita maso:* "gods that one sees with one's own eyes," as late as the second half of the nineteenth century.

It is difficult to imagine feelings such as those of Radama II, the young sovereign of whom we have just spoken, who was rather inept and in a fit of anger reproached a mistress of his for having converted to Protestantism:

> In vain do you evoke Jesus Christ! Jesus Christ is nothing but a human being; he is not God. *I* am far superior to him. God alone occupies a rank superior to mine! (*Daty Malaza* 2.43, cited in Délivré 129 and 371, note 38)

As "visible gods," the sovereigns were compared to the sun, and like the sun, they did not die. They retired in the west and reappeared in the east, and death was comparable to Ibonia's sojourn under water. Everywhere on the great

Portrait of King Merina Andrainampoinimerina. Tananarive, Queen's Palace Museum. Paris, Musée de l'Homme collection.

island, the symbolism of the special royal vocabularies is unequivocal. Take Imerina, for example: the sovereign does not die, he "turns his back"; "to hide" means to bury: "the sun is hidden" (Cousins 77). Elsewhere, in the west (the direction of death), the expression "the sky is broken" announces the sovereign's death. They also speak of a "hole in the sky" which refers to the Betsileo legend of the dead Prince who is seized by a waterspout and sucked straight up to the sky, which gapes wide open to receive him (*A.N.* 177). The waterspout and thunder, lightning, meteorites, and the rainbow are attributes of the deity.

Yet Ibonia, as he himself asserts, will experience death; he will follow "the road of all those whose door faces west" (Becker 131), but he immediately adds "his body is not one of those that are buried to rot, but one of those that are planted to grow" (ibid.).

This recalls a previous theme: even when they die, the sovereigns supposedly keep the attributes of the divine; they "die with the odor of sanctity"; their bodies do not decompose. In a supernatural tale, the young princess discovers the bodies of her two brothers, lifeless but not decomposing; "they do not smell bad, and their faces have not changed at all" (*A.N.* 69).[20]

Ranoro and Imaitsoanola: The Malagasy Mélusines

There are two reasons why the Green Princesses occupy a central place in Malagasy mythology. First, they tie together themes that otherwise appear to be distinct. Second, they allow comparisons outside of Madagascar (if only by formulating new hypotheses) that can shed light on the cultural history of this part of the Indian Ocean. This raises several points relating to the Malagasy tales and the comparative folklore of the Mélusines.

The tale of "A Thousand and One Nights," the story of Beder, the prince of Persia, and Giauhare, the princess of the kingdom of Samandal (ed. Galland, vol. 2, pp. 311–75), tells the story of the marriage of a prince with a Mélusine princess of the sea. After an initial period of time during which she maintains an obstinate silence, the princess succeeds in subjugating her husband to the point where he dismisses all the women of the harem, keeping her as his only wife. This plot occurs in a number of Malagasy tales (*A.N.*, 60–64; Renel 1.187–90; Ferrand 1893.91–92). However, four supernatural tales—"Imaitsoanala" (the green woman in the forest) and "The Hornless Cow" (Renel 1.35–45), on the one hand, and "Ifaranomby" and the already-mentioned tale of "Haitraitra . . . " (Man proposes, and God disposes: *A.N.* 90–93, 64–69), on the other—use the well-known theme of "the sovereign who has no family . . . and has only one wife," to develop the transition from polygynous marriage to monogamous marriage that Ibonia exalted. Monogamous marriage, which is characteristic of the Princes of the Center (at least from the point of view of royal succession), could be posthumous, as in the case of Ifaranomby, the assassinated wife who—in this version—does not come back to life.

"Imaitsoanala" and "The Hornless Cow," natural or adopted daughters of a monstrous mother, share the pattern of an extraordinary birth from an egg that, in one case, will take years to hatch (cf. Ibonia). The sympathetic attitude of the mothers is repaid by ingratitude when the daughters, without even asking their mothers' consent, agree to follow the Andriambahoaka princes. Quite understandably, this action provokes the mothers to anger, which leads to the pursuit of the fugitive couple and the terrible penalty with which we are familiar: flaying the bodies and gouging out the eyes of the victims. However, at the moment when the green daughters are overwhelmed with pain, just as the Andriambahoaka princes despair of accomplishing their obviously impossible tasks, the mothers—once again sympathetic—intervene, complete the prescribed tasks, and on the day of the contest, at the public appearance of all the women in the Andriambahoaka, display their daughters at the height of their beauty, dressed in the richest clothing and even, in one case, furnished with a golden throne. We know the end of "Imaitsoanala"; the plot of the hornless cow does not stop at this point but surges ahead. Feigning an illness, the rivals demand as a remedy the sacrifice of the hornless cow, who surrenders. But following the cow's instructions, her adopted daughter must gather up her bones and bury them on the site of the sacrifice, where a supernatural tree soon sprouts. Trying to get the tree's flowers and fruits of pearl and silver, just as the adopted daughter did, the rivals become leprous when they touch the tree. Still alive, they are exiled in a miserable shanty that will serve as their tomb when they die.

"Ifaranomby" and "Haitraitra" start with the jealousy of two sterile co-wives on whom the prince imposes a young rival. In "Ifaranomby" (which contains the root *omby*, "ox, cow"), taking advantage of the prince's absence, the elder daughters assassinate the lastborn daughter, who has just given birth to an only son. In order to disguise their heinous crime, they pretend that their younger sister died of shame after having delivered "objects of misfortune": an old worn-out broom and a chisel. They treat the child like a slave that they pretend to have bought. The years go by; the child plants on his mother's tomb a seedling that becomes a marvelous tree. The prince returns. Attracted from the beginning by the child, he asks him to pick the flowers of gold, silver, and coral. The failure of the first wives proves their guilt. They are driven out, and the prince stays with his son. "Haitraitra" does not contain the episode of the marvelous tree but tells of the substitution of the same objects and a burnisher for the two newborn boys and the newborn girl (*A.N.* 64–65). The children are abandoned in a box that floats down the river. Providentially, the box is picked up by Ranakombe; the rest is predictable: the two elder co-wives are put to death for their crime.

The theme of the children abandoned in the river is taken up again in the legend of the founding of Majunga, in which the Sakalava sovereign named Andriamandisoarivo, the founder of the kingdom of Boina (at the beginning of the eighteenth century), abandons one of his granddaughters in the waters of the Betsiboka River. The Antalaotra discover the box containing the young princess and proclaim her their queen (Guillain 21–22).[21] In India, the legend of Goriyā is built on the same theme: the marriage of a king to a goddess (Kālī) who soon becomes pregnant by him. His first seven wives become intensely jealous, and when she gives birth, they substitute a stone for the newborn child, whom they abandon in a box and leave to drift downstream. The box is picked up by fisherman (Gaborieau 152).

Narrated during sessions of possession, this legend is supposed to provoke trances, and if one recalls the sessions of possession that are inseparable from the previously mentioned royal rituals, this indirect connection makes possible a clearer understanding of the significance of the Malagasy supernatural tales, as well as of the mysterious propitiatory formulas that accompany their recital. The word "tale" is a very poor equivalent for the Malagasy *angano* (our corpus is referred to as the *Anganon'ny Ntaolo,* "the *angano* of the forefathers"), a word which, apparently borrowed from Swahili, expresses along with the idea of the extraordinary, that of misfortune and of calamity, which may be the reason for the awe-inspiring atmosphere that prevails in Madagascar during the recounting of these supernatural tales.

The *Tantara Ny Andriana* "The history of the kings of the Imerina" tells the legend of Andriam/Bavi/Rano, "the Princess of the Water," who fell from heaven in the form of a fragrant leaf into a lake located on the top of Mount Angavo, about twenty kilometers east of Antananarivo. The Vazimba prince, Andriamanjavona, who appears in a genealogy as the first cousin of another son of Andrianerinerina (the fallen son of God, who becomes the first Vazimba sovereign), tries to seize her and succeeds only after pronouncing the sacred phrase from tales and stories: "If, by my father and by my mother, I am *andriana* . . ." He locks the leaf in a box; it is transformed again into a goddess, according to the text, and the prince marries her.

Then we come upon the familiar plot: Andriambavirano is the victim of the hostility of the first wife, who, after bearing him two sons and a daughter, substitutes for them the same unusual objects (a used broom, a burnisher, and a polished stone). The children abandoned in a box set adrift in the water are rescued (Callet note pages 17–18).

The History of the Kings of the Imerina reproduces this legend, to which the translators add a second legend, collected in central southeastern Madagascar, that belongs to the clan of the Zaza rano, "children of the waters" (see the tale cited by Ferrand 1893: 91–92):

> The members of this clan believe that their common ancestor must have been the eldest of triplets [*sic*] born of Andriambavirano, *who was known under the name of Fatima.* . . . According to the version we have been given, *Fatima supposedly left her husband Andriambahoaka* after a marital quarrel, when he had broken the promise . . . that he made to his wife when she was dragged out of the waters of the river . . . in a fisherman's net . . . never to refer to her . . . origin. (Callet, Chapus, Ratsimba, note 15, 16–17; italics mine)

One can understand the significance of this legendary tradition of a clan known for having been originally converted to Islam and for its close ties to the Raminia dynasty. One can also understand the great advantage in this identification of the Green Princess—the Mélusine, Andriambavirano, herself considered a goddess—with Fatima.

Of course, Shiite Islam regards Fatima, the daughter of the Prophet and the wife of the fourth caliph 'Alī (whose assassination marks the origin of the Shiite sect), as the mistress of the waters, so that in their esoteric version of the Koran, most Shiites believe that verse 31 of chapter 21—"Water is the source of all life"—refers to her. As a further example, the *ta'ziye* of the Persian theater, which are dramatic enactments and commemorations of the passion of the Imam Hussayn at Karbala, follow this tradition (Calmard 73–126), according to which Fatima is said to have received from God himself authority over all the waters of the world (Virolleaud 33, 41). Mistress of the water, Fatima is also the mistress of salt (see Ranoro) (Masse 225) and her day is Friday, the Great Day, the day of sovereignty in Madagascar; all over the island the expression "wait for Friday" is endlessly repeated both in tales and in historical traditions. When Ibonia's archrival wants to put him to death, his own father forbids him with these words: "Wait . . . for Friday, Thursday is still mine" (Becker 119–20). In the same way, the last Vazimba princess, eager to set up an "arranged" succession (*fanjakana arindra*), foresees that Thursday will be for Andriamanelo—the first sovereign of the Merina dynasty—and Friday for his younger brother.

When she is dying, Fatima orders that a small box be placed on her chest and that a sealed paper should be enclosed in it on which is to be inscribed in *green ink* (italics mine) the contract stipulating the price for the blood of Hussayn, whose martyrdom is destined to redeem all Shiites (Virolleaud 40–41). Green, which in Islam is the color of paradise, has become, in opposition to the black of the Abbasids, the emblem of the descendants and partisans of 'Alī, in other words, the Shiites (Laoust 98).

We will return to Fatima, to the Green Princesses, to 'Alī, to Andrianoro, and to Shiism. For the moment, the comparative folklore of the Mélusines will allow us to shed light on other points, all of which revolve around the aforementioned fertility of the Mélusines. This fertility, which is the best guarantee of the continuity of their lineage, quite naturally connects them with agriculture, and in Madagascar particularly with rice, the grain that symbolizes agriculture most completely.

In Java, in very ancient times, a civilizing hero hunting wild birds (like certain Andriambahoaka) discovers in the middle of a dense forest a pond where celestial nymphs who have come to bathe are taking off their clothes. He approaches, steals the clothing of one of them, and takes her for his wife. Thereafter there is no shortage of rice, although the nymph from heaven never seems to refill the storehouse. On one occasion, she asks him to keep an eye on the rice that is cooking but not to lift the cover, a prohibition that the curious hero ignores. Since the Mélusine condition has been violated, the celestial nymph returns to heaven (Rassers 266–67).

The couple are regarded as the founders of the Javanese people, the woman being connected to heaven, rice, and agriculture, and the man to earth and hunting (ibid. 270–73). In the same way, the Malagasy Mélusines, notably the daughters of God, are connected to agriculture, to cultivated plants and especially to rice. Of divine origin, rice is presented (rarely) as a voluntary gift or (more often) as an involuntary gift of God, from whom it is stolen by one of his daughters, who brings it as a dowry for her human husband. A historical legend explains how rice was supposedly introduced into the Ankaratra region (the center of the island) by a daughter of God, who, as she leaves heaven, asks her father to give her the gift of a rooster and a hen. When she arrives on earth, she quickly sacrifices the rooster in order to plant the paddy contained in his gizzard. This takes place in *Am/bari/andramanitra* ("In the place of the rice of God") (Callet, Chapus, Ratsimba, note 2, 20).

In his collections, Renel has several versions, all of which emphasize the trick involved in the theft. In one case, the daughter of God hides the grains of rice in the curls of her hair (Renel 3.19–21), but two other versions repeat the sacrifice of the fowl (ibid. 29–31 and 32–36). The second one holds an even greater interest for us, since it is an exact reprise of the first part of the Andrianoro plot in which the hero, here called "the one not created by God," with the help of Ranakombe's magic and his transformations manages to seize one of the three celestial nymphs who had come to bathe in the lake. The trial in heaven is less difficult; the hero has to identify the throne of the daughter of God, which is quite obviously green. The rest of the story repeats the stratagem of the sacrificed fowl.

In all of these tales, the heroine is expressly referred to as a daughter of God. The connection between heaven and rice is evident in all Malagasy folklore. In another tale about the origin of rice, it is lightning that comes to fertilize a few grains that have accidentally fallen in a swamp (ibid. 109–10).

A text from the *Tantara ny Andriana* on the origin of the fate of men and rice (Callet, Chapus, Ratsimba, vol. 1, 30–31, note 40) verifies in its own way a "fable" reported by Flacourt on the origin of the social orders (COAM 8.14);[22] it stresses that whatever they may do, the men who belong to different social orders can think and act only in accordance with the nature of the orders to which they belong *by virtue of their line of descent*. This is a constant of thought, at least of ancient Malagasy thought as it appears in its products.

The problem is the following: Is it possible to establish correlations that will explain within this order of thinking the essential characteristics and features of the heroes of the Andriambahoaka cycle, and particularly of the Andriana, or assimilated heroes?

To the extent that we accept this determination of marriage by line of descent and by nature—always clearly spelled out—we can first note that all Andriana marriages result sometimes from a rape (more or less consented to *afterwards*), sometimes from a contest, and sometimes, as in the case of Imaitsoanala and other heroines who are the daughters of monsters, from a marriage of free will or by mutual consent. The three elements may be more or less related to one another. In India, however, these three types of marriage, among them *svayaṃvara-*, or marriage by contest, are given as characteristic of the noble class of warrior princes (Kṣatriya). No mention is made of the solemn Brahman marriage in which the father gives his daughter to the suitor, since, as we have seen, the reverse is the case here: the union has no authorization from those on whom the Princesses depend.

Although these marriages are permissible for the Kṣatriya class, the *Mānava Dharmáśāstra*, or *Laws of Manu*, nonetheless generally looks askance at them and says that the products of these unions will be "cruel and deceitful . . . hating the Vedas and the sacred law" (3.41). Among these marriages, the one by mutual consent "stems from desire and has sexual relations as its purpose" (3.32), and, what is enlightening, it is referred to as a "Gandharva marriage." The Gandharvas are aerial spirits, the husbands of the *apsarases*, or celestial nymphs (Renou 1963, 208) and nymphs of the waters (Auboyer 218–19), "whose beauty, created for the pleasure of the gods, inspired passion in men" (ibid.). Renou adds that these nymphs, inhabitants of heaven, would visit earth, where various amorous adventures would await them (Renou 1963, ibid.), and Auboyer goes on to say: "It was thought that they would be an easy catch. All one had to do was surprise them while they were bathing in a river and sneak away with their clothes for them to be at the mercy of men" (Auboyer ibid.; also Renou 97–109).

The price for the marriage by rape or mutual attraction is familiar: a moral blemish that may well be that of all the Princes whom the harsh laws of sovereignty force "not to have a family" but that in the supernatural tales often appears not as a moral blemish but as a physical defect or abnormality. European medieval folklore explains this: from the marriages of the Mélusines and human beings are born exceptional children, endowed with physical gifts (beauty for girls, strength and intelligence for boys) but blemished and unlucky (Le Goff and Le Roy Ladurie 598–99). The physical defect may appear on the face or may manifest itself in other ways, for example, by paralysis or palsy (ibid. 589).

It is useless to go any further, since Malagasy folklore does not indicate (given the current level of knowledge) a line of descent so direct that it can come full circle and make the lastborn sons, always reputed for their courage and superior intelligence, the sons of the Green Princesses and the Princes of the Center.

The Position of the Andriambahoaka Cycle

Like Andriambavirano, who is both a Princess of the Water and a Green Princess, Fatima is connected with the water that she received from God, with salt, and finally with light, which, "when she was born, emanated from her body so much that all the earth was illuminated by it" (Virolleaud 14, note 1). I have long insisted on the identity in nature and essence of the creatures of Heaven and the Andriana. This same identity makes it possible to ask whether, just as Fatima is related to the Green Princesses, their husbands, the Andriambahoaka, and particularly their sons, the Princes of Light, could not be related to 'Alī.

The two main schools of Shiism, the duodecimal and the Ismaelian, agree in seeing in 'Alī "the friend of God" and in the Imams his successors, "those who bear within themselves the light of the Prophet" (*al-nūr al-muhammadī*). This light alone bestows on them the necessary infallibility that allows them to understand the hidden, esoteric aspects of the Koran and to relate them to its explicit aspects. As descendants of the Prophet by his daughter Fatima and by 'Alī, the Imams share in the purity of the Prophet and of Fatima, who is herself the source of this light, *nūr* (for example, Nasr 199–200; Ṭabāṭab'ī 173–217).

The links with Malagasy mythology are clearest in the Persian theater, in the *ta'ziye,* the stagings of the drama of Karbala and the Passion of the Imam Hussayn, the son of Fatima and 'Alī (and thus through his mother the Prophet's grandson). The "King of lights" for all of Shiite Islam (Massé 16), 'Alī, the "light of lights," is said to have "created Muhammad with his own light," according to some extremist sects (Virolleaud 14, note 1).[23] At the same time, not to be outdone by his wife, Fatima, who had received from God as a dowry "all of the waters of the universe" (ibid. 33–39), 'Alī is presented as the "master of the waters," who distributes the waters of paradise and on earth gives the waves of the sea their thrust, just as Andrianoro's mother did. These two attributes, light and water, can be joined together: hence, the representation of 'Alī emerging from the sun while water gushes forth at his feet (ibid. 14, note 1).

There is little doubt that the Shiite conceptions that are so apparent in Malagasy mythology were brought by the Raminias. At the beginning of the seventeenth century, the Portuguese, familiar with the Sunni mode of Islam, were disconcerted by the beliefs of the Raminias and did not know whether what they saw was religion or idolatry (COAM 2.193–94). However, a century earlier, those newcomers who, Flacourt says, were despite all appearances sent "by the caliph of Mecca," made no mistake, and being zealous Sunnis, they waged a war of extermination upon the Raminias on the shores of Matitana (COAM 8.39–40). This war was, in my view, symbolized by another myth, the myth of the giant Darafify or Darafely.

Ramini, the eponymous ancestor, himself a "great prophet," marries Fatima, the daughter of Muhammad, whom a tale that we have already cited presents as the wife of an Andriambahoaka who thus establishes his identification (Callet 16–17, note 15). The exceptional nature of Ramini stems from the fact that God did not make him as a descendant of Adam like all other men, but rather "created . . . [him] on the sea, either making him come down from the sky and the stars or creating him out of the foam of the sea" (COAM 8.82), a version confirmed by Léguevel de Lacombe, who in turn shows that Ramini was said to be created "from the purest portion of the foam of the ocean . . . activated by a spark of celestial fire" (Léguevel de Lacombe 1.180).[24]

In these versions, fire is closely connected with light. Recall the miraculous birth of Ibonia and his bath in a blazing fire that similarly failed to consume the grasshopper talisman out of which he had emerged. This theme is taken up again to a large degree in the supernatural tales in which the Princesses who have come from elsewhere do not hesitate to dive into the devouring fires, while these same fires immediately consume their rivals, who are foolhardy enough to dare to imitate them (Renel 2.257).

In historical terms, the dynasties of the Andriambahoaka Raminia reigned over the east coast from the end of the twelfth century or the beginning of the thirteenth century until the beginning of the sixteenth century, after which they were confined to the southeasternmost corner of the island. Délivré believes that the first Andriana appeared on the eastern side of the forest-covered cliff in the highlands during the first third of the fourteenth century (Délivré 233–34). There is little doubt that there was a connection between the Raminia Andriambahoaka and the highlands Andriambahoaka of the Vazimba dynasty, which preceded the Merina dynasty. The Raminia genealogy indicates that the younger brother, Rakoube, fleeing from his elder brother by going up the Mananjary River, reached the highlands (COAM 8.82–89) or, according to the version found in an Arabic-Malagasy manuscript, Alasora, the cradle of the Merina dynasty (Ferrand 1910).

In mythological terms, this identity is attested by the identification of Andrianoro, Ibonia, and Imaitsoanala with the first legendary Vazimba sovereigns, for example, with the Green Princess of the Water named Andriambavirano, the wife of Andriamanjavona, the son of Andrianerinerina. This Andrianerinerina, the first sovereign of the Vazimba dynasty, was a son of God who fell because the Vazimba knowingly made him eat defiled food, for which they were condemned to serve him (Callet, Chapus, Ratsimba 13, note 7). Here the legend appears as the inverse of the myths and supernatural tales in which, by contrast, the sovereigns are "promoted" human beings. The advent of the Merina dynasty with Andriamanelo, the son of a Vazimba princess from the same village of Alasora that Rakoube reached, does not put an end to these exceptional marriages, since Andriamanelo himself marries Imaitsoanola, "the green woman of the forest," who gives birth to Ralambo. However, when it comes to circumcision, which was introduced as a fundamental innovation by Andriamanelo, it is not a matter of *the only son,* but of two other sons, who are undoubtedly legendary, if we consider their names: Ra/masy and Ra/noro, the two qualifying terms essentially connected with circumcision (ibid. 135). These points of reference, together with ethnographic fragments and what can be learned from a natural environment still covered with vast unknown and virtually unexplored forests, lead one to believe that these myths, historical legends, and the whole oral tradition that comes with them deal with the remote period of the end of the Vazimba dynasty and the beginning of the Merina dynasty which, as we have said, probably extended from the beginning of the fourteenth century to the end of the first half of the sixteenth century.

During this period, the cycle of the Andriambahoaka and the myth of Ibonia are still no more than a developing ideology that lays the groundwork for a theory of sovereignty and social stratification. This theory guarantees the incontestable superiority of the Princes of the Vazimba line and later of the Merina line, both of whom are regarded as having a divine essence. Subsequently, and starting particularly with Andriamasinavalona, the Imerina sovereigns lean on this doctrine to support their claim to hegemony. After this, the structure of the center and the cardinal points, which dancers move through successively on the occasion of royal circumcisions,[25] becomes effectively the territorial structure of the *Imerina efa-toko,* the fourfold Imerina, whose center (the heart) symbolizes both unity and totality.

This structure is repeatedly reproduced, beginning with the architectural arrangement of the *rova,* or royal residences, with their highest point occupied by the sovereign's quarters, all the way down to the construction and interior arrangements of the most humble houses. Even in the six-section Imerina of Andrianampoinimerina (the Prince in the heart of the Imerina), the military camps of the sovereign physically reproduce on the ground the structure of the center and the four parts. Indeed, the history of the Imerina is nothing but a dialectic of the center and the cardinal points with centrifugal moments of expansion and centripetal moments of coiling. At the beginning of the eighteenth century, the four sons of Andriamasinavalona, betraying the will of their father "in the heart" of the Imerina, each wanted to become a new Prince of the Center, by questioning the preeminence of the center (Callet, Chapus, Ratsimba 1.555–63; 2.306–7).

Clearly, we are dealing with a history as mythical as myth itself, and consequently one that is subject to repetition. This irregular repetition, almost a playback, takes place in the eighteenth and nineteenth centuries with the rise of the powerful *hova* among the commoners, who, gradually becoming to the Andriana what the Andriana themselves had been to the gods, "cunning" and "ready to take advantage of situations," succeed in robbing them (the Andriana) of their essential prerogative: sovereignty. It only remained to use this robbery to begin what the historians of the nineteenth century have called a "mystical marriage." In fact, these are actually unthinkable marriages, not, this time, between daughters of God and Princes of Earth, but between female sovereigns, "visible deities," often qualified with the term "suns," and obscure "commoners of the earth." Unthinkable marriages, therefore, but marriages that Rainilaiarivony, one of the most remarkable Malagasy statesmen, would repeat exactly three times, just as in the tales.

The Andriana cycle of the Andriambahoaka in most of Madagascar is coupled with another cycle that is introduced in a minor mode: the cycle of Ikoto/fetsy (Ikoto "the cunning") and Imahaka (*A.N.* 39–53; Raiandriamampandry 32–54; Ferrand 1893, 201–48). This other cycle denotes a totally different system of values; here cunning (also a prerogative of the Andriana) could be ingenious if it were not—unfortunately—too often sordid. Formidable contenders, the two accomplices spare nothing of the established order. They insult Andriana, desecrate talismans, revere ancestors who were embroiled in swindling, and commit absolutely heinous crimes against the most defenseless people: women, children, and the elderly, for whom the Andriana had always been a bulwark. To assimilate this cycle into a *hova* ideology that was thus opposed to the ideology of the Andriambahoaka would be excessively injurious to the *hova* order. In any case, this ideology, even more extreme in its rejection of the minimum of reciprocity that should normally govern human relations, makes it possible to understand the revolutionary impact of the well-known saying: "The Andriana did not fall down from heaven any more than they sprouted from the earth; it is human beings who are the origin of the Andriana" (*A.N.* 171). This is a conception very different from the one that Iboniamasiboniamanoro expressed with majesty or that the young sovereign Radama II expressed much more recently in the middle of the nineteenth century.

Once brought down from heaven to earth, perhaps in the likeness of this fallen son of God, the first Vazimba sovereign, Malagasy mythology remains first and foremost a political mythology, through the use that has been made of it. In this context, it is amazing to see how, starting with a few simple ideas developed in two or three intellectual structures, notably those of the center and the cardinal points, a whole society and a whole civilization were finally elaborated.

By coming into conflict with one another in the name of a claimed superiority, the Princes of the Center worked toward a political unification, which they actually achieved when their sphere of influence reached the seacoast on every side, in the first half of the nineteenth century.[26] By doing this, they were able to integrate more completely the heterogeneous populations that had come from various shores of the Indian Ocean. These populations, while preserving their personal and property rights along with their particular cultures, did nevertheless accept common political and religious organizations.

These same intellectual structures, remarkably effective in the past because they were so deeply internalized, remain the same today, inspiring reflections, customs, that is—since it involves a myth of sovereignty—policies. These policies are all the more surprising to us because until this century of European influence they were based on the ideological foundations of an ancient civilization, a civilization that, because we have made no effort to understand it on its own terms, has remained for us—we must confess—largely strange and unknown.

P.O./g.h.

NOTES

Despite the existence of a rich corpus and primary works, Malagasy mythology, inseparable from that of the countries bordering the Indian Ocean, still has not—doubtless for this reason—been sufficiently studied and is far from constituting the established domain which I hope will be recognized in the future. The present article inevitably reflects these uncertainties, and, because of this situation, I must warmly thank my colleagues, Michel Carayol and Daniel Roche, who, not at all disconcerted by the Green Princesses, took the trouble of reading in detail a first manuscript which by their criticism they have helped to improve greatly.

Concerning the transcription of local terms, it suffices to remember that Malagasy *o* corresponds to Arabic, Malay, or Sanskrit *u* (the French *ou*) and that the Malagasy *y* in final position is equivalent to *i*.

1. The most developed version of the legendary account of the destruction of the Saba' kingdom and the consequent dispersion of the Azdites, drawing upon verses 13 and 14 of Sura 34 of the Koran, is found in Mas'ūdi 2:473–85 (work in progress).

2. "Malagasy tale 100, p. 100," exclaimed R. Becker, translator and commentator of the version of Dahle published in the original edition of *Specimens of Malagasy Folk-Lore* (1877), revised and reprinted regularly since then under the title *Anganon'ny Ntaolo*, "Tales of the Ancients" (Dahle and Sims, eds.).

3. We have, thanks to E. Birkeli, O. Chr. Dahl, and J. Faublée, collections of the tales relating to the cycle of Zatovo for the Sakalava country of the center and southwest and the Bara of the center-south.

4. In the Zafimaniry country (the intermediary cliff of the east border of the highlands), the same concept of *manjo* designates both sterility and death.

5. Attested in parts of Indonesia that were Indianized or not affected by Islam, viewed with favor in the Austronesian world, sororal polygyny is proscribed by Islam. Common in supernatural stories, it may correspond to an Indo-Indonesian substratum prior to a second, more recent, layer marked by the interdictions of Islam. (See also note 18.)

6. The word *fianakaviana*, "family," which nowadays designates the extended family but formerly the reduced conjugal family, is based on the root *kavin* (Malay/Indonesian *kawin*), from which in this language come all the terms signifying alliance and marriage. For other examples of these cryptic etymologies used to reinforce the logic of the situations, see note 12, as well as, in the text, the developments about Andria/noro, the "Prince of Light."

7. This raises another problem, that of the "provider monsters," cadavers from which emanate goods, wealth, a whole people, which is connected with the theme of traps, nets, miraculous chests providing the magical wealth of last-born sons (cf. Ibonia, ed. Becker, 103–6). Also, in an opposite sense, the sanction by which a monster devours the doer of a misdeed: *A.M.* 125–26. In the last case, it is a serpent with seven heads (*fananim/pita/loha* from the Sanskrit *phaṅin*), the incarnation of dead Princes.

8. Often called *omby* (cattle) *baria* from the Arabic *bahr*, "sea."

9. Monogamous marriage, which in the twilight of his life Ibonia proclaimed the perfect union, which "nothing, no person, except death, can dissolve" (Becker 131).

10. In this regard, two Indian tales translated and presented by L. Renou are very explicit: Renou (1963) 73, 76, 103, 105, 108.

11. According to these Princes, the eclipses (of the moon) are caused by the aggression of a giant serpent (he supports the Earth on his coils), who would devour the moon if he were not expediently frightened by the uproar of humans. This is the theme of the *asura* Rāhu, whose name, moreover, appears in the Malagasy Rao (the same pronunciation) of the expression *hinan-dRao:* "devoured by Rao." According to Berthier, this expression is used on the fifth or sixth night, at the moment when the moon rises and presents a fringed upper edge (Berthier 56). Moreover, this legend directly evokes the water serpent Naga of Indonesian mythology, which supports the Earth and which is here assimilated to Rāhu.

12. Andrianoro assumes the status of servant (Malagasy *mpanompo*) which is, curiously, connected with the Malay etymology of son-in-law, which he is: Malagasy *vinanto,* Malay *binantu,* from a root *nantu* evoking the idea of "service" (cf. note 6)!

13. This ought to be confirmed; one must not forget that the cow is the equivalent in the animal world of humans and, like humans, it possesses a soul (*ambiroa*). It is the same in Indonesia, notably in Celebes, where *ambiroa* is *hambiruan.*

14. In Indonesian mythology, Ibonia would be a fetish man, a quality frequently attributed to the Princes. Thus, Alkema and Bezemer report that the Priest-King Singa Manga Radja, killed during a rebellion in 1910, was a fetish; "he had been seven years in the womb of his mother, his tongue was covered with hair, and a word from him could kill men and animals and devastate a whole region" (p. 156).

15. The connection of the razor and the banana directly evokes circumcision. It was customary for the mother's brother of the infant to swallow the prepuce of his sister's son in a piece of banana.

16. Dumézil, in vol. 2 of *Mythe et epopée,* as well as in *Heurs et malheurs du guerrier,* develops this theme of the Indo-European sovereign heroes whose youthful activities of a bad or an antisocial nature did not in any way prejudice their future as great civilizing sovereigns.

17. Prince Andriamahatindriarivo, who had married a young (half) sister Ra/tsipi/rano, "the blessed," literally "the sprinkled" (with holy water).

18. A permitted marriage in Indonesia, but prohibited by the Koran (cf. note 5).

19. The word of the texts is *sira,* but another, more solemn term, also of Indonesian origin, *fanasina,* is derived from *hasina,* "sacred and active power," a characteristic concept of sacred sovereignty.

20. In addition to the Andriana, the priest-diviners, guardians of the idols (mediators of another kind between Heaven and Earth, gods and men), share this privilege. The traditions report that the remains of a famous guardian idol, whom Andriamasinavalona had had put to death, had remained incorruptible: "Neither the ants nor dogs attack him: ferns grow beneath them (the remains) and envelope them." Finally, the body, like that of a sovereign, was deposited in a marsh. (Callet, Chapus, Ratsimba 1.557.)

21. This is Andriamahatantiarivo.

22. In the same way that a tale explains the creation of the world as resulting from the dismemberment of an aquatic monster (Renel 3:124–25), Flacourt reports a "*ramina* fable according to which the primordial spouses from whom the social orders would be produced were themselves drawn from different parts of the body of Adam: brains, neck, shoulder, calf, sole of the foot." In the same *ramina* conception, Eve was born from an abscess "on the flesh of the leg of Adam" (COAM 2:93–94), a version which is found in Borneo in the Iban myth of creation where, similarly, the wife of the first man was born from his calf (Jensen 75).

23. Virolleaud borrows these images from the representations of the Nuṣairiya, a Shiite sect that is considered heretical and "extremist" and that is defined by its incarnationism and its belief in the passage of the Holy Spirit into a succession of imams (Laoust 147).

24. Birth from sea foam is attested in the Malay archipelago; for example, Devic 34–35, 41.

25. It is not possible for me to expand upon this dance of royal circumcision, called *Soratra,* "of the scripture" (cf. Rasamimanana and Razafindrazaka 43–44 and figure 6; Cousins 5–7; Callet, Chapus, Ratsimba 1:142–44), nor further upon all the adjacent symbolism of the game of *fanorona,* also called *soratra andriamanitra,* "Scripture of God." Both the dance and the game are directly connected with the same structure of the center and four cardinal points, whose great productivity we have seen.

26. I refer to the "political testament" attributed to Andrianampoinimerina, who died in 1810, one of the greatest, if not the greatest, Malagasy sovereign, who declared: "The sea is the boundary of my rice field."

BIBLIOGRAPHY

Sources in Malagasy (with or without translation)

R. BECKER, *Conte d'Ibonia: Essai de traduction et d'interprétation d'après l'édition Dahle de 1877* (Antananarivo 1939), *Mémoires de l'Académie malgache.* R. P. CALLET, *Tantara ny Andriana eto Madagascar,* historical document which follows Malagasy manuscripts (2d ed., Antananarivo 1878, Presy Katolika). R. W. E. COUSINS, *Fomba Malagasy* (Antananarivo 1963, 2d ed. Trano Printy Imarivolanitra). R. DAHLE, *Specimens of Malagasy Folk-Lore* (Antananarivo 1877). R. DAHLE and J. SIMS, *Anganon'ny Ntaolo: Tantara mampiseho ny Fomban-drazana sy ny Finoana sasany nananany* (Tales of the elders: Accounts revealing their ancestral customs and beliefs) (Antananarivo 1971), numerous editions.

Firaketana ny fiteny sy ny zavatra malagasy, Boky II (Malagasy encyclopedia, book 2) (Antananarivo).

R. J. A. HOULDER, *Ohabolana ou Proverbes malgaches* (Antananarivo 1957). RAIANDRIAMAMPANDRY, *Tantara sy Fomban-drazana* (Antananarivo 1971). M. RANDRIA, *Foto-teny Malagasy Boky I,* Revio Fampitaha (Antananarivo 1968). J. RASAMIMANANA and L. RAZAFINDRAZAKA, *Fanasoavana ny tantaran'ny malagasy/ Contribution à l'histoire des Malgaches, Ny Andriantompokoindrindra* (Ambohimalaza 1957, reprint of 1909 edition). R. P. WEBBER, *Dictionnaire malgache-français rédigé selon l'ordre des racines* (île Bourton 1853).

The Malagasy text of the myth of I/bonia/masi/bonia/manoro is found in *Specimens of Malagasy Folk-lore* and in *Anganon'ny Ntaolo.* R. Becker has made a translation of the first version. We are indebted to G. S. Chapus for a second attempt at translation, but it is a very incomplete translation, which, moreover, comes from much modified versions of *Angano.* For the peripheral regions of the west and south, thanks to E. Birkeli, O. Chr. Dahl, and J. Faublée, we have collections of tales about the "Cycle of Za/tovo," other versions of the cycle of the Andriambahoaka.

On Madagascar

Among the general works, besides *L'histoire des rois,* it is necessary to emphasize the *Collection des ouvrages anciens concernant Madagascar* and the published fascicles of the *Firaketana ny Fiteny sy ny zavatra malagasy* (Encyclopedia of the Malagasy language). H. BERTHIER, *Notes et impressions sur les moeurs et coutumes du peuple malgache* (Antananarivo 1933). R. P. CALLET, G. S. CHAPUS, and E. RATSIMBA, *Histoire des rois: Traduction du Tantaran'ny Andriana* by R. P. Callet, vols. 1–2 (Antananarivo 1953, 1956). G. S. CHAPUS, *Les Imériniens dans les "Contes des anciens"* (Montpellier 1930).

The collection of ancient works about Madagascar (COAM): A. GRANDIDIER, CHARLES ROUX, H. FROIDEVAU DELHORBE, and G. GRANDIDIER, eds. (1904–20), vol. 2: Tentative d'évangélisation portugaise, 1613 à 1640; vol. 8: Histoire de la Grande Ile de Madagascar d'Étienne de Flacourt, première partie, 1642 à 1658; vol. 9: Histoire de la Grande Ile de Madagascar, deuxième partie, 1642 à 1658. R. DECARY, "Les Marofotsy, coutumes et croyances," *Bulletin de l'Académie malgache,* vol. 27. A. DELIVRE, *L'histoire des rois d'Imerina: Interprétation d'une tradition orale* (Paris 1974). G. FERRAND, *Contes populaires malgaches* (Paris 1893); "Les voyages des Javanais à Madagascar," *Journal Asiatique,* 15/2 (1910): 281–330. M. GUILLAIN, *Documents sur l'histoire, la géographie et le commerce de la partie occidentale de Madagascar* (Paris 1845). B. F. LEGUEVEL DE LACOMBE, *Voyage à Madagascar et aux îles Comores, 1823–1830,* vol. 1 (Paris 1840). H. LEITÃO, *Os dois descobrimentos da ilha de São Lourenço mandados fazer pelo vice-rei D. Jerónimo de Avezedo nos anos de 1613–1615* (Lisbon 1970). CH. RENEL, *Contes de Madagascar* (Paris 1910–30), vol. 1, "Contes merveilleux"; 2, "Fables et Fabliaux"; 3, "Contes populaires"; "Ancêtres et Dieux," *Bulletin de l'Académie malgache,* n.s. vol. 5 (1920–21).

On the Problems of Relationships (essentially the Indian Ocean, Arabo-Persian front, India, and Indonesia)

B. ALKEMA and T. J. BEZEMER, *Concise Handbook of the Ethnology of the Netherlands East Indies* (1961). J. AUBOYER, *La vie quotidienne dans l'Inde jusqu'au VIIIe siècle* (Paris 1961). G. BUHLER, ed., *The Laws of Manu* (New York 1969). J. CALMARD, "Le mécénat des représentations de Ta'ziye," in *Le monde iranien et l'Islam,* vol. 2 (Geneva 1974). M. DEVIC, *Légendes et traditions historiques de l'archipel indien: Sedjarat Malayou* (Paris 1878). G. DUMÉZIL, *Mythe et épopée* 2: *Types épiques indo-européens: Un héros, un sorcier, un roi* (Paris 1971). M. GABORIEAU, "La transe rituelle dans l'Himalaya central: Folie, avatar, méditation," *Puruṣ ārtha,* part 2 (1975). R. HEINE-GELDERN, "Conceptions of State and Kingship in Southeast Asia," paper no. 18, Cornell University (Ithaca 1956). E. JENSEN, *The Iban and Their Religion* (Oxford 1974). P. E. JOSSELIN DE JONG, "Marcel Mauss et les origines de l'anthropologie structurale hollandaise," *L'homme* 12, 4 (1972): 62–84. J. LE GOFF and E. LE ROY LADURIE, "Mélusine maternelle et défricheuse," in *Annales,* 1971, special issue *Histoire et structure* nos. 3 and 4. H. LAOUST, *Les schismes dans l'Islam: Introduction à une étude de la religion musulmane* (Paris 1968). H. MASSE, *Croyances et coutumes persanes,* 1 (Paris 1938). MAS'ŪDI, *Les Prairies d'Or,* 2 (Paris 1965). A. GALLAND, trans., "Les mille et une nuits," in *Contes arabes* (Paris 1965), 2:311–75. S. H. NASR, *Islam, perspectives et réalités* (Paris 1975). W. H. RASSERS, *Pānji, the Culture Hero: A Structural Study of Religion in Java* (The Hague 1959). L. RENOU, *Anthologie sanskrite* (Paris 1961); *Contes du Vampire: Vetālapañcaviṃśatikā* (Paris 1963). H. TABĀṬABĀ'I, *Shi'ite Islam* (London 1975). CH. VIROLLEAUD, *Le théâtre persan ou le Drame de Kerbela* (Paris 1950).

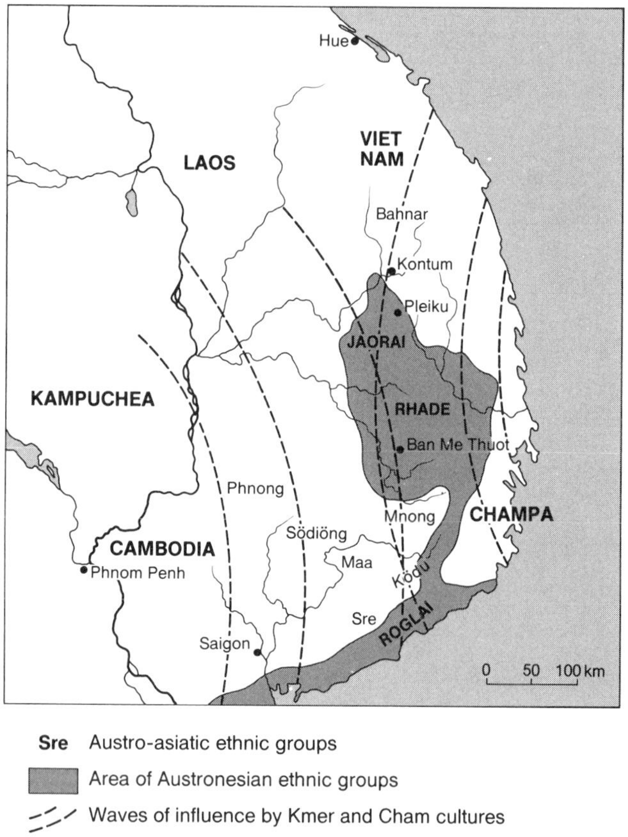

Indigenous population of southern Indochina.

The Mythology and Ritual of the Indigenous Populations of the Southern Part of the Indo-Chinese Peninsula: Orientation of Research

I. The Indigenous Indo-Chinese

The indigenous populations of the southern part of the Indo-Chinese peninsula are, by definition, neither Cambodian, nor Laotian, nor Vietnamese—or, to be more precise, they are neither Khmer, nor Lao, nor Viet, since they are all subject to one of the nations which these three peoples have constituted. Most are Vietnamese in nationality, but not at all Viet in language or culture. They are too little known for us not to present them here; they deserve a place in this work that is out of proportion with their population or their historical and political role, because they are cultures in which myth has remained alive, infusing all of existence.

The eastern part of the mountainous range between India and China is like a hand whose fingers are the ranges, valleys, and rivers (the Brahmaputra in India, the Irrawaddy in Burma, the Menam in Thailand, the Mekong in Laos and Cambodia, the Red River in Vietnam), which generally flow northwest-southeast. This seems to have been the main direction of the ancient migrations which, following these arteries, peopled the Indo-Chinese peninsula and the Pacific islands beyond. This arterial movement does not exclude certain reverse movements, like that of venous blood. Belonging to this substratum of the population, the "indigenous Indo-Chinese peoples" have been inhabitants of the peninsula the longest. They make up several ethnic groups, whose main relations were established in an east-west direction, between themselves and, farther away, with Champa (a former empire on the eastern coast) and Kampuchea (Cambodia), both Indianized states.

These groups have never formed a unit and have no common term to designate themselves. Called Phnong ("wild," the name of an ethnic group) by the Cambodians (in Khmer, *phnom* means "mountain"), Moï ("wild") by the Vietnamese, Kha ("slave") by the Laotians, they were called Montagnards ("mountaineers") by the French (hardly an appropriate name, since most of them are settled in valleys or on plateaus at 300 to 600 meters), a term picked up by the Vietnamese under the form Thüöng (since Mọi was overly pejorative). Georges Condominas has proposed "Proto-Indochinese." Each group has its own ethnic name (for example: Mnong, Eddé, Jörai, Bböhnar . . .), not to mention the distorted or entirely diferent names which their neighbors give them (Eddé becoming Rhadé, for instance, or Kreng). The groups together amount to about one million people, and so form an ethnic minority but one which has played a role in the demographic formation of the peninsula and the history of the nations that make it up.

Until the seventeenth century, the southern part of the peninsula was divided between two great empires: Kampuchea in the west, Champa in the east. The ethnic minorities in between were autonomous if not totally independent. They were not entirely foreign to these kingdoms, to the extent that the "Khmer are Hinduized Phnong" (Cœdès, 1948) and the Cham are Hinduized Jörai. The network of (east-west) relations among all these peoples was such that cultural influences went in both directions; it is dificult to distinguish, for example, what Jarai mythology owes to that of Champa, or vice versa, or whether there was a foundation common to the ancient Jarai and the proto-Cham. If there was some Indianization of the indigenous minorities on the western and eastern fringes of the two empires, it happened through cultural osmosis, in a muted echo of the peaceful Indianization of the Khmer and the Cham (the latter having then been partly Islamicized, something of which the culture of the Chamized ethnic groups bears no trace).

On the north-south axis things happened in a completely different way. The Vietnamese (Sinicized Austroasiatic peoples), after occupying the Red River delta, slipped between the coast and the cordillera as far as the Mekong delta without ever penetrating the central range, difficult of access from the east except through a few rare valley passes. They annihilated the Cham empire—Vietnamization, the daughter of Sinicization, took place through military conquest and systematic occupation. It was from the west that French colonial expansion won the back country and annexed the ethnic minorities—the last step in the occupation—without, however, entirely subjugating them. Here the only Frenchification we observe is in the form of lasting influences: political among the Eddé, where the civil administration favored an autonomist program, cultural among the Bböhnar, where the Catholic mission attacked the mythology. When they left, the French ceded the territory of the indigenous peoples to the Vietnamese who settled there, coming from the east, the south, and finally the north; assimilation to Vietnamese culture had begun.

The mythology of the ethnic groups of the interior gives evidence (at least by allusions, brief references) of relations with neighboring peoples: Khmer, Lao, or Cham, rarely Viet; if the French are ever named, it is in what are clearly very recent additions, and the tone tends to be one of mockery. The myth of the origin of writing belongs to the following schema, common to a number of groups: a celestial divinity inscribes instructions on skins (of buffalo or deer); these are meant to communicate knowledge to men. The Khmer, Lao, and Viet have carefully kept these skins; "we, too busy drinking our rice beer, we let a dog tear up that skin, that's why we don't know how to write." The Jörai variant on this theme: "The French wrote down on paper what the Master of Heaven dictated to them, the Lao wrote it down on wood, the Jörai on a skin" (then the dog comes along). The Sré make up for this by adding that it was they who brought the techniques to the French.

Within a large and entirely oral literature, this myth and several others are found among several ethnic groups. And yet the indigenous peoples of Indochina are divided into two great ethnolinguistic families: the Austroasiastic peoples (or Mon-Khmer), generally on the higher and less fertile lands, separated into northern and southern groups by the continuous mass of the Austronesian peoples (or Malayo-Polynesians). The Austronesian peoples penetrate them like a wedge, occupying the valleys and the richer lands—which suggests that their arrival was later and of eastern origin; but this is only a hypothesis, since we know nothing of the early history of these populations without documents, everything in their culture being perishable, except for speech. In the myths, every ethnic gropu claims to originate in the territory it now inhabits, after coming out of the netherworld. We find this among the Austroasiatic peoples as much as among the Austronesian peoples, although their languages are unrelated and there is no mutual comprehension between the two families.

Related linguistically to the Malayans and Indonesians (particularly to the Minangkabau of Sumatra and the Dayak of Borneo), the Austronesian people constitute groups that are strong (especially the Eddé and Jórai) and solidly structured, in a position of superiority relative to the Austroasiatic people, whom they have sometimes mistreated (Jörai against Bböhnar, for example). Yet in their material culture, their mode of life, their way of thinking and its literary expression, they are closer to the continental Austroasiatic peoples than to the insular Austronesian peoples—which permits a comparative study of the two mythologies.

The forest is the common context of their existence. It occupies a large place in the myths and provides the materials for houses (wood, bamboo, and thatch) and part of the subsistence of these peoples, hunters and gatherers, who also grow rice, maize, and some vegetables. The most remarkable productions of their material culture are weaving (cotton) and basketwork (bamboo and rattan), everyday masterpieces. The family may be matrilineal, with matrilocal residence, as among the Sré and the Jörai, or patrilineal, as among the Maa and certain Mnong groups; everywhere the mother's brother plays a privileged role. The household rather than the village constitutes a unit. The only real power is that of tradition; everyone knows what he must do to follow the path of the ancestors.

Rather than speaking of their religion as something distinct from everyday activities, it would be more correct to say that everything in their life (and all of their life) has a

Pnong warriors in a bas-relief from Angkor. Paris, Musée de l'Homme collection. Photo J. Dournes.

A Jörai warrior's dress. Paris, Musée de l'Homme collection. Photo J. Dournes.

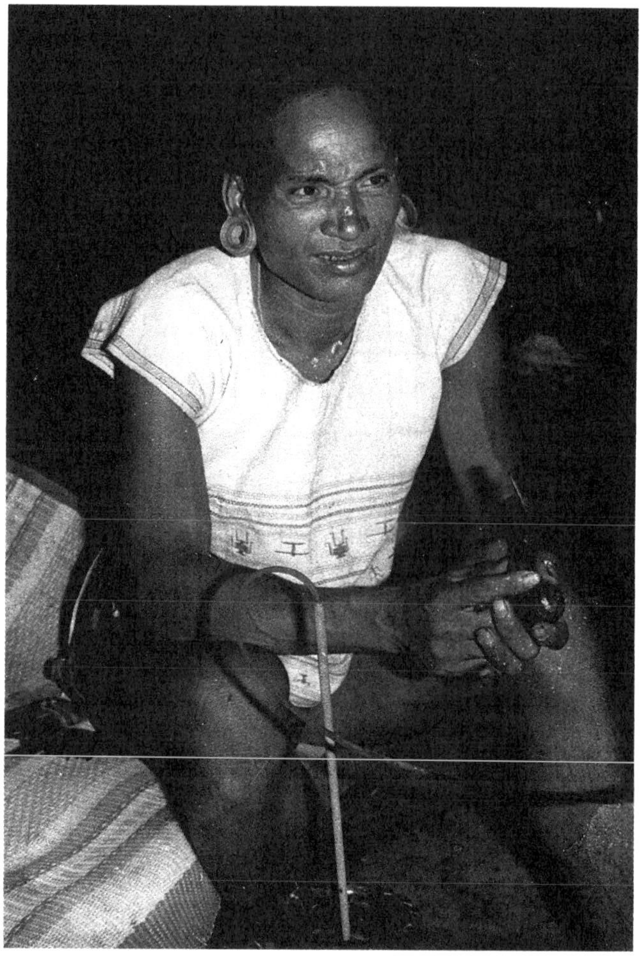

Socializing around a jar of rice beer (Mnong.) Paris, Musée de l'Homme collection. Photo J. Dournes.

religious—or, better, mythological—aspect to it, and this is true of all of the ethnic groups. Mythology is not something separate, which makes it very difficult to isolate it in cultures where everything holds together and is explained by a global world view, a unified conception of man and his place in the universe. Mythology is not limited to stories and to story time; it is also silence and the inner life. Myths are memorized by everyone (to different degrees); they bring together (and explain) the dreams and the behavior of men who never cease to live in the world that they imagine.

II. Method and Orientation of Research

The indigenous peoples of Indochina have been studied from the beginnings of colonization, chiefly by the French: explorers, military men, missionaries, then by administrative and educational functionaries, finally by ethnographers; most of their studies are limited to the ethnic group known to the writers. The mythology of these populations is scarcely known. This is easy to understand: collecting myths, understanding them to some degree, collecting commentaries, recognizing the myth's place in life and how it informs thought—all this requires long-suffering patience, great intimacy with the population studied, its confidence and its collaboration, and thus a very long stay, regular participation in daily life, an immersion in the culture that allows one to "think like them" and dream with them.

A failure to achieve this kind of knowledge of the ethnic minorities leaves the researcher with only an outside view, a view of the least essential part of their culture. The mythology of these peoples is not only the most beautiful and original of their productions, it is above all their inner life; it is the genius of these peoples, and should allow us—this is a personal opinion—to account for any trait of their culture by situating it in a totality of thought that gives it its meaning and marks it as its own. Mythology understood in this sense cannot be reduced to a collection of myths: the stories that we hear are only points of orientation, the whole set of texts collected forming a sort of map of the imaginary, a projection (into the time of recitation and the linearity of its unfolding) of the totalizing world view common to the Indo-Chinese peoples.

Their life is far from being a paradise. They have the wisdom not to make work into a value or man into a master of creation. Located in their own proper place, among other living things, they know that anything can be dangerous: the forest and its tigers, the sky and its lightning; a neighbor may be an enemy. A great pleasure is to gather around a pot of beer, to drink, smoke, and chat. It is especially in the evening that they reveal themselves: tale-tellers and orators, transmitting from generation to generation a prodigious oral literature (maxims, invocations, songs, proverbs), of which mythology is only a part. When one is lucky enough to live with populations who are not content merely to tell myths (which is itself no longer so frequent in the world), but who live them and mythicize every day, one has only to collect, transcribe, translate, interpret, and live them oneself.

Note that we are dealing with languages that are without traditional writing systems; terms borrowed from these languages are transcribed here according to the usual system used in various publications.

"Myth" is taken here in the sense of the Sré *yalyau*, or the Jörai *akhan*, that is, a traditional story, orally transmitted, without distinguishing between what we call "myth," "folktale," and "legend," and without limiting mythology, as is too often done, to "origin myths," or to stories about gods, especially since any traditional story implies the literature as a whole and reflects the global vision of the imaginary, a whole conception of the world.

Myth is also an art, the art of beautiful language, the art of telling tales, which even more than music, has its times (preferably at night) and its conditions (some stories cannot be told completely without a sacrificial ritual, as if to "excuse" oneself for revealing hidden things, serious events).

But can be speak of *a* mythology for different ethnic groups speaking different languages? This is the orientation of our ongoing research: to bring together what remains (relatively) separate in the field and then to study the reasons for similarities and the meanings of the differences. Examples will be taken primarily from two ethnic groups: the Sré, who speak an Austroasiatic language, and the Jörai, who speak an Austronesian language, with some references to other ethnic groups of the two language families. It is thus not (yet) a matter of a synthesis but of the current results of research that tend to support the hypothesis of a common culture, and to highlight the links between this southern Indo-Chinese mythology and those of other Austroasiatic and Austronesian populations (that of the Cham, in particular), which are also too little known on this level. Without disdaining the use of Western methods of formal analysis, the research is carried out mainly from inside: at the heart of a mass of texts, memorized so that they can be brought together easily, with the knowledge of what men do and think about them—a knowledge that is also a complicity.

More than one hundred texts have been collected in this way among the Sré, and more among the Jörai; whenever one or the other of these is evoked in an article, it will be given with its number in the corpus (Ms. *n* for the former; Mj. *n* for the latter), to facilitate reference to the works and articles in which they are cited, translated, or analyzed; this allows us to avoid weighing down the articles with material that is published elsewhere.

J.D./j.l.

BIBLIOGRAPHY

1. General Bibliography

J. BOULBET, *Pays des Maa', Domaine des Génies* (Paris 1967); *Dialogue lyrique des Cau Maa'* (Paris 1972). G. COEDES, *Les États hindouisés d'Indochine et d'Indonésie* (Paris 1948). G. CONDOMINAS, "Les tribus proto-indochinoises," in *Ethnologie de l'Union française*, by A. Leroi-Gourhan and J. Poirier (1953), 2:658–78; *Nous avons mangé la forêt de la pierre-génie Gôo* (Paris 1957); *L'exotique est quotidien* (Paris 1965). DAM BO (J. DOURNES), *Les populations montagnardes du Sud indochinois* (Saigon and Lyons 1950). J. DOURNES, *En suivant la piste des hommes sur les hauts plateaux du Viêtnam* (Paris 1955); *Coordonnées, structures jörai familiales et sociales* (Paris 1972); *La culture jörai*, catalogs of the Musée de l'Homme (1972). P. GUILLEMINET, "La tribu Bahnar du Kontum," *Bull. EFEO* 45, 2 (1952): 393–561. H. MAITRE, *Les régions moï du Sud indochinois* (Paris 1909); *Les jungles Moï* (Paris 1912). A. PAVIE, *Mission Pavie Indo-Chine*, 11 vols. (Paris 1901–19).

2. On Myths and Rituals

J. DOURNES, "Chants antiques de la montagnes," *Bull. Soc. Études Indoch.*, 24 (1948); "Le maître des eaux (conte sré)," *France-Asie* 91 (1953): 25–29; "Fêtes saisonnières des Sré," *Bull. EFEO* 46, 2 (1954): 599–610; *L'homme et son mythe* (Paris 1968); "L'inceste préférentiel," *L'homme* 11, 4 (1971): 5–19; "Orphelin transformé," *Archipel* 2 (1971): 168–96; "Sous couvert des Maîtres," *Arch. europ. de sociol.* 14 (1973): 185–209; "La toupie incestueuse," *L'homme* 15, 3–4 (1975): 31–53; "La fée du figuier," *L'ethnographie* 68 (1974): 79–92; 69 (1975): 81–114; "Deux versions d'un mythe," *ASEMI* 6, 4 (1975): 97–124; *Akhan, contes oraux de la forêt indochinoise* (Paris 1976); *Le parler des Jörai et le style oral de leur expression* (Paris 1976); *Trois mythes sré* (Paris 1978); *Pötao, une théorie du pouvoir chez les indochinois Jörai* (Paris 1977; *Forêt Femme Folie, une traversée de l'imaginaire jörai* (Paris 1978).

Note: Jörai myths have been published for the most part; Sré myths are being published; for the Bböhnar, thousands of pages, collected by P. Guilleminet, await publication.

The History and Function of Indo-Chinese Myth: Change and Permanence

The indigenous Indo-Chinese are not a vanished society, nor are they a primitive society frozen in some deadly archaism. Throughout the ups and downs of history, after wars and colonizations, they have managed to do more than simply survive; they live and continue to make myths. Their culture remains alive, for, while it has not ceased to change in its manifestations, this does not alter or destroy the originality of its conception. Under these conditions, a study of myths would be incomplete if it did not take into account the dynamic factor and if it did not follow the changes diachronically. Mythology is not necessarily a science of antiquity; fortunately for us (at least if the poets give it their attention), it still lives (for how long?) among people who think in myths.

The factors of change are of two kinds: the internal dynamics of the productivity of an ethnic group and contacts with other peoples and cultures. These two categories interact: the inner dynamics select what will be brought in, while outside contacts influence choices: some culture elements are retained and others abandoned, a process which can be demonstrated better in ritual than in mythology.

It is difficult to determine what the reciprocal influences were between the Austronesian peoples and the Austroasiatic peoples in prehistory. We know, for instance, that the Jarai of the north temporarily colonized the Bahnar of the south, and it is possible that they were heirs to them in somewhat the same way as the Romans were heirs to the Greeks. As for the less distant period, it may be possible, once Cham literature has been uncovered and analyzed, to recognize exchanges between it and the literatures of the eastern Indo-Chinese—a process which has already been pointed out in several studies devoted to them. Two factors should be taken into consideration: the Austronesian peoples (and their close neighbors) were "Chamized," and the Chams were Austronesian; just as the Chams assimilated Hindu cults (a statue of Śiva became the figure of the Cham king Pô-Klong-Garai; Bhagavati was adapted as Yang-Pō-Nagar, "Mistress of the country"; Indra was interpreted as Yang-In—see Mus, 1933, p. 371), the Jarai have recovered Cham deities (a Cham statue became for the Jarai a figure of Damsel Pe—see Dournes, 1970, p. 154). One can observe similar reciprocal interactions between the western Indo-Chinese and the Khmer or Laotians (Khmer is an Austroasiatic language). Before the French intervention, Sino-Vietnamese culture apparently had no impact on that of the indigenous inland peoples, although there may have been trade between them. In recent times, colonization in the Western style effected a brutal contact between the so-called modern world (because it thinks that it alone evolved) and the world of those who were called primitive. As a historical consequence of this colonization, Vietnamization became more efficient. Let us look at some examples of the effects of these changes, though it will not be possible to distinguish internal dynamics from acculturation, so closely are the two intertwined today.

Among the Jarai, who have been the most studied, myth and ritual undergoes modification in one generation. The same myth told over a period of ten or fifteen years by the same speaker or by another speaker (by an elderly woman and then by her grandson, for example) undergoes changes; passages are skipped (especially those that allude to the whole mythological corpus), elements are added (a reference to the French, to the Vietnamese), but the narrative remains recognizably Jarai and has kept its original color. The ritual changes and tends to be simplified; the great costly rituals dedicated to terrible deities give way to domestic and funeral rituals; we should also note a tendency toward rationalism: "The *Yang* always ask for sacrifices; they favor only the rich, who have all the resources and get richer and richer. We, the poor, need not offer them anything whatsoever." And in an extreme case, a simulacrum replaces the traditional ritual (a simulacrum that has nothing to do with the one that is customarily expected to be offered to possessed sorcerers).

The Catholic missions naturally encouraged this attitude, not among the Jörai (where they were not admitted) but among the Bböhnar (where they settled); strange and alien rituals replaced others, and the myths disappeared from the memories of Christians who had learned that they were devilries to be destroyed along with their remarkable ritual paintings. In their attempts to remove the *Yang*, the fathers destroyed the sacred and all resistance at the heart of the ethnic group. The effects of missions and colonization were very different depending on the populations; the Austronesian peoples, who had strong social systems, resisted on the whole.

Another phenomenon that attacks the culture of minorities from the outside is a recuperation. That is, missionaries borrow those elements that appear to them to be the least pagan and convert them (that is to say, denature them) in order to integrate them into an aseptic pagan Christianity. An administrator writes a literary work by joining bits and pieces of myths whose meaning is perverted; or he may traffic in the unwritten customary law in order to reinforce colonial power. Vietnamese publications cite the epics of the minorities and twist the meaning so as to find there the naturally "revolutionary" (we used to say "Christian") soul of people thus "prepared" to join their brothers in the struggle. A myth of the Eddé tribe thus appeared in a comic strip: the hero, who has Western features, wears a feather headdress like an American Indian chief and rebels against heaven! By working on their minorities, nations foster their naïveté, deceiving especially those who would not recognize popular local cultures in any other form.

On the other hand, there is a new and highly localized tendency among some Jörai to acquire a taste for their oral literature, to collect and transcribe their ancient myths faithfully and without attempting to modernize, politicize, or moralize them.

The literature of the indigenous Indo-Chinese is of the people and for the people; it is not limited to an elite but is merely better known by cultivated people who are not materially the most comfortable; quite the contrary. Myths are profoundly embedded within each person; mythical behavior, ritual activity, and social life are not images of one another, but the man who lives by myth, the man who performs a ritual, and the man who lives with his family are one and the same man. The mythic dimension is lived in daily life, from within. The link established between myth, ritual, and behavior is a function of what we might call "the mythological mentality," which can be seen notably in the following:

—A latent desire that "everything take care of itself," by counting more on the intervention of the *Yang* than on individual responsibility, preferring the direct result "fallen from heaven" to any human effort to produce it, waiting for the "ready-made," the gift, without active participation—which is not without political consequences, especially when one sees how "aid to the Third World" functions in this way.

—A disposition to admit what is strange and unusual (which results in great tolerance for the ways of other people), to await the marvelous and to see in it a sign of the *Yang* powers, a sign rather than a miracle or magic force (as some Westerners might be tempted to interpret it).

—An aspiration, repressed by the constraints of existence, to transgress the human condition in such things as social laws; an aspiration to be in an imaginary, distant place; the temptation of the forbidden: the woman and the forest, the sister and the fairy.

—The feeling that a certain communication is possible between domains, places, and times; more than that, a feeling that there is a kind of continuum within which man is situated. The two arts that are most practiced by the Jörai and other Indo-Chinese are the recitation of myths and music, which unfold in time and are perceived by the ear, the organ of hearing and the seat of the intelligence (whereas sculpture, painting, and weaving are blocked out in space), but only in order to go beyond the passage of time. As Lévi-Strauss has stated: "Like a musical work, myth functions on the basis of a double continuum" (1964: 24). Mythological thought establishes a particular type of relationship with the universe: man is coextensive with space (one species among others, he speaks with animals and plants), and by virtue of the timelessness of myth he is contemporary with the "paradise" of his dreams and with the stories of Drit. Myth suppresses ruptures between societies (Dournes, 1955, p. 91) and between persons (the "I" and the "you"—and is that not love?)

This leads us to emphasize what seems to be the essential function of myth: to recover, to reinvent the continuum by going beyond ambiguity (which is different from continuity but is a means of attaining it) and by opposing confusion (such as the one produced by rice beer, a mixed drug, which is said to bring about oblivion in which "husband and wife no longer recognize each other and all become confused"—but the one reciting the myth, he does not drink, at least until he has finished his story).

This continuum is signified in the ritual, which through repetition and redundancy tries to plug the holes, to do all that is possible (that is, imaginable), whether through divination in which man is on an equal footing with the *Yang*, energies that we might call supernatural, or through omens in which man is carried back to the time when he understood the language of the birds.

This continuum is represented in the myth, whose hero travels through the air and the underworld, changes himself into animals, and speaks with forest creatures and domestic objects. He leaps over mountain ranges in a single bound, stops time in its course. The theme of the day that never ends because the sun suspended its course at the hero's whim (explicit or otherwise) is a classical image of Jarai mythology (Mj. 44, 47, 110, 118); this is always for the sake of prolonging the pleasures of lovers, situated outside the bounds of time. This theme reverses that of the Mang-ling Darkness, a catastrophic period during which the sun did not show its face, which makes the sun a figure of life and happiness and, more exactly, a sign of love: beyond the oppositions and successions of life and death, day and night, lovers are freed from their limitations (both as living beings and as persons), and, no longer in need of the mediation of a third term, they attain the mythological goal of a recovered unity. Perhaps they do more. Through the imaginary, these people—so distant and yet so close to us—join and link all those on earth who know that in order to escape from the life that divides and severs, one need not die or sleep; one can also dream.

J.D./g.h.

BIBLIOGRAPHY

1. For the history: J. DOURNES, "Recherches sur le Haut Champa," *France-Asie* 201 (1970): 143–62. P. MUS, "Cultes indiens et indigènes au Champa," *Bulletin de l'École Française d'Extrême Orient*, 1933, 367–410.

2. For the evolution of the literature (modifications and variants): J. DOURNES, *Le parler des Jörai et le style oral de leur expression* (Paris 1976).

3. On the utilization of the literature: L. SABATIER, *La chanson de Damsan, légende radé du XVIe siècle* (Paris); "La chanson de Damsan," *Bulletin de l'École Française d'Extrême Orient* 33 (1934): 143–302; *Recueil des coutumes rhadées du Darlac* (Hanoi 1940); and the Vietnamese publications below.

4. On the continuum: J. DOURNES, *En suivant la piste des hommes sur les hauts plateaux du Vietnam* (Paris 1955); "Le discret et le continu," *JATBA* 18, 7–8 (1971): 274–87. C. LEVI-STRAUSS, *The Raw and the Cooked* (New York 1969); originally in French.

5. Vietnamese publications (in French): *Viêtnam* (Hanoi), November 1974, p. 11. *Giai Phong* (South Vietnam), no. 6 (1975): 14–15.

Indigenous Indo-Chinese Cosmogony

I. Ndu/Adei: The Celestial Divinity

Like most of the Austroasiatic peoples of the south (Katu, Maa, M̱nong), the Sré, in their myths and rituals, invoke ōng Ndu. Ōng is the general term used to designate men of one's grandfather's generation and those who are assimilated into that group (such as notables and elderly men whom one does not know); according to context, the term may be translated as "grandfather," "sir," or "my lord." Ndu functions as a proper name. Although he is anthropomorphized by the name and by mythic scenes that describe his appearance on earth, Ndu has no perceptible form or representation, apart from the wavy lines on top of the ritual festival pole among certain of the Röglai and Maa. He lives nowhere; he can be everywhere. He is unanimously said to be superior to all of the *yang* and is manifestly apart from all others—even if, thanks to a slip on the part of a bard who pronounced Ndu in place of Ködu (Ms. 123), it is conceivable that he may be connected with the deified mythic ancestor Ködu (*kö* is the particle which precedes all proper names of people among the Sré, but not the name of Ndu, who is thus not "personified" in this sense). He appears to be some kind of foster father, or providence: "Milk comes from Ndu; thus he fed men in the beginning. But when they grew up, milk was not sufficient, so Ndu created rice." Ndu is involved with the paddy *yang* (if not on the same plane) or in the form of Ndu *yang* (which, like banyan *yang*, expresses the sacred relation between Ndu and human beings), or still in the form of (*yang*) Ndu-Ndai—a classical rhyme word of the oral style, simply echoed for the rhythm. "We ask for rice from *yang*, and *yang* seeks it for us from Ndu." There is thus no higher order, no world beyond, except, perhaps, Sun (a heavenly divinity, and female), who, according to certain Sré, entrusted Ndu with the task of feeding humans.

Among the Austronesian groups, along with the Eddé, the Jörai use the name *öi Adei*. The term *öi* is the exact equivalent of the Sré *ōng*, and has the same uses. Adei is located above the vault of the heavens, the underside of the vault being *röngit*, the visible sky. This name is also pronounced Dei, Dai, or Diē: the reduplication ("to make an assonant balance, *pötüth*, but there is only one öi Adei") takes the form of öi Du-öi Dei (or Ködu-Ködē) in which it is easy to recognize Ndu-Ndai. It is in effect the same name, as H. Maitre once stated: "At the festival of the seed grains, all of the Mnong of diverse families offer a pot to Ndu, the supreme Spirit, the Aï Dë of the Rhadé" (Edde) (1912: 187). "He created everything," say the Jörai, "all things come from him, and without him there would be nothing." He has power over the life of everyone and stands above all; he is also invoked under the form of *yang dlong*, "on high" (as one says Elohim so as not to pronounce Yahweh), or in a parallel with *yang*: "If *yang* agrees to it, if Adei concedes it," has the sense of our "if God wills it." He has no connection with Sun, who, in Jörai thought, is *yang* manifest. Thus Adei = Ndu; it is the same word and the definition is close, but he is conceived and seen differently. To the extent that *yang* is an abstraction common to all the ethnic groups, Ndu/Adei is a variously colored mythic image: *yang* is conceived as a relationship; Ndu/Adei is perceived as a term.

In Sré mythology, Ndu intervenes in a very precise sense. "Seeing a butterfly flutter up over his house, a man recognized a manifestation of Ndu. In the night, in a dream he heard Ndu promise him assured riches. After that, he lacked nothing" (Ms. 116). "A poor man went out of a wealthy house where no one had offered him anything. A bat got caught in his hair, and wherever he went, people invited him to drink and eat; it was Ndu who accompanied him" (Ms. 117). The following account is of primary importance: "A very poor young man, Ddöi ("orphan"), goes to his mother's brother to borrow some rice. His uncle gives him nothing. On the road, he meets Ndu in the form of an old man and tells him of his troubles. Ndu then takes the form of Ddöi and brings a handful of straw to the uncle to obtain rice in exchange; the uncle chases him away. Ndu returns to Ddöi and promises to help him. Ndu gives a few seed grains to Ddöi; from this, Ddöi gets more rice than anyone in the world. The uncle wants to see the prodigious harvest; he climbs up into the rice granary, falls out of it, and breaks his bones. Then Ndu goes to look for a poor young girl who also lives alone. He brings her to Ddöi and marries them. Ndu disappears, never to be seen again. Ddöi and his wife live happily together" (Ms. 22—these texts are obviously much abridged here—cf. Dournes 1963: 52; 1971: 188). Another account, less widespread, is unique in depicting the poor man as coming to Ndu "on the border between heaven and earth"—the only case in which the man takes the initiative in the affair. The principal agrarian ritual of the Sré makes use of an element of this myth: handfuls of straw, soaked in the blood of the sacrificed she-goat, are placed at the four corners of the rice field, "the roads by which Ndu comes"; between

A Sré spirit house, *kut Ndu*. Musée de l'Homme collection. Photo J. Dournes.

the rice fields and the village, at the base of the ritual pole, they erect a "spirit house," *kut Ndu*, of bamboo and thatch, to receive Ndu at the time of his visit. Ndu is called first with whistles, then by a long invocation: "May the rice leave the other people and pile up here for us, and may we become very rich!" This is not in the spirit of the myth; here the man demands and sets his sights on wealth as if it ought to fall to him from the sky. At the time of the Sré new year festival, it is said, "Let us borrow rice from Ddöi, let us borrow paddy from Ndu"—and both are called *ŏng* in this case.

What about the people who call the kindly Ndu "Adei"? The Jarai myths introduce a son (more often the youngest of seven than the younger of two) of öi Adei (but never Adei himself) who descends to earth at the request of their father, who is moved by human misery, in order to transform the condition of a poor naked girl. In the form of a young man (sometimes deformed, to put her to the test), he asks permission to marry the poor girl, who has been raised by her grandmother Bush. He procures the means for her subsistence and gives her a child, then returns for good to the heavenly domain (Mg. 11, 13, 14, 66, 94). The reverse movement (of humans toward Adei) may be seen in several cases: (1) the type of "the child who did not want to die," who goes from village to village until he comes to the house of öi Adei, where he learns that one must die there too, but that on the border between heaven and earth one would not die, and yet one would not eat either (Mj. 70); (2) the type of the young boy who wants to avenge his uncle who has been killed by a powerful lord; he climbs to the house of öi Adei, who refashions his body so that it is ready for anything (exactly as the old woman Bush does for her protégés [Mj. 8, 20], but Adei [male] does so by forging, whereas Bush [female] does her work as a potter) and takes his own heart to put it in the body of the boy who, not surprisingly, kills the lord and takes his aunt back to him (Mj. 49); (3) the case of the epic heroes: the din of their battles disturbs öi Adei, who sends his servant girl Whirlpool (H'Kroah, the divinity of ascending whirlpools) to seize the hero, bring him up to heaven, and restore his strength (Mj. 24 and parallels); (4) Dier, the hero of a long epic: he climbs up to the house of Adei to marry his daughter and bring her back to earth with him (Mj. 109). In this text and in some others, Adei is a somewhat grotesque character, whom his wife awakens by pouring a bucketful of molten lead in his ear, something which would be unthinkable for the Sré if it were done to Ndu, but which would be quite appropriate for their demiurge, the good-natured giant Nyut.

The Jörai homologue for the Sré Ddöi would seem to be Drit (or Rit), which has the same meaning, "orphan." A whole cycle of Jörai mythology has Drit as its hero—he is, if not the national hero, at least a model for the argumentative and unpredictable Jörai. If we must reduce all these accounts to a single schema (which is painful since they are so beautiful), it might well be the following: the poor Drit lives with a grandmother Bush (who may be called Ya'-Pum) between the village and the forest (they are marginal people). An accident of the hunt puts him in contact with a beautiful fairy girl who has connections with the worlds of animals, flowers, and heavenly bodies, and who brings him a life of ease in the form of food and clothing (as though she were the initiator and introducer of technical knowledge). A local lord, *potao*, is jealous and takes her away from him. A series of trials, in which he is successful, allows Drit, who defeats the lord, to take back his beloved. In some accounts, the lord offers his own daughter in marrige to Drit, who does not want her and leaves her for the fairy of his dream;

in this case the lord functions as a father-in-law, that is, as a mother's brother who claims his right to the bride, and who thus corresponds to the evil uncle of Ddöi. Öi Adei apparently does not enter into the picture in any of this. Drit and his grandmother Bush are invoked ritually, notably in a long prayer addressed to the powerful divinities of the sources of rivers, Diö-Diung-Yung-Hmeng, who are legendary warriors charged by öi Adei with watching over the ritual activities of humans. As for öi Adei, he is invoked by the Jörai in a very different tone from that of the myths, and on the most important occasions: at fertility rites (before sowing) and during catastrophes (drought, incest—which are connected); the celebrants remain naked, in the manner of servants, to call respectfully to öi Du-öi Dei, parallel to ya'Dung-Dai (*ya'* is the feminine of *öi*).

This grandmother Dung-Dai, whose name is so similar to Du-Dei, is often explicitly said to be the wife of öi Adei. The study of many texts shows that she is interchangeable with grandmother Pum (Bush), the grandmother of Drit, who is in complicity with the fairies of the forest. This leads to the understanding that the Jörai Providence may well be female—öi Adei being no more than a very distant *deus otiosus*—and that the Jörai equivalent of the venerable Ndu of the Sré could be a pair of women, or rather a woman with two aspects: the old woman of the woods and the young fairy girl, a single female principle of fertility. This is in keeping with Jörai culture, where woman is everything and does everything. She is now visible in the moon, whose full face shows the old Bush under her banyan tree (cf. Sauer 1972: 88).

The Jörai Drit and the Sré Ddöi have the same character of "orphan"—that is, a loner, without parents or family, outside of all classifications, like Ndu/Adei—but they are not the same person: the Jörai seems more typed, with more character; the passive Ddöi resembles an ordinary Sré. Drit has more "liver"—as they say where he comes from—yet his victory and the goods he acquires come to him only through a woman—which is very Jörai. One may note another difference, which is connected with the character of the men of each ethnic group: the connections between heaven and earth are clearly sexualized among the Jörai (a son of god marries a daughter of men, or a son of men loves a daughter of a god), while they are not sexualized among the Sré—except when a son of men falls in love with a daughter of Sun (Ms. 13), and then we obtain the equation (Sré daughter of Sun = Jörai son of Sky) which makes the female Sun analogous gous to the male Adei in a chiasmic figure with the homology noted above (Ya' Dung-Dai corresponding to Ndu):

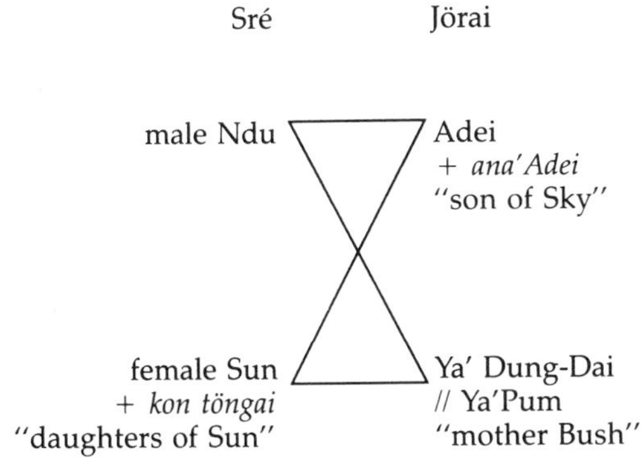

By means of cross-checking, interconnections, and intermediate figures (*mediators*), the Jarai, even more than the Sré, seem to be searching for a continuity; it appears as if the mythological figures of the two ethnic groups were weaving the same sorts of threads between them.

Ndu/Adei being a term, a separation between the distant god and the lower world would be logical; hence the *yang* relationship (abstraction) and the intermediate heroes (images) which serve to connect, to retrieve the lost unity. Such a vision nevertheless depends more on what is dreamed than on what is lived (in daily and ritual life), for only the dream voyager has no fear of straddling those distinctions which society loves so well (cf. Dournes 1975).

II. The Cosmic Ruptures

As far as origin myths are concerned, the indigenous Indo-Chinese have very little to say—although we know that this is not all there is to their mythology—apart from disconnected elements, which are nevertheless important for their representation of the universe, imagined in space and time as being marked, if not cut up, by ruptures in the initial and ideal continuum. On the occasion of traditional narrations and spontaneous conversations, it is still possible to glean diverse bits of information—a delicate operation which is worth the trouble—but more successfully among the Austroasiatic peoples than among the Austronesian peoples. The elements that follow do not reflect a rigorous chronological order.

1. *The Sré Creation and the Departure from Hell*

The Sré conceive the world as having seven levels, of which three are celestial and three infernal, with the earth in between. All was created in the heavens and then transported to the hells, where the demiurge Bung intervened on the side of Ndu; this creation is viewed as a work of the forge—a specifically masculine work. Bung brought plants, animals, man, and fire to earth out of the subterranean world, through the hole situated at Nkany. Then the giant Nyut thrust heaven still higher; since that time, it has been impossible to pass between the upper and lower worlds, which are inverse images of one another (in the hell called Brah-Ting, everything is done opposite to the way it is done on earth). "We, the sons of men, we are the sons of the seven" (the seventh world, in the middle).

2. *The Jörai Universe and the Emergence from Earth*

The Jörai believe the earth is like a round winnowing basket and the sky like another concave winnowing basket turned down on the earth; since they separated from one another, it is impossible to pass from one to the other. The sky is called the "model," *gru*, and the earth is its mirror image. Above the sky is the province of Adei; below is the world of the dead where everything is reversed. Humanity (that is, the seven Jörai clans) emerged from the earth through the hole of Dreny. Once every seven years a white buffalo is sacrificed there and its blood is poured into the hole. Only one young girl was unable to pass through because she was leading a buffalo whose horns were too wide (this detail is also found among the Sré): this is the girl of dreams whom only mythical heroes are able to join, under the earth or at the bottom of the waters. *'Mang* means at once "hole," "door," and "narrow pass"; the "hole" of Dreny, imagined as such by the Jörai and the Eddé, may actually be a narrow pass (that of Mdrak or another one) by which the ancestors of the Austronesian people entered the central Indo-Chinese plateau.

Thirteenth-century heads of statues from Champa known as H'Bia Pē and his brother. The Jörai perform a ritual in their honor. Musée de l'Homme collection. Photo J. Dournes.

3. *The Primitive Conditions of Existence*

According to the Jarai, the first man flew like a bird, did not die, and spoke with plants and animals; animals were like men and men were like *yang* (the iris filled the whole outer eye, which gave them another view of things, the *yang* view: for example, what we see as buffalo is man; what we see as spider is soul, the double of a human, according to a code of equivalences which is analogous to the code that allows for the interpretation of visions seen in dreams). And öi Adei lived with them. Hoes hoed by themselves, and man only had to feed them; and wicker carrying baskets grew on trees like fruit. This continued until ruptures in space and time interrupted the harmony. This was partly the fault of men, who got drunk and forgot to feed their axes and hoes, who revolted: "In the future, if you want the earth to produce, you will have to hew and hoe!" (and see below).

According to the Sré, primitive man lived in a state of paradise: he did not have to work, and Ndu offered him immortality. Ndu dug a shallow well and asked a couple to jump into it. But the water was freezing. The man and the woman limited themselves to soaking their hands, sprinkling water on their heads, and drinking a little: this is why the nails and hair never stop growing and there are two sets of teeth. But for having refused the water of youth, men experienced suffering, old age, and death. A serpent dove into the well; he shed his skin and reemerged completely new: this is why snakes always remain young (Ms. 114).

4. *The Destructive Flood*

In Sré, *da' ling* is the sea, the ocean: *da' ling kwo da'ling kwa* was a flood of maritime origins, which covered all of the earth. Everything was destroyed. The *yang* entered rocks and mountains; Ndu alone did not have to flee, since he lives neither here nor there. Of all mankind, only a young man and his sister, who took shelter in a drum, survived. When the water receded, the drum landed on Mount Yang-La; out of it emerged the brother and sister and all future mankind (Ms. 7—an identical tradition is found among the Austroasiatic Katu).

In Jörai, *ling* means "flood," but the legendary catastrophe is more often designated "the boiling sea." The waters inundate everything: those who cling to rocks become *yang*, and those who cling to the pods of the cottonwood tree become stars. A pregnant woman (in one variant, it is a woman with a person called Black Dog, by whom she will have a son) enters a drum. When the waters subside and leave the drum behind, she comes out, splitting open the skin of the drum. With her son, she engenders the new humanity (Mj. 73). Thus humanity is the product of incest, between brother and sister among the Austroasiatic people and between mother and son among the Austronesian peoples; this is rare among the latter, who prefer to celebrate the mythical love of a young man for his sister (and such cases occur in reality). The famous story of H'Bia Pē and her incestuous brother (Mj. 45; Dournes 1970: 154; 1971: 13), and the ritual connected with it—drought, which is catastrophic in dry tropical countries, is conceived as the consequence of incest—are explained in the context of the account of the flood.

Another famous case of incest, again among the Jarai, brought about a tragic rupture: under the effects of a philter meant for another man, Röyot's brother falls in love with her, and she dies in childbirth. Seeing this overwhelmingly sad sight, öi Adei can no longer bear to remain among men, and he returns to the heights forever. Since then, animals do not speak to men, birds sing their dirge for öi Adei, and the *Pterocarpus* (a leguminous plant) secretes blood. The heroine and her brother became rocks (the mass of stone called "mother and child" in all the languages of the region) (Mj. 55; Dournes 1971: 12). The death of Röyot rendered the earth *cölom*, "impure," which connotes rupture (from order, from the norm, from the acceptable). Every act which is *cölom*—for example, the violation, even unconscious, of a prohibition—even today necessitates a purifying sacrifice to rid oneself of impurity and to reestablish normal relationships, to renew ties with tradition (the correct succession of actions) and with every being, because *cölom* has repercussions in the universe like a stone thrown into still water.

5. *The Cold Darkness*

The theme of cold darkness, like that of the flood, is common to nearly every ethnic group. Moreover, the terms used to designate this darkness are all connected, even in unrelated languages.

In Sré, the noun *börling-börlang* designates a universal upheaval described as follows: "Tired of the battles fought by men, Sun decides not to rise. It is dark and cold, and frozen water comes otu of the earth. Because they soaked their heads in this water, the *börling* birds (Drongo) and *börlang* birds (Garrulax), so named after this catastrophe, are white on the tops of their heads. In the future there will be another *börling-börlang* day, which will be the end of this world and the beginning of a new one" (Ms. 132). This myth should be compared with that of Ms. 9 for the story of the warrior hero who was able to reach the Sun by means of a ladder (Dournes 1948: 25); and with the Jörai myths in which it is öi Adei who interrupts battles. The expression *börlang-kang* (*kang*, "obstruct") designates the rainbow (see below). A Sré woman announced the golden age of the new *börling-börlang* and ordered the sacrifice of all white animals.

The Bböhnar equivalent of this is *mang-ling*. "According to a confused tradition, the Bböhnar claim to have known an endless night that followed a disappearance of the sun. Another endless night will precede the end of the world" (Guilleminet 1963: 534). The *börlang* bird (Garrulax) seems to have no connection with this phenomenon but is used for omens. The Mnong also call this catastrophe *mang-ling* (confused with the Flood in Condominas 1953: 655 and 1957: 454). This tradition is still alive among the Ködu, who connect the *mang-ling mang-ta* with the *pörleng pörlang* birds (the same as *börling-börlang*).

In Jörai, the *ling-mang* cataclysm is described as follows: "During seven days and seven nights, the sun did not rise, the wind blew, and it was cold." This does not seem to be directly connected with the *bling* and *blang* birds (names designating the same species, here the bird-judges of tradition), but, as with the Sré, a new upheaval is awaited: the "prophet" Dam Bam announced the golden age, connected with the revolt for self-government—as is frequent in the messiansim of populations subjected to outside rule—as well as with mythical representations (the rice fields planted with a single grain of rice at each corner).

6. The Secondary Ruptures

Under the heading of secondary ruptures are grouped those phenomena that indigenous thought associates, on the level of signs, with "unique" ruptures in history.

The eclipse of the sun, whose "cause" is different from one ethnic group to another, is always frightening, especially because it is a reminder of the "Cold Darkness."

Lightning is everywhere considered to be a punishment for a fault (in general, for having put together things which should have been kept separate—and especially for incest). It is the spark of the short-circuit, which cuts off the current; it is always associated with thunderstones (prehistoric stone axes) gathered as protective talismans.

The lunar halo is interpreted as follows by the Sré: if the circle does not constitute a continuous line but is broken, for example, on the western side, then death will come from that direction.

The rainbow is, for the Sré, the manifestation of *Briang* (another form of *börlang*), a pair of celestial beings who drink blood. The upper arc is man and the lower arc woman; the colors are those of the blood that is sucked in (the red band is human blood) (Ms. 72). In Jörai it is the manifestation of tragic death, Driang, the source of ritual impurity; it causes a short-circuit by joning heaven and earth, which should be separated. Mythology endows it with an extraordinary capacity to absorb (Mj. 99). In Mnong, it is Brieng, the "eater of souls" (Condominas 1957: 128). In Bböhnar, *Bödreng* comes to drink on earth, which is an omen of tragic death. The problem of cultural contacts, or of a common origin, is once again posed by these similarities, not only between words, but even more between concepts, with the ambiguity of an arc that connotes a rupture of the norm.

J.D./d.w.

BIBLIOGRAPHY

I. The Celestial Divinity

J. BOULBET, *Pays des Maa', domaine des Génies* (Paris 1967). G. CONDOMINAS, *Nous avons mangé la forêt de la pierre-génie Gôo* (Paris 1957), indes, 450, 451, 473. J. DOURNES, "Fêtes saisonnières des Sré," *Bull. EFEO* 40 (1954): 599–609, ill.; *Dieu aime les païens* (Paris 1963); "Orphelin transformé, jalons mythologiques," *Archipel*, no. 2 (1971), 168–96, bibliography; "La toupie incestueuse, ou de la distinction nécessaire," *L'homme* 15, nos. 3–4 (1975): 31–53. H. MAITRE, *Les jungles moï* (Paris 1912). C. O. SAUER, *Seeds, Spades, Hearths, and Herds: The Domestication of Animals and Foodstuffs* (Cambridge, MA, 1972).

II. Cosmic Ruptures (Bibliography by Ethnic Groups)

1. Austroasiatic Peoples

Bböhnar: P. GUILLEMINET, *Dictionnaire bahnar-français* (Paris 1963).

Ködu: A. FERREIROS and J. DOURNES, "Deux versions d'un mythe," *ASEMI* 6, no. 4 (1975): 97–124.

Maa: J. BOULBET, *Pays des Maa', domaine des génies* (Paris 1967), 57–59.

Mnong: G. CONDOMINAS, "Les tribus proto-indochinoises," in *Ethnologie de l'Union française* (Paris 1953), 2:658–78; *Nous avons mangé la forêt de la pierre-génie Gôo* (Paris 1957).

Sré: DAM BO, *Les populations montagnardes du Sud indochinois* (Lyon 1950). J. DOURNES, "Chants antiques de la montagne," *B.S.E.I.* (1948), 4:11–111; *En suivant la piste des hommes sur les hauts-plateaux du Viêtnam* (Paris 1955).

2. Austronesian Peoples

Jörai: J. DOURNES, "Recherches sur le haut Champa," *France-Asie*, no. 201 (1970), 143–62; "L'inceste préférentiel," *L'homme* 11, no. 4 (1971): 5–19; *Coordonnées, structures jörai familiales et sociales* (Paris 1972); "La toupie incestueuse," *L'homme* 15, nos. 3–4 (1975): 31–53; "Sam Bam, le Mage et le Blanc dans l'Indochine des années trente," *L'ethnographie* 1 (1978): 85–108.

On prophecy, see also J. MIDDLETON, "Political System of the Lugbara," in *Tribes without Rulers*, Middleton and Tait, eds. (3d ed., London 1967), 225.

The Functions and Methods of Mediators and Intermediaries among the Indigenous Indo-Chinese

I. Mediators and Intermediaries—Mending Ruptures and Seeking the Continuum

As if they were traumatized by cosmic ruptures, the indigenous Indo-Chinese, in their passion for continuity and their memory of the original harmony, imagine mediations that reestablish the unity that disappeared from existence and is recovered in myth. Creatures whose condition is ambiguous, such as those who are between two realms or between two levels of the universe, are all designated for this function; among them are the birds, between heaven and earth, who have an important place, especially among the Sré.

Yai-dam-du, the son of the stars, has come down to earth and is in trouble. He asks his sister, who has remained up above, to send him food; she entrusts it to the birds: rice to the crow, vegetables to the titmouse, and water to the drongo (*Dissemurus paradiseus*) (Ms. 14). This is only one example among many. For the Jörai, this mode of mediation is realized largely on a horizontal plane, notably between the world of the forest and that of the village: thus the woodpecker and the blackbird were sent on a mission by the old woman of the woods (Mj. 30; Dournes 1975).

Mac-mai goes to join her fiancé; they are tricked by monkey people who pass themselves off as one or the other of the lovers. Ndu sends a turtledove to reveal the truth to the two heroes (Ms. 93). Sometimes this is a young girl who transforms herself into a turtledove in order to test the feelings of the man she loves (Ms. 13). In a Jörai myth, a young man is transformed into a bird so that he can tell his father about a misfortune that has befallen the father's wife (Mj. 115); in a story of the same type, a turtledove tells the boy about the place where his mother is held prisoner (Mj. 109). The bird sees, knows, and tells all; this concept is probably linked to the practice of augury based on the direction of flight and the songs of birds.

In Jörai antiquity, the drongo was the judge charged by heaven with settling disagreements among human beings (notably the incest between Pé and her brother). The strong authoritative voice of this bird with its long tail (its "loincloth") has its echo today in the elocution of Jörai judges (or rather mediators) who recite the "words of justice." In Sré antiquity, the crow and the vulture were kings on earth and demanded human sacrifices. The hero Trong son of Tre overthrew them: he struck them, they grew wings, and they fled (Ms. 27). Man became master in place of the birds, and the buffalo replaced man as the object of sacrifice.

Today there is a particular veneration for a very small primate, the *Nycticebus kukang*, the slow loris (in Jörai *kra alé*, "bamboo monkey"; in Sré *dô glé* has the same meaning and refers to the same animal, like the Bböhnar *dok glé*). This primate lives in trees, between heaven and earth; it is active only at night, but it is consulted during the day: the animal is given a little stick, which it accepts or not, thus responding to the question that it is asked; this is a form of divination. The tradition of several ethnic groups makes this primate the king (*bötaw, potao*) of animals; Jörai myths in particular (Mj. 4, 107) develop this notion: he emerges victorious from battles with elephants or rhinoceroses; he is the friend of old mother Bush, and as such is associated with Drit, the shabby little victor over all trials, and therefore, like him, is a mediator (between the animal world and the human world, and between the forest and the village). Moreover, according to Jörai evolutionism, he is regarded as the link between the animal kingdom and that of humans, and his name is invoked in a series along with the names of the ancestors.

The mythology does not lack the resources to establish bridges between the kingdoms; among the Sré as well as among the Jörai, there are many double characters: all of the *sömri* (Sré or *rökai* (Sré and Jörai), tiger-men or ogres, are ambiguous in nature and function, usually terrifying, sometimes terrified by a small child. A man reveals himself in turn as a buffalo, a deer, and then a tiger (Ms. 80); a parallel Jörai figure makes him an elephant man (Mj. 30). These characters, who really have two natures, are to be distinguished from mythological characters (especially those of Jörai origin) who appear in the form of toads, civet cats, or pythons, but in reality are young men who test their companions and then reveal that they are accomplished and courteous men. On the other hand, they may be compared with what the Jörai call "two men:" in daylight they are like everybody else, but during the night they become vampires, reduced to nothing but a head that trails its entrails behind it like the tail of a comet; they come to suck the blood (the life) of human beings, and are associated with fruit bats—which, however, are not vampires (Desmodontidae, a native American family). In any event, all of these imaginary creatures bear witness to a taste, if not a need, to go beyond distinctions, to make categories overlap, to retrieve a continuum that was dreamed of but is disquieting (people make classifications to reassure themselves), at the same time revealing what indigenous thought associates within its own zoology, where human beings are not the privileged creatures that we make of them.

On another level, the level of practical life, man can establish rituals of alliance with animals (the tiger in particular, the slow loris among the Bböhnar-Röngao—cf. Kemlin 1917) and even with plants, to indicate a continuum (indeed a complicity, notably in the case of the hunter who makes a kind of pact of mutual nonaggression with the tiger, his rival) while maintaining a distinction. These alliances are analogous to those that are made in social life, either by a marriage, which joins two families (and a young man calls his allied father-in-law "uncle," which is what the hunter calls his allies in the forest), or, especially, by those treaties that make two strangers sworn friends or even relations (with the relationship of brothers or the relationship between a mother and son). This ritual plane cuts across the mythical plane—our distinctions do not make much sense in a homogenous system—and it does so in two types of situations: (1) the case of the hero Drit, a hunter living on the margins, who makes alliances with the animals of the forest, releasing his catch so that the animals will later come to his rescue; (2) the case of real people who are driven by their phantasms to make alliances, as in marriage, with tiger women or fairies of the woods to the point where they become possessed. In an attempt to free them, the family pronounces a ritual formula of divorce—Drit may marry a dryad, and everyone can dream about it, but it is dangerous (a sign of mental confusion) to view it as though it had really happened.

More rare are ritual alliances made with deities, in a vertical rather than a horizontal direction (living beings are not arranged in a hierarchy). These alliances result from predictive dreams, and it is by means of the dream that they join together with myth, where this type of liaison is not infrequent. It is represented by a ladder among the Sré and by a thread among the Jörai: the Sun makes a beautiful woman come down a ladder to attract a hero and to make him climb up after her (Ms. 130; cf. Ms. 10, 16, 124); Heaven sends the god of whirlwinds to seize a boisterous warrior and raise him into a small boat at the end of a cord (Mj. 24). This last detail brings us back to the hero Drit, who, going the other way, descends into the netherworld inside a small tethered boat (Mj. 15). Furthermore, among the Jörai the unwound thread of a spindle is used either to reascend toward a protecting fairy (Mj. 30) or to descend to earth to join a desired beautiful woman and to bring her back up (Mj. 36, 125). One must connect the realms and the worlds by all available means (mediations), and the mythic imagination does not lack such means.

II. The Flight and the Voyage

The dream of flying is not unique to the Indo-Chinese. When dealing with such universal themes, any attempt at comparison would be futile unless the analysis drew upon the particular coloration that a culture gives such themes through an original vision.

The myths of several ethnic groups have developed the image of flying while tied to a kite, which is already less banal; but the kite originated in East Asia, from China to Malaysia. In various Austroasiatic and Austronesian languages, it is called *klang* (or *kling* in Sré), from the same noun that serves as a generic term for hawks and falcons (like the English *kite*). The sons of Lady Kling (the name is probably not gratuitous) launch a kite, attach themselves to the cord, cut off the cord beneath them, and fly off in this way to fight their enemies, who are also suspended from a kite, but one

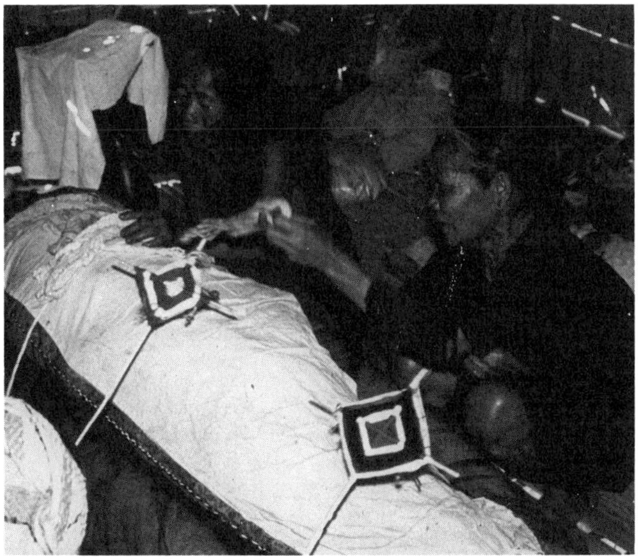

Jörai wailers around the body of a dead person in his shroud, on which flyswatters threaded with crosses have been placed (Vietnam). Paris, Musée de l'Homme collection. Photo J. Dournes.

that is tied up, which causes their downfall (Ms. 23). Drit ties himself to a loose kite to ascend from the netherworld, to which he had descended in a small tethered boat in order to win the beautiful woman whom the lord desired (Mj. 15). Another time, Drit is attached to a kite by the lord who wants to get rid of him; Drit rises through the air and flies to a marvelous country from which he brings back a talisman that allows him to overcome all difficulties (Mj. 117).

Another means of aerial transportation is the "flying horse," *aseh por* in Sré as well as in Jörai (which again underscores the probability that their myths have a common origin). It is always explicitly stated that the horse has a white coat (perhaps because such horses are rare in these regions), and it must not be too hastily assimilated to Pegasus. When Lang, the daughter of the Sun, entrusts her husband with a mission to her mother, he mounts the "flying white horse," which transports him to the Sun (Ms. 13). When a celestial girl sends her flying white horse down to earth, Drit succeeds in taming it, mounts it, and joins the beautiful girl on high (Mj. 1).

The simplest means of flying, however, is making wings for oneself, which is what the hero does, notably when the girl has the qualities of a bird. A girl of the air has come to earth to bathe in a lake; she lays her feather mantle on the ground and goes into the water. Drit suddenly appears and takes the mantle; the beautiful girl follows him back to his home, finds her hidden mantle, puts it back on, takes flight, and disappears. Drit has wings made for himself, tries to fly, arrives at the heights of the sky, and—luckier than Icarus—is reunited with the woman he loves (Mj. 16; cf. also Mj. 22, 89).

The image of flight is taken up again in a Jarai funeral rite. A flyswatter made of cross-threads, shaped in a square, is broken diagonally according to custom. The two triangular halves are placed in the coffin on either side of the corpse: "They are the body's wings," which will allow it to reach the world of the dead. Furthermore, in the course of his successive transformations, the dead person will take on the appearance of a hawk, *klang*.

To move through the air is as "natural" as to swim in the water, at least for the war heroes of the Jörai epics. Most of the single combats take place somewhere between heaven and earth, in the zone of the clouds. The two fighters step on their round shields, which transport them into the heights, when it is not the shields themselves that confront one another, as one might imagine a battle of flying saucers.

Like the shield, which is efficacious only in movement, the characters in the mythology, mainly of the epic type, cannot stand still. They engage in prodigious voyages: on earth (such as Sing-könga's tour of Jörai country); on the sea, riding on the back of a whale (as do Drit and his Sré counterpart Trong); to the realm of the river snakes in the depths of the waters; in the air to the ends of the earth and the sky; and finally even to the world of the dead, located somewhere in the west—as though everything had to be explored and nothing left out, in order to gather everything together within the global vision of the mythology taken as a whole.

To speak of a journey is to evoke a dream, and in indigenous thought, this association leads to the particular form of shamanism practiced by the indigenous Indo-Chinese.

The mythical hero transcends taboos and categories; he crosses over intervals and frontiers—in other words, he goes too far, which one might say is what myth is made for. But this game is far too dangerous for common mortals in everyday life. During sleep, the body or "appearance" (*rup* in Sré and Jörai, *rūpa* in Sanskrit) remains visible on its bed. The permanent ego, rather than the "double" (*böngat* in Jörai, *semangat* in Malay), can go out temporarily and leave on a journey; this is the dream. Everything that the *böngat* sees and does during its outing is the subject matter of the dream. It is essential not to go too far nor to venture where one must not go. It sometimes happens that the *böngat* returns late, because he is temporarily detained by a captivating vision or by a *yang* that stops it; this is illness. The relatives of the sick person try to determine by divination or through a shaman what sacrifice should be offered to what *yang* in order to free the *böngat* of the sick person and reintroduce it into his body.

This mythic voyage and this notion of the dream make it possible to explain how the indigenous Indo-Chinese see the function of the shaman, the *pöjau* (or *böjau, njau*) in all the languages of these ethnic groups. The *pöjau* is a man or woman who has experienced the "too-distant," like the Jörai hero Drit, who shares with impunity the intimacy of the sylvan deities, but not like the possessed person, who has surrendered to the charms of these deities and has become a wild creature. The *pöjau* is a marginal and hypersensitive person who has overcome his problems and the spirits that might otherwise lead him astray; he has made his voyage and has returned from it. Either after a flight into the forest, from which he has emerged unscathed, or after a premonitory dream entreating him to become a *pöjau*, in any case on recovering from a psychosomatic illness, the subject about to undertake the voyage takes up his duties, initiated by another *pöjau* or by his *yang*, also known as *gru* (Sanskrit *guru*), in the sense of "a model to reproduce" (just as heaven is the model for earth), and in the sense of "initiator."

The modes of action of the *pöjau* are multiple, the two principal ones being the dream and the voyage. If he is a specialist in the dream technique, it suffices for him to lie down with an object belonging to the sick person for whom his services are required. The symbolic contact of his body with the object will orient his dream. The shaman falls asleep and dreams, that is, his *böngat* goes out and has an adventure. In this case, he goes to meet the *böngat* of the sick person. He will then see what has happened to him and what *yang* holds him captive. When he wakes up, he will reveal the cause of the illness, and the family will know to what *yang* it should sacrifice.

The traveling shaman works in the same way, but in an altered state that is not sleep. Seated or standing and making some movements with his arms, swaying his torso and often accompanied by a musical instrument played by an assistant, he begins to invoke his *yang gru,* and then he enters into a kind of drunkenness without using alcohol or drugs. His *böngat,* that is, his self, has left. In his hut, the sick person and his relatives can only see a semblance of him and hear a voice, for "his mouth speaks." He gradually recounts all the adventures of his trip, the dangerous passage across a forest—the wild world, beyond the human world—where he meets tigers and malevolent deities. Almost exhausted, he reaches the spot where the sick person's *böngat* had ventured and is held captive by a *yang.* By virtue of his *gru* and the charm that he uses, he recaptures the lost *böngat,* makes the return trip with him, comes back victorious into the hut (which his body has never left), and finally reintroduces into the head of the sick person his *böngat,* which is occasionally materialized as an insect that the shaman holds in his hand (or pretends to hold—it matters little, it is a figurative language). Among the Jörai, especially, the quest for the distant captive is sexualized. The shaman courts forest girls and sees in the *böngat* that is to be saved a female figure (with the sexes reversed in the case of a woman *pöjau*). The scenario is analogous to the one in a series of myths in which the hero sets off on a dangerous mission to free a beautiful captive woman who is being kept prisoner by a monster or a wicked lord.

In a certain sense, the shaman's voyage reintegrates myth and dream into daily life. The character of the *pöjau* is ambiguous. Not only does he see what is on the "other side of the mirror," but he in fact stands on both sides of the mirror at the same time. He reconciles distinct realms without any confusion for himself, which is the most successful retort (both conceived and experienced) to the traumatizing ruptures that the shaman has personally overcome.

J.D./g.h.

BIBLIOGRAPHY

Mediators and Intermediaries

Bahnar-Röngao: J. KEMLIN, "Les alliances chez les Röngao," *Bull. EFEO* 17 (1917).

Jarai: J. DOURNES, "La fée du figuier," *L'ethnographie,* no. 68 (1974), pp. 79–92; no. 69, pp. 81–114; *Akhan, contes oraux de la forêt indochinoise* (Paris 1976); *Forêt Femme Folie* (Paris 1978).

Sré: J. DOURNES, "Chants antiques de la montagne," *B.S.E.I.,* 1948, 11–111; *Trois mythes sré* (Paris 1978).

The Flight and the Voyage

For the myths, see the bibliography for the article "The Mythology and Ritual of the Indigenous Populations of the Southern Part of the Indo-Chinese Peninsula."

On shamanism: G. CONDOMINAS, *Nous avons mangé la forêt de la pierre-génie Gôo* (Paris 1957), index pp. 439–40; shamanic voyage: pp. 147–55. J. DOURNES, *En suivant la piste des hommes sur les hauts-plateaux du Viêtnam* (Paris 1955), 25-26, 165–68; "Chamanisme à Mujat (Sarawak, Borneo)," *Objets et mondes,* 12, 1 (1972): 23–44; "Le chamane, le fou et le psychanalyste (introduction à une typologie des *pöjau* jörai)," *ASEMI,* 4, 3 (1973): 19–30 (the whole issue is devoted to shamanism; biblio.). P. GUILLEMINET, "Recherches sur les croyances des tribus du Haut-Pays d'Annam, les Bahnar du Kontum et leurs voisins; les magiciens," *Institut Indochinois pour l'étude de l'homme* 4 (1941): 9–33. G. MORECHAND, "Le chamanisme des Hmong," *Bull. EFEO* 54 (1968): 53–294.

The Number Seven, Even and Odd, among the Indigenous Indo-Chinese

Once there was a couple who had seven daughters. Unable to feed them, they put them in a basket and abandoned them in a river. The seven young women invoked the *yang,* who landed them on a beach. They met Drit and worked for him. One day, Drit's spear trap accidentally struck one of them, and she died of her wound. Only six remained. Subsequently, when the sky was inverted and moved away from the earth, they became the stars of the constellation known as "Seven Maidens" (Mj. 62). They are the Pleiades, and Drit's trap is what we call Orion's Belt. The two neighboring constellations are closely connected with the cultivation of rice among the Jörai and also among the Sré, who emphasize Orion's Belt, where they see seven stars (Dournes 1973, p. 122), and among many of the peoples of Southeast Asia, notably the Malays (Windstedt 1951, p. 44) and the Dayaks of Borneo ("the beautiful country of the seven stars that point to the work to be done"; Ling-Roth 1896, vol. 1, p. 307). According to a Malay legend, one of the seven Pleiades fell to earth in the region of Majapahit (Hamilton 1944, p. 122). The "inversion" to which the Jörai myth refers is suggestive: the figure of the stars is presented as inverting reality, and that reality would be the myth itself; from the Jörai viewpoint, what we see is merely the inverse of a reality that escapes us; it is not the myth that is inverting, but reality that is inverted.

There are no fewer than eight Jörai myths in which there are seven heroes (Mj. 11, 24, 42, 43, 51, 58, 62, 69), and we find a similar situation among the Sré (Ms. 10, 20, 81). They may be the seven sons of the sky (Jörai), or the seven sons of the giant Nyut (Sré), or the six sons and a daughter, the youngest (Mj. 42, Ms. 10). Whether they are the sons of the sky or warrior heroes, among the Jörai they have the same assonanced names, which suggests that there may be a system. In the series of seven, it is always the youngest who comes out on top, for seven perfects and concludes. Journeys and battles last seven days and seven nights, as does the legendary flood. The Sré universe has seven levels and a dragon with seven heads. There are seven Jörai clans. The same applies to ritual: seven is sacred and indicates abundance. In rites of exorcism, in particular, a Jörai counts to seven and then cries: "Finished!" In the most important rituals there are seven jars of beer. This character of the number is widely attested in Southeast Asia (Jaspan 1964, p. 100; Loeb 1935, p. 96; Schärer 1963, p. 26; Skeat and Blagden 1906, vol. 1, p. 349; Staal 1940, p. 61).

Next to the ubiquitous seven, mythical *pairs* can pose a problem, but a distinction needs to be made. First of all, there are onomastic doublets of the type of Adu-Adei, the celestial divinity, designating a single individual with a kind of echo for the sake of rhythm. For both Austroasiatic and Austronesian peoples, mythology abounds with heroes who are "doubled" in this way but are in fact only one. The oral style of expression, with its play of balancing, easily accounts for this. On the other hand, there are heroes who come in couples, generally presented as elder and younger brothers, who oppose each other for no reason and with no outcome unless there is a third party. Such couples include Set/Rok (northern Austroasiatic groups) and But/Tang (their counterparts among the southern Austroasiatic groups), who have no known ancestors and are sometimes said to be the "sons of the sky." Indeed, they are imagined as civilizing heroes, if they are not fantastic enemy brothers. Finally, a third possibility, two individuals "make up a pair," "like earrings or the tusks of an elephant." They are complementary and necessary to one another, to the point of being actually only one. This is explicitly described in the story of the blind man and the lame man; the lame man rides on the shoulders of the blind man and guides him, and they form a composite figure that frightens a dragon (Mj. 43; note that the blind man is the youngest and the only survivor of seven brothers). At that moment the two are reduced to one (see Lévi-Strauss 1968, p. 275ff.); composed of two elements, a pair is singular, in Jörai too.

A glance at taxonomy clarifies the arithmetic of the myth. This is not a digression, since everything in such cultures is part of the system. In Jörai, for instance, realms are designated by binomial formulas, such as wood-stone for the plant-minerals realm, next to the animal group and the human group, all of which add up to three. Plants are usually named by two terms, comparable to our genus and species, but the complete formula has three terms; the first is the category, of which there are three: tree, creeper, grass; furthermore, these series of threes intersect and overlap through intermediate species, as if to constitute a sequence without any break in continuity (Fournes 1971, p. 277ff.). Two is perfected in three in order to approach unity. We can already see a certain opposition emerging between even and odd: an even number engenders only repetition, whereas the odd number promotes concatenation. The playing of gongs provides a useful image of this: a piece will begin with two (or four) gongs playing in binary rhythms (1, 2-1, 2); a third gong joins in and then brings along the following four (or eight) gongs, and the melody is created (1, 2, 3-1, 2-1, 2); the concerts are played by seven or thirteen (sometimes twelve) gongs.

The fact that all human beings have ten fingers does not make the decimal system universal. The Jörai count on their fingers by pressing the thumb on the index finger for one, on the middle finger for two, on the ring finger, the little finger, back to the ring finger, then the middle finger, and finally the index finger, for a total of seven. The Jörai system is septimal, and their language attests to this, as do many other languages related to Malay. There is a name for each number from one to seven; eight and nine are compound words added later (Blagden 1894, p. 40; Collings 1949, p. 85). Fourteen is "two (times) seven." The Bahnar count on their fingers, pressing the thumb on each phalanx of the other four fingers, which adds up to twelve—one of the bases of their system. These two kinds of counting are connected with the solar-lunar calender of these people: the month is lunar (based on seven); the year is solar (twelve months).

Among the indigenous Indo-Chinese who hold seven in very high esteem (almost all of them), it is fascinating to hear the Jörai express (outside of the mythic formulation) their preference for odd numbers: "*Grop*, 'even,' is heavy, closed [like the syllable itself], full without being complete; it can no longer move nor be inventive. It is a stick-in-the-mud, like a man who has one woman and doesn't seek another. *Lé*, 'odd,' is light and open [like the syllable itself]; it calls for something else. It awaits a liaison; it is a sign of luck. If I want to know whether I will have good luck, I pick up a handful of small sticks at random. I hold them behind my back, and I count them. If the number is odd, I will have good luck; if not, I'll lose everything." Two, four, and six are bad luck, because they are closed into themselves; if unity is added to them, they open out to a liaison. Three connotes balance, five is the number of the higher deities and of the sky. Seven is plenitude, because it is the "last word" among odd numbers. Thus, these people, among whom the Jörai are no exception, cannot rest on binary oppositions (a sign of bad luck) and therefore tend to complete them with a third term, the lucky intermediate which reestablishes the continuum. This is one of the keys to the system formed by their mythology.

The mythical and mystical meaning of odd and even—and of seven in the first place—may have virtually universal correspondences (following Virgil, *numero deus impari gaudet*, Verlaine also "preferred the odd number"), but it does not have the same significance in all cultures. Here the odd number is conceived as able to connect, but it connects only if it has a mediating character, a strong third term; otherwise it remains up in the air like an "extra man," *mönuih röbeh*, a Jörai expression meaning useless, unclassifiable. There is the ambiguity of the odd number and of the hero Drit who appears as a marginal creature and whom society neglects, but who turns out to be the strong link that holds all things together and reunites the worlds.

J.D./g.h.

BIBLIOGRAPHY

C. O. BLAGDEN, "Early Indochinese Influence in the Malay Peninsula," *Journal of the Royal Asiatic Society, Straits Branch,* 1894, 21–56. H. D. COLLINGS, "A Temoq Word List and Notes," *Bull. of the Raffles Museum,* Singapore (December 1949), p. 85. J. DOURNES, "Le discret et le continu, notes complémentaires d'ethnobotanique jörai," *JATBA* 18, 7–8 (1971): 274–87; "Chi-Ché, la botanique des Sré," *JATBA* 20, 1–12 (1973): 1–189. A. W. HAMILTON, *Malay Pantuns* (Sydney 1944). M. JASPAN, *From Patriliny to Matriliny* (Canberra 1964). C. LÉVI-STRAUSS, *The Origin of Table Manners* (New York 1978), trans. from French. H. LING-ROTH, *The Natives of Sarawak and British North Borneo* (Singapore 1896). E. M. LOEB, *Sumatra: Its History and People* (Vienna 1935). H. SHÄRER, *Ngaju Religion, the Conception of God among a South Borneo People* (The Hague 1963). W. W. SKEAT and C. O. BLAGDEN, *Pagan Races of the Malay Peninsula* (London 1906). F. J. STAAL, "Folklore of Sadong Dayaks," *Journal of the Royal Asiatic Society, Malayan Branch* 18, 11 (1940). R. O. WINSTEDT, *The Malay Magician* (London 1951).

The Ambiguous Notion of Power among Austroasiatic and Austronesian Peoples: The *Pötao* of the Jörai

Pötao is power among Austroasiatic and Austronesian peoples, in the form of *bötau* among the Sré, for example, or in the form of *pötao* among the Jörai. But this notion of power is ambiguous.

Sré mythology conceives of power as originally exercised by cruel, carrion-eating birds. A young man stole the power from them. Since then, when one speaks of *bötau* in myths, one refers to a Cham lord (the head of a Cham principality, not necessarily the emperor of Champa) regarded as the ruler of minor indigenous chiefs and later as the intermediary between Vietnamese authority and the minorities who used to be more or less subjects of Champa. In today's common parlance, unless one refers to ancient times, the word no longer designates a person, but power or authority. It is an abstraction. The people know no lord. They deal only with an impersonal and irresponsible administration. Nothing remains now of the mythico-historical *bötau,* not even a trace in the ritual.

For the Jörai, things went very differently. The development of the notion took another direction, and the notion was completely transformed. In this respect, the Jarai are unique among the indigenous Indo-Chinese; moreover, they made *Pötao* an essential element of their concept of the universe, a bridge uniting myth, ritual, and history. The *Pötao* of myth is formidable but is ridiculed; the *Pötao* of ritual has an awesome power but is venerated; the *Pötao* of history has a different meaning depending on who speaks of it. The interplay of these meanings and transformations is difficult to grasp and requires extensive analysis (Dournes 1977); the following is the result of long research.

To this day, the entire Jörai ethnic group recognizes *Pötao* masters. There are three of them, and they are metaphorically classified as Fire, Water, and Air; the neighboring ethnic groups, the Eddé to the south and the Bahnar to the north, are not unaware of them and indeed fear them. The written literature of foreign people indicates that at least two of the *Pötao* were considered kings and chiefs of state by neighboring nations, who maintained diplomatic relations with them. For the Cambodians to the west, the Jörai rulers were *samdach,* the same title that Sihanouk used; for the Vietnamese, to the east, they were *Vua,* the same title that the emperors Gia Lông and Minh Mang used. When the French first wanted to approach the Jörai country, they understood their Laotian guides to be saying that they would have to deal with its *Somdet* (the Lao form of *samdach*), which the French changed to *Sadètes* (or *Sadet*). The *Pötao* agreed to be called *Samdach* and *Vua,* because this would promote autonomy for Jörai territory, viewed by neighboring states as a nation with kings. This move was useful to the Jörai, the only natives for whom outside powers had any consideration. But for the internal purposes of the Jörai, none of this applied: they didn't have those "kings of fire" that were embroidered in the imagination of foreigners.

Three types of myth connected with what might be called the "*Pötao* system" show how it is conceived.

1. In stories about the *kötang,* the "hard ones" or powerful ones, the hero, who was born with a sword and shield, goes to war against a local lord, sometimes called *pötao,* to rob him of his wife, his people, and his wealth. This type of epic may have been based on historical facts, notably on the struggles among Chamized principalities; certain names of Jörai warriors are akin to the names of Cham persons known through inscriptions. Through the Cham, signs of Indian influence allow us to make comparisons with epics such as the *Mahābhārata.*

2. In the cycle of Drit, the hero is exploited by a local tyrant, a *pötao,* who claims the right to appropriate for himself whatever the poor Drit obtains supernaturally with the help of the inhabitants of the forest. In particular, he claims Drit's dryad fairy, who is a symbol of woman and also of all of Jörai culture. Victorious in all of the trials imposed on him by the *pötao,* Drit finally overthrows him, but, unlike the *kötang,* he does not do this in order to seize power. Rather, he remains the poor little man, but free of coercion. In these first two types, the *pötao* have only material power, as did the lords in the old days, and they are more or less ridiculed, like the celestial ruler in the myths but unlike the *Adei* in the rituals.

3. In the stories in which the central figure is *ddau* (a "sabre" blade), either Drit or a *kötang* discovers a marvelous sword; made red-hot, it can cool only by absorbing a human being. It controls the states of matter (fire, water, air) which it subsumes in itself. It arouses the desire of nations, which fight to possess it. It finally remains with the Jörai and safeguards their peace when it is laid down and hidden. It is thus an image of power that must no longer be exercised and is preserved by the *Pötao* of today who bear the same title as those who once possessed the power. (The capital *P* here indicates the sacred character of these *Pötao,* which distinguishes them from the lords of battle.) In addition, fragments of origin myths associate them with the forge (which brings iron, fire, and water into the story and has a masculine connotation) and with pottery (which brings in earth, water, and fire and has a feminine connotation). When one realizes that the Jörai "states" are concerned rather with elements of matter, matter ignited, liquified, made into a gas, one can more easily understand the confusion wrought by foreigners.

The Jörai *Pötao,* sacred masters, are said to be Fire, Water, and Air, that is, they are "like fire, like water"; Lord Fire is to Lord Water as fire is to water. Symbolic guardians of rain, they are, as a group and without hierarchy, regulators of the weather in its relation to humans. Fire, Water, and Air form a system of reference to classify the three rulers into a coherent series and to situate them as mediators between the people and the states of matter, which in turn are connected with the cosmic forces. The triad Fire-Water-Air is congruent with the climatic states of heat-humidity-wind and has a mythological equivalent in the triad of thunder-lightning-typhoon.

The homes of Lord Fire and Lord Water are not very distant and are located on either side of the north/south line separating the waters of the east and west, respectively, where they each perform their ritual rounds; Lord Air lives slightly to the south of Lord Fire. This allocation between east (congruent with man) and west (congruent with woman) is very important to the Jörai because of the place that this axis of the compass points occupies in their conceptual system. Lord Fire is called "father" *Pötao,* Lord Water is "mother," and Lord Air is "son" (the term is also used to designate a nephew or a son-in-law). The three *Pötao* function as a representation of the geographic and social structures of the Jörai universe at its top. It is the roof under which the people live. In the house, which is oriented from north to south, the east is the place for men, the west is the place for

A view of the annual ritual of the visit to villages by the *Pötao* (Jörai). Paris, Musée de l'Homme collection. Photo J. Dournes.

south, the east is the place for men, the west is the place for women, and the south (where one enters) is associated with descendants, in opposition to the north, the direction of the cemetery and the ancestors.

The *Pötao* who belong to myth and to dated recorded history (as a result of diplomatic exchanges with neighboring courts) are simultaneously "kings" assuring autonomy for the populations that invoke them and "priests" officiating at rituals for internal use (within ethnic groups). The official activities of the *Pötao*—who are ordinary peasants when they do not exercise their functions, rather like shamans, although the resemblance ends there—are divided into three types of rituals:

1. The annual rounds made by each *Pötao* at the beginning of the rainy season, on his side of the dividing line of the waters. Surrounded by his assistants, whose names represent a microcosm of society, the *Pötao* visits his villages, stopping in the main ones, where he presides over an impressive ceremony and recites, in the course of a sacrifice, a long invocation asking for rain, fertility, and good health. This is to assure the order of succession of the seasons and to give it meaning for fixed periods.

2. The sacrifice on the mountain, offered during catastrophic circumstances (such as abnormal drought), more solemn but closed to the common people, celebrated solely by Lord Fire and his retinue before the sacred sword and other objects of the treasury. These are usually hidden but are taken out for this occasion and venerated according to the rite that Jörai thought associates with the sacrificial festivals performed at tombs.

3. The rites of election, confirmation, and burial, punctuating the existence of a *Pötao*. The periodicity of these rituals is irregular, as is that of the second type, but they are not motivated by an anomaly and are even more public than the first type, since the entire ethnic group is directly involved in them.

A more probing analysis allows us to distinguish three types of functions represented by the *pötao* system:

1. Father-Fire essentially guards the sacred sword, the symbol of power, a power no longer warlike but cosmic, associated with the forge and thus with an aspect of creation, a male function connected with the heavenly diety Adei who intervenes only in the case of very serious disorders.

2. Mother-Water subsumes in the *Pötao* of the west the female functions in society: the reproduction of food products and of the Jörai people, connected with the *yang* of the sources of rivers.

3. Son-Air watches over the sacred pebbles and potsherds that represent troops of warriors; his warrior function connects him with the "powerful ones" of long ago who are now more or less equated with the dangerous *yang,* with whom one must avoid contact.

This distribution has some analogy with the three functions identified by Georges Dumézil in the ancient Indo-European traditions.

By taking the *Pötao* system as a whole, no longer conceived according to its titles and the individuals who incarnate them, but by considering a different level, more abstract than symbolic, we discover another interplay of functions (which do not overlap with the first set):

1. The political function, as an aspect of existence in which *Pötao* joins together what myth and reality separate: the effective exercise of power (the lords of ancient history) and the tendency to give up all power (from the Drit to modern man), in the natural ambiguity of the mastery of the *Pötao* and in the uncertainty of the political situation, where the rise of a powerful man is a permanent danger.

2. The familial function, with a disjunction between love and marriage in myth and in reality, in which three *Pötao* men play the role of male procreator, female procreator, and the procreated, but transmit the power of these three to their son-in-law, which makes it possible for the woman to recover her place.

3. The religious function, which colors all of existence and appears in ritual, overlays the distinctions between the political and familial functions, the mythical and the real, as a third term that causes these couples to interpenetrate within the experience of the *Pötao* who are everything simultaneously.

We find here again the threefold organization of the universe, and we understand the necessity within this system for a third *Pötao,* Lord Air, the most "fluid" and elusive, thanks to whom two changes into three to constitute one totality, which is not only conceived as a recovered continuum but is experienced by a people with strong structures, reconciling myth and history by transcending the oppositions.

J.D./g.h.

BIBLIOGRAPHY

J. BOULBET, *Pays des Maa', domaine des génies, Pub. EFEO,* 1967, pp. 70, 133. J. DOURNES, "Pötao, les maîtres des états, position de thèse," *ASEMI,* 4, 3 (1973): xix–xxvi; "Sous couvert des maîtres, aperçu sur la pensé politique d'une ethnie indochinoise," *Arch. Europ. de Sociol.,* 1973, 185–209; *Pötao, une théorie du pouvoir chez les indochinois Jörai* (Paris 1977).

Yang: The Sacred Connection, Sacrifice, and the Ritual of Counting among the Austroasiatic and Austronesian Ethnic Groups

I. Yang, the Sacred Connection

The term *yang* is common to almost all Indo-Chinese ethnic groups (natives of the south), both Austroasiatic and Austronesian. It is a key notion in these cultures, heard in conversation, in invocations, and in mythical stories. Like many of the most current and typical words, it is very difficult to translate. Depending on the author, it means "spirits," "genies," "angles," "deities," "the Sacred." It cannot be translated by the same word in all contexts; thus "to make *yang*" is not "to make spirit" but "to make sacred," to sacrifice or to "make a connection"; it is the religious act. But *yang* has the same meaning in all languages of the area (*löh yang* in Sré is the exact equivalent of *nga' yang* in Jörai, that is, to sacrifice). The notion of *yang* can only be understood as the basis of the whole myth-making process, and this article should be read along with the other articles on the Indo-Chinese world.

In Old Cham, *yaṅ* means "god, lord" (Boisselier 1963, p. 248); in Old Malay, *hiyan* means "god, deity" (Ferrand 1919, p. 254); "*jang* is a Javanese root meaning 'spirit'" (Geertz 1960, p. 26). "In Nousantarian, the stem *iang* designates all manifestations of the deity" (Lombard 1968, p. 168), which is closest to the Indo-Chinese meaning. In Vietnamese, *dàng* means "spirit" (especially in conjunction with *thân*). In modern Malay, *yang* is a relative pronoun; another meaning is "deity." "The word *hyaṅ* belongs to the Indonesian vocabulary and designates approximately all that is sacred" (Dupont 1952, p. 152). It corresponds to the Khmer *prah/bah* and is found in this last form in several Austroasiatic languages, either instead of *yang*, among the Sedang and Stieng, or in combination with *yang*, among the Mnong, or else in the combination *brah-yang*, among the Sré. In Khmer, *preah/prah* means "divine, sacred." This list covers all of Southeast Asia and places the Indo-Chinese ethnic minorities in relation with millions of other people who think *yang*, a notion with a profound resonance in this part of the world. Comparison enhances the meaning and informs us of cultural contacts.

The *yang* have no independent existence; they have no history—with the exception of some heroes of mythology and some famous ancestors (all interrelated) who are assimilated to *yang* deities. They are abstractions that intervene only as a relation between man and nature (see Mus 1934, p. 8; Sebag 1971, p. 141). When one wants to say that a certain rock, or river, or plant "has *yang*" (i.e., that it has "a sacred character" and not a little spirit hidden within), it means that man has noticed through a sign that this object, now charged with the sacred, maintains a certain connection with him that is potentially dangerous. This connection may be temporary: we cannot say that such and such a tree is inhabited by a deity, which makes it difficult to speak of animism, a Western creation that is diametrically opposed to their reism. The universe is a continuum: minerals, plants, animals, and humans are constantly interconnected. The ambiguity of this mythological thought stems from the necessity for everything to hold together (maintain cohesion) and at the same time for everyone to keep his own place (avoid short-circuits), so that the ordered ritual may either establish beneficial connections or break harmful ones. Is this not the definition of religion itself, if we accept the etymology *religare?*

To break malevolent bonds, this bow is ready to pierce the *Yang* threatening the village (Jörai). Paris, Musée de l'Homme collection. Photo J. Dournes.

Inside a chru cemetery, vats of beer are opened on the occasion of the sculpting of a top of a tomb (foreground). Paris, Musée de l'Homme collection. Photo J. Dournes.

Yang is legion, but *yang* is uncountable, for in all the languages, a classifier must be inserted between the numeral and the numbered object, and there are appropriate classifiers for all things, from minerals to humans. A language is thus revealing, not only through its idioms but also through its silences. It is impossible to say "two, three *yang*"; like cosmic elements and abstractions, *yang* is outside all categories. *Yang* has no classifier because it is itself a classifier, not of objects but of their connections, at a sacred level (or in their sacred aspect). There are as many connections as there are individuals. Thus my forest *yang* is not necessarily that of my neighbor. *Yang* cannot be represented concretely. When a Jörai or a Sré shouts: "Oh Yang!" he no more thinks of a personified or figurative being than we think of interstellar space when we say "Heavens!" Although *yang* does not take a classifier, it does tolerate being prefixed like verbs and adjectives, particularly in Jörai: *möyang* expresses an extraordinary mode, to "make *möyang*" is to do something very unusual—a word freely combined with *mösih,* the supernatural. The expression often occurs in mythological texts when the hero gets ready to perform a supernatural feat. "May my mouth utter *möyang,* may a rich dwelling rise up in this very place!"

Yang are signs. Everything in the universe of these people can be a sign, and this is a fundamental principle of their symbolism, which diviners and shamans are very expert in interpreting. "If we get sick after cutting down a tree, we know that the tree 'has *yang*'; it has it because it has hurt us. We must then offer sacrifice to get rid of it" (the *yang* and the hurt). "If we come down with a fever after going somewhere, it is because we have come face to face with (or gone through) a *yang* aura (*höpô' yang*); divination tells us what sacrifice we must perform to get well again." A *yang* manifestation, a hierophany, is always a sign of a sacred connection that may have been injured by some excessive promiscuity. The continuum is not a confusion.

Everything may not "be *yang,*" but everything can "have *yang.*" There is therefore no need to draw up a list. It is possible, however, to identify a few notions that are widespread among the various ethnic groups and that are, at the same time, particularly striking. *Yang* are not in a hierarchy; they are not subject to comparison, since they are not individuated. Some, however, do stand out, notably, the paddy *yang* (rice in the field), which is invoked everywhere, often together with the superior deity Ndu/Adei. Paddy *yang* is the energy of vegetation of the principal grain food; it is a power, a virtue in the old sense of the term, distinct from the principle of life, or "soul," that rice has like any other living form. Among the Jörai, quite exceptionally, this *yang* is called *hri-yang,* as if it referred to a proper name—*hri* has no other use and does not mean paddy; similarly, among the Bböhnar, it is called *sri* or *hri.* This is probably the same word as *sré,* "rice field," which gave its name to an ethnic group. In Malay, Seri is the goddess of fertility, principally of rice. This Indo-Asian word comes from Sanskrit and occurs in Indo-European languages in the name of the goddess Ceres. This might explain the exceptional personification of this *yang;* we can guess that it is the product of some "Chamization," since the Hinduized culture of the Cham tended to personify as deities the notion of *yang,* which is far more abstract among the Proto-Indo-Chinese.

Water *yang* (principally in the sense of river) has in almost all ethnic groups the distinction of being imagined as a snake or a dragon (in mental representations that are not concretized in plastic art). The Sré give a reason for this: the bends of a river are the marks left by the movements of a mythical snake. Sré and notably Jörai mythologies (Ms. 24, 44, 62, 71, 99; Mj. 4, 43, 111) are rich in texts that show a dragon/serpent as master of the waters, who dwells in a rich house in the depths below, appears as a handsome adolescent, and marries a daughter of man. The connection with the Hindu *nāga* is not accidental: the word for dragon is *löngrai* in Sré, *cögrai* in Jörai, and *nögarai* in Cham, from the Sanskrit *nāga-rāja.* Here again it would appear that Hinduization (mediated through Cham) modified the entirely mental, nonfigured *yang* of the ancient natives.

The forest *yang* (of the bush, of the woods, or wild) is ambiguous, a power of attraction and repulsion for the other world (otherness connotes hostility but is also a component of love), a place where one may meet the tigers, tiger men, and ogres of mythology, but also young girls comparable to naiads and dryads, shimmering fairies who draw into the unreal all those who fall under their spell. The hunger who habitually frequents this realm has concluded some pact with this type of *yang;* the shaman who crosses it comes into contact with these *yang;* the possessed man, charmed by the forest girl, leaves his own people and lives naked in the woods; the marginal man, situated between village and forest, like Drit, a hero in the Jörai myths, can by his very nature make the link between animal girls (or plant girls), who are manifestations of *yang,* and the world of culture, through the mediation of his grandmother, who is also a tree or bird and now lives on the moon. This is the dream of recovered continuity.

Sharing meat in a Jörai cemetery. Paris, Musée de l'Homme collection. Photo J. Dournes.

Jörai tomb. Paris, Musée de l'Homme collection. Photo J. Dournes.

II. The Ritual of Counting

"Paddy from the Cham, paddy from the Ködu, paddy from among the Röglai . . . I call you, I summon you, I gather you." This sequence of ritual invocations by the Austroasiatic Ködu (indigenous Indo-Chinese) is one example among many of what may appear to be a gratuitous redundancy but is in fact a necessary enumeration. All the ethnic groups have this ritual reciting of a series of names of places, rivers, mountains, localities, and among the Jörai, where funeral rites are more important than agrarian rites, characters from mythology who are connected with the ancestors—a sequence of names that constitute genealogies and reveal classifications. This need to omit nothing could be illustrated by countless quotations (see the bibliographical references). Our purpose here, in connection with the other articles on the indigenous Indo-Chinese, is rather to account for the need, to indicate its general meaning in current scholarship, and to express that meaning here in the form of a sketch rather than a synthesis (which would be premature).

After a Jörai, in the course of a ritual to promote healing, has invoked all the imaginable *yang* in a series, rivers and woods, hills and clouds, he concludes with "and all the *yang* I do not know." In this way he manifests his almost maniacal taste for an organized totality, with a bit of trickery that allows him to cover all bets rather than a sacred awe of scrupulous worry; too much has been said about the "terror" in which "primitive" people are said to live.

The ritual invocations are traditional recitations in which there is little room for improvisation, as assonances provide the linkage between one formula and the next. As such they are pieces of eloquence and proofs of knowledge of the oral literature and of the correct thing to do. The same applies to the gestures that accompany the words, gestures that have been meticulously described in all their multiplicity and minutiae by G. Condominas (1957). One has to hedge all of one's bets, plug all the holes, show one's expertise; one must impress the people present at the ritual at least as much as the spiritual powers, of whom little is known. The need to tie everything together, as if in a continuous web, is seen in the sacrifice of the buffalo; the buffalo, which is offered as food for the *yang* and is eaten by the human participants, replaces a man, as is evidenced in the Sré myth of K'Du kon Bo (Ms. 11), the sacrificed hero, and is viewed as a man by the *yang*. On the subject of the food offered to the *yang* (who are no more cannibalistic than carnivorous), let us note the popular interpretation: when the head and giblets of a chicken have been left behind on the ground for *yang* and they are gone the next day, it is a *sign* that *yang* has accepted the sacrifice—even if a dog or a vulture has been seen taking it away; that doesn't stop people from saying, "*Yang* has eaten . . ."

During sacrificial rites, especially among Austroasiatic peoples, long boards and high festive poles are brightly decorated with painted and stylized motifs, depicting the sun, moon, stars, tiger cheeks, buffalo teeth, flowers, seeds, etc., juxtaposing and linking a large sampling of categories of beings in the same encyclopedic spirit that presides over the enumerations in the oral style. This tendency toward exhaustive signification is also found (among both Austroasiatic and Austronesian peoples) in woven bands on the borders of blankets, depicting plants, animals, and humans (and nowadays even airplanes). These productions are not strictly ritual, insofar as one can distinguish what is "ritual" from what is not. They are above all cultural manifestations of a well-organized knowledge, a mode of self-expression and perhaps also of reassurance: "everything is connected" (*ratio stat!*).

Festival pole. In the background, decorated ritual boards (Halang). Paris, Musée de l'Homme collection. Photo J. Dournes.

In a litany of invocations, when banyan *yang b* (*Ficus rumphii*) is followed by banyan *yang b'* (*Ficus glomerata*) during a plant series, the link is established not so much between *yang* and banyan as between the two species of *Ficus* (and other plants), on the one hand, and between this series and the series of humans who are making the invocation, on the other hand. *Yang* thus serves as a classifier, which is very important for the study of indigenous taxonomies, but at a level "higher" than that of the signs. The banyan tree is taken here to indicate the strength, fertility, and abundance that the invokers hope for. Between the chain of plants and the chain of humans, the collective *yang* weaves a web of connections that are both real (a symbiosis with the environment, which must be experienced in a proper equilibrium) and symbolic (the strength of some must also be the strength of the others, by means of the *yang* energy). This distinction is not explicit for the interested parties. The same applies more or less to litanies of the names of ancestors (in part mythical): the sacred character (*yang*) of the invocation establishes the continuity (in this instance a continuity in time) between the living and the creatures of the past.

It has been said even by indigenous Indo-Chinese that the ritual came from the myth and reenacted it. In the first place, it is not enough to say it, especially if it is in response to a question, for this to take place in just this way. Furthermore, one must distinguish between ethnic groups. Among the Sré, the principal agrarian ritual (Ndu) seems to come directly from the myth that explains it; among the Jörai, such a link is rarely perceptible. In any event, we do not know what happened diachronically. But we propose with more confidence, on the basis of current observations, that myth and ritual are projections of the same "calculating" thought, on various levels of expression and, moreover, most often on different occasions.

The Sré *hoé yang* is the exact equivalent of the Jörai *iau yang* (*hoé* = *iau*, "to call") and has the same meaning of ritual or sacred invocation, but the experience is different. Among the Sré, the ritual, both gestures and words, is prescribed to establish contact with the *yang*, who are expressly invited to live among humans and partake of their offerings. Among the Jörai, most of the rituals aim to get free of a bond that has become dangerous and needs to be dissolved, untied, loosened (the vocabulary is quite rich in this regard), rather than tied tightly. The *yang* are called and asked to take their share and to leave us in peace. A common saying goes, "*Yang* among themselves, the dead among themselves, the living among themselves." The Jörai are at ease when they feel that everything is connected, but since they are fiercely independent and have a great sense of humor, they avoid domination, like the weaver woman who takes care that the threads of the warp do not become tangled between any two movements of the shuttle that connects them. Their common culture ensures that both of these peoples are Southeast Asians, but the particular way of life of each group ensures that some think of themselves as Sré, others as Jörai.

J.D./g.h.

BIBLIOGRAPHY

1. Yang

C. O. BLAGDEN, "A Malayan Element in Some of the Languages of Southern Indochina," *Journal of the Royal Asiatic Society*, 1902, 2. J. BOISSELIER, *La statuaire du Champa*, Publ. *EFEO*, 1963. L. CADIÈRE, "Monuments et souvenirs Chams," *Bull. EFEO*, 1905, 194–95. P. DUPONT, "Études sur l'Indochine ancienne," *Bull EFEO*, 1952, 119–76. G. FERRAND, "Le Kouen Louen," *Journal Asiatique*, 1919, 254. C. GEERTZ, *The Religion of Java* (New York 1960). D. LOMBARD, *Histoires courtes d'Indonésie*, Publ. *EFEO*, 1968. P. MUS, "L'Inde vue de l'Est, cultes indiens et indigènes au Champa," *Bull. EFEO*, 1934, 1–44. L. SEBAG, *L'invention du monde chez les Indiens Pueblos* (Paris 1971).

2. The Ritual of Counting

J. BOULBET, "Börde au rendez-vous des Génies," *B.S.E.I.* 35, 4 (1960): 627–50. G. CONDOMINAS, *Nous avons mangé la forêt de la pierre-génie Gôo* (Paris 1957). J. DOURNES, "La religion des Montagnards du Haut-Donnaï," *B.S.E.I.* 24 (1949): 29–49; "Fêtes saisonnières des Sré," *Bull. EFEO* 46, 2 (1954): 599–610; "Le mort c'est l'autre, la geste funéraire jörai," *Objets et mondes*, 1975, 351–84. A. FERREIROS, *Les Kon-Cau de la Daa'-Nying* (microéd. univers., Paris 1973), 73-30-32. P. GUILLEMINET, "Le sacrifice du buffle chez les Bahnar de la province de Kontum," *B.A.V.H.* 2 (1942): 147–51. B. Y. JOUIN, *La mort et la tombe* (Paris 1949). JOUIN and BOTREAU-ROUSSEL, "Un sacrifice au génie des éléphants à Bandon chez l'héritière de Kundjonob," *Inst. Indoch. pour l'Étude de l'Homme* 6 (1943): 375–86. J. KEMLIN, "Les rites agraires chez les Röngao," *Bull. EFEO* 9 (1910): 493–522; 10 (1910): 131–58. MAURICE, "Trois fêtes agraires rhadé," *Bull. EFEO* 15, 1 (1952): 202–7; "L'âme du riz," *B.S.E.I.* 29, 2–3 (1954): 1–258. For the ritual role of plants, see: J. DOURNES, "Bois-Bambou, aspect végétal de l'univers jörai," *JATBA*, 1968, 89–156, 369–498; "Chi-Ché, la botanique des Sré," *JATBA*, 1973, 1–189.

VIETNAMESE MYTHOLOGY

The documents that allow us access to Vietnamese mythology come from two sources different in nature and time. The first and older of the two sources comprises accounts written mainly in Chinese by Vietnamese scholars. The second source, essentially oral, is more diversified and comes mostly from rural areas. It can, however, be said that there is little in either source on the subject of the creation of the universe and of natural phenomena. A few reasons may be advanced to explain this shortage.

Vietnamese scholars, imbued with Confucian biases, exercised great selectivity, like their Chinese colleagues whose models they imitated. They are not interested in creationist theories, avoid the question of the origins of mankind as a species, and are not awestruck by the configuration of the universe. Loath to explain the creation of the universe, they pay particular attention to extraordinary men who were deified at the time of their deaths because of their great deeds. They do, however, include the miraculous birth of the Vietnamese people, descended from a sovereign couple of mythical origin, and they thus euhemerize mythic themes. Although certain etiological themes that explain the causes of things are sometimes found in these collections, they deal with the plant kingdom but never with the creation of the first men or of the first animals.

In modern oral stories, there are some passages that deal with the early times of humanity. These are scattered scraps with no coherent system. Regarded by the lay reader as simple popular tales, they in fact contain mythological elements that show how the universe was given its shape, and how, after the sky and earth were formed, man passed from the Golden Age to life as it is now. Nevertheless, basic themes such as the birth of the human race and the creation of the universe are missing, and one gets the impression not only that the elite of the country rejected the creationist theory, but that the people in general had relatively little interest in it.

Finally, the history of Vietnam is itself partly responsible for this apparent indifference: the incessant invasions by Chinese armies, followed by lengthy occupations, led at least to the partial destruction of the Vietnamese cults and the substitution of Chinese deities. There are numerous traces of these newer Chinese cults throughout the country. For example, there is the temple of the war god Chen-Wu and the temple of General Ma Yăn, Subduer of the Seas, who conquered Vietnam in the first century A.D. In the ninth century A.D., a Chinese general named Kao Pien was known for his gifts as a magician and geomancer. He tried unsuccessfully to eliminate the sacred powers of the great local deities by ceremonies of exorcism and magic.

But the desire for self-identity and the need to discover the origin of the first founder made it possible to preserve a few legendary features of the birth of the Vietnamese people. It is not the origin of the human species that is treated here but that of the Vietnamese people. This is a semimythical genealogy rather than a cosmogony.

In our article entitled "The Origins and the First Ages in the Major Structures of Vietnamese Mythology" (see below), a new subject emerges: the gods of nature. In discussing the sky, we thought it useful to add the names of a few deities that assist in the task of governing. The choice is certainly arbitrary, for we omitted several among them that play important parts in the Chinese Taoist pantheon: the two acolytes of the heavenly emperor, Nam Tao and Bac Dau, who record births and deaths; the god of the hearth, who is responsible for reporting annually to heaven on the conduct of men; and so forth. But the fact that their images are all too faithful copies of Chinese models justifies such omissions.

L.O.M./g.h.

BIBLIOGRAPHY

R. P. CADIÉRE and LÉOPOLD, *Croyances et pratiques religieuses des Viêtnamiens,* 3 vols. (Hanoi, Saigon, Paris, 1944, 1955, 1957). CAO HUY DINH, *Hinh tuong không lô va tâp thê Anh hung dung nuoc, giu nuoc trong truyên cô dân gian Viet-Nam* (On the giant and the enculturating heroes in popular Vietnamese stories), in *Truyên thông anh hung dân tôc* (Hanoi 1971). DAO DUY ANH, *Cô su Viêt Nam* (Ancient history of Vietnam) (Hanoi 1956). DINH GIA KHANH-CHU XUAN DIEN, *Van hoc dân gian* (Folklore studies), 3 vols. (Hanoi 1962, 1972, 1973). DOAN THI DIÊM, *Truyên ky tân pha* (Marvelous legends), Vietnamese trans. (Hanoi 1962). G. DUMOUTIER, *Les cultes annamites* (Hanoi 1907), extract from the *Revue Indo-Chinoise,* 1906; a good overview of Sino-Vietnamese and Vietnamese deities. M. DURAND, *Technique et Panthéon des médiums viêtnamiens (dông)* (Paris 1959); *Imagerie populaire viêtnamienne* (Paris 1960); "Viêtnam," in *Le monde du sorcier* (Paris 1966), 331–51. M. DURAND and NGUYÊN TRÂN HUÂN, *Introduction à la littérature viêtnamienne* (Paris 1969). P. GIRAN, *Magie et religion annamites* (Paris 1962), *Hung vuong dung nuoc* (The Hung kings, founders of the kingdom), 4 vols., vols. 2 and 4 (Hanoi 1972 and 1974). A. LANDES, *Contes et légendes annamites* (Saigon 1886); this is the richest collection of legends in French translation. ÀLVAN HAO, "Les fêtes saisonnières au Viêtnam," in *Revue du Sud-Est asiatique* (1962), no. 4. LÊ VAN PHAT, "La vie d'un Annamite: Croyances diverses," *Bull. de la Société des Études Indochinoises,* no. 54 (1908). LY TÊ XUYÊN, *Viêt diên u linh tâp,* Vietnamese trans. of Lê Huu Muc (Saigon 1961). P. MUS, *La religion des Annamites,* in *Indochine,* work published by Sylvain Lévy (Paris 1931). NGÔ SI LIÊN, *Dai Viêt su ky toan thu,* Vietnamese trans. of Cao Huy giu, vol. 1 (Hanoi 1967). NGUYÊN DÛ, *Truyên ky man luc,* French trans. of Nguyên Trân Huân (Paris 1962), Vietnamese trans. of Truc Khê et Ngô van Triên (2d ed., Hanoi 1971). NGUYÊN DÔNG CHI, *Luoc khao vê Thân thoai Viet Nam* (Hanoi 1956); this was the first published collection of documents on Vietnamese mythology. NGUYÊN KHAC XUONG, *Truyên thuyêt Hung vuong* (Legends of Hung kings) (Vinh Phu 1971). NGUYÊN VAN HUYÊN, *Le culte des immortels en Annam* (Hanoi 1944). NGUYÊN VAN KHOAN, "Essai sur le Dinh et le Culte du Génie tutélaire des villages au Tonkin," *Bull. de l'École française d'Extrême-Orient* 30 (1930): 1–33. PHAN KÊ BINH, *Nam-hai di nhân liêt truyên* (new ed., Saigon 1968). P. PRZYLUSKI, "L'or et ses pouvoirs magiques," *Bull. de l'École française d'Extrême-Orient* 14 (1914). R. A. STEIN, "La légende du foyer dans le monde chinois," in *Échanges et Communications, mélanges offerts à Claude Lévi-Strauss,* 2 vols. (The Hague 1970), 1280–1305. TÔ NGUYÊT DINH, *Chuyên coô tich* (Saigon 1969). TRAN THÊ PHAP, *Linh-nam chich quai,* Vietnamese trans. of Le Huu Muc (Saigon 1961). VAN TAN-NGUYEN LINH, *Thoi dai Hung vuong* (Hanoi 1976).

The Origins and the First Ages in the Major Structures of Vietnamese Mythology

I. The Configuration of the Universe

No one knows where the sky and the earth came from. When they first appeared, they were nothing but a mass of shapeless and chaotic matter. Everything was immersed in total darkness. At that moment a giant began to detach the sky from the earth. This colossus has the name of Không Lo, borrowed from the Chinese. He also goes by other names that generally illustrate his prodigious exploits: Sir Ocean-Scooper, Sir River-Hollower, Sir Forest-Grower, and so forth. His stride is tremendous; his breath makes gusts of wind; and his cries are the rolls of thunder. First he raised the sky with his head. Then he cleared the earth in order to build a gigantic pillar to support the full weight of the sky. Thus separated from the earth by a great distance, the sky took the form of an inverted bowl and the earth that of a square plateau. This representation of the original world was undoubtedly taken from a Chinese mythological concept. It is still given expression in the etiological legend about a kind of bread made of sticky rice that the Vietnamese now eat only at the festival of the New Year: Chung bread. In this story, which is set during the mythical dynasty of the first Vietnamese sovereigns, the Hung, the throne was to revert to the prince whose offering was most highly prized. One young prince found himself at a disadvantage, since his poverty would not allow him to compete with his older brothers. But on the advice of a deity, he began to make two kinds of breads never seen before: the one that symbolized the sky was a round cake; the other was square and represented the earth.

The same giant pulled down the supporting pillar when he noticed that the sky and the earth had become solid and dry. He broke it up into pieces and violently threw the blocks of stone around him: thus the mountains and the islands were born. The huge ditches that the giant had dug in order to build the pillar received water and became the oceans. The ebb and flow of the sea were connected to the breathing of a turtle of immeasurable size that remained motionless most of the time.

In the course of arranging the universe, a new character, a female, appeared. The two of them formed a giant couple whose relationship was amorous but also full of conflicts, the outcome of which was always in favor of the woman. To begin with, she dominated her companion by her size: her sex organ was twice as big as her partner's, if we accept the terms with which people compare their genitals; their size was measured in terms of surface area. She also had greater physical strength. Since the male giant wanted to marry her, she challenged him to a contest: each of them would erect a mountain within three days. If his should surpass hers in height, she would consent to marry him. But she was the one who won, because from the summit of her mountain one could turn one's gaze to the horizon. She kicked down the mountain that her suitor had built. She also imposed another difficult task that consisted of filling a riverbed overnight.

When the male giant's labors were almost over, she imitated the cock's crow to herald daybreak and forced the giant to stop. Other tests followed, consisting now not in creating new peaks but in moving certain already existing mountains to other regions or in lining them up straight, as happened to the Annamite mountain range in central Vietnam, which was initially made up of mountains arranged haphazardly.

Gradually, the giant's creations lost their global character; for instance, when he had erected the support pillar, he then built some mountain, identified by name. He transported from the upper region toward the plain two mountains known today by the names of Ba-vi and Tam-dao. Like all peasants, he moved earth by means of a flail. According to one current theme, the straps of his baskets broke in mid-journey. Clods of earth were cast in all directions: this is how hills were first formed on earth. In certain localities stretching toward the south of central Vietnam, in order to erect some mound, the giant had to scoop out earth from the bottom of the sea and bring it back ashore. These works were intended to allow the population to take refuge there when the rivers were in spate.

Finally, he won the hand of his female companion. On the day of the wedding, he set out for her house, accompanied by one hundred people. But as night fell, they were blocked by a river. The giant stretched out his penis to form a bridge. As his men were crossing, one of them accidentally dropped hot ashes on the giant's penis and made him jump. The men lost their balance and half of them fell into the water. The woman rescued them and hid them under her dress to warm them up again. The allusion to the sex organ does not seem fortuitous. It brings to mind a ritual now performed in secret in certain villages where the inhabitants fashion a phallus from wood and a woman's sex organ from the spathe of the areca nut, and the women and girls fight over them. The performance of this ritual is thought to be indispensable to the security of the village, and the sex of the first child born after it will correspond to that of the symbol that was won.

II. Men and Animals

This is the point where the Sky might be discussed. But we shall see that its role is so closely tied to earthly events that it has no particular autonomy of its own. Besides, many legends that concern it are closely related to historical periods that are very distant from the cosmogony. We would therefore rather deal first of all with elements that seem to have a more direct relationship with the most remote times of creation. Nevertheless, we should mention that the Sky, called the Jade Emperor, has presided over a certain number of creative acts.

Once the separation of the sky and the earth was accomplished, human beings appeared. Their creation is attributed to a supreme deity, Ngoc Hoang or the Jade Emperor, a name borrowed from the Chinese. This "creator of all beings" fashioned the first men with the finest material available in the chaotic mass. On the other hand, to make the animals, he settled for rougher materials from among the remains of the sky and the earth. He took greater care in making men; that is why their intelligence is so highly developed. The twelve "Heavenly Midwives" were responsible for modeling faces. Each shaped a certain number of organs. Physical blemishes were the results of their oversights. The twelve Heavenly Midwives also presided over the birth of babies. It was their task to teach children how to talk and walk.

III. Sun and Moon

The relationships between men and the sun and the moon were far from neighborly; a number of legends about them will be found below in the discussion of the Golden Age or Lost Happiness.

Sun and Moon were both daughters of the Jade Emperor. They were commanded to light the world; they warmed the surface of the earth, but their heat was so intense that the soil dried up to the way the earth is today. Many legends attempt to explain the appearance of the moon and the marks on it. Sometimes the explanation involves a tree, the banyan, a kind of sacred fig tree that can still be seen growing near pagodas. Sometimes it involves a fistful of sand thrown to its surface in an attempt to chase the moon away, when its heat was unbearable. For long ago, the moon did not cast a light as soft as moonlight is today. On the contrary, it emitted a burning heat which brought much suffering to mankind. Every time it appeared, it created panic among human beings, who would hurl insults at it and vow to drive it away. Quai, a young man of prodigious size and strength, climbed to the top of a mountain to await the arrival of the Moon. As soon as he saw it, he threw a fistful of sand at its face. The Moon retreated far away and since then has stayed at a safe distance from the earth.

The markings that one can see on the surface of the lunar disc come from the projectiles cast by Quai. The grains of sand have greatly reduced the moon's brightness and have destroyed its burning heat. There is another explanation for these facts: in order to relieve the sufferings of mankind, the Moon's mother had to smear ashes on the face of her daughter.

It is also said that the man in the moon was Cuôi. A compulsive liar, he was exiled there and condemned to stand forever with his arms around the trunk of the lunar banyan tree. But he continued to play his tricks. The elder son of the family joined him by means of the power of a younger brother who could make his wishes come true. On the moon, Cuôi the liar handed the elder son his stone ax and advised him to chop down the lunar tree in order to find rice. But after a full day's hard labor, he discovered that his efforts were in vain. Cuôi also advised him to crush a stone to get flour to abate his hunger.

IV. The Length of the Day

To explain the greater or shorter length of days according to the seasons, two different kinds of rotation of the sun around the earth are visualized. In the first instance, "Sister Sun" is carried in her palanquin by a group of youths; as they linger on the way, the sun leaves the earth late and the day grows long. On the other hand, when she is carried by a group of old men, she returns home quickly, because these bearers take their job to heart and perform their assigned duties conscientiously, and thus the day is short.

V. Eclipses

The husband of the two sisters, the Sun and the Moon, is a bear. The eclipses of the Sun and of the Moon are interpreted in terms of the sexual relations between the bear and his wives. The eclipse constitutes a bad omen: scarcity and destruction of crops. People try to separate the bear from his wives by sounding gongs, beating drums, and striking rice mortars with pestles. The lunar eclipse is called "the bear eating the moon."

These few fragments of lunar and solar mythology do not seem to be known by the Vietnamese people as a whole, for they have been drawn from legends of different localities and collected in recent years.

On the other hand, the festival of midautumn is quite widespread. It is dedicated to the moon and takes place every year on the fifteenth day of the eighth lunar month. It has come down to us from China, and it is easy to recognize all the elements of Chinese myth. The white round cakes especially prepared for the occasion are decorated with the jade hare, the three-legged toad, and the tree of immortality. In the course of this festival, which is primarily for children, they run around the town carrying lanterns shaped like fish and crabs. They sing a round to the beat of the Ho Khoan ("Oh hoist") and perform the dance of the lion. At nightfall, groups of young men on one side and young girls on another sing the alternating verses of a long love song, a literary contest in which each seeks to outdo the other in imagination or spirit. In certain places, this festival is the occasion for worshiping the ancestors.

The appearance of the lunar disc makes possible predictions of good or bad omens: if the moon is clear, the harvest of rice of the tenth month will be good; if it is misty, the harvest of the fifth month will be abundant. If the moon is not visible, all the crops will be lost. Women and young girls especially worship the moon; by interpreting the "shadows of the face of the moon" they are able to choose the time for betrothal and marriage.

VI. The Creation of Rice and Cotton

The appearance of men and other beings was soon followed by that of rice and cotton. This was the work of the Jade Emperor: he wanted to provide human beings with food and clothing. However, the supreme deity hesitated about the actual size that he would give to the two seedlings. He called a meeting of all the animals on earth and asked their advice. Two dominant opinions emerged from the debate. One came from the large animals, who wanted the rice grain to be the length of the elephant's tail and the ear of the cotton plant to be as bulky as the head of the pachyderm. The other opinion came from the small animals, who proposed that the grain of rice and the ear of cotton plant be the size of the tail and head of the lizard, respectively. In this way there would be no waste on the part of the small animals. The Jade Emperor favored the lizard's side—and that is why the plants are the size they are.

Parallel to this legend is another one about the size of the grain of rice which is part of the etiological myths of the Golden Age.

VII. The Golden Age

It is not usually possible to dissociate the myths of the creation of the elements and natural phenomena (plants and food) from the theme of Lost Happiness, of Death, and of the search for Immortality. Every initial creation is either prevented from reaching its goal, diverted from its purpose, or destroyed once it has been achieved. The same applies to the Sun and the Moon, which were once close to human beings but were chased away or forced to distance themselves, and to the grain of rice, which was originally abundant and obtained without difficulty but which became hard to get as a result of man's negligence. The gift of immortality was stolen from man.

Once upon a time the Sun came down to the top of the trees. Similarly, the Moon liked to come close to the world of the living to see them go about their business. But people failed to take advantage of this arrangement. Out of laziness, they would expose any object to the sun and would go as far as to dry decomposed bodies and rubbish. The Sky, who is here called the Jade Emperor, withdrew the Sun to a distance of one hundred million kilometers from the earth to punish men for their negligence. The removal of the Sun plunged mankind into a total darkness that threatened its survival. The rooster, aided by the duck that carried it on its back, set out in search of the light. The rooster crossed the eastern sea and reached the Sun in his refuge. He asked the Sun to return to earth; but the request was granted only in part: the Sun appears only when men need it. To make it come up, the rooster starts to crow—and that is why the rooster's crow announces the new day.

Once upon a time a grain of rice was enormous, like a bowl (according to some), or like a dugout canoe (according to others). Moreover, it grew by itself, without needing to be cultivated. When it was ripe, the rice rolled by itself into the granary of each household. People could just help themselves to the amount they needed, and the grain immediately swelled back to its original size. Only one condition was imposed: every housewife had to keep the pathway of the grain of rice clean. But one woman out of laziness failed to sweep her yard in time. The grain refused to come in, for it could not stand to roll over filth. The furious housewife struck the grain of rice and it broke into small pieces. Then it flew into a rage and told her: "From now on, I shall return only when I am cut with a wooden handle and an iron blade, that is, with a sickle." That is how farm work first appeared in mythology and why a grain of rice is so small today.

We should note that at the turn of the century, during his ethnographic fieldwork, Father Cadière discovered vestiges of the worship of a giant rice grain. This worship took place in a "pagoda" erected in honor of the Rice Couple, whom the villagers respectfully called "Sir Rice" and "Lady Rice." They worshiped a ball of rice the size of a coconut that tradition claimed was of ancient origin. The large grain of rice had a virtually unlimited power of nutrition, for a small fragment would swell enough when it was cooked to feed an entire family.

VIII. Immortality and Death

At the beginning of time, the Celestial Emperor wanted to let men live forever. So that his wish would be fulfilled, he sent one of his messengers to earth solemnly to proclaim that when men reached old age they would shed their skins and become young again, whereas snakes, instead of shedding them, would die. But the heavenly messenger accidentally stumbled on a brood of snakes. Threatened by the snakes, he was forced to proclaim the opposite of what he had been ordered to say, that is, that men would have to die when they got old, whereas snakes would enjoy immortality by changing their skin. The agent of this counterorder was punished severely: he was excluded from the heavenly realm and exiled to earth in the shape of a dung beetle in order to compensate for the damages inflicted on the human species. The dung beetle lives in human excrement.

The themes related to the quest for immortality may be interpreted as attempts by the popular imagination to rediscover one of the primordial conditions that were so favorable to man. These are not properly myths, since they only concern a small number of people and their efficacy was fleeting. But in the course of these adventures, for a limited time, man resumes certain special contacts with the supernatural world. Such is the story of the Man in the Moon.

Cuôi, a woodcutter, accidentally witnessed a scene during which a tigress revived her cub with the help of leaves from the banyan tree. He got this power and revived a young woman, whom he later married; he also revived his dog. He planted the magic tree in his garden. One day, as he prepared to go away, he told his wife not to urinate at the foot of the tree. But she disobeyed his order, and the tree rose up toward the sky. The woodcutter arrived just then and tried to hold it back with his ax, but the tree carried him away with it to the moon. Since then, the tree can be seen on the moon, with the wretched woodcutter at its foot.

We shall cite one more example: The future god of the mountain, Tan Viên, was also a woodcutter. While he was cutting down a tree, he came in contact with a deity who handed him a magic cane that cured the sick and revived the dead. He used the power often and thus saved the son of the king of the Waters. But soon no one heard of the magic cane any more.

IX. The Sky

In the popular consciousness, the Sky represents a supreme deity who governs the whole universe. He is notably the chief of the gods of nature and the one in complete charge of human destiny. The name he bears varies according to what position a group or a personality at the heart of Vietnamese society occupies. He is commonly called Ong Troi, Sir Sky; but in a more religious and folkloric context his name is the Jade Emperor, Ngoc Hoang. The king, his civil servants, and scholars call him the Emperor from on High, Thuong-dê.

In principle, individuals do not worship him directly; this is a concern of the earthly emperor, since the latter is his agent on earth, according to Chinese concepts of kingship. Like the Chinese emperor, the Vietnamese emperor presides every three years over a ceremony of offerings in honor of the Sky and the Earth. This is the sacrifice offered in the southern outskirts of the capital, the Nam-giao, which seem to be a faithful replica of the Chinese model.

Along with a host of other deities, the Jade Emperor belongs to the Chinese Taoist pantheon. The heavenly ruler lives surrounded by his wife and children. He governs with the help of his celestial assistants, whom he convenes in council at his court. A few human beings have been able to visit his residence by the path of dreams: first, one makes a voyage through the atmosphere, crossing nine aerial levels before reaching one's destination. This is a grandiose palace with jade doors and golden walls. To reach the court one has to pass through nine gates. The inside of the palace is adorned with the peaches of immortality, with precious pearls taken from under the jaw of the black dragon, and with magic trees offered by the kings of the netherworld.

There are no longer any direct communications between heaven and earth. Nevertheless, a few hints in the folklore suggest that they once existed: someone set up a ladder to climb to heaven to ask about his fate (in a popular song); an immortal woman would send her husband and son down from the sky by means of a cord (in the legend of the morning and evening stars); another example speaks of two celestial gods who came down onto the top of a mountain.

The role played by the wife of the Jade Emperor is not known, but we know more about his sons and daughters. Some of them were sent to earth where some became rulers, others heroes or famous persons; still others spent time there in exile. It is said that the mother of the future founder of the Early Lê dynasty (tenth century) dreamed, before giving birth, that the Emperor from on High had entrusted a Golden Boy (the name given to the sons of heaven) with the mission of ruling over Vietnam. As the Golden Boy hesitated, the Emperor took a piece of jade and hit him on the forehead. The child was born with a scar on his forehead.

The goddess Liêu Hanh, whom the practitioners of the cult of mediums recognize as the most illustrious of the Holy Mothers, is the incarnation of a daughter of the Jade Emperor. She was sent into exile on earth for having indelicately broken a jade wine cup that she was supposed to serve to guests. She was married to a human, and she bore him a son. She died when her earthly exile came to an end. But memories of the human world haunted her spirit, and she returned to earth in the form of a beautiful flutist. Men who teased her knew unhappiness and pain. She was particularly fond of beautiful secluded places. Constantly traveling, she was sometimes seen in the north of the country and sometimes in the capital, where she ran a teahouse frequented by scholars. She left without a trace at each departure, and her house would miraculously disappear. Meanwhile, her husband died and was reincarnated as a great scholar. She found him again, and they lived together until the end of her second exile. She ascended to the sky and then came down to earth again, this time with her father's consent, to become the goddess of a village in Thanh-hoa. In the seventeenth century, the imperial court regarded her as a demoness and called on sorcerers and warriors to destroy her temple. But she unleashed epidemics that killed off men and decimated herds throughout the region. The imperial court was forced to rebuild her temple and to confer a royal license on her.

In popular stories, the Jade Emperor intervenes repeatedly in the organization of the primordial world of humans. In particular, he created animals, some useful and others harmful. It is not surprising that the buffalo occupies an essential place in agricultural activities since it is a celestial deity that was sent into exile on earth as a punishment for disobedience. The buffalo was ordered by the Jade Emperor to plant a handful of rice and a handful of grass, for the benefit of man. He first threw the grass and second only half of the rice; that is why grass grows in abundance but rice is scarce. The Jade Emperor became angry and turned his assistant into a buffalo. He sent him to earth to eat grass and help men in their labors.

The mouse is also of celestial origin, as is the cat. The mouse was once an officer of the Jade Emperor, in charge of watching over the granary of heaven, but he stole the grain in order to sell it or to give it to his friends. To punish him, the supreme deity sent him into exile on earth in the form of a mouse. He continued to nibble at men's rice, and they complained to the god of the hearth. In order to give them satisfaction, the Jade Emperor sent them another metamorphosed celestial officer to chase after the mouse—the cat.

Since the Jade Emperor presided over atmospheric phenomena, he sent to earth several assistants, such as the rain god, the thunder god, and so forth. These representatives discharged their duties poorly, so that men and animals suffered disastrous consequences, as the following legend shows:

The rain god left the earth and thus caused a great drought. Men and animals died in great numbers. The toad, accompanied by the fox, the bear, and the tiger, ascended to the sky to ask for rain. The toad arrogantly beat a drum at the gate of the palace. The Jade Emperor, wearied by this insolence, sent his troops against him. But his own animals were defeated, and he had to bow down before the might of his visitor. He agreed to receive him. The toad presented him with his grievances and demanded that the rains be sent down immediately. He won his case. Since then, he has been charged by the Jade Emperor with announcing rain: all he has to do is to cry out. A maxim makes him the "mother's brother" of the Sky and asks people not to mistreat him or penalties will be inflicted on them by the Sky.

It is to the thunder god, Thien Lôi, that the Jade Emperor gave the mission of chastising criminals, blasphemous sons, and all who commit serious moral faults, or who are predestined to be struck by lightning, including animals. He even killed certain animals that had become evil spirits because of their exceptional longevity. As the divine judge, he threw an ax at the head of his victims to accomplish his task. At the same time, he hit with a hammer the drums suspended from his body, thus producing rolls of thunder. People represented him as an extremely ugly creature, with the head and feet of a rooster. That is because he had originally been punished by being transformed into a piece of meat that a celestial rooster came to pick at with terrible and painful pecks. After this incarnation, he took the partial form of a rooster and experienced great fear of this animal. For this reason, people who want thunder to go away clack their lips and suck in as if they are calling fowl. They also believe that Neolithic polished stone tools are the god's instruments, of which there are two kinds: those made of bronze kill human beings; those made of stone are used to kill animals and demons. These tools of the age of polished stone and bronze constituted talismans that sorcerers used to fight against devils and sicknesses. They could be found in places where lightning had struck after three months and ten days, for at this date they rose to the surface of the ground.

We have seen the thunder god in his terrible aspect. There are a few themes in the folklore that show him as vulnerable and unintelligent, a belief that functions as a kind of collective reaction against this heavenly executioner that everyone fears. Thus, when it is discovered that a child is destined to be struck by lightning, he is made to wear one of the ax talismans. The child will escape being struck by lightning, for he is considered to have already been struck. Similarly, the thunder god is known to execute his powers within strict limits, for he strikes without discernment wherever he is told to strike. His clumsiness is such that a young girl will escape unscathed simply by squatting with her buttocks facing the sky.

The god is made the object of derision in the following legend, in which the hero defeats him by disarming him. Cuong Bao, "the violent one," refused to perform the ritual for his dead mother. Instead, he made offerings to the hearth god. To punish him for his filial impiety, the Jade Emperor sent the thunder god to him. But "the violent one," who was warned and advised by the hearth god, covered the roof of his house with "Indian spinach" and oil. The thunder god slipped on the roof and fell, dropping his ax. "The violent one" immediately picked it up. Disarmed, the thunder god had to return to the sky and announce his defeat. He ordered the rain god to send a flood to drown "the violent one." Aided again by the hearth god, the hero built a raft on which he took refuge. The waters swelled and lifted him up to the gate of heaven. The emperor felt compelled to make the waters recede, out of fear that all the people might drown. "The violent one" was once again the victor. But when he subsequently neglected the hearth god, the protection was withdrawn from him and he was struck by lightning while crossing a field.

X. The Dragon King

The Dragon King, Long-vuong or Thuy-tê, rules the world of the waters by the order of the Jade Emperor. But he apparently deals only with matters concerning the seas; he delegates his powers to his subordinates and puts them in charge of the other waterways. He thus remains far from the world of living creatures; he has only episodic contacts with them and only through the mediation of his messengers. Much like the Jade Emperor or like an earthly king, he lives at the center of his court, surrounded by his wife and children and by an army of aquatic animals. His residence is a magnificent palace that rises from the bottom of a deep pit. Sometimes the Dragon King entrusts the building of his home to a human being. On this occasion, he chooses a human carpenter of great talent and sends two messengers to invite him to his aquatic realm. When the work is completed, the King offers him precious pearls in payment. When the Dragon King invites guests, they come to him in two ways: either the king's messengers escort them and open a way for them by miraculously parting the waters, or else they move around in the water by using a rhinoceros's horn. Both King An-duong and the future god Tan Viên made use of this powerful talisman. A human being happened to reach the palace of the Dragon King. He was a fisherman, an experienced and strong diver. He met some turtles who offered him the boon of understanding the language of the animals in exchange for his promise never to reveal to living creatures what he had seen. But when he returned home, he disclosed to his wife the mysteries of the kingdom of the waters. He died immediately, vomiting blood. The reason why the world of the waters must remain unknown is that it is *âm (yin)* and is opposed to the world of living creatures, *duong (yang)*; that is also why there is a certain confusion between it and hell, one of whose names is *âm-phu*.

In popular stories, the Dragon King is presented as a being of extreme kindness. He always knows how to express his gratitude toward a human being who has saved one of his children. His sons and daughters often wander around in waterways in the form of fish or other aquatic animals, and they often get caught by fishermen. When they are released, they beg the king, their father, to invite these benefactors and to reward them. The Dragon King offers his guests gifts of magical objects or objects of great value: a book that makes wishes come true, magical claws, precious pearls, and so forth.

There are marriages between water spirits and human beings, such as Giap-Hai, who bought a turtle from a pair of boatmen and thus saved its life. Every time he goes away, a beautiful young girl comes out of the turtle's shell to prepare his dinner for him. Giap-Hai discovers the secret. He waylays the young girl and steals her shell. She is forced to admit that she is the daughter of the Dragon King. She offers to marry him in order to repay him. They get married in the kingdom of the waters. Thanks to the Dragon King, Giap-Hai receives instruction from a good master and comes in first in an examination for scholars. In another account, the daughter of the Dragon King marries a fisherman for love. She cannot return alive to her father's kingdom, for she would miss her husband and prefers to stay with him.

Another favorite theme tells the adventures of the foster parents of a sea serpent. An old childless couple found two eggs from which two serpents hatched. They brought up the serpents as though they were their own children. But when they had grown up, the serpents returned to live under water. To compensate the old couple, the real father of the serpents miraculously procured for them as much money as they desired. The two serpents became the benevolent spirits of two villages.

But not all associations with water spirits are so good. They are responsible for much misery and many catastrophes. These local "administrators," and not the sons of the Dragon King, cause calamities. They make the waters rise in order to steal wood to construct the palace. The *giai,* a kind of freshwater turtle of giant size (which must not be confused with the real turtle, who is kind), can demolish dikes. People sometimes manage to kill them by throwing rubbish at them. But the most efficacious way is to bury a metal rhinoceros under the dikes. This has the magical property of stabilizing waterways.

Even more to be feared is the *thuông-luông,* a sea serpent one hundred feet long, covered with scales and endowed with a red crest. This creature has been identified as the Chiao dragon of the Chinese, which is also known to the Vietnamese: the misdeeds of the Chiao dragon resulted in the ancient custom of tattooing. Sometimes he is encountered in a female aspect: a Chiao dragon takes the form of an old woman to probe the hearts of people, and then she makes the waters rise to drown the wicked and to save those who have treated her well. As for the *thuông-luông* we mentioned earlier, he always appears as a male and has a particular inclination for sexuality. Since he is a ferocious monster, he raises the waves to sink junks and to carry women away to his kingdom, to rape them or to force them to become his wives. One legend tells of a *thuông-luông* who devoured the people that he had shipwrecked by overturning their boats. Every year the people had to bring him a human victim. One man volunteered. He let the monster swallow him, and then he cut the monster up with a dagger and killed him.

Traces of human sacrifices to sea serpents can be found in the two following accounts. One of the emperors of the Ly dynasty (eleventh through thirteenth centuries) suffered from an eye ailment, which was connected with the overflowing of a river, according to one diviner's interpretation. To get cured, he cast a couple of oil merchants into the river as sacrificial offerings. Another emperor of the Trân dynasty (thirteenth through sixteenth centuries) had to let his favorite woman jump into the river as an offering to a Chiao dragon: the dragon, who threatened to sink the imperial junks, had demanded a human wife. Finally, King Lê Thanh-tông (fifteenth century) lodged a complaint with the chief of the kingdom of waters. The chief sent a herd of aquatic animals to punish the guilty party and to demand that he return the woman. In fact, they recovered the body of the young girl.

But the best known of all mythical animals is without any doubt the dragon. Distinct from the ferocious and sensual Chiao dragon and from the Dragon King who is the chief of the aquatic realm, the dragon represents a beneficent being, dispenser of rains, of which he became the god. His role can be compared to that of the toad during the Bronze Age of Dongson. Like the Chinese dragon, he buries himself in the earth during the off-season and arises to fly through the air in the spring; then he uses his mouth to pulverize the rains that the farmers have been awaiting. A noble animal, classed in the highest rank of the "four sacred animals," he is the emblem of royal power. He is represented on court costumes, on the throne, and on imperial junks. In 549, Triên Quang Phuc received from the Immortal Chu Dông-tu, who rode on a dragon, a claw from that animal, which made it possible for him to defeat an enemy army. The future king, Dinh Tiên-hoang, is seen as having been carried across a river by two yellow dragons when he was pursued by his uncle. Finally, the capital city Thang-long, "the Ascent of the Dragon" (Hanoi), was thus christened by the founders of the Ly dynasty (eleventh century) because a yellow dragon had risen to the sky to indicate to the king an era of prosperity.

In conclusion, with the exception of the religious representations of the deities of nature, the themes that deal with the primordial world seem at first glance to have lost their religious tenor. They are no longer stories deemed to be true so that they may be believed and actualized through rituals. Gathered indiscriminately among other folkloric documents, they appear as etiological legends rather than cosmogonic myths.

Nevertheless, if we isolate a certain number of motifs and set them next to certain elements of the mythology of neighboring peoples, particularly the mythology of the non-Vietnamese mountain tribes, we see that they are part of a more complex network of myths. Thus, the Vietnamese hunter of the Moon, Quai, evokes the Tay marksman of the twelve suns and the Chinese archer Yi, who conquered the surplus suns. The return of the sun into the world of humans took place in the same way among the Vietnamese and the same Tay: in both cases the rooster and the duck went out into the open sea to reclaim it. The theme of the giant rice grain fits into a more coherent set of myths of the first creations of the universe among the Black Tai. An analogous version of the tree of immortality that rises into the sky can be found among the Muong: it is the story of Ta Keo Rênh. As for the universal flood, no trace of it can be found among the Vietnamese, unless we see a few allusions to it in the story of "the violent one" whom the waters carried up to the sky, which implies that all of mankind was left under the waters.

These few examples lead us to believe that Vietnamese mythology did indeed exist, but that it was effaced by an imported Confucianism, and that only popular and oral traditions have been able to preserve some reminiscences of it.

L.O.M./g.h.

Civilizing Heroes and the Organization of the First Vietnamese Kingdom

1. The Mythic Origin of the Vietnamese

Ancient and modern historians have attributed the foundation of Van-lang, the first Vietnamese kingdom, to the Hung King. The documents that they cite are fragmentary and derive more from legend than from historical fact. Thus in Vietnam the mythic history of the world is identified with the setting up of the kingdom and the origins of its people. All Vietnamese readily call themselves "sons of the Dragon and grandsons of the Immortal (female)." The origin of this phrase derives from the following legend.

Lac Long-Quân, Lord Dragon of the tribe of the Lacs and the future father of the first Hung King, was a descendant of the aquatic animal of the same name. He married an Immortal of the mountain, Lady Au-Co, of marvelous beauty. After three years and ten days she miraculously gave birth to a membranous pouch, from which, seven days later, one hundred eggs emerged. From these hundred eggs were born a hundred boys. All grew up without needing to be nursed. But their mother and father could no longer live together. Lord Dragon reminded his wife that he was of the race of Dragons and lord of the aquatic element, while she was of the race of the Immortals and thus belonged to the earthly element. But the two elements water and earth (or fire) are opposed to one another. They cannot remain together. They divided their sons and each of them led away fifty boys. Lord Dragon took his sons to his kingdom of water, while Lady Au-Co went with hers to the high country.

This separation into two groups, one going toward the mountain, that is, to the northwest, and the other settling in the maritime region of the southeast, is probably an allusion to the ethnic minorities of North Vietnam, on the one hand, and to the installation of the Vietnamese themselves in the plains and coastal regions, on the other. According to this myth, the two groups have a common source.

The simultaneous birth of a hundred males not only evokes an image of fertility but also recalls the renewal of humanity described in the myths of certain neighboring peoples. Instead of a membranous pouch, we find in these myths either a piece of flesh or a gourd out of which, after the universal flood, a brother and sister come who give birth to the Vietnamese and non-Vietnamese peoples. The separation of the spouses in this legend rests on the opposition of earth and water. Moreover, the Vietnamese term for "the country," "the kingdom," is precisely "earth-water" (*dât-nouc*). It can thus be said that the union of the mythic couple already reinforces the idea of the nation.

2. The Civilizing Heroes: The Hung Vuong

The eldest of the fifty sons who followed their mother was chosen by his brothers as the first king of the Van-lang kingdom. He reigned under the title of Hung Vuong, and his dynasty included eighteen Hung kings. Recently collected legends about them reveal that they were civilizing heroes. These kings lived in close contact with their people; they taught them new techniques, discovered new food plants for their benefit and also originated new customs. Moreover, the mastery of water was and remains one of the most indispensable secrets of rice cultivation. Thus, the Hung had to battle against water monsters who started floods, destroying harvests and carrying people away.

More than twenty centuries have passed, and the Vietnamese still worship the Hung. Their temples are found especially in the province of Phu-tho (north Vietnam). In one of these temples, located on a mountain summit, a tablet can be found with the following inscription: "The tablet of the eighteen generations of holy sovereigns of the Hung family." During their annual festival, the tablets of these kings are taken out and carried in a procession, and various games are organized in their honor.

The first Hung founded his capital. He made a grand tour of the country to choose the future location of the capital. When he had found a vast, flat site, he commissioned an eagle to construct a hundred mounds and demanded that the construction work be completed in one night. When ninety-nine mounds had been finished, a cock began to crow. The eagle thought that it was already day and abandoned his work. The Hung King left this site to search for another place. He was attracted by a new site in the mountains. But a blow of his horse's hoof made a piece of a peak give way. The king judged that the site was not stable and abandoned it. He left a third site as well, for he saw a serpent there, which he considered a bad omen. Then he came upon a golden tortoise coming out of the water to greet him; the tortoise carried him on its back throughout its domain. But he found this site too narrow and decided not to choose it as a capital. Finally, one day he came upon an exceptional place and decided to settle there; he called his capital Phong-chau.

The Hung kings explored the jungle and the mountain. Myths about the Hung often suggest a mastery of the mountain and an exploration of the jungle. From there it is but one step to the idea of setting up a territory. Every time the king took part in the hunt he was accompanied by a considerable following. He took with him his sons and his daughters. The hunting party lasted several days and was interrupted by pauses for refreshments. Meals were prepared in the manner of non-Vietnamese mountain tribes.

One day the Hung King halted at the foot of a mountain. His daughters discovered some fragrant plants and brought them to their father. The king had some game covered with these fine herbs before it was roasted. He tasted it and found it much better than before. He took the herb away to plant it at his residence. Until now, people in certain places preserve a ritual that consists in offering a sacrifice to the king, a plate of chicken cooked with this herb.

The first Hung King taught the techniques of agriculture to his people. There was a time, they say, when people did not know about the plow and rice cultivation. They ate only game, roots and plants, and wild fruit. But at each flood the rivers brought new layers of fertile alluvium. The Hung King dammed up the flooded lands. With rice growing wild, he showed his people how to save its seeds and plant them. Then he went in person to pull up the young rice plants and replant them. All his subjects tried to imitate him.

This legend is accompanied by a ritual meant to reactualize the king's exploit. The ritual was preserved until very recent times in the village where the exploit is said to have occurred—Minh-nong, in the Viet-tri province in north Vietnam. The people of this village had the custom of offering a sacrifice to the Hung King. The ceremony took place under a banyan, as before. An old man was chosen to descend into a flooded rice field to repick some young rice plants symbolically. The ritual is the same as that performed during the festival to honor Than-nong, a god of agriculture among the Chinese and Vietnamese. In this substitution, then, there is an attempt to regard the ritual as being of Vietnamese origin.

The mastery of the waters took place during this protohistorical period, when the problem of water already constituted a major preoccupation. The battle against the surging floods of the water courses has been translated into mythology. The adversary was formidable and was identified with an aquatic animal. Only Lord Dragon was able to conquer it; even the Immortals failed. This fabulous beast—half-fish, half-serpent—lived in the eastern sea. It stirred up storms as it moved on its multiple paws. It sought to devour human beings. One day it changed into a white rooster and, announcing dawn, drove off the Immortals who were trying to destroy its lair. Lord Dragon, disguised as a fisherman, pretended to offer it a human victim. But instead he threw a white-hot lump of metal down its gaping beak. The beast fell, and the sovereign cut off its head and tail.

The ferocious dragon Kiao also represented hostile nature.

It devoured the inhabitants of the mountain. The Hung King understood that this fabulous animal considered the essence of people to be contrary to its own. On the advice of the king, the people tattooed themselves with figures of the monster so as to resemble him and escape his attacks. This was a way to become familiar with nature. The custom continued in all levels of society, popular as well as aristocratic, until the fourteenth century.

But the most significant example of the mastery of water is found in the legend of Son-Tinh, the Spirit of the Mountain, and Thuy-Tinh, the Spirit of Water. These two spirits struggled to obtain the hand of the daughter of the Hung King; the king did not know to which of the two he should marry the princess, for they were equal in magical power. He asked them to come back with wedding gifts; the one who brought them first would marry her. The Spirit of the Mountain brought them first and took the princess away. The Spirit of Water came late and grew furious. He led his army of aquatic animals in pursuit of his happy adversary to try to snatch the young bride away. When he came to Mount Tan-Vien, the residence of the Spirit of the Mountain, he rushed into an assault, provoking great storms. The Spirit of the Mountain stretched metal nets across the rivers in order to check their progress. The people gave him their cooperation. They built a barrier all around Mount Tan-Vien and encouraged the god with the noises of drums and rice mortars. They shot arrows in the direction of the water: the lifeless bodies of aquatic animals came floating up to the surface. This battle is taken up again every year and the floods of the seventh month are witness to it.

Tan-Vien is the beneficent god of the mountain. In the preceding legend, this god has the attributes of a divinity of nature. Later, he takes on the aspect of a divinized human being. There is a story about his miraculous conception. His mother, poor and ugly, had no husband; she became pregnant after putting her foot down on the footprint of a giant. Chased into the forest by the inhabitants of her village on account of her pregnancy, she was fed by tigers who brought her meat every day. Her son became a woodcutter and worked to help his mother. Then, one day, he received a magic wand from the hands of a god; this instrument enabled him to resuscitate the dead or kill people, depending on which end he pointed at the subject in question. In addition, this divinity charged him with guarding the mountain Tan-Vien. After this the boy brought many dead people back to life. He became a doctor as well, tending to the diseases of simple people whom he sought out himself. The people expressed their admiration for him and gave him the title of god of the mountain.

His good deeds did not stop there. A civilizing hero in the same way as the Hung kings, he brought many new techniques to the people. In one village where the inhabitants did not know how to net fish, the god taught them this technique. In another situtation, he showed his hunting companions a new way of preserving game meat. In this way the god of the mountain became the patron god of hunters. In the region of Vinh-phu where, according to a recent count, there are more than five hundred temples dedicated to the Hung family and their generals, including Tan-Vien, people offer him a sacrifice every time they return from the hunt. During these ceremonies, the hunters reenact a scene from Tan-Vien's hunt. Pigs replace game and are carried in a procession to the sound of drums and cheers; a feast is prepared in the open air. Then the participants vie with one another in tearing off pieces of red paper previously pasted onto poles stuck beside the pigs. These pieces of paper are then pasted on crossbows so that the final hunt may be more fruitful. Sacrifices are also performed to request the opening of the hunt and entrance into the forest. No one dares to go there to collect wood before this festival. It should be added that the divinity has Lord Tiger for an acolyte.

On the national level, Tan-Vien is regarded by the population as the first of the divinities of the kingdom through his great power of regulating rains and drought. His place of worship is on the peak of Mount Tan-Vien ("roundness of the parasol"), so named because it has the form of a dome. Formerly, every three years the emperor of Vietnam sent his high officials there to offer sacrifice. On this occasion, neighboring villagers would offer the divinity axes of polished stone and bronze, which they believe to be thunderstones and to which they attribute magic virtues. We are also told that during the battle against the Spirit of Water, the god Tan-Vien made these thunderstones rain down to control the floods raised by his enemy. The people sacrifice to him on the first and the fifteenth of the month. On these days, tigers, rhinoceroses, and elephants leave the jungle to come to make an act of submission to the god.

In brief, this period is marked by setting the kingdom in order. The chiefs who arranged it knew how to provide exemplary models and to furnish the qualities that characterize a civilization. The hostile natural forces were immense; they are represented by monsters. If the Hung kings were able to exterminate them, it is because they were of supernatural origin, like the multitude of generals who helped them in their task. Once the watercourses were dammed up, the land became arable and people could live in security. The rituals now observed by the Vietnamese have for their object the reactualization of the exemplary acts of the civilizing heroes of the earliest times.

L.O.M./d.g.

PART

4

East Asia and Inner Asia

Chinese Mythology

Ancient Chinese mythology has been very poorly transmitted to us, and it suffices to leaf through the ancient Chinese books to be convinced of this. Only with difficulty can we recognize in the Confucian classics the old myths, camouflaged as history: at their origins we find only sovereigns or sages who founded the civilization. In the writings of various philosophical schools, such allusions to legend as we find are always very fragmentary. In a general sense, mythology was transformed into history by scholars whose main concern was to teach an ethics and an art of government and who did so by referring to models that they sought in early antiquity. Nevertheless, there is enough ancient Chinese to offer fairly plentiful, if sporadic, data; and by drawing these together and comparing them, it is possible to recover the broad outlines of a mythology which turns out to be richer than would at first have appeared. But we have only a fragmentary and very incomplete knowledge of it, so that many of the visual representations unearthed by archaeology remain unexplained. M. Hentze is certainly correct in thinking that the motifs that decorated the ancient Yin and Zhou bronzes are not merely designs but have a religious significance even when they appear to be no more than geometric fillers. But the texts give us no explanation for this decoration of the ancient bronzes; by the same token, much later, many of the scenes represented on Han funerary sculptures remain enigmatic. On the other hand, the sculptures sometimes confirm what is related in the texts; thus the thunder god appears as he is described by Wang Chong in the *Lunheng,* with drums threaded together on a single strut. Archaeology thus remains a precious resource which may continue to offer much new information, the further study of which will enrich our knowledge of the ancient religions: witness the recent discovery, in tombs near Chang Sha, of two beautiful banners of painted silk, covered with mythological subjects (the sun, moon, fusang trees, the door of heaven, etc.).

As for written sources, the one with the most mythological data is incontestably the *Shanhai Jing* (Book of mountains and seas): this is a mythic geography whose eighteen chapters were written over different periods of time, all B.C. Tradition attributes its redaction to Yu the Great. He had nine sacred cauldrons (*ding*) made, upon which were represented the gods and demons in order that his subjects could distinguish the good and evil spirits that they risked encountering in their travels over mountains and valleys. The *Shanhai Jing,* an illustrated book, was probably composed for the same purpose, since it gives a great deal of information on the gods and demons of mountains and waterfalls, not only "within the boundaries of the seas," that is, within the empire, but also beyond, in the regions situated on the periphery of the civilized world.

Apart from the *Shanhai Jing,* it is the poems of Qiu Yuan (end of the fourth century B.C.), in the *Chuci* (Elegies of the land of the Chu), which are the richest in ancient mythological data, especially the *Lisao,* the *Jiu Ge* (Nine songs), and above all the *Tianwen* (Celestial questions). This last poem is composed of questions about mythology, but we are unfortunately not always provided with the answers to the enigmas, even with the aid of the commentaries.

Among the philosophical works, the *Huainanzi,* a text inspired by Daoism and written by the scholarly seers of the court of a king of Huainan in the second century B.C., contains fragments of myths that are not found elsewhere.

In the time of the Six Dynasties, a period of division in which the ascendancy of Confucianism was somewhat weak-

Han funerary ledger. Paris, Musée Guimet. Photo Arch. Phot. Paris/SPADEM.

ened, some collections appeared containing some fairly well preserved legends: the *Shiyiji* of Wang Jia (fourth century A.D.), the *Bownzhi* of Jhang Hua (A.D. 232–300), the Shoushenji of Gan Bao (fourth century A.D.), the *Shu chi* of Jen Fang (A.D. 460–508) and the *Shen yi ching*, attributed to the Tung fang Sho of the Han dynasty, but in fact anonymous. All of these works make it possible to flesh out the most ancient information, though we have to reckon with the literary fables and morals that their authors often inserted into their accounts.

M.K./d.w.

BIBLIOGRAPHY

M. GRANET, *Danses et légendes de la Chine ancienne* (Paris 1926); *Fêtes et chansons anciennes de la Chine* (Paris 1929); *La pensée chinoise* (Paris 1934; 2d ed., 1968); *Études sociologiques sur la Chine* (Paris 1953). H. MASPERO, "Les légendes mythologiques dans le Chou king," *Journal asiatique*, 1924; *Mythologie de la Chine moderne*, in *Mythologie asiatique illustrée* (1928), reprinted in *Le Taoïsme et les religions chinoises* (1971); *Mélanges posthumes*, vol. 1: *Les religions chinoises* (Paris 1967). W. EBERHARD, *Lokalkulturen im alten China*, 1–2 (1942); *Typen chinesischer Volksmärchen*, FF Communications 120. C. HENTZE, *Funde in Alt-China* (Göttingen 1967). K. FINSTER-BUSCH, *Das Verhältnis des Shan-hai djing zur Bildenden Kunst* (Berlin 1952). W. EICHHORN, *Die Alte Chinesische Religion und das Stattkultwesen* (Leiden and Cologne 1976). WERNER, *A Dictionary of Chinese Mythology* (1931; 2d ed., 1961). IZUSHI YOSHIHIKO, *Shina shinwa densetsu no kenkyû* (Tokyo 1943). MORI MIKISABURO, *Chûgoku kodai shinwa* (Tokyo 1969). YUAN K'E, *Zhong guo gudai Shenhua* (1957). YANG KUAN, *Zhong guo shangqushi daolun*, in *Gushi Pian* 7, 1.

Chinese Cosmogony

Ancient Chinese literature has almost no cosmogonic myths. The Confucian authors, who are little given to metaphysics, are in principle hostile to the marvelous. The Daoist philosophers, more inclined to make use of legendary traditions to illustrate their theses, also have little to say on the subject. For example, we could hardly qualify as mythological what Laozi, the *Liezi*, or the *Huainanzi* say about the beginning of the world:

> The Dao gave birth to the One,
> One gave birth to Two,
> Two gave birth to Three,
> Three gave birth to ten thousand beings;
> The ten thousand beings carry the Yin on their backs and embrace the Yang. (Laozi, 42)

The commentary of Heshang Gong on this text shows a somewhat more mythic concept of origins:

> That to which the Dao first gave birth was the Unity from which proceeded the Yin and the Yang. The Yin and the Yang produced the Three Energy Breaths: the Pure, the Impure, and the Mixed, which in turn constituted, respectively, the Sky, the Earth, and Man. Together, the Sky and Earth gave birth to ten thousand beings: the Sky furnished the seedlings, the Earth transformed them, and Man raised and nourished them.

Here, the Sky and the Earth are the Father and Mother of the creatures, and the One or the Unity is a way of designating Chaos, the original state of nondifferentiation. The *Liezi* also develops a formation of the world through stages, the starting point being the *Taiyi* (here *yi* is not the Unity, but the principle of mutations of the *Yi Jing*). But it is this *Yi* mutation that becomes the *Yi* Unity.

> By mutation, the One becomes Seven; Seven, by mutation, becomes Nine. With this ninth mutation, one returns to One. One is the beginning of the mutations of forms. That which was pure and light rose and became the Sky; that which was gross and heavy became the Earth; the intermediate breaths became man. Thanks to the seeds received by Earth from Sky, the ten thousand beings appeared through transformation. (*Liezi*, 1)

The formation of the world is the end result of a cyclic evolution, which is completely in agreement with one of the fundamental ideas of Chinese thought, for which the alternations between the Yin and the Yang and the five elemental Virtues order the life of the cosmos and of man, as well as the unfolding of history.

The *Huainanzi* (chapter 3) describes the formation of the world as follows:

> At the time when the Sky and Earth had not yet taken shape, the world was nothing more than a confused, undefinable mass, which is called the Great Beginning (*Taishi*). The Great Beginning produced the Void; this produced the Space-Time-Universe which produced the original Breath (*Yuanqi*). The original Breath was a thing without limits. Its clear and pure elements rose lightly to form the Sky; its heavy and gross elements coagulated to form the Earth. Since it is easier for clear and pure elements to become concentrated than for heavy and gross elements to coagulate, the Sky took shape before the Earth became stable. The complementary essences of Sky and Earth were the Yin and the Yang; the concentrated essences of the Yin and the Yang formed the seasons; and when the essences of the seasons diversified, they formed the ten thousand beings. The warm breath of the Yang, accumulated, came to produce fire, whose most subtle elements became the sun. The cold breath of the Yin, accumulated, came to produce water, whose most subtle elements became the moon. The most subtle of the superabundant solar and lunar elements became the stars. The Sky received the sun, moon, and stars; the Earth received the waters, rivers, ground, and dust.

In the same work, we also encounter the following text (chapter 7):

> Long ago, at a time when the Sky and the Earth did not exist, there reigned a great formless mist: such darkness, such an unmoving and silent immensity whose origins cannot be known! Two divinities were thus born out of this confusion, one regulating the movement of the Sky, the other organizing the Earth. They brought about the separation of the Yin and the Yang and established far off the eight poles of the world. The hard and the soft (the Yang and the Yin) completed each other mutually and the ten thousand beings took shape. The most gross of the fluids became the reptiles, and the most subtle of the fluids became man.

Exegetes hesitate to identify the two divinities to which the *Huainanzi* refers. Most of them contend that they are Fuxi and Nüwa. These two divinities with the bodies of serpents were nevertheless popular in the time of the Hans: they wonderfully symbolize the Yin and the Yang, and their attributes, the compass and the square, well designate them as the artisans of the round and the square, of the Sky and the Earth.

Through these Daoist texts we can see how these thinkers understood the origins of the world. But we do not know what the popular beliefs on this subject were. There seems to have been a myth of Chaos that Zhuangzi used by transposing it into a fable intended to illustrate the evil deeds of overzealous bearers of civilization:

> The lord of the southern Ocean was Shu; the lord of the northern Ocean was Hu. The lord of the Center was Chaos. Shu and Hu sometimes met in the province of Chaos, who treated them with great courtesy. They thought about the best way to repay him for his good deeds: "Everyone has seven openings for seeing, hearing, eating, and breathing. He is without these. Let us try to make these openings in him." Each day they undertook to pierce an opening in him. On the seventh day, Chaos died. (Chapter 7)

In classical literature, Hundun, Chaos, is one of the ones who are banished from Zhuen. In the *Shanhai Jing,* he is a monster who resembles a sack; and he has certain points in common with the Hundun of Zhuangzi, but he is no longer the primordial Chaos. It is not until a work of the third century A.D., the *Sanwu Liji,* that the celebrated myth of Pangu appears:

> In the time when the Sky and the Earth were a chaos resembling an egg, Pangu was born in this and lived inside it for eighteen thousand years. And when the Sky and Earth constituted themselves, the pure Yang elements formed the Sky and the gross Yin elements formed the Earth. And Pangu, who was in the midst of this, transformed himself nine times each day, sometimes into a god in the Sky, sometimes into a saint on Earth. Each day the Sky rose by one *Zhang* (ten feet), each day the Earth thickened by one *Zhang,* and each day Pangu grew by one *Zhang.* This continued for eighteen thousand years, and then the Sky reached its highest point, the Earth its lowest depth, and Pangu his greatest size.

Part of this narrative is inspired by the texts of the *Huainanzi* and *Liezi* cited above, but suddenly Pangu, who is completely unknown to earlier literature, appears on the scene. This may be explained by the southern origin of this myth, which did not become known to the Chinese until quite late. The *Shuyi Ji,* a sixth-century collection of *mirabilia,* tells another version:

> Living beings began with Pangu, who is the ancestor of the ten thousand beings of the universe. When Pangu died, his head became a sacred peak, his eyes became the sun and the moon, his fat the rivers and seas, and the hair of his head and body became trees and other plants. The ancient scholars affirm that the tears of Pangu gave rise to the Blue and Yellow rivers, that his breath was the wind, his voice thunder; the pupils of his eyes made the lightning flash, and the sky was clear when he was content and somber when he was angry. According to a belief of the Qin and Han periods, Pangu's head became the sacred peak of the East, his belly the peak of the Center, his left arm the peak of the South, his right arm the peak of the North, and his feet the peak of the West. In the (southern) lands of Wu and Chu, it is said that Pangu and his wife are the origin of the Yin and the Yang.

It is impossible to know what the author intended by "the ancient scholars," and as for his assertion that there was a belief about Pangu in the time of the Qin and the Han, this is very unlikely. The *Shuyi Ji* adds that tombs of Pangu were found in the Nanha, and temples of Pangu at Guilin. Nanha (the Southern Seas) is taken to mean the coastal regions of southern China and the lands across the sea; Guilin was in the north of Guangxi, a region completely inhabited by the Miao, Yao, and other aboriginal peoples. It is certain that these texts about Pangu do not offer us the original form of the myth: they were collected through hearsay and were for the northern Chinese nothing more than strange tales. Nevertheless, this legend must have retained enough local prestige for the Daoists to take interest in it and to take it over by replacing Pangu with a deified Laozi: "Laozi transformed himself: his left eye became the sun, his right eye became the moon, his head became Mount Kunlun, his hairs were the stars, his bones were dragons, his flesh the quadrupeds, his intestines serpents, his stomach the seas, his fingers the five sacred peaks, his body hair the plants, and his heart Mount Huagai" (*Xiaodao Lun,* sixth century A.D.).

Among the rare cosmogonic myths which came from China proper, the one about the break in communications between the Sky and the Earth must be mentioned. It was almost forgotten very early, and there remain only a few very short or distorted references to it. In the *Shu Jing* (*Lüxing*) we read: "The August Lord charged Chongli with breaking the communication between Sky and Earth, in order to halt the descents of the gods." According to the exegetes, the August Lord is Zhuanxu (regarded as a historical emperor), who is said to have introduced a religious reform. He is said to have done this in order to keep the people from giving themselves up to irregular cults in the course of which sorcerers and sorceresses invoked the spirits and caused them to "descend," i.e., caused themselves to be possessed by them. In fact, this is an old myth according to which the Sky and the Earth, too close to one another, communicated in such a way that gods were able to descend to be among men.

Although the ancient Chinese did not preserve their old cosmogonic myths, they did nevertheless have legends about heroes who repaired the damage done to the world by a rebellious monster or by a flood, the latter being the Chinese version of the Flood myth. They also have a myth about the creation of mankind:

"According to popular legend, at the time when the Sky and the Earth were created, mankind did not yet exist. Nüwa began to fashion men out of yellow earth. But she found this task to be too much for her powers; therefore she went to draw some mud, which she used to make men. It is thus that the nobles were the men fashioned from yellow earth; poor people, who live in vile and servile conditions, are the men who were drawn out of the mud" (*Fengsu Tongyi,* second century A.D.).

Nüwa appears here as the divinity who created men. It is surprising that this myth is found in only one single work, to which it is incidental, at that; perhaps this was a little-known local tradition. In a more widespread myth, Nüwa intervenes to repair the damage done when the monster Gonggong made a hole in one of the pillars of the world with a thrust of his horns. The pillar swayed, and it is for this reason that the heavenly bodies flow toward the west while on earth rivers flow toward the east. As for the Sky, "Nüwa melted the rocks of five colors in order to repair it; she cut off the legs of a great turtle to erect four pillars at the four poles, killed the black Dragon (Gonggong) to save the world, and piled up the ashes of reeds to stop the overflowing waters" (*Huainanzi*). Nüwa is one of the two mythic characters who fight against the Flood. The other is Yu the Great, a renowned hero who, though presented by historians as a sort of hydraulic engineer, was surely a demiurge who organized the world with its mountains and its sacred rivers of which he became the principal god. Nüwa and Yu, moreover, have such close mythic ties that the goddess has been assimilated to the wife of Yu, the daughter of Tushan.

M.K./d.w.

Sky and Earth, Sun and Moon, Stars, Mountains and Rivers, and the Cardinal Points in Ancient China

I. Sky and Earth

Under the Han there were at least two ways of representing the world (Sky-Earth, *Tiandi*). According to the first, the universe is a chariot covered by a canopy: the canopy is round and is the Sky; the Earth is represented by the square frame of the chariot. The Sky is supported by columns, four or eight in number. There are also eight moorings (*wei*). One of these pillars, Mount Buzou, situated to the northwest of the world, was shaken by Gonggong. According to another theory, the Sky resembles an egg and the Earth is the yolk in the center of the egg. To explain how the Earth is kept in equilibrium in this position, one *weishu* ("apocryphon") said that under the Earth there are eight columns (*Hetu Juodixiang*). But in general the eight columns were erected between the Sky and the Earth.

The Earth, a great square in whose interior there were nine provinces, was surrounded on four sides by the "Four Seas." The Four Seas were not oceans, but regions peopled by barbarians: nine kinds of Yi barbarians to the east, six kinds of Man barbarians to the south, seven kinds of Rong to the west, and eight kinds of Di to the north. All these peoples were beyond the domain of civilization, but if the Virtue (*De*) of China's sovereign was powerful enough, they were submissive and came even to the capital to bring tribute. The *Shanhai Jing* and the *Huainanzi* further enlarge the vision of the world by situating "beyond the seas" (*Haiwai*) populations which are more or less fantastic, such as the Country of Women situated beyond the western sea: all the inhabitants of this country are women (they become pregnant by washing themselves in a certain pond); the Country of the People with One Head and Three Bodies; to the south is the Country of Naked Men, the Country of Men with Feathers (who can fly, but not far), the Country of Stabbed Breasts (descendants of Fangfeng, who was stabbed in the breast while fleeing Yu), etc.

The square Earth had a center: the royal capital. The capital was also square with four gates, in the image of the world. Its principal sanctuaries were also round or square according to whether they corresponded to the Sky or the Earth. The altar of the Sky was round, that of the Earth square. The Mingtang, the Temple of Light in which the sovereign revolved like a sun to conform to the seasonal rhythms, had a square base and a round roof.

Just as the Earth, inside of the Four Seas, was divided into nine provinces, the Sky comprised nine plains. But soon the Sky was imagined as nine levels high, while the Earth was nine levels deep: at the bottom were the Ninth Springs or Yellow Springs where the land of the dead was situated. But in earlier times the Yellow Springs do not seem to have been imagined as very deep underground: libations there made their way to the surface and spirits of the dead might easily escape from it in the winter, when the ground was cracked. But when the vision of the world became larger, during the period of the Warring Kingdoms, the land of the dead was situated in the far north, in an abyss from which the waters issued from the interior of the earth.

II. The Sun and the Moon

In the myth of Pangu, the eyes of the cosmic man become the Sun and Moon. The connection of the eyes with these two luminaries is very frequent. It is found in the Daoist representation of the human body conceived as a microcosm. It is also found in other myths, such as the myth recalled by the *Xuanzonggi:* "To the north on the Mountain of the Bell, there is a stone with a head like a human head; the left eye is the Sun, the right eye the Moon; when the left eye is open, it is day; when the right eye is open, it is night." In the *Shanhai Jing,* "The spirit of the Mountain of the Bell is the Fiery Dragon who has a human face and the body of a great dragon of a thousand *li;* he stands erect, very angry, his eyes fixed. If he opens his eyes, it is day, if he closes them, it is night; if he exhales, it is winter; if he inhales, it is summer." In this variant of the myth, the eyes of the cosmic dragon are luminaries that play the role of the sun.

But according to the most widespread myth, there were ten suns and twelve moons. And each of these luminaries was inhabited by animals: crows for the sun, a toad and a hart for the moon (or moons, but the lunar animals seem to relate only to a single moon). Already in the representations of the Han period, these animals were depicted in disks of the sun and the moon; the crow was often represented with three feet.

It was therefore a time when there were ten suns. They perched on the solar Mulberry Tree, the Fusang, and appeared in turn: in fact nine suns remained on the lower branches of the tree, and one perched on the upper branch (*Shanhai Jing*). But it happened that one day they all appeared at the same time, so that creatures were in danger of being scorched. Yi the archer saved the world by destroying nine of the ten suns. Yi the archer belongs to the mythology of the ancient eastern populations of China, whose ancestor was a solar being, an expert archer and fowler. According to the *Huainanzi,* Yao ordered Yi to destroy the nine undesirable suns, as well as other monsters who were ravaging the world.

After Yi's exploit, only one sun remained. The sun travels in a chariot. The *Huainanzi* enumerates the stages of his daily voyage from the Valley of the Boiling Waters (Tangqu), where the Fusang tree is located, to the Sad Springs. It is not the Sun himself who drives his chariot, but a woman who is his mother, Xihe. Xihe is the wife of the mythical emperor Di Xun (who is identified with Shun and Di Ku); the *Shanhai Jing* speaks of a country of the Xihe, descendants of the mother of the ten suns, and says that the mother washed her children in the "Abyss of the Sweet River."

The myth of the ten suns is certainly connected with the denary cycle (the ten cyclical characters called "trunks"), which, from the period of the Yin, served to designate the days: one might think that a new sun appeared on each of these ten days. As for the twelve moons, they were the twelve lunations of the year and also the twelve branches of the duodenary series of cyclical characters.

Moon goddess. Bronze. Paris, Musée Guimet. Photo Musées nationaux.

Like the ten suns, the twelve moons have a mother who bathes them in a lake situated to the west of the world. This mother of the moons is called Changxi or Changyi or Hengnge: she is, like Xihe, a wife of Di Xun, which would make the Sun and the Moon half brother and half sister, but the mythology is very uncertain, especially since the names of the deities are rendered with orthographic variants that make it difficult to find one's bearings.

The archer Yi who destroys the solar crows appears again in a legend that explains the presence of a toad in the moon. Yi had obtained the drug of immortality from the Xiwangmu; his wife Henge stole it from him and fled to the moon; there she became the lunar toad. That is why the drug of immortality is found in the moon: the imagery generally represents the hare in the act of pounding the medicine in a mortar. The moon surely designated perenniality, because its light dies and comes to life again perpetually. This idea is found again in another popular legend, apparently later, according to which there is a great tree in the moon, a cinnamon tree. A man tries to cut it down with an ax, but the injured trunk heals after each blow. The cinnamon tree furnished the Daoists with a food that promoted long life.

Like other ancient peoples, the Chinese feared eclipses, which were baneful omens. Moralists asserted that eclipses were brought on by the irregular conduct of the sovereigns and their wives. In this case, the king had to reestablish order through a warlike commotion: "While the feudal princes are all present, if the sun happens to become eclipsed, they will come to its aid behind the Son of Heaven, each of them taking up the color and weapon appropriate to his region (in other words to the cardinal direction of his fief)" (*Li Ji,* trans. Couvreur, 1, p. 439). Eclipses were the occasion for ceremonies of exorcism in which drums were beaten and arrows were shot toward the endangered sun or moon. Eclipses were brought on by a monster that devoured the luminary concerned. In the case of the sun, it was a celestial dog or wolf; in the case of the moon, it was said to be a toad, which is not very consistent with the idea of a toad present in the moon.

To this mythological data must be added the fact that the sun and the moon are the preeminent representatives of the Yang and the Yin, whose oppositions and interactions constitute the life of the universe. The sun is the perfect Yang (*Taiyang*), and the moon the very essence of the Yin. The sun is composed of fire, and the moon of water. The fire of the sun could be collected by means of an instrument called *Yangsui,* a kind of bronze mirror; similarly, the lunar dew, also called "luminous water," was collected by means of another mirror called *Fangzhu,* which was square (whereas the *Yangsui* was, appropriately, round): the solar fire and lunar water were used in religious ceremonies.

If the sun is Yang and the moon Yin, one might wonder about the nature of the animals that inhabit them. The black crow is certainly Yin: thus the Yin is in the Yang, according to a fundamental idea that requires that each of the great cosmic principles contains a portion of the opposite principle. For the moon, the question is more subtle. Liu Xiang, in the *Wujing tongyi,* spoke of two animals in the moon and added that the hare is Yin and the toad Yang. Although this last point creates a difficulty (the toad has an affinity with water and with the night; moreover, it is a metamorphosis of Yi's wife), it is interesting that the moon is found to contain the Yin and the Yang, surely because of the alternations of its light and dark phases.

III. The Stars

Ancient China had a highly developed astrology, as can be seen, for instance, in the chapter of the "Governors of the Sky" that Sima Qian devoted to it in *The Historical Accounts* (*Shi Ji,* chap. 27, trans. Chavannes, vol. 3). There were many beliefs about the stars and their connections with human events, but relatively few myths. Among the latter, the most popular was the myth of the weaver woman and the cowherd. According to the legend, the weaver woman descended from the sky on the seventh day of the seventh month; a cowherd saw the woman and took her clothes away from her, which made it possible for him to marry her. But one day she succeeded in recovering her clothes and reascended to the sky. The cowherd pursued her, but the God of the Sky separated them with the help of the Milky Way; they can be reunited only once a year, on the seventh day of the seventh lunar month (Eberhard, *Typen,* no. 34: *Schwanenjungfrau,* following various sources). This version is late, for the ancient texts speak only of two lovers who are two stars separated by the Milky Way, which they can surmount only at the time of the festival of the seventh month; they succeed with the assistance of magpies who assemble to form a bridge (this motif already figured in the *Huainanzi,* if a citation from the *Baishe liu ti* is to be believed). The Milky Way was a celestial river and still bears the name of the Han (*Tian Han*).

The festival of the seventh day of the seventh month was a women's festival connected with fertility. In that festival, women moved wax dolls down a stream of water in order to obtain children. It was also a festival in which girls "asked for skill" in their labors and resorted to various methods of divination to find out which among them would be the most skillful. Granet connected the myth of the Weaver Woman with ancient Chinese festivals of youth, festivals in the course of which young peasant men and women met at the edge of the water and exchanged songs before coupling (*Festivals and Songs,* pp. 257–58).

IV. Mountains and Rivers

From earliest antiquity, mountains and streams of water were sacred powers to which sacrifices were offered. In the Yin period (second millennium B.C.), people sacrificed to a mountain (called Yue) and to a river (the Huanghe), both of which had the power to give rain and promote the harvest. Under the Zhou, the Son of Heaven was responsible for sacrifices to the "illustrious mountains and the great rivers," that is, to the five sacred peaks (the Wu Yue) and the four great watercourses, the Huanghe, the Yangzi, the Huai, and the Ji. The feudal lords had the right to sacrifice only to the mountains and waterways of their own territory, and they were also the only ones with the power to do so, for it was dangerous to annex a sacred mountain; the mountain might refuse the offerings of the usurper and bring on a drought instead of the rains that it normally produced. A mountain was the source of fertility for the territory that it ruled and stabilized; it protected the inhabitants of that territory and watched over the destiny of the lord of the place. For the empire as a whole, the Five Sacred Peaks had the same functions; laid out (theoretically) at the four corners of space and at the center, they were obligatory stations where the Son of Heaven had to stop to perform sacrifices when he undertook his ritual rounds. The most renowned of these mountains was Taishan, the sacred mountain of Shandong, where the principalities of Qi and Lu were situated. Lying to the east, associated with the Green Emperor, the divinity of the east who presided in the spring, this mountain, more than any other, was a source of life not only for the principalities of Qi and Lu, but for the whole of China. It was on Taishan, we believe, that seventy-two sovereigns since Fuxi performed the *feng* sacrifice, by which they announced to Heaven the complete success of their government. But on a more popular level, the god of Taishan presided over human destinies; he maintained an account of the years of life of each man in a kind of ledger. From the first century A.D., since the later Han, it was believed that the dead went to reside on Taishan, but it is not certain that the god of that mountain was already the infernal judge that he was generally acknowledged to be later.

In the *Baopuzi,* Ge Hong (283–343) said that the great mountains possessed a great divinity, the small mountains a small divinity. This was certainly already true for more ancient times. The *Shanhai Jing,* whose mythical author was Yu the Great, was an illustrated book intended to show the mountains and waterways, first of China proper, then of the regions situated in the Four Seas and beyond; it also described the minerals, plants, more or less strange animals, spirits, and deities that one might encounter there. Some chapters conclude with a recapitulation indicating, for each direction, the deities of the mountains and their half-human, half-animal aspects, as well as the offerings that should be made. But this "practical" information hardly appears to correspond to a reality; it answers rather to religious fiction.

Besides real mountains like Taishan and other sacred peaks, fabulous mountains situated to the far east and far west of ancient China captured the imagination of people in search of immortality. To the east, in the sea, off the shores of Shandong, were the "three holy mountains," which were three islands inhabited by Immortals. Magicians described their wonders to Qinshi Huangdi in these terms:

> It is said of the three holy mountains, Penglai, Fanzhang, and Yingzhou, that they are found in the middle of the Bohai; they are not remote from men, but, unfortunately, when one is on the point of getting there, the boat is pushed back by the wind and turned aside. In former times, people could get there; it is there that the Immortals are found, as well as the drug that prevents death; there all creatures, birds and quadrupeds, are white; the palaces and gates are made of gold and silver there; when these people were not yet there, they saw the mountains from a distance like a cloud; when they arrived, the three holy mountains were turned upside down under the water; when the people were very close to them, a wind suddenly brought their boat back to the open sea.

The emperor Qinshi Huangdi sent a man with a band of children, boys and girls, to search for these islands, but they found "a calm and fertile place" and did not return (see *Historical Accounts* of Sima Qian, trans. Chavannes, vol. 3, chap. 28).

The *Liezi* (chap. 5) relates the story of the islands of the blessed: there were formerly five, inhabited by Immortals who flew from one to the other. The islands drifted at the mercy of the waves and the tides. The celestial emperor commanded a spirit called Yugiang to find fifteen giant tortoises to carry the five mountains on their heads, each in turn, for sixty thousand years. But a giant arrived unexpectedly and fished for six of these tortoises and carried them off, so that two of the islands drifted away and disappeared, and only three islands remained. It is likely that the author of the *Liezi* somewhat embroidered the ancient myth.

The mythical mountain of the west is Kunlun (which has nothing to do with the mountain known by geographers). It is a purely legendary mountain, whose name (with no other information) figures first in the chapter called *Yugong* ("the tribute of Yu") of the *Shu Jing.* The *Tianwen* alludes to the "Hanging Gardens," to the nine tiers of a walled city, to gates that open on the four sides of Kunlun. The *Shanhai Jing* (chap. 11) speaks of Mount Kunlun situated to the west of the Country of Tapirs; it covers an area of eight hundred square *li;* it rises to an altitude of seven or eight thousand feet; an arborescent grain forty feet in height grows there; there are nine wells with jade balustrades, and nine gates, of which the Gate of the Dawn (Kaiming: "Opening of Light") is guarded by a tiger with nine human faces. This mountain is the earthly residence of the Celestial Sovereign and the abode of one hundred deities. Five watercourses have their source there: the Red River, the Yellow River, the Xiang River, the Black River, and finally the Ruo River (whose waters are so feeble that they cannot support even a feather). In another chapter (chap. 16), the *Shanhai Jing* has a slightly different text: Kunlun is a great mountain situated to the south of the Western Sea, at the edge of the Flowing Sands (Liusha) on the other side of the Black River: it is ruled by a spirit with a human face and a tiger's body, with nine white tails; the mountain is surrounded by the waters of the Abyss of the Ruo River; all species of creatures are found there.

In the *Huainanzi* (chap. 4), Kunlun is described in considerable detail, and its size is amplified; chiefly, it is said that plants of immortality grow on this mountain and that it is there that is found the Cinnabar River (Dan Shui), whose water prevents death if it is drunk. Kunlun comprises tiers that one must climb to mount the hierarchy of sanctity: one successively acquires immortality, spiritual power, and finally the divine condition at the moment of reaching the residence of the Supreme Emperor (Tai Di). The latter might be the Yellow Emperor, since the *Mu tianzi zhuan* relates that Mu the Son of Heaven climbed Kunlun to see the palace of Huangdi. But soon it was made the residence of the Xiwang Mu, the Queen Mother of the West who had become queen of the Immortals. Hereafter, Kunlun was a paradise of immortality. "Mount Kunlun . . . is so large that it rises higher than the Sun and the Moon. It has nine tiers separated from each other by ten thousand *li.* It is covered by irridescent clouds and when one looks at it from below, one seems to see the walls of a city with porticos. . . . Crowds of Immortals mounted on dragons or cranes frolic there" (*Shiyi Ji*). Another text, drawn from the *Shanyi Jing* and cited in the *Shuijingzhu,* speaks of Kunlun and the Xiwang Mu: on Kunlun, there is a bronze column, so high that it penetrates the Sky; it is what is called the Column of the Sky; its circumference is three thousand *li;* it is perfectly round as if it had been polished. At its foot, there is a revolving room with the nine administrations of Immortals. At its summit, there is a great bird called Xiyou; it faces south; its extended left wing covers the Dongwanggong (Venerable King of the East); its right wing covers the Xiwang Mu; on its back there is a small space without feathers that measures nineteen thousand *li;* the Xiwang Mu climbs there once a year to pay a visit to the Dongwanggong.

The text of the *Shiyi Ji* cited above adds that in the western countries, Kunlun is given the name of Sumeru. Although there may be certain resemblances between these two mythical mountains, the resemblances appear only in relatively late descriptions; the earliest descriptions, those of the *Shanhai Jing,* betray no Indian influence. In the *Yuben Ji* (*Annals of Yu*), a lost work cited by Sima Qian in his final account of chapter 123 of the *Shi Ji* (*Da yuan zhuan*), it is said that Kunlun is the place where the sun and the moon hide, each in turn, and that a brilliant light emanates from there. This image could come from the myth of Sumeru, as could the image of the rivers that spring from the four sides of the mountain. But the light attributed to Kunlun is not necessarily due to a foreign influence. In the *Shanhai Jing* (chap. 2), in connection with Mount Huaijiang where the "Hanging Gardens" of the Sovereign are found (as on Kunlun), Mount Kunlun, which can be seen far to the south, sends forth a great light and effusive vapors. The light is not unexpected, since the mountain is a way of access to Heaven, a belief confirmed by the *Lunheng,* in which one reads that people who wish to reach heaven must pass through Kunlun, for it is there, to the northwest of the world, that the Gate of the Sky is found. It is also there, according to the *Shanhai Jing* (chap. 16), that the Mountain of the Sun and the Moon is found; this mountain is the axis of the Sky and seems to be identical to the Gate of the Sky mentioned immediately after, which is the place of the passage of the Sun and the Moon. (There is a strange deity there, with a human face but no arms, and with both his feet pulled up over his head.) All of these representations are simultaneously confused and in the end rather coherent in their fundamental themes. Kunlun is in the west, with the setting sun; but it is also a way of access to the sky; it is the Column of the Sky, so it is central. It is a paradise of immortality, and after having been the earthly residence of the Celestial Sovereign or the Yellow Emperor, it became, in popular belief, the place where the palace of the Xiwang Mu and of the Immortals who surround her is situated.

Among the numerous deities of the waterways that ancient China recognized (among them several female deities), the god of the Yellow River, Hebo, is by far the most important. The name signifies properly the "Count of the River," but the sense of the epithet is uncertain. It may be a simple, respectful way of naming the deity, but it may also be a true title, for according to the *Li Ji* ("Treatises on Rites," one of the Confucian classics), sacred mountains and waterways received the titles of ministers or lords.

The river god had a name: Bingyi (or Fengyi). For Daoist authors, he was a man who, having consumed an elixir and obtained the Dao, became an "Immortal of the Water." He drowned trying to cross the river, and the Celestial Sovereign bestowed on him the office of Count of the River (*Baopuzi,* cited in the commentary on the *Chuci, Jiuge*). The *Huainanzi* describes him as one who drives a chariot in the brilliance of the sun and in a kind of whirlwind, to climb to Kunlun, where he is swallowed up by the Gate of Heaven. The *Shanhai Jing* says that Bingyi inhabits a certain abyss and that he has a team of two dragons.

One ancient legend, of which only elements remain, makes Hebo and Yi the archer adversaries, perhaps because of an amorous rivalry. Hebo's wife was the goddess of the Luo River; Yi dreamed that he had relations with this divinity and the *Tianwen* seems to say that he drew his bow against the Count of the River and took the Lady of the Luo as his wife. According to another version of this event, Hebo transformed himself into a white dragon and went for a walk in this guise at the edge of the water. Yi caught sight of Hebo and shot an arrow at him that hit him in his left eye. Hebo complained to the Celestial Sovereign, who dismissed the matter (*Tianwen* and commentary).

According to the *Huainanzi,* it is because the Count of the River killed people by drowning them that Yi shot his arrows at him and hit him in the left eye. That is entirely consistent with the belief that people who have drowned are dangerous spirits (except for the female deities of the waters, like the goddess of the Luo), but it is also consistent with the fact that Hebo required human victims. At least, there was a time when sorceresses "gave maidens in marriage to the Count of the River." They chose a girl from the population and adorned her as a married woman; she was placed on a bed that was made to float on the water of the river but then drifted from the shore and sank. This practice was suppressed by Ximen Bao when he was sent by the marquess Wen of Wei (424–387) to undertake the work of canalization at Ye, a town where the cult was established. Another cult site was at Linjin at the confluence of the Yellow River and the Luo River. In 417 B.C., the duke of Qin seized the town and "then began to give princesses to the river as wives." It is probable that there was formerly a popular cult there analogous to the cult at Ye. At Qin it was practiced to secure the god's protection and also to annex an important cult in some way.

V. The Cardinal Directions

The importance of the directions in the thought and life of the Chinese cannot be exaggerated. Each of the directions of space had its specific characteristics and each was linked by a complex system of correspondences, not only to cosmic forces, to all kinds of beings and deities, but even to the weather, for each cardinal sector corresponded to a season. Therefore, it was never a matter of indifference to know how and where a town, house, temple, or tomb was to be constructed. Such was the case from the time of the Yin, who already connected the idea of death and disease with the north. As in subsequent periods, the dead were interred toward the north. Moreover, information has been obtained from the names of the winds that figure on some inscribed

The Grand Emperors of the Five Peaks accompanying the Grand Emperor of Literature and his assistants.

fragments. There were four winds (later, there were eight), each with a name. The names are found again, as are the names of the directional sectors from which the winds originate, in ancient texts such as the *Shanhai Jing* and the *Shu Jing* (*Yaodian*). It is certain that the north wind brought epidemics. Later, the spirit of the north, Boqiang or Yuqiang, was a great demon of pestilence (*Tianwen* and commentary). The *Shanhai Jing* describes him as a spirit with a human face and the body of a bird, who has a green serpent in each ear and tramples two red serpents underfoot. The same passage speaks of a mountain at the north pole of the world, but it is rather an abyss, for it is there that the waters of the sea come to be swallowed up: it is the Tiangui (celestial *gui*). The *gui* of this expression represents, according to the *Shuowen*, which provides another, more current way of writing, the waters that flow down from the four directions and into the interior of the earth. *Gui* is also a cyclical character, the last of the denary series; it is preceded by the character *ren*, which represents an embryo. *Ren* and *gui* in conjunction correspond to the north and to winter. The north was therefore simultaneously the land of unfathomable waters, of the Yin, of death, and the region from which life springs forth. The character *zi* of the duodenary series denoted the far north; but *zi* signifies "egg" or "child." Finally, in the modern language, *Tiangui* means "menses."

From the last centuries B.C., every conception relating to the directions was governed by the theories of the Yin and the Yang and of the Five Elements. It may be recalled that Yin, the feminine principle of darkness, moisture, and cold, characterizes the west and the north; Yang, the masculine principle of light, dryness, and heat, characterizes the east and the south. As for the elements (which have very little to do with the chemical elements), they are distributed in this manner: wood = east; fire = south; earth = center; metal = west; water = north. They are further associated with the seasons: the spring corresponds to the east, the summer to the south, the autumn to the west, the winter to the north, and the center is represented by a short period at the end of summer. Finally, a color is associated with each element-direction-season: east = green; south = red; west = white; north = black; center = yellow. The association with colors had a great importance in rituals and liturgy, for clothes, ornaments, and offerings had to conform to the colors. It was essential in the arrangement of the altar of the God of the Imperial Earth: the altar was square and was composed of clays of different colors oriented as stated above. To confer a fief, the sovereign took a clod of the color corresponding to the direction of the vassal and gave it to the vassal, who added it to his own mound of earth, which therefore had only one color. The system of correspondences certainly involved other domains, in particular the organs of the body, which had consequences for medical or hygienic theories and practices that sought to make the order of the body conform to the order of the universe.

Each cardinal direction was also associated with an emblematic animal. The Four Animals figure, for example, in this passage from the *Li Ji* (*Quli*): "The soldiers on the march have the Red Bird before them, the Dark Warrior behind them; to the left the Green Dragon, to the right the White Tiger." The Dark Warrior is the epithet given to the Tortoise entwined by a serpent—but, fundamentally, the animal of the north is the Tortoise. It is clear that these soldiers are thought to have the south before them and, consequently, the north behind, the Dragon to the east, and the Tiger to the west. Such was the normal, correct orientation of any authority; it was the orientation of the sovereign who "reigns facing the south." But his subjects, in his presence, faced the north, the direction of formidable powers, from which that "Dark Warrior" originates who watches over the north. To create a protected space, it sufficed to arrange around oneself the four Animals, whether represented on banners, as in the case of soldiers on the march, or mentally, as the Daoists did in the course of their meditational exercises.

All of these ideas about the directions, the elements, and colors, also deeply concerned politics and history. In 771 B.C., a duke of Qin instituted the worship of his ancestor Shaohao, who received the ritual name of White Emperor; his sanctuary was called "the holy place of the west." Later, the princes of Qin instituted cults of the Green Emperor, the Yellow Emperor (Huangdi), the Emperor of Flames (Yandi, in other words the Red Emperor). No doubt the princes of Qin wished to secure the protection of the divinities of the territories that had been conquered, or were being conquered, in the different directions. Moreover, Zou Yan (third century B.C.) devised a theory that had great reverberations; it taught that the cosmic order is governed not only by the alternation of the Yin and the Yang, but also by a cyclical alternation of the Five Virtues, that is, by the alternate influence of the Five Elements: each sovereign or dynasty governed in conformity with one of the Virtues. According to Zou Yan, the Virtues succeed one another by overcoming one another. The Sky, moreover, sends omens that announce to the people which virtue predominates: when the time of Huangdi (the Yellow Emperor) came, the Sky caused earthworms and giant crickets to appear, which made Huangdi proclaim that the energies of the Earth were triumphing; he took yellow as his emblem and, in any enterprise, accommodated himself to the element Earth (= center). Yu received omens that made him proclaim the triumph of the element Wood (east); Tang, the founder of the Yin, ruled by the element Metal (west); King Wu of Zou ruled by the element Fire (south); a red crow holding a red written document in his beak came to perch on the altar of the Earth. The *Lüshi Chunqiu* (chap. 13, § 2), which sets forth the sequence of oriented virtues, adds that the Virtue that would replace the Virtue of Fire would necessarily be that of Water, which implies that the author foresaw that Qinshi Huangdi would choose Water and Black as emblems. This question of dynastic Virtues was to occupy a great place in the speculations of historians and philosophers of the Han dynasty.

M.K./b.f.

BIBLIOGRAPHY

E. CHAVANNES, *Le T'ai-chan* (Paris 1910). M. GRANET, 1926, 1929, 1934–68, 1953. M. KALTENMARK, "La naissance du monde en Chine," in *La naissance du monde,* Sources orientales 1 (1959). H. MASPERO, 1924. MORI MIKISABURO, 1969. M. SOYMIE, "La lune dans les religions chinoises," in *La lune, mythes et rites,* Sources orientales 5 (1962).

For full citations, see "Chinese Mythology."

Ancient Chinese Goddesses and Grandmothers

Ancient Chinese mythology includes several female figures who play a more important role in its beliefs than one would have expected from such a patriarchal society. But the patriarchal structure was the culmination of an evolution that began from a form of society in which women had a much more important position. This is demonstrated by certain aspects of the familial organization, as brought to light by Marcel Granet and confirmed by mythological data.

The heroes, and especially the founders, of royal or imperial lineages are not born like mere mortals; they have always been conceived under supernatural circumstances. This is not only true of mythical characters, for the historians relate similar miracles for numerous emperors of every period, and even for some common people. Considering only legends of antiquity (which inspired those of more recent periods), we will cite the most famous cases.

I. Fubao, the Mother of Huangdi

"A great light encircled Polaris and lit up the countryside near the city; it aroused Fubao, who gave birth to Huangdi" (*Hanzhen Wu,* an "apocryphon" of the Shi Jing). As in most of these stories, the mother of the Yellow Emperor finds herself in an uncultivated countryside (*ye*) when she conceives: it is in this sort of spot, which is also a sacred place connected with the ancestor cult, that "irregular" unions of young peasants take place at the time of agricultural festivals. The very name of Fubao evokes the idea of contact with spirits and possession.

II. The Mother of Yu the Great

The mother of Yu the Great sees a shooting star, then swallows a marvelous pearl, which is a *yi-yi* (*Coix lachryma*) seed. Her chest splits open when she gives birth to Yu (commentaries on the *Shiji*). The *Wuyue Chunqiu* specifies that Yu's mother found the seed on a certain mountain, and that when she swallowed it, she had an impression of contact with a man; she became pregnant, and her side split open so she could give birth to Yu, who is here called Gaomi. Medical treatises claim medicinal virtues for *yi-yi* seeds; they are supposed to relieve and purify the body. Here, they are also pearls made of moonlight. This is why the *Weizhou* relate that Yu's mother found, in a spring at the foot of the Rock Knot mountain, a "lunar essence" (*Yuejing*) which resembled an egg; after this she became pregnant. According to another legend, Yu was born from the Rock Knot, and his own son was also born from a rock, since its mother had been petrified and Yu was obliged to split her open with a stroke of his sword in order to have the child. Yu's mother and the Rock Knot are apparently identical.

III. The Daughter of Tushan, the Wife of Yu

"Yu, in the course of his labors, met the daughter of Tushan (Mountain of Earth). Before he met her, he had inspected the southern lands. Tushan's daughter had ordered a servant girl to wait for Yu at the southern foot of Tushan, and she sang a song which said: how handsome is he for whom I wait. This was the source of the southern songs" (*Lushi Chungiu,* chap. 6). The southern songs were love songs which the Confucian orthodoxy condemned as being too licentious. This is another instance of free love, a common theme of the songs of the *Shi Jing.* In the poem entitled *Tianwen,* of the anthology of the land of Chu (*Chuci*), Yu seems to descend from the Sky to have relations with Tushan in a place called the Mulberry Trees of the Terrace. This is certainly an allusion to the celebrated Mulberry Forest, Sanglin, the sacred place of the land of Song (which inherited the Yin cults), in which gatherings of boys and girls took place which were sexual festivals. This is the source of Yu's reputation for dissolute morals (*Lushi Chunqiu,* chap. 11).

The name of Gaomi given to Yu in the *Wuyue Chunqiu* is the

equivalent of Gaomei. Gaomei is the name of a divinity whom the ritualists generally, but not always, considered to be male. According to their explanations, the name is to be translated as "Great Matchmaker." There was a royal, and later imperial, festival of Gaomei which took place in the spring, apparently for the purpose of asking for children. Actually, Gaomei was originally a female divinity whose name probably meant, rather than "Great Matchmaker," the "Great, or First, Mother." The most illustrious of these Mothers were Nüwa, Jiandi, and Jiangyuan.

IV. Nüwa

Nüwa was most worthy of being called a Mother: she created the first men. She shaped them first with yellow soil, then with mud. The men made from yellow earth became the nobles; those made from mud were people of base condition (*Feng su tong*). But her merits do not stop there: like Yu, she battled against the overflowing waters. These had been unleashed by the rebellious monster Gonggong, who had shaken the Sky and Earth when he smashed a pillar of the sky with a thrust of one of his horns. Nüwa repaired the azure sky with stones of five colors, cut the feet off of a tortoise to set up four pillars at the four directions, killed the Black Dragon (Gonggong), and piled up ashes of burnt reeds to stop the overflowing waters (*Liezi* and *Huainanzi*).

We know that Nüwa is the wife and sister of Fuxi and that the two were represented as two serpent-bodied gods with intertwined tails. They were regarded as the inventors of marriage, and it is for this reason, we are told, that Nüwa was honored as the Divine Matchmaker, Shenmei (*Lüshi*).

The "wa" character of Nüwa is defined by the *Shuowen* (a late first-century A.D. dictionary) as "the name of a holy and divine woman of ancient times who produced the ten thousand beings through metamorphosis." The mountain on which Nüwa melted the stones used to repair the Sky is called Huangmu Shan, the Mount of the August Mother (as well as Nüwa Shan). But as Gaomei she must have been a grandmother of the royal house, as were (as we shall see below) the grandmothers of the Yin and the Zhou. This is in fact the case, since she is assimilated in several texts to the daughter of Tushan, who is Yu's wife (*Shiben, Wuyue Chunqiu*). She is thus the same Gaomei as that of the Xia dynasty.

Nüwa not only creates beings by metamorphosis, but she herself constantly changes shape (commentary on the *Tianwen*). There is a rather strange text to this effect in the *Shanhai Jing* (chap. 16): in a certain "countryside" (*ye*) there lived ten genies who were the metamorphosed entrails of Nüwa; they lay across a road, blocking it. "Ten" is perhaps erroneous here, since it would be more understandable for Nüwa's entrails (she is a serpent) to be transformed into a genie, probably a reptile. This reptile blocked a road whose destination is not mentioned in the text but that was surely that sacred "countryside" prohibited to the profane. This is undoubtedly a labyrinth theme.

V. Jiandi, Mother of the Ancestors of the Yin

Jiandi is a wife of Gaoxin (Di Ku). She goes to bathe with two other women; they see a black bird drop an egg. Jiandi picks it up and swallows it. After this she finds that she is pregnant and gives birth to Xie. The *Shiyi Ji,* a fairly late (fourth century) and fantastic work, but one which has preserved many legendary themes, relates this story and ornaments it; but it specifies that Jiandi was walking at Sangye, the Country of Mulberries—this is undoubtedly the Mulberry Forest, Sanglin. The black bird is made into a swallow. The Yin family carries the name of the Zi clan because Jiandi swallowed the egg (*zi*) of a swallow.

This myth of an egg swallowed by the mother of an ancestor appears again in the case of other families, all of which are eastern, or of eastern origin. So it is with the ancestor of the Chin: Nuxiu, a female descendant of Zhuan Xu, was weaving when a black bird dropped an egg, which she ate, after which she gave birth to Daye. In the case of Zhumang, the ancestor of the Fuyu (an ancient Korean kingdom), the myth shows certain variants: the hero's mother is the daughter of the Count of the River; his father the king locks her in a room; sunbeams strike the body of the young girl; no matter where she moves, the sunbeams follow her; she becomes pregnant and gives birth to an egg; Zhumang emerges from the egg (his later adventures show that he is a solar being). There is another variant regarding King Yan of the Hiu, who is famous for having no bones. His mother gives birth to an egg, which she throws into the water. A marvelous dog finds it and brings it back; King Yan is born from the egg. The dog that intercedes here is to be connected with the dog in the myth of Panhu.

VI. Jiangyuan, the Mother of Houzi (Prince Millet), Ancestor of the Zhou

Jiangyuan is also a wife of Di Ku. She goes out to play in the "countryside," where she sees a giant's footprint; she places her foot in it, after which she becomes pregnant. The same legend is recounted of Huaxu, the mother of Fuxi, who finds the giant's footprint in the Marshes of Thunder. The god of thunder lived there with a dragon's body and a man's head: the footprint is thus that of the thunder god. But in the case of Jiangyuan, all the exegetes affirm that this is a Sovereign from On High. The *Shi Jing* has preserved several poems that sing the virtues of Jiandi and Jiangyuan. The commentators do not fail to recall that these women miraculously conceived while on the way to a sacrifice to Gaomei, but they do not explain who Gaomei was.

A poem from the *Shi Jing* is dedicated to Bigung, which was a temple of Jiangyuan or of Gaomei, according to different glosses, but the apparent contradiction is explained if Jiangyuan was Gaomei. This Bigung temple was always closed. The *Yuanmin Bao* (an apocryphon) relates that it was at Bigung, in a place called Fusang (the Solar Mulberry tree), that Jiangyuan stepped in a footprint. Here once again is the theme of the sacred mulberry, solar tree, and holy place.

An important theme that history and poetry do not fail to recall with regard to Jiangyuan and Houzi is that of the mythic ordeal that Houzi was forced to undergo. After she had given birth to him, his mother, "judging this to be a misfortune," decided to abandon him, and exposed him successively in an alley, in a deserted forest, and on a frozen pond: Houzi emerged victorious from these ordeals with the help of the animals that protected him. Granet has shown that behind this myth, which qualifies this hero as a god of the harvest, there lies a rite that prescribed depositing the newborn child on the ground (M. Granet, *Le Dépôt de l'enfant sur le sol,* in *Études sinologiques*).

VII. Xiwang Mu, the Queen of the West

Xiwang Mu is especially known as the queen of the Daoist Immortals. A very popular figure, she is represented as a beautiful lady attended by the "Daughters of Jade." She is represented on Han sculpted stones associated with symbols

The Queen of the West: Xiwang Mu (Qing dynasty). Bronze. Paris, Musée Guimet. Photo Musées nationaux.

of long life. The *Huainanzi* tells a story of the drug of immortality that Yi the Archer obtained from Xiwang Mu and that was stolen from him by his wife Henge, who escaped to the moon. But in the *Shanhai Jing* (*Xishanjing*), this Mother is a demon of plague, who dwells on the Jade Mountain (Yushan) situated far to the west, beyond the flowing sands (Liusha). She has a leopard's tail and tiger's teeth; she wears a jade ornament in her wild hair; she reigns over the stars of plagues, ruin, and punishments. She lives in a cave on the north of Mount Kunlun. Three blue birds bring her her food.

The *Shanhai Jing* is the sole text that presents Xiwang Mu as a demoness. This is probably a survival of an archaic trait that was reinforced by the classical association of the west with punishments and with the decline of the Yang, vegetation, and life in general.

A historical legend from before the Han recounts how, in the tenth century B.C., King Mu of the Zhou met Xiwang Mu while traveling in the west: "He was pleased by her company and forgot to return" (*Shi Ji*, chap. 5). This story is related in the "Novel of the Son of the Mu Sky" (*Mu tionzi zhuan*) in which Xiwang Mu, however, is only a queen of an indeterminate land to the west of China. A commentary on the *Shi Ji* cites a third-century author according to whom the common people call the spirits who preside over the east and west and over the rising and setting of the Yin and the Yang (the sun and the moon), the royal Mother and Father (*Wang fu mu*). From the time of the later Han onward, Xiwang Mu had a consort who resided in the east: this was Dongwanggong (the Venerable King of the East). There may even have been worship offered to this god of the Yang parallel to that offered to the goddess of the Yin, Xiwang Mu (*Wu Yue Chun Qiu*). A great bird on the top of the bronze Column of Kunlun shields Xiwang Mu with his right wing and Dongwanggong with his left (*Shenyi Jing*). But Dongwanggong is much less popular than Xiwang Mu. Xiwang Mu alone is portrayed in legend and in literature, and popular devotion is addressed principally to her. The *Bowuzhi* cites a remark attributed to Laozi according to which the common people place their trust in Xiwang Mu, while the Daoists of the higher levels rely on celestial male deities. The *Bowuzhi* dates from the third century, but an event from 3 B.C. indicates that faith in Xiwang Mu was already alive among the common people at that time. In that year, there was panic among part of the population of Shandtong. Crowds of people carrying "slips of Xiwang Mu," which were probably talismans, took to the road apparently with the goal of visiting the goddess at her residence on Kunlun. The pilgrims sang and danced as they offered sacrifices to the goddess. The *Shoushenji* reports this event and adds that the people had a talismanic writing that ensured immortality to those who carried it.

Since the second century B.C., at least, Xiwang Mu has been an Immortal who has recipes for long life. In a later novel of Daoist inspiration, she wants to teach the recipes to emperor Wu of the Han and offers him marvelous peaches (*Hanwudi Neizhuan*). Daoism would make her the mother of numerous Immortals, among which there reappears an ancient divinity of the land of Chu, the divinity of Wushan, the Mount of the Sorceress.

VIII. The Goddess of Wushan

The Mount of the Sorceress was a sacred place in the land of Chu. It was the abode of a divinity to whom kings offered worship, in a sanctuary, the Gaotang, situated at the summit of the mountain; this sanctuary was the subject of a poem, the *Gaotang fu*, written by a poet from Chu. Legend related that an ancient king of Chu who visited this sanctuary located in the "countryside" (*ye*) of Yunmeng (a region of sacred marshes) saw the divinity in a dream; she revealed her name, Yaoji, to him, and told him that her soul had become a plant used in love magic. The king had relations with this goddess, who was apparently a Gaomei. She figures among the daughters of Xiwang Mu, and bears the name of Blossoming Lady of the Clouds (Yunhua furen); Yu the Great visited the Mount of the Sorceress and asked her help in controlling the waters. She entrusted talismans to him and sent spirits to help him in his task. The *Yongcheng Zixian Lu* of Du Guangting (850–933), which relates this legend, states that there was a sanctuary of the goddess at the foot of the mountain and, across the river, an "altar of the divine girl, the venerable celestial of stone" (*Shitianzun Shen nü tan*). The goddess is said to have turned into a rock. This is obviously a case of conflation with the myth of Yu's wife, which is easily explained if the two heroines were both Gaomei.

IX. Water Goddesses

Among the female deities of ancient China, certain water goddesses should be cited. These are generally women who have drowned and who become associated in legend with illustrious persons. The most famous are the goddess of the Luo River and the two goddesses of the Xiang River. While the souls of drowned persons are generally dreaded demons, these female deities of the rivers are never portrayed as dangerous.

The goddess of the Luo (Luoshen), Mifei (or Fufei), was celebrated by renowned poets. Her legend may be reduced to the following: she was the daughter of Fuxi, and she drowned in the Luo River. She dwells at the confluence of the Luo and the Yi. She was, according to certain texts, the wife of the Count of the River and perhaps the wife of Yi the Archer.

The two divinities of the Xiang are the subject of two liturgical poems of the Jiuge of the *Chu Ci* entitled *Xiangjun* (the princess of the Xiang) and *Xiang furen* (The Lady of the Xiang). The *Shanhai Jing*, 5, says that they lived on an island in Lake Dongting (the Xiang runs into this lake), that they frequented a Chasm of the Lake, and that they brought together the effluvia of the three rivers: they unleash whirlpools and torrential storms. When Qin Shi Huangdi visited the "temple of the Xiang mountain," he encountered a violent tempest and learned that this was the place in which the daughters of Yao, the wives of Shun, were buried. The *Shanhai Jing* simply says that they were the daughters of the Sovereign (from On High), but Yao may very well be taken as a celestial Di. Whatever the case, the legend would have it that Shun took a voyage to the south, and that he died there; his two wives followed him and drowned in the Xiang. In the Tang period, these two divinities of the Xiang were still worshiped.

M.K./d.w.

BIBLIOGRAPHY

W. EBERHARD 1942. L. GRANET 1929. KALTENMARK, "Notes à propos du Kao-mei," *Annuaire de l'École pratique des Hautes Études*, 5th section, 1966–67. K. SCHIPPER, *L'Empereur Wou des Han dans la légende taoïste* (Paris 1965). Full citations in "Chinese Mythology."

Mythical Rulers in China: The Three Huang and the Five Di

Ancient Chinese historians, all more or less Confucian, eschewed anything bizarre and supernatural, things that Master Kong refused to talk about. But when they had to talk about the beginning of history, if not the origin of the world, they resorted to the names of certain deities, heroes, and ancestors derived from various traditions in order to integrate them into a system. The same system was based on metaphysical, moral, and religious concepts, so that ancient myths that came from different local cultures were gradually replaced by a new mythology, an invention of scholars of the last few centuries B.C. It is a genuine mythology, for the heroes that appear have nothing historical about them and fragments of real myths are retrieved by changing their meaning. The historians' task was to extract a moral teaching and to show how the order of the world gradually deteriorated. At the beginning of history, perfect rulers ruled, while recent times have been decadent and violent. Formerly, there was harmony between man and nature, and the sovereign ruler, thanks to his virtue (*De* or *Daode*), had the blessings of Heaven, for Heaven conferred the heavenly mandate (*tianming*) only on virtuous rulers and took it back from evil monarchs. The accord between the ruler and heaven was made manifest by miracles of good omen: the appearance of supernatural animals and plants and of precious objects of talismanic value that were carefully preserved in the dynastic treasury.

Those were the happy times, when the three August Ones and the Five Emperors (*Sanhuang Wudi*) ruled successively. This expression has become a stereotype designating the beginning of history. After these two periods came the Three Kings, or rather the Three Dynasties and the Five Hegemonies (*Sanwang Wupa*). There is significance in the recurrence of the numbers three and five, numbers charged with symbolic value; three is an expression of perfection and totality, and five evokes a cross with its center and is thus an expression of universality. The three royal dynasties are the Xia, the Yin (also known as Shang), and the Zhou. The Xia Dynasty is purely mythical. With the Yin and the Zhou, we enter into history, albeit a history heavily mixed with legend.

I. The Sanhuang (Three August Ones)

Since the time of Qinshih Huangdi (221–210 B.C.) the title for the emperors of China has been *huangdi*. Before that, rulers bore the title of prince (*hou*) or king (*wang*). All of these terms once had religious meaning. *Di* was the highest deity of the Yin, probably identical with their first ancestor. The same term designated the sacrifice that was offered to him. Originally (on bronze inscriptions and in the oldest texts of the Zhou), *Huang* was only an adjectival form expressing the brightness and glory of certain divine beings: Heaven, the Ruler on High, the ancestors. As the name of a god, Huang first appears in the *Lisao* and in the *Jiuge* (The Nine Songs) of *Chuci* (a famous anthology from the land of Chu). These poems attributed to Qu Yuan (332–295 B.C.) must date from the beginning of the period of the Warring States. The *Lisao* mentions a Huang from the West (Xi Huang), and the first of the *Jiuge* (liturgical chants) is dedicated to a deity called Dong Huang Taiyi (Supreme Unity, Huang from the East). In the same poem, the god is also called Shang Huang (Huang from On High): it seems as if *Huang* in this case replaced the *di* of the classical Shangdi, that is, the supreme deity of Heaven. But the Dong Huang Taiyi is certainly the Rising Sun, so it

Fuxi. Portrait album, n.d. (Smith-Lesouef collection). Paris, Bibliothèque nationale. Photo BN.

seems that the sun is identified with the celestial deity. The Xi Huang of the *Lisao* could be the setting sun. Whatever this deity may be in the land of Chu, *Huang* soon came to designate a series of human rulers, the Three Huang. The August Ones (if we keep the translation proposed by Granet) were characterized by a complete and luminous spirituality. Virtue among the succeeding rulers steadily declined. The Di had the intelligence of the *Dao*, the Wang that of the *De;* as for the Ba (The Hegemonies), all they knew was the use of military force (*Guanzi*). The *Fengsu-tongyi* (second century A.D.) celebrates the Three Huang whose action, or rather inaction, is like that of Heaven, which does not speak or move, leaving the natural and vital rhythms free to follow their own course.

When the Zheng king of Qin had completed the unification of China, the title of the emperor was deliberated. His ministers proposed the title of *Tai Huang* (the Supreme August One), and explained that "long ago, there was the Celestial August One (*Tien Huang*), the Earthly August One (*Di Huang*), and the Supreme August One, the latter being the highest in dignity." But the emperor refused this title and declared that his title would be Huangdi, adding to *Huang* the "imperial title of high antiquity" (*di*). Qinshih Huangdi felt that he embodied the virtues of the Three August Ones and the Five Di. The *Lüshi Chunqiu* composed in Qin in 239 B.C. already spoke of the San Huang without actually identifying them. As for the Di, we shall see that they were said to be historical emperors, but also celestial deities who had played a key role in the religious history of the new emperor's own family. The Chinese of those remote periods did not distinguish ancient rulers from celestial deities; they usually assimilated them without reaching agreement as to their real identities, which differed depending on the regions. There seems to have been in Qin a series of three *Huang*, one of heaven, one of earth, and one supreme *Huang*. But this concept evolved under the Han when the *Tai Huang* was replaced by the *Huang* of Man, in keeping with an idea very much in vogue at this time, whereby heaven, earth, and man constituted a sort of triad representing the three great spiritual forces of the universe. But these rather abstract entities could not fit into the overall picture if the Three August Ones were historical rulers. Therefore the three *Huang* became three individuals chosen from among prestigious mythological figures who were later transformed into important people of antiquity. We do find, however, in the *Weishu* (apocrypha completing the Confucian classics) and in other works, several lists that diverge about one of the characters but agree in making Fuxi and Shennong two of the Three August Ones. The third is sometimes Nüwa, although she is well known in other contexts (being not only Fuxi's wife, but also an independent deity); sometimes Zhurong, a god of fire; or else Suiren, an inventor of fire and of cooked food. We shall limit our remarks here to Fuxi and Shennong.

Fuxi (or Paoxi) was from the time of the Han dynasty regarded as the oldest ruler, but, curiously enough, the historian Sima Qian makes virtually no reference to him. Yet he was famous through two separate legends. He was, first, the inventor of the eight trigrams that were the basis for the hexograms of the Yi Jing. Consequently, the great appendix to this classic, the *Xici,* refers to him in the following terms, taken from the Annals of the *San Huang,* which Sima Qian added to the *Shi Ji:* "Lifting up his head, he contemplated the figures that are in the sky; lowering his head, he contemplated the forms that are on the earth. All around him, he contemplated the brightly colored birds and animals and also what belongs to the soil. Closer to him, he considered all the parts of his body; in the distance, he considered all living creatures. He was the first to trace the eight trigrams by means of which he gained access into the potency of divine spirits and separated into distinct classes the varying natures of beings. He was the first to regulate marriage between man and woman. . . . He built nets and snares and taught hunting and fishing. . . . He built a lute with thirty-five strings." According to this text, Fuxi invented the divinatory diagrams when he was inspired by heavenly and earthly phenomena and by living creatures, including his own body. He did all this at a time when writing did not exist. Divinatory symbols in fact constituted a universal symbolism far more meaningful than any other kind of writing. He is also credited with inventing a kind of notation system that operates by means of knotted ropes. In the postscript of the *Shuowen,* this invention is attributed to Shennong, but the attribution to Fuxi is quite reasonable, since he was also the inventor of nets.

According to another mythical depiction of Fuxi, certainly a very popular one, he had the body of a snake. That is how he is depicted on several sculpted stones of the Shandong, as part of a couple with his wife Nüwa, who also has the tail of a serpent: the two tails are intertwined. In these images, Fuxi holds a carpenter's square and Nüwa, a compass; in this they are visibly a pair of demiurges who hold in their hands the symbols of their creative and civilizing virtues. But according to Chinese concepts about circles and squares (associated, respectively, with heaven and earth, and with Yang and Yin), we would normally expect Fuxi to hold the compass and

Nüwa, the carpenter's square. Here, their attributes are reversed, and this reversal may be explained by a rather subtle philosophical idea: Yin and Yang are effective only through one another, by mutual collaboration. This is also shown by the illustrated representations of the sun and the moon in which the Yang star is inhabited by a Yin animal, and the Yin star is inhabited by a Yang animal. We should, however, note that Nüwa, the wife of Fuxi (and also his sister—which brings in a different theme, the theme of the primordial couple or the couple that survived the flood), was also, and principally, an independent deity about whom there were many more legends than about Fuxi (who remains a rather dim figure).

Shennong, the Divine Plowman and the second August One, is, as his name implies, a god of farming, but he also became a god of fire because he was assimilated to the god of fire, Yandi, who was really an independent deity. The assimilation nevertheless prevailed, and Shennong became a god of the fire used to clear fields: "He struck the weeds and trees with a red whip" (*Mémoires historiques,* vol. 1, p. 13). "He was the first to test the hundred species of plants and the first to find healing drugs" (ibid.). This is the second feature of Shennong: he is the patron god of doctors and apothecaries. The first *Bencao* (treatise on medicinal plants) is attributed to him, as is the invention of markets and commercial trading. As a result of his identification with Yandi, he was made the adversary in a fight with the Yellow Emperor Huangdi, though the battle between Yandi and Huangdi itself is merely a double of the battle between Huangdi and Chiyou. But there is nevertheless a trait held in common by Shennong and Chiyou: both of them have horns; but Chiyou was most probably a fighting bull, while Shennong, the god of agriculture, was a peaceful plowing buffalo.

Shennong. Portrait album, n.d. (Smith-Lesouef collection). Paris, Bibliothèque nationale. Photo BN.

II. The Wudi (Five Emperors)

For the historian Sima Qian, the Five Emperors whose reign marks the beginning of his *History* (*Shi Ji*) were human rulers who lived in very remote times, with no particular chronology. He acknowledges that the Confucian classics, especially the *Shu Jing,* do not mention them, at least the first two, Huangdi and Zhuan Xu. For the orthodox, history begins with Yao. But Sima Qian conducted his investigation in several regions, questioning "notables and old men"; he noticed that there were other accounts besides the official versions, and that those accounts could not be neglected. He does, however, warn the reader that he has expurgated the information obtained by word of mouth or in noncanonical texts. He thus reestablishes history, free of anything supernatural and thus true to life. Fortunately, the commentaries partially compensate for this shortcoming by referring to ancient sources that sometimes betray the true character of these rulers: they were actually the divine ancestors of different clans and the heroes of many myths and legends, of which we unfortunately have only scattered fragments.

Huangdi (the Yellow Emperor). Huangdi has remained a highly popular figure to this day. He was connected with enough legends to perpetuate his memory, and he was above all the inventor of numerous crafts, so that many guilds recognized him as their patron. He was credited with treatises on medicine (among them the classic of Chinese medicine, the Huangdi Neijing), sexuality, astrology, and the martial arts. His yellow color gives him a central position with respect to the other emperors, so that, more than the others, he represents absolute sovereignty. To a great degree, he is the equivalent of the Ruler on high. In antiquity, he was the ancestor of a dozen clans.

His personal name is Xianyuan. "His mother, Fubao, went to take a walk in the country (*ye*), and saw great lightning around the Big Dipper. She was aroused, and she conceived. Twenty-four months later, she delivered Huangdi on the mound of Shou (longevity) or on the mound Xianyuan, after which he was named." This legend is built on the same model as numerous supernatural ideas that embellish the biographies of heroes or rulers. Their prototype is the mating of young peasant men and women in the "brush" (*ye,* "uncultivated fields") during spring festivals, a custom that is well described by Granet through the love songs of the *Shi Jing.* The event that marked the reign of Huangdi was the combat that he waged against a rebel, Chiyou. He is also said to have fought against Shennong, who is identified with the Emperor of Fire, but the original myth probably included only one battle. According to certain texts, Chiyou had seventy-two or eighty-one brothers. "The eighty-one brothers had the bodies of animals and human voices, brass heads, and iron foreheads. They ate sand. They invented arms" (Granet, *Danses et légendes,* p. 354, citing the *Guizang*). "The seventy-two brothers had brass heads and iron foreheads. They ate iron and stones. In the province of Ji, when one digs into the ground and finds skulls that appear to be made of brass or iron, these are the bones of Chiyou" (*Shuyi Ji*). This monstrous rebel, whose head had horns, fought with Huangdi. When he fought with his horns, no one could resist him. He was, however, defeated at Zhuolu in northern Hebei, but his tomb was thought to be in Shandong. At the

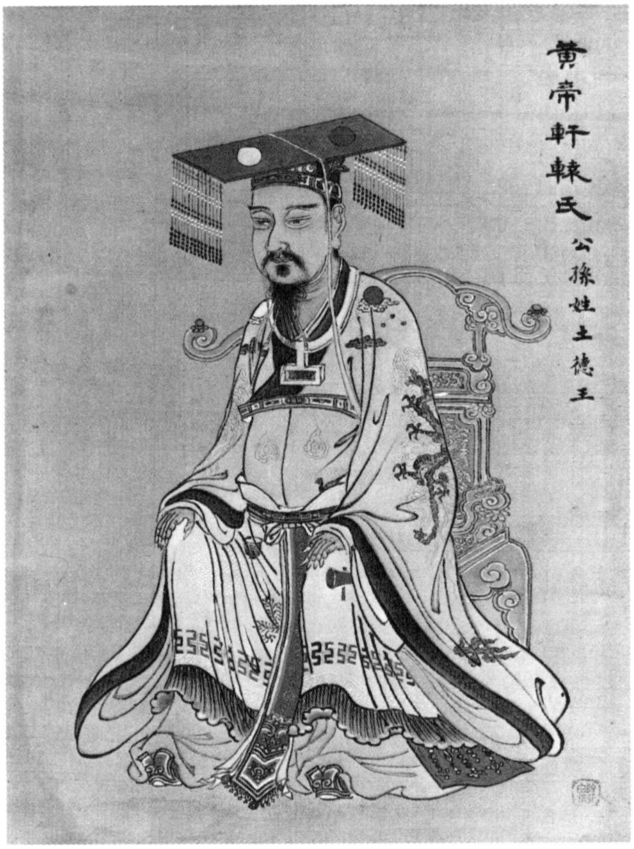

Huangdi. Portrait album, n.d. (Smith-Lesouef collection). Paris, Bibliothèque nationale. Photo BN.

battle of Zhuolu, Chiyou caused a thick fog to spread so that Huangdi and his soldiers lost their way. But Heaven sent down a "Dark Girl" (Xuannü) who taught Huangdi how to use the compass and gave him a military talisman. This was really a struggle between magic of two kinds: Chiyou called on the gods of wind and rain, but Huangdi called down a daughter of Heaven called Ba, Drought. He also enlisted the aid of a winged dragon, Yin. After the death of Chiyou, whenever trouble arose, all Huangdi had to do was draw an effigy of his defeated enemy to exact respect from the empire.

During this memorable struggle, Huangdi invented a war drum: "In the eastern sea, on Mount Liubo, there is an animal called Gui. It looks somewhat like an ox, all blue and hornless, and it has only one leg. Whenever it comes in or out, there is wind and rain. It is bright like the sun and the moon. Its roars sound like thunder. Huangdi took hold of it and used its hide to make a drum which he beat with one of the bones of the Beast of Thunder. The noise could be heard five hundred *li* away and exacted respect from the whole empire" (*Shanhai Jing* 14).

Outside of the battle of Zhuolu, the event that fired the imagination the most was the final apotheosis of Huangdi. The myth has a Daoist flavor and was in fact used by the Daoists as an exemplary story. In order to persuade Emperor Wu of the Han that he ought to follow the example of Huangdi, who was able to enter into communication with the gods and to perform the Feng sacrifice to Heaven, one of the *fangshi* (magicians) of his court tells him of this apotheosis in the following words: "Huangdi took copper from Mount Shoushan and forged it into a tripod at the foot of Mount Jing. When the tripod was finished, a dragon with a hanging dewlap beard came down to fetch Huangdi. Huangdi mounted the dragon. His ministers and his wives, numbering seventy, mounted behind him. Then the dragon rose up. The other subordinate officers, who had not been able to mount him, hung on to the dragon's beard. The strands were torn out and the officers fell; they knocked down Huangdi's bow. The crowd looked up and beheld (the apotheosis) from afar. When Huangdi reached heaven, the people below, crying out, picked up his bow and the hairs of the dewlap. This is why succeeding generations have called this place 'tripod lake' and the bow has been called 'the cry-of-the-crow'" (*Mémoires historiques*, vol. 3, p. 488). According to the *Feng su tung* and a commentary of the *Huainanzi* quoted in footnotes by Chavannes, the "cry of the crow" (*wu hao*) is the mulberry tree that is used for dye. When a crow is perched on a branch of this tree, the branch bends down to the ground; the crow does not dare to fly and cries out (*hao*); the branch is cut and an arrow is made of it; this is how the bow gets its name. This legend recalls the solar crows shot by the archer Yi. The fact that the crow is perched on a branch of the mulberry tree from which a bow is made is significant, because the mulberry tree is a solar tree. Recall, too, that during an eclipse, arrows were shot to rescue the sun. Here Huangdi reappears as a sun. Although yellow is the color of the element earth, it is also the color of gold (*huangjin*, "yellow metal"), which is a solar essence.

Zhuanxu. Zhuanxu is a less-defined individual, but he too seems to be a sun. He is called Gaoyang (the great Yang). Like the sun, he bathes in a pit. He fought against Gonggong, the rebel who threw the world into havoc and caused a great flood. He is an ancestor of the princes of Chu and of Qin. The *Pohu tong* states that he wore the *wu* sign on his head (the cyclical sign of the south). He is the ruler responsible for the separation of Heaven and Earth, because "he ordered the leader of the south, Zhong, to look after heaven and thus to have the gods under his care; he ordered the leader of the fire, Li, to look after the earth and to have the people under his care. He saw to it that [the gods and the people] observed anew the ancient rule, did not encroach on one another, and stopped being negligent" (*Mémoires historiques*, vol. 3, pp. 324–25). Zhuanxu is also known to have had three sons who became demons: one resides in the Blue River (the Yangtzi) and became a demon of fever; another became a demon of the waters and the woods; the third one dwells inside houses and frightens children. These demons were expelled in the twelfth month during the No ceremony.

Gaoxin. Gaoxin, or Emperor Gu (Di Ku), about whom the historian has virtually nothing to say, is interesting because of his wives, who are mothers of the royal races, impregnated through the action of Heaven. One of them is the mother of ten suns; another is the mother of twelve moons. Modern epigraphers assimilate this emperor to the ancestor Gui, who figures in Yin oracle inscriptions. Sometimes called Di Xun, he may have been a solar crow.

Yao. Yao is one of the principal figures of Confucianism, appearing as a model of virtue in the *Shu Jing* and other classics. With this ruler, we enter into orthodox history. The *Shu Jing* depicts him as taking pains to establish the calendar "in order to indicate the seasons carefully to the people." To this end, he made use of six individuals: Xi and He, two younger brothers of Xi, and two younger brothers of He. The first two were assigned to watch the sky and to calculate the movement of the sun and the moon. The last four were in charge of the seasons. The youngest brother of Xi lived in the east and took care of spring. The next youngest lived in the south and took care of summer. He's youngest brother lived in the west and took care of autumn; and the next youngest lived in the north and took care of winter. The youngest brother of Xi and the youngest brother of He governed "with respect" the exit and reentry of the sun (*Mémoires historiques*, vol. 1, p. 43ff.; Granet, *Danses*, vol. 1, p. 252ff.). By instituting "the offices of Xi and He," Yao "clarified the seasons and rectified measurements; as a consequence, Yin and Yang were in harmony, the wind and rain were well regulated, bounty and good influences prevailed; the people stopped suffering untimely deaths and illnesses." We have here a perfect example of the distortion of an ancient mythology in order to create a new one. The purpose is to show how a ruler worthy of this name organizes time and space, which are interdependent in Chinese thought. Originally, Xi and He were just one name, Xihe, a name borne by a goddess who was the mother of the ten suns.

In the system of basic virtues (*Wude*), according to which each ruler or dynasty reigns under the sign of one element, Yao comes under the sign of fire. His name may have some connection with fire, and the fact that he was held in fiefdom to Tao ("pottery") would associate him with the crafts of fire. But all of this remains uncertain. What is known is that the Han emperors regarded Yao as their ancestor, starting with the time when this house chose fire as the color of the dynasty.

Shun. When Yao became old, he did not transfer his power to his son but to a pious man of the people, named Shun, who is also, for Confucians, a model of virtue and especially a model of filial piety. There are many ancient legendary elements in his "biography." Before succeeding Yao, Shun underwent a certain number of trials. The first one was his own marriage: Yao gave him his two daughters as wives. He also entrusted him with his nine sons to see what kind of leader of men he was. This was a double test, good for the "inside" (*nei*), that is, private family life, and for the "outside" (*wai*), that is, public life. Shun passed both tests splendidly, and, most notably, his wives "did not insultingly boast of their nobility . . . [and] they served their parents-in-law." Unfortunately, the parents-in-law were bad. "Shun's father, Gu Sou, was blind. When Shun's mother died, the father took another wife who bore Xiang ('elephant'). Xiang was arrogant. Gu Sou loved his son by his second wife and relentlessly sought to do away with Shun." As a result, there were more trials: "Shun's parents sent him to repair the attic; they took away the ladder and Gu Sou set the attic on fire." Shun used two large hats as a parachute and escaped death. A second trial was imposed: to dig a well. When he was at the bottom, his father and brother threw in enough dirt to fill the well, but Shun escaped through a side exit that he devised. Thus he was victorious in this double test of fire and water. But he escaped these dangers with the help of his wives, the daughters of Yao, for he was able to get down from the burning attic because they had taught him "the art of the bird," and he emerged from the well because they had taught him "the art of the dragon," which made it possible for him to come out of the earth.

Shun underwent yet another trial. Yao sent him into a great forest on the mountain. "There was a violent wind, thunder, and rain; he was not troubled. Yao then recognized that Shun was worthy of being given the empire."

No sooner had Yao transferred his power to Shun than the latter proceeded to a quadruple expulsion; he eliminated four monsters or demons (depicted as rebels) that were the "harmful remnants of once Sovereign Virtues whose rule had come to an end" (Granet, after the *Tso Chuan*). This is how the *Shi Ji* summarizes the event: "When Shun went to welcome his guests at the four gates, he exiled the four criminal families and banished them to the four frontiers, so as to bring the demons under his sway. Then the four gates were opened and it was announced that there were no more criminals." The four gates are probably the gates of the capital, but they could also be the gates of the Mingtang, a kind of square temple from which the sovereign ruler regulates time-space by circling it like the sun. From his capital or his temple, Shun, the ideal sovereign, receives his vassals, who bring tribute to him, and expels to the ends of the world the agents of his predecessor, in order to subdue the demons who in this context are merely the Barbarians at the borders. But there was another version of the legend of Shun according to which he behaved quite differently toward his king and toward his father and brother: he reduced Yao to the condition of his vassal, banished his father Gu Sou, and killed his young brother (*Hanfeizi*). The old chief was thus eliminated by force, as was his elderly father, and especially his younger brother. Myths of this kind were, however, too much at variance with the Confucian ethic, and they were practically expelled from the written accounts. One would have liked to know more about the connection between Shun and elephants. His brother is an elephant; elephants plow the fields for Shun in Cangwu (in the Guangxi). Xiang the

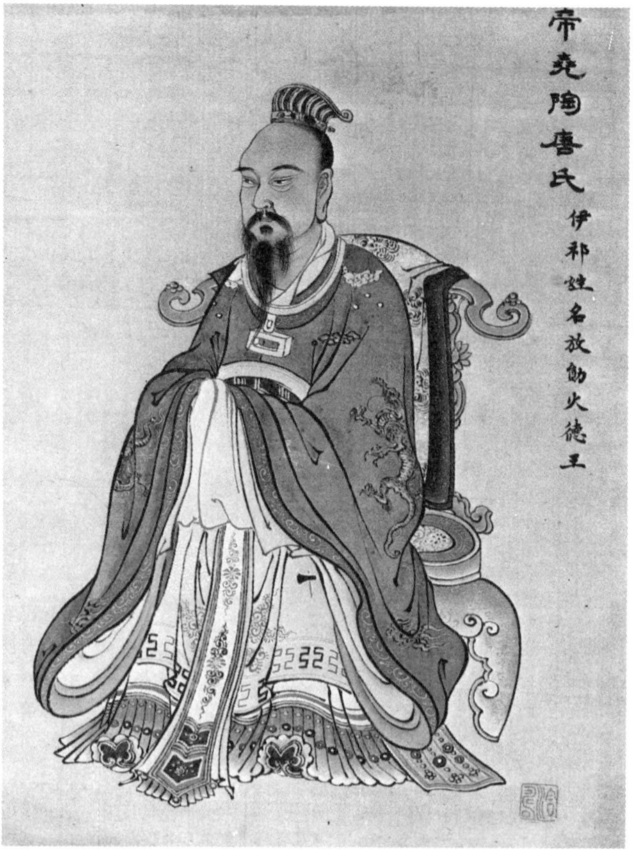

Yao. Portrait album, n.d. (Smith-Lesouef collection). Paris, Bibliothèque nationale. Photo BN.

elephant, Shun's brother, received as a fiefdom a domain called Yubi hsü (domain of the nose), where there was a temple of Xiang at the foot of a mountain (*Shuijing zhu*, 38). These legends must go back to the time of the Yin dynasty, because archaeology has shown that elephants were common then, although they are not mentioned later. This would also confirm the identification of Shun with Di Ku as the ancestor of the Yin and therefore as someone from the east. Mencius recalled that Shun was a Barbarian from the east, and he tells that in his time there were still popular traditions about him in eastern Qi, in Shandong.

Yu. Yu is one of the most renowned heroes of ancient China. He succeeded Shun, who gave his throne to him just as Yao had done for Shun. But since Yu's own son succeeded him, he (Yu) became the founder of the first dynasty, that of the Xia; that is why he is called Yu of the Xia and, often, the Great Yu or Yu the Great (Da Yu), because of his great merits. He is most famous for having fought against the unleashed waters of a great flood that suddenly struck in the time of Yao and continued during the reign of Shun. Yao had first appointed the father of Yu, Gun, to stop the flood, but Gun failed and was put to death. Yu inherited his task and succeeded at the cost of heroic efforts that left him half paralyzed and crippled.

Many texts reveal the mythical character of Gun and Yu. Both were demiurges who were the first to organize the fields (*bu tu*) and stabilize the nine provinces, that is, the entire territory of the empire. But Gun rebelled, furious for not being named minister (*sangong*). Shun had him dismembered on the Mount of Feathers. He then transformed himself into a yellow animal; it is unclear whether this animal was a bear or a turtle. As this animal went into some kind of hole, chances are it was a turtle, although the reading of "bear" is not impossible, since Yu can change into a bear at any given moment. The etymology of their names, however, suggests that Gun and Yu were aquatic animals.

According to the written tradition, Gun fought the flood by using a system of dikes, while Yu dug channels: actually, he cut through mountains. But according to many texts (*Shanhai Jing, Tianwen, Huainanzi*), Yu used the same methods as Gun, diked the waters, plugged the openings, and so forth. Gun was punished not so much for his poor technique as for stealing from the Ruler on High the magic (swelling) earth he used to build the dikes and walls. Furthermore, Yu used the same swelling earth to make great mountains. Yu appears as a true architect of the world, which he surveyed from east to west and north to south, so that one encounters "traces" of him almost everywhere (a prominent theme in the ancient literature).

After he had organized the world, Yu presided over the Great Mounts and Great Rivers (*ming shanchuan:* the sacred mountains and rivers of the territory). He summoned the deities of the mountains and rivers in a great assembly on Mount Guiji, which is his sacred mountain. At this assembly, the giant Fangfeng arrived late and was killed by Yu. Fangfeng, perhaps a wind god, had a dragon head with one eye; his descendants tried to rise up against Yu but lost their nerve and stabbed themselves in the chest. Yu revived them, and ever since then there has been a people known as "stabbed chests." As chief of the divinities of the mountains and rivers, Yu was worshiped as a "god of the soil" (*she*), just as Hou Ji, the ancestor of the Zhou, a god of farming, became the "god of the harvest" (*ji*). Together they are called Yu and Ji, just as the altars of the soil and the harvest together formed a double sanctuary that in official cults symbolized dynasty and homeland.

The fact that Yu became a god of the soil must be connected with the name of his wife, the daughter of Tushan, the mountain of the earth. This daughter was one of the "licentious" girls celebrated in the *Shi Jing* and condemned by moralists. She met Yu in the "countryside" (*ye*), among the mulberry trees, an instance of the typical theme of meetings on a holy site. This theme characterizes the "irregular" but common love affairs among young peasant men and women during seasonal festivals and is also associated with miraculous conceptions by mothers of heroes. One day Yu's wife saw her husband turn into a bear at the wrong time. She was turned to stone, but since she was pregnant, Yu had to cut her open with his saber to get his son. Yu himself was born of a stone. There is surely a connection between these split stones, the labors of Yu in drilling into mountains, and the standing stones that once adorned the mounds of the soil, along with trees, and which also constituted at least one element of the shrines of Gaomei, the Great Mediator, or Great Mother. Unfortunately, the texts say almost nothing about these sites of archaic cults, but it appears that there were female deities of the soil beside, or before, the male deities of the soil who are discussed in the classics.

The Rulers of Perdition. The Xia and Yin dynasties founded by heroes worthy of the heavenly mandate were ruined by two kings who lost the mandate because of their misbehavior. The texts tirelessly attribute the most scandalous acts and the most horrible crimes to them. Jie, the last of the Xia, and

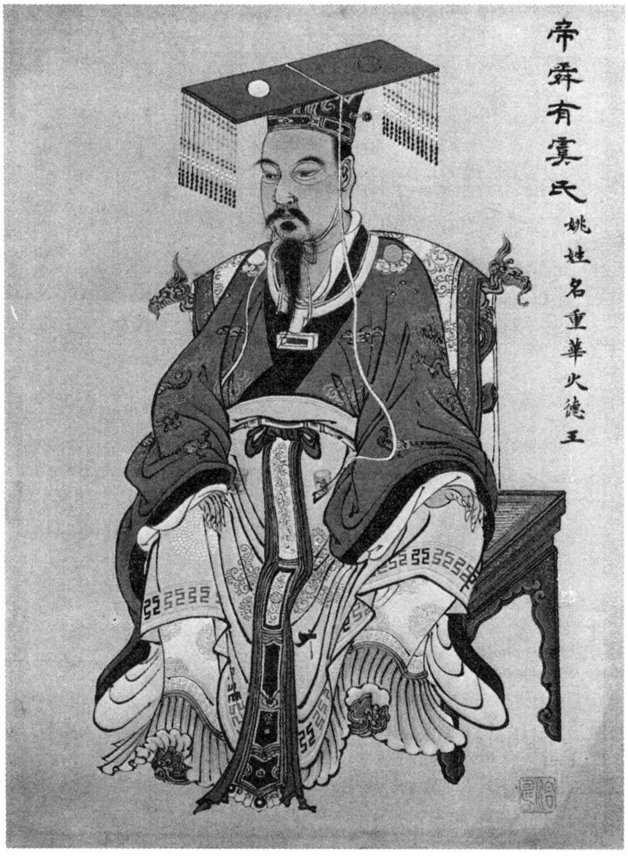

Shun. Portrait album, n.d. (Smith-Lesouef collection). Paris, Bibliothèque nationale. Photo BN.

Yu the Great. Portrait album, n.d. (Smith-Lesouef collection). Paris, Bibliothèque nationale. Photo BN.

Zhouxin, the last of the Yin, were tyrants for whom historians use the same themes. Both loved luxury and debauchery. They were excessive and "had special talents for evildoing." Zhouxin had superhuman strength; he could crush wild animals with his bare hands. He invented cruel methods of punishment and torture, such as torture on a metal beam placed over a fire. These evil rulers left their principal wives and amused themselves with beautiful captive women, like Daji, who loved to attend torture sessions. They commissioned lascivious music and dances. This music was ill-fated. When Zhouxin was defeated, his music master drowned himself in the river, and at night one could hear his melodies coming from the riverbanks, but "whoever first hears them, his kingdom shall be diminished" (*Hanfeizi*). Zhouxin "gave great parties at Shaqiu (the hill of sand where the tyrant had had parks and terraces built). He created a pond of wine; he suspended great cuts of meat so as to make them look like forests; he sent naked men and women to seek one another there; he gave orgies that lasted all night." These tyrants did not heed any remonstrances and killed the sage who voiced them. Thus the sage Bigan admonished Zhouxin, who replied, "I have heard that the heart of a sage has seven openings," and he cut Bigan in two to look at his heart. The best counselors fled: "The great tutor and the second tutor of the Yin took their sacrificial utensils and their musical instruments and took shelter with Wu, king of the Zhou." Wu took charge of a group of lords to attack Zhouxin, who lost the battle: "He [Zhouxin] climbed up on the Terrace of the Deer; he put on his clothes adorned with precious jewels, threw himself into the fire, and died. Wu, king of the Zhou, then cut off Zhouxin's head and hung it from a white standard; he killed Daji."

The fall of the tyrants was announced by disorders of nature: stars falling from the sky, earthquakes, mountains collapsing, rains of earth, women turning into men, and the appearance of two suns, one setting and symbolizing the tyrant, the other rising and symbolizing the new Son of Heaven. This final theme is not a mere image, but recalls the solar character of the ancient kings. On the list of the first eight Yin kings, it is noteworthy that the names of the second, fourth, sixth, and eighth designate four moments in the day, four positions of the sun: Zhaoming, morning; Changro, noon; Ming, evening; and Wei or Hunwei, night.

M.K./g.h.

BIBLIOGRAPHY

ERKES, *Zur Sage von Shun* (T'oung-pas 1939). E. CHAVANNES, *Les mémoires historiques de Se-ma Ts'ien,* vol. 1. M. GRANET, 1926. M. KALTENMARK, "Religion et politique dans la Chine des Ts'in et des Han," *Diogène,* no. 34 (Paris 1961). KOU KIE-KANG, "San houang k'ao," *Kou-che pien,* 7. YANG K'OUAN, *Introduction.* For full citations, see "Chinese Mythology."

THE GREAT FLOOD IN CHINESE MYTHOLOGY

The *Shu Jing,* cited in the "Historical Accounts" (*Shi Ji*) of Sima Qian, relates that in the time of the emperor Yao there was a great flood; Yao commanded Gun to struggle against the waters; Gun failed in his task and was put to death. It was Gun's son, Yu the Great, who was credited with putting an end to the flood. As it is recounted in these classical texts, the flood in the time of Yao, which continued under the reign of Shun, was a simple catastrophe such as has always occurred in China and elsewhere. There is nothing to suggest that it was a mythical Flood that was supposed to have annihilated humanity. What interested the authors was to elucidate the great virtues of these sovereigns and, in particular, the virtues of Yu, who devoted himself to the public weal, which allowed him to succeed to the throne that the aging emperor Shun ceded to him. Remaining within the context of the text of the *Shu Jing,* one would be tempted to say that the ancient Chinese were not acquainted with a myth of the Flood (which Frazer affirmed in *Folklore of the Old Testament*). One must, however, bear in mind the fact that the ancient historians were, above all, moralists who zealously applied themselves to the rationalization of ancient legends. In this edifying narrative, the flood is a rather secondary element, but one gathers from certain descriptions that it might well have been, originally, a true Flood, as is suggested in particular by that often-used expression: the enormous mass of waters "rose up to the sky." But humanity was not destroyed; the text says only that "the people below lamented," and in *Mencius:* "In the time of Yao, the waters, stopped in their courses, had overflowed and flooded the empire. The land was full of serpents and dragons; men had no place to settle. In the lowlands, they made nests for themselves (on piles); in the highlands, they hollowed out caves."

One of the points that interested the Confucian authors in the story of Gun and Yu was the opposition of two techniques and also of two moral philosophies. Gun, who is the inventor of ramparts, attempted to contain the waters by constructing barrages and dikes. Yu, by contrast, constructed outlets; he is famous for having cut the channel of Lungmen. The lesson of political ethics that might be drawn from these two attitudes is not ambiguous. In fact, in an older account of the legend, it appears that Yu employed the same methods as Gun, and that he also tried to contain the waters by damming them up. The reason the sovereign (Yao, Shun, or the Shangdi, the Sovereign from On High) punished Gun is that he had acted contrary to the sovereign's will and had stolen from him the magical earth (swelling earth) that had the property of being inexhaustible.

Another version of the Flood brings into play not only Gun and Yu, but Gonggong and Nüwa. Gonggong is a monster who, vanquished in a combat for sovereignty, had, in his fury, battered in, with thrusts of his horns, a mountain that was one of the pillars of the world: Mount Buzhou ("noncircular, cracked"). This column of the Sky was therefore shattered, and the moorings of the Earth broken; the Sky inclined toward the northwest so that the sun, moon, and stars now move in that direction, while the waterways flow toward the east, where the Earth is swallowed up. Nüwa restored the Sky with stones of five colors that she had smelted, cut off the feet of a great tortoise to erect them at the four poles, killed Gonggong, and finally heaped up the ashes of reeds to arrest the overflowing waters. The waters seem to be only one of the elements of the disaster caused by Gonggong.

The version of the myth in which Nüwa intervenes may be what led some to suspect the existence of a true Flood in the background of these legends. It should be recalled that the deity with the body of a serpent (or a dragon) forms with Fuxi a married couple and also a brother-sister pair. Now, it is through the incestuous union of a brother with his sister, the only survivors of the Flood, that humanity is saved from annihilation in numerous variants of the myth among the aborigines of southern China, and the two spouses/siblings are often called Fuxi and Nüwa. It should also be remembered that the Chinese Nüwa is the creator of humanity. Moreover, Nüwa and Yu have so many points in common that the goddess figures as a kind of female counterpart to the hero. She is assimilated to the daughter of Tushan, the wife of Yu. There is a certain relationship between the two pairs of demiurges: Yu and Tushan on the one hand, Fuxi and Nüwa on the other hand. The two great floods, that of Yu and that of Nüwa, are probably only two versions of the same myth. In both cases, the flood is not localized, but extends over the whole empire, that is, the whole Earth, thus approaching a true Flood. But it is either a natural catastrophe or a disaster caused by a demon; it does not arise as the punishment for any transgression or fault. There are, however, local legends in which this theme does occur. Before examining them, let us speak of the myth of Yi Yin.

Yi Yin is a celebrated figure who aided T'ang the Victorious, the founder of the Yin dynasty. The story of his birth is recounted thus in the commentary of the *Tianwen*:

> The mother of Yi Yin, who was pregnant, dreamed that a divine woman said to her: when the mortar and the furnace produce frogs, hurry up and get away, but without turning around. Some time later, frogs were born in the mortar and the furnace. The mother ran toward the east and turned around to look at the town: the town was completely covered by a flood. The mother drowned and was transformed into a hollow mulberry tree. When the waters had subsided, there was a small child crying on the bank of the river. Some people took him in and raised him. When he was fully grown, he distinguished himself by his exceptional gifts.

The *Lüshi Chunqiu* recounts the same legend in slightly different terms; in particular, it is just a matter of water coming from a mortar. But the version cited above is notable in that the mortar is evidently a Yin symbol, and therefore aquatic, and the furnance is a Yang symbol, and igneous. But the character *chao*, which designates the furnace, is composed of two elements: "cavern," or "hollow," and "frog." Therefore, even etymologically, there was a connection between the furnace and frogs, an essentially aquatic animal. (Frogs were used to obtain rain.)

The theme of the hollow mulberry tree that occurs here must be emphasized, for the mulberry tree is a solar tree; that is why, here, the mother of Yi Yin flees toward the east. The theme is also connected with Sanglin (the forest of mulberry trees), which was the holy place of the Yin and of their heirs, the princes of Sung: this holy place is constantly linked to the theme of miraculous conceptions.

Finally, the theme of the prohibition against turning around and the sanction (here, the metamorphosis into a hollow mulberry tree, elsewhere petrifaction) is encountered in multiple versions of a well-known legend, the legend of the Inundated Town (the theme of the town of Ys).

The most famous case was that of the town of Liyang, which was a subprefecture of the kingdom of Huainan, in the present-day province of Anhui. The *Huainanzi* (chap. 2) alludes to it, which provides the commentator Zhao Yu with the opportunity to recount the legend:

> There was (in Liyang) an old woman who always did good deeds. Two young scholars happened to pass by and said to her: this land will be flooded and will become a lake. They advised her to watch the threshold of the eastern gate of the town, and when she saw blood there, she would have to flee, climb the Northern Hill, and not turn around. From that moment, the old woman constantly went and watched the threshold of the gate. The keeper of the gate asked her why, and the old woman told him what the scholars had said. That night, the keeper killed a chicken and sprinkled its blood on the threshold of the gate. The next morning, the old woman, noticing blood on the gate, climbed the Northern Hill without delay. The whole country was inundated by the waters and became a lake in the space of one night.

A variant specifies that the old woman had turned around and that she was changed into stone. The same story is recounted, with variations, for other regions. Instead of the bloody threshold, one more often encounters a stone tortoise, or sometimes a lion, whose eyes are smeared with blood.

Among the numerous local legends on this same theme, the legend of the lake of Qiong Du, in Sichuan, deserves to be cited. This region was inhabited by "barbarian" populations in the time of the Han, and it is in connection with these peoples that the commentary on the Book of the Second Han (*Xu Han Shu*, chap. 86) relates the story of this lake. In it there were many fish whose heads are peculiarly large, so large that from a distance one would believe that they were capped with iron pots. Now, there was once a very poor old woman who lived alone. But a small horned serpent came to visit her in her bed. The old woman fed the serpent and it grew. It happened that the serpent killed the horse of the prefect. The prefect, furious, demanded that the old woman hand the serpent over to him, and since the serpent was not to be found, he had the old woman put to death. The serpent warned that it would avenge its "mother." For forty days a storm was unleashed; the people discovered that they had the heads of fish. In one night, the town and its region became a lake. Only the house of the old woman remained intact; it served thereafter as a shelter for fishermen. In clear weather, the walls and houses of the submerged town can be seen.

Here there is a frequent characteristic of the legends of towns (or sometimes of a great house) that are flooded: the residents are transformed into fish. Very often, the inundation occurs after a collective fault: the killing of an extraordinary animal, a great fish or a white buffalo, which is eaten. One woman does not participate in the feast; she is forewarned, but she turns around and is petrified. She is nonetheless venerated as a patron divinity of fishermen.

M.K./b.f.

BIBLIOGRAPHY

W. EBERHARD, 1942. IZUSHI YOSHIHIKO, 1943. H. MASPERO, 1924. MORI MIKISABURO, 1969.
For full citations see "Chinese Mythology."

Myths and Legends about the Barbarians on the Periphery of China and in the Land of Chu

The "barbarians" that surrounded the central states of ancient China had myths and legends which were entirely their own. Certain of these traditions were taken up in dynastic histories and in other texts and thus became celebrated in China itself. For the Chinese, moreover, the barbarians were the objects of beliefs that assimilated them to animals. The Chinese names for them are most often represented by written characters with the classification of quadruped or insect. Furthermore, campaigns against these peoples were considered more as hunting expeditions than as military operations. Only the civilized world was truly "human": the "Four Seas" constitute an unreliable zone in which barbarians, animals, and demons are indistinguishable from one another. At the same time, Chinese civilization slowly spread on these peripheral borderlands, assimilating certain peoples and subjugating others (these were called "cooked"), with still other peoples managing to maintain their independence and putting up greater resistance (these were called "raw"). These complex and ambiguous relationships between Chinese and barbarians are reflected in legends which the Chinese collected more or less faithfully. We may add under this heading the legends of the land of Chu, even if this is not considered to be "barbarian" in the strict sense of the word.

I. Panhu, the Ancestral Dog

Several aboriginal ethnic groups of southern China have a myth concerning an ancestor who was a dog and whose name was Panhu. There are numerous versions of this legend, of which the best known is that related in the *Hou Han Shu* ("History of the Later Han"), at the beginning of the chapter about the Man (a Chinese name, unrelated to the English word), the barbarians of the South. In the time of the (mythic) emperor Gao Xin (that is, Di Ku), the Rong Dog (the Chinese name means dog) barbarians were causing trouble and it was impossible to subdue them. The sovereign made a proclamation: anyone who brought him the head of the enemy general would receive a great reward of gold and a fief comprising one thousand households, and would receive in marriage the emperor's own youngest daughter. The emperor had a dog whose coat was of five colors; it is this dog, named Panhu, who brings back the head of the enemy. The emperor is embarrassed, but the princess persuades him that he cannot break his word. The emperor therefore gives her to Panhu, who carries her on his back and goes into the mountains of the south, where he takes refuge in a "room of stone," in a place of difficult access. The emperor does his best to send emissaries in search of his daughter, but all of these fail because they run into storms that halt their advance. The couple has six sons and six daughters who, after the death of Panhu, intermarry and give birth to the Man tribes. The emperor grants them an exemption from taxes and statute labor because of the merits of Panhu and because their mother was a Chinese princess. This legend has remained very much alive among the Yao, the Miao, and the Xiamin of the southern provinces of China, Zhojiang, Guangxi, Guizhou, Yunnan, and the mountains of Tonkin. Not only is there an altar of the ancestral dog in their houses, but his memory is also evoked through certain details of clothing and in particular through women's headdresses. According to the Xiamin version, Panhu, in the face of the emperor's hesitation to give him his daughter, advises him to place him under a golden bell for seven days and seven nights, after which he will be transformed into a man. But on the sixth day, the princess lifts up the bell: Panhu's body has already been transmuted, but his head is still that of a dog. Panhu dresses in clothing and the princess adopts a headdress like a dog's head. They then marry and go into the mountains, where they have three boys and a girl.

According to a widespread version (already cited in the commentary on *Hou Han Shu*), whose aim is to explain the name of the ancestral dog, there was in the palace of Gao Xin an old woman who had an ear disorder: from her ear a sort of cocoon is extracted; this is placed in a gourd (*hu*) which is covered with a tray (*pan*); the cocoon turns into a five-colored dog, who is named Panhu.

This legend, which is widespread in this form among the southern aboriginal peoples, leaves some problems unresolved:

a) What is the relationship between Panhu and Pangu? Pangu is the cosmic man who was born inside the primordial Chaos; he then grew so much between Heaven and Earth that they moved apart from one another, until finally the different parts of his body became the heavenly bodies, the mountains, the rivers, and the other constituents of the universe. This myth is very different from that of Panhu, yet there is certainly a connection between the two names Panhu and Pangu; in addition, the two myths belong to the same regions and the same populations. It nevertheless appears, judging from ethnological investigations, that the Panhu cult is the more widespread of the two at present, but that the two names may at times be interchanged out of confusion. Numerous tribes preserve with pictures the account of the legend of Panhu: it is important to them that the text of this account contain the exemption from taxation and statute labor that the sovereign is said to have given to their ancestors.

b) In the account in the *Hou Han Shu*, the enemy who is to confront Panhu is the general of the Rong Dogs. These peoples inhabited the Shaanxi and Shanxi. Their very name indicates that they must have had close connections with the dog. The *Shanhai Jing*, on the subject of the Rong Dogs, says that there was a genie there with an animal's body and a human face, referred to as Quanrong. And elsewhere (chap. 12), this country is also called Quanfengguo, the enfeoffed Land of the Dog. The inhabitant shown in the illustration accompanying the text had the appearance of a dog; a young woman kneeling before him offered him food and drink. It is impossible to tell whether this text is referring to the legend of Panhu. The commentary of Guopu summarizes two legends, that of the *Hou Han Shu* and another according to which Quanfengguo was a Land of Dogs whose inhabitants were descended from a pair of white dogs. There are "Lands of Dogs" in the north as often as to the south and west; if the males there are dogs, their wives are always women who dress and eat like the Chinese, whereas the Dogs (sometimes with a human body and the head of a dog) have no clothing and eat raw meat. Thus, in all of these traditions, the Dog represents the state of savagery and nature, while the woman represents culture. Yet it was a woman who prevented Panhu from becoming completely human. This brings us to another theme which will allow us to bring together the two myths of Panhu and of Pangu (cf. Eberhard, *Lokalkulturen* 2, p. 80). Pangu is born in Chaos, in Hundun. This is the cosmic egg: it is also a sack. Among the descriptions and comparisons of Hundun in the ancient texts, we find one which speaks of its resemblance to a dog whose eyes cannot see and whose ears cannot hear. A Man tribe recounts that, when Panhu died, he was placed in a tree and pierced with needles. The meaning of this act is unclear in this context, but it may recall the ancient legend of a Yin king who, in an act of defiance, had a skin bottle filled with blood and suspended so as to represent Heaven and used as a target for arrows. It is nevertheless difficult to believe that Pangu is Heaven; on the other hand, if he is Hundun or Chaos, the act of piercing him could be connected with the Hundun of Zhuangzi, in which two other divinities wished to make openings, that is, sense organs.

It is thus not impossible to find a link between Pangu and Panhu, whose myths at first glance have nothing whatsoever in common. It must be added that the myths and legends about the dog are numerous and complex and are disseminated throughout the Far East; and it is not inconceivable for legends on this subject to be encountered among peoples quite distant from one another. The writings of the Chinese certainly contributed to their dissemination as well.

II. Linjun

Linjun is the ancestor of one of the clans of the Man barbarians of Ba (eastern Sichuan). All of these peoples came from Mount Chungli, which had two caverns, one red and one black: the Ba clan came from the red cavern and the others from the black. Since they had no leader, they agreed to choose the one who could reach one of the caverns by throwing his sword. Only one man of the Ba clan succeeded, and a second ordeal was agreed upon: he who could cause a boat made of earth to float would be made leader. Again the man of the Ba clan passes this test, and he thus becomes the leader of all of the clans, under the name of Linjun (the Lord of the Granary). Sailing his earthen boat, he arrives at Yanyang, where there is saltwater and a goddess of salt who wishes to keep him there. When he refuses, the goddess transforms herself into an insect surrounded by a cloud of other insects and obscures the sun. The world is plunged into darkness for over ten days. Through a trick, Linjun succeeds in killing the goddess with an arrow, at which point "Heaven opens and shines forth." Linjun continued his voyage in his earthen boat to the place where he founded a city. When he died, his soul became a white tiger to whom human victims were sacrificed.

There were other female divinities of salt in Sichuan, and these also demanded human sacrifices. At Renzhou, in the southern part of the province, there was a fountain of salt attached to the temple of a Daughter of Jade. Since she had no husband, she was offered young boys, who were thrown into the fountain to keep it from drying up. There was also, in a mountain of the same region, a great serpent called "the God of the Western Mountain." The inhabitants periodically sacrificed to him a girl who would serve as his wife. This continued until the day when a wise governor conceived the idea of marrying the serpent god to the Daughter of Jade so that the custom of human sacrifices ceased.

III. The Kings and Heroes of Shu (Sichuan)

The most ancient king of Shu was Cancong, who was succeeded by Po-huo and Yuxiao, each of whom reigned for several hundred years. The name Cancong means "grove of the silkworms," which is not without interest, since it is in Sichuan that we find a famous legend about the origin of silkworms.

A man goes off on a voyage and his wife promises their daughter in marriage to any man who will bring her husband back. His horse brings her husband back, but instead of keeping her promise, she has the horse killed and has its skin dried in the courtyard. The hide envelops the daughter, who becomes a silk cocoon.

Cancong taught his people agriculture and the art of raising silkworms. Sacrifices are offered to him under the name of "the God of the Green Robes" (Qingyi Shen).

After the three ancient sovereigns, Duyu reigned; he took the name of Wang Di after he married a girl who came from a spring and may have been a divinity of salt. After him came Bieling, a man from the state of Jing (Chu): this was a dead man whose corpse had floated upriver to Chengdu, where he returned to life. Wang Di made him a minister because he knew how to master the floodwaters. At this point, there are two versions of the account. According to the first, Wang Di seduced the wife of Bieling; according to the second, it was, on the contrary, Bieling who seduced the wife of Wang Di. The latter cedes the throne to Bieling, or is killed by Bieling and becomes a cuckoo. The bird cries until it spits up blood. Hearing the cuckoo is inauspicious, since it portends a separation. The people know that the cuckoo is the soul of an ancient king of Shu.

Bieling is a famous hero, quite similar to Yu the Great, since he also goes through mountains. It is because of his works that the land of Shu became habitable. His name designates him as "the spirit of a tortoise." Following the abdication (or the murder) of Wang Di, he became king under the name of Kaiming ("Opening of Light").

In the time of King Kaiming five giants (Wuding Lishi) were born who could move mountains. Whenever a king died, they erected a great rock upon his tomb: these came to be called the "stone bamboo shoots" (of Chengdu). According to another legend about a Mountain of the Five Wives (Wufu Shan) at Zitong, the king of Qin had offered five beautiful girls to the king of Shu. The latter sent the five giants to meet them, but on their return trip they saw near Zitong a great serpent who entered a cave. When they tried to pull it back by the tail, the mountain collapsed, crushing the five men and the five Qin women: the mountain was thus broken up into five hills which are called "the Tombs of the Five Women" or "of the Five Giants" (*Huayang Guozhi,* chap. 3). According to another version, the five girls are changed into stones. These are some of the legends about the megaliths of Sichuan.

Another renowned hero from the land of the Shu is Li Bing. A magistrate in the region in the third century B.C., he cleansed the country by digging through a mountain to make a passage for the waters of a river so that they irrigated the plain instead of flooding it. Furthermore, he tames a water monster and himself becomes a god of the waters. The god of the confluence of two rivers near Chengdu each year demanded the sacrifice of two girls whom he made his wives. Li Bing takes the place of one of the girls, and arriving at the sanctuary of the god, offers him something to drink; but the god slips away. A combat ensues: two water buffalo are seen fighting on the shore of the river; one of them is Li Bing, and he is losing the fight. He indicates to his soldiers how they may recognize the enemy buffalo, and they kill it with their arrows. Li Bing thus became the god of the waters at Kuan-hien. Before his temple stands a stone ox who protects him from the waters (it is a common practice to erect a stone or bronze ox on the shore of a river or lake). Under the Song, Li Bing was associated with another divinity who was taken to be his own son, Erlang. Legend attributes to him the merit of having slain the buffalo-dragon against which his father had fought in the river. He became a popular divinity in every province, and is represented as a young hunter accompanied by his dog.

IV. Zhuwang, the Bamboo King

The *Hou Han Shu* speaks of an ancient barbarian kingdom of the southeast named Yelang, whose first leader is the Bamboo King. A girl of this country was bathing in a river when a great bamboo stem with three nodes passed between her feet. She heard cries coming from inside the stem. When she split it open, she found a baby inside it, whom she took home and fed. When the child grew up, he proved to have great skill in warfare and became the king of Yelang. His name was Zhu (Bamboo). The bamboo stem from which Zhuwang was born became a forest in which the sanctuary of the hero is located. Although this story as it is recounted in the *Hou Han Shu* is close to the theme of Moses (cf. the birth of Yi Yin), it is possible that in the original version this was a miraculous conception. It is also very close to the theme of the mother of the dragons. This is a woman who finds in the water an egg from which dragons are born; but according to certain variants, it is the mother herself who gives birth to the dragons after she has eaten the egg, or after she has been touched by a piece of wood (see Eberhard, *Typen,* no. 58 and no. 60). This final theme is found in the origin legend of the Ailao, a people of the Yunnan. Again, it is the *Hou Han Shu* that recounts this myth: a woman fishing in the river is struck by a piece of wood floating in the water; she becomes pregnant and gives birth to ten sons. The piece of wood transforms itself into a dragon who leaves the water and comes to demand that its children be returned. Nine of these flee when they see the dragon; the youngest cannot flee, and sits on the back of the dragon, who licks him. He is named Jiulong (Nine Dragons), but this name, in the mother tongue, means "seated on the back." Jiulong would become the first king of the Ailao.

M.K./d.w.

BIBLIOGRAPHY

W. EBERHARD, *Lokalkulturen im alten China,* 1–2 (1942). H. MASPERO, "Chinois et Tai," in *Mélanges posthumes,* 1: *Les religions chinoises* (Paris 1967).

Chinese Demons

I. The Chinese Conception of Demons and Spirits

The Chinese term for demons in general is *gui.* In rituals, *gui* is the name of the inferior soul, *po,* which is connected to the blood and bones during life but becomes more or less detached from them after death. Also after death, the superior soul (*hun*) becomes a spirit (*shen*) that leaves the body and tends to roam but must be fixed to the slab by the mourning rituals. The *po* that has turned into a *gui* becomes a dangerous ghost unless it too is fixed in a sepulcher. At the time of the sacrifices of the ancestor cult, the two souls, the *hun* and the *po,* or the *shen* and the *gui,* are reunited, and the sacrificers feel that the reconstituted ancestor is present at their side. But when people speak of *gui,* they also think of all sorts of malevolent demons and not only of ghosts. There are, moreover, many other names for the demons, but they are less general.

The Chinese have always lived in a world populated by invisible beings; some are benevolent, but more often they are alarming and dangerous. To contend with the dangerous ones, there were fortunately rites of exorcism, and, more recently, Daoism provided efficacious recipes to use against the demonic armies.

The Confucians, skeptics on principle, did not speak of demons unless to scoff at "superstitions." It is in criticizing popular beliefs that Wang Chong (first century A.D.) gives us much information on this subject. But earlier, the philosopher Mozi (fourth century B.C.), an adversary of the Confucians, was a pious man who believed in the gods and demons. In a chapter entitled *Ming gui* (Proofs of the existence of demons), he refers to the evidence and cites ancient texts that prove that spirits and demons have always been seen and heard, not only by isolated individuals, but even by whole crowds. He defends his belief in spirits for chiefly moral reasons:

1. Spirits (*guei-shen*) punish those who have killed innocent people: such was the case with two persons who were assassinated by great lords and whose phantoms returned to punish the guilty ones, in both cases in the course of hunting parties in sacred parks or marshes.

2. Spirits punish priests who have been negligent in their choice of jades and offerings: Mozi gives an example in which a spirit comes to complain of such negligence (apparently through the mouth of a sorceress) and assaults the sacrificer in the act of officiating.

3. Spirits punish perjurers. The example chosen is that of two litigants sent by a duke of Qi to the hill of the God of the Earth: they must take an oath by sprinkling the altar with the blood of a ram. The ram strikes the perjurer with his horns and kills him.

In the *Lunheng* (the chapter called *Dinggui,* Reflections on the *gui*), Wang Chong sets forth various opinions, including his own, concerning demons. He is of the opinion that the apparitions of *gui* are not caused by spirits of the dead, but by the thoughts of the living when they are ill. A sick man is afraid, and then demons appear to him. He is the victim of an obsession that Wang Chong compares to a strong mental concentration. After this rationalist opinion, he cites other explanations: a man sees demons when the "light of his eyes" is disturbed. In the state of sleep, this light turns inward and is directed toward the interior of the sleeper, who sees forms (dreams). It is the same in the case of sickness or madness. In these three cases—dreams, sickness, madness—there is fatigue and the light of the eyes turns inward. A demon is the breath, the energy (*gi*) of sickness. This breath is inharmonious and manifests itself in the illness as a demon. In reality, the demon issues from the environment: in a forest, for instance, it will be the spirit of a tree (but when the breaths of man and nature are in harmony, the spirits of nature are vivifying). The *gui* are the spirits of old things that can assume a human appearance, in particular in the case of succubi and incubi. The *gui* are beings like the others, but they originate from countries outside of China; they have human or animal form. They are seen only in the case of sickness, but they are not illusions. Thus the two spirits Shentao and Yulei catch them and feed them to tigers (see below). There are people who are possessed by demonic "breaths," such as sorcerers, mediums, and other inspired people who utter words said to be prophetic. For Wang Chong, these breaths are of solar origin (for him, the Yang, when it is excessive, is injurious).

Such were some of the more or less rational or fantastic ideas that were held to explain demons. Demons, for most people, were quite real, and the world was populated with them. Certain demons were particularly famous for having played a great role in the very distant past: they are Chiyou, Gonggong, and the Four Malefic Beings expelled by Shun.

II. The Famous Demons

Chiyou is, for history, a rebel who fought Huangdi, the Yellow Emperor. He is the inventor of arms and a god of war. The battle that placed him in opposition to Huangdi was, in fact, a contest of magic in the course of which the two adversaries were aided by all sorts of spirits. Chiyou is a monster with teeth two inches long, so solid that they cannot be broken. He has the body of a man, the hooves of a bull, four eyes, and six hands. According to one text, he had the head of an ox; according to others, he and each of his brothers (seventy-two or eighty-one) had a copper head and an iron face. He ate iron and stones. Sometimes, the "bones of Chiyou," which seem to be made of copper and iron, are found in the earth. When Huangdi had defeated him, he made an image of him to inspire terror. When sacrifices are made on his tomb (situated to the west of Shandong), a red cloud, which is called "the banner of Chiyou," issues from the tomb. There were quite diverse traditions about this monster, who sometimes appears to be a serpent who is defeated by a winged dragon. But he is above all a personification of the forge, in which arms—instruments of misery, as Laozi calls them—are made.

Gonggong is another rebel who is chiefly famous for having, with a thrust of his horn, battered in Mount Buzhou, one of the pillars of the world. This exploit caused the sky and earth to swing and the waters to overflow. The goddess Nüwa restored the sky and contended with the inundation. This labor is sometimes attributed to Yu the Great, but that is another version of the myth. Gonggong is described as a serpent with a human head and red hair. A vassal of Gonggong, called Xiangliu, looked just as terrible: he had nine heads and the body of a serpent, and he was coiled around himself. With his nine heads, he ate on nine mountains. Where he vomited, foul swamps formed. By obstructing the overflowing waters, Yu succeeded in drowning him, but on the spot where his corpse lay, there was so much putrid water that one could neither cultivate nor live there. Yu purified this ground and the emperors built terraces there (*Shanha Jing,* 17).

Marcel Granet has clearly shown how a good sovereign inaugurated his new reign. He had to establish a calendar: this is what Yao did by sending the Xi and the He to regulate space and time. Moreover, he had to expel the lapsed Virtues: this is what Shun did at the moment when Yao ceded power to him. He eliminated "four evils," four monsters that the *Shu Jing* designates by their names and the *Zuo Zhuan* by their nicknames. Among these monsters are Gonggong and Gun (the father of Yu). Gonggong is also surnamed Qiongqi, the Rogue, and Gun is called Taowu, the Stake. The other two who were expelled are Huandou, surnamed Hundun (Chaos), and San Miao, surnamed Taotie (the Glutton). We know that the masks on ancient bronzes are called Taotie, but this identification is modern.

Gun, the father of Yu, is famous for having been commanded by Yao to fight the overflowing waters and for having failed after nine years of effort. "Shun then banished Gun to the Mount of the Feather (Yushan) and dispatched him with the sword of Wu (a country celebrated for its weapons)." But the legend most often states that Gun threw himself into an abyss, where he was transformed into a yellow animal, a bear, or a tortoise; he became the god of the abyss. It seems clear that Gun was a fish spirit, as is suggested by his name, which is written with the character for fish. According to an odd tradition reported by the *Tianwen* and the *Guizang,* the body of Gun remained intact for three years; when it was opened with the sword of Wu, Yu emerged from the body. But the legend generally says that Yu was born from a stone (*Huainanzi*).

San Miao (Three Miao) were assailed by Shun because they

possessed a Virtue for disorder that "was making them lose their place in the numbers of the Calendar." But it was Yu who, holding a shield and an ax in his hands, danced between two staircases (leading to the great hall of the ancestral temple), which resulted in the submission of the Three Miao. In another version, the lord of the San Miao was slain by the Sovereign, and his people (the Miao) revolted and entered the Southern Sea (Miao is the name of an aboriginal people of southern China).

Huandou is assimilated by Chinese scholars to Danzhu (Vermilion Cinnabar), who was a son of Yao but who, quite unworthy of his father, was exiled to the bank of the river Dan (Cinnabar). In the same way, Huandou was expelled to the south, among the Man barbarians. The *Shanhai Jing* speaks of the country of Huandou, whose inhabitants have human faces but the beaks and wings of birds, and who catch fish.

In spite of the uncertainty of the texts that represent various traditions about each of the four demons, classics like the *Shu Jing* and the *Zuo Zhuan* state that they were dispersed to the four ends of the world, where they became the subduers of the demons who populate the borders of the civilized world. Perhaps one can subdue demons only by being a demon oneself.

There is, in the anthology of poets of the ancient principality of Chu, the *Chun Qiu,* a poem attributed to Song Yu (third century B.C.), entitled "Recalling the Soul," *Zhaohun.* The ritual of recalling the soul occurred, in the classical religion, just after death. A priest (or priestess) of Chu in this poem performs this recalling for a sick person: he or she calls the patient's soul by pointing out the dangers that await it in each of the directions of space, in the Sky, and on Earth. Among these dangers, the most terrible are those due to monsters and demons. The soul is therefore invited to return home, for:

To the east are giants who seek to get hold of souls to devour them. Moreover, the ten suns that emerge all at the same time cause even metals and stones to melt.

To the south is a region where the Tattooed Faces and the Black Teeth live, who make sacrifices of human flesh; there are also a great many enormous reptiles there, giant foxes, and serpents with nine heads whose greatest pleasure is to swallow people.

To the west is the country of flowing sands: you are in danger of entering the lair of the Thunder there. If you escape from there, you are lost in an immense desert inhabited by ants as big as elephants and by giant black wasps.

To the north is the land of ice and snow (the poet does not say anything more about this region).

Toward the Sky, the soul will encounter tigers and leopards that guard the entrances to the nine tiers. A giant with nine heads, accompanied by terrifying wild animals, amuses himself by snatching the imprudent who come that far and hurling them into a deep abyss.

Toward the lower world, in the Earth, is the Residence of Darkness where Tubo, the Count of the Earth, lives. He is a horned monster whose sinuous body makes "nine curves." This last expression is the very one that designates a labyrinth. This demon of the Earth and Darkness is not distinguished from the sinuous path that leads to the subterranean world and that it is his function to bar. The poem continues by showing how Tubo pursues the travelers who stray into these parts and takes possession of them by marking them with the print of his bloody fingers. The text adds a few words which commentators connect with the description of Tubo, but which appear to concern another monster with the body of a bull and three eyes. "All these demons are greedy for human flesh."

Numerous *gui* figure in the ancient literature but, as is the case for divinities and heroes, the information on the subject is confused and contradictory. In Confucian works, the *gui* become historical figures, such as Kui, who is sometimes Shun's music master, sometimes a horned demon with one leg. He is identified with the Shanxiao, demons who live in the mountains and who cause fever. These demons are very small and are naked. They have only one foot and resemble a drum, which brings us back to Kui, who, according to the *Shanhai Jing,* is a one-footed animal that Huangdi captured, later making a drum out of his skin.

The emperor Zhuanxu had three sons who died in infancy and became demons. The eldest inhabits the Yangzi Jiang and is a spirit of pestilence. A second, Wangliang, is a spirit of the mountains; he mimics a human voice to lead people astray. He resembles a small three-year-old child, but has red eyes and long ears. A third son of Zhuanxu haunts the corners of houses and loves to frighten small children. He himself is a child-demon (*Lunheng,* 22). The souls of children who died in infancy were greatly feared. The most dangerous demons look like small children.

Yu the Great, to contend with the great flood, traveled the earth and thus became acquainted with the gods and demons that are encountered during travels. Tradition attributes to him the redaction of the *Shanhai Jing,* a geography that describes spirits of all kinds who haunt various sites. These spirits were also represented on the nine caldrons that Yu cast in order that men might know "the divine things and the impure things; the Chinese can therefore go on the rivers and through the marshes, in the mountains, and in the forests without ever running afoul of hostile beings and without the Chimei and the Wangliang ever harassing them" (Granet, *Dances,* p. 489, citing the *Zuozhuan*).

More than anyone, the Daoists were people who needed to frequent uninhabited places, mountains, and forests, whether to retire there in solitude or to search there for medicinal or magical plants. Therefore they needed to know the demons that they were in danger of encountering and the means of guarding against them. Ge Hong (283–343), a physician and alchemist, provides much information about this in the *Baopuzi.* But one text was particularly important for him because it recommended methods of controlling divinities and avoiding demons. This book, the *Sanhuang Jing* or *Sanhuang Wen* (Texts of the Three Majesties), is lost, but the tradition is preserved in a late treatise on it that figures in the *Dao Zang* (fasc. 575) under the title (which we abridge) *Taiqing . . . Sanhuang nei biwen.* The first chapter of the book gives lists of divinities and demons. These last are classed in two categories, the *gui* and the *jing.*

III. A Classification of the *Gui* and the *Jing*

There are forty *gui,* eight for each of the four directions and eight for the center. These demons are rather like different kinds of policemen in the orders of celestial divinities; they pursue and punish malevolent powers and sinners. They maintain armies in their own orders to aid the "correct emanations" of Sky and Earth. The Daoist who has the proper formula to do it, moreover, can also mobilize these celestial hordes. It suffices for him to draw a certain talisman with vermilion on a yellow fabric and reduce it to ashes so that he can swallow it, and he will have the power to subjugate evil spirits. Other formulas enable him to make demons appear at will and cause them to assume all sorts of appearances. All this magic must, however, serve only for good.

Unlike the celestial *gui,* the *jing* (a term that also signifies "subtle essence"), seventy in number, are independent demons; they answer neither to the Sky nor to Earth, nor to any divinity. Each of the demons is described and its name is given. The person who knows the names of demons has a hold over them and can make them disappear. The *jing* demons clearly affect daily life more than the preceding forty *gui* do. Many of them figure in story literature, but some of them belong to the oldest tradition. The Wangliang, for instance, figures in that tradition, but he is not a very dangerous demon; he is some ten feet tall; he has eyes of fire; there is a danger of meeting him at night at the edge of water or on a deserted path; he makes people sick, but not seriously. This spirit is produced by a stone, a clod of earth, or a branch of a rotted tree, in contact with moisture.

A few examples chosen rather at random will give an idea of the richness of this collection. The first demon on the list is called "Demonic Soul, Swallower of Corpses": he looks like a beautiful young girl, but he produces all sorts of malevolent prodigies in places of habitation; he is in reality the spirit of a fox that is ten thousand years old. If this demon is encountered in the mountains, he can be recognized by a violet hair that grows from his left eyebrow. To make him disappear it suffices to call him by his name. Another demon looks like a handsome young man, but he has only one leg; he sows trouble in houses, abuses daughters and wives there, and brings stolen objects there: he is the spirit of an old servant. A certain spirit assumes the form of a very ugly old woman. By night he enters the bellies of small children and steals their souls from them, which makes them cry in the night. Certain demons are inoffensive, such as the spirit of copper ore that is a tamed tiger; he wanders at night on high summits. There is also a spirit of old gold nuggets that appears as a young girl dressed in yellow with red feet and walks at night holding a flame, but without causing any harm. There is a spirit of silver nuggets that assumes the aspect of a young boy dressed in white and walks along paths during the day, playing with a fish. (For the last two spirits, there is an inversion of the boy and the girl, for gold is Yang and silver is Yin.) But the amiable demons are exceptional; most are terrible: the soul of a man assassinated in the solitude of a mountain appears as a specter with unruly red hair and green eyes; he calls people by name and beats them to death with stones. Similarly, the soul of a drowned man who has retained too much vital power will assume the appearance of a woman who is drowning: if someone comes to her rescue, she drags them into the waves. These last two are souls who are seeking a substitute in order to be liberated (and to be able to reincarnate). The demon "Red Serpent with a White Face" is also the soul of a drowned man who walks at the edge of the water: he blows his breath on anyone who happens to pass by and that person throws himself into the water against his will. The spirit of a very old tree may lurk in an altar of the Earth (*Tudi*) and jeopardize the lives of those who come to lay down offerings. The spirit of an old carp assumes the aspect of a young girl in mourning clothes who weeps at the edge of the water. Old statues of deities, in certain houses or in temples, may become dangerous demons. A white serpent three thousand years old becomes a beautiful young girl who seduces and bewitches young men who happen to walk in deserted places, near old altars, or in abandoned houses: she enchants them by reciting poems and singing songs. But she can be recognized by a green hair in her right eyebrow.

IV. Exorcism

To contend with all the demons that populate the world, there were from antiquity numerous methods of exorcism. In more recent periods, religious Daoism elaborated a rich collection of diverse recipes: magic formulas and dances, talismans, etc. Daoist priests, when they took on the function of exorcists, knew how to summon transcendent armies that hurried from the sky or that the priests drew from their own bodies. But at the origin of certain of these Daoist rites were ancient practices that should be mentioned briefly.

Yu the Great is famous for having invented a magical dance, the "step of Yu," which is still used by Daoists. It was a sort of hopping dance (Yu, after his hydraulic labors, was paralyzed on one side) that the sorcerers danced to expel demons. But it was also danced by a certain venomous bird who thereby caused stones to split in order to dislodge serpents (Yu has close ties with cleft stones).

To expel pestilence, there was in antiquity a ceremony that was celebrated on the occasion of the new year. Granet has described in detail this ceremony, called Da Nuo (*Dances and Legends*, p. 298ff.). We can do no better than to return to those important pages and give here a brief summary. The ceremony took place in the palace and required many people: one hundred and twenty young boys, ten to twelve years old, each dressed in a red cap and a black tunic and holding a tambourine. The principal figure, the Fangxiangshe, wore a mask with four eyes. His outer apparel was black, his inner garb red; he held a lance and a shield. There were also twelve dancers disguised as horned animals. The ceremony consisted principally of a dance by the Fangxiangshe and the twelve animals. At a given moment, all of them drove out the pestilences and went to throw them in a river. The expulsion concluded, figurines of men, made from the wood of a peach tree, were arranged on the gates.

The custom of renewing the images on the gates at the new year has remained very much alive even to our time. The custom dates back to antiquity. According to one legend that has several variants, two spirits called Shentao and Yulei have the function of seizing the *gui.* They inhabit the Eastern Sea, on Mount Dushuo, and cling to an immense peach tree whose sinuous branches cover thousands of *li.* Among these branches, to the northeast is the "Gate of the *gui*" (*guimen*) by which the innumerable *gui* come in and go out. With cane ropes, the two spirits bind the *gui* that they catch and give them to tigers to eat. A variant states that they drag the *gui* with a bow made of peach wood. This tree with sinuous branches, in which the Gate of the Demons is situated, appears to be a transposition of the theme of the labyrinthian passage that, in so many mythologies, leads, but dangerously, to the world of the dead. Only here the theme is inverted; it is the *gui* who encounter the obstacle.

M.K./b.f.

BIBLIOGRAPHY

DE GROOT, *The Religious System of China,* vol. 5, part 2. K. SCHIPPER, "La démonologie chinoise," *Sources orientales* 8 (Paris 1971). KIANG CHAO-YUAN, *Le voyage dans la China ancienne* (Shanghai 1937; new ed. 1975).

See also the general bibliography for "Chinese Mythology."

The Mythology of Smelters and Potters in China

The arts of fire—smelting metals and firing ceramics—occupy an important place in ancient Chinese civilization, as may be appreciated by the magnificent ceramic and bronze objects that have been left by the Yin and the Zhou. Since bronze utensils were mainly used for cultic purposes, it is not surprising that smelters were set apart from others, and that casting was an operation that had a mystic character. The potter's art is hardly less prestigious, as the two crafts are fused in the mythology; the creation of the world is assimilated to the work of the potter and not to that of the smelter, because the potter fashions his clay on a wheel, which is not the case with the smelter. (Cf. the myth of Nüwa, who shaped men out of earth and mended the sky with the stones of five colors that she had smelted.)

The mythic sovereigns, particularly Huangdi and Yu the Great, are the smelters of sacred caldrons. When Huangdi had completed the casting of a tripod (*ding*), he rose into the sky on a dragon's back. Yu cast nine *ding* out of metals that came from the nine provinces (i.e., from the whole empire); represented on these tripods were the divinities and demons that his subjects would have wanted to know about while traveling.

It is useful to recall Huangdi's battle with Chiyou, the inventor of weapons, who was a monster with a copper head, a bronze forehead, and metal bones. Granet, starting from the fact that owls were sacrificed to Huangdi and comparing themes about this bird, came to the conclusion that the owl was the animal emblem of a royal clan of blacksmiths (*Danses et Legendes,* 2, p. 537). Eberhard refers to a tradition (drawn from a late work) according to which Chiyou's wife was an owl (*Lokalkulturen,* 1, p. 136).

Blacksmiths could distinguish the sexes of the metals they used in the manufacture of objects that went in male-female pairs. The same is the case with swords. When a magic sword is smelted, all of the gods are present: the *jiao* dragons hold up the furnace, the Red Sovereign loads it with charcoal, the Master of the Rain washes down and sweeps, and the Genie of Thunder operates the bellows of the forge. Two swords, one male and one female, were famous: Ganjiang and Moye. These two names are also those of two smiths, who were husband and wife, about whom the following legend is told: Ganjiang receives the order to forge two swords. He gathers together iron from five mountains and gold from the ten directions. He examines the Sky and the Earth, the Yin and the Yang; after three months of effort, he has not succeeded in fusing the metals. Moye recalls the principle that the transformation of metal requires a human sacrifice. Ganjiang then tells how his master had been obliged, in order to effect the fusion, to throw himself along with his wife into the furnace (according to one version, the wife alone sacrificed herself). Moye (or the two of them) sacrifices her hair and nails and orders three hundred boys and girls to operate the bellows. Moye, according to one version, jumps into the furnace alone. The smelting, following these sacrifices and sacred unions, was successful and the two swords could be completed. The male sword was named Ganjiang and the female Moye. Ganjiang hides the male sword and presents only the female sword to the king. The furious king kills Ganjiang, who had earlier told Moye, when she was pregnant, to show the son she would give birth to later the place where he had hidden the male sword.

Tripod vase. Zhou dynasty. Paris, Musée Guimet. Photo Arch. Phot. Paris/SPADEM.

The son does in fact find the sword and dreams of avenging his father. Since there is a price on the son's head, a stranger proposes to cut it off and carry it to the king, and then to kill the king. The son agrees to this, and the stranger carries his head to the king; the king tries to boil it in a caldron, but it will not cook. The stranger cuts off the head of the king, which falls into the boiling water; then the stranger kills himself, and his own head unites with the two others. At this point, the three heads cook and become indistinguishable. Three tumuli are raised and are called the tombs of the Three Kings.

Swords are not the only metal objects that are sexualized and go in pairs. The same is the case with bells, which like to fly through the air or hide in the water, as well as for bronze drums, which are sacred objects for the aboriginal populations of the south.

An apotheosis of a smelter, analogous to that of Huangdi, may be found in the *Liexian zhuan,* a Daoist hagiographic collection dating from the beginning of the first century A.D.: a person named Tao Angong was a master of the forge. One day, the flames of his forge rose up on all sides to the sky. Tao Angong prostrated himself at the foot of his forge and begged for mercy. A red bird alighted on the top of the forge and said to him, "Angong, Angong, look, your forge has entered into communication with the sky; on the seventh day of the seventh month, a red dragon will come here for you." A red dragon did come on the appointed day, and the smith climbed onto its back and flew up toward the southeast. In this story the elevation of the Daoist smith is effected through a red dragon and by following the luminous path that leads from his forge to the sky. The Daoists normally rise up on a trail of light, but in the example of Tao Angong it is the smiths who are destined to rise up into the sky in flames, especially when they sacrifice themselves in the furnace.

Ning Feng Zu, another character in the *Liexian zhuan,* was a master potter of Huangdi who had learned to produce five colors of smoke. Ning Feng Zu made a pyre and burned himself on it; he rose and fell with the puffs of smoke. It is probable that the potter was also obliged to sacrifice himself in order to succeed in firing his vases, which shows how closely the two crafts were related (*tao,* in the name of Tao Angong, means "potter").

It is not surprising that the principal god of fire, along with the Emperor of the Flames, was Zhurong. He was the "Regulator of the Fire," *Huozheng,* and his name seems to mean "Brilliance of the Forge."

M.K./d.w.

BIBLIOGRAPHY

W. EBERHARD 1942. M. GRANET 1926. L. LANCIOTTI, "Sword Casting and Related Legends in China," *East and West,* July 1955. Full citations in "Chinese Mythology."

Caves and Labyrinths in Ancient China

Numerous Chinese legends treat the theme of the labyrinth and related motifs: meander, cave, shell, pearl, and dance. Although there is no Chinese term that corresponds exactly to "labyrinth," the idea is frequently conveyed through expressions containing the character *qiu* (in the sense of "curve," "bend," "meander"), which figures in many geographical names. The course of the Yellow River traces bends that are known as the "nine curves (*jiuqu*) of the Huanghe," an expression in which "nine" is merely symbolic, or even mythic in this occurrence: the river was believed to have its source at the mountain Kunlun, a legendary mountain, which, with its nine tiers, gives access to the nine storeys of heaven. In order to attain the highest heavens the nine bends of the river had to be crossed and the nine storeys of Kunlun climbed.

Labyrinth themes are abundantly represented in Daoism. They are present in the holy places called "cave heavens" (*dong tian*). A significant and particularly celebrated example is that of Linwu dong tian, which is a cave in an island of Lake Taihu, once situated between the kingdoms of Wu and Yue. The island is called Dong ting ("salt cave") and the sacred cave is nestled in a hill named Baeshan (which can be interpreted as "mountain of the sorcerer or sorceress"). This cave is connected with a legend about some famous talismans that involves Yu the Great. A "holy man" revealed to Yu the "five talismans of the *Lingbao,*" which allowed the hero to conquer the great flood; but he commanded Yu to hide them, after he used them, in a sacred mountain. That is what Yu did: he hid the talismans in the cave of the Baeshan. Later, King Helu of Wu, a contemporary of Confucius, ordered a hermit to enter the cave. It was a real labyrinth; not until he had traversed thousands of *li* did the hermit reach a city from which a lunar light emanated. He discovered the sacred writings there and brought them back to offer them to the king. Since the talismans were enigmatic, Helu sent someone to ask Confucius what they meant.

Sacred caves, of which the cave of Linwu is a typical example, are thus labyrinths; they are, moreover, illuminated within either by a characteristic moonlight that owes nothing to the sun (*Shengao,* 2) or by an opening that allows the penetration of a ray of light coming from the sky. People go to caves containing bats—animals that know how to eat in such a way that they do not die—to search for drugs that give immortality, or even texts and talismans that offer salvation. In every case, these are principles of life that are hidden within the entrails of the earth and that must be discovered; to find them, one must undergo trials, cross difficult passages, and discover the entrances and exits of the holy places.

The theme is found again in Daoist texts about the heavens and the hells. The celestial residence (*xuandu*) comprises a terrace with nine circumvolutions (*jiuqutai*); through "ten detours and nine circumvolutions," it communicates with the eight directions of the world (*bafang*). The concise text, which describes this celestial residence and which figures in diverse works dating from the six dynasties, speaks also of communication with the world above through some sort of column or spiral emanation. In contrast, the Daoist world of the dead is the residence of the north, in the ocean of the north; a tribunal called by many names can be found there: "The Tribunal of the (Yellow River's) Sources and Windings" (*Chuanqu Zhi fu*), "The Tribunal of the Nine Shadows and the Long Night" (*Jiuyou changye zhi fu*). The theme of the Long Night is often linked with that of the orgies of the kings of hell; the orgies take place in the labyrinths. Granet has shown the meaning of the complex theme of the "long night": first in connection with the popular festivals of the winter solstice, exuberant and orgiastic, then with the legends of the "kings of hell" (those who lose their kingdom through their excesses; cf. *Civilisation chinoise,* p. 236ff.). In the background of this mythology of orgies, peasant and aristocratic, it is not difficult to find ancient rituals in which the longest night (that of the solstice) and the resurrection of life are celebrated together. The theme of the orgy in its connection with the labyrinth is perfectly illustrated by the celebrated "Pavilion of Wanderings" (*Milou*) of Emperor Yangdi of the Sui. The same themes are found earlier in the story of the platform of Gusu that King Helu had constructed to "drink the night away" (this is the same Helu who appears in the story of the labyrinth cave of Baoshan). Here there is no longer an underground cave but an elevated construction that was the scene of orgies and drinking bouts; there was no access to it, however, except through a "road with nine detours," *Jiuqu lu.* One text says that King Helu had the tower constructed in order to contemplate from afar Lake Taihu, the site of the same Baoshan with its cave where the Ling Bao talismans were discovered. But the talismans were bad luck for Helu and his kingdom. He had no right to the talismans: Yu, to whom they were revealed, is the ancestor, not of the kings of Wu, but of the kings of Yue, the rival state to Wu. Helu's desire to possess the talismans, his construction of an excessively high tower, and his ambition to reach the sky all joined together to cause the downfall of King Helu.

Thus the motifs of labyrinth, cave, and spiral tower are closely linked to the great themes of life, death, and resurrection (the theme of the orgy merely expresses the idea that all excess pushed to an extreme gives birth to a renewal). It is significant that the Daoist term denoting the male sexual organ is "nine detours," *Jiuqu,* the same expression that denotes a river's windings or Helu's labyrinthine road of Gusu.

This expression *Jiuqu* is found in a legend that strangely recalls the shell of Daedalus, when he was tested by Minos, who was pursuing him in Sicily. We hear of a pearl pierced by a winding hole and therefore called "the pearl with nine windings," *Jiuqushu.* According to one version of the legend, known only through brief allusions, Confucius knew how to pass a thread through the pearl: it was sufficient to glue the thread to an ant who would pull as it passed through the hole. In another version that figures in a late work (the *Tianzhongji* of the Ming dynasty), during a journey, Confucius meets two young girls who are gathering mulberry leaves. They warn him that he will be in danger and will have to submit to a test: he will have to pass a thread through the "pearl with nine windings." Thanks to the young girls who reveal the trick to him, Confucius got free. The story specifies that smoke is used to force the ant to penetrate the pearl.

The poet Su Dongpo makes an allusion to this pearl in a poem entitled *Xiangfusi jiuqu guandeng,* "The festival of lanterns in the labyrinth of the monastery of Xiangfu." The image of the pearl comes into the poem to describe the crowd of devotees who enliven the monastery at dawn. But this is surely also an allusion to a labyrinth game that was played in certain regions on the occasion of the festival of lanterns (the fifteenth day of the first moon). Thus, at Beijing, a labyrinth was made of Sogho mats and decorated with numerous lanterns; this was called "the lanterns of the nine windings of the Yellow River." When someone entered this construction he would get lost and wander there for a long time before getting out.

The labyrinth is associated with New Year's festivals in Sichuan, at Gui Zhou: there, the population used to go walking in a place called the "rocks of the eight cohorts" (Bazhentu). There, they say, was the famous "labyrinth of the eight cohorts" of Zhuge Liang, the celebrated hero of the Three Kingdoms: if someone entered, he would lose his way and no longer be able to get out. And women look for little rocks with holes in them which they thread and wear like amulets on their heads. The close resemblance between this fertility ritual and the *Jiuqu* pearl is obvious.

Among the numerous legends in which the themes of interest to us occur we will take up those in which Yu appears—Yu who hid the talismans at the bottom of the labyrinth cave. Other sources say that the sacred writings were revealed to him, or that he hid them in a holy mountain, Mount Guiji, or, more precisely, on one of the peaks of that mountain, the Yuanwei Shan, whose name seems to signify that it is a labyrinth. In this mountain there is a cave named after Yu. A later poet, Ai Tingtao, in a poem consecrated to a promenade in Linwu dong tian (where the five talismans were hid), in two parallel verses evokes first the "pearl with nine windings" that the ant goes through, and then Yu's Cavern, which is a labyrinth, for "he who wishes to penetrate Yu's Cavern gets lost in the east and in the west."

Another legend is told in the *Shiyi Ji* (chap. 2): Yu the Great, when he got through the Longmen pass, entered a deep cave. There was an animal there resembling a pig who had in his snout a "pearl that brightened the night," whose brilliance was like that of a torch; there was also a green dog that barked in front of the cave. Escorted by the animals, Yu finally came upon a god with a serpent's body who was none other than Fuxi; he then received the supreme initiation from this divinity. The voyage through the cave illuminated by this supernatural pearl, which is simultaneously the moon and the sun, is equivalent to climbing to the sky. This is why the sacred caves are the Caves of the Sky.

M.K./d.g.

BIBLIOGRAPHY

M. KALTENMARK, *Ling-pao: Note sur un terme du taoïsme religieux,* a collection published by the Institut des hautes études chinoises, vol. 2: *A Mythological Study on Chinese Religion. Themes of Labyrinth and Grotto* (in Japanese), Annual of the Sanko Research Institute for the Study of Buddhism, no. 2 (Tokyo 1967).

See also the general bibliography of "Chinese Mythology."

Some Legends about Laozi and the Immortals in Daoist Mythology

Religious Daoism, which must be distinguished from philosophical Daoism (Laozi, Zhuangzi, Liezi), has its own mythology, but it is not always easy to recognize the authentic legends in the midst of the theologians' artificial constructs. In this article, we shall limit ourselves to an overview of a few legends concerning Laozi and the Immortals. Speculations about the hierarchies of the heavens and the countless deities in the macrocosm and the microcosm, who are often merely names, are of only limited interest to the history of Daoism, of which we still know relatively little.

I. Laozi

The figure of the historical Laozi is so obscure that we cannot be sure that he ever really existed. The book attributed to him, the *Laozi* or *Daode Jing,* has an uncertain history, and scholars do not agree on its date. Yet it is the most famous book of ancient China, the one with the most commentaries, and it is by far the most often translated. To Daoists, it represents a particularly sacred scripture, and Laozi became a deity by the last centuries B.C.

As early as 100 B.C., Sima Qian admits in a short biography devoted to Laozi that he was able to collect only uncertain and contradictory data about him. He states that Laozi's family name was Li, that his personal name was Er, and that he was styled Dan. He was born in a village in the state of

Chu (modern Henan). As for his life, Sima Qian says that he was an archivist at the royal court of the Zhou; Confucius came to visit him; when he saw the Zhous falling into decadence, he left to go west; en route he dictated his book in two chapters (the Book of the Dao and the De) to the guardian of the Xiangu Pass; he finally vanished without a trace. But other traditions claim that Laozi had cultivated his vital forces in such a way that he lived more than two centuries. It is clear that in the time of Zima Qian, Laozi was a legendary figure.

The meeting between Laozi and Confucius is very famous; it has been told often and with many variants, and has been depicted on several sculpted funerary stones of Shandong province (second century A.D.). Confucius came to consult Laozi about rituals and was reprimanded and exhorted to adopt a Daoist attitude. He was so impressed that he compared Laozi to a dragon.

Laozi's departure for the west and his mysterious disappearance have given rise to a later legend according to which the Daoist master became the Buddha. Later still, about 300, Daoists composed an apocryphal sutra on this theme, the "Book of Laozi Who Converted the Barbarians" (*Laozi hua hu ching*). For centuries, this book has inspired violent polemics between Buddhists and Daoists.

During the Han period, the main Daoist current was called *Huang Lao Dao* ("the Dao [way, doctrine] of Huangdi and Laozi"). This school taught methods of government and techniques of longevity. The association of the Yellow Emperor with Laozi is the result of interactions between the shifting and highly complex state of the Han imperial rituals on the one hand, and on the other, popular beliefs, of which little is known, political and religious speculations of the school of Zou Yan, and beliefs about the Immortals and longevity.

The doctrine of that school revolved around both the art of governing (through "nonaction") and techniques of longevity. It is well represented by the commentary of Laozi called "of Heshang gong." In the hagiography, Laozi is expert in these techniques; it has been noted that the *Shi Ji* mentions traditions according to which he lived more than two hundred years. The *Liexian zhuan* places his date of birth under the Yin (second millennium B.C.). This ancient hagiographic collection goes on to say that he knew how to nourish his vital energies and that he attached major importance to sexual methods.

In the text of an inscription composed in 165 by order of the emperor Huan of the Han, on the occasion of a sacrifice to Laozi, there are references to exercises for mental concentration and to techniques for longevity, through which the sage was transformed into an Immortal and "shedding its skin as a cicada would, he escaped from the world." This inscription also summarizes some of the beliefs about Laozi that were current in popular circles: the sage has become a deity, a cosmic god who exists at the center of primordial chaos; his place is in the center of heaven; he transformed himself nine times in accordance with the movement of the sun and with the rhythm of the seasons; he is surrounded by the Four Emblematic Beasts (Green Dragon on the left, White Tiger on the right, Red Bird in front, and Turtle behind). He has taught the Doctrine to the Holy Sovereigns beginning with Fuxi and Shennong. In the final expression of praise in the inscription, Laozi is a radiant deity who contributes to the brilliance of the sun, moon, and stars, and who moves back and forth between heaven and earth.

It is interesting that the idea of Laozi's transformations already appears in this text, and this for two reasons. First,

Laozi leaving for the west. Qing bronze. Paris, Musée Guimet. Photo Musées nationaux.

the same theme and the same expression of "nine transformations" in connection with the sun appear in the myth of Pangu. This myth of southern origin first appears in texts from the third century A.D. We also know that the theme of the dismemberment of the cosmic man, whose body becomes the world, was transposed to Laozi. It would thus seem that this myth existed at least in the second century. But the theme of the transformations of Laozi or of a cosmic being in general is certainly Chinese, and it it hardly likely that it was borrowed (compare the myth of Nüwa, and the ideology of the *Yi Jing* as a whole). Moreover, the "nine transformations" are connected with exercises of meditation in which the practitioner used mirrors and visualized a series of nine spirits who might have been the various visible forms of Laozi. Certain texts gave detailed descriptions of him during these transformations, which were to be visualized: "Laozi has seventy-two *xiang* signs and eighty-one *hao* signs. He transforms himself nine times. During the first metamorphosis, he is six feet six inches tall, wearing the cap of the magpie and the fish and the eight-bordered clothing of the phoenix. During the second metamorphosis, he is seven feet seven inches tall, wearing a multilayered cap on his head, a white cloak with red collar and crimson sleeves . . ." (*Sandong Zhunang*, cited by A. Seidel, *La Divinisation de Lao-tseu*, p. 37). Laozi was visualized with nine names and seventy-two and eighty-one extraordinary signs marking his physical appearance. His devotee depicted him the way he was before his birth, during the period of gestation that lasted seventy-two or eighty-one years.

The second point to be made about the transformations of Laozi on the inscription of the year 165 concerns a book that has come down to us in manuscript form, the *Laozi Bianhua Jing* ("Sutra of the transformations of Laozi"). It may date from the later Han and may have originated with a popular messianic sect (see the study done on this text in A. Seidel, op. cit.). In this book, we find no exercises of meditation but rather transformations in the course of history: Laozi periodically descends into the world to teach rulers the art of governing and of becoming immortal—a theme indicated by a passing reference in the inscription. Here again, Laozi is a primordial being, "Ruler of all deities, ancestor of Yin and Yang, soul of the thousand beings, potter and founder of the void, creator-transformer." He appears in the guise of different individuals whose names are given in the text, beginning with the reigns of the three August Ones (*San Huang*), the Five Emperors (*Wu Di*), and so forth, until the end of the later Han. However, before speaking of these historical appearances, the text mentions nine transformations and gives a series of nine names: though it is not stated explicitly, these must be again the nine appearances that Laozi puts on in the course of his meditation.

There are in the legend of Laozi elements that betray the influence of Buddhism, first in the stories of his birth, particularly the fact that he was delivered from his mother's left side. On the other hand, the theme of his miraculous conception is Chinese: Laozi's mother was aroused by a shooting star, just like the mother of Yu the Great and the mothers of many other heroes. As for Laozi's appearances as the master of emperors, the resemblance to the avatars of the Buddha may lead us to suspect an Indian influence, though this need not be the case: the belief in immortality and in the condition of the *Xianren* (the Immortals) who disappear and reappear in the course of time is a very Daoist theme, and it suffices to explain the legend in question.

Laozi, deified since the Han, occupies an important place in Daoism, but he has no longer been at the summit of the pantheon since theology devised a multitude of hierarchical divine entities. Furthermore, such Daoists as Ge Hong denied his divinity and saw in him no more than an exceptional man. For others, in his aspect of Laojun (Lord Lao), he is part of a divine triad. At the top is the Yuanshi Tianzun, a kind of celestial father who reveals a doctrine of salvation to his disciple the Daojun (Lord of the Dao), who transmits it to the Laojun, who in turn spreads it all over the world, a task in keeping with his role as a savior god in close contact with mankind. These three deities are personifications of the Dao.

II. The Immortals (Xian, Xianren, Shenxian)

The Daoist ideal was to live as long as possible and even not to die. To reach this goal, they used many methods, both physical and spiritual. These methods became increasingly numerous and complicated as time went on, but many of them had been in existence since late antiquity. Physiological techniques were known to Laozi and Zhuang Zi. While Zhuang Zi taught mostly spiritual asceticism, Daoists in general did not distinguish between the two ways of conceiving the achievement of salvation. Spiritual exercises and various physical techniques went hand in hand, and both of them helped increase the power of life in such a way that the practitioner rose to a higher state, that of the *Xianren*, the Immortals. An Immortal is a quasi-divine being, for not only does he not die, but he is free from the various constraints of this lower world, his body is lightened, he becomes luminous, he frolics in space, travels on dragons and cranes, or flies on wings. Such individuals can be seen depicted on sculpted stones and on various pieces of Han bronze and lacquer ware. They are also the object of much discussion in texts. The *Lunheng* of Wang Chong explains that the Immortals are depicted in pictures with their bodies covered with down and feathers, with their arms transformed into wings, flying through the clouds. These winged Immortals are connected with the Barbarous Birds that the ancient books place somewhere in the Orient. They are discussed in the *Yu Gong* of Shu Jing, and when speaking of the land of feathered men (*Yumin Guo*) the *Shanhai Jing* states: "These men have elongated heads; feathers grow out of their bodies." About the land of men with the heads of *huan* birds (descendants of Huandiu, the minister or son of Yao, the banished ancestor of the Miao), Guopu says they are depicted as *Xianren*. In the same series of eastern peoples, the *Shanhai Jing* speaks of the "land of people who do not die," where there is a tree of immortality and a fountain of life. Also in the East were the wondrous islands accessible only to those who could fly. This entire mythology of the *Xianren* long antedates the formation of religious Daoism, but the religious movements that developed in the province of Shandong at the end of the Warring States Period and during the Han dynasty played an important role in the formation of Daoism, so that its influence on the mythology of this region is not surprising. This of course does not exclude other influences, in particular the influence of shamanistic cults of the land of Chu. The theme of the "Distant Wanderers" (*Yuanyou*), which appears in the title of a poem of the "Elegies of Chu" (*Chuci*), is already clearly Daoist: the shaman poet eats solar emanations and visits the birdmen on Cinnabar Mound: "The poet goes to find the Immortals in a brightly shining home; the Cinnabar Mound is, night and day, eternally luminous." He later adds that once a man has attained the Dao, he grows feathers on his body.

Following are some examples of biographies of *Xianren* taken from the *Liexian zhuan*, a collection of legendary biographies attributed to Liu Xiang (77 B.C.).

> Chisangzi (Red Pine Tree) was Master of the Rain in the time of Shennong. He consumed liquid jade and taught this diet to Shennong. He could walk into fire to consume himself in it. He often went to Mount Kunlun and stopped in Xiwangmu's stone chamber. Following the wind and the rain, he rose and descended. The youngest daughter of Yandi (Shennong), who ran after him, also obtained the state of an Immortal and left with him.

Chisangzi is a complex figure, a god and sorcerer of the rain, but also connected with fire. Among the procedures to make rain, those that used heat and fire were particularly effective: one could burn a mountain or a witch, or simply expose her to the heat of the sun; some Mandarins offered themselves in order to put an end to drought by being burned at the stake. This was, moreover, a way of attaining freedom from one's perishable body (*shijie*), which was surrendered to the flames. The name of Red Pine Tree is interesting because the pine, an evergreen, symbolized a great vital force. Its red color is that of the Yang, of life and vigor; it is evidently also connected with fire. One legend about the daughter of Yandi (the Emperor of the Furnaces, identified with Shennong) tells us that she was sometimes a woman and sometimes a magpie. She went to live on the top of a mulberry tree and built a nest there with twigs that she brought back in her beak. The Red Emperor (i.e., Yandi) tried to bring her back, and, failing, set her nest on fire; his daughter thereupon rose to heaven.

> Ning Feng Zi was a man who lived in the time of Huangdi. According to tradition, he was Huangdi's master potter. A spirit came to visit him and took over his fire. This genie was able to produce smoke in five colors. After some time, he taught his art to Ning Feng Zi, who built a pyre and set himself afire; following the billows of smoke, he rose and came down. When they examined his ashes, they found his bones.

The *Yunji Qiqian*, an important Daoist encyclopaedia, refers to this biography of the *Liexian zhuan* as an example of "deliverance by fire" (*huojie*), but originally it must have been about the sacrifice of the potter. As in the case of the Red Pine, it is a matter of something more than a simple *huojie*, even from the Daoist viewpoint: the column of five-colored smoke forms a road on which the Daoist climbs up and down.

> Rong Chen Gong presented himself as the teacher of Huangdi . . . He knew perfectly the technique of "repairing and leading." He used to draw up the essence in the "mysterious female." His principle was that "the living spirits that reside in the valley do not die," for this is how life and breath are sustained. His hair, once white, became black again, his teeth, which had fallen out, grew back. His techniques were identical to those of Laozi. He is also said to have been Laozi's teacher.

This mythical Daoist was famous for his sexual prescriptions for longevity. The expression "repair and lead" is one of those that designate these practices. The sentence "the living spirits that reside in the valley do not die" is taken from a famous passage in the *Daode Jing* (chapter 6) in which it refers to the universe, whereas here it refers to the microcosm with a precise physiological meaning having to do with the same sexual practices.

M.K./g.h.

BIBLIOGRAPHY

H. MASPERO, *Mélanges posthumes*, vols. 1–2; *Le taoïsme et les religions chinoises*. M. KALTENMARK, *Le Lie-sien tchouan*, translated and annotated (Beijing 1953). K. SCHIPPER, *L'empereur Wou des Han dans la légende taoïste* (Paris 1965). A. SEIDEL, *La divinisation de Lao tseu dans le taoïsme des Han* (Paris 1969).

Remarks on Japanese Religions and Mythological Beliefs

These introductory remarks will briefly summarize the major currents of Japanese religious history and provide a framework for what is treated in detail in other articles. We have identified eight major themes, which are treated in eleven articles of varying length. Here we will present some ideas and some important entities in the Japanese pantheon which in other works have often been examined too briefly or even neglected. We have not taken up questions already presented in current works, even if we could have treated them in a different or improved form. Instead, we refer the reader to the bibliography that concludes this article.

We will examine some basic concepts of the religious and mythic universe of Japan, and these in detail. The choice is necessarily subjective and includes the following: *tama* ("the vital or sensory spirit"), an idea that is certainly older than that of the *kami* ("deities"), whether these were personified or not. The *kami* will be presented in connection with the Buddhist divinities and the theory called *honji suijaku* ("state, original body" = the Buddha; and "descended trace" or "temporal manifestation" = Shinto deities, *kami*). An examination of the other world, although the subject of a separate article, is closely tied to the worship of mountains, which occupy a very important place in Japanese religious thought. The mountains, inasmuch as they represent the other world, are not only the kingdom of the dead, of the spirits of the ancestors, but are also the site of asceticism and the training of magicians. As a representative example of these shamanic magicians, if a highly complex one, we will use En no Gyōja, the semihistorical founder of mountain asceticism. But mountains are also very often associated with the world of demons; we will use as one example the concept of the *tengu*—both in general and in relation to the mountain ascetics called *yamabushi*. Finally, mountains and the mountain god play a major role in many festivals and seasonal rites; we will in particular evoke the rites of *bon* ("the festival of the dead") and of the New Year.

The bibliographies that follow each article are not exhaustive. They merely suggest certain works—in Japanese and in Western languages—which will allow readers to pursue more deeply the questions that have been raised. Under the heading of *Sources* are books which offer basic materials. *Monographs* include works entirely or principally devoted to the subject treated in the article. Finally, there are *articles* from periodicals. *Miscellaneous* brings together works which, although very useful, treat the problem addressed only in passing. At the beginning of each section are works in Western languages, but this is merely for convenience.

1. Archaeology

Many centuries before the arrival of Buddhism, the religious universe of Japan was marked by a number of notions to which the name of Shinto ("the way of the *kami*") was later given. Our knowledge of these religious notions from the earliest period of Japanese culture comes largely from archaeologists and their hypotheses. The Jōmon period (named from pottery designs made with strings) is characterized by clay statues (*dogū*) and polished stone cylinders (called *sekibō*), which have been found among piles of shells. The interpretation of the *dogū*—which often represent pregnant women—is not easy. They have often been connected with generative powers and fertility cults; other statues, whose limbs are broken, are supposed to represent wounds or diseases, which were magically transferred to the figurines. The *sekibō* are usually connected with phallic cults or interpreted as signs of authority. From the following period, the Yayoi period (named after a district in Tokyo where excavations were carried out), the famous *dōtaku*, bronze bells, have particularly captured the attention of historians, especially the bells without clappers: an enigma still far from clear. Enigmatic as well are the *magatama*, jewels in the curved shape of a comma, which date from the time of the Kofun (or the time of the "tombs"); they must have been used during outdoor prayers and ceremonies for fertility or a good crop. The presence of boats in the tombs may testify to a belief that the dead (or their souls) used a ship to reach the beyond on the other side of the sea.

2. Written Sources

The first literary sources about the life and religious concepts of the Japanese are found in the Chinese chronicles,

Sacred tree and small shrine. CERTPJ photo archive. Photo R. Stein.

notably the *Weishi* ("Chronicle of the Wei," from the end of the third century). They tell us, among other things, that divination and tattooing were once in vogue in Japan, during the reign of a queen named Himiko, who was devoted to magic and had the power to bewitch.

On the Japanese side the earliest sources date from the eighth century: the *Kojiki* (The record of ancient matters, 720), the *Nihongi* (Chronicle of Japan, 720), the *Fudoki* (Notes on the customs and provinces, middle of the eighth century), and the *Man'yōshū* (The collection of ten thousand leaves, the oldest anthology of Japanese poetry, eighth century). But these sources may go back to the sixth century for part of their contents. They are thus the foundation for all research on ancient Japanese beliefs. The order to compile the *Kojiki* was given by the Emperor Temmu (at the end of the seventh century) in the hope of assembling the oral texts and traditions of earlier epochs. Redacted from a point of view that was above all political, this work, a selection drawn from the mass of existing legends, is nevertheless a very precious source for knowledge of the customs and religious and mythic ideas of the ancient Japanese. The *Nihongi* (also called the *Nikon shoki*), completed eight years after the *Kojiki*, reveals more Chinese influence. The influence is expressed, for example, in the attempt to systematize dates on the model of Chinese chronology. Like the *Kojiki*, the *Nihongi* is based on lost works; it differs from the earlier work, however, in bringing together many more materials. From these a specific version of a myth or legend is chosen, and the others, valuable as variants, are preserved only as its "different versions." The *Fudoki* contain mainly local legends, notes on place names, and the like.

3. Mythology

In their first parts, the *Kojiki* and the *Nihongi* narrate the events of the "age of divinities" (*kamiyo*), which begins with the divine creative couple, Izanagi and Izanami. From their descendants were born Amaterasu, the sun goddess, and her brother, Susano-o. Amaterasu reigned on the high celestial plain (*Takama ga hara*), Susano-o, exiled, on the earth. From him was born the divinity Okuninushi, who ruled the land of Izumo. This *kami* finally ceded his power to Ninigi, the grandson of Amaterasu, who from then on governed the "land of the eight great islands." From Kyūshū, where Ninigi had descended, Jimmu Tennō, according to the *Kojiki* and *Nihongi*, would lead his clan toward Yamato to become the first emperor of Japan.

The sources cited above are particularly rich in information about the divinities called *kami*, forces and phenomena of nature, such as trees, animals, mountains, and the like. Strongly impregnated with magic and with animistic notions, this religion of nature did not have a well-structured pantheon; it is only when a strong clan came into power that the diverse divinities venerated by the others were grouped around Amaterasu, the sun goddess.

4. Buddhism: From Its Introduction to the Nara Period (Sixth to Eighth Centuries)

The introduction of Buddhism became the object of a controversy among several great families: on the one hand, the Mononobe and the Nakatomi, who since ancient times were in charge of the cult of the *kami*; and on the other, the Soga, who controlled the administration, finances, and so forth. A principal reason behind the receptive attitude of the Soga was a concern to assure profits and other "immediate advantages" (*genze riyaku*), which they thought this prestigious religion could give them—especially in curing illnesses. By contrast, the Mononobe, responsible for the cult of the *kami*, feared the anger and curse of their divinities.

Although the Soga eventually triumphed over their political and religious adversaries, and consequently Buddhism was favorably accepted, on the whole, and could implant itself in Japan, we should not forget the lasting opposition to the new religion, as well as to foreign influence; such a resistance was also observable in literature. Thus the first great anthology of Japanese poetry, the *Man'yōshū*, presents only very weak and sporadic traces of Buddhism (cf., for example, poems 345, 348, and 351, or even 3849 and 3850, which sing of the instability of the world). One might ask if the paucity of explicit references to Buddhism in the *Man'yōshū* is not explained by the fact that this religion was then the concern of the state, which offered it favor from above, while it was still little understood or accepted by the people. Although the nobility with the necessary financial means was charged at the beginning with the construction of sacred edifices and the organization of the rites, it was the state that, during the time of the Emperor Shomu (the first half of the eighth century), favored the expansion of the new religion into the provinces, through the construction of sanctuaries called *kokubunji*.

5. The State Buddhism of the Nara Period (Eighth Century)

The expansion of Buddhism was reinforced by the diffusion of two sutras (the *Konkō myō-kyō* and the *Ninnō-kyō*), both of which were by their very contents qualified to serve as a protection for the state. Many monks, civil servants in practice, were sent to study in China. Research on Buddhism was carried on within diverse schools, often brought together in a single monastery. Nara Buddhism thus merits the two epithets frequently attributed to it: *gokoku bukkyō* (Buddhism destined for the protection of the state) and *gakumon bukkyō* (Buddhism as an object of study). Yet for all this, Buddhism did not entirely lack popular dissemination, as is proved by the first collection of Buddhist anecdotes (*setsuwa*), the *Nihon Ryōiki* (Collection of miraculous and strange stories of Japan, from the beginning of the ninth century). In addition to its importance for the knowledge of Japanese life of the time, the *Nihon Ryōiki* is valuable for its presentation, with innumerable variants, of a concept predominant at that time—the Karmic retribution for deeds (*inga*).

Sacred tree encircled with the ritual cord, the *shimenawa*. Sumiyoshi shrine, Osaka. CERTPJ photo archive. Photo L. Frédéric.

6. Esotericism

Two new sects were transplanted to Japan at the beginning of the ninth century, Tendai and Shingon. The basic teaching of Tendai is that all beings are essentially "Buddha" (have the "Buddha nature"). From the point of view of this doctrine the most important sutra is the *Hokekyō* (the Lotus Sutra), whose teaching, for the Tendai sect, constitutes the supreme word of Shākyamuni the Buddha; everything else that he had preached was merely preparatory.

It is fitting to mention briefly here esoteric Buddhism, or *mikkyō,* a term that must be understood in opposition to *kengyō,* the "open doctrines," which are easy to understand. *Kengyō* is what the Buddha Shākyamuni has explained, but *mikkyō* was preached by the Buddha Dainichi Nyorai. The first contacts with the teachings and conceptions of *mikkyō* go back to the Nara period; it is only at the beginning of the Heian period, however, that these doctrines were presented in systematic fashion, by the Shingon sect. Shingon identified the whole world with the Buddha Dainichi Nyorai, who represents the metaphysical body (*hosshin*) of the universe. The illusory body of phenomena is purely and simply identical to the ultimate reality (*sokuji ni shin*); man may, with the help of mantras (Japanese: *shingon,* "magic formulas") and meditation, attain illumination and unite instantaneously with the Buddha (*sokushin jōbutsu*). Alongside very difficult and complex philosophical speculations, Shingon has also elaborated a detailed system of practical magic. During the Heian period, the two sects, Tendai and Shingon, rivaled one another in magical rites and exorcism at court and throughout society. Shingon elaborates the concept of the "three mysteries" (*san mitsu*), which lead to shelter from all danger and unification with the Buddha in a mysterious way—through thought, word, and acts; it has thus given birth to many rites, whose most important aspects are the formation of "seals" or gestures with the fingers (*in*) and the recitation of incantory formulas (*shingon*).

Legends soon multiplied around the Japanese founder of Shingon. According to the best-known legend, Kōbō Daishi, in a position of *samādhi* (*samai*) in his tomb in *Oko no in* on Mount Kōya, awaited the arrival of the future Buddha, Miroku (for literary traces of this belief, see songs 234 and 295 of the *Ryōjin hishō,* from the twelfth century). In the ancient traditions about mountains (*sangaku shinkō*), Mount Kōya was associated in the tenth century with the idea of *jōdo,* the "pure land." People go to this mountain on pilgrimage to purify themselves; the dead are also buried there. Beliefs and customs connected with Kōya were spread by monks called (*Kōya hijiri,* or "holy men of Mount Kōya."

7. The "Pure Land" and *Nembutsu*

Among the contributions of Buddhism to the religious thought of Japan, an important place should be given to the ideas of *gokuraku* ("paradise") and *jigoku* ("hell"). Beliefs connected with *jōdo* (the "pure land") go back to the Nara period. During the next period, the Heian, *nembutsu sanmai* was practiced on Mount Hiei; this consisted in repeating the name of Amida Buddha for ninety days in a building especially constructed for that purpose, the *jōgyō sanmai do.* Later, the *nembutsu* was interpreted as a way of achieving salvation, for Amida had once made a vow (*hongan*) to save every being who put confidence in him and invoked his name. The illustrious monk Genshin (942–1017) set forth the doctrine of *jōdo* and *ōjō* ("to become reborn in Amida's paradise") in his book *Ōjōyōshū* (The essentials for rebirth in the pure land, 984); there he depicts in full both hell and the paradise of the west, where Amida reigns. The *nembutsu* of Genshin is still rather meditative, and it is not until Hōnen (1133–1212)—after Genshin the true founder of Japanese Amidism—that the accent is put on the repetition of the name of Amida. With this type of *nembutsu,* Hōnen made access to Buddhist doctrine much easier; he opened up an "easy path" (*igyō*), a path to salvation accessible to everyone. A disciple of Hōnen, Shinran (1173–1262), the founder of the *Jōdo Shinshū* ("the true sect of pure land"), took this faith in the force of *nembutsu* a step further. If all really depends on the grace of Amida, which transcends man (*tariki,* the "force of the other"), anything else is useless for making merit. Even the repetition of the name of Amida becomes useless; it is enough to have pronounced it only once. Shinran thus rejects the final attachment to *jiriki* (or "one's own power"), a trace of which is still maintained in the concern to assure the *ōjō* in Amida's paradise securely for oneself through the effort of repetition in the *nembutsu.* These ideas of Shinran are set forth in the famous *Tannishō* (Treatise deploring heresies), compiled by one of his disciples after his death. Finally, the founder of the Jishū tradition, the monk Ippen (1239–89), propagated a form of *nembutsu* with song and dance; Ippen's thought reveals a highly syncretistic tendency.

8. The Middle Ages (Twelfth to Sixteenth Centuries)

Two notions characterize the Middle Ages, *mujō,* the instability of all things in an ephemeral world, and *mappō,* the decline of the Buddhist law. This notion of "decline," the third phase in the period since the death of the Buddha Shākyamuni, was known in China since the sixth century. It was taken up in Japan by certain Nara sects, and later by Saichō and Kūkai, the founders of the Tendai and Shingon sects. On the one hand, the concept of *mujō* inspires a need to leave the world; on the other, the concept of *mappō* facilitates access to the "easy way" propagated by Jōdo Buddhism.

9. The Edo Period (Seventeenth to Nineteenth Centuries)

The Tokugawa government, which tended to favor Buddhism as a state religion, exercised strict control over all aspects of religious life, in particular, obliging each family to belong to a temple. The sanctuaries adapted very quickly to this rule, which, among other advantages, assured them of regular revenues. Moreover, the already popular customs of *kaichō* (the exhibition of the treasures and icons of the temples) and *tomitsuki* (lotteries) guaranteed them respectable profits. But though the number of sanctuaries increased, spiritual and religious life was in decline. Buddhism and the general state of religion were severely criticized by Confucians who initiated a sort of anti-Buddhism. In the pilgrimage traditions of the medieval period, the *o-kage-mairi* to Ise answered to the religious aspirations of the people while at the same time satisfying a certain taste for travel among them. The *o-kage-mairi* helped to maintain the popular fervor for Shinto at a time when Buddhism enjoyed the protection of the state. The interest in Shinto, which from the Heian period remained alive in close connection with Buddhism, was stimulated on the one hand by the philological and literary researches of the *kokugaku* ("national studies") movement, and on the other by popular sermons, called *shintō kōshaku.*

A characteristic trait of the period is resort to magic to cure disease or to assure divine favor. *Shugendō,* Daoism, and esoteric Buddhism kept for the use of their congregation magic formulas which could banish evil and assure advantages. Tokugawa policy had particularly affected the *yamabushi,* the representatives of the Shinto-Buddhist syncretism known as *Shugendō.* And so these *yamabushi,* deprived of part of their resources, specialized even more in magical operations (*majinai*) and divination (*uranai*).

10. The Meiji Period (1868–1912)

In restoring to the emperor his ancient authority and earlier functions, the Meiji reform made him an absolute sovereign and even recognized his sanctity as a descendant of the sun goddess Amaterasu. In instigating a quasi-divine veneration of the sovereign and favoring the principle of *saisei-itchi* ("union of church and state"), the reformers were also pursuing an anti-Buddhist policy (*haibutsu kishaku*) and trying to purify Shinto, the national religion, from everything foreign, that is, Buddhist. Alongside official Shinto (the "Shinto of the sanctuaries"), which was something of an ethnocentric ideology, a religious Shinto was also tolerated. The latter was known as the "Shinto of the sects," and under this label a great number of groups and beliefs burgeoned, including the first of the "new religions" (such as Tenri-kyō, Kurozumi-kyō, and Konkō-kyō).

H.O.R./d.g.

BIBLIOGRAPHY

1. Sources

W. G. ASTON, *Nihongi: Chronicles of Japan from the Earliest Time to A.D. 697* (reprinted London 1956). B. H. CHAMBERLAIN, *Kojiki or Records of Ancient Matters,* TASJ 10, supplement 1882. K. FLORENZ, *Nihongi Zeitalter der Götter,* MOAG supplement 1901; *Die historischen Quellen der Shintō-Religion* (Göttingen 1919). D. PHILIPPI, *Kojiki* (Tokyo 1968). M. SHIBATA, *Kojiki, chronique des chose anciennes* (Paris 1969). A. R. TSUNODA, *Japan in the Chinese Dynastic Histories* (South Pasadena, CA, 1951).

Additional sources: ALLAN ANDREWS, trans., *The Teachings Essential for Rebirth: A Study of Genshin's Ojōyōshū* (Tokyo 1973). YOSHITO S. HAKEDA, trans., *Kūkai: Major Works* (New York 1972). IAN H. LEVY, trans., *The Ten Thousand Leaves: A Translation of the Man'yōshū, Japan's Premier Anthology of Classical Poetry,* vol. 1 (Princeton 1981). *The Manyōshū: The Nippon Gakujutsu Shinkōkai Translation of One Thousand Poems* (New York 1965). KYOKO MOTOMOCHI NAKAMURA, trans., *Miraculous Stories from the Japanese Buddhist Tradition: The Nihon Ryōiki of the Monk Kyōkai* (Cambridge, MA, 1973).

2. Monographs

M. ANESAKI, *History of Japanese Religions* (Tokyo 1963); *Japanese Mythology: The Mythology of All Races,* 8 (Boston 1928). W. G. ASTON, *Shintō, the Way of the Gods* (London 1905). S. ELISSEEFF, "Mythologie du Japon," in *Mythologie asiatique illustrée* (Paris 1927). W. GUNDERT, *Japanische Religionsgeschichte* (Stuttgart 1943). CH. HAGUENAUER, *Origines de la civilisation japonaise: Introduction à l'étude de la préhistoire du Japon,* part 1 (Paris 1956). G. KATŌ, *Le Shintō* (Paris 1931). J. E. KIDDER, *Japan before Buddhism* (London 1959). J. KITAGAWA, *Religion in Japanese History* (New York 1966). FR. K. NUMAZAWA, *Die Weltanfänge in der Japanischen Mythologie* (Freiburg, Switzerland, 1946). D. SAUNDERS, "Japanese Mythology," in *Mythologies of the Ancient World* (Garden City, NY, 1961). STEINILBER-OBERLIN/MATSUOKA, *Les sectes bouddhiques japonaises* (Paris 1930). R. TAJIMA, *Les deux grands mandalas et la doctrine de l'ésotérisme Shingon* (Tokyo and Paris 1959). M. W. DE VISSER, *Ancient Buddhism in Japan,* 2 vols. (Leiden 1935). S. HISAMATSU, *Kodai shiika ni okeru kami no gaisetsu* (Tokyo 1941). KANASAKI/KASAHARA, *Shūkyō-shi: Taikei Nihon shi sōsho* 18 (Tokyo 1969). T. MATSUMURA, *Nihon shinwa no kenkyū*, 4 vols. (Tokyo 1955–58). T. OBAYASHI, *Nihon shinwa no kigen* (Tokyo 1964); *Nihon shinwa no kōzō* (Tokyo 1975). S. TSUDA, *Nihon no shintō*, Tsuda Sōkichi zenshū 9 (Tokyo 1964).

Additional monographs: RICHARD M. DORSON, ed., *Studies in Japanese Folklore* (New York 1980). H. BYRON EARHART, *Japanese Religion: Unity and Diversity* (3d ed., Belmont, CA, 1982). GARY L. EBERSOLE, *Ritual Poetry and the Politics of Death in Early Japan* (Princeton 1989). ROBERT S. ELLWOOD, *The Feast of Kingship: Accession Ceremonies in Ancient Japan* (Tokyo 1973). JOSEPH M. KITAGAWA, *Understanding Japanese Religion* (Princeton 1988). MINORU KIYOTA, *Shingon Buddhism: Theory and Practice* (Los Angeles 1978). JIN'ICHI KONISHI, *A History of Japanese Literature*, vol. 1: *The Archaic and Ancient Ages* (Princeton 1986). FANNY HAGIN MAYER, *Ancient Tales in Modern Japan* (Bloomington, IN, 1985).

3. Articles

R. BEARDSLEY, "Japan before History: A Survey of the Archeological Record," *Far Eastern Quarterly* 19, 3 (1955). D. C. HOLTOM, "The Meaning of Kami," *MN* 3–4 (1940–41). J. KITAGAWA, "The Buddhist Transformation in Japan," *History of Religions* 4, 2 (1965); "Prehistoric Background of Japanese Religion," *History of Religions* 2, 2 (1963). R. PEARSON, "The Contribution of Archeology to Japanese Studies," *Journal of Japanese Studies* 2, 2 (1976). H. O. ROTERMUND, "Les croyances du Japon antique," in *Encyclopédie de la Pléiade, Histoire des Religions* 1 (Paris 1970).

Additional articles: ICHIRO HORI, "Japanese Folk-Beliefs," *American Anthropologist* 61 (June 1955): 404–24. ALAN L. MILLER, "*Ame No Miso-Ori Me* (The Heavenly Weaving Maiden): The Cosmic Weaver in Early Shinto Myth and Ritual," *History of Religions* 24, 1 (August 1984): 27–48. TARYO OBAYASHI, "The Structure of the Pantheon and the Concept of Sin in Ancient Japan," *Diogenes* 98 (Summer 1977): 117–32; "The Origins of Japanese Mythology," *Acta Asiatica* 31 (1977): 1–23.

4. Miscellany

D. SAUNDERS, *Mudra: A Study of Symbolic Gestures in Japanese Buddhist Iconography* (New York 1960). M. ANZU, *Shintō shisō ron-sō* (Tokyo 1972). R. SAWA, *Butsuzō zuten* (Tokyo 1962). SHINTŌ BUNKA KAI, ed., *Sengo shintō ronbun senshū* (Tokyo 1973). M. TAKAZAKI, *Bungaku izen* (Tokyo 1967). Y. TAKEDA, *Kami to kami wo matsuru mono to no bungaku* (Tokyo 1940).

The Vital Spirit and the Soul in Japan

Tama, which is ordinarily translated as "soul," is closer to "vital spirit": from a functional viewpoint, *tama* designates the forces that are felt behind every phenomenon, somewhat like *mana*, though the two should not be identified. Although they are attached to objects or bodies, these vital or sensory forces have the ability to distance themselves from them, to move freely, and are thus transferable. But *tama* also designated more impersonal forces, especially the *kotodama* (the power inherent in words). The conception derives from the conviction that pronouncing a name (the importance of which is stressed by the name of *zumon uta* that the *Fukuro sōshi* gives to "magical poems") enables one to obtain what one desires by virtue of the power inherent in the words. This "spirit of words" may be used for good as well as for evil, for personal gain as well as for the harm that one may inflict upon others.

The best-known example of this double character in ancient times is that of the *norito*, "the chanted prayers," which may originally have been the words of a deity, or words which were spoken to it by a man. Speaking of auspicious things, it was thought, made them become real, and the same was true of inauspicious words and things. A classical example—outside of the sphere of the *norito*—attesting to the capacity of certain words to harm, like a malediction, is the episode of the lost fishhook, as related in the *Kojiki*. The fact that certain words are placed under a taboo, and that in their place *imikotoba* are used ("taboo words," to which the earliest references are already found in the *Nihongi*), is also a result of the vast sphere encompassed by the concept of *kotodama*. The earliest examples of the term are to be found in the *Man'yōshū* (nos. 894, 2506, 3254). The phenomenon was from the start very closely associated with beliefs about the *kami*, whose words were transmitted and revealed by Shinto priests or the ruler. Over the centuries, this close—and above all religious—connection was lost, and *kotodama* came to operate without restriction and independent of the individual: anyone could invoke them, since it was in the words themselves, which were still held to be divine, that the authority of the *kami* resided. At still another stage in the history of the notion of *kotodama*, the efficacy was attributed to language in general, and its divine origin was forgotten.

Analogous to the concept of *kotodama* is that of *kotoage*, "raising the voice" (see, for example, *Man'yōshū*, nos. 3253, 4124) to speak to the deities. More precisely, it is the *kotoage* that brings the *kotodama* into play. A poorly executed *kotoage* is immediately followed by divine punishment, as, for example, in the *Kojiki* and the *Genji-monogatari*. The *Kojiki* relates that the hero Yamato-takeru (son of Emperor Keikō) met, near Mount Ibuki, the messenger of the deity of that mountain—a white boar—whom he intended to kill upon his return from the summit. At that point the deity caused it to hail so heavily that Yamato-takeru fainted, which one gloss of the *Kojiki* explains as a result of his sacrilegious *kotoage*. The *Genji-monogatari*, in the "Suma" chapter, tells how Prince Genji, exiled from the court for his carnal relations with his stepmother, observed a ritual of purification (*harae*) at Suma on the seashore, addressing himself at that time to the *kami* to tell them that he had not been conscious of having done any evil—and from this improper *kotoage* a storm arose.

We will enumerate here some examples of the act of *kotodama*, among many in the literature. The *Kojiki* contains a poem about the deity Okuninushi who is trying to appease the jealousy of his wife, Suseri-hime, at the time of his departure to the land of Izumo; the answer of Suseri-hime, which is also a poem, and especially the accounts that follow, reveal that the jealousy and anger of the goddess have in fact been dissipated. Elsewhere, a girl who had negligently given the sovereign (Yūryako Tennō) a cup of sake into which a leaf from a tree had fallen assuages his anger with a poem that eulogizes the palace and the empire (and thus the sovereign himself). Finally we cite the *Kojiki*, which contains the myth of Ame-no-waka-hiko, one of the deities sent to Japan to govern it. Upon his death, caused by an arrow fallen from the sky, a divine friend, Ajisuki-takahikone, comes to offer his condolences. When he is seen approaching, with his appearance so like that of the dead man, it is thought that the latter has been resuscitated by lamentations and by songs and dances. In his anger at having been taken for someone who was dead and also out of fear of the defilement that any association with death carries, Ajisuki-takahikone destroys the mortuary hut before departing. The poem that Taka-hime, the wife of the dead deity, then recites to calm his anger clearly brings out the importance attached to the utterance of the proper name of the god. The same magical pacification of the *tama* (*chinkon*) appears in cases of sickness and death. The *Nihongi,* in the twenty-first year of the reign of the Empress Suiko (613), describes the meeting of Prince Shōtoku (574–622, son of Emperor Yômei) with a starving mendicant. Shōtoku restores him by means of a poem and furnishes him with food and clothing (see also poems nos. 415 and 3020 of the *Man'yōshū*). When the mendicant dies, his corpse is placed in a tomb, but—is it to mark his supernatural origin?—he disappears from it shortly thereafter. A well-known poem of the poet Kakinomoto Hitomaru (late seventh century) is addressed to a dead person whom he encounters while walking (*Man'yōshū,* no. 220). The *Fukuro sōshi,* from the Heian period, mentioned a poem which protects anyone who meets a corpse. A fairly plausible explanation for these practices is that in ancient times when one accidentally came into contact with sick people or especially with the corpse of a person who had died while traveling, one performed a sort of *tamafuri* ("shaking of the *tama*") to give the sick body new *tama*—which are, as has been noted, transferable—in order to comfort and reanimate it; or to pacify the spirit of the dead which wanders without rest and is thus dangerous. The *Tsurayuki-shū* anthology presents one of the best examples of the use of a poem as an offering. The poet Ki no Tsurayuki (868?–945?) travels on horseback south of Osaka; suddenly his horse stops moving. The people explain to him that the deity Aridōshi Myōjin dwells there and is surely full of wrath against Tsurayuki for passing without making an offering to him. The poem that Tsurayuki composes at their suggestion calms the *kami,* especially through the evocation of his name. The offering of a poem is an offering of the forces of *tama* that it contains and that its recitation has liberated. An analogous idea appears in certain poems of the *Man'yōshū* (nos. 141, 1230) in which a person ensures for himself the favor of a god by evoking his name in a place name.

Related to the offering of *tama* through a recitation (which sometimes accompanies an offering) is the magical action of "knotting" (*musubi*) together grasses and branches in order to make an offering to a deity of its own *tama,* or (the distinction is a difficult one to make) to bind up a malevolent spirit. This is especially practiced by travelers, particularly upon passing through a crossroads or a mountain pass. The generally accepted etymology for the word that means pass, *tōge,* i.e., the contraction of *ta-muke* ("turning the hand"—in a movement of offering?), does not contradict this, no more than does the popular depiction of a dreaded *kami,* Sodemogisama, the "lord who tears off the sleeves." He is one of the great number of deities of passes, roads, and crossroads, who demand from those who pass before their abodes certain pieces of clothing (or the *tama* in them), failing which they are thrown to the ground and a piece of their sleeve is torn off (see also poem no. 421 of the *Kokinshū,* 905). It should be noted that the earliest offerings made to the *kami*—the *nusa*—were of cloth, which was later replaced with paper.

The *Unkin zuihitsu* (1861) tells the legend of Gyōgi *bosatsu,* who meets a merchant who has loaded his horse with mackerel for the market. When the monk finds that he has been refused even a single fish as alms, he recites a poem that makes the horse sick. When he realizes with whom he is dealing, the merchant makes amends and Gyōgi undoes the charm by modifying a word of the poem, which changes a negation into an affirmation. Numerous legends about a monk and a merchant are current in Japan. Their religious foundation seems to be the distant reflection of an ancient form of veneration of the deities of crossroads, passes, major roads, and various routes.

To return to the term *musubi,* certain poems of the *Man'yōshū* (nos. 10 and 141) attest the custom, which was alive in antiquity, of ensuring the safety of moving to a different place by the act of tying together branches or blades of grass. And many texts speak of an analogous action consisting of making a knot in the cord of one's garment (see *Man'yōshū,* no. 251). This is a case of "fixing the *tama*" (*tama musubi*), hindering them from circulating freely (see the legend of Urashima Tarō, and passages in the *Genji monogatari,* the *Ise-monogatari,* story no. 110, or poem 763 of the *Man'yōshū*). For greater security during a journey, one may fix these *tama* to something, for instance, in poem 251 of the *Man'yōshū,* to the husband's clothes when he leaves on a journey, to ensure that he returns safe and sound—since the *tama* tend to return to the vital spirits from which they depart. To undo the knot means, reciprocally, to grant leave to the *tama* and to break with their bearer (*Man'yōshū* no. 3427).

To conclude this survey of the use of *waka* (poems) as offerings, let us look at the presentation to the sovereign of *kuniburi* songs, or "songs of the provinces" (*kuni tamafuri?*), at the time of the Oname matsuri. At the time of this festival the newly enthroned ruler addresses himself for the first time to the *kami,* and the *miko* (female shamans) of various provinces offer these songs, the aim of which is to cause the *tama* of the local deities, who are captured in the different provincial toponyms, to enter the body of the emperor, whose well-being and strength one wishes to ensure, while demonstrating their submission and loyalty.

The Japanese poem is also the magical means of gaining divine assistance. Thus poem 40 of the *Kojiki* transformed, through speech, the sake that Jingū Kōgō offered to her son Ojin Tennō, on his return from Yamato, into a sake prepared by the deity Sukunabikona ("the master of medicines," who "rises like a crag in the land of the world beyond [*tokoyo*]"); into *sake,* the poem continues, that the god had sanctified and blessed and carried from the other world. Sukunabikona, coming from beyond the sea to Izumo, will aid Okuninushi to reign over Japan and to heal diseases. According to other passages in the same text, this *tama* spirit in the form of a visiting deity (*marebito*) is a kind of alter ego of Okuninushi, who comes from the other world at certain times of the year to bring good fortune and, in particular, a rich harvest. Both Okuninushi and Sukunabikona are considered to be *ishigami* ("deities of stone") and protectors against disease. The invocation of the name of the deity (see above) is supposed to bring his intercession in the presentation of sake; in the same way, certain terms, associated in the poem with the act of blessing, of sanctifying—terms interpreted as designating gestures or dances accompanying the preparation of sake (see also no. 41 in the *Kojiki*)—translate the idea of a transfer of *tama,* freed by motion and by the word, into the sake. A similar belief in the possibility of the transfer of *tama* may also be derived from the myth of the sun goddess Amaterasu in the celestial cave.

A few characteristic elements are inherent in the notion of *tamafuri* (the magical act of shaking the *tama*) already mentioned. The *tamafuri,* or *mi-tamafuri* when one is speaking of the emperor (see *Nihongi,* 24th day, 11th month, 14th year Temmu), is a magical act intended to reinforce or pacify the vital spirits, the *tama.* These dwell in objects as well as in the human body, influencing the physical condition of humans by their growth or diminution.

At one extreme, the deficiency in *tama* necessarily results in death. Thus, for the ancient Japanese, life and death were defined by a greater or lesser supply of *tama,* which was considered essentially the same in man and in nature and in certain objects (such as swords, jewels, and branches of the sacred tree called *sakaki*). Passages in both the *Kojiki* and *Nihongi* chronicles that speak of an offering of swords or jewels to the emperor may be read in the light of a magic rite consisting of offering through such objects the powers that they contain, in order to increase the sovereign's supply of *tama.* The passage of the *Nihongi* (24th day, 11th month, 14th year Temmu) cited above, that speaks—without giving details—of an act of *mi-tamafuri* performed for the benefit of the emperor, is also revealing. The two Chinese characters ("recalling of souls") in which the *Nihongi* gives this reading of *mi-tamafuri* show that, in China at least, funerary practices were at the foundation of the ritual, but this was not necessarily the case in the Japanese context; probably these rituals aimed at restoring the *tama* of the emperor (who does not die until some time thereafter).

The fact that the emperor was weakened, if not sick, and the date on which the ritual mentioned in the *Nihongi* was performed may give some information as to its probable meaning. The date is that of a festival that the imperial court would later observe under the name of *chinkonsai* ("festival of the pacification of the souls"), also called *tamashizume* ("to pacify the spirits") or *tamafuri-* ("shaking the *tama*") *matsuri,* a term that indicates the complex character of the rite. Its central element is, according to the *Ryō no gige,* the concern to comfort the *tama* (vitality) of the emperor. The performance of the *chinkonsai* coincides with the time of the winter solstice (the moment when nature is at its lowest level of strength and vitality) and seems clearly to indicate a magical ritual of consolation.

Principally undertaken by the *miko* (shamans called Sarume), the magical acts of the *chinkonsai* strikingly resemble the one that is described in the myth of the withdrawal of the sun goddess Amaterasu into the celestial cave. And since no Uzume, the shamaness of the myth, is regarded as the ancestor of the Sarume, mythologists tend to see in this story of Amaterasu and Uzume a sort of etiological myth about what would later become the *chinkonsai,* bringing together elements of magic through acts (dance) and verbal magic (songs: *chinkon-ka*).

When the goddess withdraws into the cave after the sacrilegious acts committed by her brother Susano-o, the world is plunged into darkness. The other deities, anxious to bring the wrathful goddess out, perform a divination, placing before the entrance to the cave a sacred tree (*sakaki*) to which they attach mirrors, curved jewels (*magatama*), pieces of cloth, etc.; and they recite *noritos.* The crucial element, nevertheless, is the dance executed by the goddess Ame no Uzume, which arouses the curiosity of Amaterasu to such a degree that she finally comes out of the cave. Starting from this dance, which is described as violent and lascivious, it may be possible to attempt a kind of synthesis of the different interpretations given to the myth (as an etiological myth of the *chinkonsai,* as a magical practice aimed at driving away the eclipse of the sun, as a funerary rite, etc.) by viewing it as an act with the character of a *tamafuri,* i.e., an act destined to remedy a decrease of vital forces, of nature and of man, if not to give new impulse to a declining sun. Although we are tempted to conclude that this is a myth about the eclipse of the sun, with practices analogous to those observed among numerous other peoples (dance and noise accompanying the driving out of evil spirits), the dance that we also encounter at the time of funeral ceremonies might lead us to explain the myth in connection with funerals. The funerary aspect of the myth might also be read in the allusion the text makes to the "door of the celestial cave" which scholars have associated with the stones placed at the entrance to a tomb (*kofun*). Other significant terms (*iwagakuru:* to hide in the cave of a cliff; cf. the *norito* of the "Appeasement of Fire," in the death of Izanami; or, as in poem 418 of the *Man'yōshū, iwatate:* to erect a stone = close the entrance to a tomb?) may indicate that as early as the seventh and eighth centuries the myth of Amaterasu was supposed to reflect an ancient funerary rite.

We have passed in review several important elements, including the extremely complex concept of *tama,* especially in its impersonal aspect, as expressed by the idea of *kotodama.* A final question should be posed in this context: what happens to the *tama,* particularly those of humans, after they have left the body, i.e., after death? We have said that the *tama* could move freely, that they were transferable, etc. It must be added that they are, depending on the situation, visible or invisible, as is evident from the story about Sukunabikona (see above). If they take a form, it is usually that of a bird (see song 35 of the *Kojiki,* which speaks of the death of the hero Yamato-takeru), or—as poem 148 of the *Man'yōshū* seems to suggest—of clouds.

The story of Prince Homutsu-wake (*Nihongi* 8th day, 10th month, 23rd year of Emperor Suinin) brings together clearly the principal characteristics of the *tama:* the possibility of increasing their mass through contact and/or addition, their transferability, and their transformation into a bird. The story of the *Nihongi* relates that at the moment when a swan—a vehicle of the *tama*—flew over the prince, although he was already thirty years old and still unable to speak, he finally gained the ability to express himself.

The story of Ōkuninushi and Sukunabikona also brings to light a final component of the concept of the *tama:* they come to men from beyond the sea, which seems to be confirmed by songs 71–73 of the *Kojiki.* These songs speak of a wild goose that laid its eggs in Japan; the emperor (Nintoku) demands an explanation for this phenomenon from the sage Takeuchi no Sukune, who explains it (in the form of *hogi-uta,* songs destined to bring happiness) as a favorable augury for a long reign by that sovereign. What is interesting is that this involves a wild goose, an aquatic bird that comes from Siberia to Japan over the sea; i.e., from beyond the sea, where the *tokoyo* world is situated. In this way the song of Takeuchi no Sukune quite clearly takes on the character of a magical act of the *tamafuri* type, based on the belief in vital and sensorial spirits and in the power inherent in words.

H.O.R./d.w.

BIBLIOGRAPHY

1. Monograph

G. EBERSOLE, *Ritual Poetry and the Politics of Death in Early Japan* (Princeton 1989).

2. Articles

CH. HAGUENAUER, "La danse rituelle dans la cérémonie du chinkonsai," *Journal asiatique* 216 (1930). H. O. ROTERMUND, "Les croyances du Japon antique," *Encyclopédie de la Pléiade, Histoire des religions* 1 (Paris 1970). I. HORI, "Waga kuni ni okeru reikon no kannen," *Nihon minzokugadu* 3. M. NISHITSUNOI, "Chinkon kashū toshite no Man'yōshū," *Minzoku bungaku kōza* 4, "kodai bungei to minzoku" (Tokyo 1960).

Additional articles: GARY L. EBERSOLE, "The Buddhist Ritual Use of Linked Poetry in Medieval Japan," *The Eastern Buddhist* n.s. 16, 2

(Autumn 1983): 50–71. TETSUO KURE, "Mogari no miya no genkei," *Kodai bungaku* 18 (1979): 48–54. NARIMITSU MATSUDAIRA, "The Concept of 'Tamashii' in Japan," in Richard M. Dorson, ed., *Studies in Japanese Folklore* (New York 1980), pp. 181–97. ITSUHIKO OHAMA, "Chinkon no fumi: Man'yo shiron," *Bungaku* 39, 9 (September 1971): 1–11. YUTAKA TSUCHIHASNI, "'Miru' koto no tamafuri-teki ishiki," *Man'yō* 39 (April 1961).

3. Miscellany

T. NISHIMURA, "Uta to minzokugaku," *Minzoku mingei sōsho* 6 (Tokyo 1960). M. NISHITSUNOI, *Kodai saishi to bungaku* (Tokyo 1967). Z. OTA, "Kodai Nihon bungaku shichō-ron I," *Hasshō shi no kōsatsu* (Tokyo 1967). T. SOKURA, "Nihon shiika no kigen ronsō," *Kōza Nihon bungaku no sōten* 1, Jōdai-hen (Tokyo 1969). M. TAKASAKI, "Koten to minzokugaku," *Hanawa sensho* 2 (Tokyo 1964). Y. TSUCHIHASHI, *Kodai kayō to girei no kenkyū* (Tokyo 1966).

JAPANESE CONCEPTIONS OF THE AFTERLIFE

I. Before Buddhism

It is very difficult to gain an idea of Japanese conceptions about the afterlife for the period before the first written Japanese documents.

During the period of Jōmon (4000–250 B.C.), the diversity of the modes of burial, while bearing witness to religious preoccupations, poses many problems. For instance, sepulchers have been found in which the skeleton was curled up, others in which it was stretched out, some in which stones were placed on the chest or the head. Does the fetal position, which has survived in the northwest of Japan, signify the return to the womb, or is it a precaution taken against the dead person? In addition, it might be asked if such diversity does not derive from differences in culture or social distinctions.

During the period of Yayoi (third century B.C.–third century A.D.), continental influences added another element to the preceding period's diversity of religious data. Certain archaeological discoveries indicate the existence of beliefs that are found in later periods. For example, in a tomb from the Osaka region, a wooden bird has been found which may have been attached to a baton. It may have been the image of the soul of the dead flying toward heaven, a flight comparable to the one described in the *Kojiki* in the passage on the death of the hero Yamato-takeru.

Beginning with the period of large *kofun* sepulchers (fourth to seventh century A.D.) the archaeological data may be correlated with the first written documents, which, though dating from the beginning of the eighth century, report earlier beliefs and practices.

1. The Myth of the Visit to Yomi No Kuni

Still, the problem remains complex. Although there are imposing funeral mounds such as the one attributed to Emperor Nintoku (312–399), the texts are very meager and often vague about beliefs in the afterlife or funeral practices. The only somewhat extended account in the earliest texts (*Kojiki, Nihongi*) is that of the visit paid by Izanagi to his wife Izanami in *yomi no kuni*.

In the *Kojiki* version, Izanami dies after giving birth to fire. Her husband Izanagi sets out to rejoin her in *yomi no kuni* in order to try to lead her back. But he arrives too late, for she has already eaten food cooked in the fire of *yomi no kuni*. Despite a prohibition, Izanagi lights a tooth of his comb and discovers the decomposed body of his wife. He flees, pursued by the furies, whom he holds off by throwing magical objects behind him. When he arrives at the limits of the country, *yomotsu hirasaka*, he closes the passage between the two worlds by rolling a giant stone across the entrance. Polluted by this visit, Izanagi goes to purify himself in the sea.

What does this account tell us of *yomi no kuni?* (1) It is an obscure place (the word *yomi* is formed from the same root, *yo*, as *yoru*, "night"; further, Izanagi had to light a torch in order to see his wife). (2) It is the land of impurity, symbolized by the decomposing corpse, contact with which brings pollution that requires purification. (3) There is a passage between the land of the dead and the world of the living, a passage closed by a boulder. (4) *Yomi no kuni* is inhabited by furies and thunderbolts; nevertheless it is not clearly stated who governs it: at the end of the account, Izanami is called "the great deity of *yomi*," even though at the beginning she goes to ask the advice of other deities. (5) This land is not entirely different from our world, for there is a palace there, people eat there, and trees even grow there. (6) There is never any question of judgment of the dead or of souls. This conception of a somber and impure afterworld is presented more precisely in the *norito*, collections of prayers which were written down in 905, but certain of which are much older. In the *Ho shizume no matsuri norito*, the festival of the appeasement of fire, the subterranean character of *yomi no kuni* is well marked, while it cannot be assumed in the *Kojiki* account.

The *Michi ae no matsuri norito*, the festival of the meals offered on the roads, expresses the notion of an impure land regarded as a source of diseases. Here the term *yomi no kuni* is not used, but there are two terms that are equivalent to it: *ne no kuni* (*ne* can refer to the notions of base or origin) and *soko no kuni* (*soko* has the sense of "basis," but *soko no kuni* is sometimes compared to *tokoyo no kuni*). The prayer asks the deities who protect the roads to prevent the malevolent beings who "come from the land of *ne*, the land of *soko*," from doing harm.

The conception of another world as a source of evils and calamities is preserved in the popular traditions revolving around the *dōsojin* (deities who protect the roads), who are related to the deities of diseases and whose prototype would be the boulder put in place by Izanagi. Still, it is difficult to believe that the *yomi no kuni* as it appears in the myth of the visit of Izanagi would be the only vision that the ancient Japanese had of the next world.

2. Yomi No Kuni, Ne No Kuni, and Soko No Kuni

In other contexts *yomi no kuni* seems much less somber and gloomy than in the myth just discussed. Thus, Susano-o (the brother of the solar goddess Amaterasu) refused the ocean which Izanagi assigned him to govern, in order to go to the land of his mother (Izanami), to *ne no kuni*. Why would he choose to visit a gloomy place? In a variant of the *Nihongi*, after he has been chased from *takama no hara*, the high celestial plain, Susano-o must go to *ne no kuni* where he outfits himself in a straw raincoat and a large sedge hat, that is, in the guise of a *mare bito*, a voyager coming from the next world to bring prosperity.

In the myth of Okuninushi, Susano-o governs *ne no kuni*. Although this land shelters snakes and wasps, it also contains various objects that assure sovereignty. This is also the dwelling place of the daughter of Susano-o, who will become

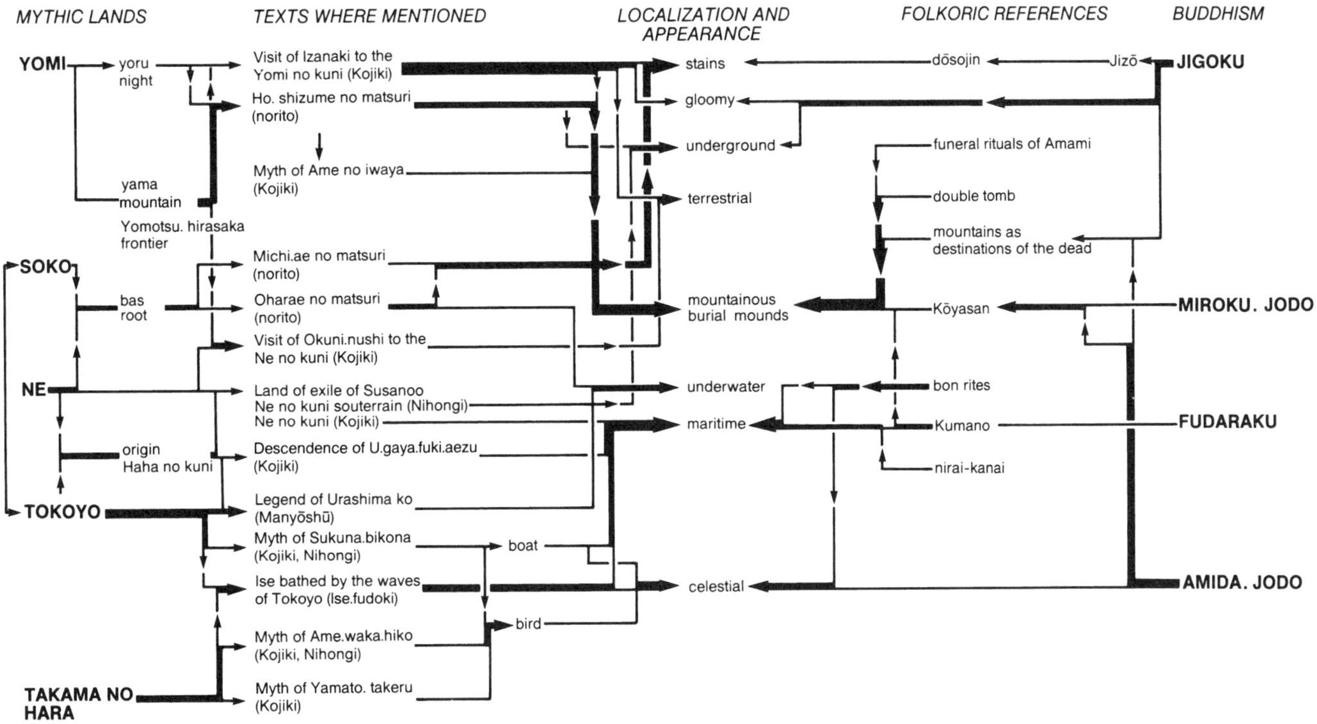

Concordance among myths, characteristics, and popular rituals concerning various forms of the afterlife. Drawing Fr. Macé.

the wife of Okuninushi. One explanation of the myth compares the trials that Okininushi undergoes to the rites of initiation, which, by a symbolic death, cause the initiate to be reborn into a new life.

In this case, death no longer brings pollution; it regenerates. The land of the dead is not only a repugnant land but the place from which the forces of life, *tama,* spring.

Ne no kuni (*yomi no kuni*), the maternal land, the land of the ancestors who come back to bring prosperity, has been compared to the *niraikanai,* the mythical world from which the inhabitants of Okinawa expect the ancestors, the heroes who bring civilization, to come. This paradisiacal land is situated beyond the seas. As we have already seen, *ne no kuni,* through the mediation of Susano-o, is also connected with the ocean. Further, in the *Ō harae no matsure norito,* the festival of the great purification, one expels pollution to the *ne no kuni* and *soko no kuni,* the land located in the oceanic plain. There the pollution disappears. This text situates *ne no kuni* in the ocean and connects it with another mythical country, also maritime, *tokoyo no kuni.*

3. Tokoyo No Kuni

The allusions to *tokoyo no kuni* in the ancient texts are brief, vague, and sometimes contradictory. One of the more illuminating is contained in the myth of Okuninushi. A female deity named Sukunabikona appears there sailing on a boat and dressed in bird feathers or butterfly wings, depending upon the version. She comes to aid Okuninushi in creating the country and then departs again for *tokoyo no kuni.* We are again dealing with a country conceived in terms rather close to that of *nirai-kanai,* the country from which civilization and prosperity come.

But *tokoyo no kuni,* in this first text, does not appear to be a place of residence for the dead, although certain indications seem to suggest this. The hypothesis has been advanced that the *tokoyo* of *tokoyo no kuni,* signifying eternity, is the same word as *tokoyo,* the eternal night.

But it seems that this comparison is after all not possible, for linguistic reasons which we will not discuss here. However, in the passage of the *Kojiki* giving the lineage of Ugaya Fuki Aezu, it is said that Mikenu sets off across the crests of the waves toward *tokoyo no kuni,* while Inai enters into the ocean, the country of his mother. These disappearances, which can be interpreted as deaths, recall those of Sukunabikona and Susano-o.

Thus there are connections between the ocean, the land of the mother, *tokoyo no kuni* and *ne no kuni* (*yomi no kuni*), which make possible the interpretation of certain archaeological remains. The famous fresco of the funeral mound of Mezurashizuka, in the province of Fukuoka, represents a boat guided by a bird, carrying a man (the dead person?): it has been suggested that this boat leads the dead person toward *tokoyo no kuni.*

4. The Mountain

But there is another difficulty. Most of the poems of the *Man'yōshū* that allude to the abodes of the dead speak of the mountains or the sky, places to which one can only cautiously attach the conceptions that have been presented concerning *yomi no kuni* or *tokoyo no kuni.* However, mountains have played an important role in the Japanese vision of the afterworld. They are the privileged locus of divine manifestations, the wild and uncultivated world in a land of rice cultivation, but also the sources of water and thus of prosperity.

For these diverse religious reasons and also because in a country as mountainous as Japan very little available space remains, the mountain was the preeminent burial place.

The first funeral mounds seem to have been gently sloping hills. Then they were designated by the term *yama,* mountain. Even during the Heian period (794–1185), when the Japanese had ceased to construct mounds for the emperors, their tombs continued to be called *yama*.

Furthermore, in the popular traditions, the mountain retained a very important place during funerals and funeral rites. In many regions of Japan, the coffin is called *yama oke*, "the box of the mountain," and the activity of digging the grave, *yama shigoto*, "mountain work." In the Amami archipelago (south of Kyushu), until recently, the body of the deceased was placed in thickets called *goshō yama*, the "mountain of the other world."

In other regions of Japan, there is or was a system of double burial: one grave in which the body is laid, which is at some distance from the village, and an empty grave near the village, which is visited on festival days. Frequently the term that denotes the first grave refers to mountains, for example, *yama no haka*, the "mountain tomb."

The mountain, the residence of the dead, is still at the center of numerous rites of the festival of *bon*. *Bon* originated as a Buddhist festival for the salvation of the souls of the dead, but many non-Buddhist elements have been incorporated into it. It lasts from the thirteenth to the sixteenth day of the seventh lunar month.

During this period, the ancestors are thought to return to their families. The rites of welcome vary according to the region, but a very large number are connected with the mountain: a fire lit on a summit, a path opened between the summit and the village, the gathering of flowers on the mountain (the flowers are regarded as the repositories of souls, as are dragonflies, which it is forbidden to capture during this period).

Many mountains have become the special centers of beliefs connected with death and are regarded as residences for the dead, such as the mountains Kōya, Asama, Osore, Tate, etc.

It seems therefore rather curious that the myths of the *Kojiki* and the *Nihongi* do not refer clearly to the residence of the dead in mountains.

Is it not possible that the *yomi no kuni* was situated in the mountain? (The word *yomi* might then be related to *yama*, "mountain.")

The subterranean position of *yomi no kuni* is but rarely specified, except, for example, in one of the versions of *Nihongi* that tells of the expulsion of Susano-o from *Takama no hara* and in the *Ho shizume no matsuri norito;* but these two texts are probably rather late. Furthermore, in this *norito*, another conception of the world of the dead is apparently juxtaposed to the first, for it is said there that Izanami, because her husband had looked at her, "shut herself in the rock grotto." In archaic texts this expression often signifies the death of important personnages.

It is probably in this sense that the term is used in the myth of the reclusion of Amaterasu. The practice might originate in an ancient custom of burial in caves. In particular, in the province of Izumo, the region in which the *Kojiki* places the entrance to *yomi no kuni*, a cave has been discovered that contains numerous skeletons from the Yayoi period. "To shut oneself in the rock grotto" may also refer to the stone rooms of the artificial mountains that are funerary mounds.

5. The Sky

As we have seen, certain poems of the *Man'yōshū* allude to a celestial residence of the dead. The account of the death of Yamato-takeru refers to the same residence. This account states that a white bird flew from the funerary mound and, after many stops, disappeared into the sky. The ascension recalls the term used in ancient texts for the death of emperors, *kamu agaru*, "ascend divinely."

Further, in the account of the funeral of Ame-no-waka-hiko, different birds play the roles of mourners, bearers of offerings, and members of the retinue. Might these birds not also be there to welcome the soul that will fly away in the form of a bird?

6. Conclusion

There are, on the one hand, various words—*yomi no kuni, ne no kuni, tokoyo no kuni, haba no kuni* (the land of the mother)—and, on the other hand, many places regarded as abodes of the dead: subterranean world, funerary mound, mountain, submarine world, ocean, sky. A single explanation could not clarify this diversity or the connections that unite the various terms.

First of all, the content of the terms seems to have changed with time, along with the expansion of continental influences. Thus, one cannot exclude the hypothesis that the words *ne* and *tokoyo* may refer to a single conception, that of a maritime afterworld, a land of ancestors, from which prosperity comes. Then, little by little, the terms *yomi, ne,* and *soko* may have come to be applied to the negative aspects of death, for example, death as a source of pollution. At the same time, the Japanese may have borrowed certain characteristics of the Chinese hell. On the other hand, *tokoyo no kuni* seems related to other Chinese conceptions, especially that of a land of immortals in which there is neither old age nor death. It is also the land to which the legendary Tajimamori goes in search of the fruits that give immortality, the land to which Urashim Taro goes to spend three years that last longer than a lifetime.

The ancient Japanese seem to have conceived of many abodes for the same dead person. For example, a provisional abode was situated in the surroundings of the tomb or the funerary shelter, where the body awaited a transformation that made possible the transfer to the final destination. On the other hand, as the rites of *bon* and the new year suggest, the souls of the ancestors must have been invited to visit their family at regular intervals. Finally, the funerary chambers of the mounds must have been constructed with the aim of assuring a certain survival which, nevertheless, did not have to be limited to a single subterranean abode.

The differences among the abodes in the next world may have been regarded as almost automatically dependent on the type of death, certain deaths being judged infamous, others glorious. Is it not here that one must seek an explanation for the gloomy character of *yomi no kuni* to which Izanami goes when she has died in childbirth (see above)? This kind of death, regarded as particularly abnormal, had for a long time been the occasion of a special mode of burial.

Another source of differentiation may have been the social order. The members of the aristocracy who could have large tombs constructed for themselves no doubt believed that in this way they assured themselves of another world that would be happy. Thus, the members of the imperial family must have hoped to reascend after their death to *Takama no hara*, the land of their ancestor Amaterasu. But since this destiny was probably not available to everyone, what could the hope of survival have been for those who were abandoned without burial?

The different origins of the populations of Japan might in part explain certain divergences in their conceptions of the afterworld. Thus, the horizontal conception of space which locates the other world beyond the seas (characteristic of the

Osore-san Mountain, Aomori prefecture, at the time of the festival of the dead (*o-bon*) in August. *Left:* The marker indicates the site of the inferno of the king of the *shuras*. *Right:* Pilgrims cross the lava field to offer "the great penitence" at the temple. CERTPJ photo archives. Photo Th. Lesoual'ch.

myths of the Izumo cycle) is opposed to the vertical representation of a world divided into three parts superimposed one upon the other: sky, earth, and underworld, a representation of the cycle of *takama no hara* that bears the ideology of the imperial clan.

Another explanation arises from the hypothesis that a people who came from the sea retained a nostalgia for the land of their ancestors. As this people penetrated the new regions, they would have gradually absorbed into their original beliefs other beliefs, particularly about mountains.

The present state of research precludes any synthesis of these hypotheses. Moreover, it is rather futile to speculate about an original condition, given the poverty of the sources available to us. On the other hand, it is very interesting to note the connections between the different abodes that have been examined. For instance, on the occasion of the *bon* festival, the welcome might be made in the form of flowers picked on a mountaintop, which connects the mountain and the sky. The souls are often brought back by placing rafts in the river or the sea. There is, therefore, a triple connection that the rites of *bon* deploy: sky, mountain, ocean. This triad is found in the fresco of the funerary mound of Mezurashizuka, an artificial mountain, where the association of a bird and a boat—just as in the myth of Sukunabikona—blurs the distinction between ocean and sky.

II. Buddhism

Buddhist beliefs arrived very early in Japan, even before the traditional official dates of 538 or 552.

However, the diffusion of Buddhist ideas about the next life seems to have been particularly slow, and the adoption of Buddhist funeral rites was very gradual. Empress Jitō at the beginning of the eighth century was the first sovereign to be cremated according to a Buddhist ritual. Though the aristocracy gradually followed her example, cremation encountered such resistance among the people that even now certain regions still do not practice it. Furthermore, even where it has been implanted, it seems to be regarded as a means of accelerating the process of separating the flesh from the skeleton, which is also the aim of the double interments as they have long been practiced in the Amami archipelago.

On the other hand, Buddhist terms have prevailed in almost the entire vocabulary dealing with death or the afterworld, to which they give their own connotation. The imprint has been so strong that Buddhist sects have a monopoly over funerals, whether they use cremation or not.

The new religion arrived in Japan with a doctrine that presented a coherent and elaborate vision of existence. Considering the resistance that it must have encountered, we may justly ask how the doctrine endured in Japan.

The conception of the cycle of rebirths seems to have turned away from its original significance. Since the Buddhist believer must attempt to break the cycle and the bonds that maintain it, some have committed suicide (double suicide, *shin jū;* suicide of vassals at the death of their lord, *junshi*) in order to create a bond that would assure a common future existence. In addition, from the Buddhist point of view, human life is devalued, considered as ephemeral, and characterized by suffering. Thus, though the consciousness of the impermanence of things has occupied an important place in Japanese sensibility and poetry, the deprecation of this world could only with difficulty become rooted in a society that honored its ancestors and therefore took care to guarantee that there would be descendants; in popular belief, the dead without families are *gaki*, "hungry ghosts," whose fate is similar to that of the damned. People who wished to die with the hope of being reborn in a better existence had to rely on the mercy of the Amida Buddha; but they could also count on the family, whose duty it was to improve the lot of the dead through their prayers and offerings—through the principle of the transfer of merit (*ekō*).

Finally, the various forms of rebirth which normally would have remained in an abstract state were often conceived of in a very concrete manner in the popular traditions.

1. Hell (Jigoku)

King Emma (Sanskrit: Yama), who, in the beginning, had ruled at the crossroads to judge the guilty and to send them back to be reborn according to their merits on one path or another, became sovereign of the eight hells, which were organized and administered according to the mode of Chinese administration. The various hells, in which the damned resided according to their crimes, are well known to us through painted scrolls and from the testimony of those who, according to tradition, have returned from them. One can indeed return from hell, since one might have been summoned there by mistake, or the Bodhisattva Jizō might intervene. Jizō, protector of roads and crossroads, advocate of the dead before King Emma, became Emma's enemy. The farces of the Middle Ages (*kyōgen*) transformed Emma into a king of demons who was deceived by every kind of trick and always lost against Jizō. Apparently *jigoku* has lost its terrifying content.

From another perspective, popular beliefs have situated *jigoku* in the mountains. The volcanic activity that was frequent in Japan must have favored such a location, as well as the role of the mountains in pre-Buddhist beliefs about the afterlife (see above). Indeed, *jigoku* is not situated in a single mountain but in the regional centers cited above as local abodes of the dead. *Jigoku* took the place, therefore, of a previous conception of the afterworld. We have confirmation of this in an account of *Nihon ryō iki*. In this account, the monk Chikō is taken to hell because of his jealousy. But the abduction is merely a warning; after he has undergone much suffering, he is sent back to earth with a final recommendation that is utterly surprising in a Buddhist text: "Do not eat the food cooked in the fire of *yomi*." Finally, the current explanation states that the ancestors arrive during the *bon* festival because the cover of the caldron of hell is ajar during this period. Taken literally, this would imply that the ancestors are among the damned.

Although they have distinct origins, the ways of the *gaki* and *ashura* (demons) have entered into the shifting development of *jigoku*.

The *gaki* are a type too close to that of the damned to be separated from them. As for the way of the *ashura*, it is reserved for those of the dead who continue to be devoured by their passion and who are transformed into demonic beings. Held back by their attachment to the world, they continue to haunt the places that were familiar to them. Their apparition would provide the material for numerous literary works, and in particular the No plays. But the success of ghost stories may also rest upon a more ancient belief that the dead remain close to the world of the living and continue to intervene in the life of their descendants.

2. The Pure Lands (Jōdo)

It seems that very early the possibility of reincarnation was envisaged only for young children, who, as a result, were not interred in the usual places, but near the house or even inside. The great hope was to be reborn in paradise, in the "pure land," *jōdo*.

One of the "pure lands," that of the Bodhisattva Miroku (Maitreya), is at the center of a legend about the monk Kūkai. The legend recounts that Kūkai had himself entombed alive in a meditation room and that, immobile, he awaited there the coming of Miroku, the Buddha of the Future. This legend incontestably reinforced the attraction that Mount Kōya already exercised as a burial place. Waiting for the reign of Miroku is also at the origin of certain mummifications, *miira*, at least those that are prepared in observance of the fast unto death. The belief in another pure land, that of the Bodhisattva Kannon, gave birth to specific practices. In order to arrive in the pure land situated toward the south, on a mountain beyond the seas, certain fervent believers went so far as to embark on boats that they set adrift on the open sea off Kumano. The choice of Kumano as a point of departure may be explained by the bonds with the afterworld that this great religious center had maintained since antiquity. Are not the banks of Ise, nearby, bathed in waves that are supposed to come from *tokoyo?*

But the pure land par excellence is that of Amida, and its success is linked to that of the Amida sects. Belief in the paradise of Amida spread through every layer of the population, from monks to laity, from people of the court of the Heian period to the lower classes influenced by the popular preachers of the Middle Ages. The most fervent among the believers, ready to commit suicide in order to go there and be reborn, at the last moment had the vision of a purple cloud and heard the celestial music of the cortege of Amida, come to welcome them (*raigō*). Popular beliefs also transposed the land of felicity known as *jodō* to mountains such as Mount Kōya.

F.M./m.s.

BIBLIOGRAPHY

1. Monographs

S. GORAI, *Kōya hijiri* (Tokyo 1975). CH. HAGUENAUER, *Origines de la civilisation japonaise: Introduction à l'étude de la préhistoire du Japon*, part 1 (Paris 1956). SH. INOGUCHI, *Nihon no sōshiki* (Tokyo 1965). Y. YOBAYASHI, *Kofun no hanashi* (Tokyo 1974). N. KOIKE, *Hito no shigo no hanashi* (Tokyo 1972). T. OBAYASHI, *Nihon shinwa no kigen* (Tokyo 1973); *Sōsei no kigen* (Tokyo 1965). T. SAKURAI, *Nihonjin no sei to shi* (Tokyo 1968). Y. SATO, *Sōsōgirei no minzoku* (Tokyo 1968). M. SAWADA, *Jigokuhen* (Kyoto 1976). T. TAMAMURO, *Sōshikibukkyō* (Tokyo 1976). SH. WATANABE, *Shigo no sekai* (Tokyo 1959). T. YAMAORI, *Nihonjin no Reikonkan* (Tokyo 1976). K. YANAGITA, *Senzo no hanashi* (Tokyo 1946); *Yamamiya kō* (Tokyo 1947).

Additional monographs: GARY L. EBERSOLE, *Ritual Poetry and the Politics of Death in Early Japan* (Princeton 1989). ICHIRO HORI, *Folk Religion in Japan* (Chicago 1968). KAZUO KASAHARA and JUNKO OGIRI, eds., *Iki-zama, shini-zama: Nihon minshū shinkōshi* (Tokyo 1979). YANAI KYUSAKU, *Ama no iwato shinwa no kenkyÿ* (Tokyo 1977). TAMURA YOSHIRO and MINAMOTO RUŌEN, eds., *Nihon ni okeru sei to shi no shisō* (Tokyo 1977).

2. Articles

CH. HAGUENAUER, "Du caractère de la représentation de la mort dans le Japon antique," in *T'oung pao*, no. 33 (1937): 158–83; "La danse rituelle dans le Chinkonsai," *Journal asiatique* (April–June 1930), 299ff. J. HORI, "Manyōshū ni arawareta sōsei to sekaikan, reikonkan ni tsuite," in *Nihonshūkyōshikenkyū* (Tokyo 1963), 2:49–93.

Additional articles: KEN AKAMATSU, "The Significance of the Formation and Distribution of *Kofun*," *Acta Asiatica* 31 (1977): 24–50. TOSHIO AKIMA, "Songs of the Dead: Poetry, Drama, and Ancient Death Rituals of Japan," *Journal of Asian Studies* 41, 3 (May 1982): 485–509.

GARY L. EBERSOLE, "The Religio-Aesthetic Complex in *Manyōshū Poetry* with Special Emphasis on Hitomaro's *Aki no no* Sequence," *History of Religions* 23, 1 (August 1983): 18–36. TAKESHI MATSUMAE, "The Heavenly Rock-Grotto Myth and the Chinkon Ceremony," *Asian Folklore Studies* 39, 2 (1980): 9–22; "Taiyō fune to tokoyo shinkō," *Kokugakuin zasshi* 62, 2–3 (February–March 1961): 23–43. TAKAYOSHI MOGAMI, "The Double-Grave System," in Richard M. Dorson, ed., *Studies in Japanese Folklore* (New York 1980), pp. 167–80. SUSUMU NAKANISHI, "The Spatial Structure of Japanese Myth: The Contact Point between Life and Death," in Earl Miner, ed., *Principles of Classical Japanese Literature* (Princeton 1985), pp. 106–29. NELLY NAUMANN, "*Sakahagi:* The 'Reverse Flaying' of the Heavenly Piebald Horse," *Asian Folklore Studies* 41, 1 (1982): 7–38. NOBUTSUNA SAIGO, "Yomi no kuni to ne no kuni: Chika no sekai ni tsuite," *Bungaku* 39, 11 (November 1971): 19–35. MASAO SUGANO, "Tokoyo-yuku shinwa no keisei," *Kokugakuin zasshi* 62, 10 (October 1962): 42–48. SHIGEKI WADA, "Mogari no kiso-teki kōsatsu," *Shirin* 52, 5 (September 1969): 32–90.

3. Multivolume Works

T. MATSUMURA, *Nihon shinwa no kenkhū*, 4 vols. (Tokyo 1954–58). *Nihon no kōkogaku*, 7 vols. (Tokyo 1965–67), vols. 4 and 5 on Kofun jidai. SH. ORIKUCHI, *Kodai kenkhū*, 6 vols. (Tokyo 1974). *Shinpojiumu Nihon no shinwa*, 5 vols. (Tokyo 1972–75).

Buddhism and Archaic Beliefs in the Shinto-Buddhist Syncretism of Japan

The rapprochement of Buddhism and archaic beliefs had already been initiated in the sixth and seventh centuries. Buddhism, introduced in Japan as a part of mainland culture, was actively supported by the rulers. The second article of the "Seventeen Article Constitution," promulgation of which is ordinarily attributed to Prince Shōtoku (574–622), recommends, for example, the veneration of the "three jewels" (*sanbō*). A decree dated the twenty-seventh day of the third lunar month of the fourteenth year of Emperor Temmu (686) orders the construction and veneration of Buddhist statues (cf. the *Nihongi*). This political support furthered the mixing of the two belief systems, since the emperors were also the highest functionaries of the national religion, Shinto. The fact that the Shinto religion did not have statues of deities made it even easier to accept Buddhist iconography and the ideas it expressed. The incorporation of Shinto deities within Buddhism, when Shinto did not have, in this encounter with Buddhism, clearly defined ethical and philosophical concepts, took place chiefly in Shingon esotericism, which affirmed that the entire universe was nothing but a manifestation of the Buddha Dainichi. Also, from the point of view of its rituals, Buddhism was attractive. It was rich, for example, in practices of exorcism which corresponded easily to the pre-Buddhist magic that was employed during prayers for rain (*amagoi*). As for the *kami*, people originally viewed them with respect and fear; when, with time, the respect gave way to fixed forms of veneration, people developed the idea that they could secure the supernatural forces of the *kami* for themselves. Soon it was common to read the sutras before the *kami*. More generally, the new form of Buddhism that the Tendai and Shingon sects represented gave an important place to the "magical" use of the sutras, accentuating tendencies that already existed in Buddhism during the Nara era.

But the rapprochement of Buddhism and Shinto had also been furthered by the proximity, if not the actual geographical identity, of the cult sites. In its concern to assure the economic equilibrium of the temples in the provinces, Buddhism hoped to rely on local cults. Although the new religion had been rapidly accepted by the aristocratic class, who most often lived in the capital, ancient Shinto always reigned in the provinces and among those who worked in the domains of the Buddhist temples. The better to protect these lands, where ancient beliefs were still alive, Buddhism sought the support of local deities and made them the protecting deities of their temples. In order to justify the construction of the temples, they forged legends according to which, for example, at such and such a place an old man—the local deity in his human aspect—had asked for the temple for himself. At the time of the construction of the "Great Buddha" of Nara, the deity Hachiman of Usa (at Kyushu) was "transferred" to the capital, probably to avert the disturbance or resentment of people alarmed by the diffusion of Buddhism, but also to further the alliance of the two religions.

In architecture the close bonds between Buddhism and Shinto were manifested in the construction of *jingūji*, Buddhist annexes to Shinto sanctuaries in front of which the sutras were recited and Buddhist ceremonies were carried out. The opening of Buddhism to other religions was at least partially the cause of the growing tendency to regard the recitation and the offering of the sutras before the *kami*—protectors of the Buddhist law—as an act that could bring salvation and joy to the *kami*. During the Nara period, it was already common practice to count the *kami* among those beings who—like the humans attached to this world of illusion and suffering—could find salvation through the Buddhist law. The next stage was to give the name and title of *bosatsu* to these Shinto deities, who were thought to have arrived at the state of a bodhisattva (Japanese *bosatsu*) through the power of the Buddhist law. The first example of such a promotion is Hachiman, who was called *Hachiman dai bosatsu* in 781. Endowed with the quality of future Buddhas (that is, of bodhisattvas), the *kami* were finally raised to the same level as a Buddha, but they are only avatars (*gongen*), and it is with this title that they are venerated by Buddhism; they are the "trace descended on earth" (*suijaku*) of the Buddhas, who themselves are the "original state" (*honji*) of the *kami*.

This same concept of the *honji suijaku*, which allowed the *kami* to be held as temporary manifestations of Buddhas, at the time of the propagation of Buddhism in China, served to mark the superiority of Buddhism over Confucianism and Daoism. In Japan, no religion could rival Buddhism, on either the ideological plane or the institutional. People therefore chiefly tried to find a new interpretation of the nature of Shinto deities in Buddhist terms. There was not yet a true syncretism during the Nara period, but during the Heian period the concept of *honji suijaku* took form, though it did not yet attribute to each deity a particular Buddha who would be its *honji*. *Kami* and Buddhas were simply thought to be identical, the Buddhas "softening the light of their wisdom" (*wakō*) to allow their emanations to descend in multiple forms upon the earth, where they adapted themselves to the unequal receptivity of beings (*dōjin*).

The Kamakura period (1185–1333) saw the most fully marked evolution of the *kami* toward Buddhism, through the concept of *honji-suijaku*. This is most apparent in the celebrated collection of *setsuwa* entitled *Shasekishū*. These didactic anecdotes show clearly the change that took place on the threshold of the Middle Ages in the vision of the *kami;* here they are described as animated by a profound desire to turn humans away from this lowly world, to take them away from seeking *genze riyaku* (immediate or material profit), and this concern is accompanied by a marked insistence on the future life (*gose*) as the only thing of value. In order to aid in the liberation from the cycle of samsara, the deities put at man's disposal the *hōben* (expedients) which facilitate access to the Buddhist path. The *kami* lost, then, the characteristics which distinguished them from Buddhas; they were assimilated functionally as well as existentially.

The primary cause of the different manifestations under which Buddhist and Shinto deities appear is Dainichi Nyorai in the metaphysical body (*hosshin*). To humble oneself through *hōben* (by compassion for beings) or, to put it another way, to conceal one's true nature as a Buddha in order to manifest oneself as a *kami* in the dust of this lowly world is the major concept of medieval Shinto, *wakō dōjin*. The term, which derives from a passage of Laozi (*Daodejing*, "masterpiece of the path and of the power"), passed into Buddhist texts, notably the famous *Maka shikan* (594) of Zhikai, founder of the Tendai sect in China. By the transmission of this text, as well as that of the sutras and other works, the notion of *wakō dōjin* was known at that time by the Japanese and taken up not only in the literature of the time (which had a strongly Buddhist tint—as in the *Hōgen-monogatari*, the *Gikeiki*, the *Taiheiki*, etc.), but also in the "words of the law" (*hōgo*) of certain monks (like Ippen), in the popular religious songs (*imayō*) of the *Ryōjin hishō*, in No plays (like *Aridōshi*). The idea of *wakō dōjin* and what it makes of the *kami* are well illustrated in the *Shasekishū*, already mentioned, in which certain of the anecdotes could even be regarded as the beginning of an evolution that ends by reversing the position of interdependence between the *kami* and the Buddha (still fixed in the *honji-suijaku*), to the detriment of the Buddha. This evolution had only begun in the *setsuwa*. The history of En no Gyōja presents Shākyamuni and Miroku *bosatsu* as inferior to a *gongen* (in this case, Zaō Gongen) in the difficult task of guiding and saving beings at the time of *mappō*. During the time of *mappō* many beings lack *dōshin*, that pious spirit whose absence is especially contrary to the will of the *kami* (fundamentally of the Buddhas). Eichō Sōzu, for example, who carries on a dialogue with the divinity of the sanctuary of Kasuga concerning the doctrines of the "nothing-but-thought" (*yuishiki*), is nevertheless told that he is incapable of seeing the august countenance, because of his lack of *dōshin*. There is the same insistence in the reactions of the *kami* to those who lack the "wide-awake heart" (*bodaishin*). The state of the spirit—a necessary condition for deliverance from samsara—is deemed more important than the maintenance of Buddhist temples. Defined by reference to the future life, this insistence on the value of *bodaishin* is also characteristic of the *kami* of the Middle Ages, as is the compassion mentioned above. The compassion (*jihi*) not only suffices to motivate all the intervention of the *kami* in the world of men but is held to be more important, finally, than the observance of traditional taboos (such as those of impurity). This is what the divinity of Yoshino teaches the monk Jōkan, who wrongly thinks that he is defiled by contact with death and thereby prevented from approaching the *kami*.

All the evidence indicates that it was the theory of the *honji-suijaku* that made possible the transfer of the virtue of compassion, originally characteristic of Buddhas and bodhisattvas, to their avatars. The diverse *engi* ("accounts of the origin," in particular of sanctuaries) contained in the *Shintōshū* (mid-sixteenth century) and the *otogi-zōshi* (popular tales of the epoch of Muromachi)—notably the *honji-mono*—go so far as to make the compassionate *kami* experience all the suffering of humans. Moreover, in order to mark clearly their disapproval of self-seeking demands (*genze riyaku*), the *kami* counter them with inertia and impotence; on the other hand, they abound in *hōben*, which are expedients to hasten beings on the path of Buddhism, and they predict, for example, particular hells (such as the hells beneath the sanctuaries of Kasuga and Hiyoshi) as places of spiritual reeducation.

In summary: at the beginning of the Middle Ages, the concepts of *honji-suijaku* and *wakō dōjin* had made it possible for Shinto deities to be regarded as avatars of Buddhas; then, finally, because of the affinity of character and function ascribed to them with the Buddhas of whom they are the emanation, they became "Buddhist" *kami*, tributaries, in their thought and their reactions, of traditional Buddhist values.

H.O.R./d.f.

BIBLIOGRAPHY

1. Sources

H. O. ROTERMUND, ed. and trans., *Collection de sable et de pierres, Shasekishū* (Paris 1979).

Additional source: ROBERT E. MORRELL, trans., *Sand and Pebbles (Shasekishū): The Tales of Muju Ichien, a Voice for Pluralism in Kamakura Japan* (Albany, NY, 1985).

2. Monographs

A. MATSUNAGA, *The Buddhist Philosophy of Assimilation: The Historical Development of the Honji Suijaku Theory*, MN Monograph (Tokyo 1969). T. HARADA, *Nihon shūkyō kōshō-shi ron* (Tokyo 1969). J. HORI, *Waga kuni minkan shinkō-shi no kenkyū*, 2 vols. (Tokyo 1953). SH. MURAYAMA, *Shinbutsu shūgō shichō*, Sara sōsho 6 (Kyoto 1964); *Honji suijaku*, Nihon rekishi sōsho 33 (Tokyo 1974). K. OYAMA, *Shinbutsu kōshō-shi* (Kōya-san 1944). T. SAKURAI, *Shinbutsu kōshō-shi kenkyū* (Tokyo 1968).

Additional monographs: J. H. KAMSTRA, *Encounter or Syncretism: The Initial Growth of Japanese Buddhism* (Leiden 1967). CHRISTINE GUTH KANDA, *Shinzō: Hachiman Imagery and Its Development*, Harvard East Asian Monographs 119 (Cambridge, MA, 1985). WATASE MASATADA, *Kakinomoto Hitomaro kenkyū*, 3 vols. (Tokyo 1976).

3. Articles

H. O. ROTERMUND, "La conception des kami japonais à l'époque de kamakura: Notes sur le premier chapitre du Sasekishū," *Revue de l'histoire des religions* 182–83 (1972).

Additional article: TOSHIO KURODA, "Shintō in the History of Japanese Religion," *Journal of Japanese Studies* 7, 1 (Winter 1981): 1–21.

MOUNTAINS IN JAPAN

Among many signs of the veneration of mountains in ancient Japan are not only archaeological finds (mirrors, vases, ritual utensils) but also literary vestiges, such as the passages of the myths in the *Kojiki* and *Nihongi* that deal with obedience to the deities of the mountains. Various classifications of mountains have been advanced (cf. Kishimoto, Ikegami, Hori, etc.), the criterion being the nature and form of the mountains or the cults observed on them. Thus, by the first criterion, volcanoes are usually considered the residences of deities; other mountains are revered as sources of water or as the place of the souls of the dead (which implies a mountain burial) or as a place of passage for souls on their way to the world beyond. Depending on the form taken by the cult practiced there, a distinction is made between mountains that are climbed at a designated time, by people who wish to go into a retreat there or to devote themselves to religious practices, and mountains that are climbed as often as possible, the climbing being an exercise in and of itself. Taking the second point of view, and placing the emphasis on the principal element of the cult, Ikegami distinguishes among the following: (*a*) mountains of pilgrimage closely associated with the spirits of the dead (for instance, Mount Osore); (*b*) mountains that are revered for themselves, the mountain being the "body of the deity" (*shintai*), a typical example of which is Mount Miwa; people do not climb these mountains but worship them from below in a hall of veneration (*haiden*); (*c*) mountains that people climb with the aim of uniting with the deity on the peak (for example, Mount Ontake and Mount Fuji); (*d*) mountains more specifically associated with multiple functions in popular belief: the place where the souls of the ancestors reside, the place of the *ujigami* and/or of the *yama no kami;* and finally (*e*) mountains suitable for *shugendō,* those that are places of religious practices and asceticism.

A word about mountains as sources of water and as the dwelling places of "deities that give water" (*mi-kumari no kami*). Since popular beliefs and many seasonal customs have been closely associated with agriculture, with the dead, and with the spirits of the ancestors in Japan from the earliest times, and since wind and rain are of major importance to the farmer, it was quite natural that religious concerns would extend to the mountains, from whose peaks the water flows that is so precious for rice cultivation. In the sanctuaries known as *mikumari,* the deities of wind and rain were worshiped. The *Engishiki* (927) informs us of the existence of four of these shrines in Yamato, in particular at Yoshino and Katsuragi. The cult of Komori Myōjin, observed in such shrines, apparently developed as the result of a phonetic confusion between *kumari* and *komori.*

The function of mountains as burial sites appears clearly in poem 165 of the *Man'yōshū,* in which Princess Oku mourns the death of her brother, Prince Otsu. The particular connection between mountains and death is also manifested in numerous terms from the vocabulary of folklore (for example, *yama shigoto,* meaning both "to work in the mountains" and "to dig a grave"), and becomes eminently clear in the *banka* (elegies) of the *Man'yōshū,* which mostly indicate that the soul rests in the mountains; a few of these poems give the sky or the clouds, the rocks or the sea, as an abode of the soul, and only a very small minority speak of anything like a hell. The importance of mountains in the religious life of the Japanese is also reflected in the presence of the *yama-miya* ("shrines in the mountains") and the *sato-miya* ("shrines in the villages at the foot of a mountain"). The rituals connected with the *ujigami* ("deity of the clan") and with the *yama-miya* shrines are explained by the belief that the souls of the dead—which gradually rise to the stage of *kami*—reside in the mountains but come down to the villages at certain times of the year. That the mountain is a place of passage to the afterlife is expressed in the concept of *shide no yama* ("the mountain of the voyage beyond the tomb"), a mountain that Buddhism has made into a dangerous place, peopled with evil demons, as seems to be indicated by a reference in poem 858 of the *Shin zoku kokin wakashū* (1439). A messenger between the world below and the world beyond, the cuckoo is supposed to pass through this same *shide no yama.* This is what is said in poem 1307 of the *Shūi Wakashū* (perhaps from the beginning of the eleventh century). Of the innumerable seasonal Japanese feast days, it is *bon* that best translates, in its diverse ritual forms, the close ties between mountains and death.

Since ancient times, Japanese sacred mountains, particularly Mount Yoshino, have been the destination points for imperial voyages. It was at Yoshino that Emperor Jimmu was blessed with a revelation in a dream; and many empresses, Jitō among others, went to Yoshino. In the first Japanese anthology of poems in the Chinese style, entitled *Kaifūsō* (eighth century: see poems 48 and 73), the sacred character of Mount Yoshino is emphasized by qualifiers that refer to the spirits and the immortals (*sen*) of Daoism. One likely explanation for these mountain visits was the quest for sacred water. Called *haraegawa* or *mitarashigawa,* the streams of water situated near sacred mountains were regarded as the boundary between our world and the world beyond. Yet another aspect of mountains in Japan is that of the fertile mother who has the (magical) power to grant life and to bring about rebirth. And this leads us to the divinity of the mountain, *yama no kami.*

Among the various classes of Japanese *kami,* the *yama no kami* is especially important, and the worship of these deities is at the heart of the *sangaku shinkō.* There are different sorts of *yama no kami,* which can remain fixed in a definite region or vary according to the social nature of the worshipers. Thus woodsmen and hunters have their own *yama no kami;* for the rural community, the *yama no kami* is above all the deity that comes down from the mountains when the season requires, in order to become the *ta no kami* or "deity of the fields"—a belief that is connected with the belief in the visiting deities who come from the world beyond in order to bring good fortune. The idea of such a visiting deity coming from the world beyond the mountains—and not, as in a more remote period, from the world beyond the sea (like the deity Sukunabikona)—seems to have taken shape at the time when the ancient Japanese began to leave the seacoast to settle farther inland. It is notably during the period when the rice is transplanted that the *yama no kami* becomes the object of attention: then they welcome him to the fields and address him with prayers for a good crop. While waiting for the crop to be garnered, the deity (who has become *ta no kami*) will remain in the plain to ensure prosperity. The custom of going right up to the mountain to welcome the deity, often taking well-designated paths and observing certain practices, as well as the fact that the mountains were places for the initiation of boys when they reached maturity, have influenced the practice of the *shugendō* known as *haru-yama* ("spring mountain").

The mountain deity is difficult to characterize in terms of external appearance. Sometimes it appears in the form of a

Yudono-san Mountain, Yamagata prefecture. A group of pilgrims (*kō*), fulfilling their ascetic duties by climbing the "three summits of Dewa" (*Dewa sanzan*) before worshiping the "body of the deity" (*shintai*) of Yudono, represented by this rock, from which mineral waters spring. In front of the rock is a stone niche in which pilgrims place and light candles. CERTPJ photo archive. Photo taken in 1936 by A. Togawa.

snake; at other times it looks more like the fabulous creature called the *tengu*. Often it is female, and representations of *yama no kami* often depict ugly features (the deity is one-eyed, one-legged, etc.) and signs of a nasty temperament (for this point of view, see the provincial chronicles: *Harima Fudoki, Hitachi Fudoki*.) The female character is underscored and is confirmed by various facts. A play from the Heian period, which is referred to in the *chinkonka* songs ("for the appeasement of souls") cited in a work entitled *Nenjūgyōji hishō* (Secret notes on seasonal rituals), mentions, for example, the belief that a female deity (O-hirume or Amaterasu) would bring "a box of souls" *tama tebako* from a sacred mountain to the new emperor (see Hori). *Juni-sama* ("the lady of the twelve months") is another name for the *yama no kami*, who is supposed to give birth once a year to twelve children, that is, the twelve months of the year. Numerous ritual practices connected with birth are also more easily interpreted in the light of a female *yama no kami*, protector of childbirth.

Nowadays it is believed that these concepts originated in an ancient belief of hunters in a mother deity of the mountains. Yanagita, for example, distinguishes three categories: (*a*) the so-called Kōya type, in which the deity and her son grant permission to build temples or houses on the mountain (this type owes its name to a legend attributing to Kūkai a meeting with Nifutsuhime, the deity of Mount Kōya: following this encounter, Kūkai is said to have obtained permission to build his monastery, but he also built one in honor of the deity and her son Kariba Myōjin, who, disguised as a hunter, had met Kūkai on the mountain and had brought him to his mother); (*b*) the Nikko type, in which we see the goddess granting the right to hunt, as reward for a good deed, to a certain Banzaburo, who will later emerge, in the region of Nikko, as the ancestor of the hunters; and (*c*) the type called Shiiba (a village in Kyushu), in which the deity *yama no shinbo* ("the mother goddess of the mountain") is disguised as a young girl, testing the character of hunters, such as the two brothers Oma and Koma, one hardhearted, the other generous.

As Hori has well demonstrated in numerous studies, beliefs about mountains have significant characteristics in common with ancient forms of shamanism. The concept of the sacred mountain as the realm of the dead, the place of passage between this world and the world beyond or the meeting place between the dead and the living, and the idea that the mountains are the domain of spirits or deities (Buddhist or Shinto), or a place where shamans practice asceticism, are the basis on which the *shugendō* was established. The existence of ties between the mountain ascetics of the *shugendō* and hunters can also be seen in certain rituals practiced by hunters.

H.O.R./g.h.

BIBLIOGRAPHY

1. Sources

Sangaku shūkyōshi kenkyū sōsho, 12 vols. (Tokyo 1975).

2. Monographs

N. NAUMANN, "Yama no kami, die japanische Berggottheit," *Folklore Studies* 22 (1963–64). K. HIGO, *Nihon ni okeru sangaku shinkō no rekishi,* Sangaku shinkō series no. 4 (Tokyo 1949). I. HORI, *Nihon ni okeru sangaku shinkō no genshi keitai,* Sangaku shinkō series no. 2 (Tokyo 1949). K. HORITA, *Yama no kami shinkō no kenkyū* (Kuwana 1966). N. MIYAJI, *Kumano sanzan no shiteki kenkyū* (Tokyo 1956); *Sangaku shinkō to jinja,* Sangaku shinkō series no. 3 (Tokyo 1949). I. OBA, *Nihon ni okeru sangaku shinkō no kōkogakuteki kōsatsu,* Sangaku shinkō series no. 1 (Tokyo 1948). SH. TAKASE, *Kodai sangaku shinkō no shiteki kenkyū* (Tokyo 1969).

Additional monographs: H. BYRON EARHART, "The Celebration of *Haru-Yama* (Spring Mountain): An Example of Folk Religious Practices in Contemporary Japan," *Asian Folklore Studies* 27, 1 (1968): 1–18. ICHIRO HORI, *Folk Religion in Japan* (Chicago 1968). YOSHIKO YAMAMOTO, *The Namahage: A Festival in the Northeast of Japan* (Philadelphia 1978).

3. Articles

H. IKEGAMI, "The Significance of Mountains in the Popular Beliefs in Japan," in *Religious Studies in Japan* (Tokyo 1959). I. HORI, "Mountains and Their Importance for the Idea of the Other World in Japanese Folk Religion," *History of Religions* 6/1 (1966). H. KISHIMOTO, "The Role of Mountains in the Religious Life of the Japanese People," *Proceedings of the Ninth International Congress for the History of Religions 1958* (Tokyo 1960). T. HARADA, "Yama no sūhai to yama no kami-toku ni yama bukkyō to no kanren ni oite," *Nihon shūkyō kōshō-shi ron* (Tokyo 1949). I. HORI, "Yama to shinkō," *Kokugakuin daigaku Nihon bunka kenkyūjo kiyō,* vol. 12 (1963). H. IKEGAMI, "Sangaku shinkō no sho keitai," *Jinrui kagaku,* vol. 12 (1960). K. KINDAICHI, "Yama no kami-kō," *Minzoku* 2/3. SH. SUZUKI, "Genshi sangaku shinkō no ikkōsatsu: Tōhoku ni okeru Hayama shinkō," *Shūkyō kenkyū,* vol. 170 (1961). A. TOGAWA, "Yama no kami to ta no kami," *Shōnai minzoku,* vol. 22 (1960). K. YANAGAWA, "Sonraku ni okeru sangaku shinkō no soshiki," *Shūkyō kenkyū,* vol. 143 (1955). K. YANAGITA, "Yama miya-kō," *Yanagita Kunio shū,* vol. 11; "Yama no kami to okoze," *Yanagita Kunio shū,* vol. 4.

Additional articles: ICHIRO HORI, "Mysterious Visitors from the Harvest to the New Year," in *Studies in Japanese Folklore,* Richard Dorson, ed. (Bloomington, IN, 1963), pp. 76–106. ITSUHIKO OHAMA, "Jitō tennō wa naze Yoshino e itta ka?" *Kokubungaku: Kaishaku to kanshō* 34, 2 (February 1969): 60–64. YOSHITAKA YOSHIDA, "Yoshino sanka to Jitō chō," *Kokubungaku: Kaishaku to kyozai no kenkyū* 28, 7 (May 1983): 122–27.

Magic in Japan

Traces of magic as a central element in popular beliefs are found in the earliest documents of Japanese literature. We know that magical action is ordinarily distinguished from verbal magic. Magical action is characterized by analogical effects (imitation, attraction between things that resemble one another), contact (action through contiguity), or sympathetic acts (those which rest on the belief in an internal relationship between things or phenomena, as is expressed, for example, by the adage *pars pro toto*). One might ask, however, if a distinction between imitative magic (for example, *amagoi:* a prayer for rain; and *taue:* the replanting of rice), magic by contact, and sympathetic magic (in the case of *hitogata:* an anthropomorphic figurine to which the blemishes and sins of men are transferred in a ritual of purification) always takes into account the complex reality of popular Japanese beliefs. One could just as well, for example, distinguish between acts of individual and collective magic, or between those acts that are executed in a clearly delineated

Kyōto. Woman with eye disease; she has touched the eye of the turtle and then her own diseased eye with the intention of healing it. CERTPJ photo archive. Photo P. Bonicel.

Daruma and *Himedaruma*, Sendai, 12 and 10 cm. Dolls of this kind, built so as always to remain upright, symbolize man's resilience in the face of difficulties. Commercially sold *darumas* have only one eye; the second eye is painted on after a wish that has been made on the doll comes true. CERTPJ photo archive, Berval collection. Photo L. Frédéric.

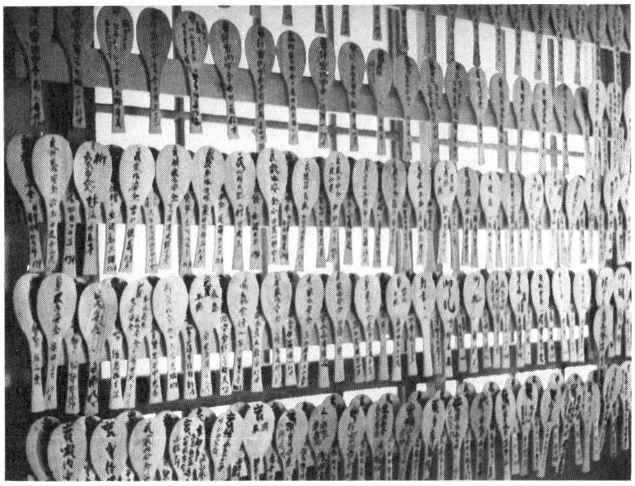

Shakushi or *shamoji*, rice spoons (Okayama prefecture), which are offered as ex-votos. Below a Sanskrit letter, they bear a votive formula, the name and age of the donor, and the date of the offering. CERTPJ photo archive. Photo H. O. Rotermund.

fashion and are always the same and those that vary with circumstances.

From the standpoint of the phenomenology of religions, magical behavior is based on the conviction that man has the capacity to manipulate his environment at will—objects, phenomena, evil spirits, demons, and even deities. This attitude is particularly illuminated by the verbal magic based on the belief in *kotodama.* From a functional standpoint, Japanese magic can be divided into three main categories: (*a*) to increase one's wealth or to make a profit; (*b*) to curse someone or harm him; and (*c*) to protect oneself from evil and calamities. In some of the latter practices, such as the *mushi-okuri,* which repels insects, or the *amagoi,* the prayer for rain, one can see elements of a therapeutic and prophylactic order grouped together. But it is not easy to distinguish the so-called magic attitude from the attitude that stems from a truly religious conviction, such as the *gankake* (vow) and the *kigan* (prayer, supplication), etc.

The whole life of the Japanese was formerly, and remains to a large extent today, punctuated by magical actions. This is especially true of birth and education (often imitative magic). It is also true of times of sickness, when magic is combined with therapy based on experience. Illnesses were often interpreted as the machinations of evil spirits, and efforts were made to chase them away, to transfer the evil to other objects or persons, to abandon it at crossroads, or even to "sell" it. Among magic objects or acts that could be used in this kind of healing are the saber, the knife, fishing, etc. Suspending a rice ladle (*shakush*) or garlic at the entrance of a house was a means of preventive therapy. Amulets (*o-fuda*) were used. Sacred ropes (*shimenawa*) were pulled. People used the *nembutsu* (notably in the form of the *hyakuman-ben nembutsu*) or a threatening *kigan.* They would force a deity to act, as in the case of Shibari Jizō ("bound Jizō"). Occasionally, the demons of diseases were dismissed (*ekibyōgami-okuri*) by simulating another time of year (notably by celebrating the New Year) or by some other way of disguising reality. Certain legendary events—as is obviously the case in the history of the teahouse on the Yu no O mountain pass—serve as the background for traditions that can often be summarized under the rubric of homophonic sympathy.

As far as death is concerned, magic rituals aimed above all to provide protection against impurity, to interrupt the relationship between the living and the dead, and to make sure that the dead would not return. While the "hunting of the demons" (demons of disease), referred to above, was carried out ad hoc in the event of illness, there were also other events, seasonal in character and propitious for such actions, including, most notably, the day of *setsubun* (the changing of the season). On that day, as on New Year's day, or on another two days known as the *kotoyōka* (the eighth day of the second and twelfth months), one could engage in a *mushi-okuri* or a *mushi-yoke,* otherwise performed right after the *taue.* The principles upon which the "insect hunt" is based have many points in common with the protective measures taken against the spirits of the dead, the *goryō* (angry spirits that inflict curses), a belief that goes back to the Heian period.

Numerous well-known practices take place at the beginning of the year, notably the *narikizeme,* a form of magic designed to ensure the fertility of trees. Most often the magical act is accompanied by the recitation of formulas (*jumon, tonaegoto, majinaiuta*), as the concept of *kotodama* demands.

H.O.R./g.h.

BIBLIOGRAPHY

1. Sources

SH. KARASAWA, *Shinbutsu hihō taizen* (Tokyo 1909). MEISHIN CHŌSA KYŌGI KAI, ed., *Nihon no zokushin,* 3 vols. (Tokyo 1952). K. ONO, *Kaji kitō himitsu taizen* (Tokyo 1970).

2. Monographs

B. FRANK, *Kata-imi et kata-tagae: Étude sur les interdits de direction à l'époque Heian,* Bulletin de la Maison Fr.-Jap., n.s., 5:2–4 (1958). H. O. ROTERMUND, *Majinai-uta.* Grundlagen, Inhalte und Formelemente japanischer magischer Gedichte des 17–20. Jahrhunderts. Versuch einer Interpretation, *MOAG*, vol. 59 (1975). Y. FUJIKAWA, *Meishin no kenkyū* (Tokyo 1932). T. HINO, *Meishin no kaibō* (Tokyo 1938). SH. INOGUCHI, *Nihon no zokushin* (Tokyo 1975). E. INOUE, *Yōkaigaku* (Tokyo 1930). T. KANEKO, *Kodai no juteki shinkō* (Tokyo 1968). E. KONNO, *Gendai no meishin*, Gendai kyōyō bunko (Tokyo 1969). Y. MIYANAGA, *Majinai no kenkyū* (Tokyo 1911). T. YOSHIDA, *Jujutsu* (Tokyo 1970). H. YOSHINO, *Nihon kodai jujutsu: Onmyōdō gogyō to Nihon genshi shinkō* (Tokyo 1975).

Additional monographs: GEOFFREY BOWNAS, *Japanese Rainmaking and Other Folk Practices* (London 1963). WINSTON DAVIS, *Dojo: Magic and Exorcism in Modern Japan* (Stanford 1980).

3. Articles

T. HARADA, "Zokushin," *Nihon minzokugaku taikei*, vol. 7 (1962). I. UENO, "Majinai ni tsuite," in *Minkan denshō*, 13:11.

Additional articles: U. A. CASAL, "Magical Vengeance in Old Japan," *Asiatische Studien* 10 (1956): 114–29. HAKU ITŌ, "Man'yōjin to kotodama," in *Man'yōshū kōza*, vol. 3 (Tokyo 1973), pp. 46–63. YOSHII IWAO, "Yamato-takeru no mikoto monogatari to majinai uta: Sono sōka ni tsuite no icki ksetsu," *Kokugo kokubun* 27, 10 (October 1958): 52–62. TSUNOSUKE NAKAGAWA, "Waka darani setsu," *Kokubungaku kō* 20 (1957): 20–29. EDWARD NORBECK, "Yakudoshi: A Japanese Complex of Supernatural Beliefs," *Southwestern Journal of Anthropology* 8, 1 (Spring 1952): 269–85.

4. Miscellany

N. MIYATA, "Kinsei no hayari-gami," *Nihonjin no kōdō to shisō*, 17 (1972). SH. ORIKUCHI, "Kodai kenkyū," *Orikuchi Shinobu zenshu*, 1–3. T. SAKURAI, *Minkan shinkō to gendai. Ningen to jujutsu*, Nihonjin no kōdō to shisō, 9 (1971).

Japanese Divination

Japanese divination is, on the one hand, the passive act of interpreting omens (*kizashi, zenchō*) and, on the other, that of prophesying the future with the help of procedures called *urani* (or *bokusen*). The first of these derives from the belief that certain omens (the presence of animals, manifestations of natural phenomena, symptoms in the human body, etc.) indicate the coming of a specific event. Thus, since ancient times, falling stars (*nagareboshi*) have been regarded as harbingers of death or imminent catastrophe, as is the cry of the raven (*karasu naki*). Peasants attempted to interpret certain meteorological phenomena out of a concern for the coming harvest: for example, snow at the beginning of the year promised a good harvest. Dreams (*yume*) are given a particular place in the interpretation of omens, and their images are perceived sometimes as good omens and sometimes as bad omens. Among the dream images that are good omens are the *takara-bune* ("treasure boat"), Mount Fuji, the animal messengers of the gods, etc. Among the evil omens are monks, the *taue* (the transplanting of rice), fishing, etc. Good dreams could be bought from another person, and those that boded ill changed for the better through certain magical acts.

The practices called *urani* actively sought knowledge of the future. One of the oldest known practices of this sort in Japan is scapulomancy (*futomani*), as attested to in the *Kojiki*, the *Nihongi*, and even the early Chinese chronicle known as the *Wei Che*. Divinatory acts, either *koboku* (the burning of turtle shells) or the use of sticks, were very popular from the earliest times, in which they were overseen by two state ministries. The people who occupy themselves professionally with this (the *ekisha*), who were especially prosperous during the three centuries of the Edo period, enjoy great popularity even today. The consulting of horoscopes (*o-mikuji*) also remains very popular, and horoscopes are sold in sanctuaries, where they are in demand especially at certain times in a life (marriage, examinations, etc.), or certain times in the year (New Year's, etc.). The *kayu-ura* ("divination through the use of rice paste")—which attempts to ascertain whether the harvest will be good—and the *mame-ura* ("divination through the use of beans," a kind of meteorology) are but two examples which testify to the vitality of the ancient traditions of divination in Japan.

H.O.R./d.w.

BIBLIOGRAPHY

1. Monographs

BAN NOBUTOMO, *Seiboku-kō*, Zenshū 2 (Tokyo 1907). SH. KANEZASHI, *Hoshi-uranai, hoshi-matsuri* (Tokyo 1974).

2. Articles

M. TSUBAKI, "Nihon ni okeru bokkotsu, bokkō, bokuhō," *Shūkyō kenkyū* 210 (1972). YANAGITA KUNIO, "Ishiura no shurui," *Yanagita Kunio shū* 30; "Toshi-ura no ni-shu," *YKS* 13; "Arata naru taiyō," *YKS* 13.

Additional article: SEY NISHIMURA, "Retrospective Comprehension: Japanese Fortunetelling Songs," *Asian Folklore Studies* 45, 1 (1986): 45–66.

3. Miscellany

K. HIGO, *Nihon ni okeru genshi shinkō no kenkyū* (Tokyo 1947). T. WAKAMORI, *Nenjū gyōji* (Tokyo 1957).

Takarabune ("boat of treasures"). Meiji period. This representation was placed beneath one's pillow on New Year's Day to guarantee a lucky dream. The animals, objects, and figures in the boat are symbols of longevity and prosperity. CERTPJ photo archive. J. P. Hauchecorne collection. Photo Frédéric/Rapho.

The *Yamabushi*, Mountain Ascetics of Japan

The term *yamabushi* ("those who sleep in the mountains," also called *shugenja*) designates ascetics and refers to one of the most peculiar forms of popular Japanese belief, *shugendō*. The *yamabushi* may be lay persons or monks; they practiced in the past and to a certain extent they still today practice the climbing of sacred mountains at certain times of the year; there, in the heights, they devote themselves to religious exercises of a psychophysical nature, acquiring in this way supernatural powers that qualify them as exorcists. *Shugendō* is "the path (the method, *dō*) for acquiring, by the practice of magico-religious exercises (*shu*)—in the mountains—supernatural forces assuring miraculous powers (*gen*)."

Our earliest information about the mountain ascetics and *shugendō* was furnished by missionaries of the second half of the sixteenth century (Lancelotti, Frois, Vilela, etc.). Their interpretation of *shugendō* is clearly influenced by Christian conceptions, resulting sometimes in a rather distorted representation. Analyzed with prudence, their accounts nevertheless preserve a good number of valuable elements. Two centuries later, it was Kaempfer who, in his *History of Japan*, was to contribute to our knowledge of the *yamabushi* and *shugendō*.

Nothing is known about the precise date when the term *shugen* was formed. A passage from the *Sandai jitsuroku* (True chronicle of the three reigns, 901) refers to a monk who had lived from his youth in the mountains of Yoshino and there acquired supernatural powers (*shugen*). In the *Konjaku monogatari-shū* (Tales of times now past, beginning of the twelfth century), a collection of Buddhist anecdotes, it is said of a monk that he "loved the *shugen*" and traversed numerous mountains, crossed the sea, and applied himself to harsh and difficult exercises. These passages clearly show that mountains were chosen by preference as the place for asceticism and the acquisition of magical powers. The word *dō* ("path") was probably added to the word *shugen* when, at the beginning of the Middle Ages, the *yamabushi* imposed upon themselves specific exercises, conceived religious categories distinct from those of other sects, and followed a training according to fixed rules: that is, at the time when a method and a tradition of *shugen* practices began to be made manifest as such. *Shugendō* was not, however, conceived in the Middle Ages as a true sect, as the terms *shugendō* and *yamabushi-dō* distinctly prove. It is really only at the beginning of the Tokugawa period (seventeenth to nineteenth centuries) that these beliefs were called *shugen-shū*, or just *zōshū*.

The central element, the most important of the characteristics of *shugendō* that date back to prehistory, is the veneration of nature, particularly the veneration of mountains (*sangaku shinkō*). The worship of mountains is certainly not limited to Japan, but there it has assumed a very important place in various popular beliefs, largely because of esoteric Buddhism (*mikkyō*), the second element constituting *shugendō*. In the course of its diffusion in India, Buddhism had already incorporated certain popular deities of Brahmanism in the same way as it had incorporated numerous religious conceptions; and it is particularly through these popular aspects that esoteric Buddhism was readily assimilated into the beliefs of the Japanese people. Copying a sutra, offering sutras, accompanied, for instance, prayers for rain (*amagoi*) or for curing illnesses and all other apotropaic acts. But pre-Buddhist magic and divination were not rejected or suppressed by Buddhism; it was rather a change of nuance.

Hall of Zaō Gonzen, Zaō-dō, at the Kinpusen-ji monastery on Mount Kinpu, Yoshino, Nara prefecture. In the foreground, preparations for the *saito-goma*, a ritual characteristic of *shugendō* that brings together apotropaic, expiatory, and sacrificial elements and is addressed either to Fudō myōō ("king of knowledge, the immutable," Acala) or to Aizenmyōō ("king of knowledge of attraction," Rāgavidyārāja). CERTPJ photo archive. Photo A. Stein.

Saito-goma of the *yamabushi* of Goryūson ryū-in. Kojima, Okayama prefecture. CERTPJ photo archive. Photo H. O. Rotermund.

"Free monks" (*shido-sō*), "holy men" (*hijiri*), *yamabushi*, etc., contributed through their pilgrimages to the diffusion of the rites and magical practices of popular esoteric Buddhism even in the remote provinces. They contributed to the amalgam with Shintoist elements. The way in which esoteric Buddhism and practices in the mountains were mingled in *shugendō* is made clear by the concept of *sokushin jōbutsu* ("to realize the nature of Buddha in our actual bodies"). For *shugendō*, that realization does not result, as in esoteric

Buddhism, from a mystic communion with the cosmic Buddha in word, action, or thought. In the manner of shamanism, rather, the spirits of the dead (ancestors), or Dainichi nyorai, in his concrete form of Fudō myōō (the "King of the Immutable Science"), are believed to take possession of the practitioner, endowing him with supernatural faculties: oracles, the power to cure illnesses, etc.

In the early period of Buddhism in Japan, that religion at first remained concentrated in the plain of Yamato and in its state-subsidized temples, where a privileged class of monks studied the doctrines. Contact with the population was limited to ascetics who mingled with the people, in whose service they often performed missionary activities. The most famous ascetic was Gyōgi, venerated later under the name of Gyōgi *bosatsu*. Like him, numerous ascetics in the mountains followed their own religious path; they often came into contact with shamanic practices reputed to confer extraordinary gifts. Among the most celebrated of these magicians are E no Ozunu and the monk Taichō. The principal region of the "Buddhism of the mountains" was Yamato, particularly the region of the Yoshino and Kumano mountains. Eventually, periods of asceticism on a mountain were vigorously encouraged as an essential part of a monk's spiritual training by Dengyō Daishi and Kōbō Daishi, the two founders of esoteric Buddhism in Japan; even before the Tendai and Shingon sects, esotericism may have had some place in the doctrines and studies of other sects. This suggests, too, that the custom of making pilgrimages in the mountains was propagated mainly by Japanese monks who had spent some time studying in China. But before the period of Dengyō and Kōbō Daishi, esotericism had been only one aspect of Buddhism. The new Buddhism of the mountains attempted to familiarize the Japanese people with ideas and conceptions proper to the "great vehicle" (*mahayana*), and in this task it was aided by the magico-religious elements of esotericism.

Esotericism established, with the help of mudra and mantra, a system of magical rites, utilized specially to protect against the many perils and dangers of daily life. Those who performed these rites and practices were "free monks," *ubasoku* (pious lay persons), "holy men" (*hijiri*), exorcists (*genja*), and finally *yamabushi*. Buddhism thus propagated was no longer pure Buddhism; it had become intertwined with non-Buddhist conceptions, such as the worship of mountains, the veneration of *yama no kami* ("deities of the mountain"), and numerous other popular beliefs. In close contact with shamans, often living at the foot of mountains, Buddhism won new domains of activity by absorbing preexistent ancient religious practices.

The shamanic aspect is another popular constituent element of *shugendō*. The life and activities of one such shamanic magician from the ancient period, living in the mountains and known for his miraculous powers, might constitute the foundation of the story in the *Shoku Nihongi*, which gives an account of E no Ozunu (En no Gyōja), the legendary ancestor of the *yamabushi*. Magic is another characteristic element of *shugendō*; the acquisition of magical powers was, as has been seen, the direct goal of exercises on a mountain. The importance attributed to the acquisition of these powers—which were then used in various domains of daily life—was expressed by the custom of a "competition of powers" (*gen kurabe*), one of the most spectacular forms of which, still practiced, is *hiwatari*, walking on fire. Such a successful demonstration of acquired powers was considered to be a guarantee of abilities to cure illnesses in a *kitō* (exorcism).

Another element constituting *shugendō*, still active today, is divination, a domain in which Daoist influences are clearly evident. Deciding the direction in which one must go and identifying lucky or unlucky days are classical aspects of it, as are also the practice of *kugadachi* (or trial by boiling water) and the rites of *yudate* (purification by boiling water). The last major element of *shugendō* is the concern for the elimination of sins (*metsuzai*), which is not foreign to Buddhism in general, but has taken in *shugendō* the specific form of an expiation by the sacrifice of life. Such suicide has been practiced by the *yamabushi*, in the form of *shashin-gyō* ("the practice of abandoning the body"), since the ninth century. That it may have been quite widespread is attested by the prohibition of its practice that is found in the *Sōni-ryō* (Code for monks and nuns, 701). The present form of *shashin-gyō*, as it is practiced on Mount Omine, is *nozoki* ("gazing into the valley").

When the period of exercises on a mountain became a criterion for acquired powers, there began to be a custom not only of "practicing" on a single mountain, but of climbing the most accessible of them, which favored a great diffusion of this kind of asceticism and also changed its character: more than the eremitic life, it was life in pilgrimage that was preferred and that became the most important characteristic of the *yamabushi*. The popularity of their pilgrimages coincided with the custom among nobles of going to Kumano, and for this kind of pious expedition the *yamabushi* were taken as guides. From the end of the Heian period they occupy an important place in the religious world of Japan. They begin then to distinguish themselves from other religious groups by outward dress and to become, on the threshold of the Middle Ages, the most characteristic figures of Japanese syncretism. In their aspect of monks in pilgrimage to the local centers of *shugendō*, they were called *kyakusō* ("monk visitors"). Often they traveled through the provinces by routes that they had opened and that they alone knew; at the beginning of the Muromachi period (fourteenth century) they were everywhere. In the course of a pilgrimage, a *sendatsu* accompanied them, a guide who also directed the ritual climbing of the mountains (*mine-iri*) and whose tasks were, in addition, to organize and perform rites during the period of the ascent and to point out certain taboos that, even today, affect the consumption of food and drink, as well as the use of certain words. When these itinerant ascetics encountered one another on the way—where they subsisted principally by *takuhatsu* ("the search for alms")—their custom was, in the Middle Ages, to practice *mondō*: ritualized dialogues, with stereotyped questions and answers. This is a custom that is sometimes still observed, but then it took place in the context of certain rites of the *yamabushi*. The tradition of such *mondō*, which in the Middle Ages were already ritualized in the *yamabushi-seppō* ("preaching of the *yamabushi*"), included the *saimon* ("ballads") from the end of the Middle Ages; in the Edo period these became the *uta-saimon* ("sung *saimon*"), already approaching entertainment, and, still later, the *Naniwa-bushi* ("expressions of Naniwa").

On the cultural plane, the role of the itinerant *yamabushi* was manifested in the literary domain (see the *otogi-sōshi*, popular stories, and the *gunki-mono*, epics of war) and in the domain of *geinō*, popular dramatic arts (as, for instance, the *yamabushi-kagura*). The art of Japanese syncretism is to some degree identical to the art of *shugendō*. This is suggested, for example, by the mandalas (graphic representations of the spiritual world of a Buddha, Bodhisattva, or other deity) or the statues of the *myōō* ("kings of knowledge"). A typical expression of the art of *shugendō* is the *kake-botoke* ("hanging Buddhas") chiseled on the back of a votive mirror.

What were the tasks of the itinerant *yamabushi*? The role of the *sendatsu* has already been mentioned. The most impor-

Yamabushi in the precincts of the temple Asakusa-dera in Tokyo, selling medicines, and performing the functions of horoscope caster and magician. CERTPJ photo archive. Photo H. O. Rotermund.

(Left) Ceremonial garb of the *yamabushi* of Mount Haguro, Dewasanzan, Yamagata prefecture. On the man's head, the *tokin;* in his right hand, the *kongōzue;* in his left hand, the *hiôgi* fan; and around his neck, the *yuigesa* stole and the *hora-(gai)* conch shell. CERTPJ photo archive. Photo H. O. Rotermund.

tant tasks of the *yamabushi* in general were until recently exorcism and divination. Curing illnesses with the help of exorcism, with specific amulets (*o-fuda*), performing magic and divination, often accompanied by *tonaegoto* ("magical formulas") or *majinai-uta* ("magical poems"), were preeminently the domain of the *yamabushi.*

When the *yamabushi* were not traveling through the provinces, they remained—particularly from the period of Edo on—in the service of a "parish" (*danna-ba*), attached to a local center of *shugendō,* unless they were in the service of a *daimyō* (feudal lord) for whom they served as a substitute (*daikan*) in pilgrimages, for instance. Once they began to establish themselves in villages and sanctuaries in this manner, to wed *miko* (kinds of female shamans) in order to divide the work, and to appropriate to a large extent the practices and rites of *ommyōdō* ("the way of the yin and the yang"), their influence on the daily life of rural communities became very strong.

H.O.R./b.f.

BIBLIOGRAPHY

1. Sources

Shugendō shōsho 1–3, in *Nihon daizōkyō* (Tokyo 1919). *Sangaku shūkyō-shi kenkyū sōsho,* 12 vols. (Tokyo 1976–).

2. Monographs

H. B. EARHART, *A Religious Study of the Mount Haguro Sect of Shugendō,* MN Monograph (Tokyo 1970). G. RENONDEAU, *Le shugendō: Histoire, doctrine et rites des anachorètes dits yamabushi* (Paris 1965). H. O. ROTERMUND, *Die Yamabushi: Aspekte ihres Glaubens, Lebens und ihrer sozialen Funktion im japanischen Mittelalter* (Monographien zur Völkerkunde 5) (Hamburg 1968). G. SCHURHAMMER, "Die Yamabushis; nach gedruckten und ungedruckten Berichten des 16. und 17. Jahrhunderts," in *Zeitschrift für Missionswissenschaft und Religionswissenschaft* 12 (1922); reprinted in *MOAG* 46 (1965). SH. GORAI, *Yama no shūkyō-shugendō* (Tokyo 1970). SH. GORAI, ed., *Konohagoromo,* Tōun rokuji, Tōyō bunko 273 (Tokyo 1975). H. MIYAKE, *Shugendō girei no kenkyū* (Tokyo 1971). T. MURAKAMI, *Shugendō no hattatsu* (Tokyo 1943). SH. MURAYAMA, *Yamabushi no rekishi,* Hanawa sensho 71 (Tokyo 1970). A. TOGAWA, *Dewa sanzan shugendō no kenkyū* (Tokyo 1973). E. UNO, *Shugendō,* Nihon shūkyō dai kōza (Tokyo 1927–28), vol. 9, 11, 17. T. WAKAMORI, *Shugendoō-shi kenkyū* (Tokyo 1943); *Yamabushi* (Tokyo 1964).

Additional monograph: CARMEN BLACKER, *The Catalpa Bow* (London 1975).

3. Articles

C. BLACKER, "Initiation in Shugendō: The Passage through the Ten States of Existence," in *Initiation: Contributions to the Theme of the Study* (Leiden 1965). I. HORI, "Self-Mummified Buddhas in Japan: An Aspect of the Shugen-dō (Mountain Asceticism) Sect," in *History of Religions,* 1, no. 2 (1961). P. LOWELL, "Occult Japan, or the Way of the Gods: An Esoteric Study of Japanese Personality and Possession," *TASJ,* vols. 21 and 22. SH. KOYANAGI, "Dōkyō to shingon mikkyō to no kankei wo ronjite shugendō ni oyobu," in *Tetsugaku zasshi* 450–51 (1924). N. KUBO, "Dōkyō to shugendō," in *Shūkyō kenkyū* 173 (1962). SH. SUZUKI, "Shugendō natsu mine-iri ni tsuite," in *Shūkyō kenkyū* 174 (1963).

Additional articles: SHIGERU GORAI, "Yūgyō no hijiri-tachi," *Dentō to gendai* 16 (July 1972): 126–37. TAMOTSU HIRUSUE, "Yūgyō-teki naru mono," *Bungaku* (1970), pp. 250–301. ICHIRO HORI, "On the Concept of Hijiri (Holy Man)," *Numen* 5 (1958): 128–60. MANABU MURAKAMI, "Setsuwa Tales and Hijiri Ascetics," *Acta Asiatica* 37 (1979): 85–103.

The *Tengu* Demons of Japan

The famous "epic of war" of the Japanese Middle Ages, the *Heike monogatari* (Tale of the Heike, thirteenth century), expresses the idea that the destiny of two rival families, the Taira and the Minamoto, which contended for supremacy on the threshold of the Middle Ages, was influenced and even directed by the two divinities Itsukushima Myōjin and Hachiman. The rise and influence of the general in chief Taira no Kiyomori (1118–81) was supposed to have been due, for instance, to Kumano Gongen, and the *Taiheiki*—another epic of war—relates that the crossing of Emperor Go Daigo (1288–1339) at Hōki was successfully achieved thanks to dragon deities. Such views express the medieval conception of the world that attributed the events of history to the action of specific deities; on the other hand, the preceding period, the Heian period (late eighth to twelfth century), identified supernatural forces either with a "destiny," not specifically determined, or with Shinto and Buddhist deities in general.

One of the characteristics of the medieval conception of the world was that the action of deities is not indicated only through oracles: divine powers appear in the open; thus the *Taiheiki* relates how Zaō Gongen, who had taken the form of a "luminous thing" (*hikari mono*), showed the way to Emperor Go Daigo on Mount Kinpu when he was fleeing to Yoshino.

In addition to the Buddhas and the Shinto deities, demons and malevolent spirits of all kinds exercised their influence over human beings. Among the "transformed beings" (*bakemono*), the best-known are the *tengu* ("celestial dogs," a literal but inexact translation, considering the connotations of this word in Japan), who are demons closely connected with the mountains. From the Heian period, innumerable anecdotes developed around the *tengu* (see, for example, *Konjaku monogatari shū* [Tales of times now past], chap. 20).

The Japanese *tengu,* whose image has remained alive until now, is, in certain regions of Japan, identified with the *yama-otoko* ("the man of the mountains," a monster) and has the traits of the *yamabito* or "people of the mountains" (who are, moreover, also called *tengu* in certain texts). It is above all in isolated mountain communities, most preoccupied with demons, that beliefs in the *tengu* have been primarily transmitted, and it is there that sanctuaries have even been consecrated to them.

In popular imagination, the *tengu* appear suddenly, and they are capable, just like foxes, of bewitching human beings. Because of this element of suddenness, any unusual and strange phenomenon came to be attributed to some machination of the *tengu.* Endowed with terrible supernatural powers (and the art of becoming invisible or of freely altering appearance), and also able to fly, the *tengu* are often represented as shunning the world of men. With some ambiguity, feelings of vengeance as well as of compassion are attributed to them, which causes them to be at the same time feared and venerated. This connects them somewhat with the "deity of the mountain" (*yama no kami*).

China had two representations of the *tengu,* one which saw in them a meteoric phenomenon (see *Shih-chi,* "Historical accounts" of Sima Qian, first century B.C.), an omen of catastrophes or wars, and the other which regarded them as fabulous beings living in the mountains (see *Shan-hai ching,* "Chronicle of the mountains and the seas," between the twelfth and second centuries?). The Japanese probably borrowed from China the concept of the *tengu* as a meteor. However, the popular milieux retained only the second conception, the idea of a demonic creature, although in Japan this creature no longer has, in a practical way, anything in common—of appearance and character—with his Chinese homologue: he is, in fact, no longer either a star or an animal, which has led certain scholars to formulate the hypothesis of a purely Japanese *tengu.* This is particularly true of Inoue Enryo, who thinks that the *tengu* were born in the mountains, where many natural phenomena (rain, wind, the falling of rocks) might seem, to the people of the plains, different from what they know, and terrible. It has also been speculated that the populations that withdrew to the mountains at the time of the unification of the country were the source of many beliefs in strange beings: encounters with woodcutters or even the *yamabushi* ("those who sleep in the mountains") might lead people to believe that they had seen supernatural beings. Finally, it is conceivable—psychologically speaking—that those who frequent mountain sanctuaries are more easily inclined to see the supernatural everywhere. This is what the scholar Hirata Atsutane (1776–1843) suggests in his *Kokon yōmi-kō* (Study on the specters of the present and the past, 1828).

The image of the modern *tengu,* with his various manifestations and functions, such as those mentioned above, is nevertheless rather remote from the concept of the medieval *tengu,* who is closely associated with the idea of proud monks (particularly the *yamabushi*) reduced to an animal existence. Some of the mountains where the *tengu* reside are well-known centers of *shugendō*—mounts Atago, Takao, Kumano, and Omine, for example—and are attested as such in medieval literature.

Karasu Tengu ("crow *Tengu*"). Wood, 14 cm. Nagano. Inscription: "Shinshû karasu tengu." CERTPJ photo archive. Berval collection. Photo L. Frédéric.

The depiction of the *tengu* has endowed these demons with the features of birds, with wings, a beak, and claws, but at other times they have a long nose and an entirely red face. The literature has many references to these features of the *tengu:* beaks and wings, for instance, in the *Konjaku monogatari shū*. The *Taiheiki* interprets the spoor of birds on mats as the sign of a gathering of *tengu.* As for dress, the *tengu* are rather like monks and *yamabushi;* but although there is no longer anything to indicate a connection with the bird, the *tengu* monk may, in certain representations, display a sign of this affinity, for example, a fan made of feathers. From numerous detailed descriptions in the literature (see *Genpei seisui-ki, Taiheiki*), one may surmise that the *tengu* look like kites, and that they wear clothes typical of the *yamabushi:* the khaki *kakigoromo* and the *tokin,* a small linen cap.

Let us now consider the nature and function of the medieval *tengu* before examining in this light their connection with the *yamabushi.* The medieval *tengu* are chiefly monks who have fallen, through the sin of pride. The *Shasekishū* (Collection of sand and pebbles, thirteenth century) distinguishes between the evil *tengu* and the good; the good ones make themselves useful to men, assist them, and sometimes transfer their supernatural abilities to them: for example, to a monk, the mantra that makes one invisible (see *Shasekishū*), while, in the *Nō Kurama Tengu,* the hero Yoshitsune learns the martial arts from the *tengu* of Mount Hurama. The *Miraiki* "ballad" (*kōwaka*) shows the *tengu* of Mount Hira as being animated by feelings of compassion toward humans. Their supernatural faculties predispose the *tengu* not only to fly and to become invisible, but also to adopt at will any appearance whatever, and to simulate, for instance, the apparition of a Buddha. But it is their evil humors and the numerous expressions of their hostility to the Buddhist law, far more than any of their positive aspects, that the texts of Japanese literature recount: they carry off children, cause objects to fall and buildings to collapse, and sow dissension. The presence of a *tengu* is often signaled—as in the *Heike monogatari*—by the sound of falling trees. Other acoustic manifestations of the presence of a *tengu,* such as the *tengu-warai* (laughter) and the *tengu-ishi* (falling stones or pebbles), also have the character of a sudden event in the solitude of the mountains or forests. The main point of the inauspicious activities of the medieval *tengu* may be described as anti-Buddhism. The *Taiheiki* and the *Kokonchomonshū* abound in stories of *tengu* who disturb the spiritual exercises of monks. These texts for the first time, as the war epics from the Muromachi period were to do later, explicitly allude to the identity of the *yamabushi* and the *tengu,* to such an extent that the terms *tengu* and *yamabushi* served equally to name those who, in these Buddhist stories, molest monks, kidnap them, or lead them away on a forced visit to their previous dwelling places. Among the narratives that have as a common theme the kidnapping of a *chigo* (a novice in a temple), see especially the *Aki no yo no naga monogatari,* a story that, the *Shasekishū* records, refers for the first time to the sufferings to which the *yamabushi-tengu* are exposed. Sometimes they are consumed by flames, sometimes demons from hell make them drink melted copper from sake cups, or put them to death, temporarily, by burning. In this context, certain sources describe a dance of the *yamabushi,* probably there a reflection of their custom of performing, after practices in the mountains (*mine-iri*), certain dances called *ennen-mai* ("dance for the prolongation of life").

Tengu from Yamagata wearing the *tokin,* the usual attribute of the *yamabushi.* The inscription on the left reads "Dewa sanzan." CERTPJ photo archive. Berval collection. Photo L. Frédéric.

Though it is easy to ascertain the close kinship between *yamabushi* and *tengu,* it is much harder to understand the reasons for it. In brief: the Heian period, strongly imbued with ideas about the existence of demons, conceived the *tengu* as a being of a terrible nature, hostile to the Buddhist Law, having the appearance of a kite. As fomenters of trouble, the *tengu* were compared to "malevolent spirits"—the *goryō*—which resulted in attributing to the *tengu* a social function analogous to the function that accrued to the *goryō.* The Kamakura period, marked by the idea of powerful forces controlling human destinies, interpreted the activities of the *tengu* as the consequences of an unforeseeable destiny.

The disorder created by warrior-monks, who moved through narrow passes to intimidate the capital, and the quarrels between temples may have appeared to be the evil work of the *tengu,* as was the haughty attitude assumed here and there by monks too sure of their power and too negligent of monastic discipline. Moreover, among the monks who fomented disorder in the Middle Ages, one must include certain *yamabushi,* who had begun in the Kamakura period (twelfth to fourteenth centuries) and the Muromachi period (fourteenth to sixteenth centuries) to organize themselves and to concentrate their forces: among the seven kinds of Japanese *tengu* enumerated in the *Tengu no sōshi* (Story of the *tengu,* thirteenth century) are the "monks of the Daigoji temple," otherwise called *yamabushi.* But the *tengu* and the *yamabushi* also shared the mountains, the *tengu* to take their kidnap victims there, to hold their meetings there, etc., and the *yamabushi* for their exercises—from which arose the suspicion that the *yamabushi* were connected with demons, were possessed by them, and in fact were one with them. The *yamabushi*—like many shamans—were often recruited among the natives of the mountains, who, as we have just seen, were sometimes confounded with the *tengu.*

But other reasons are connected with the very figure of the *yamabushi.* The mountains were, for them, the place where they strove to acquire, by various exercises and mysterious practices, supernatural gifts (among others—see the *Taiheiki*—the ability to bring the recently dead back from hell) that could not fail to hold the attention and stimulate the

Tengu in the character of a *yamabushi* at Mount Takao-san, Tokyo, Hachiōji-shi. Identifiable as attributes of the *yamabushi* are the *tokin* and the *yuigesa* stole. In his left hand the *tengu* carries a fan of feathers, symbolizing his ability to fly. CERTPJ photo archive. Photo H. O. Rotermund.

imagination. The account from the *Taiheiki* that narrates the visit of the *yamabushi* Unkei to Mount Atago, where he attended an assembly of *tengu* deliberating the fate of the world, attests, on the one hand, the *yamabushi* practice of foretelling the future and at the same time brings them closer to the *tengu*, who were thought to be able to tell the future and influence the course of the world.

Should we assume that the *yamabushi* were inclined to arrogance, conceit, and the abuse of the powers of the exorcists and diviners in contact with the supernatural world? The fate that was usually imagined for those who had committed the sin of pride was to fall among the demons. Moreover, that the *tengu-yamabushi* were, as we saw, hostile to Buddhism, that they burned down temples and molested and kidnapped monks, signifies perhaps a repugnance on the part of the *yamabushi* for other sects that, in their turn, were ready to criticize their mode of life harshly (see *Shasekishū*). With a most original point of view, Tsuda Sōkichi holds that demons, and particularly the *tengu*, were supposed to have power only over monks who were negligent in Buddhist discipline or services. It is likely that the *yamabushi* themselves—by their garb, their bizarre exercises, and their behavior—contributed to maintaining the fear that was inspired by the belief in their kinship with the terrible *tengu*. For them, this went so far as the veneration of the *tengu* (see, for example, in the *Genpei seisui-ki*, the story of the ascetic Mongaku) as patron deities of the *shugendō*.

H.O.R./b.f.

BIBLIOGRAPHY

1. Monographs

H. O. ROTERMUND, *Die Yamabushi: Aspekte ihres Glaubens, Lebens und ihrer sozialen Funktion im japanischen Mittelalter* (Hamburg 1968). M. CHIGIRI, *Tengu-kō, jōkan* (Tokyo 1974); *Tengu no kenkyū* (Tokyo 1975).

Additional monograph: CARMEN BLACKER, *The Catalpa Bow: A Study of Shamanistic Practices in Japan* (London 1975).

2. Articles

M. W. DE VISSER, "The Tengu," *TASJ* 36 (1908). E. INOUE, "Tengu-ron," *Meishin to shūkyō* (Tokyo 1916).

Additional articles: U. A. CASAL, "The Tengu," *Occasional Papers of the Kansai Asiatic Society* (Kyoto 1957); "The Goblin Fox and Badger and Other Witch Animals," *Folklore Studies* 18 (1959): 1–94. W. MICHAEL KELSEY, "The Raging Deity in Japanese Mythology," *Asian Folklore Studies* 40, 2 (1981): 213–36. TAKESHI UMEHARA, "The Genealogy of Avenging Spirits," *Diogenes* 86 (Summer 1974): 17–30.

3. Miscellany

K. YANAGITA, "Yama no jinsei," *Yanagita Kunio shū* 4 (1963).

JAPANESE SHAMANISM

In the religious life of ancient Japan, which was shared among various clans, certain persons who had shamanic traits took charge of the ritual ceremonies of the villages. Then in the sixth and seventh centuries, when a suprafamilial and supralocal organization came into being, the deities (*kami*) venerated by the diverse clans were regrouped into a genealogically ordered system and, parallel to this evolution, certain of those who had been shamans of influential clans were given new duties of a governmental nature, while others retained their earlier functions. Buddhism undoubtedly influenced the traditional practices of the shamans, introducing, for example, the use of mantras (magical formulas) which were believed to ensure peace, protect from fires, bring rain, etc. At the beginning of Japanese Buddhism, the state supervised the ordination of monks, their requests to go to the mountains to perform austerities, etc.; in short, all that concerned the new religion. This was done through the consultation of the *Sōniryō* (Code for monks and nuns, 701).

The state monks, shut into their temples where they pursued their study of Buddhist hermeneutics, lacked contact with the common people, whose religious demands and aspirations were attended to by "free monks" (*shido-sō*) who devoted themselves to magical exercises and rites outside of Buddhist orthodoxy. Close to the free monks were the *ubasoku* (lay worshipers), whose origins dated from the Nara period. They frequented the mountains and forests, performed exorcisms, recited the sutras, and practiced divination. Entering the religious life without the permission of the government, they preferred the mountains as their place of asceticism, mountains in which they encountered magicians and shamans who were often recruited from among the "people of the mountains" (*yamabito*).

In short, though there were shamans who came under the influence of Buddhism, the Buddhists, reciprocally, took on certain shamanic tasks and functions, which they carried out with equal success. Soon a stay in the mountains came to be regarded as an indispensable stage for anyone who thought he was a magician. There was a great demand for magic, and Buddhism gained ground all the more easily after a decree of 729 (*Shoku Nihongi* [Chronicle of Japan, continued, 797]) prohibited the magic and rites that were unorthodox in Buddhist eyes.

It was probably a magician of the *yamabito* sort who was at the source of the legend of En no Gyōja. This magician certainly enjoyed a great reputation, for he is mentioned in the *Shoku Nihongi;* but he is also a somewhat fantastic and syncretic person around whom numerous legends took shape. The *Shoku Nihongi* relates that he was exiled to the Izu peninsula. Renowned for his powers, he had lived on Mount Katsuragi, and a Korean from one of the higher courtly circles had even chosen him to be his master; but, jealous of the powers of En no Gyōja, he went so far as to slander him before the emperor. To this point, the account appears to be quite historical, but the traits that follow are clearly legendary: it was said of Ozunu (En no Gyōja) that he was capable of putting demons to work for him, of forcing them to draw water, to cut branches from trees, etc. If they were not obedient, he forced them to submit to his will through the use of magic powers. The passage cited in the *Shoku Nihongi* would suggest that En no Ozunu was a magician from the region of Mount Katsuragi, in the same way as there were other magicians on other mountains. But in his biography in the *Nihon Ryōiki* (Anthology of miraculous and strange stories of Japan, early ninth century), he is depicted as a true Buddhist who venerated, for example, the "three jewels" (*sanbō:* the Buddha, the law, and the monastic community). "En no Ubasoku was of the family of Kamo," states the text. "Every night he attached himself to a cloud of five colors, flew through the air in the company of the denizens of the palace of the *sen* (spirits), and frolicked in the gardens of eternal life. . . . He practiced the magic of the *kujaku* (peacock) and showed that he was possessed of a marvelous power. He chased after the *kijins* (demons) to use them as he pleased . . . [here we pass over the account of how he was slandered and exiled]. In those days he ran over the waters as if he were walking on solid ground . . . and leapt into the sky where he soared like a phoenix" (trans. Renondeau, *Shugendō*). The allusion to the flight of the phoenix betrays the tendency, already considerable in the *kōsō-den* (biographies of illustrious monks), to endow Buddhist monks with certain attributes of the *sen* (or spirits). Yet the question must be posed as to whether the flight of En no Ozunu is explicable solely in terms of the Daoist qualities of *sen.* If we are to believe the *Nihon Ryōiki,* the supernatural powers of En no Gyōja are due to the practice of the mantra of the *kujaku-ō* ("queen of the peacocks"), which was originally a variant of a formula pronounced for protection against snakes. According to Waddell, the peacock is related to an Indian sun bird that preys upon snakes. The very idea of the bird was influenced by that of the *garuda,* the mythic Indian bird who was most notably incorporated into esoteric Buddhism as a manifestation of Bonten (Brahma). Various ideas about the *garuda* also exercised a certain influence (according to de Visser) upon representations and conceptions of the Japanese *tengu.*

It is difficult to know when and for what reason En no Gyōja was proclaimed the founder of the *shugendō* and the ancestor of the *yamabushi.* There are instances of his veneration from the Middle Ages onward, but this is certainly not founded upon historical fact. The exercises and practices that were initiated by En no Gyōja may have resembled to some extent those of the *yamabushi* of later periods, and his designation as the ancestor of the *yamabushi* is not unrelated to the fact that he already enjoyed great renown as a magician in the Nara period. It is also likely that En no Ozunu had disciples. Mount Katsuragi, which is mentioned in the *Shoku Nihongi,* has an early reputation as an object of veneration, especially at the court. It was the dwelling place of the divinity Hitokotonushi ("the master of a single word," probably an oracle) and the people feared and respected those who served this deity. These disciples were the ones who, in contact with Buddhist groups, could have transmitted the exercises and practices of their master, as well as his memory. It may have been the same with Mount Kinpu in Yoshino, a renowned place of asceticism from the second half of the Nara period onward, which was destined to become even more popular than Mount Katsuragi. And this is why En no Gyōja, too, was connected with Kinpu, as his biography attests in the *Nihon Ryōiki.* One proof that the legend of En no Ozunu was influenced by Buddhists or by mountain-dwelling ascetics of Buddhist origin is the fact that, from the mountain-dwelling magician which he was in the *Shoku Nihongi,* En no Ozunu is transformed into an *ubasoku* (pious layman) in the *Nihon Ryōiki.* In this text the deity of Mount Katsuragi, Hitokotonushi, is one of the demon gods whom Ozunu triumphs over through the use of the *kujaku-ō mantra,* thus proving the superiority of Buddhist

En no Gyōja, Dorogaw Ryūsenji (Nara prefecture) at the foot of Mount Omine. At left, one of the two servants, Goki and Zenki, who are associated in legend with the ascetic En and are the demons of the mountain and subject to his magic powers. In his right hand En no Gyōja holds a *shakujō* (a stick with rings), in his left hand a sutra scroll. CERTPJ photo archives. Photo H. O. Rotermund.

magic over the powers of the *kami* (cf. Tsuda). At the same time, the anecdote of the construction of a bridge connecting Katsuragi with Kinpu evokes the meritorious social activity, often mentioned in the *Shoku Nihongi*, of certain monks of the Nara period. En no Gyōja first appears as a *gyōja*, that is, as an ascetic, in the *Sanbō-e kotoba* (Illustrated legends of the three treasures, 984); thus he has become completely Buddhist and able by virtue of his gifts to make deities appear (such as Zao bosatsu on Mount Kinpu, as related in the *Konjaku monogatari-shū*).

When the ascetics among whom the memory of En no Ozunu remained alive began to go on pilgrimages throughout the country, they could quite naturally have spread the myth of this Buddhist magician, still within the milieu of mountain-dwelling ascetics. The *shugendō* of later periods did in fact connect En no Gyōja with many mountains. Because of the distances which separated them, it is most unlikely that he climbed to the peak of every one of them, as the legends would have it; but these indications preserve the recollection of the numerous *yamabushi* ascetics who went on pilgrimages. When these ascetics organized themselves at the beginning of the Middle Ages, En no Gyōja was promoted to the rank of ancestor. In the doctrinal texts of the end of the Middle Ages and of the Edo period, he is regarded as the incarnation of the deity Fudo myōō ("the King of Knowledge," Acala, "the Immutable"), and in 1799 the Emperor Kōkaku conferred upon him the title of *Jinben daibosatsu* or "the mysteriously transformed great Bodhisattva."

H.O.R./d.w.

BIBLIOGRAPHY

H. BOHNER, "Honchō shinsen-den," in *MN* 13, nos. 1–2 (1957). H. B. EARHART, "Shugendō, the Traditions of En no Gyōja, and Mikkyō Influence," in *Studies of Esoteric Buddhism and Tantrism* (Kōyasan 1965). G. RENONDEAU, "Le Shugendō, histoire, doctrine et rites des anachorètes, dits yamabushi," *Cahiers de la Société asiatique*, 18 (1965). H. O. ROTERMUND, "Die Legende des En no Gyōja," *Oriens Extremus* 12, no. 2 (1965). T. SATO, "En no Ozunu den," *Tenri daigaku gakuhō*, 8 (1956). S. TSUDA, "En no Gyōja densetsu-kō," *Shichō 1931*, no. 1.

Additional works: CARMEN BLACKER, *The Catalpa Bow: A Study of Shamanistic Practices in Japan* (London 1975). ICHIRO HORI, "Shamanism in Japan," *Japanese Journal of Religious Studies* 2, 4 (December 1975): 231–88.

JAPANESE FESTIVALS AND SEASONAL RITES: *MATSURI* AND *NENCHŪ GYŌJI*

I. *Matsuri*

The word *matsuri*, "festival," in Japan designates any act that a worshiper accomplishes in the dwelling place of a Shinto divinity. The offerings deposited on a tomb are placed there in order to celebrate *matsuru*, the spirits of the ancestors; similarly, the processions in which the crowds fill the streets pursuing the gods are *matsuri*. More particularly, festivals carried out in honor of the principal god of a village sanctuary are generally given this name. These are called *jinja no matsuri*, festivals of the Shinto shrines, which are frequently contrasted with another sort of ritual, those of seasonal festivals, the *nenchū gyōji*.

Japanese festivals are generally well known to tourists for their picturesque character and the high spirits and enthusiasm in which they take place. The religious function of the festivals is now quite diluted, and they are becoming profane village festivals in the same way as in the West. Nonetheless, behind the display one may recover the characteristics of the festival as they are defined, for example, by Durkheim in *Sociology and Philosophy*. They are communal festivals which serve psychologically to integrate the individual into society and sociologically to reinforce the unity of the group; they commemorate the existence of the group and renew and increase its power. These are the characteristics that we propose to recover through a brief description of Japanese festivals.

1. *The Community*

The first characteristic of the festival is its communal character. In the countryside, the community is that of the village, and in the city it is that of the neighborhood, which, curiously, constitutes a sort of extension of the original agrarian community. The communal character of Japanese civilization has long been attributed to purely economic factors and regarded as a consequence of rice cultivation. But the extension of this agrarian model to the whole Japanese territory is a relatively recent phenomenon, and there are still many regions today, especially in the north of Japan, in which the economy is based on the cultivation of other cereals. Yet we find that the *matsuri* are carried out similarly

Nebuta festival (July) in Hirosaki, Aomori prefecture: ritual of exorcism preceding the festival of the dead. The rumbling of the giant drum is supposed to drive away evil spirits. CERTPJ photo archive. Photo L. Berthier.

in these areas. The impact of rice cultivation on communal beliefs cannot be denied, but it appears to be a factor that has reinforced and perpetuated the festival rather than one that created it. The agrarian character of the deity to whom the festival is addressed seems secondary.

2. *The Gods*

The Japanese gods venerated in the sanctuaries are known, depending on the village, by three different names: *uji-gami, ubusuna-gami,* and *chinju-gami.* The word *chinju,* which is of Chinese origin, names the god as guardian of a place. In principle, this is not an indigenous deity, but it is often confused with *ubusuna-gami,* the local deity associated with a place and the people that live there. The idea of *uji-gami* is slightly more complex: it is either a tutelary deity of an *uji,* a family or clan, or the ancestral deity of that *uji.* In both cases, its role is to watch over the *uji-ko,* the children of the *uji,* who are regarded as the members of the community that the deity protects or as the deity's descendants. The problem is thus one of knowing whether there is a family relationship between the god venerated at the time of the annual festival—or festivals—of the sanctuary and the community of worshipers.

Japanese belief would have it that when someone dies, his spirit becomes a god after a time of varying length. In other words, at the end of a certain period, the spirit of the dead person loses its individuality and becomes fused into the ancestral spirit of the lineage to which it belongs. It is thus logical to regard the deity as the ancestor of the villagers. But this implies that all of the inhabitants of a place belong to the same clan. The growth of villages and increasing population movements entail certain modifications in this state of affairs. When individuals from outside of the clan come to settle on its lands, they sooner or later become integrated, mainly for economic reasons, into the community of worshipers—but this does not make them descendants of the ancestral spirit. The spirit loses its ancestral character and takes on a "local" coloring; then it tends to become a protector, an *ubusuna-gami.* In a third stage, the intensification of communications spreads the cult of a given prestigious god who appears to be more powerful than the local deity; the god is then simply imported, in the role of guardian of the site, and it generally supplants its predecessor. There is thus no fundamental difference between the three categories of gods, and the festivals dedicated to them are generally thought of as a group.

The ancestral deities also seem to have an agrarian character. The sanctuary festivals are essentially celebrated on the second and eleventh months of the old lunar-solar calendar (March and December), these being periods which apparently correspond to the beginning and end of agricultural work. A frequent assimilation of the ancestral god to the *ta no kami,* the god of the rice paddy, should also be noted, along with the fact that, according to popular beliefs, the *ta no kami* comes down from the mountain in the spring and returns there at the end of autumn, when it becomes the *yama no kami,* the deity of the mountain. But in Japan the mountain is the abode of the dead. Thus, agrarian characteristics are attributed to the ancestral deity in an agrarian context, which is not surprising.

3. *Organization of Worship*

Given the ancestral character of the deity, it is natural for the entire community to take part in the festival. Traditionally, participation is obligatory, and anyone who refuses runs the risk of bringing the wrath of the deity down on him and on the whole community.

Today, the Shinto priests (*kannushi*) generally celebrate the festivals in front of the worshipers, but there are still numerous examples of festivals performed by the *uji-ko* themselves. The entire community still participates in the festival in certain villages, where life is completely interrupted throughout the rites. The most celebrated example is that of the *igomori matsuri,* "the retreat festival" of the village of Hōzono, south of Kyoto. All of the villagers respect very strict prohibitions for two days; only after the purification of all of the participants does the festival of the tutelary deity take place. The inhabitants sleep all day and stay up all night, and their life is governed by the essential rule of not making any noise. In general, there are very strict rules concerning the use of a "pure fire" lighted with flint, as well as innumerable food taboos.

Nevertheless, it is clear that the prohibitions weigh very heavily on the life of the community; it would have been natural for them to attempt to lighten the load by establishing a rotating system. This is probably the source of the system of the *tōya matsuri,* festivals performed by certain members of the community in the name of everyone, following a system of rotation. The man who is assigned to direct the rites of a village, generally over the period of a year, is called the *tōya* or *tōnin,* which means "chief" or "he whose turn it is"; he is also given the name of *ichinen kannushi,* "priest for the year," or "priest for one year." The way of naming the *tōya* varies from one village to another (by the distribution of houses, a lottery, etc.). If several villages participate in the same festival, each of them has its own *tōya.*

Another sort of local organization is the *miya-za,* which was especially widespread in the Kinki era and in Kyushu. The *miya-za,* which today appear as associations for organizing the festivals, in earlier times administered the whole of economic, social, and religious life. Their composition varies considerably among villages, but originally they were associations made up of the most influential members of the village; even today, there are certain *miya-za* in which all of the members belong to a single family which is supposed to have founded the village. Economic pressures have forced the associations to become more open, and they may include men from all the important families of the village or even all of the village men. Women and children are generally excluded from them. The *tōya* is named from among the members of the *miya-za*.

The final stage of the development of the festival community was completed with the establishment of a professional clergy. This development did not, however, follow a linear trajectory, as this discussion might lead one to believe, and there are numerous intermediary stages.

4. *The Festival Site*

When the entire community participates in the festival, it is constrained to live in the vicinity of the deity, a fact that imposes on the community all sorts of interdictions and purifications that are incompatible with a normal active life. It may be for this reason alone that sanctuaries were constructed for the yearlong residence of the deity. Although this argument may appear insufficient, it is nevertheless true—with the exception of very old sanctuaries and those of great renown such as Ise or Izumo—that the *jinja,* or Shinto sanctuary, does not appear to be essential to festivals. When there is a *tōya,* the sacred palanquin which shelters the divine symbol is transported incognito to its dwelling on the eve of the festival, to be brought back in great pomp to the sanctuary only after the rites have ended. If there is no *tōya,* the festival begins with a procession that brings the sacred palanquin to the *o-tabi-sho,* the "place of travel," where the ceremonies take place. When the ritual has ended, the palanquin generally makes a ritual tour of its territory before returning to the sanctuary at the end of the rites. The *o-tabi-sho* may be identical every year—the most common procedure today—an outstanding tree, for example, being chosen as the material support for the visiting god. It may also change with each ceremony; its placement is then in principle designated by divination. The place of travel is above all a pure area into which the deity may descend without being affected by any pollution. It is brought to the attention of the deity and of men by the *shimenawa,* strings of rice grass from which paper cutouts are suspended.

5. *Preparations*

No one may approach the festival ground unless in a state of perfect purity. To attain this ideal state, two complementary methods are used. The first, which is passive, consists in respecting the prohibitions; the other requires active purifications called *misogi*—purification through the use of water (bathing in the sea or in a given river, picking up seaweed or pebbles, and sprinkling oneself with water drawn from a spot designated by tradition, etc.)—and *harai:* taking *gohei,* sticks hung with strips of paper and symbolizing the god, and shaking them over one's head. In most cases people in mourning may not participate in the festivals, because the pollution that weighs upon them, that of death, is the most terrible and may bring the wrath of the deity upon them, or even contaminate the deity. Festivals are thus always preceded by a taboo period, *mono-imi,* whose duration varies widely, from several weeks to a few hours. Finally, in order to ensure maximum safety, the purifications are increased throughout the period, in case some pollution has become attached to anyone.

6. *Welcoming the God*

When the purifications have been completed, the god is welcomed. It may manifest itself under various forms, with its spirit "clinging" to any material support, which is called a "divine body" (*shintai*). The supports are generally classified into three categories: natural, artificial, and human. Natural supports—the oldest ones—are plants, trees, stones, mounds, mountains, animals, etc. In the case of animals, one does not always know whether these are messengers of the gods or, more directly, the appearance that the gods take on. At festivals, moreover, it is rare to see any animals but horses, which, being the mounts of the nobility, were assimilated to the mounts of the gods. People may also offer horses (in stone ex-votos, for example) or regard them as beings that are sent by the deities and that participate more or less in their divine nature.

The most common artificial supports are the *gohei,* sticks from which white paper streamers are hung. The essential part of this cultic object is the wooden handle, which is a portable miniature of the tree or pillar, the most common natural representation of the deity. Alongside these ritual objects may be found a broad diversity of instruments: brooms, mortars, pestles, baskets, shoes, ladles, sickles, chopsticks, etc. In urban festivals, the symbol of the deity and the festival site are artificially brought together: these are immense chariots (called *yama, hoko, dashi,* etc.) which are richly decorated and on which the presence of the god is generally marked by an object such as a lance or a pole. The sacred palanquins, the *mikoshi,* are so widespread today that the word *matsuri* evokes their image. These sometimes enormous golden palanquins shelter a divine symbol which may be quite simply a piece of paper stuck to its ceiling or a twig, a mirror, etc.

The final sort of support of interest to us here is human. Two clearly different categories of these may be distinguished: that of mediums, generally feminine, *miko,* who in the past went into trances in order to transmit the oracles of the gods (today, they are most often female students who learn a few dance steps for the occasion in order to earn some pocket money); and that of the *yorimashi,* children in whose bodies the deity resides at the time of the festival: so it is that a baby wearing powder and makeup rides on a horse or on a man's back. It is considered to be a good omen when the baby sleeps through the whole of the ceremonies.

The coming of the god and its welcome, *kami-mukae,* constitute the primary elements of the festival. In the beginning, the welcome took place on the night preceding the ceremonies and had a secret character, but today, especially in the cities, where the theatrics are more developed, it becomes a grandiose procession that draws a crowd of spectators—for tourism and pilgrimage are becoming more and more mixed together.

7. *Offerings and Prayers*

Once the deity has been installed in the *o-tabi-sho,* offerings are made to it in order to delight it and to win its favor. The offerings are extremely varied goods of the highest quality: marine products, fish, mountain products, vegetables, dried fruits, and especially agricultural products, rice, cooked and ground rice cakes, *mochi,* and sake. The preparation of the offerings is very complex and often constitutes the essential part of the *tōya*'s duties. When the offerings are placed before the deity, one or more *norito,* prayers that announce the requests of the worshipers, are read in front of the divine symbol. Today the prayers generally consist of stereotyped texts requesting abundant harvests and asking that the community be spared any catastrophe. Then a meal follows, the *naorai,* during which offerings are consumed and sacred sake, called *miki,* is drunk. The communal meal with the deity has the function of transmitting the energy of the deity into the *uji-ko.* Inasmuch as the ancestral deity is often considered to be the rice god, and the offerings are essentially rice or derivatives of it, the worshipers are nourishing themselves with the vital strength of the ancestral spirit.

8. Closing Rites

The final phase of the festival consists in accompanying the deity back to its dwelling or, in the majority of cases, to the *jinja;* this is the *kami-okuri,* the separation from the deity. This closing rite corresponds to the welcome described above, which it closely resembles. Offerings may be made again and some dances executed again at the sanctuary before they finally leave the deity, who is not to return to the world of men until the following festival.

9. Entertainments

The rites constitute only the skeleton of the festival, which also generally includes an element of spectacle, the *kami-waza,* whose function, it is said, is to delight or appease the spirit of the god. Most often, the *kami-waza* are regarded as kinds of spectacles offered as a "bonus" to the gods and to men; there is a dissociation between the festival itself, conducted by the priest of the *tōya,* and distractions of a purely profane character dispensed to the worshipers. Yet a study of the contents of the *kami-waza* suggests that such was not always the case. Three categories of *kami-waza* may be distinguished:

—Competitions, sumo wrestling, footraces, archery, and contests to win an object which is sometimes a symbol of the deity used to have a divinatory goal. Today, it is believed that the winners will enjoy a more favorable fate than the losers during the year; but it must be noted that the sportive aspect of the rites is much more important than their religious value.

—Dance performances present the trances of a medium who formerly gave oracles. In the course of time, the oracle itself lost its importance, which devolved instead upon the atmosphere in which it was given; the *miko* gave up divination in order to dedicate themselves to *kagura* dances, whence their name of *kagura miko.* Thus, often there are *yudate kaguras,* "dances of boiling water," in which young girls in red and white priestly robes dance, a dwarf bamboo branch in their hands, sometimes in front of caldrons of boiling water. Formerly, the steam rising from the caldrons served to create an atmosphere that was propitious for giving oracles, and the *miko,* in their trances, transmitted the god's answers to the assembled worshipers. Today, in most cases, they content themselves with dipping the dwarf bamboos into the water and shaking them in the direction of the spectators.

—Theatrical presentations underwent a special development; it is difficult to recall, when one sees a No play presented by famous professionals, that the plays of the classical repertory thus presented have an origin similar to that of the *kagura.* Alongside the No theater, there are peasant dances, marionette plays, dances and music of the court, etc.

10. The Mythic Prototype of the Festival

According to tradition, the origin of the spectacles goes back to a dance performed by the goddess Ame no Uzume no mikoto before the "celestial abode of the rock grotto," in which the sun goddess Amaterasu had shut herself when she was terrified by the injuries that her brother Susano-o had caused her. Susano-o, having skinned a colt, pierced a hole in the peak of the roof of his sister's house and threw in the animal's corpse. When she saw this, one of the goddess's friends, stupefied, died with her genitalia run through by a shuttle, according to the *Kojiki* (Records of ancient matters, 712). Another version of these events, however, reported in the *Nihongi* (Chronicle of Japan, 720), declares that it was the goddess herself who died; mythologists agree that it was in a later period, when the goddess was established as the ancestor of the imperial family, that, shocked by the idea that this powerful goddess could have died in such a way, one of her friends was substituted for her. Whatever the case, once the goddess secluded herself in a cave, the world was plunged into darkness. The gods consulted with one another to find a way to bring her out of her retreat and appealed to Uzume, who turned over an empty tub in front of the door to the cave and, carrying dwarf bamboo branches in his hand, began to dance on top of it. At the height of her dance, she uncovered her breasts and lowered the belt of her garment down to her genitalia. Seeing this, the eight hundred myriads of gods burst out laughing. Amaterasu, amazed that it was possible to rejoice in her absence, partly opened the door to her cave and saw her reflection in a mirror that was held out to her; more and more intrigued, she came out of the cave, which a deity closed behind her.

Flower festival (*hana'-matsuri*), the Temple of Shin Yakushiji at Nara (month of April). The branches, which used to be gathered in the mountains, are the symbolic support of the deities. The seated figure at the right is the Buddha as healer, Yakushi nyori; at the left is Basara daishō, one of the "twelve generals" (*jūni shinshō*) in the entourage of the Buddha Yakushi. CERTPJ photo archive. Photo L. Berthier.

This myth is interpreted as the prototype for the rites of the "appeasing of the soul" (*tama-shizume*) and for popular rites executed immediately after the death of an individual in order to restore him to life. It describes the rebirth of the sun goddess, a rebirth made possible by certain rituals. This was a fertility rite consisting of the dance of Uzume, the ancestral goddess of the *miko*, who undressed herself. It is a rite whose aim is to reunite the body with the spirit that is escaping, by making a great racket to call it back: people stamp their feet in order to drive the forces of evil into the ground and to reawaken the vital forces that are hidden in the earth. This trance makes possible the revival of supernatural spirits whose strength becomes exhausted over time. Similarly, the *matsuri* functions to increase the deity's power by means of the energy generated through the ritual; and consequently to augment the strength of the entire community which, through the communal meal taken with it, participates in its power. The role of the festival seems to be more prophylactic than propitiatory, with divination playing only a very minor role.

The *matsuri* corresponds quite closely to what Malinowski called "religious activity," as opposed to "magical activity." We would say, borrowing the anthropologist's terms, that it expresses the cohesion and consciousness of the community, but that it prefigures no future event that it would bring on or forestall. In diametrical opposition to seasonal festivals, it includes its end in itself, in the energy that it generates and projects upon the community.

II. *Nenchū gyōji*

The expression *nenchū gyōji* means "things accomplished during the year" and designates the ensemble of rituals executed in Japan throughout the twelve months of the year. Although the term appears only in texts starting from the Heian period (eighth to twelfth centuries), it encompasses a much older reality. Popular language makes use of quite diverse terms that imply the idea of ruptures in time or transitions or denote taboos. These days were experienced in a particular fashion and placed outside the daily order whose normal unfolding they ensured.

Seasonal rites have various origins. Three principal currents may be distinguished: rites of the noble class inspired by ceremonies of the court, rites of warriors, and rites of agrarian origin. This classification is arbitrary, since the three sorts of rites exerted a perceptible influence on one another and were transformed and refined under the influence of customs and the Buddhist religion that came from the continent by way of the court. The agrarian rites remain the most archaic, since these are the only ones that are truly connected to the daily necessities arising from the vicissitudes of agriculture, vicissitudes made all the more serious by the fact that today this is often the monoculture of rice.

1. *The Calendar*

A note to a Chinese text composed in the third century, the *Wajinden*, specifies that before the introduction of the Chinese calendar, the Japanese knew only two seasons: spring, the plowing season, and autumn, the harvest season. Thus they conceived of a year whose subdivisions were founded upon the rhythm of agriculture. Furthermore, the study of ancient texts, like ethnographic research, shows that rituals generally took place in the second and eleventh months, at the beginning and end of the agricultural work. Thus the real year was spread over only ten months, with the two winter months constituting a sort of blank that corresponded to a time of rest. Nowadays the rites of *koto-yōka* (rites of the eighth day of the second and eleventh months) mark the extremities of this year; the period that separates them is a ritual period rich in prohibitions and centered upon the preparation and celebration of the New Year.

With the introduction of the Chinese calendar, the Japanese began to divide the year into four seasons. The calendar is founded upon two principles: a lunar time which gives rise to a twelve-month year and a solar time yielding a year composed of twenty-four seasonal breaths. The lunar year begins on the "initial day" of the year (*ganjitsu*), while the solar year begins on "the day of the starting point of spring" (*risshun no hi*). Since the two types of years have different lengths, the *ganjitsu* and the day of *risshun* coincide only once every nineteen years.

The introduction of the Western calendar—which is one month behind the lunar-solar calendar—only aggravated the disorder created by the superposition of the Chinese calendar upon the indigenous one, and tangled the situation inextricably.

2. *Rites of the New Year*

Today the New Year is set at January 1, but it seems that in the past the Japanese considered the month to have begun at the time of the full moon, i.e., the fifteenth. So there must have been two groups of rites, those of the "Great New Year," *ōshōgatsu*, around the first day of the first month, and those of the "Small New Year," *koshōgatsu*, around the fifteenth. The rites of the former are dedicated to each family's welcoming of the deity of the year (*toshi-gami*), to whom they give offerings—essentially of rice cakes, which are placed in a small alcove (*toshi-dana*) that serves as an altar. The presence of the deity in the house is marked by a few pine branches (*kado-matsu*) artistically arranged in a pot set on the threshold of the house; the branches serve as the material support for the spirit of the deity. The nature of that deity is fairly imprecise, and the oral tradition describes it as an old man with an elongated head, a one-legged god, or a god who is mounted on a headless horse and shakes a small bell. These fantastic descriptions associate him with the god of the mountain who comes down to the plains at the beginning of the plowing in order to transform himself into a rice deity. Yet, it is still too early to begin farm work; the god is also the ancestral or tutelary deity of the clan. The ancestral deities are appealed to to protect the coming year, and propitiatory rites are carried out; the master of the house, early in the morning of the first day of the first month, draws from a well the *waka-mizu* (the water of youth) which is used to prepare the first tea and to write the first words. Rites of "the beginning of the labors" (*shigoto hajime*) are executed either by striking the ground of the rice paddy three times after making an offering of a few grains of rice to the deity or by going out to sea to enact symbolically the movements of fishing. Finally, gifts are exchanged, with superiors giving more than inferiors by way of renewing the annual contract: the deities give rice to men, who offer them a few grains in exchange, while the lords offer their vassals rice cakes, *mochi*, as a means of renewing their ties of obligation.

The Small New Year seems to be more closely related to agrarian life; it consists essentially of propitiatory rites and divination. In the rice paddies or at the sanctuary, people mime the different stages of rice cultivation (*niwa ta ue*), and chase after young married couples to spank them with long sticks (*iwai-bō*) in order that they may have many children; children run around the fields hunting moles and birds to the accompaniment of ritual phrases. Finally, divination is practiced: people grill beans to deduce, from the way they brown, the sunshine, rains, winds, and storms of the twelve months of the coming year.

The rites may take place partly on the day of *setsubun*, the eve of *risshun*, which constitutes a sort of New Year. But usually people are content to throw the beans into the house while shouting, "Fortune inside, demons out."

The deity of the New Year leaves either at the end of the Great New Year, the seventh, or at the end of the Small New Year, the fifteenth. A great fire is lit, in which all of the New Year's decorations, including the *kado-matsu*, are burned; the *toshi-gami* departs, riding the smoke that rises from the fire. Numerous traditions assert that if one is exposed to the smoke or eats rice cakes cooked in the fire, this will bring long life. The fire, which is kindled at the moment when the sun sets, is a source of life for that heavenly body, to which it imparts strength, just as it does to men. Furthermore, the destructive power of the sun drives away inauspicious spirits.

3. *The Rites of Spring*

It is with the passing (*koto-yōka*) of the eighth day of the second month that the working year begins. On this day, a one-eyed monster visits all of the houses; to drive it out, people leave objects having many "eyes" on the threshold, especially strainers. The monster wastes its time counting the eyes until it is finally too late for it to enter. This strange visitor was formerly the "visiting god" or the "rare deity" (*marōdo-gami*) who came from afar during the period of the beginning of the agricultural work. People awaited it in their homes, without moving and with respect for the prohibitions; today, perhaps because it was necessary to portray it as dangerous so that people would not leave their houses, this powerful and fearsome god has become transformed into a monster. The *marōdo-gami,* whose mythic prototypes are Susano-o, a violent god who offered men the boon of cereals, and Omononushi, a healing god, come from the world beyond to bring civilization to men.

The beginning of spring is marked by rites of propitiatory offerings. One of the most interesting, because it has an equivalent in autumn, is that of the day of the young wild boar (*Inoko*), in the second month. The deity of the rice paddies descends from the mountains onto the plain; he is offered rice and the paddy is ritually plowed. In the countryside, this is a day off from work.

It is necessary at the same time to drive away evil powers, so there are numerous exorcisms and purifications. March 3 is known today as the day of the festival of the dolls (*hina-matsuri*), celebrated in honor of little girls. The dolls dressed in brocade that today decorate tiered platforms were formerly nothing more than rag, wood, or straw effigies that were thrown into streams or the sea as scapegoats to carry off all impurities. On the fifteenth day of the third month, the rites of purification are repeated: *mochi* are placed at the entrances of houses, hooked onto dwarf bamboo branches. These are then thrown down at crossroads with sheets of paper on which is written "May the 404 diseases go away!"

Sometimes it is not until after these rites—or even later, on April 8, the Buddha's birthday—that the deity of the rice paddies is greeted. But in the country this is the day of the deity of the mountain, whom the people go to seek on the heights where they gather branches and flowers that will serve as supports for the deity when it comes to watch over the work in the fields.

4. *The Rites of Summer*

The rites of the beginning of the summer concern the transplanting of the rice, which is one of the important phases of rice culture; exorcisms and fertility rites are frequent at this time. The fifth day of the fifth month, the day of little boys, is consecrated to such rites. Samurai dolls set out on decorated tiered platforms are colorful reflections of ancient scapegoats. In the countryside, children gather armfuls of irises and slap the ground with them; they wrangle on the borders of the settlements while men and women throw stones at each other or gibe at each other. This is the only day of the year on which women may assert themselves; formerly, men were obliged to leave their homes for the night, because their wives were being visited by the rice deity who came down from the mountain for the transplanting. On this occasion, the ancestral altars are cleaned out and the deity is offered three small rice plants which are left intact in a corner of the field. The work of the first day of transplanting is done in festival costume, to the sound of the flute and drum. When the transplanting has been completed, the rice deity rises back up into the sky or onto the mountain.

Preparations are then made to welcome the second half of the year. The sixth month, essentially consecrated to the water deity, is marked by numerous rites of renewal. On the first day of this month the last rice cakes of the New Year are eaten, with the idea of once more calling upon their therapeutic virtues. People purify themselves in every way possible, this being the original sense of the *Tanabata* festival. A Chinese legend recounts that two stars of the Eagle (Aquila) and the Harp (Lyra), separated by the Milky Way upon the order of the Celestial Emperor, because of the lassitude which their love had inspired, meet only once a year, on July 7, which is the day that their reunion is celebrated throughout the country. On the sixth, in the hope of becoming skillful calligraphers, children write their wishes on strips of paper which they hang on bamboo branches placed in the gardens. On the morning of the seventh, the decorations are thrown into the river, to send their messages to the deities. This involves a necessary expulsion of evil forces and a purification, both of which are done in anticipation of the second great welcome of the ancestors, which marks the renewal of the year.

5. *The Rites of Bon*

The period of *bon* opens with the *kamabuta-tsuitachi*, the "first (day) of the lid of the caldron": on this day, the cover of the caldron of hell is partly lifted so that the spirits of the dead may come out; people can hear their cries at this time by pressing their ears to the ground. Preparations must be made to welcome them: a path is traced from the cemetery or the mountain to the village, and the tombs are cleaned. Two sorts of spirits are awaited: the ancestors and the "spirits without ties," who have no family (the *muen-botoke*) and who, many of them having died under tragic circumstances, may return to torment men. Their coming is especially marked by the fires that are kindled on their tombs and in the hills. The people rejoice with the ancestors: this is the *bon-gama*, a meal eaten outdoors where two paths cross or in a hut, and during which children sometimes eat offerings made to the ancestors. There are also the *bon* dances (*bon-odori*), which animate cities and villages for three days, on the fourteenth, fifteenth, and sixteenth. On the sixteenth, the people part from the

Wakamiya festival (*Wakamiya [on.] matsuri*), in the sanctuary of Kasuga at Nara (month of December). The *miko* are dancing in front of the "travel place" (*o-tabisho*) of the deity. At the right is the orchestra (koto, flute, drum, and mouth organ). CERTPJ photo archive. Photo L. Bernier.

ancestors; the offerings made to them are wrapped in leaves and thrown out on the edge of the village. Straw boats are set adrift, and thousands of lanterns are set afloat in streams and seas; people may also light a fire in the cemetery or on the threshold of the house.

6. *The Rites of Autumn*

Starting on the fifteenth day of the eighth month, the people welcome a person whose nature is not well understood. This must be a "visiting god," a *marōdo-gami,* whose role is played by children who steal potatoes and rice balls. The size of their thefts guarantees the abundance of the harvests. When the harvest approaches, rites of exorcism and purification are carried out.

The harvest itself is accentuated by three festivals, the *San-ku-nichi,* "the three nines," the ninth, nineteenth, and twenty-ninth of the month, which are festivals of the rice deity, of the peasants, and of the city dwellers. Offerings are made to the grain deity, but the people in the countryside are too busy to organize any large festivals. The *ni-name* rituals, the first offerings of grains, are more important. Given the name of *Tōkan-ya,* the Night of the Ten, or *Inoko,* the Day of the Young Wild Boar, these mark the departure of the rice god for the mountains. The *Ae-no-koto* rite in the region of Nōtō (district of Ishikawa) is certainly one of the most interesting. The rice god who has come down to the rice paddy on the ninth day of the first month is welcomed into the peoples' homes on the fourth or fifth day of the eleventh month. The head of the household brings home two balls of rice, which are the divine couple of rice. As soon as it has arrived, the deity, in the person of the head of the household, takes a bath and receives numerous offerings which must be named aloud for him, since he is blind because of his long sojourn underground. The offerings particularly include two huge radishes, one straight and the other forked, which are sexual symbols. It is the grains preserved in the two balls of rice that will be sown in the rice paddy in the spring. This closes the cycle of the work of rice culture.

7. *The Rites of Winter*

Agrarian rites are sparse in the winter, the most important being that of the *Taishi-kō,* the twenty-third day of the eleventh moon. Tradition consecrates this festival to the Buddhist sage Kōbō-daishi (774–835). One evening, the sage asked for hospitality at a poor house. The woman of the house, who had nothing to give him, went to steal acorns or chestnuts from her neighbors. The holy man, filled with pity, made snow fall in order to cover her footprints, which were easy to recognize since she had a limp. An older version makes the sage himself, who has nothing left to feed his numerous children, the thief. The event is celebrated by offering Kōbō rice balls and *miso* soup, which are eaten with chopsticks of unequal length in memory of the woman with the limp. The rite is addressed to the mountain deity and marks the beginning of the gathering of mountain fruits and vegetables. Since it is now nearly the winter solstice, the people eat pumpkins, whose form evokes the sun, in honor of the "winter solstice of Kōbō."

The *Shichi go san,* a festival for children three, five, and seven years old, is also celebrated. These three ages formerly marked the child's accession into the religious community (age three), the entrance into the childhood group (age five), and the attainment of that age (seven) after which the child is an entirely independent being who has the right, in case of death, to full funeral rites. This is a kind of rite of passage of the end of the year.

8. *End-of-Year Rites*

The active year ends with the *koto-yōka* of the eleventh month. Preparations for the new year begin on the thirteenth: the necessary decorations, foods, and instruments are prepared, and a period of taboo begins, which continues until January.

All preparations must be completed before the last day of the year, the *Omisoka.* Work is prohibited on the last night of the year: men, animals, and even objects, carefully laid on their sides, lie idle. In very traditional villages, the people try to stay awake as late as possible, for failing to do so brings on an early death, and they try to keep children from sleeping. People stay indoors to await, awake, the deity of the year. There is but one task which must be done during the night: to make sure that the fire in the hearth does not go out. During this time, crowds of people rush into the great sanctuaries to gather up a piece of the new fire that the ministers of the cult have kindled and with which the first meal of the new year will be cooked.

Thus the year involves two great periods of agrarian rites which run from the second to the sixth month and from the seventh to the eleventh month. The rites are separated from one another by two periods dedicated to renewing the forces of nature which are closely associated with the ancestors—who periodically return from the world beyond to watch over men, especially at the time of *bon,* whose funerary character has been accentuated through the influence of Buddhism. The rites themselves are rather monotonous despite their apparent diversity: at each pivotal time, evil forces are expelled and those which are favorable summoned and thanked once they have fulfilled their tasks. Offerings and divination allow the worshiper to enter into a contractual relationship with the beneficent powers. These are practical, effective, and indispensable rites.

L.Be./d.w.

BIBLIOGRAPHY

1. Sources

BUREAU DES AFFAIRES CULTURELLES, *Nihon minzoku chizu* 1, 1–2, *Nenchū gyōji* (Tokyo 1969). K. YANAGITA, ed., *Saiji shūzoku goi* (Tokyo 1939).

2. Monographs

Y. HASHIURA, *Tsuki goto no matsuri* (Tokyo 1966). J. MIYAMOTO, *Minkan-goyomi* (Tokyo 1942). N. MATSUDAIRA, *Matsuri no honshitsu to shosō* (Tokyo 1943–46). MINZOKU-GAKU KENKYŪ-KAI, *Nenchū gyōji zusetsu* (Tokyo 1953). M. NISHITSUNOI, "Ujigami shinkō to sairei," in *Kyōdo kenkyū kōza,* vol. 6 (Tokyo 1957–58). U. SAKAI, *Ine no matsuri* (Tokyo 1958). Y. TAKAHARA, *Nihon katei saishi* (Tokyo 1944). H. TAKEDA, *Nōson no nenchū gyōji* (Tokyo 1943). T. WAKAMORI, *Minzoku saijiki* (Tokyo 1970); *Nenchū gyōji* (Tokyo 1958). K. YANAGITA, *Nihon no matsuri* (Tokyo 1942); *Nenchū gyōji oboe-gaki* (Tokyo 1955); *Saijitsu-kō* (Tokyo 1946).

Additional monographs: FELICIA G. BOCK, trans., *Engi-Shiki: Procedures of the Engi Era, Books I–V* (Tokyo 1970); and *Engi-Shiki: Procedures of the Engi Era, Books VI–X* (Tokyo 1972). U. A. CASAL, *The Five Sacred Festivals of Ancient Japan: Their Symbolism and Historical Development* (Tokyo and Rutland, VT, 1967). FRANK HOFF, trans., *The Genial Seed: A Japanese Song Cycle* (New York 1971). YOSHIKO YAMAMOTO, *The Namahage: A Festival in the Northeast of Japan* (Philadelphia 1978).

3. Articles

B. FRANK, "Dates des *setsubun* et des commencements de saison: Les vingt-quatre souffles de l'année solaire sino-japonaise," in *Kata-imi et kata-tagae,* appendix 3, *Bulletin de la Maison franco-japonaise,* n.s., 5, nos. 2–4 (1958); "A propos de la 'vieille année' et du printemps," in *Asien Tradition und Fortschritt,* Festschrift für Horst Hammitzsch (Bochum 1971).

Additional articles: FELICIA G. BOCK, "The Rites of Renewal at Ise," *Monumenta Nipponica* 29, 1 (1974). H. BYRON EARHART, "Four Ritual Periods of Haguro Shugendō in Northeastern Japan," *History of Religions* 5, 1 (Summer 1965): 93–113. ROBERT S. ELLWOOD, "Harvest and Renewal at the Grand Shrine of Ise," *Numen* 15, 3 (November 1968): 165–90; "The Spring Prayer (Toshigoi) Ceremony of the Heian Court," *Asian Folklore Studies* 30, 1 (1971): 1–29. FRANK HOFF, "The Taue-zoshi: A Poetry of Growth," *Literature East and West* 15, 4 and 16, 1–2, pp. 680–92.

4. Miscellany

M. NISHITSUNOI, *Kagura kenkyū* (Tokyo 1934). K. HIGO, *Miya-za no kenkyū* (Tokyo 1941); *Orikuchi Shinobu zenshū,* vols. 2, 3, 15, 16, 17 (Tokyo 1954–59). K. YANAGITA, *Senzo no hanashi* (Tokyo 1946); *Yama miya-kō* (Tokyo 1947).

KOREAN MYTHOLOGY

In Korea, there are very few myths that mention the origin of the world;[1] a few oral traditions simply say that the universe was primordially a chaos, but that a crack finally appeared so that the sky could be separated from the earth. Two suns and two moons then illuminated the world, but one sun and one moon were brought down with an arrow; man was made from earth.

Archery is of great importance in the ancient beliefs of Korea. A primary abode of the Koreans was called "land of the dawn" or "earth of the bow." Their legendary ancestor is called Tangun, "lord of the birch." He is sometimes regarded as the father of the founder of Koguyuřyo, one of the three ancient kingdoms of Korea. It is not at all surprising that this last individual, named Tongmyŏng,[2] was also known as Čumong,[3] "the good archer."

The circumstances of Čumong's birth are mysterious. The *Wei chou* (chap. C) relates that the eldest daughter of the deity of the waters was bathing in a spot called the Heart of the Bear when she was surprised by Hämosu, her future husband. The birth of Čumong resulted from this encounter.

"In the capital of Eastern Fouyu, a man appeared, it is not known from where, who said his name was Hämosu,[4] and who claimed to be the son of the Heavenly Emperor who had come to found a state." The daughter of the deity of the waters explains how she came to know the son of the god of the sky: "I saw the man. After he had lured me into a house located at the spot called the Heart of the Bear . . . he made me commit adultery with him. After that, he left and never returned."

In this way the girl conceived an egg from which Čumong emerged. The same text says:

> Ryuhwa (= the name of the girl) was shut up in a room. The light of the sun fell on her. Shielding her body, she avoided it, but the light of the sun pursued her. After that, she conceived and gave birth to an egg. The king (of Fouyu) . . . had the egg thrown to a dog, and then to a pig, but neither the dog nor the pig ate it. It was abandoned on a road; cattle and horses avoided it. Later, it was left in a field; the birds covered it with their wings. The king . . . tried to break it, but without success. He gave it back to the woman (who "gave birth"). She wrapped up the egg and put it in a warm place. A boy broke its shell and emerged from it. He had beautiful features.

The miraculous birth of a legendary hero is nearly always connected, in Korean mythology, with the light of the sun and an egg. Examples of this are cited in the *Samguk yusa:* the founder of Silla,[5] a southern kingdom of Korea that rivaled that of Koguryŏ, was born from an egg that a white horse deposited on the ground when an extraordinary blast, like a lightning bolt, touched the earth (chap. 1); the six eggs, which transformed themselves into boys, of which one was the founder of the land called Karak,[6] were deposited at a spot that was touched by a violet cord that descended from the sky (chap. 2); Alji, creator of the Kim clan, one of the royal families of Silla, is no exception: "Prince Ko noticed, one night, a light which emanated from the forest called Forest of the Cock; in the midst of the purple clouds that connected the sky with the earth, a chest hung from a tree. The king had the chest opened and found a boy inside. (This boy) later took the throne of Silla" (chap. 1).

It is clear that the egg, or the chest that symbolizes it, does not yield its "fruit" until after it has been fertilized by the light of the sun. It should be noted, however, that in these cases of "miraculous" births the maternal role is insignificant; the mother is a mere celestial messenger sent to earth and may be replaced by an animal, such as the bear who gave birth to Tangun (*Samguk sagi*, chap. 1).

The passage already cited from the *Wei chou* about the abandonment of the egg[7] merits further attention. What does it mean that neither the dog nor the pig wanted to eat it, that cattle and horses avoided it, and that birds covered it with their wings? A comparison with other texts shows that this is a case of a "divine" gesture on the part of the animals. For example, it is said in the *Luen heng* (chap. 2) that the abandoned "child" was saved in succession by the pig and the horse who breathed into its mouth; and, according to the *Heu Han chu* (chap. 85), this was how it was known that this child was a deity. According to the *Wei che* (chap. 30), the chiefs of the clans of Fouyu were designated by an animal name: the horse chief, the cattle chief, the pig chief, the dog chief, etc. Each of these animals was probably venerated as the ancestor of a clan and thus Čumong inherited all of the ancestral sacred powers before he was born. The primitive Ye, the neighbors of the men of Koguryŏ, considered the tiger their god. Čumong's relationship with animals signifies the initiatory tests that he had to undergo before penetrating the new milieu dominated by the animalized spirits. This explains why the hero was as much protected as molested before his birth.

Čumong was a good archer.[8] About this, the *Samguk sagi* (chap. 13) says, "He made his own bow and arrows at the age of seven. Every time he shot, his arrows hit their target. In the popular language of the Fouyu, the word *čumong* means good archer. It is said that it was for this reason that he was given this name. Kŭmwa (= King of the Fouyu) had seven children who always played with Čumong, but whose talent was less than his. The eldest son, whose name was Täso, said to the king that his son was not the issue of a human being at all, that he had courage, and that he feared that there would be a disaster if people did not pay attention to this. Later, when the people were hunting on the plains[9] . . . because Čumong shot well, he was given a small number of arrows, but the animals he killed were great in number. The sons of the king and the vassals plotted once more to kill him. Accompanied by his three friends . . . Čumong came to a stream. They wanted to cross, but there was no bridge. Fearing that the pursuing soldiers would follow, Čumong announced to the river that his ancestor was the Heavenly Emperor, his mother, the daughter of the deity of the waters, and that today he had been forced to flee, but he did not know how to get rid of the soldiers who were pursuing him.[10] Then the fish and shellfish came out and made a bridge, but they dispersed as soon as Čumong had crossed over them, and the pursuing horsemen were unable to cross (the stream)."

But what magical power does the bow represent in Korean mythology? The *Tongguk Li Sangguk čip* (chap. 3) provides particularly valuable information on this subject; according to this text, when Čumong was ready to leave Fouyu, his mother gave him the grains of five cereals, which he lost in the course of his flight. While resting at the foot of a great tree, he noticed a pair of pigeons who had just alighted there. Telling himself that it was surely his divine mother who had sent them there, he shot an arrow that killed the pigeons, and from their throats the cereal grains fell out. After this, he threw water over the pigeons, which resuscitated them, and they flew away.

The fertility of the soil symbolized by the grains of the five cereals is connected here, through the intermediary of the bow and arrow, with the fertility of the woman, in this case the mother of Čumong, daughter of the deity of the waters. It is also significant that Čumong finds himself at the foot of a tree: like the bow, this allows him to make a magical ascension and connects the three cosmic worlds, the sky, the earth, and the subterranean world. We also understand why Čumong had to demonstrate his talent as a good archer before King Songyang, of a neighboring country, in order to prove that he was really the successor of the celestial god; the document that we have just cited (chap. 3) says that the hero succeeded in hitting the navel of a deer from a distance of one hundred steps and in breaking a jade basin from a distance of more than a hundred steps.[11]

However, to demonstrate that one really has this royal virtue, it is not enough merely to possess the power represented by the bow. So, according to the *Tongguk Li Sangguk čip* (chap. 3), Čumong, who had just founded his kingdom, laments in these terms:

> "We still do not have the ritual of the drum and the horn. The messenger (of King Songyang) . . . is arriving, and I am unable to greet him with the ritual. He will scorn us." A vassal . . . presents himself and offers to go and take the drum and the horn (from King Songyang) . . . for the great king (= Čumong). The king says "How will you take the treasures of a foreign land?" (The vassal) answers: "These are the presents of heaven. How can one not take them? Who could have thought that the great king would arrive here when he was in trouble at Fouyu? May the great king now have the courage to confront the danger of ten thousand deaths, and may he cause his name to resound. This is a fate fixed by heaven, and it shall be realized. What is there that we cannot do?" After this, (the vassal) . . . and two others left . . . and returned with the drum and the horn.

The drum was used at Koguryŏ to accompany the dance and ceremony of funerals, which suggests that the drum was used to communicate with the world beyond by means of its magical sounds, and that this instrument might have had the special quality of being an ascensional symbol for the dead. We know nothing about the horn, but that the drum had this value is evident from the fact that, according to the *Samguk sagi* (chap. 14), a prince of Koguryŏ named Hodong seduced a daughter of the commanding officer of the Chinese commandery of Lolong so that he could finally smash the officer's magical drum. The destruction of the instrument caused the total ruin of the commandery.

Once he has thus obtained this other power represented by the drum, Čumong undertakes the conquest of the land of

Flying horse. Discovered in 1976 at Kyongju, ancient capital city of the kingdom of Silla, in the tomb known as "Č'ŏnma" ("heavenly horse").

Scene of a ritual hunt. Wall painting from Koguryu. Fourth century.

King Songyang. The *Tongguk Li Sangguk čip* (chap. 3) relates that he succeeded in destroying it by inundating it with a rain that he caused by uttering an incantation before a white deer that he had captured during his campaign:

> "If the sky does not cause the rain to fall to inundate the capital of the King (Songyang) . . . , I will never release you; if you wish to escape, entreat the sky." The deer cried out sadly and his cry reached the sky, which caused to fall, over seven days, the rain that submerged the capital of King Songyang; King Čumong crossed the water with a rope made of reeds and climbed onto the back of a duck. The inhabitants of the country all grabbed the rope. With his whip, Čumong traced a line on the water which immediately dried up. Songyang came and surrendered himself and his country to him.[12]

The hero dries up the water with his whip and thus causes a resurrection. This is not a strange phenomenon for the people of Koguryŏ, whose religious beliefs gave the whip a symbolism identical to that, for example, of the bow and arrow. The exploit by Čumong would not have been accomplished if the "father" and "mother" of Čumong had not met at the spot called "Heart of the Bear." The bear represents both death and resurrection, as is shown in the myth of the birth of Tangun, the lord of the birches. The *Sambuk yusa* (chap. 1) says that the bear had to take a tuft of artemisia and twenty garlic bulbs and to avoid the light of the sun for a hundred days, in order finally to acquire the form of a human being. The hero is regarded as the son of the lord of the birches, who is himself the son of the bear. Underlying all this is the fact that Čumong is a deity endowed with a sacred power that allows him to inhabit the sky and the subterranean world which water represents, as is suggested in a passage from the *Tongguk yŏji sŭngram* (chap. 51) according to which Čumong, while living in the sky, could often pass over to the subterranean world through a cave.

The ability to join the two worlds was also necessary so that Čumong could recognize his child as his legitimate heir. The *Samguk sagi* (chap. 13) says about this:

> When Čumong formerly found himself at Jouyu, he married a woman. She became pregnant and gave birth to a child after Čumong's flight. He was named Yuri. When he was small, the child amused himself in the street by shooting at sparrows. By accident, he smashed an earthenware object that a woman was using to draw water. She insulted him, saying that the child had no father and that was why he was so mean. He asked his mother, "Who is my father? Where is he exactly?" His mother answered, "Your father is an extraordinary man. Knowing that no one wanted to have anything to do with him in this country, he fled toward a southern land, founded a state there, and made himself king. While fleeing, he asked me, if I gave birth to a boy, to reveal to him that his father had hidden an object at the foot of a pine growing out of a heptagonal stone. If the child is able to find it (he would recognize him as) his legitimate son." After hearing his mother speak in this way, Yuri left to search for the object in the valleys of the mountains, but he returned exhausted without success. One morning, when he was in the house, he had the impression that he had heard a voice between the pillars. He went to see and noticed that the pillars had seven angles. He then searched below the pillars and saw a piece of a broken sword. With this object . . . he went to see his father and presented the broken sword to him. The king brought out the other piece of the broken sword which he possessed and reunited the two fragments, which made a single sword. The king rejoiced and named the child his crown prince.

In Korea, the tree or pillar that connects the three cosmological worlds is symbolized by a pole on whose summit one or two birds are sculpted. This tradition has continued for at least two thousand years; the *Wei che* (chap. 30) says that in the southern half of the Korean peninsula, a pole was planted in a sacred and inviolable place and on its top one or more small bells were hung.[13]

In any case, Čumong's extraordinary powers are evident from the fact that, according to the *Samguk sagi* (chap. 13), three men, who entered into the service of the hero even before he could have founded his state, wore, respectively, a hemp coat, a long robe, and a uniform made from aquatic herbs. We know that these are the costumes of shamans, who would have been so differentiated because of the functions that were assigned to them in remote antiquity. Hemp is the material that is still used today for funerary dress, which suggests that the function of the man who wore this garment was communication with the world inhabited by the dead, i.e., the sky. The second type of costume was worn, until relatively recently, by Korean Buddhist monks, and was black. This was probably a Korean shamanic tradition that the Buddhists finally adopted, for the color black was often the sign of the presence of a shaman. The pole that is set up, even now, to indicate the dwelling place of a shaman, carries a black cloth ribbon at its summit. In a village festival at Čain (in the province of Kangwŏn), the inhabitants form a procession behind a great pole, the *kamsattuk,* at the top of which black ribbons are hung. These two kinds of costume are reminiscent of the distinction that is made, among the Buryats, for example, between the two categories of shamans, the black and the white. The uniform made from aquatic herbs may be compared with the costume that the shaman continues to wear today to dance in village festivals on the east coast: a bamboo belt hung with seaweed and ribbons of different colors. This costume symbolizes a descent into the water, as do the ducks' feet, designs of diving birds, etc., that are hung from the dress of Siberian shamans.

The preceding evidence suggests that Korean mythology required three kinds of specialized shamans: black and white shamans and shamans who communicated with the world of the waters. The fact that Čumong had these three shamans as servants clearly proves that he could connect the three cosmological worlds. It is evident that he inherited this power from his father, Hämosu, the son of the Heavenly Emperor. Proof of this is to be found in a passage from the *Tongguk Li Sangguk čip* (chap. 3) which shows how the deity of the waters was able to recognize Hämosu as a true son of the god of the sky, by imposing upon him a proof of metamorphosis:

> The deity of the waters transformed himself into a carp. But the king (*Hämosu*) became an otter and caught him; the deity of the waters took the form of a deer and ran away, but the king became a wolf and pursued him; the deity of the waters turned himself into a pheasant. He was attacked by the king, who had metamorphosed into a falcon; the deity of the waters thus knew that this was really a son of the Heavenly Emperor.

Such a capacity for metamorphosis was necessary to a "chief," as is proven in the myth of Sŏk T'alhä, the fourth monarch of Silla. According to the *Samguk yusa* (chap. 1), the latter could not rival the king of Karak in this art and had to leave the country without achieving his desire to conquer it.

The mythology of Čumong is divisible into three parts: the transmission of the power to communicate with the sky and the submarine world, the protection of the ancestral animal spirits, and the specialization of the functions of the shaman. The elements that play the most important role in these are sky and water, as in other myths from northeastern Asia. The mythology of Čumong has undoubtedly degenerated and does not offer a single detail about the celestial world or about the submarine world. This is equally true of all Korean myths, of both written and oral transmission; only certain novels give a more or less detailed description of the two worlds, under the influence of Chinese literature. It is thus difficult to find the original form of the Korean myths in the mythology of Čumong. Another enigma is posed by the myth about Tangun in which there is no water at all. Is this because it is earlier than those in which water is inevitably connected with the sky? It is difficult to answer this question.

But what is noteworthy is the evolution of the process of ascension into the sky. Čumong simply flew to arrive there, but the other Korean mythic heroes climb to the summit of the mountain to come near to the celestial god and to receive the message from the sky.[14] After he has undergone the test of crossing the waters, King T'alhä climbs a mountain, builds a stone cave in which he remains for seven days, and in the end discovers an "omnipotent" dwelling place at the foot of a hill which curiously resembles the crescent moon, a sign of prosperity. The first inhabitants of the land of Karak also climb to the summit of a mountain from which the voice of an invisible being had come, and upon it they discover the six eggs that are transformed into boys, of which one is the future king of the country. After a long sea voyage, the wife of the king arrives in the country and climbs the mountain to perform a rite which consists in offering her trousers to the spirits of the mountain (*Samguk yusa,* chap. 2). This should be compared to the Japanese myth of Ame no Uzume Mikoto who, in order to draw the great goddess Amaterasu from her hiding place, must expose her breasts and her sexual organ (*Kojiki,* chap. 1).

What was the concept of the earth held by the people of Koguryŏ? The Korean myths say nothing about this. The historical texts, such as the *Wei che* (k. 30), relate that the land of Koguryŏ was divided, from the time of its foundation, into five parts, the one occupied by the royal clan and the four

Pair of birds decorating a celestial pole. Third century. South Korea.

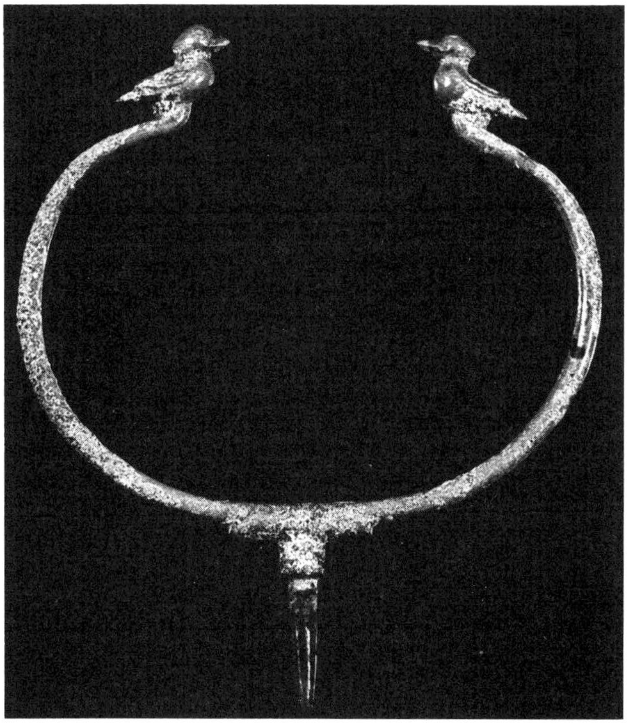

Crown discovered in 1921 at Kyongju in the tomb known as "Kŭmgwan" ("golden crown").

that surrounded it.[15] This is reminiscent of what happened at Silla where, before the creation of the kingdom, the ancient territory had been divided into four parts that bore the names of "father," "son," "mother," and "daughter" and whose locations were assumed to be to the west, east, south, and north (*Samguk yusa*, chap. 1). In this last land there were "royal" golden crowns decorated with trees that had three, or sometimes four, branches, placed one upon the other. The trees with three branches may represent religious power, with its faculty of connecting the three cosmogonic worlds, and the trees with four branches, the secular power that has the right to dominate the earth which extends toward the four cardinal points.[16] The importance that Korean mythology accords to the four reference points is shown in the myth of King T'alhä in the *Samguk yusa* (chap. 1). This king, born in the land of the dragons to the north of Silla, headed south until he finally came to a village named Sŏji ("to know the West"). And when he arrived in the capital of Silla, he climbed the mountain situated to the east of that city.

What was a Korean deity supposed to look like? The myth of Čumong indicates that he had a beautiful physiognomy. But the *Samguk yusa* (chap. 1) says that King T'alhä had a skull that was more than a meter in diameter, that his waist size was slightly less than three meters, and that his teeth were not separated but formed a single mass. After his death, the king became the god of the Eastern Mountain and returned to demand that his bones be smashed in order to make from them a statue which was to be kept at the royal palace and later in the mountain where he had constructed a cave to stay in for seven days, as was related above (ibid.). This legend must be related in some way to the surplus bone which was sought in Korea as a manifest proof of extraordinary powers; according to the *Samguk sagi* (chap. 11), Queen Činsŏng recognized a man named Ho as the crown prince because he had two bones that protruded from his back like wings.

At Koguryŏ, the country founded by Čumong, the place of worship that appears to be the most primitive is a cave in which a seat of the god was installed, upon which a wooden fire drill was placed. The eternal question of fire is posed here. This simple arrangement of the site of worship reveals that in the minds of the people of Koguryŏ fire is of divine origin and maintains contact with the god. But the worship of the god took place, according to the *Wei che* (chap. 30), on the occasion of the assembly of all the people on the tenth moon of the lunar calendar, i.e., after the harvest. It is therefore likely that the fire drill, which represents the god, symbolizes fertility. Did not the "mother" of Čumong transmit the grains of the five cereals? And among the people of Fouyu, Čumong's country of origin, the monarch was responsible for agricultural cultivation, to the point of being discharged or even killed by his people in case the harvest was bad (ibid.).

L.O./d.w.

NOTES

1. Cf. Yim Suk-jay, "Les mythes coréens de l'origine du monde," in *Revue de Corée* 29 (Summer 1976): 42–64.

2. Tongmyŏng is a translation into Chinese of many words of the language of Koguryŏ that mean "lightning from the east." This shows why the annalists wanted to give Čumong the family name of Hä, sun, or in Chinese, Gao, high, height.

3. In some Chinese documents (e.g., *Wei che*, chap. 30, etc.), Čumong is identified with Tongmyŏng, who was the founder of Fouyu, which was located to the north of Koguryŏ. This confusion probably comes from the fact that the people of Fouyu and those of Koguryŏ had the same ethnic origin, so that a mythology of the same kind was able to circulate among both of them. Since it is impossible to separate the "two" mythic personalities, Koguryŏ and Fouyu, at least from the point of view of the mythology, one must study all the descriptions of these "two" creatures who were one in the belief of the people who formed the country of Fouyu about the third century B.C. and of those who founded the kingdom of Koguryŏ in the first century B.C.

4. Hämosu could be a word composed of *hä*, "sun," and *mosu* < *mos* ≃ *mot*, "pool, gulf."

5. Cf. Li Ogg, "Pulgŏnä sinhwa-ga česihanŭn myŏt kadji čonggyosa-čŏk mundje," in *Études coréennes offertes au professeur Lee Sŏngŭn* (Seoul 1974), 189–96.

6. Cf. Li Ogg, "Suro wang sinhwa (Mythe relatif au roi Suro)," in *Mélanges commémoratifs du 60ᵉ anniversaire du professeur Č'ö Hodjin* (Seoul 1974), 139–47.

7. The story of this abandonment survived for a long time in Korea. About the beginning of the tenth century, someone named Kyŏnhuŏn, a great leader of the revolt against Silla, was suckled by a tigress when his parents, busy with their own work, left him in the forest (*Tongguk yŏdji sŭngram*, chap. 29); in the same period, the parents of Kyunyŏ (923–73), a future great Buddhist monk, abandoned him in the street because the infant was very ugly, but they were able to take him back when they saw that crows covered him with their wings (*Kyunyŏ čŏn*, appendix to *Samguk yusa*, new ed. by Č'ö Namsŏn); at the end of the tenth century or the beginning of the eleventh, Kim Tŭkpä, a future general, was protected by a tiger when he was abandoned by his parents (*Tongguk yodji sŭngram*, chap. 28).

8. Representing the quality of royalty, this weapon has often been offered as a gift to the Korean court by Manchu and Japanese envoys. The importance of the bow is indicated by the fact that in A.D. 8, a king of Koguryŏ condemned his son to death when he broke a bow offered by the king of a neighboring country (*Samguk sagi*, chap. 13).

9. The scene of the hunting ritual is represented on the fresco of the tomb of Muyŏngč'ong, built near the ancient capital of Koguryŏ; see Yi Pyongdo, *Hanguk sa* (Seoul 1968), 1: pl. 1. On the importance of the hunt, see also Hentze, "Shamankronen zur Han-zeit in Korea," *Ostasiatische Zeitschrift* 9, 5: 156–63.

10. According to other historical texts (e.g., *Wei che*, chap. 30), Čumong hit the water with his bow instead of uttering this speech; but the *Tongguk Li Sangguk čip* (chap. 3) says that Čumong pointed to the sky with his whip.

11. The arrow was evidently directed according to the will of God. The country founded by Tangun was called *kung hol*, i.e., "the land of the bow" (*Tongguk yŏdji sŭngram*, chap. 42). According to one tradition, the three deities shot the bow to find the ideal site on which to establish the capital (ibid., chap. 38).

12. Many legends recount that a dream in which one floods the world by urinating is an omen that one will conquer it (e.g., see *Samguk yusa*, chap. 1).

13. See Haguenauer, "Lieux d'asile au Japon et en Corée," *Journal asiatique*, July–September 1934, 109–24.

14. Tangun will become, after his death, the god of the mountain, and King T'alhä, the god of the eastern mountain.

15. Cf. Li Ogg, "A propos des 'pu' à Koguryŏ," in *Études franco-coréennes* 2 (1975): 67–99.

16. See the article cited in note 5, especially 193–95.

Basic Sources

1. Korean

Samguk sagi: History of the three Korean kingdoms, from the first century B.C. through the tenth century, edited by Kim Pusik (1075–1152).

Samguk yusa: Anecdotes of three Korean kingdoms, collected by the Buddhist monk Ilyŏn (1206–89).

Tongguk Li Sangguk čip: Complete works of Li Kyubo (1168–1241), known also under his nom de plume Sangguk.

Tongguk yŏdji sŭngram: Geography of Korea with historical and ethnological explanations by Ro Sadjin (1427–98).

2. Chinese

Houhanshu: History of the Chinese dynasty of the later Han (25 B.C.–A.D. 220), compiled by Fan Yi (fifth century); chap. 85 is devoted to the countries of northeast Asia.

Lunheng: Diverse treatise, edited by Wang Chong (died in 97); he collected the current opinions of his time on China and other neighboring countries.

Weishu: History of the Northern Wei of China (386–550), written by Wei Chou (551–54); chap. 100 is devoted to the "barbarians of the east," in particular, Koguryŏ, Fouyu, etc.

Wei che: Thus entitled for brevity, it is but one part of a work entitled *San Kouo che*, a history of three Chinese kingdoms from 220 to 280, Shu, Wei, and Wu, edited by Chen Shou (died in 292). Chapter 30 of the part concerning the Wei kingdom, namely, *Wei che*, gives interesting descriptions of Korea and other countries of north Asia.

BIBLIOGRAPHY

CHUGEUN CHANG, *Hanguk-ŭi sinhwa* (Seoul 1961). DUK-SOON CHANG, ed., *The Folk Treasure of Korea: Sources in Myth, Legend and Folktale* (Seoul 1970). SHIN-YONG CHUN, ed., *Folk Culture in Korea* (Seoul 1974). C. A. CLARK, *Religions of Old Korea* (New York 1932). TAE-HUNG HA and GRAFFON K. MINTZ, *Samguk Yusa: Legends and History of the Three Kingdoms of Ancient Korea* (Seoul 1972). ČEWON KIM, *Tangun sinhwa-ŭi sin yŏngu* (new ed., Seoul 1976). YŎLGYU KIM, *Sinhwa čŏnsŏl* (Seoul 1975). NŬNGHWA LI, *Čosŏn musok ko* (new ed., Seoul 1976). OGG LI, "A propos de Čumong," *International Journal of Korean Studies* 1 (1972): 65–92. SHŌEI MISINA, *Nissen sinwa densetsu-no kenkyū* (Tokyo 1972). BYENG-SEN PARK, *Le récit de la princesse abandonnée et les médiums à travers l'histoire de Corée* (Seoul 1973). ČINT'A SON, *Čosŏn mindjok minhwa-ŭi yŏngu* (Seoul 1948). FRITS VOS, *Die Religionen Koreas*, vol. 22-1 of Die Religionen der Menschet (Stuttgart 1977). YI PYONGDO, *Hanguk sa, Kodä p'yŏn* (Seoul 1959).

INTRODUCTION TO TIBETAN MYTHOLOGY

I. Mythological Survivals

Is there such a thing as a "Tibetan mythology"? If one expects to find a coherent and codified structure of divine lineages, alliances between divinities and the intrigues that accompany them, their battles, amorous adventures, and relationships with men and heroes, as is the case with the Greeks, one will be disappointed.

And yet Tibetan religion is not without its myths. There is, for example, a considerable quantity of mythological material in texts dating from the eighth and ninth centuries A.D. (even, in some cases, from the seventh century), rediscovered at the beginning of the twentieth century in Central Asia and in Dunhuang in northwest China. In some of them there are even instructions for rituals and narrations of myths entirely untouched by Buddhist influence. But it is very difficult to interpret these texts, in part because of their archaic language, in part because the manuscripts have often survived only in fragments, and, finally, because of the very form and structure of these myths, which are often disjointed, allusive, and obscure.[1]

Later sources reveal a vast religious literature that might be called "Lamaist"—in other words, the literature that was written in Tibet under Buddhist patronage during the past thousand years—numerous tales of those events that took place in primordial time and are regarded as paradigms of essential importance for the present state of society and the world. They contain myths that deal with the formation and structure of the universe and with the beings—men, animals, and gods—that inhabit it, as well as accounts of the first kings and their divine origins. Nevertheless, these myths are in no way unified or coherent; they are, rather, fragmentary, contradictory, confused. In the texts that follow the triumph of Buddhism, mythological tales are characterized by a lack of stability. Certain themes are more or less constant, but they appear in continually renewed variants, as mythology had never been subject to an effective codification. To judge by these texts, the fragments of myths they contain seem to have been often imperfectly understood and inextricably mixed up, apparently because they now had only a little or no functional importance, preserved as they were in many cases for purely "antiquarian" reasons or through a conventional deference to a distant and half-forgotten past.

However, the documents of Dunhuang suggest that at a certain period in the history of Tibetan religion the mythological dimension of religious consciousness played a much greater role than in the historical period. One gets the impression that the disparate elements that appear in later texts only as oblique rays of the light from a distant past, broken by the prism of superimposed Buddhism—the latter being a fundamentally mystical religion, and consequently nonmythological in its anthropology and its epistemology as well as in its metaphysics—at one time formed the center around which all religious life gravitated. And if we turn from these texts to contemporary popular religion, this hypothesis is confirmed, for here the mythical dimension is still fully significant. In particular there clearly appears a consciousness of the importance of origins, whether of social institutions, clans or lineages, magical substances, or rituals or instruments.

II. *Bonpo* Sources

It may therefore be said that Tibetan religion considered as a whole does not lack mythology. However, before going any further, we must deal with a problem of definition relating to the term "Tibetan religion." The majority of Tibetans refer to their religion as *chos,* which translates the Sanskrit *dharma,* a word that in the Buddhist context refers to the doctrine preached by the Buddha. And there is no doubt that the Tibetans are profoundly Buddhist and have been so for many centuries. But aside from the usage in which it is strictly applied to canonical writings of Buddhism, *chos* may refer to the Tibetan religion in its entirety, and this includes numerous elements that are genetically in no way Buddhist. It is of course these essentially non-Buddhist aspects that must provide the basis for the study of Tibetan mythology.

But the problem is complicated by the presence of another religious tradition called *bon.* The original meaning of this word is obscure; but at least from the eleventh century, if not earlier, it was used in the same sense as *chos,* that is, to refer to the totality of religious life, though only by a particular school or sect, the Bonpo (literally, those who conform to the *bon*). The religious traditions referred to by *chos* and *bon* are similar, to a degree that was not fully realized until recently, for both of them incorporate the philosophical and moral teachings of Indian Buddhism. But there is a decisive difference between them: *chos* always underscores its continuity with Indian Buddhism and tends to minimize the numerous non-Buddhist elements, which are, however, clearly identifiable in it; whereas *bon* has chosen, for reasons that are not very clear but could have been political rather than purely religious, to underscore all that ties it to pre-Buddhist religious tradition.

This fact explains the frequent distrust and occasional open hostility that opposes partisans of *bon* and *chos.* In fact, Buddhism, introduced in Tibet under the patronage of several kings in the seventh and eighth centuries, came up against fierce opposition from local priests. Among these priests there were several groups that were referred to as *bon-po;* and when these pre-Buddhist priests disappeared as an organized body in consequence of the triumph of Buddhism in the ninth century, their name—together with many of their doctrines and rituals—was passed on to the tradition that, after the dark and chaotic period that followed the collapse of the national dynasty, emerged in the eleventh century. Then, despite the close resemblance of its fundamental dogmatics to Buddhism, it chose to call its doctrines *bon,* in conscious and direct opposition to *chos.*[2]

Although the term *bon* must not be indiscriminately associated with all that is non-Buddhist or "popular" in Tibetan religion, it remains true that the Bonpo school, given its particular historical perspective, has been able to preserve numerous archaic traditions, among which are many elements of a mythological nature. We will call these sources "Bonpo," although it must be clearly understood that this does not necessarily mean that they reproduce as such the beliefs of the ancient pre-Buddhist *bon-po* priests.

These remarks indicate in barest outline the perspective in which the study of Tibetan mythology is approached here. We will not describe Tibetan religion in its entirety, whether in the Buddhist or the pre-Buddhist periods, but only certain mythological elements that appear in it, which one can assume to be indigenous, that is, not introduced by Buddhism. But we must also stress that if the texts of Tun-huang and other archaic documents indeed form a distinct category, there has never been a complete rupture as such, either literary or religious, between this material and other later documents, such as the collections of rituals dedicated to the chthonic divinities (*Klu-'bum*).[3] In addition, between the later Bonpo tradition, other Lamaist schools, and "popular" religion, the differences, although useful from the point of view of analysis, are very often unclear or even nonexistent.

P.K./t.l.f.

NOTES

1. For the study of the mythological texts of Tun-huang, see Lalou (1949, 1952, 1958), and especially Stein (1971), who includes many corrections and amplifications to the documents published by Thomas (1957).

2. Note that in this article "Bonpo" refers to the tradition of Lamaist times and "*bon-po*" to pre-Buddhist priests. On the religion of the ancient *bon-po* priests, see Lalou (1952, 1957, pp. 5–14, 1958), Stein (1962a, pp. 193–204, 1970), Snellgrove and Richardson (1968, pp. 51–59), Haarh (1969, pp. 99–125 and 327–97). The problem of the relations between *bon* and *chos* has been studied by Snellgrove (1967, introduction, pp. 1–21), Stein (1970), and Kvaerne (1972, 1974). The best synthesis of the doctrines of the Lamaist Bonpo tradition is furnished by the selection of extracts of the *gZi-brjid* from the fourteenth century, translated by Snellgrove (1967). See also Snellgrove and Richardson (1968, pp. 99–110), Karmay (1972, introduction, 1975), and Kvaerne (1971, 1973). On the pre-Buddhist religion, see Lalou (1952 and 1957, pp. 5–14); Stein (1962); Snellgrove and Richardson (1968, pp. 51–59); Haarh (1969, pp. 99–125, 327–97); Macdonald (1971); Stein (1972, pp. 229–40; 1985, with criticism of the interpretations of Macdonald 1971). Problems connected with the relationship between *bon* and *chos* have been studied by Snellgrove (1967) and Kvaerne (1972). The best presentation of the Lamaist Bonpo tradition is provided by Snellgrove (1967) and Karmay (1975).

3. This is emphasized by Stein (1971, p. 481). On the *Klu-'bum,* cf. "Cosmogonic Myths of Tibet."

BIBLIOGRAPHY

Principal Studies

J. BACOT, F. W. THOMAS, and CH. TOUSSAINT, *Documents de Touenhouang relatifs à l'histoire du Tibet* (Paris 1946). A.-M. BLONDEAU, "Le lha-'dre bka'-thaṅ," in *Études tibétaines dédiées à la mémoire de Marcelle Lalou* (Paris 1971), 29–126. G. A. COMBE, *A Tibetan on Tibet* (London 1926). E. B. COWELL, *The Jātaka or Stories of the Buddha's Former Births,* vol. 1 (London 1895). E. DARGYAY, "Zur Interpretation der mythischen Urgeschichte in den tibetischen Historikern," *Central Asiatic Journal* 16, no. 3 (1972): 161–77. S. C. DAS, ed., *dPag-bsam ljon-bzang* (Calcutta 1908). W. EBERHARD, *Kultur und Siedlung der Randvölker Chinas,* T'oung Pao, 36 suppl. (Leiden 1942). H. EIMER, "T'e'u raṅ mdos ma," in *Serta*

Tibeto-Mongolica, Festschrift Heissig (Wiesbaden 1973), 47–87. A. H. FRANCKE, *A Lower Ladakhi Version of the Kesar Saga* (Calcutta 1905–9). E. HAARH, *The Yar-luṅ Dynasty: A Study with Particular Regard to the Contribution by Myths and Legends to the History of Ancient Tibet and the Origin and Nature of Its Kings* (Copenhagen 1969). M. HERMANNS, "Schöpfungs- und Abstammungsmythen der Tibeter," *Anthropos* 41–44 (1946–49): 275–98, 817–47; *Himmelsstier und Gletscherlöwe* (Eisenach and Kassel 1955); *Die Familie der Amdo-Tibeter* (Freiburg and Munich 1959). H. HOFFMANN, *Quellen zur Geschichte der tibetischen Bon-Religion* (Wiesbaden 1950); *Die Religionen Tibets* (Munich 1956). S. HUMMEL, "Die Gesichtsbemalung der Tibeter," *Zeitschrift für Ethnologie* 83, 2 (Brunswick 1958): 281–84. J. W. DE JONG, "An Old Tibetan Version of the Rāmāyaṇa," *T'oung pao* 58 (1972): 190–202. S. G. KARMAY, *The Treasury of Good Sayings: A Tibetan History of Bon,* London Oriental Series 26 (London 1972); "A General Introduction to the History and Doctrines of Bon," *Memoirs of the Research Department of the Toyo Bunko,* no. 33 (Tokyo 1975), 171–218. B. I. KUZNETSOV, ed., *rGyal-rabs gsal-ba'i me-long,* Scripta Tibetana, vol. 1 (Leiden 1966). P. KVÆRNE, "A Chronological Table of the Bon po: The *bstan-rcis* of *Ñi ma bstan 'jin,*" *Acta Orientalia* 33 (1971): 205–82; "Aspects of the Origin of the Buddhist Tradition in Tibet," *Numen* 19 (1972): 22–40; "Bonpo Studies: The A-khrid System of Meditation," *Kailash* 1 (1973): 19–50, 247–332; "The Canon of the Tibetan Bonpos," *Indo-Iranian Journal* 16 (1974): 18–56, 96–144. M. LALOU, "Les chemins du mort dans les croyances de Haute-Asie," *Revue de l'Histoire des Religions,* (January–March 1949); "Rituel bon-po des funérailles royales," *Journal Asiatique* 240 (1952): 339–60; *Les religions du Tibet* (Paris 1957); "Fiefs, poisons et guérisseurs," *Journal Asiatique* 246 (1958): 157–201. B. LAUFER, "Über ein tibetisches Geschichtswerk der Bonpo," *T'oung Pao* 2 (1901): 24–44. J. E. VAN LOHUIZEN-DE LEEUW, "Two Notes on Mathurā Sculpture," *India Antiqua,* Festschrift Nobel (Leiden 1947), 235–39. A. MACDONALD, "La naissance du monde au Tibet," *La naissance du monde,* Sources Orientales, vol. 1 (Paris 1959), 417–52; "Une lecture des Pelliot tibétain 1286, 1287, 1038, 1047 et 1290," *Études tibétaines dédiées à la mémoire de Marcelle Lalou* (Paris 1971), 190–391. R. DE NEBESKY-WOJKOWITZ, *Oracles and Demons of Tibet: The Cult and Iconography of the Tibetan Protective Deities* (The Hague 1956). E. OBERMILLER, *History of Buddhism by Bu-ston,* part 2 (Heidelberg 1932). H. E. RICHARDSON, *Ancient Historical Edicts at Lhasa* (London 1952). W. W. ROCKHILL, *The Land of the Lamas* (London 1891). I. J. SCHMIDT, *Forschungen im Gebiete der älteren religiösen, politischen und literärischen Bildungsgeschichte der Völker Mittelasiens* (Saint Petersburg 1824). D. L. SNELLGROVE, *Buddhist Himālaya* (Oxford 1957); *The Nine Ways of Bon: Excerpts from gZi-brjid,* London Oriental Series 18 (London 1967). D. SNELLGROVE and H. RICHARDSON, *A Cultural History of Tibet* (London 1968). R. A. STEIN, "Notes d'étymologie tibétaine," *Bulletin de l'École française d'Extrême-Orient* 41 (1941–42): 203–31; *L'épopée tibétaine de Gesar dans sa version lamaïque de Ling,* Annales de musée Guimet, Bibliothèque d'Études 61 (Paris 1956); "Les K'iang des marches sino-tibétaines: Exemple de la continuité de la tradition," *Annuaire de l'EPHE 1957–1958,* pp. 1–15; *Recherches sur l'épopée et le barde au Tibet,* Bibliothèque de l'Institut des hautes études chinoises, 13 (Paris 1959); *Les tribus anciennes des marches sino-tibétaines: Légendes, classifications et histoire,* Bibliothèque de l'Institut des hautes études chinoises, 15 (Paris 1961); *La civilisation tibétaine* (Paris 1962); "Une source ancienne pour l'histoire de l'épopée tibétaine," *Journal Asiatique,* 1962, 77–106; *Annuaire de l'EPHE 1967–1968, 78–79; Annuaire du Collège de France, Résumé des cours 1968–1969,* 461–66; "Un document ancien relatif aux rites funéraires des bon-po tibétains," *Journal Asiatique* 258 (1970): 155–85; "Du récit au rituel dans les manuscrits tibétains de Touen-houang," *Études tibétaines dédiées à la mémoire de Marcelle Lalou* (Paris 1971), 479–547. F. W. THOMAS, *Tibetan Literary Texts and Documents Concerning Chinese Turkestan* (London 1951), vol. 2; *Ancient Folk-Literature from North-Eastern Tibet* (Berlin 1957). G. TUCCI, *Tibetan Painted Scrolls,* 3 vols. (Rome 1949); *The Tombs of the Tibetan Kings,* Serie Orientale Roma, vol. 1 (Rome 1950); "The Secret Characters of the Kings of Ancient Tibet," *East and West* 4 (1955): 197–205; "Die Religionen Tibets," 1–291, in Tucci/Heissig, *Die Religionen Tibets und der Mongolei* (Stuttgart 1970). M. WAIDA, "Symbolism of Descent in Tibetan Sacred Kingship and Some East Asian Parallels," *Numen* 20 (1973): 60–78. H. WENZEL, "The Legend of the Origin of the Tibetan Race," *Festgruss an Rudolf von Roth* (Stuttgart 1893), 170–72.

The Importance of Origins in Tibetan Mythology

All Tibetan mythology revolves around the notion of origin. Whether it is the beginning of a social relationship, a rite of passage from one stage of life to another, the performance of a ritual, or the use of an instrument, there is hardly a situation whose ultimate origin cannot be found in a mythical event. The myths that allude to such archetypes are thus among the most important aspects of Tibetan religion. When an event of the myth is invoked, it is as it were reactivated; it becomes coexistent with the current situation and infuses it with the dynamism and potentialities that are characteristic of all that took place in primordial time.

Thus the edicts and royal commands at the time of the great Tibetan kings of the eighth and ninth centuries were introduced by an evocation of the first Tibetan king, 'O-lde spu-rgyal, "who came from the gods of heaven to be lord of men" (Thomas 1951, p. 99). An uninterrupted line of kings descends to the current ruler whose "great dominion, good religion, and great knowledge" are thereby guaranteed and, consequently, his ability to undertake the founding of monasteries (ibid.) or to negotiate treaties with neighboring states (Richardson 1985, pp. 106–43). The same importance accorded to origins appears in the later religion. Thus the Bonpo use a ritual narrative, an "exposition" (*smrang,* cf. *smra-ba,* "to speak") of the archetype (*dpe*), to introduce rituals of exorcism, etc. (Snellgrove 1967, p. 20, p. 256 n. 9; Karmay 1975, p. 202). Such an explanation of the way in which the rite was established in the beginning guarantees its effectiveness, and a fourteenth-century Bonpo text underlines that "the exposition (*smrang*) must be done carefully and completely" (Snellgrove 1967, p. 51). A detailed study of the mythological precedent of the ritual of "recapturing the soul" (believed to have been "stolen" by a demon) of a person who is afflicted with disease or other problems is to be found in Karmay 1987, pages 107–12.

There are a great variety of these mythical tales, and we can only present a modest selection of them here (Stein 1971, pp. 535–37, gives a comprehensive bibliographical summary and discusses certain basic terms, pp. 537–45). The necessity to point out origins is not always explicitly formulated (op. cit., p. 536), but can nevertheless be assumed, at least for an archaic stage of Tibetan religion. For example, the Na-khi of western China, who are closely related to the Tibetans, stress the necessity of reciting the mythical account of the origins of a number of elements in their rituals, which are extremely complex (op. cit., pp. 535–36). For actual Tibetan texts, we can first of all mention the "explanations" (*bshad*), that, for example, of the "fool" of the New Year (*'dre-dkar*) (op. cit., pp. 434–44), of the hat of the bard (op. cit., pp. 359–66, 498), and of the horse that belongs to the hero of the epic (Stein 1956, pp. 105–6), as well as the origin of the mother of the hero (Heffler 1977, p. 95). In addition we can cite the presentation of the origin, as well as of the present state of the characters, at the beginning of theatrical performances (Stein 1959, p. 402 n. 17); the accounts of the origin of certain cultural elements, such as the knife (Stein 1971, p. 536), beer, tea, etc. (Hermanns 1955, p. 66), or of destructive substances such as poison (Karmay 1975, p. 203); and finally of marriage and the diverse customs that accompany the marriage ceremony.

A good example of this last type of relationship has been published by S. G. Karmay on the basis of a Bonpo text containing the mythical narrative of the first marriage, which was the marriage of a man with a goddess (op. cit., pp. 208–11). This goddess, named Srid-lcam 'phrul-mo-che ("Lady of the Visible World, the Great Magical One"), is the daughter of the god of the world (*srid-pa*); the man is Ling-dkar, lord of rGya. His request for the hand of the goddess is at first refused by the god of the world, but the latter is finally convinced by Ling-dkar's eloquence:

> If man and the gods come together, man will worship the gods and the gods will protect man; the one will be kind to the other. Although the sun and the moon shine in the sky, their rays fall to earth. The warm vapor is exuded from the earth and goes up into the sky as clouds. This is an example of what we are to one another.

Before the goddess leaves, she and her brother play dice for their portions of the inheritance of their parents. She asks for half of it, but since she is a girl, she gets only a third. When she leaves, her father gives her an arrow (a masculine symbol) as a parting gift, and her mother gives her a spindle (a feminine symbol). A priest carries out the ritual of the "Evocation of Fortune" in order to prevent the family's good fortune and prosperity from leaving with the bride.

The text then describes the actual marriage ritual, in the course of which a thread called the *dmu* thread (the same name as the cord that in mythical times connected the first kings of Tibet with their celestial dwelling place) is attached to the groom's sinciput, while a *g.yang* thread ("thread of fortune") is attached to the head of the bride. The suitor holds an arrow and makes offerings of beer and small conical cakes; the bride holds a spindle and offers curdled milk and flour mixed with butter. The priest offers the groom a piece of gold ("the gold of the soul"), and the bride a turquoise ("the turquoise of the soul"); then the couple and the priest together sing the story of the origins of the arrow, the spindle, and the *dmu* and the *g.yang* threads (Karmay 1975, p. 210):

> From the union of the two divine beings in the beginning of time three eggs were laid. "From the bursting of the golden egg a golden arrow with turqoise tail-feathers appeared. This is the arrow of life, 'the fish-eye of the groom.' From the bursting of the turquoise egg a turquoise arrow with golden tail-feathers appeared. This is the glorious arrow of the bride. From the bursting of the conch-white egg a golden spindle came into existence. From the light-rays of the sky and the vapours of the ocean a white clump of Bon came into existence. This was drawn out and spun by the wind. It was wound around a tree. This yarn was called the *dmu*-thread and the *g.yang*-thread."

Another version, which belongs to the popular religion of northwestern Tibet (*A-mdo*), was recorded by M. Hermanns; it evokes the archetypical marriages that took place in successive periods of the cosmos (Hermanns 1959, p. 58):

> During the first cosmic period, the great god Tshang-pa (Brahmā) gave his daughter rNam-rgyal to the ruler of the *klu* (nāgas). The priest of the bride's family was Theng-ge. In the time of the second cosmic period, when 'Jamd-byangs (Mañjuśrī) was emperor, a Chinese princess was given in marriage to the Tibetan king. The priest of the bride's family was Kong-tse. During the third cosmic period these events were taken as models.

In this example a social institution is guaranteed first through one mythological prototype, then through another that belongs to the heroic period of Tibetan history—in this case, the marriage of king Srong-btsan sgam-po, in the seventh century, to the Chinese princess Wen-ch'eng.

In the first chapter of an important Bonpo text, the "Cave of the Treasure" (*mDzod-phug*) published by Tenzin Namdak (*Mdzod phug: Basic Verses and Commentary,* Delhi 1966; a summary of its cosmogonic parts is found in Tucci 1970, pp. 237–39, and a more extensive analysis of the cosmogony and the theogony in Karmay 1975, pp. 191–94), we encounter a cosmogony followed by a theogony. In the theogony each divine figure is considered, according to the commentary, to be the origin of one of the aspects of the world: a class of spirits or of demons, a social institution, or the abilities and character traits of men. Thus all aspects of existence can be rendered meaningful through reference to a divine origin. And in the Tibetan epic, brilliantly studied by R. A. Stein (1956 for the translation and publication of the first chapters; 1959 for a detailed study of the structure, sources, and function), there is the same constant need to underline, implicitly or explicitly, the importance of a knowledge of origins. For example, the hero's horse, when it is captured and tamed for the first time, tells of its history, its pasture lands, etc. (1956, pp. 105–6).

The Tun-huang texts show the same concern to establish mythical paradigms. Here is an example of this kind of tale (Stein 1971, pp. 485–91):

> A long time ago a mare was born in the sky. But she found neither grass nor water there. Consequently she descended to Gung-thang, the land of the gods (probably a lower region of the sky), and became the property of the goddess Gung-btsun ("Lady of the Sky"). There she was given shelter, rice, flour, and molasses. But she remained rebellious. She could not be tamed, and the goddess finally chased her away. The mare then descended to the land of rDzi-lung (an even lower region of the sky, that of the winds), where she copulated and gave birth to three foals. In this land of rDzi-lung there was neither grass nor water, so that the first born of the three brothers went to the North (of Tibet) to find some. The second and third went to the pasture lands (to the south of the Northern Plain), where both grass and water were in abundance.
>
> In the North the eldest foal encountered the wild yak. Invoking the creator god Yab-lha bdag-drug, who long ago assigned the North to the yak and the pasture lands to the horse, the yak stabbed the horse with his horns and killed him. The two surviving brothers went to look for him and finally found his body in the North. The youngest exhorted his brother to avenge the murder, but the latter preferred to return to the pasture lands, to eat the grass and to drink the water. The other reproached him for his lack of courage, and decided to go to sKyi-mthing, the land of men, even though he was warned that a bit would be placed in his mouth and a saddle on his back. For, he replied, in the pasture lands his brother would be pricked by thorny weeds and chased by dogs. And he

made a pact with Man: As long as Man would live the horse would carry him, for one hundred years; and when Man would die the horse would carry him on his back through the seven thousand stars. Man then mounted the horse and went first to the pasture lands where the horse's older brother, described now as a *rkyang* (wild horse), was grazing; then he continued to the North, found the yak, pursued and killed it. Thus the horse was avenged, and his brother and the rider returned to the land of men. Later, when demons caused the death of the horse's master, the priests designated the horse to transport him to the land of the dead.

This mythical narrative serves to explain (through the remembrance of origins) and thus to justify a number of outstanding aspects of the world today: the opposition of the horse and the yak and of the domesticated horse and the *rkyang*, and the potential opposition of horse and man, overcome by the contractual relationship between them, which means that man undertakes to avenge the horse at the expense of the yak. This results, however, in man's pollution, from which he dies, while the horse appears in its funerary function, which is to help man pass into the world beyond the grave.

P.K./t.l.f.

BIBLIOGRAPHY

See the general bibliography for "Introduction to Tibetan Mythology," above.

Cosmogonic Myths of Tibet

The most fundamental origin of all is obviously that of the world, and it is thus not surprising that the religion of Tibet has cosmogonic myths. In fact, it has a large variety of cosmological themes, which may indicate borrowing from neighboring civilizations. To isolate these and find their sources is, however, a delicate task. But the parallels that a religious phenomenology brings to light between these cosmogonic myths and those of other parts of Asia are too striking to pass over in silence.

I. The Birth of the World from a Cosmic Egg

The birth of the world from a cosmic egg is one of the most frequent themes in Tibetan cosmogonies; in fact, it appears not only in cosmogonies, in the strict sense of the term, but also in other contexts. It is, furthermore, found in a great number of variants. "The number of eggs, their color, form and size, as well as the way in which they are hatched, is as varied as the number of texts" (Karmay 1986, p. 84). It has been suggested that this motif of the cosmic egg is of Indian origin (Stein 1972, p. 247); this is also the opinion of certain Tibetan authors as early as the twelfth century (Karmay 1986). There would, however, seem to be little reason to doubt that the mythical theme as such is an indigenous Tibetan one. An example as typical as it is well-known may be found in the *rLangs po-ti bse-ru,* which relates the origins and the history of one of the great and ancient families of eastern Tibet, the rLangs. Until recently, this book was accessible only in the form of citations in the *Chronicle* of the fifth Dalai Lama (seventeenth century), and in the *History* of Sum-pa mkhan-po (eighteenth century). The relevant part of the chronicle was translated by Tucci (1949, pp. 632–34), Hermanns (1949, pp. 295–97), Macdonald (1959, pp. 428–29), Haarh (1961, p. 253), and Karmay (1986, pp. 130–31).

From the essence of the five primordial elements a huge egg was formed. On the outside shell appeared the white cliff of the gods; on the inside a lake, like a whirlpool in the liquid part of the egg, with the six classes of living beings in the middle. From the yolk (?) of the egg, eighteen eggs were formed. From these, the middle one, as white as a conch shell, separated itself from the others. By the force of its own wish, this egg developed the five sensory organs as well as arms and legs, and thus was transformed into a man. From primordial time (*ye-nas*) he had formed a vow (*smon*); therefore, he gave himself the name "King Ye-smon." (The version translated by Macdonald contains a slightly different etymology.)

Two motifs will be recognized in this myth: the cosmic egg, which contains the world and the beings that populate it, and the primordial man, who appears as the metamorphosis of an egg. There is surely no reason not to consider this myth as being authentically Tibetan; but we must nevertheless note that the allusion to the "five primordial elements" and to the "six classes of living beings" points to an Indian, i.e., Buddhist, influence; and that the name of the primordial man, King Ye-smon (pronounced ye-mö), could be of Iranian origin, and is thus perhaps older than the Buddhist elements. In Iranian mythology the mythic king and first mortal man was Yima, whom we know as *Yima xshaetha,* "Yima the glorious." The etymology which the *rLangs po-ti bse-ru* offers, on the other hand, whether popular or scholarly, is certainly artificial.

An important source of cosmogonic myths is the collection of rituals used to gain the favor of the *klu,* the aquatic and chthonic beings whom the Tibetans identify with the Indian *nāgas.* This collection, known as the *Klu-'bum,* literally "The Hundred Thousand Klu," is traditionally considered to be a Bonpo text. Yet the versions which we have are the fruit of an edition made by Buddhists. On the other hand, the accounts found in the *Klu-'bum* correspond, often in a striking manner, to others in the Tun-huang manuscripts; and the contents of the *Klu-'bum* are essentially of non-Buddhist origin (Stein 1971, p. 481, n. 4; 1967–68a, pp. 78–79; 1967–68b, pp. 457–59; 1968–69, pp. 461–66). In brief, these accounts have the following overall structure (Stein 1962a, pp. 206–10): the *klu,* who inhabit the underground waters, are disturbed by the activities of man, who builds houses, plows, etc., because these break the surface of the ground and alter the landscape. The *klu* consequently make diseases spread. After the failure of various remedies, the priests, often named *bon-po,* are summoned and discover the cause of the disaster, whereupon they perform a propitiatory ritual. These accounts often include cosmogonic myths which serve to justify the rites. The following is an example

(Tucci 1949, p. 711, *Klu-'bum* fol. 117b; summary in Stein 1962a, p. 210):

> From the uncreated being a white light originated, and from the essence of that light a perfect egg came out. Outside it was luminous, it was good; it had no parts, it had no hands and no feet, but it was possessed of the power of motion; it had no wings but could fly, it had neither head nor eyes nor mouth, still a voice came out of it. After five months, this miraculous egg broke and a man came out.

His dwelling was a continent in the midst of a great ocean. He was seated upon a golden throne. The *klu* came to pay him homage and he ordered the universe, regulated the passage of time, invited the gods to protect the living, and triumphed over demons.

The basic structure here is the same as the one in the *rLangs po-ti bse-ru:* (*a*) starting from an undifferentiated beginning (*b*) an egg takes shape from which (*c*) a demiurge who has a human form—but who is also clearly conceived here as an aquatic being, a *klu*—is born. This demiurgic and beneficent being orders the universe, and is consequently known as bsKos-mkhan ("he who assigns") (Stein 1959, p. 300, n. 16; 1962a, p. 207; he translates his name as "the elect") and as Srid-pa'i mkhyen ("he who knows the visible world").

We will limit ourselves to one more example of this type of myth (Tucci 1949, p. 712, *Klu-'bum* fol. 132b): a series of transformations—from the void to a blue light, then to a rainbow, then to steam, then to a "subtle splendor"—end up producing an egg, whose different parts give birth to diverse aspects of the world: from the vapor steam and heat arise, from the skin seven golden mountains, from the creamy part space, from its heat fire, etc.; and from the inside of the egg a *klu* demiurge is born.

The egg is in fact the preeminent matrix and the place of origins. It is not only in the context of the world's coming into existence, but in many other contexts, too, that the egg symbolizes an absolute beginning. Thus the *Klu-'bum* cites the egg as the origin of the social divisions; the five classes of *klu* are born from six eggs: from a golden egg the class of kings emerges, from a turquoise egg the class of servants, from an iron egg the class of Brahmans, from a bronze egg the class of pariahs, and from a copper egg the class of animals (Tucci 1949, p. 711, *Klu-'bum* fol. 126a; summarized in Stein 1962a, p. 210). This myth clearly draws upon the Indian schema of the four social classes (Brahmans, warriors, merchants, and servants), to which are added the animals (a *klu* may have an animal form). Elsewhere, an egg may be the origin of lakes: this is the case of the four lakes that ring *Ti-se* (Kailāśa), the sacred mountain of western Tibet, lakes which are said to have come from four eggs. From a white egg came Lake Gur-rgyal lha-mo, from a turquoise egg, Ma-pham g.yu-mtsho (Mānasarovar), from a golden egg, La-ngag bsil-mo (Rākastal), and from a silver egg, Gung-chu dngul-mo (Tucci 1949, p. 712). In the Tibetan epic, the hero Ge-sar is born from an egg (Stein 1959, p. 202). Further, eggs are the source of the six primordial clans of Tibet: two birds laid eighteen eggs, divided into three groups of six: white, yellow, and blue (the colors of the sky, earth, and the underground waters). These were shattered by the smiths of the gods (*lha*), the atmospheric demons (*gnyan*), and the *klu*, respectively, while the six eggs in the middle produced the six clans (Stein 1961, pp. 21–22; cf. Hermanns 1949, p. 277). Finally, certain divinities are recognized as having been born from eggs. According to a Bonpo text, there were nine terrifying goddesses, called *byin-te*, who were born from nine eggs that were the fruit of the union of Srid-pa'i rgyal-mo ("Queen of the Visible World") and Lha-rgod thog-pa: an egg as white as a conch rose to the sky, where it was hatched by the wind of the gods (*lha*), and out of it came a white woman, gNam-gyi byin-te chen-mo ("Great *byin-te* of the Sky"); a yellow egg descended into the earth, and so forth (Nebesky-Wojkowitz 1956, pp. 313–14). Likewise, another Bonpo text, the *gZi-brjid*, describes the birth of a *wer-ma* divinity from an egg (see Snellgrove 1967, pp. 61–63). An egg may also be the source of parasites, of evil omens, of diseases, etc. (Snellgrove 1967, p. 71).

II. The Birth of the World from the Body of a Cosmic Being

Another cosmogonic motif, which is structurally connected to the cosmic egg, is the birth of the world from the body of a cosmic being, which often, but not always, entails the death of that being. The *Klu-'bum* offers a good example of this type of cosmogony (Tucci 1949, p. 712; summarized in Stein 1962a, p. 210):

> A *klu-mo* (female *klu*) born from the void . . . was named Klu-rgyal-mo srid-pa gtan-la phab-pa ("the Klu Queen who set in order the visible world"). The sky arose from the top of her head, the moon from the light of her right eye, the sun from the light of her left eye, four planets from her upper teeth. When the *klu-mo* opened her eyes, it was day; when she closed them, it was night; from the other twelve lower and upper teeth were born the lunar mansions. From her voice was born thunder, from her tongue lightning, from her breath the clouds, from her tears rain, from the fat of her tongue the hailstorms, from her nostrils the winds, from her blood the five oceans, from her veins the rivers, from her flesh the earth, from her bones the mountains, etc.

There is no question of an egg in this case: the entire cosmos arises from the body of the primordial *klu-mo*. The same theme is found in different variants, which bring into play the death and cutting into pieces of an animal or a monster. The Tibetan epic relates, for example, how a divine toad was transformed into a number of elements, all of which play a role in the setting of the epic (Stein 1959, p. 463):

> The uncreated blue toad of turquoise was carried up into the sky of Brahmā, the God of the world, but falling back to earth it shattered into several pieces from which Rin-chen dar-lu (the chief of one of the families of the Gling clan, that of the hero Ge-sar) was born; his joints, falling onto the plain, gave birth to his horse, Pha-wang drel-dkar; the toad's hairs, scattered by the wind, gave birth to the thirteen sacred junipers of the divine mountain of rMa, and the blood of the toad gave rise to the thirteen lakes of turquoise, etc.

The cosmogonic animal may also be a tiger (ibid.):

> The tigress who drank milk and ate men was captured. When her head was thrown to earth, it became the sacred mountain Ger-mjo; when her skin was spread over the plain, it became the sTag-thang khra-mo ("Spotted Plain of the Tiger"); when her tail was cut off, it became the wild gorges of lCags-nag on the rMa River; her kidneys became the ten thousand men and the hundred thousand horses of the clans of sGa and 'Bru.

As in the case of the cosmic egg, the fragmentation of the body of a mythic being does not necessarily take place in connection with the coming into being of the world in its totality, but may concern only a part of the world or, more exactly, the world as conceived from the viewpoint of a particular region or locality, as in the following account from western Tibet (Francke 1905, p. 17; discussed by Stein 1959, pp. 461–62):

> A young boy named Dong-gsum mi-la sngon-mo loved to go hunting with two dogs. One of his dogs caught a nine-headed ogre on a cliff above a hermitage. The ogre begged the boy not to kill him, and promised that he would help him both in war and in sports. The boy . . . went to ask the lama what he should do, and the lama said he should kill the ogre, from whose body the land of Gling would come into being:
> From four of its heads would be born the four walls of the Gling castle,
> from four others the four corners of the Gling castle;
> from one of its heads the floor of the castle;
> from its legs the great beams,
> from its arms the smaller beams,
> its fingers would become the roof slats,
> its ribs the thatch of the roof,
> the stomach would become the Gro-ma plain
> the entrails the rGyu-ma gorge
> the bottom of the stomach would become the sPo-mtho nang-ma hunting ground,
> and the eyes the Tshang-ya spring.

The murder of a primordial being is of course a frequent cosmogonic theme in the history of religions. Even if it is difficult to say whether Tibetan mythology was affected by foreign influences, we cannot help but think of similar motifs which appear in India as well as in China.

III. Dualist Cosmogonies

Whereas the cosmogonies considered up to this point see the world as emanating from a single preexisting substance, there are others which bring into play, at least in their most significant aspects, a dualistic schema according to which the world comes into being in the course of a combat that opposes two principles which are generally defined as "light" and "darkness." A good example of a cosmogony of this sort is found in the *Klu-'bum*. The passage in question has been translated by Tucci (1949, pp. 730–31) and by Macdonald (1959, pp. 441–46); it was summarized by Stein (1972, p. 246) and discussed by Kvaerne (1987, pp. 167–70). The following outline follows the interpretation of Kvaerne, 1987, which basically agrees with Tucci, 1949, but differs from Macdonald, 1959:

There is first of all a primeval state of nonexistence in which there is neither time (the four seasons), nor space (mountains, houses), nor living beings (animals, gods, and demons). Two lights appear all by themselves; one is white and one is black. From the rays of these lights are born a black man and a white man. The black man, the lord of nonexistence, of murder and destruction, begins to create all that is noxious and destructive: among the stars and planets he creates the demons; among the birds, the falcon; among the wild animals, the wolf; among the fish, the otter; for trees he creates the ax; for the grasses, the sickle; for men, every sort of disease, etc. The white man, the "Luminous One," or "the lord who loves the visible world," creates all that is wholesome and beneficial: he gives the sun its heat and the moon its clarity, he separates night from day, he causes plants and trees to grow and procures the well-being of every living thing. He wishes birds to be without enemies and horses without diseases, etc.; he wants Buddhist stupas and Bonpo temples to be built, scriptures to be written and recited, lamas to be venerated, etc.

Even if the references to stupas, etc., are manifestly the result of Buddhist influence, the main theme of the myth is clearly non-Buddhist. The dualistic schema that appears in it implies an idea of the world that seems to be particularly well attested in Bonpo sources. It has been suggested (Tucci 1949; Karmay 1975, p. 195) that this dualism may reflect an Iranian influence upon some stage of Tibetan religion. We are reminded here of the similar creation of the elements of good and evil by Ohrmazd and Ahriman, as it is described, for example, in the *Bundahishn*. Nevertheless, similarity does not necessarily imply historical connection, and definite textual proof of Iranian influence on Tibetan mythology has so far not been brought to light (cf. Kvaerne 1987).

The same theme of opposition between "light" and "darkness" is explicitly combined with that of the cosmic egg in an elaborate cosmogony found in a Bonpo text, the *dBu-nag mi'u 'dra-chags*, "The Origin of the Dwarfs with Black Heads," that is, of the human race (summarized in Hoffmann 1966, pp. 104–5, and translated by Karmay 1986, pp. 107–8):

Out of an initial state of void, two principles manifest themselves, the one consisting of light and paternal, the other consisting of rays and maternal. From frost and dew arises a lake which is like a mirror, and from this lake an egg appears.

Two eagles are born from this egg, one named "Bright Light" and the other "Dark Rays."

From the union of these birds come three eggs, one white, one black, and one spotted. From the white egg is born the lineage of the gods, from the black egg appear two black men, and from the spotted egg is born the primeval man, King Ye-smon.

Ye-smon creates the world in the form of three pairs of mountains and valleys, and at the same time creates three classes of divine beings. These are, in succession, the Phyva, the dMu, and the gTsug.

In this case the dualistic element is clearly present, but its function is limited. Two antagonistic principles give birth to one egg, and the three birds which result from it through incubation produce three eggs, from one of which is born the demiurge, who in turn creates three classes of divine beings.

As was the case with the other cosmogonic myths, dualistic cosmogonies may also be used to explain the origin, or to justify the employment, of rituals, instruments, etc. For example, the mythic archetype of a magical ritual is discovered in a battle between the demon (*bdud*) rNgam-rje btsan-po ("the powerful lord of rNgam," rNgam being the realm of the demons), and the god of the world (*srid-pa*), King Ye-smon. rNgam-rje mounted "a black fiendish horse with long cheeks. He headed a host of many jackals." King Ye-smon "struck him with a lump of melted bronze in the shape of a vajra and hit his feet, arms, and head. Then he bound him with an iron chain and put him upside-down inside the left horn of the yak in a place where three roads meet" (Tucci 1949, p. 717; see also Tucci 1970, pp. 259–61, and Karmay 1975, pp. 203–4).

The theme of a battle between two opposing principles is also found in epic form. Of particular interest is the combat between the lord of the demons Khyab-pa lag-ring ("Penetrating long hands") and the central figure of the later Bonpo tradition: sTon-pa gShen-rab, "Teacher, the best of the *gshen* priests." The protracted struggle is described in detail in a Bonpo work, the *gZer-mig*, which contains the biography of gShen-rab (see Hoffmann 1961, pp. 85–95, for a short summary of the whole work; a more detailed analysis of chapters 10–12, which are cited here, may be found in Blondeau 1971, pp. 34–39, and a detailed summary of a later version of the biography, the *gZi-brjid*, is provided in Kvaerne 1986):

> When they see that gShen-rab is succeeding in converting the living beings of this world, the demons are filled with despair, and Khyab-pa lag-ring leaves his castle in order to use a series of tricks to undo the activity of the Teacher: he transforms himself into various beings who try in vain to persuade gShen-rab to leave this world of sorrows. When trickery fails, brute strength is resorted to, and the demon attacks the entourage of gShen-rab. First he tries to induce the sons of the Teacher (who are of supernatural birth) to proclaim false doctrines; when this too fails, he appears before the two wives of gShen-rab in the form of seven horsemen who claim to be the sons of Brahmā and who try to convince them to return with them to the land of the *nāgas*, but with no more success. Finally, nevertheless, he manages to seduce the youngest daughter of gShen-rab, gShen-za ne'u-chung, and carries her back to the land of the demons. Later she gives birth to a pair of demonic twins before she is saved by her father.
>
> In the meantime, Khyab-pa once again prepares to attack the Teacher, and seven of his horsemen succeed in stealing his excellent horses and depart to hide them in Tibet in the region of rKong-po, in the southeast. gShen-rab, however, pursues them as fast as he can. The demons try to stop him with magic, conjuring a snowstorm, a valley of fire, a vast ocean formed from the four great rivers of Tibet, and a sandstorm, and they hurl down mountains to block his path. Each time gShen-rab comes through the ordeal, and he even succeeds in converting part of the army of the demons. Undaunted, Khyab-pa's mother and other demonesses turn themselves into a hundred girls who offer gShen-rab poison in golden bowls. But he transforms the poison into a medicine, and the girls turn into old hags. They too are converted and the horses are recovered. Khyab-pa suddenly feints submission, but in fact he tries to turn the Teacher's wives and daughters against him. When this fails, he tries to kill them, but his arrows become flowers. His only success is in burning the books of the Teachers, but this too is temporary. Other adventures follow, but when all is over, Khyab-pa is converted and becomes one of gShen-rab's disciples.

This "biography" of sTon-pa gShen-rab, which is in itself a remarkable literary document, has been interpreted in diverse ways. For our purposes, we will consider only the dualistic theme, which, even if certain parallels with the temptation of the Buddha by Māra may be noted, nevertheless has a profoundly non-Buddhist ring to it. It might be tempting to suppose that there is some Iranian influence here. The martial atmosphere and the repeated sorties of each camp against its enemy could suggest this. But to recognize in this text a systematic copy of the Manichean cosmological and soteriological mythic schema, as M. Hermanns has tried to do (1965, pp. 130–31), is to go far beyond what the document itself justifies.

Turning once again to the question of the origins of these dualistic cosmogonies, it must be noted that, beyond the possibility of there having been Iranian prototypes, the Chinese concepts of the yin and the yang may also have played a role of equal or even greater importance. This is what is suggested by the documents of Dunhuang, in which the opposition between light and darkness often appears. Referring to a mountain, one of these archaic texts speaks of "one hundred male *gshen* with white turbans on the sunny side (white) and one hundred female *gshen* with hats (?) on the shaded side (black)" (Stein 1971, p. 506), a theme which corresponds exactly, as R. A. Stein stresses, to the yin and the yang, which could in fact designate the two sides of a mountain (op. cit., p. 505, n. 74). The same text distinguishes, in connection with a funerary rite, "a superior soul (*ya-bla*) which is fixed on high in the 'castles' on the sunny side of a mountain, and an inferior soul (*ma-bla*) fixed below in the 'castles' on the shady side" (p. 510). However, in these formulas and in others like them, we are dealing not with real myths but rather with concepts and images that were later used in the creation of coherent mythological accounts in the *Klu-'bum*, the *gZer-mig*, etc. The function of these images in the ancient Dunhuang texts has been thus described by R. A. Stein:

> The terms have no absolute value in themselves. They should not be taken literally. They do not describe a real situation or an event which would be a part of an account. In K2 we see the two sorts of souls (bipartite structure: above/below) associated with the two sides of a mountain, the bright and the dark, whereas in B they are "localized" on the top and in the bottom of the valley. This was not a case of a fixed and independent cosmogonic system in which these souls occupied a determined place. This was merely a case of trying to point out a unity in their duality.

P.K./d.w.

BIBLIOGRAPHY

See the general bibliography for "Introduction to Tibetan Mythology," above.

Anthropogonic Myths of Tibet

I. The Children of the Monkey and the Ogress

Tibetan anthropogonic myths are a distinctive fusion of Buddhist and pre-Buddhist elements. In their themes, they are less varied than cosmogonic myths. Most widespread among them are those which deal with the genealogy of the Tibetan people, who are viewed as the descendants of a monkey and a female demon designated as *brag-srin-mo*, an "ogress of the cliff." There are numerous versions of this myth; Laufer (1901: 27, n. 11) gives the complete bibliography of the earliest references to them by Western authors. See also Kuznetsov (1966: xviii). One of the oldest versions dates from the twelfth century (see Macdonald 1971: 202–5); another version is found in the "Clear Mirror of the Royal Dynasties" (*rGyal-rabs gsal-ba'i me-long*), which dates from the fourteenth century. The text of this is reproduced in Kuznetsov, 1966: 42–45, and was translated by Wenzel

(1893). Here is a summary of the account as found in the "Clear Mirror of the Royal Dynasties":

> A monkey gifted with magical powers vows to become an *upāsaka* in the presence of the Bodhisattva Avalokiteśvara, who thereupon sends him to meditate in Tibet, the land of snows. While he meditates there on compassion and rejoices in the Void, a demoness passes by. Driven by the acts of her past existences, she exhibits various signs of passionate desire. Taking the form of a woman, she begs the monkey to marry her, and when she threatens to die on the spot, he permits her to sleep beside him. But she continues to implore him to marry her, and threatens that if he does not, she will unite with a demon, kill innumerable living beings, and give birth to a race of demons which will devour all of the creatures who live in the Land of Snows. Torn between compassion and his vow of chastity, the monkey transports himself magically at lightning speed to the top of Mount Potala, to the south, and presents his dilemma to Avalokiteśvara. Avalokiteśvara orders him to marry the demoness, and from the heavens the goddesses Bhṛkuṭī and Tārā give their assent, while Avalokiteśvara prophesies that in the future the doctrine of the Buddha will be preached in the Land of Snows.
>
> Six little monkeys are born shortly thereafter to the monkey and the ogress, each of them reborn from one of the six states of transmigration (gods, titans, men, animals, tormented spirits, and beings who live in the hells). The father leads his offspring into a forest and leaves them there. When he returns three years later, their number has multiplied to five hundred. As the fruits of the forest do not provide them with enough food, they beg their father to give them something to eat. Not knowing what to do, he goes again at lightning speed to Avalokiteśvara and complains bitterly: he has allowed himself to be seduced by a woman and is certainly doomed to rebirth in hell. Avalokiteśvara, however, climbs Mount Meru at the center of the earth, extracts the five kinds of grain from its interior, and scatters these over the surface of the earth so that the whole land is covered with cereal grains. The monkey leads his offspring there, and when they have eaten the grain, their fur and tails become shorter. They learn to speak, make clothing out of bark, and gradually build homes and cover the plains with planted fields. It is from them that the Tibetan people are descended.

II. Buddhist and Non-Buddhist Elements

The Buddhist elements in this myth are obvious. The most evident of these is of course the Bodhisattva Avalokiteśvara himself. His presence in this myth is by no means fortuitous. From the Lotus Sutra onward, in fact, he is described as an active divinity who intervenes to protect his devotees from every sort of danger whenever they ask his assistance. In the Tibetan tradition, he plays a determining role, since he is considered the patron saint of the country. The great monarch Srong-btsan sgam-po, who unified Tibet in the seventh century A.D., came to be regarded as an incarnation of Avalokiteśvara, and the Dalai Lamas, who at Lhasa continued the royal traditions in a theocratic form, are likewise considered to be visible manifestations of the great Bodhisattva. It is consequently quite understandable that it is Avalokiteśvara who provokes the events that lead to the appearance of the Tibetan people. It may also be noted that it is two Buddhist goddesses who give their assent to the marriage of the monkey and the demoness. Tārā in particular is considered to be the female counterpart of Avalokiteśvara. The ancestor of the Tibetans, the great monkey, is characterized in Buddhist terms. He vows to become an *upāsaka,* goes to Tibet to meditate, and tries at first to keep away the demoness who pines for his love. His principal trait is compassion, whether it is directed toward the demoness or his descendants. Finally, the reference to the six states of transmigration is purely Buddhist.

Elsewhere, however, the myth contains elements which are certainly non-Buddhist, the most striking being the very idea that the human race—or what in this context amounts to the same thing, the Tibetan people—should be the fruit of the union of a monkey and a demoness. Buddhism generally shares certain pan-Indian conceptions, among which is the belief in cosmic periods in the course of which humanity has gradually degenerated from a state of divine bliss, in which life was long, to the present condition of suffering and early death. But in this myth the movement is in the opposite direction; the monkeys become men beginning on the day on which, instead of wild fruits, they begin to eat the grain that they cultivate. In structuralist terms, we might say that the second part of this myth expresses a passage from nature to culture, with Avalokiteśvara playing the role of a kind of culture hero.

Another version of this myth appears in a fifteenth- or sixteenth-century text, the "Treasure of Explanations, the Jewel That Satisfies All Wishes" (*bShad-mdzod yid-bzhin nor-bu;* text published by Lokesh Chandra, with an introduction by E. Gene Smith, *A 15th Century Tibetan Compendium of Knowledge,* Śatapiṭaka series, vol. 78, New Delhi 1969; cf. fol. 88–100). In some respects the Buddhist elements are even clearer in this text. For example, it is stated that the monkey is a supernatural manifestation of the Bodhisattva Avalokiteśvara. It is also interesting to note that the name given to the monkey is Ha-lu-ma-da', in which may be recognized Hanumān, the monkey king who plays such an important role in the Indian epic of the *Rāmāyaṇa.* The relationship between the myth and the epic is further emphasized by this detail: the monkey is born in the land of demons, Langa-pu-rangs, which is Laṅkāpura, except that the Sanskrit *pura,* "city," was understood on the basis of its approximate homophone, *Pu-rangs,* which is a region of western Tibet.

In this version, the evil nature of the ogress is even more apparent. She attempts to devour her son, which is given as the reason his father must lead him into the forest. By contrast, the theme of the six little monkeys, each reborn from one of the states of being, is lacking. There is only one child, and he is already practically a human being, as he has neither fur nor a tail. Nevertheless, he copulates with all the female monkeys who already live in the forest, which results in the birth of the four hundred offspring who are to become the ancestors of the four primordial Tibetan clans. But these offspring of the firstborn are incapable of climbing trees to collect fruit, and it is more for this reason than because of overpopulation, as was the case in the other version of the myth, that they are at the point of dying of hunger when the Bodhisattva monkey returns after one year. Incapable of picking enough fruit for all of them, he hurries to Avalokiteśvara, who pours into the hand of the monkey the five kinds of grain (this time nothing is said of their place of origin), and the monkey returns to the Land of Snows to plant them in the center of the country, at rTse-sdang (rTse-thang) in the region of Yar-lung.

We know of still other variants of the same myth. Thus, in a rather complex version, six eggs result from the union of the monkey and the demoness, from each of which a being is born who represents one of the six states of existence. But beside these a son is also born, who is manifestly identical to the primordial man of the cosmogonic myths, since he bears the name of Ye-smon rgyal-po, King Ye-smon. It is from this last son that the Tibetan clans are descended (Hermanns 1949: 277–78). Finally, in an oral version collected recently, the offspring of the ogress and the monkey are said to have been "so numerous and diverse in character—beasts, birds, fishes, creeping things, and man—that in the course of time the children of men emigrated to Mount Kunlun, down whose four sides flowed four great rivers issuing from the mouths of a horse, an elephant, a lion, and a peacock; and following these several streams, they became widely separated and divergent in race" (Combe 1926: 36; 38, with the citation of a Bonpo informant). Of course, in this last example, there is no way of deciding whether it is a case of a well-established variant or simply the interpretation of a particular person.

No pre-Buddhist version of this myth has been preserved, and I believe that it is a Buddhist fabrication. But it is possible to isolate the non-Buddhist elements that were combined in it. There is first of all the fact that the "Scroll of the Words of the King" (*rGyal-po bka'i thang-yig*), a text which dates from the fourteenth century, but which certainly preserves older traditions, describes in one of its chapters a series of mythic beings of demonic nature who dominated Tibet before the first king rose to power. "First a black demon held sway, and the land was known as the land of devils. . . . As a result, sprites called *nyen-po* and *tsen-po* appeared. Next a devil and an ogress held sway, and the country was called the land of the two divine ogres. As a result, red-faced flesh-eating creatures appeared. Next the serpents (*klu*) and the powers (*btsan*) held sway, and the country was called the realm of Tibet with its many parts. As a result, grain appeared, active in the waters" (this translation follows that of Snellgrove 1957: 129–30; a somewhat different translation is in Tucci 1949: 732). Here it is the second generation of demonic beings that interests us. At a certain moment in its mythic prehistory, Tibet is dominated or characterized by two demons, one male and one female, the latter explicitly called *srin-mo*, "ogress." From these there arose "red-faced flesh-eating" creatures. But although this designation is often applied to demonic creatures in general, it is also used to describe and distinguish the Tibetans from other peoples, as is attested by Chinese texts of the Tang dynasty, which say that the Tibetans painted their faces red (Hummel 1958; Stein 1958: 6). Much may be said about the religious and magical significance of the color red, but one reason why the Tibetans painted themselves in this way was perhaps their belief that they were descended from red-faced beings.

This passage is also interesting for the fact that it can be connected with a third version of the anthropogonic myth, which is found in the *Maṇi bka'-'bum*. This time it is said of the six little monkeys that, "because they had a monkey for a father, their bodies were covered with fur, and their faces were red. Because they had an ogress of the cliffs for a mother, they were without tails and craved raw meat and blood." (For translation, see Rockhill 1891: 355–61; Hermanns 1949: 817–21; and Macdonald 1959: 435–39. The translation here follows Macdonald. For another version, that of dPa'o gtsug-lag 'phreng-ba, see Dargyay 1972: 164–65.) A fourth version is found in the "Book of the Words of the Ministers" (*Blon-po bka'i thang-yig*) in which it is said of the son, this time an *only* son, that he stood upright and had "a red flat face, and no tail. He ate red meat and drank warm blood" (Snellgrove 1957: 124–26). One may conclude from this that one of the components of this anthropogonic myth is the pre-Buddhist notion that Tibet, at a certain moment in mythic time, had been dominated by two demons, from the union of which arose these red-faced flesh-eating creatures.

The *rGyal-po bka'i thang-yig* indicates that the cultivation of grains appeared in the following generation. This corresponds to the anthropogonic myth in which grain appears in the first or second generations that followed the Bodhisattva monkey. The formula "active in the waters" could, if the translation is correct, signify that this concerns rice (pace Tucci 1949: 732). In this case, we are led to southern Tibet, the only region in which the cultivation of rice is possible. This is interesting, since the second component of the myth, the origin of men beginning with the monkey, comes from the region that lies between Tibet and China, where it is found among Tibeto-Burmese peoples of western China. These are peoples who are very close to the Tibetans in language and religion, but who have known the influence of Buddhism only to a very small degree.

The best known of these nations, the Chiang, in recent times has lived in the west and north of the Chinese province of Sichuan (cf. Tucci 1949: 713; he stresses the importance of these regions; the following summary is based on Stein 1958). Chiang mythology relates that they had previously lived elsewhere, and that, when they were forced to emigrate to their present territory, they had to fight and drive out beings called *Qa*. These *Qa* are described as strong but stupid, heavyset, with long teeth, a low forehead, and a long tail; in short, these are monkeys. They lived in caves and ate fruits, roots, and grasses. And it was only when a divinity revealed to the Chiang how they could keep the *Qa* away that they became capable of plowing the earth and developing social institutions; only then did they become fully human. Thereupon the Chiang named themselves the *rmi* or *rma*, "men," a word which can be associated with the Tibetan *mi*, "man." This is a passage between nature and culture which is wholly analogous to the change in condition that the children of the Bodhisattva monkey underwent as a result of the intervention of Avalokiteśvara. But there is an even more obvious connection between the Chiang myths and Tibetan anthropogonic myths. Chinese annals report that the Chiang claimed to be descended from the family of *mi* monkeys. According to Chinese dictionaries, this is a large monkey with a red face and a short tail; in other words, an anthropoid. It is also called *mu*. This makes it tempting to regard this name as a borrowing on the part of the Chinese, and to connect the word with the Tibeto-Burmese word for "man" (*mi* in Tibetan, *rmi* in Jyarong, *rme, rma* among the Chiang, etc; compare also the Tibetan clans *rMu, rMe, rMa,* etc.).

Ancient Chinese sources relate that another border people was composed of dwarfs, who had that form because they were descended from monkeys who had raped some sleeping women (Eberhard 1942: 144); this is interesting when compared with Tibetan sources which often call the first Tibetans *mi'u*, "dwarfs." In any case, the crucial role of the monkey in the present Chiang religion is remarkable. They adore a divine ancestor named Abba ("father") Mu-la ("heaven"?) Sei ("god"). This god is ritually represented by the skull of a monkey wrapped in white paper together with its lungs, liver, intestines, lips, and nails, and he is addressed as "Old Master Ancestor" (Stein 1958: 8). If we combine these notions with that of the two demons who dominated Tibet, we arrive at the anthropogonic myth of the Tibetans.

III. The Work of the Tibetan Buddhists on the Mythic Elements

The question remains: How was it possible for the Buddhists of Tibet to combine these two myths and make a Bodhisattva of this ancestral monkey? In fact, it was easy. In more than one version the monkey is named Hanumān; that is, he is identified with the brave and loyal monkey-king of the *Rāmāyaṇa*. This Indian epic was known early in Tibet, in any case before the eleventh century (de Jong 1972). Another lead may perhaps be found in the Buddhist Jātaka literature, where a wise and clever monkey who would later be reborn as the Buddha Śākyamuni is the central figure of a famous Jātaka found in the Pāli canon in the *Mahāvastu,* and in a Chinese version (van Lohuizen-de Leeuw 1947). In another Jātaka, the Bodhisattva appears, in an earlier existence, as the king of the monkeys (Cowell 1895, 1:144, Jātaka no. 58).

Another motif, although not specifically Buddhist, is of Indian origin: that of the ogress dominated by intense sexual desires. It was her insistent advances that were the direct cause of the Tibetan people. Yet the Tibetan tradition does not seem to furnish a basis for such an idea of demons, whether male or female. In the Indian tradition, by contrast, it is considered to be an established psychological truth that women have a sexual need so intense that neither reason nor morality can curb it when it has been awakened. This notion is here combined with the motif of the ascetic who during his meditation is solicited by a woman to whom he finally succumbs, which is a familiar theme of Indian religion.

Thus the myth of the origin of the Tibetans was created from diverse elements. It remains for us to show how the finishing touches were applied by the Buddhist tradition. The *Maṇi bka'-'bum* which was referred to above is particularly centered upon the cult of Avalokiteśvara. In this text, as well as in the *Blon-po bka'i thang-yig,* there is a sort of prelude to the myth, in which the Buddha Amitābha summons Avalokiteśvara and orders him to populate Tibet in such a way that the country may later be converted to Buddhism. Avalokiteśvara returns to his seat on Mount Potala, and looking over Tibet with his divine eye, causes a ray of light to shoot forth from the palm of his left hand; this ray transforms itself into a monkey. In the same way, Tārā transforms herself into an ogress, and thus it is the two gods themselves who are united in what follows. In late Buddhist tradition, for example in the chronicle of the fifth Dalai Lama, this is taken to its logical conclusion: the concupiscence of the ogress is no longer mentioned; on the contrary, the goddess "took the illusory form of a wild beast, but her heart was as immaculate as the new moon when it rises."

In the *Maṇi bka'-'bum* there is also a short epilogue in which the Buddhist propaganda is particularly transparent. But there is also a synthesis between the two versions with regard to the offspring of the monkey: on the one hand, six or four young who were monkeys first; and, on the other, a son who was semihuman but who copulated with female monkeys. This text first speaks of six baby monkeys, but also tells us that after they had received the grain which gradually rendered them human, Avalokiteśvara created once more: this time a little boy who had all the signs of a supernatural beauty. When the monkeys ask him why he is so handsome, he replies that it is because he abhors the ten sins and practices the ten virtues. At this point he instructs the monkeys in the doctrine of the Buddha, and they gradually become men (Macdonald 1959: 438–39).

One might nevertheless wonder whether the use that Buddhism made of the ancient mythic traditions for its own ends was altogether fruitful in the case of the anthropogonic myth. A Bonpo work of the fifteenth century dismisses the whole account as obviously erroneous, noting with sarcasm, "There are those who claim that the Tibetans are descended from the union of a monkey and an ogress, and that they once had tails. But this is not true, since the Tibetans do not have tails. Furthermore, it is said that there are people with tails near the border, in China, toward the east; but there is a difference between those beings and the human race" (Laufer 1901: 25). It is at least likely that the non-Buddhist elements were too conspicuous to pass unnoticed. As a consequence, this myth had to compete with another account which should perhaps be characterized rather as "legend," since it is set in a well-defined historical perspective, associating the origins of the Tibetan people with a great conflict whose historic character is beyond doubt, a conflict that appears in the *Mahābhārata.*

IV. A Rational Legend about the Origin of the Tibetans

A rational legend about the origin of the Tibetans was penned by the great Tibetan scholar Bu-ston (1290–1364) in his *History of Buddhism,* here cited in the translation of E. Obermiller (1932: 181; cf. Tucci 1949: 731; he shows that this version may be connected with a definite source, Prajñavarman's commentary on a canonical text, the *Devātiśayastotra.* Prajñavarman was an Indian translator active in Tibet in the second half of the eighth century. On Rūpati who will be mentioned here, see Haarh, 1969: 176–79. No prince of this name is mentioned in the *Mahābhārata;* cf. S. Sörensen, *An Index to the Names in the Mahābhārata,* London 1904–1925):

> As for the way in which the first men appeared in Tibet, says Bu-ston, one may read in the Commentary on the *Devātiśayastotra* that, when the five Pāṇḍavas battled with the twelve armies of the Kauravas, King Rūpati fled into the mountains of the Himālaya with a thousand warriors dressed as women. It is from these that the Tibetans are said to have descended.

Here there is no trace of the supernatural. Having provided this completely rational account, Bu-ston does nothing more than indicate without commentary the other version of the origin of the Tibetans (the tale of the monkey and the ogress), showing an attitude that is clearly nonmythological. This rationalistic attitude is carried to its logical conclusion by a Buddhist scholar of the early nineteenth century, who states that, "As for the origin of the people of the country of Tibet, it is difficult to make a decision, because they are explained by the Tibetans as having been produced from a monkey; by the Indians as having been produced by Rūpati and his army; and according to old chronicles of the Chinese as having been produced from Zan-me'o and his army." He then concludes that since there were many different clans, as well as Mongolians and Chinese, "among the kings, ministers, and translators of Tibet in former times . . . it is not certain that there was only one racial origin" (Wylie 1962: 113).

Other anthropogonic myths existed in Tibet, but were not as widely received as that of the ancestor-monkey. Thus the *rLangs po-ti bse-ru* testifies to a rather complicated genealogy that begins with the Primordial Man *Ye-smon rgyal-po* and, after numerous generations of divine beings, ends with the six original tribes of Tibet; in other words, with mankind (Macdonald 1959: 428–29). At no time in this anthropogony which is also a theogony is there any mention of a monkey, or of a monkey and an ogress, or of Avalokiteśvara. This account is, in essence at least, entirely pre-Buddhist.

P.K./d.b.

BIBLIOGRAPHY

See the general bibliography for "Introduction to Tibetan Mythology," above.

Divine Sovereignty in Tibet

According to the "Scroll of the Words of the King" (*rGyal-po bka'i thang-yig*), a fourteenth-century text, Tibet was originally governed by a succession of demoniacal beings. During each era a new element of culture was introduced—first grain, then weapons, horses, ornaments, good manners and polite conversation, and finally the first king, named sPu-rgyal btsan-po, "sPu-rgyal the Mighty" (Snellgrove 1957, pp. 129–30). Myths about the first king of Tibet and his immediate successors form a significant part of Tibetan mythology. But these are extremely complex traditions that present a confused picture, full of gaps and contradictions. We will thus introduce only the most characteristic elements of these myths, leaving aside numerous variants and secondary elements. (Detailed studies are found in Haarh 1959, notably pp. 168–288, and in Macdonald 1971.)

I. The First King: A Pre-Buddhist Version of the Myth

When the Tibetans came into contact with Buddhism in the seventh and eighth centuries, they were governed by sacred kings who constituted the focus of an elaborate cult in which priests—called *bon* and *gshen*—played a decisive role. The institution of sacred sovereignty lasted until the fall of the national dynasty in 842, that is, about a century after the effective introduction of Buddhism. Consequently, myths about the celestial origin of the first king were preserved and remembered, but as far as the later sources are concerned, only after they had passed through a reinterpretation that tended to be rationalist. We can, however, begin by studying a pre-Buddhist version of the myth, preserved in a manuscript from Tun-huang, a version in which the first king is called Nyag-khri btsan-po (which later became gNya'-khri btsan-po). (This text is found in Bacot/Thomas/Toussaint 1946, p. 81, translation pp. 85–86; cf. also Macdonald 1959, p. 426, for the first lines, and Snellgrove/Richardson 1968, pp. 24–25):

> He came from the heights of the heaven of the gods,
> the son of the six Lords, the ancestral gods
> who dwell above the mid-heaven . . .
> He came to earth as Father-of-the-Land, as Lord,
> he came as the rain that impregnates the earth.
> When he arrived at the divine mountain *Gyang-do,*
> that great mountain bowed low again and again;
> the trees came together,
> the springs rippled with their blue waters,
> and the rocks and boulders saluted him respectfully
> in order to honor him.
> He came as the lord of Tibet of six regions
> and when he came for the first time to the earth
> it was as lord of everything under heaven.
> He came to the center of the sky,
> to the center of the earth,
> the heart of the world,
> fenced round by snow-mountains.
> And after the Son-of-the-gods had lived
> as ruler in the land of men,
> he returned visibly to heaven.

The central element of this myth is found extensively in central and eastern Asia, and is perhaps of Altaic origin, for other myths, which are often surprisingly similar, are found among the Mongols, Koreans, and Japanese. The basic idea is always that the first king of the people or the tribe was an atmospheric or celestial divinity who, sometimes in response to prayers, descended through the different levels of the atmosphere to the summit of a mountain (Waida 1973 for the Korean and Japanese myths). This mountain plays the role of an *axis mundi*—in this case the king is said to come to the land that is "beneath the center of the sky"—and it is often considered, at least in Tibet, to be a divinity, and worshiped accordingly. The descent of the king from heaven takes place to establish sovereignty—that is, the social order as it is known in the present time—and simultaneously to ensure fertility on earth. It is thus evident that this Tibetan myth belongs to a very widespread mythic and cultic schema. The importance of the first king in the world view of the ancient Tibetans is attested by several inscriptions that have been preserved from the eighth and ninth centuries. Each of them is preceded by a brief account of the arrival on earth of the first king, named 'O-lde Spu-rgyal (see Richardson 1985 for a study of the entire corpus of inscriptions). Only through an invocation to the first king can the reigning king affirm his own status and authority.

The "Scroll of the Words of the Ministers" (*Blon-po bka'i thang-yig*) also offers a version of the myth which is worth translating in its entirety (Hoffmann 1950, p. 347, for the text; translation, p. 248; another translation in Tucci 1949, p. 732; and in Haarh 1969, p. 235):

> The Lady Gung-rgyal (Queen of Heaven) of the land of sPu
> gave birth to the nine *the'u-brang* brothers;
> he descended from the youngest of them, 'U-pe-ra.
> It is difficult to tell the heavy task he undertook.
> The son of Khri-rgyal-ba and Dri-dmu tri-btsan,
> gNya'-khri btsan-po was born when the moon was full (*nya*),
> so that he was also called Nya-khri btsan-po.
> At that time there were only petty kings in Tibet,
> and they could not stand up to the four great kings of the four cardinal points.
> As three maternal uncles, the minister (they were thus four),
> and two wise men of the six clans of the subjects went to find a ruler,
> the lord sKar-ma yol-sde said:
> "The son of the gods, who is called gNya'-khri btsan-po,
> who lives above the five levels of the sky,
> is the nephew of the *dmu,* so invite him then!"
> But gNya'-khri btsan-po said: "There are (in Tibet) six things to fear,
> theft, hatred, enemies, yaks, poison, and evil spells!"
> (to which replied) sKar-ma yol-sde, the "rib-god":

"Here in Tibet we have punishments for thievery,
we oppose love to hatred, we have allies against our enemies,
and against yaks we have weapons, against poisons, medicines,
against evil spells we have means by which one can be freed."
And bringing the ten *dmu* objects, (gNya'-khri-btsan-po) came.

In other words, we learn that the king is descended from a group of divine beings, the *the'u-brang,* who at a later period ended up as demons in the popular religion. But he is also associated with the *dmu,* and when he comes to earth, he carries *dmu* objects. This word, which is derived from a Tibeto-Burman root meaning "heaven," designates a group of divinities intimately associated with the Tibetan kings (Stein 1941, pp. 211–16; Tucci 1949, pp. 714–15). It is even said in other versions that the king descended to earth by means of a *dmu* cord or a *dmu* ladder. The mountain upon which he landed can itself be qualified as "the heavenly ladder" (*mtho-ris them-skas*) (Tucci 1970, p. 242).

The theme of the celestial origin of the first king, who appears on top of a mountain, was also applied to later, local dynasties. Thus the genealogical account of the kings of Derge, a principality in eastern Tibet, tells that the ancestor of the kings was a divine youth who descended to the peak of a mountain in the east; because he had come from the sky, people called him gNam-tsha-'brug, "the Dragon who is the offspring of Heaven" (Kolmaš 1968, p. 25).

II. Buddhist Rationalization

Buddhism could accept the myths of the first kings only by subjecting them to a radical process of rationalization. The myth results, for Bu-ston, the famous scholar (1290–1364), in what follows (translated by Obermiller 1932, pp. 181–82; Macdonald 1959, p. 422; and Haarh 1969, p. 179; detailed discussion in Haarh 1969, pp. 171–212):

> Regarding the Tibetan royal dynasty, there are those who say that its ancestor was the fifth descendant of Prasenajit, king of Kosala, others who say that he was the fifth descendant of sTobs-chung, the youngest son of Bimbisāra. Still others claim that when the Tibetans were oppressed by the twelve minor kings of the demons and spirits, Udayana, king of Vatsala, had a son. The eyes of this child closed from below upwards, and his fingers were joined together by a membrane. Faced with such strange signs, the king placed him in a sealed copper vessel and threw him into the Ganges. A peasant then found him and raised him, but when he had grown up the young prince was unhappy to learn what had happened, and fled into the Himalayan mountains. He arrived at the foot of the divine mountain Lha-ri yol-ba, the "Royal Plain of Four Portals." Some *bon-po* then said to each other: "He has come by way of a *dmu* cord and a *dmu* ladder; he is therefore a god." And they asked him, "Who are you?" "A King," he replied. They asked him where he came from, and he pointed to the sky. Since they did not understand what he had said, they put him on a wooden throne which four men carried on their necks. "Let him be our king!" they said, and he was given the name gNya' (neck) khri (throne) btsan-po (king).

What is most striking in this narrative is that what referred most explicitly to the divine and to the mythical times has been systematically eliminated. It is true that the central figure of the narrative is the son of a king whose unusual physical characteristics set him apart from other men. But when the Tibetans choose him as king, it is because of a misunderstanding caused by their inability to comprehend him. Furthermore, the very widespread motif of the future hero who is at first abandoned and is raised by adoptive parents (cf. for example, the lives of Moses and Kṛṣṇa) was introduced into this story. Finally, there is an evident wish to provide an explanation for the name of the king. While these explanations manifestly are the result of either learned or popular etymological speculation, one of them at least (being carried on the necks of four men) is perhaps not entirely arbitrary, for in Iranian as well as in Byzantine civilization the divine sovereignty of the king was affirmed by his being lifted on the necks of his subjects (L'Orange 1953, pp. 87–89).

Bu-ston presents the Tibetan royal dynasty as a branch of an Indian family, and Udayana, king of Vatsala, is in fact a historical personage, the contemporary of the Buddha Śākyamuni. The myth has thus been rendered completely historical and profane, while continuing to legitimize the Tibetan kings, since they are connected to India, the land of the Buddha. It is interesting to note that Tibet was later to play a similar role vis-à-vis Mongolia, Mongolian chronicles explaining the genealogy of the Khagans by linking them to Indian dynasties through the mediation of mythical Tibetan kings (Haarh 1969, pp. 92–98). In a similar fashion a fifteenth-century Bonpo text makes the first Tibetan king a son of Pāṇḍu, the father of the heroes of the *Mahābhārata,* which connects him to a period which, according to traditional chronology, precedes the life of Śākyamuni, whom the Bonpo did not accept as being the Buddha (Laufer 1901, pp. 29–30; summarized in Tucci 1949, p. 731).

Despite all these innovations, one can see that Bu-ston has kept the chronology that was consistent with the series of demoniacal beings who are said to have governed Tibet before the arrival of the first king. He has also kept the central motif of the association of this future king with a mountain, no longer, it is true, in the form of a descent from the heights of the heavens onto the top of the mountain, but using the idea of a descent from the mountain itself. He still speaks of the invitation made to the king; and when the king comes down from the mountain, he enters a plain that has "four doors," which is thus a quadrangular, sacred area where he is encountered by *bon-po* (in whom we recognize the representatives of the pre-Buddhist religion) who were apparently awaiting a divinity coming to them by means of a celestial cord or ladder. In a later version, supplied by Sum-pa mkhan-po in the eighteenth century, it is said that the king was met by "twelve men who were worshiping the local divinity" (Snellgrove 1957, p. 127). The term used here, *yul-lha,* designates the sacred mountain of the country, the one onto which the mythical ancestor-hero descends.

But other versions are even more rationalist; the future king is welcomed by "shepherds" (Kuznetsov 1966, p. 46; translation by Hoffmann 1950, p. 297), "hunters" (*La-dvags rgyal-rabs,* cited by Hoffmann 1950, p. 312), "some fortunate Tibetans" (*dPa'o gtsug-lag 'phreng-ba,* translated by Haarh, p. 175), or, in an effort of synthesis, "twelve wise men, *bon-po* and others, who were watching over their herds" (*Chronicle of the Fifth Dalai Lama,* translated by Haarh 1969, p. 182).

Thus there have been diverse traditions about the first king. In fact, the situation must have already become confused very early on, for one of the manuscripts of Tun-huang, probably from the tenth century, gives three different versions of his origin, one being that he was one of the "twelve little kings," the second connecting him, although obscurely, to a class of demons, and the third being the account of his well-known descent from the sky "above the thirteen levels of the heavens." The passage ends with the remark that "one cannot know clearly who he was" (Macdonald 1971, pp. 214–19). The subsequent tradition preserved the idea of three different versions. The "Scroll of the Words of the Ministers" classifies them thus (Hoffmann 1950, p. 247; Haarh 1969, p. 169; Macdonald 1971, pp. 206–13; Stein 1988, pp. 1420–21):

> Concerning king gNya'-khri btsan-po, who descended from the gods,
> we are told that there are several versions; one "secret," one "public" and one "ultra-secret."
> According to the "secret" version, he is descended from kings;
> this is the version of *chos* (Buddhism).
> According to the "public" version, he is descended from gods;
> this is the version of *bon*.
> According to the "ultra-secret" version, he is descended from the *the'u-brang;*
> this is the version of the people and the ministers.

Sum-pa mkhan-po, after giving the Buddhist version in great detail, mentions the other two traditions. But he cannot help adding his own commentary, which in one stroke reveals the inability to understand the ancient myths which is so characteristic of Buddhist scholasticism:

"All these tales of a descent from the sky come from the fact that the Bonpo like the sky. It would be quite wrong to pursue these falsehoods."

III. Myths about Subsequent Kings

But if we wish to "pursue these falsehoods," we must see how Tibetan mythology describes the destiny of the subsequent kings. In this connection there is a myth of quite special interest which tells how Gri-gum btsan-po, the eighth king, was the first to leave his body behind him on earth, just like ordinary mortals. This myth explains the origin of the funerary mounds that were built for kings, one of the most striking or at least best-known aspects of the pre-Buddhist religion (Tucci 1950; Haarh 1969, pp. 327–97).

We have seen that the first Tibetan king was believed to have returned bodily to heaven. Subsequent tradition specifies that this body and those of his first six successors became rainbows that faded into the sky. They were known by the collective name of the "Seven Enthroned Ones of Heaven" (gnam-gyi khri-bdun). The seventh successor, however, was Gri-gum btsan-po. The tales about this king are particularly complex; they have been studied by Haarh (1969, pp. 142–67 and 401–6). From the oldest version, which comes from a chronicle discovered in Tun-huang, one can learn the following (translation by Bacot/Thomas/Toussaint 1946, pp. 123–28; Snellgrove 1957, pp. 131–32; and Haarh 1969, pp. 401–6):

Because of a misunderstanding for which his nurse was responsible, the king was given the ominous name of Drigum btsan-po ("the mighty one killed by pollution," which in later texts always becomes Gri-gum btsan-po, ". . . killed by the sword"). Since he was descended from the gods and therefore differed from other men, he had the miraculous power to disappear into the zenith. However, he challenged his nine paternal and three maternal kinsmen to fight against him. Each one in turn declined. He then asked his chief groom, Lo-ngam, to fight with him, but when he too declined the offer, the king would not let him. Lo-ngam then said that he would fight, but only on condition that he be given the treasures of the gods: the lance that throws itself; the sword that strikes by itself; and the armor that dons itself. This the king accepted. When they met at the place set for the battle, the groom asked the king to cut the celestial cord and reverse the ladder of the nine spheres, and this too the king agreed to do. Then Lo-ngam fixed two hundred spear points on the horns of one hundred oxen and loaded ashes on their backs. The oxen fought among themselves, and the ashes were scattered everywhere, so that Lo-ngam was able to prevail in the confusion. Since the king no longer had the benefit of the *dmu* cord, he perished, and his two sons built him an earthen tomb in the shape of a tent.

From that day, kings left their bodies behind them on the day of their death. In other versions of the myth, it is explicitly said that Lo-ngam first managed by means of a ruse to get the king's tutelary divinities to abandon him, and subsequently easily triumphed over him when the king at last inadvertently cut the celestial cord (Haarh 1969, pp. 142–67; Kuznetsov 1966, p. 47; Tucci 1949, p. 733).

Thus, for the Tibetan kings death is the result of a misunderstanding or an accident. Moreover, divine revelations, supernatural powers, immortality, etc., depend on the tree, the cord, or the ladder that make communication between the sky and the earth possible. To break the *dmu* rope was a disaster. To tie it together again, in the context of a ritual, signifies life, prosperity, and the reassertion of royal power. This is why the *gZer-mig,* the biography of the Buddha of the Bonpo, the Teacher gShen-rab, states that when his parents were married, and likewise when he himself married his first wife, the *dmu* cord, among other rites, was tied by the *dmu* (Hoffmann 1950, p. 141). It is a striking example of the continuity of ideas in the history of Tibetan religion that during the marriage ritual of the Bonpo of today, a cord, called the *dmu* cord, is attached to the groom's sinciput (Karmay 1975, p. 210).

In closing, let us mention a curious ceremony that was practiced in Lhasa until the first decades of the twentieth century. During this ritual, three men of the province of gTsang slid down a rope at a terrifying speed from the roofs of the Potala to an obelisk at the foot of the palace, hundreds of feet below. In theory this ceremony took place to commemorate the defeat of a king of gTsang by the Mongols in 1641. But that defeat also had the effect of making the fifth Dalai Lama the recognized head of all Tibet, and of restoring Lhasa, the capital of the ancient kings, to its political primacy. And it is thus not absurd to see in this ceremony of the recent past an expression of the continuity of royal power which links the Dalai Lama to the earliest mythical kings of Tibet (Snellgrove 1957, pp. 133–34).

P.K./t.l.f.

BIBLIOGRAPHY

See the general bibliography for "Introduction to Tibetan Mythology," above.

The Religion and Myths of the Turks and Mongols

I. Religion

The Turks and Mongols, whose languages are related (Turkic and Mongolic are subfamilies of the Altaic family), have exerted strong influences upon one another. Their religions stem from the same system.

We do not know when that religion took shape, but it surely goes back to prehistory. The oldest word in their vocabulary that has been reconstructed with certainty, namely, the word used to designate the sky god, *tengri*, comes to us from the Xiong Nu confederacy that settled on the frontiers of China in the second century B.C. It is possible that this formation had both pre-Turkic and pre-Mongolian ethnic elements. What we know of Xiong Nu religion does not seem very different from what was to become Turco-Mongolian religion, but it also greatly resembles the religion of the Scythians. Similar phenomena must have occurred throughout the Eurasiatic steppe in the course of the first millennium B.C.

The oldest proto-Mongolian peoples seem to have appeared in the first century A.D. Among them are the Wusun, though some believe that these were Indo-Europeans; more certain are the Xianbi and the Wuhuan, heirs of the Donghu; the Ruanruan (Avar?), whose dominion stretched from Korea to the high Irtysh and to Yangi; and finally the Khitan, who made their presence felt in China from the end of the seventh century and settled there later in the tenth century under the dynasty name of Liao. The proto-Turks were represented by the Toba (Tabgach), who began to come down from the Baikal region toward the Chinese borders around A.D. 260, and the Goujiu Dingling, one branch of whom would later give rise to the Tölesh and the Uighur. Even then all of these peoples seemed to have the religious concepts that would become those of their successors. But in order to form a relatively precise idea of these concepts we must begin with the Tujue (Turks), the former vassals of the Ruanruan in Altai, who settled on the upper Orkhon in the course of the sixth century, ruled over northern Mongolia, and spread westward (the Western Tujue) to begin the "Turkization" of Transoxiana. We must then consider the other peoples who were their adversaries or their subjects, namely, the Türgesh and the Qarluq, located south and east, respectively, of Lake Balkhash; the Tölesh more to the east; the Toquz Oghuz and the Basmil living in northern Mongolia; and the Kirghiz who settled along the banks of the Yenisey. Information of considerable significance may also be garnered in the west from the Oghuz, whence came the Seljuk and the Ottomans; the successors to the western Tujue who had reached the lower course of the Syr Darya, the Ural, and the Volga; the Pecheneg or Comans, who were destroyed at the end of the eleventh century by the Byzantines; the Judaized Khazar living along the Caspian Sea, and the Qipchaq, cousins of the Kimek of Siberia; and to the east the Uighur, who were allied with the Basmil and the Qarluq and who had replaced the eastern Tujue before being expelled by the Kirghiz toward eastern Gansu and the regions of Turfan, Beshbaliq, Kucha, and Yangi, where their kingdom prevailed until the fourteenth century, but not without their conversion to Buddhism, Nestorianism, and Manichaeism at around the same time.

Despite the relative wealth of documents pertaining to the Tujue, it is only from the time of the founding of the Mongol Empire by Genghis Khan in the thirteenth century that sufficient religious data are available. A comparison of the documents of the eighth and thirteenth centuries reveals strong resemblances and leads to the conclusion that in its broad outlines the religion did not change. However, those are generally official documents concerning rulers, and it is possible that there was a popular religion that largely escapes us. There are many good reasons to think that shamanism *stricto sensu* already had in the Middle Ages some of the characteristics that we associate with it today.

There is less certainty about other religious issues. The economic ruin of Central Asia after the fourteenth century, the virtually total triumph of Islam and Buddhism, and the Chinese and Roman conquests succeeded in profoundly altering the beliefs of those rare peoples who remained shamanists. In any event, one should not expect to find perfect uniformity over a span of some two thousand years and over an area stretching from the far reaches of China to the Balkans and the Slavic territories. It is true that the contributions from neighboring China and distant Iran were harmoniously blended at the center of the first empires, but it is not at all difficult to detect regional influences here and there. We must therefore speak in terms of diversity within unity.

Contrary to widespread opinion, shamanism was not the religion of the Turco-Mongols, nor did it account for more than a part of their spiritual lives. It was not even the only means of divination or the only basis of magic. Coexisting with shamanism were haruspicy perhaps, scapulimancy for sure, and astrology, as well as other secondary techniques. The *yadaji*, experts in the art of bringing rain and storms by the use of a bezoar stone, were among others able to form a corps of magicians independent of shamanism.

The religion was a monotheism with multiple gods. The great god was the sky, Tengri, who dispensed the viaticum for the journey of life (*qut*) and fortune (*ülüg*) and watched over the cosmic order and the political and social order. People prayed to him and sacrificed to him, preferably with a white horse. The ruler, who came from him and derived his authority from him, was raised on a felt saddle to meet him. Tengri issued decrees, brought pressure to bear on human beings, and enforced capital punishment, often by striking the offender with lightning. The many secondary powers—sometimes named deities, sometimes spirits or simply said to be sacred, and almost always associated with Tengri—were the Earth, the Mountain, Water, the Springs, and the Rivers; the master/possessors of all objects, particularly of the land and the waters of the nation; trees, cosmic axes, and sources of life; fire, the symbol of the family and alterego of the shaman; the stars, particularly the sun and the moon, the Pleiades, and Venus, whose image changes over time; Umay, a mother goddess who is none other than the placenta; the threshold and the doorjamb; personifications of Time, the Road, Desire, etc.; heroes and ancestors embodied in the banner, in tablets with inscriptions, and in idols; and spirits wandering or fixed in Penates or in all kinds of holy objects. These and other powers have an uneven force which increases as objects accumulate, as trees form a forest, stones form a cairn, arrows form a quiver, and drops of water form a lake.

Animals play a major role. All species have at one time or another been valorized by religious representations, but some have had a more brilliant career than others, more

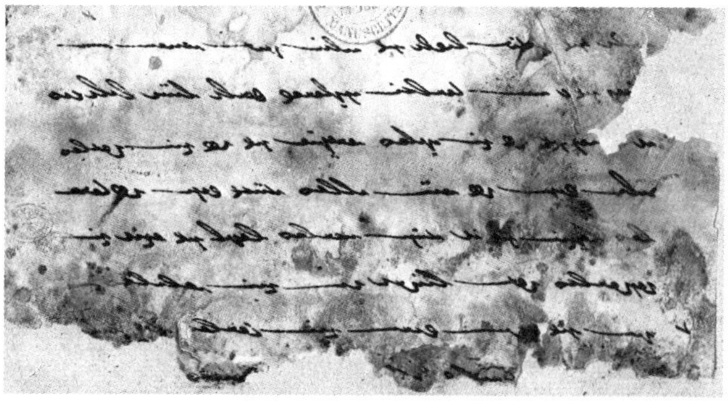

Manuscript of the Orghuz *name* (suppl. turc 1001, p. 1). Paris, Bibliothèque nationale. Photo BN.

Seljuk two-headed eagle. Konya, Indje Minareli Medrese Museum. Photo J.-P. Roux.

through historical circumstances than through their own aptitude; among these are the wolf, the lion, and the eagle. They play virtually infinite roles as classifiers, allies, or adversaries of men and particularly of shamans, as envoys or agents of the sky god, as advisers about things to come, as guides and leaders, and as sacrificial victims. Their form was the essential form, the form of human souls before birth and after death, a form that a man wanted to put on whenever he could or when he was initiated. They appear principally as ancestors, either uniting among themselves to give birth to a human or uniting with humans. This primordial union was commemorated in the form of a combat that men waged among themselves or against animals when they reached puberty.

Compared with the attention that the Turco-Mongols paid to their origins, the attention they gave to cosmogony and eschatology appears scanty. Their conceptions of the formation of the world, first made up of two, then three parallel zones, and then of successive stages, is known only from a few ancient lines and a few relatively late texts. The universe may eventually come to an end but only man's death matters. Death does not, however, put an end to life. Multiple souls go on living eternally, in the sky especially (or, in the earliest texts, on the mountain of the ancestors), or else in the tomb, in the erected stone (*balbal*), or on the banner sign. Funeral ceremonies, which never were of a uniform type (burial, cremation, exposure), were celebrated solemnly and with rituals (lamentations, mutilations, declamations, sacrifice, communal meal). The fate of the dead human or animal also depended on manner of death (with or without bloodshed) and the way in which the bones were treated, since the skeleton, the skull, and the blood contained souls.

In addition to the rituals dedicated to the sky and the funerary rituals, there were ceremonies of prayers and offerings to secondary deities and to spirits, libations of milk and koumiss, processions around a central point, animal races and fights, purification sessions, and pilgrimages. Countless prohibitions intervened in every action of daily life.

Various great universal religions undertook to conquer the Turks and the Mongols during the Middle Ages, but only Buddhism and Islam were ever to enjoy significant success. The Mongols embraced Buddhism. Henceforth known by the names of Buryat, Khalkha, Kalmuk, and Ordo, under their new official religion they kept many of the features of their former beliefs. The great majority of the Turks adopted Islam. Only a few small ethnic groups of the Altai (the Tatars) and Siberia (the Yakuts especially) preserved their primitive shamanism until the Russian revolution, not without being influenced by the Russian Orthodox church.

In 960, the Qarakhanids, Turkic dynasts of Kashgar, converted to Islam. The Oghuz Turkic masses which had already made contact with the religion preached by Muhammad entered the Muslim lands in hordes in about 1031, and from 1071 they began to colonize Asia Minor, henceforth known as Turkey. The traditions of Central Asia changed even more when they made contact with Islam, but these changes were not absolute. The Kazaks, who converted as late as the eighteenth century, the Kirghiz, and the Turks of Turkey themselves even today have many characteristics that reflect traits from the eighth century. This does not mean that everything that appears to be aberrant in Turco-Islamic civilization stems from Turkic tradition. Anatolian substrata along with Greek, Christian, Iranian, and Arab contributions have often been inextricably blended together.

Very different fates awaited the religion of the Turks in Islam depending on whether the traits fit together or were incompatible and on how vigorously they were defended by those who held them.

The ancient Altaic prescription to kill an animal without shedding a drop of its blood entailed a contradiction of the Sharia, which required that meat be bled before it was consumed, and so this prescription quickly fell into disuse. On the other hand, it seems clear that Islamic funerary art, despite the Koranic prescription that the dead be buried in the desert in an unmarked grave, was born of Turkic funerary art. The rich iconography that developed in the minor arts and in Islamic architecture starting in the twelfth century reflects above all Central Asiatic beliefs. We find, for example, a prince in his majesty sitting cross-legged, holding a goblet in his right hand which rests on his chest; a double monumental representation, in painting and in sculpture, of the great myth of the struggle against the bull that was to be told shortly thereafter in the *Kitab-i Dede Qorqut;* and pairs of animal ancestors fighting, corresponding to the blue wolf and fallow doe of the Central Asiatic empires; and other such animals, which were tirelessly reproduced by coppersmiths, ceramists, miniaturists, and sculptors. The one-headed or two-headed eagle in time sat on the top of trees of life, as is still the case in the pagan Turkic world of the Siberian Yakuts. The coat of arms, which later developed especially among the Mamluks, may have been a distant memory of totemism, as was perhaps also the immoderate use of the names of animals, especially during the Seljuk era, when the Arslan (lion), Kilich Arslan (saber lion), Toghrul (falcon), Bars Bay (rich tiger), Turumlay (merlin), Tay Boga (colt-bull), and Kurt (wolf)—all abound.

Until recently, the Sunnite Turkic world, even in its loftiest circles, preserved some customs from the pre-Islamic Turkic world: strangulation of princes, organization of ritual fights, exhumation and incineration of the corpses of enemies, self-sacrifice of a healthy man to save a sick man, wearing feathers as part of a headdress, decorating flags with the tails of yaks or horses—all of these are traits that can only be explained as shamanic representations.

The Islamization of the masses in Anatolia was slow, even when the culture spread, because the true religious propagandists—the Turkoman babas, Baba Ishaq, Barak Baba, Sari Saltuq, and many others—were clearly shamans disguised in Islamic garb. At the end of the thirteenth century, the poet Sheyyad Hamza translated and commented to his audience on the *bismillah* ("In the name of God the Merciful, the Compassionate"). At the end of the fourteenth century, a commentary on the Koran in Kastamuni Turkish deemed it necessary to explain Allah with the word *tengri*. The founder of the Bektashi order, Hadji Bektash, showed in his book, the *Vilayet Name*, that he drew heavily on the pre-Islamic tradition of the Oghuz.

Very briefly, Tengri the sky god was assimilated to Allah well before he acquired all of Allah's features. His viaticum for life, the *qut*, became grace; his order, the *yarliq*, which was expressed by the imperial authority, became intercession or pardon. Islamic notions of divine mercy and clemency remained alien for a long time. Secondary deities and master possessors did not disappear immediately, since in the *Kitab-i Dede Qorqut*, under the same circumstances and in comparable terms, prayers were still addressed to God, to the mountain, water, trees, and certain animals. Sometimes they were identified with jinn or with peris, or else they kept their original meaning by virtue of the presence, real or imagined, of a saint (numerous sites where people worship a tree, a plot of ground, a body of water near a tomb). Sometimes they were transformed under the influence of mysticism (the gate, formerly a deity, became a symbol of access to knowledge). At still other times they would vanish, leaving behind only traces of almost magical practices (placental rites inherited from the ancient goddess Umay). Islamic symbols and readings from the Koran helped the Turks preserve their traditions. The anecdote of Nemrud shooting arrows at God shows how myths of struggles against evil heavenly spirits persisted. The symbol of the soul as bird allowed free use of the euphemism "he became a gyrfalcon" to mean "he died," and probably also the belief in the notion it suggests.

But interferences from Altaic religion were not all that Turkish Islam had to contend with. The Christian substrata of Anatolia and Thrace, and, beyond those, ancient Greek substrata also intervened. Where Hellenism had taken root, its resistance to Islamization promoted within the local literature the introduction and preservation of old Asiatic legends when they had points in common with Greek legends. The legend of the petrified woman weeping over her children, the one-eyed monster Tepegöz, and the struggle between man and the angel of death survived only because of Niobe, Polyphemus, and Alcestis. Symbioses occurred. When Turkish women bathed in the ancient holy fountains of the Greeks in order to ensure their fertility, were they acting in accordance with local traditions or with those of Central Asia? Did the cult that developed in the Cavern of the Seven Sleepers of Ephesus come within an Islamic-Christian perspective or a shamanic perspective? The cult whose sanctuary was Mount Ida (*Kaz Dagi*) enriched with purely Turkic representations the complex created by the marriage of ancient myths, Mariology, and alevism.

Dragon. Thirteenth century. Konya, Inje Minareli Medrese Museum. Photo J.-P. Roux.

Drawing on stone wall of Mount Pissanaja-Jora. From Appelgren-Kivalo, *Alt-Altaische Kunstdenkmäler* (Helsinki, 1931). Paris, Bibliothèque nationale. Photo Flammarion.

The situation in Turkey is, therefore, never clear, and much work remains to be done if we are to understand it better. What already seems certain is that a true mythology is not to be found, since Islam excluded it. At most we may discover mythological vestiges which will always refer us back to a previous religious system.

II. The Deities

It is practically impossible to isolate the deities of the Turco-Mongol world, in part because they can only be manifestations of the sky god, and in part because, since everything is a force, everything may conceivably obtain divine status at any moment. Two examples follow.

The great eagle that flies near the sky and is sent by the sky is a messenger of god, but it may be regarded as a divine epiphany. The ancestor, who is a guiding spirit, becomes a true god in the tradition of the Mongols after Genghis Khan.

We must therefore consider the names of deities cautiously when we first encounter them in Paleo-Turkic texts. Öd Tengri or *Öd*, whom the *Qutadgu Bilig* later named Ödlek and depicted as Time personified, rode on horseback and acted simultaneously as the moon. Was he a "god of time," a "heavenly time," or the sky god who organizes time? Yol Tengri, also on horseback, repaired what was broken, made peace, and distributed the viaticum of life (generally a gift from heaven); he may have been a "god of the road," or a "god of fortune" (depending on the meaning given to the word *yol*), or "divine luck" ("the divine way"), or, finally, the sky god as distributor of luck. A "sacred god" (*tengri iduq*) who hears prayers such as "Lead us not astray" is even more mysterious. Today, *tengri* is the name given to the multiple deities who are often the children or the messengers of the heavenly god.

We will discuss the meaning and functions of the earth, the mountain, fire, water, and trees, which in many cases represented something very particular that it would be hard to treat as divine but that became gods not only in modern times but also in the past. The earth in particular appeared as a great goddess, often connected with the sky god. But we also find a few individuals who occupy an important position during the Tujue period.

The place of the stars in the sky does not always allow us to say whether the divine role attributed to them was independent of that of the sky. Some of them, in particular the sun and the moon, seem to have been highly venerated in themselves. Venus seems to have had a special career of her own. First named Erlik (or Erklik), the "virile one," "the valiant one," a title also given to diverse powerful individuals, she was a warrior who killed the stars at dawn. Under Buddhist influence she became a god of hell and king of demons, the equivalent of Yama, attested in Turkish as early as 1202. A tendency toward dualism led her in certain cases to enter into a rivalry with the sky.

From the eighth century, Umay, the placenta, a fertility goddess, was exceptionally well known. Held in high esteem, she was named "Empress" (*Qatun*); the sovereign queen resembled her; her role was parallel with that of the sky, and she was called upon to act along with the spirits of the earth and the water. She is sometimes confounded with the earth. Kashghari says, "If she is worshiped, a child is born." At that time, as today (when she appears among the Yakuts unchanged, except that her name has become Ayisit), she protected newborn children and mares during the first three days of life. Many placental rites of the Muslim Turkish world stem from her ancient cult.

Not until the Mongol period do we begin to see the god of the gate. According to *The Secret History of the Mongols*, he resides in the frame of the gate, which "bestows happiness." In fact, he was also situated in the wood of the threshold, on which it was forbidden to walk under penalty of death, as all travelers visiting Central Asia were quick to learn.

In the thirteenth century, too, travelers unanimously mentioned the existence of numerous idols made of felt, fabric, or wood that were suspended inside houses or displayed on carts. These idols were fed and sprinkled with milk and koumiss and were said to dispense milk and promote growth; they resemble the idols that are known from excavations as well as those that ethnographers have collected. They must have represented many things—the earth, "the wife and sons" of the earth perhaps, shepherds, the dead, the ancestors. Among these objects was a sheepskin stuffed with wool and considered to be the deity of the home. Not much is known about them, but they seem to correspond to what ethnologists today call *ongon*, idols of the hunt, medicinal idols, idols of stockbreeding, etc. In the thirteenth century, however, the word *ongon* referred to something altogether different. According to Rashid ed-din, it referred to the bird, different for each Oghuz tribe, which each tribesman knew and was forbidden to hunt. Corresponding to Rashid ed-din's list are the lists, less clear and peculiarly presented as lists of deities or of paragons of virtue, that were furnished earlier by ibn Fadhlan for the Bashkir and by al-Mada'ini or the *Qutadgu Bilig* for other Turkic peoples. Perhaps these *ongon* were represented by idols, but there is no proof of this. They may be totems, but they are certainly not gods.

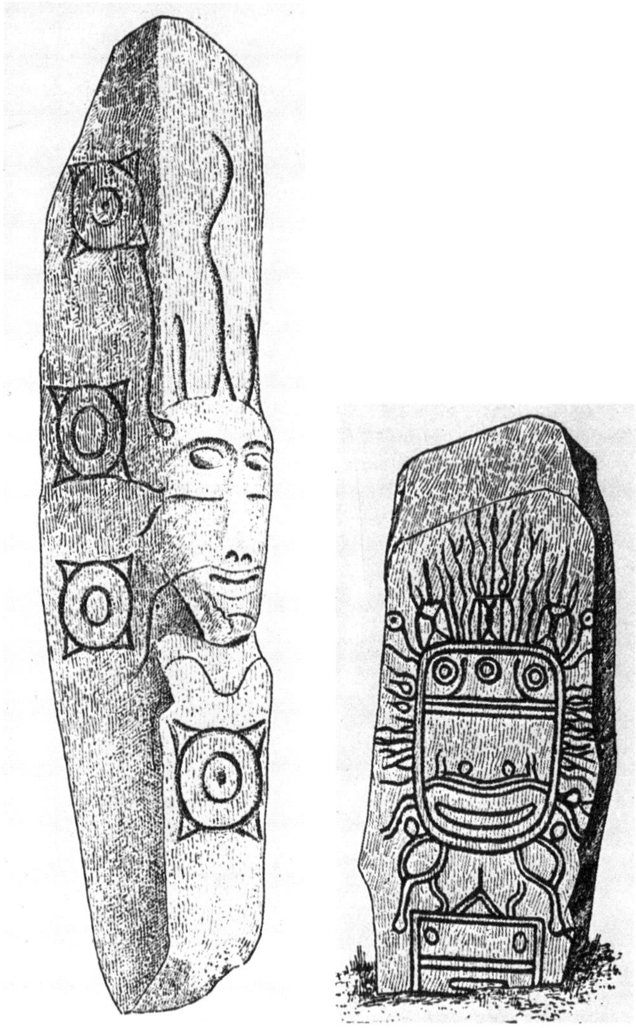

Ancient Turkic stelae. From Appelgren-Kivalo, *Alt-Altaische Kunstdenkmäler* (Helsinki, 1931). Paris, Bibliothèque nationale. Photo Flammarion.

The different *tengri* of the Turks and Mongols of the time are discussed in the chapter devoted to the sky god. We should note, however, that among the Mongols a few personalities were distinguished in importance: the god of fire, Genghis Khan, the "Old Man in White" (*Tsagan Ebügen*), the lords of the earth and the waters, the god of fertility, and the god of war (*Dayichin tengri*).

The treatment of the deities in the Turkish pantheon in Muslim Anatolia was marked by the idea, crucial in Central Asia, that what is called a "god" is above all a power that emanates from objects, comparable in some respects to what the Arabs call *baraka*. Nor did the trend toward monotheism and the existence of the sky god constitute an insuperable obstacle to Islamization. Consequently, deities did not quickly disappear, and when they finally did, they left traces that are visible today.

The *Kitab-i Dede Qorqut* presents a divine triad to whom one addressed prayers of the same nature and structure as those that were addressed to Allah. They include affirmations of faith; references to Islamic events, real or imagined, and to events of daily life; and requests from the supplicant. It is, however, unlikely that any reader of the book would have given the title of god to the members of this triad: the mountain, the water, and the tree. The same text also addresses and praises animals, notably, horses, camels, and sheep, and shows that their behavior or fate determined the behavior or fate of men. The same idea appears in certain old texts of Central Asia, and therein lies an essential fact.

Among the ancient deities that are still faithfully remembered in contemporary Turkey but that have at least officially lost divine status, let us mention the deity of the gate, which is quite explicit. At the popular level, people probably no longer know why they must not step on the threshold, nor why they must prostrate themselves in front of it and kiss it. But in mystical heterodox circles the words of Muhammad provide a basis: "I am the city of knowledge, and Ali is its gate." The gate is thereby taken as a symbol of entrance into the light of knowledge. The various parts of the gate represent the family of the Prophet: the lintel is Muhammad; one doorjamb is Hasan, the other Hussein; the threshold is Fatima; the hinge is Ali himself.

J.-P.R./g.h.

BIBLIOGRAPHY

I. Sources: Ancient and Medieval Periods

The religions of the Turks and Mongols may be known from the still incomplete data of archaeology and linguistics, from published texts, and from information of foreign origin.

We possess no religious texts as such. The eastern Tujue have left three great inscriptions on stelae in the Orkhon region, those of Ton Yuquq (725), Kül Tegin (732), and Bilge Kaghan (735), often designated, the first as the inscription of Baïn Tsokto, the latter two as inscriptions of Kocho-Tsaïdam. A fourth inscription, that of Ongin, is shorter, clearer, and undated. Written in "runic" characters, they were deciphered by W. Thomsen at the end of the nineteenth century and have been studied many times since:

W. THOMSEN, *Inscriptions de l'Orkhon déchiffrées* (Helsinki 1896); "Alttürkische Inschriften aus der Mongolei," *Zeitschrift der Deutschen Morgenländischen Gesellschaft*, 1924–25, 121–75. W. RADLOV, *Die Alttürkischen Inschriften der Mongolei* (Saint Petersburg 1895). H. N. ORKUN, *Eski Türk Yazitlari*, vol. 1 (Istanbul 1936). R. GIRAUD, *L'inscription de Baïn Tsokto* (Paris 1961). G. CLAUSON, "The Ongin inscription," *Journal of the Royal Asiatic Society*, 1957, 177–92.

Of the western Tujue, we have five brief stone inscriptions and an engraved staff from the region of Talas. Of the Kirghiz, a considerable number of small inscriptions, undated but after the seventh, indeed the eighth century, were found in the valley of the upper Yenisey. The Uighurs of Orkhon are probably responsible for ten small inscriptions from the Valley of the Hoytu Tamir:

W. RADLOV, *Atlas der Altertümer der Mongolei* (Saint Petersburg 1892–99); the plates have been retouched. S. E. MALOV, *Enisejskaja Pismennost' T'urkov* (Moscow and Leningrad 1952). H. N. ORKUN, *Eski Türk Yazitlari*, vols. 2–4 (Istanbul 1939–41). L. BAZIN, "L'inscription d'Uyug Tarliq (Iénissei)," *Acta Orientalia* 22 (1955): 1–7.

The runic alphabet is still employed by the author of a small book of omens, the *Irq Bitig* (end of the tenth century), written in a Manichaean monastery in the Tuen-huang region but conforming to the nomadic and shamanic traditions of the Turks:

W. THOMSEN, "Dr. M. A. Stein's Manuscripts in Turkish 'Runic' Script," *Journal of the Royal Asiatic Society*, 1912, 181–227. H. N. ORKUN, *Eski Türk Yazitlari* (Istanbul 1939), 2:71–93.

Almost all the manuscripts of the rich Uighur literature, written in a newly borrowed alphabet, belong to the world religions, but several preserve substrata:

W. BANG and A. VON GABAIN, *Türkische Turfan-Texte*, Akademie der Wissenschaften (Berlin 1928–31). Certain selected texts in A. VON GABAIN, *Alttürkische Grammatik* (Leipzig 1950).

The text of a version of the legend of Oghuz Khan in Uighur characters, at the Bibliothèque Nationale in Paris, is from after the thirteenth century but reveals an earlier state of the mythology:

W. RADLOV, *Das Kudatku Bilig* (Saint Petersburg 1891), 232–44. R. NOUR, *Oghouz-name, épopée turque* (Alexandria 1928). P. PELLIOT, "Sur la légende d'Uγuz Khan," *TP*, 1930, 247–358. BANG and RACHMATI, *Die Legende von Oghuz kagan* (Berlin 1932).

This legend, altered, reappeared in the Persian historians of the thirteenth century and in the seventeenth century in the Turkish author of Khiva, Abul Ghazi Bahadur Khan:

K. JAHN, *Die Geschichte des Oguzen des Rašid-ed-din* (Vienna 1969). DESMAISONS, *Histoire des Mongols et des Tartares*, 2 vols. (Saint Petersburg 1871–74). A. N. KONONOV, *Rodoslovnaia Turkmen* (Moscow and Leningrad 1958).

In the second half of the eleventh century, a Turk from Kashgar, Mahmud al-Kashgari, wrote, in Arabic, the most ancient dictionary of Turkish dialects, an inexhaustible source, especially for proverbs and archaic poems:

BROCKELMANN, *Mitteltürkischer Wortschatz nach Mahmud al-Kašγari Divan Luγat at-Turk* (Budapest and Leipzig 1928). B. ATALAY, *Divanü Lûgat-it Türk*, 4 vols. (Ankara 1939–43).

His compatriot and contemporary Yusuf Khass Khadjib is less interesting for our subject:

W. RADLOV, *Das Kudatku Bilig* (Saint Petersburg 1891). R. R. ARAT, *Kutadgu Bilig* (Istanbul 1947).

Although far less valuable than that of Kashgari, other dictionaries or glossaries often furnish complementary information:

A. BATTAL, *Ibnü Mühenna Lugati* (Istanbul 1934). K. GRÖNBECH, *Codex Cumanicus* (Copenhagen 1936); *Komanisches Wörterbuch* (Copenhagen 1942). A. CAFEROĞLU, *Abu Hayyan Kitab al-Idrak li lisan al-Atrak* (Istanbul 1931). M. TH. HOUTSMA, *Ein Türkisch-arabisches Glossar* (Leiden 1894).

Mongol sources are even less numerous than Turkish sources. The essential document is the *Histoire secrète des Mongols*, written in 1240, the text of which was reconstituted and partially translated (six chapters) by Pelliot on the basis of a Chinese version and was later recovered:

P. PELLIOT, *Histoire secrète des Mongols* (Paris 1949). P. POUCHA, *Die geheime Geschichte der Mongolen* (Prague 1956). E. HAENISCH, *Die geheime Geschichte der Mongolen* (Leipzig 1937–41). P. A. MOSTAERT, "Sur quelques passages de l'Histoire secrète des Mongols," *HJAS* 13–15. (1950–52). F. W. CLEAVES, *The Secret History of the Mongols*, vol. 1 (Cambridge, MA, 1957).

Some letters by rulers, edicts of tolerance, documents of chancellery, in Mongol and Chinese, complete our information for the thirteenth and fourteenth centuries:

CLEAVES, "The Sino-Mongolian Inscription of 1362," *HJAS*, 1949, 2–133. P. A. MOSTAERT, "Une phrase de la lettre de l'Ilkhan Argun à Philippe le Bel," *HJAS*, 1955, 200–220. P. PELLIOT, "Les Mongols et la papauté," *Revue de l'Orient chrétien* 19 (1924): 225–35; 27 (1931): 3–84. E. CHAVANNES, "Inscriptions et pièces de chancellerie chinoises à l'époque mongole," *TP*, 1904, 357–447; 1905, 1–42; 1908, 297–428.

Other chronicles are more recent and deal less with the original religious facts:

BAWDEN, *The Mongol Chronicle Altan Tobči* (Wiesbaden 1955). W. HEISSIG, "A Mongolian Source to the Lamaist Suppression of Shamanism in the 17th Century," *Ant.* 48 (1953): 1–29 and 493–536.

Almost all the rest of the classical Mongol literature is Buddhist.

The insufficiency of Turkish and Mongol sources is in part compensated for by the relative wealth of foreign sources. The earliest are the Chinese annals, which have been translated or studied for a long time but which have been truly exploitable only from the most recent and reliable versions. Hence one must be prudent with the older works:

DE GUIGNES, *Histoire générale des Huns, des Turcs et des Mongols*, 4 vols. (Paris 1756). S. JULIEN, *Documents historiques sur les Tou-kioue (Turcs)*

(Paris 1877). WIEGER, *Textes historiques chinois*, 3 vols. (Hien Hien 1905). J. J. DE GROOT, *Chinesische Urkunden zur Geschichte Asien*, 2 vols. (Berlin and Leipzig 1921). PARKER, "The Early Turks," *China Review*, vols. 24–25; *A Thousand Years of the Tartars* (London 1924).

One may rely upon:

E. CHAVANNES, *Documents sur les Tou-Kiue (Turcs) occidentaux* (Saint Petersburg 1903). EBERHARD, *Çin'in Şimal Komşulari* (Ankara 1942); "Kultur und Siedlung der Randvölker Chinas," *TP* 30–36 (1942). LIU MAU-TSAI, *Die chinesischen Nachrichten zur Geschichte der Ost-Türken (T'u-küe)*, 2 vols. (Wiesbaden 1958).

The works devoted to the Khitan are important:

R. STEIN, "Leao tche," *TP* 25:1–154. WITTFOGEL and FENG, *History of Chinese Society: Liao, 907–1125* (New York 1949).

The Greek sources, which were already given by Chavannes (*Documents sur les Tou-Kiue (Turcs) occidentaux*), are more complete in G. MORAVCSIK, *Byzantino-turcica*, 1, 2 (2d ed., Berlin 1958).

Muslim geographers, historians, and travelers often give the essential information from the ninth century (al-Mada'ini, ca. 752–840; ibn Khurdadhbeh, † 885). In the tenth century, ibn Fadlan reported extensively on his travels among the pre-Slavic Bulgars of the Volga; the *Hudad al-Alam*, Mas'udi, ibn Rusteh, Abu Dulaf Mis'ar, Maqdisi are fairly rich. Later, Gardizi, ibn Sina, Marwazi, and Idrisi remain valuable sources on certain points. In the thirteenth century, the two great Iranian historians Juvaini and Rashid ed-din are especially interesting for data on the Mongols. Wassaf and Khondemir (fourteenth–fifteenth centuries) sometimes complement them. The chroniclers of the Crusades, Western, Armenian, and Syriac, G. de Nangis, Joinville, Guiragos, Haytton, Grigor d'Akanč, Bar Hebraeus, are often less well informed, but their contributions are not useless.

BROCKELMANN, "Alttürkische Volksweisheit," in *Festschrift für Hirth* (Berlin 1920). HOMMEL, "Zu den alttürkischen Sprichwörten," in *Hirth Anniversary Volume, Asia Major* (London 1932). M. CANARD, "La relation du voyage d'ibn Fadlan," *Annales Inst. Ét. Orientales* 16 (1958): 41–146. Z. V. TOGAN, *Ibn Fadlân' Reisebericht* (Leipzig 1939). V. MINORSKY, *Hudud al-Alam* (London 1937); *Sharaf al-Zaman Tahir Marvazi* (London 1942); "Tamim ibn Bahr's Journey to the Uyghurs," *BSOAS* 12 (1947–48): 257–306. AL-MAQDISI, *Le livre de la création et de l'histoire*, translated by Huart, 6 vols. (Paris 1899–1919). AL-MAS'UDI, *Les Prairies d'Or*, text and trans. of Barbier de Meynard and Pavet de Courteille, 2 vols. (Paris 1866–77). IBN RUSTEH, *Les Atours précieux*, translated by Wiet (Cairo 1955). IBN SINA, *Le livre des directives et des remarques*, translated by Goichon (Paris 1951). AL-IDRISI, *Kitab Rojar (Géographie d'Idrisi)*, 2 vols. (Paris 1836–40). QUATREMÈRE, *Histoire des Mongols de la Perse* (Paris 1836). BLOCHET, *Introduction à l'histoire des Mongols* (Leiden and London 1910). J. A. BOYLE, *The History of the World-Conqueror*, 2 vols. (Manchester 1968); *The Successors of Gengis Khan* (New York and London 1971). K. JAHN, *Die Geschichte des Oguzen des Rašid-ed-din* (Vienna 1969). BAR HEBRAEUS, *The Chronography of Gregory Abul Faradj*, translated by E. A. Wallis Budge (London 1932). BLAKE and FRYE, "History of the Nation of the Archers (the Mongols) by Grigor of Akanč," *Harvard Journal of Asian Studies* 12 (1949): 269–399. Finally, see the collection *Recueil des historiens des Croisades* (Paris).

In the period of Mongol domination, many Western travelers visited Central Asia and made essential contributions:

L. HAMBIS, *Marco Polo: La description du monde* (Paris 1955). JEAN DE PLAN CARPIN, *Histoire des Mongols*, translated and annotated by Dom Jean Becquet and L. Hambis (Paris 1965). W. W. ROCKHILL, *The Journey of William of Rubruck* (London 1900). D. SINOR, "Un voyageur du xiiie siècle: Le dominicain Julien de Hongrie," *BSOAS* 14 (1952): 589–602.

II. Sources: Modern Period

We have much more information for the modern period. The travels in Central Asia that ceased just after the fall of the Mongol Empire resumed beginning in the seventeenth century and became more and more numerous. Among a rich literature, we cite:

OLÉARIUS, *Relation du voyage en Moscovie, Tartarie et Perse* (Paris 1666). WITSEN, *Noord en Oost Tartarye*, 2 vols. (Amsterdam 1705). STRAHLENBERG, *Der Nord- und Östliche Theil von Europa und Asien* (Stockholm 1730); *Description historique de l'empire russien*, 2 vols. (Amsterdam 1757). J. G. GEORGI, *Bemerkungen auf einer Reise in russischen Reiche* (Saint Petersburg 1755); *Beschreibung aller Nationen des russischen Reichs* (Saint Petersburg 1776). J. G. GMELIN, *Reise durch Sibirien*, 4 vols. (Göttingen 1751–52). PALLAS, *Sammlungen historischen Nachrichten über die mongolischen Völkerschaften*, 2 vols. (Saint Petersburg 1776–1801); *Reise durch verschiedene Provinzen des russischen Reichs*, 3 vols. (Saint Petersburg 1776); *Voyages en différentes provinces de l'Empire de Russie*, 5 vols. (Paris 1783–93). LEVCHINE, *Description des hordes et des steppes des Kirghiz-Kazak* (Paris 1840). HUC, *Souvenir d'un voyage dans la Tartarie, le Tibet et la Chine* (Paris 1850).

It is also interesting to read Clarke (1813), Ermann (1848), Struys (1720), Helmersen (1848), Ides-Isbrand (1699), Smith (1630), Timkowski (1827), Lebedur (1829), Middendorf (1851), Tchiahtcheff (1845), etc. From the end of the nineteenth century, the researchers collected texts and documents. Vast collections of data may be found in:

A. SCHIEFNER, *Heldensagen des Minussischen Tataren* (Saint Petersburg 1859). W. RADLOV, *Aus Sibirien*, 2 vols. (Leipzig 1884); *Proben der Volksliteratur*, 8 vols. (Saint Petersburg 1866–96). COXWELL, *Siberian and Other Folk-Tales* (London 1925). N. TH. KATANOV, *Volkskundliche Texte aus Ost-Türkistan* (Berlin 1943). P. A. MOSTAERT, *Textes oraux ordos* (Peking 1937); *Folklore ordos* (Peking 1949). RINTCHEN, *Les matériaux pour l'étude du chamanisme mongol* (Wiesbaden 1959–61).

Among others, Castagné has studied the "Survivances d'anciens cultes et rites en Asie centrale," *Revue Eth. et trad. popul.*, 1923, 245–55.

The great Kirghiz epic of Manas is an essential source on which Hatto is now working (for example: *Asia Major*, 14:2, 19:1; 18:2; CAJ, 13:3; 15:2, 4). A fragment containing the episode of Er-Töshtük has been translated into French: P. N. BORATAV, *Er Töshtük: Le géant des steppes* (Paris 1965).

III. Turkey

In the Islamic Turkish literature, which preserves rich pre-Islamic substrata, the *Book of Dede Qorqut*, known from two sixteenth-century manuscripts but edited in the fifteenth century, occupies the first place:

E. ROSSI, *Il Kitab-i Dede Qorqut* (Rome 1952). M. ERGIN, *Dede Korkut Kitabi* (Ankara 1958). J. HEIN, *Das Buch des Dede Korkut* (Zurich 1958).

Stories and epic tales from the first centuries of Islamization in Asia Minor *(Saltikname, Darabname, Kissa-i Melik Danishmend Gazi, Kissa-i Abu Muslim)* are still scarcely accessible. On the epics and epic stories, see:

P. N. BORATAV, *Köroğlu Destani* (Istanbul 1931). GÖLPINARLI and BORATAV, *Pir Sultan Abdal* (Ankara 1943). I. MELIKOFF, *Abu Muslim le Porte-Hache du Khorassan* (Paris 1962).

The work of the founder of the Bektashi order, Hadji Bektash, merits particular mention:

E. GROSS, *Das Vilâyet-nâme des Haǧǧi Bektasch* (Leipzig 1927).

It is often thought that the traditions of Central Asia were more numerous among the heterodox Alevi-Bektashi than in the Sunni majority, and they are naturally more numerous in the popular literature than in the official Ottoman literature. See:

P. N. BORATAV, *Contes turcs* (Paris 1955); *Türk Halk edebiyati* (Istanbul 1973); *Türk Folkloru* (Istanbul 1973). W. EBERHARD and P. N. BORATAV, *Typen türkischer Volksmärchen* (Wiesbaden 1953). I. BASGÖZ, *Izhali Türk Halk edebiyati Antolojisi* (Istanbul 1956).

Numerous ethnographic documents have been collected in Turkey, but chiefly in Turkish. There are numerous records in *TFA* and in *Halk Bilgisi Haberleri* (Istanbul). See also *Türkiye'de Halk ağzindan söz derleme dergisi*, 6 vols. (Istanbul 1939–52); *Türkiye'de Halk ağzindan derleme sözlüğu*, A.G., 6 vols. (Ankara 1963–72). AZRA ERHAT, *Mitoloji Sözlüğu* (Istanbul 1972). Among the monographs, we cite ALI RIZA ÖNDER, *Yaşayan Anadolu efsaneleri* (Kayseri 1955). M. ÖNDER, *Anadolu efsaneleri* (Ankara 1966). Y. Z. DEMIRCIOĞLU, *Yürük ve köylülerde hikayeler masallar* (Istanbul 1931).

For works in European languages, see the *Encyclopédie de l'Islam* (1st and 2d eds., Leiden); *Philologiae Turcicae Fundamenta*, 2 (Wiesbaden 1964). See also the monographs of J. P. ROUX, *Les traditions des nomades de la Turquie méridionale* (Paris 1970). M. NICOLAS, *Croyances et pratiques turques concernant les naissances* (Paris 1972).

IV. Studies

The religion of the Turks and Mongols (Altaic religion) is almost unknown in its ancient form. The works devoted to it are few in number, but almost all the works of history devote a chapter to the spiritual life:

VAMBERY, *Die primitive Kultur der Turko-Tatarischen Volkes* (Leipzig 1879), and *Das Türkenvolk* (Leipzig 1885) are old.

The basic work, by U. Harva, is largely outdated and full of prejudices, but it assembles many facts, generally recent:

U. HARVA, *Die Religiösen Vorstellungen der altaischen Völker* (Helsinki 1938); French trans., *Les représentations religieuses des peuples altaïques* (Paris 1959).

This author had previously published a more limited book, under the name of Holmberg:

HOLMBERG, *Siberian Mythology* (Boston 1927).

Much discussed, the works of the lamented Paulson are limited to the Arctic peoples. See his contribution in:

PAULSON, HULTKRANZ, and JETTMAR, *Die Religionen Nordeurasien und der amerikanische Arktis* (Stuttgart 1962); French trans., *Les religions arctiques et finnoises* (Paris 1965). See also the other title below.

Turkish mythology and beliefs have given birth in Turkey to two works, the second less trustworthy:

A. INAN, *Tarihte ve bugün Şamanizm* (Ankara 1954). B. ÖGEL, *Türk Mitolojisi* (Ankara 1971).

The large book edited by DIOSZEGI is a collection of articles of which some concern solely the Turks and Mongols: *Glaubenswelt und Folklore der sibirischen Völker* (Budapest 1963). There are others regrouped in a more modest volume: *Traditions religieuses et para-religieuses des peuples altaïques* (Paris 1972).

The beliefs of the ancient Turks have been studied by A. VON GABAIN, "Inhalt und magische Bedeutung der alttürkischen Inschriften," *Ant.* 48 (1953). R. GIRAUD, *Les règnes d'El-Terich, Qapghan et Bilgä, 680–734* (Paris 1960), chap. 5. J. P. ROUX, "La religion des Turcs de l'Orkhon," *RHR*, 1962, 1–24 and 199–231. Those of the Mongols, by Heissig and Pallisen especially: HEISSIG and TUCCI, *Die Religionen Tibet und der Mongolei* (Stuttgart 1970), French trans., *La religion du Tibet et de la Mongolie* (Paris 1973). N. PALLISEN, *Die alte Religion des mongolischen Volkes* (Marburg 1949). See also the reports of: J. CURTIN, *A Journey in Southern Siberia: The Mongols, Their Religion, Their Myths* (London 1909). The work of: E. DORA EARTHY, "The Religion of Gengis Khan," *Numen* 2, 3 (1955): 228–32, is bad.

Among the works that shed light on the role of the world religions among the Turks of Central Asia: P. PELLIOT, *La Haute Asie* (Paris n.d.), is brief but illuminating. A. VON GABAIN, "Die alttürkische Literatur," *Philologiae Turcicae Fundamenta*, 1964, longer, gives valuable information.

Works about the Turkish traditions of Turkey, the borrowings made by the Turks, and the contacts of the Turks of Turkey with Christianity are still insufficient. We cite: NACI KUM ATABEYLI, "Anadolu'da Oğuz destani," *Ün* 1, 5 (1934): 81–83. J. K. BIRGE, *The Bektashi Order of Dervishes* (London 1937). P. N. BORATAV, "Vestiges oghuz dans la tradition bektasi," *XXIV. Int. orient. Kongress, München 1957* (Wiesbaden 1959). C. CAHEN, *Pre-Ottoman Turkey* (London 1968). W. CROOWFOOT, "Survivals among the Kappadokian Kyzylbash," *JRAI* 30 (1900). GORDLEVSKY, *Gosudartsvo Seldzukidov Maloy Azii*, 1941. M. S. GÜNALTAY, "Selcuklarin Horasan'a indikleri zaman Islam dünyasinin siyasal, sosyal, ekonomik ve dini durumu," *Belleten* 7 (1943): 59–92. HASLUCK, *Christianity and Islam under the Sultans*, 2 vols. (Oxford 1929). M. F. KÖPRÖLÖ, *Turk edebiyatinda ilk Mutasavviflar* (Istanbul 1919; 2d ed., Ankara 1966); "Influences du chamanisme sur les ordres mystiques musulmans," *Mémoires institut turcologie Univ. Istanbul*, n.s., 1 (1920). K. E. MÜLLER, *Kulturhistorische Studien zur Genese pseudo-islamischer Sektengebilde in Vorderasien* (Wiesbaden 1967). C. S. MUNDY, "Polyphemus and Tepegöz," *BSOAS* 18, 2 (1956): 279–302. A. SOYALI, "Turks in the Middle East before the Seljuqs," *Jour. American Orient. Soc.*, 1943. O. TURAN, "Les souverains seldjoukides et leurs sujets non musulmans," *Studia islamica*, 1953. H. Z. ÜLKEN, "Infiltration des religions païennes dans les mœurs et les coutumes anatoliennes," *Traditions religieuses et para-religieuses des peuples altaïques* (Paris 1972).

On particular points, barely touched on here, see, on divination: ROUX and BORATAV, "La divination chez les Turcs," *Divination*, 2 vols. (Paris 1968), 2:279–329. A particular technique is examined by: R. ANDREA, "Scapulimantia," in *Boas Anniversary Volume* (New York 1906), 143–65. BAWDEN, "Scapulimancy among the Mongols," *CAJ* 6, 1 (1958): 1–31. On rites to produce rain, refer to BORATAV, "Istiska," *Islam Ansiklopedisi* 54:1222–24, and M. F. KÖPRÜLÜ, "Une institution magique chez les Turcs: Yat," *Actes 2e congrès Int. Histoire Relig. 1923* (Paris 1925), 440–51.

Turkish and Mongolian Cosmogony and Cosmography

We know only one ancient Turkish cosmogony, the celebrated genesis of Orkhon, of the Tujue period, which is as undidactic as can be: "When, above, the blue sky, below, the dark earth were formed, between the two appeared the sons of Kishi (= of man)." The old translations using "create" are faulty, as the verb used is the passive reflexive of *qil*, "make, form." It is the same verb that is used again later with regard to men. The problem of the origin of the universe thus little preoccupied the Turks and Mongols, who were more interested in tribal myths. The word "eternal" (*möngke*), which always accompanies the name of the sky in the period of Gengis Khan, seems opposed to the Tujue notion of a formation of the sky and the earth; this is one of the reasons why it was believed that the sky and the earth drew apart or separated.

The fact that more recent cosmogonies were influenced by foreign religions such as the Judeo-Christian tradition, as is proved by the name Ay-wa for the first woman, also tends to prove that there never was a great indigenous myth. According to an Islamic manuscript from the beginning of the fourteenth century, which was inspired by a version going back to the tenth century if not earlier, when a cave of the Kara Tag (black mountain) was flooded, a hole became filled with mud. Under the effects of heat, the mud dried up and formed the first man, Ay Ata, Father Moon. His companion was born four years later from another flood. There are some variants of this account, which demonstrate its reception. Abd al-Qadir Buda'ini relates that a Turkish sovereign of India was born during an eclipse of the moon (which is why he is named Moonbeam). A Qipchaq tradition calls the first man My Father Moon (Ay Atam). He was born from a piece of clay heated by the sun.

Unlike their ancestors, contemporary Turks and Mongols have multiple cosmogonies. The most renowned was reported by Radlov for the Altai: "Before the Earth and the Sky existed, all was water. There was no earth. There was no sky. There was no sun or moon. Then Tengere Kaira Kan, the highest of the gods, the beginning of all creation, the father and mother of the human race, created, first of all, a being resembling himself called Kishi (Man)." The Buryat say that in the beginning there existed only the gods to the west and the evil spirits to the east. The gods created men.

In Turkey, popular cosmogonies introduce certain Turkish traditions which are inserted into a strongly Islamicized context. In Istanbul, it is said that God sent the angel Gabriel to take a handful of clay to make man. The earth, knowing that man would sin and burn in hell, begged the angel to renounce his mission. A more elaborate Anatolian version says that God sent in succession the archangels Israfil, Michael, and Jebrail, who refused to take the humus. Finally Azrail, the angel of death, ignored the earth's pleas and man was created. Among the Alevi-Bektashi, it is believed that

Allah first created a green ocean out of which came a precious stone. Allah cut this in half, and one-half was the green light of Muhammad and the other the white light of Ali. Then he created an angel.

The representation of the world has undoubtedly evolved over time. It is likely that originally, since there was only the sky above and the earth below, the underworld did not yet exist and was an important later borrowing, probably from Buddhism. We do not know when the sky and, for reasons of symmetry, the underworld, sometimes called hell, came to take on seven or nine levels. The ancient texts say nothing on this subject, whereas recent texts are very prolix; but certain cave paintings may point to the existence of these levels in prehistory. The sky covers and shelters the earth which supports it. The two are connected by a central axis which is a pillar, mountain, tree, or perch, rising from the navel of the earth up to the navel of the sky. The Chinese conception of the square earth and the round sky is probably the most ancient: the disinherited peoples are not under the sky but at the four corners of the world. Later, in the western regions, the earth is a disk, which represents a radical ideological change due to Muslim influences and, beyond this, to the Ptolemaic conception. Four or five elements compose the universe. According to Theophylactus Simocattes and modern Bektashism, there are four: water, fire, earth, and air; according to Jean de Plan Carpin, if he is not mistaken, there are five: water, fire, earth, moon, and sun.

Other notions complement or embellish the essential schema; it is difficult to judge their antiquity. The sky rests upon four pillars situated at the four cardinal points; the earth is surrounded by the oceanic river—an idea which may perhaps be glimpsed in the eighth century inscription of Ton Yuquq—or by a chain of mountains; it is held up by a turtle or by the horns of a bull whose movements provoke earthquakes. The theme of the turtle who bears the world may have been borrowed from China in the first century A.D. Certain peoples have conceived of several animals, one on top of the other, beneath the earth: taking up the theme of a mythic sexual combat, they transmit a powerful cosmogonic vision. In a popular Turkish song, the majestic eagle unfurls its wings on the top of a mountain to cover the earth. This notion may be ancient, since the eagle often symbolizes the sky god.

J.-P.R./d.w.

BIBLIOGRAPHY

There is very little about cosmogony. J. P. ROUX, "La naissance du monde chez les Turcs et les Mongols," in *La naissance du monde* (Paris 1959), 283–97. P. N. BORATAV, "Le mythe turc du premier homme," in *Proceedings, 23rd Int. Congress of Orientalists* (Cambridge and London 1954), 198–99. H. ÖRDEMIR, *Die altasmanischen Chroniken als Qvelle zur türkischen Volkskunde* (Freiburg 1975). See also the manuals of HARVA and RADLOV, *Proben* (Saint Petersburg 1866), 1.

Turkish and Mongolian Demons

Evil spirits are innumerable in the Turkish and Mongolian societies of central and northern Asia, but we know little of the ancient demonology. Chinese and Western texts often mention demons that we understand poorly. Several of the demons, decidedly vague, are surely the enemies of men, occupied with leading them astray on their journeys, playing tricks on them, and stealing their souls. The shamans, the protectors of human life, struggle against these. Other spirits, from all the evidence, assist the shamans, and the term "demon" is not appropriate for them.

"Demons," "devils," "satans," according to the various meanings that the medieval glossaries give to the work *yek*, cited five times by Kashgari, seem to appear rather late. The *yek*, whose name is derived from *yemek*, "to eat," is an eater of men, perhaps the cannibal of later literature. According to an Arab-Qiptchaq vocabulary, he has the aspect of a squall accompanied by a spindrift, but he can also be any unseasonable and dangerous manifestation.

Nearly every people has a special name to designate demons, and there are few differences between them. The Yakuts apply the word *yör* to the unsatisfied and anthropophagous dead who roam the earth. The Mongols see in the *chidkür* the soul of a dead person who brings misfortune to the living. The medieval *abaji, elkin,* or *yelkin* are phantoms, specters.

Venus, under the influence of Buddhism, becomes in the eastern zones of the Turco-Mongolian world equivalent to Yama, the king of demons.

Since Islam admits the existence of various supernatural beings, angels, jinn, these beings are encountered among Muslim Turks (*jinn, peri, makir, shaytan, ifrit, dev*). The *jinn* bring on illnesses and appear chiefly in accounts that have the support of magical beliefs and operations. Specialized healers have the power of summoning them in order to attempt to win them over. The *peri,* who manifest themselves in the form of birds, often pigeons, belong rather to marvelous stories. Some demons have more personality. Al-Basti, or Al-Karisi, or Al, "the Red Woman," "the Red Mother," is a female who attacks women in childbirth and gives them puerperal fever. She rides horses during the night and abandons them in a sweat in the morning. Her prototype from Central Asia, in the thirteenth century, was equally identified by the sweat that covered the horses at dawn. It is uncertain whether she should be identified with Albiz (or Albin), a demon attested among the Ottomans from the sixteenth century and known also in Central Asia and Siberia. The Hortlak, called also by the Persian name of *jadi,* is a ghost who feeds on the flesh of the dead and digs up corpses during the night. Kara Kondjolos is a malevolent being, certainly of Greek origin (Kallikantzaros), who rages in the winter, poses questions to passersby and kills, with a comb, those who do not answer. Charshamba Karisi, "the Woman of Wednesday," is a female demon thus named because she rages only one day a week. Kara-Kura resembles a she-goat the size of a cat and pounces on men at night to suffocate them. This may be why she is identified with nightmares.

J.-P.R./b.f.

BIBLIOGRAPHY

In addition to manuals such as that of Harva, see: U. JOHANSEN, "Die Alpfrau," *ZDMG* 109 (1959). E. BENVENISTE, "Le dieu Ohrmazd et le démon Albasti," *Journal asiatique* 248 (1960). A. INAN, *Samanizm.*

The Turkish and Mongolian Ancestor Cult

The ancestor cult can to a certain extent be confused with the cult of animals, since the preeminent ancestor is an animal. We will here consider the one to whom the animal gave birth as the true founder of the tribe or family.

In the most ancient times, the ancestor cult developed in the territory of the origin myth and was therefore bound to a precise geographical site. It was performed each year by the sovereign in person or, when he was absent, by an official delegation. According to the Chinese, the Tujue sacrificed to the ancestral progenitor on the seventh day of the seventh month. This sacrifice had an importance comparable to the sacrifice offered to the sky.

In the same societies, and more generally when the burial place was not kept secret, the cult developed around the tomb, eventually in a funerary temple (Tujue, Qarluq), or at least near an inscribed stela (which the ancient Turks called the "eternal stone") and near the statue of the dead person. In the tenth century Istakhri declared that the Khazar can never pass near the royal tomb without dismounting from horseback and praying. Later, Abu'l Ghazi ascribed the origin of idolatry to the ancestor cult. The habit arose, he said, of making images of the dead, and then people began to worship them. This simplification is not devoid of sense, and several ethnographers have believed that they could prove that shamanism derived from the veneration of ancestors. At least, there have been found in dwellings statuettes of the dead which were fed, watered, and revered, or tablets upon which their name was engraved.

One of the most interesting forms of the ancestor cult is the cult of the flag. The soul of the founder of the empire, first that of the animal, then that of the man, came to dwell in the flag. According to the meaning of the word *sülde,* used in Mongolian times in the expression *tug sülde,* which designates the flag containing the good fortune of Genghis Khan, it was a "traveling companion," which guarded and protected the empire. In recognition of this, sacrifices were made to it. The incarnation of Genghis Khan in the banner gave a particular brilliance to something which was already very old: the ceremony of the deployment of flags was solemnly carried out and had such significance that it was preserved for a long time, until the Mogul Empire in India. As for the banner of the Tujue, ornamented with the head of a wolf, it seems to have been the prototype of all those which were subsequently seen in the Turkish Muslim world, the Ottomans included, and which were ornamented with yak or horse tails, embroidered with astrological and zoomorphic images.

J.-P.R./d.f.

BIBLIOGRAPHY

HEISSIG and TUCCI, *La religion du Tibet et de la Mongolie* (Paris 1973). J.-P. ROUX, *Faune et flore sacrées dans les sociétés altaïques* (Paris 1966). ZELENINE, *Le culte* (Paris 1952).

The Importance of Animals in the Religion of the Turks and Mongols: Tribal Myths and Hunting Rituals

I. Human Life and Animal Life

Animals intervene constantly in the magical and religious life of the Turks and Mongols and therefore occupy a place of primary importance in their concerns. Even though the Tujue inscriptions do not seem to reflect this, all the other documents and informants are explicit enough to allow us to be sure of this. As we move forward in time and men choose more and more often the names of animals as patronyms (this trend reached a high point during the twelfth and thirteenth centuries), we see more clearly the close relationships that were established between human and animal life. This relationship went from one of comparison to one of fusion, by way of participation and mutation, stemming from a belief in the fundamental unity of life, which was manifested in various ways, but whose ultimate reality could be seen in the animal, and whose essential form was that of the animal. Although the animal was totally other, he was also totally similar, having, as men did, a social life and an organization into clans, with their leaders and saints. With few exceptions, he was not a god, despite what certain unenlightened informants seem to say, but he is superior to man in his gifts, because he has not lost to anthropomorphism his original form, which is that of the human soul (especially in the form of birds), as is proven by the existence of the soul, before incarnation, as a small bird on a celestial tree, by its transformation into a gyrfalcon after death, or by its flight toward heaven.

Because the animal is superior to man, man utilizes the animal's power by using his organs for divination (scapulimancy, haruspicy) and for magic (bezoars for bringing rain). Alliances were made with him, so that he would agree to give his wool, milk, and meat. These alliances corresponded to conflicts regarded as tribal wars and were to be resolved by hunting rituals. The animal was considered appropriate for sacrifice to the sky, to the gods, and to the ancestors. He was thought to be the best means of classifying tribes and time; hours, days, months, and years were all determined by the Calendar of the Twelve Animals, which came from China and arrived on the Volga in about 603, but was so completely adopted by the Turks that they developed their own etiological myth around it, whereby each animal in the series entailed in his own characteristics the characteristics of the year.

Because the animal resembled man, it was thought that conversations with him were possible, that his behavior could be imitated, that certain of his physical traits could be acquired, and that he could appear in human form just as man could appear in animal form—and this was always done by the wearing of skins, feathers, wings, and horns. Feathers decorating the heads of shamans, princes, and others led to the Islamic style of decorating with feathers that is so clearly indicated on miniatures. This remarkable proximity naturally permitted matrimonial relations, which were commemorated or renewed during ritual battles and which resulted in making animals, who often came from the sky (which was identified with light), into the founders of clans, the ancestors of shamans, and then, as a result, into protectors or guides.

All of the conditions were ripe, or almost ripe, for the animal to become a totem. But totemism requires a division into phratries, while Turco-Mongolian history is a continuous attempt to establish empires at the expense of the tribal order. These empires tended to suppress the totems of vassalized clans in order to exalt their own. This explains the preponderance of certain species of animals, even though all animals, without exception, were called upon to play a role.

II. The Principal Animals

We can indicate here only the main functions of the principal animals.

The wolf, ancestor of the Tujue and the Mongols, is the most important animal figure in ancient Turco-Mongolian mythology. His role as ancestor is less frequent in modern times, but he remains the guide and protector of the Oghuz, who often have a taboo about his name. In Turkey, the traces of this cult have almost completely disappeared.

The dog is often substituted for the wolf. The dog is also the sacrificial animal of the ancient Comans and Bulgars and of certain modern-day Siberians. Held in suspicion by Islam, he lost his position bit by bit, and his untimely barking, which in the past was generally considered lucky, began to be regarded as a bad omen.

A recollection of the tiger, certainly a divinity of the ancient Siberians and in the *Irq Bitig,* is retained in the name of the Turkish hero Alp Er Tonga and in the Calendar of the Twelve Animals. During the Qarakhanid and Seljukid eras, he was replaced by the lion, whose introduction as an ancestor in the tribal myths must have come through the Uighurs and the Oghuz. Islam, which declared Ali the Lion of God, reinforced his position among the Muslim Turks.

The bear is generally considered to be a man in disguise and is often viewed as a father. His cult, very important today in Siberia (among the Yakuts), must have been found among all the Turks at one time, as vestiges are found in Turkey. In Turkey, as in Central Asia, it is believed that the bear can have sexual relations with girls. A lunar animal, he is also sometimes considered to be the master of the forest.

The stag is not always identifiable, since his name also designates game in general; but in Turkey the stag is not hunted, because he is connected with the saints and the herd leaves blessings wherever it passes. Perhaps a symbol of the earth in the ancient mythology(?), the stag maintains a relationship with the sky, which gives him the same *qut* (viaticum for the journey of life) as men. His horns are powerful talismans, which are placed in front of homes.

The horse is man's inseparable companion in life as in death and the principal animal sacrificed to the sky. In the animal calendar, the month of the horse is that of the solstice, the period when the sun is at its zenith; in Turfan, the horse is often painted blue and he is made to run in a circle about a center point. It may be concluded from this that he symbolized the Sky or the Sun. In the *Qutadgu Bilig,* he is a symbol of time. In Central Asia, as in Turkey (in the *Kitab-i Dede Qorqut* and the oral legend of Urfa), there are traditions about a horse born of the water or of an aquatic animal. Certain graves of horses are considered sacred places.

A double tradition exists regarding the camel, which must, or must not, be eaten. In the *Irq Bitig,* the spume of the camel reaches the sky and penetrates the earth; the camel wakes those who sleep. In some myths, he seems to play the role of an ancestor: camel fights, organized from prehistoric times until the present, make this hypothesis more likely. In Turkey, the skull of the camel is a talisman (*nazarlik*) that wards off evil.

The Bulgars did not kill serpents, and Bashkirs included them among the "twelve gods" who were their twelve tribal ancestors. The serpent therefore occupies a position of considerable importance, but he is especially important because of his king, the dragon. The dragon was borrowed from the Chinese under the name of *luu* and was subsequently named *ežder* or *evren;* he became acclimatized over large parts of the steppes, but certain groups (Azeri, Turkmen, Uzbek) did not accept him, replacing him on the Calendar of the Twelve Animals with the crocodile or the fish. The name *evren* refers to his basic function, which was to turn on himself (see, in the iconography, the loops of his body) and in the universe. He spends the winter underground, and he emerges in the spring to rise up to the sky. In the Bektashi traditions, Hadji Bektash flushed him from his grotto to send him into the blue. He is therefore ambivalent. This explains why he is shown on Anatolian Seljukid monuments as supporting the tree of life or as an ornament on the cornerstones of arches. His open mouth juts out, with its menacing pointed teeth, suggesting that he is a swallower of men. Later, in Turkey, he would be pictured with seven fire-breathing heads. According to a sixteenth-century tradition, still found locally today, the dragon was born of a doe. He is the protector and patron of tanners. Often in combat against men, the dragon was crushed by Hizir, the image of spring, which evokes stories about Saint George.

The boar and the pig do not appear to have received much attention except in the areas bordering on China, where they may have been regarded as ancestors. The well-known Islamic taboo canceled any possibility for their prominence in the Western world that was in contact with Islam. The same taboo affected the hare in the heterodox regions of Turkey, where this creature is held in aversion. For the Mongols, however, the hare served as a guide and was worshiped. The Qarakhanids were converted to Islam by the hare, and the Yakuts carve his image in wood, in which they see the spirit of the forest.

Birds are certainly the most numinous animals. Birds of prey, carefully distinguished by the Oghuz according to species, age, and sex, serve as emblems (*ongon*) for their twenty-four tribes. Kashgari says that their name is often carried by men, and we have innumerable historic examples of this among the Muslim Turks. Muslim Turkish texts say that falcons are "the heroes of Khorasan," and this region seems to be the area where they were most highly prized. Further east, they certainly play a role in the tribal myths of the Uighurs.

The one-headed or two-headed eagle, the latter already found on the bronzes of Ordos and placed on the headdress of Ton Yuquq, is the king of birds. He flies near the sky god, from whom he returns to earth with messages; he perches on a rock, at the top of the cosmic tree; he shades the earth. In the epic of *Er Töshtük,* he carried the hero off on a cosmic voyage. The *Kitab-i Dede Qorqut* praises individuals who have the qualities of the eagle; Seljukid iconography uses the eagle as the emblem of the king.

The goose and the swan are fused in narratives where they appear as guides and protectors and are also used as images of young girls. This metaphor may come from the ancient legend of Swan Lake (Goose Lake) known by almost all contemporary Turkish and Mongol peoples and brought to Turkey in ancient times. A man passing near a lake sees a group of naked women bathing. He steals the clothes of one

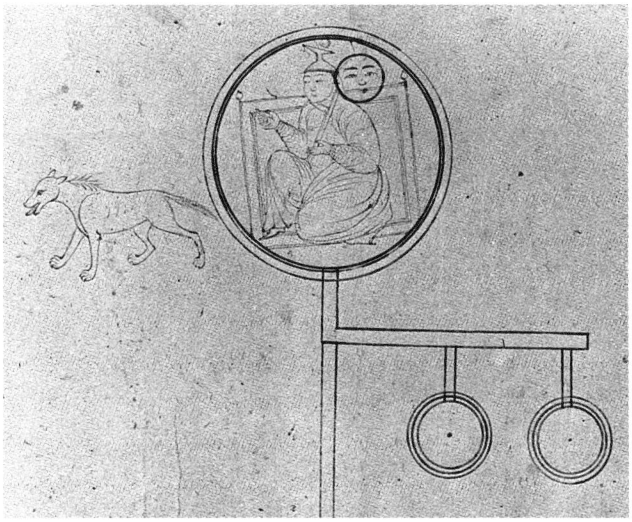

Alan Qo'a's blue wolf husband. Miniature from *Shu'b-i Panjgane.* Baysunghur album. Istanbul, Topkapi Museum. Museum photo.

of the women; the others take flight. The woman whose clothes he has taken becomes his wife and gives him children. She turns back into a swan when, through trickery, she is able to recover her clothing.

All the other birds merit our attention: the crane, worshiped by the Bashkir, the Turkish symbol of the young wife; the hen, paragon of chastity; the stork, the pilgrim father of Mecca. The rooster is notable because of the way he is represented among the heterodox peoples of Turkey: sacrificed at the tombs of saints, he is the archangel Gabriel or Selman al-Farsi, Companion of the Prophet, a friend of God, and "close to the throne" of Heaven. His morning song puts an end to the harmful activities of the jinn.

Composite or monstrous animals, such as the sphinx, the harpy, the winged lion, and the siren, are numerous and are popular subjects of Islamic art under Turkish influence. The unicorn evokes the great wild stag and destructive energy. Its horn, raised toward the sky, may serve as a symbol. Barak is a mythical dog that Kashgari says was born of a eagle and that Turkish Islam assimilated to Burak, the stallion of Muhammad's mystical ascension to heaven (*Miraj*).

III. Tribal Myths, Myths of Origin

It is likely that the primitive legend of the ancestral wolf developed in the Xiong Nu region, at an unknown date but undoubtedly very early. The legend seems to have been completely formed before the Christian era among the Wusuan of Isiq qul and Ili. The two narratives from which we know it show a female wolf nursing an abandoned child, while a crow flies above. In the fourth century A.D., the Goujiu (Dingling) take up the story, but in a slightly different form: a princess becomes the wife of a wolf. In the sixth century, the Tujue synthesized the two versions, conserving both the theme of adoption and that of the sexual union of a human with an animal: a child of a Hiong-nu tribe which was exterminated by its enemies is not put to death, but thrown into a marsh covered with grass. There he is raised by a she-wolf with whom he subsequently mates. The wolf retreats to a cave in the heart of the mountains to give birth to ten boys. From these children the Tujue descended. In memory of their origin, they decorate their standard with the head of a wolf and go each year to make sacrifices in the ancestral cave.

The breadth and duration of the Tujue empire assured the survival of this myth. It was taken up in the thirteenth century by the Mongols. According to *The Secret History,* "Gengis Khan was descended from the blue wolf (*Börte Tchino*), whose wife was the wild doe (*Qo'ai Maral*). He made his camp at the source of the river Onon, near the *Burqan Qaldun* mountain." At an undetermined date, the Kirghiz used this myth as well, but replaced the wolf with a dog who was the husband of forty young girls. There is also an echo of this myth in the Uighur legend of Oghuz Khan, where the wolf, without being specified as an ancestor, plays his role of protector and guide. A final resurgence of the myth appears in the epic of Manas (Kirghiz), during the nineteenth century, which portrays a couple made up of a wolf and an ibex, in the persons of Er Töshtük and his wife.

Other comparable myths are less frequently encountered and often come to us in an altered form. The Khitan are descended from a union between a horse and a cow who met at the junction of two rivers. The Qarakhanids may have a camel and a lion for ancestors; the Qalatch, a jackal and a woman. The Kirghiz, in addition to the dog ancestor, recognize a bull ancestor. The bull seems to have played a frequent role in the myths of origin. Oghuz Khan is himself a bull, although he may be described as having the body of a bull, a wolf, a sable, and a bear. The *Kitab-i Diyarbekriyya* (fifteenth century) reports that the ancestor of the Kara Koyunlu (eastern Turkey) was born of a woman, lost, recovered, and nursed by a cow. Themes connected with the ancestral lion are widespread in western Turkey, not without some contamination by Islam. The daughter of Qarakhanid Satuq Bughra Khan, Red Light (Ala Nur), meets a lion and faints: shortly thereafter she gives birth to a child. In the *Kitab-i Dede Qorqut* of Muslim Anatolia, Basat the child is lost, recovered, and raised by a lion; he becomes a lion and Dede Qorqut must give him a name to make him into a man. A version of this myth by Abu Bakr ben Abdallah tells that the ancestor of the Turks, the Tatars, and the Mongols is Alp Kara Arslan (Heroic Black Lion), who was born in the desert to a woman who had been raised by an eagle and carried into the mountains to the den of a lion who had him nursed by the lioness. In their most complete form (a union of two animals, of which one is often carnivorous, the other herbivorous), all of these couples resemble those depicted on the battle plaques found in the animal art of the steppe. We believe that these plaques were already illustrations of this myth.

The family of Genghis Khan, for whom we have already mentioned one myth of origin, glorified itself with a second myth, recorded in the same *Secret History.* One of the female ancestors of the emperor, Alan Qo'a, was visited every night in her tent by a shining yellow man. He came in through the smoke hole, rubbed his belly, and was engulfed by his own light; then he left, in the form of a yellow dog, by climbing the rays of the sun and the moon. From this hierophany were born three sons who were, said Alan Qo'a, "evidently the sons of Heaven."

The confusion between the animal and the ray of light is an attempt to harmonize two images completely different in appearance. According to many myths, light is responsible for the impregnation of women. We think we have found the earliest manifestation of this belief among the Tchao. Accord-

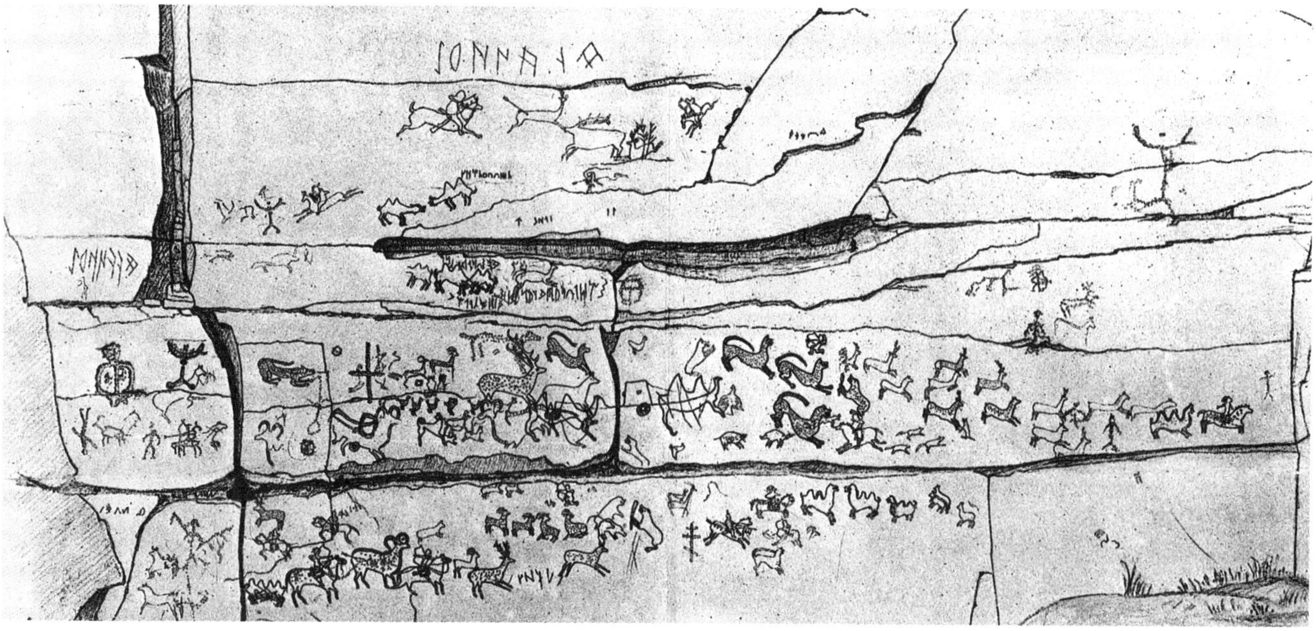

Hunting scenes. Stone from Kara Yüs. From Appelgren-Kivalo, *Alt-altaische Kunstdenkmäler* (Helsinki 1931). Paris, Bibliothèque nationale. Photo Flammarion.

ing to the Khitan, whom we have mentioned with reference to another myth, the great king A-pao-ki was conceived by the sunlight which fell into his mother's womb. Many characters from history and modern stories are named Rays of the Moon and Rays of the Sun. According to the Kalmuks, the daughter of the khan named Ray of the Sun spent the night near a tree with a minister named Moon. Elsewhere, the khan marries first a woman named Ray of the Sun and then one named Ray of the Moon. The moon impregnates women so often that the word *inal,* defined by Kashgari as "son of a prince and princess," is sometimes glossed as *Ay-nal,* Ray of the Moon.

The tree mentioned among the Kalmuks becomes a protagonist of the light in the Uighur myth of Buqu Khan. Between Tola and Selenga two trees grew. The ground rose up to form a mound on which the celestial light descended. From one day to the next, the mound increased in size, until one day it exploded and gave birth to five children. When the children were able to speak, they asked for their parents. They were shown the trees. They approached the trees and showed them the respect a child shows its parents. But the light only appears in the second part of the story. Buqu, the last of the five children, was visited by a celestial young girl, who came in through the opening in the top of his tent; he carried her off to the mountain to unite with her. The combined play of tree and light occurs again in the epic of Oghuz Khan, where one of the wives of the hero is described as a luminous girl born in a tree. In the *Book of Dede Qorqut,* the Cyclops Tepegöz is also born in a mound, but his father is the tree; according to another version, his parents are a bird-catcher woman and the son of a shepherd. In Turkish folklore, the character called Bey Börek, already known from the *Kitab-i Dede Qorqut,* marries the daughter of the white poplar.

The ingestion of various objects, generally described as coming from the sky, can cause pregnancy. Among the ancient Xianbi, a pellet of hail falls into a woman's mouth. In our day, a Siberian woman swallows an icicle cube. Quite often a solemn banquet or the chewing of an apple (Turkey) is enough to end sterility and cause the birth of a hero. In Altai and Siberia, ancestors and shamans are born from the intervention of all sorts of animals and objects. Yakut women became pregnant by eating a white worm; an old Gagauz woman, by eating lentils. One Karagasse clan is descended from a mole, another from a small fish. Among the Buryat, women united with bulls, swans, wolves, burbots, and boars. Among the Mongols, a girl who has been seduced is married to a prayer rug and her child is considered to have come from the sky.

The sexual union of the ancestors, whether both are animals, both are human, or one is human and one animal, is most often regarded as a fight between zoomorphic beings. The tribe resulting from the combat renews it in a ritual, generally at the beginning of the year. More remarkably, at the time of puberty, they organize a ritual fight against the animal, which gives the young man access to the women, allows him to make a name for himself, and makes the winner into a father almost immediately. Naturally, in Turkey and in other areas of the contemporary Muslim Turkish world, all idea of sexual and mythical union has been forgotten, but the manifestations which support it still survive. Folkloric dances make allusion to the union, and in the clans, until the beginning of the twentieth century and perhaps even today, young people are made to fight rams, bull calves, and colts.

The cult of the blue wolf is almost forgotten in Turkey, although in certain areas, sterile women call upon this beast in the hope of conceiving. On the other hand, the possibility of sexual union between bears and women is firmly believed in—a typically Siberian theme. A bear steals a young girl, marries her, and impregnates her. Her brothers come to save her, kill the animal and the children that he has given her, and take her back to their home. But the girl weeps for her lost husband.

IV. Hunting Rituals

Although innumerable hunting rituals exist today in Siberia and Central Asia, and traces remain in Turkey, Turkish and Mongol hunting rituals were little known before the eighteenth century. Yet they seem to appear on cave drawings and funeral stelae: is the game depicted there for purposes of sympathetic magic or to commemorate the hunt? In the *Irq Bitig*, we see for the first time the encirclement of the animals and the king's obligation to seize the animal with his own hand. This rite, so rich in meaning, evokes the privilege of the leader or father to hunt with dogs, the prohibition against bloodshed, and the theme of the first hunt.

The privilege of hunting with dogs arose out of the social hierarchy and the danger posed by the first kill; it was important that the one in charge be responsible for this activity. For this purpose, it was necessary for him to give the right to hunt in his name in the course of an initiation ceremony performed at puberty.

The prohibition against bloodshed, which was respected for domestic animals, was difficult to obey in the case of wild game. Efforts were made, however, to adhere to it whenever possible by hunting with falcons, putting buttons on the tips of arrows, and using traps, clubs, and stones.

The first hunt in a person's life or the first hunt of the year, since it was the most dangerous, was accompanied by many precautions, ceremonies, and rituals.

The hunter often wore the skin of the animal or imitated his cry. This was certainly a hunting trick; particularly necessary, not, as has often been written, in order to fool the animal, but in order to enter its society. In the same way, in Siberia, the fallen bear is introduced into tribal society disguised as a man: it is one of the important events of the great bear festival and an essential part of the religious life of the northern tribes. To fool the game, where that is deemed necessary, the hunter assures the animal that someone else was responsible for its death; this feature must be recent. Older perhaps is the practice of asking the animal's forgiveness for having killed it. But, in a general way, the kill is performed according to laws similar to the rules of war. The tribes do not hunt certain species that are their allies. Care is always taken not to exhaust a particular species. This involves closing the hunting season annually, as well as letting some animals escape from the closed circle of the hunting area. In contemporary societies, strict attention is paid to weapons which are only efficacious in certain conditions: the game must not be insulted, lest it refuse to allow itself to be killed; the name of the animal must not be spoken; women are generally considered dangerously impure for the hunter and his instruments. To allow the animal to come back to life, care is taken to not break any bones of his skeleton. That this is an ancient custom seems to us to be proven by Siberian and Turkish legends about the skeletons of stags that were reconstructed with ribs of wood to replace those that had been lost by accident. The ingenious hunter, killing a stag some time later, was surprised to find the rib he had made.

The custom of giving a piece of meat from the slaughtered animal to the next passerby (*pay vermek,* "to give a portion," in modern Turkish, *shirolga, sauga,* in the Middle Ages) appears widespread since ancient times.

J.-P.R./d.b.

BIBLIOGRAPHY

Rituals of the hunt are discussed in: BAWDEN, "Mongol Notes," 2: "Some 'Shamanistic' Hunting Rituals from Mongolia," *Central Asiatic Journal* 12, no. 2, 101–43. HOLMBERG, "Über die Jagdtritten der nördlichen Völker Asiens und Europas," *JSFO* 41, no. 1 (1925): 1–53. E. LOT-FALCK, *Les rites de chasse chez les peuples sibériens* (Paris 1953).

The ritual of dividing up the game is examined in: EBERHARD, "Remarks on Siralγa," *Oriens* 1, no. 2 (1948): 220–21. PELLIOT, "Sirolγa Širalγa," *TP,* 1944, 102–13. J.-P. ROUX, *Faune et flore sacrées dans les sociétés altaïques* (Paris 1966), 87–118.

This article shows the importance of the animal world among the Turks and the Mongols. Miss von Gabain did this earlier in "Über die Bedeutung frühgeschichtlicher Tierdarstellungen," in *Mélanges F. Köprülü* (Istanbul 1953).

On animals one may read especially: P. N. BORATAV, *Les histoires d'ours en Anatolie* (Helsinki 1955). G. CLAUSON, "Turks and Wolves," *Studia Orientalia* 28 (1964): 1–22. R. DANKOFF, "Barak and Buraq," *Central Asiatic Journal* 15, no. 2 (1971): 102–17. DYRENKOVA, "Bear Worship among the Turkish Tribes of Siberia," *Proceedings of the 23d International Congress of Americanists,* 1928 (New York 1930). C. M. EDSMAN, *Bärenfest in den Religionen in Geschichte und Gegenwart* (3d ed., Tübingen 1957). STERNBERG, "Der Adlerkult bei den Völkern Sibiriens," *Archiv für Religionswissenschaft* 28 (1930): 125–53. Z. TEOMAN, "Bozkurt efsanenisin Anadoludaki Izleri," *TFA* 33 (1952). M. R. GAZIMIHAL has written many notes on animal worship in Turkey: see *TFA* 147 (1961); 14 (1959); 126 (1960); etc.

Altaic totemism is discussed in: CHODZIDLO, "Spuren des Totemismus bei den Jakuten?" *Ant.* 41–44 (1946–49): 359–65. HAECKEL, "Idolkult und Dualsystem bei den Ugrien," *Archiv für Völkerkunde* 1 (1946): 95–163. JUSSIPOW, "Totemistiche Relikte bei den Kazaren Tataren," in DIOSZEGI, *Glaubenswelt.* POTAPOFF, "Traces de conceptions totémiques chez les Altaïens," in "Exposition d'art iranien," by L. MORGENSTERN, *REV. ARTS ASIATIQUES* 10 (1936): 199–210. ROUX, *Faune et flore sacrées.* ZOLOTAREV, *Perezitki totemisma u Narodov Sibirri* (Leningrad 1934). And in a rather confusing way, according to the Calendar of Twelve Animals, in OSMAN TURAN, *Oniki hayvanli Türk Takvimi* (Istanbul 1961).

On sacrifice, one may read: GAHS, "Blutige und unblutige Opfer bei den altaischen Hirtenvölker," *Semaine Int. Eth. Religieuse* (Milan 1925, Paris 1926), 217–26. BOYLE, "A Form of Horse Sacrifice amongst the 13th and 14th Century Mongols," *CAJ* 10 (1965): 145–50.

On the goose (or swan) girl, see: EBERHARD, "The Girl That Became a Bird," *Semitic and Oriental Studies* (Berkeley 1951). HATTO, "The Swan Maiden," *BSOAS* 24, no. 2 (1961): 326–52.

THE TREE OF LIFE AND THE COSMIC AXIS AMONG THE TURKS AND MONGOLS

The Turks and Mongols developed many myths and beliefs about the Great Tree, the Solitary Tree, the Dry Tree, the Old or Withered Tree, and many shrubs of lesser importance, as well as groups of trees in groves or forests. Almost all of these myths and beliefs may be reduced to two basic concepts: the tree of life and the cosmic axis.

It is difficult to prove that the deification of the tree was the result of these representations. It does appear to have taken place quite often, if one is to believe the various sources reporting a cult or a religion dedicated to a tree, or the Turkish prayers to a tree, or Kashgari's statement, "The Turks give the name Tengri (god) to all that is great to the eye like a great tree."

Many ancient Uighur, Qipchaq, and Oghuz myths assign a role in the births of great men to a tree, which is their father or mother. Sometimes the kinship between tree and man is shown by the advice that a man passes on to his children. To this day, the Yakuts believe that the first man was nursed by a woman who appeared, naked to the waist, in the cosmic tree; this myth has existed in the Sogdian region since the beginning of recorded history and can be found in a slightly different form in the *Oghuz Name*. In Anatolia they still tell the story of a woodcutter who was about to chop down a tree when a girl appeared to him in the tree trunk. This notion must have given birth to the goddess of the tree, popular in Central Asia and Siberia during the nineteenth century. The Yakuts pray to this goddess, thanking her for watching over their flocks and protecting their wild game. Among the Kazak, sterile women roll on the ground at the foot of a lone apple tree in order to have children. The Turks of Turkey spend the night at the foot of a tree and dream that an old man visits them. The power of the tree to produce offspring and its influence on human life are evident in other instances. Among the Khitan, a ceremony was held periodically at the base of a forked tree: the emperor lay on the ground while an old man tapped on a quiver and cried, "A son is born!" Among the Mongols, as in contemporary Turkey, it is believed that the man who plants a tree will have a long life; in Turkey, a peasant who chops down a tree can have no more descendants. The tree has also played a role in resurrection and eternal life. The Yakuts, among others, buried their dead under a tree, while the Mongols planted a tree for the souls of the dead. More often, the body was put up among the branches of the tree for the flesh to decompose or be eaten by beasts of prey, but also in order to place the dead person in closer proximity to the sky and to allow him to become a part of the life cycle of the tree. For this same reason, they hung up the skins of sacrificed horses, impaled them on long poles, and made a rudimentary casket from a hollowed-out trunk. The Tujue in particular waited until the leaves fell or grew again before celebrating funeral rites.

The cosmic tree, briefly documented in ancient times, is very evident in our day. The Tatars of Altai say that "at the navel of the earth and the center of all things the largest of all earthly trees grows, a gigantic pine whose top branches touch the home of Bay Ülgen (the great God)." The Yakuts tell of an enormous tree at the center of the earth whose branches cross the sky and from whose roots an eternal wave gushes, spreading as a foaming yellow liquid. If a passerby stops to drink, his fatigue and hunger disappear. In the Er-Töshtük episode of the epic of Manas (nineteenth-century Kirghiz) a splendid tree inspired the belief that the vault of the heavens rested upon it. This cosmic tree, which functions like the cosmic mountain, is thought to make it possible for the two or three levels of the universe to communicate. Sometimes it holds up the sky, and it plays an important role in shamanism. Planted at the center of the yurt so that the trunk goes through the upper opening (Tatars of Altai; Buryat), often sprouting seven or nine branches (Tatars of Altai), it is used as a ladder by the magician during his celestial voyage.

Although the tree of life and the cosmic tree retain their symbolic value in Turkey, they are not necessarily of Central Asian origin in that country. However, during the first centuries of Islamization, trees were venerated and prayed to; people would say to a man, "May your large shade tree never be cut down." They invoked a "tree without top or bottom." In an ancient Oghuz version of a myth, a legendary sovereign saw three trees growing from his navel, giving shade in all quarters and reaching to the sky; this myth reappears among the Ottomans: a tree rises from the navel of Osman, the founder of the dynasty, and the shade from its branches covers the entire earth. Today it is not only in forested regions that stories of holy trees are told. Yoruk cattle breeders and many nonmigratory groups worship the birch, the pine, the myrtle, the cedar, plane trees, very old and very large trees, and small bushes called *koca*, an ancient term meaning "powerful." Such trees are called "holy" (*yatir, evliya*). People make pilgrimages to them, walk around them, build cairns at their feet, and make vows to them, often by tying or nailing on pieces of cloth to represent an illness to be cured. These trees are not cut down. Tahtaci woodcutters call them "masters" (*rabbi*). The founder of their craft, Hajib Nadjar, whom they may really invoke by this title, is the master of trees.

The forest of the Kara Koyunlu grew from the half-burned scepter of Karajaoglan, whose name is a euphemism for "bear." Surely this medieval legend reveals a belief, known elsewhere, in a bear who is the master/owner of the forest. This owner is more usually a saint who is supposed to protect the trees. A tree planted near a sanctuary is said to acquire its virtuous qualities. Jinn may also assemble around trees and bring them to life. The theme of dead wood that becomes green again, of Old Testament origin, entered the Alevi-Bektashi tradition in the fifteenth century and is still in evidence there. In the mystical theology of this same tradition, the gallows, *dar agatch*, is a reference to the torment of the famous Mansur Halladj. In religious worship, it refers to the center of the site where this torment was enacted. There are numerous sacred groves in Turkey. They recall those of Central Asia, for which the mountainous forest of Ötüken may be the prototype.

J.-P.R./d.b.

BIBLIOGRAPHY

J.-P. ROUX, *Faune et flore sacrées dans les sociétiés altaïques* (Paris 1966); *Les traditions des nomades de la Turquie meridionale* (Paris 1970). C. KUDRET, *Karagöz* (Ankara 1969). L. BARBAR, "Baumkult der Bulgaren," *Anthropos* 30 (1935). HOLMBERG, *Der Baum des Lebens* (Helsinki 1922–23).

THE MOUNTAIN AS COSMIC AXIS AMONG THE TURKS AND MONGOLS

In the mythology of the Turks and Mongols, the mountain always played an important role. As a powerful symbol of verticality close to the sky god and sometimes holding him up, the mountain was situated at the center of the universe, where it served as a cosmic axis, the cradle of the race, its snowy woodlands inaccessible and mysterious.

Any mountain, any elevation of the terrain, however minor, could be charged with meaning, but certain summits designated by name received particular attention. Such was the case with the Red Mountain, the abode of the dead, among the Wuhuan. Among the Tujue, there was the *ötüken* (in the Khanghai), foremost among strategic spots, a sacred power (*iduq*) like earth and water, with which it was sometimes identified. There was also the mountain where the ancestral cave was found, perhaps the *Kögmen* that is cited among the divinities in the inscription of Ulan Bator, and a rather mysterious *P'o-teng-ning-li*, the Chinese transcription of *But Tengri.* Among the Khitan, the sacred mountain is the *Mu-ye,* where the founders of the race had gathered, and among the Mongols, it is the *Burqan-Qaldun,* on which Genghis Khan took refuge; since it had saved him, "He offered sacrifice to it every morning, and he invoked it every day." But there were still others, among the Chigil, the Qarluq, and probably among all the Turco-Mongolian peoples of the steppe.

The connections between the divinity of the mountain and the divinity of the earth are not very clear. The Turkish noun *ötüken* is derived from *öt,* "prayer, counsel, opinion," and seems to be the root of the words *Etüken/Itügen* (the *Itoga* and *Natigay* of Western travelers), which for the Mongols of the thirteenth century designated the earth goddess. Among the Uighur, *ötken* is the personification of the sacred homeland. As for the *P'o-teng-ning-li,* the Chinese see in it the god of the land of the Tujue.

In the course of their migration to Turkey, the Turks rebaptised a number of high places with names that they had used in Central Asia, and they established a cult there. At the same time, they regarded as holy certain summits that were sacred in native traditions: for example, Ararat, where Noah's ark landed; the Kaz Dagi (Mount of Geese); and the ancient Mount Ida, where Greek traditions about the judgment of Paris, Christian Mariolatry, and a Muslim mystical strain exalting a daughter of Fatima (herself the daughter of the Prophet), combined to form a shamanistic worship of woman. The Kaf Dagi, sometimes confused with the Kaz Dagi (which has, however, been identified with the Caucasus), was the dwelling place of the *divs* and the peris, or the wall surrounding the earth and perhaps supporting the sky. Numerous summits bear shrines dedicated to various saints, but these saints are often unknown and could be considered personifications of the mountain.

There is little doubt that the mountain kept much of its divine value during the first centuries of the Islamization of the Turks. In the *Kitab-i Dede Qorqut,* prayers were addressed to the Qazilik Tag, evoking the misfortune of its collapse and its aging. Up to our own day, especially in the Taurus mountains, natural sanctuaries are visited by pilgrims who pray or offer sacrifices there.

J.-P.R./g.h.

BIBLIOGRAPHY

See the bibliography of the article "The Earth among the Turks and Mongols." See also P. N. BORATAV, *Köroğlu destani* (Istanbul 1931). H. TANYU, *Ankara ve çevresin de adak ve adak yerleri* (Ankara 1967).

Turkish and Mongolian Shamanism

In the narrow sense of the word, shamanism is a technique specific to the Altaic (Turks, Mongols, Tungus) and Siberian peoples. It involves a representation of the world as divided into levels connected by a central axis and the use of the trance as a means to accomplish the cosmic voyage, to heal the sick, and to foretell the future. Widely documented and studied in modern times, it long appeared doubtful in antiquity and the Middle Ages. There can no longer be any doubt that shamanism has existed from a very early period, if only for the reason that the Turkish name for the shaman, *qam,* is attested in the Tang Annals on the subject of the Kirghiz peoples; but it is not certain that it held as central a position then as it subsequently came to have. Old Turkic inscriptions are silent on the subject, and foreign sources say little more. The only documents at our disposal are archaeological, and they do not permit a complete analysis. In any case, it appears that up to the end of the first millennium, if not longer, the quest for magical powers, which is today its essential constituent, did not exist. We can thus only conjecture that among the Ruanruan the cosmic voyage was carried out by the rulers of the Tujue through the personal intervention of heaven. Travelers and historians often speak of magicians or sorcerers, but without giving any details. One may see in the werewolf of pre-Slavic Bulgaria a shamanic disguise; or one may see shamans in the "priests of demons" who, in the seventh century, "accomplished marvels in the air." The now well-known relationship between the blacksmith and the shaman no doubt influenced the future evolution of the Tujue: while we do not know all their history from the time when they were vassals of the Ruanruan, we know that they forged metals for them. Several characters in ancient texts perform actions that may be shamanic. The inscriptions of Hoytu Tamir depict two individuals who live at a dangerous crossroad in order to perform rites and sacrifices. The *Irq Bitig* speaks of a man dressed in a long garment and equipped with a bowl and a cup without which he could not travel far, of an old holy woman who comes back to life by licking the edge of a spoonful of grease, and of another man in a long robe who loses his mirror (a shamanic instrument). The *Oghuz Name* presents a heroic old scholar who is the prince's interpreter of dreams.

When the information is more detailed, it reveals first the divinatory arts. Theophylactus Simocattes writes, "The Turks have priests who foretell the future." Marwazi later recounts that an individual surrounded by singers and magicians (whom we see already in 576 at the court of Dilzibul when the Byzantine ambassador Zemark comes there) is summoned by the Kirghiz every year on a fixed date. He faints, goes into convulsions, and is asked to foretell the events that will take place in the year which has just begun. Kashgari, who mentions the *qam* four times, explains that he makes predictions, tells fortunes, casts spells, and pronounces a great number of incomprehensible words. Juvaini affirms that the Uighur shamans are possessed by demons who tell them all that they wish to know. Ibn Sina, to whom we owe the most remarkable ancient description of the shamanic ceremony, writes, "(in a Turkoman tribe) when they go to consult the diviner in order to receive a prophecy, he begins to run fast in every direction, panting, until he passes out. In this state, he tells what he sees in his imagination, and those who are present take down his words."

Other accounts, briefer but no less peremptory, speak of magical healing. The *Hudad al-'Alam* describes this in the following terms, "The Oghuz hold their doctors in high esteem and, whenever they see them, venerate them. These doctors guide their lives." Juvaini says literally that the shamans attend to the sick.

Bar Hebraeus affirms that Mongol shamanism has Uighur shamanism as its source. We may believe him in part,

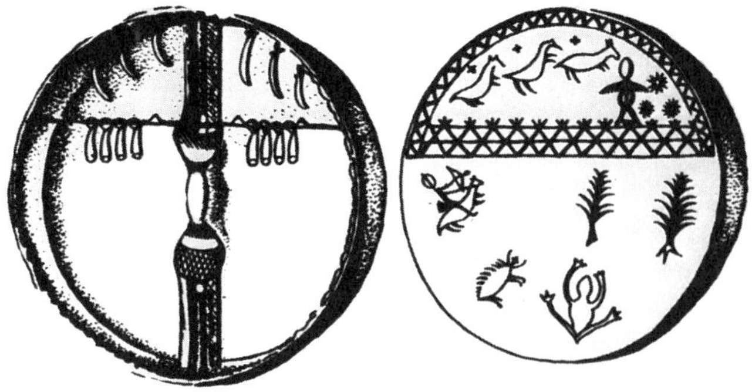

Shaman's drum. Paris, Musée de l'Homme collection. Museum photo.

because the Uighur greatly influenced the Mongols, but it would appear that their shamans were very powerful before the coming of Gengis Khan. This power would become so considerable as to force the conqueror to put to death his great shaman Teb Tenggeri (Kököchü). Male shamans (*böge, bö'e*) or female shamans (*udagan*) as shamanic pontiffs (*beki*) hold a prestigious position, playing a political role even to the point of becoming tribal leaders. Dressed in white, mounted upon white horses, covered with honors, these latter officiate as priests, preside over ceremonies of purification by fire, perform certain sacrifices, and distribute offerings to the gods. Of course, these priestly functions were monopolized by shamans of other periods as well, but it is rarer to find those who, like the Mongol shamans, infringe upon the provinces of other magicians. These practice scapulimancy, haruspicy, and possibly astrology; they are prestidigitators, they cause idols to speak, and they use the rain stone (*yada*), which renders them masters of the elements. Their principal field of action nevertheless remains shamanism. They foretell the future of newborn infants, decide which days are auspicious and which inauspicious. The magical healing that Juvaini, Rashid-ed-din, Wassaf, and Rubruck speak of is often effected by extracting from the body a piece of felt which moves like an animal, or by moistening the painful organ with magical water. The ascension into the sky is clearly attested only in the case of Teb Tenggeri, who, after his death, rises up above his tent, "once again clothed in his body." More often the spirits traffic with men by visiting them in their homes. Rubruck's description on this point is exemplary: "Cooked meat is placed at the center of the dwelling. The shaman begins to repeat his invocations. He strikes the ground violently with his drum. Finally he enters into a rage, and it becomes necessary to bind him. Then, in the darkness, the demon comes. The shaman gives him the meat to eat, and the demon responds to his questions."

Accounts of shamanic sessions become more numerous and detailed from the seventeenth century onward. They show, as would later ethnographers, that these sessions constitute a real journey which the shaman recounts step by step as he is undertaking it. He goes to search for the soul that has fled or been stolen by evil spirits, or else he drives out the spirits which have entered the body of the patient; he conducts the soul of the dead to heaven; he interrogates the Sky or the gods in order to know the future. On his path, he encounters noxious powers in the form of animals who attempt to hinder his passage, but he is helped by benevolent powers, also in the forms of animals. He is himself, with his stag or bird costume, a veritable animal. He is integrated into the world of animals and has become one of them, often by virtue of a preliminary initiation that sometimes involves ritual nudity. The dress and instruments of shamans are known to us through precise descriptions and from fragments conserved in museums. The most rudimentary of these have at least deer antlers, feathers, and wings; sometimes they have organs from other animals, such as bones, bear paws, and furs. Their essential utensils are horse-headed canes, mirrors, and especially drums decorated with designs representing the cosmos, with the two zones of the universe, the axis which joins them, and the different beings that inhabit them.

Since it is more preoccupied with daily life than with metaphysics, shamanism can easily resist the pressure of the religions which the people who practice it have come to embrace. Although destined to die out in Turkey, it would do so only after having exerted influence upon the Muslim mystic orders, on medieval literature, and on various aspects of popular life. In the Seljukid period and in the first centuries of the Ottomans, the "babas" who traveled the length and breadth of Turkey and ostensibly preached the doctrines of Islam were merely shamans in disguise. Wearing felt caps with horns on the sides, their necks adorned with bones, they carried a staff and small bells and played a drum. Barak Baba made a "terrible clamor" with this instrument.

In epics and romances, babas, heroes, and all of the saints fly up to the sky or descend through a well into the subterranean world to search for young men and women kidnapped by evil jinn or cannibals. Along the way, they fight innumerable battles with the inhabitants of upper and lower cosmic zones, helped or hindered by animals; and they meet the prophets of Islam who inhabit the heavens, who reveal to them the language spoken by the spirits, or who give them talismans against demons.

J.-P.R./d.w.

BIBLIOGRAPHY

The bibliography on shamanism in general is considerable. Almost all the works at least allude to the shamanism of Central Asia and Siberia. There are numerous bibliographic citations in the remarkable study by M. ELIADE, *Shamanism: Archaic Techniques of Ecstasy* (Princeton 1964).

See also D. BANZAROV, *Černaya vera ili šamanstva u mongolov* (Kazan 1846). N. K. CHADWICK, "Shamanism among the Tatars of Central Asia," *JRAI* 66 (1936): 75–112. V. M. MIKHAILOVSKY, "Shamanism in Siberia and European Russia," *JRAI* 24 (1894): 62–100, 126–58. G. NIORADZE, *Der Schamanismus bei den sibirischen Völkern* (Stuttgart 1925). A. OHLMARKS, *Studien zum Problem des Schamanismus* (Lund and Copenhagen 1939). A. PARTANEN, "A Description of Buriat Shamanism," *JSFO* 51 (1961). G. N. POTANIN, *Otcherki severo-zapadnij Mongolli*, 4 (Saint Petersburg 1883). J. P. ROUX, "Le chamanisme, expérience spirituelle de la vie animale," *Synthèses* 265–66 (1968): 41–46. G. SANDSCHEJEW, "Weltanschauung und Schamanismus der Alaren-Burjaten," *Ant.* 22 (1927). W. SIEROSZEWSKI, "Du chamanisme d'après les croyances des Yakoutes," *RHR* 44 (1902): 204–33, 299–338. *Studies in Shamanism*, C. M. Edsman, ed. (Stockholm 1967). *Studies in Siberian Shamanism*, M. N. Michael, ed. (Toronto 1963).

Independently of each other, Boyle and Roux have attempted to extract information about shamanism from the historical data: BOYLE, "Turkish and Mongol Shamanism in the Middle Ages," *Folklore* 83 (1972): 177–93. J. P. ROUX, "Le nom du chaman dans les textes turco-mongols," *Ant.* 53 (1958): 133–42; "Éléments chamaniques dans les textes pré-mongols," *Ant.*, 441–56; "Le chaman gengiskhanide," *Ant.* 54 (1959): 401–32; "Le chaman altaïque d'après les voyageurs européens des XVIIe et XVIIIe siècles," *Ant.* 56 (1961): 438–58.

The Sky God and the Stars among the Turks and Mongols

I. The Sky God (Tengri)

In the Chinese transcription *zhenli, tengri* represents the oldest Turco-Mongolian word that we know. Originally, it designated, on the one hand, the sky in its materiality ("the sun is in the sky"), and, on the other hand, the pan-Altaic sky god and the secondary divinities, *tengri* of time (*öd tengri*), *tengri* of the path (*yol tengri*), etc. In these latter senses, the word was used even to our time in shamanistic Central Asia and Siberia. After it came to designate the various gods of the universal religions, it became an equivalent for Allah among the Muslim Turks. The sky was later to be named after one of the adjectives applied to the sky god: *gök,* "blue."

The sky god is quite prominent in Old Turkic inscriptions and in *The Secret History of the Mongols.* He is called "high" (*üze*), which answers to cosmographic and institutional visions and at the same time emphasizes an opposition with the earth which is "below"; "blue" (Turkish *kök/gök,* Mongolian *köke*); and "strong" (*kütch*). His strength is manifested in the pressure that he exerts and even more in the delegation of his strength to the prince, jointly with the earth. Genghis Khan received his strength from the two zones of the cosmos. In the Mongolian period, the sky god's benevolent mandate was associated with this delegation. At the same time, people adopted the habit, which was not to disappear, of calling him "eternal" (*möngke,* in Mongolian).

Tengri was from the very start a national and imperial god; his people lived under him, at the center of the universe, and called him emperor (khan) or, rarely and later, father. He waged war at his will and obtained victory for his people. They were protected by him at all times; thanks to him, they avoided annihilation in times of grave danger. When the empire was extended, Tengri became the god of all the subjects of the conqueror, the god of all men: the proof of this is particularly evident under the domination of Genghis Khan.

The sovereign and high dignitaries held their power from him, were descended from him, and resembled him. They acted in his name. If they were no longer in harmony with him, there was disorder. They received his orders (*yarlik*) and echoed them. They might enter into communication with him by breaching the sky, through a voyage that the god instigated by seizing them by the top of the head, or by receiving his messengers. The common people were therefore concerned with him only indirectly and were more interested in the inferior powers. Nevertheless they received from him the viaticum of life (*qut*), sometimes represented as a gelatinous material, good fortune or chance (*ülüg*). The life and death of everyone depended on him. He chastised harshly, by killing, sometimes with lightning, and did not like those who had evil thoughts.

His creative power was not revealed until the tenth century. However, from this period, and even while Kashgari was to say, for instance, that Tengri causes plants to grow, the creator already bore another name, Balig Bayat, the Supreme Rich One or the Supreme Old One. Nothing enables us to say whether this figure was at that time distinct from Tengri, as he was to be much later.

The worship that was rendered him was not very extensive and must have chiefly concerned those in power. Among the Tujue, in the course of the enthronement ceremony for the sovereign, the latter was lifted on a carpet of felt to be presented to the Sky. The Khitan informed the Sky of the accession of a new emperor by lighting a fire. Like men, animals directed brief prayers to him. A Mongol of the thirteenth century, before leaving on a campaign, isolated himself, sought an elevated spot, dismounted, fell prostrate, and took off his cap and his sash. He prayed for twenty-four hours or three days. The same Mongols exempted from tax the pious who agreed to pray to the Sky for the longevity of the emperor. Periodically, the Sky received sacrifice; sometimes this was performed each day, sometimes each year, sometimes on fixed dates—the first, fifth, or ninth of the month—and sometimes when an important event required it. The Tujue assembled to sacrifice to the Sky in the middle ten days of the third month, on an elevation, on the bank of the Tamir or at its source. Among the T'o-pa, the sacrifice was accompanied by the circumambulation of a hillock, which was called "to go around the sky." The preferred victim was a horse; it was impaled on a slanted pole; its hide was suspended from a tree. But other animals were also immolated: oxen, dogs, sheep.

The messengers, the emanations of the Sky, are of very ancient origin. Sometimes people speak of the eagle who flies at the side of god, sometimes of enigmatic angels, or of rays of light, of dazzling maidens, of blue animals that come from him. They are today more and more numerous as Tengri recedes into inaccessible zones and tends to become otiose. Even among the Mongolian groups that always speak of *Köke Möngke Tengri,* "the Blue Eternal Sky," the celestial gods are more important than he is. He is no longer always the supreme god: he continues, however, to establish his home in the sky. His names vary with his personality. Among the Yakuts, he is called, among other names, "the White Master Creator"; among the Tatars of the Altai, "the Great One" (Ülgen) or "the Great Rich One" (Bay Ülgen). Where he exists, the other celestial gods are his daughters, his sons, or his assistants, who are also called *tengri.* There are seven or nine of them, or they may be far more numerous; there may be thirty-three or even thirty times thirty-three, whom the Buryat and others divide into the good and the evil. Elsewhere they are specialized: gods of wind, lightning, the door, vapor, anger, the four quarters, etc.

In Muslim countries, Tengri has been assimilated to Allah and has only gradually lost his primary characteristics. For a long time the Turks insisted on his lofty position, on the beauty of god, on the pressure that he exerts. They reclaimed images known from shamanism, the royal eagle who flies by the side of God, the tears that fall down from the sky to earth, the reflection of the face of God in the mirror of the lake. When Allah shows the path (*yol*) he recalls the *yol tengri,* the "god of the path" of the ancient mythology.

II. The Stars

The astrological notions of the ancient Turks seem negligible, and it is not before the beginning of the second millennium A.D. that these notions developed under Greek influence, as the vocabulary of the *Qutadgu Bilig* proves. Nevertheless, from the earliest times, the seven and nine planets (by considering Venus and Mars vesperal and matinal) and the apparent movement of the sky were at the foundation of many representations and rites. It was important that life be organized like the cosmos and unfold according to its rhythm. That is why great importance was accorded to the numbers seven and nine and to their derivatives, chosen whenever possible for funerals, the numbers of tribes, etc., or arbitrarily conceived, before the twelve months of the year placed the number twelve in competition with them. That is why multiple circumambulations around a center were performed, a repetition of the movement of the stars around the polestar, which was later regarded as the stake of the heavens to which horses are attached, or even as its navel, connected by the cosmic axis to the navel of the earth. And that is why, from the period of the Xiungnu, people waited until the moon was full to begin expeditions, and they oriented themselves in the direction of the rising sun.

The only stars that played a recognized role in the eighth century were "the Good Pleiades," *Ülker,* who were used to divide the year and occasioned the fine season, whereas Argal heralded the bad season. This was probably the source of the myths of the impregnation of the wild she-goat by the constellation, myths still known in Turkey. Another important star was Venus, *Erklik,* who was a powerful warrior destined to become a god.

From the eleventh century, a greater number of stars were included in the mythology, while animals began to populate the sky. Venus ceased to be a warrior and became a star of light, then *Cholban,* the Brilliant One, a word which was to be confounded with *Choban,* the Shepherd, of Iranian origin. The Great Bear was represented as an assembly of seven khans. Jupiter or Libra constituted the Heroes in Harmony; Sirius was the White Stallion; the Milky Way was the Path of the Bird, probably with reference to the path that souls follow going to the Sky. The Kirghiz believed that Mars bore evil influences. Certain stars were "worshiped" or "venerated," Sirius in particular (informants say that the Turks called it the Lord of Lords), Gemini, Saturn, and, naturally, the moon and the sun.

These two luminaries became the emblems of the king in the monarchies as they were becoming Islamicized, and it was perhaps as such that they often figured prominently on the cornerstones of the arches in the Seljukid monuments of Turkey. Their cult and the images to which they laid claim were, however, very ancient. The Turks and Mongols never ceased to respond to the symbol of the moon, which is born, grows, dies, and comes to life again, and to the symbol of the sun, which sets and rises. The gender of these luminaries was unstable. The creative power of the sun caused the Turks and Mongols to regard it as a female being, and the moon, in consequence, was most often male. Even today in Turkey the moon is called *Ay Dede,* "Grandfather Moon." But in the Mongolian period, the moon was said to be engendered by the sun because the moon receives its light from the sun. In return, the figures who were called Rays of the Moon were innumerable, evoking all those who are born miraculously from the power of its light. The name of the bear, *ayi,* has an entirely different etymology but had been brought into connection with the name of the moon, *ay,* because the bear had the reputation of impregnating women, and because it hibernates.

The worship rendered to the moon, well attested, was less frequent than the worship rendered to the sun. Among the Khitan, it was specified that one worships the sun but not the moon. To the star of the day, offerings were made, prayers were said when it rose, when it set, and at its fullness. Genghis Khan ascended the *Burqan Qaldun,* prayed, and prostrated himself nine times in the direction of the sun.

In the modern Altaic world, the cult of the stars has lost nothing of its relevance. The Yakuts say that the stars that move are living beings, that the planets are windows of the sky. Among the constellations venerated by the Mongols, the Great Bear, *Dolugen Ebügen,* receives sacrifices. A myth of the hunt is connected with Orion. A Turkish name of the Pleiades, misunderstood, has made them celestial apes.

J.-P.R./b.f.

Genghis Khan praying to the sun on the Kipchak steppe. Iran, Imperial Library of Tehran. Photo Forman Archive, London.

BIBLIOGRAPHY

Despite his importance, the sky god has been little studied: J. P. ROUX, "Tängri, essai sur le Ciel-Dieu des peuples altaïques," *RHR* 149:49–82, 197–230; 150:27–54, with additional notes; *RHR* 154:32–66. P. PELLIOT, "Tangrim-Tarim," *TP,* 1944, 165–85. P. W. SCHMIDT, *Der Ursprung der Gottesidee,* vol. 9 (Freiburg 1949).

Qut is included in: L. BAZIN, "Le nom propre d'homme Qorqut," *UAJ* 36:278–383. BOMBACI, "Qut-luγ. bolsun!" *UAJ* 36, nos. 3–4: 384–91. KOTWICZ, "Formules initiales des documents mongols," *RO* 10:131–37. SCHAEDER, "Über einige mitteliranische und osttürkische Abteilungen," *ZDMG* 7 (1928): 114–16.

On the stars: L. BAZIN, "Les noms turcs et mongols de la constellation des 'Pléiades,'" *AOAH* 10, no. 3 (1960): 295–97; "Über die Sternkunde in alttürkischer Zeit," *Akad. d. Wissenschaft und Literatur* 5 (1963): 571–82.

Water among the Turks and Mongols

Water is one of the four or five elements which make up the universe. Antagonistic to the fire which it extinguishes (and it is forbidden to pour any on the hearth), it is also the complement of fire, since fire comes from wood, which in turn grows with water. Water's role in fertility is well known, and it appears in certain myths of creation (a ditch in human form which fills up with water, hailstones), in certain funeral rites (funerals held under a river, near a spring). It also acquires a specific value as a special drink, comparable to milk; in the mystic Alevi-Bektashi sect of Turkey, the Water of Life (*Ab-I Hayat*) must be drunk by those who seek knowledge. But it was as a symbol of purity that water struck the Turks and Mongols most of all. In most political communities of Central Asia (pre-Slavic Bulgarians, Oghuz, eighteenth-century Mogols, modern-day Siberians and Altaians) and in certain heterodox religious communities in Turkey, it is forbidden to soil water with waste, whether by bathing or by washing laundry or household utensils. Bathing or ritual washing may therefore take on a significant meaning, which brings us back to the theme of fertility. The immersion of Turkish women who wish to become pregnant may stem from local traditions (the persistence of this rite in places visited by the Greeks in earlier times) just as easily as from those of Central Asia.

Water evidently had its "master/possessors," but this does not mean that there was a water god, although certain medieval informants speak of its worship. The accumulation of water (*Köl Irkin*, in Turkish) is for Kashgari a symbol of the great intelligence that princes were supposed to have. Its "master/possessors" are referred to as "Lords," just as are the masters of the earth in *The Secret History of the Mongols.* Earlier, among the Tujue, "the sacred lands and waters" may have been the group of the master/possessors of the sacred territory, these territories themselves or only certain ones among them. They had exceptional power.

We know of a certain number of aquatic regions, lakes, rivers, and springs that had their own cults. Among the Tujue, the spring of the Tamir (and perhaps others) was worshiped. According to Chinese sources, in the second ten days of the fifth month, people gathered on the banks of the river to sacrifice to the sky god. Among the Mongols, worship was marked by invocations to the Selenga, Onon, Kerulen, and Ili rivers. For the Yakuts, each river had its own master; the Karagasses brought him offerings so that he would give them fish. This master is sometimes imagined as a bull living in the water. The Tatars of Altai say that the prince (khan) of the Abakan River is the dispenser of rain.

J.-P.R./d.b.

BIBLIOGRAPHY

P. N. BORATAV, *Halk hikâyeleri ve halk hikâyeciliğ* (Ankara 1946); *Türk folkloru* (Istanbul 1973. See also INAN, HARVA, ROUX.

Turkish and Mongolian Eschatology: The End of the World and the Fate of Man after Death

The Turks and Mongols tell us little about the end of the world. Allusions found in the Tujue texts lead one to believe that the sky could collapse and the earth fall into ruin. But the destiny of the universe and the human race did not preoccupy them any more than did their genesis. In Turkey, Islam imposed its vision of the end, on which certain themes were grafted whose origins are unknown to us: the end of the world will be announced by such unusual events as a pact between the wolf and the lamb, the sterility of women, the shrinking of roads, and the multiplication of constructed surfaces. In the contemporary traditions of Central Asia and Siberia, Christian and Buddhist influences are perceptible and are no doubt responsible for eschatologies (the universal flood and Noah's ark).

On the other hand, the fate of man after death received great attention. Death does not put an end to life, even if rarely used expressions such as "he became nothing" in the sense of "he died" may incline one to think otherwise. The place most often indicated as the residence after death is the sky, probably because all great men, since they came from the sky, return to it, and our information is essentially connected with such men. One reaches the sky by flying up to it, perhaps by taking on the appearance of a bird. Subsequently, people spoke of a fly that leaves the body (Er Toshtük) or of a pigeon (Abu Muslim), and people made use of the formula "he became a gyrfalcon." This idea enjoyed great success for a long time among Muslim Turks. The word for flight (*utch-*) combined with the verbal suffix *maq* forms *utchmaq* ("take flight"), which was confused with the Soghdian *utchmaq,* "paradise." Thus, from the eleventh century onward, this word served to designate that particular region of the other world, which had previously been unknown. This is prefigured in the special area that was the region in which the ancestors lived and to which, according to certain pre-Tujue peoples, the dead are supposed to return: the Red Mountain of the Wu-huan, the home of the dead, might have taken the place of the Sky.

Life in the sky is similar to life on earth, which is why it is necessary to take there the greatest possible number of worldly goods, servants, and women. Hell (*tamu/tamuk*) was introduced recently under the influence of a foreign religion, and could not have been an ancient home of the dead. The notion of retribution is unknown, offenses being punished on earth. Hell and retribution have nevertheless entered greatly into more recent representations.

There is reason to think that the ruler reaches the sky by his own means, and almost ineluctably. By contrast, from an early period the aid of a shaman must have been necessary for ordinary mortals, whose fate is less certain. The failure to complete rites, the abduction of the dead person by an evil spirit, or his capture by a victorious enemy may have an influence on his eternity. The shedding of blood, which contains a soul, prohibited for members of the royal family and for sacrificial animals, and the required treatment of bones indicate that even the powerful are not entirely assured of reaching the sky without injury. It was a widely practiced custom—even in Muslim lands up to the seventeenth century—to exhume enemies in order to burn their bones. This act destroyed all of the bonds that they still maintained with the earth, and in particular the power that they maintained there. It is thus evident that the dead could also partially live in the lower world. In fact, the gift of ubiquity is general and is explained by the multiplicity of souls that every individual has. Each of these would be summoned to survive in a different place: in the tomb; in the *balbal*, a formless stone or a wooden pole set up by the slayer in order to fix his victim there; in "cushions" that take the place of the *balbal* in Mongol times when the *balbal* had disappeared; in funerary statues (which researchers have often confused with *balbal*); in idols of household gods; and in banners. Still others were able to return to their houses or wander through space in the form of unsatisfied demons. Resurrection or reincarnation are ill-defined, but seem to have been at least sporadically accepted for humans (even in Turkey, as among the Tahtaci), as they were for animals. In modern times, the abode of the dead and the visions it inspires have become further diversified. The Yakuts seem to survive in a hell "below," which may mean "to the north." Others believe that everything is reversed in the other world.

As we often see, death is a punishment, and whatever one's destiny is, the fate of the deceased is not enviable. Death is an inescapable necessity that is personified and encountered ("He found the necessity" *kergek*) when one's viaticum of life (*qut*) and one's favorable fate (*ülüg*) are exhausted and have not been "renewed" by God. In Islamic societies in Turkey, the red-winged Azrail, the angel of death, the actualization of Necessity, comes in search of the *qut*, which has become a soul. In order not to abandon it to him, the Turks of Turkey, probably like their Central Asian predecessors, enter into battle with Azrail or bargain with God or, like the Mongols, find a volunteer to die in their place (as in the episodes of the death of Tului and the death of Babur Shah in the *Kitab-i Dede Qorqut*). People seek to delay this grim deadline by every means possible. Genghis Khan goes in search of a medicine of immortality and has priests of every confession pray for his longevity.

J.-P.R./d.w.

BIBLIOGRAPHY

P. N. BORATAV, *Türk folkloru* (Istanbul 1973); "Notes sur Azraïl dans le folklore turc," *Oriens* 4 (1951). See also HARVA, RAVLOV, and IMAN, and the bibliography of the article "Turkish and Mongolian Funerary Customs."

Turkish and Mongolian Master Spirits (Ejen and Izik)

The master/possessors, also named master spirits, are known primarily through ethnography, which designates them with the Mongolo-Tungus word *ejen* or the Turkish *izik*, derived from the ancient *idhi*, which is connected with *iduq*. Today the master spirits are innumerable, since every object and every being is animated by a spirit or belongs to an invisible power.

Kashgari clearly explains what is meant by *iduq*: "Anything that is blessed/sacred. This name is given to every animal that is set free. One may not burden it with a load, or milk it, or shear its wool. It is protected by a vow made by its owner." The *Irq Bitig* offers an interesting detail when it says that the *iduq* is a white animal, which will be generally confirmed by what follows. We are quite familiar with animals "set apart, in Mongol times and after." At the same time, it is not certain that the *iduq* was originally an animal. Old Turkic inscriptions designate by this word "the earth and water," "the forest or mountain of Ötüken," "the spring" or "the springs" (of the Tamir): in other words, a series of sacred territories. These territories are sacred because they are "left free"; that is, because no transaction may be undertaken there, because an absolute respect surrounds all that is found there, including the animals that live there and the plants that grow there. We do not know whether the contagion of the numinous moves from living beings into the ground or from the ground into living beings. Documents of the Mongol period, in speaking of the "lords of the earth and of the waters," place the master spirits in higher relief, but do not resolve the problem. Rites of consecration of immaculate animals, isolated from the herd, are widely practiced at this time.

The religious manifestation of the *iduq* in the Tujue and Mongol periods is never that of an animal or a plant, but that of a place, and this undoubtedly means the master/possessor of a place. This takes place most often in conjunction with the Sky, or the Sky, Earth, and *Umay*, when the whole tribe, and not merely the leaders, are concerned. Yet we find that the Chinese masters of the earth and of the waters demonstrated violently against a prince of the family of Genghis Khan when the Mongols brought war to China.

One might envisage the master spirits as taking up residence in cairns (*obo*) set up in determined places, often on hilltops and crossroads, but it is more likely that these are particular master spirits, those of rocks—indeed, an entirely different manifestation of power.

In modern times, the *ejen* and the *izik* are not distinct animals or plants or a group of holy places but, as we have said, the animators of every object. Their importance is thus a function of the interest that a given tribe may take in a given object. They are the source of the innumerable precautions that must be taken with the tools one uses and of nearly every prohibition. It is no exaggeration to claim that they underlie all deities, mountains, springs, fire, etc. In Turkey, they could be quite easily assimilated to the jinn and, to a certain extent, to the saints whose real or imagined tombs lend *baraka* to neighboring objects.

J.-P.R./d.w.

BIBLIOGRAPHY

Idols (*ongon*) are the subject of the interesting but debatable work of ZELENINE, *Le culte des idoles en Sibérie* (Paris 1952), translated from Russian. See also: A. INAN, "Ongon ve tös kelimeleri hakkinda," *Türk tarih, arkeologya ve etnografya Dergisi*, 2 (1934): 277–85. Some describe the Master Spirits. On these, see E. LOT-FALCK, "La notion de propriété et les esprits-maîtres en Sibérie," *RHR*, 1953, 172–97. For the survivals in Turkey, see M. NICOLAS, "Les pèlerinages," in *Traditions religieuses et parareligieuses* . . . J. P. ROUX, *Traditions des nomades* . . .

The Cult of Fire Among the Turks and Mongols

So unclear is the place that fire occupied for the Turks of the seventh and eighth centuries that it was possible to doubt the existence of a cult of fire there in spite of the testimony by Theophylactus Simocattes, who said, "The Turks honor fire in an extraordinary manner." It is unlikely that no such cult existed. The fire cult is pan-Altaic and becomes clearer and clearer as more documents appear. Today, in the shamanistic milieus of Central Asia and Siberia, it is one of the principal divinities. Fire was nevertheless originally not a god but a power that played an important role.

Regarded as one of the four or five elements of the universe, fire had no known origin in the early period. The Mongols still hold it to be one of the oldest manifestations of life. It is also said to have come down from the sky, sometimes in the form of lightning, as a dangerous and inauspicious, yet sometimes beneficial, manifestation of power. Some individuals have the reputation of having discovered or tamed it. These civilizing heroes are theriomorphic among the Buryat, Teleuts, and Yakuts.

The ascensional power of fire is attested from 907 among the Khitan, who burn wood to announce to the sky the coming of a prince. Today it is exalted in hymns: "O fire! May your brilliance spread and rise up to the ninety-nine *tengri!*" The smoke goes up the axis mundi formed by the hearth, which is placed at the center of the yurt, and the upper opening of the tent; it is itself an axis mundi. As a destructive element, fire conveys with it all that it has consumed, particularly offerings, bodies, and especially the bones of the dead whose presence on earth is to be obliterated.

Fire purifies. Menander already relates how the Turks made the Byzantine ambassador Zemarchus go around a bed of coals. In the Mongol period, European travelers related that they had to pass between two fires before they could enter the camp, and that it was customary to offer tribute and gifts at such places. These travelers and other sources show that this same rite was used for mourners and for objects that the dead left behind, as well as for thieves and violators of minor taboos. Much later, other applications were found in Central Asia, Siberia, and Turkey. Among the Mongols, it is the young daughter-in-law who is purified by fire; in Turkey, people try to heal the sick by having them leap over the fireplace or pass between two fires. In Turkey, as in Siberia, rooms are fumigated with burning juniper branches to drive away spirits.

Fire is used for divination, sometimes when the colors of the flames are examined and sometimes when it roasts the scapulae of sheep. It forges weapons, giving a particular status to the smith, who is also a manipulator of iron—a luminous substance.

These principal functions—its trance, its hesitant departure, its exaltation and extension, and its powers to keep animals and spirits at a distance—give fire a very marked shamanic aspect and make it the alter ego of the shaman. Like the shaman, the Muslim Turkish saint is a master of fire and is able to walk on live coals or pick up embers in his hands.

The law code of Genghis Khan (the *yasaq*) determined the proper behavior to be observed toward fire. It is forbidden to place a knife in it, to touch it with metal—so as not to injure it or cut off its head—or to spill water on the hearth. These prohibitions are prior to the *yasaq* and are found in exactly the same form in Muslim Turkey. They prove the respect that people have for fire. The majority of medieval observers speak of the adoration or veneration of fire, describing the customs of the Ephthalites, Oghuz, Uigurs, Kimek, Pechenegs, pre-Slavic Bulgars, Khazars, etc. Some of these peoples may have practiced Zoroastrianism, but our information is too general to allow us to assign all of these phenomena to that religion. Elsewhere, certain findings are more specific: in some places people speak of a god of fire (*ot tengri*); among the Khitan, this god is especially venerated in the winter.

As a symbol of the home and guarantor of the perpetuity of the family (the term used in Central Asia for "destroy one's offspring" is "extinguish one's fire"), fire is apparently of the male gender and has had, since an early time, a high priest in the person of the youngest son, the *ejen* or *ottchigin* ("Prince of the Fire"). This son never leaves the paternal home and inherits the authority and all the possessions of the family. However, at present and even though the *ottchigin* has not disappeared either in Siberia or in the heterodox Turkish tribes, in several regions fire is a female divinity with a female priestess. It may thus be called "Mother Fire" or "Grandmother." Since 1594, we have records of young wives worshiping it. For Mongolia, it has been possible to establish a line of demarcation between north and south; on the one side fire is masculine and its priest male; on the other it is feminine and has a priestess. Prayers and offerings, consisting solely of firstfruits, are offered to this divinity by the Yakuts, Teleuts, Soyotes, Golds, etc. It causes the growth of grass and the productivity of herds. The oldest known text of prayers is thought to be the one collected by Pallas in 1768; this is sufficient to show that the fire cult is hardly perceptible at an early date. Allusions made to the performance of sacrifices are not specific enough for us to decide whether these were made for the fire itself or, through the intermediary of fire, for some other power, such as the Sky. It is undoubtedly fire that is concerned in the Khitan ceremony, later taken up by the Mongols, which consisted of burning food in the earth.

J.-P.R./d.w.

BIBLIOGRAPHY

Doubt has been cast upon the cult of fire by R. GIRAUD (*Les règnes . . .*); the cult has also been treated by N. POPPE, "Zum Feuerkultus bei den Mongolen," *Asia Major* 2 (1925), and J. P. ROUX, "Fonctions chamaniques et valeurs du feu chez les peuples altaïques," *RHR* (1976), 1:67–101. See also P. A. MOSTAERT, "A propos d'une prière au feu," *American Studies in Altaic Linguistics* (Bloomington, IN, 1962), 211–13. Numerous materials in RINTCHEN, *Les matériaux . . .*

Turkish and Mongolian Funerary Customs

The funerary customs of the Turks and Mongols show no uniformity whatsoever. Abandonment or exposure of the corpse in trees, cremation, and burial have been practiced simultaneously or in turn. It seems, nevertheless, that the former methods have persisted into modern times only among isolated and relatively undeveloped peoples, and that burial gradually supplanted cremation. A change must have taken place around 628, since the Annals of the Suei say at

Funerary stelae. From Appelgren-Kivalo, *Alt-altaische Kunstdenkmäler.* (Helsinki 1931). Paris, Bibliothèque nationale. Photo Flammarion.

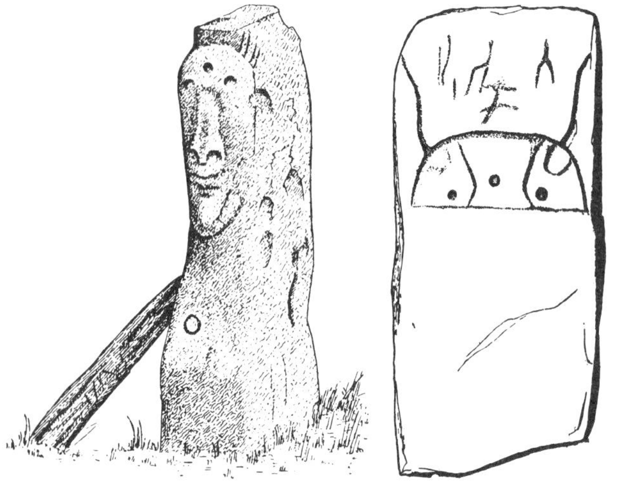

Funerary stelae. From Appelgren-Kivalo, *Alt-altaische Kunstdenkmäler.* (Helsinki 1931). Paris Bibliothèque nationale. Photo Flammarion.

this date that "In the past the custom (among the Turks) was to burn the dead. Now tombs are built for them." However, here, as elsewhere, it may have been the ashes that were interred. As for exposing the dead, this did not exclude placing the skeleton in the earth or burning it, since this was done (as was scraping the bones) in order to get rid of the flesh.

Some rites may have been common to the funerals of all the Altaic peoples: the exposing of the corpse in a mortuary tent, visits of "contemplation" paid to it, laying out the body, and wrapping it in a shroud. Similarly, they all seem to have organized their funerary rites in three periods: the day of death, the day of the funeral, and the days of commemoration.

On the day of the death, the people lamented with wild, dreadful cries, gashing their faces and ears. They walked around the funeral tent and made horses run. At this time, or later, they cut their hair, at least at an early period.

The time and place of the funeral rites were carefully chosen. The Tujue waited until the leaves fell from the trees or appeared on them; this is why, as among the Toba, Kirghiz, and others, the corpse was temporarily exposed when it was not immediately mummified. Among all of these peoples, the preference is always to bury the dead on the banks of rivers, on knolls, and in the forests. There are references to the immersion of the body or the rerouting of a watercourse so that it then passes over the sepulcher. Sometimes the place of burial was kept secret (Mongol emperors); sometimes it was indicated by a temple, an inscribed stela, *balbals,* or statues. When the sepulcher was kept secret, its builders were massacred as a precautionary measure. More often, the widows, slaves, and animals of the dead man were immolated so that they could accompany him. The custom of immolating widows was short-lived and was replaced by that of widow remarriage to the son-in-law, who was charged by her father with maintaining her. Objects were buried, burned, or placed on the tomb. When there was a temple, scenes from the life of the dead man were depicted upon it; his elegy (*agit*), sculpted upon a stela, contained a summary of his exploits or of abstract signs which included the *tamga,* or clan markings, and drawings of animals or objects.

Statues of the dead man or woman were supposed to be expressive. Quite different were the *balbals,* stones or pieces of wood stuck into the ground, representing the enemies killed by the dead man during his life or executed at his death, sometimes in great numbers. The custom of making *balbals* appears not to have survived long after the year 1000.

A great crowd, coming from a great distance, took part in the funeral. Specialized groups, such as the *sagditch,* the close friends, or the *sigiltchi,* the public mourners, played an important particular role. Around the freshly dug grave, the people would again take up their lamentations, lacerate their faces, mutilate themselves, and make the horses run. The *agit,* or elegy—which is still in use in Turkey and of which we have preserved some ancient references in short Old Turkic inscriptions—were sung or chanted. These *agit* were sometimes composed in the first person, as if the dead person himself were speaking. He proclaimed his manly virtue, his wealth, and his honor. An interesting allusion made to the accompanying ritual says that these virtues had to be proclaimed while standing up and while fasting. The sacrifice was accompanied by a communal meal, which may have been followed by orgies. The *yog* (funeral meal), which represented the most important moment in the ceremony, came to designate the obsequies themselves in the Turkish language.

The commemorations, of which we still find more than traces in Turkey—various rites can be found there that are performed in Central Asia—generally took place on the third, seventh, and fortieth days, and at the end of one year. On these days, people began to do again what had been done on the day of the funeral. Some documents say that they opened the bier to look once again at the dead man, which implies that the tomb was not completed until sometime later. Others speak of an evocation of the dead person (*ang,* in Turkish), who is supposed "to come down among his own."

If the commemorations were repeated beyond the end of the first year, they gradually became an ancestor cult.

J.-P.R./d.w.

BIBLIOGRAPHY

Funerary customs have been studied by CASTAGNÉ, *Les monuments funéraires de la steppe des Kirghizes* (Orenburg 1911). JAWORSKI, "Quelques remarques sur les coutumes funéraires turques," *RO* 4:225–61. KATANOV, "Über die Bestattungsgebräuche bei den Türkstämme," *Keleti Szemle* (Budapest 1900). KOTWICZ, "Les tombeaux dits Kereksür en Mongolie centrale," *RO* 4:60–170. NACHTINGALL, "Die erhohte Bestattung in Nord- und Hochasien," *Ant.* 48 (1953): 44–70. PASSEK and LATYNINE, "Sur la question des kammenye baby," *Eurasia septentrionalis antiqua* 4 (1929): 290–311. PAULSON, "Seelvorstellungen und Totenglaube bei nordeurasischen Völkern," *Etnos* 35, 1–2. J. P. ROUX, *La mort chez les peuples altaïques anciens et médiévaux* (Paris 1963). TOMKA, "Les termes de l'enterrement chez les peuples mongols," *AOAH,* 1965.

HEROES OF THE TURKS AND MONGOLS

Oghuz Khan. Manuscript from 1317. Istanbul, Topkapi Museum. Museum photo.

The range through which the numerous Turkish and Mongolian heroes are known can be either universal or local. All peoples of all tribes create legendary characters for themselves, historical or not, ancient shamans, conquerors, initiators, and ancestors to whom are attributed special powers and who are imagined to have performed marvelous feats. In extreme cases, they can become quasi deities.

There are far too many of these heroes to mention each by name. It seems that the oldest of all was A-se-na, the founder of the Tujue dynasty, known only through the Chinese transcription of a dubious word. Born of a she-wolf and a young Hiong-nu, he married the daughters of the gods of summer and winter, unknown elsewhere. The greatest of these heroes, however, must be Alp Er Tonga, "Courageous Tiger Man," still known in the eleventh century through fragments of poems collected by Kashgari. At that time, Alp Er Tonga was associated with Afrasiyab, the legendary hero of the Iranian world.

The Uighur Buqu Khan of the Tolesh tribe, born through the union of two trees, in a knothole, under the action of a ray of light, may have rivaled Alp Er Tonga in fame. The sovereign Qarakhanid, Satuk Bughra Khan, who was the first of the Turks of Central Asia to convert to Islam (960), on the recommendation of a hare, seems to have been known only among the Muslim Turks. The birth of this Camel-Prince, whose myth of origin was embellished with traditions about a lion, was accompanied by miracles, earthquakes, the appearance of springs, and the blooming of gardens. His daughter Ala Nur, Red Light, was impregnated by a ray of light, a manifestation of the lion, but identified by Muslims with Ali, the Lion of God.

Oghuz Khan, the eponymous ancestor of the Oghuz from whom the Seljukids and the Ottomans descended, probably owes his reputation to the importance of this last dynasty. Numerous *oghuz name* recounted his exploits, but few have survived until our time. We know that he married two female deities and had six children with them: Sun, Moon, Star, Sky, Mountain, and Sea. His name was understood to mean Colostrum, because he drank only the first milk of his mother, but it means Young Bull, which is what he is.

The two greatest Mongolian heroes are Genghis Khan, the founder of the thirteenth-century empire, and Geser Khan, of Tibetan origin. Both were deified. Genghis Khan was incarnated in the banner which is worshiped, and temples were erected to him. In the temple of the Eight White Tents in Ordos, he was until recently worshiped as a god of initiation. Geser Khan was the oppressor of demons and the god of shepherds and warriors.

It is probable that the episodes of the *Kitab-i Dede Qorqut* depict the various famous heroes of the Oghuz world surrounding the shaman who gives his name to this book. The memory of many of them survives today in certain regions of Turkey. Among them, one can cite Bayindir Khan, supreme ruler of the confederation, who is said by certain traditions to have been the contemporary of the Prophet. Before his conversion to Islam, he is said to have frightened Muhammad, who dug a hole into the wall and hid inside it, thus creating the first mihrab. Then there was Basat, who was fed by a lion and conquered the Cyclops, and Dumrul, whose wife wanted to give her soul to Azrail in exchange for his own and who fought with the angel of death. The Islamic saints, Old Testament characters as well as Koranic and Irano-Arabic, appropriated pre-Islamic myths, such as that of Ali, the fourth caliph of Islam who was very important in Turkey, and Abu Muslim, head of a popular Iranian movement during the Abassid era. Hizir and Ilyas, who drank the Water of Life, protected men on land and water, respectively. They are honored together during the feast of Hidrellez (Hizir-Ilyas). Hizir borrowed some of the attributes of certain nature cults connected with spring (his name means verdure) and in certain traits he resembles the Christian Saint George.

J.-P.R./d.b.

BIBLIOGRAPHY

See the articles by P. N. BORATAV in *Encyclopédie de l'Islam* (2d ed.), on Khidr-Ilyas, and *Islam Ansiklopedisi,* on Hizir. HEISSIG, *La religion* (Paris 1973).

The Turkish and Mongolian Ritual of the Blood Oath

It is among the ancient Turks that we can best understand the value that Altaic peoples attribute to blood. In fact, the uneasiness that menstrual blood and a few other images connected with blood evokes among the Siberian peoples today is secondary.

The oldest custom that we know connects blood with taking an oath. The Comans and Bulgars of the Volga swore on the blood of a dog whose throat had been cut and made alliances by drinking a few drops of their own blood from golden goblets. Similar performances existed among the Scythians, the Xiong Nu, and the Tujue, who drank blood from the gilded or skin-covered skulls of enemy chiefs. In Turkey, "to drink," *and itchmek,* remains the expression used to say "to swear." During the Mongol period, especially, we see clear evidence of a fraternal alliance between strangers who then were to treat one another as born of the same parents. These blood brothers (Turkish *kan kardesh,* Mongolian *anda,* derived from *ant,* "oath," in Turkish) exchanged blood, often by cutting their wrists. The exchange of important objects such as knucklebones and arrows could also have the same effect. This institution is very old indeed and has left behind more than mere memories in Turkey. It is already mentioned in the inscription of Begre and later by Kashgari, who states that perjury would be punished by the iron sword, "for iron is considered a sacred substance."

What must have justified these rituals and practices was the idea that blood contains the soul or one of the souls of every living being. The respect owed to princes meant that no blood could be shed when they were executed; instead, they were smothered, strangled, drowned, or trampled to death. Among the Ottomans, when members of the imperial family were executed they were strangled by a bow string around the throat. Because there was concern about the resurrection of animals, it was also forbidden to make them bleed when they were sacrificed, and even when they were hunted. When immolations took place, the sacrificer put his arm right on the victim's heart and squeezed it with his hand. Al-Umari's description of this operation during the Middle Ages corresponds almost word for word with those reported by travelers in the seventeenth and eighteenth centuries.

J.-P.R./g.h.

BIBLIOGRAPHY

On the interdiction against bloodshed, M. F. KÖPRÜLÜ, "La proibizione di versare il sangue," *Annali Istituto Univer. Orientale di Napoli,* 1940, 15–23, has given an incomplete preliminary sketch.

The Earth among the Turks and Mongols

The earth, called *yer* in the Genesis of the Orkhon, is there presented as one of the two cosmic zones, the one below formed at the same time as the sky. It may already have been a deity, as it would be later for the Khitan, Uighurs, and Mongols. The Chinese said that the Tujue had a god of the earth who appeared as a mountain, Podengringli (= But Tengri). In the inscriptions, this god gave orders jointly with the sky, but less frequently than the sky did. The same texts also use the word *yer* in the expression *iduq yer sub* ("sacred lands and waters") which defined certain numinous places animated by "master/possessors." The connections between *yer* in *iduq yer* and *yer* as a zone of the universe are not clear.

Among the Khitan, the earth was a complement of the sky; the earth, in the form of an old woman riding a gray ox, was worshiped at the same time as the sky. The earth goddess is found among the Mongols of the thirteenth century under the name of Etügen/Itügen, probably derived from Ötüken, the holy mountain of the Tujue. Marco Polo, who named her Natigay, saw her as a male deity, since he gave the deity a wife. Both husband and wife guarded the herds, grain, and earthly places. They were represented by images made of felt. At that time, the earth was regarded as male, as it was among the Buryat, who described the earth as an old man with gray hair to whom a sacrifice had to be made at the end of the harvest; but more generally the earth was regarded as female. Among the Yakuts, the earth promoted the growth of grass and the birth of babies. The Mongols prayed to her for fertility, fecundity, and the growth of the herd; they offered her milk, koumiss, and tea. A certain confusion may have arisen between the earth and other divinities, particularly between her and the goddess Umay, who also had the functions of a mother.

In Turkey, the earth is bivalent, simultaneously pure and clean, for it shakes itself to get rid of its impurities (an idea whose origin may perhaps be found in the Muslim principle of *teyemmüm,* according to which one could replace the water from ablutions with earth), and at the same time a symbol of offense, humiliation, servitude, putrefaction, and death. No memory of the ancient earth goddess would remain if there were no "earths of strength," small plots of land located on a holy site (often near a tomb) to which people come to dig up clay and eat it. This rite may, however, have another origin.

J.-P.R./g.h.

BIBLIOGRAPHY

A. E. DIEN, "A Possible Early Occurrence of Altaic Iduγan," *CAJ* 2, 1, pp. 12–20. E. LOT-FALCK, "A propos d'Etugen, déesse mongole de la terre," *RHR* 149 (1956): 157–96. P. A. MOSTAERT, "Le mot Natigay-Nacigay chez Marco Polo," in *Oriente Poliano* (Rome 1957), pp. 95–101. PELLIOT, "Le mont Ötükän chez les anciens Turcs," *TP* (1929) 212–19. RINTCHEN, "Explication du nom Burqan Qaldun," *AOAH* 1 (1950): 189–90.

The mother goddess Umay has been singled out for study by L. BAZIN, "La déesse-mère chez les Turcs pré-islamiques," *Bull. Sté E. Renan* 2 (1953): 124–26 (continuation of *RHR*).

The Personification of Thunder among the Turks and Mongols

Storms with such spectacular manifestations as thunder and lightning deeply impressed the ancient Turks and Mongols. Kashgari said that storms were provoked by the sky god himself. A few facts show that violent and repeated thunder was considered a divine punishment which could be provoked by the violation of a taboo such as that against washing one's clothes in running water. This idea is also found in Turkey among the Tahtajis and before that in the jokes of Nasrettin Hodja. Among the Bulgars of the Volga, when lightning struck a house, no one ever approached it again; it was abandoned with all of its contents. Among Genghis Khan's Mongols, anything struck by thunder had to be purified by passing it between two fires. Later, according to Pallas, an animal struck by lightning could not be eaten.

Thunder must have been personified very early. When lightning struck, Uighurs would shoot arrows at the sky. Shooting at the sky was also practiced by the Ruanruan, Oghuz, Mongols, and Yakuts, but they did not always shoot at thunder. In Turkey, this practice made its way into the Islamized cycle of Nemrud, who wanted to kill God. More often, the target was the tree of life.

One could also pray to thunder. The Mongols would sprinkle milk and koumiss on the ground and ask the thunder to spare their cattle. Later, they sacrificed on the spot where lightning had struck, or they offered a white horse to the thunder god. In Siberia today, thunder is often given the form of a bird; the people make an image of it from wood and place it on a perch. Among the Teleuts, it is said that Ilyas is the maker of thunder. Others see it in the form of a dragon. Among the Buryat, one of the most powerful makers of thunder is Esen Sagan, who fights demons with his fiery arrows and is often thought to ward off evil spirits. Turkish traditions held that thunder materialized into stone or metal. From this metal, Köroglu was thought to have forged a saber with supernatural qualities.

J.-P.R./g.h.

BIBLIOGRAPHY

See HARVA, *Rel. Vorstellungen*. P. N. BORATAV, *Köroğlu destaru* (Istanbul 1931); *Türk folkloru* (Istanbul 1973). J. P. ROUX, *Les traditions* (Paris 1970).

Gods and Myths of the Abkhaz, the Cherkess, and the Ubykh of the Northern Caucasus

The Abkhaz and the Cherkess live to the north of the Caucasus mountains. At the beginning of the nineteenth century, before the Russian conquest, their territory extended all along the coast of the Black Sea to the Sea of Azov. The Ubykh must be included as well, being geographically, culturally, and linguistically midway between the other two groups, though they are no longer found in the Caucasus and only a few representatives remain in Turkey.

These three peoples were converted to Islam in the eighteenth century (the end result of a process which began in the fifteenth century). Their own religion disappeared relatively quickly, surviving only in certain fragmentary beliefs, which are insufficient to allow us to reconstruct the original system.

It appears that they must have worshiped, as did other Caucasians (Georgians and Ossets), a supreme god, of whom little more than a name remains. However, there is one name that does allow us to guess at some very interesting theological concepts, though these unfortunately can barely be glimpsed.

The supreme God of the Abkhaz was Anc°a. The name can be broken down as follows: *a-*, definite article; *-n-*, particle, "there," and *-c°a*, plural suffix. Literally, it means "the theres," or the group of divine parts believed to be present everywhere in the universe but united in a single Whole. This multiplicity of the One would correspond well with what we know of the Georgian supreme god, Morige. This is the purely verbal trace of a theology which may be as complex as others more famous.

Among the Ubykh and the Cherkess, the functions of the supreme God are separated and assigned to two entities, of which we know only that one was apparently benevolent toward man, while the other inspired fear. This was not a dualism of the Zoroastrian type but rather a sharing of roles reminiscent of the Indo-European dyad of sovereign gods.

For the Ubykh, the difference is not only onomastic, but seems also to have been vaguely perceived. They distinguish between a God who is invoked for blessings and a God who is invoked only in curses. The first God, who was benevolent, was Wa in the formulaic language, Waba elsewhere. This word is probably derived from a root seen in the Cherkess word *We*, "sky." The original name of God would therefore be simply "Sky," as it was among the Turks before the advent of Islam. The terrible God was Wašx°a, doubtless related to the storm, as the etymology indicates: *wa*, "sky," and *šx°a*, "gunpowder," yielding the "thundering sky."

The same division is found among the Cherkess, who once distinguished between The, today the only name given to the supreme God, and Wašhe, invoked exclusively for curses. His name certainly contains the word "sky," *we* or *wa*, and "big" or "high," *še*.

I. Storm Gods

The Cherkess name for storm god is the same as their word for lightning: Shyble, a pictorial term which literally means "horse-serpent." Among the Abkhaz too, the name of the god becomes confused with the name of the natural phenomenon over which he presides: Afy. As is proved by several formulaic expressions, Afy, like the supreme God Anc°a, is seen as being simultaneously one and many.

The cult dedicated to the storm god is identical, except for a few details, among the two peoples. As in Georgia and Ossetia, death by lightning was interpreted as a sign of divine favor and a good omen, whether it happened to a human being or to an animal. Both underwent the same ritual treatment. Outside the village, generally in the forest or at the end of a woods, a kind of very high scaffolding was erected, consisting for the most part of an armature of four large alder branches (or stripped young trees) stuck in the ground and attached to crosspieces of the same wood. At the top of the structure, alder branches with their leaves were arranged to form a kind of litter. The body, human or animal, was placed here and covered with leaves. Several victims, preferably white goats, had their throats cut near the scaffolding, and as soon as their heads were cut off they were fastened on top of the posts that were set in the ground. Songs, dances, and feasts went on for several days. When the ritual was completed, the area remained untouched for several days, at least three (seven in certain areas). Only at the end of this period was the corpse of the person struck by lightning, if a human, taken down and buried.

This custom, still observed at the beginning of the twentieth century, resembles the funeral practices of the inhabitants of Colchis, as described by several authors of antiquity. The northern part of Colchis coincides with the present-day territory of the Abkhaz. According to Apollonius of Rhodes, in the third century B.C., the Colchians considered it blasphemous to cremate or bury male corpses. Instead, they wrapped them in untanned cowhide and tied them high in a tree with ropes. Nicholas de Damas (first century B.C.) gives the same information: "Colchians do not bury their dead, but hang them in trees"; so does Claudius Ellien three centuries later: "Colchians sew their dead in skins and hang them in trees."

In the seventeenth century, Archangelo Lamberti noted that the Abkhaz "cut a tree trunk in the shape of a coffin, where they place the body, tying it to a treetop with vines." Other travelers observed the same practice in the eighteenth century.

According to every indication, the temporary exposure of the dead on a scaffolding of alder bushes represents the attenuation and limitation of archaic funeral rites which must originally have applied to all corpses, or at least to all dead males.

II. Blacksmith Gods

The Cherkess and the Abkhaz (unlike the Georgians) never had a sacerdotal caste. The function of a priest was performed either by the oldest member of a clan, lineage, or extended family, or, more often, by the blacksmith. Among these peoples, the god of the forge therefore had a high position and his services extended into many areas beyond those of his technical expertise.

Shashw was both one and many, as was common in Abkhaz theology. He was invoked as a single god, but various formulas of cursing treated him linguistically as plural (for example, *š'as° 'ry-lax,* "the curse of the Shashws").

The Cherkess god, Tlepsh (λ'epš'), was himself a "well-tempered" blacksmith, able to fuse metal together with his bare hands. His forehead was decorated with seven horns. At his forge he made objects, especially weapons, which had magical properties and value, but only when his work was performed with no witnesses. He plays an important role in the Nart epic (particularly among the Ossets, who call him Kurdalägon), fashioning fabulous weapons for heroes and literally tempering the metallic demigod, Batraz.

Among the two peoples, the forge is a sanctuary and the site of various cults. The Abkhaz made their most serious vows there. The Cherkess used the space to perform rituals to change the weather, usually to make rain. The blacksmith god is linked to storms through his obvious affinities with fire, and is a parallel to Shyble, the lightning spirit. He also has power over the fertility of women and the birth and raising of children, especially sons. For example, in case of a difficult birth, the woman in labor would drink water that had been used to temper a sword. The newborn infant received a kind of baptism at the forge: he was "tempered" by being immersed in water normally used by the smith to cool objects that had been heated white-hot. Among the Abkhaz, the newborn infant was left on the hearth of the forge, on the same bed of coals (fortunately cooled) where weapons and tools were usually fashioned (see the apparently strange treatment to which the Osset blacksmith god subjects young Batraz, according to Osset legend).

Long and complex rituals were performed in honor of this god. For this purpose, the Abkhaz used, not the ordinary forge, but a miniature workshop, situated in a tiny building and including all the blacksmith's tools, reproduced in miniature. The day before the main ritual, which lasted three days, the smith, accompanied by his entire family, led a kid to the toy forge and sacrificed it at sunset, "when the god is in his house." In addition, a rooster was sacrificed by a man, and a hen by a woman. During the days which followed, many shells were fired, for the smith god intercedes in the techniques of hunting and makes them successful (the divinities of the hunt preside over the game, rather than over the actual activity of hunting with dogs; see the discussion of Caucasian gods of the hunt, in section V, below).

It is noteworthy that the cult of the forge was divided into two parts: the real workshop constitutes a sanctuary for all rites not directly involved with the professional activity of the smith, while that activity gives rise to a cult which takes place in a miniature forge, set apart from the true forge.

III. Ahyn and the Cow Who Offers Herself for Sacrifice

Ahyn (*axyn,* or *axym* in some dialects) is the Cherkess patron god of animal breeding. As such, he has an important place in the pantheon of these peoples, for whom livestock played a primary economic role, to the point where several sources consider him the supreme god of the Cherkess. He is the only northern Caucasian deity to be named in the following mythological fragment:

A long time ago, at the edge of the Black Sea near Touapse, there lived a man whose daughter was of unequaled beauty. The father decided to give his daughter in marriage to the man who could jump from one mountain to the other, crossing the valley in a single bound. The only man to succeed at this test was a giant named Ahyn, thanks to his normal means of locomotion: a pole one hundred "sajēnes" long (226 meters), which he set in the valleys to propel himself from one mountain to the next. The father was horrified at the idea of such a peculiar son-in-law, but the giant pleased the young girl, and she married him.

Later, Ahyn announced his intention to visit his father-in-law. Terrified at this prospect, the father fled with all his belongings and began to stalk the giant, intending to kill him by sawing through his enormous pole while he was asleep. In the meantime, Ahyn, unsuspecting, continued along his way, accompanied by all his herds, so numerous that they entirely covered all the surrounding mountains. It was the giant's habit to sleep one week out of two; taking advantage of this long sleep, his father-in-law had no trouble sawing through Ahyn's pole in several places. When the giant awoke and tried to jump from one summit to the next, the pole broke and Ahyn sank forever beneath the waves of the river. His immense herds disappeared at once.

A sacred tree, dwelling place of a god. The horns evoke the cow that offers herself as a sacrifice.

Since that time, and, it is said, even today, to commemorate the event and to allow the Cherkess to atone for their mistake by means of a sacrifice, each year on the same date a cow appears, the cow of Ahyn. She emerges from the forest and moves toward a sacred grove. She knows where to stop and nothing and no one can interrupt her progress. Everyone follows the cow respectfully until she reaches the place where she stops of her own accord and offers herself spontaneously to her sacrificer's knife. Her throat is cut in the place she has chosen, and she is then taken to a second area to be skinned, a third to be cut up, a fourth to be cooked, and a fifth for her flesh to be eaten.

The last part of the myth, concerning "the cow who comes forth by herself" (according to the Cherkess expression), has merged with a ritual which was still practiced at the beginning of the twentieth century. The same belief, along with the cult and the practices attached to it, is widespread among the Abkhaz and the Mingrelians (inhabitants of ancient Colchis).

The legend of the god Ahyn and his death caused by the destruction of his pole includes several variations, not only among the Cherkess but also among their neighbors the Ubykh. G. Dumézil succeeded in documenting one of these variations among the Turkish Ubykh as late as 1930.

Ahyn's pole entered into other Caucasian myths, particularly the Abkhaz legends of Abrskil and the Georgian legends of Amirani; it allows us to explain certain important symbols that would be undecipherable without recourse to their Cherkess source.

IV. Shewzerysh

Shewzerysh (or Sewserysh) is especially important because of the possible links between his cult and the great hero of the Nart epic, Sosryko (Sawsyryq°e among the Cherkess and Soslan among the Ossets).

He seems to have been the protector of the grain at all stages of its production and storage. His cult was celebrated in the spring according to some sources, after the harvest or in winter according to others, and always in the presence of and by means of the knotty trunk of the young plane tree or pear tree, or a column shaped from one of these. The evening before "the night of Shewzerysh," the trunk or log of the plane tree is placed outside, in front of the door. It becomes confused with the deity himself, as it is also addressed by the name "Shewzerysh." The crucial moment of the ritual is the "entrance of the tree" into the house. This practice is reminiscent of the *arbor intrat* of Asiatic religions and the role of the pine tree in the cult of Atys (cf. Frazer, *Attis and Osiris*). This connection suggests the presence of an eschatological element which may be confirmed by the mythology of this god (if indeed this mythology belongs to him; cf. Soslan among the Ossets). The Cherkess say that he was once a man who was endowed with marvelous powers, in particular the ability to walk on water. God punished him for his excessive pride by taking away his legs.

The legend of the Nart hero, Soslan, still has definite traces of a "mythology of Shewzerysh" which has been forgotten today.

V. Gods of the Hunt

In the Caucasus, hunting was once an autonomous economic activity, and it still is today in several mountainous regions. This explains its firm grip on pagan religion and mythology.

All of the Caucasian peoples still know the "masters of game," often female, who simultaneously protect the activity of the hunters and the ecological conservation of the wild animals who are their legitimate property. Like our modern-day forestry administration, the gods of the hunt simultaneously encourage and limit the killing of wild game.

In Ossetia, the "god of the hunt" and "master of wild beasts" is the masculine spirit Aefsati (the same name is attributed to one of the Svana hunting gods, Apsat). Game is called "Aefsati's cattle" (*aefsatijy fos*). He is invoked before the hunt and is thanked after a successful hunt, before the flesh of the slain animal is consumed.

The patron of the Cherkess hunt (a goddess among the Kabards, western Cherkess) is the "forest god," Mezythe (or Mezeth in Kabard), from *mez,* "forest," and *the,* "god." His body is covered with silver, like a kind of organic armor. He has silver horns, his mustache is made of golden flames, and he is the size of an elephant. Dressed in chamois skins, he is armed with a bow of hazelwood, with dogwood arrows. Mezythe rides a gigantic boar with golden bristles, escorted by forest stags and does who are pastured and milked by the girls in his service (his own daughters, according to Abkhaz beliefs). He is fed exclusively on the blood of the animals which hunters offer him in their sacrifices.

It is important to emphasize that for all Caucasian peoples, a hunt is the equivalent of a sacrifice, each animal killed becoming a victim offered up to the master of game.

Cherkess hunters use a secret language among themselves, the "language of the forest," whose "secret" consists of adding meaningless suffixes after each open syllable.

The Abkhaz have two deities of the hunt who are related to one another by marriage: Ajrg and Azhwajpshaa. The first has daughters who are eternally young and who are dedicated to the care of the does of the forest. These daughters marry no one but the sons of Azhwajpshaa.

G.C./d.b.

BIBLIOGRAPHY

A.A., *Religioznye verovanija abxazcev*, Sbornik svedenii o kavkazskix gorcax, 5 (Tbilisi 1971). G. ÇURSIN, *Materialy po êtnografii Abxazii* (Sukhumi 1956). N. DUBROVIN, *Çerkesy (adyge)* (Krasnodar 1927). G. DUMÉZIL, *La langue des Oubykhs* (Paris 1931); *Loki* (Paris 1947); *Mythe et épopée*, 1, part 3 (Paris 1968); *Romans de Scythie et d'alentour* (Paris 1978). N. DŽANASIA, "Iz religioznyx verovanii abxazov," *Xristianskij Vostok* 4 (Saint Petersburg 1915). D. I. GULIA, *Božestva oxoty u abxazov* (Sukhumi 1926); *Kul't Kozla u abxazov* (Sukhumi 1928). S. INAL-IPA, *Abxazy* (Sukhumi 1965); *Kabardinskij fol'klor* (Moscow and Leningrad 1936). M. KOSVEN, *Etnografija i istorija Kavkaza* (Moscow 1961). L. I. LAVROV, "Doislamskie verovanija adygejcev i Kabardincev," in *Issledovanija i Materialy po voprosam pervobytnyx religioznyx verovanij* (Moscow 1959). L. L'JUL'E, *Cerkessija* (Krasnodar 1927). S. NOGMOV, *Istorija adygejskogo naroda* (Nal'čik 1947). S. X. SALAKAJA, *Abxazskij narodnyj geroičeskij êpos* (Tbilisi 1966). E. M. ŞILLING, "Religioznye verovanija narodov SSSR," *Çerkesy*, 2 (Moscow and Leningrad 1931). STAL', *Etnografičeskij očerk čerkesskogo naroda*, Kavkazskij sbornik, 21 (Tbilisi 1900).

SOULS AND THEIR AVATARS IN SIBERIA

Man has many souls. Their number varies in different populations and, within a single population, in different groups. According to the Western Tungus, as studied by G. M. Vasilevič, the Tungus have two souls: the *been*, the corporal soul which descends into the world of the dead after death, and the *omi*, the permanent vital principle which is reincarnated and thus assures the reproductive capacity of the clan. The *been* is the basis of individuality, while the *omi* is merely a clan soul. Vasilevič, contrary to other authors, does not count the *xanjan*, the shadow and the reflection in water or a mirror, as a soul.

After death, while the *been* retires along the river which descends to the lower world, the *omi* flies into the higher world and perches on the mythical tree with the other *omi* of the clan. In a few years, it redescends to the earth and drops into a tent through a smoke hole. After falling into the fire, it penetrates the womb of a woman, who becomes pregnant.

According to variants collected by other authors, the western Tungus have three souls: the *been*, the corporeal soul; the *omi*, the surviving soul; and the *maïn*, the soul-destiny of more recent creation. Certain informants conceive of the *maïn* as a thread that stretches from the head of an individual to the hand of Seveki, the master spirit of the higher world. When an evil spirit cuts the thread, the man dies. According to others, the *maïn* remains a soul exterior to the body of its owner and, under a human guise, leads the life of a hunter in the swamps of the higher world, full of game, and the adventures which it experiences are reflected in the life of the earthly hunter. In this case, as in the other, the soul does not seem to play any role after death. When a man dies, his *been* descends into the village of the dead ruled by Mangi, the chief of the ancestors. He receives the *been*, but he also desires the soul which, in the version recorded by Anisimov, carries the name of *xanjan* during the life of the individual on earth but becomes *omi* after the individual's death. Mangi thus goes to search for the *xanjan*. He catches up with it at the sources of the mythical river and forces it to turn around. But the *xanjan* suddenly transforms into a bird. He takes the name of *omi* again and flies toward the tree of the higher world from which he will redescend to be reincarnated upon the earth in his time.

It seems curious that an irregularity serves to establish the rule. Nevertheless, we can compare this *xanjan*, which carries the *omi* in essence, to the great soul of the Gilyak, which includes the small mobile soul charged with survival. However, the Gold, a Tungus group of the Amur basin, have elaborated a similar system. The *omi* becomes incarnate in a newborn child, and when the infant reaches the age of one year, it takes the name of *ergeni* (the swallow according to Lopatin, but more probably a derivation from *erga*, "breath"). When the individual dies, the *ergeni* becomes *fanja* (a phonetic variation of *xanjan*). The *fanja* descends to the world of the dead with a shaman as guide. Later, the *fanja* becomes *omi* again (it is not specified by what process this occurs) and is reincarnated. If the infant dies before it is one year old, its *omi* reascends immediately to the tree of the young birds.

The Oroč, neighbors and relatives of the Gold, have in addition a unique soul which traverses the lower world before ascending back to the higher world, from which it will descend to be reincarnated. After death, this soul (whose name is unknown) goes to the world of the dead, where it waits patiently for four generations. Then it sets out once again for the higher world. It arrives there after being transformed successively into an old man made of iron, an iron arrow, and a metallic duck, then into glass, and then into a butterfly in order to fly to the moon, which here represents the higher world. It lives several years on the moon in the territory of the old mistress of the bear or that of the tiger (this division of the moon into two halves, each having a different master spirit, is probably a survival of a dual organization among the Oroč). Fed on charcoal, the soul is transformed into a mushroom and then thrown to the earth, where it is reincarnated in a newborn child. Then the cycle begins again.

The Tungus of Manchuria have a system which is related to the Gold system. When it is still in its mother's womb, the infant is given an *omi* soul. When it is born, it receives the *erga*, "breath," which is taken here to mean not soul but rather life. During the first year the *omi* of the baby is always ready to take flight toward the higher world; that is, nursing babies are always on the edge of death in these populations. To protect the soul of the infant, it is placed in a small anthropomorphic wooden cradle called *anjan*. When the infant has grown and become conscious, one says that its *omi* is stabilized and it now possesses the *susi* soul. The *susi* is composed of three elements "unified like the nail, the skin, and the bone of a finger," say the Tungus of Manchuria.

The first element, the *fanjanga* (root *fanja/anjan*), linked to consciousness, causes death by its departure, but its ultimate fate is unknown. The second element descends into the world of the dead (according to certain informants, it some-

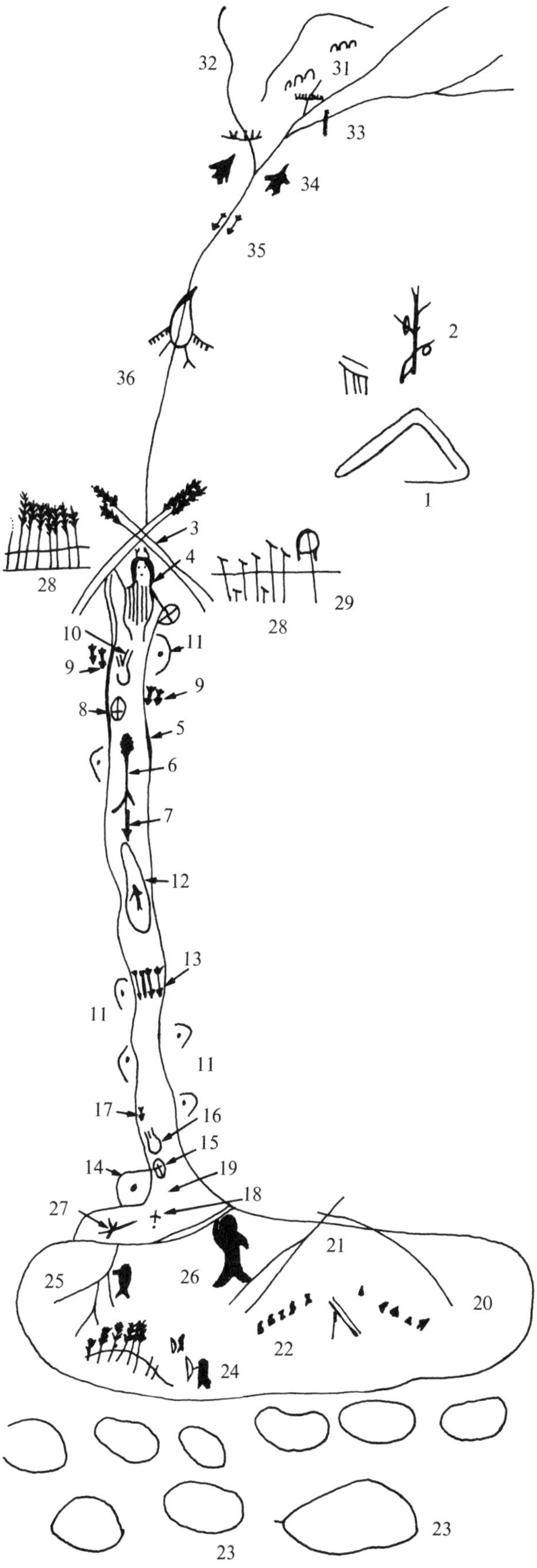

times returns to be reincarnated on earth in a human or animal form). The last element is regarded as the soul of the afterlife; it returns after death to the higher world and waits there to redescend into a new embryo. This soul is the *omi*.

In fact, what is essential among the Tungus is not the variable number of what may be called "souls" for lack of a better term, but the voyages of the soul, which continues to be reincarnated from the higher world to the earth in the middle, and passes through the lower world.

The shaman's route along the great mythic river, leading the soul of the deceased to the netherworld.

1. The abandoned tent of the deceased.
2. The platform on which the corpse of the deceased lies. The personal effects of the deceased are hung from the branches of a nearby tree so that they can accompany the deceased into the afterlife.
3. The tent of the shaman, with the items needed for the ritual.
4. Intil'gun, the old shaman of the Kordujal' clan leads the *been*, the physical soul of the deceased, into the netherworld.
5. The mythic river.
6. The spirit of the larch sweeps the path before the shaman.
7. The spirit of the loon guides the shaman.
8. The shaman's drum serves as a boat to carry him down the river.
9. The spirits that protect the shaman.
10. The physical soul of the deceased on its platform (which has now become a raft) follows the shaman.
11. The encampments of the old mistresses of the route to the netherworld. The shaman stops at each encampment to ask which path to follow.
12. The island of the old mistress of the river, where the shaman rests; he too consults her about the remainder of the route he must follow.
13. Narrow passage of the river, where the shaman has set up a barrier of protective spirits.
14. The encampment of one of the old mistresses of the route—the final stopping place on the shaman's journey. From here, he calls the inhabitants of the village of the dead, on the other side of the river, to come for the soul, but the shaman himself does not cross the estuary.
15. The shaman's drum, serving as a boat.
16. The soul of the deceased.
17. The reindeer offered as a sacrifice.
18. The loon that guides the shaman.
19. The estuary beyond which is the netherworld proper.
20. The island where the dead of the clan live.
21. The village of the dead of the clan.
22. The dead women sitting around a fire, doing various domestic tasks.
23. The nine mountains where the shaman ancestors live. Mangi, the chief of the ancestors, lives on the highest mountain.
24. The dead of the clan hunting.
25. The dead making a dam for fishing.
26. The old mistress of the village makes a sign for the dead to fetch the soul from the other side of the estuary.
27. One of the dead leaves by boat to fetch the soul.
28. The shamanistic spirits that block access to the netherworld.
29. The reindeer pelt offered as a sacrifice.
30. The *omiruk*, the reserve for the *omi* souls, the souls in the afterlife in the world above.
31. The *omi* souls.
32. The tributaries of the mythic river in the world above.
33. The barrier of protective spirits installed by the shaman in the world above to protect the *omiruk*.
34. The bird spirits that protect access to the *omiruk* by air.
35. Barrier formed by the salmon protective spirits.
36. The *omi* soul of the deceased being transformed into a bird in order to escape from Mangi, flying off to the *omiruk*, where it will wait for several generations before descending again to be reincarnated on earth.

Representation of a Tungus or Altaic shamanic ancestor, found in the Stanovoi mountains by the explorer Joseph Martin at the end of the nineteenth century. Wood, with a leather cape and yellow glass beads for eyes. Paris, Musée de l'Homme collection. Museum photo.

I. The Souls of the Dead That Have Reached the World of the Dead

The soul of the dead leaves the world of the living with regret. The route that awaits him is dangerous: a river with turbulent rapids for the Western Tungus, a dusty, rock-strewn road for the Eastern Tungus. On each of these routes, baneful spirits lie in wait to kill as the souls of the dead pass. The shaman is charged with guiding the souls through these dangers to the village of the dead. For certain groups, he is content to guide the soul from afar through directions transmitted by his bird messengers. This definitive separation of the dead from the living is one of the fundamental tasks of the shaman.

When the soul of the dead arrives in the world of the dead, he leads there a life similar to the one he knew on earth, with the difference that this new universe is cold and dark, barely illuminated by one-half of a frozen sun.

The dead keep their names and their individuality until the fourth generation. Always a little jealous of the living, they tend to be harmful to them. A Tungus of Manchuria had had eczema, his legs had swelled, and then his two horses died; he wondered who among the dead had sent him all these ills: his father, his mother, or his younger brother who had recently died? The shaman can restabilize the situation by offering a sacrifice to the angry dead in question. The dead then stop their malevolent activities and even help the shaman with advice and predictions about the future of the clan. Besides, the dead have a less evil character than the shaman's other auxiliary spirits. Thus a shaman of eastern Siberia agreed to chant on a phonographic record (in the 1920s) an invocation to the ancestral spirits, which he ended with these words: "Do not come. I am chanting only for the machine." But he refused categorically to disturb the auxiliary spirits called *séven* in the same offhanded way.

When four generations have passed, the soul of the deceased joins the swelling crowd of anonymous ancestors that have become incapable of good or evil. According to another variant, it falls into a world situated further down, the *ellamrak* for the Western Tungus, the *ela gurum* for the Eastern Tungus, and there disintegrates definitively. The Oroč explain the tragic depopulation of their group by this definitive destruction.

Nevertheless, not all the dead are reduced to impotence with time. Some very distant ancestors form the active and benevolent category of the protector spirits of the family. These spirits, of great help in daily life in warding off illnesses and aiding in the hunt, are of an ancestral origin. Indeed, the term for them among the Western Tungus—*muxdy*—comes from *mugdy,* "ancestor." *Mugdy* is itself formed from *mudge,* "trunk," for the Tungus used to place their dead in the hollowed-out trunks of trees.

Each family has at least one protector spirit, who resides in an anthropomorphic statue of wood, horn, metal, or rags. The statuette of the *Muxdy* of the Western Tungus is a stylized representation of a man. The *Džuli* of the Gold, although male, is provided with breasts prominent enough for certain Soviets to conclude that the *Džuli* was formerly female, at a supposedly matriarchal period. But in Siberia the protector spirits of the family are not necessarily masculine. Among the Ket, for example, the *Alel* are imagined in the form of old women.

The figurines are handed down in the male line in all the populations. Among the Tungus it is apparently the men who feed them. On the eve of every new moon and when he returns from a successful hunt, the senior male of a Tungus family coats the *Muxdy* with grease, blood, or marrow. The Gold master of the house, just as he leaves his family for many months of hunting in the forest, bows to the earth in front of the statue of the *Džuli* guardian spirit and asks it to watch over his return and his possessions. If, upon his return, he finds everything in good order, bowing down once again, he offers to the *Džuli* broth, alcohol, and Chinese wine.

Among the Ket, in contrast to the Tungus, the women are charged with the care of the *Alel.* Each year, at the end of summer, just before the great hunting season, the Ket women dress the statuette in a new garment of fur or cloth so that the *Alel* will continue to work at night, maintaining the fire, caressing the children and braiding their hair, sharpening the fishhooks, playing with the dogs or making them bark at the approach of danger.

The guardian spirits, like the other Siberian spirits that were kept inside a pillar, were treated according to their merits. They were honored and fed as long as their services were hoped for. At every change of camp, at the opening of the hunting and fishing season, upon the birth of a child, they were taken out of the ritual sack or sacred sleigh and were set out to be rubbed with food. On a journey, the white reindeer consecrated to the celestial spirit would transport them. But whenever these spirits did not keep their promises, and when ill fortune struck the household, they would be left without food and sometimes abused. If a Gold suffered a violent kidney pain, the *Džuli* would be taken outside and buried to the waist, and would remain in that position until the illness was healed.

II. The Souls of the Dead That Have Not Arrived at the World of the Dead

The souls of the dead that have not arrived at the world of the dead are the miserable and starving souls that wander the earth. For one reason or another, they cannot be guided to the lower world, because they have been deprived of ritual funerals.

Numerous in forests and swamps, they flutter about in the form of will-o'-the-wisps or lurk in tree trunks. When a tree is cut down, they cry: "*Onoï!* What pain!" and drive the logger mad. They whistle with the wind in the branches, creak with the ice on frozen rivers, and respond with the echo. Easily startled, they pose no danger to the brave: the crackling of a fire or the barking of a dog puts them to flight.

Much more formidable are the souls of those who have died a violent death. Those who have died from suicide, drowning, freezing, being crushed under a tree, or falling into an abyss seek to lure the hunter to a death identical to theirs. The Gold envision suicides—who are the most jealous of the happiness of the living and therefore the most dangerous—as black birds with iron feathers and metallic beaks.

These spirits generally become the master spirits of the localities in which they died. If the shaman succeeds in mastering them, they enter into the category of the *séven,* spirits who, in exchange for offerings and compliments, agree to aid the shaman. As for souls who have been led to the lower world, but who have managed to escape and to slip back again onto the earth, they lurk in hiding for the souls of the living. Their very name describes them: among the Western Tungus they are called *nevi,* "those who seek a glance."

L.D./m.s.

The Sky, the Great Celestial Divinity of Siberia

The sky, the great celestial divinity of Siberia, is the supreme divinity of all the ethnic groups of Siberia. From the summit of the sky, he superintends the proper course of the universe. For many of the groups his name originally meant "sky": Buga (Tungus), Es (Ket), Nga (Enc), Turum/Torym (Ostyak), Num (Selkup). This figure sometimes undergoes a change of status in different groups. A great celestial god for some (Ket, Enc, Eastern Tungus), he becomes a spirit-lord for others (Western Tungus), and even a collectivity of spirits (Buryat, Yakut). Nevertheless, he appears most frequently as an incarnation of the sky who superintends the mechanism of the universe without interfering in human affairs, and, ordinarily, neither prayers nor sacrifices are addressed to him.

In spite of his essentially indifferent and inaccessible character, certain groups have more or less anthropomorphized him. The Tungus offer two extreme examples. For the Eastern Tungus, Buga remains so remote that they have no idea of his appearance and even their shamans maintain no connection with him. By contrast, the Western Tungus of the Yenisey have conceived an anthropomorphic spirit who interferes in the life of men, who intervenes in their hunts, in the birth of infants, and in the reproduction of the herds of domesticated reindeer.

Under the various names of Seveki, Xovoki, Ekśeri, or Maïn, the celestial spirit of the Western Tungus governs the upper world. Further, he holds in his closed fist the ends of *maïn* threads, the soul-destiny according to some, the soul-breath according to others. Each of these threads is connected to the head of an individual, and if a malevolent spirit cuts the thread, the person dies unless a shaman succeeds in tying a knot. The celestial spirit also holds the *maïn* of plants and trees that he causes to grow by pulling from above. According to certain variants, he also casts onto the earth the souls, *omi,* of men and the souls of domesticated reindeer in the form of blades of grass and hairs, when the time has come for them to become incarnate in a baby or a fawn. Moreover, since the spirit-lords who bestow game are subordinate to him, he can thwart or favor the hunt. That is why the Western Tungus hook white ribbons to trees as an offering to the celestial spirit to obtain abundant game.

It seems that among the Western Tungus this figure exercises two functions: the function of organizer of the world and the function of dispenser of game. In this last role he evokes the Toman of the Ket, the beautiful female symbol of the south, who, each spring, climbs to the top of a cliff and shakes her white sleeves above the Yenisey. Down escapes from them and is transformed into geese, swans, and ducks, who fly north toward Ket.

The celestial spirit of the other ethnic groups is situated between these two extremes. Among the Ket, Es, under the aspect of a bearded old man, is content to inspect the universe on the longest day of summer. At that time the stars and the earth draw near to his home. He gives them his benediction with his orders for the year and wishes them a pleasant journey.

Nga, among the Enc, regulates the course of the seasons and determines the date when he will grant a favorable time for the hunt, for, it is said, if he allowed perpetually fine weather to prevail, men would take all the fish and kill all the game. Nga seems, nevertheless, a little less removed from men than his Ket homologue, for he takes the trouble to send them dreams to inform them of their destiny. Nga is married to D'ja Menjuu, the mother of vegetation, who while moving through the sky spreads out the lower part of her mantle to form the rainbow.

Organizers who ensure the equilibrium of the world, these spirits are very rarely creators. The indigenous peoples of Siberia seem to be little concerned with the creation of the world. They regard it generally as given from the very beginning. In the most widespread myth of creation, an immensity of water covers everything. In the beginning, the Tungus recount, there was water everywhere. Ekśeri, the celestial divinity, flew above the waters with his duck. Ekśeri, tired, asked his bird to dive and fetch him some mud in its bill. The duck disgorged the mud onto the surface of the water, which formed the earth.

The Tungus add that this benevolent divinity had an evil elder brother who eventually became master of the lower world and spoiled his younger brother's creation. According to a myth of the Yeniseian people, this benevolent creator fashioned human souls out of earth and stones. He put them on a board to dry under the protection of a dog who, at that time, had no fur. The elder brother succeeded in persuading the dog to let him see the souls in exchange for fur. As soon as he caught sight of them, the evil one spit on the souls, and that is why men die. On his return, the younger brother punished the dog by condemning him to feed upon ordure. In northern variants of this myth, the unfaithful guardian is a crow who allows himself to be bribed with the promise of a liver to eat.

Other Siberian pantheons, for the most part, also include a benevolent demiurge associated by close bonds of kinship with the spirit responsible for disease and death. Among the Tungus, as we have seen, it is a pair of brothers; among the Ket, Es has the malevolent Xosadam for a wife, the incarnation of the north, mistress of cold, darkness, and disease. On her lifeless island, at the northern extremity of the world, where white mosses and twisted trees grow, in the midst of gusts of wind and the doleful cries of black birds with serpent heads, the Kyns, bearers of illness and robbers of souls, Xosadam devours human souls. It is she who sends the tempests, the epidemics, and all the calamities that befall men.

As for the Enc, they make Todomé, the evil divinity of the lower world, the son of Nga, the sky. Todomé chases human souls the way hunters pursue game. Sometimes his gluttony is such that he tries to devour even his mother, D'ja Menjuu. She then ascends and asks Nga to show their son the "people for eating."

L.D./b.f.

Siberian Master Spirits and Shamanism

I. Master Spirits

Master spirits are of primary importance for the economic life of hunters; they are the masters of certain species of animals, of territories in which game lives, and of natural phenomena such as fire, lightning, etc.

As a general rule, the spirits are addressed directly, without the mediation of the shaman. However, when a master spirit manifests a particular animosity and refuses to grant game for several days or weeks at a time, the shaman directs a rite to appease and propitiate the spirit. On the occasion of certain ceremonies proper to the Western Tungus, the shaman visits the master spirits of the clan territories in order to ask for the souls of the game which the clan may slay in the course of the hunting season. The intercession of the shaman nevertheless remains reserved for exceptional cases, which has led some to think that the master spirits existed before the establishment of shamanism.

1. *The master spirit of fire.* The great majority of Siberian peoples depict the master spirit of fire, a very ancient spirit, as an old woman who is sitting bent over in the flames of the hearth. Each family jealously guards this spirit, which is essentially a clan spirit, and who lives in the center of the tent. The Tungus never allow an outsider to carry away an ember or even to light a pipe from the household fire, for in the flames of the hearth dance the souls of children who are yet to be born, who have fallen from the sky through the smoke hole and who are waiting to enter into the body of one of the women of the house. One of the most important moments of marriage among the Gold consists in the presentation of the fiancée to the "Grandmother Fire" of her new home; she is asked to grant her "a good life and many children."

As the attentive protector of the family, Grandmother Fire takes care of the herd of domesticated reindeer and patronizes the hunt. Before each meal, the mistress of the house feeds her by throwing a few pieces of meat into the fire and saying "Eat, satisfy your hunger. Give game, so that all may be satisfied." She is fed more abundantly at the beginning of the hunting and fishing seasons and when there is a big take: reindeer, elk, or bear.

To express her thanks, she counsels the hunter, shows him the path to follow, and forewarns him of his future success or failure by crackling and throwing sparks. If the fire sputters in a certain way, the hunters, certain that they will have no success, cancel their expedition. Fire helps the hunter in another, no less effective way, by purifying his traps, his weapons, and his clothes. The purification of objects with fire is regularly practiced in everyday life as well as in shamanic ritual. Fire's role as mediator with the supernatural is not limited to this: she transmits the offerings of men to other spirits, the most widespread method of sending grease or alcohol to the spirits consisting in pouring them into the fire.

Women are specially charged with caring for Grandmother Fire and making sure that she is never extinguished. At night, they leave a glowing birch log to burn. While traveling, they carry a brand from the last camp in a birch bark receptacle padded with wet moss, or else they slip a pinch of ashes into the lining of their sleeve. Before lighting the fire at a new camp, they shake the ash or the firebrand there as they ask Grandmother Fire to establish herself there. In times of war, they extinguished the fires of enemy clans and thus symbolically pledged their death.

In order to not offend Grandmother Fire, they carefully observe a series of taboos. One must never throw water or garbage into the hearth, as such things would glue her eyes together with soot. Neither should one stir up the fire too roughly or agitate a knife in the flames, for fear of wounding her. Most importantly, they are careful that tufts of hair from game do not fall into the flames. Yakut hunters are so cautious as to conceal the head of the fox under their hats in order to hide it from Grandmother Fire.

The master spirit of the fire abhors all that comes from the forest. The master spirits are in perpetual battle with them, but the antagonism is particularly virulent between the master spirit of the household fire and that of the forest. It is not that the forest dreads the fire that destroys it, as some people would explain it, but that fire, as a domestic symbol, is opposed to the forest as a symbol of the savage world and sometimes even of the world beyond. (Thus, in the forest, the realm of all kinds of spirits, the bear that the hunter

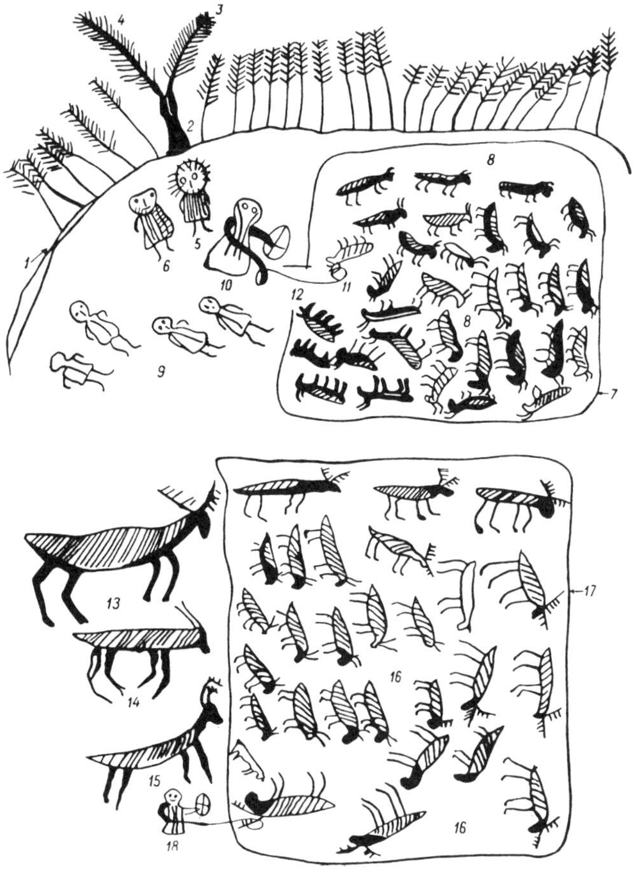

The shaman Pilja at the dwelling of the old mistress of the clan's territory (above) and at the dwelling of the old mistress of the clan (below), catching game for the hunters of the clan. (Šingkelavun ritual). Western Tungus drawing. After Anisimove, *Religija Evenkov* (1958).

Upper drawing

1. The mountain Uromi.
2. The clan's sacred tree.
3–4. The cedar (3) and the pine (4) that grow from the trunk of the sacred tree.
5. The mistress of the territory, Dunne Mušun or Dunne Enin.
6. Her old husband.
7. The stockade that encloses the Dunne's herd of deer.
8. The herd of the Dunne, made up of "souls," which, at the Dunne's command, will incarnate themselves in the reindeer and the elk of the forest.
9. The assistants of the Dunne's husband, who help him care for the herd.
10. The shaman Pilja, in the Šingkelavun ritual, lassoing the souls of the animals that the hunters will kill during the season.
11. The drum beater has been transformed into a leather lasso for the catch. The shaman will carry off the souls, which have become strands of wool and fur for the trip, in his drum.
12. The entrance to the enclosure.

Lower Drawing

13–15. The old mistress of the clan, Bugady Enintyn, represented in the form of three enormous female reindeer or elk.
16. The herd guarded on earth by the three Bugady.
17. The stockade around the enclosure.
18. The shaman Pilja lassoing the animals that his clan's Bugady has awarded him.

encounters is not an animal but a dead relative who has come to visit his descendants in a bearskin.) Although the meat of domestic reindeer may be grilled directly on the coals in the hearth, it is proper to put a receptacle between deer meat and the flames. This opposition reappears even in the killing of domestic reindeer and wild reindeer, which the Tungus do not kill in the same way, since the souls of wild reindeer come from the place of the master spirit of the forest, while those of domestic reindeer, like those of the people of the clan, are descended, under the surveillance of the celestial spirit, from territories which the clan possesses in the higher world.

2. *The master spirit of the forest*. The master spirit of the forest rules the species of animals that concern the hunters; it is he who drives into the hunter's traps a sable or fox taken in his preserves. It should be noted that the Yakut master spirit grants only animals hunted by means of traps, snares, or pitfalls, not those killed with the bow and, later, the gun.

The master spirit of the forest is named differently by different groups, but is best known in the literature by the Yakut name of Baj Bajanaj, "the rich Bajanaj." Among the Tungus he often has the name of Bainača or Bajan Ami, "the rich father." The master spirit of the Tungus forest so closely resembles his Yakut and Altaic homologues that it is believed that this personage was created at a time when these groups were still in close contact.

He appears sometimes as a bear or a sable of remarkable beauty, and sometimes as an old man dressed in sumptuous furs, who rides a reindeer, a dog, a bear, or a tiger, according to the region. The Tungus have preserved in their southern myths the memory of a master spirit of the forest who was a ravishing woman accompanied by a cortege of bears who took the place of dogs. Other Tungus myths speak of a woman who flees with the game at the slightest tinkling of metal. But this very ancient female character has disappeared from the pantheons of the nineteenth and twentieth centuries.

According to certain specialists, there were originally several master spirits, each specializing in an animal species or a type of trap, but they gradually became confused and combined into the present image of an old man who sometimes metamorphoses into a superb animal. One finds traces of these polyvalent Bajanajes among the Yakuts, where informants account for as many as seven, or sometimes eleven, Bajanajes, of which nine are brothers and two are sisters.

Possessed of a very acute sense of hearing, the master spirit of the forest demands that the departure for the hunt take place in utmost silence, and that all noise cease at the camping place. The same respectful silence should be observed at the time of offerings. On the other hand, when the hunter observes an animal caught in his trap, he should rejoice loudly and thank the Bajanaj with great bursts of laughter. In the evening in the forest, the Bajanaj comes to hear the stories told by the hunters around the fire. If the hunters succeed in making him laugh, the Bajanaj will send them abundant game the following day. This liberating power of laughter, which causes game to be released, has been attested with numerous mythic beings, from Sedna of the Eskimos, who lives at the bottom of the sea, to Gargantua of French folklore.

Being very cheerful, the Bajanaj also likes overstated praise. When he sends a musk deer, the Yakuts are supposed to act as if they think the animal is so huge that it cannot fit

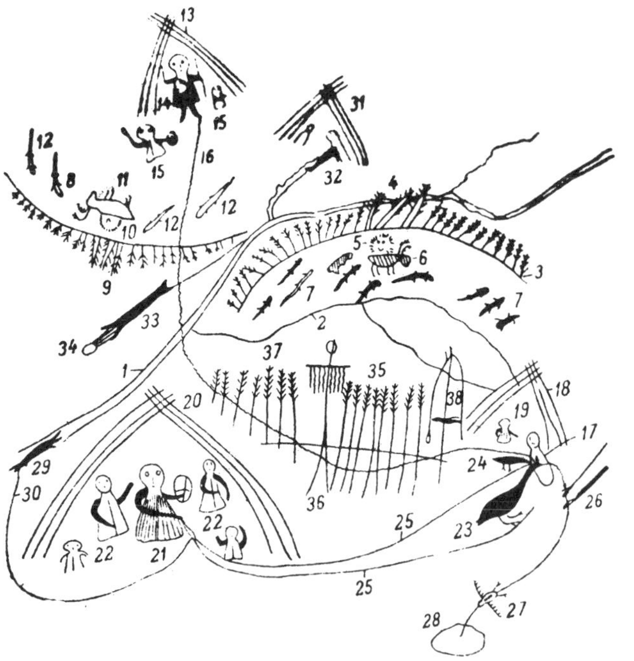

The shaman of the Momol' clan roots out the evil spirit sent by a shaman of the Njurumnal' clan. In revenge, he sends another evil spirit to steal the soul of one of the Njurumnal' clan. Western Tungus drawing. After Anisimov, *Religija Evenkov* (1958).

1. The Tongousska Pierreuse, a tributary of the Iémosséi.
2. Its tributaries.
3. The Momol' clan's territory.
4. The *bugady*, the sacred trees that mark the site where the religious ceremonies take place.
5. The master spirit of the Momol' clan's territory.
6. The guardian spirit of the Momol' clan.
7. The *maryija*, a barrier of protective spirits that prevent evil spirits from entering clan territory.
8. The Njurumnal' clan's territory.
9. The site where Nujurumnal' clan rituals take place.
10. The guardian spirit of the Nujurumnal' clan.
11. The shaman of the Nujurmnal' clan.
12. The *maryija* of the Nujurmnal' clan.
13. The text of the Nujurmnal' clan's shaman.
14. The shaman of the Nujurmnal' clan.
15. The shaman's assistants.
16. The path of the evil spirit, causing sickness, that the shaman of the Nujurmnal' clan has sent to the Momol' clan.
17. The evil spirit, in the form of a worm, slips into the intestines of a man of the Momol' clan and eats away at his bodily soul.
18. The tent of the sick man.
19. His wife.
20. The tent of the shaman of the Momol' clan.
21. The Momol' shaman working his magic to learn the cause of the sickness.
22. Those of the Momol' clan who attend the *kamlanie*.
23. The goose spirit of the shaman.
24. The woodcock spirit and the goose spirit plucking out the spirit from the sick man with their beaks.
25. The path of the shamanistic spirits.
26. The spear spirit and the lance spirit, which must kill the evil spirit when it leaves the sick man.
27. The owl spirit, which, after swallowing the evil spirit, will expel it into the netherworld.
28. The entrance to the netherworld.
29. The pike with two heads that the shaman of the Momol' clan has sent to the Njurumnal' clan in revenge.
30. The route of the pike with two heads.
31. The tent of the sick man of the Njurumnal' clan.
32. The pike spirit tears out the bodily soul of the sick man of the Njurumnal' clan.
33. The pike spirit carries away this soul.
34. The soul of the sick man of the Njurumnal' clan.
35. The stockade of larch spirits erected by the Momol' shaman where the evil spirit passed by.
36. The spear spirit positioned by the Momol' shaman on the path followed by the evil spirit.
37. Pelts hung up as offerings on larches.
38. A reindeer pelt offered as a sacrifice to the spirits of the world above.

through the door, and they pretend to be knocking down the doorposts.

In order to propitiate him, the people address frequent prayers to him before, during, and after the hunt. Furthermore, they revere him in the course of the hunt by silently laying down a small offering in the form of permanent supports for the spirit (a piece of birch bark on which are engraved eyes and a mouth) placed in mountain gorges and in isolated places where game is plentiful. The shaman, as we have seen, intercedes only in cases of continued bad luck in hunting, through rituals involving larger offerings.

The master spirit of the forest asks that the hunter show respect for animals. Traps should kill instantly, without useless suffering. It is proper to conserve the parts in which the soul of the animal lives—the nose, the lips, and the long bones—in order to allow for their resurrection. A language of the hunt, which excludes the usual terms for animals, is obligatory.

Taboos concerning women are particularly strict. Women are prohibited from eating certain parts of the animal, and they must be careful not to step over the fur of the elk or the wild reindeer or the clothing of the hunter, so as not to communicate their impurity to them.

The master spirit of the forest also rules over nervous disorders which he sends out or withdraws at will. Ruling simultaneously over a disease and a type of game is also characteristic of the numerous little auxiliary spirits of the hunt, which have less prestige. For example, the Muxa of the Gold assists in hunting the sable, but causes stomachaches by moving around in the stomachs of the sick. Doonte, the bear, is propitiated at the time of Siberian sturgeon fishing and in case of pains in the arms or complications following childbirth. Ambaseon, the tiger, grants game, but causes stomachaches, etc.

3. *The master spirit of water.* The master spirit of water, often conceived as an old man with algae for hair, lurking at the bottom of the waters, plays a less important role in daily life than do the great master spirits of fire and of the forest.

He owns the fish and the aquatic game of lakes and rivers. Before fishing, people make offerings to him on the shore. These offerings are more solemn at the very beginning of the fishing season, when river ice breaks up. The offerings consist of products which the spirit does not own himself: domestic animals, game, and forest roots. Permanent supports are erected for him on riverbanks, and the statue of the "Old Man of the Ob," erected by the Ostyaks at the confluence of the Ob and the Irtysh, had a bow and arrows and a lance so that the spirit might defend himself in his frequent battles with other master spirits.

4. *Master spirits of clan territories.* The master spirit of the territory which each Tungus clan has is an old woman named Dunne Enin, "territory mother," whose protection is asked with each change that the clan makes. The mistress of the

A Tungus shaman. Nerchinsk. USSR. Transbaikalia. Paris, Musée de l'Homme collection. Photo Kobizeff-Angarski.

house leaves her as an offering an old piece of cloth or a used object when the clan leaves a camp. When a new tent is erected, or the new fire is lit, women ask her permission to sit there and ask her protection.

If the spirit becomes angry with an individual, that person falls ill or returns from the hunt empty-handed. To appease her, the person then offers her two pieces of cloth which are hung close to the tent: a black ribbon for her and a white ribbon for her celestial homologue; for the territory that the clan possesses on earth has its reflection in the higher world and in the lower world (*infra*).

Territory mother Dunne Enin supplies her protégés with game. At the opening of the hunt, the Tungus shaman of Yenisey celebrates the *šingkelavun* rite: he goes down to ask the Dunne for the souls of the game that the clan will kill that year. In the course of a dialogue which all of the hunters of the clan who are assembled for the ritual follow passionately, the shaman begs the Dunne to grant him reindeer, elk, and deer. The Dunne begins by refusing as she recalls all of the taboos concerning fire and the physiology of women that had been broken by the people of the clan. The shaman, with the active support of his spectators, protests and implores. The Dunne finally agrees to release game onto the taiga on condition that the Bugady Enintyn agrees.

Bugady Enintyn may be translated as "the mother of the sacred locality of the clan." *Buga* means (1) sky, (2) universe, (3) homeland, and (4) locality. The last two senses of *buga* intersect with those of the Dunne. The *bugady* are the sacred places of the clan, either the grove of trees or the heap of rocks where the people gather to do certain rituals that concern the clan.

The Bugady Enintyn lives beneath these rocks or in the roots of the trees, sometimes as a female wild reindeer or elk and sometimes as an old woman. She is considered to be the mythic mother of the people of the clan and of the animals that populate the clan territory. Probably it is she who, under the name of the animal mother, swallows the soul of the shaman at the time of his initiation, in order to return it to the world in an animal form. Thanks to this zoomorphic soul, or animal double, the shaman is able to perform his rituals.

After drawing close to the Bugady, who has taken on the guise of a female reindeer, the shaman catches in his drum the souls of the wild reindeer, elk, and deer that the Bugady keeps in her subterranean enclosure. The shaman deposits them in his drum where they take on the appearance of tufts of hair. After again passing close to the Dunne to obtain her assent, the shaman returns to earth and shows the hunters the hairs that represent the game they will kill in the course of the coming hunting season. The hunters protest, not finding them numerous enough. The shaman therefore returns to the Bugady and offers to delouse her. She then takes on her anthropomorphic guise and takes off her blouse. The shaman takes advantage of this to steal from the little bag that she carries on her body other hairs which, this time, are enough to satisfy the hunters.

It appears that these two old clan mistresses, whose names are sometimes confused and exchanged by informants, are so close to one another that they sometimes seem to be the same personage, doubled into a human and an animal form. Nevertheless, certain differences may be seen: the Dunne is more the incarnation of the clan territory, while the Bugady, located at the heart of the clan, beneath the sacred trees, appears more as the mother of the clan, including its game, men, and shaman. From the zoomorphic aspect of the Bugady, Soviet researchers have derived arguments in support of their thesis of a primitive matriarchy that was combined with totemism.

5. *Master spirits of sites.* Apart from Dunne Enin, the mistress of the whole of the clan territories, the master spirit of the forest, and the master spirit of water, each site has its own master spirit, whether it be a picturesque place, a geographical irregularity, a simple valley, the meandering of a stream, or the flank of a mountain.

The spirits are varied in nature. They may be particular spirits, such as Kadar, the spirit of the rocks among the Eastern Tungus; the souls of deceased shamans; or the souls of those who have died a bad death. The last, accident victims or suicides, are the most terrible. Full of rancor, they try to draw the traveler into a death similar to their own. When a hunter enters into their territory, he deposits an offering—a pinch of tobacco, a piece of cloth, or a twig—at the foot of their support (generally a heap of rocks or a piece of bark engraved with a stylized face), in order that the spirits not attack him but, on the contrary, grant him game.

6. *Master spirits of mythic territories.* The mythic universe of the Tungus is divided into three layered worlds. At the center is the world of the middle, i.e., the earth, where men

and animals live. The earth is flat and it floats, held up by gigantic serpents, on the subterranean waters. Above and below, the higher and lower worlds are arranged symmetrically.

The higher world is composed of seven or nine superimposed skies, with the master spirit living above all of these. The lower world is striated into seven or nine layers as well, with the master spirit of the lower world living below all of the layers. The master spirit of the lower world, named Xargi among the Western Tungus, is regarded as either the oldest of the shamanic ancestors of the clan or the inauspicious older brother of the good creator. Sometimes he bears the name of Mangi, and then the Tungus see him in the aspect of a bear. (The bear, in numerous Tungus myths, is the elder brother of man and is accidentally killed by him.)

The term Mangi is the name of an aboriginal population with which the Tungus were united at the time of their arrival in the region. Also known under the name of Mangi, the bear is the culture hero who taught men to domesticate reindeer, and he is the mythic hunter who pursues into the sky the celestial elk Xeglun, tracing the Milky Way with his skis.

Next to this universe of three-tiered worlds, which is common to many Siberians, the Tungus of the Yenisey have developed a more recent concept in which the universe is seen as symbolized by a colossal river that has its source in the higher world to the south, and that crosses the middle world and flows out into the lower world, to the north, at the entrance to the village of the dead. In the course of this mythic river—which is oriented from the southeast to the north—one may see the memory of the ancient migrations of the Tungus who descended the Yenisey at the end of the first millennium A.D.

Tungus shaman's costume. Göttingen, Museum für Völkerkunde. Museum photo.

Seveki, the master spirit of the higher world, lives above the sources of the Yenisey. Further down, in swamps rich in lichens, pass the souls of domesticated reindeer who wait to descend to the earth and to become incarnate in the herds of the clan. Not far away, the mythic tree of the clan extends its branches, upon which warble the fledgling souls of future babies of the clan.

In the lower world, each of several master spirits reigns over a part of the territory. Along the river route leading to the village of the dead are posted seven old female shamans, master spirits of the shores, who guard the way. The oldest and most powerful of these lives on an island just before the mouth of the river. In a dream that he has during his initiation, the novice shaman comes to her to be instructed in shamanic knowledge.

It is also an old shaman who is the mistress of the village of the dead where the dead men and women of the clan continue to fish, sew, and cook as they did when they were alive. Many Soviet researchers see in these old goddesses of the lower world the trace of a predominantly female pantheon dating from an original matriarchy, which the coming of the patriarchy drove down to the lower world.

At the very bottom, well below the village of the dead, is found the shamanic earth reserved for dead shamans, of which Xargi is the master spirit. Each clan has its own village of the dead and its own tributary which connects the village to the great mythic river common to all of the Tungus clans. In the same way, each clan has its own swamps in the higher world for the souls of its herds of reindeer and its tree which is reserved solely for the souls of its clan. Each Tungus clan thus reconstitutes its miniature mythic world, with its territory on earth and in the world beyond set aside for its members alone, whether they are alive on earth, awaiting reincarnation in the higher world, or gone to the world of the dead. As the great celestial divinity remains distant and indistinct, a vast conception of the universe seems to leave these hunters indifferent, since the local spirits which supply them with game are more important to them than all the others.

II. The Shaman and the Shamanic Spirits

1. *The shaman.* The shaman serves as mediator between men and spirits. Spirits cause disease and then death by stealing the souls of individuals or by entering, most often in the form of a worm, into a man's body, which they gnaw through gradually. Although certain spirits provoke death and diseases, others possess the animals of the forest and the fish of lakes and streams which they grant to the hunter according to their pleasure.

Thus, the health and livelihood of men depend upon the spirits. As a consequence, the shaman who knows how to manipulate them and take back the souls they have stolen or obtain the souls of game animals appears as the protector of the physical and economic well-being of his people.

The rites which the shaman uses on the spirits, known as shamanic seances, or *kamlanie* (a Russian neologism formed from Turkish *kam,* "shaman"), are more or less complex. Nevertheless, they generally take place according to the following schema. They take place at night, close to the glowing hearth fire, and may last for a few hours in several successive nights. The shaman, dressed in a special costume with numerous fringes and shreds of cloth where the spirits perch, begins by summoning his auxiliary spirits, to the accompaniment of his slowly beating drum.

After incorporating his spirits (through his armpits, anus, forehead, or mouth), the shaman sends his soul, i.e., his animal double, into the mythic territories of the other world to bring back a sick person's soul that has been taken there by a spirit, or to steal the fledgling soul of a baby, which he will bring to a sterile woman, or to conduct the soul of a dead person to the lower world, or else to deal with spirits in other transactions to obtain game or to heal a sick person.

As he sings and dances, this time in a frantic mode, the shaman mimics his extraterrestrial voyages and his combats with spirits. Catatonic trances are rare, but when they occur, it is the shaman's assistant who explains to the listener the adventures of the shaman in the other world. When his mission is terminated, the soul of the shaman is reintegrated into his body. Before dismissing his auxiliary spirits, the shaman asks them for some information for the use of the spectators, most often about the hunt and weather conditions. He then thanks them and sometimes offers them a sacrifice. A session of purification ends the *kamlanie.*

The shaman is paid in kind for his work, according to the prosperity of the family. The payment ranges from a precious fur to some ribbons for the shaman to hang from his costume. Far from being prosperous, shamans are relatively poor in comparison with other families, since their relationships with the spirits often hinder them from going off to hunt at the best time. The gifts which he receives are more a compensation than a profit. A Tungus shaman of the Yenisey, charged with executing several seances in succession for a sick woman during the squirrel hunting season, asked the husband for squirrel pelts as recompense. Only false shamans, charlatans, those who allied themselves with the kulaks at the beginning of the Revolution, would seek to extort profits, according to the great Soviet specialist on the Tungus, G. M. Vasilievič.

Tungus shamans do not seek their vocation. On the contrary, it is imposed upon them by a spirit—an ancestor shaman, as a rule—in the course of an illness that may last for years, of which the symptoms (melancholy, flight into the forest, insomnia, etc.) are similar throughout Siberia. The spirit may choose either a boy or a girl, most often during adolescence. Once the chosen one is resigned to becoming a shaman, the future shaman is gradually healed by songs performed to summon the spirits and by their incorporation.

The seance has therapeutic power not only for the sick person treated by the shaman, but also for the shaman. If shamans go long without officiating, their spirits torment them until they take their drum in hand. It should not be deduced from this that shamans are hysterics, as numerous nineteenth-century authors assumed somewhat too easily. Although one finds a few cases of imbalance or instability among the shamans, the great majority of them are perfectly healthy. On the other hand, in order for a shaman to be effective and appreciated, he or she must be endowed with an artistic temperament, for the shaman's seances are the only theater in the forest, and this is a theater that is all the more exciting because it involves the health and the subsistence of its spectators.

The gifted shaman sees his power increase in the course of time through a series of consecrations during which he receives new accessories in a determined order: paddle, drum, breastplate, boots, mittens, overcoat, headdress of chamois leather, and finally a headdress crowned with iron antlers.

The shaman cannot abandon his priestly office of his own will, even when he becomes old or falls ill. Nevertheless, the nervous tension and the exaltation of the seance are such that one has seen very old shamans, weak and trembling, begin to leap and dance with vigor when possessed by the spirits.

The death of a shaman is felt by his clan to be a catastrophe, for his shamanic spirits, after losing their master, are set free and think no more about defending the clan against invasion by the malevolent spirits that prowl in search of souls to carry off. Furthermore, the shamanic spirits, when they return to their essentially malevolent spiritual nature, attack the members of the clan and bring them insanity, anguish, and bad luck in hunting. It is understandable that the clan waits impatiently for the appearance of the next shaman, so he may overcome the auxiliary spirits and once again fulfill the functions of diviner, doctor, psychopomp, bringer of game, and organizer of entertainment.

2. *The shamanic spirits.* (*a*) The shamanic ancestors. At the bottom of the lower world, the dead shamans choose among their living descendants on earth that male or female who is to become a shaman. It appears to be unusual among the Tungus that an individual feels called to the shamanic office without having shamanic ancestors. At the time of the mythic initiation of the shaman into the other world, the spirits dismember the candidate and count his bones in order to verify that he has the "extra bone" without which he cannot become a shaman. The extra bone, the name and position of which are never specified, symbolizes the obligatory shamanic ancestry.

Among the Western Tungus, once the future shaman has been chosen, the earliest of the shamanic ancestors (named Mangi or Xargikakum, "the very great Xargi," according to informants) assigns him a particular ancestral Xargi. This ancestor will go to the future shaman in a dream and announce his election. He will whisper into his ear the words and tune of his shamanic songs, which the elected one is to repeat as he sways. After instructing him, the Xargi continues to counsel the shaman throughout his career. At the time of shamanic seances, he will reveal to him the names of the spirits of diseases and the paths by which they have come and will direct the shaman's battles against them, battles curiously similar to the ambush wars that take place between enemy tribes in the taiga.

The support of the Xargi, hooked to the shaman's dress, is a small human figure punched into a metal plate. Yet, at the time of his interventions in *kamlanies,* he is often described as half-man, half-animal (half-wolf, half-bear, half-wolverine, or half-reptile).

It is perhaps because of this zoomorphic aspect that the Xargi is sometimes confused with the shaman's animal double, which is brought into the world by the animal mother at the time of his initiation. When the future shaman has been chosen, his soul descends into the root of the sacred tree of the clan, the dwelling of the animal mother, who is often conceived as a female reindeer or elk (very likely an avatar of the Bugady Enintyn). She swallows the shaman's soul and returns it to the world in the form of a reindeer or elk fawn. The animal mother can also be a bear, eagle, burbot, etc. Then the new soul of the shaman belongs to that

Tungus shaman in a Tungus village. Engraving (Witsen, 1750–80). Paris, Musée de l'Homme collection. Museum photo.

species. The shaman's soul emerges strengthened by this metamorphosis, which gives him new qualities. After this, it is this shaman's animal double that brings to a successful conclusion the shaman's performance during his seances.

Some sources do not speak of the animal mother. In this case, the shaman's soul is rendered more resistant by the ancestral spirits who forge it in iron as they preserve its human appearance. According to some traditions, the dismembered body of the shaman is boiled in a caldron and then offered to the spirits who rule over various illnesses. The more spirits there are to eat him, the more powerful the shaman will be, because he will know how to heal the disease ruled by the spirit who has tasted his flesh. During the ordeals that take place in the other world, the shaman remains stretched out and immobile in his tent, eating and drinking nothing; this state may last for a week.

The ancestors grant the novice shaman a troop of zoomorphic auxiliary spirits who serve as messengers, scouts, mounts, spies, or warriors during his seances. It is again the ancestors who decide when the shaman becomes worthy to receive his accessories: paddle, drum, jacket, boots, headdress. The accessories are obtained in a determined order, and with them the shaman acquires the power of the spirits that animate them and that communicate to him a more extensive power of clairvoyance and greater capacities for movement and battle.

In the final analysis, the shaman is nothing without his ancestors. All of his power—his zoomorphic soul brought into the world by the animal mother (very probably an ancestral spirit), his metallic soul forged by dead shamans, or the troop of auxiliary spirits given to him by the same shamans, along with the accessories of the ritual—all of the power of the Western Tungus shaman comes to him from his ancestors.

A peculiarity of the Gold shaman has been stressed by Sternberg. According to his informant, the electing spirit will choose a young man after having sexual relations with him, and female shamans are elected by male spirits. We find traces of this marriage between the shaman and his principal spirit among other Tungus groups, but probably one should not generalize such instances, as Sternberg does.

(*b*) The zoomorphic spirits, servants of the shaman. One must not confuse these mere servants, who are stripped of any personal life and exist solely as a function of the shaman, with the independent spirits who take on animal forms on occasion. The birds, fish, and mammals given by the ancestors to the novice shaman are given by the Western Tungus the collective name of *etan*, i.e., diverse. They are the symbol of the quality that characterizes their species, and the shaman uses them in ways appropriate to those qualities.

Sometimes the shaman incorporates them during the *kamlanie* in order to appropriate this quality for himself: the strength of the tiger, the quick movement of the deer, the combativeness of the reindeer in rut, the power of the bear, the distant vision of the lizard who climbs into the treetops, the ability of the fox and the sable to slip by unnoticed, the birds' ability to fly, the fishes' ability to swim, and so forth.

Sometimes he puts them to use in roles in which the qualities appear to be necessary: he dispatches the hare as a messenger, and that animal's confusing footprints lead astray the evil spirits sent out after it; he sends carnivorous pike ahead as scouts when he descends the great mythic river on his drum, which becomes a boat for the occasion; he sends the goose to seize, with its long beak, the evil spirit at the bottom of a sick person's intestines.

However, the essential uses of the zoomorphic spirits are as mounts and sentinels. Swans, geese, and eagles carry the shaman up to the higher world. Loons, reindeer, and bears carry him down to the lower world. The burbot, grayling, and salmon help him to cross lakes. The animals most preferred for use are those which belong to several elements and are thus most able to facilitate passage from one world to another. Thus, the loon, the characteristic spirit of Tungus shamanism, swims as well as it flies, and the frog is found painted, embroidered, or carved on nearly every accessory of the Amur basin.

As for warrior sentinels, their abundance is noteworthy. The first thing that a newly named Yenisey shaman does is to establish a line of guardian spirits: birds in the air, fish in the streams, and quadrupeds in the woods, who watch to see that no malevolent spirits penetrate the borders of the clan territories. The mythic territories of the clan are also protected by birds and fishes which constantly patrol them. In the higher world, the approaches to the tree that bears the souls of the clan and the celestial swamps where the souls of future reindeer graze are sheltered behind several lines of birds. In the lower world, the entrance to the small stream that leads to the village of the dead is defended by a dam of fish spirits.

The animal spirits do not content themselves with merely watching over the clan territories, but also care for the souls of the people of the clan. Beneath the gills of pike spirits, the western shaman hides the souls of the spectators at the beginning of the great *kamlanie* in the course of which he will travel into the world beyond and encounter all sorts of malevolent spirits. The shaman returns the souls to their owners at the end of the seance when all danger has been warded off. These precautions show to what degree the Tungus feel themselves to be surrounded by fearsome, ever-watchful spirits, which are always on the prowl for a soul to steal.

(*c*) Spirits susceptible to being mastered by the shaman. With the exceptions of the great celestial divinity and the master spirits of fire, the forest, and water, all spirits are susceptible to the mastery of the shaman. According to certain informants, the shaman of the Western Tungus could even master the master spirits.

By "master" we mean that the shaman incorporates the spirit through his mouth, armpits, anus, or forehead, or else that he introduces it into a support, a rough depiction of the spirit hastily carved into wood, cut from birch bark, embroidered on chamois leather, or wrought in iron. No aesthetic concern inspires the sculptor; only effectiveness counts. It is enough for the support to offer sufficiently meaningful lines that the spirit recognizes that this "seat" is meant for him.

When the spirit is enclosed in the support, he becomes dependent upon men. The spirit then becomes easy to feed by rubbing the support with grease, blood, etc.; or, on the contrary, easy to get rid of by throwing the support into a stream or the depths of the forest. It is for this reason that supports are made both for the guardian spirits of the household who are fed daily and for the malevolent spirit that one wishes to send far away.

A shaman incorporates a spirit when he wishes to borrow from it its appearance and its virtues in order to bring his travels and battles in the other world to a successful conclusion. He also incorporates it in order to establish the dialogue by which he learns how to render the spirit favorable through fine words and promises of offerings, or, on the contrary, to frighten it and send it away with threats.

The shaman is free to add to the very long list of spirits known and transmitted from generation to generation other spirits of his own invention, new spirits which he or a member of his clan has encountered in the course of his travels over the taiga.

Beyond this, the shaman borrows, according to his own taste, the spirits of other groups. It is sufficient that they appear to him to be efficacious. They have thus adopted the Sumu spirit (Mongolian *süme,* "temple"), Saint Nicholas, Lenin, and even the French Communards.

Sometimes the shaman buys auxiliary spirits from another shaman. A Tungus thus acquires Koryak spirits which continue to speak Koryak throughout the *kamlanie,* since the spirits speak their native languages. If the shaman does not know the language, he jabbers a few mangled words, which are sufficient for his audience.

Once the spirits have been mastered, they become the shaman's auxiliaries, his *séven,* a term common to all of the Tungus dialects; it originally meant "to throw fat into the fire," this being the oldest means of propitiating the spirits. The spirits, which are harmful in essence, do not lose this nature when they are mastered by the shaman. They are merely compelled by him to come to his aid.

This native spitefulness of the spirits may perhaps explain in part the existence of shamans who eat souls. The shaman who eats souls is a shaman who is powerful enough to steal the soul of another person and thus cause his death. The shaman who eats the souls of his enemies in the course of the frequent battles between neighboring groups is not regarded by members of his clan as a malevolent shaman. Only the shaman who attacks his own people is an authentic eater of souls, hated and feared.

Ordinarily, the shaman agrees with his spirit to do evil. An old shaman of the Eastern Tungus had caused so much unhappiness in the course of his life, killing babies and horses, that four shamans decided to rid the clan of him. The old shaman, in order to defend himself, practiced shamanism for three days and three nights. In vain. When he knew he was dying, he predicted to his clan, "Don't worry, you'll all follow me!" And in fact, after his death, his principal auxiliary spirit visited one family after another, bringing to each its lot of calamities.

However, it sometimes happens that the spirit acts without the knowledge of its master and sometimes against his or her will. A Yakut female shaman had as spirits two extremely ferocious dogs who had devoured the souls of her young nephews. The shaman, who was said to have "thoughts of the sun," grieved over the death of the children and descended into the lower world to muzzle her dogs.

Not satisfied with being harmful to men, the spirits fight among themselves and steal each others' sacrifices. This brings an endless series of problems to the unlucky individual who has offered the sacrifice, on whom the spirit who was robbed takes his revenge. The spirits, whose greed is insatiable, are always searching for food. A Buryat who bemoaned the existence of spirits exclaimed, "They are as greedy as sheep!" They never stop demanding offerings of fat, milk, alcohol, and meat, and along with these they must also have praise, flattery, and compliments. At least once a year, the shaman must offer a great banquet to all of his spirits. Certain shamans have spirits that are more demanding than others. When they feel they have been neglected, they torment their master until he takes care of them. The shaman then performs a *kamlanie* alone in his tent, for the sole purpose of calming his spirits.

Fortunately, it is very easy to scare the spirits and ward them off. Any metallic or pointed object—bells, claws, hooks, or porcupine quills—sends them into flight. A cry or an insult makes them disappear. Certain Gold spirits had a particular terror of insults shouted in Russian. It is even easier to trick them. One need only change the names of things, and the spirits cannot find them. The symbolic language of humans is completely hermetic to them, whence

Tungus shaman. Nineteenth-century lithograph. Paris, Musée de l'Homme collection. Museum photo.

the frequency of tabooed words and the use of substitute terms, especially during the hunt or important rites, such as that of the bear cult. In order to combat them, the shaman uses trickery more often than strength. An Ul'č female shaman wanted to do away with a spirit who devoured all of the young children of a family. She had a wooden doll made, which she laid in the cradle. The spirit did not notice the difference and entered the doll. The shaman then simply crushed it with a hammer.

Wicked, greedy, boastful, stupid, and fearful, these spirits bear a surprisingly close resemblance to the devils that appear in our own medieval tales.

L.D./d.w.

Siberian Religion and Myths: The Example of the Tungus

I. The Peoples of Siberia

The various ethnic groups which populate Siberia belong to five great families. West of the Yenisey and in the Taimyr peninsula are the Finno-Ugric peoples, represented by the Ugrians (Xant) and the Samoyeds (Nenc, Enc, Nganasan, and Selkup). The Altaic family is made up of the Buryats, of Mongolian origin, who live around Lake Baikal, the Turks (among them the Yakut, who live on either side of the Lena, while the Altaic peoples, Tuvs, Tofalar, Šor, and Xaka populate the Altai mountains), and the Tungusic-Manchu branch (comprising Tungus [Evenk] extending from the Yenisey to the Sea of Okhotsk, Lamut [Even], Gold [Nanaj or Nanai], Ul'č, Udege, Orok, and Orochon living in the Amur River valley). The Paleo-Arctic peoples (Chukchee, Koryak, Kamchadals, and Yukaghir) wander as nomads on the northeasternmost corner of Siberia, and the Gilyaks live on the island of Sakhalin and at certain points on the opposite shore. Small groups of Eskimos are located near the Bering straits. Finally, a few Ket clans are situated on the middle Yenisey.

Though each ethnic group has elaborated its own pantheon and created its own spirits, they all have three basic categories of spirits: the great deity of the sky, the master spirits, and the shamanic spirits. They have all also developed a method of acting upon the spirits, namely, shamanism. The basic principles of this system, which make it possible to remedy the malevolent actions of the spirits and to obtain from some of them good hunting or fishing, remain similar throughout Siberia. Only the details vary: thus, the Chukchee shamans use hallucinogenic mushrooms to promote the trance, whereas in the rest of Siberia shamans attain this state without any help other than musical rhythm. Certain Paleo-Arctic shamans dress in women's clothing and live maritally with men, a practice that seems to be unknown elsewhere.

In order to illustrate Siberian beliefs, we prefer to describe the mythology of a single group, with all of its details and its particular flavor, rather than to offer an overview that would outline only the skeleton common to these mythologies. This will not, however, prevent us from occasionally mentioning other ethnic groups to point out basic resemblances.

We have chosen for this purpose a people typical of the Taiga, the Tungus. In addition to their features representative of hunters and reindeer breeders, the Tungus are the only people who are found scattered over the entire territory of Siberia, from the banks of the Yenisey to the shores of the Sea of Okhotsk by way of the forests of the Transbaikal.

Tungus shaman with his drum and his embroidered plastron made of reindeer skin. Paris, Musée de l'Homme collection. Photo Encyclopédie française/Daniel.

Before the revolution of 1917, the Tungus were hunters and breeders of reindeer and were organized into patrilineal clans. The clan was a union of relatives, all descendants of the same ancestor and possessing a common territorial hunting ground; it had a council of elders at its head. Besides the old men, three individuals enjoyed great prestige: the shaman of the clan, the civil chief who led the collective hunts, and the military chief who was in charge of the warring expeditions that were very frequent among the Tungus.

The Tungus lived in tents made of poles set into the ground in a circle and joined at the top, covered with reindeer skins in the winter and with birch bark in the summer. These two raw materials, skin and bark, were also used to make most clothing and household utensils.

Very broadly speaking, their economy might be characterized as one that depended on hunting in the winter and fishing and gathering in the summer. It is possible to distinguish three separate groups of Tungus, according to their way of life:

—the vagabond Tungus, who change their campsites in response to the vagaries of hunting and the pursuit of game;

—the nomadic Tungus, who breed reindeer and horses in the Transbaikal and go back and forth between their winter and summer campsites;

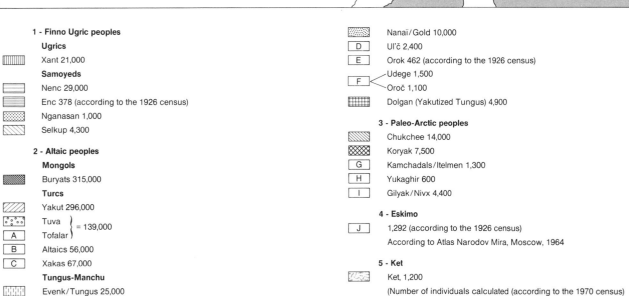

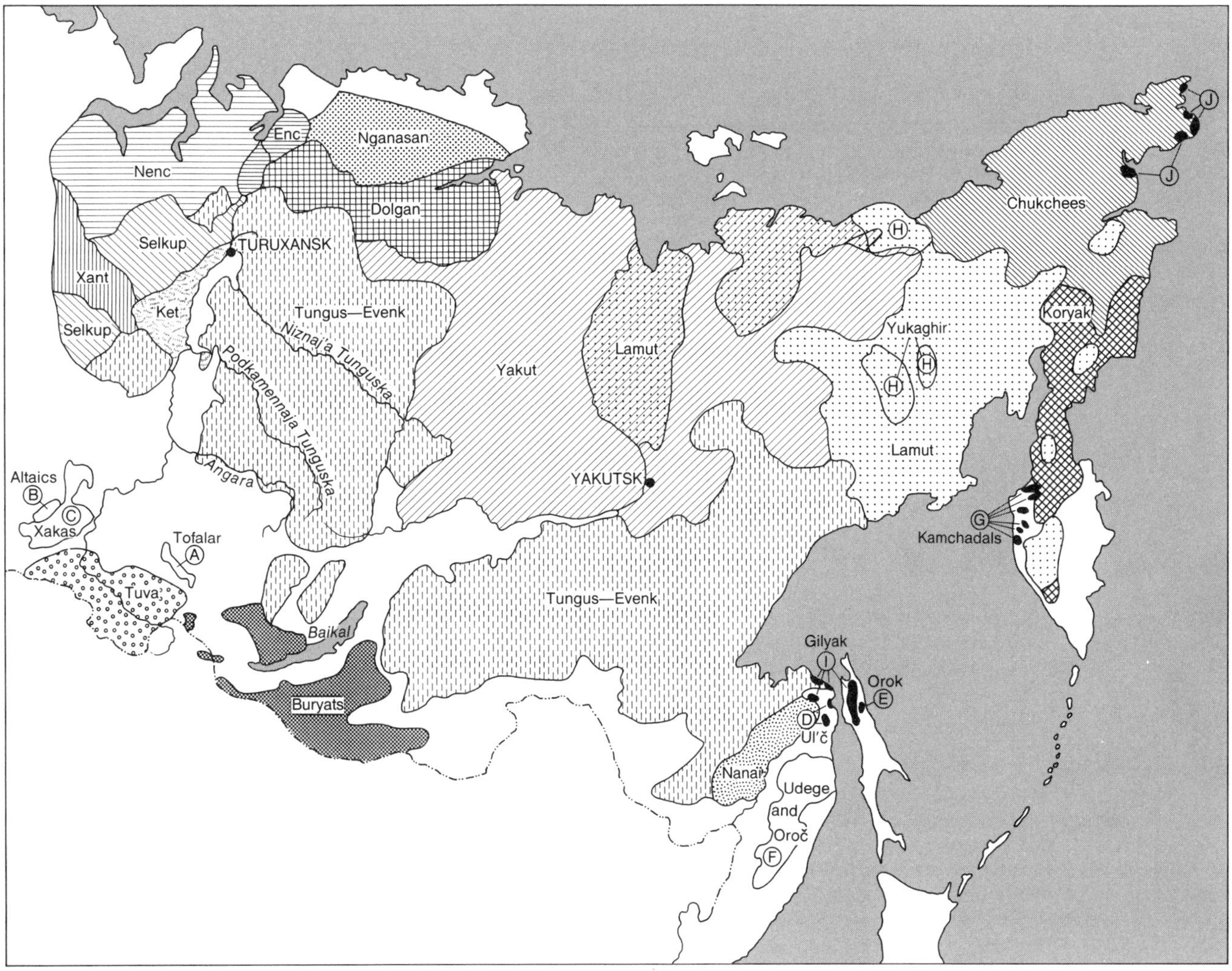

1 - **Finno Ugric peoples**

Ugrics

Xant 21,000

Samoyeds

Nenc 29,000

Enc 378 (according to the 1926 census)

Nganasan 1,000

Selkup 4,300

2 - **Altaic peoples**

Mongols

Buryats 315,000

Turcs

Yakut 296,000

Tuva } = 139,000
A Tofalar }

B Altaics 56,000

C Xakas 67,000

Tungus-Manchu

Evenk/Tungus 25,000

Evenk/Lamut 12,000

Nanaï/Gold 10,000

D Ul'č 2,400

E Orok 462 (according to the 1926 census)

F Udege 1,500
Oroč 1,100

Dolgan (Yakutized Tungus) 4,900

3 - **Paleo-Arctic peoples**

Chukchee 14,000

Koryak 7,500

G Kamchadals/Itelmen 1,300

H Yukaghir 600

I Gilyak/Nivx 4,400

4 - **Eskimo**

J 1,292 (according to the 1926 census)

According to Atlas Narodov Mira, Moscow, 1964

5 - **Ket**

Ket, 1,200

(Number of individuals calculated (according to the 1970 census)

Bronze mirror worn as part of a shaman's costume. Paris, Musée de l'Homme collection. Museum photo.

—the sedentary Tungus, who have settled on the shores of great lakes or large rivers: in good weather, the entire family takes part in fishing; in the winter, the men leave to hunt in the forest, leaving behind the old, the women, and the children in their winter homes.

A caravan of reindeer that carries or pulls luggage accompanies the Tungus in their moves. Depending on the group, the Tungus ride their reindeer or walk beside them.

East of the Lena in the far north, the Orochon, that is, the "Reindeer Tungus," cross their females with wild males and thus obtain a larger and more robust breed for riding. They never kill their reindeer for food except in case of extreme famine, but use their herds exclusively for transportation and dairy products. These substantial herds occupy such an important place in their economic life that the summer migration is solely for pasture.

West of the Lena, the Tungus practice a much more rudimentary kind of breeding. Each family owns only a few reindeer which no one except children and the elderly ever ride. In the autumn, these Tungus do not hesitate to slaughter their domesticated reindeer when there is a shortage of food.

II. The Religious Problem

To summarize briefly the impression that one gathers from the Tungus pantheon, one must first recognize the undeniable presence of a large number of female spirits: grandmother fire, the mothers of the clan and of the territory of the clan, the animal mother, the old female shamans who guard the river route in the netherworld, and the mistress of the village of the dead. Nevertheless, it seems wrong to claim, as Soviet authors do, that Tungus communities were once matriarchal.

Similarly, survivals of phenomena connected with totemism have been recorded in Siberia. The Gold clans notably bear the names of certain animals (bears, tigers) whom they particularly revered and regarded as their ancestors, and whose meat was taboo. But these phenomena are not numerous enough for us to join the Soviets who, faithful to evolutionist theory, claim that totemism existed among all the Siberian peoples at the time of the matriarchy. That is possible, but it has yet to be proved.

Aside from this problem, what is striking in this system of beliefs is the Tungus fear of the spirits, a fear indicated by the abundance of rites and actions in daily life designed to keep the spirits at bay or to make them favorable. One cannot begin a meal, however hungry one may be, without first throwing a mouthful to the spirits. This is the only ritual action that has been preserved until today throughout Siberia. Siberians continue to throw a few drops of wine into the fire before meals, even if the deep meaning of this act has dissipated. And the same request is always made: "Grant us good game!" addressed to the master spirit of the fire, the master spirit of the forest, the guardian spirit of the house, the mother of the territory, the mother of the clan, and the ancestors.

There are innumerable spirits who look after the game. The master spirits of the forest, of the clan territory, of the locality, of a particular mountain slope, of a particular bend in a river—they all rule over territories that blend together and overlap. Even the spirits who have no territories have the right to watch over the same game. Beyond a certain confusion that is inherent in any pantheon elaborated by a people who have no written tradition and are spread over such a vast expanse, this also reveals an obsession with famine. One could never have enough game even if one asked everyone for it.

The shaman is there to appease the fear, the hunger that afflicts and traps the hunters lost in the taiga. Through his battles against the spirits, the shaman makes every effort to sustain the precarious life of his group and to remedy the effects of natural accidents. Without promising either paradise or a better world, he confronts the evil forces to wrest health and food from them. But the fighter must be on his guard, because the jealous deity keeps watch. And if he oversteps his rights, this second Prometheus will be defeated, as was the Buryat shaman who dared to create a human soul and was condemned to dance on a stone until his own body was worn away and completely disappeared.

L.D./g.h.

BIBLIOGRAPHY

1. Mythology of Siberia in General

C. F. COXWELL, *Siberian and Other Folk-Tales,* Primitive literature of the empire of the Tzars, collected and translated with an introduction and notes (London 1925) (translations of tales by Chukchee, Yukaghir, Koryak, and Gilyak). V. DIÓSZEGI, ed., *Popular Beliefs and Folklore Tradition in Siberia* (Bloomington 1968). (This remarkable book contains thirty-one articles on the shamanism of different Siberian groups, written by Soviet specialists.) K. DONNER, *La Sibérie,* trans.

from Finnish by L. Froman (Paris 1946). M. ELIADE, *Shamanism: Archaic Techniques of Ecstasy* (Princeton 1964). (This well-known book, first published in French in 1951, presents a very personal view of shamanism.) H. FINDEISEN, "Sibirisches Schamanentum und Magie," *Institut für Menschen- und Menscheitskunde* (Augsburg 1953); *Schamanentum, dargestellt am Beispiel der Besessenheitspriester nordasiatischer Völker* (Stuttgart 1957). A. FRIEDRICH and G. BUDDRUSS, *Schamanengeschichten aus Siberien* (Munich 1955). U. HARVA, *Die religiösen vorstellungen der altaischen Völker* (Helsinki 1938) (also in French). U. HOLMBERG, "The Shaman Costume and Its Significance," *Annales Universitatis Fennicae Aboensis,* ser. B, 1, 2 (1922). E. LOT-FALCK, *Les rites de chasse chez les peuples sibériens* (Paris 1953). H. N. MICHAEL, ed., *Studies in Siberian Shamanism,* Arctic Institute of North America, Anthropology of the North, trans. from Russian sources, 4 (Toronto 1963) (translation of fundamental Russian articles on Siberian shamanism, particularly Tungus shamanism). G. NIORADZE, *Der Schamanismus bei den Sibirischen Völkern* (Stuttgart 1925). I. PAULSON, Å. HULTKRANTZ, and K. JETTMAR, *Les religions arctiques et finnoises* (Siberians, Finns, Lapps, and Eskimos) (Paris 1965) (originally German). A. POPOV, *Materialy dlja bibliografii russkoj literatury po izučeniju šamanstva severo-azjatskix narodov* (Leningrad 1932). (A very important bibliography for those interested in Siberian shamanism, containing over seven hundred titles of Russian works on shamanism of all the Siberian groups.) E. D. PROKOF'EVA, "Šamanskie kostjumy narodov Sibiri," *Sbornik Muzeja Antropologii i Etnografii* 27 (1971): 5–100 (many illustrations of Siberian shamanic costumes). L. STERNBERG, "Divine Election in Primitive Religion," *XXIe Congrès international des Américanistes,* 1924 (Göteborg 1925), 472–512. D. K. ZELENINE, *Le culte des idoles en Sibérie,* trans. from Russian by Welter (Paris 1952).

2. Studies of Various Ethnic Groups

(a) The Finno-Ugrians

(i) Ugrians

Xant/Ostyak F. K. KARJALAINEN, "Der Religion der Jugra-Völker (Ostjaken und Wogulen)," *Folklore Fellows Communications,* 41, 44, 63 (Helsinki 1921–27). NIPPGEN, "Les divinités des eaux chez les peuples finno-ougriens. 1: Les Ostiaques et les Vogouls" (Paris 1925), extracts from *La revue d'ethnographie et des traditions populaires,* no. 22 (1925).

(ii) Samoyeds

H. UFER, *Religion und Religiösen Sitte bei den Samojeden* (Erlangen 1930).

Enc/Samoyeds of Yenisey E. D. PROKOF'EVA, "Materialy po religioznym predstavlenijam Encev," in *Sbornik Muzeja Antropologii i Etnografii* 14 (1953): 194–230.

Nenc/Yurak T. LEHTISALO, "Entwurf einer Mythologie der Jurak-Samojeden," in *Mémoires de la Société finno-ougrienne* 53 (1924); "Der Tod und die Wiedergeburt des künftigen Schamanen," *Journal de la Société finno-ougrienne* 48 (1936–37).

Nganasan B. O. DOLGIX, *Legendy i skazki nganasanov* (Krasnoyarsk 1938).

Selkup/Samoyed-Ostyak G. N. PROKOF'EV, "Ceremonija oživlenija bubna u ostjako-samojedov," *Izvestija Leningradskogo Gosudarstvennogo Universiteta* 2 (1929). E. D. PROKOF'EVA, "Kostjum sel'kupskogo (ostjako-samojedskogo) šamana," *Sbornik Muzeja Antropologii i Etnografii* 11 (1949): 335–76.

(b) The Altaic Peoples

(i) Mongols

Buryats N. N. AGAPITOV and M. N. XANGALOV, "Materialy dlja izučenija šamanstva v Sibiri (šamanstvo u Burjat)," *Izvestija Vostočnogo-sibirskogo otdelenija Russkogo Geografičeskogo Obščestva* 14, nos. 1–2 (1883). M. N. XANGALOV, "Skazanija Burjat, zapisannye raznymi sobirateljami," in *Zapiski Vostoňo-Sibirskogo otdelenija Russkogo Geograficeskogo Obščestva po otdeleniju etnografii,* 1, fasc. 2 (1895).

(ii) Turks

Yakut W. JOCHELSON, "The Yakut," *Anthropological Papers of the American Museum of Natural History* 33 (New York 1933). V. L. SIEROSZEWSKI, "Du chamanisme d'après les croyances des Yakoutes," *Revue de l'histoire des religions* 46 (1902). V. F. TROŠČANSKIJ, "Evoljucija černoj very (šamanstva) u Jakutov," *Učenye Zapiski Kazanskogo Universiteta* 4 (1903).

Tuva/Sojot/Urjanxaj V. BOUNAK, "Un pays de l'Asie peu connu: Le Tanna-Touva," *Internationales Archiv für Ethnographie* 29 (1928): 1–16; "La république de Tanna-Touva," *Anthropos,* 1929, 1–117. V. DIÓSZEGI, "Der Werdegang zum Schamanen bei den nördöstlichen Sojoten," in *Acta Etnographica Academiae Scientiarum Hungaricae* 8, 3–4 (1959); "Tuva Shamanism: Intraethnic Differences and Analogies," ibid., fasc. 1–2 (1962): 145–90. L. P. POTAPOV, "K izučeniju šamanizma u narodov Sajano-Altajskogo nagor'ja," in *Pamjati Vladimircova,* 1958.

Tofalar/Tubalar/Karagas I. EVSENIN, "O religioznyx verovanijax karagasov," *Bezbožnik,* no. 2 (1929).

Altaic Peoples (comprising the southern Altaic peoples or Altaic peoples proper: Telengit and Teleut, and the northern Šor, Čelkan, Kumandin) A. V. ANOXIN, "Materialy po šamanstvu u altajcev," in *Sbornik Muzeja Antropologii i Etnografii* 4, fasc. 2 (1924). N. P. DIRENKOVA, *Šorskij fol'klor* (Moscow and Leningrad 1940); "Materialy po šamanstvu teleutov," in ibid. 10 (1949): 107–91. U. HARVA, *Die Religiösen Vorstellungen der Altaischen Völker,* trans. from Finnish (Helsinki 1938) W. RADLOFF, *Aus Sibirien,* vols. 1–11 (Leipzig 1884). W. SCHMIDT, "Die Asiatischen Hintervölker: Die primären Hintervölker Alt-Türken, der Altai und Abacan-Tataren," *Der Ursprung der Gottesidee,* vol. 11 (Freiburg 1949).

Xakas/Kirghiz of the Yenisey (comprising the Kačin, Koïbal, Kyzyl, Beltir, and Sagaj) N. COHN, *Gold Khan and Other Siberian Legends,* 1946 (selection and trans. of texts collected by Castren and Titov from Koïbal, Kačin, and Sagaj). V. DIÓSZEGI, "How to Become a Shaman among the Sagais," *Acta Orientalia Hungaricae* 15, fasc. 1–3 (1962). N. F. KATANOV, *Xakasskij fol'klor* (Abakan 1963).

(c) Tunguso-Manchu

Tungus (comprising the Evenk [Tungus proper], the Even/Lamoutes, the Nanaj/Gold, the Dolgan, Negidal, Ul'č, Udege, Orok, Oroč) A. F. ANISIMOV, *Religija evenkov v istoriko-genetičeskom izučenii i problemy proisxoždenija pervobytnyx verovanij* (Moscow and Leningrad 1958). G. V. KSENOFONTOV, *Legendy i rasskazy o šamanax u Jakutov, Burjat i Tungusov* (Irkutsk 1928). L. A. LOPATIN, "Tales from the Amur Valley," *Journal of American Folklore* 46 (1933): 201–56; "A Shamanistic Performance to Regain the Favor of the Spirit," *Anthropos* 35–36 (1940–41): 352–55. A. A. POPOV, *Dolganskij fol'klor* (Leningrad 1936). S. M. SHIROKOGOROV, *Psychomental Complex of the Tungus* (London 1935). P. P. ŠIMKEVIČ, "Materialy dlja izučenija šamanstva u Gol'dov," in *Zapiski Priamurskogo Otdela Russkogo Geografičeskogo Obščestva* 2 (1896). L. STERNBERG, *Giljaki, oroči, gol'dy, negidal'cy, ajny* (Khabarovsk 1933). G. M. VASILEVIČ, *Evenki: Istoriko-etnografičeskie očerki XVIII načalo XX v* (Leningrad 1969).

(c) The Paleo-Arctic Peoples

(i) Chukchee

W. BOGORAS, "Idées religieuses des Tchouktchis," J. Denniker, trans. *Bulletins et mémoires de la Société d'anthropologie de Paris,* 5th ser., nos. 3–4 (1904); "Religious Ideas of Primitive Man, from Chukchee Material," *XIVe Congrès international des américanistes* (1904), 1:129–35; "Chukchee Mythology," *Memoirs of the American Museum of Natural History* 12, part 1 (New York and Leiden 1910); "Chukchee Tales," *Journal of American Folklore* 41, no. 161 (1928): 297–452. H. KUNIKE, *Märchen aus Sibirien* (Jena 1940) (German trans. of tales from the Chukchee, Čuvancy, Koryak, Yukaghir, and Kamchadal). *Tundra Tales,* Nola M. Zobarskas, ed. (New York 1967) (Chukchee, Koryak, and Eskimo tales).

(ii) Koryak/Nymylan

W. JOCHELSON, "The Mythology of the Koryak," *American Anthropologist* 6 (1904): 413–26; "The Koryak," *Memoirs of the American Museum of Natural History* 10, part 1 (Leiden and New York 1908). G. KENNAN, *Tent Life in Siberia and Adventures among the Koryaks and Other Tribes in Kamchatka and Northern Asia* (New York and London 1871). H. KUNIKE,

Märchen aus Sibirien (Jena 1940). F. LITKE (or F. LÜTKE), "Die Tschuktschen," *Archiv für die Wissenschaftliche Kunde von Russland* 3 (1843): 446–64.

(iii) Kamchadal/Itelmen

S. P. KRASHENINNIKOV, *La description du Kamtchatka,* Voyage en Sibérie 2 (Paris 1768). H. KUNIKE, *Märchen aus Sibirien* (Jena 1940).

(iv) Yukaghir

W. BOGORAS, "Tales of Yukaghir, Lamut and Russianized Natives of Eastern Siberia," *American Museum of Natural History, Anthropological Papers* 20 (New York 1918): 1–148. W. JOCHELSON, "The Jukaghir and Jukaghirized Tungus," *Memoirs of the American Museum of Natural History* 12 (New York and Leiden, part 1, 1910; part 2, 1924; part 3, 1926). H. KUNIKE, *Märchen aus Sibirien* (Jena 1940).

(v) Gilyak/Nivx

E. A. KREJNOVIČ, "Očerk kosmogoničeskix predstavlenij Giljak o. Saxalina," *Etnografija* 8, 1 (1929): 78–102. B. PILSUDSKI, "Schwangerschaft, Entbindung und Fehlgeburt bei den Bewohnern der Insel Sachalin," *Anthropos* 5 (1910): 756–74. L. ŠRENK, *Ob inorodcax Amurskogo kraja,* 3 vols. (Saint Petersburg 1883–1903). L. STERNBERG, "Die Religion der Giljaken," *Archiv fr̈ Religionswissenschaft* 8 (Leipzig 1905); *Materialy po izučeniju giljackogo jazyka i fol'klora* (Saint Petersburg 1908).

(d) The Eskimo

W. BOGORAS, "Eskimo of Siberia," *Memoirs of the American Museum of Natural History* 12 (New York 1910). E. NELSON, *The Eskimo about Bering Strait* (Washington 1900). A. OLLIVIER, "Sur les Esquimaux d'Asie," *Bulletin de la Société d'anthropologie,* 2d ser., 12 (1879). E. S. RUBCOVA, *Materialy po jazyku i fol'kloru eskimosov* (Moscow and Leningrad 1927).

(e) The Ket/Yenisey/Ostyak of Yenisey

E. A. ALEKSEENKO, *Kety: Istoriko-etnografičeskie očerki* (Leningrad 1967). V. I. ANUČIN, "Očerk šamanstva u enisejskix ostjakov," *Sbornik Muzeja Antropologii i Etnografii* 2, fasc. 2 (1914). K. DONNER, "Ethnological Notes about the Jenisey-Ostyak," *Mémoires de la Société finno-ougrienne* 66 (1933). H. FINDEISEN, "Zur Problematik des Seelenglaubens," *Europäischer Wissenschaftsdienst,* 1944; "Indochinesen in Nordsibirien," *Atlantis* 12:58–62.

Finno-Ugrian Myths and Rituals

I. The Finno-Ugrian Peoples

From the Atlantic to the Taimyr peninsula, the "archipelago" of Uralian peoples is strung across the whole of northern Europe and western Siberia as the vestiges of a continent which the increasing tide of Scandinavians, Russians, and Turko-Tartars has never ceased to wash over for the last two thousand years. Uprooted from their ancestral land by waves of backwash which stirred the people of the steppes beginning in the high Middle Ages, only the Magyar horsemen—apparently natives of present-day Bachkiria who were strongly Turkized by several centuries of contact with the Bulgars of the Volga and other southern neighbors—were able to found a state which was stable, durable, and soon to be Christian, in the heart of Europe before the year 1000. Finland—in which Swedish, although only a minority language, would remain the sole true language of the culture if not of the civilization until the end of the nineteenth century—would not obtain its independence until 1918. As for Estonia, it was only during the brief interval between the two world wars that it would escape, however briefly, from Russian power. All of the other peoples would only be independent at a period which was a prehistoric one for them—like the independence of the American Indians before the coming of the white man. All would remain more or less without writing until the revolution of 1917.

It is estimated that it was around 4000 B.C. that the two branches of the Uralic family—Samoyeds on the one hand and Finno-Ugrians on the other—separated. The Samoyeds—about 30,000 in all—are today spread over the immense stretch of tundra bordering the Arctic Ocean between the White Sea and the Taimyr peninsula; there remain only four Samoyed language groups, of which Nieniets, or Yurak, which is spoken by approximately 25,000 speakers, is by far the largest.

Several groups would successively break away from the common Finno-Ugrian: (1) At the beginning of the second millennium B.C., an Ugrian branch today represented by the Hungarians, on the one hand, and the Ugrians of the Ob—the Voguls and the Ostyaks (Mansi and Hanti)—on the other. (It should be noted that the majority of the non-Russian peoples of the Soviet Union are today officially designated by their names for themselves in their own languages. This reform, which followed the 1917 revolution, was made necessary by the often pejorative connotations attached to the names used by the Russians. Outside of the USSR, the old names borrowed from the Russians nevertheless remain in use by the majority of the Finno-Ugrians. We shall conform to this usage, indicating the indigenous ethnonym in parentheses when such is necessary.) (2) A Permian branch (from the city of Perm in the Urals) today represented by two languages: Zyrian (Komi) and Votyak (Udmurt), spoken, respectively, by 350,000 and 700,000 persons. (3) A Volgic branch, whose present-day branches, spoken in the region of the great bend of the Volga, are Cheremis (Mari) and Mordwin, with the latter subdivided into Erza Mordwin and Moksha Mordwin. There are approximately 500,000 Cheremis; the Mordwins, who number 1.3 million, are the third largest Finno-Ugrian people, after the Finns and the Hungarians, but before the Estonians. (4) Lapp, which is fragmented into numerous groups and whose position continues to give rise to much controversy. (5) The Balto-Finnic languages (previously referred to as the Finnish languages of the Baltic) of which the two largest groups are by far Finnish (4.5 million speakers), the primary language of Finland and also recognized, along with Russian, in the Karelian Republic in the USSR; and Estonian, spoken by 1 million people as their official language—alongside Russian, the federal language—of the Estonian Republic. Other Balto-Finnic languages are Veps, spoken by some 16,000 people in the Onega Lake region; Vote, spoken by certain families in the Leningrad district; and finally, Livonian, which, gone from Livonia, survives in some ten villages in Northern Kurland.

The linguistic connection uniting these different peoples in no way implies that they belong to a racial or cultural community. Ethnically the Hungarians are closer to their German, Slavic, or Latin neighbors than they are to any Finno-Ugrian people. The Finns and the Estonians more closely resemble the Scandinavians, Baltic peoples, and northern Russians—all of these being speakers of Indo-

Detail of a disk-shaped hair ornament discovered at Rakamaz; the representation is possibly of the *touroul*, the mythic bird of the ancient Hungarians. The birds it holds in its talons may be either souls that it is carrying to earth or symbols of its power. Nyíregyháza (Hungary). Josa Andras Museum. Photo Kalman Konya—Ed. Corvina, Budapest.

European languages—than they do their linguistic cousins, the Lapps. The Ugrians of the Ob and the Samoyeds are strongly Mongoloid. The hypothesis has even been advanced that the Lapps, and even the Ugrians of the Ob and the Samoyeds, may have replaced their own languages with Uralic languages.

If we also bear in mind that the Uralians, whatever their historical fortunes may have been, have nearly always been in a position of weakness and have never ceased to borrow from the ways of life, technical knowledge, beliefs, demons, and gods of their invaders and neighbors, it should not surprise us that the common foundation of Uralic mythology and religion is quite difficult to discern beneath the innumerable strata left by foreign contributions.

The task of the comparativist is made all the more difficult by the fact that we often have a very poor knowledge—or no knowledge at all—of the myths and rites of the ancient peoples under whose influence the Uralians fell. This is the case with the various Iranian peoples of the steppe—Cimmerians, Sarmatians, and Scythians—who are known to us especially through archaeological discoveries and the often unverifiable accounts of Herodotus. This is the case with the Baltic peoples, whose ancient religion has reached us only through vestiges of folklore and the hardly comprehensive testimonies of missionaries regarding their "pagan" superstitions. This is the case to a great extent with the Turko-Tartars, through the mediation of whom Islam exerted an influence upon the Cheremis and the southern Votyaks. To these one may add the possibility of a Paleoarctic substratum underlying the religions of the Lapps, Samoyeds, and Ugrians of the Ob.

II. The Sources

The documents which we have at our disposal for the study of Finno-Ugrian mythologies are relatively numerous but of very unequal antiquity, depending on whether these peoples were more or less distant from the seats of civilization. Their religion per se was first described from the outside by travelers or by missionaries charged with extirpating that religion.

The oldest written sources are also those which treat those beliefs which disappeared the earliest. The first allusions to the Hungarians appear in Arabic and Greek documents before the conquest of the Danubian homeland: these are rare, brief, and uncertain. More consistent are the testimonies contained in the Latin chronicles of the Middle Ages; much later than Christianization, they are nevertheless too often dictated by reasons of state.

The first written document on the religion of the Finns is a fairly dry and highly controversial versified compendium on the "gods" adored by the Hämians—the inhabitants of the province of Häme in western Finland—and by the Karelians. It is contained in the preface to the Finnish translation of the Psalter published in 1551 by Michael Agricola, the bishop of Turku. The first study dedicated to the religion of the ancient Finns is the *De superstitione veterum Finnorum theoretica et practica* of Chr. Lencqvist, which was published in 1782, and which was followed in 1789 by the *Mythologia fennica* of Chr. Ganander.

The Lapp religion was known fairly early, thanks mainly to Johann Scheffer of Strasburg (under his Latin name Johannes Schefferus), who, in his *Lapponia,* published in 1674 and immediately translated into German, English, French (1678), and Dutch, painted a remarkable tableau of beliefs and rites—based on his own observations but also taking into account all earlier sources—in which he devoted an entire chapter, complete with engravings, to what is today known as shamanism.

With the exception of a short hagiography of Saint Steven, apostle to the Zyrians in the fourteenth century, and of an allusion made to the customs of the Mordwins in a fifteenth-century Italian travel account, our first information about the religion of the eastern Finno-Ugrians dates mainly from the seventeenth and eighteenth centuries. In the nineteenth century, systematic studies were carried out, principally by Finns and Russians. The great name is that of Uno Harva—Holmberg before 1927—who published a series of monographs in German and Finnish whose authority still remains unquestioned. Under the title *Finno-Ugric, Siberian,* he published in English the first study of the ensemble of Finno-Ugrian religions.

Contrary to widespread general opinion outside of Finland, the *Kalevala*—that inspired compilation in which Lönnrot contributed so profoundly to the national consciousness of his people—is not a source which may be used directly in a scientific approach to ancient Finnish mythology. What Lönnrot wanted—and he succeeded magnificently—was to compose, drawing on oral poetry, an epic which would make the Finnish community proud of its traditions and which, by giving it a prehistory, would root it in history. To this end, he undoubtedly drew upon authentic folk texts, a great number of which he had collected himself in the course of his wanderings through the country. But he interpreted, interpolated, and wove them together with verses of his own making; and he restored them following the image which he himself had, influenced by the ideas of his century—notably those related to the origin of the Homeric poems—regarding a hypothetical ancestral epic of which the oral tradition would have passed on only certain sparse and corrupted fragments. He particularly eliminated all which did not appear to him to be sufficiently archaic, beginning with all that related to Christianity—introduced in Finland in its Roman Catholic form at least four centuries before the Reformation. The same reservations hold for the *Kalevipoeg*, the Estonian national epic which was compiled slightly later by Kreutzwald in imitation of the *Kalevala*.

Under its rough exterior, folklore by contrast offers researchers an exceptionally rich field of inquiry. Thanks especially to Finnish, Hungarian, and Estonian scholars, immense collections of oral texts (incantations, mythological poems, funerary lamentations, folktales, etc.) were collected throughout the Finno-Ugrian world. Customs and superstitions were—and continue to be—cataloged, analyzed, and compared. The interpretation of certain of these is not without its risks. Elements belonging to various cultural strata occur in them in a tangled form and are not always easy to isolate and date. The Finnish school has earned a deserved international reputation in this domain.

Vogul mask used in the ritual of the bear festival. Budapest, Ethnographic Museum. Photo Ferenc Cservenka.

Complementing this basic survey of written sources and oral tradition, paleolinguistics, the study of etymologies and layers of vocabulary, also affords important information which sheds light upon the depths of an even more distant past. This method has been especially applied to the Finnish (Joki, E. Itkonen, M. Kuusi) and Hungarian (Pais) spheres.

Finally, even though the culture of the Finno-Ugrian peoples was mainly based upon wood, a perishable material, it is likely that archaeology may be able to furnish us with very precious data for the reconstruction of the religious history of these peoples. It is certainly regrettable that entire regions, notably western Siberia, have been very inadequately explored. We may console ourselves by pointing out the importance of discoveries made in Hungary on several village sites and of necropolises dating from the time of the conquest.

III. Rituals and Myths of Hunting and Fishing

The rituals and myths of hunting and fishing belong to an archaic economy to which agriculture and herding—including the raising of reindeer in the great north—were added without ever wholly obliterating the manifestations of the archaic economy anywhere. The diversification of the master spirits is certainly not as great in northern Europe as in Siberia, where hunting and fishing even recently still constituted the principal, and sometimes nearly the only, sources of food.

The great keeper of game is the master of the forest. Thus we find among the Finns the names of Tapio and Hiisi which were mentioned by Agricola—the latter under the name of Hittavainen—in his double list of the gods of Häme and Karelia. The same function is fulfilled by the man of the forest, the Zyrian *vörsa-mort* or the Votyak *n'ules murt*, who was imagined to be "taller than the tallest tree" and highly enterprising with women. The Votyaks claimed that he was capable of growing and shrinking in size at will. He was also said to have only one eye. In this regard, the Cheremis and the Moksha Mordwins know of a couple made up of the Old Man and the Old Woman of the Forest. Among the Erza Mordwins, it was especially the latter who was invoked.

In a parallel fashion, all of the Finno-Ugrian peoples know of a master spirit of the water and of fish. Sometimes they even know of several, as in the case of the Cheremis, for whom every lake was until recently the domain of a particular spirit. This water spirit is generally anthropomorphic, sometimes male and sometimes female, but also capable of metamorphosing into a fish, most often the pike. It is fitting to offer it sacrifices, particularly the first catch of the fishing season. As with the Russians' *vod'anoï*, this is an often dreadful personage whose wrath is to be avoided.

The most spectacular and complex of the rituals of the hunt is certainly the bear cult, whose Finnish ritual was still being practiced in the nineteenth century and which continues even today among the Ugrians of the Ob and among the Samoyeds. The hunt, the kill, moving the animal to the village, cutting it up, and consuming it all take place according to a ceremony whose principal aim is to absolve the hunters of guilt in the eyes of the victim and to free them from guilt in their own eyes. The bear, whose real name is taboo—among the Voguls, for example, the name given to

Place of Samoyed worship. Engraving from Nordenskiöld, *Vegas färd* (1880).

the bear by men is not the same as that used by women—is often called the "man" or the "master of the forest." The dead bear is treated with deference. Women are absent during the greater part of the ceremony, probably because of the sexual power attributed to that arctic animal which most closely resembles man. The bear's skeleton is generally reconstituted and buried in order to allow for its resurrection; the skull is hung separately in a tree, outside the reach of wild animals; or else, as with the Voguls, strung from a post which is placed in the center of the village and constitutes the principal cultic site.

The worship of the bear should not be regarded as belonging exclusively to ancient Uralic culture, any more than the other rituals of the hunt. It may also be found among all of the Paleoarctic peoples of Europe, Asia, and America, and its prehistoric extension may have been much greater.

Myths and rituals of hunting and fishing are probably not the only vestiges of the ancient beliefs of these peoples. The cult of rocks, which is characteristic of the Uralic peoples of the Arctic, is undoubtedly also a legacy of the distant past. The best known example of this is the cult of the Lapps, who used to worship, under the name of *seite,* crags or mountains which were particularly outstanding for their shape, location, or size. Quite often the *seite* was to be found in a region which was said to be a part of the world of the dead.

The antiquity of various beliefs in domestic spirits is more difficult to determine. These beliefs gave rise everywhere to practices and rites which were generally very close to those which may also be found among the Scandinavians and the Russians. The house in which people live (or the nomads' tent), as well as the barn, the stable, the threshing area, and the sauna, each have their spirits. A domestic cult which is more complex than in other places is that which developed especially among the Votyaks and Cheremis. Its sanctuary is the sacrificial hut, which is connected to family and clan. Offerings destined for the spirit of the hut were generally placed unburned on the sacred board, which was regarded simultaneously as a domestic altar and the abode of the spirit. This spirit was connected with the earth.

IV. Shamanism

Shamanism, in the strict sense of the word, makes up an integral part of the Paleoarctic culture of Eurasia and America. Its prehistoric range seems to have been even wider: has it not been surmised that the famous and mysterious "staffs of command" found in certain prehistoric sites in France might have in fact been the "drumsticks" of a shamanic drum?

It was in this circumpolar culture that the widely attested shamanism of the northernmost Uralic peoples—the Lapps, Samoyeds, and Ugrians of the Ob—participated. It was, in fact, in its Lappish variant—which no longer exists today—that it was first described, although under the name of magic or sorcery.

Northern European and western Siberian shamanism hardly differ in their essentials from what is properly known as Siberian shamanism, as described elsewhere in this work. The shaman is first and foremost a mediator, healer, and diviner, capable of going into ecstasy and of communicating with the beyond. Not everyone who wants to can be a shaman, and the shamanic vocation is said to be connected to certain neurotic predispositions. Much has been said about Arctic hysteria. Shamans, however, are the exact opposite of psychopaths or the possessed. They are rather persons who "possess" spirits, whom they make their auxiliaries. If the depressive state which accompanies the first signs of a calling is troublesome and first provokes a movement of rejection on the part of the elected, the shaman later appears as an individual whose exceptional equilibrium originates from having mastered his initiatory neurosis.

We know of no Uralic shamanic customs that are analogous to those found, for example, among the Tungus. They are reduced to a minimum: a particular belt among the Lapps, a special hair style among the Samoyeds and the Ugrians of the Ob. On the other hand, the drum was indispensable. "Taking away our drums is like depriving you of your compasses," is what a Lapp is reported to have said once to the ecclesiastical authorities ordered to extirpate sorcery from the northern deserts. These drums were of different types according to the region. Four may be distinguished among the Lapps alone. The figures drawn with alder sap on the skin of the drum were more or less numerous and ordered. Sometimes two horizontal lines divided the surface into two or three "storeys," corresponding to the sky, the earth, and the subterranean world. The drum helped to provoke the shaman's ecstasy. It was also used in divination. This function explains the sometimes very high number—up to one hundred—of figures drawn on the drum. On the drum were placed—generally on the representation of the sun—a set of rings which were caused to move by striking the drumskin with a sort of drumstick made from a reindeer horn in the shape of a Y or a T. In this way one could know the future and also know to which god it was proper to sacrifice and which offerings were most acceptable. The drum was sometimes regarded as the vehicle of the shaman. The Lapp word *kannus,* which is used for a drum with an angular frame, means "spur" in Finnish.

According to our oldest sources on Lapland, adult women could not touch the drum. At the time of migrations, it was carried in the last sled, sometimes even by a different route which was far from any customary trail, in order to avoid the possibility of the great danger that might befall a woman from another community were she, in ignorance, to take the same route during the next three days.

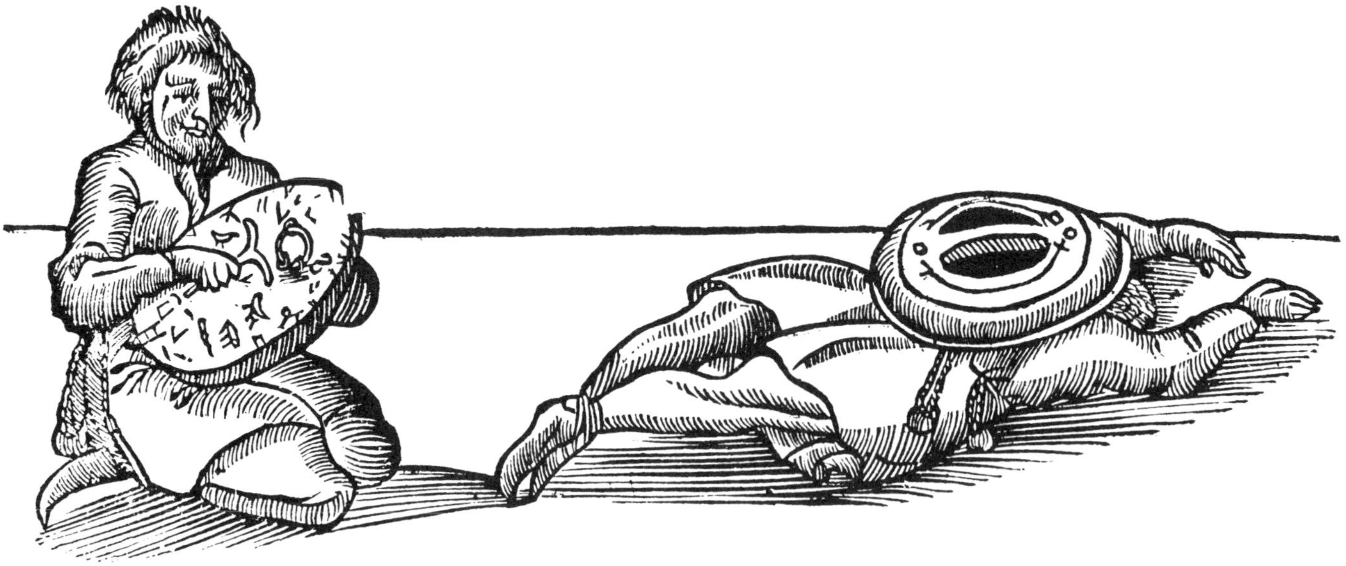

Lapp practicing divination with his shaman's drum and then throwing himself on the ground, his head almost completely covered by the drum. From Schefferus, *Lapponia* (1673).

In Lapland, the use of the drum was formerly the prerogative of the male head of the community; thus it is possible to speak of a sort of domestic shamanism. In serious or delicate cases, people nevertheless called upon individuals who were particularly known for their talents and their powers. Shamans did not, however, constitute a particular caste.

Shamanism appears to have an archaic legacy among the Uralic peoples. The same word for shaman is found in the Balto-Finnic languages (Finnish *noita*, Estonian *nõid*), in Lapp (*noaidi*), and in Vogul (*n'ait*). A number of traces of this religious complex seem be perpetuated in folklore, particularly in popular tales and in the superstitions of other Finno-Ugrian peoples, including the Hungarians. Does this give us the right to designate as shamans the *táltos* (pronounced *taltoś*) of the Magyar conquerors of the tenth century? This is uncertain, unless one takes the meaning of the word "shaman" in a very extended—perhaps overextended—sense.

V. The Gods

We know almost nothing of the common Finno-Ugrian pantheon. It is certainly possible to find gods whose functions are more or less the same from one people to another: what archaic religion did not know of a sky god or an earth spirit? But the names of the gods—which are, moreover, often of foreign provenance—are never found in all the languages of the Finno-Ugric family. Only three names are common to at least two language groups: (1) the name of the god represented by the Finnish *Jumala* and the Lapp *Ibmel* (if the latter is not merely a borrowing, pure and simple, from the Finnish) (which today designate in both cases the god of the Christians) as well as by the Cheremis Jumo (which is unknown in Mordwin); (2) the name of the Lappish god Tiermes, who is generally identified with the Numi-Tõrem of the Ugrians of the Ob, but whose name has on numerous occasions been connected with that of the Celtic Taranis and the Scandinavian Thor; (3) the name of the Votyak god Inmar, which seems to be the same as the god Ilmari (Ilmarinen in the *Kalevala*) of the ancient Finns, although the derivation in both cases is anything but clear. Curiously, all of these are supreme gods, or at least gods of the sky or of storms. No less curious is the Indo-European word which yielded the Latin *deus* and the French *dieu*, which in Finnish is *taivas*, "sky," borrowed from a Baltic language.

According to Agricola's testimony (which uses the word *jumala* only in a Christian sense) the most important god of the ancient Finns was *Ukko*—whose name means "goodman" or "old man"—a god of vegetation, rain, and thunder. His cult, together with that of Sampsa Pellervoinen—perhaps the Saint Samson of Orthodox Christianity, another divinity connected with agriculture—was celebrated in the course of a festival called "the basket of Ukko" (*Ukon vakka*) and seems to have been the occasion for orgies quite possibly of a ritual nature. Pellonpoika ("Peter-of-the-fields"?) was the god of barley and of beer. Rongoteus—whose name was, according to Haavio, a form of that of Saint Stephen the Martyr—was the god of rye. Virokannas—"John-of-the-incense"?—was the god of oats. Köndös—Saint Urban?—was the god of cleared ground. Ägräs was the god of turnips, peas, and beans. Although the etymologies which have been offered for these names are often fragile, it is likely that Agricola's list includes a number of Catholic saints who were forced into hiding by the Reformation and whose names were distorted by the popular language. It is important to stress that this is a double list: the dichotomy which opposes the "gods of the Hämeans" to the "gods of the Karelians" may be in part explained by the fact that Hämia and Karelia were, respectively, under the control of Sweden and thus of Rome, and within the sphere of influence of Novgorod and thus of Byzantium. It is nearly certain that the religion of the Balto-Finnic peoples of this period was a syncretism between ancient indigenous beliefs and the Christianity introduced by the Crusades. A similar syncretism continued into recent times, and even today it subsists here and there among the Lapps, the Votyaks, and the Ugrians of the Ob.

At times several syncretisms have succeeded one another. The Lapps incorporated several ancient Scandinavian gods into their most archaic gods, followed by—if we may allow ourselves the use of the plural—the "Christian gods."

On the first drum described by Scheffer are represented: on the higher "storey" Thor and the god the Lapps called "the Great Governor" (*Storjunkare*), each accompanied by a servant; below were Christ and the apostles; further down was the sun. No ancient god figures on the second drum (with the exception of the sun, an ambivalent figure), which shows only God the Father, Jesus, the Holy Spirit, and Saint John. On the fourth drum there are no Christian figures, but only "the god Tiuri," "the god Thor," "Thor's hammer," "the Great Governor," "a divine figure made of wood," and naturally, the sun.

What makes any comparison difficult is that it seems as if the gods of the Uralians, as a whole, had no proper names. Perhaps the supreme god was more or less the only one to dwell far enough away from men to be able to be called by his name without danger. Whatever is the case, the gods and spirits are nearly always designated by common names or by paraphrases. In other cases, the name used is often of an incontestably foreign source.

The sovereign god of the Lapps is called Tiermes only in the east. Elsewhere he is known as Radien ("the sovereign"), Veraldenradien, or Veraldenolmai ("sovereign of the world," "man of the universe"), which are names of Scandinavian origin. He is still called Atjek ("the old one, father"). Horagalles—whose name probably means "the old man of Thor"—is sometimes confused with him. The very name of Inmar, the supreme god of the Votyaks, seems to derive from the word *in/inm-*, "the sky." The same relationship exists in Finnish between the name of Ilmarinen and the word *ilma*, "air, sky." Inmar is constantly called *kildiśin*, "creator," *vordiś*, "feeder," etc.

The only thing that can be said for certain is that gods or spirits whose functions are comparable may be found among all of the Uralic peoples with few exceptions, as is also the case among their non-Uralic neighbors.

The elements and meteorological phenomena naturally have their divinities or their spirits; there are too many to list them here. Agricola mentions a "mother of the water." The Lapps honored a "man of the wind" (Pieggolmai) in olden times, who was called Ilmaris (cf. the Finnish god Ilmarinen) in the west, but who was perhaps influenced by the Scandinavian Njord. They also worshiped the sun, but, as far as we know, they never gave it a particular name.

The gods, like humans, often have families. Of course, divine couples are to be found, such as that formed among the Votyaks by *Inmar ataï* ("Inmar the father") and *Inmar anaï* ("Inmar the mother"), undoubtedly in the image of God the Father and the Mother of God. It is also undoubtedly Christian influence that gave rise here and there to the formation of trinities. Uno Harva reports that in the sacrificial formulas of the Votyaks of the old circle of Glazov, the trinity is called *Inmar-kildiśin-kuaź*, a compound in which *Inmar* means "God"; *kildiśin*, "the creator"; and *kuaź* ("air, sky, founder") designates the Holy Spirit.

The earliest sources mention a trinity among the Lapps made up of Radien-attje, "the reigning father" (a sovereign god who is identical to Ibmel), Radien-kieddi, his son, and Radien-akka, his wife, to whom is sometimes added Rananeida ("the maiden of the grass"), a goddess of renewal who is regarded as the daughter of the father god.

Just as the god of the sky is a man, the earth is everywhere "mother earth." The earth, however, was created by God. On the other hand, in every cosmogony water is considered to be the primordial and uncreated maternal element. This, as we have seen, does not stop lakes and rivers from harboring male and female water sprites, masters and mistresses of fishes to whom it is proper to pay homage. We should also point out that the Votyaks once honored a "mother sun" (*Śundy-mumy*) and a "mother thunder" (*Gudiri-mumy*), whose equivalents are not to be found elsewhere. Certain scholars, especially from the USSR, view these as traces of an ancient matriarchal society.

On the subject of the devil, Manker writes that the name of the devil in the Lapp language was a late borrowing from Finnish, and that "there does not appear to have originally been a being corresponding to the devil in Lapp mythology." This reasoning, which may be applied to all of the Finno-Ugrian peoples, is only partly convincing when one thinks of the force of vocabulary taboos regarding a character of such a dreadful nature.

VI. Agrarian Rites

The fertility of animals and plants depended upon the union of sky and earth—whose concrete manifestation was seen by the Estonians in spring lightning. Accordingly, the agrarian rites consisted primarily of prayers, offerings, and

Shaman's drum, with commentary by J. Schefferus (*Lapponia*, 1673) as follows: "Drum A: *a*, Thor; *b*, his servant; *c*, the great *Junker*; *d*, his servant; *e*, birds; *f*, stars; *g*, Christ; *h*, the apostles; *i*, a bear; *k*, a wolf; *l*, a reindeer; *m*, a bull; *n*, the sun; *o*, a lake; *p*, a fox; *q*, a squirrel; *r*, a serpent. Drum B: *a*, God the Father; *b*, men; *c*, the Holy Spirit, *d*, Saint Peter; *e*, difficult death; *f*, an oak; *g*, a squirrel; *h*, the sky; *i*, the sun; *l*, a wolf; *m*, a lavaret; *n*, a wood grouse; *o*, friendship with the wild reindeer; *p*, Anund, son of Erik, the owner of this drum, kills a fox; *q*, gifts; *r*, an otter; *s*, friendship with other Lapps; *t*, a swan; *v*, symbol allowing one to find out something about others, for example, whether someone who is ill can be cured; *x*, a bear; *y*, a pig; β, a fish; γ, a psychopomp. The T-shaped objects are the beaters for the shaman's drum." The three rings shown at the bottom of the illustration are placed on the drum and used for divination.

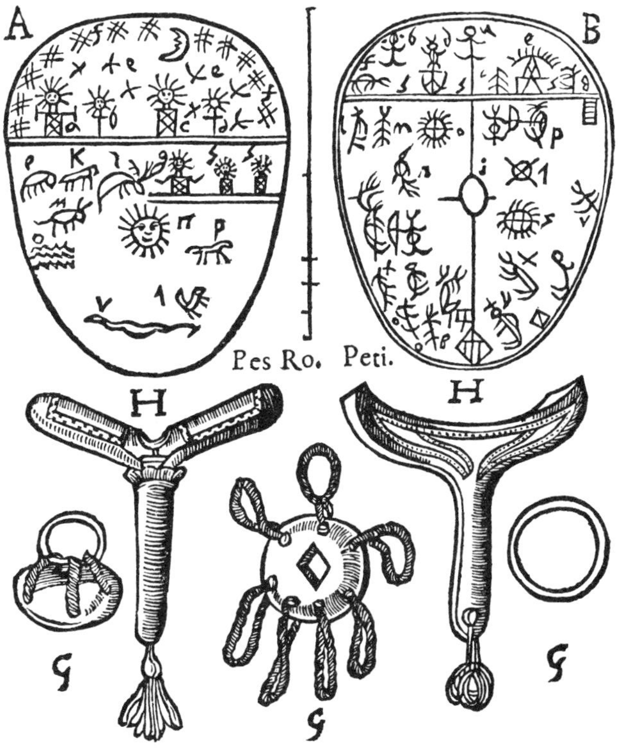

Cheremis priests kneeling in the sacred wood. Photographed by U. Harva, 1913. Helsinki, Suomalaisen Kirjallisuuden Seura. In Lehtinen and Kukkonen, *Iso Karhu–The Great Bear* (Helsinki 1980).

sacrifices addressed to the celestial powers: thunder, wind, and sun, and chthonic powers—especially the earth, but also, according to different peoples, the different "mothers" of grain, barley, cereals, and grass, or else the "father of the field"; these would later give rise to their Christian substitutes, of whom the most important were Saint George and Saint Elias.

Prayers were either simple formulas, incantations, or long mythological poems whose recitation was sometimes combined with an elaborate dramatic performance.

In a very widespread custom, white animals were sacrificed to the celestial powers, and brown or black animals to those of the earth. This custom is found not only among the agriculturalists of the forests, but also among the reindeer herders of the tundra and the nomads of the steppe who were the ancient Hungarians: the Lapps sacrificed white reindeer to the sun, and the sacrifice of a white horse is well documented among the Magyars of Árpád. The same symbolism is undoubtedly found in the milk libations offered by the Estonians to thunder gods in earlier times.

The earth was felt to be a living being. The Livonians forbade the spilling of boiling water upon it or the setting of the blade of a knife into it, for fear of wounding it. In order to remain fertile, the earth asked to be fed. The Cheremis had the custom of sacrificing a black cow to it, or sometimes a bull, whose skin and bones were then buried in order to help the springtime resurrection. In the Vyatka region, each peasant then went out into his field and placed an egg on it or poured out a spoonful of soup as he said, "Eat, earth, and bring us a good harvest."

But man could also, by means of a phenomenon of cosmic contagion, contribute to setting in motion the process of fertility. Such was the meaning of the great annual festivals that were connected to the principal moments of agricultural life: planting, bringing in the harvest, the summer and winter solstices, etc. The ritual meals and the sexual excesses which sometimes more or less licitly accompanied them—they are stigmatized by Agricola—accelerated the circulation of food, sap, and blood. In certain regions of Finland the planter was supposed to be naked. (Virgil wrote in his *Georgics,* "Make yourself naked for plowing and sowing!"). But magic worked both ways. At the feast of Saint John, the festival of the summer solstice, young girls in search of a husband rolled about naked in the fields of rye so that the night dew, by moistening their skin, would make them irresistible. Mircea Eliade believes that this custom was aimed at activating the growth of young plants. The participants seem also to have sought to appropriate the erotic power of vegetation for themselves.

VII. The Mythic Narratives

Naturally all of the Finno-Ugrian peoples know a certain number of origin myths, on the subject of which comparative studies still have been made in only a partial way. It is in the Finnish domain that these myths have been most carefully analyzed, and it is also in this domain that we have the greatest number of documents at our disposal. Popular Finnish poetry even distinguishes a particular genre, that of "birth" (*synty*), a narrative poem which related the creation *in illo tempore* of a being, an animal, an element, a substance, etc. Knowledge of the conditions in which prototypes were created gives man power over the representatives of such genera. In the *Kalevala,* Väinämöinen, the "eternal knower," recites the "birth" of iron in order to stop blood from flowing from wounds caused by iron.

The creation of the world is accounted for in an archaic myth which has innumerable variants but which in essence holds that a bird—often an eagle, but sometimes a diver—lays an egg in the primordial sea, or sometimes on an island; that the egg breaks, and that the two halves of its shell become the sky and earth, with the white and yolk giving birth to the moon and sun.

The myth known as the myth "of the great oak," a gigantic tree whose branches obscure the light of the sun, moon, and stars, and which could only be cut down by a little man who came out of the sea, is common among Balto-Finnic and Volga-Finnic peoples, but is also found among the Baltic peoples from whom it was undoubtedly borrowed. Among the Indo-Europeans, the oak is related to the god of thunder. The Baltic name of this god, Perkunas—which is also found in Perun, the name of the principal god of the Slavs, in the mysterious Scandanavian god Fjörgyn, and in the Finnish name of the devil, Perkele—may be derived from the ancient name of the oak represented by the Latin *quercus.* But the fact that the world tree was an oak for the Finnic peoples does not necessarily mean that this representation was not known to their ancestors under the form of a fir or a birch, for example, as is the case for numerous peoples further east. The memory of a mythic tree which is simultaneously the tree of life, the world tree, and the shamanic tree seems to have echoes even in popular Hungarian folktales.

Representations of the earth, sky, and heavenly bodies are most often generally the same for the Finno-Ugrians as for their neighbors. The sky is often described as a cover or as the fabric of a tent, of which one side, which was left to flap, provoked the birth of the wind by its movements. Several groups believed that the sky was lower toward the south and that only a narrow passage allowed migratory birds to return to their mythic abode, known in Finnish as *lintukotolainen,* "the house of the birds." They imagined that, at the place at which the sky met the earth, a land existed that was peopled by minuscule men; some would see in this an echo of much more southern beliefs about the Pygmies.

In the late spring, the Votyaks (Udmurts) sacrifice two sheep, a white one and a black one. First the white sheep is sacrificed to Inmar, the sky god. Photographed by U. Harva, 1911. Helsinki, Suomalaisen Kirjallisuunden Seura. In Lehtinen and Kukkonen, *Is Karhu—The Great Bear* (Helsinki 1980).

If by myths we mean a more or less sanctified archetypal representation, many legendary or marvelous accounts are not really myths. It is nevertheless often difficult to decide, since ancient myths could also survive in a degenerate form, as is often the case with folktales. On the other hand, accounts of historical acts may become obscured with time so as to become invested with all the functions of myth. How is one to classify, for example, the account of the death and resurrection of the Lemminkäinen or the cycle of the forging and abduction of the *sampo*, episodes which are well known through the *Kalevala?* Yet another problem is that of the legendary accounts of the birth of the Hungarian nation and the discovery, through the agency of a marvelous deer, of the new Danubian homeland.

VIII. The Cult of the Dead

The Finno-Ugrians, as has been shown by Ivar Paulson and others, early made the distinction between a "free soul" and a "corporal soul." The former was conceived as the extracorporal manifestation of an individual, his alter ego, which, in this life, could at certain times separate from the body and lead an independent existence, as occurs in dreams, in the shamanic trance, or in the "loss of the soul," by which a certain group of diseases were explained. The corporal soul, attached to the body for the duration of its terrestrial life, could sometimes be broken down into a "vital soul," the "breath," charged with the functions of physical life, and an "I soul," corresponding to the psyche.

The cult of the dead was practiced in various forms, apparently by all the Finno-Ugrian peoples. The free soul of the dead was supposed to lead in the beyond a life which was most often imagined as a reverse image of the terrestrial life. It was sometimes thought that the dead were rejuvenated, and that after becoming very small, they were reborn among the living. Elsewhere it was believed that the dead lived with their heads below their feet. In several Hungarian sepulchers dating from the time of the Conquest, it has been possible to ascertain that the position of the buttons on the clothing of the dead had been reversed; similarly, the sword was placed on the right side rather than on the left. We should again point out the custom—which is also well documented among the Russians—of sacrificing to the dead "backwards." The ceremonies took place, not "in the direction of the sun," but "against the sun." Thus one turned toward the west, and not the east, to say the prayers. The clothes of the participants were worn inside out and backwards.

The living were responsible for assuring the well-being of the dead through prayers, offerings, and sacrifices. The normal mode of disposal of the dead was inhumation; cemeteries have been extremely important aspects of ritual always and everywhere. Among the Karelians, the dead person was laid out in a kind of small wooden house with "windows" through which one could supply the dead person with food and other offerings. The Samoyeds and Uralians of the Ob used to have the custom of exposing their dead in trees. It is nevertheless probable that the aim of this custom was to place the remains of the dead out of the reach of wild animals while awaiting the thaw that would allow for inhumation. But the practice was connected with one that continued in Karelia into recent times: to hang the offerings for the dead in trees which were specially pruned and were regarded as sacred, trees called *karsikko* in Finnish. Among the Votyaks, all the members of the clan, that is, all the inhabitants of several villages, participated in certain ceremonies. Sacrifices in memory of the dead took place on the third, seventh, and fortieth days after the funeral. A very important ceremony took place on Holy Thursday.

It does not appear that the Finno-Ugrians had—before their first contacts with Christianity or at least with Islam—an idea of a differentiated afterlife made up of a paradise for the just and a hell for the wicked. The dead were above all physically present in their sepulchers. The tomb was the house of the dead, and the cemetery was a village whose inhabitants formed families, were married, procreated, and died; the "old one," a mythic ancestor and the first occupant of these places, held authority there.

Although the coexistence of these two representations appears contradictory, several Finno-Ugrian peoples imagined that there was also a "land of the dead," far to the north or west. The best-known example of this is *Tuonela*, which is so richly treated, as we know, in the *Kalevala*.

J.-L.M./d.w.

BIBLIOGRAPHY

A. ALFÖLDI, *Medvekultusz és anyajogú társadalmi szervezet Eurázíában* (Nyk 1936); "An Ugrian Creation Myth on Early Hungarian Phalerae," *American Journal of Archaeology* 73 (1969). E. ARBMAN, "Shamanen, extatisk andebesvärjare och visionär," in Å. HULTKRANTZ, *Primitiv religion och magi* (Stockholm 1955); Underjord och heliga fjäll i de skandinaviska lapparnas tro. Arv, Bd. 16 (Uppsala 1960). P. ARISTE, Vadja rahva usund. V 36 (1932). I. I. AVDJEJEV, "Dramatičeskije predstavljenija na mjedvjež'jem prazdnike u mansi," *Sovjetskij Sjevjer*, nos. 3–4 (1935). Ö. BEKE, "Tscheremissische Texte zur Religion und Volkskunde," Oslo Etnografiske Museum, bulletin 4 (1931); "Texte zur Religion der Osttscheremissen," *Anthropos* 29 (1934). BERGSLAND and CHRISTIANSEN, "Norwegian Research on the Language and Folklore of the Lapps," *JAI*, 80 (1950). J. W. BOECLER and F. R. KREUTZWALD, *Der Ehsten abergläubische Gebräuche, Weisen und Gewohnheiten* (Saint Petersburg 1854). P. BOGAJEVSKIJ, "Očerki religioznykh predstavljenij votjakov," EO 1980 (1890). M. A. CASTRÉN, "Föreläsningar i Finsk Mytologi," *Nordiska resor och forskningar* (Helsinki 1853). V. A. ČERNJECOV, "Predstavljenija o duše u obskikh ugrov," *Issljedovanija i matjerialy po voprosam pervobytnykh religioznykh vjerovanij*, Trudy Instituta Etnografii 51 (1959). B. COLLINDER, *The Lapps* (Princeton 1949). I. DIENES, *Les Hongrois conquérants*, Corvina, ed. (Budapest 1972). V. DIÓSZEGI, "A sámánhit emlékei a magyar népi müveltségben" (Budapest 1958); a résumé of theses presented in this work has been published in German in *Acta Ethnographica* 7 (1958): 97–135; "A Pogány magyarok hitvilága" (Budapest 1967); A honfoglaló magyarság hitvilágának történeti rétegei. A világfa. Népi kultura—népi társadalom, 2–3 (1969). C. M. EDSMAN, Studier i jägarens förkristna religion: Finska björnjaktsriter, Kyrkohistorisk Årsskrift (Uppsala 1954); "Bear Rites among the Scandinavian Lapps," *Proceed. of the IXth Intern. Congress for the History of Religions* (Tokyo 1960); *Studies in Shamanism* (Stockholm 1967). M. ELIADE, *Shamanism: Archaic Techniques of Ecstasy* (Princeton 1964). J. ERDÖDI, Uráli csillagnevek és mitológiai magyarázatuk, Budapest, A Magyar Nyelvtud. Társaság kiadványai, no. 124 (1970). FJELLSTROM, *Kort berättelse om Lapparnas Björna-fänge* (Stockholm 1755). CHR. GANANDER, *Mythologia fennica* (Åbo 1789). B. GAVRILOV, "Povjer'ja, obrjady i obyčai votjakov Mamadyšskogo ujezda," *Trudy IV arkheologičeskogo sjezda* (Kazan 1891). G. GJESSING, "Sjamanistisk of Laestadiansk ekstase hos samene," SS, V (Oslo 1953). M. HAAVIO, *Suomalaiset kodinhaltiat* (Porvoo and Helsinki 1942); *Väinämöinen, Eternal Sage*, FFC 144 (1952); *Karjalan jumalat* (Porvoo and Helsinki 1959); *Heilige Haine in Ingermanland*, FFC 189 (1963); "Suomalainen mytologia," WSOY (1967). P. HAJDU, *Uráli népek* (1975), a work by a double team of Finnish and Hungarian specialists under the direction of P. Hajdu. A. HÄMÄLÄINEN, "Ihmisruumiin substanssi suomalais-ugrilaisten kansojen taikuudessa," *MSFOu* 47 (1920); Der voršud-mudor-Kult der Votjaken, ESA 6 (1931); "Das kultische Wachsfeuer der Mordwinen und Tscheremissen," *JSFOu* 32 (1937). U. HARVA (originally Uno Holmberg), "Die Wassergottheiten der finnisch-ugrischen Völker,"

MSFOu 32 (1913); "Permalaisten uskonto," *SU* 4 (1914); "Über die Jagdriten der nördlichen Völker Asiens und Europas," *JSFOu* 41 (1925); Die Religion der Tscheremissen, FFC 61 (1926); *Finno-Ugric, Siberian: The Mythology of All Races,* vol. 4 (Boston 1927); *Suomalaisten muinaisusko* (Porvoo and Helsinki 1948); *Die religiösen Vorstellungen der Mordwinen,* FFC 142 (1952); "Lappalaisten uskonto," *SU* 2 (Helsinki 1915). J. HAUTALA, "Myytit ja kvasimyytit," *Kalavalaseuran vuosikirja* 37 (Porvoo 1957). L. HONKO, Krankheitsprojektile, Untersuchung über eine urtümliche Krankheitserklärung, FFC 178 (1959); Geisterglaube in Ingermanland, 1, FFC 185 (1962); *De finsk-ugriska folks religion,* Illustreret Religionshistorie 1 (Copenhagen 1968); "Role Taking of the Shaman," *Temenos* 4 (1969). M. HOPPÁL, A mitológia mint jelrendszer, Jel és közösség (Budapest 1975). Å. HULTKRANTZ, "Swedish Research on the Religion and Folklore of the Lapps," *JAI* 85 (1955). A. IPOLYI, *Magyar Mythologia* (Eger 1854). T. I. ITKONEN, "Heidnische Religion und späterer Aberglaube bei den finnischen Lappen," *MSFOu* 87 (1946). G. JAKOVLJEV, *Religioznyje obrjady čeremis* (Kazan 1887). C. JOHANSSON, Om kultplatser och heliga områden i Torne och Lule lappmarker, Svenska Landsmål (Uppsala 1944). *Kalevala:* French translation by J. L. Perret (Stock 1931), also in English. K. KANDRA, *Magyar Mythologia* (Eger 1897). K. F. KARJALAINEN, *Die Religion der Jugra-Völker,* 1–3 (Porvoo 1922–27). R. KARSTEN, *Samefolkets religion* (Helsinki 1952). L. KETTUNEN, "Tähelepanekuid vepslaste mütoloogiast," *EK,* 1925; "Vermlannin suomalaisten uskomuksia, taruja ja taikoja," *KV* 88 (1935). M. G. KHUDJAKOV, "Kul't konja v Prikam'i," *IGAIMK* 100 (1932). J. KROHN, "Suomen suvun pakanallinen jamalanpalvelus," *SKST* 83, 1 (1894); "Suomalaisten runojen uskonto," *SU* 1 (1914); *Skandinavisk mytologi* (Helsinki 1922); *Zur finnischen Mythologie,* 1, FFC 104 (1932). M. KUUSI, *Kirjoittamaton kirjallissus,* vol. 1 of Suomen kirjallisuus, Suomenkirjallisuuden Seura/Otava (Helsinki 1963). T. LEHTISALO, *Entwurf einer Mythologie der Jurak-Samojeden* (Helsinki 1924); *Der Tod und die Wiedergeburt der künftigen Schamanen* (Helsinki 1937). CHR. E. LENCQVIST, *De superstitione veterum Fennorum theoretica et practica* (Aboae 1782). A. LOMMEL, *Shamanism: The Beginnings of Art* (New York and Toronto 1967). O. LOORITS, *Liivi rahva usund,* 3 vols. (Tartu 1926–28), includes German summary, *Der Volksglaube der Liven; Estnische Volksdichtung und Mythologie* (Tartu 1932); *Gedanken-, Tat-, und Worttabu bei den estnischen Fischern* (Tartu 1939); *Eesti rahvausundi maailmavaade* (Stockholm 1948); *Grundzüge des estnischen Volksglaubens,* 3 vols. (Lund 1949–60); *Hauptzüge und Entwicklungswege der uralischen Religion,* Folklore-Studies 17 (Tokyo 1958). EVELINE LOT-FALCK, *Les rites de chasse chez les peuples sibériens* (Paris 1953). J. LUKKARINEN, Inkeriläisten kotijumalista, SMA 26 (1912); Inkeriläisten praasnikoista, S4: 11 (1912); "Inkeriläisten vainajainpalveluksesta," *MSFOu* 35 (1914); Tietoja susiihmisistä Inkerissä (1914). W. MAINOV, "Les restes de la mythologie mordvine," *JSFOu* 35 (1889). E. MANKER, *Die lappische Zaubertrommel,* 2 vols. (Stockholm and Thule 1938, 1950); "Några lapska kultplatser," *Ymer* 66, 2 (1946); *Lapparnas heliga ställen* (Stockholm 1957); *Fangstgropar och Stalotomter* (Stockholm 1960). C. MÉRIOT, "Une réponse religieuse à une situation de dépersonnalisation ethnique en Laponie: Le mouvement laestadien," *Cahiers du Centre d'études et de recherches ethnologique de l'Université de Bordeaux,* 2, no. 3 (1975). H. H. MICHAEL, *Studies in Siberian Shamanism* (Toronto 1963). R. MITUSOVA, Mjedvježij prazdnik u aganskikh ostjakov Surgutskogo rajona. Tobol'skij kraj, no. 1 (1926). B. MUNKÁACSI, Seelenglaube und Totenkult der Wogulen. Keleti Szemle (1905); "Volksbräuche und Volksdichtung der Wotjaken," *MSFOu* 102 (1952). V. NALIMOV, Njekotoryje čerty iz jazyčeskogo mirosozercanija zyrjan, *EO* 57 (1903); Zagrobnyj mir po vjeronanijam zyrjan, *EO* 72–73 (1907). H. PAASONEN, "Über die ursprünglichen Seelenvorstellungen bei den finnischugrischen Völkern und die Benennungen der Seele in ihren Sprachen," *JSFOu* 26-4 (1909). D. PAIS, *A magyar ösvallás nyelvi emlékeiböl,* Akadémiai kiadó (Budapest 1975). I. PAULSON, Å. HULTKRANTZ, and J. JETTMAR, *Les religions arctiques et finnoises* (Paris 1965). I. PAULSON, *Die primitiven Seelenvorstellungen der nordeurasischen Völker* (Stockholm 1958); "Die Tierknochen im Jagdritual der Nordeurasischen Völker," *ZE,* 84, 2 (1959); Seelenvorstellungen und Totenglaube bei nordeurasischen Völkern, *E,* 1960, 1–2; Schutzgeister und Gottheiten des Wildes (der Jagdtiere und Fische) in Nordeurasien, AUS-SSCR 2 (1961); *Himmel und Erde in der Agrarreligion der finnischen Völker* (Stockholm 1963); "Der Mensch im Volksglauben der finnischen Völker," *ZE* 88-1 (1963); "Seelenvorstellungen und Totenglaube der permischen und wolga-finnischen Völker," N. Vol. 9, 2 (1964); "Outline of Permian Folk Religion," *Journal of the Folklore Institute* 2 (1964); Le gibier et ses gardiens surnaturels chez les peuples ouraliens, *SFU* (1965); "Die Wassergeister als Schutzwesen der Fische im Volksglauben der finnischugrischen Völker," *AEthn,* 1966. O. PETTERSON, "Jabmek and jabmeaimo," Lunds Universitets Årsskrift, vol. 52, 6 (Lund 1957); "Tirmes-Dierbmes-Horagalles-Thor," in *Knut Lundmark och världsrymdens erövring* (Lund 1961). F. V. PLESOVSKIJ, O vozniknovjenii i razvitii kosmogoničeskikh mifov komi i udmurtov, *VKFU* (Syktyvkar 1965). G. N. PROKOFIEF, Ceremonija oživljenija bubna u ostjakov-samojedov, Izv. Leningradskogo gos. Universiteta, 2 (1929). JE. D. PROKOFIEVA, Kostjum sel'kupskogo šamana, Sbornik muzjeja antropologii i etnografii AN SSSR (1950). J. OVIGSTAD, *Kildeskrifter til den lappiske Mythologi* (Trondheim 1903, 1910); Lappische Opfersteine und heilige Berge in Norwegen, Oslo Etnografiske Museums skrifter, vol. 1, 5 (Oslo 1926). G. RANK, "Zum Problem des Sippenkultes bei den Lappen," *AV* 9 (1954); "Lapp Female Deities of the Madder-akka Group," *SS.,* 6 (Oslo 1955); *Die heilige Hinterecke im Hauskult der Völker Nordosteuropas und Nordasiens,* FFC 137 (1949). A. V. RANTASALO, *Der Ackerbau im Volksaberglauben der Finnen und Esten,* FFC 30–32 (1919–20). E. REUTERSKIÖLD, *Källskrifter till lapparnas mytologi, Bidrag till vår odlings häfder,* vol. 10 (Stockholm 1910); *De nordiska lapparnas religion* (Stockholm 1912). S. RHEEN, En kortt Relation om Lapparnes Lefwarne och Sedher, etc., Svenska Landsmål, vol. 17, 1 (Uppsala 1897). G. RÓHEIM, *Hungarian and Vogul Mythology* (Locust Valley, NY, 1954). A. SAUVAGEOT, "Mythologies des peuples de langue ouralienne," in *Mythologies des steppes, des forêts, et des îles* (Paris 1963); *Les anciens Finnois* (Paris 1961). J. SCHEFFERUS, *Lapponia* (Frankfurt 1673). TH. SEBEOK and RR. J. INGEMANN, *Studies in Cheremis: The Supernatural* (New York 1956). W. STEINITZ, "Totemismus bei den Ostjaken in Sibirien," *Ethnos,* nos. 4–5 (1938). D. STRÖMBACK, "The Realm of the Dead on the Lappish Magic Drums," in *Arctica: Essays Presented to Ake Campbell* (Uppsala 1956). A. TURUNEN, "Über die Volksdichtung und Mythologie der Wepsen," *SF* 6 (1952); *Kalevalan Sanakirja,* 1953. Z. ÚVÁRI, Az agrárkultusz kutatása a magyar és az európai folklórban (Debrecen 1969). J. VASILJEV, Übersicht über die heidnischen Gebräuche, Aberglauben und Religion der Wotjaken, *MSFOu* 18 (1902). V. M. VASILJEV, Matjerialy dlja izučenija vjerovanij i obrjadov čeremis, 10 5, 10 (1915). A. VILKUNA, *Das Verhalten der Finnen in "heiligen" Situationen,* FFC 164 (1956); Über den finnischen haltija "Geist, Schutzgeist," *AUSSSCR (SON)* 1 (1961). K. VILKUNA, Vuotuinen ajantieto, Otava (Helsinki 1968). G. VJERJEŠ-ČAGIN, Staryje obyčai i vjerovanija votjakov, *EO* 83 (1910); Votskije bogi, JAOIRS, 1911, 7. W. VON UNWERTH, *Untersuchungen über Totenkult und Odinverehrung bei Nordgermanen und Lappen* (Breslau 1911). M. WARONEN, *Vainajainpalvelus muinaisilla suomalaisilla* (Helsinki 1898). Y. WICHMANN, "Tietoja votjakkien mytologiasta," *S* 3 (1893): 6. K. B. WIKLUND, "En nyfunnen skildring av lapparnas björnfest," *MO,* 6 (1912); "Saivo: Till frågan om de nordiska beståndsdelarna i lapparnas religion," *MO,* 10 (1916). D. ZELENIN, "Tabu slov u narodov vostočnoj Jevropy i sjevjernoj Azii, I," *SMAE* 7 (1929).

Index

Page numbers in italics refer to illustrations

A

B

C

D

J

K

L

M

N

O

P

T

U

V